Commentary on
ROMANS

Commentary on ROMANS

FREDERIC L. GODET

KREGEL PUBLICATIONS
Grand Rapids, Michigan 49501

Commentary on Romans, by Frederic Louis Godet. Published in 1977 by Kregel Publications, a division of Kregel, Inc., P. O. Box 2607, Grand Rapids, MI 49501. All rights reserved.

Library of Congress Cataloging-in-Publication Data

Godet, Frederic Louis, 1812-1900.
   Commentary on the Epistle to the Romans.
   (Kregel Reprint Library series)
   Originally published in 1883 under title:
Commentary on St. Paul's Epistle to the Romans.
   Reprint of the 1956 ed. published by Zondervan Publishing House, Grand Rapids, in series: Classic commentary library.

   1. Bible. N.T. Romans—Commentaries. I. Title.

BS2665.G55   1977   227'.1'07   77-79189
                                                                               CIP
ISBN 0-8254-2732-0 (paperback)
ISBN 0-8254-2715-0 (deluxe hardback)

    4 5 6 7 8 Printing/Year 95 94 93 92 91

Printed in the United States of America

CONTENTS

	Page
Introduction to the American Edition	ix
Preface	xv

INTRODUCTION

1. The Apostle Paul 3
   - A. Before His Conversion 3
   - B. His Conversion 7
   - C. His Apostleship 13

2. The Church At Rome 36
   - A. Foundation 36
   - B. Composition and Tendency 41

3. The Epistle to the Romans 45
   - A. Author 45
   - B. Date 46
   - C. Aim 47
     - 1). Apologetic 48
     - 2). Polemic 51
     - 3). Didactic 54

4. Arrangement and Plan 59

5. Preservation of the Text 65
   - A. Principal Commentators 69
   - B. Title Authentic 71

COMMENTARY

1. Preface (1:1-15) 73
   - A. The Address (1:1-7) 73
   - B. Paul's Interest in Christians at Rome (1:8-15) . 85

2. Treatise (1:16-15:13) 91
   - A. Statement (1:16, 17) 91
   - B. Excursus on dikaioūv, to Justify 95

3. Fundamental Part (1:18 - 5:21)
   - A. First Section — God's Wrath on All (1:18-3:20) 99

vi / Contents

	Page
1). God's Wrath on the Gentiles (1:18-32)	99
2). God's Wrath Suspended over Jewish People (2:1-29)	113
3). Jewish Prerogative — No Exemption from Judgment (3:1-8)	131
4). Scriptures Proclaim Universal Condemnation (3:9-20)	139
B. Second Section — Justification by Faith Acquired by All (3:21-5:11)	145
1). The Fact by Which Justification by Faith is Acquired (3:21-26)	146
2). Excursis — The Expiation	160
3). This Mode of Justification Harmonious With Meaning of the Law (3:27-31)	162
4). Abraham Justified by Faith (4:1-25)	167
5). Certainty of Believers Final Salvation (5:1-11)	185
C. Third Section — Universal Death and Salvation (5:12-21)	200
Universality of Salvation in Christ is Proved by Universality of Death in Adam (5:12-21)	200
4. Supplementary Part 1 — Sanctification (6:1-7:25)	231
A. First Section — Its Principal Contained in Justification by Faith (6:1-7:6)	235
1). Sanctification in Christ Dead and Risen (6:1-14)	235
2). Excursus — To Die Unto Sin	237
3). Infant Baptism	241
4). The Power to Deliver from Sin (6:15-23)	253
5). Emancipation from the Law (7:1-6)	263
B. Second Section — The Law Powerless to Sanctify Man (7:7-25)	270
Law Powerless to Extricate . . . (7:7-25)	270
C. Third Section — The Work of the Holy Spirit (8:1-39)	294
1). Victory Over Sin and Death (8:1-11)	295
2). Adoption (8:12-17)	307
3). The Completion of Salvation (8:18-30)	311
4). Hymn of Assurance of Salvation (8:31-39)	329
5. Supplementary Part 2: The Rejection of Israel (9:1-11:36)	336
1). The Freedom of God (9:1-29)	338
2). Cause of Israel's Rejection (9:30-10:21)	367
3). God's Plan in History of Salvation (11:1-36)	391

Page

6. Practical Treatise
   A. General Part — Life in Salvation (12:1-13:14) .   421
      1). Foundation of Christian Activity (12:1, 2)   424
      2). Believer as a Member of the Church (12:3-21)   428
      3). Believer as a Member of the State (13:1-10)   439
      4). Awaiting Christ's Return — Motivation for
           Christian Living (13:1-14)   448
   B. Special Part — Direction Regarding Difference of
      View in Church at Rome (14:1-15:13) . .   452

7. Concluding Epistle (15:14-16:27)   475
   A. Personal Explanations (15:14-33)   475
   B. Recommendations and Warning (16:1-24) . .   487
   C. The Look Upward (16:25-27)   502

CONCLUSIONS
  Appendix
    A. Probation After Death   517
    B. The Christian Conflict   522
    C. Foreordination   524
    D. Freedom and Sovereignty   526
    E. The Mystery Respecting Israel's Future . .   529

INTRODUCTION
TO THE AMERICAN EDITION

Reverend Frederic Louis Godet, D.D., was born on October 25, 1812, at Neufchatel, Switzerland. He was educated at the University of Neufchatel, Berlin, and Bonn, in philosophy and theology. After completing his studies, in 1837, he became an assistant pastor of Valawjin. The next year, 1838, Prince William of Prussia (later Emperor of Germany) appointed Godet to direct the education of his only son, Frederick William (later, Kaiser Frederick Wilhelm of Germany). A lasting friendship developed during the six years (1838-44) they studied together.

In 1845, he became pastor of a church in Val de Ruy, and by 1850, he was considered one of the outstanding pastors of that area. God, in His graciousness, gave to His maturing pastor an unusual acceptability in the pastorate of his home area. Simultaneously, he was a professor of Biblical exegesis and dogmatic theology in the local Swiss Reformed College. While pastoring and teaching, he received his D.D. degree from the University of Basle, Switzerland. During this time, Godet became one of the most influential leaders against the growing liberalism in academic scholarship and Protestant theological circles. In 1873, he became the prominent leader of the faculty of the Free Evangelical University of Neufchatel. Here he became the outstanding professor of New Testament exegesis. It was during this time that he wrote this Commentary on Romans.

Godet is certainly not a novice, having been a leader of study, discussion groups, investigations, development of theological opinions, and a scholarly defense of scriptural authority. God had uniquely prepared this chosen scholar enabling him to distinguish, clarify, defend truth, or oppose erroneous views by his stating substantial scriptural evidences of the truth defended through his study and knowledge of the original texts. He consistently and dogmatically used the *Textus Receptus* when he disagreed with his critics; he was careful to cite his evidence from the *Textus Receptus* for his differing opinions.

He was known by his contemporaries (one of whom was Dr. Philip Schaff) to be a man of enthusiastic scholarship, a real patriot, and a sincere Christian. His contemporaries believed him to be a very qualified writer of this commentary because of his hearty sympathy with the book of Romans and his experience with the power and blessedness of its Holy Spirit-taught truths. Godet could not only picture sin in relationship to the Lord, Jesus Christ, but also accept the grace and glory of complete forgiveness. Because of this, he replaces what could be considered by some to be a dry, boring, mechanical regurgitation of facts with the deep feeling of the Psalmist as he cries, "How sweet are Thy words unto my taste! Yea, sweeter than honey to my mouth" (Psalm 119:103).

He is known best throughout the English-speaking world for his Commentaries on John (1864-65), Luke (1871), Romans, (this volume, 1879-80), and I Corinthians (1886). They were all readily received and translated into English almost immediately. This volume of Romans is considered by many the most difficult to exegete, and, in some opinions, his best and most conclusive systematic piece of work. We believe this commentary has endured the criticism and proven itself a classic tool available on the Book of Romans. It is very scholarly written, as the reader will readily recognize. Godet not only examines x / Introduction to the American Edition

very critically the original text, but unfolds with understanding the doctrines involved and graphically shows the correlation and relationship with other truths. Therefore, this volume is highly valued for scholars, pastors, teachers, and christian workers, aiding them in their study and presentation of the Book of Romans.

Like the sweet drippings of a honeycomb which entice the appetite for more and more, Godet challenges, stimulates, and entices the reader to search the Scriptures. Even if the reader does not agree, Godet will inspire him to dig out the truth which will lead to the bedrock of conviction. The inexhaustible riches of the God-breathed Scriptures should cause each generation of Bible scholars to clarify even more the insights, concepts and principles set forth by the Holy Spirit to practical application for the day in which they live. Godet, already having built the foundation, enables the reader to peer deeper into spiritual truth, that may lead to practical holy living.

The first American edition appeared in 1883. The introduction was written by Talbot W. Chambers. He also wrote an extended appendix as an explanation of his disagreement with certain aspects of Godet's Commentary. In order not to break the continuity of this current edition and yet include Mr. Chambers' views, it is placed at the end of this volume. I trust it will shed additional light upon the subjects considered.

This new American edition is sent forth with the prayer that the Holy Spirit will use the unfolding of Romans to expose the person and purpose of our Lord Jesus Christ to each reader. May all who read and study this commentary be brought to the conclusion "To God only wise, be glory through Jesus Christ forever. Amen" (Romans 16:27).

Greenville, Michigan, 1977 　　　　　　　　　　　　　　　　　J. ARNOLD FAIR

PREFACE

No one will deny that there is room for some emotion in giving to the public a Commentary on the Epistle to the Romans. It avails nothing that the author is only the interpreter of a given text. The contents of that text, accepted or rejected, affect his readers so decisively, that the author, who serves them as a guide, feels himself at every step under a burden of the gravest responsibility.

This consideration cannot weigh with me, however, to prevent me from offering to the church, and especially to the churches of the French language, this fruit of a study which, in the course of my theological teaching, I have been called again and again to renew.

I shall here state frankly an anxiety which fills my mind. I believe the divine conception of salvation, as expounded by St. Paul in this fundamental work, to be more seriously threatened at this moment than ever it was before. For not only is it assailed by its declared adversaries, but it is abandoned by its natural defenders. In these divine facts of expiation and justification by faith, which formed, according to the apostle's declaration, *the gospel which he received by the revelation of Jesus Christ* (Gal. i), how many Christians see nothing more, and would have the church henceforth to see nothing more, than a theological system, crammed with Jewish notions, which St. Paul himself conceived by meditating on Jesus Christ and upon His work!

It will not be long, I fear, ere we see what becomes of the life of individuals and of the church, as soon as its roots cease to strike into the fruitful soil of apostolical revelation. A religious life languishing and sickly, a sanctification without vigor or decision, and no longer distinguished by any marked feature from the simple morality of nature—such will be the goal, very soon reached, of that rational evolution on which the church, and particularly our studious youth, are invited to enter. The least obscuration of the divine mind, communicated to the world by means of apostolical revelation, has for its immediate effect a diminution of spiritual life and strength.

Must the church of France, in particular, lose the best part of its strength at the very moment when God seems at length to be bringing France into its arms? This would be the last tragedy of its history—sadder still than all the bloody but heroic days of its past.

It is neither the empty affirmations of free thought, nor the vague teachings of a semi-rationalism—which does not know itself whether it believes in a revelation or not—which will present a sufficient basis for the religious elevation of a whole nation. For there is needed a doctrine which is firm, positive, divine, like *the gospel of Paul*.

When the Epistle to the Romans appeared for the first time, it was to the church a word in season. Every time that, in the course of the ages, it has recovered the place of honor which belongs to it, it has inaugurated a new era. It was so half a century ago, when that revival took place, the powerful influence of which remains unexhausted to this hour. To that movement, which still continues, the present Commentary seeks to attach itself. May it also be in some measure to the church of the present a word in season!

I may be justly charged with not having more completely ransacked the immense library which has gradually formed round St. Paul's treatise. My answer is: I might have . . . but on condition of never coming to an end. Should I have done so?

And as I have been obliged to set a limit to my study, I have been obliged to restrict also the exposition of the results of my labor. If I had allowed myself to cross the boundaries of exposition properly so called, to enter more than I have sometimes done into the domain of dogmatic developments, or into that of practical applications, the two volumes would have been soon increased to four or six. It was better for me to incur the charge of dryness, which will not repel any serious reader, than to fall into prolixity, which would have done greatly more to injure the usefulness of the Commentary.

The pious Sailer used to say: "O Christianity, had thy one work been to produce a St. Paul, that alone should have rendered thee dear to the coldest reason." May we not be permitted to add: And thou, O St. Paul, had thy one work been to compose an Epistle to the Romans, that alone should have rendered thee dear to every sound reason.

May the Spirit of the Lord make all *of His own* that He has deigned to put into this work, fruitful within the church, and in the heart of every reader!

THE AUTHOR

INTRODUCTION

Coleridge calls the Epistle to the Romans "the profoundest book in existence." Chrysostom had it read to him twice a week. Luther, in his famous preface, says: "This Epistle is the chief book of the New Testament, the purest gospel. It deserves not only to be known word for word by every Christian, but to be the subject of his meditation day by day, the daily bread of his soul. . . . The more time one spends on it, the more precious it becomes and the better it appears." Melanchthon, in order to make it perfectly his own, copied it twice with his own hand. It is the book which he expounded most frequently in his lectures. The Reformation was undoubtedly the work of the Epistle to the Romans, as well as of that to the Galatians; and the probability is that every great spiritual revival in the church will be connected as effect and cause with a deeper understanding of this book. This observation unquestionably applies to the various religious awakenings which have successively marked the course of our century.

The exposition of such a book is capable of boundless progress. In studying the Epistle to the Romans we feel ourselves at every word face to face with the unfathomable. Our experience is somewhat analogous to what we feel when contemplating the great masterpieces of mediæval architecture, such, for example, as the Cathedral of Milan. We do not know which to admire most, the majesty of the whole or the finish of the details, and every look makes the discovery of some new perfection. And yet the excellence of the book with which we are about to be occupied should by no means discourage the expositor; it is much rather fitted to stimulate him. "What book of the New Testament," says Meyer, in his preface to the fifth edition of his commentary, "less entitles the expositor to spare his pains than this, the greatest and richest of all the apostolic works?" Only it must not be imagined that to master its meaning nothing more is needed than the philological analysis of the text, or even the theological study of the contents. The true understanding of this masterpiece of the apostolic mind is reserved for those who approach it with the heart described by Jesus in His Sermon on the Mount, the heart *hungering and thirsting after righteousness*. For what is the Epistle to the Romans? The offer of the *righteousness of God* to the man who finds himself stripped by the law of his *own righteousness* (i. 17). To understand such a book we must yield ourselves to the current of the intention under which it was dictated.

M. de Pressensé has called the great dogmatic works of the Middle Ages "the cathedrals of thought." The Epistle to the Romans is the cathedral of the Christian faith.

Sacred criticism, which prepares for the exposition of the books of the Bible, has for its object to elucidate the various questions relating to their origin; and of those questions there are always some which can only be resolved with the help of the exegesis itself. The problem of the composition of the Epistle to the Romans includes several questions of this kind.

We could not answer them in this introduction without anticipating the work of exegesis. It will be better, therefore, to defer the final solution of them to the concluding chapter of the commentary. But there are others, the solution of which is perfectly obvious, either from the simple reading of the Epistle, or from certain facts established by church history. It cannot be other than advantageous to the exposition to gather together here the results presented by these two sources, which are fitted to shed light on the origin of our Epistle. It will afford an opportunity at the same time of explaining the different views on the subject which have arisen in the course of ages.

An apostolical epistle naturally results from the combination of two factors: the personality of the author, and the state of the church to which he writes. Accordingly, our introduction will bear on the following points: 1. The Apostle Paul; 2. The Church of Rome; 3. The circumstances under which the Epistle was composed.

In a supplementary chapter we shall treat of the preservation of the text.

THE APOSTLE PAUL

If we had to do with any other of St. Paul's Epistles, we should not think ourselves called to give a sketch of the apostle's career. But the Epistle to the Romans is so intimately bound up with the personal experiences of its author, it so contains the essence of his preaching, or, to use his own expression twice repeated in our Epistle, *his Gospel* (ii. 16, xvi. 25), that the study of the book in this case imperiously requires that of the man who composed it. St. Paul's other Epistles are fragments of his life ; here we have his life itself.

Three periods are to be distinguished in St. Paul's career : 1. His life as a Jew and Pharisee ; 2. His conversion ; 3. His life as a Christian and apostle. In him these two characters blend.

A. *St. Paul before his Conversion*

Paul was born at Tarsus in Cilicia, on the confines of Syria and Asia Minor (see his own declarations, Acts xxi. 39, xxii. 3). Jerome mentions a tradition, according to which he was born at Gischala in Galilee.[1] His family, says he, had emigrated to Tarsus after the devastation of their country. If this latter expression refers to the devastation of Galilee by the Romans, the statement contains an obvious anachronism. And as it is difficult to think of any other catastrophe unknown to us, the tradition is without value.[2]

Paul's family belonged to the tribe of Benjamin, as he himself writes, Rom. xi. 1 and Phil. iii. 5. His name, Saul or Saül, was probably common in this tribe in memory of the first king of Israel, taken from it. His parents belonged to the sect of the Pharisees ; compare his declaration before the assembled Sanhedrim (Acts xxiii. 6) : "I am a Pharisee, the son of a Pharisee," and Phil. iii. 5. They possessed, though how it became theirs we know not, the right of Roman citizens, which tends, perhaps, to claim for them a somewhat higher social position than belonged to the Jews settled in Gentile countries. The influence which this sort of dignity exercised on his apostolic career can be clearly seen in various passages of Paul's ministry (comp. Acts xvi. 37 et seq., xxii. 25-29, xxiii. 27).

The language spoken in Saul's family was undoubtedly the Syro-Chaldean, usual in the Jewish communities of Syria. But the young Saul does not seem to have remained a stranger to the literary and philosophical culture of the Greek world, in the midst of which he passed his childhood. "Tarsus," even in Xenophon's time, as we find him relating (*Anab.* i. 2. 23), was "a city large and prosperous." In the age of Saul it disputed the empire of letters with its two rivals, Athens and Alexandria. In what degree Greek culture is to be ascribed to the apostle, has often been made

---
[1] *De Vir. illust.* c. 5.
[2] It is not quite exact to say, as Lange has done in Herzog's *Encyclopedia,* art. "Paulus," that Jerome retracted this assertion in his *Commentary on the Epistle to Philemon.* The phrase, *talem fabulam accepimus,* implies no intention of the kind (see Hausrath in Schenkel's *Bibel-lexicon,* art. "Paulus").

3

matter of discussion. In his writings we meet with three quotations from Greek poets : one belongs both to the Cilician poet Aratus (in his *Phœnomena*) and to Cleanthes (in his *Hymn to Jupiter*) ; it is found in Paul's sermon at Athens, Acts xvii. 28 : " As certain also of your own poets have said, We are also his offspring ;" the second is taken from the *Thaïs* of Menander ; it occurs in 1 Cor. xv. 33 : " Evil companionships corrupt good manners ;" the third is borrowed from the Cretan poet Epimenides, in his work on *Oracles;* it is found in the Epistle to Titus i. 12 : " One of themselves, a prophet of their own, said : The Cretans are always liars, evil beasts, slow bellies." Are these quotations proofs of a certain knowledge of Greek literature which Paul had acquired ? M. Renan thinks not. He believes that they can be explained as borrowings at second hand, or even from the common usage of proverbs circulating in everybody's mouth.[1] This supposition might apply in all strictness to the second and third quotation. But there is a circumstance which prevents us from explaining the first, that which occurs in the discourse at Athens, in the same way. Paul here uses this form of citation : " *Some* of your poets have said . . ." If he really expressed himself thus, he must have known the use made by the *two* writers, Aratus and Cleanthes, of the sentence quoted by him. In that case he could not have been a stranger to their writings. A young mind like Paul's, so vivacious and eager for instruction, could not live in a centre such as Tarsus without appropriating some elements of the literary life which flourished around it.

Nevertheless it cannot be doubted that his education was essentially Jewish, both in respect to the instruction he received and to the language used.[2] Perhaps he was early destined to the office of Rabbin. His rare faculties naturally qualified him for this function, so highly honored of all in Israel. There is connected with the choice of this career a circumstance which was not without value in the exercise of his apostolical ministry. According to Jewish custom, the Rabbins required to be in a position to gain their livelihood by means of some manual occupation. This was looked upon as a guarantee of independence and a preservative from sin. The received maxim ran thus : " The study of the law is good, provided it be associated with a trade. . . . Otherwise, it is useless and even hurtful."[3] Saul's parents chose a trade for him which probably connected with the circumstances of the country where they dwelt, that of *tentmaker* (σκηνοποιός, Acts xviii. 3), a term which denoted the art of making a coarse cloth woven from the hair of the Cilician goats, and used in preference to every other kind in the making of tents. The term used in the Book of the Acts thus denotes the work of weaving rather than tailoring.

When we take account of all the circumstances of Saul's childhood, we understand the feeling of gratitude and adoration which at a later date drew forth from him the words, Gal. i. 15 : " God, who *separated me from my mother's womb.*" If it is true that Paul's providential task was to free the gospel from the wrappings of Judaism in order to offer it to the Gentile world in its pure spirituality, he required, with a view to this mission, to unite many seemingly contradictory qualities. He needed, above all, to come from the very heart of Judaism ; only on this condition could he thoroughly know life under the law, and could he attest by his own experience the powerlessness of this alleged means of salvation. But, on the other hand, he required to be exempt from that national antipathy to the Gentile world with which Palestinian Judaism was imbued. How would he have been able to open the gates of the kingdom of God to the Gentiles of the whole world, if he had not lived in one of the great centres of Hel-

---

[1] *Les Apôtres, p.* 167.
[2] Hausrath has with much sagacity collected the facts which establish the influence of the Aramaic language on the style of Paul (*Bibellex.*, art. " Paulus," IV. 409).
[3] *Pirkê Abot*, II. 2.

lenic life, and been familiarized from his infancy with all that was noble and great in Greek culture, that masterpiece of the genius of antiquity? It was also, as we have seen, a great advantage for him to possess the privilege of a Roman citizen. He thus combined in his person the three principal social spheres of the age, Jewish legalism, Greek culture, and Roman citizenship. He was, as it were, a living point of contact between the three. If, in particular, he was able to plead the cause of the gospel in the capital of the world and before the supreme tribunal of the empire, as well as before the Sanhedrim at Jerusalem and the Athenian Areopagus, it was to his right as a Roman citizen that he owed the privilege. Not even the manual occupation learned in his childhood failed to play its part in the exercise of his apostleship. When, for reasons of signal delicacy, which he has explained in chap. ix. of his first Epistle to the Corinthians, he wished to make the preaching of the gospel, so far as he was concerned, *without charge*, in order to secure it from the false judgments which it could not have escaped in Greece, it was this apparently insignificant circumstance of his boyhood which put him in a position to gratify the generous inspiration of his heart.

The young Saul must have quitted Tarsus early, for he himself reminds the inhabitants of Jerusalem, in the discourse which he delivers to them, Acts xxii., that he had been "brought up in this city." In chap. xxvi. 4 he thus expresses himself not less publicly: "All the Jews know my manner of life from my youth at Jerusalem." Ordinarily it was at the age of twelve that Jewish children were taken for the first time to the solemn feasts at Jerusalem. They then became, according to the received phrase, "*sons of the law.*" Perhaps it was so with Saul, and perhaps he continued thenceforth in this city, where some of his family seem to have been domiciled. Indeed, mention is made, Acts xxiii. 16, of a son of his sister who saved him from a plot formed against his life by some citizens of Jerusalem.

He went through his Rabbinical studies at the school of the prudent and moderate Gamaliel, the grandson of the famous Hillel. "Taught," says Paul, "at the feet of Gamaliel, according to the perfect manner of the law of our fathers" (Acts xxii. 3). Gamaliel, according to the Talmud, knew Greek literature better than any other doctor of the law. His reputation for orthodoxy nevertheless remained unquestioned. Facts will prove that the young disciple did not fail to appropriate the spirit of wisdom and lofty prudence which distinguished this eminent man. At his school Saul became one of the most fervent zealots for the law of Moses. And practice with him kept pace with theory. He strove to surpass all his fellow-disciples in fulfilling the traditional prescriptions. This is the testimony which he gives of himself, Gal. i. 14; Phil. iii. 6. The programme of moral life traced by the law and elaborated by Pharisaical teaching, was an ideal ever present to his mind, and on the realization of which were concentrated all the powers of his will. He resembled that young man who asked Jesus "by the doing of what work" he could obtain eternal life. To realize the law perfectly, and to merit the glory of the kingdom of heaven by the righteousness thus acquired—such was his highest aspiration. Perhaps there was added to this ambition another less pure, the ambition of being able to contemplate himself in the mirror of his conscience with unmixed satisfaction. Who knows whether he did not flatter himself that he might thus gain the admiration of his superiors, and so reach the highest dignities of the Rabbinical hierarchy? If pride had not clung like a gnawing worm to the very roots of his righteousness, the fruit of the tree could not have been so bitter; and the catastrophe which overturned it would be inexplicable. Indeed, it is his own experience which Paul describes when he says, Rom. x. 2, 3, in speaking of Israel: "I bear them record that they have a zeal of God, but not according to knowledge. For they, being ignorant of God's righteousness, and going about to establish their own

6 / Introduction

righteousness, have not submitted themselves unto the righteousness of God " [that which God offers to the world in Jesus Christ].

Three natural characteristics, rarely found in union, must have early shown themselves in him, and attracted the attention of his masters from his student days : vigor of intellect—it was in this quality that he afterwards excelled St. Peter ; strength of will—perhaps he was thus distinguished from St. John ; and liveliness of feeling. Everywhere we find in him an exuberance of the deepest or most delicate sensibility, taking the forms of the most rigorous dialectic, and joined to a will fearless and invincible.

In his exterior Saul must have been of a weakly appearance. In 2 Cor. x. 10 he reproduces the reproach of his adversaries : " His bodily appearance is weak." In Acts xiv. 12 et seq. we see the Lycaonian crowd taking Barnabas for Jupiter, and Paul for Mercury, which proves that the former was of a higher and more imposing stature than the latter. But there is a wide interval between this and the portrait of the apostle, drawn in an apocryphal writing of the second century, the *Acts of Paul and Thecla*, a portrait to which M. Renan in our judgment ascribes far too much value.[1] Paul is described in this book as " a man little of stature, bald, short-legged, corpulent, with eyebrows meeting, and prominent nose." This is certainly only a fancy portrait. In the second century nothing was known of St. Paul's apostolate after his two years' captivity at Rome, with which the history of the Acts closes ; and yet men still know at that date what was the appearance of his nose, eyebrows, and legs ! From such passages as Gal. iv. 13, where he mentions a sickness which arrested him in Galatia, and 2 Cor. xii. 7, where he speaks of a *thorn in the flesh*, a *messenger of Satan* buffeting him, it has been concluded that he was of a sickly and nervous temperament ; he has even been credited with epileptic fits. But the first passage proves nothing ; for a sickness in one particular case does not imply a sickly constitution. The second would rather go to prove the opposite, for Paul declares that the bodily affliction of which he speaks was *given* him—that is to say, inflicted for the salutary purpose of providing the counterpoise of humiliation, to the exceeding greatness of the revelations which he received. The fact in question must therefore rather be one which supervened during the course of his apostleship. Is it possible, besides, that a man so profoundly shattered in constitution could for thirty years have withstood the labors and sufferings of a career such as that of Paul notoriously was ?[2]

Marriage takes place early among the Jews. Did Saul marry during his stay at Jerusalem ? Clement of Alexandria, and Eusebius among the ancients, answer in the affirmative. Luther and the Reformers generally shared this view. Hausrath has defended it lately on grounds which are not without weight.[3] The passages, 1 Cor. vii. 7 : " I would that all men were even as I myself" (unmarried), and ver. 8 : " I say to the unmarried and widows, It is good for them if they abide even as I," do not decide the question, for Paul might hold this language as a widower not less than if he were a celibate. But the manner in which the apostle speaks, ver. 7, of the *gift* which is granted him, and which he would not sacrifice, of living as an unmarried man, certainly suits a celibate better than a widower.

Had Saul, during his sojourn at Jerusalem, the opportunity of seeing and hearing the Lord Jesus ? If he studied at the capital at this period, he can hardly have failed to meet Him in the temple. Some have alleged in favor of this supposition the passage, 2 Cor. v. 16 : " Yea, though we have

---

[1] *Les Apôtres*, p. 170.
[2] In an interesting article (*Revue Chrétienne*, March, 1878) M. Nyegard has taken up and supported the view of several German theologians, and of Rückert in particular (Gal. iv. 14), that the weakness in question was a disease of the eyes. The argument of this writer is ingenious. But none of his proofs seem to us convincing.
[3] *Bibellex.*, art. "Paulus."

known Christ *after the flesh*, yet now henceforth know we Him no more." But this phrase is rather an allusion to the pretensions of some of his adversaries, who boasted of their personal relations to the Lord ; or more simply still, it denotes the carnal nature of the Messianic hope current among the Jews. As there is not another word in Paul's Epistles fitted to lead us to suppose that he himself saw the Lord during His earthly life, Renan and Mangold have concluded that he was absent from the capital at the time of the ministry of Jesus, and that he did not return to it till some years later, about the date of Stephen's martyrdom. But even had he lived abroad at that period, he must as a faithful Jew have returned to Jerusalem at the feasts. It is certainly difficult to suppose that St. Paul did not one time or other meet Jesus, though his writings make no allusion to the fact of a knowledge so purely external.

Saul had reached the age which qualified him for entering on public duties, at his thirtieth year. Distinguished above all his fellow-disciples by his fanatical zeal for the Jewish religion in its Pharisaic form, and by his hatred to the new doctrine, which seemed to him only a colossal imposture, he was charged by the authorities of his nation to prosecute the adherents of the Nazarene sect, and, if possible, to root it out. After having played a part in the murder of Stephen, and persecuted the believers at Jerusalem, he set out for Damascus, the capital of Syria, with letters from the Sanhedrim, which authorized him to fill the same office of inquisitor in the synagogues of that city. We have reached the fact of his conversion.

B. *His Conversion.*

In the midst of his Pharisaical fanaticism Saul did not enjoy peace. In chap. vii. of the Epistle to the Romans, he has unveiled the secret of his inner life at this period. Sincere as his efforts were to realize the ideal of righteousness traced by the law, he discovered an enemy within him which made sport of his best resolutions, namely lust. "I knew not sin but by the law ; for I had not known lust except the law had said, Thou shalt not covet." And thus he made the most important experience of his life, that which he has expressed in these words of the Epistle to the Romans (iii. 20) : "By the law is the knowledge of sin." The painful feeling of his powerlessness to realize virtue was, if I may so call it, the negative preparation for the crisis which transformed his life. His soul, hungering and thirsting after righteousness, found the attempt vain to nourish itself with its own works ; it did not succeed in satisfying itself.

Another circumstance, fitted to prepare for the change in a more positive way, occurred at this period. An inactive witness of Stephen's martyrdom, Saul could calmly contemplate the bloody scene—see the brow of the martyr irradiated with heavenly brightness, and hear his invocation addressed to the glorified Son of man, in which was revealed the secret of his love and triumphant hope. His soul was no doubt deeply pierced in that hour ; and it was with the view of cicatrizing this wound that he set himself with redoubled violence to the work of destruction which he had undertaken. "The hour shall come," Jesus had said to His apostles, "in which whosoever shall kill you will think that he renders God worship." It was really with this thought that the young persecutor raged against the Christians. Nothing but an immediate interposition on the part of Him whom he was thus persecuting could arrest this charger in his full career, whom the sharp prickings by which he felt himself inwardly urged only served to irritate the more.

The attempt has been made in modern times to explain in a purely natural way the sudden revolution which passed over the feelings, convictions, and life of Saul.

Some have described it as a revolution of an exclusively inward charac-

8 / Introduction

ter, and purely moral origin. Holsten, in his work on the *Gospel of Peter and Paul* (1868), has brought to this explanation all the resources of his remarkable sagacity. But his own master, Baur, while describing the appearing of Jesus at the moment of Saul's conversion as " the external reflection of a spiritual process," could not help acknowledging, after all, that there remains in the fact something mysterious and unfathomable : " We do not succeed by any analysis, either psychological or dialectical, in fathoming the mystery of the act by which God revealed His Son in Saul." [1]

The fact is, the more we regard the moral crisis which determined this revolution, as one slowly and profoundly prepared for, the more does its explanation demand the interposition of an external and supernatural agent. We cannot help recalling the picture drawn by Jesus, of " the stronger man" overcoming " the strong man," who has no alternative left save to give himself up with all that he has into the hands of his conqueror. Saul himself had felt this sovereign interposition so profoundly, that in 1 Cor. ix. he distinguishes his apostleship, as the result of constraint, from that of the Twelve, which had been perfectly free and voluntary (vv. 16-18 comp. with vv. 5, 6). He, Paul, was taken by force. He was not asked : Wilt thou ? It was said to him, *Woe to thee, if thou obey not!* For this reason it is that he feels the need of introducing into his ministry, as an afterthought, that element of free choice which has been so completely lacking in its origin, by voluntarily renouncing all pecuniary recompense from the churches, and imposing on himself the burden of his own support, and even sometimes that of his fellow-laborers (comp. Acts xx. 34). This fact is the striking testimony borne by the conscience of Paul himself to the purely passive character of the transformation which was wrought in him.

The account given in the Acts harmonizes with this declaration of the apostle's conscience. The very shades which are observable in the three narratives of the fact contained in the book, prove that a mysterious phenomenon was really perceived by those who accompanied Saul, and that the fact belongs in some way to the world of sense. They did not discern the person who spoke to him, so it is said, Acts ix. 7, but they were struck with a brightness surpassing that of ordinary sunlight (xxii. 9, xxvi. 13); they did not hear distinctly the words which were addressed to him (Acts xxii. 9), but they heard the sound of a voice (Acts ix. 7).[2] Sometimes these striking details of the narrative have been alleged as contradictions. But the hypothesis has become inadmissible since criticism, by the pen of Zeller himself, has established beyond dispute the unity of authorship and composition characterizing the whole book. Supposing even the author to have used documents, it is certain that he has impressed on his narrative from one end to the other the stamp of his style and thought. In such circumstances, how could there possibly be a contradiction in a matter of fact ? It must therefore be admitted that while Saul alone *saw* the Lord and *understood* His words, his fellow-travellers observed and heard something extraordinary ; and this last particular suffices to prove the objectivity of the appearance.

Paul himself was so firmly convinced on this head, that when proving the reality of his apostleship, 1 Cor. ix. 1, he appeals without hesitation to the fact that he has *seen the Lord*, which cannot apply in his judgment to a simple vision ; for no one ever imagined that a vision could suffice to confer apostleship. In chap. xv. of the same Epistle, ver. 8, Paul closes the enumeration of the appearances of the risen Jesus to the apostles with that which was granted to himself ; he therefore ascribes to it the same reality as to those, and thus distinguishes it thoroughly from all the visions with

---

[1] *Das Christenthum und die christliche Kirche der drei ersten Jahrhunderte*, 3d ed. p. 45.
[2] It is to be observed that in the former of the two passages the writer uses the accusative (τὴν φωνήν), and in the latter the genitive (τῆς φωνῆς) ; in the former case he had in view the penetration of the *meaning* of the words ; in the latter, the confused perception of the sound of the voice.

which he was afterward honored, and which are mentioned in the Acts and Epistles. And the very aim of the chapter proves that what is in his mind can be nothing else than a bodily and external appearing of Jesus Christ; for his aim is to demonstrate the reality of our Lord's *bodily* resurrection, and from that fact to establish the reality of the resurrection in general. Now all the visions in the world could never demonstrate either the one or the other of these two facts: Christ's bodily resurrection and ours. Let us observe, besides, that when Paul expressed himself on facts of this order, he was far from proceeding uncritically. This appears from the passage, 2 Cor. xii. 1 et seq. He does not fail here to put a question to himself of the very kind which is before ourselves. For in the case of the Damascus appearance he expresses himself categorically, he guards himself on the contrary as carefully in the case mentioned 2 Cor. xii. 1 et seq. against pronouncing for the external or purely internal character of the phenomenon: "I know not; God knoweth," says he. Gal. i. 1 evidently rests on the same conviction of the objectivity of the manifestation of Christ, when He appeared to him as *risen*, to call him to the apostleship.

M. Renan has evidently felt that, to account for a change so sudden and complete, recourse must be had to some external factor acting powerfully in Saul's moral life. He hesitates between a storm bursting on Lebanon, a flash of lightning spreading a sudden brilliance, or an increase of ophthalmic fever producing in the mind of Saul a violent hallucination. But causes so superficial could never have effected a moral change so profound and durable as that to which Paul's whole subsequent life testifies. Here is the judgment of Baur himself, in his treatise, *Der Apostel Paulus*,[1] on a supposition of the same kind: "We shall not stop to examine it, for it is a pure hypothesis, not only without anything for it in the text, but having its obvious meaning against it." M. Reuss[2] thus expresses himself: "After all that has been said in our time, the conversion of Paul still remains, if not an absolute miracle in the traditional sense of the word (an effect without any other cause than the arbitrary and immediate interposition of God), at least a psychological problem insoluble to the present hour."

Keim, too, cannot help acknowledging the objectivity of the appearance of Christ which determined so profound a revolution. Only he transports the fact from the world of the senses into the not less real one of the spirit. He thinks that the glorified Lord really manifested Himself to Paul by means of a spiritual action exercised over his soul. This explanation is the forced result of these two factors: on the one hand, the necessity of ascribing an objective cause to the phenomenon; on the other, the predetermined resolution not to acknowledge the miracle of our Lord's bodily resurrection. But we shall here apply the words of Baur: "Not only has this hypothesis nothing for it in the text, but it has against it its obvious meaning." It transforms the three narratives of the Acts into fictitious representations, since, according to this explanation, Saul's fellow-travellers could have seen nothing at all.

If Paul had not personally experienced our Lord's bodily presence, he would never have dared to formulate the paradox, offensive in the highest degree, and especially to a Jewish theologian (Col. ii. 9): "In Him dwelleth all the fulness of the Godhead *bodily*."

With Saul's conversion a supreme hour struck in the history of humanity. If, as Renan justly says, there came with the birth of Jesus the moment when "the capital event in the history of the world was about to be accomplished, the revolution whereby the noblest portions of humanity were to pass from paganism to a religion founded on the divine unity,"[3] the conversion of Paul was the means whereby God took possession of the

---

[1] 2d ed. p. 78.   [2] *Les Epîtres Pauliniennes*, p. 11.   [3] *Vie de Jésus*, p. 1.

man who was to be His instrument in bringing about this unparalleled revolution.

The moment had come when the divine covenant, established in Abraham with a single family, was to extend to the whole world, and embrace, as God has promised to the patriarch, *all the families of the earth.* The universalism which had presided over the primordial ages of the race, and which had given way for a time to the particularism of the theocracy, was about to reappear in a more elevated form and armed with new powers, capable of subduing the Gentile world. But there was needed an exceptional agent for this extraordinary work. The appearing of Jesus had paved the way for it, but had not yet been able to accomplish it. The twelve Palestinian apostles were not fitted for such a task. We have found, in studying Paul's origin and character, that he was the man specially designed and prepared beforehand. And unless we are to regard the work which he accomplished, which Renan calls " the capital event in the history of the world," as accidental, we must consider the act whereby he was enrolled in the service of Christ, and called to this work, as one directly willed of God, and worthy of being effected by His immediate interposition. Christ Himself, with a strong hand and a stretched-out arm, when the hour struck, laid hold of the instrument which the Father had chosen for Him. These thoughts in their entirety form precisely the contents of the preamble to the Epistle which we propose to study (Rom. i. 1-5).

What passed in the soul of Saul during the three days which followed this violent disturbance, he himself tells us in the beginning of chap. vi. of the Epistle to the Romans. This passage, in which we hear the immediate echo of the Damascus experience, answers our question in the two words : A death, and a resurrection. The death was that of the self-idolatrous Saul, death to his own righteousness, or, what comes to the same thing, to the law. Whither had he been led by his impetuous zeal for the fulfilling of the law ? To make war on God, and to persecute the Messiah and His true people ! Some hidden vice must certainly cleave to a self-righteousness cultivated so carefully, and which led him to a result so monstrous. And that vice he now discerned clearly. In wishing to establish his own righteousness, it was not God, it was himself whom he had sought to glorify. The object of his adoration was his *ego*, which by his struggles and victories he hoped to raise to moral perfection, with the view of being able to say in the end : Behold this great Babylon which I have built ! The disquietude which had followed him on this path, and driven him to a blind and bloody fanaticism, was no longer a mystery to him. The truth of that declaration of Scripture, which he had till now only applied to the Gentiles, was palpable in his own case. " There is not a just man, no, not one " (Rom. iii. 10). The great fact of the corruption and condemnation of the race, even in the best of its representatives, had acquired for him the evidence of a personal experience. This was to him that death which he afterwards described in the terms : " I through the law am dead to the law" (Gal. ii. 19).

But, simultaneously with this death, there was wrought in him a resurrection. A justified Saul appeared in the sphere of his consciousness in place of the condemned Saul, and by the working of the Spirit this Saul became a *new creature* in Christ. Such is the forcible expression used by Paul himself to designate the radical change which passed within him (2 Cor. v. 17).

Accustomed as he was to the Levitical sacrifices demanded by the law for every violation of legal ordinances, Saul had no sooner experienced sin within him in all its gravity, and with all its consequences of condemnation and death, than he must also have felt the need of a more efficacious expiation than that which the blood of animal victims can procure. The bloody death of Jesus, who had just manifested Himself to him in His glory as the Christ, then presented itself to his view in its true light. Instead of seeing in it, as hitherto, the justly-deserved punishment of a false Christ, he recognized in it the great expiatory sacrifice offered by God Himself to wash away the sin of the world and his own. The portrait of the Servant of Jehovah drawn by Isaiah, of that unique person on whom God lays the iniquity of all . . . he now understood to whom he must apply it. Already the interpretations in the vulgar tongue, which accompanied the reading of the Old Testament in the synagogues, and which were afterward preserved in our *Targums*, referred such passages to the Messiah. In Saul's case the veil fell; the cross was transfigured before him into the instrument of the world's salvation; and the resurrection of Jesus, which had become a palpable fact since the Lord had appeared to him bodily, was henceforth the proclamation made by God Himself of the justification of humanity, the monument of the complete amnesty offered to our sinful world. "My *righteous* Servant *shall justify* many," were the words of Isaiah, after having described the resurrection of the Servant of Jehovah as the sequel of His voluntary immolation. Saul now contemplated with wonder and adoration the fulfilment of this promise, the accomplishment of this work. The new righteousness was before him as a free gift of God in Jesus Christ. There was nothing to be added to it. It was enough to accept and rest on it in order to possess the blessing which he had pursued through so many labors and sacrifices, peace with God.

He entered joyfully into the simple part of one accepting, believing. Dead and condemned in the death of the Messiah, he lived again justified in His risen person. It was on this revelation, received during the three days at Damascus, that Saul lived till his last breath.

One can understand how, in this state of soul, and as the result of this inward illumination, he regarded the baptism in the name of Jesus which Ananias administered to him. If in Rom. vi. he has presented this ceremony under the image of a death, burial, and resurrection through the participation of faith in the death, burial, and resurrection of Jesus, he has, in so expressing himself, only applied to all Christians his own experience in his baptism at Damascus.

To the grace of justification, of which this ceremony was to him the assured seal, there was added that of regeneration by the creative operation of the Spirit, who transformed his reconciled heart, and produced a new life within it. All the energy of his love turned to that Christ who had become his substitute, guilty, in order to become the author of his righteousness, and to the God who had bestowed on him this unspeakable gift. Thus there was laid within him the principle of a true holiness. What had been impossible for him till then, self-emptying and life for God, was at length wrought in his at once humble and joyful heart. Jesus, who had been his substitute on the cross, in order to become his righteousness, was easily substituted for himself in his heart in order to become the object of his life. The free obedience which he had vainly sought to accomplish under the yoke of the law, became in his grateful heart, through the Spirit of Christ, a holy reality. And he could henceforth measure the full distance between the state of a slave and that of a child of God.

From this experience there could not but spring up a new light on the true character of the institutions of the law. He had been accustomed to regard the law of Moses as the indispensable agent of the world's salvation; it seemed to him destined to become the standard of life for the whole race, as it had been for the life of Israel. But now, after the experience which he had just made of the powerlessness of this system to justify and sanctify man, the work of Moses appeared in all its insufficiency. He still saw in it a pedagogical institution, but one merely temporary. With the Messiah, who realized all that he had expected from the law, the end of the Mosaic discipline was reached. "Ye are complete in Christ" (Col. ii. 10); what avails henceforth that which was only the *shadow* of the dispensation of Christ (Col. ii. 16, 17)?

And who, then, was He in whose person and work there was thus given to him the fulness of God's gifts without the help of the law? A mere man? Saul remembers that the Jesus who was condemned to death by the Sanhedrim was so condemned as a blasphemer, for having declared Himself the Son of God. This affirmation had hitherto seemed to him the height of impiety and imposture. Now the same affirmation, taken with the view of the sovereign majesty of Him whom he beheld on the way to Damascus, stamps this being with a divine seal, and makes him bend the knee before His sacred person. He no longer sees in the Messiah merely a son of David, but the Son of God.

With this change in his conception of the Christ there is connected another not less decisive change in his conception of the Messiah's work. So long as Paul had seen nothing more in the Messiah than the Son of David, he had understood His work only as the glorification of Israel, and the extension of the discipline of the law to the whole world. But from the time that God had revealed to him in the person of this son of David according to the flesh (Rom. i. 2, 3) the appearing of a divine being, His own Son, his view of the Messiah's work grew with that of His person. The son of David might belong to Israel only; but the Son of God could not have come here below, save to be the Saviour and Lord of all that is called man. Were not all human distinctions effaced before such a messenger? It is this result which Paul himself has indicated in those striking words of the Epistle to the Galatians (i. 16): "When it pleased God, who separated me from my mother's womb and called me by His grace, to *reveal His Son* in me,[1] *that I might preach Him among the heathen* . . ." His Son, the heathen: these two notions were necessarily correlative! The revelation of the one must accompany that of the other. This relation between the divinity of Christ and the universality of His kingdom is the key to the preamble of the Epistle to the Romans.

The powerlessness of the discipline of the law to save man, the freeness of salvation, the end of the Mosaic economy through the advent of the Messianic salvation, the divinity of the Messiah, the universal destination of His work—all these elements of Paul's new religious conception, of *his gospel*, to quote the phrase twice used in our Epistle (ii. 16, xvi. 23),[2] were thus involved in the very fact of his conversion, and became more or less directly disentangled as objects of consciousness in that internal evolution which took place under the light of the Spirit during the three days following the decisive event. What the light of Pentecost had been to the Twelve as the sequel of the contemplation of Jesus on the earth, which they had enjoyed for three years, that, the illumination of those three days following the sudden contemplation of the glorified Lord, was to St. Paul.

Everything is connected together in this masterpiece of grace (1 Tim. i. 16). Without the external appearance, the previous moral process in Paul would have exhausted itself in vain efforts, and only resulted in a withering blight. And, on the contrary, without the preparatory process and the spiritual evolution which followed the appearance, it would have been with this as with that resurrection of which Abraham spoke, Luke xvi. 31: "If they hear not Moses and the prophets, neither would they believe though one rose from the dead." The moral assimilation being wanting, the

---

[1] Baur and his school have used the phrase *in me* to set aside the idea of an outward revelation in the matter of his conversion. Not only would this interpretation make Paul contradict himself, as we have shown, but, moreover, it mistakes the real bearing of the phrase *in me*. It denotes not the fact of the appearance, but the whole inner process connected with it, and which we have sought to reproduce in these pages. The *revelation of the Son* in Paul's heart is not identical with His visible appearing; it was the consequence of it.

[2] Elsewhere only in 2 Tim. ii. 8.

sight even of the Lord would have remained unproductive capital both for Paul and the world.

C. *His Apostleship*

St. Paul became an apostle at the same time as a believer. The exceptional contemporaneousness of the two facts arose from the mode of his conversion. He himself points to this feature in 1 Cor. ix. 16, 17. He did not become an apostle of Jesus, like the Twelve, after being voluntarily attached to Him by faith, and in consequence of a freely-accepted call. He was taken suddenly from a state of open enmity. The divine act whereby he was made a believer resulted from the choice by which God had designated him to the apostleship.

The apostleship of St. Paul lasted from twenty-eight to thirty years; and as we have seen that Paul had probably reached his thirtieth year at the time of his conversion, it follows that this radical crisis must have divided his life into two nearly equal parts of twenty-eight to thirty years each.

Paul's apostolic career embraces three periods: the first is a time of preparation; it lasted about *seven* years. The second is the period of his active apostleship, or his three great missionary journeys; it covers a space of *fourteen* years. The third is the time of his imprisonments. It includes the two years of his imprisonment at Cæsarea, and the two of his captivity at Rome, with the half-year's voyage which separated the two periods; perhaps there should be added to these *four* or *five* years a last time of liberty, extending to one or *two* years, closing with a last imprisonment. Anyhow, the limit of this third period is the martyrdom which Paul underwent at Rome, after those five or seven years of final labor.

1

An apostle by right, from the days following the crisis at Damascus, Paul did not enter on the full exercise of his commission all at once, but gradually. His call referred specially to the conversion of the Gentiles. The tenor of the message which the Lord had addressed to him by the mouth of Ananias was this: "Thou shalt bear my name before the Gentiles, and their kings, and the children of Israel" (Acts ix. 15). This last particular was designedly placed at the close. The Jews, without being excluded from Paul's work, were not the first object of his mission.

In point of fact, it was with Israel that he must commence his work, and the evangelization of the Jews continued with him to the end to be the necessary transition to that of the Gentiles. In every Gentile city where Paul opens a mission, he begins with preaching the gospel to the Jews in the synagogue. There he meets with the proselytes from among the Gentiles, and these form the bridge by which he reaches the purely Gentile population. Thus there is repeated on a small scale, at every step of his career, the course taken on a grand scale by the preaching of the gospel over the world. In the outset, as the historical foundation of the work of Christianization, we have the foundation of the Church in Israel by the labors of Peter at Jerusalem and in Palestine—such is the subject of the first part of the Acts (i.-xii.); then, like a house built on this foundation, we have the establishment of the church among the Gentiles by Paul's labors—such is the subject of the second part of the Acts (xiii.-xxviii.).

Notwithstanding this, Baur has alleged that the course ascribed to Paul by the author of the Acts, in describing his foundations among the Gentiles, is historically inadmissible, because it speaks of exaggerated pains taken to conciliate the Jews, such as were very improbable on the part of a man like St. Paul.[1] But the account in the Acts is fully confirmed on

[1] *Paulus*, 2d ed. I. pp. 368, 369.

14 / Introduction

this point by Paul's own declarations (Rom. i. 16, ii. 9, 10). In these passages the apostle says, when speaking of the two great facts, salvation in Christ and final judgment : "To the Jews *first.*" He thus himself recognizes the right of priority which belongs to them in virtue of their special calling, and of the theocratic preparation which they had enjoyed. From the first to the last day of his labors, Paul ceased not to pay homage in word and deed to the prerogative of Israel.

There is nothing wonderful, therefore, in the fact related in the Acts (x. 20), that Paul began immediately to preach in the Jewish synagogues of Damascus. Thence he soon extended his labors to the surrounding regions of Arabia. According to Gal. i. 17, 18, he consecrated three whole years to those remote lands. The Acts sum up this period in the vague phrase "many days" (ix. 23). For the apostle it doubtless formed a time of mental concentration and personal communion with the Lord, which may be compared with the years which the apostles passed with their Master during His earthly ministry. But we are far from seeing in this sojourn a time of external inactivity. The relation between Paul's words, Gal. i. 16, and the following verses, does not permit us to doubt that Paul also consecrated these years to preaching. The whole first chapter of the Epistle to the Galatians rests on the idea that Paul did not wait to begin preaching the gospel till he had conferred on the subject with the apostles at Jerusalem, and received their instructions. On the contrary, he had already entered on his missionary career when for the first time he met with Peter.

After his work in Arabia, Paul returned to Damascus, where his activity excited the fury of the Jews to the highest pitch. The city was at that time under the power of Aretas, king of Arabia. We do not know the circumstances which had withdrawn it for the time from the Roman dominion, nor how many years this singular state of things lasted. These are interesting archæological questions which have not yet found their entire solution. Nevertheless, the fact of the temporary possession of Damascus by King Aretas or Hareth at this very time cannot be called in question, even apart from the history of the Acts.[1]

At the close of this first period of evangelization, Paul felt the need of making the personal acquaintance of Peter. With this view he repaired to Jerusalem. He stayed with him fifteen days. It was not that Paul needed to learn the gospel in the school of this apostle. If such had been his object, he would not have delayed three whole years to come seeking this instruction. But we can easily understand how important it was for him at length to confer with the principal witness of the earthly life of Jesus, though he knew that he had received from the Lord Himself the knowledge of the gospel (Gal. i. 11, 12). What interest must he have felt in the authentic and detailed account of the facts of the ministry of Jesus, an account which he could not obtain with certainty except from such lips ! Witness the facts which he recites in 1 Cor. xv., and the sayings of our Lord which he quotes here and there in his Epistles and discourses (comp. 1 Cor. vii. 10 ; Acts xx. 35).

For two weeks, then, Paul conferred with the apostles (Acts ix. 27, 28) ; the indefinite phrase : *the apostles,* used in the Acts, denotes, according to the more precise account given in the Epistle to the Galatians, Peter and James. Paul's intention was to remain some time at Jerusalem ; for, notwithstanding the risk which he ran, it seemed to him that the testimony of the former persecutor would produce more effect here than anywhere else. But God would not have the instrument which He had prepared so carefully for the salvation of the Gentiles to be violently broken by the rage of the Jews, and to share the lot of the dauntless Stephen. A vision of the

[1] The fact is established by the interruption of the Roman coins of Damascus under Caligula and Claudius, and by the existence of a coin of this city stamped "of Aretas the Philhellene" (see Renan, *Les Apôtres,* p. 175).

Lord, which Paul had in the temple, warned him to leave the city immediately (Acts xxii. 17 et seq.). The apostles conducted him to the coast at Cesarea. Thence he repaired—the history in the Acts does not say how (ix. 30), but from Gal. i. 21 we should conclude that it was by land—to Syria, and thence to Tarsus, his native city ; and there, in the midst of his family, he awaited new directions from the Lord.

He did not wait in vain. After the martyrdom of Stephen, a number of believers from Jerusalem, from among the Greek-speaking Jews (*the Hellenists*), fleeing from the persecution which raged in Palestine, had emigrated to Antioch, the capital of Syria. In their missionary zeal they had overstepped the limit which had been hitherto observed by the preachers of the gospel, and addressed themselves to the Greek population.[1] It was the first time that Christian effort made way for itself among Gentiles properly so called. Divine grace accompanied the decisive step. A numerous and lively church, in which a majority of Greek converts were associated with Christians of Jewish origin, arose in the capital of Syria. In the account given of the founding of this important church by the author of the Acts (xi. 20-24), there is a charm, a fascination, a freshness, which are to be found only in pictures drawn from nature.

The apostles and the church of Jerusalem, taken by surprise, sent Barnabas to the spot to examine more closely this unprecedented movement, and give needed direction. Then Barnabas, remembering Saul, whom he had previously introduced to the apostles at Jerusalem, went in search of him to Tarsus, and brought him to this field of action, worthy as it was of such a laborer. Between the church of Antioch and Paul the apostle there was formed from that hour a close union, the magnificent fruit of which was the evangelization of the world.

After laboring together for a whole year at Antioch, Barnabas and Saul were sent to Jerusalem to carry aid to the poor believers of that city. This journey, which coincided with the death of the last representative of the national sovereignty of Israel, Herod Agrippa (Acts xii.), certainly took place in the year 44 ; for this is the date assigned by the detailed account of Josephus to the death of this sovereign. It was also about this time, under Claudius, that the great famine took place with which this journey was connected, according to the Acts. Thus we have here one of the surest dates in the life of St. Paul. No doubt this journey to Jerusalem is not mentioned in the first chapter of Galatians among the sojourns made by the apostle in the capital which took place shortly after his conversion, and to explain this omission some have thought it necessary to suppose that Barnabas arrived alone at Jerusalem, while Paul stayed by the way. The text of the Acts is not favorable to this explanation (Acts xi. 30, xii. 25). The reason of Paul's silence about this journey is simpler, for the context of Gal. i., rightly understood, does not at all demand, as has been imagined, the enumeration of *all* the apostle's journeys to Jerusalem in those early times. It was enough for his purpose to remind his readers that his *first* meeting with the apostles had not taken place till long after he had begun his preaching of the gospel. And this object was fully gained by stating the date of his *first* stay at Jerusalem subsequent to his conversion. And if he also mentions a later journey (chap. ii.), the fact does not show that it was the second journey absolutely speaking. He speaks of this new journey (the third in reality), only because it had an altogether peculiar importance in the question which formed the object of his letter to the churches of Galatia.

---

[1] The received reading : *to the Hellenists*, absolutely falsifies the meaning of the passage (Acts xi. 20). It has already been corrected in our translations in the English *Grecians*, should be *Greeks*; the reading should be : *to the Hellenes*, according to the oldest manuscripts (*Sinaiticus, Alexandrinus*, etc.), and according to the context, which imperatively demands the mention of a fact of a wholly new character.

2

The second part of the apostle's career includes his three great missionary journeys, with the visits to Jerusalem which separate them. With these journeys there is connected the composition of Paul's most important letters. The fourteen years embraced in this period must, from what has been said above, be reckoned from the year 44 (the date of Herod Agrippa's death) or a little later. Thus the end of the national royal house of Israel coincided with the beginning of the mission to the Gentiles. Theocratic particularism beheld the advent of Christian universalism.

Paul's three missionary journeys have their common point of departure in Antioch. This capital of Syria was the cradle of the mission to the Gentiles, as Jerusalem had been that of the mission to Israel. After each of his journeys Paul takes cares to clasp by a journey to Jerusalem the bond which should unite those two works among Gentiles and Jews. So deeply did he himself feel the necessity of binding the churches which he founded in Gentile lands to the primitive apostolic church, that he went the length of saying: "lest by any means I had run, or should run, *in vain*" (Gal. ii. 2).

The first journey was made with Barnabas. It did not embrace any very considerable geographical space; it extended only to the island of Cyprus, and the provinces of Asia Minor situated to the north of that island. The chief importance of this journey lies in the missionary principle which it inaugurates in the history of the world. It is to be observed that it is from this time Saul begins to bear the name of *Paul* (Acts xiii. 9). It has been supposed that this change was a mark of respect paid to the proconsul Sergius Paulus, converted in Cyprus, the first-fruits of the mission to the Gentiles. But Paul had nothing of the courtier about him. Others have found in the name an allusion to the spirit of humility—either to his small stature, or to the last place occupied by him among the apostles (παῦλος, in the sense of the Latin *paulus, paululus, the little*). This is ingenious, but far-fetched. The true explanation is probably the following: Jews travelling in a foreign country liked to assume a Greek or Roman name, and readily chose the one whose sound came nearest to their Hebrew name. A *Jesus* became a *Jason*, a *Joseph* a *Hegesippus*, a *Dosthai* a *Dositheus*, an *Eliakim* an *Alkimos*. So, no doubt, Saul became Paul.

Two questions arise in connection with those churches of southern Asia Minor founded in the course of the first journey. Are we, with some writers (Niemeyer, Thiersch, Hausrath, Renan in *Saint Paul*, pp. 51 and 52), to regard these churches as the same which Paul afterward designates by the name of churches of Galatia, and to which he wrote the *Epistle to the Galatians* (Gal. i. 2; 1 Cor. xvi. 2)? It is certain that the southern districts of Asia Minor, Lycaonia, Pisidia, etc., which were the principal theatre of this first journey, belonged at that time, administratively speaking (with the exception of Pamphylia), to the Roman province of Galatia. This name, which had originally designated the northern countries of Asia Minor, separated from the Black Sea by the narrow province of Paphlagonia, had been extended by the Romans a short time previously to the districts situated more to the south, and consequently to the territories visited by Paul and Barnabas. And as it cannot be denied that Paul sometimes uses official names, he might have done so also in the passages referred to. This question has some importance, first with a view to determining the date of the Epistle to the Galatians, and then in relation to other questions depending on it. According to our view, the opinion which has just been mentioned falls to the ground before insurmountable difficulties.

1. The name Galatia is nowhere applied in Acts xiii. and xiv. to the the-

atre of the first mission. It does not appear till later, in the account of the second mission, and only after Luke has spoken of the visit made by Paul and Silas to the churches founded on occasion of the first (xvi. 5). When Luke names Phrygia and *Galatia* in ver. 6, it is unquestionable that he is referring to different provinces from those in which lay the churches founded during the first journey, and which are mentioned vv. 1–5.

2. In 1 Peter i. 1, Galatia is placed between Pontus and Cappadocia, a fact which forbids us to apply the term to regions which are altogether southern.

3. But the most decisive reason is this: Paul reminds the Galatians (iv. 13) that it was sickness which forced him to stay among them, and which thus led to the founding of their churches. How is it possible to apply this description to Paul's first mission, which was expressly undertaken with the view of evangelizing the countries of Asia, whither he repaired with Barnabas?

From all this it follows that Paul and Luke used the term Galatia in its original and popular [1] sense ; that the apostle did not visit the country thus designated till the beginning of his second journey, and that, consequently, the Epistle to the Galatians was not written, as Hausrath thinks, in the course of the second journey, but during the third, since this Epistle assumes that *two* sojourns in Galatia had taken place previously to its composition.[2]

A second much more important question arises when we inquire what exactly was the theoretic teaching and the missionary practice of Paul at this period. Since Rückert's time, many theologians, Reuss, Sabatier, Hausrath, Klöpper, etc., think that Paul had not yet risen to the idea of the abrogation of the law by the gospel.[3] Hausrath even alleges that the object which Paul and Barnabas had in Asia Minor was not at all to convert the Gentiles—were there not enough of them, says he, in Syria and Cilicia?—but that their simple object was to announce the advent of the Messiah to the *Jewish* communities which had spread to the interior. He holds that it was the unexpected opposition which their preaching met with on the part of the Jews, which led the two missionaries to address themselves to the Gentiles, and to suppress in their interest the rite of circumcision. To prove this view of the apostle's teaching in those earliest times, there are alleged : (1) the fact of the circumcision of Timothy at this very date (Acts xvi. 3) ; (2) these words in Gal. v. 11 : " If I *yet* preach circumcision, why do I *yet* suffer persecution ? Then is the offence of the cross ceased ;" (3) the words, 2 Cor. v. 16 : " Yea, though we have known Christ after the flesh, we know Him in that manner *no more.*"[4]

Let us first examine the view of Hausrath. Is it credible that the church of Antioch, itself composed chiefly of Christians of Greek origin and uncircumcised (comp. the very emphatic account of this fact, Acts xi. 20 et seq.), would have dreamt of drawing the limits supposed by this critic to the commission given to its messengers ? This would have been to deny the principle of its own foundation, the free preaching of the gospel to the *Greeks.* The step taken by this church was accompanied with very solemn circumstances (a revelation of the Holy Spirit, fasting and prayer on the part of the whole church, an express consecration by the laying on of hands, Acts xiii. 1 et seq.). Why all this, if there had not been the consciousness that they were doing a work exceptionally important and in certain re-

---

[1] "The inscriptions," says Renan himself, "prove that the old names remained " (p. 50).
[2] "Ye know how on account of sickness I preached the gospel unto you *at the first*" (πρότερον, the first of two times).
[3] Reuss, *Hist. de la théol. chrét.* I. 345 et seq. ; Sabatier, *L'Apôtre Paul,* pp. 3–6. Renan in *Saint Paul,* p. 72, says : "Paul, who *in the earliest part of his preaching,* as it seems, preached circumcision, *now* declared it useless.
[4] Comp. especially Klöpper, *Das zweyte Sendschreiben an die Gemeinde zu Korinth,* pp. 286–297.

spects new ? And instead of being a step in advance, this work would be in reality, on the view before us, a retrograde step as compared with what had already taken place at Antioch itself ! The study of the general course of the history of the Acts, and of the progress which it is meant to prove, forces us to the conclusion that things had come to a decisive moment. The church undertook for the first time, and with a full consciousness of the gravity of its procedure, the conquest of the Gentile world.

The question, what at that time was the apostle's view in regard to the abrogation of the law, presents two aspects, which it is important to study separately. What did he think of subjecting the Gentiles to the institutions of the law ? and did he still hold its validity for believing Jews ?

According to Gal. i. 16, he knew positively from the first day that if God had revealed *His Son* to him in so extraordinary a way, it was " that he might proclaim Him *among the Gentiles.*" This conviction did not follow his conversion ; it accompanied it. Why should the Lord have called a new apostle, in a way so direct and independent of the Twelve, if it had not been with a view to a new work destined to complete theirs ? It is with a deliberate purpose that Paul, in the words quoted, does not say *the Christ,* but *His Son.* This latter expression is tacitly contrasted with the name *Son of David,* which designates the Messiah only in His particular relation to the Jewish people.

Now it cannot be admitted that Paul, knowing his mission to be destined to the Gentiles, would have commenced it with the idea of subjecting them to the discipline of the law, and that it was not till later that he modified this point of view. According to Gal. i. 1 and 11-19, the gospel which he now preaches was taught him *by the revelation of Jesus Christ,* and without human interposition. And when did this revelation take place ? Ver. 15 tells us clearly : " when it pleased God to reveal His Son to him," that is to say, at the time of his conversion. His mode of preaching the gospel therefore dates from that point, and we cannot hold, without contradicting his own testimony, that any essential modification took place in the contents of his preaching between the days following his conversion and the time when he wrote the Epistle to the Galatians. Such a supposition, especially when an Epistle is in question in which he directly opposes the subjection of the Gentiles to circumcision, would imply a reticence unworthy of his character. He must have said : It is true, indeed, that at the first I did not think and preach on this point as I do now ; but I afterward changed my view. Facts on all sides confirm the declaration of the apostle. How, if during the first period of his apostleship he had circumcised the Gentile converts, could he have taken Titus *uncircumcised* to Jerusalem ? How could the emissaries who had come from that city to Antioch have found a whole multitude of believers on whom they sought to impose circumcision ? How would the Christians of Cilicia, who undoubtedly owed their entrance into the church to Paul's labors during his stay at Tarsus, have still needed to be reassured by the apostles in opposition to those who wished to subject them to circumcision (Acts xv. 23, 24) ? Peter in the house of Cornelius does not think of imposing this rite (Acts x. and xi.) ; and Paul, we are to suppose, was less advanced than his colleague, and still less so than the evangelists who founded the church of Antioch !

It is more difficult to ascertain precisely what Paul thought at the beginning of his apostleship as to the abolition or maintenance of the Mosaic law for believing Jews. Rationally speaking, it is far from probable that so sequacious a thinker as St. Paul, after the crushing experience which he had just had of the powerlessness of the law either to justify or sanctify man, was not led to the conviction of the uselessness of legal ordinances for the salvation not only of Gentiles, but of Jews. This logical conclusion is confirmed by an express declaration of the apostle. In the Epistle to the

Galatians, ii. 18-20, there are found the words : "*I through the law* am dead *to the law*, that I may live unto God ; I am crucified with Christ." If it was *through* the law that he died *to* the law, this inner crisis cannot have taken place till the close of his life under the law. It was therefore in the very hour when the law finished its office as a schoolmaster to bring him to Christ, that this law lost its religious value for his conscience, and that, freed from its yoke, he began to *live* really *unto God* in the faith of Christ crucified. This saying, the utterance of his inmost consciousness, supposes no interval between the time of his personal breaking with the law (a death) and the beginning of his new life. His inward emancipation was therefore one of the elements of his conversion.[1] It seems to be thought that the idea of the abrogation of the law was, at the time of Saul's conversion, a quite unheard-of notion. But what then had been the cause of Stephen's death ? He had been heard to say "that Jesus of Nazareth would destroy this temple and change the institutions which Moses had delivered" (Acts vi. 13, 14). Among the accusers of Stephen who repeated such sayings, Saul himself was one. Stephen, the *Hellenist*, had thus reached before Paul's conversion the idea of the abolition of the law which very naturally connected itself with the fact of the destruction of the temple, announced, as was notorious, by Jesus. Many prophetic sayings must have long before prepared thoughtful minds for this result.[2] Certain of the Lord's declarations also implied it more or less directly.[3] And now by a divine irony Saul the executioner was called to assert and realize the programme traced by his victim !

The gradual manner in which the Twelve had insensibly passed from the bondage of the law to the personal school of Christ, had not prepared them so completely for such a revolution. And now is the time for indicating the true difference which separated them from Paul, one of the most difficult of questions. They could not fail to expect as well as Stephen and Paul, in virtue of the declarations already quoted, the abrogation of the institutions of the law. But they had not perceived in the cross, as Paul did (Gal. ii. 19, 20), the principle of this emancipation. They expected some external event which would be the signal of this abolition, as well as of the passage from the present to the future economy ; the glorious appearing of Christ, for example, which would be as it were the miraculous counterpart of the Sinaitic promulgation of the law. From this point of view it is easy to explain their expectant attitude as they considered the progress of Paul's work. On the other hand, we can understand why he, notwithstanding his already formed personal conviction, did not feel himself called to insist on the practical application of the truth which he had come to possess in so extraordinary a way. The Twelve were the recognized and titled heads of the church so long as this remained almost wholly the Jewish-Christian church founded by them. Paul understood the duty of accommodating his step to theirs. So he did at Jerusalem, in the great council of which we are about to speak, when he accepted the compromise which guarded the liberty of the Gentiles, but supported the observances of the law for Christians who had come from Judaism. And later still, when he had founded his own churches in the Gentile world, he did not cease to take account with religious respect of Jewish-Christian scruples relating to the Mosaic law. But it was with him a matter of charity, as he has explained 1 Cor. ix. 19-22 ; and this wise mode of action does not authorize the supposition that at any time after his conversion his teaching was contrary to the principle so exactly and logically expressed by him : " Christ is the end of the law" (Rom. x. 4).

The circumcision of Timothy in Paul's second journey, far from betray-

---

[1] The same result is reached by analyzing the passage Phil. iii. 4-8.
[2] Jer. xxxi. 31 et seq. ; Mal. i. 11, etc.   [3] Mark ii. 18, vii. 15, 16, xiii. 1, 2, etc.

ing any hesitation in his mind on this point, is wholly in favor of our view. Indeed, Paul did not decide on this step, because he still regarded circumcision as obligatory on believing Jews. The point in question was not Timothy's salvation, but the influence which this young Christian might exercise on the Jews who surrounded him : " Paul took and circumcised him," says the narrative, "*because of the Jews who were in those regions.*" If this act had been dictated by a strictly religious scruple, Paul must have carried it out much earlier, at the time of Timothy's baptism. The latter, indeed, was already a Christian when Paul arrived at Lystra the second time and circumcised him. ("*There was there a disciple,*" we read in Acts xvi. 1.) At the beginning of the second journey, Timothy was therefore a believer and a member of the church, though not circumcised. This fact is decisive. It was precisely because the legal observance had become in Paul's estimation a matter religiously indifferent, that he could act in this respect with entire liberty, and put himself, if he thought good, " under the law with those who were under the law, that he might gain the more." [1] Such was the course he followed on this occasion.

The words, Gal. v. 11 : " If I *yet* preach circumcision, why do I *yet* suffer persecution ?" on which Reuss mainly supports his view, do not warrant the conclusion drawn from them by means of a false interpretation. Paul is supposed to be alluding to a calumnious imputation made by his adversaries, who, it is said, led the Galatians to believe that previously, and elsewhere than among them, Paul had been quite ready to impose circumcision on his Gentile converts. Paul, according to the view in question, is replying to this charge, that if to the present hour he *yet* upheld circumcision, as he had really done in the earliest days after his conversion, the Jews would not continue to persecute him as they were still doing. But the reasoning of Paul, thus understood, would assume a fact notoriously false, namely, that he had only begun to be persecuted by the Jews after he had ceased to make the obligatoriness of circumcision one of the elements of his preaching of the gospel. Now it is beyond dispute that persecution broke out against Paul immediately after his conversion, and even at Damascus. It was the same at Jerusalem soon after.[2] It is therefore absolutely impossible that Paul could have thought for a single instant of explaining the persecutions to which he was subjected by the Jews, by the fact that he had *ceased* at a given point of his ministry to preach circumcision, till then imposed by him. Besides, if Paul had really been accused in Galatia of having acted and taught there differently from what he had done previously and everywhere else, he could not have confined himself to replying thus in passing, and by a simple allusion thrown in at the end of his letter, to so serious a charge. He must have explained himself on this main point in the beginning in chap. i. and ii., where he treats of all the questions relating to his person and apostleship.

We therefore regard the proposed interpretation as inadmissible. The change of which the apostle speaks is not one which had taken place in his system of preaching ; it is a change which he might freely introduce into it now if he wished, and one by which he would immediately cause the persecution to which he was subjected to cease. " If I would consent to join to my preaching of the gospel that of circumcision, for which I was fanatically zealous during the time of my Pharisaism, the persecution with which the Jews assail me would instantly cease. Thereby the offence of the cross would no longer exist in their minds. Transformed into an auxiliary of Judaism, the cross itself would be tolerated and even applauded by my adversaries." What does this signify ? The apostle means, that if he

[1] 1 Cor. ix. 19-22.—The situation was evidently quite different when it was attempted to *constrain* him to circumcise Titus at Jerusalem. Here the question of *principle* was at stake. In this position there could be no question of concession.
[2] Acts ix. 23-29.

consented to impose circumcision on those of the Gentiles whom he converted by the preaching of the cross, the Jews would immediately applaud his mission. For his conquests in Gentile lands would thus become the conquests of Judaism itself. In fact, it would please the Jews mightily to see multitudes of heathen entering the church on condition that all those new entrants by baptism became at the same time members of the Israelitish people by circumcision. On this understanding it would be the Jewish people who would really profit by Paul's mission ; it would become nothing more than the conquest of the world by Israel and for Israel. The words of Paul which we are explaining are set in their true light by others which we read in the following chapter (Gal. vi. 12) : "As many as desire to make a fair show in the flesh, they constrain you to be circumcised, only that they may not be persecuted for the cross of Christ." Certain preachers therefore, Paul's rivals in Galatia, were using exactly the cowardly expedient which Paul here rejects, in order to escape persecution from the Jews. To the preaching of the cross to the Gentiles they added the obligatoriness of circumcision, and the Jews easily tolerated the former in consideration of the advantage which they derived from the latter. This anti-Christian estimate was probably that of those intriguers at Jerusalem whom Paul calls, Gal. ii., *false brethren unawares brought in*. Christianity, with its power of expansion, became in their eyes an excellent instrument for the propagation of Judaism. So we find still at the present day many liberalized Jews applauding the work of the Christian church in the heathen world. They consider Christianity to be the providential means for propagating Israelitish monotheism, as paving the way for the moral reign of Judaism throughout the whole world. And they wait with folded arms till *we* shall have put the world under *their* feet. The difference between them and St. Paul's adversaries is merely that the latter allowed themselves to act so because of the theocratic promises, while modern Jews do so in name of the certain triumph to be achieved by their purely rational religion.

Thus the words of Paul, rightly understood, do not in the least imply a change which had come over his teaching in regard to the maintenance of circumcision and the law.

As to the passage 2 Cor. v. 16, we have already seen that the phrase : *knowing Christ no more after the flesh*, does not at all refer to a new view posterior to his conversion, but describes the transformation which had passed over his conception of the Messiah in that very hour.

We are now at the important event of the *council of Jerusalem*, which stands between the first and second journey.

Subsequently to their mission to Cyprus and Asia Minor, which probably lasted some years, Paul and Barnabas returned to Antioch, and there resumed their evangelical work. But this peaceful activity was suddenly disturbed by the arrival of certain persons from Jerusalem. These declared to the believing Gentiles that salvation would not be assured to them in Christ unless they became members of the Israelitish people by circumcision. To understand so strange an allegation, we must transport ourselves to the time when it was given forth. To whom had the Messianic promises been addressed ? To the Jewish people, and to them alone. Therefore the members of this people alone had the right to appropriate them ; and if the Gentiles wished to share them, the only way open to them was to become Jews. The reasoning seemed faultless. On the other hand, Paul understood well that it cut short the evangelization of the Gentile world, which would never be made Christian if in order to become so it was first necessary to be incorporated with the Jewish nation. But more than all else, the argument appeared to him to be radically vicious, because the patriarchal promises, though addressed to the Jews, had a much wider range, and really concerned the whole world.

Baur asserted that those who maintained the particularistic doctrine at

22 / Introduction

Antioch represented the opinion of the Twelve, and Renan has made himself the champion of this view in France. Baur acknowledges that the narrative of the Acts excludes, it is true, such a supposition. For this book expressly ascribes the lofty pretensions in question to a retrograde party, composed of former Pharisees (Acts xv. 1–5), and puts into the mouth of the apostles the positive disavowal of such conduct. But the German critic boldly solves this difficulty, by saying that the author of the Acts has, as a result of reflection, falsified the history with the view of disguising the conflict which existed between Paul and the Twelve, and of making the later church believe that these personages had lived on the best understanding. What reason can Baur allege in support of this severe judgment passed on the author of the Acts? He rests it on the account of the same event given by Paul himself in the beginning of Gal. ii., and seeks to prove that this account is incompatible with that given in the Acts. As the question is of capital importance in relation to the beginnings of Christianity, and even for the solution of certain critical questions relative to the Epistle to the Romans, we must study it here more closely. We begin with the account of Paul in Galatians; we shall afterward compare it with that of the Acts.

According to the former (Gal. ii), in consequence of the dispute which arose at Antioch, Paul, acting under guidance from on high, determined to go and have the question of the circumcision of the Gentiles decided at Jerusalem by the apostles (ver. 1). "A proof," observes Reuss, "that Paul was not afraid of being contradicted by the heads of the mother church."[1] This observation seems to us to proceed on a sounder psychology than that of Renan, who asserts, on the contrary, that at Antioch "there was a distrust of the mother church." It was in the same spirit of confidence that Paul resolved to take with him to Jerusalem a young Gentile convert named Titus. The presence of this uncircumcised member in the church assemblies was meant to assert triumphantly the principle of liberty. This bold step would have been imprudence itself, if, as Renan asserts, the church of Jerusalem had been "hesitating, or favorable to the most retrograde party."

Paul afterward (ver. 2) speaks of a conference which he had with the persons of most repute in the apostolic church—these were, as we learn from the sequel, Peter and John the apostles, and James the Lord's brother, the head of the council of elders at Jerusalem; Paul explained to them in detail (ἀνεθέμην) the gospel as he preached it among the Gentiles, free from the enforcement of circumcision and legal ceremonies generally. He completes the account, ver. 6, by subjoining that his three interlocutors found nothing to add to his mode of teaching (οὐδὲν προσανέθεντο). In Greek, the relation between this term *added* and that which precedes (*explained*) is obvious at a glance. Paul's teaching appeared to them perfectly sufficient. Paul interrupts himself at ver. 3, to mention in passing a corroborative and significant fact. The *false brethren brought in*, maintained that Titus should not be admitted to the church without being circumcised. In other circumstances, Paul, in accordance with his principle of absolute liberty in regard to external rites (1 Cor. ix. 20), might have yielded to such a demand. But in this case he refused; for the question of principle being involved, it was impossible for him to give way. Titus was admitted as an uncircumcised member. True, Renan draws from the same text an entirely opposite conclusion. According to him, Paul yielded for the time, and Titus underwent circumcision. This interpretation, which was Tertullian's, is founded on a reading which has no authorities on its side except the most insufficient;[2] as little can it be maintained in

---

[1] *Hist. de la Théol. chrét.* II. p. 310.
[2] The omission of οὐδὲ, ver. 5, in the *Cantabrigiensis*, two Codd. of the old Latin translation, and in some Fathers, exclusively Greco-Latin authorities.

view of the context. As to the apostles, they must necessarily have supported Paul's refusal, otherwise a rupture would have been inevitable. But not only were the bonds between them not broken ; they were, on the contrary, strengthened. Paul's apostolic call, with a view to the Gentiles, was expressly recognized by those three men, the reputed heads of the church (vv. 7-9) ; Peter in his turn was unanimously recognized as called of God to direct the evangelization of the Jews. Then the five representatives of the whole church gave one another the *hand of fellowship*, thus to seal the unity of the work amid the diversity of domains. Would this mutual recognition and this ceremony of association have been possible between Paul and the Twelve, if the latter had really maintained the doctrine of the subjection of the Gentiles to circumcision ? St. Paul in the Epistle to the Galatians (i. 8) makes this declaration : " Though we or an angel from heaven preach any other gospel unto you than that which we have preached unto you, let him be accursed !" Now the contents of this preaching of the gospel by Paul are also found thus stated in the Epistle (vv. 2–4) : " Behold, I say unto you, that if ye be circumcised, Christ shall profit you nothing." And he would have recognized, he, Paul, as coming from God equally with his own, the apostleship of Peter, and the teaching of Peter (ii. 7, 8), of Peter preaching circumcision ! The result flowing from Paul's narrative is not doubtful. The liberty of the Gentiles in respect of circumcision was expressly recognized at Jerusalem by the apostles and the church. The narrow Judaizers alone persisted in their obstinacy, and formed a minority ever more and more hostile to this apostolic course.

It is less easy to know from Paul's account what was agreed on in regard to converts from among the Jews. The apostle's entire silence on this point leads us to suppose that the question was not once raised. Paul was too prudent to demand a premature solution on so delicate a point. His silence indicates that the old practice, according to which Jewish-Christians continued to observe the law, was tacitly maintained.

We pass now to the account given in Acts. Luke does not speak of the revelation which determined Paul to submit the question to the jurisdiction of the apostles. Natural as it is for Paul to mention this biographical detail, the explanation of its omission in a history of a more general character is equally easy.

Acts presents the picture of a plenary assembly of the church before which the question was discussed, especially by Peter and James. This account differs from that of Galatians, in which we read only of a private conference. Reuss does not think that this difference can be explained. But a private talk between the leaders of two negotiating parties does not exclude a public meeting in which all interested take part. After mentioning the exposition which he gave of his teaching, without saying exactly to whom, ver. 2, Paul adds an explanatory remark in the words : " and that *privately* to them which were of reputation." [1] By this remark it would seem that he desires tacitly to contrast the private conversation which he relates with some other and more general assembly which the reader might have in his mind while perusing his narrative. The conclusion was therefore prepared in the private conversation, and then solemnly confirmed in the plenary council. Luke's narrative is the complement of Paul's. The interest of Paul, in his attitude to the Galatians, was to prove the recognition of his gospel and apostleship by the very apostles who were being opposed to him ; hence the mention of the private conference. Luke, wishing to preserve the deeply interesting and precious document which emanated from the council of Jerusalem, required above all to narrate the latter.

[1] Δέ is here taken in the same exegetical sense as Rom. iii. 22 (*to wit*). This is also Baur's understanding.

According to Luke, the speeches of Peter and James conclude alike for the emancipation of the Gentiles. This is perfectly in keeping with the attitude ascribed to them by St. Paul : " *they added nothing* to my communication." James speaks of it in the Acts, at the close of his speech, as a matter of course, and about which there is no need of discussion, that as to the Christians of Jewish origin, the obligation to live conformably to the observances of the law remains as before. Now we have just seen that this is exactly what follows from Paul's silence on this aspect of the question.

Finally, in its letter to Gentile believers, the council asks them to abstain from three things, meats offered to idols, animals that have been strangled, and impurity (vv. 28, 29). Is not this demand in contradiction to the words of Paul : *they added nothing to me ?* No, for the apostolical letter in the Acts immediately adds : "From which things if ye keep yourselves, *ye shall do well.*" The phrase used would have been very different if it had been meant to express a condition of salvation added to Paul's teaching. The measure which is here called for is so on the ground of the interests of the church.

In fact, this was the price paid for union between the two parties of which Christendom was composed. Without the two former conditions, the life of Gentile believers continued, in the view of Jewish Christians, to be polluted with idolatry, and penetrated through and through with malign, and even diabolical influences.[1] As to the third demand, it figures here because impurity was generally considered among the Gentiles to be as indifferent, morally speaking, and consequently as allowable, as eating and drinking (1 Cor. vi. 12-14). And we can the better understand why licentiousness is specially mentioned in this passage, when we remember that the most shameless impurities had in a manner their obligatory and religious part in idolatrous worships.[2]

As to the delicate question whether this compromise should be merely temporary, or if it had a permanent value in the view of the church of Jerusalem, no one even thought of suggesting the alternative. They moved as the occasion demanded. Every one thought that he had fulfilled his task by responding to the necessities of the present situation. The really important fact was, that the emancipation of the Gentiles from legal observances was irrevocably recognized and proclaimed by the Jewish-Christian church. Paul might assuredly congratulate himself on such a result. For though Jewish believers remained still tacitly subject to the Mosaic ritual, no positive decision had been passed on the subject, and the apostle was too far-seeing not to understand what must eventually follow the liberty granted to the Gentiles. Once these were set free from the Mosaic discipline, it was thereby established that the Messianic salvation was not bound up with the institutions of the law. Entrance into the church was independent of incorporation with Israel. All that Paul desired was implicitly contained in this fact. Levitical ritual thus descended to the rank of a simple national custom. By remaining faithful to it, believing Jews kept up their union with the rest of the elect people, an indispensable condition of the mission to Israel, till the day when God, by a striking dispensation, should Himself put an end to the present order of things. Paul

---

[1] According to certain Jewish theories represented by the *Clementine Homilies* (viii. 15), animal food renders man ὁμοδίαιτος (*commensal*), the table companion of demons as well as paganism and its diabolical feasts. Blood in particular, as the vehicle of souls, must be carefully avoided.

[2] All that has been said with the view of identifying these three demands laid down at Jerusalem with the so-called *Noachian* commandments, as well as the conclusions drawn therefrom—for example, the assimilation of the new converts to the former Gentile proselytes (see Reuss especially—has not the slightest foundation in the text. One is forced, besides, by this parallel to give a distorted meaning to the word πορνεία, *unchastity*, as if in this decree it denoted marriages within certain degrees of relationship which were forbidden by the law and allowed in heathendom. But there is nothing here to warrant us in giving to this word so frequently used a different meaning from that which it has throughout the whole of the New Testament.

was too prudent not to content himself with such a result, the consequences of which the future could not fail to develop.

The conclusion to which we are thus brought, on this important and difficult question, is in its general features at one with that which has been recently stated by three men of undoubted scientific eminence, Weizsäcker, Harnack, and even Keim. The first, in his admirable treatise on the church of Corinth,[1] thus expresses himself on the question : " The apostles remained Jews, and confined themselves to the mission among the Jews. But they granted to Gentile Christianity so thorough a recognition, that we must conclude that their religious life had its centre no longer in the law, but in their faith as such. . . . In fact, Paul never reckoned the Twelve among his adversaries. He always distinguished them expressly from these, both before the conflict, by choosing them as arbiters, and after it" (Gal. ii.). Harnack, the man of our day who perhaps best knows the second century, thus expressed himself recently : " The apocalyptic writings are the last strongholds within which a once powerful party still intrenches itself, whose watchword was : either Jewish-Christian or Gentile-Christian (the Tübingen school). The influence of Jewish-Christianity on the catholic church in the course of formation, must henceforth be estimated at an almost inappreciable quantity."[2] Keim, in a recent work,[3] demonstrates the general harmony of the narratives given by Paul and Luke, except on one point (the conditions imposed on Gentile-Christians in the Acts, which he holds to be a gloss added to the original account) ; and he appreciates almost exactly as we do the mutual attitude of Paul and the Twelve. Impartial science thus returns to the verdict of old Irenæus : " The apostles granted us liberty, us Gentiles, referring us to the guidance of the Holy Spirit ; but they themselves conformed piously to the institutions of the law established by Moses."[4] The exposition of Renan, given under Baur's influence, is a mere fancy picture.

Returning to Antioch, Paul and Barnabas took with them Silas, one of the eminent men belonging to the church of Jerusalem, who was charged with delivering the reply of the council to the churches of Syria and Cilicia.[5] Soon afterward Paul set out with Silas on his *second missionary journey*, after separating from Barnabas on account of Mark, the cousin of the latter (Col. iv. 10.) The texts give no ground for supposing that this rupture took place on account of any difference of view regarding the law, as some critics of a fixed idea have recently alleged. Barnabas and Paul had gone hand in hand in the conferences at Jerusalem, and the sequel will prove that this harmony continued after their separation. Paul and Silas together crossed the interior of Asia Minor, visiting the churches founded in the course of the first journey. Paul's destination now was probably Ephesus, the religious and intellectual centre of the most cultivated part of Asia. But God had decided otherwise. The country whose hour had struck was Greece, not Asia Minor ; Paul understood this later. The two heralds of the gospel were arrested for some time, by an illness of St. Paul, in the regions of Galatia. This country, watered by the river Halys, was inhabited by the descendants of a party of Celts who had passed into Asia after the inroad of the Gauls into Italy and Greece, about 280 B.C. This illness led to the founding of the churches of Galatia (Gal. iv. 14). When they resumed their journey the two missionaries were

---

[1] *Jahrb. für deutsche Theologie*, 1876.
[2] *Theol. Literaturzeitung* (review of the publication of the Ascension of Isaiah, by Dillmann), 1877.
[3] *Aus dem Urchristenthum*, I. pp. 64-89.
[4] *Adv. Hær.* iii. 12. 15: *Gentibus quidem* (apostoli) *libere agere permittebant, concedentes nos spiritui sancto ; . . . ipsi religiose agebant circa dispositionem legis quæ est secundum Mosem.*
[5] The arguments of M. Renan (*Saint Paul*, p. 92) against the authenticity of this, the oldest document of the church, are too easily refuted to require that we should examine them in this sketch.

26 / Introduction

arrested in the work of preaching by some inward hindrance, which prevented them from working anywhere. They thus found themselves led without premeditation to Troas, on the Egean Sea. There the mystery was cleared up. Paul learned from a vision that he was to cross the sea, and, beginning with Macedonia, enter on the evangelization of Europe. He took this decisive step in company with Silas, young Timothy, whom he had associated with him in Lycaonia, and, finally, the physician Luke, who seems to have been at Troas at that very time. This is at least the most natural explanation of the form *we* which here meets us in the narrative of the Acts (xvi. 10). The same form ceases, then reappears later as the author of the narrative is separated from the apostle, or takes his place again in his company (xx. 5, xxi. 1 et seq., xxviii. 1 et seq.). Renan concludes from the passage, xvi. 10, without the least foundation, that Luke was of Macedonian extraction. We believe rather (comp. p. 15) that he was a native of Antioch. Such also is the tradition found in the *Clementine Recognitions* and in Eusebius.

In a short time there were founded in Macedonia the churches of Philippi, Amphipolis, Thessalonica, and Berea. St. Paul was persecuted in all these cities, generally at the instigation of the Jews, who represented to the Roman authorities that the Christ preached by him was a rival of Cæsar. Constantly driven forth by this persecution, he passed southward, and at length reached Athens. There he gave an account of his doctrine before the Areopagus. Thereafter he established himself at Corinth, and during a stay of about two years, he founded in the capital of Achaia one of his most flourishing churches. We may even conclude from the inscription of 2 Corinthians (i. 1 : " To the church of God which is at Corinth, with all the saints which are *in all Achaia*") that numerous Christian communities were formed in the country districts round the metropolis.

After having concluded this important work, the founding of the churches of Greece, Paul went up to Jerusalem. There is mention in the Acts of a vow fulfilled before his departure from Greece (xviii. 18). By whom ? By Aquila, Paul's companion ? So some commentators have held. But if Aquila is the nearest subject, Paul is the principal subject of the clause. Was the religious act called a vow contrary to the spirituality of the apostle ? Why should it have been so more than a promise or engagement (comp. 1 Tim. vi. 12–14) ? Anyhow, Acts xxi. shows us how he could find himself in a state of life so full of complications that Christian charity constrained him to find his way out of it by concessions of an external nature. From Jerusalem Paul went to Antioch, the cradle of the mission to the Gentiles.

Here we must place an incident, the character of which has been not less misrepresented by criticism than that of the conferences at Jerusalem. Peter was then beginning his missionary tours beyond Palestine ; he had reached Antioch. Barnabas, after visiting the Christians of Cyprus along with Mark, had also returned to this church. These two men at first made no scruple of visiting the Gentile members of the church, and eating with them both at private meals (as had been done before by Peter at the house of Cornelius) and at the love-feasts. This mode of acting was not strictly in harmony with the agreement at Jerusalem, according to which believers of Jewish origin were understood to keep the Mosaic law. But, following the example of Christ Himself, they thought that the *moral* duty of brotherly communion should, in a case of competing claims, carry it over *ritual* observance. Peter probably recalled such sayings of Jesus as these : " Not that which goeth into the man defileth the man, but that which goeth forth from the man ;" or, " Have ye not heard what David did when he was an hungered, and they that were with him . . .?" (Matt. xii. 1–4). Finally, might he not apply here the direction which he had received from above at the time of his mission to Cornelius (Acts x. 10 et seq.) ? As to Barnabas, since his mission in Asia, he must have been accustomed to subordinate Levitical prescriptions to the duty of communion with the Gentiles. Thus all went on to the general satisfaction, when there arrived at Antioch some believers of Jerusalem, sent by James. Their mission was, not to lay more burdens on the Gentiles, but to examine whether the conduct of Jewish-Christians continued true to the compromise made at Jerusalem. Now, according to the rigorous interpretation of that document, Peter and Barnabas, both of them Jews by birth, were at fault. They were therefore energetically recalled to order by the newcomers.

We know Peter's character from the Gospel history. He allowed himself to be intimidated. Barnabas, whose natural easiness of disposition appears in the indulgence he showed to his cousin Mark, could not resist the apostle's example. Both were carried the length of breaking gradually with the Gentile converts.

Here we have a palpable proof of the insufficiency of the compromise adopted by the council of Jerusalem, and can understand why Paul, while accepting it as a temporary expedient (Acts xvi. 4), soon let it fall into abeyance.[1] This agreement, which, while freeing the Gentiles from Mosaic observances, still kept Jewish Christians under the yoke of the law, was practicable no doubt in churches exclusively Jewish-Christian, like that of Jerusalem. But in churches like those of Syria, where the two elements were united, the rigorous observance of this agreement must result in an external separation of the two elements, and the disruption of the church. Was this really meant by James, from whom those people came ? If it is so, we ought to remember that James was the brother of Jesus, but not an apostle ; that blood relationship to the Lord was not by any means a guarantee of infallibility, and that Jesus, though He had appeared to James to effect his conversion, had not confided to him the direction of the church. He was raised to the head of the flock of Jerusalem—nothing more. But it is also possible that the newcomers had gone beyond their instructions. Paul instantly measured the bearing of the conduct of his two colleagues, and felt the necessity of striking a decisive blow. He had gained at Jerusalem the recognition of the liberty of the Gentiles. The moment seemed to him to have arrived for deducing all the practical consequences logically flowing from the decision which had been come to, and without which that decision became illusory. Insisting on the previous conduct of Peter himself at Antioch, he showed him his inconsistency. He who for weeks had eaten with the Gentiles and like them, was now for forcing them, unless they chose to break with him, to place themselves under the yoke of the law, a result which had certainly not been approved at Jerusalem ! Then Paul took advantage of this circumstance at last to develop openly the contents of the revelation which he had received, to wit, that the abrogation of the law is involved in principle in the fact of the cross when rightly understood, and that it is vain to wait for another manifestation of the divine will on this point : " I am crucified with Christ ; and by that very fact dead to the law and alive unto God " (Gal. ii. 19, 20). Baur and his school, and Renan with them, think that this conflict proves a contrariety of principles between the two apostles. But Paul's words imply the very reverse. He accuses Peter of not *walking uprightly*, according to the truth of the gospel—that is to say, of being carried away by the fear of man. This very rebuke proves that Paul ascribes to Peter a conviction in harmony with his own, simply accusing him as he does of being unfaithful to it in practice. It is the same with Barnabas. For Paul says of him, that he was carried away into the same *hypocrisy*. Thus

[1] This is one of the principal reasons for which M. Renan attacks its authenticity. The reason is not a solid one, as our account shows.

the incident related by Paul fully establishes the conclusion to which we had come, viz. that Peter did no more than Paul regard the observance of the law as a condition of salvation, even for the Jews. And it is evidently to draw this lesson from it that Paul has related the incident with so much detail. For what the disturbers of the Gentile Christian churches alleged was precisely the example and authority of the Twelve.

After this conflict the apostle entered on his *third journey*. This time he realized the purpose which he had formed when starting on his previous journey, that of settling at Ephesus, and carrying the gospel to the heart of the scientific and commercial metropolis of Asia Minor. He passed through Galatia. He found the churches of this country already disturbed by the solicitations of some Judaizing emissary, who had come no doubt from Antioch, and who by means of certain adepts sought to introduce circumcision and the other Mosaic rites among the Christians of the country. For the time being Paul allayed the storm, and, as Luke says (Acts xviii. 23), " he *strengthened* all the disciples" in Galatia and Phrygia. But this very word proves to us how much their minds had been shaken. At Ephesus there awaited him his faithful friends and fellow-workers, Aquila and his wife Priscilla ; they had left Corinth with him, and had settled in Asia undoubtedly to prepare for him. The two or three years which Paul passed at Ephesus form the culminating point of his apostolical activity. This time was in his life the counterpart of Peter's ministry at Jerusalem after Pentecost. The sacred writer himself seems in his narrative to have this parallel in view (comp. Acts xix. 11, 12 with v. 15, 16). A whole circle of flourishing churches, that very circle which is symbolically represented in the apocalyptic description by the image of seven golden candlesticks with the Lord standing in the midst of them, rises amid those idolatrous populations : Ephesus, Miletus, Smyrna, Laodicea, Hierapolis, Colosse, Thyatira, Philadelphia, Sardis, Pergamos, and other churches besides, mentioned in the writings of the second century. The work of Paul at this period was marked by such a display of the power of the Holy Spirit, that at the end of those few years paganism felt itself seriously threatened in those regions, as is proved by the tumult excited by the goldsmith Demetrius.

But this so fruitful period of missionary activity was at the same time the culminating point of his contention with his Judaizing adversaries. After his passage through Galatia they had redoubled their efforts in those regions. These persons, as we have seen, did not oppose the preaching of the cross. They even thought it well that Paul should Christianize the Gentile world, provided it were to the profit of Mosaism. In their view the law was the real end, the gospel the means. It was the reversal of the divine plan. Paul rejected the scheme with indignation, though it was extremely well fitted to reconcile hostile Jews to the preaching of Christ. Not being able to make him bend, they sought to undermine his authority. They decried him personally, representing him as a disciple of the apostles, who had subsequently lifted his heel against his masters. It is to this charge that Paul replies in the first two chapters of the Epistle to the Galatians. Next, they maintained the permanence of the law. Such is the doctrine which Paul overthrows in chap. iii. and iv., by showing the temporary and purely preparatory character of the Mosaic dispensation. Finally, they denied that a doctrine severed from all law could secure the moral life of its adherents. Such is the subject of the last two chapters, which show how man's sanctification is provided for by the life-giving operation of the Holy Spirit, the consummation of justification, much better than by his subjection to legal prohibitions. This letter was written shortly after Paul's arrival at Ephesus (comp. the phrase : *so soon*, i. 6). The passage, 1 Cor. xvi. 1, seems to prove that it succeeded in re-establishing the authority of the apostle and the supremacy of the gospel in Galatia.

But the Judaizing emissaries followed Paul at every step. Macedonia does not seem to have presented a favorable soil for their attempts; they therefore threw themselves upon Achaia. They were careful here not to speak of circumcision or prescriptions about food. They knew that they had to do with Greeks; they sought to flatter their philosophical and literary tastes. A speculative gospel was paraded before the churches. Next, doubts were sown as to the reality of the apostleship of Paul, and by and by even as to the uprightness and purity of his character. The First Epistle to the Corinthians gives us all throughout, as Weizsäcker has well shown, the presentiment of a threatening storm, but one which the apostle seeks to prevent from bursting. Severe allusions are not wanting; but the didactic tone immediately becomes again the prevailing one. It is in the second letter that the full violence of the struggle is revealed. This letter contains numerous allusions to certain personal encounters of the utmost gravity, but posterior to the sending of the first. It obliges the attentive reader to suppose a sojourn made by Paul at Corinth *between* our two letters preserved in the canon, and even a lost intermediate letter posterior to this visit.[1] The interval between the dates of First and Second Corinthians must, if it is so, have been more considerable than is usually held; the general chronology of Paul's life does not, as we shall see, contradict this view. The lost letter intermediate between our two canonical Epistles must have been written under the influence of the most painful experiences and the keenest emotions. Paul then saw himself for some time on the eve of a total rupture with that church of Corinth which had been the fruit of so many labors. Led away by his adversaries, it openly refused him obedience. Some dared to raise the gravest imputations against his veracity and disinterestedness; his apostleship was audaciously ridiculed; Paul was charged with being ambitious and boastful; he pretended to preach the gospel without charge, but he nevertheless filled his purse from it by means of his messengers: all this was said of the apostle of the Corinthians at Corinth itself, and the church did not shut the mouths of the insolent detractors who spoke thus! But who then were they who thus dared to challenge the apostle of the Gentiles in the midst of his own churches? Paul in his Second Epistle calls them ironically *apostles by way of eminence* [*chiefest*, Eng. transl.]. This was, no doubt, one of the titles with which their adherents saluted them. Baur and his school do not fear to apply this designation to the Twelve in Paul's sense of it. "These *apostles by way of eminence,*" says the leader of the school,[2] "undoubtedly denote the apostles themselves, whose disciples and delegates the false apostles of Corinth professed to be." Hilgenfeld says more pointedly still:[3] "The apostles by way of eminence can be no other than the original apostles." This opinion has spread and taken root. We should like to know what remains thereafter of the apostleship of Paul and of the Twelve, nay, of the mission of Jesus Himself? Happily, sound criticism treats such partial and violent assertions more and more as they deserve. We have already stated the conclusion which has now been reached on this question by such men as Weizsäcker, Keim, Harnack. It is easy, indeed, to prove that the phrase: "apostles by way of eminence," which St. Paul employs, borrowing it ironically from the language used at Corinth, could not designate the Twelve. 1. We read, 2 Cor. xi. 6, that Paul was described at Corinth as a *man of the commonalty* (ἰδιώτης, *rude*, Eng. transl.) *in language*, as compared with the superior apostles. Now, what reasonable man could have put the Twelve above Paul in the matter of speech? Comp. Acts iv. 13, where the apostles are called *men of the commonalty*, or *unlettered*, while

---

[1] Such at least is the conviction to which we have been led by the attentive study of the texts, in more or less entire harmony with several critics of our day.
[2] *Paulus*, I. 309.
[3] *Einl. in's N. T.* p. 298.

Paul was regarded as a man of high culture and vast knowledge (Acts xxvi. 24). 2. If it had been wished to designate the Twelve by the phrase: "the more eminent apostles," the very word would have made a place beneath them for an apostle of an inferior order. And for whom, if not for Paul? Now, his adversaries were not content at this time to make him an apostle of an inferior order; they contrasted him with the Twelve, as a false apostle with the only true. We are thus led to conclude that the apostles *par excellence*, who were being exalted at Corinth in order to blacken Paul, were no other than those lofty personages from Jerusalem who, in the transactions related Acts xv. and Gal. ii., had openly resisted the apostles, and affected to give law to them as well as to the whole church, those very persons whom Paul has designated in Galatians as *false brethren brought in*. In Acts it is related that after Pentecost many priests (vi. 7) and Pharisees (xv. 5) entered the church. These new Christians of high rank and great theological knowledge brought with them their pretensions and prejudices, and they ill brooked the authority of simple and uncultured men like the Twelve. They looked upon them as narrow-minded. They treated them with disdain; and from the height of their theological erudition thought it deplorable that so glorious a work, from which they might have drawn so much advantage, had fallen into such poor hands. They therefore tried audaciously to snatch the direction of the church from the apostles. Thus, apostles by way of eminence, arch-apostles, far from being a name intended to identify them with the Twelve, was rather meant to exalt them above the apostles. It was they who, after the council of Jerusalem, in opposition to the Twelve no less than to Paul, though under their name, had organized the counter mission which Paul soon met in all the churches founded by him. Most commentators justly hold that these people and their adherents at Corinth formed the party which in 1 Cor. i. 12 is named by Paul the party *of Christ*. In this case it is easy to understand the meaning of the designation. It means, in contradistinction to those who were carried away with enthusiasm for this or that preacher, those who would not submit either to Paul or the Twelve, and who appealed from them to the authority of Christ alone. Thus the party called *that of Christ* is contrasted (1 Cor. i. 12) with that of Peter, as well as with that of Paul or Apollos.[1]

At the time when Paul wrote our Second Epistle to the Corinthians, the hottest moment of the conflict was past. This Epistle in many of its parts is a shout of victory (comp. especially chap. vii.). It was intended, while drawing closely the bond between the apostle and the portion of the church which had returned into communion with him, finally to reduce the rebellious portion to submission or powerlessness;[2] and it appears to have gained its end. Paul, regarding this church as henceforth restored to him, came at length, in the end of the year 58, to make his long-expected sojourn among them; he passed the month of December of this year at Corinth, and the first two months of the following year. Then he set out, shortly before the feast of Passover, on a last visit to Jerusalem. For some time past vast plans filled his mind (Acts xix. 21). Already his thoughts turned to Rome and the West. Paul was in the highest degree one of those men who think they have done nothing so long as anything remains for them to do. The East was evangelized; the torch of the gospel was at least lighted in all the great capitals of Asia and Greece, Antioch, Ephesus, Corinth. To these churches it fell to spread the light in the countries which surrounded them, and so to continue the apostolic work. Egypt and Alexandria had

---

[1] There is nothing more curious than to see how Baur seeks to get rid of this distinction between the party of Christ and that of Peter, which is absolutely destructive of his system: "The partisans of Peter and of Christ," he says, "were not two different parties, but only two different names for one and the same party," *Paulus*, I. 297, 298.

[2] The last four chapters are, as it were, the ultimatum addressed to this party.

probably been visited, perhaps by Barnabas and Mark after their journey to Cyprus. The West remained. This was the field which now opened to the view and thoughts of the apostle. But already the gospel has preceded him to Rome. He learns the fact . . . What matters it ? Rome becomes to him a mere point of passage. And his goal, receding with the rapid march of the gospel, will now be Spain.[1] His Christian ambition drives him irresistibly to the extremity of the known world. A duty, however, still detained him in the East. He wished to pay Jerusalem a last visit, not only to take leave of the metropolis of Christendom, but more especially to present to it, at the head of a numerous deputation of Gentile Christians, the homage of the whole pagan world, in the form of a rich offering collected in all the churches during these last years in behalf of the Christians of Jerusalem. What more fitted to cement the bond of love which he had endeavored to form and keep up between the two great portions of Christendom !

All the deputies of the churches of Greece and Asia, his travelling companions, were already assembled at Corinth to embark with him for Syria, when he learned that the freighted vessel and its cargo were threatened with dangers by sea. He therefore took the way by Macedonia, celebrated the Passover feasts at Philippi, and hastened the rest of his journey so as to arrive at Jerusalem for Pentecost. There he solemnly deposited the fruit of the collection in the hands of the elders of the church presided over by James. In the conference which followed, James communicated to him the prejudices with which he was regarded by the thousands of believing Jews who were daily arriving at Jerusalem to celebrate the feast. Paul had been represented to them as a deadly enemy of the law, whose one aim was to destroy Mosaism among the Jews throughout the whole world. James proposed to him to give the lie to these rumors, by himself carrying out a Levitical ceremony in the temple before the eyes of all. The proposal was that he should join some Jews who were then discharging a vow of *Nazariteship*, and take upon himself the common expense.

M. Renan represents St. Paul as if he must have been greatly embarrassed by this proposition, because he could not conceal from himself that the rumor spread against him was thoroughly well founded. To consent to James's proposal was therefore deliberately to create a misunderstanding, "to commit an unfaithfulness toward Christ." Yet this writer thinks that Paul, under constraint of charity, managed to overcome his repugnance ; as if charity authorized dissimulation ! M. Reuss seems to hesitate between two views : either Luke, incapable of rising to the height of Paul's pure spirituality, has not given an exact representation of the facts, or we must blame Paul himself : "If things really passed as the text relates, . . . it must be confessed that the apostle lent himself to a weak course of which we should hardly have thought him capable ; . . . for the step taken was either a profession of Judaism or the playing of a comedy."[2] Both alternatives are equally false, we answer with thorough conviction. In fact, Paul could with perfect sincerity give the lie to the report spread among the Jewish-Christians of the East. If, on the one hand, he was firmly opposed to every attempt to subject Gentile converts to the Mosaic law, on the other, he had never sought to induce the Jews to cast it off arbitrarily. This would have been openly to violate the Jerusalem compromise. Did not he himself, in many circumstances when he had to do with Jews, consent to subject himself to legal rights ? Have we not already quoted what he wrote to the Corinthians : "To those that are under the law I became as under the law" (1 Cor. ix. 20) ? The external rite being a thing indifferent in his eyes, he could use it in the service of charity. And if he sometimes conformed to it, it is perfectly certain that he could never allow him-

---

[1] Observe the delicate expression of this thought, Rom. xv. 24.
[2] *Hist. apostol.* pp. 208, 209.

self to become its fanatical adversary. He left it to time to set free the conscience of his countrymen, and did not dream of hastening the hour by a premature emancipation. And therefore, whatever may be said to the contrary, he could protest without weakness and without charlatanism against the assertion which represented him in the East as the deadly destroyer of Mosaism among all the members of the Jewish nation.

The circumstance to which we have been referring was, as is well known, the occasion of his being arrested. Here begins the last period of his life, that of his *imprisonments*.

3

After his imprisonment and a show of trial at Jerusalem, Paul was transferred to Cesarea. In this city he passed two whole years, vainly expecting to be liberated by the governor Felix. In the year 60 the latter was recalled ; and either in this year, or more probably the following, his successor, Festus, arrived. Here is the second principal date in the apostle's life, which, with the aid of the Roman historians, we can fix with tolerable certainty. In the year 61 (some say 60) Paul appeared before Festus, when, to put an end to the tergiversations of the provincial authority, he appealed to the imperial tribunal. It was a right which his Roman citizenship gave him. Hence his departure for Rome in the autumn following the arrival of Festus. We are familiar with the circumstances of his voyage, and of the shipwreck which detained him at Malta for the winter. He did not arrive at Rome till the following spring. We learn from the last two verses of the Acts that he continued there for two years as a prisoner, but enjoying much liberty of action. He could receive his fellow-workers who traversed Europe and Asia, who brought him news of the churches, and in return carried to them his letters (Colossians, Ephesians, Philemon, Philippians).

Here Luke's history closes abruptly. From this time we have nothing to guide us except patristic traditions of a remarkably confused character, or suppositions still more uncertain. Some assert that Paul perished, like Peter, in the persecution of Nero, in August of the year 64 ; on the other hand, certain statements of the Fathers would lead us to think that Paul was liberated at the close of the two years mentioned in the Acts ; that he was able to fulfil the promise which he had made to Philemon and to the Philippians to visit them in the East (Philem. 22 ; Phil. ii. 24) ; and that he accomplished his final purpose, that of carrying the gospel to Spain. If the pastoral Epistles are really by the apostle, as we cannot help thinking, they are the monument of this last period of his activity. For it does not seem to us possible to place them at any period whatever of Paul's ministry anterior to his first captivity at Rome.

As no church in Spain claims the honor of being founded by the apostle, we must hold, on this supposition, that he was seized shortly after his arrival on Iberian soil, and led prisoner to the Capital to be judged there. The Second Epistle to Timothy would, in that case, be the witness of this last captivity ; and Paul's martyrdom, which, according to the testimony of the Roman presbyter Caius (second century), took place on the Ostian Way, must be placed about the year 66 or 67. This is the date indicated by Eusebius.[1]

We have thus, for fixing the chronology of the life of the apostle, two dates which are certain : that of his journey to Jerusalem with Barnabas at the time of Herod Agrippa's death (Acts xii.), in 44 ; and that of his appearing before Festus on the arrival of the latter in Palestine (Acts xxv.), in 61 (or 60). It remains to us, by means of those fixed points, to indicate the approximate dates of the principal events of the apostle's life.

---

[1] But while erroneously placing the persecution of Nero in that year.

Festus died the same year as he arrived in Palestine, consequently before the Passover of 62.

Paul cannot therefore have been sent by him to Rome, at the latest, till the autumn of the year 61. Paul's arrest at Jerusalem took place two years earlier, at Pentecost, consequently in the spring of 59.

The third missionary journey, which immediately preceded this arrest, embraces his stay at Ephesus, which lasted about three years (Acts xix. 8, 10, xx. 31), and various journeys into Greece besides, perhaps more important and numerous than is generally thought. If to this we add his stay in Achaia (Acts xx. 3), and the last journey to Jerusalem, we are led backward to the autumn of the year 54 as the beginning of his third journey.

His second mission, the Greek one, of which Corinth was the centre, cannot have lasted less than two years, for the Book of Acts reckons eighteen months and one or two more to his sojourn at Corinth alone (Acts xviii. 11, 18). We may therefore ascribe to this second missionary journey the two years between the autumn of 52 and that of 54.

The council of Jerusalem, which was held very shortly before this time, must consequently be placed at the beginning of 52, or about the end of 51.

The first missionary journey, that of Paul and Barnabas in Asia Minor, as well as the two sojourns at Antioch before and after, filled the few years preceding.

Thus, going back step by step, we reach the other date which must serve as a guiding-point, that of Herod Agrippa's death, in 44. Now the time at which we arrive, following Paul's career backwards, is exactly the date when Barnabas seeks him at Tarsus, to bring him to Antioch, where they labored together in the church, and whence they were delegated to Jerusalem in regard to the approaching famine; the date of Herod Agrippa's death, in 44.

The length of Paul's stay at Tarsus before Barnabas sought him there is not exactly indicated, but it seems to have been considerable. We may reckon it at three or four years, and we come to the year 40 as that in which Paul's first visit to Jerusalem, after his conversion, took place.

This visit was preceded by Paul's journey to Arabia (Gal. i. 18), and his two sojourns at Damascus before and after it; he himself reckons this period at three years (i. 18). Paul's conversion would thus fall about the year 37.

Paul must then have been at least thirty years of age. We may therefore place his birth about the year 7; and if he died in 67, assign to his earthly life a duration of sixty years.

This entire series of dates appears to us in itself to be clear and logical. But, more than that, history in general presents a considerable number of points of verification, which very interestingly confirm this biographical sketch. We shall mention six of them.

1. We know that Pilate was recalled from his government in the year 36. This circumstance serves to explain the martyrdom of Stephen, which is intimately connected with Saul's conversion. Indeed, the right of pronouncing sentence of death having been withdrawn from the Jews by the Roman administration prior to the death of Jesus, it is not likely that they would have indulged in so daring an encroachment on the power of their masters as that of putting Stephen to death, if the representative of the Roman power had been in Palestine at the time. There is therefore ground for thinking that the murder of Stephen must be placed in the year 36, the time of the vacancy between Pilate and his successor. An event of the same kind took place, according to Josephus, about the year 62, when the high priest Ananias put James the brother of Jesus to death, in the interval which separated the death of Festus from the arrival of Albinus his successor. The absence of the governor, it would seem, awoke in the heart of

34 / Introduction

the people and their leaders the feeling of their ancient national independence.

2. The journey of Paul and Barnabas to Jerusalem, recorded in Acts xi. and xii. (on occasion of the famine announced by Agabus), must have taken place, according to our chronology, in the year 44 (Herod Agrippa's death). Now we know from the historians that the great famine overtook Palestine in the reign of Claudius, in 45 or 46, which agrees with the date assigned to this journey.

3. St. Paul declares, Gal. ii. 1, that it was fourteen years *after his conversion* (such is the most probable meaning of the passage) when he repaired to Jerusalem with Barnabas to confer with the apostles (Acts xv.). If, as we have seen, this conference took place in 51, it really falls in the fourteenth year after the year 37, the date of the apostle's conversion.

4. We have been led to the conclusion that the apostle arrived at Corinth about the end of the year 52. Now it is said (Acts xviii. 1) that Paul on arriving at this city made the acquaintance of a family of Jewish origin, that of Aquila and Priscilla, who had recently come from Italy in consequence of the decree of the Emperor Claudius commanding the expulsion of Jews from Rome. " Claudius," says Suetonius, " banished from Rome the Jews, who were perpetually raising insurrections." From various indications furnished by Roman historians, this decree must belong to the last days of the life of Claudius. Now this emperor died in 54 ; the date of the decree of banishment thus nearly coincides with that of Paul's arrival at Corinth.

5. Towards the end of his stay at Corinth, Paul was charged before the proconsul of Achaia, called Gallio. This proconsul is not an unknown personage. He was the brother of the philosopher Seneca, a man of great distinction, who plays a part in his brother's correspondence. He was consul in the year 51 ; his proconsulship must have followed immediately thereafter. Gallio was thus really, at the time indicated in Acts, proconsul of Achaia.

6. Josephus relates that, while Felix was governor of Judea, an Egyptian excited several thousands of Jews to insurrection, and proceeded to attack Jerusalem. The band was destroyed by Felix, but the leader escaped. Now we know from Acts that, towards the end of Felix's government, the Roman captain who was commanding at Jerusalem suspected Paul of being an Egyptian who had incited the people to rebellion (Acts xxi. 38). All the circumstances harmonize. It was the very time when the escaped fanatic might have attempted a new rising.

If we recapitulate the principal dates to which we have been led, we find that the apostle's life is divided as follows :—

From 7–37 : His life as a Jew and Pharisee.

From 37–44 : The years of his preparation for his apostleship.

From 44–51 : His first missionary journey, with the two stays at Antioch, before and after, and his journey to the council of Jerusalem.

From 52–54 : His second missionary journey ; the founding of the churches of Greece (the two Epistles to the Thessalonians).

From 54–59 : The third missionary journey ; the stay at Ephesus, and the visits to Greece and to Jerusalem (the four principal Epistles, Galatians, 1st and 2d Corinthians, Romans).

From 59 (summer) to 61 (autumn) : Arrest at Jerusalem, captivity at Cesarea.

From 61 (autumn) to 62 (spring) : Voyage, shipwreck ; arrival at Rome.

From 62 (spring) to 64 (spring) : Captivity at Rome (Colossians, Ephesians, Philemon, Philippians).

From 64 (spring) to 66 or 67 : Liberation, second captivity, martyrdom (pastoral Epistles).

How are we to account for the institution of this extraordinary apostleship side by side with the regular apostleship of the Twelve?

The time had come, in the progress of the kingdom of God, when the particularistic work founded in Abraham was at length to pass into the great current of humanity, from which it had been kept apart. Now, the normal mode of this unparalleled religious revolution would have been this: Israel itself, with the work of the Messiah before it, really and joyfully proclaiming throughout the whole world the completion of salvation, and the end of the theocratic economy. It was to prepare Israel for this task, the glorious crown of its history, that Jesus had specially chosen the Twelve. Apostles to the elect nation, they were to make it the apostle of the world.

But man seldom answers completely to the task which God has destined for him. Instead of accepting this part, the part of love, in the humility of which it would have found its real greatness, Israel strove to maintain its theocratical prerogative. It rejected the Redeemer of the world rather than abandon its privileged position. It wished to save its life, and it lost it.

Then, in order to replace it, God required to call an exceptional instrument and found a special apostleship. Paul was neither the substitute of Judas, whom the Twelve had prematurely replaced (Acts ii.), as has been thought, nor that of James the son of Zebedee, whose martyrdom is related Acts xii. He is the substitute for a converted Israel, the man who had, single-handed, to execute the task which fell to his whole nation. And so the hour of his call was precisely, as we have seen, that, when the blood of the two martyrs, Stephen and James, sealed the hardening of Israel and decided its rejection.

The calling of Paul is nothing less than the counterpart of Abraham's.

The qualities with which Paul was endowed for this mission were as exceptional as the task itself. He combined with the power of inward and meditative concentration all the gifts of practical action. His mind descended to the most minute details of ecclesiastical administration (1 Cor. xiv. 26–37, *e.g.*] as easily as it mounted the steps of the mystic ladder whose top reaches the divine throne (2 Cor. xii. 1–4, *e.g.*).

A not less remarkable combination of opposite powers, which usually exclude one another, strikes us equally in his writings. Here we meet, on the one hand, with the dialectical rigor which will not quit a subject till after having completely analyzed it, nor an adversary till it has transfixed him with his own sword; and, on the other, with a delicate and profound sensibility, and a concentrated warmth of heart, the flame of which sometimes bursts forth even through the forms of the severest argumentation. The Epistle to the Romans will furnish more than one example.

The life of St. Paul is summed up in a word: a unique man for a unique task.

2

THE CHURCH AT ROME

AFTER having made acquaintance with the author of our Epistle, it is important for us to form a just idea of the church to which it was addressed. Three questions arise here :—1. How was the church of Rome founded ? 2. Were the majority of its members of Jewish or Gentile origin ? 3. Was its religious tendency particularistic or Pauline ?

These three subjects, the *foundation, composition*, and *tendency* of the church, are undoubtedly intimately related. They may, however, be studied separately. To avoid repetition, we shall treat the last two under a common head.

A. *Foundation of the Roman Church.*

Among the apostolic foundations mentioned in the Book of Acts, that of the church of Rome does not appear. Reuss sees a lacuna in this silence. But is not the omission a proof of the real course of things ? Does it not show that the foundation of the Roman church was not distinguished by any notable event such as the historian can lay hold of ; that it took place in a sort of stealthy manner, and was not the work of any individual of mark ?

What are the oldest known proofs of the existence of a Christian church at Rome ?

In the first place, our Epistle itself, which assumes the existence, if not of a completely organized church, at least of several Christian groups in the capital ; in the second place, the fact related in the first part of Acts xxviii. On his arrival at Rome in the spring of the year 62, Paul is welcomed by *brethren* who, on the news of his approach, come to receive him at the distance of a dozen leagues from the city. How was such a Christian community formed ?

Three answers are given to the question.

I. The Catholic Church ascribes the founding of the Church of Rome to the preaching of Peter. This apostle, it is said, came to Rome to preach the gospel and combat the heresies of Simon the magician, at the beginning of the reign of the Emperor Claudius (41–54). But it is very probable that this tradition rests in whole or in part on a gross mistake, of which Justin Martyr is the first author.[1] If the apostle had really come to Rome so early, and had been the first to propagate the gospel there, Paul evidently could not write a long letter to this church without mentioning its founder ; and if we consider that this letter is a didactic writing of great length, a more or less complete exposition of the gospel, we shall conclude that he could not, in consistency with his own principles, have addressed it to a church founded by another apostle. For he more than once declares that it is contrary to his apostolic practice " to enter into an-

---

[1] *Apol.* i. c. 26. Justin takes a statue raised to a Sabine god (*Semo Sancus*) in an island of the Tiber for a statue erected to the magician Simon of the Book of Acts. This statue was rediscovered in 1574 with the inscription : SEMONI SANCO DEO FIDIO. Such at least is one of the sources of the legend. Eusebius (ii. 14) has followed Justin.

other man's labors," or "to build on the foundation laid by another" (Rom. xv. 20 ; 2 Cor. x. 16).

Strange that a Protestant writer, Thiersch, is almost the only theologian of merit who still defends the assertion of Peter's sojourn at Rome in the beginning of the reign of Claudius. He supports it by two facts : the passage Acts xii. 17, where it is said that, delivered from his prison at Jerusalem, Peter went *into another place*,—a mysterious expression used, according to this critic, to designate Rome ; and next, the famous passage of Suetonius, relative to the decree of Claudius banishing the Jews from Rome, because they ceased not " to rise at the *instigation of Chrestus*." [1] According to Thiersch, these last words are a vague indication of the introduction of Christianity into Rome at this period by St. Peter, and of the troubles which the fact had caused in the Roman synagogue. These arguments are alike without solidity. Why should not Luke have specially named Rome if St. Peter had really withdrawn thither ? He had no reason to make a mystery of the name. Besides, at this period, from 41 to 44, Peter can hardly have gone so far as Rome ; for in 51 (Acts xv.) we find him at Jerusalem, and in 54 only at Antioch. Paul himself, the great pioneer of the gospel in the West, had not yet, in 42, set foot on the European continent, nor preached in Greece. And the author of the Acts, in chaps. vi.-xiii., enumerates very carefully all the providential circumstances which paved the way for carrying the gospel into the Gentile world. Assuredly, therefore, Peter had not up to that time crossed the seas to evangelize Rome. As to the passage of Suetonius, it is very arbitrary to make *Chrestus* a personification of Christian preaching in general. The true Roman tradition is much rather to be sought in the testimony of a deacon of the church who lived in the third or fourth century, and is known as a writer under the name of Ambrosiaster or the false Ambrose (because his writings appear in the works of St. Ambrose), but whose true name was probably Hilary. He declares, to the praise of his church, that the Romans had become believers " without having seen a single miracle *or any of the apostles*." [2] Most Catholic writers of our day, who are earnest and independent, combat the idea that Peter sojourned at Rome under the reign of Claudius.

After all we have said, we do not mean in the least to deny that Peter came to Rome about the end of his life. The testimonies bearing on this stay seem to us too positive to be set aside by judicious criticism.[3] But in any case, his visit cannot have taken place till after the composition of the Epistle to the Romans, and even of the letters written by Paul during his Roman captivity in 62 and 63 (Col. Phil. Eph. Philem.). How, if Peter had at that time labored simultaneously with him in the city of Rome, could Paul have failed to name him among the preachers of the gospel whom he mentions, and from whom he sends greetings ? Peter cannot therefore have arrived at Rome till the end of the year 63 or the beginning of 64, and his stay cannot have lasted more than a few months till August 64, when he perished as a victim of the persecution of Nero. As Hilgenfeld says : " To be a good Protestant, one need not combat this tradition." [4]

It is even probable that, but for the notoriety of this fact, the legend of the founding of the church of Rome by St. Peter could never have arisen and become so firmly established.

II. The second supposition by which it has been sought to explain the existence of this church—for in the absence of everything in the form of narrative one is reduced to hypothesis—is the following : Jews of Rome who had come to Jerusalem at the time of the feasts were there brought

---

[1] *Claud.* c. 25 : *Judæos impulsore Chresto assidue tumultuantes Româ expulit.*
[2] *Commentaria in XIII. epistolas Paulinas.*
[3] The testimonies are those of Clement of Rome, Clement of Alexandria, Dionysius of Cor., the author of the Fragment of Muratori, Irenæus, Tertullian, and Caius.
[4] *Einl.* p. 624.

into contact with the first Christians, and so carried to Rome the seeds of the faith. Mention is made indeed, Acts ii. 10, of Roman pilgrims, some Jews by birth, the others proselytes, that is to say, Gentiles originally, but converted to Judaism, who were present during the events of the day of Pentecost. At every feast thereafter this contact between the members of the rich and numerous Roman synagogue and those of the church of Jerusalem must have been repeated, and must have produced the same result. If this explanation of the origin of the church of Rome is established, it is evident that it was by means of the synagogue that the gospel spread in this city.

M. Mangold, one of the most decided supporters of this hypothesis,[1] alleges two facts in its favor—(1) the legend of Peter's sojourn at Rome, which he acknowledges to be false, but which testifies, he thinks, to the recollection of certain original communications between the apostolic church, of which Peter was the head, and the Roman synagogue ; (2) the passage of Suetonius, which we have already quoted, regarding the troubles which called forth the edict of Claudius. According to Mangold, these troubles were nothing else than the violent debates raised among the members of the Roman synagogue by the Christian preaching of those pilgrims on their return from Jerusalem.

But, as we have seen, the legend of Peter's preaching at Rome seems to have an entirely different origin from that which Mangold supposes ; and the interpretation of the passage of Suetonius which he proposes, following Baur, is very uncertain. According to Wieseler and many other critics, Chrestus—the name was a very common one for a freedman—simply designates here an obscure Jewish agitator ; or, as seems to us more probable, Suetonius having vaguely heard of the expectation of the Messias (of the *Christ*) among the Jews, regarded the name as that of a real living person to whom he ascribed the constant ferment and insurrectionary dispositions which the Messianic expectation kept up among the Jews. The word *tumultuari, to rise in insurrection*, used by the Roman historian, applies much more to outbreaks of rebellion than to intestine controversies within the synagogue. How could these have disturbed the public order and disquieted Claudius ?

There are two facts, besides, which seem to us opposed to this way of explaining the founding of the church of Rome.

1. How comes it that no circumstance analogous to that which on the above hypothesis gave rise to the Roman church, can be proved in any of the other great cities of the empire ? There were Jewish colonies elsewhere than at Rome. There were such at Ephesus, Corinth, and Thessalonica. Whence comes it that, when Paul arrived in these cities, and preached in their synagogues for the first time, the gospel appeared as a thing entirely new ? Is there any reason for holding that the Christianity of Palestine exercised a more direct and prompt influence on the synagogue of Rome than on that of the other cities of the empire ?

2. A second fact seems to us more decisive still. It is related in Acts xxviii. that Paul, three days after his arrival at Rome, called together to his hired house, where he was kept prisoner, the rulers of the Roman synagogue. The latter asked him to give precise information as to the doctrine of which he was the representative. " For," said they, " we have heard this sect spoken of, and we know that it meets with opposition everywhere" (in every synagogue). The narrative does not state the inference drawn by them from these facts ; but it was evidently this : " Not knowing the contents of this new faith, we would like to learn them from lips so authoritative as thine." What proves that this was really the meaning of the Jews' words is, that they fixed a day for Paul when they would come to converse

---

[1] *Der Römerbrief und die Anfänge der römischen Gemeinde*, 1866.

with him on the subject. The conference bore, as is stated in the sequel of the narrative, "on the kingdom of God and concerning Jesus," taking as the starting-point "the law of Moses and the prophets" (ver. 23). Now, how are we to understand this ignorance of the rulers of the synagogue in respect of Christianity, if that religion had really been preached among them already, and had excited such violent debates as to provoke an edict of banishment against the whole Jewish colony ?

It has been sought to get rid of this difficulty in different ways. Reuss has propounded the view that the question of the rulers of the synagogue did not refer to Christianity in general, but to Paul's individual teaching, and the opposition excited against him by the Jewish-Christian party.[1] But this view would have imperatively demanded the Greek form ἃ σὺ φρονεῖς, and not merely ἃ φρονεῖς. Besides, the sequel of the narrative very clearly shows that Paul's exposition bore on the kingdom of God and the gospel in general, and not merely on the differences between Paulinism and Judaizing Christianity.

Others have taken the words of the Jews to be either a feint, or at least cautious reserve. They measured their words, it is said, from the fear of compromising themselves, or even, so Mangold thinks, from the desire of extorting some declaration from the apostle which they might use against him in his trial. The rest of the narrative is incompatible with these suppositions. The Jews enter very seriously into the discussion of the religious question. On the day fixed they come to the appointed place of meeting in greater numbers than formerly. During a whole day, *from morning till night*, they discuss the doctrine and history of Jesus, referring to the texts of Moses and the prophets. On the part of men engaged in business, as must have been the case with the rulers of the rich Jewish community established at Rome, such conduct testifies to a serious interest. The result of the interview furnishes like proof of the sincerity of their conduct. This result is twofold ; some go away convinced, others resist to the last. This difference would be inconceivable if they had come to Paul already acquainted with the preaching of the gospel merely to lay a snare for him.

Olshausen has proposed a different solution. According to him, the banishment of the Jews by Claudius led to a complete rupture between the synagogue and the Jewish-Christians. For the latter naturally sought to evade the decree of expulsion. And so it happened that, when the banished Jews returned to Rome, there was no longer anything in common between them and the church ; the Roman Jews soon lost all recollection of Christian doctrine. But Baur and Mangold have thoroughly refuted this supposition. It ascribes much more considerable effects to the edict of Claudius than it can ever have had in reality. And how could a short time of exile have sufficed to efface from the minds of the Jewish community the memory of Christian preaching, if it had already made itself heard in full synagogue ?

Baur has discarded all half measures. He has struck at the root of the difficulty. He has pronounced the narrative of the Acts a fiction. The author desired to pass off Paul as much more conciliatory to Judaism than he really was. The true Paul had not the slightest need of an act of positive unbelief on the part of the Jews of Rome, to think himself authorized to evangelize the Gentiles of the capital. He did not recognize that alleged *right of priority* which the Jewish-Christians claimed in favor of their nation, and which is assumed by the narrative of the Acts. This narrative therefore is fictitious.[2] The answer to this imputation is not difficult : the Paul of Acts certainly does not resemble the Paul of Baur's theory ; but he is assuredly the Paul of history. It is Paul himself who proves this to

---

[1] Again quite recently in his *Histoire Apostolique*, pp. 247, 248.
[2] *Paulus*, I. 367 et seq. Hilgenfeld likewise : "The narrative of the Acts is not credible."

us when he writes thrice with his own hand, at the beginning of the Epistle to the Romans (i. 16, ii. 9, 10), the : "to the Jews *first*," which so completely confirms the course taken by him among the Jews of Rome, and described so carefully by the author of the Acts.

All these explanations of the account, Acts xxviii., being thus untenable, it only remains to accept it in its natural meaning with the inevitable consequences. The rulers of the synagogue of Rome had undoubtedly heard of the disputes which were everywhere raised among their co-religionists by the preaching of Jesus as the Christ. But they had not yet an exact acquaintance with this new faith. Christianity had therefore not yet been preached in the Roman synagogue.

III. Without altogether denying what may have been done in an isolated way for the spread of Christianity at Rome by Jews returning from Jerusalem, we must assign the founding of the Roman church to a different origin. Rome was to the world what the heart is to the body, the centre of vital circulation. Tacitus asserts that " all things hateful or shameful were sure to flow to Rome from all parts of the empire." This law must have applied also to better things. Long before the composition of the Epistle to the Romans, the gospel had already crossed the frontier of Palestine and spread among the Gentile populations of Syria, Asia Minor, and Greece. Endowed as it was with an inherent force of expansion, could not the new religious principle easily find its way from those countries to Rome? Relations between Rome and Syria in particular were frequent and numerous. Renan himself remarks them : " Rome was the meeting-point of all the Oriental forms of worship, the point of the Mediterranean with which the Syrians had most connection. They arrived there in enormous bands. With them there landed troops of Greeks and Asiatics, all speaking Greek. . . . It is in the highest degree probable that so early as the year 50 some Jews of Syria already become Christian entered the capital of the empire."[1] In these sentences of Renan we have only a word to correct. It is the word *Jews*. For it is certain that the churches of Antioch and Syria were chiefly composed of *Greeks*. Those Christians of Gentile origin might therefore very soon make their way to Rome. And why should it have been otherwise with members of the Christian communities of Asia and Greece, who were much nearer still?

There are some facts which serve to confirm the essentially Gentile origin of the Roman church. Five times, in the salutations which close our Epistle, the apostle addresses groups of Christians scattered over the great city.[2] At least five times for once to the contrary, the names of the brethren whom he salutes are Greek and Latin, not Jewish. These bear witness to the manner in which the gospel had gained a footing in the capital. This wide dissemination and those names of Gentile origin find a natural explanation in the arrival of Christians of Greece and Asia, who had preached the word each in the quarter of the city where he lived. The course of things would have been quite different had the preaching of the gospel proceeded from the synagogue. A still more significant fact is related in the first part of Acts xxviii. On hearing of St. Paul's approach, the brethren who reside at Rome haste to meet him, and receive him with an affection which raises his courage. Does not this prove that they already loved and venerated him as their spiritual father, and that consequently their Christianity proceeded directly or indirectly from the churches founded by Paul in Greece and Asia, rather than from the Jewish-Christian church of Jerusalem? Beyschlag, in his interesting work on the subject before us,[3] raises the objection that between the composition of the

[1] *Saint Paul*, pp. 97, 98.
[2] We shall afterwards examine the question whether those salutations really form part of the Epistle to the Romans.
[3] " Das geschichtliche Problem des Römerbriefs," *Stud. und Kritik.* 1867.

Epistle to the Romans, about the end of the year 57 or 58, and the founding of the churches of Greece, about 53 or 54, too little time had elapsed to allow the gospel to spread so far as Rome, and to make it possible for the *whole world* to have heard of the fact (Rom. i. 8). But the latter phrase is, of course, somewhat hyperbolical (comp. 1 Thess. i. 8 ; Col. i. 6). And if the founding of the churches of Syria goes back, as we have seen, to about the year 40, and so to a date eighteen or nineteen years before the Epistle to the Romans, the time thus gained for this Christian invasion is certainly not too short. Even the five or six years which intervene between the evangelization of Greece and the composition of our Epistle sufficed to explain the arrival of the gospel at Rome from the great commercial centres of Thessalonica and Corinth.

It may be asked, no doubt, how came it, if it did so happen, that the representatives of the Christian faith in the capital had not yet raised the standard of the new doctrine in the synagogue ? But it must be remembered that for such a mission it was not enough to be a sincere believer ; one required to feel himself in possession of scripture knowledge, and of a power of speech and argument which could not be expected from simple men engaged in commerce and industry. We read in Acts (xviii. 26 et seq.) that when Apollos arrived at Ephesus, and when, supported by his eminent talents and biblical erudition, *he made bold*—such is the word used—to speak in the synagogue, Aquila, the disciple and friend of Paul, did not attempt to answer him in the open assembly, but thought it enough to take him *unto him* to instruct him privately in the knowledge of the gospel. This is easily understood ; it was a paradoxical proclamation which was in question, being, as St. Paul says, *to the Greeks foolishness*, and still more *to the Jews a stumbling-block*. The first-comer was not fitted to proclaim and defend it before the great Rabbins of capitals such as Antioch, Ephesus, or Rome. So true is this, that some expressions in the Epistle to the Romans would lead us to suppose that Paul himself was accused of shrinking from the task. Is it not indeed to a suspicion of this kind that he is alluding, when, after speaking of the delays which had hitherto prevented his visit to Rome, he declares (i. 16) " that *he is not ashamed* of the gospel of Christ " ? Only a very small number of men exceptionally qualified could essay an attack such as would tell on the fortress of Roman Judaism, and not one of those strong men had yet appeared in the capital.

We have in the Book of Acts an account of the founding of a church entirely analogous to that which we are supposing for the church of Rome. It is that of the church of Antioch. Some Christian emigrants from Jerusalem reach this capital of Syria shortly after the persecution of Stephen ; they turn *to the Greeks*, that is to say, the Gentiles of the city. A large number believe, and the distinction between this community of Gentile origin and the synagogue is brought out so pointedly that a new name is invented to designate believers, that of *Christian* (Acts xi. 19-26). Let us transfer this scene from the capital of Syria to the capital of the empire, and we have the history of the founding of the church of Rome. We understand how Greek names are in a majority, such being borne by the most distinguished of the members of the church (in the salutations of chap. xvi.) ; we understand the ignorance which still prevailed among the rulers of the synagogue in relation to the gospel ; we understand the extraordinary eagerness with which the Christians of Rome come to salute Paul on his arrival. All the facts find their explanation, and the narrative of the Acts is vindicated without difficulty.

B. *Composition and Tendency of the Roman Church*

It was generally held, till the time of Baur, that the majority of the Roman church was of Gentile origin, and consequently sympathized in its tendency with the teaching of Paul ; this view was inferred from a certain number of passages taken from the Epistle itself, and from the natural enough supposition that the majority of the church would take the general character of the Roman population.

But Baur, in a work of remarkable learning and sagacity,[1] maintained that on this view, which had already been combated by Rückert, it was absolutely impossible to explain the aim and construction of the Epistle to the Romans ; that such a letter had no meaning except as addressed to a church of Jewish-Christian origin, and of Judaizing and particularistic tendency, whose views Paul was concerned to correct. He sought to give an entirely different meaning from the received one to the passages usually alleged in favor of the contrary opinion ; and he succeeded so well in demonstrating his thesis, that he carried with him the greater number of theologians (MM. Reuss, Thiersch, Mangold, Schenkel, Sabatier, Holtzmann, Volkmar, Holsten, etc.). Even Tholuck, in the fifth edition of his *Commentary*, yielded, up to a certain point, to the weight of the reasons advanced by the Tübingen critic, and acknowledged the necessity of holding for the explanation of the Epistle the existence at Rome, if not of a majority, at least of a very strong minority of Judaizers. Philippi made a similar concession. Things had come so far three years ago, that Holtzmann could assert without exaggeration that "Baur's opinion now hardly found any opponent."[2]

Yet even in 1858 Theodore Schott, while making large concessions to Baur's view regarding the tendency and arrangement of the Epistle, had energetically maintained that there was a Gentile-Christian majority in the church of Rome.[3] Several theologians have since then declared for the same view ; so Riggenbach in an article of the *Zeitschrift für die Lutherische Theologie* (1866), reviewing Mangold's work ; Hofman (of Erlangen) in his *Commentary* on our Epistle (1868) ; Dietzsch in an interesting monograph on Rom. v. 12–21, *Adam und Christus* (1871) ; Meyer in the fifth edition of his *Commentary* (1872). Even Hilgenfeld in his *Introduction* (p. 305) has thought right to modify Baur's opinion, and to acknowledge the existence of a strong Gentile-Christian and Pauline element in the Roman church ; finally, in the very year in which Holtzmann proclaimed the final triumph of Baur's view, two authors of well-known erudition and independence as critics, Schultz and Weizsäcker, declared in the *Jahrbücher für deutsche Theologie* (1876) for the preponderance of the Gentile-Christian element.

After all these oscillations an attempt at conciliation was to be expected. Beyschlag[4] has proposed such a solution in a work in which the facts are grouped with a master-hand, and which concludes, on the one side, that the majority of the Roman church, in conformity with Paul's express statements, was of Gentile origin ; but, on the other, that this Gentile majority shared Judaizing convictions, because it was composed of former proselytes.

According to the plan which we have adopted, and not to anticipate the exegesis of the Epistle, we shall not here discuss the passages alleged either for or against the Gentile origin of the majority of the readers ;[5] either for or against the Judaizing tendency of this majority.[6]

But outside the exegesis properly so called we have some indications which may serve to throw light on the double question of the composition and tendency of the majority of the church.

---

[1] "Ueber Zweck und Veranlassung des Römerbriefs," in the *Zeitschrift für Wissenschaft liche Theologie*, 1836 (reproduced in his *Paulus*, I. 343 et seq.).
[2] *Jahrbücher für protestantische Theologie*.
[3] *Der Römerbrief, seinem Zwecke und Gedankengange nach, ausgelegt.*
[4] See the article already quoted, p. 68.
[5] *For*: i. 6, 13, xi. 13, xv. 14 et seq. *Against*: ii. 17, iv. 1, vii. 1.
[6] *Against*: i. 8, 11, 12, vi. 17, xiv. 1-xv. 13, xvi, 17-19, 25. *For*: the whole polemic against the righteousness of the law.

1. The letter itself which we have to study. St. Paul, who would not build on the foundation laid by another, could not write a letter like this, containing a didactic exposition of the gospel, except to a church which he knew belonged to him at least indirectly in its composition and tendency as well as origin.

2. The ignorance of the rulers of the synagogue in regard to the gospel. Baur himself, in rejecting Luke's narrative as a fiction of the author of the Acts, has acknowledged the incompatibility of this fact with the preponderance of a majority in the Roman church having a Jewish-Christian tendency.

3. The persecution of Nero in 64. This bloody catastrophe smote the church of Rome without touching the synagogue. "Now," says Weizsäcker, " if Christians had not yet existed at Rome, except as a mere Jewish party, the persecution which fell on them, without even ruffling the surface of Judaism, would be an inexplicable fact both in its origin and course." [1]

4. The information given by the apostle as to the state of the church in the beginning of his Roman captivity in Phil. i. He tells how the somewhat drowsy zeal of the Christians of the capital had been reawakened by his presence. And in this connection he mentions *some* Christians (τινές) who set themselves fervently to preach, but from envy (ver. 15). Who are they? The common answer is: the Judaizers of the Roman church. Well and good. But in that case, as they form an exception to the majority of the faithful whom Paul has just mentioned (τοὺς πλείονας, *the majority*, ver. 14), and who have received a holy impulse from confidence in his bonds, the Judaizers can only have been a minority. Here, then, is an express testimony against the prevalence of Jewish-Christianity in the church of Rome. Against it is Weizsäcker, who exhibits this proof in all its force.

5. The composition of Mark's Gospel. It is generally admitted that this narrative was composed at Rome, and for the Christians of the capital. Now the detailed explanations contained in the book as to certain Jewish customs, and the almost entire absence of quotations from the Old Testament, do not sanction the view that its author contemplated a majority of readers of Jewish origin.

6. The Epistle of Clement of Rome. This writing, which is some thirty odd years posterior to the Epistle to the Romans, breathes in all respects, as Weizsäcker says, the spirit of the Gentile-Christian world. Such is also the judgment of Harnack in his introduction to the Epistle.[2] No doubt it is far from the strong spirituality of Paul, but still it is substantially his conception of Christianity. Now, the national type of this great church cannot, as Weizsäcker says, have become transformed in so short a space of time. This writing is therefore a new proof of the predominance of the Gentile element in this church from its origin.

7. The Easter controversy of the second century. Rome put herself at the head of all Christendom to root out the Paschal rite established in the churches of Asia Minor. And whence came the offence caused by the mode of celebrating Easter in those churches? From the fact that they celebrated the holy Easter supper on the evening of the 14th Nisan, at the same moment when the Jews, in obedience to the law, were celebrating their Paschal feast. Certainly, if the Roman church had been under the sway of a Judaizing tradition, it would not thus have found itself at the head of the crusade raised against them.

8. The catacombs of Rome. There are found at every step in those burying-places names belonging to the noblest families of the city, some of them even closely related to the imperial family. The fact shows the access which Christianity had found from the first to the upper classes of Roman

---

[1] Article quoted, p. 163.
[2] In the edition of the *Apostolic Fathers*, published by Gebhardt, Harnack, and Zahn

44 / Introduction

society, who assuredly did not belong to Judaism. Another proof, the full force of which has been brought out by Weiszäcker.

To support his view, Baur has quoted the passage of Hilary, which we have already mentioned, p. 37, and particularly the following words : " It is certain that in the time of the apostles there were Jews dwelling at Rome. Those of them who had believed, taught the Romans to profess Christ, while keeping the law." [1] But the contrast which the passage establishes between *Jews* and *Romans* shows clearly that Hilary himself looked on the latter, who, according to him, formed the great body of the church, as of Gentile origin. So the fact is precisely the reverse of what Baur affects to prove from the words. And as to the legal tendency which, according to Hilary, the Jewish-Christian instructors had inculcated on the Romans, it is clear that in the third or fourth century this writer possessed no tradition on the subject ; nothing positive was known at Rome in the second century regarding facts otherwise of great importance, such as Paul's journey to Spain. It was therefore a conclusion which he drew from the anti-Jewish polemic which he thought he could trace in the Epistle to the Romans.

If any one is entitled to appeal to this passage, it would seem to be not Baur, but Beyschlag. Yet even that would not be exact ; for Hilary nowhere says that those Romans who had been converted by the believing Jews of Rome formerly belonged to Judaism as proselytes. The contrary is rather to be inferred from the words he uses. Besides, Beyschlag's solution, during the twenty years that have elapsed since it was proposed, has found only a single supporter, M. Schürer (in his review of Hilgenfeld's *Introduction*).[2] And the fact is easily understood. For either the gospel reached Rome through the synagogue—and then how would the proselytes have been in such a majority that the church could have been, as Beyschlag admits, regarded as an essentially Gentile-Christian community ? or the gospel spread to the capital from the churches of Greece and Asia Minor, in which the spiritualism of Paul was supreme—and in that case whence came the legal character with which Beyschlag supposes it to have been impressed ? The hypothesis asserts too much or too little. So Weizsäcker and Schultz have not stopped for an instant to refute it.

The result of our study is, that the Roman church was mostly of Gentile origin and Pauline tendency, even before the apostle addressed our letter to it. The formation of the church was indirectly traceable to him, because its authors proceeded for the most part from the churches of the East, whose existence was due to his apostolic labors. Besides, the recruiting of the church having taken place chiefly in the midst of the Roman, that is to say, Gentile population, Paul was entitled to regard it as belonging to the domain of the Apostle of the Gentiles. Of course this solution will not be valid until it has passed the ordeal of the texts of the Epistle itself.

The result which we have just reached renders it at once more difficult and more easy to explain the course adopted by the apostle in writing such a letter to this church.

For if it is easier to explain how he could by writing instruct a church which came within the domain assigned to him by the Lord, on the other hand it is more embarrassing to say with what view he could repeat in writing to this church all that which it should already have known.

---

[1] *Constat temporibus apostolorum Judæos . . . Roma habitasse, ex quibus hi qui crediderant, tradiderunt Romanis ut Christum profitentes legem servarent.*
[2] *Studien und Kritiken,* 1876.

THE EPISTLE 3

To study the composition of this Epistle, which establishes for the first time a relation between the apostle and the church, we shall have three points to consider :—(1) the author ; (2) the circumstances of his life in which he composed the letter ; (3) the aim which he set before him. We shall continue to avoid interrogating our Epistle except in so far as the data which it may furnish are obvious at a glance, and demand no exegetical discussion.

A. *The Author*

The author declares himself to be Paul, the apostle of the Gentiles (i. 1-7, xi. 13, xv. 15-20). The sending of the letter pertains, in his view, to the fulfilling of the commission which he has received, " to bring all the Gentiles to the obedience of the faith" (i. 5).

The unanimous tradition of the church is in harmony with this declaration of the author.

Between the years 90 and 100 of our era, *Clement*, a presbyter of the church of Rome, reproduced in chap. xxxv. of his Epistle to the Corinthians the picture of the vices of the Gentiles, such as it is traced in Rom. i.; in chap. xxxviii. he applies to the circumstances of his time the exhortations which are addressed to the strong and the weak in chap. xiv. of our Epistle. Our letter was therefore preserved in the archives of the church of Rome, and recognized as a work of the apostle whose name it bears.

It cannot be doubted that the author of the Epistle called the *Epistle of Barnabas* (written probably in Egypt about 96), when writing his third chapter, had present to his mind Rom. iv. 11 et seq. : " I have set thee to be a father of the nations believing in the Lord in uncircumcision." [1]

The letters of *Ignatius* again and again reproduce the antithesis in the twofold origin of Jesus as Son of David and Son of God, Rom. i. 3, 4.

In the *Dialogue with Trypho*, chap. xxvii., Justin, about the middle of the second century, repeats the enumeration of the many biblical passages whereby Paul, Rom. iii., demonstrates the natural corruption of man.

The *Epistle to Diognetus* says, chap. ix., not without allusion to Rom. v. 18, 19 : " That the iniquity of many may be covered through righteousness, and that the righteousness of one may justify many sinners."

The *churches of Lyon and Vienne*, in their letter to the churches of Pontus (about 177), speak of their martyrs (Eus. v. 1) : " Really proving *that the sufferings of this present time*," etc. (Rom. viii. 18).

Many features of the picture of Gentile infamies, Rom. i., reappear in the *Apologies of Athenagoras* and of *Theophilus*, shortly after the middle of the second century. The latter quotes Rom. ii. 6-9, and xiii. 7, 8 textually.

The so-called *Canon of Muratori* (between 170 and 180) places the Epistle to the Romans among the writings which the church receives, and which should be read publicly.

---

[1] As in Rom. : Τῶν πιστευόντων δἰ ἀκροβυστίας (nothing similar in the passage of Gen. xvii. 5).

The quotations made by *Irenæus* (56 times), *Clement of Alexandria*, and *Tertullian*, are very numerous. It is only from this time forward that Paul is expressly named in these quotations as the author.

In the third century *Origen*, and in the fourth *Eusebius*, do not mention any doubt as expressed on the subject of the authenticity of our Epistle.

The testimony of heretics is not less unanimous than that of the Fathers.

Basilides, *Ptolemæus*, and very particularly *Marcion*, from the first half of the second century onward, make use of our Epistle as an undisputed apostolical document.

Throughout the whole course of the past centuries, only two theologians have contested this unanimous testimony of the church and the sects. These are the English author *Evanson*, in a work on the Gospels, of the last century, and *Bruno Baur*, in our own day, in Germany. They ask :—
1. Why does the author of the Acts of the Apostles not say a word about a work of such importance ? As if the Book of Acts were a biography of the Apostle Paul ! 2. How are we to understand the numerous salutations of chap. xvi. addressed to a church in which Paul had never lived ? As if (granting that this page of salutations really belongs to our Epistle) the apostle could not have known all these persons in Greece and the East who were now living at Rome, as we shall prove in the case, for example, of Aquila and Priscilla ! 3. How can we hold the existence of a church at Rome so considerable as our Epistle supposes before the arrival of any apostle in the city ? As if the founding of the church of Antioch did not furnish us with a sufficient precedent to solve the question !

Thus there is nothing to prevent us from accepting the testimony of the church, which is confirmed, besides, by the grandeur which betrays a master, and the truly apostolic power of the work itself, as well as by its complete harmony in thought and style with the other writings acknowledged to be the apostle's.

B. *The Date*

The external circumstances in which this letter was composed are easily made out.

1. Paul had not yet visited Rome (i. 10-13) ; this excludes every date posterior to the spring of the year 62, when he arrived in the city.

2. The apostle is approaching the end of his ministry in the East. From Jerusalem to Illyria he has filled every place with the preaching of the gospel of Christ ; now he must seek a field of labor westward, at the extremity of Europe, in Spain, xv. 18-24. Paul could not have written these words before the end of his residence at Ephesus, which lasted probably from the autumn of 54 to the Pentecost of 57.

3. At the time he wrote he was still free ; for he was discussing his plans for travelling, xv. 23-25. It was therefore at a period previous to his arrest at Jerusalem (Pentecost of the year 59).

The interval which remains available is thus reduced to the short period from the year 57 to 59.

4. At the time when he wrote, he was about to start for Jerusalem, at the head of a numerous deputation charged with carrying to the mother church the fruits of a collection organized on its behalf in all the churches of the Gentile world (Rom. xv. 24-28). When he wrote his first Epistle to the Corinthians (Pentecost 57), and a year and a half later (unless I am mistaken) his second (summer 58), the collection was not yet finished, and he did not know at that time whether it would be liberal enough to warrant his going himself to present it to the church of Jerusalem (1 Cor. xvi. 1-4 ; 2 Cor. viii. and ix.). All is completed when he writes the Epistle to the Romans, and the question of his taking part personally in the mission is decided (xv. 28). This indication brings us to the time immediately pre-

ceding Paul's departure from Corinth for Jerusalem, which took place in March 59.

5. Finally, we are struck with the sort of anxiety which appears in the words used, xv. 30-32 : " Strive together with me in your prayers to God for me, that I may be delivered from them that do not believe in Judea." We recognize in this passage the disquieting presentiments which came out in all the churches at that point in the apostle's life, when he went to face for the last time the hatred of the inhabitants and authorities of Jerusalem (comp. Acts xx. 22, 23, xxi. 4, 10-12). The Epistle to the Romans was therefore written very shortly before his departure for that city.

To fix the point exactly, it remains only to attempt to determine the *place* of its composition.

1. xvi. 1, he recommends Phebe, a deaconess of Cenchrea, the port of Corinth, on the Egean Sea. It is therefore probable that if this passage really belongs to the Epistle to the Romans, Paul wrote from Corinth or its neighborhood.

2. He names Gaius as his host (xvi. 23). This is probably the same person as is mentioned in the first Epistle to the Corinthians (i. 14) as being one of the earliest converts of that city.

3. He sends a greeting from Erastus, treasurer of the city, xvi. 23. It is probable that this person is the same as we find mentioned, 2 Tim. iv. 20, in these words : " Erastus abode *at Corinth*."

These indications lead us to conclude with great probability that Corinth was the place of composition. This result agrees with the preceding one relative to the date. In fact, mention is made in Acts xx. 2 of a three months' stay made by Paul in Hellas, that is to say, in the southern part of Greece, of which Corinth was the capital. This stay immediately preceded Paul's departure for Jerusalem, and took place, consequently, in the months of December 58, and January and February 59.

So it was during this time of repose that the apostle, after so many anxieties and labors, found the calm necessary for composing such a work. The time was solemn. The first part of his apostolic task was finished. The East, wholly evangelized in a way, lay behind him ; he had before him the West still enveloped in the darkness of paganism, but which belonged also to the domain assigned him by the Lord. In the midst of this darkness he discerns a luminous point, the church of Rome. On this he fixes his eye before entering on the journey to Italy in person.

We shall see if the Epistle to the Romans corresponds to the solemnity of the situation.

C. *The Aim.*

Critics differ as much in regard to *the aim* of our Epistle as they are agreed about its date and authenticity. Since Baur's time the subject has become one of the most controverted in the whole range of New Testament criticism.

The question stands thus : If we assign a special practical aim to the Epistle, we put ourselves, as it seems, in contradiction to the very general and quasi-systematic character of its contents. If, on the contrary, we ascribe to it a didactic and wholly general aim, it differs thereby from the other letters of St. Paul, all of which spring from some particular occasion, and have a definite aim. The author of the oldest critical study of the New Testament which we possess, the so-called *Fragment of Muratori*, wrote thus about the middle of the second century : " St. Paul's letters themselves reveal clearly enough, to any one who wishes to know, in what place and *with what view* they were composed." If he had lived among the discussions of our day, he would certainly not have expressed himself thus about our Epistle. What increases the difficulty is, that the letter is not addressed to a church which Paul had himself founded, and cannot be regarded, like his other Epistles, as the continuation of his missionary work. Let us add, finally, the sort of obscurity which, as we have seen, rests on the founding of this church, and consequently on the nature of its composition and its religious tendency, and we shall understand how an almost numberless multitude of opinions should have been broached, especially in the present day, regarding the intention of the letter. It seems to us possible to distribute the proposed solutions into three principal groups.

The first starts from the fact that all the other Epistles of the apostle owe their origin to some special occasion, and ascribes to this one a practical and definite aim. In the situation of Paul's work, and at the time when he was preparing to transfer his mission to the West, it concerned him to acquire or to make sure of the sympathy of the Roman church, destined as it was to become his point of support in those new countries, as Antioch had been in the East. Our Epistle, on this view, was the means chosen to obtain this result. Its aim was thus *apologetic*.

Diametrically opposed to this first group is a second, which takes account especially of the general and systematic character of the Epistle. Such contents do not seem to be compatible with the intention of obtaining a particular practical result. The apostle, it is therefore held, simply proposed to instruct and edify the church of Rome. The aim of the letter was *didactic*.

Between these two groups stands a third, which admits, indeed, the aim of teaching, but that with a definite intention, namely, to combat the legal Jewish-Christianity which was already dominant, or at least threatening to become so, within the Roman church. Our Epistle, consequently, had a *polemic* intention.

We proceed to review these three groups, each containing numerous shades of opinion. That which we have indicated in the third place, evidently forming the transition between the other two, we shall treat second in the following exposition.

FIRST GROUP : APOLOGETIC AIM

The way was opened in this direction at one and the same time (1836) by Credner and Baur.[1] The apostle wishes to prepare for himself a favorable reception in the principal church of the West; such is the general viewpoint, which is variously modified by the different adherents of this conception.

I. The most precise and sharply defined situation is that supposed by Baur. The church of Rome, being in the great majority of its members Jewish-Christian by origin, and particularistic in tendency, could not look on Paul's mission to the Gentiles otherwise than with dislike. No doubt, Jewish-Christianity no longer desired at Rome, as it had done formerly in Galatia, to impose circumcision on the Gentiles; it did not attack, as at Corinth, Paul's apostolic dignity and moral character. But the Christians of Rome asked if it was just and agreeable to God's promises to admit the Gentiles *en masse* into the church, as Paul was doing, before the Jewish people had taken their legitimate place in it. It was not wished to exclude the Gentiles. But it was maintained that, in virtue of the *right of priority* granted to Israel, they ought not to enter till the chosen nation had done so. Paul feels deeply that a church so minded cannot serve as the point of

---

[1] Credner, *Einleitung in das N. T.* 1836, § 142. Baur, *Tübinger Zeitschrift*, 3 Heft : Ueber Zweck und Veranlassung des Römerbriefs. This forms the original work which the author reproduced in his *Paulus*, 1st edition, 1845, and afterward completed in the *Theol. Jahrb.* 1857. The author gradually softened his first conception; this is most of all apparent in his last exposition : *Das Christenthum und die Christl. Kirche*, etc., 1860, p. 62 et seq.

support for his mission in the West, that it will rather put a hindrance in his way. And hence, at the last stage of his sojourn in Greece, during the three months of rest which are allowed him at Corinth, he writes this letter to the Romans, with the view of completely rooting out the prejudice from which their repugnance to his mission springs. Not only has the right of priority, to which Israel pretends, no existence, since the righteousness of faith has now for all time replaced that of the law, but the conversion of the Gentiles, for which Paul is laboring, will be the very means which God will use to bring back the hostile Jews to Himself. It will be seen that, on this view, the great outline of the ways of God, ix.–xi., far from being, as is commonly thought, a simple appendix, forms the central part of the letter, that in which its true intention is expressed. The whole preceding exposition of the righteousness of faith forms its admirable preface.[1]

The treatise of Baur produced at the time of its appearance an effect similar to that caused eight years afterward by a like work on the Gospel of John. The learned world was as it were fascinated; men thought they were on the eve of a sort of revelation. From the dazzling effect then produced criticism is only slowly recovering at the present day. Credner's work was less developed and less striking; he only added to the idea which we have just indicated in the form presented by Baur an original feature, which has recently been revived by Holsten. We mean the relation between the composition of the Epistle to the Romans and the large amount of the collection made in behalf of the church of Jerusalem at the same period. At the very time that he was endeavoring by this work of love to influence the metropolis of Jewish-Christianity in the East, his practical genius sought by means of our Epistle to acquire a point of support for his mission in the most important Jewish-Christian church of the West. So understood, the letter becomes an *act*, a real and serious work, as is naturally to be expected from a man like Paul composing such a treatise.

The following, however, are the reasons which have prevailed with science more and more to reconsider its verdict:

1. It has been found impossible to accept the very forced explanations by which Baur has labored to get rid of the passages attesting the Gentile origin and the Pauline tendency of the church of Rome.—2. An attempt at conquest, such as that which Baur ascribes to Paul, has been felt to be incompatible with the principle professed by him in our very Epistle, not *to build on another man's foundation*. In this case Paul would be doing even worse; he would be introducing himself into a house wholly built by strange hands, and would be seeking to install himself in it with his whole staff of apostolic helpers; this, no doubt, with a view to the work of Christ, but would the end justify the means?—3. The idea which Baur ascribes to the Christians of Rome, that of restricting the preaching of the gospel to the Jews until the whole elect people should become believers, is a strange and monstrous conception, of which there is not the slightest trace either in the New Testament or in any work of Christian antiquity. The Judaizers, on the contrary, strongly approved of the conversion of the Gentiles, insisting only on the condition of circumcision (Gal. v. 11, vi. 13). To refuse to the Gentiles the preaching of salvation till it should please the Jews to become converts, would have been an aggravation, and not at all, as Baur says, an attenuation of the old Jewish pretensions.—4. It is impossible from this point of view to account for the detailed instruction with which the Epistle opens (i.–viii.), and in particular for the description of

---

[1] Baur expresses himself thus: "The apostle's intention is to refute Jewish particularism so radically that it shall remain like an uprooted tree in the consciousness of the age.... The absolute nullity of every claim founded on particularism: such is the fundamental idea of the Epistle" (*Paulus*, 2d ed. I. p. 380).

the corruption of the Gentiles (chap. i.). If all that was only intended to provide a justification of the missionary course followed by the apostle, stated ix.-xi., was not Schwegler right in saying "that such an expenditure of means was out of proportion to the end in view?" It is not less difficult to explain from this standpoint the use of the moral part, especially of chap. xii.—5. In general, the horizon of the Epistle is too vast, its exposition too systematic, its tone too calm, to allow us to ascribe to it the intention of making a conquest, or to see in it something like a mine destined to spring the ramparts of a hostile position.—6. This explanation comes very near to compromising the moral character of Paul. What Baur did not say, his disciple Holsten frankly confesses in our day.[1] After quoting these words of Volkmar: "that the Epistle to the Romans is the maturest fruit of Paul's mind," this critic adds: "But it must, at the same time, be confessed that it is not its *purest* work. Under the *pressure of a practical want*, that of reconciling the Jewish-Christians to his gospel . . ., Paul has not kept—*and he knows it well himself*—at the height of his own thought . . . ; he has *blunted the edge of his gospel.*" If, to bear out the exposition of Baur and his school, one must go the length of making the Epistle to the Romans a work of Jesuitism, we think that this solution is judged.

Baur has cited the testimony of Hilary (*Ambrosiaster*), who says of the Romans: "Who, having been wrongly instructed by the Judaizers, were immediately corrected (by this letter)."[2] But even on this point it has been shown that Hilary's opinion was wholly different from Baur's; since, according to the former, the Judaizers, who had led the Romans into error in regard to the law, were absolutely the same as those who had troubled Antioch and Galatia;[3] while, according to Baur, those of Rome made entirely different pretensions.

II. The difficulties which had led even Baur to modify his view have forced critics who are attached in the main to his opinion to soften it still more considerably. The critic whom we may regard as the principal representative of Baur's corrected exposition is Mangold.[4] According to this author, the church of Rome, while Jewish-Christian in its majority and legal in its tendency, had not the strictly particularistic conception which Baur ascribes to it. It was merely imbued with certain prejudices against Paul and his work; it did not know what to think of that wide propagation of a gospel without law in the Gentile world. The general abandonment of Mosaism, which the missionary action of the apostle brought in its train, appeared to it to endanger the Lord's work, and even the morality of those multitudes of believing Gentiles. Paul, therefore, on the eve of transferring his activity to the West, felt the need of reassuring the Romans as to the spirit of his teaching, and the consequences of his work. In i.-viii. he seeks to make them understand his *doctrine;* in ix.-xi. he explains to them his *mission*. He hopes thereby to succeed in gaining a powerful auxiliary in his new field of labor.—This view has obtained a pretty general assent; it is found wholly or in part in Thiersch, Holtzmann, Ritschl, Beyschlag, Hausrath, Schenkel, Schultz, as also in Sabatier.[5] It has its best support in the anti-Judaistic tendency, which may, with some measure of probability, be ascribed to various parts of the Epistle. But it has not the perfect transparency of Baur's view; it is hard to know wherein those prejudices of the Roman church against Paul's work consist, neither springing from Judaizing legality, properly so called, nor from the exceptional point of view imagined by Baur.—Besides, as directed to a

---

[1] In his article: "Der Gedankengang des Römerbriefs," *Jahrb. f. prot. Theol.* 1879.
[2] *Qui, male inducti, statim correcti sunt.* . . .
[3] Philippi has quoted these words: *Hi sunt qui et Galatas subverterant.* . . .
[4] In the work already quoted, *Der Römerbrief*, etc., 1866.
[5] *L'apôtre Paul*, p. 159 et seq.

church not strictly Judaizing, what purpose would be served by the long preface of the first eight chapters, pointed against the righteousness of the law? What end, especially in the line of justifying Paul's missionary practice, would be served by the moral part, xii.-xiv., which has not the slightest connection with his work? Here, certainly, we can apply the saying of Schwegler, "that the expenditure of means is disproportioned to the end." There remain, finally, all the reasons which we have alleged against the Jewish-Christian composition of the church.

III. While acknowledging the Gentile origin of the majority of the church, and the Pauline character of its faith, Schott and Riggenbach [1] think that the object of the Epistle is simply to awaken and quicken its sympathy with Paul's work, on the eve of his passing to the West.—But in that case the extravagance of the means employed becomes still more startling. To demonstrate in the outset in eight long chapters the truth of Paul's gospel to a Pauline church, in order to obtain its missionary co-operation, would not this be idle work—labor lost?

It is true that Schott, to meet this difficulty, images an objection raised at Rome to Paul's future mission in the West. The East, says he, was full of Jewish communities; so that, while laboring in these countries for the Gentiles, Paul was at the same time laboring, up to a certain point, in the midst of Jews, and for their good. But it was wholly otherwise in the West, where the Jews were not so plentifully scattered. Here Paul's work must necessarily be severed from action on the Jewish people. Paul, anticipating the accusations which would arise from this fact, writes the Epistle to the Romans in order to obviate them.—But the difference which Schott lays down on this head between the East and the West does not rest on any historical proof. And, as Beyschlag rightly asks, "What strange believers those Christians of Rome must have been, who, while themselves enjoying the blessings of salvation, notwithstanding their Gentile origin, imagined that those same blessings could not be offered to the other Western Gentiles till after Israel had been wholly converted!"

IV. Hofmann has given to the apologetic intention an altogether particular complexion. Our letter, he would have it, is the *personal* justification of Paul in reference to the long delays which had retarded his arrival at Rome. It was intended to prove that a gospel such as his leaves no room in the heart of its apostle for feelings of shame or lukewarmness. And thus it sought to secure a favorable reception for his person and mission. The object of his letter is consequently to be found revealed in i. 14-16.— But is it possible to conceive so broad and authoritative a scheme of doctrine as that of the Epistle to the Romans, given with a view so narrow and personal? The passage, i. 14-16, may have served as a preface for Paul to his subject; but it cannot express the *aim* of the Epistle.

In general, Paul might certainly expect, as a fruit of this letter, an increase of sympathy for his person and mission; and the great change which was about to pass over his life and work would naturally lead him to desire this result. But it must have been a more urgent reason which led him to take pen in hand, and to give a fuller and more systematic exposition of his gospel than he had bestowed on any other church.

SECOND GROUP : POLEMIC AIM

The authors belonging to this group do not find in our Epistle the proof of any aim relating to the apostle himself and to his missionary work. The aim of the letter, in their view, is to be explained solely by the state of the church to which it is addressed. The object to be accomplished was

---

[1] Schott, work quoted. Riggenbach, *Zeitschrift für lutherische Theologie und Kirche* (review of Mangold's work), 1866.

52 / Introduction

to destroy the legal tendency at Rome, or to render its introduction impossible ; and so, according to some, to bring about union and peace between the two parties of the church.

I. Thus Hilary spoke in this direction : " The Christians of Rome had allowed Mosaic rites to be imposed on them, as if full salvation were not to be found in Christ ; Paul wished to teach them the mystery of the cross of Christ, which had not yet been expounded to them." Similar words are to be found in many of the Fathers, as well as in some Reformers and modern theologians (Augustine, Melanchthon, Flatt, etc.). The opinion of Thiersch is also substantially the same : " The church of Rome having been left by Peter in a state of doctrinal inferiority, Paul sought to raise it to the full height of Christian knowledge." Volkmar, too, would seem to adhere to this opinion. He calls our Epistle " *a war and peace treatise*, intended to reconcile a strictly Jewish-Christian church to the free preaching of the gospel." This explanation suits the grave and didactic character of the fundamental part, i.–viii., as well as the express statement of the theme, i. 16, 17. Only it is not easy to understand how Paul could have congratulated his readers on the *type of doctrine* according to which they had been taught, as he does xi. 17, if his intention had been to substitute a new conception of the gospel for theirs. We have found, besides, that the majority of the church was not Jewish-Christian in tendency.

II. From early times down to our own day, many have thought that Paul's polemic against Jewish legalism was intended to bring about the union of the two parties at Rome. We shall cite in particular, in the Middle Ages, Rabanus Maurus and Abélard ; in modern times, Eichhorn (partly), Flatt, Hug, Bleek, Hilgenfeld, Hodge, etc. Hug thinks that after the Jews, who had been banished from Rome by the edict of Claudius, returned, a new treaty of union became necessary between the Christians of Gentile and those of Jewish origin. This *Eirenicon* was the Epistle to the Romans, which revolves entirely round this idea : " Jews and Gentiles are equal before God ; their rights and weaknesses are similar ; and if any advantage existed in favor of the one body, it was abolished by Christ, who united all in one universal religion." Hilgenfeld ascribes to Paul the intention of uniting the rich Jewish-Christian aristocracy with the numerous *plebs* of Gentile origin. Hodge, the celebrated American commentator, denies the prevalence of a Judaizing tendency in the church of Rome, but thinks, nevertheless, " that conflicts now and again arose, both regarding doctrine and discipline, between the believers of the two races," and that this was the occasion of our Epistle. The view of Baumgarten-Crusius is almost the same : " This exposition of the Pauline conception is intended to unite believing Jews and Gentiles in forwarding the common work." [1] From this point of view the passage, xiv. 1–xv. 13, must be regarded as containing the aim of the Epistle. But this piece, bearing as it does the character of a simple appendix, cannot play so decisive a part ; and it would be inconceivable that, up to that point, Paul should have given neither in the preface nor in the course of the letter the least sign of this conciliatory intention ; for, finally, when he demonstrates the complete parity of Gentiles and Jews, both in respect of the condemnation under which they lie and of the faith which is the one condition of salvation for all, he nowhere thinks of bringing Jews and Gentiles into union with one another, but of glorifying the greatness of salvation and the mercy of God its author.

III. Weizsäcker (see at p. 42) also holds the anti-Jewish tendency of our Epistle. But as he recognizes the Gentile-Christian composition of the

---

[1] Holsten, too, has words to the same effect : " At the height of his triumph at Corinth, Paul felt for the first time the want and the necessity of a reconciliation between Gentile-Christian Christianity and that of the Jewish-Christians. The Epistle to the Romans is the first of those letters of peace and union which sought to satisfy this want of the new religion."

church, and cannot consequently admit the predominance of the legal spirit in such a community, he supposes that the time had come when the Judaizing attack which had assailed all the churches of Paul was beginning to trouble it also. "The church was not Judaizing, but it was worked by Judaizers." This situation, supposed by Weizsäcker, is perfectly similar to that described in Phil. i. Paul's aim, accordingly, was this: he does not wish to *attack*, as Baur thought, but to *defend;* he wishes to preserve, not to acquire. Thus the fundamental part on the righteousness of faith and the sanctification flowing from it (i.-viii.) finds an easy explanation. Thus, too, we have no difficulty in understanding the famous passage, ix-xi., which is intended, not, as most modern critics since Baur suppose, to justify the missionary practice of Paul, but to solve this problem raised by the progress of events: How does it happen, if this gospel of Paul is the truth, that the Jews, the elect people, everywhere reject it?

One has a feeling of satisfaction and relief after reading this excellent work, so judicious and impartial; one feels as if he had reached shelter from the sweeping current, the spirit of prejudice which has swayed criticism for forty years. And yet it is impossible for us to accept this solution. How, if our Epistle was occasioned by a violent Judaizing aggression, is there no trace of the fact throughout the whole of the letter, and especially in the introductory passsge, i. 8–15? St. Paul there congratulates the Romans on their faith, and yet makes not the slightest allusion to the dangers which it runs at that very moment, and which form the occasion of his writing! How could the moral part, from chap. xii. onward, present no trace whatever of this polemical tendency? Weizsäcker confesses the fact, but explains it by saying that Jewish legalism had only just been imported into the church, and had not yet affected its moral life. This answer is not sufficient; for it is precisely by forms and observances that ritualism strives to act. In the Epistle to the Galatians, written in a similar situation to that which Weizsäcker supposes, the anti-Judaistic polemic is quite as emphatically brought out in the moral part as in the doctrinal exposition; comp. v. 6 et seq.; then ver. 14, and especially the interjected remarks, ver. 18-: "If ye are led by the Spirit, ye are not under the law;" ver. 23: "The law is not against such things" (the fruits of the Spirit); comp. also Gal. vi. 12–16. We shall have to examine elsewhere in the course of exposition the passage, Rom. xvi. 17-20, where Paul puts the church on its guard against the arrival of Judaizers as a probable fact, but one yet to come. Finally, notwithstanding all the ability of this critic, we think that he has not entirely succeeded in explaining the complete difference between the Epistle to the Romans, so calm and coldly didactic, and that to the Galatians, so abrupt and vehement in its tone.

IV. There is a view which to some extent gives weight to these objections, while still maintaining the anti-Judaistic character of the Epistle. We mean the solution which was already propounded at the time of the Reformation by Erasmus, and reproduced in our day by Philippi, Tholuck (last edition), and in a measure by Beyschlag. Paul, who found himself pursued by Judaizing emmissaries at Antioch, in Galatia, and at Corinth, naturally foresees their speedy arrival at Rome; and as, when a city is threatened by an enemy, its walls are fortified and it is prepared for a siege; so the apostle, by the powerful and decisive teaching contained in our Epistle, *fortifies* the Roman church, and puts it in a condition to resist the threatening attack victoriously. Nothing more natural than this situation and the *preventive* intention of our Epistle connected with it; the explanation harmonizes well with the term *strengthening*, which the apostle frequently uses to express the effect which he would like to produce by his work within the church (i. 11, xvi. 25). The only question is, whether so considerable a treatise could have been composed solely with a view to a future and contingent want. Then there is not in the whole letter more than a single allusion to the possible arrival of the Judaizers (xvi. 17-20). How could this word thrown in by the way at the close, after the salutations, reveal the intention which dictated the letter, unless we are to ascribe to the apostle the course which ladies are said to follow, of putting the real thought of their letter into the postscript?

V. An original solution, which also belongs to this group of interpretations, has been offered by Ewald.[1] According to him, Christianity had remained hitherto enveloped in the Jewish religion; but Paul began to dread the consequences of this solidarity. For he foresaw the conflict to the death which was about to take place between the Roman empire and the Jewish people, nov. becoming more and more fanaticized. The Epistle to the Romans is written with the view of breaking the too close and compromising bond which still united the synagogue and the church, and which threatened to drag the latter into foolish enterprises. The practical aim of the writing would thus appear in chap. xiii. in the exhortation addressed to Christians *to obey the higher powers ordained of God* in the political domain; and the entire Epistle would be intended to demonstrate the profound incompatibility between the Jewish and the Christian spirit, and so to establish this application. One cannot help admiring in this theory the originality of Ewald's genius, but we cannot make up our mind to attach such decisive importance to the warning of chap. xiiii.; for this passage is only a subdivision of the moral instruction, which is itself only the second part of the didactic exposition. So subordinate a passage cannot express the aim of the Epistle.

We are at the end of the solutions derived from the danger which the Roman church is alleged to have been then incurring from the legal principle, whether as a present enemy or a threatening danger. And we are thus brought to the third class of explanations, composed of all those which despair of finding a local and temporary aim for Paul's Epistle.

THIRD GROUP: DIDACTIC AIM

According to the critics who belong to this group, the Epistle to the Romans is a systematic exposition of Christian truth, and has no other aim than to enlighten and strengthen the faith of the Christians of Rome in the interest of their salvation.

Thus the author of the ancient Muratori Fragment says simply: "The apostle expounds to the Romans the plan of the Scriptures by inculcating the fact that Christ is their first principle."

The ancient Greek expositors, Origen, Chrysostom, Theodoret, with those of the Middle Ages, such as John of Damascus, Oecumenius, Theophylact, seek no more mysterious aim than this: to guide men to Christ. But why especially address such instruction to the church of Rome? Theophylact answers: "What does good to the head, thereby does the same to the whole body." This answer betrays a time when Rome had come to occupy the central place in the church.

Our Reformers and their successors have almost the same idea of our Epistle: "The whole of this Epistle," says Calvin, "is composed methodically."[2] Paul, says Melanchthon, has drawn up in the Epistle to the Romans "the summary of Christian doctrine,[3] though he has not philosophized in this writing either on the mysteries of the Trinity, or on the mode of the incarnation, or on creation active and passive. Is it not in reality on the law, on sin, and on grace, that the knowledge of Christ depends?"

---

[1] *Die Sendschreiben des Apostels Paulus.* 1857. [2] "*Epistola tota methodica est.*"
[3] "*Doctrinæ christianæ compendium*" (Introduction to the *Loci communes* of 1521).

Grotius thus expresses himself : "Though addressed strictly speaking to the Romans, this letter contained all the supports (*munimenta*) of the Christian religion, so that it well deserved that copies of it should be sent to other churches." So he thinks he can explain the use of the Greek instead of the Latin language. He thus anticipates a recent hypothesis, of which we shall speak by and by. Tholuck in his first editions, and Olshausen in his excellent commentary, also think that Paul's aim was wholly general. He wished to show how the gospel, and the gospel only, fully answers to the need of salvation attaching to every human soul, a want which neither paganism nor Judaism can satisfy. Glöckler, Köllner, Reiche, and de Wette likewise adhere to this view ; the latter at the same time establishing a connection between the evangelical universalism expounded in our Epistle, and the position of Rome as the centre of the empire of the world. Meyer also, while fully sharing this view, feels the need of showing how the teaching was rooted in actual circumstances. He thinks that Paul has here expounded the gospel as it appeared to him at the close of the great struggle with Judaism from which he had just emerged, and as he would have preached it at Rome had he been able to go thither personally.

M. Reuss in his last work (*Les épîtres pauliniennes*) escapes from Baur's view, which had previously exercised a very marked influence over him. The absence of all polemic in our Epistle indicates, he thinks, that the apostle addresses this exposition of the essence of the gospel to an *ideal public*. In reality, are not the wants of all the churches substantially the same ? Only he ascribes to the apostle the special desire of making the church of Rome "the focus of light for the West."

M. Renan explains our Epistle by the importance of the church of Rome and the apostle's desire to give it a token of his sympathy. "He took advantage of an interval of rest to write in an epistolary form a sort of *résumé* of his theological teaching, and he addressed it to this church, composed of Ebionites and Jewish Christians, but embracing also proselytes and Gentile converts." This is not all. The careful analysis of chap. xv. and xvi. leads M. Renan to conclude that the letter was simultaneously addressed to three other churches, that of Ephesus, that of Thessalonica, and a fourth church unknown. This writer draws a picture of Paul's disciples all occupied in making copies of this manifesto intended for the different churches (*Saint Paul*, p. 481).

The force of all these explanations lies in the general and systematic tenor of the Epistle to the Romans. It is this characteristic which distinguishes it from all the others, except that to the Ephesians. But the weakness of these solutions appears—1. In the difference which they establish between this letter and Paul's other writings. "Such an Epistle," says Baur, "would be a fact without analogy in the apostle's career. It would not correspond to the true Pauline epistolary type." 2. In the fact that all these explanations utterly fail satisfactorily to answer the question : Why this systematic teaching addressed to Rome and not elsewhere ? 3. In the serious omissions from the system. Melanchthon was struck with this. We instance two of them especially : the omission of the doctrines relating to the person of Christ and to *the end of all things*, Christology and Eschatology.

But these objections do not appear to us to be insoluble. What, indeed, if these two characteristics which seem to be mutually contradictory, the local destination and the generality of the contents, were exactly the explanation of one another ? In the so varied course of apostolic history might there not be found a *particular* church which needed *general* teaching ? And was not this precisely the case with the church of Rome ?

We know that Paul did not omit, when he founded a church, to give those who were attracted by the name of Christ profound and detailed instruction regarding the gospel. Thiersch has thoroughly demonstrated this fact.[1] Paul refers to it in the question so frequently repeated in his Epistles : *Know ye not that . . .* ? which often applies to points of detail on which a pastor does not even touch in our day in the instruction which he gives to his catechumens.[2] The Book of Acts relates that at Ephesus Paul gave a course of Christian instruction in the school of the rhetorician Tyrannus *every day* for *two whole years.* What could be the subject of those daily and prolonged conferences, and that in a city like Ephesus? Most certainly Paul did not speak at random ; he followed some order or other. Starting from the moral nature of man, his natural powers of knowledge and his indestructible wants,[3] he showed the fall of man, the turpitude of the Gentile world,[4] and the inadequacy of Judaism to supply an efficacious remedy for human misery.[5] Thus he came to the means of salvation offered by God Himself.[6] From this point he cast a look backwards at the ancient revelation and its several aspects, the patriarchal promise and the Mosaic law.[7] He showed the essential unity and the radical difference between the law and the gospel.[8] In this retrospective glance he embraced the entire history of humanity, showing the relation between its fall in one man and its restoration in one.[9] Finally, on this basis he raised the edifice of the new creation. He revealed the mystery of the church, the body of the glorified Christ, the sanctification of the individual and of the family,[10] the relation between Christianity and the State ;[11] and unfolding the aspects of the divine plan in the conversion of the nations,[12] he led up to the restitution of all things, physical nature itself included, and to the glory to come.[13]

He did what he does in his Epistles, and particularly in the most systematic of all, the Epistle to the Romans. Baur has alleged that the apostles had no time, in the midst of their missionary labors, to systematize the gospel, and to compose a Christian dogmatic. But could Baur suppose that a mind of such strength as Paul's was could have lectured for two years before an audience like the cultivated class of the Ephesian population,[14] without having at least traced an outline of Christian doctrine ?

Now, this apostolic instruction which Paul gave with so much care in the churches which he founded, and which was the real basis of those spiritual edifices, he had not given at Rome. Thessalonica, Corinth, and Ephesus had enjoyed it ; the church of the Capital of the world had been deprived of it. Here the message had preceded the messenger. A community of believers had been formed in this city without his assistance. No doubt he reckoned on being there himself soon ; but once more he might be prevented ; he knew how many dangers attended its approaching journey to Jerusalem. And besides, should he arrive at Rome safe and sound, he had too much tact to think of putting the members of such a church as it were on the catechumen's bench. In these circumstances, how natural the idea of filling up by means of writing the blank which Providence had permitted, and of giving, in an *epistolary treatise* addressed to the church, the Christian instruction which it had missed, and which was indispensable to the solidity of its faith ! The apostle of the Gentiles was not able to establish the church in the metropolis of the Gentile world . . ., the work was taken out of his hands ; what shall he do ? He will found it anew. Under the already constructed edifice he will insinuate a powerful substruction—to wit, his apostolic doctrine systematically arranged, as he expounds it everywhere else *viva voce.*

---

[1] *Versuch zur Herstellung des histor. Standpunkts*, p. 91 et seq.
[2] The coming of Antichrist, 2 Thess. ii. 15 ; the judgment of angels by believers, 1 Cor. vi. 2, 3.
[3] Rom. i. 19, 20, ii. 14, 15.
[4] Rom. i. 23-31.
[5] Rom. ii. 1-iii. 20.
[6] Rom. iii. 21-26.
[7] Gal. iii. 15-17.
[8] Rom. iv., x.
[9] Rom. v. 12-21.
[10] Rom. xii.; Eph. i. iv. 1-vi. 9.
[11] Rom. xiii.
[12] Rom. ix.-xi.
[13] Rom. viii. ; 1 Cor. xv.
[14] See Acts xix. 31.

If such is the origin of the Epistle to the Romans, we have in it nothing less than the course of religious instruction, and in a way the dogmatic and moral catechism of St. Paul. In this explanation there is no occasion for the question why this instruction was addressed to Rome rather than to any other church. Rome was the only great church of the Gentile world to which Paul felt himself burdened with such a debt. This is the prevailing thought in the preface of his Epistle, and by which he clears the way for the treatment of his subject (i. 13-16). After reminding the Romans that they too, as Gentiles, belong to the domain confided to his apostleship, i. 1-6, he accounts, from ver. 8, for the involuntary delays which have retarded his arrival at Rome; and so comes at length to speak of the evangelical doctrine which he desired to impart *viva voce*, and which he now addresses to them in writing. Nothing could explain more naturally the transition from ver. 15 to ver. 16. The systematic form of the *treatise* which begins here, the expressly formulated theme which serves as its basis (i. 16, 17), the methodical development of the theme, first in a dogmatic part, i.-xi., then in a moral part, xii.-xv. 13 (which is not less systematically arranged than the former),—all these features demonstrate that the author here intends to give a didactic exposition.

No doubt there are blanks, as we have already acknowledged, in this summary of Christian truth, and we cannot in this respect compare it with our modern dogmatic systems. But the limits which Paul traced for himself are not difficult to understand. They were indicated by those of the personal revelation which he had received. The phrase: *my gospel*, which he uses twice in this Epistle (and only once again in his other letters), sufficiently indicates the domain within which he intended to confine himself. Within the general Christian revelation with which all the apostles were charged, Paul had received a special part, his lot, if one may so speak. This is what he calls, Eph. iii. 2, "the measure of the grace which had been committed to him." This part was neither the doctrine of the person of Christ, which belonged more particularly to the apostles who had lived with Him, nor the delineation of the *last things*, which was the common property of the apostolate. His special lot was the way of *gaining possession* of the Christian salvation. Now Paul wished to give to the church only that which he had himself received " through the teaching of Christ, without the intervention of any man" (Gal. i. 11, 12). And this is what has naturally determined the contents of the Epistle to the Romans. The limit of his divinely received gospel was that of this Epistle. This certainly did not prevent its contents from touching at all points the general teaching of the apostles, which included Paul's, as a wider circumference encloses a narrower. One sees this in the christological and eschatological elements contained in the Epistle to the Romans, and which harmonize with the general apostolic teaching. But it is not from this source that the substance of our Epistle is derived. The apostle wishes to give to the Romans *his* gospel, and, if I may so speak, his Paul.

From this point of view we can also account for the elements of anti-Jewish polemic which have misled so many excellent critics, Mangold and Weizsäcker for example, as to the aim of his letter. Paul wished to expound the mode of individual salvation; but could he do so without taking account of the ancient revelation which seemed to teach a different way from that which he was himself expounding? Could he at this moment of transition, when the one of two covenants was taking the place of the other, say: *by faith*, without adding: *and not by the law?* The anti-legal tendency belonged inherently to his teaching, as much as the anti-papal tendency belonged to Luther's. Would a Reformer have been able, even without intending to write polemically, to compose a system of dogmatics without setting aside the merit of works? The aim of Paul's treatise was didactic and world-wide; the introduction proves this (the description of the corruption of the Gentile world) ; the middle confirms it (the parallel between Adam and Jesus Christ) ; the close completes the demonstration (the systematic exposition of morals, without any allusion to the law). But beside this way of salvation, which he was anxious to expound, he saw another which attempted to rival it, and which professed also to be divinely revealed. He could not establish the former without setting aside the latter. The anti-Judaizing pieces do not therefore oblige us to ascribe this tendency to the whole letter. They have their necessary place in the development of the subject of the Epistle.

It need hardly be said that our explanation does not exclude what truth there is in the other proposed solutions. That Paul desired by this system of instruction to secure a favorable reception at Rome ; that he hoped to strengthen this church against the invasion of Judaizers, present or to come ; that he had it before him to gather into his letter the whole array of biblical and logical arguments which a hot conflict and incessant meditation had led him to collect during the years which were just closing ; that this treatise was like a trophy raised on the field of battle, where he had gained such signal triumphs, since the opening of hostilities at Antioch to his complete victory at Corinth ; and that, finally, no part of the world appeared to him more suitable for receiving this monument erected by him than the church of the Capital of the world,—of all this I make no doubt. But it seems to me that those various and particular aims find their full truth only when they are grouped round this principal one : to found afterhand, and, if one may so speak, morally to *refound* the church of Rome.

To set free the kingdom of God from the Jewish wrapping which had served as its cradle, such was the work of St. Paul. This task he carried out by his life in the domain of action, and by the Epistle to the Romans in the domain of thought. This letter is, as it were, the theory of his missionary preaching, and of his spiritual life, which is one with his work.

Does the course of the Epistle really correspond to the aim which we have now indicated ? Has it the systematic character which we should be led to expect from a strictly didactic purpose ?

ARRANGEMENT and PLAN OF THE EPISTLE   4

LIKE St. Paul's other letters, the Epistle to the Romans begins with a *preface* (i. 1–15), which includes the address and a thanksgiving, and which is intended to form the relation between the author and his readers. But in this letter the *address* is more elaborate than usual. This difference arises from the fact that the apostle did not yet know personally the church to which he was writing. Hence it is that he has strongly emphasized his mission to be the *Apostle of the Gentiles;* for on this rests the *official* bond which justifies the step he is taking (vv. 1–7). The *thanksgiving* which follows, and which is founded on the work already accomplished among them, leads him quite naturally to apologize for not yet having taken part in it himself, and to express the constant desire which he feels of being able soon to exercise his apostleship among them, as well for the confirmation of their faith and his own encouragement, as for the increase of their church (vv. 8–15).

After this preface of an *epistolary* character, there begins, as in the other letters, the treatment of the subject, the *body of the writing.* But here again the Epistle to the Romans differs from all the rest, in having the central part detached from the two epistolary pieces, the introduction and the conclusion, much more sharply. The Epistle to the Romans is thus, properly speaking, neither a treatise nor a letter ; it is a treatise contained in a letter.

The treatise begins with ver. 16, the first words of which form the skilfully-managed transition from the introduction to the treatment. The latter extends to xv. 13, where the return to the epistolary form indicates the beginning of the conclusion.

1:16, 17

Before entering on the development of his subject, the apostle *expounds* it in a few lines, which are, as it were, the *theme* of the entire treatise. This summary is contained in vv. 16, 17. The apostle proposes to show that the salvation of every man, whoever he may be, rests on the *righteousness which faith procures;* he supports this proposition immediately by a scripture declaration.

With ver. 18 the development of the subject begins ; it is distributed under two heads, the one relating to *principles,*—this is the doctrinal treatise ; the other containing the *application,*—this forms the moral treatise. The first proceeds from i. 18 to the end of chap. xi.; the second from xii. 1 to xv. 13.

The *doctrinal treatise* is the positive and negative demonstration of the *righteousness of faith.* It comprehends three parts : the one fundamental, from i. 18 to the end of chap. v. ; the other two supplementary (chap. vi.–viii. and ix.–xi.).

1:18-5:21

In this first part Paul gives the *positive* demonstration of justification by faith. He develops the three following thoughts :—

1. i. 18–iii. 20. The *need* which the world has of such a righteousness. For the whole of it is under the wrath of God ; this fact is obvious as to the Gentiles (chap. i.) ; it is not less certain in regard to the Jews (ii.), and that in spite of their theocratic advantages (iii. 1-8). The Holy Scriptures come, over and above, to shut the mouth of all mankind (vv. 9-20). Summary : Wrath is on all, even on the Jews.

2. iii. 21–v. 11. The free and universal *gift* of the righteousness of faith given by God to men. This gift has been made possible by the expiatory work of Jesus Christ (iii. 21-26). It is offered to Gentiles as well as Jews, in accordance with the principle of Jewish monotheism (vv. 27-31). This mode of justification is, besides, in keeping with the decisive example, that of Abraham (iv.). Finally, the believer is assured that, whatever may be the tribulations of the present, this righteousness of faith will never fail him. It has even been provided by the faithful mediation of Jesus Christ, that it shall suffice in the day of final wrath (v. 1-11). Summary : the righteousness of faith is for all, even for the Gentiles.

3. v. 12-21. This universal condemnation and this universal justification (which have formed the subject of the two preceding sections) are both traced up to their historical points of departure, Adam and Christ. These two central personalities extend their opposite influences, the one of condemnation and death, the other of justification and life, over all mankind, but in such a way that the saving action of the one infinitely exceeds the destructive action of the other.

The righteousness of faith without the works of the law is thus established. But a formidable objection arises : Will it be able to found a *rule of holiness* comparable to that which followed from the law, and without having recourse to the latter ? After having excluded the law as a means of justification, are we not obliged to return to it when the end in view is to lay a foundation for the moral life of believers ?

The answer to this question is the subject of *the first* of the two supplementary parts (vi.–viii.).

6:1-8:39

This part, like the preceding, contains the development of three principal ideas :—

1. vi. 1–vii. 6. The relation to Christ on which justification by faith rests, contains in it a principle of holiness. It carries the believer into communion with that death to sin and life to God which were so perfectly realized by Jesus Christ (vi. 1-14). This new principle of sanctification asserts its sway over the soul with such force, that the flesh is disposed to regard this subjection to holiness as slavery (vv. 15-23). And the believer finds in this union with Christ, and in virtue of the law itself, the right of breaking with the law, that he may depend only on his new spouse (vii. 1-6)

2. vii. 7-25. This breaking with the law should occasion us neither fear nor regret. For the law was as powerless to *sanctify* man as it showed itself (see the first part) powerless to *justify* him. By discovering to us our inward sin, the law exasperates it, and slays us spiritually (vv. 7-13). Once it has plunged us into this state of separation from God, it is powerless to deliver us from it. The efforts which we make to shake off the

yoke of sin serve only to make us feel more its insupportable weight (vv. 14–25).

3. Chap. viii. But the Spirit of Christ is the liberating power. It is He who realizes in us the holiness demanded by the law, and who, by rescuing our bodies from the power of the flesh, consecrates them by holiness for resurrection (vv. 1–11). It is He who, by making us sons of God, makes us at the same time *heirs* of the glory which is to be revealed (vv. 12–17). For the sufferings of the present do not last always. The universal renovation, which is prayed for by the threefold sigh of creation, the children of God, and the Holy Spirit Himself, draws near; and, notwithstanding the tribulations of the present hour, this state of glory remains as the assured goal of God's eternal plans in favor of His elect (vv. 18–30).

As at the end of the preceding part the apostle, in his parallel between Adam and Christ, had cast a comprehensive glance over the domain which he had traversed; so, from the culminating point which he has just reached, he embraces once more in one view that entire salvation through the righteousness of faith which is rendered for ever indestructible by the sanctification of the Spirit; and he strikes the triumphant note of the assurance of salvation (vv. 31–39).

But now that this first objection has been solved, there rises another more formidable still: If salvation rests on the righteousness of faith, what becomes of the promises made to the people of Israel, who have rejected this righteousness? What becomes of the *divine election* of which this people was the object? Is not the faithfulness of God destroyed? *The second supplementary part* (ix.–xi.) is intended to throw light on this obscure problem.

9:1-11:36

St. Paul resolves this objection by three considerations, the details of which we cannot reproduce here even approximately.

1. The freedom of God cannot be restricted by any limit external to itself, nor in particular by any acquired right or privilege (chap. ix.).

2. The use which God has made of His liberty in this case has a perfectly good reason: Israel obstinately refused to enter into His mind; Israel determined to maintain its own righteousness, and rejected the righteousness of faith, which it should have possessed in common with the Gentiles (chap. x.).

3. The partial and merely temporary rejection of Israel has had the most salutary consequences for the world, and shall one day have the same for Israel itself. For the unbelief of this people has opened wide the gate of salvation to the Gentiles, and their salvation will be the means to that of Israel; so that these two halves of mankind, after having both in their turn made the humiliating experience of disobedience, shall be reunited in the bosom of eternal mercy (chap. xi.).

Thus God was *free* to reject His people; in doing so He used His freedom *justly;* and this exercise of it, limited in all respects as it is, will be *salutary*, and will show forth the wisdom of God. All the aspects of the question are exhausted in this discussion, which may be called the masterpiece of the philosophy of history. In closing it, the apostle, casting his look backwards a third time from this new culminating point, and surveying the labyrinths of ways and judgments by which God realizes His plans of love, breaks out into a cry of adoration over this ocean of light (xi. 32–36).

Justification by faith, after having been positively established, has come forth triumphant from the two trials to which it has been subjected. The question was asked: Could it produce holiness? It has shown that it could, and that it was the law which, in this respect, was powerlessness itself. The question was, Could it explain history ? It has proved that it could. What remains to be done ? One thing only : To show the new principle grappling with the realities of existence, and to depict *the life of the believer* who by faith has obtained justification. Such is the subject of the second of the two courses of instruction contained in the body of the Epistle, that is to say, of the *moral treatise*.

12:1-15:13

In the piece vi.-viii., St. Paul had laid the foundations of Christian sanctification. He describes it now as it is realized in everyday life.

Two grave errors prevail in the estimate ordinarily formed of this portion of the Epistle. Most people regard it as a simple appendix, foreign to the real subject of the work. But, on the contrary, it rests, not less than the doctrinal exposition, on the theme formulated i. 17. For it completes the development of the word *shall live*, begun in the part, chap. vi.-viii. The other error which is fallen into not less frequently, is to see in these chapters only a series of practical exhortations, without any logical concatenation. But Calvin's epithet on our Epistle : *Methodica est*, applies not less to the practical than to the doctrinal instruction, as we shall immediately see. The moral treatise embraces a *general* part (xii. 1-xiii. 14) and a *special* part (xiv. 1-xv. 13).

12:1-13:14

In this passage four principal ideas are expounded.

1. xii. 1, 2. The apostle lays down, as the *basis* and point of departure for the redeemed life, the living *sacrifice* which the believer, moved by the mercies of God, makes of his body, in order to do His perfect will, which is revealed more and more to his renewed understanding.

2. xii. 3-21. This gift of himself the believer accomplishes, in the first place, as a *member of the church*, the body of Christ, by *humility* and *love*.

3. xiii. 1-10. He carries it out, in the second place, as a *member of the state*, the social body instituted by God ; and he does so in the two forms of *submission* to the authorities, and *justice* to all.

4. xiii. 11-14. What sustains and animates him in this double task, as a Christian and a citizen, is the *point of view* which he has unceasingly before him, Christ coming again, and with Him the day of salvation breaking,— a day which shall be such only for those who are found *clothed with Christ*.

This moral teaching thus forms a complete whole. It sets forth clearly, though briefly, the *starting-point*, the *way*, and the *goal* of the life of the redeemed.

To this general teaching the apostle adds a supplementary part, which is a sort of example side by side with precept. It is an application of the great duty of self-sacrifice, in the forms of humility and love, to the existing circumstances of the church of Rome (xiv. 1-xv. 13).

14:1-15:13

A divergence of views was manifested at Rome between the majority, who were heartily spiritual and Pauline, and the minority, who were timorous and Judaizing. Paul points out to each party what its conduct should be according to the law of love, of which Christ has left us the model (xiv. 1-xv. 7) ; then, contemplating in spirit the sublime unity of

Arrangement and Plan of the Epistle / 63

the church realized in this way of love, he once more sounds the note of adoration (vv. 8–13).

This local application, while closing the practical treatise, restores the author and his readers to the midst of the church of Rome; it thus forms the transition to the *epistolary conclusion*, which corresponds to the introduction (i. 1–15). From ver. 14, indeed, the style again becomes that of a letter.

15:14-16:27

This conclusion treats of five subjects.

1. xv. 14–33. After having anew justified the very considerable didactic work which he had written them by the commission which he has received for the Gentiles, the apostle reminds the Romans that his apostolic work is now finished in the East. He hopes, therefore, soon to arrive at Rome, on his way to Spain. This piece corresponds exactly to the passage, i. 8–15, of the preface.

2. xvi. 1–16. He recommends to his readers the bearer of his letter, and charges them with greetings for all the members of the church known to him. To these personal salutations he adds, for the whole church, those with which he has been charged by the numerous churches which he has recently passed through.

3. Vv. 17–20. He invites them in passing, and in a sort of postscript, to be on their guard against the Judaizing emissaries, who will be sure to make their appearance as soon as they hear of a work of the Lord at Rome.

4. Vv. 21–24. He transmits the greetings of those who surround him, and even lets his secretary Tertius have the word, if one may so speak, to greet them in his own person.

5. Vv. 25–27. He closes with a prayer, which corresponds to the desire with which he had opened his letter, when he said, i. 11, how much he longed to be able to labor for their *strengthening*. He did what he could with this view by sending them such a letter. But he knows well that his work will not produce its fruit except in so far as God himself will do His part in working by it : " Now to Him that is of power to stablish you according to my gospel." . . .

PLAN OF THE EPISTLE.

EPISTOLARY INTRODUCTION (I. 1–15)

THE BODY OF THE WORK (I. 16–xv. 13)

SUMMARY : i. 16, 17

I. THE DOCTRINAL TREATISE (i. 18–xi. 36).
Salvation by the righteousness of faith.

FUNDAMENTAL PART : i. 18–v. 21
The righteousness of faith without the works of the law.

FIRST SUPPLEMENTARY PART : vi.–viii
Sanctification without the law.

SECOND SUPPLEMENTARY PART : ix.–xi
The rejection of Israel.

II. The Practical Treatise (xii. 1–xv. 13).
The life of the justified believer.

General Part : xii. 1–xiii. 14.
Exposition of Christian holiness.

Special Part : xiv. 1–xv. 13.
Divergences among Christians.

epistolary conclusion (xv. 14–xvi. 27)

Such is the plan or scheme which the apostle seems to me to have had steadily before him in dictating this letter.

If such is the method of the work, it could not correspond better to the object which, on our supposition, its author had in view.

PRESERVATION OF THE TEXT 5

CAN we flatter ourselves that we have the text of our Epistle as it proceeded from the apostle's hands?

1. A preliminary question has been raised on this head : Is not our Greek text the translation of a Latin original? This view is given forth so early as by a Syrian scholiast on the margin of a manuscript of the Peshito (Syrian translation), and it has been received by some Catholic theologians. But this is a mere inference, founded on the erroneous idea that in writing to Romans it was necessary to use the Latin language. The literary language at Rome was Greek. This is established by the numerous Greek inscriptions in the catacombs, by the use of the Greek language in the letter of Ignatius to the church of Rome, in the writings of Justin Martyr composed at Rome, and in those of Irenæus composed in Gaul. The Christians of Rome knew the Old Testament (Rom. vii. 1) ; now they could not have acquired this knowledge except through the Greek version of the LXX. Besides, it shows the utter want of philological discernment to call in question the original character of the Greek of our Epistle, and to suppose that such a style is that of a translation.

2. A second question is this : Have there not been introduced into the text of our Epistle passages which are foreign to the work, or even composed by another hand than Paul's? No doubt the exposition which we have just given of the method of the work seems to exclude such a suspicion by showing the intimate connection of all its parts, and the perfectly organic character of the entire letter. Nevertheless, doubts have been raised from the earliest times in regard to some passages of the last parts of the Epistle ; and these suspicions have been so aggravated in the most recent times, that from chap. xii., where the moral part begins, all at the present day is matter of dispute.

It is often alleged that Marcion, about 140, in the edition of ten of Paul's Epistles, which he published for the use of his churches, rejected from the Epistle to the Romans the whole conclusion (our chaps. xv. and xvi.). Origen says of him as follows (*ad* xvi. 24) : " Marcion entirely rejected (*penitus abstulit*) this piece ; and not only that, but he also lacerated (*dissecuit*) the whole passage from the words : *Whatsoever is done without faith is sin* (xiv. 23), to the end." But was not F. Nitzsch justified [1] in bringing out the difference between the words *lacerate* (*dissecuit*) *and wholly reject* (*penitus abstulit*) ? It is quite possible, therefore, that Marcion only rejected the doxology which closes the Epistle, xvi. 25–27, and that in xv. and xvi. he had only made some excisions to accommodate them to his system. Such was his course in regard to the biblical books which he used. An expression of Tertullian's has also been advanced (*adv. Marcion*, v. 14), which speaks of the passage, xiv. 10, as belonging to the *clausula* (the conclusion of the Epistle). But it is not to be supposed that Tertullian himself agreed with his adversary in rejecting the last two chapters, and xiv. is so

---

[1] *Zeitschr. f. histor. Theol.* 1860. Comp. also the excellent work of E. Lacheret, *Revue Théologique*, Juillet 1878, p. 66.

66 / Introduction

near the end of the Epistle that nothing whatever can be proved from this phrase.[1] What appears certain is—(1) that Marcion rejected the final doxology, xvi. 25-27, for it seemed in contradiction to his system from the way in which it mentions the *prophetical writings;* (2) that he cut and carved freely on the same principle in chaps. xv. and xvi.

Yet the many conclusions which are found at the close of our Epistle— no less than five are reckoned (xv. 13, 33, xvi. 16, 20, 24-27)—the textual displacements in the manuscripts, the greeting so difficult to explain, have awakened the doubts of criticism, and till now have not been satisfactorily settled.

Semler, at the end of the last century, supposed that the Epistle closed at xiv. 23, which explains, he thinks, why the final doxolgy, xvi. 25-27, is found here in several manuscripts. The passage containing the salutations, xvi. 3-16, he holds to have been a special leaf committed to the bearers of the letter, to indicate the persons whom they were to greet in the different churches through which their journey led them. Hence the phrase : " *Salute* N. N." . . . And what more was contained in those two chapters was addressed to the persons saluted, and was intended to be transmitted to them with a copy of the letter.

Paulus saw in chaps. xv. and xvi. a supplement intended solely for the leaders and the most enlightened of the members of the Roman church.

Eichhorn and a great number of theologians in his train have held that the whole of chap. xvi., or at least the passage xvi. 1-20 or 3-20 (Reuss, Ewald, Mangold, Laurent), could not have been addressed to Rome by the apostle. It is impossible to explain these numerous greetings in a letter to a church where he never lived. Thus we have here a fragment which has strayed from an Epistle addressed to some other church, either Corinth (Eichhorn) or Ephesus. But there remained a difficulty : How had this strange leaf been introduced from Asia or Greece into the copies of a letter addressed to the church of Rome ?

Baur boldly cut the knot. Founding on the alleged example of Marcion, he declared xv. and xvi. wholly unauthentic. " They present," he said, " several ideas or phrases incompatible with the apostle's anti-Judaistic standpoint." One cannot help asking, however, how the Epistle to the Romans could have closed with the passage xiv. 23. A conclusion corresponding to the preface is absolutely indispensable.

Schenkel (*Bibellexikon,* t. v.) thinks he finds this conclusion in the doxology, xvi. 25-27, which he transposes (with some documents) to the end of xiv., and the authenticity of which he defends. Chap. xv. is, according to him, a letter of recommendation given to Phœbe for the churches through which she was to pass on her way from Corinth to Ephesus, and from Ephesus to Rome.

Scholten holds as authentic only the recommendation of Phœbe (xvi. 1, 2) and the greetings of Paul's companions, with the prayer of the apostle himself (vv. 21-24).

Lucht [2] adheres to Baur's view, while modifying it a little. The Epistle could not close with xiv. 23. Our chaps. xv. and xvi. must therefore contain something authentic. The true conclusion was so severe on the ascetic minority combated in xiv., that the presbyters judged it prudent to suppress it ; but it remained in the archives, where it was found by a later editor, who amalgamated it by mistake with a short letter to the Ephesians, thus forming the two last chapters.

Of this theory of Lucht, Hilgenfeld accepts only the unauthentic character of the doxology, xvi. 25-27. For his part, with the exception of this passage, he admits the entire authenticity of xv. and xvi.

M. Renan has given forth an ingenious hypothesis, which revives an idea

---

[1] See another solution in Meyer, Intr. to chap. xv.
[2] *Ueber die beiden letzten Capitel des Rœmerbr.* 1871.

of Grotius (p. 55). Starting from the numerous conclusions which these two chapters seemingly contain, he supposes that the apostle composed this Epistle from the first with a view to *several churches*, four at least. The common matter, intended for all, fills the first eleven chapters. Then come the different conclusions, intended for each of the four churches. For the first, the church of Rome, chap. xv. ; for the second, that of Ephesus, xii.-xiv., and the passage, xvi. 1-20 ; for the third, that of Thessalonica, xii.-xiv., and the greeting, xvi. 21-24 ; and for the fourth, unknown, xii.-xiv., with the doxology, xvi. 25-27. Thus, indeed, all is Paul's ; and the incoherence of the two last chapters arises only from the amalgamation of the various conclusions.[1]

Volkmar presents a hypothesis which differs little from that of Scholten. The Epistle properly so called (composed of a didactic and hortatory part) closed at xiv. 23. Here came the conclusion which must be discovered among the unauthentic conglomerates of xv. and xvi. And Volkmar's sagacity is at no loss. The three verses, xv. 33, xvi. 2, and the four verses, xvi. 21-24, were the real conclusion of the Epistle. All the rest was added, about 120, when the exhortation of xiv. was carried forward by that of xv. 1-32, and when the passage xvi. 3-16 was added. Later still, between between 150 and 160, there was added the warning against heresy, xvi. 17-20.

Finally, Schultz has just proposed a very complicated hypothesis.[2] He ably maintains that all the particular passages are composed by the apostle, starting in his argument from xvi. 17-20, passing therefrom to vv. 3-16, to vv. 21-24, to vv. 1, 2, and, finally, to xv. 14-33. But it is to demonstrate immediately afterward that xvi. 17-20 can only have been addressed to a church instructed and founded by Paul, which was not the case with that of Rome. Hence he passes to the numerous salutations of chap. xvi., which can only have been addressed to a church known by the apostle, probably Ephesus. Thus there existed a letter of Paul to the Ephesians which closed with these many greetings (xvi. 3-20). But they could not be more than the conclusion of a fuller letter. Where was this letter ? In chapters xii. xiii., xiv. xv. 1-6, and in the conculsion, xvi. 3-20, of our Epistle. This letter was written from Rome by the apostle during his captivity. A copy, left in the archives of the church, was joined, after the persecution of Nero, with our Epistle to the Romans. Hence the form of our present text. The probability attaching to this hypothesis at the first glance is so slight that we can hardly suppose its author to have propounded it with much assurance.

Let us sum up our account. Opinions on chaps. xv. and xvi. fall into four classes :—1. All is Paul's, and all in its right place (Tholuck, Meyer, Hofmann, etc.). 2. All is Paul's, but with a mixture of elements belonging to other letters (Semler, Eichhorn, Reuss, Renan, Schultz). 3. Some passages are Paul's, the rest is interpolated (Schenkel, Scholten, Lucht, Volkmar). 4. All is unauthentic (Baur).

We shall have to examine all those opinions, and weigh the facts which have given rise to them (see on xv. and xvi.). Meanwhile, we may be allowed to refer to the account we have given of the general course of the Epistle, and to ask if the entire work does not produce the effect of a living and healthful organism, in which all the parts hold to and dovetail into one another, and from which no member can possibly be detached without arbitrary violence.

3. The reader of a commentary is entitled to know the origin of the text which is about to be explained to him.

The text from which our oldest editions and our versions in modern tongues have been made (since the Reformation) is that which has been pre-

---

[1] *Saint Paul*, pp. 63-74.   [2] *Jahrbücher für deutsche Theologie*, 1877.

served, with very little divergence, in the 250 copies of Paul's Epistles in cursive or minuscular writing, later consequently than the tenth century, which are found scattered among the different libraries of Europe. It was from one of these manuscripts, found at Basle, that Erasmus published the first edition of the Greek text ; and it is his edition which has formed for centuries the groundwork of subsequent editions. It is obvious that the origin of what has so long borne the name of the *Received text* is purely accidental.

The real state of things is this. Three classes of documents furnish us with the text of our Epistle : the ancient *manuscripts*, the ancient *versions*, and the quotations which we find in the works of *ecclesiastical writers*.

1. *Manuscripts.*—These are of two kinds : those written in majuscule letters, and which are anterior to the tenth century ; and those which have the cursive and minuscular writing, used since that date.

The *majuscules* in which Paul's Epistles have been preserved are eleven in number :

Two of the fourth century : the *Sinaïticus* (ℵ) and the *Vaticanus* (B) ;
Two of the fifth century : the *Alexandrinus* (A) and the *Cod. of Ephrem* (C) ;
One of the sixth century : the *Claromontanus* (D) ;
Three of the ninth century : the *Sangermanensis* (E), a simple copy of the preceding ; the *Augiensis* (F) ; the *Bœrnerianus* (G) ;
Three of the ninth to the tenth century : the *Mosquensis* (K), the *Angelicus* (L), and the *Porfirianus* (P).

We do not mention a number of *fragments* in majuscular writing. We have already spoken of the documents in *minuscular* characters. As soon as men began to study these documents a little more attentively, they found three pretty well marked sets of texts, which appear also, though less prominently, in the Gospels : 1. The *Alexandrine* set, represented by the four oldest majuscules (ℵ A B C), and so called because this text was probably the form used in the churches of Egypt and Alexandria ; 2. The *Greco-Latin* set, represented by the four manuscripts which follow in order of date (D E F G), so designated because it was the text circulating in the churches of the West, and because in the manuscripts which have preserved it it is accompanied with a Latin translation ; and, 3. The *Byzantine* set, to which belong the three most recent majuscules (K L P), and almost the whole of the minuscules ; so named because it was the text which had fixed and, so to speak, stereotyped itself in the churches of the Greek empire.

In case of variation these three sets are either found, each having its own separate reading, or combining two against one ; sometimes even the ordinary representatives of one differ from one another and unite with those, or some of those, of another set. And it is not easy to decide to which of those forms of the text the preference should be given.

Moreover, as the oldest majuscules go back no farther than the fourth century, there remains an interval of 300 years between them and the apostolic autograph. And the question arises whether, during this long interval, the text did not undergo alterations more or less important. Fortunately, in the two other classes of documents we have the means of filling up this considerable blank.

2. *The Versions.*—There are two translations of the New Testament which go back to the end of the second century, and by which we ascertain the state of the text at a period much nearer to that when the autographs were still extant. These are the ancient Latin version known as the *Itala*, of which the Vulgate or version received in the Catholic Church is a revision, and the Syriac version, called *Peshitto*. Not only do these two ancient documents agree as to the substance of the text, but their general agreement with the text of our Greek manuscripts proves on the whole the

purity of the latter. Of these two versions, the Itala represents rather the Greco-Latin type, the Peshitto the Byzantine type. A third and somewhat more recent version, the *Coptic* (Egyptian), exactly reproduces the Alexandrine form.

But we are in a position to go back even further, and to bridge over a good part of the interval which still divides us from the apostolic text. The means at our command are—

3. The quotations from the New Testament in the *writers of the second century*.—In 185, Irenæus frequently quotes the New Testament in his great work. In particular, he reproduces numerous passages from our Epistle (about eighty-four verses).—About 150, Justin reproduces textually a long passage from the Epistle to the Romans (iii. 11–17).—About 140, Marcion published his edition of Paul's Epistles. Tertullian, in his work against this heretic, has reproduced a host of passages from Marcion's text, and especially from that of the Epistle to the Romans. He obviously quoted them as he read them in Marcion's edition.[1] In this continuous series of quotations (L.V. cc. 13 and 14), embracing about thirty-eight verses, we have the oldest known evidence to a considerable part of the text of our Epistle. Tertullian himself (190–210) has in his works more than a hundred quotations from this letter.

One writer carries us back, at least for a few verses, to the very age of the apostle. I mean Clement of Rome, who, about the year 96, addresses an Epistle to the Corinthians in which he reproduces textually (c. 35) the entire passage, Rom. i. 28–32. The general integrity of our text is thus firmly established.

As to variations, I do not think it possible to give an *a priori* preference to any of the three texts mentioned above. And in supporting the Alexandrine text *as a rule*, Tischendorf, I fear, has made one of his great mistakes. When publishing this seventh edition he had to a certain extent recognized the error of his method, which had gradually become prevalent since the time of Griesbach. But the discovery of the *Sinaiticus* threw him into it again more than ever. This fascination exercised by the old Alexandrine documents arises from several causes: their antiquity, the real superiority of their text in a multitude of cases, and, above all, the reaction against the groundless supremacy of the Byzantine text in the old *Textus receptus*.

Any one who has had long experience in the exegesis of the New Testament will, I think, own three things:—1. That all preference given *a priori* to any one of the three texts is a prejudice; 2. That the sole *external* reason, having some probability in favor of a particular reading, is the agreement of a certain number of documents of *opposite* types; 3. That the only means of reaching a well-founded decision, is the profound study of the context.

In conclusion, it must be said the variations are as insignificant as they are numerous. I know only one in the Epistle to the Romans—a work so eminently dogmatic—which could exercise any influence on Christian doctrine, that of viii. 11. And the point to which it refers (to wit, whether the body is raised *by* or *on account of* the Spirit who dwells in us) is a subject which probably no pastor ever treated, either in his catechetical instruction or in his preaching.

PRINCIPAL COMMENTATORS

Ancient church: Origen (third century), in Latin translation. Chrysostom (fourth century), thirty-two homilies. Theodoret (fifth century).

---

[1] He says himself: "Whatever the omissions which Marcion has contrived to make even in this, the most considerable of the Epistles, suppressing what he liked, the things which he has left are enough for me."—*Adv. Marc.* v. 13.

70 / Introduction

Ambrosiaster, probably the Roman deacon Hilary (third or fourth century). Œcumenius (tenth century). Theophylact, bishop of Bulgaria (eleventh century). Erasmus (sixteenth century), *Annotationes in N. T.*
After the Reformation: Calvin and Theodore Beza. Luther (his celebrated *Preface*). Melanchthon, *Annotationes* (1522) and *Commentarii* (1532). Bucer, *Enarrationes* (1536). Grotius, *Annotationes* (1645). Calov, *Biblia illustrata* (1672). Bengel, *Gnomon* (1742).
Modern times : Tholuck (1824, 5th ed. 1856). Rückert (1831, 2d ed. 1839). Stuart, American theologian (1832). Olshausen (1835). De Wette (1835, 4th ed. 1847). Hodge, of Princeton (1835, published in French 1840). Fritzsche (1836). Meyer (1836, 5th ed. 1872). Oltramare, chaps. i.–v. 11 (1843). Philippi (1848). Nielsen, Dane (1856). Umbreit (1856). Ewald, *die Sendschreiben des apostels Paulus* (1857). Theod. Schott (1858). Lange and Fay in the *Bibelwerk* (1865, 3d ed. 1868). Hofmann (1868). Ph. Schaff, work published in English after Lange's *Commentary* (1873). Volkmar (1875). Bonnet, *le Nouveau Testament*, 2d ed. *Epîtres de Paul* (1875). Reuss, *La Bible, Epîtres pauliniennes* (1878). [Shedd, 1879.]
Here we mention in addition three remarkable monographs, two of them on the passage, v. 12–21. Rothe, *Neuer Versuch einer Ausl. der paul. Stelle*, v. 11–21 (1836), and Dietzsch, *Adam und Christus* (1871). The third is the work of Morison, of Glasgow, *Critical Exposition of the Third Chapter of Paul's Epistle to the Romans* (1866).
The ancient *Commentaries* are well known ; to attempt to characterize them would be superfluous. I shall say a word on the most-important of the moderns. *Tholuck* was the first, after the blighting epoch of rationalism, who reopened to the church the living fountains of evangelical truth which spring up in our Epistle. *Olshausen*, continuing his friend's work, expounded still more copiously the treasures of salvation by faith, which had been brought to light again by Tholuck. *De Wette* has traced the links of the apostle's reasoning with admirable sagacity. *Meyer* has brought to the study of our Epistle all the resources of that learned and vigorous philology, the application of which *Fritzsche* had demanded in the study of our sacred books ; to these he has added a sound exegetical sense and an understanding of Christian truth which makes his work *the indispensable Commentary.* *Oltramare* has a great wealth of exegetical materials ; but he has not elaborated them sufficiently before composing his book. *Ewald*, a paraphrase in which the original spirit of the author lives again. *Theod. Schott ;* his whole work turns on a preconceived and unfortunately false point of view. *Lange ;* every one knows his characteristics, at once brilliant and arbitrary. *Hofmann* brings a mind of the most penetrating order to the analysis of the apostle's thought, he does not overlook the slightest detail of the text ; his stores of philological knowledge are not inferior to those of Meyer. But he too often lacks accuracy ; he dwells complacently on exegetical discoveries in which it is hard to think that he himself believes, and to appreciate the intrinsic clearness of the style requires a fourth or fifth reading. *Schaff* happily remedies Lange's defects, and completes him in an original way. *Volkmar's* treatise is an analysis rather than an interpretation. The best part of it consists of criticism of the text, and of a beautiful reprint of the Vatican text. *Bonnet*, on the basis of very thoroughgoing exegetical studies, has, with considerable self-denial, composed a simple *Commentary* for the use of laymen.[1] *Reuss* explains the essential idea of each passage, but his plan does not admit of a detailed exegesis. *Morison's* monograph, as it seems to me, is a *unique* specimen of learning and sound exegetical judgment.

---

[1] We call the attention of non-theological readers to the interesting and thoroughgoing work of M. Walther : *Paraphrase de l'épître aux Romains* (1871).

TITLE OF THE EPISTLE

The authentic title is certainly that which has been preserved in its simplest form in the seven oldest Mjj., the four Alex., and the three Greco-Latin : Πρὸς 'Ρωμαίους, *to the Romans*. In later documents there is a gradual increase of epithets, till we have the title of L : Τοῦ ἁγίου καὶ πανευφήμου ἀποστόλου Παύλου ἐπιστολὴ πρὸς 'Ρωμαίους (*Epistle of the holy and everywhere blessed Apostle Paul to the Romans*).

COMMENTARY

The framework of the Epistle to the Romans is, as we have seen, the same as that of the most of Paul's other Epistles: 1. An epistolary preface; 2. The body of the letter; 3. An epistolary conclusion.

PREFACE

1:1-15

This introduction is intended to establish a relation between the apostle and his readers which does not yet exist, inasmuch as he did not found the church, and had not yet visited it. It embraces: 1. The address; 2. A thanksgiving for the work of the Lord at Rome.

FIRST PASSAGE (1:1-7)

The Address

The form of address usual among the ancients contained three terms: " N. to N. *greeting.*" Comp. Acts xxiii. 26 : " Claudius Lysias unto the most excellent governor Felix greeting." Such is the type we have here, but modified in execution to suit the particular intention of the apostle. The subject, *Paul*, is developed in the first six verses; the persons addressed, *to the Christians in Rome*, in the first half of ver. 7, and the object, *greeting*, in the second.

One is surprised at the altogether extraordinary extension bestowed on the development of the first term. It is very much the same in the Epistle to the Galatians. The fact is accounted for in the latter writing by the need which Paul felt to give the lie at once to the calumnies of his Judaizing adversaries, who denied his divine call to the apostleship. His object in our Epistle is wholly different. His concern is to justify the exceptional step he is taking at the moment, in addressing a letter of instruction like that which follows, to a church on which he seemed to have no claim.

In these six verses, 1-6, Paul introduces himself; first, as an *apostle* in the general sense of the word, as called directly by God to the task of publishing the message of salvation, vv. 1, 2; then he indulges in an apparent digression regarding the *object* of his message, the person of Jesus Christ, who had appeared as the Messiah of Israel, but was raised by His resurrection to the state of the Son of God, vv. 3, 4; finally, from the person of the Lord he returns to the apostleship, which he has received from this glorified Lord, and which he describes as a *special* apostleship to the *Gentile* world, vv. 5, 6.

Vv. 1, 2. "*Paul, a servant of Christ Jesus,*[1] *an apostle by* [his] *call, separated unto the gospel of God, which he had promised afore by his prophets in the Holy Scriptures.*"—Paul introduces himself in this ver. 1 with the utmost solemnity ; he puts his whole letter under the authority of his apostleship, and the latter under that of God Himself. On the name *Paul*, see Introd. p. 16. After having thus presented his personality, he effaces it, as it were, immediately by the modest title of δοῦλος servant. We need not translate this term by the word *slave*, which in our modern languages suggests a more painful idea than the Greek term. The latter contains the two ideas of *property* and of *obligatory service*. It may consequently be applied to the relation which *every Christian* bears to the Lord (1 Cor. vii. 22). If we take it here in this sense, the name would imply the bond of *equality* in the faith which unites Paul to his brethren at Rome. Yet as this letter is not a simple fraternal communication, but an apostolic message of the highest importance, it is more natural to take the word *servant* in a graver sense, the same as it certainly has in the address of the Epistle to the Philippians i. 1 : "Paul and Timotheus, the *servants of Jesus Christ*, to all the saints in Christ Jesus which are at Philippi." The term *servant*, thus contrasted with the term *saints*, evidently denotes a special ministry. In point of fact, there are men who are called to exemplify the general submission which all believers owe to the Lord, in the form of a particular office ; they are *servants* in the limited sense of the word. The Received reading : *of Jesus Christ*, sets first in relief the historical person (*Jesus*), then His office of Messiah (*Christ*). This form was the one which corresponded best to the feeling of those who had first known Jesus personally, and afterward discovered Him to be the Messiah. And so it is the usual and almost technical phrase which prevailed in apostolic language. But the *Vat.* and the *Vulg.* read : Χριστοῦ Ἰησου, *of Christ Jesus;* first the office, then the person. This form seems preferable here as the less usual. It corresponded to the personal development of Paul, who had beheld the glorified Messiah before knowing that He was Jesus. The title *servant* was very general, embracing all the ministries established by Christ ; the title *apostle* denotes the *special* ministry conferred on Paul. It is the most elevated of all. While Christ's other servants build up the church, either by extending it (*evangelists*) or perfecting it (*pastors* and *teachers*), the apostles, with the *prophets* (Christian prophets), have the task of founding it ; comp. Eph. iv. 12. Paul was made a partaker of this supreme charge. And he was so, he adds, by way of *call*. The relation between the two words *called* and *apostle* is not that which would be indicated by the paraphrase : "Called *to be* an apostle." This meaning would rather have been expressed by the participle (κληθείς). In ver. 7, the corresponding phrase : *called saints*, has quite another meaning from : called *to be* saints (which would assume that they *are* not so). The meaning is : saints *by way of call*, which implies that they are so in reality. Similarly, Paul means that he is an apostle, and that he is so in virtue of the divine vocation which alone confers such an office. There is here no polemic against the Judaizers ; it is the simple affirmation of that supreme dignity which authorizes him to address the church as he is now doing ; comp. Eph. i. 1 ; Col. i. 1. These two ideas, *apostle* and *call*, naturally carry our minds back to the time of his conversion. But Paul knows that his consecration to this ministry goes farther back still ; and this is the view which is expressed in the following phrase : ἀφωρισμένος, *set apart*. This word, in such a context, cannot apply to any human consecration, such as that which he received along with Barnabas at Antioch, with a view to their first mission, though the same Greek term is used, Acts xiii. 2. Neither does it express the notion of an eternal election, which would have been denoted by the compound προωρισμένος, destin-

---

[1] B, Vulg. Aug. read Χριστου Ιησου instead of Ιησου Χριστου, which the other documents read.

ed *beforehand*," as in the other cases where a decree anterior to time is meant. The expression seems to me to be explained by the sentence, Gal. i. 15, which is closely related to this: "But when it pleased God, who *had separated me* (ἀφορίσας με) *from my mother's womb, and called me* (καλέσας με) *by His grace.*" In this passage of the Galatians he comes down from the *selection* to the *call*, while here he ascends from the call to the selection. Let the reader recall what we have said, Introd. pp. 4 and 5, as to the providential character of all the previous circumstances of Saul's life. The apostle might well recognize in that whole chain the signs of an original destination to the task with which he saw himself invested. This task is expressed in the words: *unto the gospel of God*, εἰς εὐαγγέλιον Θεοῦ. If by the word *gospel* we understand, as is usually done, *the contents* of the divine message, then we must place the notion of preaching in the preposition εἰς, *in order to*, and paraphrase it thus: "*in order to proclaim* the gospel." This meaning of the word *gospel* is hardly in keeping with the living character of primitive Christian language. The word rather denotes in the New Testament the *act* of gospel preaching; so a few lines below, ver. 9, and particularly 1 Thess. i. 5, where Paul says: "Our gospel came not unto you in word only, but also in power, and in the Holy Ghost, and in much assurance; as ye know what manner of men we were among you." These words have no sense unless by *our gospel*, Paul means, our preaching of the gospel. In this case the preposition *for* preserves its simple meaning. The absence of the article before the words *gospel* and *God*, give to the words a sort of descriptive sense: *a message of divine origin*. The genitive Θεοῦ, *of God*, here denotes the author of the message, not its *subject;* for the subject is Christ, as is mentioned afterward. Paul thus bears within him the unspeakably elevated conviction of having been set apart, from the beginning of his existence, to be the herald of a message of grace (εὖ ἀγγέλλειν, *to announce good news*) from God to mankind. And it is as the bearer of this message that he addresses the church of Rome. If the apostle does not add to his name that of any fellow-laborer, as he does elsewhere, it is because he is doing this act in his official character as the apostle of the Gentiles, a dignity which he shares with no other. So it is Eph. i. 1 (in similar circumstances).

But this preaching of salvation by the apostles has not dropped suddenly from heaven. It has been prepared or announced long before; this fact is the proof of its decisive importance in the history of humanity. This is what is expressed in ver. 2.

Several commentators think that the words: *which He had promised afore*, had no meaning, unless the word gospel, ver. 1, be taken as referring to *salvation* itself, not as we have taken it, to the act of preaching. But why could not Paul say that the act of evangelical preaching had been announced beforehand? "Who hath believed *our preaching?*" exclaims Isaiah (liii. 1), "and to whom is the arm of the Lord revealed?" And lii. 7: "How beautiful are the feet of him who bringeth good tidings, and who publisheth peace!" Finally, xl. 1, 2: "Comfort ye my people, your God will say . . . Cry unto Jerusalem, that her set time is accomplished." The apostle himself quotes these passages, X. 15, 16. The preaching of the gospel to Jews and Gentiles appears to him a solemn act marking a new era, the hour of universal salvation long expected; so he characterizes it also, Acts xvii. 30; Eph. iii. 5–7; Tit. i. 3. It is not wonderful that his feelings rise at the thought of being the principal instrument of a work thus predicted! He thereby becomes himself a predicted person, continuing as he does the work of the prophets by fulfilling the future they announced. The πρό, *beforehand*, added to the word *promise*, is not a pleonasm; it brings out forcibly the greatness of the fact announced. The pronoun αὐτοῦ, "*His* prophets," denotes the close relation which unites a prophet to God, whose instrument he is. The epithet *holy*, by which their writings are characterized, is related to this pronoun. Holiness is the seal of their divine origin. The absence of the article before γραφαί, *scriptures*, has a descriptive bearing: "in scriptures which have this character, that they are holy."

Baur and his school[1] find in this mention of the prophetic promises a proof of the Judeo-Christian origin of the majority of the church, and of the desire which the apostle had to please it. But the Old Testament was read and known in the churches of the Gentiles; and the object with which the apostle refers to the long theocratic preparation which had paved the way for the proclamation of salvation, is clear enough without our ascribing to him any so particular intention.—This mention of prophecy forms the transition to ver. 3, where Jesus is introduced in the first place as the Jewish Messiah, and then as the Son of God.

Vv. 3, 4. "*Concerning his Son, born of the race of David according to the flesh; established as the Son of God with power, according to the Spirit of holiness, by his resurrection from the dead: Jesus Christ our Lord.*"—The apostle first designates the subject of gospel preaching in a summary way: it is Jesus Christ viewed as the Son of God. The preposition περί, *concerning*, might indeed depend on the substantive εὐαγγέλιον (*gospel*), ver. 1, in virtue of the verbal meaning of the word; but we should require in that case to take ver. 2 as a parenthesis, which is by no means necessary. Why not make this clause dependent on the immediately preceding verb: *which He had promised afore?* This promise of the preaching of the gospel related to His Son, since it was He who was to be the subject of the preaching.— Here begins a long period, first expressing this subject in a general way, then analyzing it in parallel propositions, which, point by point, form an antithesis to one another. They are not connected by any of the numerous particles in which the Greek language abounds; their simple juxtaposition makes the contrast the more striking.—It has been sought to explain the title *Son of God* merely as an official name: the *theocratic King* by way of eminence, the Messiah. The passages quoted in favor of this meaning would suffice, if they were needed to refute it: John i. 50, for example, where the juxtaposition of the two titles, Son of God and King of Israel, so far from demonstrating them to be synonymous, refutes the view, and where the repetition of the verb *thou art* gives of itself the proof of the contrary; and Ps. ii. 7, where Jehovah says to the Messiah: "Thou art my Son, this day have I begotten Thee." This last expression is applied to the installation of the Messiah in His kingly office. But *to beget* never signifies to establish as king; the word denotes a communication of life.

Some explain the title by the exceptional *moral perfection* of Jesus, and the unbroken communion in which He lived with God. Thus the name would include nothing transcending the limits of a simple human existence. But can this explanation account for the passage, viii. 3: "God *sending His own Son* in the likeness of sinful flesh"...? It is obvious from this phrase that Paul ascribes an existence to the Son anterior to His coming in the flesh.

The title *Son* is also explained by our Lord's *miraculous birth*. So, for example, M. Bonnet: "In consequence of His generation by the Holy Spirit, He is really the Son of God." Such, indeed, is the meaning of the term in the message of the angel to Mary: "The Holy Ghost shall come upon thee... *wherefore* that holy thing which shall be born of thee shall be called the Son of God." But the passage, viii. 3, just quoted, shows that the apostle used the name in a more elevated sense still, though the notion of the miraculous birth has obviously a very close connection with that of pre-existence.

Several theologians of our day think that the title Son of God applies to Jesus only on account of *His elevation* to divine glory, as the sequel of His

---

[1] *Paulus*, I. 372; Hilgenfeld, *Einl.* 311, etc.

earthly existence. But our passage itself proves that, in the apostle's view, the divine state which followed His resurrection is a *recovered* and not an *acquired* state. His personal dignity as Son of God, proceeded on from ver. 3, is anterior to the two phases of His existence, the earthly and the heavenly, which are afterward described.

The idea of Christ's *divine pre-existence* is one familiar to St. Paul's mind, and alone explains the meaning which he attached to the term *Son of God*. Comp. (besides viii. 3) 1 Cor. viii. 6 : "One Lord Jesus Christ, *by whom are all things*, and we by Him;" Paul thus ascribes to Him the double creation, the physical and the spiritual; 1 Cor. x. 4 : "For they drank of that spiritual Rock that followed them: and that Rock was Christ;" Paul thus regards Christ as the Divine Being who accompanied the Israelites in the desert, and who, from the midst of the cloud, wrought all their deliverances; Phil. ii. 6 : "Who, *being in the form of God*, . . . emptied Himself, and took upon Him the form of a servant, and was made in the likeness of men." Add 2 Cor. viii. 9 : "Who, though He was rich, yet for your sakes became poor, that ye through His poverty might be rich." The *riches* of which He stripped Himself, according to the last of these passages, are, according to the preceding, the *form of God* belonging to Him, His divine mode of being anterior to His incarnation; and the *poverty* to which He descended is nothing else than His *servant form*, or the human condition which he put on. It is through His participation in our state of dependence that we can be raised to His state of glory and sovereignty. There remains, finally, the crowning passage on this subject, Col. i. 15–17.—Son of God essentially, Christ passed through two phases, briefly described in the two following propositions. The two participles with which they both open serve as points of support to all the subsequent determining clauses. The fundamental antithesis is that between the two participles γενομένου and ὁρισθέντος ; to this there are attached two others ; the first : *of the race of David* and *Son of God ;* the second : *according to the flesh* and *according to the Spirit of holiness*. Two phrases follow in the second proposition, *with power* and *through His resurrection from the dead*, which seem to have no counterpart in the first. But the attentive reader will have no difficulty in discovering the two ideas corresponding to them. They are those of *weakness*, a natural attribute of the *flesh* and of *birth ;* for His *resurrection* is to Jesus, as it were, a second birth. Let us first study the former proposition by itself. The word γενομένου may bear the meaning either of *born* or *become*. In the second case, the word relates to the act of incarnation, that mysterious change wrought in His person when He passed from the divine to the human state. But the participle γενομένου being here construed with the preposition ἐκ, *out of, from*, it is simpler to take the verb in the sense of *being born*, as in Gal. iv. 4 : "*born of a woman*" (γενόμενον ἐκ γυναικός). The phrase κατὰ σάρκα, *according to the flesh*, serves, as Hofmann says, "to restrict this affirmation to that side of His origin whereby He inherited human nature." For the notion of a different origin was previously implied in the phrase Son of God.—What are we to understand here by the term *flesh ?* The word has three very distinct meanings in the Old and the New Testaments.[1] 1. It denotes the muscular and soft parts of the body, in opposition both to the hard parts, *the bones*, and to the liquid parts, *the blood ;* so Gen. ii. 23 : "This is bone of my bones, and flesh of my flesh ;" and John vi. 56 : "He that eateth my flesh and drinketh my blood." 2. The word often denotes the entire human (or animal) *body*, in opposition to the *soul ;* for example, 1 Cor. xv. 39 : "There is one flesh of men, another flesh of beasts," a saying in which the word *flesh*, according to the context, denotes the entire organism. In this second sense the part is simply taken for the whole. 3. By the same sort of figure, only

---

[1] Comp. Wendt's remarkable dissertation : *Die begriffe Fleisch und Geist im biblischen Sprachgebrauch* (1878).

still more extended, the word *flesh* sometimes denotes the whole of *man*, body and soul, in opposition to God the Creator and His omnipotence. So Ps. lxv. 2 : " Unto *Thee* shall all *flesh* (every creature) come ;" Rom. iii. 20 : "No *flesh* (no man) shall be justified in *His* sight." The first of these three meanings is inapplicable in our passage, for it would imply that Jesus received from His ancestor David only the fleshy parts of His body, not the bones and blood ! The second is no less so ; for it would follow from it that Jesus inherited from David only His bodily life, and not the psychical, the higher powers of human life, feeling, understanding, and will. This opinion is incompatible with the affirmation of the full humanity of Jesus, as we find in the writings of Paul (comp. v. 15 ; 1 Tim. ii. 5) and of John. For the latter, as well as Paul, ascribes to Jesus a human *soul*, a human *spirit ;* comp. xii. 27 : "My *soul* is troubled ;" xi. 33 : "He groaned in His *spirit*." There remains, therefore, only the third meaning, which suits the passage perfectly. As a *human creature*, Jesus derives His origin from David. All that is human in Him, *spirit*, *soul*, and *body* (1 Thess. v. 23), so far as these elements are hereditary in mankind in general, this whole part of His being is marked by the Davidic, and consequently Jewish character. This royal and national seal is impressed not only on His physical nature and temperament, but also on His moral tendencies and aspirations ; and this hereditary life could alone form the basis of His Messianic calling, without, however, obliging us to forget that in the Jew there is always the man, under the national, the human element. This meaning which we give to the word *flesh* is absolutely the same as that in the passage of John, which forms, as it were, the text of his Gospel : "The Word was made flesh ($\sigma\grave{\alpha}\rho\xi\ \grave{\epsilon}\gamma\acute{\epsilon}\nu\epsilon\tau o$)," John i. 14.

Relation of this saying to the miraculous birth.— In expressing himself as he does here, does St. Paul think of Jesus' Davidic descent through Joseph or through Mary ? In the former case the miraculous birth would be excluded (Meyer and Reuss). But would this supposition be consistent, on the one hand, with the idea which the apostle forms of Jesus' *absolute* holiness ; on the other, with his doctrine of the transmission of sin to the whole human race ? He says of Jesus, viii. 3 : " Sent in the *likeness of sinful flesh ;*" 2 Cor. v. 21 : "He who *knew no sin ;*" he ascribes to Him the part of an *expiatory victim* ($\hat{\iota}\lambda\alpha\sigma\tau\acute{\eta}\rho\iota o\nu$), which excludes the barest idea of a *minimum* of sin. And yet, according to him, all Adam's descendants participate in the heritage of sin (v. 12, 19, iii. 9). How reconcile these propositions, if his view is that Jesus descends from David and from Adam absolutely in the same sense as the other descendants of Adam or David? Paul thus necessarily held the miraculous birth ;[1] and that so much the more, as the fact is conspicuously related in the Gospel of Luke, his companion in work. A contradiction between these two fellow-laborers on this point is inadmissible. It is therefore through the intervention of Mary, and of Mary alone, that Jesus, according to Paul's view, descended from David. And such is also the meaning of the genealogy of Jesus in Luke's Gospel (iii. 23).[2] Thus there is nothing to prevent us from placing the *beginning* of the operation of the Holy Spirit on the person of Jesus (to which the words : *according to the Spirit of holiness*, ver. 4, refer) at His very *birth*.

Yet this mode of hereditary existence does not exhaust His whole being. The title *Son of God*, placed foremost, contains a wealth which transcends the contents of this first assertion, ver. 3, and becomes the subject of the second proposition, ver. 4. Many are the interpretations given of the participle $\acute{o}\rho\iota\sigma\theta\acute{\epsilon}\nu\tau o\varsigma$. The verb $\acute{o}\rho\acute{\iota}\zeta\epsilon\iota\nu$ (from $\acute{o}\rho o\varsigma$, *boundary*) signifies : *to draw a limit*, to separate a domain from all that surrounds it ; to distinguish a person or a thing. The marking off may be only in thought ; the verb then signifies : *to destine to, decree, decide.* So Luke xxii. 22, and perhaps Acts x. 42 and

---

[1] See this proof beautifully developed in Gess : *Christi Person und Werk*, 2d ed. t. II. p. 210 et seq.
[2] See the explanation of the passage in my *Commentary*.

xvii. 31. Or the limitation may be traced in words; the verb then signifies: *to declare*. Or, finally, it may be manifested in an external act, a fact obvious to the senses, which leads to the meaning: *to install, establish*, or *demonstrate* by a sign. The first meaning: *to destine to*, has been here attempted by Hofmann. But this sense is incompatible with the clause: *by the resurrection*, and it would certainly have been expressed by the word προορισθέντος, *destined beforehand* (comp. viii. 29, 30; 1 Pet. i. 20), it being impossible that the divine decree relative to the glorification of Jesus should be posterior to his mission to the world. Founding on the second meaning, many (Osterv., Oltram.) translate: "*declared* to be the Son of God." But the notion of *declaration*, and even the stronger one of *demonstration*, are insufficient in the context. For the resurrection of Jesus not only manifested or demonstrated what He was; it wrought a real transformation in His mode of being. Jesus required to pass from His state as son of David to that of Son of God, if He was to accomplish the work described in ver. 5, and which the apostle has in view, that of the calling of the Gentiles. And it was His resurrection which introduced Him into this new state. The only meaning, therefore, which suits the context is the third, that of *establishing*. Peter says similarly, Acts ii. 36: "God hath made (ἐποίησε) that same Jesus, whom ye have crucified, both Lord and Christ." Hofmann has disputed the use of the verb ὁρίζειν in this sense. But Meyer, with good ground, adduces the following saying of a poet: σὲ Θεὸν ὥρισε δαίμων, "destiny made thee God." Not that the apostle means, as Pfleiderer would have it, that Jesus *became* the Son of God by His resurrection. He was restored, and restored wholly—that is to say, with His human nature—to the position of Son of God which He had renounced on becoming incarnate. The thought of Paul is identical with that of the prayer of Jesus on the eve of His death, as we have it in John's Gospel (xvii. 5): "Father, glorify Thou me with the glory which I had with Thee before the world was." Jesus always *was* the Son: at His baptism, through the manifestation of the Father, He recovered His *consciousness* of Sonship. At His resurrection He was re-established, and that as man, in His state of Sonship. The antithesis of the two terms, *born* and *established*, so finely chosen, seems thus perfectly correct.

Three clauses serve to determine the participle *established*. The first indicates the manner: ἐν δυνάμει, *with power;* the second, the moral cause: κατὰ πνεῦμα ἁγιωσύνης, *according to the spirit of holiness;* the third, the efficient cause: ἐξ ἀναστάσεως νεκρῶν, *by His resurrection from the dead*. *With power*, signifies: in a striking, triumphant manner. Some have thought to take this phrase as descriptive of the substantive *Son of God;* "the Son of God in the glory of His power," in opposition to the weakness of His earthly state. But the antithesis of the two propositions is that between the Son of God and the son of David, and not that between the Son of God in power and the Son of God in weakness. The phrase: *with power*, refers therefore to the participle *established:* established by an act in which the power of God is strikingly manifested (the resurrection, wrought by the *glory of the Father*, Rom. vi. 4). The second clause: *according to the spirit of holiness*, has been explained in a multitude of ways. Some have regarded it as indicating the *divine nature* of Jesus in contrast to his humanity, the spirit of holiness being thus the second person of the Trinity; so Melanchthon and Bengel. But, in this case, what term would be left to indicate the third? The second divine person is designated by the names Son or Word, not Spirit. According to Theodoret, what is meant is the *miraculous power* which Jesus possessed on the earth; but how are we to explain the complement *of holiness?* and what relation is there between the virtue of working miracles, possessed by so many prophets, and the installation of Jesus in His place as Son of God? Luther understood by it the effusion of the Holy Spirit on the church, effected by Christ glorified. Then it would be necessary to translate: "*demonstrated* to be the Son of God by the spirit of holiness, whom he poured out." But this meaning does not suit the third clause, whereby the resurrection is indicated as the means of the ὁρίζειν, not Pentecost. No doubt one might, in this case, translate: "*since* the resurrection." But Pentecost did not begin *from* that time. Meyer and others regard the spirit of holiness as meaning, in opposition to the flesh: the *inner man* in in Jesus, the *spirit* as an element of His human nature, in opposition to the outer man, the body. But, as we have seen, the human nature, body and soul, was already embraced completely in the word flesh, ver. 3. How, then, could the *spirit*, taken as an element of human nature, be contrasted with this nature itself? Is, then, the meaning of the words so difficult to apprehend? The term spirit (or breath) *of holiness* shows clearly enough that the matter here in question is the action displayed on Christ by the Holy Spirit during his earthly existence. In proportion as Jesus was open to this influence, his whole human nature received the seal of consecration to the service of God—that is to say, of holiness. Such is the moral fact indicated Heb. ix. 14: "*Who through the eternal Spirit* offered himself without spot to God." The result of this penetration of his entire being by the breath of the Holy Spirit was this: at the time of His death there could be fully realized in Him the law expressed by the Psalmist: "Thou wilt not suffer thy Holy one to see corruption" (Ps. xvi. 10). Perfect holiness excludes physical dissolution. The necessary corollary of such a life and state was therefore the resurrection. This is the relation expressed by the preposition κατά, *according to, agreeably to*. He was established as the Son of God in a striking manner by His resurrection from the dead, *agreeably to the spirit of holiness*, which had reigned in Him and in His very body. In the passage, viii. 11. the apostle applies the same law to the resurrection of believers, when he says "that their bodies shall rise again, in virtue of the Holy Spirit who dwells in them." Paul is not therefore seeking, as has been thought, to establish a contrast between inward (πνεῦμα, *spirit*) and *outward* (σάρξ, *flesh*), nor between *divine* (the *Holy Spirit*) and human (the *flesh*), in the person of Jesus, which would be a needless digression in the context. What he contrasts is, on the one hand, the naturally Jewish and Davidic form of his earthly appearance; and, on the other, the higher form of being on which he entered at the close of this Jewish phase of his existence, in virtue of the principle of holy consecration which had marked all his activity here below. For this new form of existence is the condition on which alone He could accomplish the work described in the verse immediately following. The thought of the apostle does not diverge for an instant, but goes straight to its aim.—The third clause literally signifies: *by a resurrection from the dead* (ἐξ ἀναστάσεως νεκρῶν). He entered upon his human life by a simple *birth;* but in this state as a son of David he let the spirit of holiness reign over him. And therefore he was admitted by a *resurrection* into the glorious life of Sonship. The preposition ἐξ, *out of*, may here signify either *since* or *in consequence of*. The first meaning is now almost abandoned, and undoubtedly with reason; for the idea of a simple succession in time does not suit the gravity of the thought. Paul wishes to describe the immense transformation which the facts of his death and resurrection produced in the person of Jesus. He has left in the tomb his particular relation to the Jewish nation and the family of David, and has appeared through his resurrection freed from those wrappings which he had humbly worn during his earthly life; comp. the remarkable expression: *minister of the circumcision*, xv. 8. Thus it is that, in virtue of his resurrection and as the Son of God, he was able henceforth to enter into connection with all mankind, which he could not do so long as he was acting only as the son of David; comp. Matt. xv. 24: "I am not sent but unto the lost sheep of the house of Israel." The absence of the article before the word *resurrection* and before the plural *dead* is somewhat strange, and must be explained in the way indicated by Hofmann : "By an event such as that which takes place when the dead rise again." There needed a death and resurrection, if he was to pass from the state of son of David to that of Son and Christ of humanity. It is therefore on the *character* of the event that the apostle insists, rather than on the fact itself.

Before passing to the subject of the calling of the Gentiles, which is the direct consequence of this transformation in the person of the Messiah wrought by the resurrection, Paul sums up in three terms the analysis of his person which he has just given : *Jesus ;* this name denotes the historical person, the common subject of those different forms of existence ; the title *Christ* or Messiah, which sums up ver. 3 (Son of David), and that of *Lord* —that is to say, the representative of the divine sovereignty—which follows from his elevation to the position of *Son* (ver. 4). On the title of *Lord*, see 1 Cor. viii. 6 ; Phil. ii. 9–11. When he says *our*, Paul thinks of all those who by faith have accepted the sovereignty of Jesus.

The intention of the passage, vv. 3, 4, has been strangely misunderstood. Some say : it is a summary of the gospel doctrine which the apostle means to expound in this treatise. But a summary is not stated in an address. The true summary of the Epistle, besides, is found i. 17. Finally, *christological* doctrine is precisely one of the heads, the absence of which is remarkable in our Epistle. Gess says : "One must suppose that the apostle was concerned to sum up in this introduction the most elevated sentiments which filled his heart regarding the Mediators of salvation." But why put these reflections on the person of Christ in the address, and between what Paul says of his apostleship in general (vv. 1, 2), and what he afterward adds regarding his apostleship to the Gentiles in particular (vv. 5, 6) ? Hofmann thinks that Paul, in referring to the relation between Jesus and the old covenant, wishes to indicate all that God gives us new in Christ. But this observation would suit any other place rather than the address. The most singular explanation is Mangold's : "A Jewish-Christian church like that of Rome might be astonished at Paul's addressing it as if it had been of Gentile origin ; and the apostle has endeavored to weaken this impression by reminding it (ver. 2) that his apostleship had been predicted in the Old Testament, and (ver. 3) that the object of his preaching is above all the Messiah, the Son of David." So artificial an explanation refutes itself. The apostle started (vv. 1, 2) from the idea of his apostleship, but in order to come to that of his apostleship to the Gentiles, which alone serves to explain the step he is now taking in writing to the Christians of Rome (vv. 5, 6). To pass from the first of these ideas to the second, he rises to the author of his apostleship, and describes Him as the Jewish Messiah, called to gather together the lost sheep of the house of Israel (ver. 5) ; then as the Son of God raised from the dead, able to put Himself henceforth in direct communication with the Gentiles through an apostolate instituted on their behalf (ver. 4). In reality, to accomplish this wholly new work, Jesus required to be set free from the form of Jewish nationality and the bond of theocratic obligations. He must be placed in one uniform relation to the whole race. This was the effect of the transformation wrought in His person by His death and resurrection. Thus there is no difficulty in understanding the transition from ver. 4 to ver. 5.

Vv. 5, 6 : "*By whom we have received grace and apostleship, with a view to the obedience of faith among all the Gentiles, for the glory of His name: among whom are ye, also, the called of Jesus Christ.*" The words δι' οὗ, *by whom,* exactly express the transition which we have just indicated. It is from His heavenly glory and from His state as Son of God that Christ has founded the new apostolate, and called him whom He has invested with it (comp. Gal. i. 1).—The plural ἐλάβομεν, *we have received*, is explained by some : *I and the other apostles;* by Hofmann : *I and my apostolical assistants* (Barnabas, Silas, Timothy, etc.). But the first meaning is inadmissible, because the matter in question here is exclusively the apostleship *to the Gentiles;* and the second is equally so, because Paul, speaking here in his *official* character, can associate no one with him in the dignity which the Lord has conferred on him personally. What we have here is therefore the *plural of category*, which the Greeks readily use when they wish to put the person out of view, and to present only the principle which he represents, or the work with which he is charged. The words : χάριν καὶ ἀποστολήν, *grace and apostleship*, are regarded by some (Chrys., Philippi) as equivalent to : *the grace of apostleship*. But if this had been Paul's meaning, it would have been easy for him to express it so. Hofmann applies the two terms to the *ministry* of the apostle, as presenting it, the former, in connection with his own person—it is a *grace* conferred on him ; the latter, in its relation to others—it is his *mission* to them. But if the term *grace* be referred to Paul's person, it seems to us much simpler to apply it to the gift of *salvation* which was bestowed on himself ; the second term, *apostleship*, comes thus quite naturally to designate his mission for the salvation of the world. We have seen (Introd. p. 13) how these two gifts, personal salvation and apostleship, were, in Paul's case, one and the same event. The object of Christ in according him grace and calling him to the apostleship, was to spread the *obedience of faith*. It is impossible to understand by this *obedience* the *holiness* produced by faith. For, before speaking of the effects of faith, faith must exist ; and the matter in question is precisely the calling of the apostle destined to lay the foundation of it. Meyer's meaning is still more inadmissible, submission *to the faith*. In that case, we should require to give to the term *faith* the meaning of : *Christian truth* (objectively speaking), a meaning the word never has in the New Testament, as Meyer acknowledges. So he understands obedience to the inward sentiment of faith ! This is a form of speech of which it would be still more difficult to find examples. The only possible meaning is : the obedience *which consists in* faith itself. By faith man performs an act of obedience to the divine manifestation which demands of him submission and co-operation. The refusal of faith is therefore called, x. 3, a *disobedience* (οὐχ ὑπετάγησαν). The clause following : *among all the Gentiles*, might be connected with the word *apostleship*, but it is simpler to connect it directly with the preceding, the obedience of faith : "an obedience *to be realized* among all Gentiles." The term ἔθνη, which we translate by *Gentiles*, has been taken here by almost all critics who hold the Jewish origin of the Christians of Rome, in a wider acceptation. They give it the general meaning of *nations*, in order to include under it the Jews, who are also *a nation*, and consequently the Christians of Rome. This interpretation has been defended chiefly by Rückert and Baur. But it is easy to see that it is invented to serve an *a priori* thesis. The word ἔθνη undoubtedly signifies strictly: *nations*. But it has taken, like the word *gojim* in the Old Testament (Gen. xii. 3 ; Isa. xlii. 6, etc.), a definite, restricted, and quasi-technical sense : *the nations* in opposition *to the* chosen *people* (ὁ λαός, *the people*). This signification occurs from beginning to end of the New Testament (Acts ix. 15, xi. 1, 18, xxviii. 28 ; Gal. i. 16, ii. 7-9, iii. 14, Eph. ii. 11, iii. 6).[1] It is applied in the most uniform manner in our Epistle (ii. 14, 15, iii. 29, xi. 13, xv. 9, 11). Besides, the context imperatively demands this limited sense. Paul has just been explaining the institution of a special apostleship to the Gentiles, by a transformation in the Lord's mode of existence ; the whole demonstration would be useless if his aim were to prove what the believers of Rome, *though Jewish Christians*, belong also to the domain of his mission. Mangold feels the difficulty ; for, in order to remain faithful to Baur's view as to the composition of the Roman church, without falling into his false interpretation of the word ἔθνη, he tries to take it in a purely geographical sense. He

---

[1] I mention only some thoroughly characteristic passages.

thinks that by *the nations*, Paul means to contrast the inhabitants of the world in general, whether Jews or Gentiles, with the Jews strictly so called *dwelling in Palestine*. The apostle means to say: "The church of Rome, though composed of Judeo-Christians, belongs *geographically* to the world of the Gentiles, and consequently comes within my domain as the apostle of the Gentiles." But what in this case becomes of the partition of domains marked out in Gal. ii. ? It must signify that Peter reserved for himself to preach *in* Palestine, and Paul *out of* Palestine ! Who can give this meaning to the famous passage, Gal. ii. ? Besides, as Beyschlag well says, this partition between the apostles rested on a difference of *gifts*, which had nothing to do with geography, and evidently referred to the religious and moral character of those two great divisions of mankind, Jews and Gentiles. It must therefore be allowed that the words : *among all nations*, refer to Gentiles, and to Gentiles as such. Baur has sought to turn the word *all* to account in favor of his interpretation ; but Paul uses it precisely to introduce what he is going to say, ver. 6, that the Romans, though so remote, yet formed part of his domain, since it embraces *all* Gentiles without exception. It matters little, therefore, that they are still personally unknown to him, he is their apostle nevertheless.—The third clause : ὑπὲρ τοῦ ὀνόματος, *for, in behalf*, or *for the glory of His name*, depends on the whole verse from the verb *we have received*. Paul does not forget that this is the highest end of his apostleship : to exalt the glory of that name by extending the sphere of his action, and increasing the number of those who invoke it as the name of their Lord. The words sound like an echo of the message of Jesus to Paul by Ananias : " He is a chosen vessel *to carry my name to the Gentiles ;*" comp. 3, John 7. By this word Paul reveals to us at once the aim of his mission, and the inward motive of all his work. And what a work was that ! As Christ in His own person broke the external covering of Israelitish form, so he purposed to break the national wrapping within which the kingdom of God had till then been inclosed ; and to spread the glory of His name to the very ends of the earth, He called Paul.

Ver. 6 may be construed in two ways : either the κλητοὶ 'I. X. may be taken as a predicate : " in the midst of whom (Gentiles) *ye are the called of Jesus Christ*," or the last words may be taken in apposition to the subject : " of the number of whom ye are, *ye who are called of Jesus Christ*." The former construction does not give a simple meaning ; for the verb *ye are* has then two predicates which conflict with one another : " ye are in the midst of them," and : " ye are the called of Jesus Christ." Besides, is it necessary to inform the Christians of Rome that they live in the midst of the Gentiles, and that they are called by Jesus Christ? Add the καὶ, *also*, which would signify : like all the other Christians in the world, and you have an addition wholly superfluous, and, besides, far from clear. What has led commentators like De Wette, Meyer, etc., to hold this first construction is, that it seemed to them useless to make Paul say : " ye are among, or ye are of the number of the Gentiles." But, on the contrary, this idea is very essential. It is the minor premiss of the syllogism within which Paul, so to speak, incloses the Romans. The major : Christ has made me the Apostle of the Gentiles ; the minor : ye are of the number of the Gentiles ; conclusion : therefore, in virtue of the authority of that Christ who has called you as He has called me, ye are the sheep of my fold. The καὶ, *also*, from this point of view is easily explained : " of the number of whom (Gentiles) ye *also* are, ye Romans, falling consequently like the other Gentiles called by me personally to my apostolical domain." The title κλητοὶ 'I. X., *called of Jesus Christ*, corresponds to the title which Paul gave himself, ver. 1 : κλητὸς ἀπόστολος, "*an apostle by calling.*" They are bound to hear him in virtue of the same authority under which he writes to them, that of Jesus Christ. The complement : "*called of Jesus Christ*," may be taken as a genitive of possession : " called ones *belonging to* Jesus Christ." But it is better to regard it as a genitive of cause: "called ones, whose calling *comes from* Jesus Christ." For the important thing in the context is not the commonplace idea that they belong to the Lord; it is the notion of the act by which the Lord Himself acted on them to make them believers, as on Paul to make him their apostle. The idea of *calling* (of God or Christ), according to Paul's usage, includes two thoughts, an outward solicitation by preaching, and an inward and simultaneous drawing by the Holy Spirit. It need not be said that neither the one nor the other of these influences is irresistible,[1] nor that the adhesion of faith remains an act of freedom. This adhesion is here implied in the fact that the Romans are members of the church and readers of these lines.

If we needed a confirmation of the Gentile origin of the majority of this church, it would be found in overwhelming force in vv. 5 and 6, especially when taken in connection with ver. 4; and really it needs far more than common audacity to attempt to get out of them the opposite idea, and to paraphrase them, as Volkmar does, in the following way: "I seem to you no doubt to be only the apostle of the Hellenes; but, nevertheless, I am called by Jesus Christ to preach the gospel to all nations, even to the non-Hellenes such as you, believers of Jewish origin!"

We come now to the second and third parts of the address, the indication of the readers and the expression of the writer's prayer.

Ver. 7. " *To all the well-beloved of God who are at Rome,*[2] *saints by way of call: Grace be given you and peace on the part of God our Father, and the Lord Jesus Christ.*"—The dative: *to all those,* might be dependent on a verb understood: *I write,* or *I address myself;* but it is simpler to connect it with the verb implied in the statement of the prayer which immediately follows: " To you all *may there be given.*" The adjective *all* would be quite superfluous here if Paul had not the intention of widening the circle of persons spoken of in ver. 6 as being *of the number of the Gentiles.* Paul certainly has no doubt that there are also among the Christians of Rome some brethren of *Jewish* origin, and by his *to all* he now embraces them in the circle of those to whom he addresses his letter. We need not separate the two datives: *to all those who are at Rome* and *to the well-beloved of God,* as if they were two different regimens; the dative: *well-beloved of God,* is taken substantively: *to all the well-beloved of God who are at Rome.* The words denote the entire number of Roman believers, Jews and Gentiles. All men are in a sense *loved of God* (John iii. 16); but apart from faith, this love of God can only be that of compassion. It becomes an intimate love, like that of father and child, only through the reconciliation granted to faith. Here is the first bond between the apostle and his readers: the common love of which they are the objects. This bond is strengthened by another: the internal work which has flowed from it, consecration to God, holiness: κλητοῖς ἁγίοις, *saints by way of call.* We need not translate either: *called to be* saints, which would imply that holiness is in their case no more as yet than a destination, or *called and holy* (Ostervald), which would give to the notion of calling too independent a force. Paul means that they *are* really saints, and that if they possess this title of nobility before God, it is because Christ has honored them with His call, by drawing some from the defilements of paganism, and raising others from the external consecration of God's ancient people to the spiritual consecration of the new. Under the old covenant, consecration to God was hereditary, and attached to the external rite of circumcision. Under the new economy, consecration is that of the will first of all, and so of the entire life. It passes from within outward, and not from without inward; it is real holiness. The words ἐν ʹΡώμῃ, *at Rome,* are omitted in the Greek text of

---

[1] Yet it is certainly effectual, which, however, does not hinder faith from being an act of freedom.—T. W. C.

[2] The words εν Ρωμη are wanting in G g.

the Cod. *de Bœrner.* (G), as well as in the Latin translation accompanying it (*g*). This might be regarded as an accidental omission, if it were not repeated in ver. 15. Rückert and Renan think that it arises from manuscripts intended for other churches, and in which accordingly, the indication of the readers had been left blank. But in this case would it not occur in a larger number of documents? Meyer supposes that some church or other, having the letter copied for its own special use, had intentionally suppressed the words. But it needs to be explained why the same thing did not take place with other Epistles. Perhaps the cause of the omission in this case was the contrast between the general character of the contents of the letter and the local destination indicated in the suppressed words, the second fact appearing contradictory to the first (see ver. 15).

Why does the apostle not salute this community of believers, as he does those of Thessalonica, Galatia, and Corinth, with the name of *church?* The different Christian groups which existed at Rome, and several of which are mentioned in chap. xvi., were perhaps not yet connected with one another by a common presbyterial organization.

The end of ver. 7 contains the development of the third part of the address, *the prayer.* For the usual term χαίρειν, *joy and prosperity*, Paul substitutes the blessings which form the Christian's wealth and happiness. *Grace*, χάρις, denotes the love of God manifested in the form of pardon toward sinful man; *peace*, εἰρήνη, the feeling of profound calm or inward quiet which is communicated to the heart by the possession of reconciliation. It may seem that the title: *well-beloved of God*, given above, included these gifts; but the Christian possesses nothing which does not require to be ever received anew, and daily increased by new acts of faith and prayer. The Apocalypse says that "salvation flows from the throne of God and of the Lamb;" it is *from God* and *from Jesus Christ* that Paul likewise derives the two blessings which he wishes for the believers of Rome; from God as *Father*, and from Jesus Christ as *Lord* or Head of the church. We need not explain these two regimens as if they meant "*from* God *through* Christ." The two substantives depend on a common preposition: *on the part of.* The apostle therefore has in view not a source and a channel, but two sources. The love of God and the love of Christ are two distinct loves; the one is a father's, the other a brother's. Christ loves with *his own* love, Rom. v. 15. Comp. John v. 21 (*those whom he will*) and 26 (*he hath life in himself*). Erasmus was unhappy in taking the words: *Jesus Christ our Lord*, as a second complement to the word *Father:* "our Father and that of Jesus Christ." But in this case the complement *Jesus Christ* would have required to be placed first, and the notion of God's fatherhood in relation to Christ would be without purpose in the context. The conviction of Christ's divine nature can alone explain this construction, according to which His person and that of the Father are made alike dependent on one and the same proposition.

It is impossible not to admire the prudence and delicacy which St. Paul shows in the discharge of his task toward this church. To justify his procedure, he goes back on his apostleship; to justify his apostleship to them, Gentiles, he goes back to the transformation which the resurrection wrought in Christ's person, when from being Jewish Messiah it made Him *Lord* in the absolute sense of the word. Like a true pastor, instead of lording it over the conscience of his flock, he seeks to associate it with his own.

SECOND PASSAGE (1:8-15)

The Interest long taken by the Apostle in the Christians of Rome

The address had drawn a sort of *official* bond between the apostle and the church. But Paul feels the need of converting it into a *heart* relation;

and to this end the following piece is devoted. The apostle here assures his readers of the profound interest which he has long felt in them, though he has not yet been able to show it by visiting them. He begins, as usual, by thanking God for the work already wrought in them, ver. 8 ; then he expresses his lively and long cherished desire to labor for its growth, either in the way of strengthening themselves spiritually, vv. 9–12, or in the way of increasing the number of believers in the city of Rome, vv. 13–15.

Ver. 8. "*First, I thank my God through Jesus Christ* [1] *on account of you all, that your faith is spoken of throughout the whole world.*"—The apostle knows that there is no more genuine proof of sincere affection than intercession ; hence he puts his prayer for them first. The word $\pi\rho\hat{\omega}\tau o\nu$, *in the first place* (especially with the particle $\mu\acute{\epsilon}\nu$), leads us to expect a *secondly* ($\check{\epsilon}\pi\epsilon\iota\tau a$ $\delta\acute{\epsilon}$). As this word does not occur in the sequel, some have thought it necessary to give to $\pi\rho\hat{\omega}\tau o\nu$ the meaning of *above all*. This is unnecessary. The second idea the apostle had in view is really found in ver. 10, in the prayer which he offers to God that he may be allowed soon to go to Rome. This prayer is the natural supplement of the thanksgiving. Only the construction has led the apostle not to express it in the strictly logical form : *in the second place*.—In the words "*my God*," he sums up all his *personal* experiences of God's fatherly help, in the various circumstances of his life, and particularly in those of his apostleship. Herein there is a particular revelation which every believer receives for himself alone, and which he sums up when he calls God *his* God ; comp. the phrase *God of Abraham, of Isaac, and of Jacob*, and more especially the words Gen. xxviii. 20, 21. Paul's thanksgiving is presented through the mediation of *Jesus Christ ;* he conveys it through Christ as head of the church, and more immediately his own. Meyer thinks that Christ is rather mentioned here as the *author* of the work for which Paul gives thanks ; but this is not the natural meaning of the phrase : I thank *through ;* comp. besides, viii. 34. The propagation of the gospel at Rome appears to Paul a service rendered to him personally, as apostle of the Gentiles.—The phrase : *on account of you all*, seems a little exaggerated, since he does not know them all personally. But would there be a human being at Rome gained for Christ, known or unknown, whose faith was not a subject of joy to Paul ! The preposition $\dot{\upsilon}\pi\acute{\epsilon}\rho$, *in behalf of*, which is found in the T. R. (with the latest Mjj.), would express more affection than $\pi\epsilon\rho\acute{\iota}$, *on account of ;* but the latter is more simple, and occurs in some Mjj. of the three families. What increases Paul's joy is, that not only do they believe themselves, but their faith, the report of which is spread everywhere, opens a way for the gospel to other countries ; comp. a similar passage addressed to the Thessalonians (1 Thess. i. 8). The $\delta\tau\iota$, *because*, serves to bring into relief a special feature in the cause of joy already indicated ; comp. 1 Cor. i. 5 (the $\delta\tau\iota$ in its relation to ver. 4). The phrase : *throughout the whole world*, is hyperbolical ; it alludes to the position of Rome as the capital of the world ; comp. Col. i. 6.

Vv. 9, 10. "*For God is my witness, whom I serve with my spirit in the gospel of His Son, how without ceasing I make mention of you, making request in all my prayers, if perhaps now at length I might have a prosperous journey by the will of God to come unto you.*"—This thanksgiving of the apostle was an inward action of which none but God could have knowledge ; and as the words, ver. 8, might seem chargeable with exaggeration, he appeals to the one witness of his inner life. Paul thinks of those times of intimate intercourse which he has daily with his God in the exercise of his ministry ; for it is at His feet, as it were, that he discharges this task. He says : "*in my spirit*, that is to say, in the most intimate part of his being, where is the organ by which his soul communicates with the divine

---

[1] The T. R. Reads υπερ, with E G L P and the Mnn. Περι is found in ℵ A B C D K and 10 Mnn.

world. The *spirit* is therefore here one of the elements of his human nature (1 Thess. v. 23) ; only it is evidently thought of as penetrated with the Divine Spirit. When Paul says : *in the gospel of His Son*, it is clear that he is not thinking of the *matter*, but of the *act* of evangelical preaching. This is for him a continual act of worship which he performs only on his knees. The words : *of His Son*, bring out the supreme gravity of the act. How, in fact, can one take part in a work which concerns *the Son*, otherwise than in concert with God Himself ! The ὡς need be translated neither by *that* (the *fact*), which expresses too little, nor by *how much* (the *degree*), which is too strong, but by *how*. The word refers to the *mode* of this inward worship, as it is developed in what follows. The expression : *without ceasing*, explains the : "I give thanks *for you all*," which had preceded (ver. 8). Hence the *for* at the beginning of the verse.

Ver. 10. With the thanksgiving there is connected, as a second matter which he has to communicate to them, his not less unwearied *prayer* that he might be able soon to visit them. The words : *always in my prayers*, refer certainly to the following participle : *making request*, and not to what precedes, a sense which would lead to a pleonasm. Not one of the intimate dealings of the apostle with his God, in which this subject does not find a place.—'Επί, strictly speaking, *on occasion of*. The conjunction εἴπως, *if perhaps*, indicates the calculation of chances ; and the adverbs *now, at length*, the sort of impatience which he puts into his calculation. The term εὐοδοῦν strictly signifies : *to cause one to journey prosperously*, whence in general : *to make one succeed* in a business ; comp. 1 Cor. xvi. 2. As in this context the subject in question is precisely the success of a *journey*, it is difficult not to see in the choice of the term an allusion to its strict meaning : " if at length I shall not be *guided prosperously in my journey* to you." By whom ? The words : *by the will of God*, tell us ; favorable circumstances are the work of that all-powerful hand. Vv. 11, 12 indicate the most immediate motive of this ardent desire.

Vv. 11, 12. " *For I long to see you, that I may impart unto you some spiritual gift, to the end that ye may be established ; or to speak more properly, that I may be encouraged with you in the midst of you, by the mutual action of our faith, yours and mine.*"—Enriched with the gifts of God as he was, could the apostle help feeling the need of imparting some of them to a church so important as that of Rome ? There is in the verb ἐπιποθῶ, along with the expression of the *desire* which goes out toward them, one of *regret* at not having been able to come sooner. A χάρισμα, gift, is a concrete manifestation of grace (χάρις). The epithet *spiritual* shows the *nature* and *source* of the gift which he hopes to impart to his readers (the spirit, the πνεῦμα). The word ὑμῖν, *to you*, is inserted between the substantive and the adjective to bring out the latter more forcibly. The apostle hopes that by this communication they will receive an increase of divine *strength* within them. He puts the verb in the passive : *that ye may be strengthened*. We need not translate : *to confirm you* (Oltram.); on the contrary, Paul uses the passive form to put out of view the part he takes personally, and to exhibit only the result ; it is God who will strengthen. There would be a degree of charlatanism in the choice of the word *strengthen, confirm*, if, as Baur, and following him, Mangold, Sabatier, etc., think, the apostle's object in this letter was to bring about a radical change in the existing conception of the gospel at Rome. To strengthen, is not to turn one into another way, it is to make him walk firmly on that on which he is already. But Paul was too sincerely humble, and at the same time too delicate in his feelings, to allow it to be supposed that the spiritual advantage resulting from his stay among them would all be on one side. He hastens to add that he hopes himself to have his share, ver. 12. The first words of this verse have generally been misunderstood ; there has been given to them the meaning of the phrase τοῦτ' ἐστι, *that is to say* (Ostervald, Oltram.). It is forgotten that the δέ which is added here (τοῦτο δέ ἐστι) indicates not a simple explanatory repetition, but a certain modification and progress in the idea. The meaning, therefore, is: *or to speak more properly.* In point of fact, Paul had yet to add to the idea of the good which he reckoned on doing, that of the good which he hoped himself to receive. This is precisely what he has in view in the strange construction of the words which immediately follow. There is no doubt that the preposition σύν, *with,* in the compound verb συμπαρακληθῆναι, *to be encouraged with,* signifies: "I *with you,* Christians of Rome." For the subject of the verb can be no other than the apostle, on account of the words which follow: *in the midst of you.* Fritzsche attempts to give it a *you* for its subject, ὑμᾶς understood; Meyer and Hofmann would make this infinitive directly dependent on the word *I desire,* ver. 11: "I desire to see you, and to be encouraged in the midst of you." But this is to mistake the evident relation between the two passive infinitives, so closely connected with one another. "To the end that *ye* may be strengthened; and, to speak more correctly, that *with you* I may be encouraged among you." The "*with* (you)" brings out the notion of *their* strengthening, to add to it immediately, and that in the same word (in Greek) the notion of the encouragement derived by *Paul* himself, as being one with theirs; for is not the strengthening of others the means of encouraging himself? One shares in the strength which he imparts. The apostle seems to say that there is in his desire as much holy selfishness as holy zeal. The substitution of the word *encourage* (in speaking of Paul) for that of *strengthen* (in speaking of them) is significant. In Paul's case, the only thing in question is his subjective feeling, which might be a little depressed, and which would receive a new impulse from the success of his work among them; comp. Acts xxviii. 15 (*he took courage,* ἔλαβε θάρσος). This same delicacy of expression is kept up in the words which follow. By the *among you,* the apostle says that their mere presence will of itself be strengthening to him. This appears literally in what follows: "*by my faith and yours one upon another.*" These lasts words express a *reciprocity* in virtue of which his faith will act on theirs and theirs on his; and how so? In virtue of their having that faith *in common* (by the faith *of you and of me*). It is because they live in this common atmosphere of one and the same faith that they can act and react spiritually, he on them, and they on him. What dignity, tact, and grace in these words, by which the apostle at once transforms the active part which he is obliged to ascribe to himself in the first place into a receptive part, and so to terminate with the notion which unites these two points of view, that of reciprocity in the possession of a common moral life! Erasmus has classed all this in the category of *pia vafrities* and *sancta adulatio.*[1] He did not understand the sincerity of Paul's humility. But what Paul wishes is not merely to impart new strength to the Christians of Rome while reinforcing his own, it is also to aid in the increase of their church. He comes as an apostle, not only as a Christian visitor; such is the meaning of the words which follow (vv. 13-15).

Vv. 13, 14. "*Now I would not have you ignorant, brethren, that oftentimes I purposed to come unto you (but was hindered hitherto), that I might gather some fruit*[2] *among you also, even as among the other Gentiles. I am debtor both to the Greeks, and to the Barbarians; both to the wise, and to the ignorant.*" —His readers might ask with some reason how it happened that Paul, having been an apostle for more than twenty years, had not yet found time to come and preach the good news in the Capital of the world. The phrase: *I would not have you ignorant,* has something slightly mysterious about it, which will be explained presently. The δέ, *now,* expresses a gradation, but not one from the simple *desire* (ver. 11) to the *fixed purpose* (ver. 13). The right connection in this sense would have been: *for indeed,*

---
[1] *Pious fraud and holy flattery.*
[2] The T. R. reads καρπον τινα, with some Mnn. All the Mjj.: τινα καρπον.

and not *now*. Paul rather passes here from the *spiritual* good, which he has always desired to do among the believers of Rome, to the *extension* of their church, to which he hopes he may contribute. Let his work at Corinth and Ephesus be remembered; why should he not accomplish a similar work at Rome? He means, therefore: "*I shall confess to you my whole mind;* my ambition aims at making some new conquests even in your city (at Rome)." This is what he calls *gathering some fruit*. The phrase is as modest as possible. At Corinth and Ephesus he gathered full harvests; at Rome, where the church already exists, he will merely add *some handfuls* of ears to the sheaves already reaped by others. Καρπὸν ἔχειν, literally, *to have fruit*, does not here signify: *to bear* fruit, as if Paul were comparing himself to a tree. The N. T. has other and more common terms for this idea: καρπὸν φέρειν, ποιεῖν, διδόναι. The meaning is rather to secure fruit, like a husbandman who garners a harvest. The two καί, *also*, of the Greek text, "*also* among you, as *also* among the other Gentiles," signify respectively: "among you quite as much as among them;" and "among them quite as much as among you." St. Paul remembers what he has succeeded in doing elsewhere. No reader free from prepossession will fail to see here the evident proof of the *Gentile* origin of the great majority of the Christians of Rome. To understand by ἔθνη, *nations* in general, including the Jews as well, is not only contrary to the uniform sense of the word (see ver. 5), but also to the subdivision into *Greeks* and *Barbarians* given in the following verse: for the Jews, according to Paul's judgment, evidently did not belong to either of these two classes. If he had thought of the Jews in this place, he must have used the classification of ver. 16: *to the Jews and Greeks*.

Ver. 14. No connecting particle. Such is always the indication of a feeling which as it rises is under the necessity of reaffirming itself with increasing energy: "Yea, I feel that I owe myself to all that is called Gentile." The first division, into *Greeks* and *Barbarians*, bears on the *language*, and thereby on the *nationality;* the second, into *wise* and *ignorant*, on the degree of *culture*. It may be asked in what category did Paul place the Romans themselves. As to the first of these two classifications, it is obvious that he cannot help ranking among the Greeks those to whom he is writing at the very time in the Greek language. The Romans, from the most ancient times, had received their culture from the Greek colonies established in Italy. So Cicero, in a well-known passage of the *De finibus* (ii. 15), conjoins *Græcia* and *Italia*, and contrasts them with *Barbaria*. As to the second contrast, it is possible that Paul regards the immense population of Rome, composed of elements so various, as falling into the two classes mentioned. What matters? All those individuals, of whatever category, Paul regards as *his creditors*. He owes them his life, his person, in virtue of the grace bestowed on him and of the office which he has received (ver. 5). The emotion excited by this thought is what has caused the asyndeton [1] between vv. 13 and 14.

Ver. 15. "*So, as much as in me is, I have the lively desire to preach the gospel to you also, to you that are at Rome.*"[2]—Of the three explanations by which it has been sought to account for the grammatical construction of this verse, the simplest seems to me to be that which gives a restricting sense to the words κατ' ἐμέ: *for my part*, that is to say: "*so far as depends on me*, so far as external circumstances shall not thwart my desire," and which takes τὸ πρόθυμον as a paraphrase of the substantive προθυμία; the meaning is: "So far as I am concerned, the liveliest desire prevails in me to"... Such is the explanation of Fritzsche, Reiche, Philippi. De Wette and Meyer prefer to join τό with κατ' ἐμέ in the same sense as we have just given to κατ' ἐμέ alone, and to take πρόθυμον as the subject: "As

---

[1] The absence of any logical particle.   [2] G g omit τοις εν Ρωμη.

far as I am concerned, there is an eagerness to " . . . Some have made τὸ κατ' ἐμέ a periphrasis for ἐγώ, as the subject of the proposition, and taken πρόθυμον as a predicate : "My personal disposition is eagerness to announce to you " . . . The meaning is nearly the same whichever of the three explanations be adopted. The οὕτω, *so*, very obviously stands as a concluding particle. This eagerness to preach at Rome no less than elsewhere is the *consequence* of that debt to *all* which he feels lying upon him. The meaning : *likewise*, would not be so suitable. The word to *evangelize*, literally, to proclaim good *news*, seems to be inapplicable to a church already founded. But we have just seen that the apostle has here in view the *extension* of the church by preaching to the unbelieving population around it. Hence the use of the word. We must therefore take the words : *you that are at Rome*, in a wider sense. It is not merely the members of the church who are denoted by it, but the whole population of the great city represented in the eyes of Paul by his readers. As Hofmann says : "He is here considering the members of the church as Romans, not as Christians." The words *at Rome* are omitted by Codex G, as in ver. 7. Volkmar explains their rejection by the fact that some *evangelistarium* (a collection of the pericopes intended for public reading) suppressed them to preserve the universal character of our Epistle. This explanation comes to the same as that which we have given on ver. 7.

Here for the present the *letter* closes and the *treatise* begins. The first proposition of ver. 16 : *I am not ashamed of the gospel*, is the transition from the one to the other. For the words : *I am not ashamed*, are intended to remove a suspicion which might be raised against the profession Paul has just made of eagerness to preach at Rome ; they thus belong to the *letter*. And, on the other hand, the word *gospel* sums up the whole contents of the didactic *treatise* which immediately opens. It is impossible to see in this first proposition of ver. 16 anything else than a transition, or to bring out of it, as Hofmann attempts, the statement of the object of the whole Epistle.

TREATISE

1:16-15:13

THIRD PASSAGE (1:16, 17)

The Statement of the Subject

VER. 16. "*For I am not ashamed of the gospel:*[1] *for it is a power of God unto salvation to every one that believeth; to the Jew first,*[2] *and also to the Greek.*"—The long delays which had prevented the apostle's visit to Rome did not arise, as might have been thought, from some secret anxiety or fear that he might not be able to sustain honorably the part of preacher of the word on this stage. In the very contents of the gospel there are a grandeur and a power which lift the man who is charged with it above feelings of this kind. He may indeed be filled with fear and trembling when he is delivering such a message, 1 Cor. ii. 3; but the very nature of the message restores him, and gives him entire boldness wherever he presents himself. In what follows the apostle seems to say: "And I now proceed to prove this to you by expounding in writing that gospel which I would have wished to proclaim with the living voice in the midst of you." When he says: *I am not ashamed*, Paul does not seem to have in view the opprobrium attached to the preaching of the Crucified One; he would have brought out this particular more distinctly. Comp. 1 Cor. i. 18, 23. The complement τοῦ Χριστοῦ, *of Christ*, which is found in the T. R. along with the Byz. MSS., is certainly unauthentic; for it is wanting in the documents of the other two families, in the ancient Latin and Syriac Vss., and even in a larger number of Mnn. The word *gospel* denotes here, as in vv. 1 and 9, not the matter, but the *act* of preaching; Calvin himself says: *De vocali prædicatione hic loquitur*. And why is the apostle not ashamed of such a proclamation? Because it is the mighty arm of God rescuing the world from perdition, and bringing it salvation. Mankind are, as it were, at the bottom of an abyss; the preaching of the gospel is the power from above which raises out of it. No one need blush at being the instrument of such a force. The omission of the article before the word δύναμις, *power*, serves to bring out *the character* of the action rather than the action itself. Hofmann says: "*Power*, for the gospel can do something; power *of God*, for it can do all it promises." The word σωτηρία, *salvation*, contains two ideas: on the one side, deliverance from an evil, perdition; on the other, communication of a blessing, eternal life in communion with God. The possession of these two privileges is man's health (σωτηρία, from the adjective σῶς, *safe and sound*). The life of God in the soul of man, such is the normal state of the latter. The preposition

---

[1] The T. R. here reads the words του Χριστου (*of Christ*), with K L P and the Mnn. The words are wanting in all the other Mjj., in *Ital.* and *Pesch.* and in some Mnn.
[2] The word πρωτον is omitted in B G g; according to Tertullian, it was wanting in Marcion.

εἰς, *to*, or *in* (salvation), denotes not only the *purpose* of the divine work, but its immediate and certain result, wherever the human condition is fulfilled. This condition is faith,*to every one that believeth*. The word *every one* expresses the universal efficacy of the remedy, and the word *believeth*, its entire *freeness*. Such are the two fundamental characteristics of the Christian salvation, especially as preached by Paul ; and they are so closely connected that, strictly speaking, they form only one. Salvation would not be for *all*, if it demanded from man anything else than *faith*. To make work or merit a condition in the least degree, would be to exclude certain individuals. Its universal destination thus rests on its entire freeness at the time when man is called to enter into it. The apostle adds to the word *believing* the article τῷ, *the*, which cannot be rendered in French by the *tout* (all) ; the word means *each* individual, provided he believes. As the offer is universal, so the act of faith by which man accepts is individual ; comp. John iii. 16. The *faith* of which the apostle speaks is nothing else than the simple acceptance of the salvation offered in preaching. It is premature to put in this moral act all that will afterwards flow from it when faith shall be in possession of its object. This is what is done by Reuss and Sabatier, when they define it respectively : " A personal, inward, mystical union between man and Christ the Saviour " (*Ep. paulin.* II. p. 43) ; and : "the destruction of sin in us, the inward creation of the divine life" (*L'ap. Paul*, p. 265). This is to make the effect the cause. Faith, in Paul's sense, is something extremely simple, such that it does not in the least impair the *freeness* of salvation. God says : I give thee ; the heart answers : I accept ; such is faith. The act is thus a receptivity, but an active receptivity. It brings nothing, but it takes what God gives ; as was admirably said by a poor Bechuana : "It is the hand of the heart." In this act the entire human personality takes part : the understanding discerning the blessing offered in the divine promise, the will aspiring after it, and the confidence of the heart giving itself up to the promise, and so securing the promised blessing. The preaching of free salvation is the act by which God lays hold of man, faith is the act by which man lets himself be laid hold of. Thus, instead of God's ancient people who were recruited by birth and Abrahamic descent, Paul sees a new people arising, formed of all the individuals who perform the personal act of faith, whatever the nation to which they belong. To give pointed expression to this last feature, he recalls the ancient distinction which had till then divided mankind into two rival religious societies, Jews and Gentiles, and declares this distinction abolished. He says : *to the Jew first, and to the Greek*. In this context the word Greek has a wider sense than in ver. 14 ; for there it was opposed to *Barbarian*. It therefore designated only a *part* of Gentile humanity. Here, where it is used in opposition to *Jew*, it includes the whole Gentile world. Greeks were indeed the *élite* of the Gentiles, and might be regarded as representing the Gentiles in general ; comp. 1 Cor. i. 22–24. This difference in the extension of the name *Greeks* arises from the fact that in ver. 14 the only matter in question was *Paul's* ministry, the domain of which was subdivided into civilized *Gentiles* (Greeks) and *barbarian* Gentiles ; while here the matter in question is the gospel's sphere of action in general, a sphere to which the whole of mankind belong (*Jews* and *Gentiles*). The word πρῶτον, *first*, should not be interpreted, as some think, in the sense of *principally*. It would be false to say that salvation is intended for the Jews *in preference* to the Greeks. Paul has in view the right of *priority in time* which belonged to Israel as the result of its whole history. As to this right, God had recognized it by making Jesus to be born in the midst of this people ; Jesus had respected it by confining Himself during His earthly life to gathering together *the lost sheep of the house of Israel*, and by commanding his apostles to begin the evangelization of the world with Jerusalem and Judea, Acts i. 8 ; Peter and the Twelve remained strictly faithful to it, as is proved by the first part of the Acts, chaps. ii.-xii.; and Paul himself had uniformly done homage to it by beginning the preaching of the gospel, in every Gentile city to which he came as an apostle, in the synagogue. And, indeed, this right of priority rested on the destination of Israel to become itself the apostle of the Gentiles in the midst of whom they lived. It was for Jewish believers to convert the world. For this end they must needs be the first to be evangelized. The word πρῶτον (*first*) is wanting in the *Vat.* and the *Bœrner.* Cod. (Greek and Latin). We know from Tertullian that it was wanting also in Marcion. The omission of the word in the latter is easily explained; he rejected it simply because it overturned his system. Its rejection in the two MSS. B and G is more difficult to explain. Volkmar holds that Paul might ascribe a priority to the Jews in relation to *judgment*, as he does ii. 9, but not in connection with *salvation*; the πρῶτον of ii. 10 he therefore holds to be an interpolation from ii. 9, and that of our ver. 16, a second interpolation from ii. 10. An ingenious combination, intended to make the apostle the relentless enemy of Judaism, agreeably to Baur's system, but belied by the missionary practice of Paul, which is perfectly in keeping with our *first* and with that of ii. 10. The omission must be due to the carelessness of the copyist, the simple form: *to the Jew and to the Greek* (without the word *first*), naturally suggesting itself. While paying homage to the *historical* right of the Jewish people, Paul did not, however, intend to restore particularism. By the τε καί, *as well as*, he forcibly maintains the radical religious *equality* already proclaimed in the words: *to every one that believeth.*

It concerns the apostle now to explain how the gospel can really be the *salvation of the world* offered to all believers. Such is the object of ver. 17. The gospel is salvation, because it offers *the righteousness of God.*

Ver. 17. "*For therein is the righteousness of God revealed by faith for faith: as it is written, But the just shall live by faith.*"—The first part of this verse is a repetition of ver. 16, in more precise language. Paul explains how *this power unto salvation*, which should save the believer, acts: it *justifies* him. Such is the fundamental idea of the Epistle.

The term *righteousness of God* cannot here mean, as it sometimes does, for example, iii. 5 and 25, an *attribute* of God, whether His perfect moral purity, or His retributive justice. Before the gospel this perfection was already distinctly revealed by the law; and the prophetic words which Paul immediately quotes: "*The just* shall live by faith," prove that in his view this justice of God is a condition of man, not a divine attribute.

In what does this state consist? The term δικαιοσύνη, *justice,* strictly designates the moral position of a man who has fully met all his obligations (comp. vi. 13, 16; Eph. v. 9; Matt. v. 17, etc.). Only here the complement: *of God*, and the expression: *is revealed by the gospel*, lead us to give the term a more particular sense: the relation to God in which a man would naturally be placed by his righteousness, if he were righteous, and which God bestows on him of grace on account of his faith. Two explanations of this notion meet us. They are well stated by Calvin: "Some think that *righteousness* consists not merely in the *free pardon* of sins, but *partly* also in the grace of *regeneration.*" "For my part," he adds, "I take the meaning to be that we are restored to life, because God *freely reconciles* us to Himself." On the one hand, therefore, an inward regeneration on the ground of which God pardons; on the other, a free reconciliation on the ground of which God regenerates. In the former case: God acting first *as Spirit* to deposit in the soul the germ of the new life (*to render* man effectually *just*, at least virtually), and afterwards as *judge* to pardon; in the latter, God acting first as *judge* to pardon (*to declare* man *just*), and afterwards as *Spirit* to quicken and sanctify.

The first of these views is that of the Catholic Church, formulated by the

Council of Trent,[1] and professed by a number of Protestant theologians (among the earlier, Osiander ; Beck, in our day). It is the point of view defended by Reuss and Sabatier. The latter defines justification : " the creation of spiritual life."[2] The second notion is that round which the Protestant churches in general have rallied. It was the soul of Luther's religious life ; and it is still the centre of doctrinal teaching in the church which claims the name of this Reformer. We have not here to treat the subject from a dogmatical or moral point of view. We ask ourselves this one thing : Which of the two views was the apostle's, and best explains his words ?

In our verse the verb *reveals itself*, or *is revealed*, applies more naturally to a righteousness which is *offered*, and which God attributes to man in consequence of a *declaration*, than to a righteousness which is *communicated* internally by the gift of the Spirit. The instrument of appropriation constantly insisted on by the apostle, *faith*, also corresponds better to the acceptance of a *promise* than to the acceptance of a real communication. The contrast between the two evidently parallel phrases : " *The righteousness of God is revealed*," ver. 17, and : " *The wrath of God is revealed*," ver. 18, leads us equally to regard the *righteousness of God* as a state of things which He founds in His capacity of *judge*, rather than a new life conveyed by His Spirit. The opposite of the new life is not the *wrath* of the judge, but the *sin* of man.—In iv. 3, Paul justifies his doctrine of the *righteousness of God* by the words of Moses : " Now Abraham believed God, and it was *counted* to him *for righteousness* " (counted as the equivalent of a righteous and irreproachable life). The idea of *counting* or *imputing* applies better to a sentence which ascribes than to an act of real communication.—In the same chapter, vv. 7, 8, the notion of the *righteousness of God* is explained by the terms *pardon* and *non-imputation* of sin. There is evidently no question there of positive communication, of a gift of spiritual life.—In chap. v. 9, 10, Paul contrasts with *justification* by the *blood* of Christ and with *reconciliation* by His *death*, as the foundation of salvation, *deliverance* from wrath (in the day of judgment), by the communication of His *life*, as the consummation of salvation. Unless we are to convert the copestone into the basis, we must put justification by the blood first, and the communication of life by the Spirit second ; the one, as the condition of entrance into the state of salvation here below ; the other, as the condition of entrance into the state of glory above.—The very structure of the Epistle to the Romans forbids us to entertain a doubt as to the apostle's view. If the communication of spiritual life were, in his judgment, the condition of pardon, he must have begun his Epistle with chaps. vi.-viii., which treat of the destruction of sin and of the gift of the new life, and not with the long passage, i. 18-v. 21, which refers wholly to the removal of *condemnation*, and to the conditions, objective and subjective, of *reconciliation*.—Finally, it is contrary to the fundamental principle of Paul's gospel, *entire freeness* of salvation, to put regeneration in any degree whatever as the basis of reconciliation and pardon. It is to make the effect the cause, and the cause the effect. According to St. Paul, God does not *declare* man righteous after having *made* him righteous ; He does not *make* him righteous till He has first *declared* him righteous. The whole Epistle to the Romans excludes the first of these two principles (which is no other than the Judaizing principle ever throwing man back *on himself*), and goes to establish the second (the evangelical principle which detaches man radically from himself and throws

---

[1] Sess. vi. c. 7 : [Justificatio] non est sola peccatorum remissio, *sed et sanctificatio et renovatio* interioris hominis per voluntariam susceptionem gratiæ.
[2] *L'apôtre Paul*, p. 261. Let it be remembered that the author whom we are quoting defined faith (p. 265) " the inward creation of the divine life." Does Paul's language allow us to give a definition identically the same of faith and justification?

him *on God*).[1] See the transition from chap. v. to chap. vi.—We add here, as a necessary supplement, a study on the meaning of the word δικαιοῦν, *to justify*.

Excursus on the use of the word δικαιοῦν, to justify.[2]—The question is this: Are we to understand the word δικαιοῦν, *to justify*, in the sense of *making* just or *declaring* just?

Verbs in οω have sometimes the meaning of *making*: δηλόω, *to make clear*; δουλόω, *to make a slave*; τυφλόω, *to make blind*. But this use of the termination οω does not form the rule; this is seen in the verbs ζημιόω, *to punish*; μισθόω, *to hire*; λουτρόω, *to bathe*; μαστιγόω, *to scourge*.

As to δικαιόω, there is not an example in the whole of classic literature where it signifies: *to make just*. With accusative of things it signifies: *to think right*. The following are examples: Thucyd. ii. 6: "*Thinking it right* (δικαιοῦντες) to return to the Lacedemonians what these had done them." iv. 26: "He will not *form a just idea* of the thing (οὐκ ὀρθῶς δικαιώσει)." Herod. i. 133: "*They think it good* (δικαιεῦσι) to load the table." Justin, *Cohort. ad Gentil.* (ii. 46, ed. Otto): "When *he thought good* (ἐδικαίωσε) to bring the Jews out of Egypt." Finally, in ecclesiastical language: "It has been *found good* (δεδικαίωται) by the holy Council."

With accusative of persons this verb signifies: *to treat justly*, and most frequently *sensu malo, to condemn, punish*. Aristotle, in *Nicom.* v. 9, contrasts ἀδικεῖσθαι, *to be treated unjustly*, with δικαιοῦσθαι, *to be treated according to justice*. Eschylus, *Agam.* 391–393, says of Paris, that he has no right to complain if he is *judged unfavorably* (δικαιωθείς); let him reap what is his due. Thucyd. iii. 40: "You *will condemn* your own selves (δικαιώσεσθε)." Herod. i. 100: "When any one had committed a crime, Dejoces sent for him and *punished* him (ἐδικαίευ)." On occasion of the vengeance which Cambyses wreaked on the Egyptian priests, Herodotus says (iii. 29): "And the priests *were punished* (ἐδικαιεῦντο)." So we find in Dion Cassius: δικαιοῦν; and in Elian: δικαιοῦν τῷ θανάτῳ, in the sense of *punishing with death*.

Thus profane usage is obvious: *to think just*, or *treat justly* (most frequently by *condemning* or *punishing*); in both cases establishing the right by a sentence, never by communicating justice. Hence it follows that, of the two meanings of the word we are examining, that which comes nearest classical usage is undoubtedly *to declare*, and not *to make* just.

But the meaning of the verb δικαιοῦν, *to justify*, in the New Testament, depends less on profane Greek than on the use of the Old Testament, both in the original Hebrew and in the version of the LXX. This, therefore, is what we have, above all, to examine. To the term *justify* there correspond in Hebrew the Piel and Hiphil of *tsadak, to be just*. The Piel *tsiddek*, in the five cases where it is used, signifies not *to make just* inwardly, but *to show* or *declare* just.[3] The Hiphil *hits'dik* appears twelve times;[4] in eleven cases the meaning is to justify *judicially* is indisputable; for example, Ex. xxiii. 7: "For I *will* not *justify* the wicked," certainly means: I *will not declare* the wicked *just*; and not: I will not make him just inwardly; Prov. xvii. 15: "He that *justifieth* the wicked, and he that condemneth the just, are abomination to the Lord." Any other meaning than that of *declaring* just is absurd. So with the others. In the twelfth passage only, Dan. xii. 3, the word *may* be understood either in the sense of *making just*, or of *presenting as just*. (The LXX. translate differently altogether, and without using the word δικαιοῦν.)

It is on this almost uniform meaning of the verb *tsadak* in the Piel and Hiphil

---

[1] It is clear what we must think of M. Sabatier's vehement attack on the doctrine of *imputed* (or, as he calls it, *forensic*) righteousness: "Paul would not have had words severe enough to blast so gross an interpretation of his meaning" (p. 260)!—Holsten himself cannot avoid doing homage to exegetical truth. He says: "Righteousness is an *objective* state, in which man is placed by a divine act."

[2] To avoid endless quotations, I refer once for all to Morison's dissertation in his *Commentary* on Rom. iii. in connection with the word δικαιωθήσεται, ver. 20 (pp. 161–200). I do not think that, in all theology has produced on this subject, there is anything better thought out or more complete. The following study is little more than an extract from it.

[3] Job xxxii. 2, xxxiii. 32; Jer. iii. 11; Ezek. xvi. 51, 52.

[4] Ex. xxiii. 7; Deut. xxv. 1; 2 Sam. xv. 4; 1 Kings viii. 32; 2 Chron. vi. 23; Job xxvii. 5; Ps. lxxxii. 3; Prov. xvii. 15; Isa. i. 8, v. 23, liii. 11; Dan. xii. 3.

that Paul and the other writers of the New Testament founded their use of the word δικαιοῦν, *to justify*. For this word δικαιοῦν is that by which the Hebrew word was constantly rendered by the LXX.[1]

The use of the word δικαιοῦν, *to justify*, in the New Testament, appears chiefly from the following passages :—Rom. ii. 13 : the subject is the last judgment ; then, one is not *made*, but *recognized* and *declared just;* iii. 4 : God is the subject ; God is not *made*, but *recognized* or *declared* just by man ; iii. 20 : to be justified *before God* cannot signify : to be *made* just *by* God ; the phrase *before God* implies the judicial sense ; iv. 2 : to be justified *by works;* this phrase has no meaning except in the judicial sense of the word *justify;* 1 Cor. iv. 4 : Paul is not conscious of any unfaithfulness ; but for all that *he is not* yet *justified ;* a case where it is impossible to apply any other meaning than the judicial. The reader will do well to consult also Matt. xi. 19 and Luke vii. 35 ("wisdom [God's] is *justified* of her children "") ; Luke vii. 29 (the publicans *justified* God); Matt. xii. 37 (" by thy words thou shalt be *justified*, and by thy words thou shalt be *condemned*") ; Luke x. 29 (" he, wishing *to justify himself*"), xvi. 15 ("ye are they *who justify yourselves*"), xviii. 14 ("the *justified* publican"") ; Acts xiii. 39 ("to be *justified from the things* from which they could not have been *justified* by the law") ; Jas. ii. 21, 24, 25 ("to be *justified by works*").[2]

There is not a single one of these passages where the idea of an *inward communication* of righteousness would be suitable. In favor of this meaning the words, 1 Cor. vi. 11, have sometimes been quoted. If the passage be carefully examined in its context, vi. 1–10, it will clearly appear that it forms no exception to the constant usage of the New Testament, as it has been established by the collective showing of the passages just quoted.

That from a dogmatic point of view this notion of justification should be rejected as too external and forensic, we can understand,[3] though we are convinced that thereby the very sinews of the gospel are destroyed. But that, exegetically speaking, there can possibly be two ways of explaining the apostle's view, is what surprises us.

The notion of the *righteousness of God*, according to Paul, embraces two bestowals of grace : man treated—(1) as if he had never committed any evil ; (2) as if he had always accomplished all the good God could expect from him. The sentence of justification which puts man in this privileged state in relation to God is the δικαίωσις, the *act of justification*. In virtue of this act "man has henceforth," as Hofmann says, "the righteousness of God for him, and not against him."

What is the meaning of the genitive Θεοῦ, *of God*, in the phrase : *righteousness of God ?* Luther's interpretation, maintained by Philippi, is well known : a righteousness *valid before* God (iii. 20 ; Gal. iii. 11). But this meaning of the complement is very forced. Baur makes it a genitive of *quality :* a righteousness agreeable to the *nature* of God. Is it not simpler to take it as a genitive of *origin :* a justice which has God Himself for its author ? We are led to this sense also by the parallel expressions : " The righteousness that *cometh from God* " (ἡ ἐκ Θεοῦ δικαιοσύνη), Phil. iii. 9 ; " *the righteousness of God* " (ἡ τοῦ Θεοῦ δικαιοσύνη) opposed to our *own* righteousness, Rom. x. 3. Of course a righteousness of which God is the author must correspond to His essence (Baur), and be accepted by Him (Luther).

The word ἀποκαλύπτεται, *is revealed* or *reveals itself*, denotes the act whereby a thing hitherto veiled now bursts into the light ; compare the parallel but different expression, πεφανέρωται, *has been manifested*, iii. 21. The present, *is being revealed*, is explained here by the regimen *in it*, ἐν αὐτῷ—

---

[1] The LXX. sometimes use δικαιοῦν where some other Hebrew verb occurs, and in these cases eight times in the strictly judicial sense ; seven times, as Morison says, in a semi-judicial sense. Once they use it in the sense of *purifying*. Ps. lxxiii. 13: "I have cleansed (*ziqqiti*) my heart (ἐδικαίωσα τὴν καρδίαν μου)." This is the only case where δικαιοῦν has this meaning throughout the whole version of the LXX.

[2] To complete the list we have only to quote Rom. vi. 7, viii. 30, 33 ; Gal. ii. 16, 17, iii. 8, 11, 24, v. 4. The only case where discussion could arise is Rom. vi. 7, where δικαιοῦν, in any case, cannot signify *to make just* inwardly (see on the passage).

[3] On the *judicial* point of view in general, and the notion of *right* as applied to God, see on iii. 25.

that is to say, in the gospel. This substantive should still be taken in the active sense which we have given it: the *act* of evangelical preaching. It is by this proclamation that the righteousness of God *is* daily *revealed* to the world.—The expression ἐκ πίστεως εἰς πίστιν, *from faith to faith*, has been interpreted very variously. Most frequently it has been thought to signify the idea of the *progress* which takes place in faith itself, and in this sense it has been translated: *from faith on to faith*. This progress has been applied by some Fathers (Tert., Origen, Chrysost.) to the transition from faith in the Old Testament to faith as it exists in the New. But there is nothing here to indicate a comparison between the old and new dispensations. The Reformers have taken the progress of faith to be in the heart of the individual believer. His faith, weak at first, grows stronger and stronger. Calvin: *Quotidianum in singulis fidelibus progressum notat*. So also thought Luther and Melanchthon; Schaff: "Assimilation by faith should be continually renewed." But the phrase thus understood does not in the least correspond with the verb *is revealed;* and, what is graver still, this idea is utterly out of place in the context. A notion so special and secondary as that of the progress which takes place in faith is inappropriate in a summary which admits only of the fundamental ideas being indicated. It would even be opposed to the apostle's aim to connect the attainment of righteousness with this objective progress of the believer in faith. It is merely as a curiosity of exposition that we mention the view of those who understand the words thus: by faith *in faith*—that is to say, in the faithfulness of God (iii. 3). Paul's real view is certainly this: the righteousness of God is revealed by means of the preaching of the gospel as *arising from faith* (ἐκ πίστεως), in this sense, that it is nothing else than faith itself reckoned to man as righteousness. The ἐκ, strictly speaking, *out of*, which we can only render by means of the preposition *by*, expresses *origin*. This clause is joined to the verb *is revealed* by the phrase understood: *as being*. This righteousness *of* faith is revealed at the same time as being *for faith*, εἰς πίστιν. This second clause signifies that the *instrument* by which each individual must personally appropriate such a righteousness is likewise faith. To make this form of expression clear, we have only to state the opposite one: *Our own righteousness* is a righteousness of *works* and *for works*—that is to say, a righteousness arising from works done and revealed with a view to works to be done. Our formula is the direct opposite of that which described legal righteousness. To be exact, we need not say that *to faith* here is equivalent to: *to the believer*. Paul is not concerned with the person appropriating, but solely with the instrument of appropriation, and his view in conjoining these two qualifying clauses was simply to say: that in this righteousness faith is everything, absolutely everything; in essence it is faith itself; and each one appropriates it by faith. These two qualifying clauses meet us in a somewhat different form in other passages; iii. 22: "The righteousness of God *through* faith in Christ *unto (and upon)* all them that believe;" Gal. iii. 22: "That the promise *by* faith of Jesus may be given *to* them that believe;" Phil. iii. 9: "Having the righteousness which is *by* faith in Christ, the righteousness of God *for* faith." We need not, however, paraphrase the words *for faith*, with some commentators, in the sense: *to produce* faith. The εἰς *for*, seems to us to indicate merely the *destination*. It is a righteousness of faith offered to faith. All it has to do is to take possession of it. Of course we must not make a merit of faith. What gives it its justifying value is its object, without which it would remain a barren aspiration. But the object laid hold of could have no effect on man without the act of apprehension, which is faith.

The apostle is so convinced of the unity which prevails between the old and new covenants, that he cannot assert one of the great truths of the gospel without quoting a passage from the Old Testament in its support.

He has just stated *the theme* of his Epistle ; now comes what we may call the *text:* it is a passage from Habakkuk (ii. 4), which had evidently played an important part in his inner life, as it did decisively in the life of Luther. He quotes it also Gal. iii. 11 (comp. x. 37). With all that prides itself on its own strength, whether in the case of foreign conquerors or in Israel itself, the prophet contrasts the humble Israelite who puts his *confidence* in God alone. The former will perish ; the latter, who alone is *righteous* in the eyes of God, *shall live*. The Hebrew word which we translate by *faith, emounah*, comes from the verb *aman, to be firm;* whence in the Hiphil : *to rest on, to be confident in*. In the Hebrew it is : *his* faith (*emounatho*) ; but the LXX. have translated as if they had found *emounathi, my* faith (that of God), which might signify either my *faithfulness*, or faith *in me*. What the translators thought is of small importance. Paul evidently goes back to the original text, and quotes exactly when he says : "*his* faith," the faith of the believer in his God. In the Hebrew text it is agreed by all that the words *by his faith* are dependent on the verb *shall live*, and not on the word *the just*. But from Theodore Beza onwards, very many commentators think that Paul makes this subordinate clause dependent on the word *the just;* " *The just by faith* shall live." This meaning really seems to suit the context more exactly, the general idea being that righteousness (not life) comes by faith. This correspondence is, however, only apparent ; for Paul's saying, thus understood, would, as Oltramare acutely observes, put in contrast the *just by faith*, who shall live, and the *just by works*, who shall not live. But such a thought would be inadmissible in Paul's view. For he holds that, if one should succeed in being righteous by his works, *he would certainly live by them* (x. 5). We must therefore translate as in the Hebrew : The just *shall live by faith;* and the meaning is this : " the just shall live by faith " (by which he has been made just). Paul might have said : *the sinner* shall be saved by faith. But the sinner, in this case, he calls *just* by anticipation, viewing him in the state of righteousness into which his faith shall bring him. If he lives by his faith, it is obviously because he has been made just by it, since no one is saved except as being just. The word ζήσεται, shall live, embraced in the prophet's view : 1. *Deliverance* from present evils (those of the Chaldean invasion), and, in the case of posterity, deliverance from evils to come ; 2. The *possession* of divine grace in the enjoyment of the blessings of the Promised Land. These two notions are, of course, spiritualized by Paul. They become : deliverance from perdition and the possession of eternal life. It is the idea of σωτηρία, *salvation*, ver. 16, reproduced. The word *shall live* will also have its part to play in the didactic exposition which now begins, and which will develop the contents of this text. In fact, to the end of chap. v. the apostle analyzes the idea of the *righteousness of faith;* the word *shall live* serves as a theme to the whole part from chaps. vi.–viii., and afterwards, for the practical development, chaps. xii.–xiv.

The exposition of the *righteousness of faith*, which begins in the following verse, comprises three great developments : the description of universal condemnation, i. 18–iii. 20 ; that of universal justification, iii. 21–v. 11 ; and, following up this great contrast as its consummation, parallel between Adam and Christ (v. 12–21). The idea of this entire part, i.–v., taken *as a whole*, is therefore : *the demonstration of justification by faith.*

FUNDAMENTAL PART

1:18-5:21

THE principal subdivision of this part is indicated by the somewhat amplified repetition of ver. 17, which we shall find iii. 21, 22. There we again meet with the phrase *righteousness of God ;* the verb *was manifested* evidently corresponds to the word *is revealed ;* and the two secondary clauses : *by faith of Jesus Christ,* and : *unto and upon all them that believe,* are the development of the phrase *from faith to faith.* It follows from this parallel that the apostle did not mean immediately to study this great truth of justification by faith ; but he felt the need of preparing the way for this exposition by laying bare in human life the reasons for this so extraordinary and apparently abnormal mode of salvation. Such, indeed, is the subject of the first section, i. 18–iii. 20 : If the gospel reveals the righteousness of God, it is because there is another revelation, that of the *wrath of God,* and because this latter, unless mankind be destined to perish, requires the former.

FIRST SECTION (1:18-3:20)

THE WRATH OF GOD RESTING ON THE WHOLE WORLD.

In chap. i., from ver. 18, St. Paul is undoubtedly describing the miserable state of the *Gentile world.* From the beginning of chap. ii. he addresses a personage who very severely judges the Gentile abominations just described by Paul, and who evidently represents a wholly different portion of mankind. At ver. 17 he apostrophizes this personage by his name : it is *the Jew ;* and he demonstrates to him that he also is under the burden of wrath. Hence it follows that the first piece of this section goes to the end of chap. i., and has for its subject : the need of salvation demonstrated by the state of the contemporary Gentile world.

FOURTH PASSAGE (1:18-32)

The Wrath of God on the Gentiles

According to Paul's usual style, the first verse contains summarily all the ideas developed in the following piece. The study of the verse will thus be an analysis by anticipation of the whole passage.

Ver. 18. " *For the wrath of God is revealed from heaven against all ungodliness and unrighteousness of men, who hold the truth captive unrighteously.*"— The transition from ver. 17 to ver. 18, indicated by *for,* can only be this : There is a *revelation of righteousness* by the gospel, because there is a revelation of *wrath* on the whole world. The former is necessary *to save the world* (comp. σωτηρία, *salvation,* ver. 16) from the consequences of the latter.— From the notion of *wrath,* when it is applied to God, we must of course remove all that pollutes human wrath, personal resentment, the moral perturbation which gives to the manifestations of indignation the character of revenge. In God, who is the living *Good,* wrath appears as the holy disapprobation of evil, and the firm resolve to destroy it. But it is false to say, as is often done, that this divine emotion applies only to the evil and not to the evil-doer. In measure as the latter ceases to oppose the evil and voluntarily identifies himself with it, he himself becomes the object of wrath and all its consequences.[1] The absence of the article before the word ὀργή, *wrath*, brings into prominence the category rather than the thing itself: manifestation there is, whose character is that of wrath, not of love.—This manifestation proceeds *from heaven*. Heaven here does not denote the atmospheric or stellar heaven; the term is the emblematical expression for the invisible residence of God, the seat of perfect order, whence emanates every manifestation of righteousness on the earth, every victorious struggle of good against evil. The visible heavens, the regularity of the motion of the stars, the life-like and pure lustre of their fires, this whole great spectacle has always been to the consciousness of man the sensible representation of *divine order*. It is from this feeling that the prodigal son exclaims: "Father, I have sinned *against heaven* and in thy sight." Heaven in this sense is thus the avenger of all sacred feelings that are outraged; it is as such that it is mentioned here.—By ἀσέβεια, *ungodliness*, Paul denotes all failures in the religious sphere; and by ἀδικία, *unrighteousness*, all that belong to the moral domain. Volkmar very well defines the two terms: "Every denial either of the *essence* or of the *will* of God." We shall again find these two kinds of failures distinguished and developed in the sequel; the first, in the refusal of adoration and thanksgiving, ver. 21 et seq.; the second, in the refusal of the knowledge of moral good proceeding from God, ver. 28*a*.—'Επί, *upon, against*, has here a very hostile sense.—The apostle does not say: *of men*, but literally: *of men who repress*. As Hofmann says: "The notion *men* is first presented indefinitely, then it is defined by the special characteristic: *who repress*" ... We may already conclude, from this absence of the article τῶν (*the*) before the substantive, that Paul is not here thinking of all humanity. And, indeed, he could not have charged the Jews with *holding captive* the truth which had been revealed to them, comp. ii. 19–21, while he proceeds to charge this sin directly on the Gentiles. We must therefore regard ver. 18 as the theme of chap. i. only, not that of i. and ii. Besides, the wrath of God was not yet *revealed* against the Jewish world; it was only accumulating (ii. 5).—Certainly the apostle, in expressing himself as he does, does not overlook the varieties in the conduct of the Gentiles, as will appear in the sequel (ii. 14, 15). He refers only to the general character of their life.—*The truth held captive* is, as vv. 19 and 20 prove, the *knowledge of God* as communicated to the human conscience. *To hold it captive*, is to prevent it from diffusing itself in the understanding as a light, and in the conduct as a holy authority and just rule. The verb κατέχειν, *to hold back, detain*, cannot here have the meaning which some interpreters would give it, *to keep, possess*, which the word sometimes has; for example, 1 Cor. xv. 2; 1 Thess. v. 21. In that case we should require to place the charge brought against the Gentiles not in this verb, but in the qualifying clause ἐν ἀδικίᾳ : "who possess the truth *in unrighteousness*" (that is, while practising unrighteousness). But the sequel proves, on the contrary, that the Gentiles had not *kept* the deposit of truth which had been confided to them; and the simple clause: *in unrighteousness*, would not suffice to characterize the sin charged against them, and which is the reason of the divine wrath. We must therefore take the word κατέχειν, *to detain*, in the sense in which we find it 2 Thess. ii. 6, 7, and Luke iv. 42 : *to keep from moving, to repress*. Oltramare: "They hindered it *from breaking forth*."—Some translate the words ἐν ἀδικίᾳ : *by unrighteousness;* they paralyze the truth in them by the love and practice of evil. But why in this case not again add the notion of ungodliness to that of unrighteousness? The literal meaning is, not *by unrighteousness*, but *by way of unrighteousness;* this clause is therefore taken in the adverbial sense: *unrighteously, ill and wickedly*. In reality, is there

---

[1] We refer to an appendix placed at the end of this verse for an examination of Ritschl's theory respecting the wrath of God.

not perversity in paralyzing the influence of the truth on one's heart and life?

To what manifestations does the apostle allude when he says that wrath *is revealed from heaven*? Does he mean simply the judgment of *conscience*, as Ambrose and others, with Hodge most recently, think? But here there would be no patent fact which could be taken as a parallel to the preaching of the gospel (ver. 17). Bellarmine, Grotius, etc., think that Paul means *this preaching* itself, and that the words *from heaven* are synonymous with the ἐν αὐτῷ, *in it* (the gospel), ver. 17. But there is, on the contrary, an obvious antithesis between these two clauses, and consequently a *contrast* between the revelation of righteousness and that of wrath.—The Greek Fathers, as also Philippi, Ewald, and Ritschl in our own day, regard this manifestation as that which shall take place at the *last judgment*. This meaning is incompatible with the verb in the present: *is revealed*; not that a present may not, in certain cases, denote *the idea* of the action, independently of the time of its realization; so the very verb which Paul here uses is employed by him 1 Cor. iii. 13. But there the future (or ideal) sense of the present is plainly enough shown by all the futures surrounding the verb (γενήσεται, δηλώσει, δοκιμάσει), and the context makes it sufficiently clear. But in our passage the present *is revealed*, ver. 18, corresponds to the similar present of ver. 17, which is incontrovertibly the *actual* present. It is not possible, in such a context, to apply the present of ver. 18 otherwise than to a present fact. Hofmann takes the word *is revealed* as referring to that whole multitude of *ills* which constantly oppress sinful humanity; and Pelagius, taking the word *from heaven* literally, found here a special indication of the *storms* and tempests which desolate nature. But what is there in the developments which follow fitted to establish this explanation? The word *is revealed*, placed emphatically at the head of the piece, should propound the theme; and its meaning is therefore determined by the whole explanation which follows.—We are thus brought to the natural explanation. At ver. 24 mention is made of a divine chastisement, that by which men have been given over to the power of their impure lusts. This idea is repeated in ver. 26, and a third time in ver. 28: " God *gave* them *over* to a reprobate mind." Each time this chastisement, a terrible manifestation of God's wrath, is explained by a corresponding sin committed by the Gentiles. How can we help seeing here, with Meyer, the explanation, given by Paul himself, of his meaning in our verse? Thereby the purport of the following description and its relation to ver. 18 become perfectly clear; *the truth* is explained in vv. 19, 20; it is God's revelation to the conscience of the Gentiles, the notion: *to repress* the truth, is explained in vv. 21-23 (and 25); these are the voluntary errors of paganism; finally, the idea of the *revelation of divine wrath* is developed in vv. 24-27; these are the unnatural enormities to which God has given the Gentiles up, and by which He has avenged His outraged honor. All the notions of ver. 18 are thus resumed and developed in their logical order, vv. 19-27: such is the first cycle (the ἀσέβεια, *ungodliness*). They are resumed and developed a second time in the same order, but under another aspect (the ἀδικία, *unrighteousness*), vv. 28-32. The meaning of the words *is revealed from heaven*, is not therefore doubtful. It has been objected that the term *to reveal* always refers to a *supernatural* manifestation. We do not deny it; and we think that Paul regards the monstrous degradation of pagan populations, which he is about to describe (vv. 24-27 and 29-32), not as a purely natural consequence of their sin, but as a solemn intervention of God's justice in the history of mankind, an intervention which he designates by the term παραδιδόναι, *to give over*.—If ver. 18 contains, as we have said, three principal ideas: 1. The Gentiles knew the truth; 2. They repelled it; 3. For this sin the wrath of God is displayed against them,—the first of these ideas is manifestly that which will form the subject of vv. 19 and 20.

The Wrath of God, according to Ritschl.

In his work, *Die Christliche Lehre von der Rechtfertigung und Versöhnung* (II. 123-138) (The Christian Doctrine of Justification and Reconciliation), Ritschl ascribes to Pharisaism the invention of the idea of *retributive justice*, and denies its existence in Holy Scripture. Thus obliged to seek a new meaning for the notion of the *wrath of God*, he finds the following: In the Old Testament the wrath of God has only one aim: to preserve the divine covenant; the *wrath of God* therefore only denotes the sudden and violent chastisements with which God smites either the enemies of the covenant, or those of its members who openly violate its fundamental conditions,—in both cases not with the view of punishing, but of maintaining here below His work of grace. In the New Testament the idea is substantially the same, but modified in its application. The wrath of God cannot have any other than an *eschatological* application; it refers to the last judgment, in which God will cut off the enemies of salvation (not to punish them) but to prevent them from hindering the realization of His kingdom (1 Thess. i. 10; Rom. v. 9). As to our passage, which seems irreconcilable with this notion, this critic deals with it as follows:—We must wait till ii. 4, 5, to find the development of the idea of the *wrath of God*, enunciated in ver. 18. The whole passage, ver. 19-ii. 3, is devoted to setting forth the *sin* of the Gentiles, the fact of their κατέχειν τὴν ἀλήθειαν, *holding the truth captive*. The description of *chastisement (the revelation of wrath)* is not developed till after ii. 5; now this passage evidently refers to the last judgment. Thus it is that the ingenious theologian succeeds in harmonizing our passage with his system. But I am afraid there is more ability than truth in the mode he follows:—1. Ritschl will not recognize an inward *feeling* in the wrath of God, but merely an outward *act*, a *judgment*. But why in this case does Paul use the word *wrath*, to which he even adds, ii. 8, the term θυμός, *indignation*, which denotes the *feeling* at its deepest? 2. We have seen that the present *is revealed*, forming an antithesis to the tense of ver. 17, and giving the reason of it (γάρ, *for*), can only denote a time *actually* present. 3. Is it not obvious at a glance that the phrase thrice repeated: *wherefore He gave them over* (vv. 24, 26, 28), describes not the *sin* of the Gentiles, but their *chastisement*? That appears from the term *give over:* to give over is the act of the *judge; to be given over*, the punishment of the culprit. The same follows also from the *wherefores;* by this word Paul evidently passes each time from the description of the sin to that of the punishment, that is to say, to the *revelation of wrath*. 4. As to ii. 4, 5, these verses do not begin with a *wherefore*, as would be necessary if the apostle were passing at this part of the text from the description of sin to that of chastisement. These verses, on the contrary, are strictly connected with ver. 3, as continuing the refutation of Jewish security in relation to the last judgment, a refutation begun at ver. 3 with the words: "*Thinkest thou* . . . ?" and carried on to ver. 4 with these: "*Or* [indeed] *despisest thou* . . . ?" How can we regard this as the beginning of a new idea, that of chastisement succeeding that of sin? For the examination of the explanation of ver. 32 given by Ritschl, by which he seeks to justify all the violence he does to the text of the apostle, we refer to the verse itself.

With the term ὀργή, *wrath*, before us, applied to the Gentiles first, ver. 18, and afterwards to the Jews, ii. 5, we are justified in holding to the notion of that divine feeling as explained by us, pp. 164, 165.

Vv. 19, 20. "*Seeing that that which may be known of God is manifested in them; for God hath manifested it unto them. For the invisible perfections of God, his eternal power and his divinity are spiritually contemplated, since the creation of the world, in his works, that they may be without excuse.*"—The truth of which Paul wished to speak in ver. 18, was that revelation of God's person and character which He had given to men. The διότι, *because* (for διὰ τοῦτο ὅτι, *for the reason that*), carries the thought to that which follows as the reason of what precedes, in contrast to διό, *on account of which* (ver. 24), which points to

what precedes as the reason for what follows.—The meaning of this διότι, *seeing that*, is as follows : they quenched the truth, *seeing that* the truth had been revealed to them (vv. 19, 20), and they changed it into a lie (vv. 21-23) (25).
—The term γνωστόν, strictly, *what can be known*, usually signifies in the New Testament *what is really known* (γνωστός) ; this is its probable meaning in Luke ii. 44 ; John xviii. 15 ; Acts i. 19, xvii. 23. Yet it is not quite certain that the first meaning may not also be given to the word in some of the passages quoted ; and in classic Greek it is the most usual sense (see the numerous examples quoted by Oltramare). What decides in its favor in our passage is the startling tautology which there would be in saying : "*what is known* of the being of God *is manifested.*" There is therefore ground for preferring here the grammatical and received meaning in the classics. Paul means : " *What can be known* of God without the help of an extraordinary revelation is clearly manifested within them." A light was given in their conscience and understanding, and this light bore on the existence and character of the Divine Being. This present fact : *is manifested*, is afterwards traced to its cause, which is stated by the verb in the aorist : "for God *manifested* it to them ;" this *state* of knowledge was due to *a* divine *act* of revelation. God is not known like an ordinary object ; when He is known, it is He who gives himself to be known. The knowledge which beings have of Him is a free act on His part. Ver. 20 explains the external means by which He wrought this revelation of Himself in the conscience of men.

Ver. 20. He did so by *His works* in nature. By the term τὰ ἀόρατα, *the invisible things*, the apostle designates the essence of God, and the manifold attributes which distinguish it. He sums them up afterwards in these two : *eternal power and divinity*. Power is that which immediately arrests man, when the spectacle of nature presents itself to his view. In virtue of the principle of causality innate in his understanding, he forthwith sees in this immense effect the revelation of a great cause ; and the *Almighty* is revealed to him. But this power appears to his heart clothed with certain moral characteristics, and in particular, wisdom and goodness. He recognizes in the works of this power, in the infinite series of means and ends which are revealed in them, the undeniable traces of benevolence and intelligence ; and in virtue of the *principle of finality*, or the notion of *end*, not less essentially inherent in his mind, he invests the supreme cause with the moral attributes which constitute what Paul here calls *divinity*, θειότης, the sum total of qualities in virtue of which the creative power can have organized such a world.—The epithet ἀίδιος, *eternal* (from ἀεί, *always*), is joined by some with both substantives ; but power alone needed to be so defined, in order to contrast it with that host of second causes which are observed in nature. The latter are the result of anterior causes. But the first cause, on which this whole series of causes and effects depends, is *eternal*, that is to say, self-causing. The adjective is therefore to be joined only with the first of the two substantives ; the second required no such qualification. These *invisible things*, belonging to the essence of God, have been made visible, since by the creation of the universe they have been externally manifested. Τοῖς ποιήμασι is the dative of instrument : *by the works* of God in nature ; ἀπό, *since*, indicates that the time of creation was the point of departure for this revelation which lasts still. The complex phrase νοούμενα καθορᾶται, *are spiritually contemplated*, contains two intimately connected ideas : on the one hand, a viewing with the outward *sense ;* on the other, an act of *intellectual* perception, whereby that which presents itself to the eye becomes at the same time a revelation to our consciousness. The animal *sees* as man does ; but it lacks the νοῦς, *understanding* (whence the verb νοεῖν, νοούμενα), whereby man ascends from the contemplation of the work to that of the worker. These two simultaneous sights, the one sensible, the other rational, constitute in man a single act, admirably characterized by the expression *spiritual contemplation*, used by the apostle.

We have here a proof of Paul's breadth of mind and heart. He does not disparage, as the Jews did, and as Christian science has sometimes done, the value of what has been called *natural theology*. And it is certainly not without reason that Baur (*Paulus*, II. p. 260) has regarded this passage as laying the first basis of the apostle's universalism. This same idea of a universal revelation appears again in Paul's discourses at Lystra and Athens (Acts xiv. 17, xvii. 27, 28); so also in 1 Cor. i. 21, and in our own Epistle iii. 29 : " Is God not also the God of the Gentiles ?" a question which finds its full explanation in the idea of a primordial revelation addressed to all men.

The last words of the verse point out the *aim* of this universal revelation : *that they may be without excuse.* The words are startling : Could God have revealed Himself to the Gentiles only to have a reason for the condemnation with which He visits them ? This idea has seemed so revolting, that it has been thought necessary to soften the sense of the phrase εἰς τὸ . . . and to translate *so that* (Osterv.), or : "they are *therefore* inexcusable " (Oltram.). It is one great merit of Meyer's commentaries that he has vigorously withstood this method of explanation, which arbitrarily weakens the meaning of certain prepositions and particles used by Paul. Had he wished to say *so that*, he had at command the regular expression ὥστε εἶναι. And the truth, if his thought is rightly understood, has nothing so very repulsive about it : in order that, he means, if after having been thus enlightened, they should fall into error as to God's existence and character, they may be without excuse. The first aim of the Creator was to make Himself known to His creature. But if, through his own fault, man came to turn away from this light, he should not be able to accuse God of the darkness into which he had plunged himself. One might translate somewhat coarsely : that in case of going astray, they might not be able to plead ignorance as a pretext. In these circumstances there is nothing to prevent the *in order that* from preserving its natural meaning.

Vv. 19 and 20 have explained the word ἀλήθεια, *the truth*, of ver. 18. Vv. 21–23 develop the phrase : κατέχειν τὴν ἀλήθειαν, *to hold this truth captive.*

Ver. 21. " *Seeing that, when they knew God, they glorified Him not as God, neither gave Him thanks ; but were struck with vanity in their reasonings, and their foolish heart was darkened.*"—The *because that* bears on the idea of *inexcusableness*, which closes ver. 20, and reproduces the feeling of indignation which had dictated the ἐν ἀδικίᾳ, *hurtfully and maliciously*, of ver. 18 : "*Yes*, inexcusable, because of the fact that " . . . How can the apostle say of the Gentiles that they *knew* God ? Is it a simple possibility to which he is referring ! The words do not allow this idea. Ver. 19 declared that the light was really put within them. Paganism itself is the proof that the human mind had really conceived the notion of God ; for this notion appears at the root of all the varied forms of paganism. Only this is what happened : the revelation did not pass from the passive to the active form. Man confined himself to receiving it. He did not set himself to grasp it and to develop it spontaneously. He would have been thus raised from light to light ; it would have been that way of knowing God *by wisdom* of which Paul speaks, 1 Cor. i. 21. Instead of opening himself to the action of the light, man withdrew from it his heart and will ; instead of developing the truth, he quenched it. No doubt acts of worship and thanksgiving addressed to the gods were not wanting in paganism ; but it is not without meaning that the apostle takes care to put the words in front : *as God*. The task of the heart and understanding would have been to draw from the contemplation of the work the distinct view of the divine worker, then, in the way of adoration, to invest this sublime being with all the perfections which He displayed in His creation. Such a course would have been to glorify God *as God*. For the highest task of the understanding is to assert God freely, as He asserts Himself in His revelation. But if this act of reason failed, the heart at least had another task to fulfil: *to give thanks.* Does not a child even say thanks to its benefactor? This homage failed like the other. The word ἤ, *or*, must be understood here, as it often is, in the sense of: *or at least.* The words *as God* also depend logically on *were thankful*, which we have not been able to express in French[1] [nor in English].—Now man could not remain stationary. Not walking forwards in the way of *active religion*, he could only stray into a false path, that of impiety, spoken of ver. 18. Having neglected to set God before it as the supreme object of its activity, the understanding was reduced to work *in vacuo;* it was in some sort *made futile* (ἐματαιώθησαν); it peopled the universe with fictions and chimeras. So Paul designates the vain creations of mythology. The term ἐματαιώθησαν, *were struck with vanity*, evidently alludes to μάταια, *vain things,* which was the name given by the Jews to idols (comp. Acts xiv. 15; Lev. xvii. 7; Jer. ii. 5; 2 Kings xvii. 15). The term διαλογισμοί, *reasonings*, is always taken by the writers of the New Testament in an unfavorable sense; it denotes the unregulated activity of the νοῦς, *understanding*, in the service of a corrupt heart. The corruption of the heart is mentioned in the following words: it went side by side with the errors of reason, of which it is at once the cause and the effect. The *heart*, καρδία, is in the New Testament as in the Old (*leb*), the central seat of personal life, what we call *feeling (sentiment)*, that inner power which determines at once the activity of the understanding and the direction of the will. Destitute of its true object, through its refusal *to be thankful* to God *as God*, the heart of man is filled with inspirations of *darkness;* these are the guilty lusts inspired by the egoistic love of the creature and self. The epithet ἀσύνετος, *without understanding*, is often explained as anticipating what the heart was *to become* in this course: "in such a way as to become foolish." But was there not already something senseless in the ingratitude described in ver. 21? Thus the want of understanding existed from the beginning. In the form of the first aorist passive ἐσκοτίσθη, *was darkened* (as well as in the preceding aorist ἐματαιώθησαν), there is expressed the conviction of a divine dispensation, though still under the form of a natural law, whose penal application has fallen on them.

To this first stage, which is rather of an inward kind, there has succeeded a second and more external one.

Vv. 22, 23. "*Professing to be wise, they became fools, and changed the glory of the incorruptible God into the likeness of the image of corruptible man, and of birds, and fourfooted beasts, and creeping things.*" Futility of *thought* has reached the character of *folly*. What, in fact, is Polytheism, except a sort of permanent hallucination, a collective delirium, or as is so well said by M. Nicolas, *a possession on a great scale?* And this mental disorder rose to a kind of perfection among the very peoples who, more than others, laid claim to the glory of wisdom. When he says: *professing to be wise*, Paul does not mean to stigmatize ancient philosophy absolutely; he only means that all that labor of the sages did not prevent the most civilized nations, Egyptians, Greeks, Romans, from being at the same time the most idolatrous of antiquity. The popular imagination, agreeably served by priests and poets, did not allow the efforts of the wise to dissipate this delirium.

When good is omitted, there always comes in its place an evil committed. As, in respect of the understanding, the refusal of adoration (*they did not glorify*) became a vain laboring of the mind (*they became vain*), and, finally, complete estrangement from truth, folly (*they became fools*); so in respect of the *heart*, ingratitude was first transformed into *darkness;* and, finally— such is the last term described ver. 23—into monstrous and debasing fetish-

---

[1] M. Oltramare: "They neither glorified nor blessed Him as God."

ism. The ungrateful heart did not stop short at not thanking God, it degraded and dishonored Him, by changing Him into His opposite.

The *glory* of God is the splendor which His manifested perfections cast into the heart of His intelligent creatures ; hence, a bright image which is to man the ideal of all that is good. This image had been produced within them. What did they make of it ? The sequel tells. While holding the divine person, they wrapped it up, as it were, in *the likeness* of its opposite ; it would have been almost better to leave it in silence, it would not have been so great an affront. The preposition ἐν (which corresponds here to the Hebrew ב) exactly describes this imprisonment of the divine glory *in a form* ignoble and grotesque. This meaning seems to us preferable to that of commentators who, like Meyer, translate ἐν, *by*, which is less natural with a verb such as *change*. It is simpler to say "change *into*," than "change *by*." The epithet *incorruptible* is, as it were, a protest beforehand against this degradation ; we need not then translate, with Oltramare, *immortal*. Paul means to say that the glory of God is not reached by this treatment which it has had to undergo. In the phrase : *the likeness of the image*, we should certainly apply the first term to the material likeness, and the second to the image present to the artist's mind when he conceives the type of God which he is going to represent. The worship of *man* especially characterizes Greek and Roman Polytheism ; that of the different classes of animals, Egyptian and Barbarian paganism. We need only refer to the worship of the bull Apis, the ibis, the cat, the crocodile, etc., among the Egyptians.

Thus idolatry, according to Paul, is not a progressive stage reached in the religious thought of mankind, starting from primeval fetichism. Far from being a first step toward the goal of Monotheism, Polytheism is on the contrary the result of degeneracy, an apostasy from the original Monotheism, a darkening of the understanding and heart, which has terminated in the grossest fetichism. The history of religions, thoroughly studied as it is nowadays, fully justifies Paul's view. It shows that the present heathen peoples of India and Africa, far from rising of themselves to a higher religious state, have only sunk, age after age, and become more and more degraded. It proves that at the root of all pagan religions and mythologies, there lies an original Monotheism, which is the historical starting-point in religion for all mankind.[1]

This statement of the apostle has been regarded as a reflection of that contained in the Book of Wisdom (comp. for example, the passages, Wisd. xiii. 1–8 and xiv. 11–20). But what a difference between the tame and superficial explanation of idolatry, which the Alexandrian author gives to his readers, and the profound psychological analysis contained in the preceding verses of St. Paul ! The comparison brings out exactly the difference between the penetration of the author enlightened from above, and that of the ordinary Jew seeking to reconstruct the great historic fact of idolatry by his own powers.

The apostle has developed the two terms of ver. 18 : *truth, and repressing the truth*. After thus presenting, on the one hand, the divine revelation, and, on the other, the sin of man in quenching it, it remains to him only to expound the third idea of his text : the terrible manifestation of *God's wrath* on that sin, in which the whole of human *impiety* was concentrated.

Vv. 24, 25. " *Wherefore God also*[2] *gave them up to uncleanness through the lusts of their own hearts, to dishonor their own bodies between themselves :*[3] *who travestied the truth of God into a lie, and worshipped and served the creature instead of the Creator, who is blessed for ever. Amen.*" — In these words there is expressed the feeling of indignation raised in the heart of the apostle

---

[1] See the complete demonstration of this fact in the treatise of Pfleiderer, *Jahrbücher f. Prot. Theol.* 1867.

[2] א A B C omit the και after διο, which is found in the T. R., with D E G K L P and the most of the Mnn.

[3] א A B C D : εν αυτοις ; T. R., with E G K L P, the Mnn. : εν εαυτοις.

Romans 1:24, 25 / 107

by the thought and view of the treatment to which God has been subjected by the creature to whom He revealed Himself so magnificently. The verses have something of that παροξυσμός, that *exasperation of heart*, of which the author of the Acts speaks (xvii. 16) when describing Paul's impressions during his stay at Athens. This feeling is expressed forcibly by the two conjunctions διὸ καί, *wherefore also*. Διό, literally, *on account of which*, that is to say, of the sin just described; this first conjunction refers to the justice of punishment in general; the second, καί, *also*, brings out more especially the relation of *congruity* between the nature of the punishment and that of the offence. They sinned, *wherefore* God punished them; they sinned by degrading God, wherefore *also* God degraded them. This καί has been omitted by the Alex.; a mistake, as is plain, for it expresses the profoundest idea of the whole piece. No one would have thought of adding it. The word *gave over* does not signify that God *impelled* them to evil, to punish the evil which they had already committed. The holiness of God is opposed to such a sense, and *to give over* is not *to impel*. On the other hand, it is impossible to stop short at the idea of a simple *permission*: "God *let* them give themselves over to evil." God was not purely passive in the terrible development of Gentile corruption. Wherein did His action consist? He positively withdrew His hand; He ceased to hold the boat as it was dragged by the current of the river. This is the meaning of the term used by the apostle, Acts xiv. 16: "He *suffered* the Gentiles *to walk* in their own ways," by not doing for them what He never ceased to do for His own people. It is not a case of simple abstention, it is the positive withdrawal of a force. Such also is the meaning of the saying, Gen. vi. 3: "My Spirit shall not always strive with man." As Meyer says: "The law of history, in virtue of which the forsaking of God is followed among men by a parallel growth of immorality, is not a purely natural order of things; the power of God is active in the execution of this law." If it is asked how such a mode of action harmonizes with the moral perfection of God, the answer undoubtedly is, that when man has reached a certain degree of corruption, he can only be cured by the very excess of his own corruption; it is the only means left of producing what all preceding appeals and punishments failed to effect, the salutary action of repentance. So it is that at a given moment the father of the prodigal son lets him go, giving him even his share of goods. The monstrous and unnatural character of the excesses about to be described confirms this view.

The two prepositions, ἐν, *through*, and εἰς, *to*, differ from one another as the current which bears the bark along, once it has been detached from the shore, differs from the abyss into which it is about to be precipitated. Lusts exist in the heart; God abandons it to their power, and then begins that fall which must end in the most degrading impurities. The infinitive τοῦ ἀτιμάζεσθαι might be translated: to the impurity *which consists* in dishonoring. But as the whole passage is dominated by the idea of the "manifestation of divine wrath," it is more natural to give this infinitive the notion of end or aim: *in order to* dishonor. It is a condemnation: "You have dishonored me; I give you up to impurity, that you may dishonor your own selves." Observe the καί, *also*, at the beginning of the verse. The verb ἀτιμάζεσθαι is found in the classics only in the passive sense: *to be dishonored*. This meaning would not suit here, unless we translate, as Meyer does: "that their bodies *might be dishonored* among them" (the one by the other). But this meaning does not correspond with the force of the apostolic thought. The punishment consists not merely in being dishonored, but especially in dishonoring *oneself*. Ἀτιμάζεσθαι must therefore be taken as the middle, and in the active sense: "to dishonor their bodies in themselves." If this middle sense is not common in the classics, it is accidental, for it is perfectly regular. The clause *in themselves* looks superfluous at first sight; but Paul wishes to describe this blight as

108 / Justification by Faith

henceforth inherent in their very personality: it is a seal of infamy which they carry for the future on their forehead. The meaning of the two readings ἐν αὐτοῖς and ἐν ἑαυτοῖς does not differ; the first is written from the writer's point of view, the second from the viewpoint of the authors of the deed.

The punishment is so severe that Paul interrupts himself, as if he felt the need of recalling how much it was deserved. With the οἵτινες, *those who*, ver. 25, he once more passes from the punishment to the sin which had provoked it. God has dealt so with them, as *people who* had dealt so with Him. Such is the meaning of the pronoun ὅστις, which does not only *designate*, but *describe*. The verb μετήλλαξαν, *travestied*, through the addition of the preposition μετά, enhances the force of the simple ἤλλαξαν, *changed*, of ver. 23: the sin appears ever more odious to the apostle, the more he thinks of it.—The *truth of God* certainly means here: the true notion of His being, the idea which alone corresponds to so sublime a reality, and which ought to be produced by the revelation of Himself which he had given; comp. 1 Thess. i. 9, where the *true God* is opposed to idols. As the abstract term is used to denote the true God, so the abstract word *lie* here denotes idols, that ignoble mask in which the heathen expose the figure of the All-perfect. And here comes the height of insult. After travestying God by an image unworthy of him, they make this the object of their veneration (ἐσεβάσθησαν). To this term, which embraces all heathen life in general, Paul adds ἐλάτρευσαν, *they served*, which refers to positive acts of *worship*.—Παρά, *by the side of*, signifies with the accusative: *passing beyond*, leaving aside with contempt (to go and adore something else).—The doxology which closes this verse: *who is blessed for ever*, is a homage intended to wash off, as it were, the opprobrium inflicted on God by heathenism. On account of its termination, εὐλογητός may either signify: who *ought to be* blessed, or: *who is* blessed. The second meaning is simpler and more usual: just because He ought to be so, He is and will be so, whatever the heathen may do in the matter. The term εἰς τοὺς αἰῶνας, *for ever*, contrasts God's eternal glory with the ephemeral honor paid to idols, or the temporary affronts given to God.— Ἀμήν, *amen*, comes from the Hebrew *aman, to be firm*. It is an exclamation intended to scatter by anticipation all the mists which still exist in the consciousness of man, and darken the truth proclaimed.

Ver. 25 was an interruption extorted from Paul by the need which his outraged heart felt to justify once more the severity of such a punishment. He now resumes his exposition of the punishment, begun in ver. 24; and this time he proceeds to the end. He does not shrink from any detail fitted to bring out the vengeance which God has taken on the offence offered to His outraged majesty.

Vv. 26, 27. "*For this cause God gave them up unto dishonoring passions: for even their women did change the natural use into that which is against nature: and likewise*[1] *also the men, leaving the natural use of the woman, burned in their lust one toward another; men with men working infamy, and receiving in themselves*[2] *the well-merited recompense of their error.*"—Ver. 26 resumes the description begun in ver. 24, and which Paul had interrupted to ascend, ver. 25, from the punishment to its cause. The διὰ τοῦτο, *for this cause*, relates to ver. 25, and has the same logical bearing as the διό, *wherefore*, in ver. 24, which referred to ver. 23 (reproduced in ver. 25). It is therefore perfectly natural that the verb of the two propositions, vv. 24 and 26, should be one and the same (παρέδωκεν, *He gave over*).—The complement ἀτιμίας, *of dishonor*, is a genitive of quality (*dishonoring, vile*). This word goes back on the end of ver. 24: to *dishonor* their bodies among

---
[1] A D G P read ὁμοίως δε instead of ὁμοίως τε, which all the others read.
[2] Instead of ἐν ἑαυτοῖς, B K read ἐν αὐτοῖς.

themselves. The term πάθη, *passions*, has something still more ignoble in it than ἐπιθυμίαι, *lusts*, in ver. 24 ; for it contains a more pronounced idea of moral passivity, of shameful bondage.—The picture which follows of the unnatural vices then prevalent in Gentile society is confirmed in all points by the frightful details contained in the works of Greek and Latin writers. But it is asked, How can Paul give himself up, with a sort of complacency, to such a delineation? The answer lies in the aim of the whole passage to show the divine wrath displayed on the Gentile world ; comp. the term ἀντιμισθία, *meet recompense*, ver. 27. A law broods over human existence, a law which is at the same time a divine act : Such as thou makest thy God, such wilt thou make thyself.—The expressions ἄρρενες, θήλειαι, literally, *males, females*, are chosen to suit the spirit of the context.—The whole is calculated to show that there is here a just *recompense* on the part of God. The μετήλλαξαν, *they changed, travestied*, corresponds to the same verb, ver. 25, and the παρὰ φύσιν, *contrary to nature*, to the παρὰ τὸν κτίσαντα of the same verse.—There is in the ὁμοίως τε an idea of equality : *and equally so*, while the reading ὁμοίως δέ of four Mjj. contains further an idea of progress, as if the dishonoring of man by man were an intensification of that of woman.—In the ἣν ἔδει, which we have translated by "*well-merited* recompense" (literally, the recompense *which was meet*), one feels, as it were, the indignant breathing of God's holy wrath. Justice could not let it be otherwise ! The *error*, πλάνη, is not that of having sought satisfaction in such infamies ; it is the voluntary lie of *idolatry*, the lie (ψεῦδος) of ver. 25, the quenching of the truth, ver. 18 ; for this is what explains the ἀντιμισθία, the withering *retribution* just described. Once again the clause *in themselves* brings out the depth of this blight ; they bear it in themselves, it is visible to the eyes of all.

The moral sentiment in man is based on the conception of the holy God. To abandon the latter, is to paralyze the former. By honoring God we ennoble ourselves ; by rejecting Him we infallibly ruin ourselves. Such, according to the apostle, is the relation between heathenism and moral corruption. Independent morality is not that of St. Paul.

He has described the *ungodliness* of the Gentile world, idolatry, and its punishment, unnatural *impurities*. He now describes the other aspect of the world's sin, *unrighteousness*, and its punishment, the overflowing of monstrous *iniquities* committed by men against one another, and threatening to overwhelm society.

Ver. 28. "*And even as they did not think good to retain God in their knowledge, God* [1] *gave them over to a mind void of discernment, to do those things which are not fitting.*"—The ungodliness of the Gentiles was accompanied by a depth of iniquity : the refusal to let the thought of the perfect God rule human life. *To retain God as an object of distinct knowledge* (the literal sense of Paul's words), is to keep alive within the mind the view of that holy Being, so that His will shall give law to our whole conduct. This is what the Gentiles refused to do. Ceasing to contemplate God and His will, they were given over to all unrighteousness.—Καθώς, *even as* (literally, *agreeably to which*), indicates anew the exact correlation between this unrighteousness and the punishment about to be described.—Νοῦς ἀδόκιμος, which we translate : *a mind void of discernment*, corresponds to the οὐκ ἐδοκίμασαν, *they did not think good ;* having refused to appreciate God, they lost the true sense of moral appreciation, and this loss with all its consequences is a judgment, as well as the unnatural passions described above. Such is the force of the παρέδωκεν, *gave over*, corresponding to the same verb in vv. 24 and 26.—The phrase : *those things which are not fitting*, to express *evil*, is well suited to the notion *of appreciation* which is included in the verb δοκιμάζειν, *to judge good*, and the adjective ἀδόκιμος. Evil is here char-

---

[1] ℵ A here omit ὁ Θεός.

acterized as moral *incongruity*, calculated to revolt the νοῦς, *reason*, if it were not deprived of its natural discernment. The infinitive ποιεῖν, *to do*, is almost equivalent to a Latin gerund "*in doing.*" The subjective negation μή with the participle signifies : *all that is ranked* in the class designated by the participle.—Remark, finally, the intentional repetition of the substantive ὁ Θεός, *God:* "As thou treatest *God, God* treateth thee." It is by mistake that this second *God* is omitted in the *Sinait.* and *Alex.*—Volkmar makes ver. 28 the beginning of a new section. He would have it that the subject begun here is Jewish, in opposition to Gentile guiltiness (vv. 18–27). But nothing, either in the text or in the thought, indicates such a transition ; the καί, *also*, is opposed to it, and the charge raised by the apostle in the following verses, and especially ver. 32, is exactly the opposite of the description which he gives of the Jews, chap. ii. The latter appear as the *judges* of Gentile corruption, while the men characterized in ver. 32 *give it their applause*.

Ver. 29a. "*Being filled with every kind of unrighteousness,*[1] *perverseness, maliciousness, covetousness.*"[2]—In the following enumeration we need not seek a rigorously systematic order. Paul evidently lets his pen run on as if he thought that, of all the bad terms which should present themselves, none would be out of place or exaggerated. But in this apparent disorder one can detect a certain grouping, a connection through the association of ideas.—The first group which we have detached in our translation embraces four terms ; according to the T. R., five. But the word πορνεία, *uncleanness*, should evidently be rejected ; for it is wanting in many Mjj. ; it is displaced in some others ; finally, the subject has been exhausted in what precedes.—The phrase : "all sort of *unrighteousness*," embraces collectively the whole following enumeration : πονηρία, *perverseness*, denotes the bad instinct of the heart ; κακία, *maliciousness*, the deliberate wickedness which takes pleasure in doing harm ; πλεονεξία, *covetousness* (the desire of having more πλέον ἐχειν), the passion for money, which does not scruple to lay hold of the possessions of its neighbor to augment its own. The participle πεπληρωμένους, *filled*, at the head of this first group, is in apposition to the understood subject of ποιεῖν.

The four terms of this first group thus refer to injustices committed against the well-being and *property* of our neighbor.

Ver. 29b. "*Full of envy, murder, strife, deceit, bitterness.*"—These five terms form again a natural group, which embraces all the injustices whereby the *person* of our neighbor is injured. The adjective μεστούς, *full of* (properly, *stuffed*), on which this group depends, indicates a change of idea from the preceding. As an adjective, it denotes solely the present attribute, while the preceding participle implied the *process of growth* which had led to the state described. The similarity of sound in the two Greek words : φθόνον, *envy*, and φόνον, *murder*, has led to their being often combined also in the classics ; besides, envy leads to murder, as is shown by the example of Cain. If envy does not go the length of making away with him whose advantages give us umbrage, it seeks at least to trouble him with deception in the enjoyment of his wealth ; this is expressed by ἔρις, *strife*, quarrelling ; finally, in this course one seeks to injure his neighbor by deceiving him (δόλος, *deceit*), or to render his life miserable by bitterness of temper (κακοήθεια).

Ver. 30a. "*Whisperers, backbiters, haters of God, despiteful, proud, boasters.*"—The dispositions expressed in the six terms of this group are those of which pride is the centre. There is no reason for reducing them to four, as Hofmann would, by making the second term the epithet of

---

[1] After αδικια (*unrighteousness*) the T. R. reads πορνεια (*uncleanness*), with L only ; D F G place πορνεια after κακια (*maliciousness*) ; ℵ A B C K reject it entirely.
[2] These three last terms are transposed in the MSS. (ℵ A : πονηρια κακια πλεονεξια ; B L : πον., πλεον., κακ. ; C : κακ., πον., πλεον.).

the first, and the fourth that of the third; this does not suit the rapidity of the enumeration and the need of accumulating terms.—Ψιθυριστής, *whisperer*, the man who pours his poison against his neighbor by whispering into the ear; κατάλαλος, the man who blackens publicly; θεοστυγής signifies, in the two classical passages where it is found (Euripides), *hated of God*, and Meyer therefore contends that the passive sense ought to be preserved here, while generalizing it; the name would thus signify all hardened malefactors. But this general meaning is impossible in an enumeration in which the sense of each term is limited by that of all the rest. The active signification: *hating God*, is therefore the only suitable one; it is the highest manifestation of pride, which cannot brook the thought of this superior and judge; one might say: the most monstrous form of calumny (the malediction of Providence); Suidas and Œcumenius, two writers nearer the living language than we, thought they could give to this word the active signification, a fact which justifies it sufficiently. To insolence toward God (the sin of ὕβρις among the Greeks) there is naturally joined *insult* offered to men: ὑβριστής, *insolent, despiteful*. The term ὑπερήφανος (from ὑπέρ, φαίνομαι), *proud*, designates the man who, from a feeling of his own superiority, regards others with haughtiness; while ἀλαζών, *boaster*, denotes the man who seeks to attract admiration by claiming advantages he does not really possess.

Vv. 30*b*, 31. " *Inventors of evil things, disobedient to parents, without understanding, covenant-breakers, without tenderness,*[1] *without pity.*"—The last group refers to the extinction of all the natural feelings of humanity, filial affection, loyalty, tenderness, and pity. It includes six terms. The first, *inventors of evil things*, denotes those who pass their lives meditating on the evil to be done to others; so Antiochus Epiphanes is called by the author of 2 Macc. (vii. 31), πάσης κακίας εὑρετής, and Sejanus by Tacitus, *facinorum repertor*. People of this stamp have usually begun to betray their bad character in the bosom of their families—they have been *disobedient to their parents*.—'Ασύνετος, *without understanding*, denotes the man who is incapable of lending an ear to wise counsel; thus understood, it has a natural connection with the previous term; Hofmann cites Ps. xxxii. 8, 9.—'Ασύνθετος, which many translate *irreconcilable*, can hardly have this meaning, for the verb from which it comes does not signify *to reconcile*, but *to decide in common*, and hence *to make a treaty*. The adjective therefore describes *the man who without scruple violates the contracts he has signed*, the faithless man.—'Αστοργος, *without tenderness*, from στέργειν, to cherish, caress, foster; this word denotes the destruction even of the feelings of natural tenderness, as is seen in a mother who exposes or kills her child, a father who abandons his family, or children who neglect their aged parents. If the following word in the T. R., ἀσπόνδους, *truce-breakers*, were authentic, its meaning would be confounded with that of ἀσυνθέτους, rightly understood.—'Ανελεήμων, *without pity*, is closely connected with the preceding ἀστόργους, *without tenderness;* but its meaning is more general. It refers not only to tender feelings within the family circle; here it calls up before the mind the entire population of the great cities flocking to the circus to behold the fights of gladiators, frantically applauding the effusion of human blood, and gloating over the dying agonies of the vanquished combatant. Such is an example of the unspeakable hardness of heart to which the whole society of the Gentile world descended. What would it have come to if a regenerating breath had not at this supreme moment passed over it? It is in this last group that the fact which the apostle is concerned to bring out is most forcibly emphasized, that of a divine judgment manifesting itself in this state of things. In fact, we have no more before us iniquities which can be explained by a simple natural egoism.

[1] The T. R. here adds, with C K L P, ασπονδους (*without good faith*); but the word is omitted by א A B D E G.

They are enormities which are as unnatural as the infamies described above as the punishment of heathenism. Thus is proved the abandonment of men to a mind *void of discernment* (the ἀδόκιμος νοῦς of ver. 28).

Ver. 32. "*Who, knowing*[1] *the judgment of God, that they which commit such things are worthy of death, not only do the same, but applaud*[2] *those who do them.*"—The relation of this verse to what precedes has been very generally misunderstood, hence probably the corrections of the text attempted in some MSS.—The most serious misunderstanding is that of Ritschl. This theologian regards the men to whom this verse and the four following (ii. 1–4) refer as forming a class by themselves, and wholly different from the sinners described from ver. 19 onward. The men *who repress the truth,* ver. 18, are according to him divided into two classes: "those who through heathenism have quenched the feeling of divine revelation (vv. 19–31)," and "those who, while judging the immoralities produced by paganism, nevertheless take part in them by their conduct (ver. 32–ii. 4)." But it is easy to see that this construction is devised solely with the view of finding the development of the idea of *divine wrath,* ver. 18, in the passage ii. 5 et seq., and not in the παραδιδόναι, *giving over,* of vv. 24, 26, and 28 (see p. 168). This construction, proposed by Ritschl, is impossible. 1. Because judging with a view to *approve,* ver. 32, is not the same thing as judging to *condemn,* ii. 1, 2. 2. On account of the obvious relation between the terms of ver. 32: *though knowing the judgment of God,* and those of ver. 28: *they did not keep God in their knowledge.* 3. The uniform sense of the pronoun οἵτινες, *as people who,* forces us to seek in the description of ver. 32 the *justification* of the judgment described from ver. 28. Far, then, from indicating a change of persons, this pronoun expresses the *moral qualification* by which the individuals just described have drawn on them so severe a punishment. It is an exact parallel to the οἵτινες of ver. 25. The latter justified the judgment of idolaters by recalling to mind the greatness of their offence. The former in the same way justifies the punishment which has overtaken the resistance of man to the revelation of moral good (ver. 28a): "They had well deserved to be given over to this deluge of iniquities, *they who* had acted thus toward God when He revealed his will to them." The terms which follow and explain the pronoun *they who,* set forth this radical iniquity through which men quenched the sentiment of moral truth revealed in them; comp. ver. 28a. Τὸ δικαίωμα, strictly, *what God establishes as just;* here: *His just sentence;* ἐπιγνόντες denotes the clear discernment which men had of it. The word recalls the γνόντες τὸν Θεόν, *knowing God,* of ver. 21: *moral* light was produced in them as well as *religious* light. The words following indicate the contents of that sentence which God had taken care to engrave on their heart. What appeals to God's justice do we not find in the writings of Gentile historians and philosophers! What a description in their poets of the punishment inflicted on malefactors in Tartarus! The phrase *worthy of death* has been applied by some, and recently again by Hofmann, to the *punishment of death* as executed by human judges. But this penalty would suit only one term in the whole preceding enumeration, viz., φόνος, *murder;* and the τὰ τοιαῦτα, *such things,* does not allow so restricted an application. *Death* therefore here denotes death as God only can inflict it, the pains of Hades, which the Gentiles also recognized, and which Paul, designating things from his own point of view, calls *death.* The second part of the verse leads from the offence to the punishment. It is *the mind deprived of discernment,* to which God has given up men, in its most monstrous manifestation; not only doing evil, but applauding those who do it! This is true to fact. Had not the Caligulas and Neros found advocates, admirers, multitudes always ready to offer them

---

[1] Instead of επιγνοντες, B reads επιγινωσκοντες.—To the participle επιγνοντες, D E add the verb ουκ ενοησαν, and G: ουκ εγνωσαν. Further on D adds γαρ after ου μονον.
[2] In place of the two verbs ποιουσιν, συνευδοκουσιν, B reads ποιουντες, συνευδοκουντες.

incense ? The *not only, but even*, rightly assumes that there is more guilt in approving in cold blood of the evil committed by others, than in committing it oneself under the force and blindness of passion. Such a mode of acting is therefore the last stage in the corruption of the moral sense.

The reading of the *Cantab.* would signify : "They who, knowing the sentence of God, *did not understand* that those who do such things are worthy of death ; *for* not only do they do them, etc." . . . This meaning would be admissible, but the contents of the sentence of God would remain absolutely unexplained, which is far from natural. The reading of the *Vatic.* would give the following translation : "They who, knowing the sentence of God, that those who do such things are worthy of death, not only *doing* those things, but *approving* those who do them." The construction in this case demands the doubling of the verb εἰσίν, *are* (first, as verb of the proposition ὅτι, *that those who ;* then as verb of the proposition οἵτινες, *they who*). This construction is very forced ; it is very probable, as has been supposed, that the reading of B is only an importation into the apostolic text of a form of quotation found in the Epistle of Clemens Romanus. This Father, quoting our passage, says : "They who practice these things are abominable in the sight of God ; and not only they who do them (οἱ πράσσοντες), but those also who approve them (οἱ συνευδοκοῦντες)." The "*did not understand*," and the *for* added by the *Cantab.*, appear to be mere attempts to correct the reading of the *Vaticanus.* In the whole of this chapter the apostle evidently distinguishes two degrees in the sin of the Gentile world ; the one active and internal, the other passive and external ; the one a natural result of depraved instinct, the other having the character of unnatural monstrosity. The first is chargeable on man, it is his guilt ; the second is sin as a punishment, the manifest sign of God's wrath. This great historical fact is developed in two aspects. First, from the *religious* point of view : man quenches his intuition of the Divine Being, and clothes God in the form of an idol ; his punishment in this connection is self-degradation by monstrous impurities. Then in the *moral* point of view : man quenches the light of conscience, and as a punishment his moral discernment is so perverted that he puts the seal of his approbation on all the iniquities which he should have condemned and prevented. This is the worst of corruptions, that of the conscience. Thus is fully justified the great thought of ver. 18 : The wrath of God displayed on the Gentile world to punish the voluntary darkening of the religious sense (*ungodliness*) and of the moral sense (*unrighteousness*), which had been awakened in man by the primeval revelation of God.

FIFTH PASSAGE (2:1-29)

The Wrath of God suspended over the Jewish People

In the midst of this flood of pollutions and iniquities which Gentile society presents to view, the apostle sees one who like a judge from the height of his tribunal sends a stern look over the corrupt mass, condemning the evil which reigns in it, and applauding the wrath of God which punishes it. It is this new personage whom he apostrophizes in the following words :

Ver. 1. " *Wherefore thou art inexcusable, O man, whosoever thou art that judgest : for wherein thou judgest another, thou condemnest thyself ; for thou that judgest doest the same things.*"—Whom is the apostle addressing ? Gentile magistrates, say the old Greek commentators. But a magistrate is appointed to judge crimes ; he could not be reproached for filling his office. The best of the Gentiles, say the Reformers, and Hofmann in our own day. But what purpose would be served, in this vast survey of the general state of mankind, by such a slight moral warning given to the best and wisest of the Gentiles not to set themselves to judge others ? Besides, this precept could not be more than a parenthesis, while it is easy to see that ver. 1 is exactly like ver. 18 of chap. i., the theme of all the development which immediately follows chap. ii. Evidently the person apostrophized in these terms : *O man* . . ., forms an exception among *those men* (ἄνθρωποι, i. 18) who hurtfully and wickedly reject the truth. He does not repress, on the contrary he proclaims it ; but he contents himself with applying it to others. The true name of this collective personage, whose portrait Paul proceeds to draw without yet naming him, will be pronounced in ver. 17 : "Now if thou *Jew*." The apostle knows how delicate the task is which he is approaching, that of proving to the elect people that divine wrath, now displayed against the Gentiles, is likewise suspended over them. He is about to drag to God's tribunal the nation which thinks itself at liberty to cite all others to its bar. It is a bold enterprise. The apostle proceeds cautiously. He first expresses his thought abstractly : *thou who judgest, whosoever thou art,* to unveil it fully afterward. Chap. ii. is thus the parallel of the passage i. 18–32 ; it is the trial of the Jewish after that of the Gentile world. And the first two verses are its theme.

The course followed by the apostle is this :—In the first part, vv. 1–16, he lays down the principle of God's *true* (impartial) *judgment*. In the second, vv. 17–29, he applies it directly to the Jew.—The first part contains the development of three ideas. 1. Favors received, far from forming a ground for exemption from judgment, aggravate the responsibility of the receiver, vv. 1–5. 2. The divine sentence rests on the *works*, vv. 6–12. 3. Not on *knowledge*, vv. 13–16.

The διό, *wherefore*, which connects this passage with the preceding, presents a certain difficulty which Hofmann and Ritschl have used to justify their far from natural explanations of the preceding. Meyer takes this connecting particle as referring to the whole preceding description from ver. 18. For if a man is guilty, if he commits such things without judging them, it follows that he is still more guilty if he commit them while judging them. Ver. 1 might, however, be connected more particularly with ver. 32. In point of fact, if sinning while applauding the sin of others is criminal, would not men be more inexcusable still if they condemned the sin of others while joining in it ? In the former case there is at least agreement between thought and action—the man *does* what he expressly *approves*—while in the second there is an internal contradiction and a flagrant hypocrisy. In the act of judging, the judge condemns his own *doing*.— The word *inexcusable*, here applied to the Jews, is the counterpart of the same epithet already applied to the Gentiles, i. 20.— *Whosoever thou art* (πᾶς) : whatever name thou bearest, were it even the glorious name of Jew. Paul does not say this, but it is his meaning.—It is enough that thou judgest, that I may condemn thee in this character of judge ; for thy judgment recoils on thyself. The Jews, as we know, liked to call the Gentiles ἁμαρτωλοί, *sinners*, Gal. ii. 15.—'Εν ᾧ, *wherein*, signifies : "Thou doest two things at once ; thou condemnest thy neighbor, and by condemning him for things which thou doest, thou takest away all excuse for thyself." This meaning is much more pungent than Meyer's : *in the same things which* —that is to say, in the things which thou doest, and which at the same time thou condemnest. There was undoubtedly a difference between the moral state of the Jews and that of other nations, but the passage vv. 17–24 will show that this difference was only relative. The repetition of the words : *thou who judgest*, at the end of the sentence, brings out strongly the exceptional character in virtue of which this personage is brought on the scene. The apostle confronts the falsehood under which the man shelters himself with a simple luminous truth to which no conscience can refuse its assent.

Ver. 2. "*Now*[1] *we know that the sentence of God is according to truth upon them which commit such things.*"—We might give the δέ an adversative sense: "*But* God does not let Himself be deceived by this judgment which thou passest on others." It is more natural, however, to translate this δέ by *now*, and to take this verse as the major of a syllogism. The minor, ver. 1: thy judgment on others condemns thee; the major, ver. 2: now the judgment of God is always true; the conclusion understood (between vv. 2 and 3): therefore thy hypocritical judgment cannot shelter thee from that of God. The connecting particle γάρ, *for*, in two Alex. is inadmissible. This *for*, to be logical, must bear on the proposition: *thou condemnest thyself*, which is unnatural, as a new idea has intervened since then.—What is the subject in *we know?* According to some: we, *Christians*. But what would the knowledge of Christians prove against the Jewish point of view which Paul is here combating? Others: we, *Jews*. But it was precisely the Jewish conscience which Paul was anxious to bring back to truth on this point. The matter in question is a truth inscribed, according to the apostle, on the human conscience as such, and which plain common sense, free from prejudices, compels us to own: "But every one knows."—The term κρῖμα does not denote, like κρίσις, the *act* of judging, but its *contents*, the sentence. The sentence which God pronounces on every man is agreeable *to truth*. There would be no more truth in the universe if there were none in the judgment of God; and there would be none in the judgment of God, if to be absolved ourselves, it were enough to condemn others.—The words κατὰ ἀλήθειαν have sometimes been explained in the sense of *really:* "that there is *really* a judgment of God against those who" ... But what the Jews disputed was not *the fact* of judgment; it was its impartiality—that is to say, its *truth*. They could not get rid of the idea that in that day they would enjoy certain immunities due to their purer creed, and the greatly higher position which they held than that of other nations.—*Such things*, that is to say, those referred to by the same word, ver. 32.—But the apostle is not unaware that in the Jewish conscience there is an obstacle to the full application of this principle; it is this obstacle which he now labors to remove. Vv. 3–5 develop the words: *they who do such things* (whoever they are, should they even be Jews); vv. 6–16 will explain what is meant by *a judgment according to truth*.

Ver. 3. "*But thou countest upon this, O man, that judgest them which do such things, and doest the same, that thou shalt escape the judgment of God?*" —We might, with Hofmann, take the verbs λογίζῃ and καταφρονεῖς (*thou countest, thou despisest*) in an affirmative sense. But the ἤ, or *indeed*, at the beginning of ver. 4 would rather incline us, following Paul's ordinary usage, to interpret these words in the interrogative sense; not, however, that we need translate the former in the sense of: *thinkest thou?* The interrogation is less abrupt: "thou thinkest no doubt?" The word λογίζεσθαι, *to reason*, well describes the false calculations whereby the Jews persuaded themselves that they would escape the judgment with which God would visit the Gentiles. Observe the σύ, *thou:* "that *thou wilt escape, thou*," a being by thyself, a privileged person! It was a Jewish axiom, that "every one circumcised has part in the kingdom to come." A false calculation. Such, then, is the first supposition serving to explain the security of the Jew; but there is a graver still. Perhaps this false calculation proceeds from a moral fact hidden in the depths of the heart. Paul drags it to the light in what follows.

Vv. 4, 5. "*Or despisest thou the riches of His goodness and forbearance and long-suffering; not knowing that the goodness of God leadeth thee to repentance? But, according to thy hardness and impenitent heart, treasurest up unto thyself wrath for the day of wrath and of the revelation*[2] *of the righteous judgment of*

---

[1] ℵ C read γαρ instead of δε.
[2] The correctors of ℵ and D, and the Mjj. K L P, insert a και after αποκαλυψεως.

116 / Justification by Faith

God."—'Η, *or even.* The meaning is : is there something even worse than an illusion ; is there contempt ? The case then would be more than foolish, it would be impious ! The *riches of goodness*, of which the apostle speaks, embrace all God's benefits to Israel in the past : that special election, those consecutive revelations, that constant care, finally, the sending of the Messiah, all that constituted the privileged position which Israel had enjoyed for so many ages. The second term, ἀνοχή, *patience* (from ἀνέχεσθαι *to restrain oneself*), denotes the feeling awakened in the benefactor when his goodness is put to the proof by ingratitude. Paul has in view no doubt the murder of the Messiah, which divine justice might have met with the immediate destruction of the nation. The third term, μακροθυμία, *long-suffering*, refers to the incomprehensible prolongation of Israel's existence, in spite of the thirty consecutive years of resistance to the appeals of God, and to the preaching of the apostles which had elapsed, and in spite of such crimes as the murder of Stephen and James (Acts vii. and xii.). The three words form an admirable climax. The last (*long-suffering*) characterizes this treasure of grace as exhausted, and that of wrath as ready to discharge itself. The notion of *contempt* is explained by the fact that the more God shows Himself good, patient, and meek, the more does the pride of Israel seem to grow, and the more does the nation show itself hostile to the gospel.—'Αγνοῶν may be translated : *ignoring*, or *mistaking ;* the first meaning is simpler and may suffice, for there is a voluntary ignorance, the result of bad faith, in consequence of which we do not see what we do not care to see ; it is this ignorance which is referred to here.—The phrase τὸ χρηστὸν τοῦ Θεοῦ is touching : *what is good*, sweet, gentle in God (χρηστός, strictly : *that may be handled, what one may make use of*, from χράομαι). The form : " what good there is" . . . leaves it to be inferred that there is something else in God, and that He will not let Himself be always treated thus with impunity. The time will come when He will act with rigor.—The word ἄγειν, *to lead*, implies the power possessed by man of yielding to or resisting the attraction exercised over him. If he could not resist it, how could the Jews be accused of committing this offence at this very time ? Μετάνοια, *repentance*, is the act whereby man goes back on his former views, and changes his standpoint and feeling.

Ver. 5. The δέ, *but*, contrasts the result of so many favors received with the divinely desired effect. The contrast indicated arises from the fact that the Jews in their conduct are guided by a wholly different *rule* from that to which the mercy of God sought to draw them. This idea of *rule* is indeed what explains the preposition κατά, *according to*, which is usually made into a *by*. The word denotes a line of conduct long followed, the old Jewish habit of meeting the calls of God with a hard and impenitent heart ; what Stephen so forcibly upbraided them with, Acts vii. 51 : " Ye stiffnecked (σκληροτράχηλοι) and uncircumcised in heart and ears, ye do always resist the Holy Ghost ; as your fathers did, so do ye."—*Hardness* relates to insensibility of heart to divine favors ; *impenitence*, to the absence of that change of views which the feeling of such goodness should have produced.—But it must not be thought that these favors are purely and simply lost. Instead of the good which they should have produced, evil results from them. Every favor trampled under foot adds to the *treasure of wrath* which is already suspended over the heads of the impenitent people. There is an evident correlation between the phrase *riches of goodness*, ver. 4, and the Greek word θησαυρίζειν, *to treasure up*. The latter word, as well as the dative (of favor !) σεαυτῷ, *for thyself*, have certainly a tinge of irony. What an enriching is that ! *Wrath* is here denounced on the Jews, as it had been, i. 18, on the Gentiles. The two passages are parallel ; there is only this difference between them, that among the Gentiles the thunderbolt has already fallen, while the storm is still gathering for the Jews. The time when it will burst on them is called *the day of wrath*. In this phrase two ideas are combined : that of the great national catastrophe which had been predicted by John the Baptist and by Jesus (Matt. iii. 10 ; Luke xi. 50, 51), and that of the final judgment of the guilty taken individually at the last day. The preposition ἐν ("*in* the day") may be made dependent on the substantive *wrath:* "the wrath *which will have its full course* in the day when" . . . But it is more natural to connect this clause with the verb : "thou art heaping up a treasure which shall be paid to thee in the day when" . . . The writer transports himself in thought to the day itself ; he is present then : hence the ἐν instead of εἰς.—The three Byz. Mjj. and the correctors of the *Sinaït.* and of the *Cantab.* read a καί, *and*, between the two words *revelation* and *just judgment*, and thus give the word "day" *three* complements : day of *wrath*, of *revelation*, and of *just judgment*. These three names would correspond well with the three of ver. 4 : *goodness, patience, long-suffering ;* and the term *revelation*, without complement, would have in it something mysterious and threatening quite in keeping with the context. This reading is, however, improbable. The καί (*and*) is omitted not only in the Mjj. of the two other families, but also in the ancient versions (Syriac and Latin) ; besides the word *revelation* can hardly be destitute of all qualification. The apostle therefore says : *the revelation of the righteous judgment ;* thus indicating that wrath (righteous judgment) is still veiled so far as the Jews are concerned (in contrast to the ἀποκαλύπτεται, *is revealed,* i. 18), but that then it will be fully unveiled in relation to them also.—Only two passages are quoted where the word δικαιοκρισία, *just judgment*, is used : in a Greek translation of Hos. iv. 5, and in the *Testaments of the twelve patriarchs.* The word recalls the phrase of ver. 2 : "The judgment of God *according to truth.*" It dissipates beforehand the illusions cherished by the Jews as to the immunity which they hoped to enjoy in that day in virtue of their theocratic privileges. It contains the theme of the development which immediately follows. The *just judgment* of God (the judgment *according to truth*, ver. 2) will bear solely on the *moral life* of each individual, vv. 6–12, not on the external fact of being *the hearer* of a law, vv. 13–16. These are the positive and negative characteristics of a judgment according to righteousness. —It would be unaccountable how Ritschl could have mistaken the obvious relation between vv. 5 and 4 so far as to connect ii. 5 with the notion of *wrath*, i. 18, had not a preconceived idea imposed on him this exegetical violence.

Ver. 6. " *Who will render to every one according to his deeds.*"—No account will be taken of any external circumstance, but solely of the aim which has governed the man's moral action. It has been asked how this maxim can be reconciled with the doctrine of justification by faith. Fritzsche finds in them two different theories presenting an insoluble contradiction. Others think that in the judgment the moral imperfections of believers will be covered by their faith ; which would convert faith into a means of sinning with impunity. What a *just judgment* that would be ! Melanchthon, Tholuck, and others hold that this standard is purely hypothetical ; it *would be* the standard which God would have applied if redemption had not intervened. But the future, "*will render*," is not a conditional (*would render*). Besides, *judgment according to the deeds done,* is attested by many other passages, both from Paul (Rom. xiv. 12 ; 2 Cor. v. 10 ; Gal. vi. 6), from Jesus Himself (John v. 28, 29 ; Matt. xii. 36, 37, etc.), and from other writings of the New Testament (Rev. xx. 13). Ritschl thinks that throughout this passage it is a Pharisee whom Paul introduces as speaking, and who starts from a narrow idea of divine justice—the idea, viz., of retributive justice. But what trace is there in the text of such an accommodation on the apostle's part to a standpoint foreign to his own ? The logical tissue of the piece, and its relation to what precedes and follows, present no breach of continuity. There is only one answer to the question raised, unless we admit a flagrant contradiction in the apostle's teaching: that justification by faith alone applies to the time of *entrance* into salvation through the free pardon of sin, but not to the time of judgment. When God of free grace receives the sinner at the time of his conversion, He asks nothing of him except faith ; but from that moment the believer enters on a wholly new responsibility ; God demands from him, as the recipient of grace, the fruits of grace. This is obvious from the parable of the talents. The Lord commits His gifts to His servants freely ; but from the moment when that extraordinary grace has been shown, He expects something from their labor. Comp. also the parable of the wicked debtor, where the pardoned sinner who refuses to pardon his brother is himself replaced under the rule of justice, and consequently under the burden of his debt. The reason is that faith is not the dismal prerogative of being able to sin with impunity ; it is, on the contrary, the means of overcoming sin and acting holily ; and if this life-fruit is not produced, it is dead, and will be declared vain. " *Every* barren tree will be hewn down and cast into the fire" (Matt. iii. 10). Comp. the terrible warnings, 1 Cor. vi. 9, 10, Gal. vi. 7, which are addressed to believers. —The two following verses develop the idea of the verb ἀποδώσει, *will render*.

Vv. 7, 8. " *To them who, by patient continuance in well-doing, seek for glory and honor and immortality,* [to such] *eternal life: but for them that are contentious, and do not obey the truth, but obey unrighteousness,* [for such] *wrath and indignation!*" [1]

The Jews divided men into circumcised, and consequently saved, and uncircumcised, and consequently damned. Here is a new classification, which Paul substitutes, founded solely on the moral aim. —There are two principal ways of construing ver. 7. Sometimes the three words : *glory, honor, immortality*, are made the objects of the verb : *will render* (ver. 6), understood. The phrase : *patient continuance in well-doing*, is thus taken to qualify the pronoun τοῖς μέν, *to them*, and the last words : ζητοῦσιν κ.τ.λ., become merely an explanatory appendix : " to wit, to them who seek eternal life." The meaning of the verse thus taken is : " to them who live in patient continuance in well-doing [He will render] glory and honor and immortality, [to wit, to those] who seek eternal life." But this construction is very forced. 1. The subordinate clause : " in continuance," is rather the qualification of a verb than of a pronoun like τοῖς μέν. 2. The participle ζητοῦσι would require the article τοῖς, and would make a clumsy and superfluous appendix. The construction, as given in our translation, is much more simple and significant. The regimen καθ' ὑπομονήν, literally, *according to the standard of patient continuance in well-doing*, corresponds with the *seek*, on which it depends ; seeking must be in a certain line. And the weighty word *eternal life*, at the close of this long sentence, depicts, as it were, the final and glorious issue of this long and laborious practice of goodness. This accusative is the object of the verb : *will render*, understood (ver. 6). —The notion of *patient continuance* is emphasized here, not only in opposition to the idea of intermittent moral efforts, but to indicate that there are great moral obstacles to be met on this path, and that a persistent love of goodness is needed to surmount them. The apostle says literally : perseverance in *good work*. In ver. 6 he had used the plural *works*. He now comprehends this multiplicity of works in the profound principle which constitutes their unity, the permanent determination to realize goodness. What supports a man in this course is the goal which he has constantly before him : *glory*, an existence without defilement or weakness, resplendent throughout with the divine brightness of holiness and power ; *honor*, the approbation of God, which forms the eternal honor of its object ; *immortality* (*incorruptibility*), the absolute

---

[1] T. R., with K L P, places οργη after θυμος.

impossibility of any wound or interruption or end to this state of being. The *ands*, καί, before the last two substantives, show a certain degree of emotion; the accumulation of terms arises from the same cause. In all human conditions there are souls which contemplate the ideal here described, and which, ravished with its beauty, are elevated by it above every earthly ambition and the pursuit of sensual gratifications. These are the men who are represented under the figure of the merchant seeking *goodly pearls*. For such is the pearl of great price, *life eternal!* This last word, laden as it were with all divine riches, denotes the realization of the ideal just described; it worthily closes this magnificent proposition.

But is it asked again, where, in this description of a normal human life, are faith and salvation by the gospel to be found? Does Paul then preach salvation by the work of man? The apostle has not to do here with the means whereby we can really attain to *well-doing;* he merely affirms that no one will be saved apart from the doing of good, and he assumes that the man who is animated with this persistent desire will not fail, some time or other, in the journey of life, to meet with the means of attaining an end so holy and glorious. This means is faith in the gospel—a truth which Paul reserves for proof at a later stage. "*He that doeth truth*," said Jesus to the same effect, "*cometh to the light*," as soon as it is presented to him (John iii. 21; comp. vii. 17). The love of goodness, which is the spring of his life, will then lead him to embrace Christ, the ideal of goodness; and, having embraced Him, he will find in Him the triumphant power for well-doing of which he was in quest. The desire of goodness is the acceptance of the gospel by anticipation. The natural corollary of these premisses is the thought expressed by Peter: the preaching of the gospel before the judgment to every human soul, either in this life or in the next (1 Pet. iii. 19, 20, iv. 6).[1] Comp. Matt. xii. 31, 32. And if the apostle has spoken of patient continuance in this pursuit, it is because he is well aware of that power of self-mastery which is needed, especially in a Jew, to break with his nation, and family, and all his past, and to remain faithful to the end to the supreme love of goodness.

The other class of men is described ver. 8. The regimen ἐξ ἐριθείας can without difficulty serve to qualify the pronoun τοῖς δέ; comp. the construction ὁ or οἱ ἐκ πίστεως, iii. 26; Gal. iii. 7. The meaning is: "but for those who are under the dominion of the spirit of contention."—The word ἐριθεία, *contention*, does not come, as has been often thought, from ἔρις, *disputation*, but, as Fritzsche has proved, from ἔριθος, *mercenary;* whence the verb ἐριθεύειν, "to work for wages," then, "to put oneself at the service of a party." The substantive ἐριθεία therefore denotes the spirit which seeks the victory of the party which one has espoused from self-interest, in contrast to the spirit which seeks the possession of the truth. Paul knew well from experience the tendency of Rabbinical discussions, and he characterizes it by a single word. The term *truth* is here used abstractly; but Paul has, nevertheless, in view the concrete realization of this notion in the gospel revelation. *Unrighteousness*, which he contrasts with *truth* (exactly as Jesus does, John vii. 18), denotes the selfish passions, vain ambitions, and unrighteous prejudices, which lead a man to close his eyes to the light when it presents itself, and thus produce unbelief. Unrighteousness leads to this result as certainly as moral integrity leads to faith. Jesus develops precisely the same thought, John iii. 19, 20. The words *wrath and indignation*, which express the wages earned by such conduct, are in the nominative in Greek, not in the accusative, like the word *eternal life* (ver. 7). They are not, therefore, the object of the verb *will render*, which is too remote. We must make them either the subject of a verb understood (ἔσται, *will be, there will be*), or, better still, an exclamation: "for them, wrath!"

---

[1] See Appendix A.

The three Byz. Mjj. follow the psychological order, "*indignation and wrath!*" First the internal emotion (*indignation*), then the external manifestation (*wrath*); but the other two families present the inverse order, and rightly so. For what is first perceived is the manifestation; then we pass upward to the feeling which inspires it, and which gives it all its gravity. Θυμός is the emotion of the soul; ὀργή comprehends look, sentence, chastisement.—Why does the apostle once again repeat this contrast of vv. 7 and 8 in vv. 9 and 10? Obviously with the view of now adding to each term of the contrast the words: *to the Jew first, and also to the Greek*, which expressly efface the false line of demarkation drawn by Jewish theology.

Vv. 9, 10. "*Tribulation and anguish upon every soul of man that effecteth evil, of the Jew first, and also of the Greek; but glory and honor and peace to every man that doeth good, to the Jew first, and also to the Greek!*"—The asyndeton indicates, as it always does, the more emphatic reassertion of the previous idea: "*Yes,* tribulation and anguish!"—The antithesis of vv. 7, 8 is reproduced in inverse order, not only to avoid the monotony of a too exact parallelism, but chiefly because, following up ver. 8 (*wrath and indignation*), the idea of ver. 9 (*tribulation and anguish*) presented itself more naturally than that of ver. 10 (*glory and honor and peace*); comp. the same arrangement, Luke i. 51–53. The terms *tribulation* and *anguish* describe the moral and external state of the man on whom *the indignation* and *wrath* of the judge fall (ver. 8). Tribulation is the punishment itself (corresponding to *wrath*); anguish is the wringing of the heart which the punishment produces; it corresponds to the judge's *indignation*. The *soul* is mentioned as the seat of feeling. The phrase, *every soul of man*, expresses the equality and universality of the treatment dealt out. Yet within this equality there is traced a sort of preference both as to judgment and salvation respectively (ver. 10), to the detriment and advantage of the Jew. When he says *first*, the apostle has no doubt in view (as in i. 16) a priority in time; comp. 1 Pet. iv. 17. Must we not, however, apply at the same time the principle laid down by Jesus, Luke xii. 41–48, according to which he who receives most benefits is also the man who has the heaviest responsibility? In any case, therefore, whoever escapes judgment, it will not be the Jew; if there were but one judged, it would be he. Such is the apostle's answer to the claim alleged, ver. 3: ὅτι σὺ ἐκφεύξῃ, *that thou, thou alone, shalt escape.*

Ver. 10. The third term: *peace*, describes the subjective feeling of the saved man at the time when glory and honor are conferred on him by the judge. It is the profound peace which is produced by deliverance from wrath, and the possession of unchangeable blessedness. The simple ἐργάζεσθαι, *to do*, is substituted for the compound κατεργάζεσθαι, *to effect* (ver. 9), which implies something ruder and more violent, as is suited to evil;[1] comp. the analogous though not identical difference between ποιεῖν and πράσσειν, John iii. 20, 21.—On the word *first*, comp. the remarks made i. 16, ii. 9.

Here again the apostle indicates the result finally reached, whether evil or good, without expressly mentioning the means by which it may be produced; on the one hand, the rejection of the gospel (ver. 9), as the supreme sin, at once the effect and the cause of evil-doing; on the other, its acceptance (ver. 10), as effect and cause of the determination to follow goodness and of its practice. But what is the foundation of such a judgment? One of God's perfections, which the Jew could not deny without setting himself in contradiction to the whole Old Testament, *the impartiality of God*, whose judgment descends on evil wherever it is found, *with* or *without law* vv. 11, 12).

---

[1] The only difference between the simple verb and the compound is that the former means *to work*, the latter, to *effect by working*. The original has *faire* and *parfaire*.—T. W. C.

Vv. 11, 12. *"For there is no respect of persons with God. For all those who have sinned without law shall also perish without law: and all those who have sinned in the law shall be judged by the law."*—The principle stated in ver. 11 is one of those most frequently asserted in the Old Testament; comp. Deut. x. 17; 1 Sam. xvi. 7; 2 Chron. xix. 7; Job xxxiv. 19. Accordingly, no Jew could dispute it.—The phrase πρόσωπον λαμβάνειν, literally: *to accept the countenance*, to pay regard to the external appearance, belongs exclusively to Hellenistic Greek (in the LXX.); it is a pure Hebraism; it forcibly expresses the opposite idea to that of *just judgment*, which takes account only of the *moral* worth of persons and acts. *With God* signifies, in that luminous sphere whence only just sentences emanate. But is not the fact of the law being given to some, and refused to others, incompatible with this divine impartiality? No, answers ver. 12; for if the Gentile perishes, he will not perish for not having *possessed* the law, for no judgment will cause him to be sifted by the Decalogue and the Mosaic ordinances; and if the Jew should sin, the law will not exempt him from punishment, for the code will be the very standard which judgment will apply to all his acts. Thus the want of the law no more destroys the one than its possession saves the other. The aorist ἥμαρτον, *sinned*, transports us to the point of time when the result of human life appears as a completed fact, the hour of judgment. The καί, *also* (" will *also* perish without law"), brings out the congruity between the mode of the sin and that of the perdition. In the second proposition, this *also* is not repeated, for it is a matter of course, that where there is a law men should be judged by it. The absence of the article in Greek before the word *law*, makes this word a categorical term, " A mode of living over which a law presides ;" as applied :- the Mosaic law.—Διὰ νόμου, *by law*, that is to say, by the application of a positive code (the Mosaic code). We must beware of regarding the difference between the two verbs: ἀπολοῦνται, *shall perish*, and κριθήσονται, *shall be judged*, as accidental (Meyer).[1] The very thing the apostle wishes is by this antithesis to emphasize the idea that the Jews *alone* shall be, strictly speaking, subjected to a judgment, a detailed inquiry, such as arises from applying the particular articles of a code. The Gentiles shall perish simply in consequence of their moral corruption; as, for example, ruin overtakes the soul of the vicious, the drunken, or the impure, under the deleterious action of their vice. The rigorous application of the principle of divine impartiality thus brings the apostle to this strange conclusion: the Jews, far from being exempted from judgment by their possession of the law, shall, on the contrary, be the *only people judged* (in the strict sense of the word). It was the antipodes of their claim, and we here see how the pitiless logic of the apostle brings things to such a point, that not only is the thesis of his adversary refuted, but its opposite is demonstrated to be the only true one.—Thus all who shall be found in the day of judgment *to have sinned* shall perish, each in his providential place, a result which establishes the divine impartiality.

It is evident that in the two propositions of this verse there is the idea understood: unless the amnesty offered by the gospel has been accepted, and has produced its proper fruits, the fruits of holiness (in which case the word ἥμαρτον, *sinned*, would cease to be the summing up and last word of the earthly life).—And why cannot the possession of the law preserve the Jews from condemnation, as they imagine? The explanation is given in ver. 13, and the demonstration in vv. 14–16.

Ver. 13. *"For not the hearers of the[2] law are just before God; but the doers*

---

[1] But no contrast can be intended here, for the former verb is used in 2 Cor. ii. 15, of those who are lost under the Gospel. It cannot therefore be explained as meaning merely a natural consequence.—T. W. C.

[2] Τοῦ before νόμου is found in T. R. with K L P; the others omit it.

of the[1] *law, they shall be justified.*" — Why *hearers* rather than possessors or readers? To describe the position of the Jews who *heard* the reading of the law in the synagogue every Sabbath, and who for the most part knew it only in this way (Luke iv. 16 et seq.; Acts xiii. 15, xv. 21). — *Before God*, says Paul; for before men it was otherwise, the Jews ascribing righteousness to one another on account of their common possession of the law. If such a claim were well founded, the impartiality of God would be destroyed, for the fact of knowing the law is a hereditary advantage, and not the fruit of moral action. The judicial force of the term δικαιωθῆναι, *to be justified*, in Paul's writings, comes out forcibly in this passage, since in the day of judgment no one is *made* righteous morally speaking, and can only be *recognized* and *declared* such. This declarative sense appears likewise in the use of the preposition παρά (*before* God), which necessarily refers to an act of God as *judge* (see on i. 17). The article τοῦ before νόμου, *law*, in the two propositions, is found only in the Byz. Mjj.; it ought to be expunged: the *hearers*, the *doers of a law*. No doubt it is the Mosaic law which is referred to, but as law, and not as Mosaic. Some think that this idea of justification by the fulfilment of the law is enunciated here in a purely hypothetical manner, and can never be realized (iii. 19, 20). Paul, it is said, is indicating the *abstract* standard of judgment, which, in consequence of man's sin, will never admit of rigorous application. But how in this case explain the future "*shall be* justified"? Comp. also the phrase of ver. 27: "uncircumcision when it *fulfils* the law," words which certainly refer to concrete cases, and the passage viii. 4, in which the apostle asserts that the δικαίωμα τοῦ νόμου, what the law declares righteous, is *fulfilled* in the believer's life. It will certainly, therefore, be required of us that we *be* righteous in the day of judgment if God is to *recognize* and *declare* us to be such; *imputed* righteousness is the beginning of the work of salvation, the means of entrance into the state of grace. But this initial justification, by restoring communion between God and man, should guide the latter to the *actual* possession of righteousness—that is to say, to the fulfilment of the law; otherwise, this first justification would not stand in the judgment (see on ver. 6). And hence it is in keeping with Paul's views, whatever may be said by an antinomian and unsound tendency, to distinguish two justifications, the one initial, founded exclusively on faith, the other final, founded on faith *and its fruits*.[2] Divine imputation beforehand, in order *to be* true, must necessarily *become* true—that is to say, be converted into the *recognition* of a real righteousness. But if the maxim of ver. 13 is the rule of the divine judgment, this rule threatens again to overturn the principle of divine impartiality; for how can the Gentiles fulfil the law which they do not possess? Vv. 14 and 15 contain the answer to this objection.

Vv. 14, 15. "*For when Gentiles, which have not the law, do*[3] *by nature the things which the law prescribes, these, having not the law, are their own law unto themselves: for they show thereby the work of the law written in their hearts, their conscience also bearing witness to it, and their thoughts accusing or else excusing them one with another.*" — There are four principal ways of connecting ver. 14 with what precedes.

1. Calvin goes back to ver. 12a: "The Gentiles *will perish justly*, though they have not the law (ver. 12); for they have a law in their hearts which they knowingly violate" (ver. 14). The explanations of Neander, de Wette, Hodge, etc. are to the same effect. But the number of important intermediate propositions and ideas intervening between this and ver. 12a renders it unnatural to connect the "*for*" of ver. 14 with this declaration.

---

[1] T. R., with E K L, reads του before νομου.
[2] A more accurate statement would be to say a faith shown to be genuine by its fruits.— T. W. C.
[3] T. R., with E K L P, reads ποιη; but ℵ A B read ποιωσιν, and D G ποιουσιν.

Besides, was it necessary to prove to the Jews the righteousness of the punishment which would be inflicted on the Gentiles !

2. Meyer connects the *for* with the immediately preceding proposition, 13*b*: "It is only doers of the law who can be justified, for this rule can be applied even to the Gentiles, since they too have a law engraved on their hearts." The connection is simple and logical. But can the apostle really mean to say that a Gentile can obtain justification by observing the law of nature? That is impossible. We should require in that case to revert to the purely abstract explanation of ver. 13*b*, to regard it as a hypothetical maxim, and consequently to take vv. 14, 15 as an abstract proof of an impracticable maxim. These are too many abstractions.

3. Tholuck, Lange, Schaff likewise join the *for* with 13*b*; but they hold at the same time that this *for* will be veritably realized: "The doers of the law shall be justified, for God will graciously take account of the *relative* observance of the law rendered by the Gentiles" (here might be compared Matt. xxv. 40, x. 41, 42); so Tholuck. Or: "Those Gentiles, partial doers of the law, will certainly come one day to the faith of the gospel, by which they will be fully justified;" so Lange, Schaff. But these are expedients; for there is nothing in the text to countenance such ideas. In ver. 15, Paul takes pains to prove that the Gentiles *have* the law, but not that they *observe it;* and about faith in the gospel there is not a word. This could not possibly be the case if the thought were an essential link in the argument.

4. The real connection seems to me to have been explained by Philippi. The *for* refers to the general idea of ver. 13: "It is not having heard the law, as the Jews think, but having observed it, which will justify; for if the hearing of it were enough, the Gentiles also could claim this advantage, since positive features in their moral life testified to the existence of a law engraved on their hearts, and the very definite application of it which they are able to make." This connection leaves nothing to be desired; and Meyer's objection, that it is necessary in this case to pass over 13*b* in order to connect the *for* with 13*a*, is false; for the idea of 13*b* is purely restrictive: "The doers of the law shall *alone* be justified," while the real affirmation is that of 13*a*: "Those who had been only hearers shall not be justified." It is on this essential idea of ver. 13 that the *for* of ver. 14 bears.—Ὅταν, *when it happens that.* These are sporadic cases, happy eventualities.—The word ἔθνη, *Gentiles*, has no article: "people belonging to the category of the Gentiles."—The logical relation included in the subjective negative μή is that which we should express by: "*without having* the law," or: "*though* they have it not."—Τὰ τοῦ νόμου, literally: *the things which are of the law*, agreeable to its prescriptions. They do not observe the precept as such, for they have it not; but they fulfil its contents; for example, Neoptolemus in Philoctetes, when he refuses to save Greece at the expense of a lie; or Antigone, when she does not hesitate to violate the temporary law of the city to fulfil the eternal law of fraternal love; or Socrates, when he rejects the opportunity of saving his life by escaping from prison, in order to remain subject to the magistrates. Sophocles himself speaks of these *eternal laws* (οἱ ἀεὶ νόμοι), and contrasts this internal and divine legislation with the ever-changing laws of man.—Φύσει, *by nature*, spontaneously, by an innate moral instinct. This dative cannot be joined with the preceding participle (ἔχοντα); it qualifies the verb ποιῇ, *do;* the whole force of the thought is in this idea: do instinctively what the Jew does in obedience to precepts. The readings ποιῶσιν and ποιοῦσιν may be corrections of ποιῇ with the view of conforming the verb to the following pronoun οὗτοι; the Byz. reading ποιῇ may also, however, be a correction to make the verb agree with the rule of neuter plurals. In this case the plural of the verb is preferable, since Paul is speaking not of the Gentiles *en masse*, but of certain individuals among them. Hence also the

following οὗτοι, *these Gentiles*. This pronoun includes and repeats all the qualifications which have just been mentioned in the first part of the verse; comp. the οὗτος, John i. 2.—The logical relation of the participle μὴ ἔχοντες, "*not having law*," and of the verb εἰσίν, "*are law*," should be expressed by *for;* not having law, they therefore serve as a law to themselves. The negative μή, placed above *before* the participle and the object (τὸν νόμον), is here placed *between* the two. This separation is intended to throw the object into relief: "*This law* (τὸν νόμον), for the very reason that they have it not (μὴ ἔχοντες), they prove that they have it in another way." This delicate form of style shows with what painstaking care Paul composed. But so fine a shade can hardly be felt except in the original language. The phrase: *to be a law to oneself*, is explained in ver. 15.

The descriptive pronoun οἵτινες, "as people who," is meant to introduce this explanation; it is in consequence of what is about to follow that Paul can affirm what he has just said of them, ver. 14. The relation of the verb ἐνδείκνυνται, *show*, and its object ἔργον, *the work* of the law, may be thus paraphrased: "show the work of the law (*as being*) written;" which would amount to: prove that it is written. But it is not even necessary to assume an ellipsis (ὡς ὄν). What the Gentile shows in such cases is the law itself written (as to its contents) within his heart. Paul calls these contents *the work of the law*, because all the law commanded was meant to become *work;* and he qualifies νόμον by the article (*the* law), because he wishes to establish the identity of the Gentile's moral instinct with the contents of the *Mosaic* law strictly so called. But this phrase: *the work of the law*, does not merely designate, like that of ver. 14, τὰ τοῦ νόμου (*the things agreeable to the law*), certain isolated acts. It embraces the whole contents of the law; for ver. 15 does not refer to the accidental fulfilment of some good actions; it denotes the totality of the moral law written in the heart. The figure of a *written law* is evidently borrowed from the Sinaitic law graven on the tables of stone. The *heart* is always in Scripture the source of the instinctive feelings from which those impulses go forth which govern the exercise of the understanding and will. It is in this form of lofty inspiration that the law of nature makes its appearance in man. The plural: *their heart*, makes each individual the seat of this sublime legislation. The last propositions of the verse have embarrassed commentators not a little. They have not sufficiently taken account of the starting-point of this whole argument. St. Paul, according to the connection of ver. 14 with ver. 13, does not wish merely to prove that the Gentile *possesses* the law; he means to demonstrate that he *hears* it, just as the Jew heard it at Sinai, or still hears it every Sabbath in the synagogue (ἀκροατής, *hearer* of the law, ver. 13*a*). And to this idea the appendix refers which closes ver. 15. That the Gentile *has* the law (is a law to himself), is already demonstrated. But does he hear this law distinctly? Does he give account of it to himself? If it were not so, he would certainly remain inferior to the Jew, who brings so much sagacity to bear on the discussion of the sense and various applications of the legal statute. But no; the Gentile is quite as clever as the Jew in this respect. He also discusses the data of the moral instinct which serves as his guide. His conscience joins its approving testimony afterhand to that of the moral instinct which has dictated a good action; pleaders make themselves heard within, for and against, before this tribunal of conscience, and these discussions are worth all the subtleties of Rabbinical casuistry.—Συνείδησις, *the conscience* (from συνειδέναι, to know with or within oneself). This word, frequently used in the New Testament, denotes the understanding (the νοῦς, for it is a *knowing*, εἰδέναι, which is in question), applied to the distinction of good and evil, as reason (the διάνοια) is the same νοῦς applied to the discernment of truth and falsehood. It is precisely because this word denotes an act of knowledge that it describes a new fact different from that of the moral instinct described above.

What natural impulse dictated without reflection, conscience, studying it afterward, recognizes as a good thing. Thus is explained the σύν, *with*, in the compound verb συμμαρτυρεῖν, *to bear witness with another*. Conscience joins its testimony to that of the heart which dictated the virtuous action by commending it, and proves thereby, as a *second* witness, the existence of the moral law in the Gentile. Volkmar: "Their conscience bears testimony besides the moral act itself which already demonstrated the presence of the divine law." Most really, therefore, the Gentile has a law—law not only published and *written*, but *heard* and understood. It seems to me that in the way in which the apostle expresses this assent of the conscience to the law implanted within, it is impossible not to see an allusion to the *amen* uttered aloud by the people after hearing the law of Sinai, and which was repeated in every meeting of the synagogue after the reading of the law.—But there is not only *hearing*, there is even *judging*. The Rabbins debated in opposite senses every kind of acts, real or imaginary. The apostle follows up the comparison to the end. The soul of the Gentile is also an arena of discussions. The λογισμοί denote the *judgments* of a moral nature which are passed by the Gentiles on their own acts, either (as is most usually the case) acknowledging them guilty (κατηγορεῖν, *accusing*), or *also* sometimes (such is the meaning of ἢ καί; comp. ver. 14: *when it happens that* . . .) pronouncing them innocent. Most commonly the voice within says: That was bad! Sometimes also this voice becomes that of defence, and says: No, it was good! Thus, before this inner code, the different thoughts accuse or justify, make replies and rejoinders, exactly as advocates before a seat of judgment handle the text of the law. And all this forensic debating proves to a demonstration not only that the code is there, but that it is read and understood, since its application is thus discussed.—The μεταξὺ ἀλλήλων, *between them* (*among themselves*). Some, like Meyer, join this pronoun with αὐτῶν, *the Gentiles;* he would refer it to the debates carried on *between Gentiles and Gentiles* as to the moral worth of an action. But it is grammatically more natural, and suits the context better, to connect the pronoun *between themselves* with λογισμῶν, *judgments*. For this internal scene of discussion proves still more clearly than a debate of man with man the fact of the law *written in the heart*. Holsten proposes to understand the participle συμμαρτυρούντων (borrowed from συμμαρτυρούσης) with λογισμῶν: "their conscience bearing witness, and the judgments which they pass on one another's acts in their mutual relations also bearing witness." This construction is very forced, and it seems plain to us that the two participles *accusing or else excusing* refer to the *thoughts*, just as the participle *bearing witness* referred to *their conscience*.

How can one help admiring here, on the one hand, the subtle analysis whereby the apostle discloses in the Gentile heart a real judgment-hall where witnesses are heard for and against, then the sentence of the judge; and, on the other hand, that largeness of heart with which, after drawing so revolting a picture of the moral deformities of Gentile life (chap. i.), he brings into view in as striking a way the indestructible moral elements, the evidences of which are sometimes irresistibly presented even by this so deeply sunken life?

Ver. 16. "*In the day when*[1] *God shall judge the hidden things of men by Jesus Christ according to my gospel.*"—In this final proposition there is expressed and summed up the idea of the whole preceding passage (from ver. 6), that of the *final judgment*. But what is the grammatical and logical connection of this dependent proposition? It would seem natural to connect it with what immediately precedes (ver. 15), as Calvin does: "Their inward thoughts condemn or approve them in the day when" . . . for: "till the day when" . . . But this sense would have required ἕως τῆς

---

[1] T. R., with almost all the MSS., reads εν ημερα οτε ; B: εν η ημερα ; A : εν ημερα η.

ἡμέρας. Tholuck and Philippi employ another expedient ; they understand : "and that *especially* in the day when" . . . ; or : "and that *more completely still* in the day when" . . . Others : "*as will be seen clearly* in the day when" . . . But if Paul had meant to say all that, he would have said it. Hofmann and Lange, also connecting this proposition with ver. 15 (Hofmann especially with ἐνδείκνυνται, *manifest*), regard the judgment of ver. 16 as being only the internal and purely moral judgment which is produced in the human conscience every time the gospel is preached to man. They read κρίνει, *judges*, and not κρινεῖ, *will judge*. The phrase : *in the day when*, would therefore denote, not the last judgment, but every day that a man hears the gospel for the first time. There is a context in which this explanation would be possible ; but here, where the dominant idea from ver. 6 has been the final judgment, it is inadmissible. Besides, the phrase : *by Jesus Christ*, is not exactly suitable to any but the last judgment ; comp. the words, Acts x. 42, xvii. 31 ; Matt. xxv. 31 et seq. ; and especially the very similar phrases in 1 Cor. iv. 5. Moreover, ver. 29 can leave no doubt as to the apostle's meaning. The only tolerable explanation, if it were wished to connect ver. 16 with ver. 15, would be to take the verbs of ver. 15 as expressing the permanent present of the idea : "The manifestation of the presence of the law, written within their hearts, *takes place*, for : *will certainly take place*, in the day when" . . . ; but this meaning of the verbs in the present in ver. 15 could not be guessed till after reading ver. 16. The time of the manifestation would have required to be indicated immediately to prevent a misunderstanding. The only natural connection of the words : in the day when, is to join them to the end of ver. 13 : "The doers of the law shall be justified . . . *in the day when*" . . . No doubt vv. 14, 15 thus become a sort of parenthesis. But, notwithstanding, Paul has not deviated for a moment from his principal thought. These two verses contained an explanatory remark, such as we nowadays would put in a note ; it was intended to show that the Gentiles also would be entitled to believe themselves justified, if all that was necessary for this end were to possess and hear a law without doing it. This false idea set aside, Paul resumes the thread of his discourse at ver. 16. To explain this verse, there is clearly no need of the two expedients proposed, the one by Ewald, to join it with ver. 4, the other by Laurent, to regard it as an interpolation.— The phrase : *hidden things*, is to be explained only by the understood contrast to external works, legal or ceremonial, in which the Jews put their confidence. None of those fine externals of piety or morality will deceive the eye of God in that day of truth. He will demand holiness of heart ; comp. the expression, ver. 29 ; ὁ ἐν τῷ κρυπτῷ Ἰουδαῖος, *the Jew who is one inwardly*, and : *the circumcision of the heart ;* comp. also, in the Sermon on the Mount, Matt. v. 20–48, and vi. 1–18. This idea was indispensable to complete what had been said of judgment *according to deeds*.—The word *men* sets the whole body of the judged face to face with the Judge, and reminds the Jews that they also will be there, and will form no exception.—At the first glance the phrase : *according to my gospel*, is surprising, for the expectation of the final judgment by Jesus Christ belongs to the apostolic teaching in general, and not to *Paul's gospel* in particular. Nevertheless, it is this apostle who, in consequence of his personal experience, and of the revelation which had been made to him, has brought out most powerfully the contrast between the ἔργα νόμου, legal and purely external *works*, wanting the truly moral principle of love and *good* works, the fruits of faith working by love (Eph. ii. 9, 10 ; Gal. v. 6). This antithesis was one of the foundations of Paul's preaching.—The last words : *by Jesus Christ*, recall all the sayings in which Jesus announced His advent as judge. If it is really He who is to preside in the great act of final judgment, it is plain that, being such as He has made Himself known to us, He will not be satisfied with a parade of external righteousness, and that He will demand a holiness like that which He realized Himself, which, taking its origin in consecration of heart, extends over the whole life.

The *second part* of the chapter, vv. 17–29, contains *the application* of the principles laid down in the first. After expressing himself in a general and more or less abstract way, Paul addresses himself directly to the person whom he had in view from ver. 1, and finally designates him by name. Yet he still proceeds with the utmost caution ; for he knows that he is giving a shock to inveterate prejudices, prejudices which he long shared himself. The way is slowly paved for the conclusion which he wishes to reach ; hence the length of the following sentence, which contains as it were the preamble of the judgment to be pronounced.

Vv. 17–20. "*Now if*[1] *thou who art called a Jew, and restest in the law, and makest thy boast of God, and knowest His will, and canst discern the things that differ, being instructed out of the law ; and esteemest thyself to be the guide of the blind, the light of them which are in darkness, the instructor of the foolish, the teacher of babes, because thou hast the formula of knowledge and of the truth in the law*". . . .—Instead of ἰδέ, behold, which the T. R. reads, with a single Mj., we must certainly read εἰ δέ, *now if ;* this is the natural form of transition from principles to their application ; the other reading seems to be a consequence of *itacism* (pronouncing ει as ι).—Where are we to find the principal clause to which this *now if* is subordinate ? Some, Winer for example, think that the same construction continues as far as the beginning of ver. 21, where it is abandoned on account of the length of the sentence, and where an entirely new proposition begins. But we must at least meet again somewhere in the sequel with the idea which was in the apostle's mind when he began with the words *now if*. Meyer regards ver. 21 itself as the principal clause ; he understands the οὖν, *therefore*, as a particle of recapitulation. But, in an argument like this (*now if*, ver. 17), this meaning of *therefore* is unnatural. It is better than, with Hofmann, to hold that the series of propositions dependent on *now if* is prolonged to the end of ver. 24, where the principal proposition resulting from all these considerations is understood as a self-evident consequence : what good *in this case* (that of such *sins*, vv. 21–24) will accrue to thee from *all those advantages* (vv. 17–20) ? It is to this understood conclusion, which we would replace with lacuna-points (. . .), that the *for* of ver. 25 very naturally refers. By this figure of rhetoric (aposiopesis) the apostle dispenses with expressing a conclusion himself, which must spring spontaneously from the conscience of every reader.

The propositions dependent on "*now if*," taken together, embrace two series of four verses each ; the one, that from vv. 17–20, is intended to enumerate all the *advantages* of which the Jew boasts ; the other, from vv. 21–24, contrasts the *iniquities* of his conduct with those advantages.

The advantages are distributed into three categories. 1. *The gifts* of God, ver. 17. 2. The superior *capabilities* which these gifts confer on the Jew, ver. 18. 3. *The part* which he somewhat pretentiously thinks himself thereby called to play toward other nations, vv. 19, 20. There is something slightly ironical in this accumulation of titles on which the Jew bases the satisfaction which he feels as he surveys himself.

Ver. 17. The name *Jew*, Ἰουδαῖος, is probably not used without allusion to its etymological meaning : *Jehoudah, the praised one*. The preposition ἐπί, which enters into the composition of the verb, converts this name into a real *title*. But Israel possesses more than a glorious name ; it has in its hands a real *gift : the law*. Here is a manifest sign of the divine favor on which it may consequently *rest*. Finally, this token of special favor makes God *its* God, to the exclusion of all other nations. It has therefore whereof *to glory* in God. To the gradation of the three substantives : *Jew*,

---

[1] T. R. reads, with L : ιδε (*behold*) ; the other authorities: ει δε (*now if*).

law, God, that of the three verbs perfectly corresponds : *to call oneself, to rest, to glory.*

Hence there result (ver. 18) two capabilities which distinguished the Jew from every other man. He *knows* God's will, and so succeeds in *discerning* what to others is confused. One is always entitled to be proud of *knowing ;* but when that knowing is of *the will*, that is to say, the absolute and perfect will which ordains all, and judges of all sovereignly, such a knowledge is an incomparable advantage. By this knowledge of the divine will the Jew can *discern* and *appreciate* (δοκιμάζειν) the most delicate shades of the moral life—Τὰ διαφέροντα might signify the things that are *better (meliora probare)*, from the meaning of *surpass*, which is often that of the verb διαφέρειν. But here it is better to translate : the things that *differ* (from the sense of *differing*, which is also that of διαφέρειν) ; for the apostle seems to be alluding to those discussions of legal casuistry in which the Jewish schools excelled, as when the two eminent doctors Hillel and Schammai gravely debated the question, whether it was lawful to eat an egg laid by a hen on the Sabbath day.—The last words of the verse : *instructed out of the law*, indicate the source of that higher faculty of appreciation. The term κατηχούμενος, from κατηχεῖσθαι, *to be penetrated by a sound*, makes each Jew law personified.

From this knowledge and faculty of appreciation flows the part which the Jew claims in regard to other men, and which is described in vv. 19, 20 with a slight touch of ridicule. The first four terms set forth the moral treatment to which the Jew, as the born physician of mankind, subjects his patients, the Gentiles, to their complete cure. The term πέποιθας, *thou art confident*, describes his pretentious assurance. And first, he takes the poor Gentile by the hand as one does *a blind man*, offering to *guide* him ; then he opens his eyes, dissipating his *darkness* by the *light* of revelation ; then he *rears* him, as one would bring up a being yet *without reason ;* finally, when through all this care he has come to the stage of the *little child*, νήπιος *(who cannot speak ;* this was the term used by the Jews to designate proselytes ; see Tholuck), he initiates him into the full knowledge of the truth, by becoming his *teacher.*—The end of the verse serves to explain the reason of this ministry to the Gentile world which the Jew exercises. He possesses in the law the precise *sketch* (μόρφωσις), the exact outline, the rigorous formula of the *knowledge* of things which men should have (the idea which every one should form of them), and of *the truth*, that is to say, the moral reality or substance of goodness. *Knowledge* is the subjective possession of *truth* in itself. The Jew possesses in the law not only the truth itself, but its exact formula besides, by means of which he can convey this truth to others. We need not then, with Oltramare, make these last words an appendix, intended to disparage the teaching of the Jew : "though thou hast but the shadow of knowledge." The drift of the passage demands the opposite sense : "as possessing the truth in its precise formula."

Vv. 21-24. "*And if, then, thou who teachest another, teachest not thyself, if preaching a man should not steal, thou stealest, if, while saying a man should not commit adultery, thou committest adultery, if, abhorring idols, thou robbest temples, if thou that makest thy boast of the law, dishonorest God through breaking the law ; for the name of God is blasphemed among the Gentiles because of you, as it is written*" . . .—On the one side, then, the Jews are proud of the possession of their law ; but, on the other, how do they put it in practice ? it is to set forth this contradiction that the second series of propositions is devoted, vv. 21-24. The οὖν, *then*, ironically contrasts the *real* practical *fruit* produced in the Jews by their knowledge of the law, and that which such an advantage should have produced. The term *teach* includes all the honorable functions toward the rest of the world which the Jew has just been arrogating. Ὁ διδάσκων : Thou, the so-great teacher !— The apostle chooses two examples in the second table of the law, theft and adultery : and two in the first, sacrilege and dishonor done to God. Theft comprehends all the injustices and deceptions which the Jews allowed themselves in commercial affairs. Adultery is a crime which the Talmud brings home to the three most illustrious Rabbins, Akiba, Mehir, and Eleazar. Sensuality is one of the prominent features of the Semitic character. The pillage of sacred objects cannot refer to anything connected with the worship celebrated at Jerusalem; such, for example, as refusal to pay the temple tribute, or the offering of maimed victims. The snbject of the proposition: *thou who abhorrest idols*, proves clearly that the apostle has in view the pillage of *idol* temples. The meaning is: "Thy horror of idolatry does not go the length of preventing thee from hailing as a good prize the precious objects which have been used in idolatrous worship, when thou canst make them thine own." The Jews probably did not pillage the Gentile temples themselves; but they filled the place of receivers; comp. besides, Acts xix. 37. The dishonor done to God arises from their greed of gain, their deceits and hypocrisy, which were thoroughly known to the Gentile populations among whom they lived. Paul weaves the prophetic rebuke into the tissue of his own language, but by the *as it is written* he reminds his readers that he is borrowing it from the inspired Scriptures. His allusion is to Isa. lii. 5 (which resembles our verse more in the letter than the sense), and to Ezek. xxxvi. 18–24 (which resembles it more in the sense than in the letter).

We have regarded the whole passage, vv. 17–24, as dependent on the conjunction εἰ δέ, *now if*, ver. 17: "Now if thou callest thyself . . . (vv. 17–20); and if teaching so and so, thou . . . (vv. 21–24)." Thereafter, the principal clause is easily expressed as a proposition to be understood between vv. 24, 25: "What advantage will this law be to thee, of which thou makest thy boast before others, and which thou dost violate thyself with such effrontery?" For, in fine, according to the principle laid down, ver. 13, it is not those who *know* the law, but those who *do* it, who shall be pronounced righteous by the judgment of God. The idea understood, which we have just expressed, is that to which the *for* of ver. 25 refers: "For it is wholly in vain for thee, if thou art disobedient, to reckon on circumcision to exculpate thee. A disobedient Jew is no better before God than a Gentile, and an obedient Gentile becomes in God's sight a true Jew." Such is the meaning of the following passage, vv. 25–29.

Vv. 25–27. "*For circumcision verily profiteth, if thou keep the law: but if thou be a breaker of the law, thy circumcision is made uncircumcision. If then the uncircumcised keep the ordinances of the law, shall not his uncircumcision be counted for circumcision? And shall not he who, though uncircumcised by nature, fulfils the law, judge thee, who in full possession of the letter and circumcision, dost transgress the law?*"—Paul knocks from under the Jew the support which he thought he had in his theocratic position, with its sign circumcision. We have seen it; the adage of the rabbins was: "All the circumcised have part in the world to come," as if it were really enough to be a Jew to be assured of salvation. Now, circumcision had been given to Israel as a consecration to circumcision *of heart*, an engagement to holiness, and not as a shelter from judgment in favor of disobedience and pollution. Taken then in this sense, and according to the mind of God, it had its use; but employed in the Rabbinical sense, it formed only an external wall of separation requiring to be overturned. The prophets never ceased to work in this direction; comp. Isa. i. 10–15 and lxvi. 1 et seq.—Γέγονε, strictly: "*has become, and remains* henceforth uncircumcision," in the eyes of God the righteous judge.

Vv. 26, 27 describe the opposite case: the transformation of the obedient Gentile into a Jew, according to the judgment of God. This transformation, being the logical consequence of the preceding, is connected by οὖν, *then*, with ver. 25.—The apostle is not now speaking, as in vv. 14, 15, of a simple sporadic observance of legal duties. The phrase is more solemn:

keeping the just ordinances of the law (δικαίωμα, all that the law declares righteous). In viii. 4, the apostle uses a similar expression to denote the observance of the law by the Christian filled with the Holy Spirit. How can he here ascribe such an obedience to a Gentile ?[1] Philippi thinks he has in view those many proselytes whom Judaism was making at this time among the Gentiles. Meyer and others seek to reduce the meaning of the phrase to that of ver. 14. This second explanation is impossible, as we have just seen ; and that of Philippi falls to the ground before the preceding expressions of the apostle, which certainly contain more than can be expected of a proselyte (*keep, fulfil* the law, φυλάσσειν, τελεῖν τὸν νόμον, vv. 26, 27). The comparison of viii. 4 shows the apostle's meaning. He refers to those many Gentiles converted to the gospel who, all uncircumcised as they are, nevertheless fulfil the law in virtue of the spirit of Christ, and thus become the *true* Israel, *the Israel of God*, Gal. vi. 16. Paul expresses himself in abstract terms, because here he has to do only with the principle, and not with the means by which it is realized ; compare what we have said on vv. 7, 10. The future λογισθήσεται, *will be counted*, transports us to the hour of judgment, when God, in order to *declare* a man righteous, will demand that he *be* so in reality.

We might begin ver. 27 as an affirmative proposition : *and so He will judge thee.* But perhaps it is more in keeping with the lively tone of the piece to continue in ver. 27 the interrogation of ver. 26, as we have done in our translation : "And so (in virtue of this imputation) will not He judge thee" . . . ? The thought is analogous to Luke xi. 31, 32, and Matt. xii. 41, 42, though the case is different. For there it is Gentiles who condemn the Jews by the example of their repentance and their love of truth ; here, it is the case of Christians of Gentile origin condemning the Jews by their fulfilment of the law.—Ostervald and Oltramare substitute for *judge*, used by the apostle, the term *condemn*. This is wrong ; for the claim of the Jews is to escape, not only from condemnation, but from judgment ; and it is bitter for them to hear, not only that they shall be judged *like* the Gentiles, but that they shall be judged *by* them.—Τὸν νόμον τελεῖν, to *fulfil the law*, is a phrase expressing real and persevering fulfilment. The love which the gospel puts into the believer's heart is in fact the *fulfilment of the law*, Rom. xiii. 10.—The preposition διά, strictly (*across the length of*) : *through*, here denotes, as it often does, the *state*, the circumstances in which an act is accomplished ; comp. 2 Cor. ii. 4 ; 1 Tim. ii. 15 ; Heb. ii. 15. So : "in full possession of the letter and circumcision."

This double transformation of the disobedient Jew into a Gentile, and of the obedient Gentile into a Jew, in the judgment of God, is explained and justified by vv. 28 and 29.

Vv. 28, 29. "*For he is not a Jew, which is one outwardly, neither is that circumcision, which is outward in the flesh : but he is a Jew, which is one inwardly, and circumcision is of the heart, by the Spirit, and not by the letter ; its praise is not of men, but of God.*"—The double principle laid down here by Paul was the sum of prophetic theology ; comp. Lev. xxvi. 41 ; Deut. x. 16 ; Jer. iv. 14 ; Ezek. xliv. 9. And hence it is that the apostle can make it the basis of his argument. Ver. 28 justifies the degradation of the Jew to the state of a Gentile, proclaimed in ver. 25 ; and ver. 29 the elevation of the Gentile to the rank of a Jew, proclaimed in vv. 26 and 27. The two words which justify this double transformation are ἐν τῷ κρυπτῷ, *in secret, inwardly*, and καρδίας, ἐν πνεύματι, *of the heart, by the spirit*. For if there is a principle to be derived from the whole of the Old Testament, it is that God has regard *to the heart* (1 Sam. xvi. 7). Paul himself referred in ver. 16 to the fact that in the day of judgment by Jesus Christ, it would

---

[1] But the Greek expression being participial (ἡ τελοῦσα) has a conditional force, which is well given in the English Bible, "if it fulfil."—T. W. C.

be the *hidden things* of men which would form the essential ground of His sentence. There is only one way of explaining naturally the grammatical construction of these two verses. In ver. 28, we must borrow the two subjects Ἰουδαῖος and περιτομή from the predicate ; and in ver. 29, the two predicates Ἰουδαῖός (ἐστι) and περιτομή (ἐστι) from the subject.—The complement καρδίας, *of the heart*, is the *gen. object.*: the circumcision which cleanses the heart ; the clause ἐν πνεύματι, *in spirit*, denotes the means : by the Holy Spirit.[1] The Spirit is the superior force which, by transforming the feelings of the heart, produces true inward purification. *The letter*, on the contrary, is an outward rule which does not change either the heart or the will ; comp. vii. 6. Meyer thinks we should take οὗ, *of which*, as a neuter, referring to *Judaism* in general. But to what purpose would it be to say that the praise of Judaism comes not from men, but from God ? That was sufficiently obvious of itself, since it was God who had established it, and all the nations detested it ; we must therefore connect this pronoun with *the Jew* which precedes, and even with the feminine term *circumcision*, which is used throughout this whole piece for *the person circumcised*.—The word *praise* is again an allusion to the etymological meaning of the word Ἰουδαῖος, *Jew* (see on ver. 17) ; comp. Gen. xlix. 8. God, who reads the heart, is alone able to allot with certainty the title *Jew* in the true sense of the word—that is to say, *one praised*. The idea of praise coming from God is opposed to all that Jewish vainglory which is detailed vv. 17–20.—What a remarkable parallelism is there between this whole passage and the declaration of Jesus, Matt. viii. 11, 12 : " Many shall come from the east and from the west, and shall sit down in the kingdom of heaven," etc. . . . And yet there is nothing to indicate imitation on Paul's part. The same truth creates an original form for itself in the two cases.

Yet the apostle anticipates an objection to the truth which he has just developed. If the sinful Jew finds himself in the same situation in regard to the wrath of God as the sinful Gentile, what remains of the prerogative which divine election seemed to assure to him ? Before going further, and drawing the general conclusion following from the two preceding passages, i. 18–32 and ii. 1–29, Paul feels the need of obviating this objection ; and such is the aim of the following passage.

SIXTH PASSAGE (3:1-8)

Jewish Prerogative does not imply Exemption from Judgment

The order of thought in this piece, one of the most difficult, perhaps, in the Epistle, is as follows :

1. If the Jew is judged absolutely, as the Gentiles are, what advantage has he over them ? Answer : The possession of the divine oracles (vv. 1, 2).

2. But if this possession has not realized the end which it was intended to serve (the faith of Israel in the Messiah), is not the faithfulness of God toward this people annulled ? Answer : By no means ; it will rather be glorified thereby (vv. 3, 4).

3. But if God makes use of human sin to glorify Himself, how can He yet make sinners the objects of His wrath ? Answer : If the advantage which God derives from the sin of man prevented Him from punishing sinners, the final judgment would become impossible (vv. 5–8).

It is obvious that the reasoning is consecutive, even very compact, and that there is no need of expressly introducing an opponent, as many commentators have done. Paul does not here make use of the formula : *But*

---

[1] It is more natural, with Shedd, to take the phrase as denoting the inner man in opposition to the outer man, expressed by ἐν σαρκί in the previous verse.—T. W. C.

some one will say. The objections arise of themselves from the affirmations, and Paul puts them in a manner to his own account.

Vv. 1, 2. "*What then is the advantage of the Jew? or what is the profit of circumcision? Much every way: foremost,*[1] *in that unto them were committed the oracles of God.*"—It was a thing generally granted that the elect people must have an advantage over the Gentiles ; hence the article τό, *the*, before the word *advantage*. The Greek term περισσόν literally denotes what the Jews have *more than others*. If they are judged in the same category as these, as the apostle in chap. ii., and particularly in vv. 25–29, had just shown, what have they then *more* than they ? The οὖν, *then*, precisely expresses this relation. One might infer from what precedes that every advantage of the Jew was denied.—The second question bears on the material symbol of Israel's election : circumcision. " Will the people whom God has *elected* and marked with the *seal* of this election be treated exactly like the rest of the world ?" This objection is of the same nature as that which would be made in our day by a nominal Christian, if, when put face to face with God's sentence, he were to ask what advantage there accrues to him from his creed and baptism, if they are not to save him from condemnation ?

Ver. 2. Though the advantage of the Jew does not consist in exemption from judgment, he has an advantage, nevertheless, and it is very great.— The adjective πολύ, which we have translated by *much*, properly signifies *numerous*. As neuter, it is connected with the subject of the first proposition of ver. 1 : *the advantage ;* the second question was in reality only an appendix calculated to strengthen the first.—By adding *every way*, Paul means that the advantage is not only considerable, but very varied, " extending to all the relations of life" (Morison).—Of these numerous and varied advantages he quotes only one, which seems to him, if one may so speak, central. Commentators like Tholuck, Philippi, Meyer, suppose that when the apostle wrote the word πρῶτον, *first*, he purposed to enumerate all the other advantages, but that he was diverted from fully expressing his thought. To exemplify this style there are quoted, besides i. 8 et seq., which we have had already before us, 1 Cor. vi. 12, 13, and xi. 18 et seq. But the apostle has too logical a mind, and his writings bear the mark of too earnest elaboration, to allow us to admit such breaches of continuity in their texture. In the view of a sound exegesis, the passages quoted prove absolutely nothing of the kind. Others think that we may here give to *first* the meaning of *chiefly ;* but the Greek has words for this idea. The preceding words : *every way*, suggest the translation ; they signify : " I might mention many things under this head ; but I shall confine myself to one which is in the front rank." This form of expression, far from indicating that he purposes to mention others, shows, on the contrary, why he will not mention them. They all flow from that which he proceeds to indicate. Neither has the particle μέν (from μένειν, *to remain*) its ordinary counterpart (δέ) in the sequel. It therefore means : " Though this advantage were the only one, it nevertheless remains perfectly real." The γάρ, *for*, is omitted by several Mjj. of both families, and by the old Vss. If it were kept, the ὅτι which follows would require to take the meaning of *because*, which is unnatural.—It is better, therefore, to reject it, and to translate ὅτι by *in that*.—This advantage, which takes the lead of all the others, so that after it, it is useless to announce them also, is the dignity granted to the Jews of being the *depositaries* of the divine oracles. The subject of ἐπιστεύθησαν is οἱ Ἰουδαῖοι understood, according to a well-known Greek construction ; comp. 1 Cor. ix. 17. The meaning of the verb in the passive is strictly : " to be esteemed faithful, so that men will confide to

---

[1] B D E G Syr^sch It^aliq omit the γαρ, which the T. R., with the other documents, reads after μεν.

you a deposit."—The deposit here is *the divine oracles*. The term λόγιον, *oracle*, has a graver meaning than λόγος, *word*, of which it is not at all a diminutive (Philippi) ; for it comes from the adjective λόγιος, *eloquent*. It always denotes even in the classics, a *divine* saying ; so Acts vii. 38, the law of Moses ; Heb. v. 12, the gospel revelation ; 1 Pet. iv. 11, the immediate divine communications with which the church was then favored. In our passage, where the subject in question is the privilege granted to the Jews over the Gentiles, the word must be taken as referring to the whole Old Testament ; but it is nevertheless true that the apostle thinks specially of the *Messianic promises* (Volkmar).—If Paul had intended to set forth the beneficial religious and moral influence exercised by these divine revelations on the national, domestic, and individual life of the Israelites, it is evident that he would have had a multitude of things to say. But it is equally clear that he would have been thus diverted from the object of this discussion. And hence he confines himself to establishing the point from which all the rest flows. This is the first phase of the discussion.—But an objection immediately rises : Has not this advantage, the possession of the Messianic promises, been rendered void by Israel's unbelief ? Here begins the second phase.

Vv. 3, 4. " *For what shall we say ? If some did not believe, shall their unbelief make void the faithfulness of God? Let it not be: yea, let God be found true, and every man a liar ; as it*[1] *is written : That Thou mightest be justified in Thy sayings, and mightest overcome*[2] *when Thou comest into judgment.*"—Here again Paul is not introducing any opponent ; the objection which he states springs logically from the fact he has just affirmed.—It would be possible to put the point of interrogation after the word τινές, *some* : " For what are we to think, if some did not believe ?" But we think it preferable to put the point after γάρ, *for :* " *For what is the fact ?*" and to connect the proposition : " If some did not believe," with the following question (see the translation). Paul likes these short questions in the course of discussion : *for what ? but what ?* fitted as they are to rouse attention. If he here uses the particle *for* instead of *but*, it is because he wishes from the first to represent the objection as no longer subsisting, but already resolved.—What is the unbelief of the Jews which the apostle has here in view ? According to some, Philippi for example, it is their old unbelief in respect of the ancient revelation. But the aorist ἠπίστησαν, *did not believe*, refers to a particular historical fact rather than a permanent state of things, such as Jewish unbelief had been under the old covenant. Besides, the faithfulness of God toward Israel, when formerly unbelieving and disobedient, was a fact which could not be called in question, since God by sending them the Messiah had nevertheless fulfilled all His promises to them in a way so striking. Finally, the future *will it make void ?* does not suit this sense ; Paul would rather have said : *did it make void ?* The subject in question, therefore, is a positive fact, and one which has just come to pass, and it is in relation to the consequences of this fact that the question of God's faithfulness arises. What is this fact ? We find it, with the majority of commentators in Israel's rejection of Jesus, its Messiah ; and we might even add : in the persevering rejection of apostolic preaching. The hostile attitude of Israel in relation to the gospel was now a decided matter.—The pronoun τινές, *some*, may seem rather weak to denote the mass of the people who had rejected the Messiah ; but this pronoun denotes a part of the whole irrespectively of the proportion. In chap. xi. 17, the unbelieving Jews are called " *some* of the branches ;" in Heb. iii. 16, the whole people, Caleb and Joshua only excepted, are described by this same pronoun ; comp. 1 Cor. x. 7. The phrase of Plato is also cited :

---

[1] א B read καθαπερ instead of καθως.
[2] T. R., with B G K L, reads νικησης ; א A D E: νικησεις (the same variation is found in the LXX.).

τινὲς καὶ πολλοί γε. Morison rightly says : " Many are only some, when they are not the whole."—Questions introduced by a μή always imply an answer more or less negative; so it is in this case : "This unbelief will not, however, make void " . . . ? Answer understood : "Certainly not." Hence the *for* at the beginning of the verse, which referred to this foreseen negative answer.—The verb καταργεῖν, which we have translated by *make void*, signifies literally : *to deprive of action*, or *efficacy ;* and the phrase πίστις τοῦ θεοῦ, in contrast to ἀπιστία, *unbelief*, can only designate the *faithfulness* of God Himself, in a manner His good faith. This perfection consists in the harmony between God's words and deeds, or between His past acts and His future conduct; it is his adherence to order in the line of conduct followed by Him. The question thus signifies : " Can Jewish unbelief in regard to the Messiah invalidate God's faithfulness to His people ?" The question might be asked in this sense: "If the Jews have not taken advantage of the salvation which the Messiah brought to them, will it follow that God has not really granted them all He had promised ? Will any one be able to accuse Him of having failed in His promises ?" The sense may also be : "Will He not remain faithful to His word in the future, even though after such an act on their part He should reject them ?" For, in fine, His word does not contain promises only, but threatenings ; comp. 2 Tim. ii. 13 : "If we believe not, He abideth faithful " (by punishing unbelief, as He has said).—The first of these meanings does not agree naturally with the future καταργήσει, *will make void*, which points us not to the past, but to the future. The second might find some countenance in ver. 4, where the example of David's sin and punishment is referred to, as well as in the term *righteousness* (taken in the sense of *retributive* justice) and in the term *wrath*, ver. 5. Yet the very severe meaning which in this case must be given to the phrase *God's faithfulness*, would not be sufficiently indicated. We are led to another and more natural meaning : "From the fact that Israel has rejected the Messianic salvation, does it follow that God will not fulfil all his promises to them in the future ? By no means ; His faithfulness will find a means in the very unbelief of His people of magnifying itself." The apostle has before him the perspective, which he will follow to its termination in chap. xi., that of the final salvation of the Jews, after their partial and temporary rejection shall have been instrumental in the salvation of the Gentiles.

The negative answer to this question, as we have seen, was already anticipated by the interrogative μή. When expressing it (ver. 4), the apostle enhances the simple negative. He exclaims : " *Let that not be* (the faithfulness of God made void) !" And to this forcible negation he adds the counter affirmation : " May the contrary be what shall happen : truth, nothing but truth, on God's side ! All the lying, if there is any, on man's side !"—There is an antithesis between μὴ γένοιτο, *that be far removed* (the *chalilah* of the Hebrews), and the γινέσθω δέ, *but let this come to pass!* The imperative γινέσθω, *may be* or *it become*, is usually understood in the sense : "May God be *recognized* as true" . . . ! But the term γίνεσθαι, *to become*, refers more naturally to the fact in itself than to the recognition of it by man. The veracity of God *becomes*, is revealed more and more in history by the new effects it produces. But this growing realization of the true God runs parallel with another realization, that of human falsehood, which more and more displays man's perversity. *Falsehood* denotes in Scripture that inward bad faith wherewith the human heart resists known and understood moral good. The apostle seems to allude to the words of Ps. cxvi. 11 : "I said in my haste : All men are liars." Only what the Psalmist uttered with a feeling of bitterness, arising from painful personal experiences, Paul affirms with a feeling of composure and profound humiliation in view of the sin of his people. He says even *all men* and not only all

Israelites; all men rather than God. If the principle of falsehood is realized in history, let all that bears the name of man be found capable of falseness, rather than that a tittle of this pollution should attach to the divine character. For the idea of *faithfulness* (ver. 3) there is substituted that of *veracity*, as for the idea of *unbelief* that of *falsehood*. In both cases the second is wider than the first, and includes it.—The conflict between the promises of God and His veracity, raised by the present fact of Israel's unbelief, must issue in the glory of the divine faithfulness. This necessary result is expressed by the apostle by means of a saying of David, uttered on the occasion of one of his gravest infidelities, Ps. li. 6 : " *That according as it is written* . . ." Alarm has been taken at the *that;* it has been sought to make it a simple *so that* (Osterv., Oltram.), as if what was spoken of were an effect, not an end. The wish was to avoid making David say he had sinned *in order that* God might be glorified. It cannot really be supposed that David means to ascribe to God responsibility for his trespass in any degree whatever, and that in a passage where he expressly affirms that the purity of the divine character must appear with new brightness on occasion of it. Hengstenberg and after him Philippi, have recourse to the distinction between the sinful *will* of David, which belongs wholly to him, and the *form* in which his sin was outwardly realized, a form which falls under the direction of Providence. But this distinction, which the theologian can make, could not present itself to the mind of David at the time, and in the disposition in which he composed his psalm. To explain the *that*, we have simply to take into account the manner in which David expresses himself in the foregoing words. He had said not only : " I have sinned," but : " I have sinned *against Thee ;*" not only : " I have done the evil," but : " I have done that which *is displeasing in Thy sight*." It is with the two ideas *against Thee* and *what is displeasing in Thy sight*, which aggravate the confession : *I have sinned*, that the *that* is connected. David means : " I was clear as to what I was doing ; Thou hadst not left me ignorant that when sinning I was sinning against Thy person, which is outraged by such misdeeds, and that I was doing what Thou hatest—*that* if, in spite of this knowledge, I nevertheless did it, Thou mightest be pure in the matter, and that the guiltiness might belong to me only." This idea of the knowledge of the divine will possessed by David, is that which is anew forcibly expressed in ver. 6 : " Thou didst teach me wisdom in the hidden part." God had instructed and warned David *that* if he sinned, he sinned, he might be the only guilty one, and might not be able to accuse God. The *that* has therefore nearly the same meaning as the : " to the end they might be without excuse," i. 20. We thus recognize the analogy of situation between David and Israel, which leads the apostle to quote these words here. Israel, the depositary of the divine oracles, had been faithfully instructed and warned, *that* if later, in spite of these exceptional revelations, giving themselves up to the falsehood (voluntary blindness) of their own hearts, they came to miss recognizing the Messiah, they should not be able to accuse God for their rejection, but should be declared, to the honor of the divine holiness, the one party guilty of the catastrophe which might follow.—The words : " that Thou mayest be justified *in* or *by* Thy words," signify : " that Thou mayest be *acknowledged righteous*, both in respect of the warnings which Thou hast given, and in the sentences which Thou wilt pronounce (on David by the mouth of Nathan, on Israel by their rejection)." In the Hebrew, the second proposition refers exclusively to those sentences which God pronounces ; for it said : " and that Thou mayest be found pure *when Thou judgest*." But the LXX. have translated : " that Thou mayest be victor (gain Thy case) when Thou art judged," or : " when Thou hast a case at law." It is probably this last meaning to which the apostle adapts his words, giving the verb κρίνεσθαι the middle sense, which it has in so many passages ; for example, Matt. v. 40 ; 1 Cor. vi. 1, 6 : " that

Thou mayest gain Thy case if Thou hast one to plead." Paul has obviously in view the accusation against God's faithfulness which might be raised from the fact of the unbelief and rejection of the chosen people.

But this very thought, that the veracity of God will come forth magnified from Israel's unbelief, raises a new objection, the examination of which forms the third phase of this discussion.

Vv. 5, 6. *"But if our unrighteousness establish the righteousness of God, what shall we say? Is not God unrighteous when He inflicts wrath? I speak as a man. Let it not be: for then how shall God judge the world?"*—From the *that*, ver. 4, it seemed to follow that God wills the sin of man for His own glory. But in that case, has He the right to condemn an act from which He reaps advantage, and to be angry with him who commits it? This objection might be put in the mouth of a Jew, who, placing himself at Paul's view-point, and hearing him say that Israel's rejection of the Messiah will glorify God's faithfulness, and conduce to the accomplishment of His plans, judged God highly unjust for being angry with Israel on account of such conduct. *Our unbelief* would then signify the unbelief of us Jews. But the contrast which prevailed in ver. 4 was that between *God* and *every man*, and not between Jew and Gentile. It is therefore more natural to apply the term *our* unrighteousness to *human* unrighteousness in general, undoubtedly with special application to the Jewish unrighteousness which gives rise to the objection. It is from the depths of the human conscience that the apostle fetches his question. Is it righteous on God's part to judge an act which He turns to His own advantage? As Paul had previously substituted the idea of *truth* for that of (God's) *faithfulness*, he here substitutes *righteousness* for *truth*. This term in its most general sense denotes the perfection in virtue of which God cannot become guilty of any wrong toward any being whatever. Now this is what He seems to do to the sinner, when He at once condemns and makes use of him. It is from the word ὁ that Thou mayest be acknowledged *righteous*, ver. 4, that Paul derives the term *righteousness*, ver. 5.—Συνιστάναι, strictly: *to cause to stand together*, whence: *to confirm, to establish*. The question τί ἐροῦμεν, *what shall we say?* does not occur in any other letter of the apostle's; but it is frequent in this (iv. 1, vi. 1, vii. 1, viii. 31, ix. 14, 30). It serves to fix the mind of the reader on the state of the question, at the point which the discussion has reached. If it had been in the interest of a certain school of criticism to deny the authenticity of the Epistle to the Romans, it is easy to see what advantage it would have taken of this form so exclusively characteristic of this treatise.—The interrogative form with μή assumes, as it always does, that the answer will be negative: "God is not, however, unjust in" . . . ? It is certainly the apostle who is speaking, and not an opponent; for the objection is thus expressed in the outset as one resolved in the negative. The phrase: *to inflict wrath*, alludes to ii. 4, 5, where the apostle threatened Israel with divine *wrath* against the *day of wrath;* but the question is nevertheless put in a perfectly general sense.—There is always something revolting to a conscience enlightened from above, in joining the epithet *unrighteous* with the word *God*, even hypothetically. This is why Paul adds : *I speak as a man.* By *man* he here understands man left to himself and his own reason, speaking with lightness and presumption of the ways of God. Some commentators would join this explanatory remark with what follows. But the following exclamation (μὴ γένοιτο, *let it not be so*), is absolutely opposed to this.

The argument of ver. 6, according to Meyer, is this : How would God be disposed to judge the world, if there was no righteousness in Him? For the troublesome consequences of sin could not impel Him to it, since He can turn them to good. It must be confessed that this would be a singularly wiredrawn argument. To go to prove God's righteousness by the fact of the judgment, while it is the fact of the judgment which rests on divine righteousness ! If the apostle had reasoned thus, Rückert would have been right in declaring that the argument was insufficient. But the reasoning is quite different. Meyer might have found it clearly stated by Olshausen : " If God's drawing a good result from a bad deed were enough to destroy His right to judge him who committed it, the final judgment would evidently become impossible ; for as God is always turning to good the evil which men have devised, every sinner could plead in his defence : My sin has after all served some good end."—One might be tempted to apply the word *the world* exclusively to the Gentile world, which would lead us to the explanation whereby ver. 5 is put into a Jewish mouth. To this Jewish interlocutor, excusing the sin of his nation by the good fruits which God will one day reap from it, Paul would then answer : But at this rate God could as little judge the Gentiles (*the world*). For He brings good fruits from their sins also. This meaning is very plausible in itself. But yet it does not correspond with the apostle's thought. For the word τὸν κόσμον, *the world*, would then have such an emphasis (as forming an antithesis to the Jews), that it would necessarily require to be placed before the verb. The idea is therefore more general : No final judgment is any longer possible if the beneficial consequences of sin, human or Jewish, justify the sinner. This idea is exactly that which is expounded in the two following verses.

Vv. 7, 8. " For [1] *if the truth of God hath abounded through my lie unto His glory ; why yet am I also judged as a sinner? And not, Let us do evil—as we are accused of doing, and as some falsely pretend that we teach—that good may come? whose condemnation is just.*"—Many commentators (Calvin, Grotius, Philippi) have fallen into a strange error in regard to ver. 7. They imagine that this verse reproduces once more the objection of ver. 5. The *for* serves, they say, to justify the question : " Is not God unrighteous ?" In reality the apostle is made to add : after the advantage which He has derived from my lie for His glory, how does He still judge me ? But for what reason should the *for* relate to ver. 5 rather than ver. 6, which immediately precedes ? This would be to forget the answer given in ver. 6, and so to confess its weakness ! In this case we should require rather to adopt the reading εἰ δέ, *but if*, of the *Sinaït.* and *Vatic.*, and to make ver. 7 an objection to the answer given in ver. 6. But this reading is inadmissible, because this new objection raised would remain without answer in the sequel. This same reason tells also against the explanation which makes ver. 7 a simple reaffirmation of the objection of ver. 5. How could an objection, reproduced so forcibly, possibly be left without any other answer than the relegating of those who dare to raise it to the judgment of God (ver. 8) ? For a mind like Paul's this would be a strange mode of arguing ! Ver. 7 is simply, as the *for* indicates, the confirmation of the answer given in ver. 6 : " How would God judge the world ? In reality (*for*) every sinner might come before the judge and say to Him, on his own behalf : And I too by my lie, I have contributed to Thy glory. And he must be acquitted."—By the phrase *truth of God* Paul returns to the beginning of the discussion (vv. 3 and 4). What is in question is the moral uprightness of God ; in like manner the term *lie* brings us back to the *every man a liar* (ver. 4). *This* lie consists in voluntary ignorance of goodness, to escape the obligation of doing it. The verb ἐπερίσσευσεν, *has abounded*, strictly : *flowed over*, denotes the surplus of glory which God's moral perfection extracts from human wickedness in each case. Ἔτι, *yet*, signifies : even after so profitable a result has accrued from my sins. Κἀγώ, *I also*: " I who, as well as all the rest, have contributed to Thy glory." It is as if one saw the whole multitude of sinners appearing before the judgment-seat one after the other, and throwing this identical answer in God's face ; the judgment

---

[1] א and B read εἰ δέ instead of εἰ γάρ.

is therefore brought to nothing. Thus is confirmed the answer of ver. 6 to the objection of ver. 5.—This so suitable meaning appears to us preferable to a more special sense which might present itself to the mind, especially if one were tempted to apply the term *the world* (ver. 6) to the *Gentile*, in opposition to the *Jewish* world (ver. 5). The sense would be: "For the judgment comes to nought for me Gentile, as well as for thee Jew, since I can plead the same excuse as thou, my Gentilehood contributing to glorify God's truth as much as thy unbelief to exalt His righteousness." For the application to the Gentiles of the two expressions: *God's truth*, and *lie*, see i. 25. But to make this meaning probable, Paul would require to have brought out in chap. i. the idea that idolatry had contributed to God's glory; and as to the restricted meaning of τὸν κόσμον, *the world*, see at p. 137.

The apostle pushes his refutation to the utmost (ver. 8) · Why even not go further? Why, after annihilating the judgment, not say further, to be thoroughly consequent: "And even let us furnish God, by sinning more freely, with richer opportunities of doing good! Will not every sin be a material which He will transform into the pure gold of His glory?" The words καὶ μή, *and not*, should properly be followed by the verb: *let us do evil?* ποιήσωμεν τὰ κακά, as we have translated it. But in Greek the sentence is interrupted by the insertion of a parenthesis, intended to remind the reader that such is precisely the odious principle which Paul and his brethren are accused by their calumniators of practising and teaching. And when, after this parenthesis, he returns in ver. 8 to his principal idea: ποιήσωμεν, *let us do*, instead of connecting it with the conjunction, *and (that) not*, he makes it depend directly on the last verb of the parenthesis, *teach:* "As we are accused of teaching, *let us do evil*." The ὅτι, *that*, is the ὅτι recitative so common in Greek (transition from the indirect to the direct form of discourse). The construction which we have just indicated is a form of anacolouthon, of which numerous examples are found in classic authors.—The verb *we are accused* has for its object the understood clause: *of doing so*, of practising this principle. If we understood: "Accused *of teaching*," the following words would be a mere superfluous repetition. The term βλασφημεῖσθαι seems deliberately chosen to suggest the idea that the principle calumniously imputed to him is itself blasphemous in its nature. The second part of the parenthesis adds the idea of *professing* (λαλεῖν) to that of *practising*. The words form a climax, for it is graver to lay down a blasphemous maxim as a principle than to put it into practice in a few isolated cases. Hofmann has proposed another construction; he understands ἐστιν after καὶ μή, and makes the following καθώς dependent on it: "And *it is* not the case with me, as we are accused of practising and teaching, that it only remains to do evil that" . . . But it is harsh to make the καθώς depend on ἐστί; and Meyer rightly observes that Paul would have required to say καὶ οὔ, and not καὶ μή; comp. the interrogations, 1 Cor. vi. 7; Luke xix. 23, etc.—The sort of malediction which closes the verse is applied by most commentators to those who really practise and teach the maxim which is falsely applied to Paul. But the apostle would not have confined himself in that case to the use of the simple relative pronoun ὧν, *whose;* he would necessarily have required to indicate, and even characterize, the antecedent of the pronoun, which cannot refer to any substantive expressed or understood in the preceding proposition. It must have for its antecedent the preceding τινές, *some*, and we must apply this severe denunciation to the calumniators of the apostle's life and teaching. Those who raise such accusations wrongly and maliciously against his person and doctrine themselves deserve the condemnation which they call down on the head of Paul. But it should be well observed that the apostle does not express himself thus till he has satisfied all the demands of logical discussion.

Observations on the passage, iii. 1-8.—Notwithstanding its temporary application to the Jewish people, this passage, which will find its complete explanation in chap. xi., has a real permanent value. It has always been sought to justify the greatest crimes in history by representing the advantages in which they have resulted to the cause of humanity. There is not a Robespierre who has not been transformed into a saint in the name of utilitarianism. But to make such a canonization valid, one would require to begin by proving that the useful result sprang from the evil committed as its principle. Such is the teaching of Pantheism. Living Theism, on the contrary, teaches that this transformation of the bad deed into a means of progress, is the miracle of God's wisdom and power continually laying hold of human sin to derive from it a result contrary to its nature. On the first view, all human responsibility is at an end, and the judgment becomes a nullity. On the second, man remains fully responsible to God for the bad deed as an expression of the evil will of its author, and despite the good which God is pleased to extract from it. Such is scriptural optimism, which alone reconciles man's moral responsibility with the doctrine of providential progress. The apostle has laid the foundations of this true *theodicée* in the remarkable piece which we have just been studying.—It is curious to see how Holsten seeks to explain this passage, the meaning of which has, as we think, been made so clear, by a polemical intention against the alleged Jewish-Christianity of the Christians of Rome. We do not waste time in giving a refutation which seems to us to arise of itself from the preceding.

The apostle has drawn in two great pictures the reign of God's wrath—(1) over the Gentile world (chap. i.) ; (2) over the Jewish people (chap. ii.) ; and by way of appendix he has added a passage to this second picture, intended to sweep away the objections which, from the ordinary Jewish point of view, seemed opposed to the statement that this elect people could possibly become, notwithstanding their unbelief, the object of divine animadversion. Now, to the judgment which follows from the preceding context with respect to the whole of *mankind*, he affixes the seal of *Scripture sanction*, without which he regards no proof as finally valid.

SEVENTH PASSAGE (3:9-20)

Scripture proclaims the fact of Universal Condemnation

After a general declaration, repeating the already demonstrated fact of the condemnation of Jews and Greeks (ver. 9), the apostle quotes a series of Scripture sayings which confirm this truth (vv. 10-18) ; then he formally states the conclusion (vv. 19 and 20).

Ver. 9. " *What then ? are we sheltered ?* [1] *Certainly not :* [2] *for we have before proved* [3] *all men, both Jews and Greeks, that they are under sin.*"—If the words τί οὖν, *what then,* be taken as an independent question, the meaning will be : " *What, then, is the state of things ?* To what result are we thus brought ?" But many commentators connect these two words with the following sentence, so as to form a single question. The meaning in that case is, according to the different acceptations of the verb προέχεσθαι : *What have we to allege as an excuse ?* or : *In what, then, are we superior ?* But neither of these meanings agrees with the answer following. Indeed, instead of *in no wise.* it would require to be *none whatever,* or *in nothing.* There are therefore two questions, and not merely one.—What is the sense of the verb προεχόμεθα, which by itself forms the second question ? We should first testify to the correctness of the Received reading. All the MSS. are at one on this point except A L, which read the subjunctive instead of the indicative, obviously to convert the word into an exhortation, and

---

[1] Instead of προεχομεθα, A L read προεχωμεθα; D G : προκατεχομεν περισσον.

[2] D G P omit ου παντως.   [3] D G read ητιασαμεθα instead of προητιασαμεθα.

D G, which read προκατέχομεν while adding the object περισσόν ; these last, at the same time, reject the words οὐ πάντως. This is the text which Chrysostom and Theodoret seem to have followed, as well as the Itala and Peshito. The meaning would be : *What superiority do we possess ?* It is simply an attempt to escape from the difficulty of the Received reading.—The verb προέχειν has two principal meanings in the active : *to hold before* (in order to protect), and *to hold the first place*. In the passive, the first meaning changes into *to be protected ;* the second meaning, as being intransitive, has no passive. In the middle, the verb signifies, according to the first meaning : *to protect oneself, to shelter oneself, to hold out a pretext ;* according to the second : *to place oneself at the head, to surpass*. It is logically impossible to apply here the idea of *superiority*, either in the passive form : *Are we preferred ?* or in the middle form : *Do we surpass ?* Undoubtedly these two interpretations have both found their defenders ; Osterv., for example : *Are we preferable ?* Oltram. : *Have we some superiority ?* But the question of ascribing a superiority to the Jews had been put at ver. 1 ; the apostle had resolved it affirmatively from the *theocratic* standpoint. If, then, he now resolves it negatively, as he does in the following answer, it can only be from the *moral* point of view. But in this case he could not fail to indicate this distinction. The only appropriate meaning, therefore, is that of *sheltering*, which is also the most frequent in classic Greek : " Have we a shelter under which we can regard ourselves as delivered from wrath ?" This meaning seems to us to be perfectly suitable. The apostle has demonstrated that the Jewish people, as well as the Gentile world, are under God's wrath. He has put to himself the objection : But what in this case becomes of the Jew's advantage ? And he has proved that this advantage, perfectly real though it be, cannot hinder the rejection and judgment of this people. "What then ?" he now asks as a consequence from what precedes, " can we flatter ourselves that we have a refuge ?" "In no wise," such is his answer. All is closely bound together in the reasoning thus understood.—The phrase οὐ πάντως strictly signifies : *not altogether ;* comp. 1 Cor. v. 10. When Paul means : *not at all*, he uses, in conformity with Greek custom, the form πάντως οὐ ; comp. 1 Cor. xvi. 12. But the first meaning is evidently too weak after the preceding argument, and in consequence of that which follows. Meyer even finds himself obliged here to abandon his philological rigorism, and to take the second meaning. And, in reality, this meaning is not incorrect. It is enough, as Morison says, to make a pause in reading after οὐ, *not*, adding πάντως, *absolutely*, as a descriptive : *no, absolutely ;* or better : *no, certainly*. This meaning is that of the entirely similar phrase οὐ πάνυ in Xenophon, Demosthenes, Lucian, and even that of οὐ πάντως in two passages quoted by Morison, the one taken from classic Greek, the other from patristic.[1]

The apostle demonstrates this negation, which refers specially to the Jews, by summing up in the following proposition the result of the long preceding indictment against the two divisions of mankind. The term αἰτιᾶσθαι, *to accuse, incriminate*, belongs to the language of the bar. The προ, *before, previously*, which enters into the composition of the verb, reminds the reader of the two great pictures which Paul had just drawn.—The phrase : *to be under sin*, does not merely signify : to be under the *responsibility* (the guilt) of sins committed, but also to be under the *power* of sin itself, which like a perpetual fountain constantly reproduces and increases this guilt. These two meanings, sin as a *trespass*, and sin as a *power*, are both demanded by the context, the first by the preceding, and the second by the succeeding context. In point of fact, God's wrath is not based solely on trespasses committed, which have something external and acci-

---

[1] Theognis, 305: "The wicked are *certainly not* born wicked (οὐ πάντως)." The translation: *not altogether*, is inadmissible.—Ep. to Diogn. c. 9 : "*Certainly not* taking pleasure in our sins (οὐ πάντως), but bearing them." The meaning *not altogether* would be absurd.

dental in their character; it is founded, above all, on the permanent state of human nature as it is about to be described by Scripture. So long as the Scriptures had not spoken, Paul might be regarded as a simple accuser. But as soon as the voice of this judge shall be heard, the case will be determined, and the sentence pronounced. Vv. 10–18 enumerate, if one may so speak, the grounds of judgment; vv. 19 and 20 give the sentence.

Paul first reminds his readers, in scriptural terms, of *the most general characteristics* of human corruption, vv. 10–12. Then he presents two particular classes of the *manifestations* of this corruption, vv. 13–17. Finally, he closes this description by a decisive feature which goes back to the very *fountain* of evil, ver. 18.

Vv. 10–12. "*As it is written, There is none righteous, no, not one: there is none*[1] *that understandeth, there is none that seeketh*[2] *after God. They are all gone out of the way, they are together become useless; there is none that doeth*[3] *good, no, not even one.*"—These six sentences are taken from Ps. xiv. 1–3. At the first glance, this psalm seems to be depicting the wickedness of the *Gentiles* only; comp. ver. 4: "They eat up *my people*, as if they were eating bread." But on looking at it more closely, it is clear that the term *my people* denotes the true people of Jehovah, "the afflicted" (ver. 6), in opposition to the proud and violent as well within as without the theocracy. This delineation therefore applies to the moral character of man, so long as he remains beyond the influence of divine action.—Ver. 10 contains the most general statement. Instead of the word *righteous*, there is in the Hebrew: the man *that doeth good*, which comes to the same thing.—The two terms which follow in ver. 11 have a more particular sense. The first is related to the understanding: the knowledge of the Creator in His works; the second to the will: the aspiration after union with this perfect being. The Sinaït., like most of the Mjj., reads the article ὁ before the two participles. This article is in keeping with the meaning of the psalm. God is represented as seeking *that* one *man* and not finding him. We may accentuate συνιῶν as an unusual participle of συνιέω, or συνιών, from the verb συνίω, which sometimes takes the place of the verb συνίημι.—In the case where positive good is not produced (seeking after God), the heart immediately falls under the dominion of evil; this state is described in general terms, ver. 12.

Ἐκκλίνειν, *to deviate*, to go in a bad way, because one has voluntarily fled from the good (ver. 11). Ἀχρειοῦσθαι, *to become useless*, unfit for good, corresponds to the Hebrew *alach*, *to become sour*, to be spoiled.—The sixth proposition reproduces, by way of *resumé*, the idea of the first. Mankind resembles a caravan which has strayed, and is moving in the direction opposite to the right one, and whose members can do nothing to help one another in their common misery (*do good*).

Here begins a second and more particular description, that of human wickedness manifesting itself in the form of *speech*.

Vv. 13, 14. "*Their throat is an open sepulchre; with their tongues they have used deceit; the poison of asps is under their lips: whose mouth is full of cursing and bitterness.*"—These four propositions refer to the different *organs* of speech, and show them all exercising their power to hurt, under the dominion of sin. The *throat* (larynx) is compared to a sepulchre; this refers to the language of the gross and brutal man, of whom it is said in common parlance: it seems as if he would like to eat you. The characteristic which follows contrasts with the former; it is the sugared *tongue*, which charms you like a melodious instrument. The imperfect ἐδολιοῦσαν (Alex. form) denotes the action as continually repeated. These two features are borrowed from Ps. v. 9, where they describe the behavior of

---

[1] A B G omit the ο before συνιων.   [2] B G omit ο before εκζητων (B: ζητων).
[3] א D E read the article ο before ποιων.

David's enemies. The third proposition is taken from Ps. cxl. 3, which treats of the same subject ; what is meant is that calumny and falsehood which malignant *lips* give forth, as the serpent infuses its poison. The fourth (ver. 14) describes the wickedness which is cast in your face by a *mouth* full of hatred or bitterness ; it is borrowed from Ps. x. 7, where the contrast is between the weak godly man and the powerful wicked man within the theocracy itself.

This picture of human depravity manifesting itself in word is completed by the description of the same wickedness shown in *deeds*.

Vv. 15–18. "*Their feet are swift to shed blood: oppression and misery are in their ways: the way of peace they have not known: there is no fear of God before their eyes.*"—Of these four propositions the first three are borrowed from Isa. lix. 7, 8, in which chapter the prophet confesses the corruption of Israel. The *feet*, as the emblem of walking, symbolize the whole conduct. Man acts without regard to his neighbor, without fear of compromising his welfare and even his life ; a saying taken from Prov. i. 16. He oppresses ($\sigma \acute{v}ντριμμα$) his brother, and fills his life with misery ($ταλαιπωρία$), so that the way marked out by such a course is watered with the tears of others.—No *peace* can exist either in the heart of such men, or in their neighborhood (ver. 17). And this overflow of depravity and suffering arises from a void : the absence of that feeling which should have filled the heart, *the fear of God* (ver. 18). This term is the normal expression for piety in the Old Testament ; it is that disposition in man which has always God present in the heart, His will and judgment. The words : *before their eyes*, show that it belongs to man freely to evoke or suppress this inward view of God, on which his moral conduct depends. This final characteristic is borrowed from Ps. xxxvi. 1, which marks the contrast between the faithful and the wicked even in Israel.

The apostle in drawing this picture, which is only a grouping together of strokes of the pencil, made by the hands of psalmists and prophets, does not certainly mean that each of those characteristics is found equally developed in every man. Some, even the most of them, may remain latent in many men ; but they all exist in germ in the selfishness and natural pride of the *ego*, and the least circumstance may cause them to pass into the active state, when the fear of God does not govern the heart. Such is the *cause* of the divine condemnation which is suspended over the human race.

This is the conclusion which the apostle reaches ; but he limits the express statement of it, in vv. 19, 20, to the Jews ; for they only could attempt to protest against it, and put themselves outside this delineation of human corruption. They could object in particular, that many of the sayings quoted referred not to them, but to the Gentiles. Paul foresees this objection, and takes care to set it aside, so that nothing may impair the sweep of the sentence which God pronounces on the state of mankind.

Vv. 19, 20. "*Now we know that what things soever the law saith,*[1] *it speaketh*[2] *for them who are under the law: that every mouth may be stopped, and all the world may become subject to judgment before God. Seeing that by the deeds of the law there shall no flesh be justified in his sight: for by the law is the knowledge of sin.*"—By his *we know*, Paul appeals to the common sense of his readers. It is obvious, indeed, that the Old Testament, while depicting to the Jews the wickedness of the Gentiles, did not at all mean to embitter them against the latter, but to put them on their guard against the same sins, and preserve them from the same judgments ; a proof that God saw in their hearts the same germs of corruption, and foresaw their inevitable development if the Jews did not remain faithful to Him. Thus, while none of the sayings quoted might refer *to them*, they were nevertheless all uttered *for them*.— The *law* here denotes the whole Old Testament, as being throughout the

---

[1] Or. : λαλει for λεγει.   [2] D F G L : λεγει for λαλει.

rule for Israelitish life ; comp. John x. 34 ; 1 Cor. xiv. 21, etc.—The difference of meaning between the words λέγειν, *to say*, and λαλεῖν, *to speak*, comes out clearly in this passage—the first referring to the *contents* of the saying, the second to the fact of its *utterance*.—There is no reason for weakening the sense of the conjunction ἵνα, *in order that*, and making it signify *so that*. The *object* of all those declarations given forth by Scripture regarding the wickedness of the natural man, was really to close his mouth against all vainglory, as that to which a man filled with self-satisfaction gives himself up. *Every mouth*, even the Jews'. Καί : *and that thus. All the world :* all mankind, Jew and Gentile ; ὑπόδικος, *placed under the stroke of justice*, like one whom the judge has declared guilty, and who owes satisfaction to the law he has violated. The word is frequently used in this sense in the classics ; it is a judicial term, corresponding to the word Paul had used to denote the accusation (αἰτιᾶσθαι, ver. 9). The last word : *to God*, is full of solemnity ; it is into the hands of His justice that the whole guilty world falls.

The *all the* is so true that the only possible exception, that of the Jewish people, is excluded (ver. 20). This people, indeed, could have alleged a host of ritualistic and moral works performed daily in obedience to the divine law. Did not such works establish in their case special merit and right to God's favor ? The apostle sets aside such a claim, Διότι : *for the reason that*. *No flesh :* no human creature (see on i. 3).—Here for the first time we meet with the expression ἔργα νόμου, *works of the law*, one of the important terms in the apostle's vocabulary. It is found, however, only in the Epistles to the Romans (iii. 28, ix. 32) and to the Galatians (ii. 16, iii, 2, 5, 10). But, nevertheless, it expresses one of the ideas which lie at the root of his experience and of his view of Christian truth. It sums up the first part of his life. It may be understood in two ways. A *work of law* may mean : a work exactly conformed to the law, corresponding to all the law prescribes (Hodge, Morison, etc.) ; or it may mean : such a work as man can accomplish under the dispensation of the law, and with such means only as are available under this dispensation. In the first sense it is certainly unnecessary to explain the impossibility of man's finding his righteousness in those works by an imperfection inherent in the moral ideal traced by the law. For Paul himself says, vii. 14, that "*the law is spiritual ;*" vii. 12, that "*the law is holy*, and the commandment is *holy, just, and good ;*" viii. 4, that "the work of the Holy Spirit in the believer consists in fulfilling what the law has determined to be righteous." Much more, he goes the length of affirming positively, with Moses himself (Lev. xviii. 5), that if any one exactly fulfilled the law he would live by his obedience (Rom. x. 5 ; Gal. iii. 12). Taking this meaning, then, why cannot *the works of the law* justify ? It can only be man's powerlessness to do them. St. Paul would then say : " No man will be justified by the works of the law, because works really conformed to the spirit of the law are beyond his power to realize." Thus the kind of works referred to in the declaration : "not being justified by the works of the law," would be ideal and not real. This meaning is far from natural. From Paul's way of speaking of the works of the law, we cannot help thinking that he has a fact in view—that he is reckoning with a real and not a fictitious value. We must therefore come to the second meaning : works such as man can do when he has no other help than the law—that is to say, in fact, in his own strength. The law is perfect in itself. But it does not provide fallen man with the means of meeting its demands. Paul explains himself clearly enough on this head, Gal. iii. 21 : "If there had been a law given which could have given life, verily righteousness should have been by the law." In other words, the law does not communicate the Spirit of God, and through Him the life of love, which is the fulfilling of the law (Rom. xiii. 10). Works wrought in this state, notwithstanding their external conformity to the letter of the law, are not therefore its real fulfilment. Though agreeable to the legal statute, they are destitute of the moral disposition which would give them value in the eyes of God. Paul himself had groaned till the time of his conversion over the grievous contrast in his works which he constantly discerned between the appearance and the reality ; comp. the opposition between the state which he calls, vii. 6, *oldness of the letter* and *newness of spirit*. He gives his estimate of the works of the law when, after saying of himself before his conversion, Phil. iii. 6 : "As to the righteousness which is under the law, blameless," he adds, ver. 7 : "But what things were gain to me (all this from the human point of view blameless righteousness), these I counted loss for Christ's sake."—There remains one question to be examined. Is it true, as Theodoret,[1] Pelagius, and many modern critics have thought, that Paul is speaking here only of *ceremonial* works imposed by the law, and not of works implying moral obedience? The meaning of the verse would then be this : "The whole world is condemned ; for the Jews themselves cannot be justified by the observance of the ceremonies which their law prescribes." But such a distinction between two kinds of works is opposed to the context; for the apostle does not contrast work with work—he contrasts work with faith. Then how could he add immediately, that by the law is the knowledge of sin? From vii. 7, 8, it appears that this saying applies above all to the moral law. For it was the tenth commandment which led the apostle to discern covetousness in his heart, and it was this discovery of covetousness which convinced him of sin. Hence it appears that the last words of our verse refer to the moral, and not the ceremonial law, which decides the meaning of the term : *the works of the law*. Besides, the expression *all flesh*, which evidently embraces the Gentiles, could not be applied to them if the law were here taken as the ceremonial law, for in this sense they have never had it. In general, the distinction between the ritual and the moral elements of the law is foreign to the Jewish conscience, which takes the law as a divine unity.—It follows from this saying of the apostle, that man ought never to attempt to put any work whatever between God and himself as establishing a right to salvation, whether a work wrought before his conversion proceeding from his natural ability, for it will lack the spirit of love which alone would render it *good* in God's sight ; or even a work posterior to regeneration and truly good (ἔργον ἀγαθόν, Eph. ii. 10), for as such it is the fruit of the Spirit, and cannot be transformed into a merit of man. —The declarative meaning of the verb δικαιοῦν, *to justify*, appears clearly here from the two subordinate clauses : *by the works of the law*, and *before him* (see on i. 17).

By a short proposition (20*b*) the apostle justifies the principle affirmed 20*a*. Far from having been given to sinful man to furnish him with a means of justification, the law was rather given to help him in discerning the sin which reigns over him ; ἐπίγνωσις, *discernment*, proof.—This thought is only indicated here ; it will be developed afterward. Indeed, Paul throughout the whole of this piece is treating of sin as *guilt*, forming the ground of condemnation. Not till chap. vii. will he consider sin as a *power*, in its relation to the law, and in this new connection ; then will be the time for examining the idea with which he closes this whole passage.

Judaism was living under a great illusion, which holds it to this very hour, to wit, that it is called to save the Gentile world by communicating to it the legal dispensation which it received through Moses. "Propagate the law," says the apostle, "and you will have given to the world not the means of purifying itself, but the means of seeing better its real corruption." These for us are commonplaces, but they are become so through our Epistle itself. At the time when it was written, these commonplaces

---

[1] Not Origen and Chrysostom, as Calvin erroneously says. (See the rectification in Morison.)

were rising on the horizon like divine beams which were to make a new day dawn on the world.

On the order of ideas in this first section, according to Hofmann and Volkmar.—Hofmann finds the principal division of this section between vv. 4 and 5 of chap. iii. Up to ver. 4, the apostle is proving that God's wrath rests on mankind, whether Gentile (i. 18–ii. 8) or Jewish (ii. 9–iii. 4); but from that point all the apostle says applies specially to Christians, thus: "As we are not ignorant, *we Christians* (iii. 5), that man's sin, even when God is glorified by it, can be justly judged (vv. 5–7), and as we do not teach, as we are accused of doing, that the good which God extracts from evil excuses it (ver. 8), we bow, with all other men, before the Scripture declarations which attest the common sin, and we apply to ourselves the sentence of condemnation which the law pronounces on the whole world. Only (iii. 21 et seq.) we do not rest there; for we have the happiness of knowing that there is a righteousness of faith through which we escape from wrath."—This construction is refuted, we think, by three principal facts—1. The man who judges, ii. 1, is necessarily the Jew (see the exegesis). 2. The objection, iii. 5, is closely connected with the quotation from Ps. li., and cannot be the beginning of a wholly new development. 3. The question: "What then? have we a shelter?" (ver. 9), is too plainly a reference to that of ver. 1 ("what then is the advantage of the Jew?") to be applied otherwise than specially to the Jew. This is confirmed by the end of ver. 9, in which the apostle gives the reason for the first proposition in this general sentence: "*For* we have proved *both Jews and Greeks*." It is clear, therefore, that as chap. i. from ver. 18 describes the wrath of God displayed on the Gentiles, chap. ii. describes and demonstrates the wrath of God as accumulating over the Jewish world, and that the passage iii. 1–8 is simply intended to set aside the objection which the Jew might draw from his exceptional superiority. Vv. 9–20 are the scriptural *resumé* and demonstration of this double condemnation of Jews and Gentiles.—According to Volkmar, chap. i. from ver. 18 describes the wrath of God against *all sin*, and chap. ii. that same wrath against *all sinners*, even against the Jew, notwithstanding his excuses (ii. 1–16) and his advantages, which he is unable to turn to moral account (vv. 17–29), and finally, notwithstanding the greatest of his privileges, the possession of the Messianic promises (iii. 1–8). Here, iii. 9, Volkmar places the beginning of the new section, that of the righteousness of faith. "Since the whole world is perishing, vv. 9–20, God saves the world by the righteousness of faith, which is confirmed by the example both of Abraham and Adam, the type of Christ." This construction differs from ours only in two points, which are not to its advantage, as it appears to me—(1) The antithesis between *all sins* (chap. 1.) and *all sinners* (chap. ii.), which is too artificial to be apostolical; (2) The line of demarkation between the preceding and the new section fixed at iii. 9 (instead of iii. 21), a division which awkwardly separates the section on *wrath* in its entirety (i. 18–iii. 8) from its scriptural summary (vv. 9–20).

SECOND SECTION

3:21-5:11 —JUSTIFICATION BY FAITH ACQUIRED FOR THE WHOLE WORLD

In this section, which forms the counterpart of the preceding, three principal ideas are developed.

1. The *historical fact* by which justification by faith is acquired for the world, iii. 21–26.
2. The *harmony* of this mode of justification with the revelation of the Old Testament, iii. 27–iv. 25.
3. The certainty of justification, not for the present only, but for all the *future*, embracing the last judgment, v. 1–11.

Thus the sentence of condemnation is effaced by that of absolution.

EIGHTH PASSAGE (3:21-26)

The Fact by which Justification by Faith is acquired for us.

We have already proved that ver. 21 is directly connected in sense with i. 17 (see p. 99). In the interval from. 18 to iii. 20, the apostle has shown that the wrath of God rests on mankind, whence it follows that if the world is not to perish, a divine manifestation of an opposite kind, and able to overcome the first, is indispensable. It is this new revelation which forms the subject of the following passage. Vv. 21 and 22 contain the theme of the first piece, and at the same time of the whole section. Ver. 23 once more sums up the thought of the preceding section ; and vv. 24-26 are the development of the subject, the exposition of the new way of justification.

Vv. 21, 22a. "*But now the righteousness of God is manifested without the law, being witnessed by the law and the prophets ; even the righteousness of God by faith in Jesus Christ* [1] *for all and upon all them* [2] *that believe.*"—The δέ, *but*, is strongly adversative ; it contrasts the revelation of righteousness with that of wrath. The former is presented as a new fact in the history of mankind ; so that one might be led to give the word *now* a *temporal* sense ; comp. the *at this time*, ver. 26, and Acts xvii. 30. This, however, is only apparent. The contrast with the preceding is *moral* rather than temporal ; it is the contrast between the condemnation pronounced by the law (ver. 20) and the new righteousness acquired without the law (ver. 21). It is therefore better to give the word *now* the *logical* meaning which it has so frequently in the New Testament (vii. 17 ; 1 Cor. xiii. 12, xiv. 6, etc.) and in the classics : "The situation being such." The words : *without the law*, stand foremost, as having the emphasis. They evidently depend on the verb *is manifested*, and not on the word *righteousness* (*a righteousness without law*, Aug.). The absence of the article before the word *law* does not prove that the apostle does not mean the term to denote the *Mosaic* law ; only the law is excluded from co-operating in the new righteousness not because it is *Mosaic*, but because it is *law*. Under the old dispensation, righteousness came to man through the thousand channels of legalism ; in the new, righteousness is given him without the least co-operation of what can be called a law.—We know what Paul calls the *righteousness of God :* it is the state of reconciliation with God in which man is placed by the sentence which declares him just (see on i. 17).—The verb φανεροῦν, *to put in the light*, differs from the verb ἀποκαλύπτειν, *to reveal*, used i. 17, in the figure, not in the sense. The second applies to an object which was hidden by a veil, and which is made known by withdrawing the veil ; the former, to an object placed in the shade, and on which rays of light are let fall. The only real difference from i. 17 is therefore this : there, the verb was in the *present*, for it denoted the permanent revelation of the gospel by means of evangelical preaching ; while here, the verb is in the *perfect*, because it refers, as Morison says, "to the fact itself, which that preaching proclaims." That fact now finished is the subject expounded in vv. 25 and 26 ; it is through it that the righteousness of God is set in the light for all times.

But if legal observances are excluded from all co-operation in this righteousness, it does not follow that the latter is in contradiction to the Old Testament revelation in its double form of law and prophecy. These two manifestations of the divine will, commandment, and promise, understood in their true sense, contain, on the contrary, the confirmation of the righteousness of faith, as the apostle will prove in the sequel of this section, ver.

---

[1] Marcion omitted the word Ιησου, which is also rejected by B.
[2] The words και επι παντας are omitted by ℵ A B C P, Copt., but are read in D E F G K L, Syr. Vulg. and the Fathers.

27–iv. 25. The law by unveiling sin opens up the void in the heart, which is filled by the righteousness of faith ; prophecy completes the work of preparation by promising this righteousness. Thus there is no objection to be drawn from the old revelation against the new. As the new fulfils the old, the latter confirms the former.

Ver. 22. The new righteousness, then, being given without any legal work, what is the means by which it is conferred? Ver. 22 answers: *faith in Jesus Christ*. Such is the *true* means opposed to the false. The δέ, *now*, which the translation cannot render, is explanatory, as ix. 30 ; Gal. ii. 2 ; Phil. ii. 8, etc. It takes the place of a *scilicet, to wit*. Osterv. and Oltram. have well rendered it by : *say I:* "The righteousness, *I say*, of God." Here, again, the absence of the article serves to indicate the category : *a* righteousness of divine origin, in opposition to the legal dispensation, in which righteousness proceeds from human works.—This righteousness is granted *to faith*, not assuredly because of any merit inherent in it—for this would be to fall back on *works*, the very thing which the new dispensation wishes to exclude—but because of the *object* of faith. Therefore it is that this object is expressly mentioned : *Jesus Christ*. The omission of the word *Jesus* by Marcion is perhaps to be explained by the fact that this heretic denied the humanity of Jesus, and attached importance only to His Christship. The omission of this word in the one Mj. B, cannot bring it into suspicion. It has been attempted to make this complement : *Jesus Christ, a gen. subjecti:* the faith *which Jesus Christ Himself had*, whether His faith *in God* (Benecke : His *fidelity* to God) or His *fidelity to us* (Lange). The parallel, i. 17, suffices to refute such interpretations. The only possible sense is this : *faith in Jesus Christ ;* comp. Mark xi. 22 ; Gal. ii. 16 ; Jas. ii. 1, etc.—This clause : *by faith in Jesus Christ*, is the reproduction and development of the first clause : ἐκ πίστεως, *by faith*, i. 17. The following : *for and upon all them that believe*, is the development of the second clause in the same verse : εἰς πίστιν, *for faith*. Faith, indeed, as we have seen, plays a double part in justification. It is the disposition which God accepts, and which He imputes as righteousness ; and it is at the same time the instrument whereby every one may appropriate for his own personal advantage this *righteousness of faith*. The first office is expressed here by the clause : *by faith ;* the second by the clause : *for and upon all them that believe.*—The words καὶ ἐπὶ πάντας, *and upon all them*, are wanting in the four Alex., but they are found in the Mjj. of the other two families (except P), and in the ancient Vss. Meyer and Morison justly remark that it would be impossible to account for their interpolation, as there was nothing in the clause : *for all them*, to demand this explanatory addition. It is easy to understand, on the contrary, how these words were omitted, either through a confusion of the two πάντας by the copyists—the *Sinaït.*, in particular, abounds in such omissions [1]—or because this clause seemed to be a pleonasm after the preceding. It is quite in keeping with Paul's manner thus to accumulate subordinate clauses to express by a change of prepositions the different aspects of the moral fact which he means to describe. These two aspects in this case are those of general *destination* (εἰς, *for*) and personal *application* (ἐπί, *upon*) : "As to this righteousness, God sends it *for* thee that thou mayest believe in it ; and it will rest *on* thee from the moment thou believest." Comp. Phil. iii. 9. Theodoret, Bengel, etc. have thought that the clause : *for all them*, applied to the Jews, and the clause : *upon all them*, to the Gentiles. But the very object the apostle has here in view is to efface every other distinction save that of believing. This same reason prevents us also from allowing the explanation of Mori-

---

[1] How Tischendorf, in his 8th edition, could yield to the authority of this ms. to the extent of rejecting these words, which he had preserved in the text of the 7th, is incomprehensible. The shorter reading is supported by the four oldest uncials.—T. W. C.

son, who, after Wetstein, Flatt, Stuart, puts a comma after εἰς πάντας, *for all*, that is to say, for *all men*, absolutely speaking, inasmuch as this righteousness is really universal in *destination*, and who applies the participle : *them that believe*, only to the second clause : *upon all*, inasmuch as *real participation* in this righteousness is granted to believers only. But in this case the second πάντας, *all*, should of course have been omitted. Then we shall see in ver. 25 that the condition of faith is included from the beginning in the very decree of redemption. Finally, these two clauses : *for all them*, and *upon all them that believe*, are plainly the unfolding of the contents of the words εἰς πίστιν, *for faith*, i. 17 ; whence it follows that the words *who believe* belong equally to the two pronouns *all*.—To pronounce one righteous, God does not then any more ask : Hast thou kept the law ? but : Believest thou, thou, whoever thou art ? The first clause : *for all*, contrasts this believer, Jew or Gentile, with the Jews, who alone could attain to the righteousness of the law. The second clause : *upon all*, contrasts this righteousness as a gift of God fully made, with that of the law of which *man* himself must be the maker.

These two verses are, as we shall see, the theme which will be developed in the whole following section. But, first, ver. 23 sums up the preceding section by restating the ground on which every human being needs the righteousness of faith.

Vv. 22*b*, 23. "*For there is no difference: for all have sinned, and are deprived of the glory of God.*"[1]—By denying *all difference*, the apostle means here that there are not two ways by which men can be justified, the one that of works, the other of faith. The first is closed against all, even the Jews, by the fact of universal condemnation, which has just been demonstrated. The second, therefore, alone remains open. The old Genevan version, Ostervald, and Martin put all ver. 23 into ver. 22, and thus reckon only thirty verses instead of thirty-one in the chapter. The object of this change was to make ver. 23 a simple parenthesis, that the participle *being justified* might be directly connected with ver. 22. But this grammatical connection is certainly incorrect, and we should preserve the reckoning of the verses as it stands in the Greek text.

Ver. 23. This absence of difference in the mode of justification rests on the equality of all in respect of the fact of sin. In the aorist ἥμαρτον, *have committed sin*, no account is taken of the question whether they have done so once or a hundred times. Once suffices to deprive us of the title of righteous, and thereby of the *glory of God*.—Καί, *and in consequence*.—The verb ὑστερεῖσθαι, *to lack*, expresses in general the idea of a *deficit*, which consists either in remaining below the normal level, or in being behind others. Paul therefore means that they all want more or less a normal state, which he calls the *glory of God*. By this term some have understood the favorable *opinion* which God has of the just man, His approbation or favor (Grot. Turret. Fritzsche). This meaning is far from natural ; John xii. 43 does not suffice to justify it. Others understand by this expression : *glory in God's sight*, that which we should possess if we were righteous (Mel. Calv. Philippi). This meaning is not much more natural than that which appears sometimes in Luther : the act of *glorying in God ;* or than that of Œcumenius and Chalmers : the destination of every man to *glorify God*. There are really only two senses possible. The first is that of the many commentators who understand the *glory of God* as the future and eternal glory (Beza, Morison, Reuss, etc.). But in this case we must give to the verb ὑστερεῖσθαι a very forced meaning : *to lack the necessary qualifications for obtaining* this glory. The second meaning, and the only one which we think admissible, is this . the divine splendor which shines forth from God

---

[1] The literal rendering is, *For all sinned and fall short*, etc. The second verb is in the present tense, and denotes the continuing consequence of the act in the past denoted by the first.—T. W. C.

Himself, and which He communicates to all that live in union with Him (see Hofmann, Meyer). This meaning includes that of Rückert and Olshausen, who understand it too specially, no doubt, to mean the original image of God in man. The complement Θεοῦ, *of God*, is at once a *gen. possess.* and a *gen. auctor.* God can communicate this glory, because He possesses it Himself, and it belongs to His nature. He had communicated a ray of it to man when He created him pure and happy ; it was intended to shine more and more brightly in him as he rose from innocence to holiness. By sinning, man lost both what he had received of it and what he was yet to obtain. A dispossessed king, the crown has fallen from his head.—The consequence of this state of things is indicated, in close connection with the context, in ver. 24.

Ver. 24. "*Being justified as a pure gift by His grace through the redemption that is in Christ Jesus.*"—The participle δικαιούμενοι, *being justified*, takes us by surprise. Why give this idea, which is the principal one in the context, a subordinate place, by using a participle to express it ? To explain this unexpected form, it must be remembered that the idea of justification had already been solemnly introduced, vv. 21, 22. Ver. 23 had afterward explained it by the fact of the fall ; and now it can reappear as a simple corollary from this great fact. We might paraphrase : "being *consequently* justified, *as we have just declared*, freely" . . . The *present* participle (δικαιούμενοι) refers to every moment in the history of mankind when a sinner comes to believe. There is no need therefore to add, as Ostervald and others do, a new conjunction : "and *that* they are justified." Neither is it necessary to take this participle, with Beza and Morison, as the *demonstration* of the fact of sin, ver. 23. It is impossible that the essential idea of the whole passage should be given in proof of a secondary idea. The most erroneous explanation seems to us to be that of Oltramare, who here begins a wholly new period, the principal verb of which must be sought in ver. 27 : "Since we are justified freely . . . is there here, then, any cause for boasting?" The most important passage in the whole Epistle, vv. 24-26, would thus be degraded to the rank of a simple incident. And, moreover, *the asyndeton* between vv. 23, 24 would be without the slightest justification.

This notion : *being justified*, is qualified in three directions : those of the *mode*, the *origin*, and the *means*. The mode is expressed by the adverb δωρεάν, *gratuitously*. It is not a matter of wages, it is a free gift.—The origin of this gift is : *His grace*, God's free goodwill inclining him to sinful man to bestow on him a favor. There is no blind necessity here ; we are face to face with a generous inspiration of divine love. The means is the *deliverance* wrought *in Jesus Christ*. The Greek term ἀπολύτρωσις denotes etymologically, a deliverance obtained by way of *purchase* (λύτρον, *ransom*). No doubt the New Testament writers often use it in the general sense of *deliverance*, apart from all reference to a price paid ; so viii. 23 ; Luke xxi. 28 ; 1 Cor. i. 30. But in these passages, as Morison observes, the matter in question is only one of the particular *consequences* of the fundamental deliverance obtained by Christ. The idea of the latter is usually connected with that of the ransom paid to obtain it ; comp. Matt. xx. 28, where it is said that Jesus gives his life a ransom (λύτρον), in the room and stead (ἀντί) of many ; 1 Tim. ii. 6, where the term signifying *ransom* forms one word with the preposition ἀντί, *in the place of* (ἀντίλυτρον) ; 1 Pet. i. 18 : "Ye were *ransomed* as by the precious blood of the Lamb, without spot." This notion of *purchase*, in speaking of the work of Christ, appears also in 1 Cor. vi. 20, vii. 23 ; Gal. iii. 13. It is obvious that this figure was most familiar to the apostle's mind ; it is impossible to get rid of it in the present passage.— The title *Christ* is placed before the name *Jesus*, the main subject here being his mediatorial office (see on i. 1).—After thus giving the general idea of the work, the apostle expounds it more in detail by defining exactly the

150 / Justification by Faith

ideas he has just stated. That of divine *grace* reappears in the words : *whom he had set forth beforehand*, ver. 25 ; that of deliverance, in the words : *to be a propitiation through faith ;* that of *Christ Jesus*, in the words : *in His blood ;* and, finally, the principal term : *being justified*, in the last words of ver. 26 : *the justifier of him who believeth in Jesus*. This conclusion thus brings us back to the starting-point of the passage.

Vv. 25, 26. " *Whom He had established beforehand as a means of propitiation through faith*,[1] *by His blood, for the demonstration of His justice, because of the tolerance shown toward sins done aforetime, during the forbearance of God, for the demonstration*[2] *of His justice at the present time ; that He might be just, and justifying him who is of the faith in Jesus*."[3]—It is not without reason that these two verses have been called "the marrow of theology." Calvin declares "that there is not probably in the whole Bible a passage which sets forth more profoundly the righteousness of God in Christ." And yet it is so short that the statement seems scarcely to have begun when all is said, within so few lines are the most decisive thoughts concentrated ! It is really, as Vitringa has said, "the brief summary of divine wisdom."[4]

It is God Himself who, according to this passage, is to be regarded as the *author* of the whole work of redemption. The salvation of the world is not therefore wrested from Him, as is sometimes represented by the mediation of Christ. The same thought is expressed elsewhere ; for example, 2 Cor. v. 18 : "All *is of God*, who hath reconciled us to Himself by Jesus Christ ;" and John iii. 16 : " God so loved the world, that He gave His only-begotten Son." This point should never be forgotten in the idea which we form of expiation.—The verb προτιθέναι, *to put before*, may signify in the middle, either : *to exhibit*, present *publicly* (in view of oneself), or *to set before oneself* in the innermost shrine of the spirit ; to decide, to design *beforehand* within oneself. For the preposition πρό may have the local meaning *in front of*, or the temporal meaning *before*. Both significations of the verb have been used here, and in favor of both numerous examples may be quoted in classic Greek. The second sense is obviously the prevailing one in the New Testament ; comp. Rom. i. 13, Eph. i. 9, etc., as well as the common use of the word πρόθεσις to denote God's *eternal plan* (viii. 28 ; Eph. iii. 11) ; see also Acts xxvii. 13. In favor of the first meaning, there may be quoted, indeed, the phrase ἄρτοι τῆς προθέσεως, *the shewbread*, in the LXX. If we use it here, it would make the apostle say : "whom God set forth publicly as a propitiatory victim." This act of public showing forth would refer either to the exhibition of Jesus on the cross, or to the proclamation of His death by the apostolic preaching. The middle form (to set forth *for oneself*) would find its explanation in the clause following : " for the demonstration of *His justice*." This meaning is not impossible. It is adopted by the Vulgate, Luth., Beng., Thol., de Wette, Philip., Meyer, Hofm., Morison. But this idea of a public exhibition of the person of Jesus appears to us to have it something at once

---

[1] ℵ C D E F G omit της before πιστεως.
[2] ℵ A B C D P read την before ενδειξιν.
[3] D E L read Ιησουν instead of Ιησου.—Ιησου is omitted in F G Italig.
[4] We may be allowed here to borrow from Morison the account of an experience of the illustrious poet Cowper, calculated to give an impression of the wealth of this passage. It was a time when Cowper was brought to the very verge of despair. He had walked up and down in his room a long while profoundly agitated. At last he seated himself near his window, and seeing a Bible there he opened it, to find if possible some consolation and strength. "The passage which met my eye," says he, " was the twenty-fifth verse of the third chapter of Romans. On reading it I immediately received power to believe. The rays of the Sun of Righteousness fell on me in all their fulness ; I saw the complete sufficiency of the expiation which Christ had wrought for my pardon and entire justification. In an instant I believed and received the peace of the gospel." "If," adds he, " the arm of the Almighty had not supported me, I believe I should have been overwhelmed with gratitude and joy ; my eyes filled with tears ; transports choked my utterance. I could only look to heaven in silent fear, overflowing with love and wonder." But it is better to describe the work of the Holy Spirit in his own words : "it was *the joy* which is *unspeakable and full of glory*" (1 Pet. i. 8).—*Life of Cowper*, by Taylor.

theatrical and superfluous. Independently of what we have just been saying of the ordinary meaning of the words προτιθέναι, πρόθεσις, in the New Testament, the context speaks strongly in favor of the other meaning. The fundamental idea of the passage is the contrast between the time of God's forbearance in regard to sin, and the decisive moment when at once He carried out the universal expiation. It is natural in this order of ideas to emphasize the fact that God had *foreseen* this final moment, and had provided Himself *beforehand* with the victim by means of which the expiation was to be accomplished. Thus the phrase : *to set forth beforehand*, already gives a hint of the contrast : *at the present time*, ver. 26. Placed as it is at the head of the whole passage, it brings out forcibly, at the same time, the incomparable gravity of the work about to be described. The middle of the verb refers to the *inward* resolution of God. In adopting this meaning, we find ourselves at one with the ancient Greek interpreters, Chrys., Œcum., Theoph. ; see, among the moderns, Fritzsche.[1] The word ἱλαστήριον, *propitiatory*, belongs to that host of Greek adjectives whose termination (ηριος) signifies *what serves to*. The meaning therefore is : "what serves to render propitious, favorable." The verb ἱλάσκεσθαι corresponds in the LXX. to *kipper*, the Piel of *kaphar, to cover*. Applied to the notion of *sin*, this Piel has a double sense : either to *pardon*—the subject is then the *offended one* himself, who, as it were, covers the sin that he may see it no more, for example, Ps. lxv. 4—or to *expiate*—the subject is then the victim which covers (*effaces*) the sin with its blood, that the judge may see it no more, for example, Ex. xxix. 36. In the New Testament this verb occurs twice, Luke xviii. 13, where the publican says to God : ἱλάσθητι, *show Thyself propitious* to me, which is equivalent to : forgive me ; and Heb. ii. 17 : εἰς τὸ ἱλάσκεσθαι τὰς ἁμαρτίας, *to expiate the sins of the people*. We find in these same two passages the two meanings of the term in the Old Testament. The etymology of this verb ἱλάσκεσθαι is the adjective ἵλαος, *favorable, propitious* (probably connected with ἔλεος, *merciful*). To explain the word ἱλαστήριον in our text, very many commentators, Orig., Theoph., Er., Luth., Calv., Grot., Vitringa, and among the moderns, Olsh., Thol., Philip., etc., have had recourse to the technical meaning which it has in the LXX., where it denotes the *propitiatory*, or lid of the ark of the covenant. With this meaning the substantive understood would be ἐπίθεμα, *lid*, which is sometimes joined to the adjective, for example, Ex. xxv. 17. As is well known, the high priest, on the day of atonement, sprinkled this lid with the blood of the victim (Lev. xvi. 14 et seq.). On this account these commentators hold that it was here regarded by Paul as the type of Christ, whose shed blood covers the sin of the world. The term is found in this sense, Heb. ix. 5. We do not, however, think this interpretation admissible. 1. If the matter in question were a well-known definite object, the only one of its kind, the article τό could not be omitted. 2. The Epistle to the Romans is not a book which moves, like the Epistle to the Hebrews, in the sphere of Levitical symbolism ; there is nothing here to indicate that the term is applied to an object belonging to the Israelitish cultus. 3. Gess justly observes that if this type had been familiar to St. Paul, it would have been found elsewhere in his letters ; and if it were not so, the term would have been unintelligible to his readers. 4. In all respects the figure would be a strange one. What a comparison to make of Jesus Christ crucified with a lid sprinkled with blood ! 5. Give to the verb προέθετο whichever of the two meanings you choose, the figure of the propitiatory remains unsuitable. In the sense of *exhibiting publicly*, there is a contradiction between this idea of publicity and the part assigned to the propitiatory in the Jewish cultus ; for this object remained concealed in the sanctuary, the

---

[1] Still, the former meaning is better suited to the connection, and has been generally adopted by modern interpreters.—T. W. C.

high priest alone could see it, and that only once a year, and through a cloud of smoke. And if the verb be explained in the sense which we have adopted, that of *establishing beforehand*, it is still more impossible to apply this idea of an eternal purpose, either to a material object like the propitiatory itself, or to its typical connection with Jesus Christ. We must therefore understand the word ἱλαστήριον in a very wide sense : *a means of propitiation*. After reading Morison, we cannot venture to define more strictly, and to translate : *a victim of propitiation*, as if there were to be understood the substantive θῦμα (*victim*).[1] For this meaning of the term used here does not seem to be sufficiently proved by the passages alleged (see the examples quoted by Thol., de Wette, Meyer, with Morison's criticism). The English commentator himself takes the word ἱλαστήριον as a *masculine* adjective, agreeing with the relative ὅν : " Jesus Christ, whom God set forth as *making propitiation*." Such is the explanation of the Peshito, Thomas Aquinas, Er., Mel., etc. It is certainly allowable. But in this sense would not Paul rather have used the masculine substantive ἱλαστής ? The word ἱλαστήρια is indeed found, not ἱλαστήριοι (Hofm.). We therefore hold by the generally received interpretation, which makes the term ἱλαστήριον a neuter substantive (originally the neuter of the adjective ; comp. σωτήριον, χαριστήριον, etc.). As to the idea of sacrifice, if it is not in the word itself, it follows from its connection with the following clause : *by His blood* (see below). For what is a *means of propitiation by blood*, if it is not a sacrifice ? A question may here be raised : if it is God himself who, as we have just said, has established this means of pardon *of His free grace*, what purpose then was this means to serve ? For it cannot obtain for us anything else than we possessed already, the Divine love. This objection rests on the false idea that expiation is intended to originate a sentiment which did not exist in God before. What it produces is such a change in the relation between God and the creature, that God can henceforth display toward sinful man one of the elements of His nature rather than another. The feeling of the divine mind shows itself in the foundation of the expiatory work as *compassion*. But the propitiation once effected, it can display itself in the new and higher form of *intimate communion*. As Gess says : " Divine love manifests itself in the gift of the Son, that it may be able afterward to diffuse itself in the heart by the gift of the spirit." There are therefore—1. The love which precedes the propitiation, and which determines to effect it ; and 2. Love such that it can display itself, once the propitiation is effected.

The clause διὰ [τῆς] πίστεως, *by faith*, is wanting in the *Alex.*, which, however is not enough to render it suspicious. Five Mjj. (Alex. and Greco-Lat.) omit the article τῆς (*the*, before *faith*). It would be impossible to explain why this word had been rejected if it existed originally in the text. It has therefore been added to give the notion of *faith* a more definite sense : *the* well-known faith in Jesus. But it was not on this or that particular faith the apostle wished here to insist ; it was on *faith* in its very idea, in opposition to works. — On what does the clause depend : διὰ πίστεως, *by faith ?* According to some ancients and Philippi : on προέθετο (*He set forth*, or *established beforehand*). But it is difficult to conceive what logical relation there can be between the ideas of *setting forth* or *establishing*, and a clause such as *by faith*. The only natural connection of this clause is with the word ἱλαστήριον (*means of propitiation*) : " God has established Jesus beforehand as the means of propitiation through faith," which signifies that the efficacy of this means was from the first bound by the divine decree to the condition of faith. God eternally determined within Himself the means of pardon, but as eternally He stipulated with Himself that the condition on which this means should become available

---

[1] This view is sustained by Schaff and Riddle in the "Popular Commentary of N. T." *l.c.* —T. W. C.

for each individual should be faith, neither more nor less. This idea is important ; the subjective condition of faith entered as an integral element into the very decree of amnesty (the πρόθεσις). This is what we shall find afterward expressed in the words οὓς προέγνω, *whom He foreknew* (as His own by faith), viii. 29. The clause following: *in* or *by His blood*, is connected by most commentators (Luth., Calv., Olsh., Thol., Morison) with the word *faith:* "*by faith in His blood.*" Grammatically this connection is possible ; comp. Eph. i. 15. And it is the interpretation, perhaps, which has led to the article τῆς being added before πίστεως. But it should certainly be rejected. The idea requiring a determining clause is not *faith*, which is clear of itself, but the *means of propitiation*. In a passage entirely devoted to the expounding of the fact of expiation, Paul could not possibly fail to indicate the manner in which the means operated. We therefore find the notion of *propitiation* qualified by two parallel and mutually completing clauses : the first, *by faith*, indicating the subjective condition ; and the second, *by His blood*, setting forth the historical and objective condition of the efficacy of the means. Propitiation does not take place except through faith on the part of the saved, and through blood on the part of the Saviour. The attempt of Meyer, Hofmann, etc., to make this clause dependent on προέθετο ("He set Him forth or established Him beforehand . . . *through His blood*") is unnatural. To present or establish a person through or in his blood, would not only be an obscure form of speech, but even offensively harsh. — According to Lev. xvii. 11, the soul of man, the principle of life, is in the blood. The blood flowing forth is the life exhaling. Now the wilful sinner has deserved death. Having used the gift of life to revolt against Him from whom he holds it, it is just that this gift should be withdrawn from him. Hence the sentence : "In the day thou sinnest, thou shalt die." Every act of sin should thus, in strict justice, be followed by death, the violent and instant death of its author. The sinner, it is true, no longer understands this ; for sin stupefies the conscience at the same time that it corrupts the heart and perverts the will. Such, then, is the law which must be set in the light of day before pardon is granted, and that it may be granted. Otherwise the sovereign majesty of God on the one side, and the criminal character of the sinner on the other, would remain shrouded in the conscience of the pardoned sinner ; and such a pardon, instead of laying a foundation for his restoration, would consummate his degradation and entail his eternal ruin. Thus are justified the two qualifications of the means of propitiation indicated here by the apostle : *in blood* and *by faith ;* in other terms — 1. The judgment of God on sin by the shedding of *blood ;* 2. The adherence of the guilty to this judgment by *faith*. The apostolic utterance may consequently be paraphrased thus : "Jesus Christ, whom God settled beforehand as the means of propitiation on the condition of faith, through the shedding of His blood."

Blood does not certainly denote the holy consecration of life in general. It is purely arbitrary to seek any other meaning in the word than it naturally expresses, the fact of a violent and bloody death. This signification is specially obvious in a passage where the word is found in such direct connection with ἱλαστήριον (*propitiation*), in which there is concentrated the whole symbolism of the Jewish sacrifices.

The relation commonly maintained between *propitiation* (the act which renders God favorable) and *blood* is this : the blood of the Messiah, shed as an equivalent for that of sinners, is the indemnity offered to God's justice to purchase the pardon granted by love. But it must be observed that this relation is not stated by the apostle himself, and that the term ἱλάσκεσθαι, *to render propitious*, does not necessarily contain the idea of an indemnity paid in the form of a quantitative equivalent. The word denotes in general the act, whatever it be, in consequence of which God, who was displaying His wrath, is led to display His grace, and to pardon. This propitiatory act is, Luke xviii. 13, 14, the cry of the penitent publican ; Ps. li. 17, the sacrifice of a broken and contrite heart. In the supreme and final redemption which we have in Christ, the way of propitiation is more painful and decisive. The apostle has just told us in what it consists ; he proceeds in the words which follow to explain to us its object : *for the demonstration of His justice.*

The term *demonstration* is remarkable. If the apostle had in view a *payment* offered to justice in *compensation* for the death which sinful men have merited, he would rather have said : "for the *satisfaction* of His justice." The word *manifestation* seems to belong to a somewhat different order of ideas. But let us begin with fixing the meaning of the principal expression : *the righteousness of God.* Luther has connected it with *justification.* But in this case the contrast with the time of God's *long-suffering*, ver. 26, becomes unintelligible, and the two last terms of the same verse : "that He might be *just* and the *justifier*," could not be distinguished from one another. So all interpreters agree to take the word as indicating a divine attribute which, long veiled, was put in the light of day by the cross. Which attribute is it ? *Justice* sometimes denoting *moral perfection* in general, each commentator has taken the term used by Paul as expressing the special attribute which agreed best with his system in regard to the work of redemption. It has been taken to express—(1) *Goodness* (Theodor., Abel., Grot., Seml., etc.) ; (2) *Veracity* or *fidelity* (Ambr., Beza, Turret.) ; (3) *Holiness* (Nitzsch, Neand., Hofm., Lipsius); (4) Righteousness as *justifying* and sanctifying (the Greek Fathers, Mel., Calv., Oltram.) — this meaning is almost identical with Luther's ; (5) Righteousness in so far as it carries the salvation of the elect to its goal ; such is the meaning of Ritschl, which comes very near No. 3 ; (6) *Retributive justice* in God, considered here specially as the principle of the punishment of sin (de Wette, Mey., Philip.). The first five meanings all fall before one common objection ; the Greek language, and Paul's vocabulary in particular, have special terms terms to express each of those particular attributes : χρηστότης, *goodness* ; ἀλήθεια, *veracity* ; πίστις, *faithfulness* ; χάρις, *grace* ; ἁγιωσύνη, *holiness*. Why not use one of these definite terms, instead of introducing into this so important didactic passage a term fitted to occasion the gravest misunderstandings, if it was really to be taken in a sense different from its usual and natural signification ? Now this signification is certainly that of No. 6 : justice, as the mode of action whereby God maintains the *right* of every being, and consequently *order* throughout the whole moral universe, blessing him who has respect to this order, visiting with punishment him who violates it. The essence of God is the absolute love of the good, His *holiness* (Isa. vi. 3 : "Holy, holy, holy" . . .). Now, the *good* is order, the normal relation between all free beings,[1] from God Himself to the last of them. The attribute of *justice*, eternally latent in holiness, passes into the active state with the appearance of the *free* creature. For in the fact of freedom there was included the *possibility* of disorder, and this possibility soon passed into reality. God's abhorrence of evil, His holiness, thus displays itself in the form of justice preserving order and maintaining right. Now, to maintain order without suppressing liberty, there is but one means, and that is punishment. Punishment is order in disorder. It is the revelation of disorder to the sinner's conscience by means of suffering. It is consequently, or at least may be, the point of departure for the reestablishment of order, of the normal relation of free beings. • Thus is explained the notion of the *justice of God,* so often proclaimed in Scripture (John xvii. 25 ; 2 Thess. i. 5 ; 2 Tim. iv. 8 ; Rev. xvi. 5, xix. 2, 11, etc.) ; and especially Rom. ii. 5 et seq., where we see the δικαιοκρισία, the *just judg-*

---

[1] See E. Naville, *Le problème du mal, first discourse.*

ment, distributing among men *wrath* and *tribulation* (vv. 8, 9), *glory* and *peace* (vv. 7-10).—This meaning which we give with Scripture to the word *justice*, and which is in keeping with its generally received use, is also the only one, as we shall see, which suits the context of this passage, and especially the words which follow.

How was the cross the *manifestation of the justice of God?* In two ways so closely united, that either of them separated from the other would lose its value. 1. By the very fact of Christ's sufferings and bloody death. If Paul does not see in this punishment a *quantitative* equivalent of the treatment which every sinner had incurred, this is what clearly appears from such sayings as 2 Cor. v. 21 : " God *made Him sin for us ;*" Gal. iii. 13 : " Christ hath redeemed us from the curse of the law, being *made a curse for us.*" Now, herein precisely consists the *manifestation* of the righteousness wrought out on the cross. God is here revealed as one against whom no creature can revolt without meriting death ; and the sinner is here put in his place in the dust as a malefactor worthy of death. Such is the *objective* manifestation of righteousness. 2. This demonstration, however striking, would be incomplete without the *subjective* or moral manifestation which accompanies it. Every sinner might be called to die on a cross. But no sinner was in a condition to undergo this punishment as Jesus did, accepting it as deserved. This is what He alone could do in virtue of His holiness.[1] The calm and mute resignation with which He allowed Himself to be led to the slaughter, manifested the idea which He Himself formed of the majesty of God and the judgment He was passing on the sin of the world ; from His cross there rose the most perfect homage rendered to the righteousness of God. In this death the sin of mankind was therefore doubly judged, and the righteousness of God doubly manifested—by the external fact of this painful and ignominious punishment, and by the inward act of Christ's conscience, which ratified this dealing of which sin was the object in His person.—But now it will be asked what rendered such a demonstration necessary : *Because,* says St. Paul, *of the tolerance exercised in regard to sins done aforetime.*

For four thousand years the spectacle presented by mankind to the whole moral universe (comp. 1 Cor. iv. 9) was, so to speak, a continual scandal. With the exception of some great examples of judgments, divine righteousness seemed to be asleep ; one might even have asked if it existed. Men sinned here below, and yet they lived. They sinned on, and yet reached in safety a hoary old age ! . . . Where were the *wages of sin ?* It was this relative impunity which rendered a solemn manifestation of righteousness necessary. Many commentators have completely mistaken the meaning of this passage, by giving to the word πάρεσις, which we have translated *tolerance,* the sense of *pardon* (Orig., Luth., Calv., Calov. ; see also the Geneva translation of 1557, and, following it, Osterv. etc.). This first mistake has led to another. There has been given to the preposition διά the meaning of *by,* which it cannot have when governing the accusative, or it has been translated *in view of*, which would have required the preposition εἰς. The first error lies in confounding the term πάρεσις *(tolerance, impunity)* with ἀφεσις *(remission, pardon).* The second of these substantives comes from the verb ἀφιέναι, *to send away, dismiss,* pardon *(remittere)* ; while the first used here comes from the verb παριέναι, *to let pass,* neglect, not to occupy oneself with (*prœtermittere*) ; nearly the same idea as that expressed by the word ὑπεριδεῖν, *to close the eyes to,* Acts xviii. 30. The signification of the verb παριέναι appears clearly from the two following passages : Sir. xxiii. 2 : "Lest sins should remain unpunished (μὴ παριῶνται τὰ ἀ μαρτήματα);" and Xenophon, *Hipparchic.* vii. 10 : "Such sins must not be allowed to pass unpunished (τὰ οὖν τοιαῦτα

---

[1] "O *righteous* Father, the world hath not known Thee; but I have known Thee," John xvii. 25.

ἁμαρτήματα οὐ χρὴ παριέναι ἀκόλαστα)." It is worthy of remark also that in these two places sin is designated by the same word ἁμάρτημα as Paul employs in our passage : sin in the form of positive fault, *transgression*. The real sense of πάρεσις is therefore not doubtful. It has been given by Theodor., Grot., Beng. ; it is now almost universally received (Thol., Olsh., Mey., Fritzs., Rück., de Wette, Philip. etc.). [1] The διά can thus receive its true meaning (with the accusative) : *on account of ;* and the idea of the passage becomes clear : God judged it necessary, on account of the impunity so long enjoyed by those myriads of sinners who succeeded one another on the earth, at length to manifest His justice by a striking act ; and He did so by realizing in the death of Jesus the punishment which each of those sinners would have deserved to undergo.—Ritschl, who, on account of his theory regarding the righteousness of God (see on i. 18), could not accept this meaning, supposes another interpretation (II. p. 217 et seq.). Tolerance (πάρεσις) is not, according to him, contrasted with merited *punishment*, but with the *pardon* which God has finally granted. Ver. 25 would thus signify that till the coming of Jesus Christ, God had *only* exercised patience without pardoning, but that in Christ the justice of God (His faithfulness to the salvation of His elect) had advanced so far as to give complete pardon. But where then, asks Gess, is this *only*, so necessary to indicate the advance from tolerance to pardon ? The natural contrast to impunity is not pardon, but punishment ; comp. ii. 4, 5, and the parallel passage to ours, Acts xvii. 30, 31 : "*The times of ignorance God winked at*, but now commandeth men to repent, *because* He hath appointed a day in which He will *judge* the world *in righteousness.*" Finally, it is impossible on this interpretation to give a natural meaning to the words *on account of*. For pardon was not given *because of* the impunity exercised toward those sins. Paul would have required to say, either : *because of* those sins themselves, or : *following up* the long tolerance exercised toward them.

Several commentators (Calovius, for example) refer the expression : *sins done aforetime*, not to the sins of *mankind* who lived before Christ, but to those committed by every believer *before his conversion*. It is difficult in this sense to explain the words which follow : *at this time*, which form an antithesis to the former. We must apply them to the moment when each sinner in particular *believes*. But this meaning does not correspond to the gravity of the expression : *at this time*, in which the apostle evidently contrasts the period of completion with that of general impunity, and even with the eternal decree (the πρόθεσις).

It may be further asked if these *sins done aforetime* are those of all mankind anterior to Christ, or perhaps, as Philippi thinks, only those of the Jews. The argument which this commentator derives from the meaning of ἱλαστήριον, the lid of the ark, the *propitiatory* so called, has of course no weight with us. Might one be found in the remarkable parallel, Heb. ix. 15 : "The transgressions that were *under the first testament* " ? No, for this restricted application follows naturally from the particular aim of the Epistle to the Hebrews (comp. for example, ii. 16). It may even be said that the *demonstration* of which the apostle speaks was less necessary for Israel than for the rest of mankind. For the sacrifices instituted by God were already a homage rendered to his justice. But this homage was not sufficient ; for there was wanting in it that which gives value to the sacrifice of Christ ; the victim *underwent* death, but did not *accept* it. Hence it was that the death of the Messiah necessarily closed the long series of the Levitical sacrifices. No more can we receive the opinion of Beza, Cocceius,

---

[1] Morison (p. 323) refers to the strange misunderstanding of Chrysostom, reproduced by Œcumen., Theophyl., Phot., which makes πάρεσις (strictly : relaxation of the muscles) denote here the *paralysis*, the spiritual death of the sinner. Hence probably the reading πωρωσις (MS. 46).

Morison, who think the *sins that are past* are those of the faithful of the Old Testament whom God pardoned from regard to the future sacrifice of Christ. The article τῶν ("*the* sins") does not admit of this restriction, which there is nothing else to indicate. And the sacrifice of Christ cannot be explained here by an end so special.

But if it is asked why Paul gives as the reason for this sacrifice only the *past* and not the *future* sins of mankind, as if the death of Christ did not apply equally to the latter, the answer is easy, from the apostle's standpoint: the righteousness of God once revealed in the sacrifice of the cross, this demonstration *remains*. Whatever happens, nothing can again efface it from the history of the world, nor from the conscience of mankind. Henceforth no illusion is possible: all sin must be pardoned—or judged.

Regarded from the point of view here taken by the apostle, the death of Jesus is in the history of humanity, something like what would emerge in the life of a sinner had he a time of perfect lucidity when, his conscience being miraculously brought into one with the mind of God regarding sin, he should judge himself as God judges him. Such a moment would be to this man the starting-point of a total transformation. Thus the demonstration of righteousness given to the world by the cross of Christ at the close of the long economy of *sin tolerated*, founded the new epoch, and with the possibility of pardon established the principle of the radical renewal of humanity.

Ver. 26. The first words of this verse: *during the forbearance of God*, depend naturally on the word πάρεσισ, *tolerance:* "the tolerance (shown) during the forbearance of God." It is less simple to connect this clause with the participle προγεγονότων: "committed formerly during the forbearance of God." For the principal idea in what precedes, that which needs most to be explained, is that of the *tolerance*, and not that expressed by this participle. Meyer gives to the preposition ἐν the meaning of *by:* "the tolerance exercised toward the sins that are passed *by* the forbearance of God." But the following antithesis: *at this time*, imperatively requires the *temporal* meaning of the clause ἐν τῇ ἀνοχῇ.—At the first glance it seems strange that in a proposition of which *God* is the subject, the apostle should say, not: "during *his* forbearance," but: "during the forbearance *of God*." The reason of this apparent incorrectness is not, as has been thought, the remoteness of the subject, nor the fact that Paul is now expressing himself as it were from his own point of view, and not from that of God (Mey.). Rather it is that which is finely given by Matthias: by the word *God* the apostle brings more into relief the contrast between *men's* conduct (their constant *sins*) and *God's* (His long-suffering).

We have seen that ver. 26 should begin with the words reproduced from ver. 25: *for the demonstration of His justice*. To what purpose this repetition? Had not the reason which rendered the demonstration of righteousness necessary been sufficiently explained in ver. 25? Why raise this point emphatically once more to explain it anew? This form is surprising, especially in a passage of such extraordinary conciseness. De Wette and Meyer content themselves with saying: Repetition of the εἰς ἐνδειξιν (*for the demonstration*), ver. 25. But again, why the change of preposition: in ver. 25, εἰς; here, πρός? We get the answer: a matter of style (Mey.), or of euphony (Gess), wholly indifferent as to meaning. With a writer like Paul—our readers, we hope, are convinced of this—such answers are insufficient. Rückert and Hofmann, to avoid these difficulties, think that the words: *for the demonstration* . . . should not be made dependent, like the similar words of ver. 25, on the verb προέθετο, *had established*, but on the substantive *forbearance:* "during the time of His forbearance, a forbearance which had in view the manifestation of His justice at a later period." De Wette replies, with reason, that were we to connect these words with so subordinate an idea, the reader's mind would be diverted from the essential thought of the entire passage. Besides, how can we fail to see in the πρὸς ἔνδειξιν (*for the manifestation*) of ver. 26 the resumption of the similar expression, ver. 25? The fact of this repetition is not, as it seems to us, so difficult to explain. The moral necessity of such a manifestation had been demonstrated by the tolerance of God in the *past;* for it had thrown a veil over the righteousness of God. But the explanation was not complete. The object to be gained in the *future* by this demonstration must also be indicated. And this is the end served by the repetition of this same expression in ver. 26 : "for the demonstration, I say, *in view of*" ... Thus at the same time is explained the change of preposition. In ver. 25 the demonstration itself was regarded as an *end:* "whom he set forth beforehand as a propitiation *for* the demonstration (εἰς, with a view to)" ... But in ver. 26 this same demonstration becomes a *means*, with a view to a new and more remote end : "*for* the demonstration of His justice, *that He might be* (literally, *with a view to being*) just, and the justifier" ... The *demonstration* is always the end, no doubt, but now it is only the near and immediate object—such is exactly the meaning of the Greek preposition πρός, which is substituted for the εἰς of ver. 25—compared with a more distant and final end which opens up to view, and for which the apostle now reserves the εἰς (with a view to) : "*with a view to* being just, and the justifier.'' Comp. on the relation of these two prepositions, Eph. iv. 12 : "*for* (πρός) the perfecting of the saints *with a view to* a (εἰς) work of ministry." Here we may have a convincing proof that nothing is accidental in the style of a man like Paul. Never did jeweller chisel his diamonds more carefully than the apostle does the expression of his thoughts. This delicate care of the slightest shades is also shown in the addition of the article τήν before ἔνδειξιν in ver. 26, an addition sufficiently attested by the four Alex. Mjj., and by a Mj. from each of the other two families (D P). In ver. 25 the notion of demonstration was yet abstract : "*in demonstration* of righteousness.'' In ver. 26 it is now known ; it is a concrete fact which should conspire to a new end ; hence the addition of the article : " for that manifestation of which I speak, with a view to" ... The following words : *at this time*, express one of the gravest thoughts of the passage. They bring out the full solemnity of the present epoch marked by this unexampled appearance, preordained and in a sense awaited by God Himself for so long. For without this prevision the long forbearance of the forty previous centuries would have been morally impossible ; comp. Acts xvii. 30 (in regard to the Gentiles), and Heb. ix. 26 : " But now once in the end of the ages hath He appeared, to put away sin by the sacrifice of Himself " (in regard to Israel).

And what was the *end* with a view to which this demonstration of righteousness was required at this time ? The apostle answers : *that he might be just and justifying*—that is to say, " that while being and remaining just, God might justify. It was a great problem, a problem worthy of divine wisdom, which the sin of man set before God—to remain just while justifying (declaring just) man who had become unjust. God did not shrink from the task. He had even solved the difficulty beforehand in His eternal counsel, before creating man free ; otherwise, would not this creation have merited the charge of imprudence ? God had beside Him, in Christ (προέθετο, ver. 25 ; comp. Eph. i. 3, 4), the means of being at once *just* and *justifying*—that is to say, just while justifying, and justifying while remaining just.—The words : that He might *be just*, are usually understood in the logical sense : "that He might *be known* to be just." Gess rightly objects to this attenuation of the word *be*. The second predicate : *and justifying*, does not suit this idea of *being known*. If God did not once *show Himself* perfectly just, *would* He be so in reality ? Gess rightly says : " A judge who hates evil, but does not judge it, *is* not just : if the righteousness of God did not show itself, it would not exist." In not smiting those sinners at once with the thunderbolt of His vengeance, those who had lived during the time of forbearance, God had not *shown* Himself just ; and if He had continued to act thus indefinitely, mankind and the entire moral universe would have had good right to conclude that He *was* not just. It is obvious that the words : *that He might be just*, do not, strictly speaking, express a new idea : they reproduce in a different form the reason for the demonstration of righteousness already given in ver. 25 in the words : "because of the tolerance exercised toward sins done aforetime." If this tolerance had not at length issued in a manifestation of justice, justice itself would have been annihilated. The thought is nevertheless of supreme importance here, at the close of this exposition. Men must not imagine, as they might easily do, especially with pardon before them, that the justice of God is somehow completely absorbed in His grace through the act of justifying. There is in the firm and immovable will of God to maintain right and order in the universe—His justice, that is to say—the principle of the *justification* of believers no doubt, but not less certainly that of the *judgment* of the impenitent. Now, if God did not show Himself *just* at the moment when He justifies the unjust, there would be in such a pardon what would plunge sinners into the most dangerous illusion. They could no longer seriously suppose that they were on their way to give in an account ; and judgment would burst on them as a terrible surprise. This is what God could not desire, and hence He has exercised the divine privilege of pardon only through means of a striking and solemn manifestation of His justice. He would really have given up His justice if, in this supreme moment of His manifestation, He had not displayed it brightly on the earth.

After having secured His righteousness, He is able to *justify* the unjust ; for He has, in Christ, the means of *justifying* him *justly*. We have seen that the cross re-establishes order by putting each in his place, the holy God on His throne, rebellious man in the dust. So long as this homage, making reparation for the past, remains without us, it does not save us ; but as soon as we make it ourselves *by faith in Jesus*, it avails for us, and God can *justly* absolve us. This is what is expressed by the last words, to which the passage pointed from the first : *and justifying him who is of the faith in Jesus*. By adhering to this manifestation of divine righteousness accomplished in Jesus, the believer makes it morally his own. He renders homage personally to the right which God has over him. He sees in his own person the malefactor worthy of death, who should have undergone and accepted what Jesus underwent and accepted. He exclaims, like that Bechuana in his simple savage language : Away from that, Christ ; that's my place ! Sin is thus judged in his conscience, as it was in that of the dying Jesus—that is to say, as it is by the holiness of God himself, and as it never could have been by the ever imperfect repentance of a sinner. By appropriating to himself the homage rendered to the majesty of God by the Crucified One, the believer is himself crucified as it were in the eyes of God ; moral order is re-established, and judgment can take end by an act of absolution. As to the impenitent sinner, who refuses to the divine majesty the homage contained in the act of faith, the demonstration of righteousness given on the cross remains as the proof that he will certainly meet with this divine attribute in the judgment.—The phrase : *to be of the faith*, has nothing surprising in Paul's style ; comp. the εἶναι ἐκ, ii. 8 ; Gal. iii. 7, 10, etc. It forcibly expresses the new mode of being which becomes the believer's as soon as he ceases to draw his righteousness from himself and derives it wholly from Jesus.—Three Mjj. read the accusative Ἰησοῦν, which would lead to the impossible sense : "and the justifier of Jesus by faith." This error probably arises from the abridged form ΙΥ in the ancient Mjj., which might easily be read ΙΝ. Two MSS. (F G) wholly reject this name (see Meyer).[1] The phrase : "him who is of the faith," without any indication of

---

[1] Tischendorf, eighth edition, does not mention this omission. Could he have found it to be not the fact ? No, for Westcott and Hort mention it in the Appendix to their New Testament.—T. W. C.

the object of faith, would not be impossible. This reading has been accepted by Oltramare. But two MSS. of the ninth century do not suffice to justify it. Nothing could better close this piece than the name of the historical personage to whose unspeakable love mankind owes this eternal blessing.

The Expiation.

We have endeavored to reproduce exactly the meaning of the expressions used by the apostle in this important passage, and to rise to the sum of the ideas which it contains. In what does the apostolical conception, as we have understood it, differ from the current theories on this fundamental subject?

If we compare it first with the doctrine generally received in the church, the point on which the difference seems to us to bear is this : in the ecclesiastical theory God demands the punishment of Christ as a satisfaction to Himself, in so far as His justice ought to have an equivalent for the penalty merited by man, to permit divine love to pardon. From the point of view to which the exposition of the apostle brings us, this equivalent is not intended to *satisfy* divine justice except by *manifesting* it, and in *re-establishing* the normal relation between God and the guilty creature. By sin, in short, God loses *His supreme place* in the conscience of the creature ; by this demonstration of justice He recovers it.[1] In consequence of sin, the creature no longer comprehends and feels the *gravity* of his rebellion ; by this manifestation God makes it palpable to him. On this view it is not necessary that the sacrifice of reparation should be the equivalent of the penalty incurred by the multitude of sinful men, viewed as the *sum* of the merited sufferings ; it is enough that it be so as regards the physical and moral *character* of the sufferings due to sin in itself.

The defenders of the received theory will no doubt ask if, on this view, the expiation is not pointed simply to the conscience of the creature, instead of being also a reparation offered to God Himself. But if it is true that a holy God cannot pardon, except in so far as the pardon itself establishes the absolute guilt of sin and the inviolability of the divine majesty, and so includes a guarantee for the re-establishment of order in the relation between the sinner and God, and if this condition is found only in the punishment of sin holily undertaken and humbly accepted by Him who alone was able to do so, is not the necessity of expiation in relation to the absolute Good, *to God Himself*, demonstrated? His holiness would protest against every pardon which did not fulfil the double condition of glorifying His outraged majesty and displaying the condemnation of sin. Now, this double end is gained only by the expiatory sacrifice. But the necessity of this sacrifice arises from His whole divine character, in other words, from his holiness, the principle at once of His love and justice, and not exclusively of His justice. And, in truth, the apostle nowhere expresses the idea of a conflict between justice and love as requiring the expiation. It is grace that saves, and it saves by the demonstration of justice which, in the act of expiation, restores God to His place and man to his. Such is the condition on which divine love can pardon without entailing on the sinner the final degradation of his conscience and the eternal consolidation of his sin.

This view also evades the grand objection which is so generally raised in our day against a satisfaction made to justice by means of the substitution of the innocent for the guilty. No doubt the ordinary theory of expiation may be defended by asking who would be entitled to complain of such a transaction : not God who establishes it, nor the Mediator who voluntarily sacrifices Himself, nor man whose salvation is affected by it. But, in any case, this objection does not apply to the apostolic conception as we have expounded it. For whenever the question ceases to be one of legal satisfaction, and becomes a simple demonstration of God's right, no ground remains for protesting in the name of justice. Who could accuse God of injustice for having made use of Job and his sufferings to prove to Satan that he can obtain from the children of the dust a disinterested homage, a free submission, which is not that of the merce-

---

[1] This view is nearly equivalent to what is called the governmental theory of the Atonement. It is superficial, and falls very far below the apostle's thought and words. Justice is one thing, and the re-establishment of order is quite another.—T. W. C.

nary? Similarly, who can arraign the divine justice for having given to sinful man, in the person of Jesus, a convincing demonstration of the judgment which the guilty one deserved at his hand? Deserved, did I say? of the judgment which will visit him without fail if he refuses to join by faith in that homage solemnly rendered to God's rights, and rejects the reconciliation which God offers him in this form.

It seems to us, then, that the true apostolical conception, while firmly establishing the fact of expiation, which is, historically speaking—as no one can deny—the distinctive feature of Christianity, secures it from the grave objections which in these days have led so many to look on this fundamental dogma with suspicion.

But some would perhaps say: Such a view rests, as much as the so-called orthodox theory, on notions of *right* and *justice*, which belong to a lower sphere, to the *legal* and *juridical* domain. A noble and generous man will not seek to explain his conduct by reasons taken from so external an order; how much less should we have recourse to them to explain that of God?—Those who speak thus do not sufficiently reflect that we have to do in this question not with God in His essence, but with God in His relation to free man. Now, the latter is not holy to begin with; the use which he makes of his liberty is not yet regulated by love. The attribute of justice (the firm resolution to maintain order, whose existence is latent in the divine *holiness*) must therefore appear as a necessary safeguard as soon as liberty comes on the stage, and with it the possibility of disorder; and this attribute must remain in exercise as long as the educational period of the life of the creature lasts, that is to say, until he has reached perfection in love. Then all those factors, right, law, justice, will return to their latent state. But till then, God, as the guardian of the normal relations between free beings, must keep by law and check by punishment every being disposed to trample on His authority, or on the liberty of His fellows. Thus it is that the work of righteousness necessarily belongs to God's educating and redeeming work, without which the world of free beings would soon be no better than a chaos, from which goodness, the end of creation, would be forever banished. Blot out this factor from the government of the world, and the free being becomes Titan, no longer arrested by anything in the execution of any caprice. God's place is overthrown, and the creatures destroy one another mutually. It is common to regard *love* as the fundamental feature of the divine character; and in this way it is very difficult to reach the attribute of justice. Most thinkers, indeed, do not reach it at all. This one fact should serve to show the error in which they are entangled. *Holy, holy, holy,* say the creatures nearest to God, when celebrating His perfection (Isa. vi.), and not *good, good, good.* Holiness, such is the essence of God; and holiness is the absolute love of the good, the absolute horror of evil. Hence it is not difficult to deduce both love and justice. Love is the goodwill of God toward all free beings who are destined to realize the good. Love goes out to the individuals, as holiness to the good itself which they ought to produce. Justice, on the other hand, is the firm purpose of God to maintain the normal relation between all these beings by his blessings and punishments. It is obvious that justice is included no less necessarily than love itself in the fundamental feature of the divine character, holiness. It is no offence therefore to God to speak of His justice and His rights. The exercise of a right is only a shame when the being who exercises it makes it subservient to the gratification of his egoism. It is, on the contrary, a glory to one who, like God, knows that in preserving His place He is securing the good of all others. For, as Gess admirably expounds it, God, in maintaining His supreme dignity, preserves to the creatures *their most precious treasure,* a God worthy of their respect and love.

Unjustifiable antipathy to the notions of right and justice, as applied to God, has led contemporary thought to very divergent and insufficient explanations of the death of Christ.

Some see nothing more in this event than an inevitable historical result of the conflict between the holiness of Jesus and the immoral character of his contemporaries. This solution is well answered by Hausrath himself: "Our faith gives to the question: Why did Christ require to die on the cross? another answer than that drawn from the history of His time. For the history of the ideal cannot be an isolated and particular fact; its contents are absolute; it has an eternal value which does not belong to a given moment, but to the whole of mankind. Every man should recognize in such a history a mystery of grace consummated *also for him*" (*Neutest. Zeitgesch.* I. 450).

Wherein consists this mystery of grace contained in the Crucified One for every man? In the fact, answer many, that here we find the manifestation of divine love to mankind. "The ray of love," says Pfleiderer, "such is the true saviour of mankind. . . . And as to Jesus, He is the sun, the focus in whom all the rays of this light scattered elsewhere are concentrated" (*Wissensch. Vorträge über religiöse Fragen*). On this view, Jesus sacrificed himself only to attest by this act of devotion the full greatness of divine love. But what, then, is a devotion which has no other object than to witness to itself? An exhibition of love, which might be compared to that of the woman who committed suicide, a few years ago, to awake, as she said, the dormant genius of her husband by this token of her love. Besides, how could the sacrifice of his life made by a man for his fellow-men demonstrate the love of God? We may, indeed, see in it the attestation of *brotherly* love in its most eminent degree, but we do not find the love *of the Father*.

Others, finally, regard the death of Christ only as the culminating point of His consecration to God and men, of His holiness. "These texts," says Sabatier, after quoting Rom. vi. and 2 Cor. v., "place the value of the death of Jesus not in any satisfaction whatever offered to God, but in the *annihilation of sin*, which this death brings about" (*L'ap. Paul*, p. 202). To the same effect M. de Pressensé expresses himself thus: "This generous suffering, which Jesus voluntarily accepts, is an act of love and obedience; and hence its restoring and redeeming character. . . . In the name of humanity Christ *reverses the rebellion of Eden; He brings back the heart of man to God*. . . . In the person of a holy victim, humanity returns to the God who waited for it from the first days of the world" (*Vie de Jésus*, pp. 642 and 643). Most modern theories (Hofmann, Ritschl), if we mistake not, are substantially the same, to wit, the spiritual resurrection of humanity through Christ. By the holiness he so painfully realized, and of which His bloody death was the crown, Jesus has given birth to a humanity which breaks with sin, and gives itself to God; and God, foreseeing this future holiness of believers, and regarding it as already realized, pardons their sins from love of this expected perfection. But is this the apostle's view? He speaks of a demonstration of *justice*, and not only of *holiness*. Then he ascribes to *death*, to *blood*, a peculiar and independent value. So he certainly does in our passage, but more expressly still in the words, v. 10: "If, when we were enemies, we were reconciled (*justified*, ver. 9) *by His death* (His blood, ver. 9), much more, being reconciled, we shall be saved *by His life* (*through him*, ver. 9)." It is by His death, accordingly, that Jesus reconciles or justifies, as it is by his life that he sanctifies and perfects salvation. Finally, the serious practical difficulty in the way of this theory lies, as we think, in the fact that, like the Catholic doctrine, it makes justification rest on sanctification (present or future), while the characteristic of gospel doctrine, what, to use Paul's language, may be called *its folly*, but what is in reality its divine wisdom, is its founding justification on the atonement perfected by Christ's blood, to raise afterward on this basis the work of sanctification by the Holy Spirit.[1]

NINTH PASSAGE (3:27-31)

The Harmony of this Mode of Justification with the true Meaning of the Law

The apostle had asserted, ver. 21, that *the law* and *the prophets* themselves

[1] We would not hold Professor Gess bound to all the views which we have expressed in this excursus. But we must say, that if we have succeeded in throwing any light on this passage of St. Paul, and on the fact of the atonement (*that depth into which the angels desire to look*, 1 Pet. i. 12), we owe it chiefly to that eminent theologian; comp. especially, the two articles entitled, "Zur Lehre von der Versöhnung," and "Die Nothwendigkeit des Sühnens Christi," in the *Jahrbücher für Deutsche Theol.* 1857, 1858, and 1859.

bear witness to the mode of justification revealed in the gospel. This he demonstrates, first generally, from the spirit of the law, then specially, from the example of Abraham, in the two following pieces: chap. iii. 27–31 and chap. iv. As the theme of the preceding piece was expressed in the words of vv. 21 and 22: *righteousness of God revealed without law . . . by faith in Jesus Christ*, that of the following development is found in the words of ver. 21: *witnessed by the law and by the prophets*. We see how rigorously the apostle adheres to order in his work.

The piece, vv. 27–31, argues from all that precedes to the harmony of justification by faith with the Old Testament—1. Inasmuch as the law and the gospel equally exclude justification by works, vv. 27 and 28; this is the negative demonstration; and 2. Inasmuch as only justification by faith harmonizes with the Monotheism which is the doctrinal basis of the whole Old Testament, vv. 29–31; such is the positive demonstration.

Vv. 27, 28. "*Where is the*[1] *boasting then? It is excluded. By what law? of works? Nay, but by that of faith. For*[2] *we judge that man is justified by faith*[3] *without works of law.*"—Οὖν, *then:* in consequence of the great fact which has been explained, and of the means of justification which it implies (vv. 23–26).—Καύχησις, *boasting*, vainglory; this term denotes not the *object* boasted of, but the *act* of self-glorification. The article ἡ, *the*, marks this boasting as well known; it is therefore the boasting of the Jews which is referred to. The word might be connected with the καυχᾶσθαι ἐν Θεῷ, ii. 17, and understood of the glory which the Jews sought to borrow from their exceptional position; but the context, and especially the following verse, prove that the apostle has in view the pretension of the Jews to justify themselves by their own works, instead of deriving their righteousness from the work of Christ.—This pretension has been excluded forever by the work described, vv. 24–26. There remains nothing else for man to do than to lay hold of it by faith. This question has something of a triumphant character; comp. the similar form, 1 Cor. i. 20. The self-righteousness of the Jews is treated here as the wisdom of the Greeks is in that passage. The apostle seeks it, and before the cross it vanishes. Hofmann understands this exclamation of the vainglory to which even Christians might give themselves up: "Have we then, we Christians, thus justified, whereof to boast?" This interpretation is bound up with that of the same author, according to which the question, iii. 9: "Have we any advantage (over those whom judgment will overtake)?" is also put in the mouth of Christians. But it is evident that, like the question of ver. 9, this refers specially to Jewish prejudice; for it is expressly combated in the following words, ver. 29, and it is alluded to by the article ἡ, *the*, before καύχησις.—Only the question arises, What leads the apostle to put such a question here? The answer seems to us to be this. His intention in these few verses is to show the profound harmony between the law and the gospel. Now the conclusion to which he had been led by the searching study of the law, vv. 9–20, was, that it was intended to shut the mouths of all men, and of the Jews in particular, before God, by giving them the knowledge of sin. Hence it followed that the mode of justification which best agreed with the law was that which traced the origin of righteousness not to the works of the law, by means of which man thinks that he can justify himself, but to faith; for, like the law itself, the righteousness of faith brings all boasting to silence, so that the righteousness of works, which lays a foundation for boasting, is contrary to the law, while that of faith, which excludes it, is alone in harmony with the law. And this is exactly what Paul brings out in the following

---

[1] F G It., Or. (Lat. trans.) Aug. add σου after καυχησις (*thy* boasting).
[2] ℵ A D E F G, It.: γαρ, *for*, instead of ουν, *then*, which T. R. reads, with B C K L P, Syr.
[3] T. R. places πιστει before δικαιουσθαι, with K L P, Syr., while all the rest place δικαιουσθαι before πιστει.

questions.—In these two questions the term *law* is taken in a general sense. This word is often used by Paul to denote a *mode of action* which is imposed on the individual, a rule to which he is subject, a principle which determines his conduct. Sometimes when thus understood it is taken in a good sense; for example, viii. 2 : "the law of the spirit of life which is in Jesus Christ;" again it is used in a bad sense; so vii. 23 : "the law which is in my members;" or, again, it is applied in both ways, good and bad at once; comp. vii. 21. As Baur well says, the word *law* denotes in general " a formula which serves to regulate the relation between God and man." The genitive τῶν ἔργων, *of works*, depends on a νόμον understood, as is proved by the repetition of this word before πίστεως.

That glory which man derives from his self-righteousness, and which the law had already foreclosed, has been finally excluded. And by what means? By a rule of works? Certainly not, for such a means would rather have promoted it, but by that of faith (ver. 26.) The apostle thus reaches the striking result that the rule of works would contradict the law, and that the rule of faith is that which harmonizes with it.—He here uses the word νόμος, *rule*, probably because he was speaking of *excluding*, and this requires something firm.

Ver. 28. The relation between this verse and the preceding rests on the contrast between the two ideas καύχησις and πίστει δικαιοῦσθαι, boasting and *being justified by faith*. "We exclude boasting in proportion as we affirm justification by faith."—Several commentators read οὖν, *then*, after T. R., which is supported by the *Vat.* and the Byzs. In that case this verse would form the conclusion from what precedes : " We conclude, then, that man" . . . But if the apostle were *concluding* finally in ver. 28, why would he recommence to argue in the following verse? We must therefore prefer the reading of the other Alexs. and the Greco-Lats., γάρ, *for :* "For we deem, we assert that" . . . Another question is, Whether, with the Byzs., we are to put the word πίστει, *by faith*, before the verb δικαιοῦσθαι, *to be justified*, or whether it is better to put it after, with the other two families, and so give the idea of justification the dominant place over that of the means of obtaining it. The connection with ver. 27 certainly speaks in favor of the Byz. reading, which has the Peshito for it. It is the idea of being justified *by faith*, and not that of *being justified* in general, which excludes boasting.—It is worth remarking the word ἄνθρωπον, man. This general term is chosen designedly : "whatever bears the name of man, Jew as well as Gentile, depends on the justification which is of faith, and can have no other." If it is so, it is plain that boasting is *finally excluded*. The apostle adds : "*without works of law*, that is to say, without participation in any of those works which are wrought in the servile and mercenary spirit which prevails under the rule of law (see on ver. 20). The matter in question here is neither final salvation nor works as fruits of faith (*good works*, Eph. ii. 10 ; Tit. iii. 8). For these will be necessary in the day of judgment (see on ii. 13).

If it were otherwise, if the works of the law had not been *excluded* by the great act of expiation described vv. 24–26, and by the *rule of faith* involved in it, it would be found that God provided for the salvation of a *part* of mankind only, and forgot the rest. The unity of God is not compatible with this difference in his mode of acting. Now the dogma of the unity of God is the basis of the law, and of the whole of Judaism. On this point, too, therefore, the law is at one with faith, vv. 29–31.

Vv. 29, 30. " *Or is he the God of the Jews only?*[1] *is he*[2] *not also of the Gentiles? Yes, of the Gentiles also : seeing*[3] *it is one God, who shall bring out the justification of the circumcised from faith, and who shall bring about*

---
[1] B and several Fathers : μονων instead of μονον.
[2] T. R. reads δε after ουχι with L P only.
[3] Instead of επειπερ, which T. R. reads, with D E F G K L P, we find ειπερ in ℵ A B C.

that of the uncircumcised by the faith."—The meaning of the ἤ, *or*, when prefixed to a question by Paul, is familiar to us : *"Or* if you do not admit that" . . . ? This question therefore goes to show that the negation of what precedes violates the Monotheism so dear to the Jews, and in which they gloried. The genitive 'Ιουδαίων, *of Jews*, used without the article, denotes the category. Meyer refuses to take this word as the complement of the predicate Θεός, *God*, understood ; but wrongly ;. the natural meaning is : "Is God *the God* of the Jews ?" Comp. ii. 29, 1 Cor. xiv. 33, and Luke xx. 38 (with Matt. xxii. 32). Otherwise we should require to apply here the phrase εἶναί τινος, *to be the property of* (to belong to), which does not correspond to the relation between God and man.—To the question : *Is He not also the God of the Gentiles?* Paul could answer with assurance : *yes, of the Gentiles also ;* for the entire Old Testament had already drawn from Monotheism this glorious inference. The psalms celebrated Jehovah as the God of all the earth, before whom the nations walk with trembling (Ps. xcvi.–xcviii., c.). Jeremiah called Him (x. 7) the *King of nations ;* and the apostle himself had demonstrated in chap. i. the existence of a universal divine revelation, which is the first foundation of universalism.

Ver. 30. The Alex. read εἴπερ : *if truly.* This reading might suffice if the apostle were merely repeating the principle of the unity of God as the basis of the preceding assertion : "*if indeed* God is one." But he goes further ; this principle of the unity of God serves him as a point of departure from which to draw important inferences expressed in a weighty proposition : "*who will justify.*" To warrant him in doing so, it is not enough that he has asserted the unity of God as an admitted supposition : "*if indeed.*" He must have laid it down as an indubitable fact which could serve as a basis for argument. We must therefore prefer the reading of the other two families : ἐπείπερ, *seeing that.* [1] Monotheism has as its natural corollary the expectation of one only means of justification for the whole human race. No doubt this dogma is compatible with a temporary particularism, of a pedagogic nature ; but as soon as the decisive question arises, that of final salvation or condemnation, the unity must appear. A dualism on this point would imply a duality in God's essence : "*who* (in consequence of His unity) *will justify.*" The future : *will justify,* has been variously explained. Some think that it expresses *logical* consequence (Rück. Hofm.) ; others, that it refers to the day of judgment (Beza, Fritzs.) ; a third party refer it to *all the particular cases* of justification which have taken or shall take place in history. The last sense seems the most natural : the whole new development of history, which is now opening, appears to the apostle as the consequence of the fundamental dogma of Judaism.—Meyer alleges that the difference of the two prepositions ἐκ and διά, *from* and *by* (which we have sought to render in our translation), is purely accidental. Is it also accidental that the article τῆς, *the*, which was wanting in the first proposition before the word πίστεως, *faith*, is added in the second ? Experience has convinced us that Paul's style is not at the mercy of chance, even in its most secondary elements. On the other hand, must we, with Calvin, find the difference a pure irony : "If any one insists on a difference between Jews and Gentiles, well and good ! I shall make over one to him ; the first obtains righteousness *from* faith, the second *by* faith." No ; it would be much better to abandon the attempt to give a meaning to this slight difference, than to make the apostle a poor wit. The following, as it seems to me, is the shade of meaning which the apostle meant to express. With regard to the Jew, who laid claim to a *righteousness of works*, he contrasts category with

---

[1] The other reading, however, is better supported, and is adopted by Tisch., Treg., and Westcote and Hort.—T. W. C.

category by using the preposition ἐκ, *from, out of*, which denotes origin and nature : *a righteousness of faith*. Hence, too, he omits the article, which would have described the concrete fact, rather than the quality. But when he comes to speak of the Gentiles, who had been destitute till then of every means of reaching any righteousness whatever, he chooses the preposition διά, *by : by means of*, which points to faith simply as the *way* by which they reach the unexpected end ; and he adds the article because faith presents itself to his mind, in this relation, as *the* well-known means, besides which the Gentile does not dream of any other.

The harmony between the Mosaic law and justification by faith has been demonstrated from two points of view—1. That of the *universal humiliation* (the exclusion of all boasting), which results from the former and constitutes the basis of the latter (vv. 27, 28). 2. That of *the unity of God*, which is the basis of Israelitish Mosaism and prophetism, as well as that of evangelical universalism (vv. 29, 30). Thereafter nothing more natural than the conclusion drawn in ver. 31.

Ver. 31. "*Do we then make void the law through faith ? That be far from us ! Much rather we establish*[1] *the law.*"—This verse has been misunderstood by most commentators. Some (Aug., Luth., Mel., Calv., Philip., Rück.) apply it to the sanctification which springs from faith, and by which the gospel finally realizes the fulfilment of the law. This is the thesis which will be developed in chaps. vi.–viii. We do not deny that the apostle might defer the full development of a maxim thrown out beforehand, and, as it were, by the way ; comp. the sayings, iii. 3 and 20*b*. But yet he must have been logically led to such sentences by their necessary connection with the context. Now this is not the case here. What is there at this point to lead the apostle to concern himself with the sanctifying power of faith ? Let us remark, further, that ver. 31 is connected by *then* with what precedes, and can only express an *inference* from the passage, vv. 27–30. Finally, how are we to explain the *then* at the beginning of chap. iv. ? How does the mode of Abraham's justification follow from the idea that faith leads to the fulfilment of the law? Hofmann offers substantially the same explanation, only giving to the word *law* the meaning of *moral law* in general (instead of the Mosaic law). But the difficulties remain absolutely the same.—Meyer and some others regard ver. 31 as the beginning, and, in a manner, the theme of the following chapter. The term *law*, on this view, refers to the passage of Genesis which the apostle is about to quote, iv. 3 : "The harmony of justification by faith with the law is about to be explained by what the law says of Abraham's justification." But it is difficult to believe that Paul, without the slightest indication, would call an isolated passage of the Pentateuch *the law*. Then, if the relation between ver. 31 and iv. 1 were as Meyer thinks, it should be expressed logically by *for*, not by *then*. Holsten, if we understand him rightly, tries to get rid of these difficulties by applying the term *law* in our verse to the *law of faith* (ver. 27), in which he sees an absolute rule of righteousness holding good for all men, and consequently for Abraham. One could not imagine a more forced interpretation. Our explanation is already indicated ; it follows naturally from the interpretation which we have given of the preceding verses. Paul's gospel was accused of making void the law by setting aside legal works as a means of justification ; and he has just proved to his adversaries that it is his teaching, on the contrary, which harmonizes with the true meaning of the law, while the opposite teaching overturns it, by keeping up the vainglory of man, which the law was meant to destroy, and by violating Monotheism on which it is based. Is it surprising that he concludes such a demonstration with the triumphant affirmation : " Do we then overturn the law, as we are accused of doing ?

---

[1] T. R., with E K L P : ιστωμεν ; ℵ A B C D : ιστανομεν.

On the contrary, we establish it." The true reading is probably ἱστάνομεν ; the most ancient form, which has been replaced by the later form ἱστῶμεν. The verb signifies, not *to preserve, maintain*, but to cause to stand, *to establish*. This is what Paul does with regard to the law ; he *establishes* it as it were anew by the righteousness of faith ; which, instead of overturning it, as it was accused of doing, faithfully maintains its spirit in the new dispensation, the fact which he had just proved.

This verse forms a true period to the whole passage, vv. 21–30. The law had been called to give witness on the subject of the doctrine of universal condemnation ; it had borne witness, vv. 7–19. It has just been cited again, and now in favor of the new righteousness ; its testimony has not been less favorable, vv. 27–31.

After demonstrating in a general way the harmony of his teaching with Old Testament revelation, the apostle had only one thing left to desire in the discussion : that was to succeed in finding in the Old Testament itself a saying or an illustrious example which, in the estimation of the Jews, would give the sanction of divine authority to his argument. There *was* such a saying, and he was fortunate enough to find it. It was written by the hand of the legislator himself, and related to what was in a manner the typical example of justification with the Jews. It therefore combined all the conditions fitted to settle the present question conclusively. Thus it is that Gen. xv. 6 becomes the text of the admirable development contained in chap. iv. This piece is the counterpart of the scriptural demonstration which had closed the delineation of universal condemnation, iii. 9–20. It belongs, therefore, to the exposition of the thesis of ver. 21 : the righteousness of faith *witnessed* by the law and the prophets.

TENTH PASSAGE (4:1-25)

Faith the Principle of Abraham's Justification

Abraham being for the Jews the embodiment of salvation, his case was of capital moment in the solution of the question here treated. This was a conviction which Paul shared with his adversaries. Was the patriarch justified, by faith and by faith alone, his thesis was proved. Was he justified by some work of his own added to his faith, there was an end of Paul's doctrine.

In the first part of this chapter, vv. 1–12, he proves that Abraham owed his righteousness to his faith, and to his faith alone. In the second vv. 13–16, he supports his argument by the fact that the inheritance of the world, promised to the patriarch and his posterity, was conferred on him independently of his observance of the law. The third part, vv. 17–22, proves that that very posterity to whom this heritage was to belong was a fruit of faith. In the fourth and last part, vv. 23–25, this case is applied to believers of the present. Thus *righteousness, inheritance, posterity*, everything, Abraham received by faith ; and it will be even so with *us*, if we believe like him.

1. Vv. 1–12

Abraham was justified *by faith*, vv. 1–8, and by faith *alone*, vv. 9–12.

Vv. 1, 2. " *What shall we say then that Abraham our first father*[1] *has found*[2] *according to the flesh ? For if Abraham were justified by works, he hath whereof to glory ; but not in relation to God.*"—The question with which this

[1] ℵ A B C read προπατορα, while T. R., with D E F G K L P It. reads : πατερα.
[2] ℵ C D E F G It., Or. (Lat. trans.) place ευρηκεναι immediately after τι ερουμεν, while T. R. places it, with K L P, Syr. after πατερα ημων ; B omits it.

exposition opens is connected with the preceding by *then*, because the negative answer anticipated is a logically necessary consequence of the demonstration given iii. 27–31. The particular case of Abraham is subordinate to the general principle which has just been established.—It is not proper to divide this verse, as some have done, into two questions : " What shall we say ? That Abraham has found [something] according to the flesh ?" For then it would be necessary to understand an object to the verb *has found*, righteousness, for example, which is extremely forced. Or it would be necessary to translate, with Hofmann : " What shall we say ? That *we have found* Abraham as our father according to the flesh ?" by understanding ἡμᾶς, *we*, as the subject of the infinitive verb *to have found*. But this ellipsis of the subject is more forced still than that of the object ; and what Christian of Gentile origin—for the expression *have found* could not be applied to the Jewish-Christians—would have asked if he had become a child of Abraham in the way of the flesh ? Ver. 1 therefore contains only one question (see the translation). The apostle asks whether Abraham by his own action found some advantage in the matter of salvation. In the Received reading, which rests on the Byzs., the verb *has found* separates the words *our father* from the others : *according to the flesh*, so that this latter clause cannot apply to the substantive *father*, but necessarily qualifies the verb *has found*. It is otherwise in the Alex. and Greco-Latin readings, where the verb *has found* immediately follows the words : *What shall we say ?* whereby the words *our father* and *according to the flesh* are found in juxtaposition, which might easily lead the reader to take the two terms as forming a single description : *our father according to the flesh*. But this meaning cannot be the true one ; for the matter in question here is not yet the *nature* of Abraham's paternity, which is reserved to a later point, but the manner in which Abraham became *righteous* (vv. 2, 3). The reading was probably falsified by the recollection of the frequent phrases : *father* or *child according to the flesh*.—The *flesh* denotes here human activity in its state of isolation from the influence of God, and consequently in its natural helplessness so far as justification and salvation are concerned. The meaning is therefore : " What has Abraham found *by his own labor ?*"[1] The word *flesh* is probably chosen in reference to circumcision, which became the distinctive seal of the elect family.—The term προπάτωρ, *first father*, which occurs here in the Alex. instead of the simple πατήρ (in the two other families), is strange to the language of the New Testament and of the LXX. ; but this very circumstance speaks in favor of its authenticity. For the copyists would not have substituted so exceptional a term for the usual word. Paul probably used it to bring out the proto-typical character of everything which transpired in Abraham's person.—Does the pronoun *our* imply, as is alleged by Baur, Volkmar, etc., the Jewish origin of the Christians of Rome ? Yes, if the translation were : *our father according to the flesh*. But we have seen that this interpretation is false. It is not even right to say, with Meyer) who holds the Gentile origin of the church of Rome), that the pronoun *our* refers to the Judeo-Christian minority of that church. For the meaning of this pronoun is determined by the *we*, which is the subject of all the preceding verbs (*make void, establish, shall say*) ; now this refers to Christians in general. Is not the whole immediately following chapter intended to prove that Abraham is the father of believing Gentiles as well as of believing Jews (comp. the categorical declarations of vv. 12 and 16) ? How, then, should the word *our* in this verse, which is as it were the theme of the whole chapter, be used in a sense directly opposed to the essential idea of the entire piece ? Comp., besides, the use of the expression *our fathers* in 1 Cor. x. 1. What is the understood reply which Paul expected to his question ? Is it, as is often assumed : *nothing at all ?*

[1] This view is sustained by the connection, by the chief of modern critics, and by the American reading of the Revised N. T.—T. W. C.

Perhaps he did not go so far. He meant rather to say (comp. ver. 2) : nothing, *so far as justification before God is concerned ;* which did not exclude the idea of the patriarch having from a human point of view found certain advantages, such as riches, reputation, etc.

Ver. 2. Some commentators take this verse as the logical proof (*for*) of the negative answer which must be understood between vv. 1 and 2 : "*Nothing ; for,* if he had been justified by his works, he would have whereof to glory, which is inadmissible." But why would it be inadmissible? This is exactly the matter to be examined. The reasoning would then be only a vicious circle. The verse must be regarded, not as a proof of the negative answer anticipated, but as the explanation why Paul required to put the question of ver. 1 : "I ask this, because if Abraham had been justified by his works, he would really have something of which to glory ; and consequently the boasting which I declared to be excluded (iii. 27) would reappear once more as right and good." Did not Abraham's example form the rule ?—The expression *by works* is substituted for that of ver. 1 : *according to the flesh,* as the term *being justified* replaces the *having found.* In both cases, the term appearing in ver. 2 indicates the concrete result (*works, being justified*), as that in ver. 1 expressed the abstract principle (*the flesh, finding*). The word καύχημα signifies a *matter for glorying in,* which is quite a different thing from καύχησις, *the act* of glorying. Paul does not say that Abraham would really glory, but only that he would have matter for doing so. But how can the apostle express himself at the end of the verse in the words : *but not before God,* so as to make us suppose that Abraham was *really* justified by his works, though not before God ? Some commentators (Beza, Grot., de Wette, Rück., Philip.) think themselves obliged to weaken the sense of the word *justified,* as if it denoted here justification in the eyes of men : "If Abraham was justified by his works (in the judgment of men), he has a right to boast (relatively to them and himself), but not as before God." But would such an attenuated sense of the word *justify* be possible in this passage, which may be called Paul's classical teaching on the subject of justification? Calvin, Fritzsche, Baur, Hodge, assert that we have here an incomplete syllogism ; the major : "If Abraham was justified by works, he has whereof to glory ;" the minor : "Now he could not have whereof to glory before God ;" the conclusion (understood) : "Therefore he was not justified by works." But the minor is exactly what it would have been necessary to prove ; for what had been said, ver. 27, of the exclusion of boasting or of justification by works, was again made a question by the discussion on the case of Abraham. Besides, the conclusion was the important part, and could not have been left to be understood. . The apostle has not accustomed us to such a mode of arguing. Meyer, after some variations in his first editions, has ended by siding with the explanation of Chrysostom and Theodoret, which is to the following effect : "If Abraham was justified by his works, he has undoubtedly something whereof to glory in his own eyes ; but in this case he has received no favor from God, nothing which honors him as the object of divine grace ; and his justification not coming from God, he has no cause to glory in relation to God." This meaning is very ingenious ; nevertheless it is untenable ; for—1. The term *glorying* would require to be taken in a good sense : glorying in a real favor received from God, while throughout the whole piece it is applied to an impure boasting, the ground of which man finds in himself and in his own work. 2. Paul must have said in this sense : ἐν Θεῷ, *in God,* rather than πρὸς τὸν Θεόν, *in relation to* God, comp. ii. 17. 3. Ver. 3 does not naturally connect itself with ver. 2 when thus understood, for this verse proves not what it should (*for*), to wit, that Abraham has no cause for boasting in the case supposed, but the simple truth that he was justified by his faith. Semler and Glöckler have had recourse to a desperate expedient, that of taking πρὸς τὸν Θεόν as the exclamation of an oath : "But no, *by God,* it is not so." But this sense would have required πρὸς τοῦ Θεοῦ ; and what could have led Paul to use such a form here? The turn of expression employed by the apostle is certainly singular, we shall say even a little perplexed. He feels he is approaching a delicate subject, about which Jewish national feeling could not but show itself very sensitive. To understand his meaning, we must, after the words : "If he was justified by works, he hath whereof to glory," add the following : "and he has really great reason for glorying ; it is something to have been made an Abraham ; one may be proud of having borne such a name, *but* " . . . Here the apostle resumes in such a way as to return to his theme : "but all this glorying has nothing to do with the account which he had to render to God." The words : *in relation to God*, πρὸς τὸν Θεόν, are evidently opposed to a corresponding : *in relation to man*, understood. In comparing himself with men less holy than he, Abraham might have some cause for glorying ; but the instant he put himself before God, his righteousness vanished. This is exactly the point proved by the following verses.

Vv. 3–5. "*For what saith the Scripture? Now Abraham believed God, and it was counted unto him for righteousness. Now to him that worketh his reward is not reckoned as of grace, but as of debt. But to him that worketh not, but believeth on him that justifieth the ungodly, his faith is counted for righteousness ;*"—By the words of ver. 2 : "*But it is not so in relation to God,*" the apostle gave it to be understood that he knew the judgment of God Himself on Abraham's works. Ver. 3 explains how he can pronounce regarding a fact which seems to lie beyond the reach of human knowledge. Scripture contains a declaration in which there is revealed the judgment of God respecting the way in which Abraham was justified. This saying is to be found in Gen. xv. 6. Called by God out of his tent by night, he is invited to contemplate the heavens, and to count, if he can, the myriads of stars ; then he hears the promise : "so numerous shall thy seed be." He is a centenarian, and has never had children. But it is God who speaks ; that is enough for him : *he believed God*. Faith consists in holding the divine promise for the reality itself ; and then it happens that what the believer has done in regard to the promise of God, God in turn does in regard to his faith : He holds it for righteousness itself.—The particle δέ, *now*, takes the place of the καί, *and*, which is found in the LXX., though their reading is not quite certain, as the *Sinaït.* and the *Vatic.* have a blank here. It is possible, therefore, that, as Tischendorf thinks, the generally received reading in Paul's time was δέ, *now*, and not καί. For it is evident that if the apostle preserves this particle, which is not demanded by the meaning of his own text, it is to establish the literal character of the quotation. It is not said : he believed *the promise of God*, but : *God*. The object of his faith, when he embraced the promise, was God Himself —His truth, His faithfulness, His holiness, His goodness, His wisdom, His power, His eternity. For God was wholly in the promise proceeding from Him. It little matters, indeed, what the particular object is to which the divine revelation refers at a given moment. All the parts of this revelation form but one whole. In laying hold of one promise, Abraham laid hold of all by anticipation ; for he laid hold of the God of the promises, and henceforth he was in possession even of those which could only be revealed and realized in the most distant future.—The Hebrew says : "*and God counted it* to him for righteousness." The LXX. have translated by the passive : *and it was counted to him;* Paul follows them in quoting. The verb λογίζειν, λογίζεσθαι, signifies : *to put to account;* comp. 2 Sam. xix. 19 ; 2 Cor. v. 19 ; 2 Tim. iv. 16 ; and Philem. ver. 18 (where Paul uses the analogous term ἐλλογεῖν, because he is speaking of an account properly so called : "If he has done thee any wrong, put it to my account"). It is possible to put to one's account what he possesses or what he does not possess. In the first case it is a simple act of justice ; in the second, it is a matter of grace. The latter is Abraham's case, since God reckons his *faith* to him for what it is not: for *righteousness*. This word *righteousness* here denotes perfect obedience to the will of God, in virtue of which Abraham would necessarily have been declared righteous by God as *being* so, if he had possessed it. As he did not possess it, God put his faith to his account as an equivalent. Why so? On what did this incomparable value which God attached to his faith rest? We need not answer: on the moral power of this faith itself. For faith is a simple receptivity, and it would be strange to fall back on the sphere of meritorious work when explaining the very word which ought to exclude all merit. The infinite worth of faith lies in its object, God and His manifestation. This object is moral perfection itself. To believe is therefore to lay hold of perfection at a stroke. It is not surprising that laying hold of perfection, it should be reckoned by God as righteousness. It has been happily said: Faith is at once the most moral and the most fortunate of strokes (*coups de main*). In vv. 4 and 5, the apostle analyzes the saying quoted. This analysis proves that Abraham was justified not in the way of a man who had done works (ver. 4), but in the way of a man who has not done them (ver. 5); which demonstrates the truth of the affirmation of ver. 2: "but it is not so in relation to God."—The two expressions: ὁ ἐργαζόμενος, *he that worketh*, and ὁ μὴ ἐργαζόμενος, *he that worketh not*, are general and abstract, with this difference, that the first refers to any workman whatever in the domain of ordinary life, while the second applies only to a workman in the moral sense. To the hired workman who performs his task, his reward is reckoned not as a favor, but as a debt. Now, according to the declaration of Moses, Abraham was not treated on this footing; therefore he is not one of those who have fulfilled their task. On the other hand, to the workman (in the moral sense) who does not labor satisfactorily, and who nevertheless places his confidence in God who pardons, his faith is reckoned for righteousness. Now, according to Moses, it is on this footing that Abraham was treated; therefore he belongs to those who have not fulfilled their task. These two harmonious conclusions—the one understood after ver. 4, the other after ver. 5—set forth the contents of the declaration of Moses: Abraham was treated on the footing not of a good, but of a bad workman.—The subjective negation μή before ἐργαζόμενος is the expression of the logical relation: *because*, between the participle and the principal verb: "*because* he does not do his work, his faith is reckoned to him as work."—Paul says: He who justifieth the *ungodly*. He might have said the sinner; but he chooses the more forcible term to designate the evil of sin, that no category of sinners, even the most criminal, may think itself excluded from the privilege of being justified by their faith. It has sometimes been supposed that by the word *ungodly* Paul meant to characterize Abraham himself, in the sense in which it is said (Josh. xxiv. 2) that "Terah, the father of Abraham, while he dwelt beyond the flood, had *served other gods*." But idolatry is not exactly equivalent to ungodliness (impiety), and Paul would certainly never have called Abraham ungodly (impious).—To impute to the believer righteousness which he does not possess, is at the same time not to impute to him sins of which he is guilty. Paul feels the need of completing on this negative side his exposition of the subject of justification. And hence, no doubt, the reason why, to the saying of Moses regarding Abraham, he adds one of David's, in which justification is specially celebrated in the form of the *non-imputation* of sin.

Vv. 6-8. "*As*[1] *David also exactly celebrateth the blessedness of the man, unto whom God imputeth righteousness without works: Blessed are they whose iniquities are forgiven, and whose sins are covered. Blessed is the man to whom*[2] *the Lord does not impute sin.*"—It need not be supposed that David

---

[1] Instead of καθαπερ, D E F G read καθως.   [2] Instead of ω, ℵ B D E G read ου.

here plays the part of a *second* example, side by side with Abraham. The position of the patriarch is unique, and Paul will return to it after this short interruption. He merely adduces a saying of David, the inspired singer, which seems to him to complete the testimony of Moses about Abraham.—The conjunction of comparison καθάπερ is more forcible than καθώς: it indicates an intrinsic and striking agreement: *exactly as.*—The word μακαρισμός, which we have translated by *blessedness*, strictly signifies: *the celebration of blessedness.* The verb λέγει, *says*, of which this word is the object, signifies here: *he utters* (this beatification). The following words are, as it were, the joyful hymn of the justified sinner. This passage is the beginning of Ps. xxxii., which David probably composed after having obtained pardon from God for the odious crimes into which passion had dragged him. Hence the expressions: *transgressions pardoned, sins covered, sin not imputed.* Here, then, is the negative side of justification, the evil which it removes; while in regard to Abraham it was only the positive side which was under treatment, the blessing it confers. Thus it is that the two passages complete one another.

This observation made, the apostle returns to his subject. It was not enough to prove that Abraham owed his justification to his faith. For the defenders of works might say: True; but it was *as one circumcised* that Abraham obtained this privilege of being justified by his faith. And so we have works driven out by the door, and returning by the window. The answer to the question of ver. 1: "What hath Abraham found by the way of the flesh?" would no more be: *nothing*, but: *everything.* For if it was to his circumcision Abraham owed the favor whereby God had reckoned his faith to him for righteousness, everything depended in the end on this material rite; and those who were destitute of it were *ipso facto* excluded from justification by faith. The nullity of this whole point of view is what Paul shows in the following passage, where he proves that the patriarch was not only justified by faith, but by faith *only.*

Vv. 9, 10. "*Is this beatification then for the circumcision, or for the uncircumcision also? for we say:*[1] *Faith was reckoned to Abraham for righteousness. How was it then reckoned? when he was in a state of circumcision, or of uncircumcision? Not in a state of circumcision, but of uncircumcision.*"—The *then* serves merely to resume the discussion: "I ask *then* if this celebration of the blessedness of the justified applies only to the circumcised, or also to the uncircumcised." On this everything really depended. For, on the first alternative, the Gentiles had no way left of admission to the privilege of justification by faith except that of becoming Jews; and there was an end of Paul's gospel. M. Reuss regards all this as an example "of the scholasticism of the Jewish schools of the day," and of a "theological science" which could supply the apostle only with "extremely doubtful modes of argument." We shall see if it is really so.—The second part of the verse: *for we say* ... is intended to bring back the mind of the reader from David to Abraham: "For, in fine, we were affirming that Abraham was justified by faith. How is it then with this personage, whose example forms the rule? How was he justified by faith? as uncircumcised or as circumcised?" Such is the very simple meaning of ver. 10. The *then* which connects it with ver. 9 is thus explained: "To answer the question which I have just put (9*a*), let us *then* examine how the justification of Abraham took place."—The answer was not difficult; it was furnished by Genesis, and it was peremptory. It is in chap. xv. that we find Abraham justified by faith; and it is in chap. xvii., about fourteen years after, that he receives the ordinance of circumcision. The apostle can therefore answer with assurance: "not as circumcised, but as uncircumcised." There was a time in Abraham's life

---

[1] ℵ B D omit the ὅτι, which T. R. reads with all the other documents.

when by his uncircumcision he represented the Gentiles, as later after his circumcision he became the representative of Israel. Now, it was in the first of these two periods of his life, that is to say, in his Gentilehood, that he was justified by faith . . . the conclusion was obvious at a glance. Paul makes full use of it against his adversaries. He expounds it with decisive consequences in the sequel.

Vv. 11, 12. "*And he received the sign of circumcision,*[1] *as a seal of the righteousness of the faith which he had yet being uncircumcised: that he might be at once the father of all them that believe while in a state of uncircumcision, in order that righteousness may be imputed unto them also; and the father of the circumcised, of them who not only are of the circumcision, but who also walk in the steps of the faith which our father Abraham had in uncircumcision.*"
—Καί, *and*, signifies here: "and in consequence of the justification thus found."—Περιτομῆς, *of circumcision*, may be made a genitive of apposition: "the sign *which* is circumcision," or a genitive of quality: "a sign in the form of circumcision." The former is the simpler sense. In any case, the reading περιτομήν in two Mjj. is a correction. Circumcision appears even in Gen. xvii. 11 as the *sign of the covenant* between God and His people. The Rabbins express themselves thus: "God put the sign of love in the flesh." The term σημεῖον, *sign*, relates to the material thing; the term σφραγίς, *seal*, to its religious import. Far, then, from circumcision having been the antecedent condition of Abraham's justification, it was the mark, and consequently the effect of it.—The article τῆς (after the words *righteousness of faith*), which we have translated by: *which he had*, may relate to the entire phrase *righteousness of faith*, or to the word *faith* taken by itself. If we consider the following expression: "father of all *believers*" (not of all the justified), and especially the end of ver. 12, we cannot doubt that the article applies to the word faith taken alone: "the faith which he had yet being uncircumcised." The *in order that* which follows should not be taken in the weakened sense of *so that*. No doubt Abraham in believing did not set before himself the *end* of becoming the spiritual father of Gentile believers. But the matter in question here is the intention of God who directed things with this view which was His from the beginning of the history. The real purpose of God extended to the Gentiles; the theocracy was only a means in His mind. Had He not said to Abraham, when calling him, that "in him should all the families of the earth be blessed"? Gen. xii. 3.—On the meaning of διά, *in the state of*, see on ii. 27.—The last words: *that righteousness might be imputed unto them*, should not be regarded as a new end of the: *he received the sign*, to be added to the first already mentioned (that he might be the father . . .). The verb is too remote: we must therefore make the *that* . . . depend on the participle πιστευόντων. *them that believe* (though they be not circumcised); not certainly in Hofmann's sense: "who have faith *in the fact that* it will be imputed to them," but in the only grammatically admissible sense: "them who believe *in order that* righteousness may be imputed to them." There is a desire in faith. It seeks reconciliation with God, and consequently justification.— The pronoun αὐτόν, *he* ("that he might be, *even he*"), is intended to bring the person of Abraham strongly into relief, as called to fill, he, this one solitary man, the double place of father of believing Gentiles (ver. 11) and of believing Jews (ver. 12). It is very remarkable that the apostle here puts the believers of Gentile origin first among the members of Abraham's posterity. But was it not they in fact who were in the condition most similar to that of the patriarch at the time when he obtained his justification by faith? If, then, a preference was to be given to the one over the other, it was certainly due to them rather than to circumcised Christians. What a complete reversal of Jewish notions!

---

[1] Instead of περιτομης, A D, Syr. read περιτομην.

Ver. 12. There can be no doubt that this verse refers to believers of Jewish origin, who formed the other half of Abraham's spiritual family. But it presents a great grammatical difficulty. The Greek expression is such that it seems as if Paul meant to speak in this same verse of *two* different *classes* of individuals. It appears as if the literal translation should run thus : "father of circumcision, in respect of those who are not only of the circumcision, *but also* in respect of those who walk in the steps of " . . . Proceeding on this translation, Theodoret; Luther, and others have applied the first words : " in respect of those who are not only of the circumcision," to *Jewish* believers, and the following words : "in respect of those who walk in the footsteps of Abraham's faith," to *Gentile* believers. But why then return to the latter, who had already been sufficiently designated and characterized in ver. 11 ? And how, in speaking of Jewish believers, could Paul content himself with saying that they are not of circumcision only, without expressly mentioning faith as the condition of their being children of Abraham? Finally, the construction would still be incorrect in this sense, which would have demanded οὐ τοῖς . . . μόνον (*not only for those who belong* to the circumcision) instead of τοῖς οὐ . . . μόνον (*for those who not only belong to* . . .). This ancient explanation must therefore certainly be abandoned. There can be here only one class of persons designated by *two* distinct *attributes*. The first is circumcision, and the second, a faith like Abraham's. But in this case the Greek construction seems again faulty in the second member. This is acknowledged by Tholuck, Meyer, etc. Philippi is fain to satisfy himself with the reflection that negligences of style are found in the best writers ; which is true, but does not help us here ; for the faultiness would be a real want of logic. On the other hand, the expedients recently devised by Hofmann and Wieseler are so farfetched that they do not deserve even to be discussed. And yet the apostle has not accustomed us to inexactness unworthy even of an intelligent pupil ; and we may still seek to solve the difficulty. This is not impossible, as it appears to us ; we need only take the first τοῖς to be a pronoun (*those who*), as it incontestably is, but regard the second not as a second parallel pronoun (which would, besides, require it to be placed before the καί), but a simple definite article : "*the* (individuals) *walking* in the steps of " . . . The meaning thus reached is to this effect : " those who are not only of the circumcision, but who *are also*, that is to say, at the same time, *the* (individuals) *walking* in the steps of " . . . This article, τοῖς, *the*, is partitive. It serves to mark off clearly within the mass of the Jewish people who possess the sign of circumcision, a much narrower circle : *those walking in the faith*, that is to say, the Jews, who to circumcision add the characteristic of faith. These latter do not form a second class alongside of the first ; they form within this latter a group apart, possessing beside the common distinction, an attribute (faith) which is wanting to the others ; and it is to draw this line of demarkation accurately within the circumcised Israel that the article is used.[1] The τοῖς is here simply an article analogous to the τοῖς before πιστεύουσιν.

Paul is not satisfied with saying : "who also walk in the footsteps of Abraham's faith ;" he expressly reminds us—for this is the point of his argument—that Abraham had this faith *in the state of uncircumcision*. What does this mean, if not that Abraham was still ranked as a Gentile when "he believed and his faith was counted to him for righteousness?" Hence it follows that it is not, properly speaking, for Gentile believers to enter by the gate of the Jews, but for Jewish believers to enter by the gate of the Gentiles. It will be allowed that it was impossible for one to overwhelm his adversary more completely. But such is Paul's logic ; it does

---

[1] The complete Greek phrase would be as follows : οἱ οὐκ ἐκ περιτομῆς μόνον [ὄντες], ἀλλὰ καὶ [ὄντες] οἱ στοιχοῦντες.

not stop short with refuting its opponent, it does not leave him till it has made it plain to a demonstration that the truth is the very antipodes of what he affirmed.

We find in these two verses the great and sublime idea of *Abraham's spiritual family*, that people which is the product, not of the flesh, but of faith, and which comprises the believers of the whole world, whether Jews or Gentiles. This place of father to all the believing race of man assigned to Abraham, is a fundamental fact in the kingdom of God ; it is the act in which this kingdom takes its rise, it is the aim of the patriarch's call : " *that he might be the father of* . . . (ver. 11), *and of* " . . . (ver. 12). Hofmann says rightly : " Abraham is not only the first *example* of faith, for there had been other believers before him (Heb. xi.) ; but in him there was *founded* forever the community of faith." From this point the continuous history of salvation begins. Abraham is the stem of that tree, which thenceforth strikes root and develops. For he has not believed simply in the God of creation ; he has laid hold by faith of the God of the promise, the author of that redeeming work which appears on the earth in his very faith. The notion of this spiritual paternity once rightly understood, the filiation of Abraham in the physical sense lost all importance in the matter of salvation. The prophets, John the Baptist, Jesus (John viii.), were already at one in *laying down* the truth which the apostle here *demonstrates :* faith as constituting the principle of life, as it were the life-blood of Abraham's family, which is that of God on the earth. Because, indeed, this principle is the only one in harmony with the moral essence of things, with the true relation between the Creator who gives of free grace, and the creature who accepts freely.—And this whole admirable deduction made by the apostle is to be regarded as a piece of Rabbinical scholasticism !

The apostle has succeeded in discovering the basis of Christian universalism in the very life of him in whose person theocratic particularism was founded. He has demonstrated the existence of a time when he represented Gentilism, or, to speak more properly, mankind in general ; and it was during this period, when he was not yet a Jew, but simply a man, that he received salvation ! The whole gospel of Paul was involved in this fact. But a question arose : after receiving justification, Abraham had obtained another privilege : he had been declared, with all his posterity, to be the future possessor of the world. Now this posterity could be none else than his issue by Isaac, and which had been put in possession of circumcision and of Canaan. Through this opening there returned, with banners displayed, that particularism which had been overthrown in the domain of justification. Thus there was lost the whole gain of the preceding demonstration. Paul does not fail to anticipate and remove the difficulty. To this question he devotes the following passage, vv. 13–16.

2. Vv. 13-16

Vv. 13, 14. " *For the promise, that he should be the heir of the*[1] *world, was not made to Abraham, or to his seed, by the law, but by the righteousness of faith. For if they which are of the law be heirs, faith is made void, and the promise annulled.*"—The *for* bears on the understood objection which we have just explained : " For it need not be imagined that the promised inheritance is to be obtained by means of the law, and that the people of the law are consequently assured of it." Paul knew that this thought lay deep in the heart of every Jew. He attacks it unsparingly, demonstrating that the very opposite is the truth ; for the law, far from procuring the promised

---

[1] T. R., with K L P, reads του before κοσμου ; omitted by all the others.

inheritance for the Jews, would infallibly deprive them of it.—The *possession of the world*, of which the apostle speaks, had been promised to Abraham and his posterity in three forms.—1. In the promise made to the patriarch of the *land of Canaan*. For, from the prophetic and Messianic point of view, which dominated the history of the patriarchal family from the beginning, the land of Canaan was the emblem of the sanctified earth ; it was the point of departure for the glorious realization of the latter. In this sense it is said in the *Tanchuma :*[1] "God gave our father Abraham possession *of the heavens and earth.*" 2. Several promises of another kind naturally led to the extension of the possession of the promised land to that of the whole world ; for example, the three following, Gen. xii. 3 : "In thee shall all families of the earth be blessed ;" xxii. 17 : "Thy seed shall possess the gate of his enemies ;" ver. 18 : "In thy seed shall all the nations of the earth be blessed." The two expressions : *in thee*, and *in thy seed*, alternate in these promises. But they are combined, as in our passage, in the verses, xxvi. 3, 4, where we also again find the two ideas of the possession of Canaan, and the blessing of the whole world through Israel. 3. Above all these particular promises there ever rested the general promise of the Messianic kingdom, the announcement of that descendant of David to whom God had said : "I have given thee the uttermost parts of the earth for an inheritance" (Ps. ii. 8). Now Israel was inseparable from its Messiah, and such an explanation led men to give to the preceding promises the widest and most elevated sense possible. Israel had not been slow to follow this direction ; but its carnal spirit had given to the universal supremacy which it expected, a yet more political than religious complexion. Jesus, on the contrary, in His Sermon on the Mount and elsewhere, had translated this idea of dominion over the world into that of the humble love which rules by serving : "Blessed are the meek ; for they shall inherit the earth." The apostle does not here enter on the question of *how* the promise is to be fulfilled ; he deals only with the condition on which it is to be enjoyed. Is the law or faith the way of entering into the possession of this divine inheritance, and consequently are the people of law or of faith the heirs ?—The word *inheritance*, to express *ownership*, reproduces the Hebrew name *Nachala*, which was used to designate the land of Canaan. This country was regarded as a *heritage* which Israel, Jehovah's first-born son, had received from his heavenly Father.

To prove that the inheriting seed is not Israel, but the nation of believers, Jews or Gentiles, Paul does not use, as Meyer, Hodge, and others suppose, the same argument as he follows in Gal. iii. 15 et seq. He does not argue here from the fact that the law was given subsequently to the patriarchal covenant, and could make no change in that older contract, which was founded solely on the promise on the one hand, and faith on the other. The demonstration in our passage has not this historical character ; it is, if one may so speak, dogmatic in its nature. Its meaning is to this effect : If the possession of the world were to be the reward of observing the law, the promise would thereby be reduced to a nullity. This declaration is *enunciated* ver. 14, and proved ver. 15. The inference is drawn ver. 16.

Ver. 14. If, in order to be *heir of the world*, it is absolutely necessary to come *under the jurisdiction of the law*, and consequently to be its faithful observer—otherwise what purpose would it serve ?—it is all over at a stroke both with *faith* and with the *promise :* with faith, that is to say, with the hope of that final heritage, since the realization of that expectation would be bound to a condition which sinful man could not execute, the fulfilment of the law, and since faith would thus be deprived of its object (literally, *emptied*, κεκένωται, from κενός, *empty*) ; and next, with the

---

[1] *Commentary on the Pentateuch*, probably of the ninth century.

promise itself: for, an impossible condition being attached to it, it would thereby be paralyzed in its effects (κατήργηται). Proof and conclusion, vv. 15, 16.

Vv. 15, 16. "*For the law worketh wrath: and, indeed,[1] where no law is, there is no transgression. Therefore it is of faith, that it might be by grace; to the end the promise might be sure to all the seed; not to that only which is of the law, but also to that which is of the faith of Abraham, who is the father of us all;*—Faith deprived of its object, the promise made void for those who are under the law, why all this? Simply because the law, when not fulfilled, brings on man God's disapprobation, *wrath*, which renders it impossible on His part to fulfil the promise. This passage, like so many others already quoted, is incompatible with the idea which Ritschl forms of divine wrath. This critic, as we know (see on i. 18), applies the term *wrath*, in the Old Testament only, to the sudden punishment with death of exceptional malefactors, who by their crime compromised the existence of the covenant itself. But in these words the apostle evidently starts from the idea that whatever is under the law is *ipso facto* the object of wrath, which applies to the entire people, and not to a few individuals only. Melanchthon applied the term wrath in this verse to the irritation felt by condemned *man* against the judgment of God. He forgot that the loss of the divine inheritance results to the sinner, not from his own wrath, but from that of the judge. — The article ὁ, *the*, before the word *law*, proves that the subject here is *the law* properly so called, the Mosaic law. — It would be improper to translate: "for *it is* the law *which* produces wrath," as if wrath could not exist beyond the jurisdiction of the law. Chap. i. proves the contrary. But the law produces it inevitably where it has been given. The preponderance of egoism in the human heart once granted, the barrier of the law is certain to be overpassed, and transgression is sure to make wrath burst forth.

T. R., with the Byzs., the Greco-Latins, and the oldest versions, connects the second part of this verse with the first by γάρ, *for*. This reading appears at the first glance easier than that of the Alex.: δέ (*now*, or *but*). But this very circumstance is not in its favor. The three γάρ, which have preceded, may have also led the copyists to write the same particle again. The context, carefully consulted, demands a δέ rather than a γάρ. For what says the second member? That without a law transgression is not *possible*. Now this idea does not logically prove that the law *necessarily* produces wrath. This second proposition of ver. 15 is not therefore a proof, but a simple observation in support of the first; and this connection is exactly marked by the δέ, which is the particle here not of opposition (*but*), but of gradation (*now*), and which may be rendered by *and indeed*. This second proposition is therefore a sort of parenthesis intended to strengthen the bearing of the fact indicated in the first (15*a*): "In general, a law cannot be the means fitted to gain for us the favor of God; on the contrary, the manifestations of sin, of the evil nature, acquire a much graver character through the law, that of *transgression*, of positive, deliberate violation of the divine will, and so increase wrath." Παράβασις, transgression, from παραβαίνειν, *to overpass*. A barrier cannot be crossed except in so far as it exists. So without law there is no sin in the form of transgression.—The article ὁ is wanting here before νόμος, *law*. And rightly so; for this saying is a general maxim which does not apply specially to the Jews and the Jewish law (as 15*a*). The Gentiles have also a law (ii. 14, 15), which they can observe or violate. In the latter case, they become objects of wrath (chap. i.) as well as the Jews, though in a less degree.

Ver. 16. If, then, the promise of the inheritance was serious, there was

---

[1] Instead of γαρ, which T. R. reads, D E F G K L P, It. Syr., we read in ℵ A B C, Or. (Lat. trans.): δε.

only one way to its fulfilment—that the inheritance should be given by the way of faith and not of law. This consequence is expounded in ver. 16, which develops the last words of ver. 13 : *by the righteousness of faith*, as ver. 15 had developed the first : *not by the law.*—*Therefore :* because of that condemning effect which attaches to the law. The verb and subject to be understood in this elliptical proposition might be : *the promise was made.* But the words following : *that it might be by grace*, do not allow this ; the subject in question is evidently the fulfilment. What we must supply, therefore, is : *the promise will be fulfilled*, or : *the heritage will be given.* The inheritance, from the moment of its being granted to faith only, remains a gift of pure grace ; and while remaining a gift of grace, it is possible for it not to be withdrawn, as it must have been if its acquisition had been attached to the fulfilment of the law. It is very important not to efface the notion of *aim* contained in the words εἰς τὸ εἶναι (*that the promise might be*), by translating, as Oltramare does, *so that.* There was positive *intention* on God's part, when He made the gift of inheritance depend solely on faith. For He knew well that this was the only way to render the promise *sure* (the opposite of *being made void*, ver. 14). And sure for whom ? For all the seed of Abraham, in the true and full sense of the word ; it was the fulfilment of those terms of the promise : "to thee and *to thy seed*." After what precedes, this term can only designate the patriarch's *spiritual* family—all believers, Jew or Gentile. Faith being the *sole condition* of promise, ought also to be the *sole characteristic* of those in whom it will be realized. These words : *sure for all the seed*, are developed in what follows. The apostle embraces each of the two classes of believers contained in this general term : "sure," says he, "*not only to that which is of the law*," believers of Jewish origin who would lose the inheritance if it was attached to the law, "*but also to that which is of faith*," Christians of Gentile origin to whom the promise would cease to be accessible the instant it was made to depend on any other character than that of faith. It is plain that the expression used here has a wholly different meaning from the apparently similar form employed in ver. 12. There are *two classes* of persons here, and not *two attributes* of the same persons. The second τῷ is a pronoun as well as the first. It may be objected, indeed, that in designating the first of these two classes *Paul* does not mention the characteristic of *faith*, and that consequently he is still speaking of Jews simply, not believing Jews. But after all that had gone before, the notion of faith was naturally implied in that of *Abraham's seed*. And to understand the apostle's words, we must beware of connecting the μόνον, *only*, exclusively with the words ἐκ τοῦ νόμου, *of the law :* "those who are *of the law only*," that is to say, who are simply Jews, and not believers. The μόνον refers to the whole phrase : τῷ ἐκ τοῦ νόμου, *only that which is of the law*, as is shown in the following context by the position of the καί, *also*, *before* the second τῷ : "*not only that* which is of the law, *but also that which*" . . . that is to say : not only believers who were formerly under the law, but also Gentile believers. The attribute of *faith* is expressly mentioned in the case of the last, because it appears in them free from all legal environment, and as their sole title to form part of Abraham's descendants.— The last words : *who is the father of us all*, sum up all that has been developed in the previous context. Believing Jews and Gentiles, we all participate by faith not only in justification, but also in the future possession of the world ; for the true seed to whom this promise was made was that of faith, not that according to the law. Abraham is therefore the sole stem from which proceed those two branches which form in him one and the same spiritual organism.—But after all a Jew might still present himself, saying : "Very true ; but that this divine plan might be realized, it was necessary that there should be an Israel ; and that there might be an Israel, there must needs come into the world an Isaac. Now this son is born to Abraham in the way of natural, physical generation ; and what has this mode of filiation in common with the way of faith?" Here in an instant is the domain of the *flesh* reconquered by the adversary; and to the question of ver. 1: "What has Abraham found by the flesh?" it only remains to answer: His son Isaac, consequently the chosen people, and consequently *everything*. A mind so familiarized as Paul's was with the secret thoughts of the Israelitish heart, could not neglect this important side of the question. He enters into this new subject as boldly as into the two preceding, and sapping the last root of Jewish prejudice by Scripture, he demonstrates that the birth of Isaac, no less than the promise of the inheritance and the grace of justification, was the effect of faith. Thus it is thoroughly proved that Abraham found *nothing* by the flesh; *quod erat demonstrandum* (ver. 1). This is the subject of the third passage, 17–21.

3. Vv. 17–21

The birth of Isaac was the work of faith; the apostle proves it by the Scripture narrative, the memory of which was present to the mind of all his readers, and which was intended to be recalled to them by the declaration of ver. 3 relative to Abraham's justification.

Ver. 17. "*According as it is written, I have made thee a father of many nations, before God whom he believed, as him, that quickeneth the dead, and calleth those things which be not as though they were.*"—This verse is directly connected with the end of ver. 12; for the last words of ver. 16: *who is the father of us all*, are the reproduction of the last words of ver. 12: *the faith of our father Abraham*. The development, vv. 13–16, had only been the answer to an anticipated objection. First of all, the general paternity of Abraham in relation to all believers, Jew or Gentile, so solemnly affirmed at the end of ver. 16, is proved by a positive text, the words of Gen. xvi. 5. The expression: *father of many nations*, is applied by several commentators only to the Israelitish tribes. But why in this case not use the term *Ammim* rather than *Gojim*, which is the word chosen to denote *the Gentiles* in opposition to Israel? The promise: "Thy seed shall be as the stars of heaven for multitude," can hardly be explained without holding that when God spoke thus His view extended beyond the limits of Israel. And how could it be otherwise, after His saying to the patriarch: "In thee shall *all the families of the earth* be blessed (or shall bless themselves)"? The full light of the Messianic day shone beforehand in all these promises.—But there was in this divine saying an expression which seemed to be positively contradicted by the reality: *I have made thee.* How can God speak of that which shall not be realized till so distant a future as if it were an already accomplished fact? The apostle uses this expression to penetrate to the very essence of Abraham's faith. In the eyes of God, the patriarch *is* already what he shall become. Abraham plants himself at the instant on the viewpoint of the divine thought: he regards himself as being already in fact what God declares he will become. Such, if we mistake not, is the idea expressed in the following words which have been so differently explained: *before God whom he believed.* This *before* is frequently connected with the words preceding the biblical quotation: *who is the father of us all.* But this verb in the present: *who is*, was evidently meant in the context of ver. 16 to apply to the time when Paul was writing, which does not harmonize with the expression *before*, which transports us to the very moment when God conversed with Abraham. It seems to me, therefore, better to connect this preposition with the verb: *I have made thee*, understanding the words: "*which was already true* before the God whom" . . .; that is to say, in the eyes of the God who was speaking with Abraham, the latter *was* already *made* the father of those many nations. There are two ways of resolving the construction κατεναντι οὗ . . . Θεοῦ; either: κατέναντι τοῦ Θεοῦ κατέναντι οὗ ἐπίστευσε (before the God before whom he believed); or: κατέναντι τοῦ Θεοῦ ᾧ ἐπίστευσε (before the God whom he believed). Perhaps the first explanation of the attraction is most in keeping with usage (anyhow there is no need to cite in its favor, as Meyer does, Luke i. 4, which is better explained otherwise). But it does not give a very appropriate meaning. The more natural it is to state the fact that Abraham *was there* before God, the more superfluous it is to mention further that it was in God's presence *he believed.* The second explanation, though less usual when the dative is in question, is not at variance with grammar; and the idea it expresses is much more simple and in keeping with the context; for the two following participles indicate precisely the two attributes which *the faith* of Abraham lays hold of : "before the God whom he believed as *quickening* . . . and *calling."* [1]—Two Mjj., F G, and the *Peshito* read ἐπίστευσας, thou *didst believe.* Erasmus had adopted this meaning in his first editions, and it passed into Luther's translation. These words were thus meant to be a continuation of the quotation. It would be best in this case to explain the κατέναντι οὗ in the sense of ἀνθ' οὗ : " *in respect of the fact that* thou didst believe." But this meaning is without example, and the reading has not the shadow of probability.—The two divine attributes on which the faith of Abraham fastened at this decisive moment, were the power to *quicken* and the power to *create.* It was, indeed, in this twofold character that God presented Himself when He addressed to him the words quoted : *I have made thee*—here is the assurance of a resurrection—*father of many nations*— here is the promise of a creation. Faith imagines nothing arbitrarily; it limits itself to taking God as He offers Himself, but wholly.—The first attribute, the power to *quicken* (or *raise again*), has sometimes been explained in relation to facts which have no direct connection with the context, such as the resurrection of the *dead,* spiritually speaking (Orig. Olsh.), or the conversion of the Gentiles (Ewald), or even the sacrifice of Isaac (Er. Mangold)! But ver. 19 shows plainly enough what is the apostle's meaning. It is in the patriarch's own person, already a centenarian, and his wife almost as old as he, that a resurrection must take place if the divine promise is to be fulfilled.—In the explanation of the second predicate, the far-fetched has also been sought for the obvious; there has been given to the word *call* a spiritual signification (calling to salvation), or it has even been applied to the primordial act of creation (καλεῖν, *to call,* and by this call to bring out of nothing). But how with this meaning are we to explain the words ὡς ὄντα, *as being?* Commentators have thus been led to give them the force of ὡς ἐσόμενα or εἰς τὸ εἶναι, *as about to be,* or *in order to their being;* which is of course impossible. The simple meaning of the word call : *to invite one to appear,* is fully sufficient. Man in this way calls beings which are; on the summons of the master the servant presents himself. But it belongs to God to call beings to appear which are not, as if they already were. And it is thus God speaks to Abraham of that multitude of future nations which are to form his posterity. He calls them up before his view as a multitude already present, as really existing as the starry heaven to which he compares them, and says : "*I have made thee* the father of this multitude." The subjective negative μή before ὄντα expresses this idea : "He calls as being *what he knows himself* to be non-existent." The two present participles, *quickening* and *calling,* express a permanent attribute, belonging to the essence of the subject. The passage thus understood admirably teaches wherein faith consists. God shows us by his promise not only what he wills to exist for us, but what he wills us to become and what we already are in his sight; and we abstracting from our real state, and by a sublime effort taking the position which the promise assigns us, answer : Yea, I will be so ; I am so. Thus it is that Abraham's faith corresponded to the promise of the God who was speaking to him face to face. It is this

---

[1] Godet's explication is a possible one, but the other is far more grammatical.—T. W. C.

true notion of faith which the apostle seeks to make plain, by analyzing more profoundly what passed in the heart of the patriarch at the time when he performed that act on which there rested the foundation of the kingdom of God on the earth.

Ver. 18. "*Who against hope believed in hope, in order to become the father of many nations, according to that which was spoken, So shall thy seed be.*"— The word *hope* is used here in two different senses, the one subjective: hope as a feeling (in the phrase: *in hope*), the other objective: hope to denote the *motive* for hoping (in the phrase: *against hope*). It is nearly the same in viii. 24, with this difference, that hope in the latter passage, taken objectively, does not denote the *ground* of hoping, but the *object* of hope (as in Col. i. 5). The apostle therefore means: without finding in the domain of sense or reason the least ground for hoping, he nevertheless believed, and that by an effort of hope proceeding from a fact which the eye did not see nor the reason comprehend, God and His promise. This is the realization of the notion of faith expressed Heb. xi. 1, a notion which is so often wrongly contrasted with the conception of Paul. Instead of: *he believed in hope*, it seems as if it should have been: he hoped on (the foundation of) his faith. But the ἐπί is taken here nearly in the same sense as in the frequent phrases: ἐπ' εὐνοίᾳ, ἐπ' ἐχθρᾳ, *in goodwill, in hatred;* ἐπὶ ξενίᾳ, *in hospitality*. His faith burst forth in the form of hope, and that in a situation which presented no ground for hope.— Translators generally weaken the expression εἰς τὸ γενέσθαι, *in order to become*, by suppressing the idea of intention: "and *thus it is that* he became" (Oltram.), or: "and he *believed that* he would become" (Osterv.). This substitution of the result for the intention is grammatically inadmissible. He really believed with the *intention* of becoming. If he grasped the promise with such energy, it certainly was *in order that* it might be realized. It is therefore unnecessary to ascribe this notion of aim to God, as Meyer does.—The following verses develop the two notions: *against hope* (ver. 19), and *in hope* (vv. 20, 21).

Vv. 19, 20. "*And being not weak in faith, he considered*[1] *his own body now*[2] *dead—he was about an hundred years old—and the old age of Sarah's body; but having regard to the promise, he doubted not through unbelief; but grew in strength by faith, giving glory to God.*"—Abraham is represented in this passage as placed between two opposite forces, that of sight, which turns to the external circumstances (ver. 19), and that of faith, which holds firmly to the promise (ver. 20). The δέ, *but*, of ver. 20, expresses the triumph of faith over sight.—We find in ver. 19 one of the most interesting various readings in the text of our Epistle. Two of the three families of MSS., the Greco-Latin and the Byz., read the negative οὐ before κατενόησε: *he considered not*. The effect of the subjective negative μή before ἀσθενήσας, *being weak*, on the principal verb would then be rendered thus, *because:* "because he was not weak in faith, he considered not" . . . The meaning is good: the look of faith fixed on the promise prevented every look cast on the external circumstances which might have made him stagger, as was the case with Peter, who, as long as he looked to Jesus, regarded neither the winds nor the waves. But the Alex. family, with the Peshito this time on its side, rejects the οὐ. The meaning is then wholly different: "not being weak in faith, he looked at (or considered) his deadened body . . . but for all that (δέ, ver. 20) he staggered not" . . . This reading seems to be preferable to the preceding, for it better explains the contrast indicated by the δέ, *but*, of ver. 20. The meaning is also more forcible. He considered . . . but he did not let himself be shaken by the view, discouraging as it was. The μή before ἀσθενήσας may be explained either as a

---

[1] The ου, which T. R. reads here, with D E F G K L P, It., is rejected by ℵ A B C, Syr. Or. (Lat. trans.).
[2] B F G, It. Syr. Or. omit ηδη, which is found in all the rest.

reflection of the author intended to bring out a *circumstance* which accompanied this view (he considered *without being weak*), or, what is better, as indicating the *negative cause*, which controls all that follows (vv. 19, 20): "*because* he was not weak in faith, he regarded . . . but did not stagger." In favor of the Received reading: "he considered not," . . . the passage has been alleged: "Abraham laughed, and said in his heart, Shall a child be born unto him that is an hundred years old? and shall Sarah, that is ninety years old, bear?" (Gen. xvii. 17); a passage which, according to this view, gave occasion to the rejection of the negative οὐ. This is not wholly impossible. But the time to which this passage (Gen. xvii.) applies is not the same as that of which the apostle here speaks (Gen. xv.).

Ver. 20. The δέ, *but*, denotes the contrast to the possible and natural result of this consideration. Strictly speaking, the antithesis would have been the ἐνεδυναμώθη, *he strengthened himself;* but the apostle feels the need of reminding us first, in a negative form, of what might have been so easily produced under such conditions.—The εἰς τὴν ἐπαγγελίαν, *in regard to the promise*, stands foremost. It was the object in contrast to that which was presented to his view by the effeteness of his own body and Sarah's. For the force of εἰς, comp. xvi. 19.—The verb here: διακρίνεσθαι, *to doubt*, properly signifies *to be parted*, or to be divided into two men, one affirming, the other denying; one hoping and giving himself up, the other waiting to see: "but in regard to the promise, there was no division in him." The complement: *of God*, brings out that which gave the promise this full power over his heart.—In the clause: *through unbelief*, the Greek substantive is preceded by the article: through *the* unbelief common among men, the well-known unbelief.—The ἀλλά, *but*, is more strongly adversative than the δέ: "But quite the contrary." This word forcibly contrasts the idea of the strength drawn from the promise with the weakness arising from doubt. The verb ἐνεδυναμώθη may be translated as a passive: *he was strengthened;* comp. Heb. xi. 34; but it may also be taken in the middle and reflective sense: *he strengthened himself*, reinvigorated himself, Acts ix. 22; Eph. vi. 10. The antithesis of the διακριθῆναι, *to doubt*, speaks rather in favor of the middle sense, unless we recur to the simply intransitive meaning: *he grew in strength;* this shade would perhaps be preferable; it harmonizes with the preposition ἐν, which enters into the composition of the verb, and denotes a growth of *inward* strength. In proportion as he contemplated the promise with a fixed regard, in which he put, so to speak, his whole soul, his entire being, body and spirit, was penetrated with a new force, the principle of the complete resurrection in which he had made bold to believe (ver. 17).

The clause *by faith* is usually connected with the verb *he was strengthened;* but so understood, these words do little more than repeat what has already been sufficiently expressed. It is better, therefore, to join them with the following participle: "by faith (by *this* faith) giving glory to God." The position of this word, heading the clause to which it is thus joined, corresponds with the importance of the idea of faith in the whole piece. Man was created to glorify God. He did not do so by his obedience. It is *by faith*, at least, that in his state of sin he can return to the fulfilment of this glorious destination.—*To give glory to God* means in Scripture, to render homage either by word or deed, to one or other of God's attributes, or to His perfection in general. Wherein, in this case, did the homage consist? The apostle tells us in ver. 21: in the firm conviction which he cherished of God's faithfulness to His word and of His power to fulfil it.

Vv. 21, 22. "*Being*[1] *fully convinced that, what He has promised, he is able also to perform. Wherefore*[2] *also righteousness was imputed to him.*"—

---

[1] E F G. It. omit the καί here, which all the others read. It is clearly entitled to a place in the text—.T. W. C.
[2] B D F G, Syr omit καί after διό.

Πληροφορεῖν, *to fill a vessel to the brim ;* this word used in the passive applies to a man filled with a conviction which leaves no place in his heart for the least doubt. It is the opposite of the διακρίνεσθαι, *to be inwardly divided,* of ver. 20. If the relation between the two participles : *giving glory* and *being convinced,* is as we have said, we should probably omit the καί, *and,* which begins this verse in the Alex. and Byz., and prefer the Greco-Latin reading which rejects it.—As to the καί, *also,* before ποιῆσαι, *to do,* it well expresses the inseparable relation which the moral perfection of God establishes between His *saying* and His *doing.* If His power were not equal to the height of His promise, He would not promise.

Ver. 22 sums up the whole development relating to Abraham's faith, vv. 1-21, to clear the way for the final application which Paul had in view. Διό, *wherefore,* refers to what has just been said of the confidence with which Abraham laid hold of God's promise, ver. 21. God ascribed to that confidence which glorified Him the worth of perfect righteousness. The καί, *also* ("wherefore also"), found in the Alex. and Byz. Mjj., points to the moral relation which exists between faith and the imputation made of that faith. The subject of ἐλογίσθη, *was counted,* might be the πιστεῦσαι, *believing,* understood ; but it is simpler to regard the verb as impersonal : "there was in relation to him an imputation of righteousness." This saying is more expressly connected with the first of the three subjects treated in this chapter, Abraham's justification, vv. 1-12 ; but it sums up at the same time the two others, the inheritance of the world and the birth of Isaac, which are, so to speak, its complements. Thus is introduced the fourth part, which contains the application to existing believers, vv. 23-25.

4. Vv. 23-25

Vv. 23, 24. "*Now it was not written for him only, that it was imputed to him ; but for us also, to whom it shall be imputed, when we believe on him that raised up Jesus our Lord from the dead.*"—The apostle extracts the permanent principle contained in Abraham's case to apply it to us. The δέ, *now,* marks this advance. Δι' αὐτόν, *for him* (strictly : on account of him), does not signify *to his honor* (Beza, Thol.). The idea is that the narrative was written not merely to relate a fact belonging to Abraham's history, but also to preserve the knowledge of an event which should take place in ours. So it will be on the condition expressed by the following participle τοῖς πιστεύουσιν, *for us who believe,* the meaning of which we have rendered freely in the translation (*when we believe*). Every time this condition shall be fulfilled, the same imputation *will certainly take place ;* such is the meaning of the word μέλλει, *is to.*—But what in our position now will be the object of faith ? Faith in the biblical sense can only have one object. Whether Abraham or we be the parties in question, this object, always the same, is God and His manifestation. But in consequence of the unceasing progress which takes place in the divine work, the *mode* of this manifestation cannot but change. In the case of Abraham God revealed Himself by the promise of an event *to be accomplished ;* the patriarch required therefore to believe in the form of *hope,* by cleaving to the divine attribute which could realize it. In our position now we are in presence of an *accomplished fact,* the display of the almighty grace of God in the resurrection of Jesus. The object of faith is therefore different in form and yet the same in substance : God and His manifestation, then in word, now in act. What closely binds the two historical facts brought into connection, though so distant, the birth of Isaac and the resurrection of Jesus, is that they are the two extreme links of one and the same chain, the one the point of departure, the other the consummation of the history of salvation. But it must not be imagined that, because it falls to us to believe in an accomplished fact, faith is now nothing more than historical credence given to the reality of this fact. The apostle at once sets aside this thought when he says, not: "when we believe in the resurrection of Jesus," but: "when we believe in *God who raised Jesus;*" comp. Col. ii. 12. He excludes it likewise when he designates this Jesus raised from the dead as *our Lord*, one who has been raised by this divine act to the position of representative of the divine sovereignty, and especially to the Headship of the body of the church. He gives it to be understood, finally, by unfolding in the following verse the essential contents of this supreme object of faith.

Ver. 25. " *Who was delivered on account of our offences, and was raised again on account of our justification.*"—In the title *our Lord* there was involved the idea of a very intimate relation between Jesus and us. This mysterious and gracious solidarity is summed up in two symmetrical clauses, which in a few clear and definite terms present its two main aspects. *He was delivered on account of our offences.* Perhaps Paul means by the phrase: *being delivered*, to remind us of the description of the servant of Jehovah, Isa. liii.: "His soul was delivered ($\pi\alpha\rho\epsilon\delta\delta\theta\eta$) to death" (ver. 12). He who delivers Him, according to Rom. viii. 32, is God Himself: "who spared not His own Son, but delivered Him up for us all." Paul has told us, iii. 25, for what end this act was necessary. It was required to manifest conspicuously the righteousness of God. Every sinner needed to be brought to say: See what I deserve! Thus justice was satisfied and pardon possible. *And He was raised again on account of our justification.* Commentators are unanimous, if I mistake not, in translating: *for our justification*, as if it were $\pi\rho\delta\varsigma$ or $\epsilon\iota\varsigma$, and not $\delta\iota\alpha$ (*on account of*). This *for* is explained in the sense that the resurrection of Christ was needed in order that faith might be able to appropriate the expiation which was accomplished, and that so justification, of which faith is the condition, might take place. But what a roundabout way of arriving at the explanation of this *for!* And if the apostle really meant *for (with a view to)*, why repeat this same preposition $\delta\iota\alpha$ which he had just used in the *parallel* proposition, in its natural sense of *on account of*, while the language supplied him with prepositions appropriate to the exact expression of his thought ($\pi\rho\delta\varsigma$, $\epsilon\iota\varsigma$, iii. 25, 26)? I am not surprised that in this way several commentators have found in this symmetry established between the facts of salvation nothing more than an artificial distribution, belonging to the domain of rhetoric rather than to that of dogmatics, and that one has even gone the length of reproaching the apostle "for sacrificing to the mania of parallelism." If we were shut up to the explanation referred to, we could only join regretfully in this judgment. But it is not so. Let us take the $\delta\iota\alpha$ in its natural sense, as we are bound to do by its use in the first proposition. In the same way as Jesus died because of our offences, that is, our (merited) condemnation, *He was raised because of our* (accomplished) *justification.* Our sin had killed Him; our justification raised Him again. How so? The expiation of our trespasses once accomplished by His death, and the right of God's justice proved in earnest, God could pronounce the collective acquittal of future believers, and He did so. Over the blood of the sacrifice a sentence of justification was pronounced in favor of guilty man; his condemnation was annulled. Now, in view of this divine fact, a corresponding change must necessarily be wrought in the person of Christ Himself. By the same law of solidarity whereby our condemnation had brought Him to the cross, our justification must transform His death into life. When the debtor is proved insolvent, his security is thrown into prison; but as soon as the latter succeeds in clearing the debt, the debtor is legally set free, and his security is liberated with him. For he has no debt of his own. Such is the bond of solidarity formed by the plan of God between Christ and us. Our lot is as it were interwoven with His: we sin, He dies; we are justified, He lives again. This is the key to the declaration, 1 Cor. xv. 17:

"If Jesus be not risen, ye are yet in your sins." So long as the security is in prison, the debt is not paid ; the immediate *effect* of payment would be his liberation. Similarly, if Jesus were not raised, we should be more than ignorant whether our debt were paid ; we might be certain that it was not. His resurrection is the *proof* of our justification only because it is the necessary *effect* of it. What Paul required to say, therefore, was διά, *on account of*, and not εἰς, *with a view to*. If in Christ dead humanity disappeared condemned, in Christ raised again it appears acquitted.[1] And now what is the part of *faith* in relation to the resurrection thus understood ? Exactly that of Abraham in regard to the divine promise. On hearing the promise, he no longer saw himself as he was, but he considered himself as the promise made him. So, the resurrection of Christ once completed, we have no longer to see ourselves as we are in ourselves, but as this fact reveals us to our view : justified. For this resurrection is the incarnation of my justification. If death is the payment of my debt, resurrection is, as it were, the acknowledgment of it.

We must beware, therefore, if we would not efface from the Scriptures their most magnificent revelation, of giving to the word δικαίωσις, *justification*, as several commentators, Döllinger for example, the entirely arbitrary sense of *sanctification :* Jesus was raised with a view to our moral amelioration !—or of bringing in here, as some Protestant commentators do (Calv., Thol., Philip.) with the notion of the resurrection, those of the heavenly dominion and the intercession of Christ. The resurrection is here presented by Paul in express terms in its relation to what preceded, namely, His death, not the glorified existence which followed.

Thus is finished the demonstration of the harmony between the revelation of the Old Testament and the justification by faith revealed in the gospel. The grand truth of the righteousness of faith, summarily *enunciated* iii. 21, 22, was first *placed* on its historical foundation, the work of God in Christ, iii. 23-26 ; then it was *confirmed* by its harmony with the Old Testament ; first with the spirit of the law, iii. 27-31, then with the example of Abraham, iv. 1-24. One question might yet be raised : Will this justification by faith, which saves us at present, hold good in the future ? Can it assure us of salvation even before the judgment-seat ? It is to the solution of this so grave question that the following piece is devoted. Thus will be closed the didactic exposition of justification by faith.

ELEVENTH PASSAGE (5:1-11)

The Certainty of final Salvation for Believers

The title which we have just given to this piece suffices to indicate the difference between the idea which we form of its scope and aim, and that which prevails on the subject in the commentaries. Commentators, except Meyer to some extent, and Th. Schott more completely, see in the following piece the exposition of the *fruits* of justification by faith ; to wit, *peace*, ver. 1 ; *the hope* of glory, ver. 2 ; *patience*, ver. 3 et seq. ; and the feeling of the love of God, ver. 5, et seq.[2] But, first, such a juxtaposition of effects

---

[1] This ingenious and striking view is, I think, peculiar to the author. It is better to render thus : *for the sake of* (to take away) *our offences : for the sake of* (to secure) *our justification*. Compare xiii. 5.—T. W. C.

[2] Calvin : " The apostle begins to demonstrate what he has affirmed of justification *by its effects*."—Tholuck entitles this passage : " the beneficent pathologico-religious influence of this means of salvation."—Olshausen : *of the fruits of faith*, adding at the same time that the apostle could of course only sketch these consequences of faith here, but that he will develop them afterward.—Philippi : " the beneficent consequences of justification."—Reuss says : " the piece describes the effects of justification on the man who is its object."—Lange and Schaff : " the fruit of justification."—Hodge : " the consequences of justification : 1. Faith ; 2. Free access

so diverse would not correspond with the nature of Paul's genius. Then chaps. vi.–viii. are intended, as all allow, to expound Christian sanctification as the fruit of justification by faith. But if the piece v. 1-11 were the beginning of the description of the *fruits of justification*, why interrupt the delineation by the parallel of Adam and Christ, which does not naturally belong to it? One cannot be surprised, if it is so, at the judgment of Reuss, who alleges that in the matter of systematic order our Epistle leaves something to be desired (*Gesch. d. N. T. Schr.* § 108). To escape this difficulty, Lange and Schaff, following Rothe's example, think we should close the exposition of justification at v. 11, and make the parallel of the two Adams the opening of a new division, that relating to sanctification. We shall state the exegetical reasons which absolutely prevent us from referring the passage v. 12-21 to the work of sanctification. Here we merely call the attention of the reader to the particle διὰ τοῦτο, *wherefore*, v. 12, by which the second part of our chapter is closely joined to what precedes, and which makes the following piece not the opening of a new part, but the close of that which we are studying (i. 18-v. 11). As to the disorder which Reuss attributes to the apostolic doctrine, we think we can show that the author of the Epistle is entirely innocent, and that it is solely chargeable on his expositors. The apostle never thought of explaining, in the piece which we are about to study, *the fruits* of justification; he simply finishes treating the subject of justification itself. What good, indeed, would be served by an argument in regular form like that which we find in vv. 6-8 and in vv. 9, 10, which are real syllogisms, to demonstrate what is obvious at a glance: that peace with God flows from justification? Was it not enough to indicate the fact? The view of the apostle is therefore entirely different. From this point he turns his attention to the *future* which opens up before the justified soul. It is not at its goal; a career of trials and struggles awaits it. Will its state of justification hold good till it can possess the finished salvation? The apprehension of divine wrath exists in the profound depths of man's heart. A trespass suffices to reawaken it. What justified one will not sometimes put the anxious question, Will the sentence by which my faith was reckoned to me for righteousness be still valid before the judgment-seat; and *in the day of wrath* (ver. 9) will this salvation by grace, in which I now rejoice, still endure? It is the answer to this ever-reviving fear which the following piece is intended to give. We are still, therefore, engrossed with the subject of justification. The exegesis, I hope, will prove the truth of this view, which makes this piece an essential waymark in the progress of the Epistle. As is usual with Paul, the theme of the whole passage is expressed in the first words, vv. 1 and 2.

Vv. 1, 2. "*Therefore, being justified by faith, we have*[1] *peace with God through our Lord Jesus Christ: by whom also we have obtained access by faith*[2] *into this grace wherein we stand, and triumph in the hope of the glory of God.*"—The meaning of ver. 1 is as follows: "Since, then, we have obtained by means of faith our sentence of justification from God, we find ourselves transferred relatively to Him into a state of peace, which henceforth displaces in our minds the fear of wrath."—The form of expression:

to God; 3. Our afflictions auxiliary to hope; 4. The certainty of final salvation."—Renan says: "the fruit of justification is peace with God, hope, and consequently patience."—Hofmann sums up thus: "Let us enter into this relation of peace with God, in which we have the hope of glory, consolation in trials, love to God, and the certainty of deliverance from final wrath." Bossuet: "the happy fruits of justification by faith."—Meyer better: "Paul now expounds *the blessed certainty of salvation for the present and future.*"—Holsten has some expressions which approach this point of view.—Schott is the only one with whom I find myself entirely in accord in the understanding of this piece. He entitles it: *The certainty of the believer's preservation in salvation, and of the final consummation of this salvation* (p. 234).

[1] T. R. reads εχομεν, with the F G P (and besides the first corrector of א and the third of B). The eight other Mjj. It. Syr. read εχωμεν.
[2] The words τη πιστει are omitted by B D E F G, Or. (Lat. trans.).

εἰρήνην ἔχειν πρός, is common in classic Greek (see Meyer). But must we not read, with the great majority of Mjj. and Vss., the subjunctive ἐχωμεν, *let us have*, instead of ἔχομεν, *we have, we possess?* This reading is adopted by Hofm., Gess, Volkm.; it makes this ver. 1 an exhortation. But how happens it that immediately afterward the didactic tone recommences and continues uniformly to the end of the piece, without any resuming of the exhortation? This reading certainly arises from a mistaken correction, which owes its origin to the erroneous idea which has been formed of the piece (see above). Perhaps, also, it is due to the fact that a liturgical reading began with this verse. No exegete has been able to account satisfactorily for this imperative suddenly occurring in the midst of a didactic development.¹—The words: *through our Lord Jesus Christ*, are explained by commentators, and even by Meyer, as referring to the work of expiation previously described. We cannot admit this view, for the following reasons: 1. The work of expiation is cited in ver. 2 as a benefit wholly distinct from that to which ver. 1 refers; δι' οὗ καί, *by whom also*, are the words in the beginning of ver. 2. It is therefore impossible, without useless repetition, to explain the two expressions, *through our Lord*, ver. 1, and *by whom also*, ver. 2, in reference to the same mediation. Now the mediation of ver. 2 is undoubtedly that which Jesus effected by the atonement. That of ver. 1 must therefore refer to another work. 2. The mediation of which ver. 2 speaks is mentioned as an accomplished fact, the verb being in the perfect: ἐσχήκαμεν, *we have obtained*, while the present, ἔχομεν, *we have*, refers to a present and permanent taking in possession. 3. If the clause: *through our Lord Jesus Christ*, referred to the work of expiation, it would probably be joined to the participle δικαιωθέντες, *having been justified*, rather than to the verb *we possess*. The mistake of exegesis arises from the fact that there has not been recognized in this verse the theme, and, so to speak, the title of the whole piece (on to ver. 11), a piece which refers not to the act of justification, but *to the present and future of the justified*.¹ When he says: *we have peace with God*, the apostle means: we can henceforth regard God with entire serenity, not only as to the past, but also in view of the future, and even of the judgment; for—this is the thought with which he closes the exposition about to follow—we have in Christ, besides the mediation of *His death*, by which we have already been justified (δικαιωθέντες), that of *His life*, by which we shall be maintained in this state of salvation; comp. vv. 9 and 10, which are the authentic explanation of the clause: *through our Lord Jesus Christ*, ver. 1. In this way ver. 2, which refers to the atonement, ceases to have the effect of a repetition.—Schott says to the same purpose: "As it is to the person of Christ that we owed access into grace (ver. 2), it is the same person of Christ which assures us of the perfecting of salvation (ver. 1)."

Ver. 2. Paul here reminds us that the Jesus who henceforth makes our salvation sure (*by his life*), is no other Mediator than the Jesus who has already purchased our justification (*by his death*). Thus is explained the δι' οὗ καί, "by whom *also*." The blessing of reconciliation by His death, explained above, was the foundation of the new grace he had in view throughout the whole piece. Comp. a similar return to a past development intended to serve as the starting-point of a new one, iii. 23. Before passing to the new grace he is concerned to recall the former, to impress the conviction that we owe all, absolutely all, to this Jesus only. The perfect ἐσχήκαμεν expresses an act of taking possession already past, though the possession continues. — The term προσαγωγή, which we have translated by the word *access*, sometimes signifies *the act of bringing* or *introducing*; it may, for example, designate the manoeuvre by which engines of war are brought

---

¹ This view is taken by the American portion of the Revision Committee. It is one of the rare cases in which preponderating MSS. evidence is outweighed by internal grounds.—T. W. C.

close to the walls of a besieged city (comp. Meyer). It might be understood in this sense: "by whom we have obtained *introduction into this grace.*" But the word has also sometimes an intransitive meaning: the *right of entering, access.* The other substantives compounded from the same verb have often an analogous meaning; thus ἀναγωγή, *setting out to sea;* περιαγωγή, *circular motion.* And certainly this intransitive meaning is preferable here. The first would be suitable if the matter in question were introduction to an individual, a sovereign for example; but with an impersonal regimen, such as *grace,* the meaning of *access to* is more natural. It is in this sense also that the word is taken Eph. ii. 18 and iii. 12, if we are not mistaken. The words τῇ πίστει, *by faith,* are wanting in the Vat. and the Greco-Latins. If they are authentic, they simply remind us of the part previously ascribed to faith in justification. But it is improper, with some commentators, to make the clause: *to this grace,* dependent on it. Such a form of speech: πίστις εἰς χάριν, would be without example in the New Testament. The words: *to this grace,* complete the notion of *access to:* "At the time when we believed (τῇ πίστει) we had access to this grace in which we are now established." — The perfect ἕστηκα signifies: I have been placed in this state, and I am in it. This word, which has the meaning of a present, recalls us to the ἔχομεν, *we have* henceforth, of ver. 1, and forms the transition to the following idea: "and (in this state) we glory." — This last proposition (ver. 2) might be made dependent on the relative pronoun *in which.* The meaning would be: "this grace in which we henceforth stand and glory." But this construction is somewhat awkward. Ver. 2 being already a sort of parenthesis, in the form of an incidental proposition, it is unnatural to prolong the appendix still further. We therefore connect the words: *and we triumph,* with the principal idea of ver. 1: *we have peace.* It is a climax: "not only do we no longer dread any evil at the hand of God, but we have even when we think of Him the joyful hope of all blessing." It is the feeling of security raised to the anticipated joy of triumph. These last words confirm our explanation of the ἔχομεν, "we have henceforth," ver. 1. For they express more obviously still the conviction of the justified man in relation to his future. In reality, the object of this triumphant conviction is the certain hope *of glory.* The phrase: *the glory of God,* denotes the glorious state which God Himself possesses, and into which He will admit the faithful; see on iii. 23. — The καυχᾶσθαι, *to triumph,* is the blessed conviction and *energetic* (but humble, 1 Cor. i. 31) profession of assurance in God. But some one will ask the apostle: And what of the tribulations of life? Do you count them nothing? Do they not threaten to make you lower your tone? Not at all; for they will only serve to feed and revive the hope which is the ground of this glorying. This reply is contained and justified in the following verses.

Vv. 3, 4. "*And not only so, but*[1] *we triumph on account of tribulations also: knowing that tribulation worketh constancy; and approval; and hope.*" — This passage being, strictly speaking, the answer to an unexpressed objection, it is natural that it should recur (end of ver. 4 and 5) to the idea of *hope.* The participle καυχώμενοι, *and even triumphing,* which is found in B C, would correspond very well with the digressive character evidently belonging to these verses. But it is probable that this form has been borrowed from that of ver. 11. — The phrase *we triumph,* literally translated, would be: *in* afflictions. But this translation would not render the idea of the text in our language [French]. It would express the circumstances *in the midst of which* the believer triumphs, while the Greek phrase denotes *the object* itself *of which* he boasts; comp. 1 Cor. i. 31: "to triumph *in* the Lord," for: *on account of the possession of the Lord;* 2 Cor. xii. 9: "to triumph *in* his weaknesses," for: to extract triumph *from* his very weaknesses. Thus Paul

---

[1] B C read καυχώμενοι instead of καυχώμεθα.

means here : to make his afflictions themselves a reason of triumph. This strange thought is explained by what follows ; for the climax which is about to be traced proves that it is tribulations that make hope break forth in all its vigor. Now it is this feeling which is the ground for καυχᾶσθαι (*to glory*). — The words *knowing that* introduce the logical exposition of the process whereby affliction becomes transformed in the believer into hope. First, affliction gives rise to *constancy*, ὑπομονήν. This Greek word, coming from ὑπό and μένειν, literally : *to bear up under* (a burden, blows, etc.), might be translated by *endurance*. From want of this word [in French] we say *constancy*. — Ver. 4. Endurance in its turn worketh *approval*, δοκιμήν. This is the state of a force or virtue which has withstood trials. This force, issuing victorious from the conflict, is undoubtedly the faith of the Christian, the worth of which he has now proved by experience. It is a weapon of which henceforth he knows the value. The word δόκιμος frequently denotes in the same sense the *proved* Christian, the man who has shown what he is, comp. xiv. 18, and the opposite, 1 Cor. x. 27. We find in the New Testament two sayings that are analogous, though slightly different : Jas. i. 3, where the neuter substantive δοκίμιον denotes, not like δοκιμή here, the state of the thing proved, but the *means* of proof, tribulation itself ; and 1 Pet. i. 7, where the same substantive δοκίμιον seems to us to denote that which in the faith of the believer has held good in suffering, has shown itself real and effective, the gold which has come forth purified from the furnace. — When, finally, the believer has thus experienced the divine force with which faith fills him in the midst of suffering, he feels his *hope* rise. Nothing which can happen him in the future any longer affrights him. The prospect of glory opens up to him nearer and more brilliant. How many Christians have declared that they never knew the gladness of faith, or lively hope, till they gained it by means of tribulation ! With this word *hope* the apostle has returned to the end of ver. 2 ; and as there are deceitful hopes, he adds that the one of which he speaks (*the hope of glory*, ver. 2) runs no risk of being falsified by the event.

Ver. 5. "*Now hope maketh not ashamed ; because the love of God is shed abroad in our hearts by the Holy Ghost which was given unto us.*"—This verse is the central saying of the entire passage. On the one hand, it is directly connected with the two first verses : " We no longer feel any fear ; nay, rather, we triumph in the hope of glory, a hope which is rendered brighter even by sufferings." On the other hand, this verse contains all that follows. This hope will not be falsified in the end by the event ; this is what the second part of the passage proceeds to prove (vv. 6–11).—The word *make ashamed* refers to the non-realization of the hope when the hour of glory has struck. The present *maketh not ashamed* is the present of the idea. This falsification, inflicted on the hopes of faith by facts, and the possibility of which is denied by the apostle, is not that with which the truth of materialism would confound them. This idea is foreign to the mind of Paul. The matter in question in the context is the terrible position of the justified man who in the day of judgment should find himself suddenly face to face with unappeased wrath. Paul declares such a supposition impossible. Why ? Because the source of his hope is the revelation of God Himself which he has received, of the love of which he is the object. The reawakening of wrath against him is therefore an inadmissible fact.—The *love of God* cannot denote here *our love* for God, as Hofmann would have it. It is true this critic thoroughly recognizes the imperfections always attaching to our love. But he thinks that Paul is here looking at the believer's love to his God only as a *mark* of our renewal by the Holy Spirit. Nevertheless, this meaning must be rejected ; first, on account of the choice of the verb ἐκκέχυται, *is shed abroad* (see below) ; next, because the following verses (6–8), joined by *for* to ver. 5 develop the idea of God's love to us, not that of our love to God ; finally, because the syllogism finished in vv. 9,

10 would want its basis (its minor) if the fact of God's love to us had not been established in the preceding context. *The love of God* is therefore the love with which God loves us. The verb translated by *is shed abroad*, literally signifies : *to be poured out of*. Paul means : out of the heart of God, where this love has its source, into ours. The perfect used here signifies that there was a time when this effusion took place, and that since then it has not been withdrawn. It is this meaning of the perfect which explains the use of the preposition of rest, ἐν (*in*, without the idea of motion), instead of εἰς (*into*, with motion). This preposition refers to the whole state which has resulted from the effusion. There was an act of revelation in the heart of believers, the fruit of which is the permanent impression of the love which God has for them. The medium of this transfusion of the divine love into their heart was the Holy Spirit. We see, 1 Cor. ii. 10–12, that this Divine Being, after having sounded the depths of God, reveals them to the man to whom he imparts himself. Thereby we become privy to what is passing in God, in particular, to the feeling which he cherishes toward us, just as we should be to a feeling which we might ourselves cherish toward another. In general, the work of the Spirit consists in breaking down the barrier between beings, and placing them in a common luminous atmosphere, in which each hears the heart of his neighbor beat as if it were his own. And this is the relation which the Spirit establishes not only between man and man, but between man and God Himself ; comp. John xiv. 19, 20. The aorist participle δοθέντος, *which was given to us*, reminds us of two things : the time when this heaven was opened to the believer, and the objective and perfectly real character of this inward revelation. It was not a case of exalted feeling or excited imagination ; it was God who imparted himself ; comp. John xiv. 21 and 23.—The transition from ver. 5 to 6 seems to me to be one of the points on which exegesis has left most to be desired. Commentators confine themselves in general to saying that ver. 6 gives the external proof, the proof from fact, of that divine love shed abroad in our hearts, and that the proof is the sacrifice of Christ, vv. 6–8. But this inorganic juxtaposition of the internal proof, ver. 5, and the external proof, ver. 6, is not satisfactory ; and this explanation does not correspond to the use of the particle *for*, which implies a much more intimate relation of ideas. The object is to *prove* that this hope of glory, whose source is the inward revelation of the love of God, will not be falsified by the event in the hour of judgment. For this end, what does the apostle do ? He does not merely allege an external fact already past ; he penetrates to the essence of that internal revelation of which he has just been speaking in ver. 5. He analyzes, so to speak, its contents, and transforming this ineffable feeling into a rigorous syllogism, he deduces from it the following argument, which is that of the Spirit Himself in the heart of the believer : God loved thee when thou wast yet a sinner, giving thee a proof of love such as men do not give to one another, even when they respect and admire one another the most, and when the devotion of love is carried among them to its sublimest height (vv. 6–8). Such is the minor, the divine love already manifested in the fact of redemption. The understood major is to this effect : Now the love which one has testified to his enemies does not belie itself when these have become better than enemies, friends. The conclusion is expressly stated, vv. 9, 10 : If, then, God testified to thee, to thee when yet an enemy, a love beyond all comparison, how shouldst thou, once justified and reconciled, have to fear falling back again under wrath ? It is obvious that to the end of the passage, from ver. 6, the whole forms one consecutive reasoning, and this reasoning is joined by *for* to ver. 5, because it serves only to expound in a logical form the language which the Holy Spirit holds to the heart of the believer, and by which He sustains his hope, even through earthly tribulations.

Vv. 6–8. "*For when we were yet[1] weak[2] in due time Christ died for the ungodly. For hardly for a righteous man will one die:[3] for peradventure for goodness some would even dare to die. But God establisheth His own love towards us, in that, while we were yet sinners, Christ died for us.*"—The *for* might be rendered by *in fact*. The inward revelation of divine love, whereby the Holy Spirit certifies to the believer that his hope of glory shall not be deceived, is now to be set in full light. The authenticity of this *for* is sufficiently attested—(1) By the reading of the Alex., Byz. : ἔτι γάρ ; (2) By that of the Greco-Latin : εἰς τί γάρ ; (3) By that of the *Vat*. itself, which reads εἴγε ; for this γ seems to be a remnant of the primitive γάρ. The reading of the Alex. and Byz. MSS., which put the ἔτι, *yet*, at the head of the sentence, is likewise authentic. For, to the weight of the authorities there is added the decisive importance of this little word, in which there is concentrated the whole force of the following verses : "God testified His love to us when we were yet in a state which rendered us wholly unworthy of it. . . . ! The Greco-Latin reading : εἰς τί γάρ, *for what end?* is a corruption of this not understood ἔτι. A question relative to the *end* of divine love would be out of place in this argument, where it is not the end, but the particular *character* of the love which is in question. It is wholly different with the reading of the *Vat*. : εἴγε, *if at least*, which perfectly suits the meaning of the passage, whether the *if* be made dependent on the proposition : *hope maketh not ashamed*, ver. 5—and to this the *at least* points—or whether it be taken as the beginning of the following argument : "If Christ died . . . with much stronger reason . . . (ver. 9)." This construction, adopted by Ewald, is excellent ; only it obliges us to make vv. 7 and 8 a parenthesis, which is complicated and unnecessary, since the reading ἔτι, *yet*, gives in a simpler form exactly the same sense : "When we were yet without strength, Christ died . . . ; with much stronger reason . . . ver. 9." Ver. 6 describes the miserable condition in which we were at the time when divine love was extended to us. We were *weak*, ἀσθενεῖς. The word often means *sick* (1 Cor. xi. 30). Here it expresses total incapacity for good, the want of all moral life, such as is healthy and fruitful in good works. It was certainly not a state fitted to win for us the sympathy of divine holiness. On the contrary, the spectacle of a race plunged in such shameful impotence was disgusting to it. Seven Mjj. read after ἀσθενῶν the word ἔτι, *yet* (five of them read it previously in the beginning of the verse). If this somewhat strange reading be admitted, the comma need not be placed where Tischendorf puts it (8th edition), after this ἔτι, to connect it with what precedes, but before, to join it to the following word : κατὰ καιρόν, *yet in time*. What led Tischendorf to this construction was, that he mistakenly connected the first ἔτι, in the opening of the verse, with the verb : Christ *died*. Neither the sense nor grammar is favorable to this connection. But, on the other hand, if the second ἔτι were joined to κατὰ καιρόν, *yet in time*, there would be too marked an emphasis on an idea in the passage which is purely secondary. We conclude, therefore, that the second ἔτι should be rejected from the text. It is, as Meyer thinks, a mistaken repetition arising from the fact that this little word did not appear suitable in the beginning of the passage, especially if a liturgical lesson commenced with ver. 6. So copyists have first transposed it after the ἀσθενῶν, then doubled it by combining the two readings.—The words : *in due time, at the right moment*, may contain an allusion to the eternal plan, iii. 25 : "at the *hour fixed beforehand* by divine wisdom." Or they express the idea of the suitability of this time in relation

---

[1] Three principal readings : T. R. with ℵ A C D E K P, the Mnn. Marc. Or. (Lat. trans.) Syr. read ετι γαρ ; F G, It. : εις τι γαρ ; B : ει γε.
[2] ℵ A B C D E F G read ετι after ασθενων (consequently ℵ A C D E read this word twice).
[3] Instead of δικαιον, which all the documents read, the Syriac translation seems to have read αδικων.

to the state of mankind, either because having now made full trial of their misery, they might be disposed to accept with faith the salvation of God ; or because it was the *last hour*, when, the time of forbearance having reached its limit (iii. 26), God, if He did not pardon, must judge. This last meaning seems to us, from iii. 25, 26, to be the one which best corresponds to the mind of the apostle.—The incapacity of mankind for good, their moral sickness, arose from their separation from God, from their voluntary revolt against Him. This is what the apostle brings out in the words : *for ungodly ones*, which indicate the *positive* side of human perversity. Their malady inspires disgust ; their ungodliness attracts wrath. And it was when we were yet plunged in this repulsive state of impotence and ungodliness that the greatest proof of love was given us, in that Christ died for us. The preposition ὑπέρ, *for*, can only signify : *in behalf of*. It neither implies nor excludes the idea of substitution (*in the room of*) ; it refers to the *end*, not at all to the *mode* of the work of redemption.

To shed light on the wholly exceptional character of the love testified to mankind in this death of Christ, the apostle compares the action of God in this case with the noblest and rarest proofs of devotion presented by the history of our race ; and he bids us measure the distance which still separates those acts of heroism from the sacrifice of God, vv. 7 and 8.

In ver. 7 he supposes two cases in the relations of man to man, the one so extraordinary that it is hardly (μόλις, *hardly*) conceivable, the other difficult indeed to imagine, but yet supposable (τάχα, *peradventure*). The relation between those two examples has been variously understood. According to the old Greek commentators, Calv., Beza, Fritzs., Mey., Oltram., etc., the relation is that of complete identity ; the expression : ὑπὲρ τοῦ ἀγαθοῦ, *for the man who is good*, in the second proposition, designating no essentially different character from the ὑπὲρ δικαίου, *for a righteous man*, in the first. The second proposition on this view is simply the justification of that remnant of possibility which was implied in the word *hardly* in the first : "hardly will one die for a just man ; I say, hardly ; for after all I do not absolutely deny that for such a man of probity one might be found willing to sacrifice his life." But if such were really the apostle's meaning, why substitute in the second proposition for the word δικαίον, *the just man*, the term ἀγαθοῦ, *the good man* (or *goodness*) ? Why prefix the article to the latter, which did not stand before the former : *a just* . . . *the good* (or *goodness*) ? Why put the word ἀγαθοῦ first in the proposition obviously indicating the purpose to establish an antithesis between the two ideas : *the good man* (or *goodness*), and *a just man* ? Why, finally, in the second proposition add the word καί, *even*, which establishes a gradation, and consequently a difference between the two examples quoted ? We are aware of the reason that has led so many commentators to this explanation, which is inconsistent with all the details of the text. It is the difficulty of pointing out a satisfactory distinction between the two words δικαίον, *righteous*, and ἀγαθοῦ, *good*. According to Olshausen, the first denotes the man who does no evil to any one ; the second, the man who does positive good, that is to say, more than men have a right to exact from him. According to De Wette, the one is the simply just man, the other the man who, to justice, adds nobleness. According to Hodge, the one is the man who does everything the law demands, and whose character commands *respect ;* the other, the man whose conduct is directed by love, and inspires *love*. According to Ewald, the *just* man is he who is acknowledged innocent in regard to some specific charge ; the *good* man, one who is irreproachable in all respects. Philippi thinks that the *righteous one* is the honest man, and the *good*, the generous and amiable man who does good to those about him, in his family, his city, his country, in a word, the *pater patriæ*. Tholuck, finally, arrives at a clearer and more precise distinction, by giving, like many other commentators, to ἀγαθός, *good*, the meaning of a beneficent man, first, and then by derivation, that of *benefactor*. In this latter case the article *the* is explained by saying that the person meant is *the* benefactor of the man who devotes himself to death, or rather, according to Tholuck himself, by the rhetorical use of the article ὁ, *the*, in the sense of our phrase : *the* man of virtue, *the* philanthropist. This latter explanation of the article might be applied also to the other meanings. But, despite the enormous erudition displayed by the defenders of these various distinctions to justify them from classic writers, all that is gained by most of them is to father a subtlety on the apostle ; and all that is gained by the last, the only one which presents a clear contrast between the two terms, is to make him say what he has not said. To express, indeed, this idea of *benefactor*, he had in Greek the hallowed terms ἀγαθοποιός or εὐεργέτης. Why not use them ? Besides, the addition of the article finds no natural explanation in any of these senses. Reuss has even resolutely sacrificed it in his translation : " one may dare to die for *a* man of virtue." Jerome, and after him Erasmus, Luther, Melanchthon, have taken the two terms, the just and the good, in the neuter sense : *justice, goodness*. But as to the former, this meaning would have absolutely demanded the article ; the meaning of ὑπὲρ δικαίου can be nothing else than : *for a just man*.—This last explanation, however, brings us within reach of the solution. Nothing in fact prevents us from applying Jerome's idea to the second of the two terms, and taking ὑπὲρ τοῦ ἀγαθοῦ in the sense of : *for goodness* (and not for the *good man*).[1] This is the explanation which Rückert in particular has defended, and which Hofmann has finally adopted. Not that we understand, with the former, *the good*, in the sense of the *useful*. The idea of the whole passage would be falsified if there were introduced into it a notion foreign to the purely moral domain. *The good* here, in opposition to ἀσεβεῖς, *the ungodly*, ver. 6, and ἁμαρτωλοί, *sinners*, ver. 8, can only signify a *holy* cause ; for example, the fulfilment of a sacred duty to which one sacrifices his life, like Antigone ; or the defence of the law to which one remains faithful even unto death, like the martyrs in the time of the Maccabees ; or the deliverance of our country for which so many men have sacrificed themselves, even among the heathen ; or the good of humanity in general, which has inspired so many deeds of heroic devotion. It is in this way that Julius Müller, in his *Christl. Lehre v. d. Sünde*, ends by returning to the masculine meaning of τοῦ ἀγαθοῦ, applying the adjective to Him who is *good* par excellence, to God : " For a righteous man one will hardly die ; but, *for God*, yes, peradventure such a thing will occur." This meaning would be excellent, and the contrast striking : " Hardly will men die for God, the perfectly good, and God puts Christ to death for men the ungodly !" Nevertheless, we believe that if the apostle had thought of God personally, he would have designated Him more clearly. In any case, this last sense would coincide with that of Rückert, since God is *the good* in the absolute sense of the word.—The reading of the Peshito ὑπὲρ ἀδίκων, *for unrighteous men*, in the first proposition, gives a very simple meaning, only too simple, and one which completely enervates the force of the contrast to the terms *ungodly*, and *sinners*, in vv. 6 and 8. It is condemned, besides, by all the documents.—Τολμᾶν, to dare, to have courage for ; hence, to resolve to.—Καί : it is a case which is *also* supposable. See, then, how far, in some exceedingly rare cases, the devotion of man in its sublimest manifestations can rise. To sacrifice his life for one whose honorable character inspires respect ; hardly ! to sacrifice yourself on the altar of a cause whose grandeur and holiness have possessed you ; perhaps also (καί) ! And now for the contrast between these supreme acts of human devotion and God's conduct toward us.

---

[1] This is very flat, and very unlikely in the connection. It is far better to take "good" in the sense of *kind* (cf. Acts xi. 24), which makes an obvious and appropriate gradation.— T. W. C.

Ver. 8. The δέ, *but*, indicates this contrast. What man hardly does for what is most worthy of admiration and love, God has done for that which merited only His indignation and abhorrence. On the verb συνιστάναι, see on iii. 5 ; here it is the act whereby God *establishes* beyond question the reality of His love. The apostle says τὴν ἑαυτοῦ ἀγάπην : His *own* love, or the love that is peculiar *to Him*. The expression contrasts God's manner of loving with ours. God cannot look above Him to devote Himself, as we may, to a being of more worth than Himself. His love turns to that which is beneath Him (Isa. lvii. 15), and takes even the character of sacrifice in behalf of that which is altogether unworthy of Him.—Ὅτι, *in that*, is here *the fact* by which God has proved His peculiar way of loving. —In the word ἁμαρτωλός, *sinner*, the termination ωλος signifies abundance. It was by this term the Jews habitually designated the Gentiles, Gal. ii. 15. The ἔτι, *yet*, implies this idea : that there was not *yet* in humanity the least progress toward the good which would have been fitted to merit for it such a love ; it was *yet* plunged in evil (Eph. ii. 1-7).—The words : *Christ died for us*, in such a context, imply the close relation of essence which unites Christ and God, in the judgment of the apostle. With man sacrificing himself, Paul compares God sacrificing Christ. This parallel has no meaning except as the sacrifice of Christ is to God the sacrifice of Himself. Otherwise the sacrifice of God would be inferior to that of man, whereas it must be infinitely exalted above it.—Finally, it should be observed how Paul places the subject Θεός, *God*, at the end of the principal proposition, to bring it beside the word ἁμαρτωλῶν, *sinners*, and so brings out the contrast between our defilement and the delicate sensibility of divine holiness.

In vv. 6-8 the minor premiss of the syllogism has been explained : God loved us when wicked, loved us as we ourselves do not love what is most excellent. Here properly the major should stand : Now, when one has done *the most* for his *enemies*, he does not refuse *the least* to his *friends*. But Paul passes directly to the conclusion, introducing into it at the same time the idea of the major. Reuss says, in passing from ver. 8 to 9 : "Finally, hope is also founded on a *third* consideration." The apostle does not compose in so loose a style.

Vv. 9, 10. " *Much rather then, being now justified by His blood, we shall be saved from wrath through Him. For if, when we were enemies, we were reconciled to God by the death of His Son, much rather, being reconciled, we shall be saved by His life.*"—The οὖν, *then*, concludes from the proof of love already received to the proof of love to be hoped for. The πολλῷ μᾶλλον is certainly taken here in the logical sense : much more *certainly*, and not : much more *abundantly*.—Meyer is right in saying that the conclusion proceeds not from *the least to the most*, but from *the most to the least*. The work already finished is summed up in the words : *being now justified by His blood*. The word *now* contrasts the present state of justification, on the one hand, with the former state of condemnation (the : *yet* sinners of ver. 8) ; and, on the other, with the state of future salvation (*we shall be saved*). The state in which we now are is greatly more inconsistent with final wrath than that from which we have *already* been rescued.—But what is that *wrath* from which we have yet to be delivered ? That spoken of by Paul, ii. 5, 6, in the words : "the day of wrath and revelation of the righteous judgment of God," the day when "God will render to every one according to his deeds ;" comp. 1 Thess. i. 10 ; 2 Thess. i. 8. Our Lord speaks, Luke xii. 47, 48, of the punishment in store for the servant who knew the will of his master and did it not : *he shall be beaten with many stripes*. "To whomsoever much is given, of him shall much be required." A ground this for serious vigilance on the part of the justified man, but not of fear. Paul explains why : there is in Christ more than the expiation (the blood) by which He has introduced us into the state of justification ;

there is His living person, now glorified, and consequently able to interpose in new ways in behalf of the justified, and to bring to a successful end the work of salvation so well begun in them. Such is the meaning of the words : "we shall be saved *through Him* (δι᾽ αὐτοῦ)." Comp. viii. 34 : "Who died, *yea rather*, that is risen again ; who is at the right hand of God, who *also* maketh intercession for us ;" Gal. ii. 20 : "I live, yet not I, but Christ in me ;" Heb. vii. 25 : "Ever living to make intercession for us ;" John xiv. 19 : "Because I live, ye shall live also." Paul here explains himself clearly regarding the double mediation indicated (vv. 1 and 2) by means of the two διά, *through :* "*through* our Lord . . . (ver. 1), *through* whom *also* . . . (ver. 2)." The one expressed in ver. 1 was that which was implied here in the words *through Him :* we are delivered from all fear through Him (as to our future). The other, expressed in ver. 2 ("*through whom also* we have obtained access" . . .), was that of His blood, through which we have been justified, delivered from condemnation (as to the past). It is obvious how profoundly the apostle's work is weighed, and that we were not mistaken in alleging that in the words : "We have peace with God," he had his eyes already turned to the future, the final salvation.

Ver. 10 is, strictly speaking, only a stronger repetition of the argument of ver. 9. Paul makes the reasoning more evident—1. By adding the term *enemies*, which renders the *a fortiori* character of the proof more striking ; 2. By substituting for *justified* (ver. 9) the term *reconciled*, which corresponds better with the word *enemies ;* 3. By describing the death of Christ as that of the *Son of God*, which presents its value more impressively ; 4. By explaining the indefinite term : *through him* (ver. 9), by the more precise expression : *by his life*.—The *for* is explained by the new force which the argument derives from these various changes. It is our *en effet* (in fact) ; comp. the relation between vv. 3 and 5 in John iii.—Three stages are indicated : *enemies, reconciled, saved*. Divine love, which has brought us from the first to the second, will yet more certainly bring us from the second to the third. — The terms : *weak, ungodly, sinners* (vv. 6 and 8), are here summed up in the word *enemies*. Does this word denote man's enmity to God, or that of God to man ? Hating God (*Dei osores*), or hated of God (*Deo odiosi*) ? The first notion would evidently be insufficient in the context. The enmity must above all belong to Him to whom *wrath* is attributed ; and the blood of Christ, through which we have been *justified*, did not flow in the first place to work a change in our dispositions Godward, but to bring about a change in God's conduct toward us. Otherwise this bloody death would have to be called a demonstration of *love*, and not of *righteousness* (iii. 25). Here, besides, the saying xi. 28 should be compared, where the term *enemy* of God is contrasted with the title *beloved* of God ; the first therefore signifies : one not loved, or hated of God ; comp. Eph. ii. 3 : "by nature *children of wrath*." We must obviously remove from this notion of divine enmity every impure admixture, every egoistic element, and take this hatred in the sense in which Jesus speaks of His disciple *hating* his father, mother, wife, children, and *his own life*, Luke xiv. 26. This hatred is holy ; for it is related only to what is truly hateful to ourselves and others, evil, and what is fitted to lead to it. But yet it is not enough to say, with many commentators, that what God hates in the sinner is the sin and not the person. For, as is rightly observed by Oltramare (who on this account rejects the passive sense of the word *enemies*, which we defend), it is precisely hatred against *the sinners*, and not against *the sin*, which meets us in the expression *enemies of God*, if it be taken in the sense : *hated of God*. The truth is, as it appears to me, that God first of all hates sin in the sinner, and that the sinner becomes at the same time the object of this holy hatred in proportion as he voluntarily identifies himself with sin, and makes it the principle of his personal life. Undoubtedly, so long as this development remains unfinished, the sinner is still the object of divine compassion, inasmuch as God continues to regard him as His creature destined for good. But the co-existence of these two opposite sentiments, of which, xi. 28, we have a very striking particular example, can only belong to a state of transition. The close of the development in good or evil once reached, only one of the two sentiments can continue (see on i. 18). While maintaining as fundamental the notion of *divine* enmity in the term *enemies of God*, we do not think it inadmissible to attach to it as a corollary that of man's enmity to God. Our heart refuses to embrace the being who refuses to embrace us. It is in this double sense that the word *enemy* is taken in common language. It implies a reciprocity ; comp. the expression ἐν ἔχθρᾳ ὄντες, used of Pilate and Herod (Luke xxiii. 12).—A somewhat analogous question arises as to the meaning of the expression κατηλλάγημεν τῷ Θεῷ, *we were reconciled to God.* The words may signify two things : either that man gives up the enmity which had animated him against God, or that God gives up His enmity to man. Taken in themselves, the two meanings are grammatically possible. The words 1 Cor. vii. 11 present a case in which the reconciled person becomes so by giving up his own enmity (" if the woman depart, let her remain unmarried, or, *be reconciled to* her husband ") ; 1 Sam. xxix. 4 and Matt. v. 24 offer two examples of the opposite sense. In the first of these passages, the chiefs of the Philistines, suspecting the intentions of David, who asks permission to join them in fighting against Saul, say to their king : " Wherewith should he reconcile himself (διαλλαγήσεται, LXX.) to his master (τῷ κυρίῳ αὐτοῦ), if not with the heads of our men ?" In the second, Jesus exhorts the man who would bring his offering to the altar, and who remembers that *his brother has something against him*, to go and first *be reconciled* to him. In both cases it is evident that the enmity, and consequently the giving up of the enmity, are ascribed to the man *with whom* the reconciliation has to take place (Saul, and the neighbor who thinks himself offended). In our passage the true meaning does not seem to us doubtful. The word *being reconciled* reproducing the *being justified* of ver. 9, it follows from this parallelism that it is God, and not man, who gives up His enmity. In the same way as by justification God effaces all condemnation, so by reconciliation He ceases from His wrath. This meaning results also from that of the word ἐχθρός, *enemy*, which we have just established, as well as of the term *wrath*, ver. 9. If it is God who is *hostile* and *provoked*, it is in Him first of all that the act of reconciliation must take place. This view is confirmed by the main passage, iii. 25. If it was man who had to be brought first to abandon his hostility, the reconciling act would consist, as we have just said in speaking of the word *enemy*, in a manifestation of love, not of righteousness. Finally, as Hodge observes, to make these words signify that it is we who in the reconciliation lay down our enmity to God, is to put it in contradiction to the spirit of the whole passage. For the apostle's object is to exhibit the greatness of the love testified by God to unworthy beings, in order to conclude therefrom to the love which will be testified to them by the same God in the future. The whole argument thus rests on God's love to man, and not on man's to God. On the other side it is true, as Oltramare remarks, that the expression *to be reconciled* is nowhere applied to God. It is only said, 2 Cor. v. 19 : "that He *reconciled the world unto Himself*, not imputing their trespasses unto them." How explain this fact ? Certainly the sacred writers felt that it is impossible to compare the manner in which God becomes reconciled to men, with the manner in which one man becomes reconciled to another. It was God Himself who began by doing everything to establish His righteousness and secure the majesty of His position, that He might then be able to pardon. Here there was a mode of action which does not enter into human processes of reconciliation ; and hence the apostles, in speaking of God, have avoided the ordinary expression.

If for the word *blood* ver. 10 substitutes *death,* which is more general, it is in order to call up better the Passion scene as a whole. The words: *of His Son,* exhibit the immensity of the sacrifice made for *enemies !* Conclusion : If God (humanly speaking) did not shrink from the painful sacrifice of His Son in behalf of His enemies, how should He refuse to beings, henceforth received into favor, a communication of life which involves nothing save what is ineffably sweet for Himself and for those who receive it ! Thus is proved the certainty of final salvation (salvation in the day of wrath), toward which everything pointed from the first words : *we have peace.*—The clause ἐν τῇ ζωῇ αὐτοῦ, *by His life,* must not be regarded as indicating the *object* of the being saved (introduced into His life). The ἐν, *in,* can only have the instrumental sense, like that of the ἐν τῷ αἵματι, *in* His blood, ver. 9 ; saved *through* His life, from which ours is henceforth drawn ; comp. viii. 2 : "The law of the spirit of life in Christ Jesus hath made me free from the law of sin and death." In fact, justification is not the whole of salvation ; it is the entrance on it. If sin continued to reign as before, wrath would reappear at the close. For "without holiness no man shall see the Lord," Heb. xii. 14. But the mediation *of the life* completes that of the blood, and makes sure of holiness, and thereby of final salvation. Comp. chaps. vi.-viii., intended to develop the thought which is here merely enunciated in connection with the grace of justification. The expression *be saved* therefore denotes *salvation* in the full sense of the word—the final sentence which, along with justification, assumes the restoration of holiness. A sick man is not *saved* when the trespass which has given rise to his malady has been pardoned ; he must also be cured. There are therefore, as we have elsewhere [1] shown, a sentence of *initial* grace—*justification,* in the ordinary sense of the word—founded solely on faith ; and a sentence of *final* grace, which takes account not only of faith, but also of the fruits of faith. The first is the fruit of Christ's *death ;* the second flows from participation in His *life.* For both of these graces *faith* is and remains, of course, the permanent condition of personal appropriation. If this is not expressly mentioned in our passage, it is because it refers solely to *believers* already justified (ver. 1).

We cannot help remarking here, with Olshausen, how entirely at variance with the view of the apostle is the Catholic doctrine, which is shared by so many Protestants of our day, and which bases justification on the *new life* awakened in man by faith. In the eyes of St. Paul, justification is entirely independent of sanctification, and precedes it ; it rests only on faith in the *death* of Christ. Sanctification flows from the *life* of Christ by the work of the Holy Spirit.

At the end of ver. 2, Paul had passed from the absence of fear ("*we have peace,*" ver. 1) to the positive *hope of glory,* in which already we triumph. This same gradation is reproduced here from the passage from ver. 10 to ver. 11, after which the theme contained in the first two verses will be exhausted, and the proposition : " hope maketh not ashamed " (ver. 5), fully demonstrated.

Ver. 11. "*And not only* [*so*],[2] *but even glorying*[3] *in God through our Lord Jesus Christ, by whom we have now received the reconciliation.*"—The general gradation from ver. 10 to ver. 11 is well explained by Philippi : " Salvation is not merely negative : deliverance from wrath ; we hope for better : participation in glory." It was by this idea of triumphant entrance

---

[1] *Etudes bibliques,* II. pp. 150, 229 et seq. (3d ed.).
[2] D E F read τουτο after δε.
[3] Instead of καυχωμενοι, L, 30 Mnn. It. Syr. read καυχωμεθα ; F G: καυχωμεν.

into glory that the apostle behooved to crown this whole exposition of justification. For then it is that it will become complete and final.—The construction presents a difficulty. What are we to make of the participle καυχώμενοι, *glorying*, which does not rest on any finite verb? The ancients and several moderns (Thol., Philip., Rück., Fritzs., Hodge) regard it as the equivalent of a finite verb, understanding ἐσμέν, *we are* glorying, for *we glory*. This is the meaning indicated by the reading of L and of the ancient Versions. In this case, we must understand another finite verb after *not only*, which can be no other than the : *we shall be saved*, of ver. 10. The meaning is : "and not only shall we be saved, but we glory in God even now over this assured salvation." The logical progress is from the future to the present. It has been objected that it is impossible to make a simple participle a finite verb, at least in prose, (for poetry furnishes numerous examples of such license). But how otherwise are we to explain 2 Cor. vii. 5 ? The real difficulty is to resolve the disagreement between the future *we shall be saved* and the present *we glory*. It seems that if the gradation in the mind of the apostle really bore on the matter of time, the νῦν, *now*, which occurs in the following proposition, should have been placed in this : "not only *shall* we *be* saved, but we are so certain of it that *now* already we triumph in God." If Paul has not expressed himself so, it is because this was not his meaning. A second construction is adopted by Meyer, Hofmann, and others : it consists in supplying after *not only*, not: the verb σωθησόμεθα, *we shall be saved*, but the participle καταλλαγέντες, *being reconciled*, so that this participle as well as the καυχώμενοι, *glorying*, rest both of them on the *we shall be saved* of ver. 10 : "We shall be saved, and that not only *as reconciled*, but also *as glorying*." The gradation in this case is not from the future to the present, but from the joy of reconciliation to that of triumph. The objection to this construction is this : The participle *being reconciled*, in ver. 10, is not a simple qualification of *we shall be saved* ; it is a participle of *argumentation*, as is well said by Oltramare (see also Philippi). It cannot therefore be made logically parallel with the participle *glorying*. What is to be done if we will not return to the first construction ? It only remains, as it seems to me, to derive from the verb σωθησόμεθα, *we shall be saved*, the idea of *salvation*, by supplying the participle σωζόμενοι, *saved*, after *not only*, and to refer this participle, as well as the following καυχώμενοι, *glorying*, to the time of final salvation : "Much more certainly shall we be saved (ver. 10), and that not only as *saved*, but as *glorying in God*." The meaning is almost the same as in the preceding construction, but more precise : "And when this hour of salvation shall come, it will not be as men barely saved, like those rescued from shipwreck or a deserved death, that we shall cross the threshold of eternal salvation : it will be in the triumphant attitude of men whom the Son of God has crowned with His own holiness and renewed in His glorious image, and whom the Father has marked with the seal of His adoption, viii. 15, 29." It may be objected, no doubt, that by referring this participle *glorying* to the final hour, we depart from the meaning of the same verb in ver. 2, which contains the theme of the whole passage. But Paul, on reaching the close of this development, may easily substitute for the present glorying in hope, the song of triumph at the moment of entrance into glory.—*To glory in God* was the privilege of which the Jews boasted in virtue of their monotheistic revelation (ii. 17). St. Paul here applies this expression to the sanctified Christian who has not only nothing to fear from God, but who as *His child* is also *His heir* (viii. 17).—Yet he takes care in the same breath to cast down all that might be opposed to humility in this hope of future triumph, by adding : *through our Lord Jesus Christ*. Even in the possession of perfect holiness and on the threshold of glory, it will be impossible for the Christian to forget that it is to Christ he owes all his eternal triumph as well as his past reconciliation, which was its condition. The last words : *by whom we have now received the reconciliation*, might be taken to remind the believer in what a sad state he was found, and by what painful means he needed to be rescued from it. The word *now* would then contrast his present with his *past* state. But this meaning is not the most natural after the preceding context. In closing, Paul rather contrasts the present with the future state : " through whom ye have *now already* received the reconciliation," that first pledge of the deliverance to come. He who acquired for us the first of these favors by His sufferings, even that which is the condition of all the others, will not fail to carry the work to its completion, if we remain attached to Him by persevering faith. This : *by whom we have received*, is the parallel of the *by whom also* of ver. 2, as the *through our Lord Jesus Christ*, which precedes, is the parallel of the same words in ver. 1. The cycle is closed. It is now demonstrated by this summary argument, that justification by faith includes the resources necessary to assure us of the final justification—that spoken of ii. 13— and even of final triumph, and that, consequently, the grace of justification is complete.

After thus expounding in a first section (i. 18–iii. 20) *universal condemnation*, in a second section (iii. 21–v. 11) *universal justification*, there remains nothing more for the apostle to do than to compare these two vast dispensations by bringing together their two points of departure. Such is the subject of the third section, which closes this fundamental part.

Hofmann thinks that, after describing divine wrath in the section i, 17–iii. 4, the apostle from iii. 5–iv. 25 contrasts with it the state of justification which Christians enjoy without cause of boasting ; this teaching is entirely in keeping with monotheism, strengthens moral life instead of weakening it (iii. 31), and is not at all invalidated by the case of Abraham. The conclusion is drawn v. 1-11, namely, to lead believers to enjoy this blessed state fearlessly and full of hope. This construction breaks down before the following facts : iii. 5 cannot begin a new section ; iii. 9 cannot be a question of the Christian conscience ; iii. 31 does not refer to the moral fulfiling of the law : Abraham's case cannot have so slight a bearing as that which Hofmann is obliged to ascribe to it ; v. 1 is not an exhortation in the form of a conclusion.—The construction of Volkmar is wholly different. According to him, the *exposition* of justification by faith, begun iii. 9, closes at iii. 30. Here begins the *confirmation* of this mode of justification by the Old Testament. It goes from iii. 31–viii. 36. And, first, confirmation by the *book* of the law, chap. iv. (the text of Genesis relating to Abraham) ; then, confirmation by the *law* itself, the biblical narrative of the condemnation of all in Adam, which corresponds to the doctrine of the justification of all in Christ, v. 1-21 ; finally, confirmation by the harmony of the moral consequences of justification with the *essence* of the law, vi.–viii. But, independently of the false sense given to iii. 31 as a general title of iv.–viii., how are we to place the piece v. 1-11 in one and the same subdivision with the parallel between Adam and Jesus Christ, and how are we to see in this last piece only a confirmation of justification by faith, by means of the narrative of the fall in the Old Testament? Finally, this distinction between the *book* of the law, the *law* and the moral *essence* of the law, is certainly foreign to the mind of the apostle. Holsten rightly says : "It is unnecessary to prove that these thoughts and this order belong to Volkmar, not to Paul." Our construction approaches much nearer to that which Holsten himself has just published (*Jahrb. für protest. Theol.* 1879, Nos. 1 and 2). The essential difference begins only with the following piece regarding Adam and Christ. This passage, while stating the result of the preceding part, belongs nevertheless, according to Holsten, to the following part, chap. vi.–viii , of which it is in his view the foundation.

Without failing to perceive a certain *transitional* character in this passage, we must regard it mainly as a *conclusion*. Thus it is regarded also by Lipsius in his recent work on the Epistle to the Romans (*Protestanten-Bibel*).

THIRD SECTION

TWELFTH PASSAGE (5:12-21)

The Universality of Salvation in Christ proved by the Universality of Death in Adam

Justification by faith had just been expounded; the historical foundation on which it rested, its harmony with the Israelitish revelation, the certainty of its enduring to the end—all these points had been illustrated; and the major part of the theme, iii. 21 and 22, was thus developed. One idea remains still, and that the most important of all, which was expressed in the theme in the striking words: εἰς πάντας καὶ ἐπὶ πάντας τοὺς πιστεύοντας, *for all and upon all who believe*. Universalism was the peculiar character of Paul's gospel; justification by faith, the subject of exposition thus far, was its necessary condition. To omit expressly developing this decisive feature would have been to leave the fruit ungathered after laboriously cultivating the tree. The apostle could not commit such a mistake. He performs this final task in the last piece, the very peculiar nature of which suffices to demonstrate its importance.

Commentators have understood the idea and object of the passage in various ways. According to Baur and his school, as well as several other commentators, the apostle has in view the Jewish-Christianity reigning in the Roman Church. He wishes at once to refute and gain it, either by expounding a conception of history in which the law finds no more place (Baur), or by proving that salvation, like condemnation, depends in no degree on the conduct of individuals and their works, but solely on an objective standard, on the unconditional and absolute appointment of God (Holsten). But this piece does not answer exactly either to the one or other of these two views. The observation made in ver. 20 on the secondary part played by the law, cannot express the intention of the entire piece. This remark, rendered indispensable in this universal survey by the important place filled by the Mosaic law in the religious history of mankind, is thrown out too much by the way to allow of its concentrating upon itself the interest of so vast an exposition. The other view, that of the absolute determinism which Holsten ascribes to St. Paul, would no doubt serve to cut by the roots the system of justification by works; but it would be one of those remedies which destroy the suffering by killing the sufferer. For determinism excludes human merit only by suppressing moral liberty and responsibility. It is not so that Paul proceeds. In any case, it is easy to see that the apostle's direct aim in this piece is not to exclude legal righteousness; he has done with this idea. It is the universality of the Christian salvation which he wishes to demonstrate. Ewald, Dietzsch, and Gess rightly advance the striking difference which there is between the argument of the Epistle to the Galatians and the teaching of the Epistle to the Romans. In the former, where Paul is attacking Jewish-Christianity, his argument starts from the theocratic history, from Abraham; in the latter, which expounds the relation of the gospel to human nature, Jewish and Gentile, the argument starts from general history, from Adam, the father of all mankind. From the very beginning of the Epistle the point of view is universal (Gentiles, chap. i.; Jews, chap. ii.).

Very many commentators hold the opinion that the apostle's purpose is to ascend to the source of the two currents, whether of condemnation and death, or of justification and life, which sway the life of mankind; or, as Dietzsch puts it, to the very powers which determine present facts, the lot of individuals. The practical aim of this investigation would thus be that indicated by Chrysostom in the words: "As the best physicians turn their whole attention to find out the root of maladies, and thus reach the very source of the evil, so it is that Paul acts." Every reader would thus be invited by the passage to break the bond of oneness (solidarity) which naturally unites him to the head of lost humanity, and to contract by faith the new bond whereby he can have fellowship with the head of justified humanity. This view is the most widely spread, and we do not conceal from ourselves the measure of truth which it contains. But two difficulties arrest us when we attempt to make this idea the key to the whole passage. It is perfectly obvious from ver. 12 that the apostle is rather concerned with the origin of death than with that of sin, and that he mentions the latter only to reach the former. It is also to the fact of death that he returns most frequently in the course of this piece, comp. vv. 15–18, 21. Would it be so if his direct aim were to ascend to sin, the *source* of evil? Then we find him nowhere insisting on the gravity of sin and on the necessity of faith for salvation. No exhortation to the reader to form a personal union with the new Adam reveals this directly practical intention which is ascribed to him, especially by Hofmann and Th. Schott. We are therefore forced to conclude that we are not yet on the right track.

Rothe starts from the idea that the first part of chap. v. has already begun the exposition of *sanctification* as the fruit of justification by faith, an exposition which continues in chap. vi. The passage from vv. 12–21 would thus be a simple episode intended to prove that as men became *sinners* in common by the sin of one, so they can only become *saints* in common—that is to say, in Christ. The piece would thus treat of the *moral assimilation*, either of corruption or holiness, by individual men. Such is also the opinion of Lange and Schaff, who make chap. v. 12 begin the part of the Epistle relating to moral regeneration by the appropriation of the holy life of the new Adam (vi.–viii.). There is certainly mention of sanctification in the passage, v. 1–11; we grant this to Rothe (comp. vv. 9, 10: *by Him; by His life*), but, as we have seen, only in relation to final justification, which rests on the continuance of the action of the living Christ in the justified soul. As to the subject of sanctification thus announced beforehand, it is not actually treated till chap. vi. The relations to vi.–viii. are no doubt real and profound. Lange proves them perfectly. But it is exaggerating their scope to make them a reason for detaching the passage v. 12–21 from the preceding context, in order to make it the preface to the doctrine of sanctification. The dominant ideas in the passage are not those of sin and of the new life; they are only, as we shall see, those of condemnation and justification, which had been the subject of the whole preceding part. This piece must therefore be regarded as its conclusion.

By the first term of the comparison (our common condemnation in Adam) this parallel certainly recalls the whole section of the ὀργή, *wrath*, i. 18–iii. 20, as by the second (common salvation in Christ) it recalls the subject of the second section, *the righteousness of faith*, iii. 21–v. 11. But this resemblance is far from exhausting the connection of this piece with all that precedes. The two terms of comparison, Adam and Christ, are not only put in juxtaposition with one another; they are put in logical connection, and it is in this living relation that the true idea of the piece is contained. With a boldness of thought which it is scarcely possible to imagine, Paul discovers, in the extension and power of the mysterious condemnation pronounced in Adam, *the divine measure* of the extension and power of the salvation bestowed in Christ, so that the very intensity of the effects of the fall becomes transformed, in his skilful hands, into an irresistible demonstration of the greatness of salvation. And this final piece is thus found to be at one and the same moment the counterpart of the first section (condemnation) and the crowning of the second (justification).

The following parallel falls, as it were, of itself into four distinct paragraphs :
1. V. 12–14 : the universal diffusion of death by the deed of one man.
2. V. 15–17 : the superiority of the factors acting in Christ's work over the corresponding factor in the work of Adam.
3. V. 18, 19 : the certainty of equality in respect of extension and effect between the second work and the first.
4. V. 20, 21 : the indication of the true part played by the law between these two universals of death and righteousness.

Exegesis has been led more and more to the grouping which we have just indicated (see Dietzsch, and especially Hodge), though the idea of those four paragraphs and their logical relation are still very variously understood.

I. Vv. 12–14

Ver. 12. " *Wherefore, even as by one man sin entered into the world, and death by sin ; and so death* [1] *passed upon all men, for that all have sinned ;*"— The logical connection between this piece and the preceding is expressed by διὰ τοῦτο, *wherefore.* Some, like Meyer, make this expression refer solely to the last words of ver. 11 : *we have received the reconciliation.* But we have seen that this incidental proposition, which the context itself did not require, was added there with the view of recapitulating the whole previous section, before and with the view of passing to the following passage. The very term καταλλαγή, *reconciliation,* which contains an allusion to the name ὀργή, *wrath,* is chosen so as to remind us not only of the second section (that of justification), but also of the first (that of condemnation) ; so that in reality to say that the *wherefore* refers to the last proposition of ver. 11 is to admit, with Tholuck, Rückert, Holsten, etc., that it bears on all the preceding context from i. 17 : "Since, condemned as we all were, we have found reconciliation in Christ, there is therefore between our relation to Him and our relation to the head of natural humanity the following resemblance." Hofmann and Schott make the *wherefore* refer to the piece v. 1–11 only : "On account of this assurance of final salvation which we possess in Christ" . . . According to Hofmann, the verb which is wanting should contain an exhortation to realize holiness (the contents of viii. 1 et seq.), an exhortation judged to correspond with that of the alleged ἔχωμεν, *let us have,* of v. 1. This is all pure romance. Schott derives the verb more naturally from the preceding : "Wherefore we shall be saved by Him alone (vv. 9, 10), as we perished by Adam" . . . (But see below).

The ὥσπερ, *even as,* has been construed grammatically in a multitude of ways.—1. It has been thought that the principal proposition (the verb of the *wherefore*) had been forgotten by the apostle, distracted as he was by the host of thoughts which presented themselves successively to his mind (see Rückert and Hofmann for example). I hope our readers are convinced that such an explanation, or rather absence of explanation, is impossible. We have had sufficient proof hitherto that the apostle did not compose without having fully taken account of what he meant to say.—2. The main correlative proposition is supposed to be understood ; requiring to be inferred from what precedes. De Wette adduces in this sense Matt. xxv. 14, where we find an *even as,* to which there is no corresponding principal clause, and which depends simply on the preceding sentence. Lange almost in the same way derives the understood verb from ver. 11 : " Wherefore we have reconciliation by Christ, as by one sin and death came upon all ;" Umbreit and Schott, from ver. 10 : " We shall be saved by Christ, as we perished in Adam ;" van Hengel simply understands the verb : " Where-

---

[1] D E G, It. omit the words ὁ θάνατος (*death*).

fore *it is the same in Christ* as it was in Adam." Dietzsch fills up the ellipsis by taking the verb from what follows: "*Wherefore life came by a man*, in the same way as by a man sin and death came." De Wette's explanation breaks down under the *wherefore*, which distinguishes our passage from the one quoted. In the other views the question arises, How in a didactic piece so severely composed, the apostle, instead of making such an ellipsis and holding the mind of the reader in suspense to the end as he does without satisfying him after all, did not simply write like this: διὰ τοῦτο ἐγένετο ἐν Χριστῷ ὥσπερ. . . . "Wherefore it is the same in Christ as in Adam" . . .—3. The principal verb on which ὥσπερ depends is sought in the words which follow; Erasmus and Beza, in the clause: "*and death by sin*," giving to καί the meaning of *also*. Taken rigorously, the construction would be admissible, though it would have been more correct to write οὕτως καί, or to put the καί after the clause (*thus also*, or *by sin also*); but this meaning is absolutely excluded by the fact that Paul does not think of comparing the entrance of sin with that of death. It is evident that when he wrote the *as*, he had in view as the second term of the comparison the entrance of justification and life by Christ. A similar reason is also opposed to the explanation of those who, like Wolf, find the principal point in the more remote words: "and so death passed upon all." Paul has as little thought of comparing the mode in which death entered with that of its diffusion. Besides, this would have required οὕτως καί, and not καὶ οὕτως.— 4. A more generally admitted explanation is that of Calvin (Thol., Philip., Mey., Holst.), who finds the principal point indicated, at least so far as the sense goes, at the close of ver. 14, in the words: "who is the type of Him that was to come." The meaning of these words is to this effect: "*Even as*, . . . *so by a new Adam, of whom he was the type*, justification came on mankind." We must hold on this view that the explanation interposed in vv. 13 and 14 led Paul away from finishing the construction begun in ver. 12. But it would be a strange style to give the principal proposition, which the reader was expecting after the *as* of ver. 12, in the form of this incidental proposition: *who is the type of Him that was to come.* Then in what immediately follows, ver. 15, Paul does not expound this idea of the equality between Adam and Christ, which had been announced by the *as*, and which in its substance the last proposition of ver. 14 was meant to recall. He explains, on the contrary, the difference between the two terms of comparison, so that he only raises (end of ver. 14) the idea of equality to abandon it at the same instant (vv. 15-17); what an unnatural proceeding!—5. We pass rapidly over the hypotheses of Mehring and Winer, who seek the chief clause, the former in the first proposition of ver. 15 by taking it interrogatively, the latter in the second proposition of the same verse; two equally impossible attempts, since ver. 15*a* cannot be an interrogation (see below), and since ver. 15*b* can only correspond to the subordinate proposition which precedes in the same verse: "*for if*"—etc. —There is only one explanation admissible, that of Grotius, Bengel, Flatt, best defended by Hodge, who finds the principal clause in ver. 18. It is there, indeed, that we have the close of the comparison begun in ver. 12 in the form of equality. Vv. 13 and 14 have been an explanation required by the last words of ver. 12, one of those digressions which, in our modern fashion, we put in a note. Vv. 15-17 have been brought in by the expression: "type of Him that was to come" (end of ver. 14), which demanded an immediate modification or restriction, so that it is not till ver. 18 that the apostle is free to finish the comparison he has begun. The proof that in ver. 18 Paul at length resumes the idea of ver. 12, is found in these two characteristic features: (*a*) the ἄρα οὖν, *so therefore*, which indicates the resuming of a previously expressed idea; (*b*) the reappearance of the contrast between *one* and *all* (εἰς and πάντες), which was that of ver. 12, but which had been dropped in the interval for the contrast between *one* and *many* (εἰς and οἱ πολλοί, vv. 15-17). As to the idea, it is evident that ver. 18 logically completes ver. 12. The words : *as by one fall condemnation came upon all men*, reproduce the idea, *even as*, etc., of ver. 12 ; and the following : *so also by one righteousness justification of life came upon all*, are manifestly the long delayed second term of the comparison. As to the end of ver. 14, in which so many commentators have found the principal idea, it was simply a way of announcing to the reader this second part of the comparison, which was to be still further prefaced (vv. 15-17) before being enunciated (ver. 18).

Ver. 12 describes the entrance of *death* into the world. The emphasis is on the words : *by one man*. Adam is here characterized not merely as the *first* of sinners, but as the one who laid human life open to the power of sin. If Paul does not speak of Eve, as in 2 Cor. xi. 3, *et al.*, it is because the fall of the race was not necessarily bound up with that of the woman. Adam alone was the true representative of mankind still included in him at that time.—The term *sin* should be taken here in its greatest generality. The apostle is not speaking specially of sin either as a tendency or an act, either as an individual act or as a collective fact ; but of the principle of revolt whereby the human will rises against the divine in all its different forms and manifestations. Holsten sees in *sin* an objective power controlling human existence even in Adam. But from the Bible standpoint sin exists only in the will. It has no place in objective existence and outside the will of the creature. Julius Müller reaches a result almost the same by starting from an opposite point of view ; according to him, the will of individual men has been corrupted by a free transgression previously to their earthly existence. On both of these views the apostle should have said : sin *appeared with* or *in* the first man ; but not : *sin entered by him*. The word *entered* indicates the introduction of a principle till then external to the world, and the word *by* throws back the responsibility of the event on him who, as it were, pierced the dike through which the irruption took place ; comp. the term *disobedience*, ver. 19.—The word κόσμος, *the world*, evidently denotes here, as in John iii. 16, *et al.*, only the domain of human existence. Paul certainly holds, with Scripture, the previous existence of evil in a superhuman sphere.—Assuredly no subsequent transgression is comparable to this. It created a state of things here below which subsequent sins only served to confirm. If the question is asked, how a being created good could perpetrate such an act, we answer that a decision like this does not necessarily suppose the existence of evil in its author. There is in moral life not only a conflict between good and evil, but also between good and good, lower good and higher good. The act of eating the fruit of the tree on which the prohibition rested, was not at all illegitimate in itself. It became guilty only through the prohibition. Man therefore found himself placed—and such was the necessary condition of the moral development through which he had to pass—between the inclination to eat, an inclination innocent in itself, but intended to be sacrificed, and the positively good divine order. At the instigation of an already existing power of revolt, man drew from the depths of his liberty a decision whereby he adhered to the inclination rather than to the divine will, and thus created in his whole race, still identified with his person, the permanent proclivity to prefer inclination to obligation. As all the race would have perished with him if he had perished, it was all seized in him with the spirit of revolt to which in that hour he had adhered. We are nowhere told, however, that his descendants are individually responsible for this diseased tendency. It is in proportion as each individual voluntarily resigns himself to it that he becomes personally responsible for it.—But was it compatible with divine perfection to let this succession of generations, stained with an original vice, come into the world ? God certainly might have annihilated the perverted race in its head, and replaced it by a new one ; but this would have been to confess Himself vanquished by the adversary. He might, on the contrary, accept it such as sin had made it, and leave it to develop in the natural way, holding it in His power to recover it; and this would be to gain a victory on the field of battle where He seemed to have been conquered. Conscience says to which of these two courses God must give the preference, and Scripture teaches us which He has in reality preferred.

But the point which Paul has in view in this declaration is not the origin of sin, but that of death. And hence he passes immediately, understanding the same verb as before, to the second fact: *and death by sin.* It would have been wholly different had he meant to begin here to treat the subject of sanctification; he would in that case have at least stopped for a moment at this grave fact of the introduction of sin. If sin is not mentioned by him except by way of transition to death, this is because he is still on the subject of justification, the corresponding fact to which is condemnation, that is to say, death. Death is the monument of a divine condemnation, which has fallen on mankind.—The term *death* is used by Scripture in three senses—1. *Physical* death, or the separation of soul and body; in consequence of this separation from its life principle, the body is given over to dissolution. 2. *Spiritual* death, or the separation of the soul from God; in consequence of this separation from its principle of life, the soul becomes corrupt in its lusts (Eph. iv. 22). 3. *Eternal* death, or the *second death;* this is in the human being the consummation of his separation from God by the separation of the *soul* from the *spirit*, the soul's faculty for the divine. The soul and body then deprived of this superior principle, the native element of the soul, become the prey of the *worm which dieth not* (Mark ix. 43–48). Of these three meanings, the last does not suit this passage; for the second death does not begin till the judgment. The second is equally inapplicable, because the idea of *death* would then be compounded with that of *sin*, which is distinguished from it in this very passage.[1] There remains, therefore, only the first meaning. It is confirmed, besides, by the obvious allusion to the narrative of Genesis (ii. 17, iii. 19), as well as by the explanation contained in the following verses (13 and 14), where the word *death* is evidently taken in its strict sense. We should add, however, that death, even when taken simply as physical death, always implies an abnormal state in relation to God, a state which, if it continues and develops, cannot fail to draw after it fatal consequences to man.

What, according to the apostle's view, is the relation between sin and death contained in the preposition διά, *by*, which he uses a second time? It might be said that death is simply the natural consequence of sin, since, God being the source of moral and physical life, once the bond is broken between Him and man, man must die. But in ver. 16 the apostle makes death the consequence of sin through a positive sentence, which proves that if we have to do here with a natural consequence, it is one which is also willed. It is true, two objections may be urged against this opinion, which makes death a consequence of sin. The first is what Paul himself says, 1 Cor. xv. 42, that our earthly body is sown in *corruption, weakness*, and *dishonor*, and that because it is *psychical*. A little further on, ver. 47, alluding to Gen. iii. 19, he adds that the first man is *of the earth, earthy*, which seems to make the dissolution of his body a natural consequence of his *nature*. The second objection is this: Long before the creation of man, the existence of death is proved in the domain of animal life. Now the body of man belongs to the great sum total of animal organization, of which he is the crown; and therefore the law of death must already have extended to man, independently of sin. Paul's words in the Epistle to the Corinthians, as well as those of Genesis, the sense of which he reproduces, prove

---

[1] But the contrast with "life" in verses 17, 18, 21 make it plain that throughout the passage death includes all physical and moral evil, cf. vi. 23.—T. W. C.

206 / Justification by Faith

beyond doubt the natural *possibility* of death, but not its necessity. If man had remained united to God, his body, naturally subject to dissolution, might have been gloriously transformed, without passing through death and dissolution. The notion of the *tree of life*, as usually explained, means nothing else. This privilege of an immediate transformation will belong to the believers who shall be alive at the time of our Lord's return (1 Cor. xv. 51, 52) ; and it was probably this kind of transformation that was on the point of taking effect in the person of the Lord Himself at the time of His transfiguration. This privilege, intended for holy men, was withdrawn from guilty man ; such was the *sentence* which gave him over to dissolution. It is stated in the words : "Thou art dust (that is to say, thou *canst* die), and to dust shalt thou return (that is to say, thou *shalt* in fact *die*)." The reign of death over the animals likewise proves only this : that it was in the *natural* condition of man to terminate in dissolution. Remaining on the level of animalism by the preference given by him to inclination over moral obligation, man continued subject to this law. But had he risen by an act of moral liberty above the animal, he would not have had to share its lot (see also on viii. 19–22).

From the origin of sin, and of death by sin, the apostle passes to a third idea : the *diffusion* of death. Once entered among mankind, death took hold of all the beings composing the race. The two prepositions $εἰς$ (*into*) and $διά$ (*through*) in the two verbs $εἰσῆλθεν$ and $διῆλθεν$, indicate exactly this connection between entrance and propagation. As poison once swallowed penetrates to all parts of the body, so it happened in Adam, in whom the whole race was virtually contained ; in him the tendency to dissolution victoriously asserted itself over all the individuals that were to come, so that every one of them was born dying. The word $οὕτως$, *so*, may be explained in three ways : either it repeats, as Dietzsch, Hofm. think, the notion : *by one man:* "death, after having entered by one, spread *in the same manner* (by this one)." Or, as is held by Meyer and Philippi, this *so* alludes to the relation of cause and effect, which has just been pointed out between sin and death : "and so, by reason of this connection between sin and death, death passed on all," which assumes as a premiss the understood idea that sin also extended to all. Or, finally, is it not more natural to explain the word *so* by the connection between the two verbs ? "And *once entered*, it gained by its very entrance the power of passing on all." The threshold crossed, the enemy could strike immediately all the inmates of the house. What mode would have presented the opposite of that characterized by the *so*, if death had reached each man individually by a door which he himself had opened ? The *all* is expressly emphasized in contrast to *one*, because in this contrast between one and all there is concentrated the idea of the whole passage. The Greco-Latin MSS. here omit ὁ θάνατος, *death*. In this case we must either take the verb $διῆλθεν$ in an impersonal sense : "and so *it* (this connection between sin and death) happened to all ;" or, what would be preferable, take the whole following proposition as the subject : "and so there passed on all, that *in consequence of which*, or *in virtue of which*, all have sinned." Both of these constructions are obviously forced. It is probable that the omission of ὁ θάνατος has arisen, as van Hengel well suggests, from the fact that the whole of the verse was connected with *sin;* the words : *and death by sin*, being consequently regarded merely as incidental or parenthetical, and so there was given as a subject to $διῆλθε, ἡ ἁμαρτία$, *sin*, of the first proposition.

But why does Paul add the last words : ἐφ' ᾧ πάντες ἥμαρτον, which we have translated by : *for that all have sinned ?* They seem to contradict the idea expressed in the first part of the verse, and to ascribe the death of each man not to the sin of Adam, but to his own. The numerous explanations which have been given of these words may, it seems to us, be reduced to three principal heads ; they amount in fact to one or other of these three ideas—1. The death of individual men results wholly from their own sins. 2. The death of individual men results partly from Adam's sin and partly from their own sins. 3. The death of all individual men arises solely from Adam's sin.

Let us begin with the study of the form ἐφ' ᾧ.[1] In the New Testament it is found in the local sense (Luke v. 25) ; in the moral sense, it is applied either to the *object* : ἐφ' ᾧ πάρει, "*with what object* art thou here ?" or to the determining *cause* of the action or feeling ; so without doubt 2 Cor. v. 4 : ἐφ' ᾧ οὐ θέλομεν ἐκδύσασθαι, *for that* we would not be unclothed, but clothed upon ;" probably also Phil. iii. 12 : ἐφ' ᾧ καὶ κατελήφθην, "I seek to apprehend, *because that* also I have been apprehended ;" perhaps also Phil. iv. 10 : ἐφ' ᾧ καὶ ἐφρονεῖτε, " (I say so), *because that* ye also thought ;" but this ἐφ' ᾧ may also be understood as a pronoun connected with what precedes : "as regards what concerns me, *with which* ye were also occupied." It is easy to see, in fact, that the phrase may have two different meanings, according as we take it as *pronominal* or *conjunctive*. In the former case, it bears on what precedes : *on account of*, or *in view of which*, that is to say, of the idea just expressed (*propterea*). In the second, it bears on what follows : *because*, or *in view of the fact that*, that is to say, of the idea just about to be enunciated (*propterea quod*). The difference is analogous to that of διό and διότι. We shall have need, as will appear, of all these meanings in the study of the following phrase.

The first explanation is that which makes the apostle explain the death of all by the individual sin *of all*. This is the meaning adopted by Calvin, Melanchthon, and several others, particularly by Reuss. The latter expresses himself thus : "No question here of the imputation of Adam's sin or hereditary sin ; these are scholastic theses. All have been visited with the same punishment as Adam, therefore they must all have merited it like him." The idea would thus be that all men die in consequence of their individual sins. There are three reasons which render this explanation impossible—1. The καὶ οὕτως, *and so*, evidently signifies that each individual dies in consequence of the entrance of sin, and therefore of death, into this world *by one man*. 2. This idea would be in contradiction to the very aim of the whole passage, which is to make the death of all rest on Adam, even as the righteousness of all rests on Christ. 3. The death of infants would be inexplicable on this interpretation ; for they have certainly not brought death on themselves by their individual sins. Calvin, Tholuck, and others on this account apply the ἥμαρτον, *have sinned*, not to particular acts, but to the evil disposition : *have become sinners*, which might be said also of infants who have died without actual sins. But the verb ἁμαρτάνειν cannot have this meaning. It always denotes sin as an act, not as a state. Paul would have said : ἁμαρτωλοὶ ἐγενήθησαν, or, as in ver. 19 : ἁμαρτωλοὶ κατεστάθησαν. Mangold alleges that Paul did not take account of infants when he expressed himself thus, and that he meant only to speak of mankind, so far as they really sin. But Paul is not explaining the death of this or that individual ; he is explaining the fact of death in itself. If there are examples of death, and that in great number, which do not come under the explanation he gives, it is not enough to say that he does not take account of them ; his explanation must be declared insufficient.

A second class of commentators seek to modify the preceding and evidently inadmissible explanation ; they give a restricted or determinate sense to ἐφ' ᾧ, making it signify : *seeing that besides*, or *on this condition that*, or *in so far as ;* so Julius Müller, Rothe, Ewald. The object of all these

---

[1] Ἐπί with the dative denotes—1. In its primitive (*local*) meaning : the object *on* or *near* which a thing is placed ; thus ἐφ' ᾧ κατέκειτο, the couch *on which* he lay ; ἐπὶ ταῖς θύραις, *near*, or *at the door*. 2. In the sense *of time : at the date of*, in the lifetime of ; for example : ἐπὶ Μωϋσῆ, *in the time of* Moses ; ἐπὶ νεκροῖς, *when one is dead*. 3. In the *moral* sense : *on the ground of*, that is to say, *by reason of*, or *on condition of*, or *in view of*. 4. In the *logical* sense : *as may be seen by* . . . All these different meanings may be applied to the phrase ἐφ' ᾧ.

attempts is to get at this idea : that the diffusion of death in the world, in consequence of Adam's sin, took place only on a certain condition, and on account of a subsidiary cause, the particular sins committed by each man. There is on this view a personal act of appropriation in the matter of death, as there is one, namely faith, in the matter of salvation. But such a meaning of ἐφ᾽ ᾧ cannot be demonstrated ; it would have required ἐφ᾽ ὅσον, or some other phrase. Then this meaning is opposed to ver. 16, which directly contrasts condemnation as a thing which has come *by one*, with the gift of grace as applying to the sins of the many. Besides, would it be possible for Paul to seek to establish no logical relation between these two causes, the one principal, the other secondary, and to content himself with putting them in juxtaposition, notwithstanding their apparent contradiction ?

The third class of interpretations may be divided into two groups—1. Those which take ἐφ᾽ ᾧ as a relative pronoun. So Hofmann, who makes θάνατος (*death*, in the physical and moral sense) the antecedent, and gives to ἐπί and ἐφ᾽ ᾧ the temporal sense : "during the existence, or in the presence of which (death) all have sinned"—that is to say, that when all individual men sinned, the reign of death was already established here below, which proves clearly that it was so not in consequence of our particular sins, but on account of Adam's sin. Dietzsch interprets almost in the same way as Hofmann, only he sets aside the *temporal* meaning of ἐπί, to substitute for it the notion of the *condition* on which, or the state of things in which, the fact takes place. The same relation of the ἐφ᾽ ᾧ to θάνατος is followed by Gess, except that he understands the word θάνατος of *spiritual death*, sin : "Upon all (spiritual) death has come, on the ground of which all individual men have consequently committed sin." We omit other less comprehensible shades.[1] But why have recourse to this form of expression ἐφ᾽ ᾧ, which has usually a quite different sense in Paul, and not say simply, if such was his meaning, that death here below preceded individual sins, and consequently is not their effect ? Besides, the fact itself, here ascribed to the apostle, is not strictly true. For the first death on the earth, that of Abel, was certainly preceded by a multitude of particular sins. In Gess's explanation the idea is much simpler : "In Adam death came upon all, moral corruption, as a consequence of which all since have sinned individually." But this idea lies without the context ; for Paul, as we have seen, is not treating here of the origin of *sin*, but of the origin of *death*, and of death taken in the *physical* sense. Death appears here as the visible proof of the invisible judgment which hangs over mankind. Vv. 13, 14, as well as 15 and 17, leave no doubt on this head. In this way it would seem to us simpler to give to ἐφ᾽ ᾧ the neuter sense : *on which, in consequence of which*, all have sinned. Only this meaning of ἐφ᾽ ᾧ would be, we fear, without precedent. 2. The second mode of interpretation in this third class takes the ἐφ᾽ ᾧ as a conjunctive phrase : *for that*, and connects it with the idea following : *all have sinned*. How sinned ? Through this one man who introduced sin. So Bengel : *quia omnes*, ADAMO PECCANTE *peccaverunt*. It must be allowed that the thought of the δι᾽ ἑνὸς ἀνθρώπου, *by one man*, which begins the verse, so controls the mind of the apostle that he does not count it necessary expressly to repeat it. This meaning is in harmony with the best established use of the ἐφ᾽ ᾧ in the New Testament (see above) and in the classics (see Meyer). And the idea expressed in this proposition thus understood, appears again without doubt in the first part of ver. 15 : "through the offence of one *many* be dead ;" and in that of ver. 17 : "by one man's offence death reigned *by one ;*" comp. 1 Cor. xv. 22 : "as in Adam *all die*." No doubt it is objected that the essential idea in this

[1] So Wendt, p. 196, who, if we understand him rightly, makes Paul say : "On all there has come death, *by which it may be seen* that all have sinned (ideally, that is to say, have been treated as sinners without really being so)." It is impossible for us to comprehend this meaning of ἐφ᾽ ᾧ.

case: "*in Adam*," is omitted; but we think we have accounted for the omission. And we find, as Bengel has already remarked, a somewhat similar ellipsis in the analogous though not parallel passage, 2 Cor. v. 15: "If one died for all, then all died;" understand: in him.—True, the question is asked, if it is possible that the eternal lot of a free and intelligent person should be made dependent on an act in which he has taken no part with will and conscience. Assuredly not; but there is no question here about the *eternal* lot of individuals. Paul is speaking here above all of *physical* death. Nothing of all that passes in the domain in which we have Adam for our father can be decisive for our eternal lot. The solidarity of individuals with the head of the first humanity does not extend beyond the domain of natural life. What belongs to the higher life of man, his spiritual and eternal existence, is not a matter of species, but of the individual. —The Vulgate has admitted an interpretation of this passage, set in circulation by Origen and spread by Augustine, which, in a way grammatically false, yet comes to the same result as ours. 'Εφ' ᾧ is taken in the sense of ἐν ᾧ: "*in whom*" (Adam). But ἐπί cannot have the meaning of ἐν, and even if ᾧ were a relative pronoun here, it would neither refer to Adam, who has not been named, nor to *one man*, from which it is separated by so many intermediate propositions.

The most impenetrable mystery in the life of nature is the relation between the individual and the species. Now to this domain belongs the problem raised by the words: "*for that* (in this one man) *all have sinned.*" Adam received the unique mission to represent the whole species concentrated in a single individual. Such a phenomenon cannot be repeated, at least in the domain of nature. The relation of each of us to that man, the incarnation of the species itself, has nothing in common with the relation which we have to sustain to any other man. In the revelation of salvation given to the apostle this mysterious connection was assumed, but not explained. For it belongs to a sphere on which the revealing ray does not fall. And therefore it is that in the two following verses the apostle thinks it necessary to *demonstrate* the reality of the fact which he had just announced: the death of all through the sin of one. We shall see that the meaning of these two verses comes out only when we approach them with the explanation just given of the last words of ver. 12; this will be the best proof of its truth.

Vv. 13, 14. "*For until the law sin was in the world: but sin is not imputed if there is no law; and nevertheless death reigned from Adam to Moses, even over them that had not sinned*[1] *after the resemblance of Adam's transgression, who is the figure of Him that was to come.*"—According to the first two interpretations of the preceding proposition, which lay down the sins committed by each individual as the sole or secondary cause of his death, the argument contained in vv. 13, 14 would be this: "All die because they have all sinned; for even during the time which elapsed down to the giving of the law sin was in the world; now sin is *undoubtedly* not reckoned in the absence of law. *Nevertheless*, that did not prevent sin from reigning during all the interval between Adam and Moses, which proves certainly that it was nevertheless imputed in some measure. How could that be? Because of the law of nature written even in the *heart* of the Gentiles." Such is De Wette's interpretation, also that of Lange and Reuss. In this sense the second proposition of ver. 13 must be taken as an objection made to Paul on which he raises himself. Then he would be made to answer in the sequel by confining himself to stating the very fact of the reign of death. But the explanation of death is the very point in question; how could the fact itself be given in proof? Then a simple δέ would not have sufficed to indicate such a shifting in the direction of the

---

[1] Mnn. several Lectionaries, Or. omit μη before αμαρτησαντας.

thought. The text rather produces the impression of a consecutive argument. Finally, at the close of such an argument, the apostle could not have left to be understood the solution which he himself gave of the problem, namely, the natural law written in the heart of the Gentiles. This idea, on which everything rested, was at once too essential and too unfamiliar to the minds of his readers to be passed over in silence as self-evident. It has been sought to meet these difficulties by giving to the word ἐλλογεῖν, *to put to account*, a purely subjective meaning, and so to make the proposition, ver. 13*b*, a simple observation interjected by the way. Ambrose and Augustine, then Luther, Calvin, and Melanchthon, and in our days Rückert, Rothe, and J. Müller, do in fact apply the imputation expressed by ἐλλογεῖν not to the judgment of God, but to the reckoning which the sinner makes to himself of the trespass which he has committed : " Every one died for his own sin, for sin existed even before the law, though the sinners did not take account of it, nor esteem themselves guilty. But death, which nevertheless reigned, proved that God on His part imputed it to the sinner." But this purely subjective signification of the term ἐλλογεῖν cannot be justified. It would require to be indicated in some way. How, besides, could Paul have affirmed in terms so general that the sinners between Adam and Moses did not impute their sins to themselves, after saying of the Gentiles, ii. 15, that " their thoughts mutually accuse or excuse one another," and i. 32, that these same Gentiles " knew the judgment of God, that those who do such things are worthy of death " ? Finally, the idea that, notwithstanding this want of subjective imputation, the divine imputation continued ever in force, would have required to be more strongly emphasized in ver. 14. In general, all these modes of interpretation, according to which Paul is held to explain the death of individuals by their own sins, run counter to the object which he had before him in this whole passage, the parallel between the justification of all in one, and the condemnation of all in one.

Let us then resume our explanation of the end of ver. 12 ; and let us seek from this viewpoint to give account of vv. 13, 14 : " Death passed upon all, for that (in Adam) all sinned." The course of the following argument at once becomes easy to understand : " *Sin was assuredly in the world* at that time (and you might consequently say to me : it was for that reason men died) ; but I answer : *sin is not imputed if there is no law* (it could not therefore be the cause of the death with which every individual was visited) ; *and yet death reigned even over those who had not like Adam violated a positive law.*" The conclusion is obvious : " Therefore all these individuals died, not for their own sin, but because of Adam's," which had been affirmed in the close of ver. 12, and which was to be proved. We might in our own day argue in exactly the same manner to explain the death of the heathen or of infants : Since they are still without law, they die, not because they have sinned personally, but because they all sinned in Adam. It is clear also how the argument thus understood is in keeping with the object of this passage. All having been, as is proved by the death of all, condemned in Adam, all can likewise be really justified in Christ. Hofmann and Dietzsch, who have explained ἐφ' ᾧ in the sense of : " on the ground of which (death) all have sinned," are of course obliged to interpret vv. 13 and 14 differently from us, though to arrive at the same result. We think it useless to discuss their explanation, which falls to the ground of itself, with that which they give to the last words of ver. 12.[1]

---

[1] Let us note two other explanations which, while differing considerably from ours come near it in their result, those of Tholuck and Holsten. According to the first, Paul would prove in vv. 13 and 14 the fact of *original sin*. He does so by the existence of death during the time between Adam and Moses. For the sin which certainly existed at that period was not imputable in the absence of law. Now that men died then, is certain : this could therefore only be in consequence of the predisposition to death which they had inherited from Adam, by

Having explained the argument as a whole, let us return to the details of the text itself. The *for*, at the beginning of ver. 13, bears not only on the proposition of which it forms part, but on the entire argument to the end of ver. 14.—The words ἄχρι νόμου, *until the law*, might signify, as the old commentators would have it: "as long as the law existed," that is to say, from Moses to Jesus Christ. For ἄχρι may have the meaning of *during*. But ver. 14, which paraphrases the words thus: "from Adam to Moses," excludes this meaning.—The absence of the article before νόμου, *law*, certainly does not prevent it here from denoting the Mosaic law; comp. ver. 14: *until Moses*. But it is not as Mosaic law, but as law strictly so called, that the Jewish law is here mentioned. And so the translation might well be: *till a law*, that is to say, a law of the same kind as the commandment which Adam violated. The absence of the article before ἁμαρτία, *sin*, has a similar effect; there was sin at that period among men. In the following proposition it is again sin as a category which is designated (being without article). If the substantive ἁμαρτία, *sin*, is repeated (instead of the pronoun), it is because, as Meyer says, we have here the statement of a general maxim.—The verb ἐλλογεῖν is not found elsewhere except in the Epistle to Philemon, ver. 18, where Paul asks this Christian *to put to his account*, his, Paul's, what Onesimus, whom he is recommending, may still owe to him. Between this term and λογίζειν, which he more frequently uses, the one shade of difference is that of the ἐν, *in*, which enters into the composition of ἐλλογεῖν: to inscribe *in* the account book. It is wholly arbitrary to apply this word to the subjective imputation of conscience. The parallel from the Epistle to Philemon shows clearly what its meaning is. But does the apostle then mean to teach the irresponsibility of sinners who, like the Gentiles, have not had a written law? No; for the whole book of Genesis, which describes the period between Adam and Moses, would protest against such an assertion. The matter in question is an immediate and personal imputation, resting on a threatening like this: "In the day thou eatest thereof thou shalt die." The infliction of the punishment of death in the sense of this divine saying necessarily supposes a positive law violated; it supposes in general a theocratic government set up. Only in such circumstances can the violator be brought to account to be immediately judged and subjected, either to capital punishment, or to the obligation of providing an expiatory act, such as sacrifice (taking the place of the punishment of death). Outside of such an organization there may be other great dispensations of a collective and disciplinary character, such as the deluge, the overthrow of Sodom and Gomorrah, or the abandonment of the Gentiles to their own corruption (chap. i.). These historical dispensations are vast pedagogical measures taken in respect of the whole human race;

receiving from him the disposition to sin. So at least it is that we understand this commentator. But this explanation breaks down—1. On the meaning of ἥμαρτον, which cannot signify *became sinners;* and, 2. On the whole context, which goes not to demonstrate the fact of original sin, but to explain the universality of death.—According to Holsten, the sin of which Paul here speaks, and in which he sees the cause of death, exists first in human nature as an *objective principle;* it does not become personal sin (παράβασις) until the latent principle passes into an anti-legal act, as in Adam. Now between the time of Adam and Moses that was impossible. Sin existed objectively, but without personal transgression, properly so called. If, therefore, sin reigned then, it could only be as a punishment of that objective sin manifested for the first time as transgression in Adam's sin, and not as a punishment of subjective or individual sins. But, 1. The sin of Adam, according to Paul, was the *introduction*, and not a first *manifestation* of sin. Wendt justly says: "To enter into the world signifies that something which was not there arrives in it, and not that something shows itself" (p. 194). 2. The very fact which Paul exhibits as the *cause* of death is Adam's sin, which on Holsten's explanation is completely lost in objective sin. 3. Holsten's idea, expressed in common language, amounts to this: human nature has sin inherent in it from its origin, and sin has death for its necessary consequence. Therefore death is not explained by the sin of individuals, but belongs essentially to the human species. These are propositions belonging to Determinism and Pantheism, but not to the Theism of St. Paul.

Yet these two interpretations, that of Tholuck, by laying stress on the universality of sin as a disposition, and that of Holsten, by making death an element of human nature, are *negatively* at one with ours, inasmuch as they exclude, as we do, the explanation of death by the sin of individuals.

212 / Justification by Faith

they have not the character of judicial and individual sentences, like those which rest on some article of a code violated by an individual with full knowledge of the law ; comp. the contrast between the ἀπολοῦνται, *shall perish*, and the κριθήσονται, *shall be judged*, ii. 12.—The subjective negative μή before ὄντος νόμου represents the fact as it exists in the mind of the author of the maxim.

Ver. 14. 'Αλλά : *and nevertheless ;* a strongly emphasized contrast to the idea of non-imputation (ver. 13).—The word *reign* denotes a power firmly established, resting on the immovable foundation of the divine sentence pronounced over the whole race. *Death* cannot denote more here than the loss of life in the ordinary sense of the word. There is no reference either to spiritual death (sin, Gess), or to the sufferings and infirmities of life (Hodge), but simply to the fact that between Adam and Moses men *died* though there was no law. This imputation of Adam's sin, as the cause of death to every individual man, would be absolutely incomprehensible and incompatible with the justice of God, if it passed beyond the domain of natural life marked off by the mysterious relation between the individual and the species. The sequel will show that as soon as we rise to the domain of spiritual life, the individual is no longer dependent on this solidarity of the species, but that he holds his eternal destiny in his own hands.—The words : "*also*, or (*even*) over them that had not sinned," are taken by Meyer as referring to a part only of the men who lived between Adam and Moses, those, namely, who did not enjoy the positive revelations granted during this period, the Noachian commandments, for example, Gen. ix. 1-17. Thus understood, Paul reminds us of the fact that the men of that time who were without those precepts were, as well as their contemporaries who enjoyed such light, subjected to death. But the whole passage, on the contrary, implies the absence of all positive law which could have been violated between Adam and Moses ; consequently, the phrase : "*even* over them who sinned not," etc., embraces the whole human species from Adam to Moses without distinction ; mankind during this interval are contrasted with Adam on the one hand, and with the people of Israel from Moses on the other. All these who were not under conditions of a capitally penal kind (ver. 13) died nevertheless.—The words : "*after the resemblance of Adam's transgression*," are certainly not dependent, as the old Greek expositors thought, on the word *reigned:* "death reigned on the ground of a sin similar to that of Adam." This sense leaves the words : *even over them that sinned not*, without any reasonable explanation. We must therefore bring this clause under καὶ ἐπὶ τοὺς μὴ ἁμαρτήσαντας, in this sense : "*even over them that did not sin after the fashion of Adam's sin*," that is to say, by transgressing as he did, a positive prohibition.—Hofmann insists on the strict meaning of the word which Paul uses, ὁμοίωμα, *the object* like (differing from ὁμοιότης, *the resemblance*), and, taking the genitive παραβάσεως as a subjective genitive, he explains : *according to the form which was that of . . .* or *on the type presented by the transgression of . . .* To render this shade into English, we must translate, not *after the resemblance*, but *after the fashion of* Adam's transgression.

From this whole argument it appeared that Adam had been the sole author of the reign of death, and herein precisely was he the counterpart of Him who was to come to be the sole principle of life here below. Thus it is easy to understand why the apostle, after explaining the origin of death, closes with these words, appropriately introducing the statement of the other member of the parallel : *who is the type of the Adam that was to come.* It is improper, with Bengel, to give to the participle μέλλοντος the neuter sense : *of that which* was to come (by regarding the masculine ὅς as a case of attraction from τύπος). The word Adam, immediately preceding, more naturally leads us to make μέλλων a masculine. One might more easily, with Hofmann, regard this participle as a masculine *substantive: Him* who should come, in the sense in which the Messiah is called the ἐρχόμενος, *the coming one*. The meaning is not essentially different. If the Rabbinical sayings in which the Messiah is designated as the second or the last Adam were older than the seventh century of our era (*Targum* of the Psalms), or the sixteenth (*Nevé schalom*), it might be inferred from these passages that the description of the Messiah as the Adam to come was already received in the Jewish schools, and that the phrase of the apostle is a reference to this received notion. But it is quite possible that these sayings themselves were influenced by the texts of the New Testament. So Renan says positively : "In the Talmudic writings *Adam ha-rischôn* simply denotes the first man, Adam. Paul creates *Ha-adam ha-aharôn* by antithesis." We must certainly set aside De Wette's idea, which applies the phrase : *the future Adam*, to Christ's *final* advent. The term μέλλων, *future*, is related to the time of the *first Adam*, not to the time when the apostle writes.— The word *type* denotes in Scripture language (1 Cor. x. 11) an event, or a person realizing a law of the kingdom of God which will be realized afterward in a more complete and striking manner in a corresponding future event or person. Adam is the type of the Messiah, inasmuch as, to quote Ewald, " each of them draws after him all mankind," so that " from what the one was to humanity we may infer what the other is to it" (Hofmann). —This proposition is a sort of provisional apodosis to the *even as* of ver. 12. It reminds the reader of the comparison which has been begun, and keeps the thought present to his mind till the comparison can be finished and grammatically completed by the true principal clause (ver. 18).

2. Vv. 15-17

A certain superiority of action is ascribed to Christ's work as compared with Adam's, in these three verses. What object does the apostle propose to gain by this demonstration ? Why interrupt in this way the statement of the *parity* between the two works begun ver. 12 ? It has been thought that Paul is simply gratifying a want of his heart by displaying in the outset the infinite superiority of the second work over the first, that he may not compromise its dignity by abandoning himself without reserve to the idea of equality. But whatever overflow of feeling there may be in St. Paul, it is always regulated, as we have seen, by the demands of logic. We think, therefore, that these three verses, which are among the most difficult of the New Testament, will not be understood till we succeed in making them a necessary link in the argument.

It may be said that the sagacity of commentators has exhausted itself on this passage. While Morus holds that from vv. 15-19 the apostle merely repeats the same thing five times over in different words ; while Rückert supposes that Paul himself was not quite sure of his own thoughts, Rothe and Meyer find in these verses traces of the most profound meditation and mathematical precision. Notwithstanding the favorable judgment of the latter, it must be confessed that the considerable variety of expositions proposed to explain the course and gradation of the thoughts seem still to justify to some extent the complaints of the former. Tholuck finds in ver. 15 a contrast of *quantity* between the two works, and in vv. 16, 17 a contrast of *quality* (the contrast between *right* and *grace*). Ewald thinks that the contrast of ver. 15 bears on the *thing* itself (a sad effect and a happy effect—this would be the *quality*), that of ver. 16 on the *number* and *kind* of the persons interested (*one* sinner condemned, *thousands* justified) ; then he passes on to ver. 17 with the simple remark : "to conclude," and yet there is a *for*. Meyer and Holsten find in ver. 15 the contrast of *effects* (*death* and the *gift of grace*), in ver. 16 a *numerical* contrast, as Ewald does, and in ver. 17 the *seal put* on the contrast of ver. 16 by the certainty of the future life. Dietzsch finds the gradation from ver. 15 to ver. 16 in the transition from the idea of *grace* to that of the *re-establishment of holiness* in pardoned believers ; so he understands the δικαίωμα of ver. 16. Reuss sees in ver. 15 the contrast between *just recompense* and *free grace* (a contrast of *quality*), in ver. 16 that between *a single* sinner and a whole *multitude* of sinners (a contrast of *quantity*), and in ver. 17, finally, one as to the *degree of certainty* (a *logical* gradation). Hodge finds in ver. 15 the contrast between the *more mysterious* character of condemnation and the *more intelligible* character of pardon in Christ (a contrast evidently imported into the text), and in ver. 15 the idea of Christ's delivering us from a *culpability greater* still than that of Adam's sin—that is to say, besides that of Adam, He takes away what we have added to it ourselves ; finally, in ver. 17, he finds this gradation, that not only does Christ save us from *death*, but He introduces us into a state of *positive* and eternal *felicity*.—After all this, one needs a certain measure of courage to enter this double labyrinth, the study of the text and that of the exegetical interpretations.

We have seen that the apostle's argument aims at proving the *parity* between the two works. This is the idea of ver. 12 (*even as . . . death . . . upon all . . .*), as well as of ver. 18 which completes it (*so . . . on all to justification of life*). From this connection between ver. 12 and ver. 18 it follows that the development of the superiority of action belonging to Christ's work, vv. 15-17, must be a *logical means of demonstrating the equality of extension and result*, which forms the contents of the conclusion expressed in vv. 18 and 19. The relation between the first proposition of ver. 15 and the first of ver. 16 leads us to expect two contrasts, the first expounded in ver. 15, the second in vv. 16, 17.

Ver. 15. "*But not as the offence, so is the act of grace. For if through the offence of one the many be dead, much rather the grace of God, and the gift by grace, which is by one man, Jesus Christ, hath abounded unto the many.*"— What the apostle here compares is not, as some have thought, the abundance of the effects, but rather the *degree of extension* belonging to the two works ; for the emphasis is on the term *the many*, of the two sides of the parallel ; and this degree of extension he measures very logically according to the degree of abundance in the factors—a degree indicated on the one side by the subordinate clause of the first proposition : *through the offence of one*, on the other by the subject of the second : *the grace of God*, and *the gift through this grace of one man*. From the contrast between these factors it is easy to arrive at this conclusion : If from the first factor, so insignificant in a way—the offence of one !—there could go forth an action which spread over the whole multitude of mankind, will not the conclusion hold *a fortiori* that from the two factors acting on the opposite side, so powerful and rich as they are, there must result an action, the *extension* of which shall not be less than that of the first factor, and shall consequently also reach the whole of that multitude ? Such is the general idea of this verse. It may be illustrated by a figure. If a very weak spring could inundate a whole meadow, would it not be safe to conclude that a much more abundant spring, if it spread over the same space of ground, would not fail to submerge it entirely ?

The term παράπτωμα, *fall, offence*, is not synonymous with παράβασις, *transgression*. It is applied, Eph. i. 7, ii. 1, to the sin of the Gentiles. It has something extenuating in its meaning ; it is, as it were, a mere false step. Such is the active principle in the first case. On the other hand, it is the χάρισμα, *the act of grace*, whose contents Paul will state in the double subject of the principal proposition. Some commentators have taken this first proposition of ver. 15 interrogatively. But the construction of the sentence does not lead naturally to the idea of an interrogation. And what is still more strongly opposed to this explanation is, that the sentence so understood would express the development of an analogy, while the rest of the verse states a difference. The two parallel members present a common term: οἱ πολλοί, literally, *the many*. This term has often been ill understood, or badly rendered; so when Oltramare translates by *the majority* in the first proposition, and *a greater number* in the second, which gives rise to more than one kind of ambiguity. Ostervald translates: *many*, which is as far from being exact. By this form Paul denotes, just as much as he would have done by the pronoun *all*, the totality of the human race. This is proved by the article οἱ, *the*, which he prefixes for the very purpose of indicating the idea of a totality to πολλοί, *many*. Only this term *many* is chosen with the view of establishing the contrast to the *one* from whom the influence went forth. *All* would be opposed to *some*, and not to *one*. It would not be suitable here. Paul will return to it at ver. 18. He is dealing in ver. 15 with the possibility of the action of *one* on *many*. We have sought to render the meaning of this οἱ πολλοί, by translating: *the many (the multitude)*. — An offence of one, says the apostle, sufficed to bring about the death of this multitude. This expression confirms the sense which we have given of the last clause of ver. 12; it is clearly through Adam's sin, and not through their own, that men die. This fact, established by the demonstration of vv. 13 and 14, serves as a point of support for the conclusion drawn in the following proposition. — The term χάρισμα, *act of grace*, used in opening the verse, combined the two ideas which Paul now distinguishes: the *grace* of God and the *gift* by which it is manifested, Jesus Christ. Grace is the first source of salvation. The richness of this source, which is no other than the infinite love of God Himself, at once contrasts with the weakness of the opposite factor, the offence of one. But how much more striking is the contrast, when to the love of God we add the gift whereby this love is displayed! Comp. John iii. 16. The substantive ἡ δωρεά, *the gift*, denotes not the thing given (δώρημα, ver. 16), but *the act* of giving, which is more directly related to the idea of grace. — Commentators differ as to the grammatical relation of ἐν χάριτι, *in* (or *by*) *the grace of the one man*. Meyer and others make these words depend on the verb ἐπερίσσευσεν: "The gift *flowed over through the grace of the one man, Jesus Christ*." But the expression: *the gift*, can hardly remain without an explanatory clause. And the idea: *through the grace*, connected with the verb *overflowed*, weakens the meaning of the clause instead of strengthening it. For it diverts the thought from the essential word: *unto the many*. Meyer alleges that there must be in the second member a counterpart to the words: *through the offence of one*, in the first, and that this counterpart can only be found in these: *through the grace of the one, Jesus Christ*. He thus misses one of the greatest beauties of our verse—I mean the reversal of construction introduced by the apostle in passing from the subordinate to the principal proposition; there, the intransitive form: *By . . . many are dead;*[1] here, the active form: *the grace of God, and the gift . . . have abounded to the many*. In the first case, there was a disagreeable accident involuntarily experienced: *the many* fell stricken with death; in the second, on the contrary, they are the objects of a double personal action put forth in their behalf. In reality, then, the counterpart of the expression: *through the offence of one*, is found in the second member, but as the subject, and no longer as a simple phrase. We shall again find a similar change of construction in ver. 17. Comp. also 2 Cor. iii. 9. The clause ἐν χάριτι is therefore the qualification of the word *the gift*: "*the gift consisting in the grace* of the one man, Jesus Christ." The love of God is a love which gives another love; it is the grace of a father giving the love of a brother. The absence of the article between δωρεά and ἐν χάριτι is explained by the intimate relation subsisting between

---

[1] But the force of the aorist is given much better by the rendering *the many died*.—T. W. C.

these two substantives, which express, so to speak, a single notion. The idea of the *grace of Christ* is developed in all its richness, 2 Cor. viii. 9 : " Ye know the grace of our Lord Jesus Christ, that, though He was rich, yet for your sakes he became poor, that ye through his poverty might be rich." This relation of solidarity and fraternity between Christ and us is strongly brought out by the phrase : *of the one man,* ἐνὸς ἀνθρώπου. Comp. the similar expressions, 1 Cor. xv. 21 : " *By man* (δι' ἀνθρώπου) came death, and by man (δι' ἀνθρώπου) the resurrection of the dead ;" and 1 Tim. ii. 5 : "There is one Mediator . . . *the man* Christ Jesus." The incarnation has had for its effect to raise the whole human race to the rank of His family. The adjective ἑνός, *of one,* is prefixed to contrast Christ, as well as Adam, with *the many.* And after these accumulated descriptions, all calculated to display the greatness of the gift of divine grace, there is at length pronounced the name which in the history of mankind is the only one that can figure side by side with that of Adam : *Jesus Christ.* Comp. John i. 17, where this name, long delayed, is proclaimed at last with special solemnity (in contrast to Moses) ; and John xvii. 3, where it is joined, as here, with the name of God, to describe the source of salvation and the supreme object of faith. What must have been the impression produced by the appearance of Jesus on His contemporaries, when, only twenty odd years after His death, He could be put with the avowal of the entire church —for the apostle evidently reckons on the absolute assent of his readers— on a parallel with the father of the first humanity ! The clause εἰς τοὺς πολλοὺς is placed immediately before the verb, because it is on this idea that the emphasis rests. — Ἐπερίσσευσεν, *abounded ;* it might be translated : *overflowed.* This verb properly denotes the outflow of a liquid lapping over a vessel more than filled. Christ is the vessel filled with grace, whence salvation overflows on *the many.* The aorist indicates an already accomplished fact ; the subject, then, is not a future grace, but the work of justification expounded from iii. 21. If Adam's offence was sufficiently influential to tell in the form of death on the whole multitude of the race, much more should a grace like that of God, and a gift like that of Jesus, be capable of acting on the same circle of persons ! The superiority of abundance in the factors of Christ's work thus establishes an *a fortiori* conclusion in the view of the apostle in favor of the *equality* of extent belonging to the two works here compared. Hence it follows that the πολλῷ μᾶλλον, *much rather,* should be understood in the logical sense : *much more certainly,* and not in the *quantitative* sense : *much more abundantly* (as is the opinion of Er., Calv., Rück., Rothe, Hofm., and Dietzs.). Chrysostom, Meyer, and Philippi have been led to the same view as ours. The apostle is not at all concerned to demonstrate that there is more grace in Christ than there was of death in Adam. What he wishes to prove is, that if a slight cause could bring sentence of death on all mankind, this same mankind will experience in its entirety the salutary effect of a much more powerful cause. The idea of superabundant quantity (*more richly*) is not in πολλῷ μᾶλλον, as has been thought by so many interpreters, misled by the relation between this adverb and the verb ἐπερίσσευσε, *abounded.* It is merely indicated as a premiss of the argument in the double subject of the second proposition (the grace of God and the gift of Christ) ; at the most, a sort of involuntary indication of it may be seen in the meaning of the verb ἐπερίσσευσε, *abounded.* — We have already seen the logical sense of πολλῷ μᾶλλον in vv. 9 and 10 of our chapter. It is found perhaps also in 2 Cor. iii. 7, 9, 11.

The reasoning is extremely bold ; it is as if one were to argue thus : Adam's offence has reached down to me, having had the power of subjecting me to death ; how much more certainly will the grace of God and the grace of Christ combined have the power of reaching to me **to save me !**

A second difference is evidently *announced* in the first words of ver. 16 ; the end of ver. 16 is intended to *expound* it, and ver. 17 to *demonstrate* it.

Ver. 16. *"And the gift is not as by one that sinned:*[1] *for the judgment is by one to condemnation, but the free gift is of the offences of many unto justification."*—Most expositors hold with us that the apostle is here expounding a second contrast between Adam's work and Christ's ; only it should be remarked that the form of ver. 16 is very different from that of ver. 15. We no longer find here the *a fortiori* argument there indicated by the πολλῷ μᾶλλον, *much rather*, while, strange to say, this same form of reasoning reappears in ver. 17, which is thus presented as a stronger reproduction of the argument of ver. 15. This difference between vv. 16 and 15, and this quite peculiar relation between vv. 17 and 15, prevent us from regarding ver. 16 as a second argument entirely parallel to that of ver. 15, so as then to make ver. 17 *the conclusion* of both. Hofmann is so well aware of this that he refuses to see in the first words of ver. 16 the announcement of a second contrast, and has connected them directly with the close of ver. 15. In fact, he uniformly supplies in the three propositions of ver. 16 the verb and the regimen : *abounded unto many*, of ver. 15 : " And *the gift did not abound unto the many*, as in that case in which the imputation took place through one who had sinned ; *for judgment abounded from one to many* in condemnation, and *the gift of grace abounded from one to many* in justification." It is obvious how such an ellipsis thrice repeated burdens and embarrasses the course of the argument. What of truth there is in this view is that *the gift* mentioned in ver. 16 is no other than that referred to in the words of ver. 15 : ἡ δωρεὰ ἐν χάριτι . . ., *the gift by grace of* . . ., and that consequently the second contrast, vv. 16 and 17, should be regarded as serving to bring out a particular aspect of the general contrast pointed out in ver. 15. The καί, *and*, at the beginning of the verse is thus equivalent to a sort of *nota-bene:* "And mark well this circumstance" . . . An objection might be made to the πολλῷ μᾶλλον, *much more certainly*, of ver. 15. One might say : True, the factors acting on Christ's part (15*b*) are infinitely more abundant than the weak and solitary factor acting on Adam's part (15*a*) ; but, on the other hand, was not the work to be wrought on Christ's part much more considerable than that accomplished in Adam ! If the source was richer, the void to be filled was deeper : In Adam a single actual sinner—all the rest playing only an unconscious and purely passive part ; in Christ, on the contrary, a multitude of sinners to be justified, equally conscious and responsible with the first, having all voluntarily added their own contingent of sins to the original transgression. Undoubtedly, answers the apostle ; but in the matter of salvation the part of those interested is also quite different. In the one case they were passively and collectively subjected to the sentence of death ; here, we have to do with beings who lay hold individually and personally of the sentence which justifies them. There, a single and solitary condemnation, which embraces them all through the deed of one ; here, a justification, collective also, but appropriated by each individually, which is transformed into as many personal justifications as there are believing sinners, and which cannot fail to establish the kingdom of life more firmly still than the kingdom of death was founded on the condemnation of all in Adam. This antithesis established as a *fact* in ver. 16, is demonstrated in ver. 17 by an *a fortiori* argument, entirely similar to that of ver. 15.

Nothing more is to be understood in the first proposition than the verb γίνεται, *comes about:* " And the gift does not *come about* by one sinner" (as the condemnation had done). Some have supposed a more extensive ellipsis : "The gift did not come about by one (*as the condemnation had done*),

---

[1] T. R. reads, with A B C K L P. Mnn., αμαρτησαντος ; D E F G, It. Syr. Or. (Lat. trans.) read αμαρτεματος. ℵ is doubtful, the syllable which follows τη being wanting.

by one sinner." But this ellipsis is unnecessary, and even impairs somewhat the meaning of the contrast, for the words: *by one who sinned*, depend directly on the verb: *does not come about*. The reading ἁμαρτήματος ("by one *sin*"), though supported by the ancient versions, is a correction, the origin of which is easily understood; it is borrowed from the ἐκ πολλῶν παραπτωμάτων which follows, understood in the sense of: *of many sins*. The idea *of one sin* seemed to contrast better than the idea *of one sinner* with the expression thus understood. The contrast which Paul has now in view certainly demands the Received reading. With "*the offence* of one," ver. 15, he has contrasted the grace of God and of Jesus Christ in its double fulness. Now, with the *one* sinner, in the first case, he contrasts the *multitude* of sinners who are the objects of justification in the second. What a difference between the power of the spark which sets fire to the forest by lighting a withered branch, and the power of the instrument which extinguishes the conflagration at the moment when every tree is on fire, and makes them all live again!

The substantive δώρημα denotes the concrete gift, the blessing bestowed; here it is the gift of justification by Christ, as described iii. 21–v. 11.—The two propositions develop the contrast announced (*for*). The term τὸ κρῖμα properly signifies: *the judicial act*, the sentence pronounced, in opposition to χάρισμα, *the act of grace* (in the second proposition).—The clause ἐξ ἑνός, *of one*, indicates the point of departure for this judicial act, the material on which it operated. This *one* is not neuter (one *offence*), but masculine, agreeably to the reading ἁμαρτήσαντος: *the one* who had committed the act of sin, and whose sin had become the object of judgment. It is on the word ἐξ ἑνός that the emphasis lies. Its counterpart in the second proposition is ἐκ πολλῶν παραπτωμάτων, which may be translated either by: *of many sins*, or by making πολλῶν a pronoun and a complement: *of the sins of many*. In the former case, each of those numerous offences must be regarded as the summary indication of the fall of a particular individual, in opposition to *one sinner*. But in the second the contrast is clearer: the plurality of individuals is exactly expressed by the pronoun πολλῶν, *of many*. Dietzsch denies that this last construction is possible.[1] But it is found very probably in Luke ii. 35 (ἐκ πολλῶν καρδιῶν, *of the hearts of many*) and 2 Cor. i. 11.—As the preposition ἐκ relates to the matter of the judgment, εἰς denotes the result in which it issues: "*to* condemnation." The reference is to the sentence of death pronounced on mankind because of one who had sinned; for this one contained in him the entire race.—The antithesis to this κατάκριμα, *sentence of condemnation*, appears in δικαίωμα, which must be translated by *sentence of justification*. This meaning arises from the contrast itself, as well as from the meaning of the words δικαιοῦν and δικαιοσύνη (*justify, righteousness*) throughout this part of the Epistle, and with St. Paul generally. Only the question may be asked, whether the apostle has in view here the justification granted to the sinner at the very hour of his believing, or justification in the absolute sense, as it will be pronounced in the day of judgment (ii. 13). Two reasons seem to us to decide in favor of the second alternative—1. The passage, v. 1–11, in which the final sentence of acquittal is represented as the indispensable complement of the righteousness of faith, this becoming eternally valid only by means of the former. 2. Ver. 17, which is connected by *for* with ver. 16, and the second part of which refers to the most distant future (*the reign in life*). Hence we must conclude that the term δικαίωμα, *sentence of justification*, also embraces that supreme sentence of acquittal whereby we shall conclusively escape from *wrath* (v. 9, 10). This parallel between Adam and Christ manifestly assumes the whole doctrine of justification from iii. 21, including the final

---

[1] It certainly is so unusual and unlikely that it should not be adopted without necessity, which does not exist in this case. Godet's citations do not sustain his view.—T. W. C.

passage on the justification to come, v. 1–11. The *absolute* meaning which we here give to δικαίωμα, is thus in keeping with the position of the whole passage. Dietzsch is certainly mistaken in applying this word δικαίωμα to the sanctification of the sinner by the Holy Spirit. It is nevertheless true that if we extend the meaning of this term to the final justification, on entering upon glory, it involves the work of sanctification as finished (see on v. 9, 10). But this does not in the least modify the sense of the word itself (*a justificatory sentence*), as appears from the meaning of the word δικαιοῦν and from the context (in contrast to κατάκριμα, *a condemnatory sentence*).—It is unnecessary to refute the divergent constructions proposed by Rothe and Dietzsch, according to which τὸ μέν and τὸ δέ are taken as the subjects of the two propositions having κρῖμα and χάρισμα either as predicates (Rothe), or in apposition (Dietzsch).—It has often been thought that the emphasis in this verse was on the idea of the contrast between the nature of the two results : *condemnation* and *justification*. It is not so. The real contrast indicated by the Greek construction is that between ἐξ ἑνός, *one (who sinned)*, and ἐκ πολλῶν παραπτωμάτων, the sins of *many*. There, by a judicial act, condemnation goes forth *from one sinner ;* here, by the act of grace, *from the offences of a multitude,* there proceeds a justification.—We come now to the most difficult point of the whole passage : the relation of ver. 17 to what precedes, and the exposition of the verse itself.

Ver. 17. "*For if by the one*[1] *man's offence death reigned by this one ; much rather they who receive the superabundance of grace and of the gift of righteousness shall reign in life by the one, Jesus Christ.*"—The *for* beginning this verse has been the torture of expositors, for it seems as if it should rather be *therefore*, since this verse appears to give the conclusion to be drawn from the difference indicated in ver. 16. Meyer seeks to get over the difficulty of the *for* by making it bear on the idea of δικαίωμα, ver. 16, and finding in the certainty of the *future reign* (end of ver. 17) the joyful confirmation of the grace of *justification* (ver. 16); Philippi almost the same : "The justified shall reign in life (ver. 17), which proves that they are really justified (ver. 16)." But is it logical to argue from a future and hoped-for event to demonstrate the certainty of a present fact? Is not justification at least as certain as the future reign of the justified ? Hofmann here alleges a forced turn in the dialectic. According to him, ver. 17 does not prove the fact alleged in ver. 16, but the reasoning of ver. 17 is intended to demonstrate that the second part of ver. 16 (from τὸ μὲν γὰρ . . ., *for the judgment* . . ., to the end) has really proved the truth of the first (καὶ οὐχ ὡς . . ., and the gift did not come about as by . . .). The meaning he holds to be : "I have good reason to say that it is not so with the judgment . . . as with the gift of grace . . .; for if . . . (ver. 17)." Dietzsch rightly answers that the demonstration given in ver. 16 would be very weak if it needed to be propped with the complicated reasoning of ver. 17. Dietzsch himself, starting from his sense of δικαίωμα, *the restoration of holiness*, ver. 16, thus understands the argument : "This holiness will be really restored in believers ; for, according to the divine promises, they are one day to enter into the kingdom of life (ver. 17), which cannot take place without holiness." Everything is erroneous in this explanation—1. The meaning of δικαίωμα ; 2. The intervention of the divine promises, of which there has been no mention in the context ; 3. The idea of sanctification, which is out of place in this passage. Rothe has given up in despair the attempt to discover a logical connection between vv. 17 and 16. He has accordingly attempted to refer the *for* of ver. 17 to the argument of ver. 15, making ver. 16 a sort of parenthesis. There is something seductive about this solution. We have already seen in vv. 9,

---

[1] Instead of τω του ενος, which T. R. reads, with ℵ B C K L P, Syr. It[aliq], there is found in A F G : εν ενι παραπτωματι, and in D E, It[aliq] : εν τω ενι παραπτωματι.

10 of this chapter, two verses which followed one another, both beginning with *for*, and the second of which was merely the repetition (reinforced with some new elements) of the first, and so its confirmation. It might therefore be supposed that it is the same in this case, only with the difference that ver. 16 would be inserted in order to enunciate those new elements which are to play a part in ver. 17. So it was that, following the path opened by Rothe, we long flattered ourselves that we had solved the difficulty. Yet we have been obliged to abandon this solution by the following considerations :—1. Can the *for* of ver. 17, after the insertion of a new contrast specially announced, ver. 16*a*, and expounded, ver. 16*b*, be purely and simply parallel to the *for* of ver. 15 ? 2. How happens it that in ver. 17 there is no further mention of the *many*, nor consequently of the extent of the two works, but solely of the equality of the *effect produced* (on the one side a *reign of death*, on the other a *reign in life*), and specially, that instead of the past ἐπερίσσευσεν (ver. 15), we are all at once transported into the future by the words : *they shall reign* (end of ver. 17) ? Finally— and we long held to this idea also—the *for* of ver. 17 might be taken to refer to the affirmation (vv. 15*a*, 16*a*) of the two differences : "*It is not with the offence as with the gift* . . . (ver. 15*a*) ;" "*the gift did not come about* . . . (ver. 16*a*)." But the second part of ver. 16 would thus be sacrificed ; now it is too important to be only a parenthesis. We must therefore revert to the attempt of Meyer and Philippi, which consists in connecting the *for* with ver. 16 ; this is, besides, the only probable supposition ; only we must seek to justify, better than they have done, the logical relation established by this *for*. And that does not seem to us impossible if what we have observed regarding the meaning of δικαίωμα, *the sentence of justification*, ver. 16, be borne in mind. The parallel between Christ and Adam strikes its roots into the whole previous doctrine regarding *the righteousness of faith*, iii. 21–v. 11 ; witness the *wherefore* (v. 12). Now Paul had demonstrated, v. 1-11, that once justified by the death of Christ, all the more may we be certain of being saved and glorified by His life. It is this very idea which forms the basis of the second part of ver. 17, which thus contains the paraphrase of the term δικαίωμα, *sentence of justification*, at the end of ver. 16. The relation between vv. 16, 17 is therefore as follows : Two facts are set forth in ver. 16 parallel to one another : *one* sinner, the object of the act of condemnation ; *a multitude* of sinners, the objects of the act of justification. The reality of the first of these facts was demonstrated by vv. 12-14. It remained to demonstrate that of the second. This is the object to which ver. 17 is devoted. The mode of reasoning is as follows : The apostle starts (ver. 17*a*) from the first fact as certain, and *by means of it* he infers (17*b*) *the still more certain reality* of the second. Ver. 17 has thus its logical place between the two propositions of ver. 16 to prove *by the first* the truth of the second. Not only so. But in reproducing ver. 16*a* in the first proposition of 17*a*, he combines with 16*a* the contents of the first proposition of ver. 15 (15*a*) ; and in reproducing, in the conclusion 17*b*, the second proposition of ver. 16 (16*b*), he combines with it the contents of the second proposition of ver. 15 (15*b*), and that in order to give *double* force to the *a fortiori* reasoning whereby from the premiss he reaches the conclusion ; in other words, 16*a*, supported by 15*a*, serves him as a premiss in 17*a* to reach the conclusion 17*b*, containing 16*b* combined with 15*b* by a double *a fortiori*. The meaning of this masterly logic, simpler than would have been thought possible, is as follows : If a *weak* cause, the single sin (15*a*) of one sinner (16*a*), *passively* endured, could bring about the death of every man (17*a*), *much more certainly* shall the *more powerful* cause (16*b*), assimilated by each one *personally* (16*b*), produce in him *an effect* not *inferior* to the effect produced by the first cause (17*b*). If a weak deleterious cause passively endured by me has been able to produce my death, a life-giving cause much more powerful,

which I actively appropriate to myself, will far more certainly give me life.—We thus apprehend at the same time the relation between vv. 16, 17 and ver. 15. Ver. 15 relates to the two *circles* influenced; they must cover one another perfectly (*the many*, of the two sides); for the more powerful cause cannot have extended less widely than the weaker. In vv. 16, 17 the subject is the *result* obtained in *every individual* belonging *to the many* in the direction either of death or of life. The second of these effects (life) cannot be less real than the first (death), for it has been produced by a cause *more powerful* and *individually appropriated*. Ver. 15 : *as many individuals;* vv. 16, 17 : as much *effect produced* in each one. Let us now enter upon the detailed study of this verse, in which the apostle has succeeded in combining with the argument which he was following the full riches of the antithesis already contained in vv. 15, 16.

In the first clause there is a difference of reading. Instead of : *by one man's offence*, some Greco-Latin copyists have written : *by one offence*, or again : *by the one single offence*. This reading, opposed to that of the two other families, and also of the Peshitto, can only be regarded as an erroneous correction. The idea *of one* (sinner) has been rejected, because it seemed to involve a repetition when taken with the immediately following words : *by this one*. But it has been overlooked that the terms : *by one man's offence*, are intended to reproduce the idea of the first proposition of ver. 15, as the words : *by this one*, reproduce the idea of the 'ξ ἑνός, *of one*, in the first proposition of ver. 16. These expressions have something extenuating about them : only one act, only one actor. The apostle means to contrast the weakness of these causes with the greatness of the result : a *reign of death* established in the world. We see a whole race of slaves with their heads passively bent, through the solitary deed of one, under the pitiless sceptre of death. The words : *by one*, are added as by an after-thought, in order to emphasize the *passivity* of the individuals subjected to this order of things. The apostle does not here mention, as in ver. 15, *the many*, in opposition to *this one*. He has not in view *the extent* of the reign of death, but the *part played by the individuals* in relation to this tragical situation. He sees them all as it were absorbed in the one being who has acted for all.—The expression : *death reigned*, denotes a firmly established order of things against which, for individuals, there is no possibility of resistance. Nothing more desperate in appearance than this great historical fact of the reign of death, and yet it is this very fact which becomes in the eyes of the apostle a principle of the most powerful encouragement and the most glorious hope. For this terrible reign of death, established on the weak foundation of a single sin and a single sinner, may serve as a *measure* to establish the greater certainty of the reign of life which will come to light among the justified by the freely accepted gift of God. Such is the idea of the second part of the verse. Instead of this impersonal multitude involved in the act, and thereby in the condemnation of a single sinner, Paul contemplates a plurality of distinct individuals appropriating to themselves, consciously and freely, the fulness of the gift of righteousness ; and he asks himself, with a tone of triumph, whether a glorious reign of life will not spring up under similar conditions more certainly still than the sinister reign of death established itself on the weak foundation which he has just mentioned.—The salient expression in this second part of the verse is the οἱ λαμβάνοντες, *they who receive* (literally, the receivers or accepters). The verb λαμβάνειν may signify *to take, to lay hold of*, or again : *to receive* (more or less passively). As it here evidently denotes the act of *faith*, it expresses the idea of a *taking in possession* resting on a free *acceptance* (see on i. 17). The form of the present participle is variously explained. According to Philippi, it denotes the *continuousness* of the acceptance of salvation by believers during the whole period of grace. Meyer and others take the present as referring to the epoch *now in progress*, as the intermediate station between the natural order of things and the future kingdom. But what have these two ideas to do with Paul's intention in the context? It seems to me that this present is rather that of *moral condition* relatively to the state which ought logically to arise from it. Whoever joins the number of *those accepters*, shall reign in life.—The definite article οἱ, *the*, presents all these accepters as distinct persons, individually capable of accepting or rejecting what must decide their lot. It is no longer that undistinguished mass which had disobeyed and perished in one. Here we meet again those πολλοί, the many sinners, mentioned in ver. 16, who, under the burden of their personal offences, have accepted for themselves the act of grace, and shall become individually the objects of the δικαίωμα, the sentence of justification. It is to be remarked that even in ver. 16 the article has ceased to be prefixed to the word πολλῶν (*many;* not "*the* many"), and that Paul does not even speak of πολλοί, *many*. The accepters are not the *totality* of men condemned to die; Paul does not even say that they are necessarily numerous. His thought here is arrested by *each* of them, whatever shall be their number. In this fact, taken by itself, of individual acceptance, on the side of grace there is a complete difference of position as compared with the passivity of the individuals on the opposite side. It is a first difference fitted to establish an *a fortiori* conclusion. But there is another fact, which combines with it the infinitely greater power of the cause, on the same side. The apostle had already remarked it in ver. 15: *the grace of God, and the gift of Jesus Christ*. It is easy to see the connection of the expressions used with those of 15*b*: And first: τὴν περισσείαν, *the abundance*, which reproduces the idea of the verb ἐπερίσσευσε, *hath abounded;* then τῆς χάριτος, *of the grace*, which goes back upon *the* double grace of God and *of the one man Jesus Christ;* finally, the term δωρεά, *the gift*, which appears in both verses. The complement τῆς δικαιοσύνης, *of righteousness*, is alone added here, because the subject in question is the gift accepted by faith and transformed into individual righteousness. The destination (ver. 15) has become possession. Thus the thought of the apostle is clear: as the term οἱ λαμβάνοντες, *the receivers*, forms an antithesis to διὰ τοῦ ἑνός, *by this one*, so the expressions: *the abundance of grace, and of the gift of righteousness*, form an antithesis to the: *by the offence of one*. Not only, then, is there on this side individual appropriation (ver. 16), but this appropriation rests on a more powerful cause (ver. 15).

Thus is seen the justice of the observation: that in this ver. 17 there are designedly combined to establish a double *a fortiori*, the two previously described contrasts: "If a weak objective cause, without personal appropriation on the part of those interested, has been able to establish a reign of death, with stronger reason should it be certain that a still more powerful objective cause, and one individually appropriated, will be capable of establishing a glorious reign of life." Περισσεία: *abundance*, or more strictly *superabundance*, so that the superfluity flows over; χάριτος, *of grace*, applies at one and the same time, according to ver. 15, to the love of God and to that of Jesus Christ. The *gift of righteousness* is that justification objectively realized in Christ *for the many* (mankind), and apprehended by the faith of every receiver. When the empty vessel of the human heart has once become filled by faith with this fulness of grace and righteousness, the sinner is raised to the place of a *king in life*. This last expression also forms an antithesis to an analogous one in the first proposition: *death reigned*. But the apostle has too lively a conviction of spiritual realities to say here: *life shall reign*. Death reigns; it is a tyrant. But life does not reign; it has not subjects; it makes kings. Besides Paul transforms his construction, as he had already done with a similar intention in ver. 15. This change admirably suits the thought of the context. Instead of the sombre state of things which bears sway as a reign of death, it is here the individuals themselves who, after having personally appropriated righteousness, reign personally in the luminous domain of life. Comp. on this reign what Paul said, iv. 13, of *the inheritance of the world;* then the καυχώμενοι, *glorying,* v. 11 ; finally, viii. 17.

The clause ἐν ζωῇ, *in life,* does not denote a period, as when we say : in eternal life. If the word *life* were taken in this sense, it would undoubtedly be defined by the article τῇ. The preposition ἐν must not be taken in the instrumental sense, as in v. 10 (*by* life). Contrasted as it is to this : *reign of death,* the expression denotes the *mode* or *nature* of the reign of believers. A new, holy, inexhaustible, and victorious vitality will pervade those *receivers of righteousness,* and make them so many kings. If the collective condemnation could make each of them a subject of death, the conclusion therefrom should be that their individual justification will make each of them a king in life.—The meaning of πολλῷ μᾶλλον, *much more,* is, as in ver. 15, purely logical : *much more certainly.* Unquestionably there is no doubt that there is a greater abundance of life in Christ than there was of death-power in Adam. But this is not what the apostle says here. He is not aiming to establish either a contrast of *quality* (between *life* and *death*) or a contrast of *quantity* (*more* of life *than* of death). It is a higher degree of *certainty* which he enunciates and demonstrates. Justified, we shall reign still *more certainly* in Christ, than as condemned we are dead in Adam. Our future glory is more certain even than our death ; for a more powerful cause, and one individually assimilated, will make us live *still more certainly* than the weak unappropriated cause could make us die.

There remains a last word which, put at the close of this rich and complicated period, has peculiar solemnity : *by the one, Jesus Christ.* Τοῦ ἑνός, *the one,* is a pronoun, and not an adjective : the only one, opposed to the other only one. The name *Jesus Christ* is in apposition : " by the one *who is* Jesus Christ.'' These final words remind us that He has been the sole instrument of the divine love, and that if the *receivers* have a righteousness to appropriate, it is solely that which He has acquired for them.

Again, at this point (vv. 15, 16) the reasoning of the apostle is amazingly bold. It is as if a justified sinner dared to find in the very power of the miserable lust which dragged him into evil, the irrefragable proof of the power which will more certainly still be exercised over him by the grace of God and of Jesus Christ, to save him and raise him to the throne.

Let us sum up this passage, unique as it is of its kind.

Ver. 15 demonstrates the *universal destination* of justification in Christ. The argument runs thus : If a cause so weak as Adam's single offence could influence a circle so vast as that of the entire *multitude* of mankind, with greater reason must a far richer cause (the double grace of God and of Jesus Christ) extend its action over *this same multitude.*—It is the *universalism of the gospel,* the εἰς πάντας, *for all* . . ., of iii. 22, proved by the very universality of death.

Vv. 16 and 17 demonstrate the full reality and quickening efficacy of the *personal application* which every beliver makes of the justification obtained by Christ. Affirmed in ver. 16, this individual efficacy is proved in ver. 17 : One single agent, serving as the instrument of a very weak cause, could bring about the death of so many individuals who had not personally taken part in his act. Consequently, and *much more certainly,* will each of those same individuals, by *personally* appropriating a force *far superior* in action to the preceding, become thereby a possessor of life.—Here is *the individualism of the gospel,* the ἐπὶ πάντας τοὺς πιστεύοντας, *upon all that believe,* of iii. 22, fully established by the very fact of their individual death in Adam.

We have thus reached the complete demonstration of these two words πάντι and τῷ (πιστεύοντι), *all* and *every* (believer), which are the essential characteristics of Paul's gospel, according to i. 16.

As the argument of vv. 12-14 was a necessary logical premiss to that of

vv. 15–17, the latter was a no less indispensable premiss for the conclusion finally drawn by the apostle, vv. 18, 19. In fact to be entitled to affirm, as he does in these two verses, the universality of justification in Christ as the counterpart of the universality of death in Adam, he must prove, first, that all men died in Adam and not through their own deed—such are the contents of vv. 12–14 ; then, that from this universal and individual death in Adam there followed *a fortiori* the certainty of the universal destination, and of the individual application of justification in Christ—such are the contents of vv. 15–17. It remains only to draw this conclusion : *all* (as to destination) and *each* (by faith) are justified in Christ (ver. 18) ; this conclusion is at the same time the second and long-delayed part of the comparison begun in ver. 12. The apostle could not state it till he had logically acquired the right to do so.

3. Vv. 18, 19

Vv. 18, 19. "*So then as by one offence there was condemnation for all men ; so also by one act of justification there was for all men justification of life. For as by one man's disobedience the many were constituted sinners ; so by the obedience of one shall the many be constituted righteous.*"—The result on the side of righteousness is at least equal to that which history attests on the side of condemnation : the apostle could make this affirmation after the previous demonstration, and at length close the parallel opened at ver. 12.—The ἄρα, *in consequence*, introduces this declaration as a conclusion from the argument which precedes, and the οὖν, *therefore*, takes up the thread of the sentence broken since ver. 12. These two particles combined thus exhaust the logical connection of this verse with all that prepared for it.

The first proposition is the summary reproduction of ver. 12. The understood verb is ἀπέβη, *issued*, here taken in an impersonal sense (*there came about, res cessit*, Mey.). Philippi takes ἑνός as a masculine pronoun : "by *one's* offence." But in that case we must take the ἑνός of the second proposition in the same sense, which, as we shall see, is impossible.—The κατάκριμα, *sentence of condemnation*, denotes the condemnation to death which has overtaken mankind, the : "Thou art dust, and to dust shalt thou return." There is no reference here to eternal condemnation (the ἀπώλεια).

The particles οὕτω and καί, *so* and *also*, refer, the one to the moral *analogy* of the two facts, the other, simply to the repetition of the two similar facts. Many commentators apply the expression : *by one act of righteousness*, δι' ἑνός δικαιώματος, to the *holy life* of Jesus, which was throughout, as it were, one great act of righteousness, or to His *expiatory death*, as the culminating point of that perfect life. The meaning of the Greek term, which Aristotle (Nicom. v. 10) defines : ἐπανόρθωμα τοῦ ἀδικήματος, *a reparation of injury*, might suit either the one or the other of these senses. They are, however, both inadmissible for the following reasons : 1. It is not natural to depart from the meaning the word has in ver. 16 ; now there it forms (in a rigorously symmetrical proposition) the antithesis of κατάκριμα, *sentence of condemnation ;* this positively determines its meaning : *sentence of justification*. 2. If this term be applied to the holy life or expiatory death of Jesus Christ, there arises a complete tautology with the second proposition of ver. 19, where ὑπακοή, *obedience*, has the very meaning which is here given to δικαίωμα. And yet the *for*, which connects the two verses, implies a logical gradation from the one to the other. 3. In Paul's terminology it is God and not Jesus Christ who is *the justifier*, viii. 33 (Θεὸς ὁ δικαιῶν). By ἓν δικαίωμα we must therefore understand a divine act. It is therefore *the one collective sentence of justification*, which in consequence of the death of Christ has been pronounced in favor of all sinners, of which, as we have seen, iv.

25, the resurrection of Jesus was at once the effect and proof. It is ever this same divine declaration which takes effect in the case of every sinner as he believes. If such is the meaning of the word δικαίωμα, the ἑνός is obviously an adjective and not a pronoun : " by *one act* of justification."— The verb to be understood is neither in the present nor the future : *there is,* or *there will be.* For the matter in question is an accomplished fact. It is therefore the past : *there was,* as in the first member.—The sentence already passed is *destined for* all men with a view to their personal justification. It is this *destination* which is expressed by the εἰς δικαίωσιν ζωῆς, *to justification of life,* exactly like the εἰς πίστιν, i. 17, and the εἰς πάντας (*for all*), iii. 22. The apostle does not say that all *shall be* individually justified ; but he declares that, in virtue of the one grand sentence which has been passed, all *may* be so, on condition of faith. The strongly active sense of the word δικαίωσις (the act of justifying) fits it peculiarly to denote the individual sentence by which the collective justification is applied to *each* believer.— The genitive ζωῆς is the genitive of effect : "the justification which produces life." By this word *life* Paul here denotes above all spiritual life (vi. 4, 11, 23), the re-establishing of holiness ; then, in the end, the restoration and glorification of the body itself (viii. 11). The word thus hints beforehand the entire contents of the following part (chap. vi.–viii.).

Ver. 19. At the first glance this verse seems to be a mere useless repetition of the foregoing. Looking at it closely, we see that, as the γάρ, *for,* indicates, it is meant to state the moral cause which gives rise to the two facts put parallel to one another in ver. 18. In fact, ver. 19*a* serves to explain 18*a*, and 19*b* to explain 18*b*. This logical relation accounts for two modifications, apparently accidental, which are introduced into the parallel expressions in ver. 19. For the simple ὡς, *as,* of ver. 18, there is substituted here ὥσπερ, which is more emphatic and precise, *for precisely as.* For the new contrast is meant to give the key to the preceding one. Then, for the antithesis of *one* offence, of *one* sentence of justification, to the notion of *universality,* (*all*), ver. 18, there is substituted the antithesis between εἰς and οἱ πολλοί, *one* and *the many.* Why the reappearance of this expression used in ver. 15, but abandoned since vv. 16 and 17 ? It is because the apostle would here ascend from historical effects to moral causes or hidden principles. Two historical facts sway the life of mankind (ver. 18) : the condemnation which kills it, and the justification which quickens it. These two great facts rest on two individual moral acts : an act of *disobedience,* and an act of *obedience.* Now in both cases the extension to *all* of the effect produced can be explained only on one condition : the possibility, namely, of the action of *one* on *many.* This second antithesis : *one* and *many,* belongs therefore to the exposition of *the cause* (ver. 19), as the first : *one act* and *all,* belong to the exposition of the historical fact (ver. 18). Hence the reason why in ver. 15, where he had to do with the antithesis between the two *causes,* the apostle had dropped the pronoun πάντες, *all,* used in ver. 12, to apply the form εἰς and οἱ πολλοί, *one* and *the many,* and why he reverts to it here, where he is ascending from the effect to the cause. New proofs of the scrupulous care with which the apostle watched over the slightest details of his writings.—This word παρακοή, *disobedience,* denotes the moral act which provoked the sentence of condemnation (ver. 18*a*). There had been in the case of Adam ἀκοή, *hearing ;* a positive prohibition had sounded in his ears. But this prohibition had been for him as it were null and non-existent (παρακοή).—The verb κατεστάθησαν, which we have translated literally by *were constituted,* signifies, when it is applied to an office : *to be established* in it (Luke xii. 14 ; Acts vii. 10, 27 ; and even Heb. v. 1) ; but when it is applied, as here, to a moral state, the question arises whether it is to be taken in the sense of *being regarded and treated as* such, or *being rendered* such. The second meaning, if I am not mistaken, is the most common in classic Greek : τινὰ εἰς ἀπορίαν καθιστάναι, *to put one into a* *state of embarrassment;* κλαίοντα καταστῆσαί τινα, *to make one weep,* etc. In the two principal examples taken from the New Testament there is room for some hesitation; Jas. iv. 4 : "Whosoever will be a friend of the world is made the enemy of God," may signify : "*is proved,* or *is rendered* the enemy" . . . The last sense is the more natural. In 2 Pet. i. 8 : "Such virtues will make you neither barren nor unfruitful," the second meaning is the more probable. It is also the meaning which the context appears to me to demand here. The apostle is explaining the moral cause of the fact stated 18*a*. The meaning : *to be regarded,* or *treated as* . . ., will only yield a tautology with the fact to be explained. The real gradation from the one verse to the other is as follows : "They were *treated* as sinners (by the sentence of death) (ver. 18) ; for they were really *made* sinners in Adam (ver. 19)." The last words of ver. 12 already involved the same idea. "They all participated mysteriously in the offence (ἐφ' ᾧ πάντες ἥμαρτον) ;" the first fact whence there resulted the inclination to sin affirmed in our ver. 19. Moreover, the διά construed with the genitive (*by*) would suffice to demonstrate the *effective* sense of the καθιστάναι, *to constitute,* in ver. 19. With the other sense, the διά with the accusative (*on account of*) would have been more suitable.[1]

With the disobedience of one there is contrasted the *obedience* of one. Some understand thereby the *expiatory sacrifice* of Jesus. But as in the Levitical *cultus* the victim required to be without blemish, so in the true expiatory sacrifice the victim required to be without sin. It is impossible, therefore, to isolate the death of Christ here from His holy life ; and the term *obedience* embraces both ; comp. Phil. ii. 8.—If the word δίκαιοι, *righteous,* denoted here a moral state, like the ἁμαρτωλοί, *sinners,* in the first proposition, the same question would be raised here as to the meaning of καθίστασθαι. But if the word *righteous* is applied, as the sense of this whole part requires, to *imputed* righteousness, then the verb naturally takes the meaning of *being constituted righteous,* though there would be nothing to hinder us from translating it, as in the first member, by : *being rendered righteous.* For as the case in question is a state obtained in a declaratory way, *being rendered* amounts to the same thing as *being constituted.* The future : *will be rendered,* or *constituted* righteous, is referred by some to the successive justification of those sinners who during the present economy come to faith ; by others, to the final declaration of the judgment day. In the passages 16*b* and 17*b* the apostle transported himself, as we have seen, to the *close* of the economy of probation. This connection decides in favor of the second meaning. The time in question is that described v. 9–11. If, then, the idea of *moral righteousness* is not that of this word *righteous,* as Dietzsch and others will have it, the fact of sanctification is nevertheless involved in the supreme absolution to which the second part of this verse refers.—The expression : *the many,* or *the multitude,* cannot have the same extension in the second member as in the first. For it is not here as in ver. 15, where the question was only of the destination of righteousness. This passage refers, as is proved by the future : *will be made righteous,* to the effectual *application.* Now, nowhere does St. Paul teach universal salvation. There are even passages in his writings which seem expressly to exclude it ; for example, 2 Thess. i. 9 ; Phil. iii. 19. On the other hand, the pronoun *the many* cannot denote a simple *plurality* (the majority) ; for, as we have seen in vv. 15 and 19*a*, the article οἱ, *the*, implies a *totality.* The totality must therefore be restricted to those whom, ver. 17, Paul called *the accepters,* οἱ λαμβάνοντες, and of whom he said : *they shall reign in life.* This future : *shall reign,* is in close connection with the

---

[1] A better sense is that of "setting down in a class or under a category." This can be carried through all the passages. "Constituted," not by a causative, but by a declarative act of God.—T. W. C.

future : *will be made*, in our verse ; for the declaration of righteousness (ver. 19) is the condition of reigning in life (ver. 17).

We cannot hold, with the school of Baur, that this parallel between Adam and Christ was inspired by a polemical intention in opposition to a legal Jewish-Christianity. But it is nevertheless evident that in so vast a survey of the principal phases of the religious development of mankind, a place, however small, could not fail to be granted to the Mosaic institution. The part of the *law* is therefore briefly indicated ver. 20 ; ver. 21 is the general conclusion.

4. Vv. 20, 21

Vv. 20, 21. "*Now the law was added, that the offence might abound. But where sin abounded, grace superabounded more: that as sin hath reigned unto death, even so might grace reign through righteousness unto eternal life by Jesus Christ our Lord.*"—Νόμος (the) *law*, undoubtedly denotes the Mosaic law ; but as positive law in general (regard being had to the absence of the article), we might almost translate : *a law.*—The Jews attributed a particularly important part to this institution in the history of mankind ; they claim to make it the means of education and salvation of the whole world (ii. 17-20). Paul shows that it plays only a secondary part. It was *added* during the era of sin and death to prepare for the era of justification and life. It is from want of a more exactly corresponding term that we translate παρεισῆλθεν by *was added*. It should be : *came alongside of*. Compounded of the word εἰσέρχεσθαι, *to enter*, to appear on the stage (ver. 12), and the preposition παρά, *by the side of*, it applies to an actor who does not occupy the front of the stage, and who appears there only to play an *accessory* part. It is a mistake, therefore, to ascribe to this verb the notion attached to it by the *Vulgate*, when it translates *subintravit, came in*, as it were *stealthily*, a meaning which, besides, is incompatible with the solemn promulgation of the law. Calvin finds in this verb the notion of an *intermediate* which took its place *between* Adam and Christ, and Chrysostom, that of a *passing* appearance. But παρά signifies neither *between* nor *in passing*. The true meaning of the word is : *by the side of*, and this is also the meaning which best suits the passage. The Mosaic economy was, as it were, a *side* economy, an institution parallel to the economy of sin ; as Philippi says, "it is a particular economy by the side of the great general economy." It might be compared to a canal flowing by the side of the river which feeds it.—And why this special economy ? *That the offence might abound*. If, instead of the word παράπτωμα, *offence, fall*, the apostle had said παράβασις, *transgression*, the thought would be easily understood. For he has himself said (iv. 15) : "Where no law is, there is no transgression ;" that is to say, in that case sin does not present itself as the violation of a positive command. The sense would consequently be this : The law was given to Israel that in this particular field of fallen humanity sin might take a graver and more pronounced character; that of *transgression*, and so manifest completely its malign nature ; a process which should be the means of its cure. But this sense would require the use of the term παράβασις (*transgression*). The term chosen : παράπτωμα, *offence*, has a wider meaning (see on ver. 15). The word, indeed, denotes every *particular act of sin* committed under the law or without the law. This meaning is, on the other hand, more restricted than that of the word ἁμαρτία, *sin*, which comprehends, besides, the external acts, the corrupt *inward disposition*. The apostle therefore did not mean to say that the law was given to increase *sin* itself. Not only would the word ἁμαρτία have been required in this sense, but this thought would also be incompatible with divine holiness. Neither do I think the expression can be explained exactly by the passage, Rom. vii. 10–13, which refers to the use made of the law by *sin ;*

while Paul is here speaking of its providential object. The meaning rather is: that the law by multiplying prescriptions also gives rise to much more frequent occasions of offence. Now, each of these particular offences requiring to be expiated either by a sacrifice or a penalty, human guilt is thus more clearly manifested, and condemnation (apart from the intervention of grace) better founded. Man does not thereby necessarily become worse than he was; he only shows what he is already. Yet, if we went no further, we should still fail to apprehend the full thought of the apostle. Throughout the whole of this passage (vv. 15, 17, 18) the term τὸ παράπτωμα, *the offence*, has a sort of technical meaning: *the offence of Adam*. Is it not natural to take the word here in this definite acceptation? The meaning is therefore as follows: By the law it has come about that the offence of the first man has multiplied, or in a sense reproduced itself among his descendants in a multitude of particular acts of sin, like a seed which reappears in a harvest of fruits like itself. Those acts of sin are *the offences of many*, spoken of in ver. 16, and which are the object of individual justification. And the end of the law in making the manifestation of sin abound in Israel in this concrete form was to prove the inward malady, and to pave the way for its cure. How? The sequel will explain.—In connection with what precedes, the οὗ (δέ) (*but*) *where*, cannot have the general meaning of *wherever* . . ., as if the saying which follows were a maxim of universal application. The connection between the first and second part of the verse requires that the word *where* be taken in a strictly local and limited sense: *where*, that is to say, in the domain where the law has done its work, and made the offence abound in Israel. Against this view, Meyer urges the general character of the whole passage, and especially that of ver. 21, and, like Schott and many others, he refers the words: *where* . . ., to the whole world. This objection ignores the fact stated in ver. 21, that the experiment made in Israel was intended to profit the whole world. As to the *temporal* meaning given to the word *where* by Grotius, De Wette, etc., *at the time when*, it would suit the idea perhaps. But this use of οὗ is without example in the New Testament, and cannot even be demonstrated with certainty in the classics (ἀφ' οὗ is different). The sense is therefore that given by Abélard in the words: *in eodem populo quo* . . .—As the law gave more frequent occasion in Israel of proving individual guiltiness, by that very means it gave occasion to grace to manifest itself in a manner more abundant and extraordinary (ii. 4). Among the manifestations of mercy referred to by these last words of our verse: *grace superabounded*, we cannot but suppose that the apostle places foremost the great expiatory act on which all the sins of Israel converged (Heb. ix. 15). As in the expression: *sin abounded*, he naturally thinks of the greatest crime of the Jewish people, that in which was concentrated their whole spirit of revolt, the murder of their Messiah, their deicide, the catastrophe of their history; so in the following words there is presented to the rapt view of the apostle the advantage which divine mercy has taken of this crime, by making it immediately the instrument of salvation for Israel themselves and all mankind. The word *where* might thus receive a yet stricter application than that which we have been giving to it till now. Golgotha, that theatre where human sin displayed itself as nowhere else, was at the same time the place of the most extraordinary manifestation of divine grace. The term ὑπερεπερίσσευσε, *superabounded over*, is explained by Hofmann in the sense of: *grace abounded beyond itself*; it, as it were, surpassed itself. This meaning is far-fetched. It would be better to refer the ὑπέρ, *over*, to the sin which was, as it were, submerged under this flood of pardon. But if Paul had meant to state this relation, he would certainly have repeated the same verb as he had just used in speaking of sin. It seems most natural to me to take this ὑπέρ, *over*, as expressing the superlative of the verbal idea: Grace overflowed beyond all measure, to infinity. Philippi accurately observes that πλέον in πλεονάζειν is a comparative (*the more*) : while ὑπέρ (in ὑπερπερισσεύειν) expresses not only a *more*, but a superlative of abundance.

Ver. 21. This verse declares the *universal* end of this divine dispensation which seemed at first to concern only Israel. Paul thus returns to the general idea of the entire passage. The *that*, as well as perhaps the ὑπέρ in the verb of the preceding sentence, implies that what was passing in Israel contemplated the establishment of a reign of grace capable of equalling and surpassing in mankind generally the reign of sin founded in Adam. This is what the legal dispensation could never effect. Far from bringing into the world the grace of justification, the law taken in itself made the offence and condemnation abound. The passage, Gal. iii. 13 and 14, is also intended to point out the relation between the curse *of the Jewish law*, borne by the Messiah, and the gift of grace made *to the Gentiles*. This superabounding of pardon brought to bear on this superabounding of sin in the midst of the Jewish people, had therefore for its *end* (ἵνα, *that*) to display grace in such a way as to assure its triumph over the reign of sin throughout the whole earth, and to replace one economy by another.—Ὥσπερ, *absolutely as*. The work of grace must not remain, either in extent or efficacy, behind that of sin.—The words ἐν τῷ θανάτῳ, *in death*, remind us that the reign of sin is present ; it manifests itself, wraps, as it were, and embodies itself *in* the palpable fact of *death*. The meaning : *by* death, would not give any clear idea. Far from sin reigning by death, it is death, on the contrary, which reigns by sin.—The antithesis to the words *in death* is distributed between the two terms : *through righteousness*, and *to life*. The first has no reference whatever, as one whole class of exegetes would have it, to *moral* righteousness ; for in this case its meaning would trench upon that of the following term. The word denotes, as in this whole part, of which it contains the summary, the righteousness freely granted by God to faith. Hence the apostle says : "that grace may reign through righteousness." It is in fact by free justification that grace establishes its reign.—The *end* of justification is *life*; εἰς, *unto*, is opposed to "*in* death," as the future is to the present. But this word *eternal life* does not refer merely to future *glory*. It comprehends the holiness which from this time forward should flow from the state of justification (comp. vi. 4, 11, 23). If the word *through righteousness* sums up the whole part of the Epistle now finished, the words : *unto eternal life*, are the theme of the whole part which is now to begin (vi–viii). —The last words : *by Jesus Christ our Lord*, are the final echo of the comparison which formed the subject of this passage. We understand the object of this piece : By the collective and individual fact of death in one, Paul meant to demonstrate the reality of universal and individual justification in one—universal as to destination, individual through its application to each believer. And now—so this last word seems to say—Adam has passed away ; Christ alone remains.

Adam and Christ.—It is to be borne in mind, if we are not to ascribe to the apostle ideas which nothing in the doctrine of this passage justifies, that the consequences which he deduces from our solidarity with Adam belong to a wholly different sphere from those which flow, according to him, from our solidarity with Christ. We are bound to Adam by the fact of *birth*. Every man appears here below in some sort as a fraction of that first man in whom the entire species was personified. Adam, to use the expression of the jurist Stahl, is "*the substance* of natural humanity ;" and as the birth by which we emanate from him is a fact outside of consciousness, and independent of our personal will, all that passes in the domain of this natural existence can have no other than an educational, provisional, and temporary character. So, too, *the death* of which St. Paul speaks in this whole passage is, as we have seen, not eternal damnation, but death in the ordinary sense of the word. Sin itself, and the proclivity to evil which attached to us as children of Adam, as well as the individual faults which we may commit in this state, place us no doubt in a critical position, but are not yet the cause of final perdition.[1] These facts only constitute that imperative need of salvation which is inherent in every human soul, and to anticipate which divine grace advances with love. But on reaching the threshold of this superior domain, we find ourselves face to face with a new and wholly different solidarity, which is offered to us in Christ. It is not contracted by a natural and unconscious bond, but by the free and deliberate act of *faith*. And it is here only, on the threshold of the domain of this new life, that the questions relative to the eternal lot of the individual are raised and decided. To use again the words of the writer whom we just quoted: " Christ is the *divine idea* of humanity ;" He is this idea perfectly realized. The first humanity created in Adam, with the characteristic of *freedom* of choice, was only the outline of humanity as finally purposed by God, the characteristic of which, as of God Himself, is *holiness*. The man who by faith draws his righteousness and life from the new Head of humanity is gradually raised to His level, or, as St. Paul says, to His *perfect stature;* this is *life eternal*. But the man who refuses to contract this bond of solidarity with the second Adam, remains for that very reason in his corrupt nature: he *becomes* answerable for it because he has refused to exchange it for the new one which was offered him, while he is at the same time responsible for the voluntary transgressions added by him to that of his first father ; and, corrupting himself more and more by his lusts, he moves onward through his own fault to eternal perdition, to the *second death*.

We have reached the close of the fundamental part of the treatise which forms the body of the Epistle. In the first section Paul had demonstrated universal condemnation. In the second, he had expounded universal justification obtained by Christ and offered to faith. The third section has furnished the demonstration of the fact of the condemnation of all in one, rendered indubitable by the reign of death, and proceeding, in the way of an *a fortiori* argument, to establish the fact of the justification of all in one. The question now arises, whether the mode of justification thus expounded and demonstrated can secure the moral renewal of mankind, and explain the theocratic history of which it is the consummation. Such is the subject of the two following parts.

[1] Surely this is a very careless use of words. If sin is not the cause of final perdition, what then is the cause ?—T. W. C.

SUPPLEMENTARY PART 1

6:1-8:39

SANCTIFICATION

By faith in the expiatory sacrifice of Jesus Christ the believer has obtained a sentence of justification, in virtue of which he stands reconciled to God. Can anything more be needed for his salvation? It seems not. The didactic treatise, intended to expound salvation, seems thus to have reached its close. Why then a new part?

The attentive reader will not have forgotten that in the first part of chap. v. the apostle directed our attention to a day of *wrath*, the day of the judgment to come, and that he dealt with the question by anticipation, whether the justification now acquired would hold good in that final and decisive hour. To settle this question, he brought in a means of salvation of which he had not yet spoken: participation in the *life of Christ;* and it was on this fact, announced beforehand (v. 9, 10), that he based the assurance of the validity of our justification even in the day of supreme trial. When uttering those words, Paul marked out in advance the new domain on which he enters from this time forward, that of *sanctification*.

To treat this matter is not to pass beyond the limits traced in the outset by the general thesis expressed i. 17: "The just shall live by faith." For in the expression *shall live*, ζήσεται, there is comprehended not only the grace of *righteousness*, but also that of the new life, or of *holiness*. To live is not merely to regain peace with God through justification; it is to dwell in the light of His holiness, and to act in permanent communion with Him. In the cure of the soul, pardon is only the crisis of convalescence; the restoration of health is sanctification. Holiness is true life.

What is the exact relation between these two divine blessings which constitute salvation in its real nature: justification and holiness? To put this question is at the same time to inquire into the true relation between the following part, chaps. vi.-viii., and the portion of the Epistle already studied. The understanding of this central point is the key to the Epistle to the Romans, and even to the whole Gospel.

1. In the view of many, the relation between these two blessings of grace ought to be expressed by a *but*. "No doubt you are justified by faith; *but* beware, see that you break with the sin which has been forgiven you; apply yourselves to holiness; if not, you shall fall into condemnation again." This somewhat prevalent conception of the relation between justification and sanctification seems to us to find instinctive expression in the words of Th. Schott: "Here we enter upon the domain of the *preservation* of salvation." According to this view, salvation consists essentially of justification, and sanctification appears solely as the condition of not losing it.

2. Other expositors make what follows, in relation to what precedes, a *therefore*, if one may so speak: "You are justified freely; *therefore*, impelled by faith and gratitude, engage yourselves now to renounce evil, and do what is well-pleasing to God." This mode of understanding the relation between justification and holiness is probably that followed by most of the readers of our Epistle at the present day.

3. According to others, Reuss and Sabatier for example, the connection sought would require to be expressed by a *for*, or *in fact:* If faith justifies you, as I have just shown, it is because *in fact*, by the mystical and personal union which it establishes between Christ and us, it alone has the power to sanctify us. The gift of pardon flows, on this view, from that of holiness and not the reverse ; or, to speak the truth, these blessings of grace are confounded with one another. "Paul knows nothing," says Sabatier expressly, "of the subtle distinction which has given rise to so many disputes between *declaring righteous* and *making righteous, justum dicere* and *justum facere.*"[1] So thought also Professor Beck of Tübingen. This is the opinion which was elevated by the Council of Trent to the rank of a *dogma* in the Catholic Church.

4. Finally, in these last days a bold thinker, M. Lüdemann,[2] has explained the connection sought after a wholly new fashion. The appropriate form for expressing the connection is, according to him : *or rather.* This author will have it that the first four chapters of our Epistle expound a wholly *juridical* theory of justification, of purely Jewish origin, and not yet expressing the real view of the apostle. It is a simple accommodation by which he seeks to gain his Judeo-Christian readers. His true theory is of Hellenic origin ; it is distinguished from the first by its truly *moral* character. It is the one which is expounded chaps. v.-viii. Sin no longer appears as an *offence* to be effaced by an arbitrary pardon ; it is an objective *power* which can only be broken by the personal union of the believer with Christ dead and risen. By the second theory, therefore, Paul rectifies and even retracts the first. The notion of justification is suppressed, as in the preceding view, at least from the standpoint of Paul himself ; all that God has to do to save us is to sanctify us.

We do not think that any of these four solutions exactly reproduces the apostolic view ; the two last even contradict it flatly.

1. Sanctification is more and better than a restrictive and purely negative *condition* of the maintenance of the state of justification once acquired. It is a new state into which it is needful to penetrate and advance, in order thus to gain the complete salvation. One may see, x. 10, how the apostle distinguished precisely between the two notions of *justification* and *salvation.*

2. Neither is it altogether exact to represent sanctification as *a consequence* to be drawn from justification. The connection between the two facts is still more intimate. Holiness is not an obligation which the believer deduces from his faith ; it is a fact implied in justification itself, or rather one which proceeds, as well as justification, from *the object* of justifying faith, that is, Christ dead and risen. The believer appropriates this Christ as his *righteousness* first, and then as his *holiness* (1 Cor. i. 30). The bond of union which connects these two graces is not therefore logical or subjective ; it is so profoundly impressed on the believer's heart only because it has an anterior reality in the very person of Christ, whose holiness, while serving to justify us, is at the same time the principle of our sanctification. Reuss justly observes in this relation, that from the apostle's point of view, we have not to say to the Christian : " Thou shalt sin no more ;" but we must rather say : "The Christian sins no more."

3. As to the third view, which finds in sanctification *the efficient cause* of pardon and justification, it is the antipodes of Paul's view. Why, if he had understood the relation between the two in this way, would he not have commenced his didactic treatise with the part relating to sanctification (vi.-viii.), instead of laying as its foundation the exposition of justification (i.-v.) ? Besides, is not the *then* (vi. 1) : " What shall we say *then ?*" enough to show the contradiction between this view and the apostle's con-

---

[1] *L'apôtre Paul*, p. 220.   [2] *Die Anthropologie des Apostels Paulus*, 1872.

ception? He must have said: "*For* (or *in fact*) what shall we say?" Finally, is it not evident that the whole deduction of chap. vi. assumes that of chap. iii., and not the reverse? If the opinion which the works of Reuss have contributed to accredit in the Church of France were well founded, we must acknowledge the justness of the charge which this writer brings against the apostle of "not having followed a rigorously logical course, a really systematic order."[1] But it is a hundred to one when a reader does not find the Apostle Paul logical, that he is not understanding his thought; and this is certainly the case with the critic whom we are combating. The apostle knew the human heart too well to think of founding faith in reconciliation on the moral labors of man. We need to be set free from ourselves, not to be thrown back on ourselves. If we had to rest the assurance of our justification, little or much, on our own sanctification, since this is always imperfect, our heart would never be wholly made free Godward, absolutely set at large and penetrated with that filial confidence which is itself the necessary condition of all true moral progress. The normal attitude Godward is therefore this: first *rest* in God through justification; thereafter, *work* with Him, in His fellowship, or sanctification. The opinion before us, by reversing this relation, puts, to use the common expression, the cart before the horse. It can only issue in replacing the church under the law, or in freeing it in a manner far from salutary, by setting before it a degraded standard of Christian holiness.

4. The fourth view, while equally at variance with the doctrine of the gospel, compromises, besides, the loyalty of the apostle's character. Who can persuade himself, when reading seriously the first part of the Epistle relating to justification by faith, that all he demonstrates there with so much pains, and even with so great an expenditure of biblical proofs (iii. and iv.), is a view which he does not adopt himself, and which he proposes afterward to set aside, to substitute in its room one wholly different? To what category morally are we to assign this process of substitution presented (vi. 1) in the deceptive form of a *conclusion* (*then*) and so ably disguised that the first who discovers it turns out to be a professor of the nineteenth century? Or perhaps the apostle himself did not suspect the difference between the two orders of thought, Jewish and Greek, to which he yielded his mind at one and the same time? The antagonism of the two theories perhaps so thoroughly escaped him that he could, without suspecting it, retract the one while establishing the other. Such a confusion of ideas cannot be attributed to the man who conceived and composed an "Epistle to the Romans."

Sanctification, therefore, is neither a *condition* nor a *corollary* of justification: nor is it its *cause*, and still less its *negation*. The real connection between justification and Christian holiness, as conceived by St. Paul, appears to us to be this: justification by faith is the *means*, and sanctification the *end*. The more precisely we distinguish these two divine gifts, the better we apprehend the real bond which unites them. God is *the only good;* the creature, therefore, cannot do good except *in Him*. Consequently, to put man into a condition to sanctify himself, it is necessary to begin by reconciling him to God, and replacing him in Him. For this purpose, the wall which separates him from God, the divine condemnation which is due to him as a sinner, must be broken down. This obstacle once removed by justification, and reconciliation accomplished, the heart of man opens without reserve to the divine favor which is restored to him; and, on the other hand, the communication of it from above, interrupted by the state of condemnation, resumes its course. The Holy Spirit, whom God could not bestow on a being at war with Him, comes to seal on his heart the new relation established on justification, and to do the work of a real and free

---

[1] *Les Epîtres pauliniennes*, t. II. p. 14, and *Gesch. der Neu-Testam. Schr.* § 108.

inward sanctification. Such was the end which God had in view from the first; for holiness is salvation in its very essence. Justification is to be regarded as the *strait gate*, through which we enter on the *narrow way* of sanctification, which leads to glory.

And now the profound connection between the two parts of the Epistle, and more especially between the two chaps. v. and vi., becomes manifest. It may be expressed thus: Even as we are not *justified* each *by* himself, but all *by one, by Jesus Christ our Lord* (comp. v. 11, 17, 21); so neither are we *sanctified* each *in* himself, but all *in one, in Jesus Christ our Lord* (vi. 23, viii. 39).

The *course of thought* in the following part is this: In the first section the apostle unfolds the new principle of sanctification contained in the very object of justifying faith, Jesus Christ, and shows the consequences of this principle, both as to sin and as to law (vi. 1–vii. 6).

In the second, he casts a glance backward, in order to compare the action of this new principle with the action of the old, the law (vii. 7–25).

In the third, he points to the Holy Spirit as the divine agent who causes the new principle, or the life of Christ, to penetrate the life of the believer, and who by transforming him fits him to enjoy the future glory, and to realize at length his eternal destiny (viii. 1–39).

In three words, then: holiness *in Christ* (vi.–vii. 6), *without law* (vii. 7–25), *by the Holy Spirit* (viii. 1–39). The great contrast on which the thought of the apostle moves here is not, as in the previous part, that between *wrath* and *justification;* but the contrast between *sin* and *holiness.* For the matter in question is no longer to efface sin, as *guilt*, but to overcome it as a *power* or disease.

The apostle was necessarily led to this discussion by the development of his original theme. A new religious conception, which offers itself to man with the claim of conducting him to his high destiny, cannot dispense with the demonstration that it possesses the force necessary to secure his moral life. To explain this part, therefore, it is not necessary to assume a *polemic* or *apologetic* intention in relation to a so-called Jewish-Christianity reigning in the Church of Rome (Mangold), or to some Jewish-Christian influence which had begun to work there (Weizsäcker). If Paul here compares the moral effects of the gospel (chap. vi.) with those of the law (vii.), it is because he is positively and necessarily under obligation to demonstrate the right of the former to replace the latter in the moral direction of mankind. It is with Judaism, as a preparatory revelation, that he has to do, not with Jewish-Christianity, as in the Epistle to the Galatians. Here his point of view is vastly wider. As he had discussed (chap. iii.) the question of the value of the law in relation to *justification*, he could not but take up the same subject again in connection with the work of sanctification (vii.). Besides, the tone of chap. vi. is essentially *didactic;* the *polemical* tendency does not come out till chap. vii., to give place again in viii. to positive teaching, without the slightest trace of an apologetic or polemic intention.

It is equally plain how palpably erroneous is the view of those who would make the idea of *Christian universalism* the subject of the whole Epistle, and the principle of his plan and method.[1] The contrast between universalism and particularism has not the slightest place in this part, which would thus be in this exposition wholly beside the subject.

How bold was the apostle's undertaking, to found the moral life of mankind on a purely spiritual basis, without the smallest atom of legal element! Even to this hour, after eighteen centuries, how many excellent spirits hesitate to welcome such an experiment! But Paul had had a convincing personal experience, on the one hand, of the powerlessness of the law to

---

[1] If we are rightly informed, this was the idea of the venerated and lamented Professor Beck in his courses on this Epistle.

sanctify as well as to justify; and, on the other, of the entire sufficiency of the gospel to accomplish both tasks. This experience he expounds under the guidance of the Spirit, while generalizing it. Hence the personal turn which his exposition takes here in particular (comp. vii. 7–viii. 2).

FIRST SECTION (6:1-7:6)

THE PRINCIPLE OF SANCTIFICATION CONTAINED IN JUSTIFICATION BY FAITH

This entire section is intended to lay the foundations of Christian sanctification. It includes three portions.

The first (vi. 1–14) unfolds the *new principle* of sanctification in the very object of justifying faith.

The second (vi. 15–23) exhibits the intrinsic *power* possessed by this principle, both to free the believer from sin, and to subject him to righteousness.

In the third (vii. 1–6), Paul infers from this double fact the right henceforth possessed by the believer to renounce the use of the former means, the law. The new morality is thus solidly established.

THIRTEENTH PASSAGE (6:1-14)

Sanctification in Christ dead and risen

The apostle introduces this subject by an *objection* which he makes to his own teaching, ver. 1; he gives it a *summary answer*, ver. 2, and *justifies* this answer by appealing to a known and tangible fact, namely baptism, vv. 3 and 4. Then he gives a complete and didactic exposition of the contents of his answer, vv. 5–11. Finally he applies it to the practical life of his readers, vv. 12–14.

Ver. 1. "*What shall we say then? Should we continue*[1] *in sin, that grace may abound?*"—The meaning of this question: *What shall we say then?* can only be this: What consequence shall we draw from the preceding? Only the apostle's object is not to draw a true consequence from the previous teaching, but merely to reject a false conclusion which might be deduced by a man still a stranger to the experience of justifying faith. It need not therefore be concluded from this *then* that the apostle is now passing from the principle to its consequences. In that case he would have said directly: "Shall we then continue" . . . ?—This question is usually connected with the declaration, v. 20: "Where sin abounded, grace did much more abound." But this saying referred solely to the part played by the law in the midst of the Jewish people, while the question here put is of universal application. We should rather be inclined to hold that Paul was alluding to the saying, v. 16. There, he had pointed to all the offences committed by the many sinners, terminating through the act of grace in a sentence of universal justification; and he may well, consequently, ask himself, in the name of those who do not believe in such a divine act, whether believers will not abuse it in the line of the question proposed. But even this connection would still be too narrow. If account is taken of the meaning of the whole previous part,

---

[1] T. R., with some Mnn., only: επιμενουμεν; A B C D E F G L: επιμενωμεν; ℵ K P: επι μενομεν.

236 / Sanctification

and of the calumnious accusation already expressed iii. 8, it will rather be concluded that the question bears on the whole doctrine of justification by grace, chaps. i–v. As to believers justified in the way described above, it is evident that they will never put this alternative: Shall I sin or shall I not sin? For the seal of holiness has already been impressed on their inner and outer life by the manner of their justification. This is what the apostle proceeds to show while answering the objection suggested.

The reading of the T. R., ἐπιμενοῦμεν, *shall we continue?* has no critical authority; it probably arises from the preceding ἐροῦμεν. The reading of the *Sinait.* and of two Byz., ἐπιμένομεν, *let us continue!* or *we continue*, expressing either an exhortation or a resolution, would make believers hold a language far too improbable. That of the Alex. and of the Greco-Lats., ἐπιμένωμεν, *that we should continue!* or *should we continue?* is the only admissible one. Hofmann takes it in the first of these two senses as a mutual exhortation, and with this view supplies a new: *Shall we say?* understood before the second question. But this invitation to sin, which believers would thus be made to address to one another, is too improbable a supposition; and the ellipsis of the verb: *Shall we say?* is arbitrary and superfluous. The second of the two meanings of ἐπιμένωμεν, *should we continue?* (the deliberative conjugation), is the only natural one: Should we take the resolution of continuing in our old state of sin? The following conjunction: *that*, corresponds well with this deliberative meaning. It is a calculation: the more sins committed, the more material will grace find on which to display itself.—'Ἐπιμένειν, *to continue, persevere*, in a state to which a decisive circumstance ought to have put an end.—The reply is forcible and summary. A fact has taken place which renders this calculation absolutely impossible.

Ver. 2. "*Let it not be so! We who are dead to sin, how shall we live* [1] *any longer therein?*"—Just as a dead man does not revive and resume his former occupations, as little can the believer return to his old life of sin; for in his case also there has been a *death*.—The phrase μὴ γένοιτο, *let it not be so!* expresses the revolting character of the rejected assertion, as well as a conviction of its falsehood.—The pronoun οἵτινες is the relative of quality: *people such as we*. We have a quality which excludes such a calculation: that of beings who have passed through death. To what fact does the phrase relate: *we are dead*, literally, *we have died?* It is obvious at a glance that there can be no reference here to the condemnation which came upon us in Adam ("dead *through* sin"). It is difficult to understand how the Swiss version could have committed such an error. All that follows (the being buried with Christ, ver. 3; participation in His death and resurrection with Him, vv. 4—8; and especially the expression: *dead unto sin, alive unto God*, ver. 11) leaves no doubt as to the apostle's thought. The clause τῇ ἁμαρτίᾳ, *to sin*, is the dative of relation; comp. the expressions: *to die to the law*, vii. 4, Gal. ii. 19; *to be crucified to the world*, Gal. vi. 14. The words therefore denote the absolute breaking with sin. It is the opposite of *persevering in sin*, ver. 1.—This figure of *dying* is generally applied to baptism. But we shall see that baptism is the consequence of the death spoken of by Paul in ver. 2, not that death itself. What proves it, is first the οὖν, *therefore*, of ver. 4, then the ἐθανατώθητε, *ye were put to death*, vii. 4—an expression which, accompanied with the words: *through the body of Christ*, sets aside every attempt to identify the death undergone by believers with their baptism. The fact in the mind of the apostle is of a purely moral nature. It is the appropriation of our Lord's expiatory death. The sentence of death with which God visited the sin of the world in Christ is reproduced in the conscience of every sinner. The instant he applies the expiation to himself, it becomes in him the sentence of death

---

[1] C F G L: ζήσωμεν (*should we live?*) instead of ζήσομεν (*shall we live?*).

on his own sin. He could not appropriate Christ to himself as dead *for* his sin, without finding himself die, through this death undergone for him, *to* sin itself. It was under this impression that the believing Bechuana exclaimed : "The cross of Christ condemns me to be holy."

The *righteousness of God*, in pronouncing this sentence of death on the sin of the world, the *consciousness of Jesus* in accepting and submitting to this sentence in the tortures of the cross and the agonies of His abandonment by God, and in ratifying it with a humble submission in the name of humanity which He represented, have thus smitten sin in the consciousness of every believer with a mortal blow. Such is the unparalleled moral fact which has put an end to the former life of the world in general, and which puts an end to the life of sin in every individual believer. And this result is so thoroughly implied in that of justifying faith, that Paul appeals to it in our passage as a fact already known by his readers (comp. chaps. i.-v.), and understood as a matter of course.

On the meaning of the expression: To die unto sin.—We find ourselves here met by four interpretations, which seem to us more or less false, and which it is well to set aside.

1. Many find in this and the relative expressions in the following verses nothing more than simple figures, metaphors signifying merely the duty of imitating the example of virtue which Christ has left us. Even Ritschl declares (II. p. 225) that "this reasoning of the apostle makes rather too strong an appeal to the powers of imagination." But we think we have just demonstrated the grave moral reality of the relation by which Christ brings the believer into the fellowship of His death. We shall see immediately the not less grave reality of the relation through which He communicates to him His own heavenly life, and thus makes him a risen one. The death and resurrection of Jesus are metaphors, not of rhetoric, but of action ; it is divine eloquence.

2. R. Schmidt[1] regards the death to sin of which Paul speaks as of a purely *ideal* nature, and as exercising no immediate influence whatever on the moral state of believers. The apostle simply means, according to him, that to the divine mind they appear as dead in Christ. He would have it that participation in the life of the Risen One is the only real fact, according to the apostle. But we do not find Paul making such a distinction in the sequel. He regards participation in the death of Christ as being as real, and even more so (for he puts it in the past. vv. 4, 6, 8) ; and fellowship in His life, which is represented as a future to be realized (vv. 4, 8) ; and in ver. 11 he puts the two facts exactly on the same footing.

3. Death to sin is regarded by most commentators as expressing figuratively the act of will by which the believer undertakes for himself, and promises to God, on the blood of reconciliation, henceforth to renounce evil. This would make it an inward resolution, a voluntary engagement, a consecration of the heart. But St. Paul seems to speak of something more profound and stable, "which not only *ought to be*, but *which is*" (as Gess says). This appears clearly from the passive form : *ye have been put to death*, vii. 4 ; this expression proves that Paul is thinking above all of a divine act which has passed on us in the person of another (*by the body of Christ*), but which has its counterpart within us from the moment we appropriate it by faith. It is not, then, an *act* merely which is in question, but a *state* of will determined by a fact performed without us, a state from which our will cannot withdraw itself from the time that our being is swayed by the power of faith in the death of Christ for us.

4. It was attempted, in the religious movement which stirred the church so deeply a few years ago, to represent the effect produced on the believer by the death of Christ as a fact achieved in us once for all, existing in us henceforth after the manner almost of a physical state, and as outside of the will itself. From this point of view men spoke daringly of a *death of sin*, as if this were identical with Paul's expression : *death to sin*. We appreciate the intention of those who promoted this style of teaching ; their wish was to bring back the

---

[1] *Paulinische Christologie*, p. 66 et seq.

church to the true source and the full reality of Christian sanctification. But they committed, if we mistake not, a grave and dangerous exaggeration. This *mirage* of an absolute deliverance, which had been reflected on the eyes of so many souls thirsting for holiness, soon vanishing before the touch of experience, left in them a painful disappointment and even a sort of despair. The death to sin of which the apostle speaks is a *state* no doubt, but a state *of the will*, which continues only so long as it keeps itself under the control of the fact which produced it, and produces it constantly—the death of Jesus. As at every moment Jesus could have withdrawn Himself from death by an act of His own will (Matt. xxvi. 53), so the believer may at any moment free his will from the power of faith, and take up the thread of that natural life which is never completely destroyed in him.

If it were otherwise, if ever the believer could enter into the sphere of absolute holiness, a new fall, like that of Adam, would be needed to remove him from it. If ever sin were entirely extirpated from his heart, its reappearance would be something like the resurrection of a dead man. At what point, besides, of the Christian life would such a moral event be placed? At the time of conversion? The experience of all believers proves the contrary. At some later period? The New Testament teaches us nothing of the kind. There is found in it no particular name for a second transformation, that of the convert into a perfect saint.

We conclude by saying that death to sin is not an absolute cessation of sin at any moment whatever, but an absolute breaking of the will with it, with its instincts and aspirations, and that simply under the control of faith in Christ's death *for* sin.

The practical application of the apostle's doctrine regarding this mysterious death, which is at the foundation of Christian sanctification, seems to me to be this : The Christian's breaking with sin is undoubtedly gradual in its realization, but absolute and conclusive in its principle. As, in order to break really with an old friend whose evil influence is felt, half measures are insufficient, and the only efficacious means is a frank explanation, followed by a complete rupture which remains like a barrier raised beforehand against every new solicitation ; so to break with sin there is needed a decisive and radical act, a divine deed taking possession of the soul, and interposing henceforth between the will of the believer and sin (Gal. vi. 14). This divine deed necessarily works through the action of faith in the sacrifice of Christ.

Ver. 3. " *Or know ye not, that so many of us as were baptized into Jesus Christ*[1] *were baptized into His death ?*"—The ἤ, *or*, or indeed, ought, according to the usual meaning of the phrase : *or know ye not*, to be paraphrased thus : Or, *if you do not understand what I have just said* (that there has been among you a death to sin), know you not then what was signified by the baptism which ye received ? If you understood that rite, you would know that it *supposes* a death, and *promises* a second birth, which removes every possibility of a return to the old life. It has been generally concluded, from this mode of expression : *Or know ye not* . . . ? that baptism was represented as being itself the death spoken of by St. Paul in ver. 2. I believe it is thereby made impossible to explain satisfactorily the whole of the following passage, especially the words : " *Therefore* we are buried with Him by baptism into His death." According to these words, it is not to death, it is to the *interment of the dead*, that Paul compares baptism. And, indeed, just as the ceremony of interment, as a visible and public fact, attests death, so baptism, in so far as it is an outward and sensible act, attests faith, with the death to sin implicitly included in faith. As to the phrase : *Or know ye not ?* it finds a still more natural explanation if baptism is regarded as the *proof* of death, than if, as is constantly done, to the detriment of the sense of this beautiful passage, baptism is identified with it. St. Paul means : " Ye know not that ye are dead . . . ? Well

---

[1] B and some Mnn. and Fathers reject Ἰησουν.

then, ye are ignorant that as many of you as there are, are men *interred* (baptized)! People do not bury the living." The ὅσοι, a pronoun of quantity: *as many individuals as*, differs from the pronoun of quality οἵτινες, *a kind of people who*. The point in question here is not, as in ver. 2, one of quality, but of quantity: "Ye know not then that as many baptized (buried) persons as there are, so many dead are there."—Some take the word *baptize* in its literal sense of *bathing, plunging*, and understand: "As many of you as were *plunged into Christ*." But in the similar formula, 1 Cor. x. 2: "*to be baptized into Moses* (εἰς τὸν Μωσῆν βαπτίζεσθαι)," the meaning is certainly not: *to be plunged into Moses*. The word *baptized* is to be taken in its technical sense: *to be baptized with water* (by the fact of the passage through the sea and under the cloud), and the clause must consequently signify: *in relation to Moses*, as a typical Saviour—that is to say, in order to having part in the divine deliverance of which Moses was the agent. Such is likewise the meaning of the *being baptized into Christ Jesus*, in our passage: "Ye received *baptism with water* in relation to the person of Jesus Christ, whose property ye became by that act." Comp. the phrase: *being baptized*, εἰς τὸ ὄνομα, *into the name of* (Matt. xxviii. 19 and 1 Cor. i. 13), which should be explained in a similar manner. One is not plunged into a name, but into water *in relation to* (εἰς) a name—that is to say, to the new revelation of God expressed in a name. It is to the God revealed under this form that the believer consecrates himself externally by baptism.—The title *Christ* is placed here, as i. 1, before the name of the historical person (*Jesus*). The idea of the office evidently takes precedence in the context of that of the person. Yet Paul adds the name *Jesus*, which is wrongly omitted by the *Vatic.*, for this name is closely connected with the fact of the *death* which is about to be brought into relief. —In this expression: *being baptized into death*, the sense *plunged* would be less inadmissible than in the preceding phrase; for an abstract object like *death* lends itself better to the notion of *plunging into*, than a personal one like Moses or Christ. But if such had been the apostle's meaning, would he not rather have said: *into His blood*, than *into His death?* We think, therefore, that here too it is more exact to explain: "*baptized* with water in relation to His death." When one is baptized into Christ, it is *in virtue of His death* that the bond thus formed with Him is contracted. For by His blood we have been *bought with a price*. Baptism serves only to give him *in fact* what belongs to him *in right* by this act of purchase. Baptism thus *supposes* the death of Christ and that of the baptized man man himself (through the appropriation of Christ's death). Hence the conclusion drawn in ver. 4. and which brings the argument to a close.

Ver. 4. "*Therefore we are buried with Him by baptism into death: in order that as Christ was raised up from the dead by the glory of the Father, even so we also should walk in newness of life.*"—If baptism *were*, or *represented*, the death of which Paul had spoken, the *therefore* would be very hard indeed to explain (see the commentaries). But if baptism is in his view the external proof of death, as burial is the proof of decease, he can take up again the course of his argument and say: "In consequence of this death to sin undergone in Christ, we have *therefore* been buried with Him . . . in order also to rise with him," which signifies: "buried with Him, not with the aim of remaining in the tomb or of issuing from it to return to the past life, but to penetrate into a new life, whence a return to the old is definitely precluded." The clause *into death* cannot depend on the verb *we are buried*, as Grot., Hofm., and Ostervald's version would have it. How could it be said of one interred that he thereby descends into death? The converse would be the truth. This clause, therefore, must be made directly dependent on the word *baptism:* "by baptism into death." The substantive βάπτισμα, *baptism*, like those generally derived from verbs in ιζω, has a forcible meaning which allows it easily to have this position and the relation between the notions expressed by the two substantives is so close, that no article was needed to connect them. What also guides us quite naturally to make the words *into death* dependent on the word *baptism*, is ver. 3 : *We were baptized into his death.* Undoubtedly we must explain the phrase : *baptism into death,* like the similar ones preceding : " baptism (with water) in relation to death." Our versions translate : " into *His* death" (Osterv., Oltram.). But if this had been the apostle's view, he would have expressed it by adding the pronoun αὐτοῦ, *of Him.* He evidently wished to leave the notion of *death* in all its generality, that the word might be applied at once to *His* death, and *ours* included in His. It is in relation to these two deaths which have taken place that the believer is baptized.[1]—Modern commentators are not at one on the question whether the apostle means to allude to the external form of the baptismal rite in the primitive church. It seems to us very probable that it is so, whether primitive baptism be regarded as a complete immersion, during which the baptized disappeared for a moment under water (which best corresponds to the figure of *burial*), or whether the baptized went down into the water up to his loins, and the baptizer poured the water with which he had filled the hollow of his hands over his head, so as to represent an immersion. The passage, Mark vii. 4, where the term βαπτισμός, *a washing, bath, lustration, baptism* (Heb. vi. 2), is applied not only to the cleansing of cups and utensils, objects which may be *plunged* into water, but also to that of couches or divans, proves plainly that we cannot insist on the sense of *plunging*, and consequently on the idea of total immersion, being attached to the term baptism. It is nevertheless true, that in one or other of these forms the going down into the water probably represents, in Paul's view, the moral burying of the baptized, and his issuing from the water, his resurrection.—The relation between the two facts of burial and baptism indicated by the apostle is this : Burial is the act which consummates the breaking of the last tie between man and his earthly life. This was likewise the meaning of our Lord's entombment. Similarly by baptism there is publicly consummated the believer's breaking with the life of the present world, and with his own natural life.

It is a mistake to represent the idea of the first proposition of the verse as entirely isolated from all that follows. Paul means, not only that we have been buried with Christ, but that we have been so, like Him, *in order to rise again.*—The ἵνα, *in order that*, is the essential word of the verse. In the case of an ordinary death, the man is inclosed in the tomb, to remain there ; but he who is *buried with Christ* is buried with one who died and *rose*, consequently with the intention of rising also. This idea is essential to the apostle's argument. Indeed, the believer's death, even with the baptism which seals it, would not suffice for a sure guarantee that he will not return to his old life of sin. Did not Lazarus come forth from the tomb to resume life ? What, for one dead, renders his return to an earthly existence definitively impossible, is his passing to a new and higher life by the way of a resurrection. Now, such is precisely the believer's case. By being buried with Christ by baptism, he does not intend to remain thereafter inactive and lifeless, any more than Christ Himself, when giving Himself up to the grave, thought of remaining in it. As Christ gave His life *to take it again* (John x. 17, 18), the believer renounces his life of sin for Him only to receive from Him another and wholly different life (Luke

---

[1] We recall a fact which proves how these sayings of the apostle, apparently so mysterious, find an easy explanation under the light of the lively experiences of faith. The missionary Casilis told us that he was one day questioning a converted Bechuana as to the meaning of a passage analogous to that before us (Col. iii. 3). The latter said to him : "Soon I shall be dead, and they will bury me in my field. My flocks will come to pasture above me. But I shall no longer hear them, and I shall not come forth from my tomb to take them and carry them with me to the sepulchre. They will be strange to me, as I to them. Such is the image of my life in the midst of the world since I believed in Christ."

xvii. 33). His baptism, which supposes his death, tends to life. To die to sin, is it not to die to death, and consequently to spring to life? As, then, by His burial Christ broke the last tie with His earthly life and entered on a higher life, so the believer, by his baptism, finds himself placed between a life which has taken end, and a wholly different one which opens before him. Paul knew by experience the situation indicated by his ἵνα, *in order that*. In Acts ix. we behold him placed between death on the one hand (vv. 8, 9), and the burial of baptism, followed by resurrection through the Holy Spirit, on the other (vv. 17, 18). Comp. also the position of the penitents of Pentecost, to whom Peter says: "Be baptized for the pardon of your sins, and ye shall receive the Holy Spirit." It is therefore true, as the end of the verse says, that what the resurrection was to Christ, renewing by the Holy Spirit is to believers. And in this last fact there is found the answer to the question of ver. 2 : "How shall we, who are dead to sin, live any longer therein?" Perhaps, if we were *no more than* dead, it would not be possible to answer this question so positively. But if, being dead, we have penetrated to a higher life, the relation to the old life is most certainly terminated. The conjunction ὥσπερ, *even as*, indicates only an analogy, a resemblance. The sequel will bring out the internal necessity on which this resemblance rests.—The expression: *from the dead*, is an allusion to the state of death to sin in which the believer receives baptism, and which paves the way for his spiritual resurrection.—*The glory of the Father by which* Christ was raised, is not the display of His power apart from His other perfections; but, as usual, that of all the divine attributes combined. For they have all contributed to this masterpiece of the revelation of God on the earth, righteousness as well as mercy, wisdom as well as holiness. Speaking of the resurrection of Lazarus, Jesus said to Martha: "Thou shalt see the glory *of God.*" But here we have to do with the resurrection *of the Son ;* and therefore Paul says: by the glory *of the Father.*—The word *so* expresses the analogy of the second fact with the first, irrespectively of the individuals in whom it is realized ; the *we also* sets forth the living personalities in whom the prototype is reproduced.—In speaking of believers, the apostle does not rest, as in the case of Christ Himself, on the bare fact of their resurrection, but solely on its permanent consequence, the new life which flows from it : *that we should walk in newness of life*. He does so because, in regard to believers, he wishes solely to shut out their return to their former life ; now this result springs from life in a state of complete realization, rather than from the act by which it is entered on.—The term περιπατεῖν, *to walk*, is a frequent figure with Paul for moral conduct.—Paul says : *newness of life*, instead of *new life*. By this turn of expression he gives less prominence to the idea of life (in contrast to that of *death*) than to the new nature of the second life in contrast to the nature of that which it excludes. The slightest detail of style is always strictly determined in his writing by the principal thought.

Infant baptism does not seem to me to be either *assumed* or *excluded* by this passage. The baptism *assumed* here is certainly that of adults, and adults only. The act of baptism is put *between* faith (with death to sin through faith) on the one hand, and renewing by the Holy Spirit on the other. Baptism, thus understood, therefore involves the actual fact of faith and of death to sin, as much as burial implies the death of the buried. But, at the same time, it is clear that Paul adduces the rite of baptism such as it exists at the time of his writing. The baptism of adults was that which, from the nature of things, suited the first generation of believers, as the parents required to belong to the church before there could be any question of introducing their children into it. The apostle does not therefore think of *excluding* a form which may arise when, circumstances having changed, family life shall have become an integral element in that of the church. The only question is, whether this modification is in keeping with the spirit of the gospel. And this is a question which it seems to me impossible to examine here without breaking the plan of our exegesis.

Ver. 5. "*For if we have become one and the same plant [with Him] through the likeness of His death, we shall be also partakers of His resurrection;*"—The apostle had used the rite of baptism to illustrate the impossibility experienced by the believer of continuing in his former life. Now he expounds the same truth didactically. The *in order that* of ver. 4 becomes as it were the text of this development (vv. 5–11), of which ver. 5 contains the summary.—The *for* bears directly on this *in order that*. The idea of ver. 4 was: "We were buried by baptism only *with the intention* of rising again." This intention is demonstrated by the moral fact formulated ver. 5: "The man who participates in the death of Christ cannot but participate in His resurrection." There is much said in a certain theological school about the possession of the life of Christ. This vague phrase seems intended to take the place of all Christian doctrine. Does it really mean what St. Paul understood by it? I do not examine the subject here. But in any case it should not be forgotten, as is usually done from this view-point, that the participation in the life of Christ of which the apostle speaks, has as its necessary and preliminary condition, participation in His death. The docile acceptance of the cross is the only pathway to communion in the life of the Risen One. Forgetfulness of this point of departure is full of grave consequences. For the second fact has no reality save in connection with the first.—The construction of each of the two propositions of this verse has been understood in a variety of ways. Bisping has proposed to make τοῦ θανάτου, *of death*, the complement not of τῷ ὁμοιώματι (*the likeness*), but of σύμφυτοι (*partakers*), while taking τῷ ὁμοιώματι as an adverbial clause, meant to indicate the *means* or *mode* of this participation: "If we were made partakers of His death *in a likeness;*" this notion of resemblance being applied either to the figurative rite of baptism, or to the internal fact of death to sin, which would thus be as it were the moral copy of Christ's death. This construction would enable us to establish an exact parallelism between the two propositions of the verse, for the genitive τῆς ἀναστάσεως (*of the resurrection*) in the second proposition would depend on σύμφυτοι (*partakers*), exactly as τοῦ θανάτου (*of death*) in the first on this same adjective. But one cannot help feeling how harsh and almost barbarous this construction is. Besides, it is now abandoned. The complement *of death* depends naturally on τῷ ὁμοιώματι, *the likeness*, as has been acknowledged by Chrys., Calv., Thol., Rück., Olsh., de Wette, Mey., Philip., Hofm. By this *likeness* may be understood either the external act of baptism, as representing figuratively the death of Christ, or our own death to sin as spiritually reproducing it. But whether in the one sense or the other, it is surely uncouth to connect so concrete a term as σύμφυτος, *born with*, *partaking*, with an abstract notion such as *likeness*. One is made a partaker not of the likeness of a thing, but of the thing itself. Besides, baptism is not the representation of death, but of burial (see above). It therefore appears to us, that the only admissible construction is to join the adjective σύμφυτοι with the understood regimen σὺν αὐτῷ, *with Him;* "*born with Him, united to Him*, by the likeness of His death." This is the opinion of Er., Grot., and others. The ellipsis of this pronoun arises naturally from the preceding phrase: *we were buried with Him*, ver. 4; it reappears obviously in ver. 6 (συνεσταυρώθη, *was crucified with*). The expression: *through the likeness of His death*, refers, according to what precedes, to the inner fact by which the death of Christ *for sin* is reproduced in us, that is to say, to our own death *to sin* implied in the act of faith.—The term σύμφυτος (in classic Greek more commonly συμφυής) is derived from the verb συμφύω, *to be born, to grow together.* This adjective, therefore, denotes the organic union in virtue of which one being shares the life, growth, and phases of existence belonging to another; so it is that the existence, prosperity, and decay of the branch are bound up with the state of the stem. Hence we have ventured to translate it: *to be made one and the same plant with Him.* Not a case of death to sin passes in the church which was not already included in the death of Christ, to be produced wherever faith should be realized; not a spiritual resurrection is effected within the church, which is not Christ's own resurrection reproduced by His Spirit in the heart which has begun by uniting itself to Him in the communion of His death.—It must, however, be remarked (and we shall meet with this characteristic again in the sequel of the passage) that the fact of participation in the death is put in the past (*we have become one and the same plant* . . .), while participation in the resurrection is expressed in the future: *we shall be partakers* . . . Some of the Fathers have concluded from this change of tense, that in the latter words the apostle meant to speak of the *future* resurrection, of the bodily glorification of believers. But this idea is foreign to the context, which is governed throughout by reference to the objection of ver. 1 (the relation of the believer to sin). The expression, therefore, denotes only sanctification, the believer's moral resurrection. The contrast indicated between the past and the future must find an entirely different explanation. As the communion of faith with Christ crucified is the condition of sharing in His life as risen, the apostle speaks of the first event in the past, and of the second in the future. The one *having taken place,* the other *must follow.* The past and future describe, the one the principle, the other the consequence. We begin with union to the person of Christ by faith in that mysterious: *He for me,* which forms the substance of the gospel; then this union goes forward until His whole being as the Risen One has passed into us. Gess makes τῷ ὁμοιώματι a dative of aim: "We have been united to Him *in order to the likeness* of His death," to be made conformable to it (Phil. iii. 10). But this meaning does not harmonize with ver. 2, where the reproduction of the death is looked upon as wrought in the believer by the fact of his death to sin implied in his faith.

The words ἀλλὰ καί, which connect the two propositions of the verse, might here be rendered: *well then also!* The second fact stands out as the joyous consequence of the first.—The genitive τῆς ἀναστάσεως, *of the resurrection,* cannot depend on the verb ἐσόμεθα, *we shall be:* "we *shall be of* the resurrection," meaning: we shall infallibly have part in it (in the sense of the expressions: *to be of the faith, to be of the law*). Such a mode of speech would be without ground in the passage; and the term resurrection is not taken here in the general sense; it refers solely to Christ's personal resurrection. Meyer and Philippi, true to their explanation of the first proposition, here supply the dative τῷ ὁμοιώματι: "As we have shared in the likeness of His death, we shall share also *in the likeness* of His resurrection."[1] This ellipsis is not impossible, but it renders the phrase very awkward. Following the construction which we have adopted in the first clause, it is simpler merely to understand σύμφυτοι in this second, making the genitive τῆς ἀναστάσεως, *of the resurrection,* dependent on this adjective: "Well, then, we shall be partakers also of His resurrection!" This solution is possible, because the word σύμφυτος is construed indifferently with the genitive or dative, like our English word *to partake* (to partake *of* or *in*). This direct dependence (omitting the idea of *likeness*) is according to the nature of things. Jesus does not communicate to us His death itself; we possess only its likeness in our death to sin. It is otherwise with His resurrection and His life as risen. It is this life itself which he conveys to us: "And I live; yet not I, but Christ in me" (Gal. ii. 20). "Because I

[1] It is hard to see the awkwardness, and certainly the parallelism of the clauses is better preserved in this way.—T. W. C.

live, ye shall live also" (John xiv. 18). The believer being once ingrafted into Christ by faith in His death, and thereby dead to His own life, lives again through the Holy Spirit on the very life of the risen Christ. Thus the difference of form between the first and second propositions is perfectly explained.—This summary demonstration of the truth of the *in order that* (ver. 4) required to be developed. Vv. 6 and 7 expound the contents of 5*a ;* vv. 8–10 those of 5*b*.

Ver. 6. " *Understanding this, that our old man has been crucified with Him, that the body of sin might be destroyed, that henceforth we should not serve sin.*"—Why introduce abruptly the notion of *subjective knowledge* into a relation which ver. 5 seemed to have laid down as objectively necessary ? This phenomenon is the more remarkable because it is reproduced in ver. 9 in the εἰδότες, *knowing that*, and even in the λογίζεσθε, *reckon that* (ver. 11). Meyer thinks that the believer's subjective experience is cited here to *confirm* the moral bond indicated in ver. 5 as necessary in itself : " We shall certainly be partakers . . ., *a fact besides which we cannot doubt*, for we know that" . . . This appendix so understood has all the effect of an excrescence. Philippi, on the contrary, finds a consequence to be drawn indicated by this participle : " *And thus* (in proportion as the *we shall be* of 5*b* is realized in us) we shall know experimentally that" . . . But the present participle does not naturally express a relation of consequence. There would rather have been needed καὶ γνωσόμεθα, *and thus we shall know*. Hofmann paraphrases : " And we shall make the experience that that has really happened to us, and happened in order that" . . . We do not see much difference between this meaning and that of Philippi whom this author criticises. The relation between the participle *understanding*, and the verb *we shall be* (ver. 5*b*), is rather that of a moral condition, a means. As Gess puts it : " Our participation in Christ's resurrection does not take place in the way of a physical and natural process. That such a result may take place, there is needed a moral co-operation on the part of the believer." And this co-operation of course supposes a *knowledge*, knowledge of the way (ver. 6) and of the end (ver. 8). The believer understands that the final object which God has in view in crucifying his old man (ver. 6) is to realize in him the life of the Risen One (vv. 8, 9), and he enters actively into the divine thought. Thereby only can this be realized. This notion of subjective knowledge, expressed by the words : *understanding this*, was contained in the previous ἵνα, *in order that*, of ver. 4 : " We were buried with Him *with the aim* of rising with Him, *understanding* that" . . . The whole piece, beginning with the *or know ye not that* of ver. 3, transports us into the inmost consciousness of the believer, as it has been formed in the school and through the personal assimilation of the death of Christ. The believer knows certainly that he is called to die, but to die in order to live again.—The expression : *our old man*, denotes human nature such as it has been made by the sin of him in whom originally it was wholly concentrated, fallen Adam reappearing in every human *ego* that comes into the world under the sway of the preponderance of self-love, which was determined by the primitive transgression. This corrupted nature bears the name of *old* only from the viewpoint of the believer who already possesses a renewed nature.—This old man *has been crucified* so far as the believer is concerned in the very person of Christ crucified. The apostle does not say that He has been *killed*. He may exist still, but like one crucified, whose activity is paralyzed. Up to the solemn hour of believing, sin puts on the behavior of triumphant independence, or presents itself to us as an excusable weakness. The instant we contemplate it in Christ crucified, we see it as a malefactor condemned and capitally punished by the justice of God ; and its sentence of death pronounced in our conscience is the same to it within us as the cross was to Christ—not an immediate death certainly, but the reduction of it to powerlessness.—The purpose of this moral execution, included in the very fact of faith, is *the destruction of the body of sin*. There ought to be a complete difference between this second fact indicated as the aim and the foregoing one. What the apostle calls *the body of sin*, cannot therefore be identical with what he calls *our old man*. Must we, with several, understand *the body* in the strict sense of the word, the apostle seeing in it the *principle* of evil in our human nature? But the sequel proves that he does not at all regard sin as inherent in the body and inseparable from it; for in ver. 13 he claims the body and its members for the service of God, and represents them as under obligation to become *instruments of righteousness*. It is the same in 2 Cor. iv. 10-12, where the life of Jesus is spoken of as displaying itself in *the body*, the *mortal flesh* of believers, which has become the organ of this heavenly life. So far is the apostle from regarding our bodily nature as the cause of sin, that in 2 Cor. vii. 1 he contrasts the defilements *of the spirit* with those of the flesh. And herein he is perfectly at one with the Lord, who, Matt. xv. 19, declares that "*from the heart* proceed evil thoughts, murders, adulteries, thefts, false witness, blasphemies." The very fact of the real incarnation of our Lord Jesus Christ, as taught by Paul, Rom. viii. 3 (see on the passage), suffices to refute the opinion which would hold the body to be the principle of sin. These considerations have led several commentators (Calv., Olsh., J. Müller, Philippi, Baur, Hodge) to understand the word *body* here in a figurative sense. According to them, it denotes sin itself as a heavy *mass*, or even as an *organism*, a *system* of evil dispositions, which keeps the soul under its yoke. The complement of *sin* they take as a genitive of apposition. One can easily understand in this sense how Paul should demand the destruction of this *body of sin*, that is to say, of sin itself. But it is impossible to harmonize this meaning with vv. 12 and 13, in which Paul, applying our passage, evidently speaks of the holy consecration of the *body*, taking the term in its strict sense. Besides, it would be difficult to escape from a tautology between this and the preceding proposition. There remains a third explanation found with varying shades in Meyer, Hofm., etc. It regards the genitive *of sin* as a complement of property or quality: the body so far as it serves as an instrument of sin in human life. This meaning is certainly the one which corresponds best with the thought of the apostle.[1] Only, to understand the genitive *of sin*, we must add the idea: that from our birth there exists between our body and our sinful will that intimate relation whereby the two elements are placed in mutual dependence. This relation is not a simple accident; it belongs to the fallen state into which our soul itself has come.—The verb καταργεῖν, which we translate by *destroy*, strictly signifies: *to deprive of the power of action;* and hence *to make needless* or *useless*, as in Luke xiii. 7, Rom. iii. 3; or *to annul bring to an end, destroy*, as in 1 Cor. xiii. 8, 10; 1 Cor. vi. 13; Eph. ii. 15, etc. Neither the meaning: *to render inactive*, nor *to destroy*, could be applied to the body, if we had to understand thereby the physical organism in itself. But the apostle has no thought here of recommending bodily asceticism to believers. It is not of the body as such that he is speaking; it is of the *body* so far as it is an instrument in the service *of sin*. Of the body in this special relation, he declares that it should be *reduced to inaction*, or even *destroyed*. It is obvious that in this application the two meanings of the word καταργεῖν amount nearly to the same. But the translation *destroyed* probably renders the thought best. A body, that of sin, is destroyed that another may take its place, the body which is an instrument of righteousness (ver. 13).—In the third proposition, which expresses the final aim of this inward labor, the apostle introduces a third subject:

---

[1] Yet it is open to the objection that it confuses the literal sense and the figurative of the term *body*.—T. W. C.

we, ἡμᾶς, a term which denotes the entire moral personality independently of the question whether it is or is not under the dominion of sin. This third subject differs wholly from that of the first proposition : *the old man*, as well as from that of the second : *the body of sin*. The old man is crucified by faith in Christ's crucifixion ; the body of sin is destroyed, because in consequence of the crucifixion of the old man the corrupt will which formerly used the body for its own satisfaction is paralyzed, and so can dispose of it no more. And the *ego*, the true I, the moral personality in its essence, is thus set free at once, both from the power of the old nature and of the body its instrument, and can consequently consecrate this last to a wholly new use. The apostle illustrates the truth of this moral situation by an example taken from common life.

Ver. 7. "*For he that is dead*[1] *is of right freed from sin.*"—Many commentators, from Erasmus to Thol., De Wette, Philip., Hodge, Gess, etc., take the participle ἀποθανών, *he that is dead*, in the figurative sense (comp. the similar expressions in vv. 6 and 8). But these critics divide immediately as to the meaning of the term δεδικαίωται, literally, *is justified ;* some applying it to deliverance from *guilt* and punishment (Hodge for example)—as the ordinary meaning of the word *justify* by Paul seems to demand—the others to deliverance from the *power* of sin, in the sense that he who is dead is no longer subject to this master, no longer owes him anything. Yet neither of these meanings is satisfactory. The first would take us back to the subject of justification, which was concluded at the end of chap. v. According to Gess, Paul means to express the idea that "the believer's absolution from sin (*justification*) takes place only on condition of his death to sin." That would result in making sanctification the principle of justification. The other meaning would be more suitable in some respects : "He who is dead spiritually (in the sense of ver. 6), is thereby set free from the *power* of sin." Undoubtedly in a general way this is the apostle's meaning in ver. 7 ; the context demands it. But we do not think that this interpretation accounts exactly for the expressions used. The word δικαιοῦν, even with the preposition ἀπό, cannot signify : *to free from the power of*, or, at least if we reach this meaning, it must be shown in what legitimate way that is possible. Then the participle ὁ ἀποθανών, *he that is dead*, not being accompanied by any qualification, is rather to be understood in the strict sense, and the more so as in the following verse, when the apostle returns to the spiritual meaning, he expressly indicates the change by adding the words σὺν Χριστῷ, *with Christ*.[2] It is therefore a maxim borrowed from common life which the apostle expresses here, leaving it to the reader to apply it immediately to the corresponding fact of the moral life, which is precisely that just described by him in ver. 6. It follows that the word *justify*, δικαιοῦν, must have a somewhat different meaning from its ordinary dogmatic sense in Paul's writings ; for the domain to which he here applies it is altogether different. One who is dead, he means to say, no longer having a body to put at the service of sin, is now legally exempted from carrying out the wishes of that master, who till then had freely disposed of him. Suppose a dead slave ; it will be vain for his master to order him to steal, to lie, or to kill. He will be entitled to answer : "my tongue and hands and feet no longer obey me." How, then, could he be taken to task for refusing to serve ? Such is the believer's position after the crucifixion of his own will (of his *old man*) has reduced his *body of sin* (ver. 6) to powerlessness. He can no longer serve sin in the doing of evil, any more than the slave deprived of his body by death can continue to execute the orders formerly given him by his wicked

---

[1] So Dr. Godet renders, but surely the true version of the aorist participle is, *he that died* or *hath died*.—T. W. C.
[2] So Matthew Henry: "Death makes a mighty change; such a change doth sanctification make in the soul, it cuts off all correspondence with sin."—T. W. C.

master. The verb δικαιοῦσθαι, *to be justified*, signifies in this connection : to be free from blame in case of disobedience ; to be legally entitled not to obey. The idea of *legality* is in the word δικαιοῦν, *to justify*, that of *liberation* in the preposition ἀπό, *from*. Taking the term ὁ ἀποθανών in the literal sense, as we have done, commentators have sometimes restricted its application to the malefactor, who, by submitting to the punishment he deserved, has effaced his guilt, and can no longer be apprehended for the same crime. But the words : *he who is dead*, are too general to bear so special an application, and the sentence thus understood would reopen the subject of justification, which is exhausted.—The case of the dead slave described in ver. 7, as we understand it, is the exact counterpart of the believer's moral situation described in ver. 6. The apostle leaves the reader to make this application himself, and passes in the following verses from the negative side of sanctification, crucifixion with Christ, to the positive side of this great truth, resurrection with Him. This second side is the necessary complement of the first. For the sinful will being once crucified in Christ, and its organ the body reduced to inaction, the believer's moral personality cannot remain inert. It must have a new activity ; the body itself demands a new employment in the service of this activity. We have seen how this idea was contained in the *in order that* of ver. 4. The believer dies, not to remain dead, but *in order to* rise again ; and this he knows well, for in the person of Him with whom he dies, the Risen One, he beholds beforehand the moral necessity of the event. This relation of thought, already indicated vv. 4, 5, is now developed vv. 8-10 ; comp. Gal. ii. 20.

Vv. 8-10. "*Now, if we be dead with Christ, we believe that we shall also live*[1] *with him :*[2] *knowing that Christ after being raised from the dead dieth no more ; death hath no more dominion over Him. For the death that He died, He died unto sin once for all : and the life that He liveth, He liveth unto God.*"—The δέ, *now*, marks the progress to be made from participation in Christ's death to communion in His life. This gradation corresponds exactly with the force of the *well then also*, ἀλλὰ καί, ver. 5. As, indeed, vv. 6 and 7 were the didactic paraphrase of 5*a*, so vv. 8-10 are that of 5*b*. Participation in death is mentioned as a *past* event, included in the fact of faith (*we are dead with Him ;* comp. 5*a*), while participation in the life is described as an event *to come : we shall also live* with Him. The first, indeed, is to every true believer an object of experience ; it is not yet so with the second. At the time of baptism, the view-point of the apostle (vv. 3, 4), the new life is yet an object of hope and faith. Hence, in relation to the former, the term γινώσκοντες, *knowing*, ver. 6, and in relation to the latter, πιστεύομεν, *we believe*, ver. 8. The baptized one stands between the death which he experienced on believing, and the life which he awaits with certainty as a gift from Him who is not only dead, but risen again.—*To live with Christ*, συζῆν αὐτῷ, is to share His life as one risen and glorified. Jesus, from the depths of His heavenly state, communicates Himself to the man who has appropriated His death by faith, and thus fills up with His holy life the void formed in us by the renunciation of our own life. This is our Pentecost, the aualogue of His resurrection.

Ver. 9. This faith, this firm expectation of the believer who is dead with Him. is not a vain imagination. It rests on a positive fact, the resurrection of Christ Himself : εἰδότες, *knowing that*. This participle justifies the *we believe* of ver. 8. *We believe* that our spiritual resurrection will come about, because *we know* that His resurrection has taken place, and that irrevocably. Now the latter gives us assurance of the former. But faithful to his original subject, the apostle, instead of developing the idea of the new life of Jesus, confines himself to expressing this consequence : *that He dieth no*

---

[1] C K P: συζήσωμεν instead of συζήσομεν.
[2] D E F G, It. Syr^sch : τῳ Χριστῳ instead of αυτω.

more. It is easy to see the logical relation between this purely negative turn of expression, and the question put in ver. 2 : "How shall we who are dead to sin live any longer therein?" There is no return backward for the risen Jesus ; how should there be one for us, from the time that we share His life as the Risen One? No doubt, his death alone would not have rendered His return to an earthly life impossible ; but His entrance upon a celestial life absolutely excludes such a retrograde step. Thus mere communion with His death would not suffice to furnish an unhesitating answer to the question of ver. 2, while participation in His new life settles it once and forever.—The last words of ver. 9 form an independent proposition. This break in the construction throws the idea more into relief. The time having passed when death was permitted to stretch its sceptre over him, He is freed from its power forever.

Ver. 10. The first proposition of ver. 10 unfolds the reason why death was allowed to reign over Him for a moment ; the second explains the reason why this cannot be repeated.—The two pronouns ὅ, *that which*, may be taken either as a determining expression : *in that so far as*, or as the direct object of the two verbs : *that which He died*, *that which he lived*. For in Greek it is allowable to say : to die a death, to live a life ; comp. Gal. ii. 20. This parallel and the sense itself appears to us to decide in favor of the second construction. The first would seem to indicate a power of *partial* rather than *temporary* death, which is not natural in the context.— The short-lived power of death over Jesus is explained by the regimen τῇ ἁμαρτιᾳ, *to sin*. The relation which Jesus sustained to sin was the soul cause of His subjection to death. As in this piece *death unto sin* denotes an absolute breaking with it (ver. 2), it might be attempted here to give the meaning : Jesus struggled victoriously against sin during His whole life, not granting it for a moment the right of existing in His person. But the adverb ἐφάπαξ, *once*, forbids us to extend the application of the term *dying unto sin* to His whole life. Besides, the commentators who, like Meyer and Hofmann, adopt this meaning, limit the expression to the moment of death : with *the end* of His life His struggle with sin ended ; from that moment sin (in the form of temptation) exercised no more power over His person. This meaning would certainly account to some extent for the ἐφάπαξ, *once*. But it forces us to take the word *die* in two wholly different senses in the same sentence, and it is not easy to get a clear idea of this *dying unto sin* ascribed to Jesus. Does it refer to his struggle against temptation ? The phrase *dying unto sin* is unsuitable. One dies to a real, not a possible fact. Are we to think of the struggle against sin outside of Him ? But this struggle continues to this very hour. Is it a personal breaking with evil which is meant ? He did nothing else during His whole life. The only possible meaning, therefore, seems to me to be that adopted by Grot. and Olsh. : He died to *expiate* sin, a sense connected quite naturally with that given by Chrys., Calv., etc. : and *to destroy* it. There was a moment in His existence in which He bore its penalty, and thereby established its defeat. But this moment was short, and remains single and alone. Such is the force of the term ἐφάπαξ, *once for all*. It was a transient necessity which He consented to encounter ; but such a crisis will not be renewed. The debt once paid is so completely and forever ; comp. Heb. vii. 27, ix. 12, 26, 28, x. 10 ; 1 Pet. iii. 18. The dative τῇ ἁμαρτίᾳ, *unto sin*, thus signifies : *unto the service of sin*, that is to say, to accomplish all that was demanded by the entrance and destruction of this fact among mankind. It is obvious from the *once for all* that the death of Jesus occupies a place by itself in His work, and should not be regarded merely as the culminating point of His holy life.—This crisis once past, Jesus no longer owes anything to sin, and His life may manifest itself without hindrance as an instrument of the life of God.—*To live to God*, is to live solely to manifest and serve Him, without having to submit any more to certain obligations imposed by a contrary principle. The meaning of this expression is, as Meyer says, exclusive : to God *only*. The glorified Jesus lives and acts for no other object than to manifest in the heart of men by the Holy Spirit the life of God which has become His life, life eternal ; comp. John xvii. 2 : " As Thou hast given me power over all flesh, that I should give eternal life to as many as Thou hast given me." Thus it is that He serves and glorifies God.

As Christ, then, once entered upon this life and glorious activity, does not depart from it to return back again, so the believer, once dead to sin and alive to God in Christ, cannot return to his old life of sin. Ver. 11 explicitly draws this conclusion, held in suspense since ver. 8, and prepared for in vv. 9 and 10.

Ver. 11. " *Thus also reckon ye yourselves to be*[1] *dead indeed unto sin, and alive unto God in Christ Jesus our Lord.*"[2]—The οὕτω, *likewise,* indicates the inference to be drawn from the conformity between the case of believers and that of Jesus.—*Ye also:* ye, as well as he.—Λογίζεσθε, reckon, con*sider,* is evidently an imperative, not an indicative : comp. the following imperatives, vv. 12 and 13. The apostle means : Behold, in consequence of what you witness in Jesus Himself, the view-point at which you ought to put yourselves when you regard your own case. You have no longer to see your condition as you were in yourselves : slaves of sin, dead unto God. You have to regard yourselves as you are in Christ, as I have just explained to you : dead to sin, alive to God. Beside and above the old man which still lives in him, the believer possesses a new *ego* contained in Christ who lives in him ; this *ego* has broken with sin, it is wholly consecrated to God. Such is the being whom he ought henceforth to regard as his true self ; he ought consequently to appropriate it subjectively by constantly substituting it for his natural self, which is henceforth denied at the foot of the cross. Such is the divine secret of Christian sanctification, which distinguishes it profoundly from simple natural morality. The latter says to man : Become what thou wouldst be. The former says to the believer : Become what thou *art* already (in Christ). It thus puts a positive fact at the foundation of moral effort, to which the believer can return and have recourse anew at every instant. And this is the reason why his labor is not lost in barren aspiration, and does not end despair. The believer does not get disentangled from sin gradually. He breaks with it in Christ once for all. He is placed by a decisive act of will in the sphere of perfect holiness ; and it is within it that the gradual renewing of the personal life goes forward. This second gospel paradox, sanctification by faith, rests on the first, justification by faith.

After having shown the believer how he is to regard himself in virtue of his union with Christ, the apostle calls him not to let this new position be a mere matter of theory, but to work it into his real life, to make it his life from moment to moment. As Philippi says, Christians ought to begin with discerning what they are, and then labor to manifest it. Such is the subject of vv. 12–14.

Vv. 12, 13. " *Let not sin therefore reign in your mortal body, that ye should obey its lusts.*[3] *Neither yield ye your members to sin as instruments of unrighteousness : but yield yourselves unto God, as*[4] *those that have become alive from the dead, and your members as instruments of righteousness for God.*"—In Christ all is done. In the believer all is doing and can be done only with

---

[1] The verb ειναι is placed by T. R. and K L P after νεκρους μεν ; by ℵ B C after εαυτους ; the word is rejected by A D E F G, It.
[2] A B D E F G omit the words τω κυριω ημων, found in T. R., with ℵ C K L P.
[3] Three readings : T. R. reads, with K L P : εις το υπακουειν αυτη εν ταις επιθυμιαις αυτου ; the Greco-Lat. D E F G, Ir. Or. Tert. read : εις το υπακουειν αυτη, omitting the words : εν ταις επιθυμιαις αυτου ; the Alex. ℵ A B C, Syr^sch Vg. read : εις το υπακουειν ταις επιθυμιαις αυτου, omitting αυτη.
[4] Instead of ως, A B C read ωσει.

the concurrence of his will. Hence the following exhortation which is connected by *therefore*.—It might have been thought from certain previous expressions, that Paul did not admit the existence of sin any longer in the believer; but he far from giving himself up to such exaggerations. The very word : " Let not sin *reign*," assumes that it *is* still there. But it ought no longer to be there as sovereign : for it has lost its powerful instrument and auxiliary, *the body;* the latter has become in Christ the instrument of God. These two aspects of the sanctification of the body, its liberation from sin and its consecration to God correspond respectively to vv. 6 and 7 and vv. 8–10, and are developed, the former in vv. 12 and 13*a*, and the latter in ver. 13*b*.

The imperative μὴ βασιλευέτω, *let it not reign,* is addressed grammatically to sin, but in meaning to the believer himself ; for it is he who has the task of bringing this reign to an end. The exhortation thus placed as the sequel of what precedes, reminds us of the passage Col. iii. 5 : " Ye *are dead* (ver. 3) ; *mortify therefore* (ver. 5) your members, which are upon the earth." It is because *we are dead* to sin in Christ that we can *mortify* it in ourselves in daily life. The present imperative, with the negative μή, implies the notion of a state which existed till now, but which must terminate.—We must not, as some do, give to the ἐν, *in*, the meaning of *by*, as if the apostle meant that the body was *the means by which* sin exercises its dominion over us. The natural meaning is : "*in* your mortal body." The body is the *domain*, as it were, in which the dominion of sin is exercised, in this sense, that when once the will has been subjugated by sin, it gives the body of which it disposes over to sin, and this master uses it for his pleasure.

The epithet θνητῷ, *mortal*, must bear a logical relation to the idea of the passage. The object of this term has been understood very variously. Calvin regards it as expressive of contempt, as if Paul meant to say that man's whole bodily nature hastens to death, and ought not consequently to be pampered. Philippi thinks that the epithet refers rather to the fact of sin having *killed* the body, and having thus manifested its *malignant* character. Flatt thinks that Paul alludes to the *transient* character of bodily pleasures. Chrysostom and Grotius find in the word the idea of the *brevity of the toils*, which weigh on the Christian here below. According to Tholuck, Paul means to indicate how evil lusts are inseparable from the present state of the body, which is destined by and by to be glorified. According to Lange and Schaff, the sanctification of the mortal body here below is mentioned as serving to prepare for its glorification above. It seems to us that this epithet may be explained more naturally : It is not the part *destined to die* which should rule the believer's personality ; the higher life awakened in him should penetrate him wholly, and rule that body even which is to change its nature. — It is obvious that in the last proposition of the verse, the Received reading : *to obey it in its lusts*, does not yield a simple meaning. To obey sin in its lusts is an artificial and forced expression. The Greco-Latin reading : *to obey it*, is rather superfluous ; what would this regimen add to the idea expressed by the previous words : "Let not sin reign in your body"? The Alexandrine reading : *to obey its lusts* (αὐτοῦ, *the body's*), so far as the meaning is concerned, is preferable to both the others ; and it has the advantage besides, as we shall show, of explaining easily how they arose. — The *lusts of the body* are its instincts and appetites, which, acting on the soul, determine within it the passionate and disorderly motions of sin. The term ἐπιθυμία, *lust* (from ἐπί, *upon, toward*, and θυμός, *the heart, feeling, passion*), denotes the violence with which, under the dominion of bodily appetite, the soul is carried to the external objects, which can satisfy the desires excited within it. Although, then, it is still sin, the egoistical instinct of the soul, which reigns in the body and directs its use, it thus happens that the appetites of the latter become the masters of conduct ; for they present themselves to the soul as the means of satisfying the ardent desire of enjoyment with which it is consumed. In this way the beginning and end of the verse harmonize, the reign of sin over the body, and the supremacy of the body over the person himself. But this relation of ideas was not understood by the copyists. As at the beginning of the verse *sin* was the subject of the verb *reign*, it seemed to them that the obedience spoken of in the following words was meant to be rendered to it also, and they added (as in the Byz.) the pronoun αὐτῇ, *it* (sin), which necessitated the adding also of the preposition ἐν, *in*, before the word ταῖς ἐπιθυμίαις, *the lusts*. Such is the origin of the Received reading. Or, again, they rejected all this final clause, which did not seem to be in keeping with the beginning; and thus was formed the Greco-Latin reading.

Ver. 13. After speaking of the body in general, the apostle in ver. 13*a* mentions the *members* in particular. Philippi, who, with Calvin, has understood the body in ver. 12, not of the body properly so called, but of the body and soul united (in so far as the latter is not under the influence of the Holy Spirit), gives also to the word *members*, ver. 13, a moral as well as physical sense. It is not only the eyes, hands, feet, tongue, etc., but also the heart, will, understanding. There could be nothing more arbitrary than this extension to the soul of the meaning of the words *body* and *members*. The members of the body correspond to the various *lusts*, ver. 12, and are the particular instruments of their gratification. The term ὅπλα may be translated by *arms* or by *instruments*. Meyer insists strongly on the first meaning, the only one, according to him, used in the New Testament (comp. 2 Cor. vi. 7, x. 4). But we doubt much whether this observation applies to Rom. xiii. 12 (see on the passage); and the meaning: *instrument*, seems to us much more suitable here, as there is no reference to war, but to the gratification of *lusts*.[1] — The present imperative παριστάνετε, *present*, *yield*, like the βασιλευέτω of ver. 12, denotes the *continuance* of an actual state. With the negative μή, it therefore signifies: *cease from yielding*, as you have done till now. The verb παριστάνειν signifies: to present in order to put at the disposal of.[1] The word ἀδικία, *unrighteousness*, here embraces all acts contrary to moral obligation in general. — It may be doubted whether the dative τῇ ἁμαρτίᾳ, *to sin*, depends on the verb *yield*, or on the substantive *instrument*. Perhaps it should be connected with both at once. — Vv. 12 and 13*a* have expounded the notion of the sanctification of the body from a negative point of view. Ver. 13*b* expounds it positively. It is the same gradation as we have from 5*a* to 5*b*, and from ver. 7 to ver. 8. The apostle here uses the aorist παραστήσατε instead of the present παριστάνετε, ver. 13*a*. Critics are not agreed as to the meaning and intention of this form. Meyer takes this imperative aorist as indicating the *instantaneousness* with which the consecration of the body should be carried out. Fritzsche finds in it the notion of the continual *repetition* of the acts in which this consecration takes effect. Philippi thinks that this form expresses the idea of a consecration accomplished *once for all*. As the aorist strictly denotes the passing into action, the imperative aorist strongly calls upon the individual to accomplish without delay the act indicated by the verb (almost the meaning indicated by Meyer). The difference between this aorist imperative and the present imperatives preceding is therefore this: the latter were an exhortation not to continue the old state; the former insists on an immediate transition to the new state (comp. Hofmann, p. 246). This change should affect not the body only, but the whole person: *yield yourselves*. The consecration of the body and of the members is included in that of the person. The *as* which follows does not signify: *as if* (ὡσεί, Alex. reading), but: *as being really* (ὡς, Byz. reading).—The

---

[1] But the verb *present* seems to be employed in the military sense of presenting in line and before officers, and the apostle is fond of expressions taken from usages of war.--T. W. C.

expression *dead* has been understood here in two ways. Some, like Philippi, have found in it the notion of spiritual death, in which the sinner still lies, comp. Eph. ii. 1 and 5. The apostle is thought to be contrasting the old state of estrangement from God, in which the Romans formerly were, with their present state of life in God. Others, on the contrary, like Meyer, starting from the comparison between vv. 2 and 11, think that the subject in question is the *death to sin* consummated by faith in Christ. The apostle is thought to be contrasting the state of the body's inactivity at the time when the believer is only experimentally dead with Christ (vv. 6, 7), with his new activity from the time that he receives a new life (vv. 8–10), through experimental acquaintance with the Lord's resurrection. This second meaning is obviously forced; the first, simpler in itself, also agrees better with the contrast between the believer's new and old state (vv. 12 and 13*a*). The term δικαιοσύνη, *righteousness*, in contrast to ἀδικία, *iniquity*, can only denote here moral righteousness, the fulfilment of all human obligations.—The dative Θεῷ, *to God*, does not depend probably on the understood verb *yield*, since it would have been useless in this case to repeat this clause already expressed in the previous line. It must therefore be connected with the expression ὅπλα δικαιοσύνης, *instruments of righteousness for God*. All those works of righteousness which God could not execute Himself here below without constant miraculous interventions, He accomplishes by believers, who eagerly lend their bodies and members to Him as instruments for this end.

Ver. 14. "*In fact, sin will not*[1] *have dominion over you: for ye are not under the law, but under grace.*"—We have not here a disguised exhortation, expressed by a future taken in the sense of an imperative : " Let not sin reign any more " . . . ! Why would the apostle not have continued the imperative form used in the preceding verses? It is a future fact made sure to the believer as a glorious promise : " What I have just asked of you (to die unto sin and consecrate yourselves to God), ye will certainly be able to do ; for it will be impossible for sin to hold its place longer in you ; it will no longer be able to reign over you." This promise is the justification of the command given ver. 12 : " Let not sin reign " . . . ! Ver. 14 is thus the transition from the preceding exhortation to the subsequent development which treats of the believer's emancipation.—The promise contained in the first proposition is justified in the second. The state of grace, χάρις, reconciliation to God, the enjoyment of His favor and the possession of His Spirit, communicate to the soul a victorious power all unknown to the legal state. In this latter there reign the feeling of sin, the fear of condemnation, and the servile spirit, which are the opposite of inward consecration.—And hence sin can be overcome *under grace*, while it reigns inevitably *under law*. The apostle has not put the article before the word νόμον, *law ;* for, though he is thinking substantially of the Mosaic law, it is as *law* that he wishes to designate it here, and not as *Mosaic* law. What he affirms applies to every institution having the character of an external commandment.—But why use the preposition ὑπό, *under*, and not the preposition ἐν, *in*, which seems more suitable to a notion like that of *the state of grace ?* Is grace, then, a yoke, as well as the law ? Is it not, on the contrary, an inner life, a power? In other connections Paul would certainly have made use of the preposition ἐν, *in*, with the word *grace*. But the idea of the whole passage about to follow is precisely that of the decisive control which grace exercises over the believer to *subject him* to righteousness with an authority not less imperious, and even more efficacious than the law (vv. 15–23). And it is this idea which is expressed and summed up by the preposition ὑπό, *under*.—In the same way, indeed, as the second passage of the section (vv. 15–23) is the development of the words *under*

---

[1] ℵ K read οὐκέτι (*no more*) instead of οὐ (*not*).

grace, the third (vii. 1–6), as we shall see, will be the development of the words, *no more under the law*. And the logical connection of the three passages is consequently this : After demonstrating in the first that faith in Christ crucified and risen contains in it the principle of a reign of holiness (vi. 1–14), the apostle proves that this principle is not less powerful than a law to subdue man to itself (vv. 15–23), and that in consequence of this moral subjugation the believer can henceforth without danger renounce the yoke of the law (vii. 1–6).

FOURTEENTH PASSAGE (6:15–23)

The Power of the new Principle of Sanctification to deliver from Sin

The new principle had just been laid down. The apostle had found it in the object of justifying faith. But could a principle so spiritual, apart from every external and positive rule, take hold of the will with power enough to rule it thoroughly ? To this natural objection, formulated in ver. 15, St. Paul answers as follows : by the acceptance of grace *a new master* has been substituted for the former, sin (vv. 16–19) ; and the believer feels himself obliged to serve this new master with the more fidelity because he rewards his servants by communicating *life* to them, whereas the former master pays his by giving them *death* (vv. 20–23). Thus it is proved that the new principle is clothed with sufficient, though purely internal authority, to control the believer's entire life.

Ver. 15 : " *What then ? should we sin,*[1] *because we are not under the law, but under grace ? Let it not be so !* "—The question of ver. 15 is not a repetition of that in ver. 1. The discussion has advanced. The principle of holiness inherent in salvation by grace has been demonstrated. The apostle only asks himself whether it will have the power necessary to rule man without the assistance of a law ? This is the point at which the question τι οὖν, *what then*, resumes the discussion. Thus is explained the difference of style between the question of ver. 1 and that of ver. 15. In the former, Paul asked : Should we continue in sin ? Here he says simply : *should we sin*, ἁμαρτήσωμεν. There is no doubt that the Received reading : *shall we sin*, ἁμαρτήσομεν, should be rejected, for it is not found in a single majuscule. The aorist subjunctive ἁμαρτήσωμεν does not denote, as the present would do, the permanent state, but the isolated act, which is perfectly suitable here. The question is no longer, as in ver. 1, whether the justified believer will be able to continue the life of sin which he formerly led. The answer has been given in vv. 1–14. But the matter in question is whether the new dominion will be strong enough to banish sin *in every particular case*. Hence the form of the aorist subjunctive : *should we commit an act of sin ?* Could we act thus voluntarily in a single instance ? And, in point of fact, a believer will not easily say : By grace I shall remain without any change what I have been till now. But he will find himself only too easily regarding some particular leniency toward sin as admissible, on account of the freeness of pardon. The gradation between the question of ver. 1 and that of ver. 15 makes itself also felt in the form of the motive alleged in favor of unfaithfulness. The apostle does not say now : " *that* grace may abound," words which could only come from a heart yet a stranger to the experiences of faith ; but he says here : "*because* we are under grace." The snare is less gross in this form. Vinet one day said to the writer of these lines : " There is a subtle poison which insinuates itself into the heart even of the best Christian ; it is the temptation to say : Let us sin, not *that* grace may abound, but *because* it abounds." Here there is no

---

[1] All the Mjj. read ἁμαρτησωμεν instead of ἁμαρτησομεν, which is read by T. R. with some Mnn. only.

longer an odious calculation, but a convenient let alone.—Where would be the need of holding that the apostle, to explain this question, has in view an objection raised by legal Jewish-Christianity? The question arises of itself as soon as the gospel comes in contact with the heart of man. What proves clearly that the apostle is not thinking here of a Jewish-Christian scruple, is the fact that in his reply he does not make the least allusion to man's former subjection to the law, but solely to the yoke which sin laid upon him from the beginning. And the literal translation of our verse is not: "For ye are no more under *the* law," but: "For ye are no more under *law*, but *under grace*." It is understood, of course, that when he speaks of *law* he is thinking of the Mosaic dispensation, just as, when speaking of *grace*, he is thinking of the revelation of the gospel. But he does not mention the institutions as such; he designates them only by their moral *character*.

Vv. 16–19 describe the new subjection (*to righteousness*) by which grace displaces the old subjection (*to sin*).

Ver. 16. "*Know ye not, that in respect of Him to whom ye devote yourselves as servants to obey, ye are henceforth His servants who owe Him obedience; whether it be sin unto death, or obedience unto righteousness?*"—The question of ver. 15 arose from an entirely erroneous way of understanding the relation between the moral will of man and the acts in which it is manifested. It seemed, according to the objection, that an act of liberty is merely an isolated fact in human life, and that an act of God's grace is enough to annul it, so that not a trace of it shall remain. Thus it is that a superficial Pelagianism understands moral liberty. After the doing of each act, it can return to the state in which it was before, exactly as if nothing had passed. But a more serious study of human life proves, on the contrary, that every act of will, whether in the direction of good or of evil, as it passes into reality, creates or strengthens a tendency which drags man with increasing force, till it becomes altogether irresistible. Every free act, then, to a certain degree determines the future. It is this psychological law which the apostle here applies to the two principles: of sin on the one hand, and grace on the other. He calls attention to the fact that he is appealing to an experiment which every one can make: *Know ye not that?* ... ? Jesus had already expressed this law when He uttered the maxim: "Whosoever committeth sin is the servant [of sin]," John viii. 34.—The words: *him to whom ye devote yourselves as servants*, refer to the first steps taken in one or other of the two opposite directions. At this point, man still enjoys a certain degree of moral liberty in relation to the principle which tends to master his will; he therefore *devotes himself*, as the apostle says. But in proportion as he yields himself to this principle by certain acts of compliance, he falls more and more under its sway: *ye are the servants of him whom ye obey*. These last words characterize the more advanced state of things, in which, the bond of dependence once formed, the will has lost all power of resistance, and exists only to satisfy the master of its choice. The words: ᾧ ὑπακούετε, *whom ye obey*, are strictly speaking a pleonasm; for this idea was already contained in the expression: δοῦλοί ἐστε, *ye are servants;* but yet they are not superfluous. They signify: "to whom obedience is now the order of the day, whether ye will or not." A man does not put himself at the service of a master to do nothing for him. In other words, *absolute* liberty cannot be the condition of man. We are made, not to create our guiding principle, but simply to adhere to one or other of the higher moral powers which solicit us. Every concession freely made to either is a precedent which binds us to it, and of which it will avail itself to exact more. Thus there is gradually and freely established the condition of dependence spoken of by the apostle, and which issues, on the one side, in the absolute incapacity of doing evil (1 John iii. 9), the state of true liberty: on the other, in the total incapacity either to will or to do good (Matt. xii. 32), the state of final perdition. Since Paul is not speaking as a philosophical moralist, but as an apostle, he immediately applies this truth to the two positive principles which he is here contrasting with one another, namely, as he says in the second part of the verse, *sin* and *obedience*. Of the two disjunctive particles ἤτοι (*whether certainly*) and ἤ (*or*), the first is somewhat more emphatic, as if the apostle meant to rely more strongly on the first alternative : Whether *certainly* of sin unto death, or, if this result do not suit you, of obedience unto righteousness."—Sin is put first, as the master to whom we are naturally subject from infancy. It is its yoke which faith has broken ; and consequently the Christian ought ever to remember that should he make any one concession to this principle, he would thereby begin to place himself anew under its dominion, and on the way which might guide him back to the goal of his previous life : death. The word *death* here cannot denote physical death, for the servants of righteousness die as well as the servants of sin. We are no longer in that part of the Epistle which treats of condemnation, and in which death appeared as a doom pronounced on the first sin, consequently as death strictly so called. It is the contrast between sin and holiness which prevails in this part, chap. vi.-viii. The matter in question, therefore, is *death* in the sense of moral corruption, and consequently of separation from God here and hereafter ; such is the abyss which sin digs ever more deeply, every time that man, nay, that the believer, even gives himself over to it. —Why, in opposition to sin, does the apostle say in the second alternative : *of obedience*, and not : *of holiness ;* and why, in opposition to : *unto death*, does he say : *unto righteousness*, and not : *unto life ?* *Obedience* is frequently understood in this passage as obedience to good or to God, in a general way. Obedience in this sense is certainly opposed to sin ; and if Paul were giving a course of morals, instead of an exposition of the Gospel, this meaning would be the most natural. But in the following verse there can be no doubt that the verb *obey* denotes the act of *faith* in the teaching of the Gospel. We have already seen, i. 5, that the apostle calls faith an *obedience*. It is the same xv. 18, where he designates the faith of the Gentiles by the name of obedience. Faith is always an act of docility to a divine manifestation, and so an obedience. Thus, then, it is faith in the gospel which the apostle here designates by the word *obedience ;* and he can perfectly contrast it with sin in this sense, because it is faith which terminates the revolt of sin and establishes the reign of holiness.[1] Every time the gospel is preached to the sinner, he is challenged to decide between *the obedience* (of faith) or the carnal independence of sin. Man does not escape from his state of sin by the simple moral contemplation of good and evil, and their respective effects, but solely by the efficacy of faith.—The words : *unto righteousness*, have been applied by some—Meyer, for example —to the sentence of *justification* which will be passed on the sanctified Christian at the last day. This interpretation has been adopted from the contrast between this term and the preceding : *unto death.* But we have just seen the term *righteousness* used, ver. 13, in the sense of *moral* righteousness ; and this is also the most suitable meaning here, where the object is to point out the holy consequences which will flow from the principle of faith. The antithesis to the term *death* also finds a simple explanation with this meaning. As death, the fruit of sin, is separation from God ; so righteousness, the fruit of faith, is spiritual communion with God. The former contains the idea of moral corruption, as the *way*, and the latter includes the idea of life, as the *goal.* If it were wished to render the contrast completely, we should have to say : " whether of *sin*, unto *unrighteousness* which is *death*, or of *obedience*, unto *righteousness* which is *life.*" By expressing himself as he does, Paul wishes, on the one hand, to inspire a

---

[1] Still, this reasoning does not show faith and obedience to be convertible terms.—T. W. C.

horror of sin, whose fruit is *death;* on the other, to bring into relief the essentially moral character of faith, the fruit of which is *righteousness.*

Vv. 17, 18. *"Now God be thanked that ye were the servants of sin, but ye obeyed from the heart that type of doctrine which was delivered you; then*[1] *being made free from sin, ye became the servants of righteousness."*—Ver. 16 established the necessity of choosing between the two masters: sin which leads to death, and faith which produces righteousness. The apostle declares in ver. 17—and he gives God thanks for it—that the Romans have already made their choice, and that the good one. The exclamation: *thanks be to God,* is not an oratorical form; it is a cry of gratitude from the depths of the apostle's heart for the marvellous work which God has wrought without him among those former Gentiles.—But can he give thanks because they were formerly *servants of sin?* There are two ways of understanding the form used here by St. Paul: either the thanksgiving is made to bear only on the second proposition, and the first is regarded as serving only to bring out by contrast the excellence of the change which has passed over his readers: "God be thanked that *whereas formerly ye were* servants . . ., ye have now obeyed" . . . Or it is held that the first proposition belongs also to the contents of the thanksgiving; for this view it is enough to emphasize strongly the imperfect *were:* "because ye *were,* that is to say, are no longer." In this sense the analogous expressions are compared, 1 Cor. vi. 11; Eph. v. 8 (see Meyer, Philippi). The second explanation is supported by the fact, that in the first meaning the contrast could not fail to be indicated by the particle μέν, as well as by the prominent position occupied at the beginning of the sentence by the verb ἦτε, *ye were.* But the use of the particle μέν is much rarer in the New Testament than in profane Greek. The place of the verb would undoubtedly be a more valid reason; in any case it explains how the apostle could follow up the expression: *thanks be to God,* immediately with the idea: *servants of sin.* But it is nevertheless true that the first meaning remains the simplest and most natural. Numerous examples of this mode of expression can be cited.—The imperfect ἦτε, *ye were,* brings out the *duration* of the past state; the aorist ὑπηκούσατε, *ye obeyed,* refers to the decisive fact by which they adhered to the gospel and broke with that former state.—The expression ἐκ καρδίας, *from the heart,* indicates their inward readiness, and the absence of all constraint. The gospel answered to a moral want within them.—The following proposition may be construed in three ways: 1. τῷ τύπῳ διδαχῆς εἰς ὃν παρεδόθητε, *because ye obeyed the form of doctrine to which ye were given over* (Chrys., Thol., De W., Mey., Philip., Winer); 2. εἰς τὸν τύπον διδαχῆς ὃν παρεδόθητε, *because ye gave obedience to* (or: *in relation to*) *the form of doctrine which was transmitted to you* (ὃς παρεδόθη ὑμῖν); so Hofmann: 3. εἰς τὸν τύπον διδαχῆς εἰς ὃν παρεδόθητε (combining the meanings of the previous constructions). Of these three constructions the first alone is admissible, because *to obey any one* or *anything* is expressed in Greek by ὑπακούειν with the dative, and not with the preposition εἰς; the latter would denote quite a different thing (the *aim* of the obedience). Paul congratulates the Romans on the fact that they have adhered with faith, docility, and eagerness to the form of Christian doctrine which was brought to them by those who first communicated to them the knowledge of the gospel. Does this *form of doctrine* denote Christianity in general, or a more special form of Christian teaching? In the former case, would not Paul have simply said: "because from the heart ye obeyed Christ or the gospel?" The choice of so exceptional a term, and so unique as that which he thinks good to use here, leads us rather to think of a special and precisely-defined form of Christian teaching. The reference is to that *gospel of Paul* (ii. 16, xvi. 25) which the first propagators of the gospel at Rome had preached there. Paul

---

[1] ℵ C read ουν instead of δε.

knew well from his own experience it was only in the pure spirituality of "his gospel" that the true power of Christian sanctification was to be found, and that every concession to the legal principle was at the same time a barrier interposed to the operation of the Holy Spirit. Hence his heartfelt joy because of the *form of doctrine* which had marked with its profound impress the moral life of the Christians of Rome. Could he without charlatanism have expressed himself thus, if, as so many critics think, the doctrine received by those Roman Christians had been of a Judaizing nature, and in contradiction to his own?—All the terms are, as it were, deliberately chosen to express the receptive condition of the readers. And first the word τύπος, *type, form* (from τύπτειν, *to strike*), which denotes an image deeply engraved, and pitted to reproduce its impress; comp. Acts xxiii. 25, where this word denotes the *exact tenor* of a missive, and the analogous term ὑποτύπωσις, 2 Tim. i. 13, used almost in the same meaning as here. Then the passive παραδοθῆναι, literally, *to be given over*, which strongly expresses the sort of moral subjection which results from the power of Christian truth once accepted. One is free to acquiesce in it or to reject it; but the Christ received becomes a master who instantly dispossesses the previous master.

If it is asked wherein exactly consisted this precise form of the truth of the gospel of which the apostle was here thinking, it seems to us that we find it best summed up in 1 Cor. i. 30, where Christ is presented, first, as *our righteousness*, then as *our sanctification*, lastly, *our* final *redemption*. It may be said that the whole didactic part of our Epistle is embraced in these three terms: chap. i.–v. in the first (δικαιοσύνη, *righteousness*), chap. vi. 1 to viii. 11 in the second (ἁγιασμός, *holiness*), and the end of chap. viii. in the third (ἀπολύτρωσις, *redemption*).

Some critics regard ver. 18 as the conclusion of the argument; but instead of the particle δέ, *now*, it would require to have been οὖν, *therefore*, which is found indeed in two Mjj., led astray by this supposition. We are not yet at the conclusion. The assertion: *ye were made subject to righteousness*, belongs still to the premises of the argument. Here in fact is the reasoning as a whole: In ver. 15 the objection: Will the believer wish to sin even once? From ver. 16 to ver. 18 the answer. Ver. 16, the major: Man cannot be absolutely free; he cannot help choosing between two masters, sin or righteousness. Vv. 17, 18, the minor: Now when you decided for faith (ver. 17), you accepted subjection to righteousness (ver. 18). The conclusion follows of itself. Therefore your progress in goodness is henceforth a matter of necessity. Accordingly, the objection started is resolved: you could not sin even once without renouncing the new principle to which you have given yourselves. We thus see how Paul has succeeded in rediscovering a law even in grace, but a law inward and spiritual, like his whole gospel. It is Christ Himself who, after having freed us from sin by His death, by uniting us to His life as the Risen One, has made us subject to righteousness.

But the apostle, in his exposition of the relation between the believer and his new master, had used an expression which jarred on his own sense of propriety, and which he feels the need of excusing and explaining. It was the word *servitude* (*slavery*), applied to the believer's dependence on *righteousness*. Is then the practice of goodness a servitude? Is it not, on the contrary, the most glorious freedom? Most certainly, and to this thought the remark applies which begins ver. 19; after which, in the second part of the verse, the apostle concludes this development with a practical exhortation.

Ver. 19. "*I speak after the manner of men because of the infirmity of your flesh: for as ye have yielded your members servants to uncleanness, and to iniquity unto iniquity; even so now yield your members servants to righteousness unto holiness.*"—Several critics (Beng., De Wette, Mey., Philip.) refer the *fleshly infirmity* of the Romans, of which the apostle here speaks, to their *intellectual* weakness, their inability to apprehend religious truth adequately. This is the reason which has led him to make use of a *human* mode of speaking, calling the fulfilment of righteousness a *servitude*, which, from the divine point of view, is, on the contrary, true liberty. What is well-founded in this explanation is the application of the first words of ver. 19 to the term *servitude* used in ver. 18. But what seems to me inexact, is to apply the expression *weakness of the flesh* to a defect of understanding. Does not this explanation contradict what the apostle recognizes in such forcible terms, xv. 14: the high degree of Christian knowledge to which the Church of Rome has already attained? *Weakness of the flesh* (more literally: *proceeding from the flesh*) must therefore denote a general state shared by the Romans with the great majority of the members of the Christian Church, consequently a moral rather than an intellectual state; and this is really what the expression used by the apostle naturally indicates. If the obligation to practice righteousness seems to the greater number of believers to be a subjection to a strange principle, it is not in consequence of a want of understanding; the cause is deeper; it is because *the flesh*, the love of the *ego*, has not yet been completely sacrificed. From this moral fact there arises even in the Christian the painful impression that perfect righteousness is a most exacting, sometimes even a harsh master, and that the obligation to conform in all points to the will of God makes him a slave. Such is the imperfect moral condition to the impressions of which Paul accommodates his language in the expressions used in ver. 18. The ancient Greek interpreters thought this remark, ver. 19*a*, should be connected with what follows, giving it the meaning: "I do not mean to ask of you what goes beyond your human weakness, caused by the flesh; yield your members only to righteousness *in the same measure* as you formerly yielded them to sin. I do not ask more of you." But it is evident that the apostle, in a passage in which he is describing the standard of Christian holiness, cannot think of abating aught of the demands of the new principle. The exhortation which follows cannot be less absolute than that which preceded, vv. 12, 13, and which was unaccompanied by any such clause. Hofmann and Schott take the two words ἀνθρώπινον λέγω, *I speak as a man*, as a parenthesis, and join the regimen διὰ τὴν ἀσθένειαν, *on account of the weakness of the flesh*, to the verb: *ye became subject*, ver. 18. According to this view Paul recognizes that the practice of goodness *is* really a servitude for the believer, subjection to a strange will; and that arising from the persistence of the old nature, and from the fact that the flesh requires to be constantly subdued. But it is very doubtful whether the apostle here seriously called by the name of servitude that Christian life which he represents always, like Jesus Himself, as the most glorious emancipation. Undoubtedly, in 1 Cor. ix. 27, he uses the expression δουλαγωγεῖν, *to bring into subjection*, but in a figure, and in relation to the *body*.

The imperative *yield* proves that the second part of the verse is an exhortation. But in this case why attach it with a *for* to what precedes? Can an exhortation serve to demonstrate anything? Does it not require itself to be founded on a demonstration? To understand this strange form, we must, I think, change the imperative *yield* into the form: "*ye are held bound* to yield." We can then understand how this idea may be connected by *for* with ver. 18: "Ye were made subject to righteousness henceforth, since, in fact (*for*), it remains to you only to yield your members." It must not be forgotten, indeed, that the exhortation: *yield your members*, was already expressed previously in vv. 12 and 13, and that as logically based on all that preceded (*therefore*, ver. 12), and that consequently the transition from ver. 18*b* to 19*b* may be thus paraphrased: "ye became the servants of righteousness, for, in fact, as I have shown you, ye have now nothing else to do than to yield your members to righteousness." The only difference between the exhortation of vv. 12 and 13 and that of 18*b* is that Paul said in the former : *do ;* while here, in keeping with the object of this second passage, he says : "And *ye cannot* do otherwise." By this relation between the *for* of ver. 19*b* and ver. 18, it may be proved that 19*a* is indeed, as we have seen, an interjected observation.

There is a slightly ironical touch in the meaning of the second part of ver. 19. It concerns the readers to be now in the service of their new master, righteousness, as active and zealous servants as they formerly were in the service of their old master. "Ye were eager to yield your members to sin to commit evil, be ye now as eager to yield them to righteousness to realize holiness. Do not inflict on this second master the shame of serving him less faithfully than the first." The old master is denoted by the two terms ἀκαθαρσία, *uncleanness,* and ἀνομία, *lawlessness,* life going beyond all rule, licentiousness.. The first of these terms characterizes sin as personal degradation, the second as contempt of the standard of right written in the law on every man's conscience (ii. 14, 15). This distinction seems to us more natural than that laid down by Tholuck, who takes the term *uncleanness* in the strictly proper sense of the word, and who takes *lawlessness* to be sin in general. The broad sense which we give to the word *uncleanness* appears clearly from 1 Thess. iv. 7. The two expressions therefore embrace each, as it seems to us, the whole sphere of sin, but from two different points of view.—From sin as a principle, the apostle passes to sin as an effect.[1] The regimen εἰς ἀνομίαν, *unto lawlessness,* signifies : to do all one's pleasure without being arrested in the least by the line of demarkation which separates good from evil. This expression ἀνομία, *lawlessness,* so expressly repeated, and this whole description of the previous life of the readers, is evidently more applicable to men formerly Gentiles than to believers of Jewish origin.—With sin characterized as an evil disposition, as an inward *principle,* in the two forms of degradation and lawlessness, there is contrasted goodness, also as a principle and as a moral disposition, by the term δικαιοσύνη, *righteousness.* This is the will of God, moral obligation accepted by the believer as the absolute rule of his will and life. Then with sin as an *effect* produced in the form of ἀνομία, the rejection of every rule in practice, there is contrasted goodness as a result obtained, by the term ἁγιασμός : this is the concrete and personal realization of goodness, the fruit of perpetual submission to the principle of righteousness, *holiness,* or *sanctification.* The word ἁγιασμός is usually translated by *sanctification,* and this is represented as the progressive amelioration of the individual resulting from his moral self-discipline. It is certain that Greek substantives in μος or σμος are, as Curtius says (*Schulgramm.* § 342), *nomina actionis,* denoting properly an action put forth, rather than a state of being. But we must not forget two things : 1. That, from the Scripture point of view, the author of the act denoted by the term *sanctify* is God, and not man ; this is established, as it seems to me, by 1 Pet. i. 2, 2 Thess. ii. 13, and 1 Cor. i. 30, where this act is ascribed to the Holy Spirit and to Christ. 2. That even in the Old Testament the term ἁγιασμός seems to be used in the LXX. to denote not the progressive work, but its result ; thus Amos ii. 11, where the LXX. use this word to translate *nezirim, the consecrated ones ;* and Ezek. xlv. 4, where it seems to be taken in the same sense as *mikdasch, sanctuary.* In the New Testament, likewise, it more naturally denotes the result reached than the action put forth, in the following passages : 1 Thess. iv. 3 ; 1 Tim. ii. 15 ; Heb. xii. 14. We are thus led to translate it rather by the term *holiness.* And this seems to be confirmed by the preposition εἰς, *for, unto,* which expresses the goal rather than the way. If it is asked wherein the term ἁγιασμός, taken in the sense of *holiness,* still differs from ἁγιότης. (Heb. xii. 10) and ἁγιωσύνη (i. 4 ; 1 Thess. iii. 13 ; 2. Cor. vii. 1), which

---

[1] That is, as an abiding state.

seem to be completely synonymous, the indication of the shade may be found in the form of the terminations : ἁγιότης denotes holiness as an abstract idea ; ἁγιωσύνη, as a personal quality, an inward disposition ; ἁγιασμός, as a work which has reached the state of complete realization in the person and life, the result of the divine act expressed by ἁγιάζειν.

The apostle has thus reminded the church of the two principles between which it has finally made its choice, and the necessity laid on the believer to be as thoroughgoing in his new master's service as he had been in that of the former ; he now labors to strengthen this choice and decision by presenting the consequences of the one and the other condition of dependence. On the one side, shame and death ; on the other, holiness and life. Here is the second part of the passage : vv. 20 and 21 describe the consequences of the service of sin to their extreme limit ; ver. 22 gives the consequences of dependence on God also to their final goal ; ver. 23, in an antithesis full of solemnity, formulates this double end of human life.

Vv. 20, 21. "*For when ye were the servants of sin, ye were free in respect of righteousness. What fruit therefore had ye then? Things of which ye are now ashamed ; for certainly*[1] *their end is death.*"—We must seek the counterpart of ver. 20, not in ver. 18, which belongs to a passage now concluded, but in ver. 22. In ver. 20, indeed, there begins the description of the *consequences* of the two services. The *for* bears on the exhortation contained in ver. 19*b*. It would be impossible to depict the degrading character of the former dependence in which his readers had lived, more keenly than the apostle does in the words : *free in respect of righteousness*. The conviction of what is righteous did not for a moment hamper them in their course of life. This was an annoyance which they did not feel ! To use the expression of Scripture, they drank iniquity as one drinketh up water.

Ver. 21. And what was the result of this shameful liberty ? The apostle analyzes it into a *fruit*, καρπός, and an *end*, τέλος. *What fruit had ye then?* he asks literally. The verb ἔχειν, *to have*, no more here than in i. 13, signifies *to produce*. Paul would rather have used for this meaning one of the verbs φέρειν or ποιεῖν. By saying that they *have* this fruit, he wishes to express not only the idea that they produce it, but that they possess and keep it in themselves, that they drag it with them as forming part of their own moral life. "Their works follow them," as is said. Commentators are not at one as to the meaning of the following words : *things of which ye are now ashamed*. Some, like the Peshitto, Theod., Theoph., Er., Luth., Mel., Thol., De W., Olsh., Philip., take these words as the answer to the question put : "This is the fruit, namely, acts of which, now that ye are in Christ, ye cannot think without confusion ; for ye now see clearly that the goal to which they were leading you inevitably was death." But some commentators (Chrys., Grot., Beng., Fritzs., Mey.) regard these words as a continuation of the preceding question : "What fruit did ye derive from those things of which ye are now ashamed ?" The answer in this case would be understood. According to Meyer, it would simply be : *none*, of course taking the word *fruit* in an exclusively good sense. Or the answer might be supposed to be : *a very evil fruit*, finding the proof of this evil quality in the following words : "For their end is death." But whatever may be the answer which is sought to be supplied, this construction, by prolonging the question with this long incidental proposition, has the disadvantage of taking away from its vivacity, and making the sentence extremely heavy. Besides, we must supply before the relative ἐφ' οἷς, *of which*, some antecedent or other, such as ἐκείνων or ἐξ ἐκείνων, which is not very natural. If account is taken of the very marked contrast between the two adverbs of time, *then* and *now*, τότε and νῦν, we shall be led rather to

---

[1] B D E F G read here μεν (το μεν γαρ) ; T. R., with ℵ A C K L P, omits the μεν.

see here two distinct propositions than only one. Finally, we find in ver. 22 the result described under two distinct aspects: as *fruit*, καρπός, and as *end*, τέλος. Should it not be the same in our verse, to which ver. 22 corresponds? This would not be the case in the sense preferred by Meyer. It would be necessary to make τέλος (*end*) almost the synonym and explanation of καρπός (*fruit*). This commentator relies especially on the fact that the apostle gives to the word *fruit* only a good sense; so Gal. v. 19 and 22, where he speaks of the *works* of the flesh and the *fruit* of the Spirit, and Eph. v. 11, where he characterizes the *works* of darkness as being *without fruit* (ἄκαρπα). But Meyer does not take into consideration that the mind of the apostle is here moving in the domain of a *sustained figure*, which he applies successively to the two opposite servitudes. On both sides he sees: 1. A *master* (sin, God); 2. A *servant* (the natural man, the believer): 3. Some *work* or other in the service of the master; 4. *Fruit*, which is the immediate product of the labor, the work itself (the things of which the workers are ashamed, or those which lead to holiness); 5. An *end*, as retribution at the hand of the master (death, eternal life). It is therefore evident that the figure of *fruit* is in place on the one side as well as on the other. So thoroughly is this the thought of the apostle, that in ver. 22 he says to the believer: Ye have "*your fruit*," in evident contrast to that which they had previously as sinners. As to those who to the question: *What fruit had ye?* understand this wholly different answer: a *bad, detestable* fruit, it is impossible for them to explain so important an ellipsis. We do not therefore hesitate to prefer the first of the two explanations proposed: "What fruit did ye then derive from your labor in the service of sin? Such fruit, that now when ye are enlightened, it only fills you with shame," ἔργα τοῦ σκότους (the works of darkness), Eph. v. 11.[1]

The *for* which connects the last proposition with the preceding bears on the notion of *shame*. In point of fact, the final result of those things, their τέλος (*end*), which is *death*, demonstrates their shameful nature. "It is most fitting indeed that ye should blush for them now; for their end is death." In this fact: death, as the end, there is expressed the estimate of God Himself. I regard as authentic the particle μέν, which is read here by five Mjj. It seems to me impossible that it should have been added; its omission, on the contrary, is easily explained. It is the particle known under the name of μέν *solitarium*, to which there is no corresponding δέ, and which is merely intended expressly to reserve a certain side of the truth which the reader is guarded against forgetting: "For (whatever may be the virtue of grace) it remains nevertheless true that" . . .—The *end* differs from the *fruit* in that the latter is the immediate result, the very realization of the labor, its *moral* product; while the *end* is the manifestation of God's approval or displeasure.—*Death* here evidently denotes *final* death, eternal separation from God, ἀπώλεια (*perdition*).

Ver. 22. "*But now, being made free from sin and become servants to God, ye have your fruit holiness, and your end everlasting life.*"—For the abstract master designated above, namely righteousness, Paul here substitutes *God* Himself; for in Christ it is to the living God the believer is united. The form of expression used by Paul, literally rendered, would be: "Ye have your fruit in the direction of holiness." It is to the state of holiness that ye are brought. Such, in fact, is the result of action constantly kept up in dependence on God. Every duty discharged is a step on the way at the end of which God's servant sees the sublime ideal of ἁγιασμός, completed holiness, shining.—To this *fruit* God is pleased to add what Paul calls the *end:* eternal life. Besides holiness, this expression embraces glory, imperishable happiness, perfect activity.

---

[1] Both constructions are grammatical and yield a good sense, and have divided interpreters from an early period; but the second is the more simple and natural, and has been favored by the majority of critics and editors.—T. W. C.

In ver. 23 the apostle sums up in a few definite strokes those two contrasted pictures.

Ver. 23. "*For the wages of sin is death; but the gift of God is eternal life in Jesus Christ our Lord.*"—On the one side, *wages*, something earned. The word ὀψώνιον strictly denotes *payment in kind*, then the payment in money which a general gives his soldiers. And so it is obvious that the complement τῆς ἁμαρτίας, *of sin*, is not here the genitive of the object: the wages paid *for* sin, but the genitive of the subject: the wages paid *by* sin. Sin is personified as man's natural master (vv. 12, 14, 22), and he is represented as paying his subjects with *death*. This term, according to the apostle, does not seem to denote the annihilation of the sinner. To pay any one is not to put him out of existence; it is rather to make him feel the painful consequences of his sin, to make him reap in the form of corruption what he has sowed in the form of sin (Gal. vi. 7, 8; 2 Cor. v. 10).—In the second proposition the apostle does not speak of *wages*, but of a *gift of grace* (χάρισμα). This term is taken here in its most general sense; it comprehends the *fulness of salvation*. Everything in this work, from the initial justification to the final absolution, including sanctification and preparing for glory, is a free gift, an unmerited favor, like that Christ Himself who has been made unto us righteousness, holiness, and redemption. "Hell," says Hodge, "is *always* earned; heaven, *never*." The apostle closes with the words: *in Christ Jesus our Lord;* for it is in Him that this entire communication of divine mercy to the faithful takes place. Here, again, for the διά, *by*, which was the preposition used in the preceding part (for example, v. 1, 2, 11, 17, 21), Paul substitutes the ἐν, *in*, which is more in keeping with the mode of sanctification. After being justified *by Him*, we are sanctified *in Him*, in communion of life with Him.

It is commonly thought that this twenty-third verse, as well as the whole passage of which it is a summary, applies to the *believer* only from the view-point of the second alternative, that of eternal life, and that the unconverted only are referred to by the apostle when he speaks of the *service* of sin and of its fatal goal, *death*. But the tenor of ver. 15 proves how erroneous this view is. What is the aim of this passage? To reply to the question: "Shall we sin because we are under grace?" Now this question can only be put in reference to believers. It is to them, therefore, that the reply contained in this whole passage applies. Neither could Paul say in respect of unconverted sinners what we find in ver. 21: "those things whereof we are now ashamed." It is therefore certain that he conceives the possibility of a return to the service of sin—a return which would lead them to eternal death as certainly as other sinners. It follows, even from the relation between the question of ver. 15 and the answer, vv. 16-23, that such a relapse may arise from a single voluntary concession to the continual solicitations of the old master, sin. A single affirmative answer to the question: "Shall I commit an act of sin, since I am under grace?" might have the effect of placing the believer again on the inclined plane which leads to the abyss. A striking example of this fact occurs in our very Epistle. In chap. xiv. 15 and 20, Paul declares to the man who induces a weak brother to commit an act of sin contrary to his conscience, that thereby he may *cause that brother to perish for whom Christ died*, and *destroy in him the work of God*. Such will infallibly be the result, if this sin, not being quickly blotted out by pardon and restoration, becomes consolidated, and remains permanently interposed between him and his God.[1]

---

[1] This entire paragraph and the reasoning it contains seem to be purely gratuitous, neither required nor suggested by the apostle's words.—T. W. C.

FIFTEENTH PASSAGE (7:1-6)

The Believer is set free from the Law at the same Time that he is set free from Sin

AGREEABLY to the proposition stated vi. 14 : " Sin shall no more have dominion over you : for ye are under grace," the apostle had just expounded emancipation from sin by subjection to grace. But he had said : " For ye are *not under the law*, but under grace." And the words underlined required a special explanation. It is this demonstration which is furnished by the following passage. In his view the two emancipations, that from sin and that from the law, are two closely connected facts, so that the one is the complement of the other. Also between the descriptions of the two deliverances there is to be remarked a parallelism of figures which extends to the slightest details of the two descriptions. It is easy to see how exactly vii. 1–4 corresponds to vi. 16–19, and vii. 5, 6, to vi. 21–23. Only the general figure in the two cases is borrowed from different domains of social life. The law being a nobler master than sin, the apostle in speaking of it substitutes for the degrading relation of *servitude*, the more exalted one of *marriage;* and hence also in vv. 5 and 6 for the figure of *fruits* (of labor) he puts that of *children* (the issue of marriage).

To prove the believer's emancipation from legal bondage, Paul supports his argument by an article of the law itself, which he applies spiritually, vv. 1–4 ; then he shows that the believer makes use of this right, not to yield himself more freely to sin, but to serve God better than he would have done under the law (vv. 5, 6). His emancipation in relation to the law is therefore legitimate—more than that, it is morally beneficial and necessary.

The first three verses adduce the example cited from the law, and the fourth applies it.

Vv. 1, 2. "*Or are ye ignorant, brethren (for I speak to them that know the law), that the law hath dominion over a man for as long time as he liveth ? For the married woman is bound by the law to her living husband ; but if the husband have died, she is loosed from the law*[1] *of the husband.*"—We are familiar with the meaning of Paul's question : *Or are ye ignorant ;* it explodes the negation of the expounded truth by an indisputable truth. The meaning here is therefore : Or, if ye are afraid, in the work of your sanctification, to yield yourselves solely to this new master, grace, and think that ye cannot dispense with an external rule like that of the law, know ye not that . . . ? The form of address : *brethren*, had not occurred, as Hofmann observes, since i. 13. The apostle is about to have recourse to a more familiar mode of teaching than he had hitherto used in his Epistle ; hence he approaches his readers addressing them by this title, which gives to what follows the character of a conversation.—In the parenthesis : *for I speak to those who . . .*, the *for* refers to the negative answer which is to be supplied after the question : *are ye ignorant:* " No, ye cannot be ignorant of the legal prescription which I am about to quote" . . .—We must avoid translating as if the article τοῖς stood before the participle γινώσκουσι : "*to those among you who know the law.*" The grammatical form proves that the apostle here, as well as by the word *brethren*, is addressing the whole of the church of Rome. This is one of the passages from which many conclude that this church was almost exclusively composed of Jews (Baur, Holtzmann), or at least of proselytes (De Wette, Beyschl.). Nevertheless, even Mangold

---

[1] T. R. omits the words του νομου without any authority ; a simple oversight.

264 / Sanctification

allows (p. 73) that "this expression may apply also to Christians of Gentile origin, as the O. T. was received and read throughout the whole church as a document of revelation." One might even go farther, and maintain that it would be superfluous to remind those who had been Jews that they are such as *know the law*. Very early the reading of the O. T. passed from the worship of the synagogue to that of the church. The Epistles addressed to the churches of the Gentiles prove to what an extent the apostles assumed their readers to be acquainted with the history and oracles of the O. T. St. Paul thus interrogates the Galatians, who certainly were not of Jewish origin (iv. 21) : "Tell me, ye that desire to be under the law, understand ye not the law ?"—Now, here is one of the articles of that law, which, spiritually applied, solved the question of the relation between the Christian and the law. The code, in case of death, allowed the surviving spouse to remarry. If, consequently, it is a fact that there was a death in the case of the believer, it follows, according to the law itself, that he is set free from the law, his former spouse. Such is the summary of the following verses.—So true is it that ver. 1 is still connected with ver. 14, and gives the development of the words of that verse : *not under the law*, that the term κυριεύειν, *to be master*, to have power over, is borrowed from that verse.—The term *man*, ἄνθρωπος, may designate either sex. In ver. 2, where the case of the female is specially in question, Paul uses another word (ἀνήρ) to denote the husband.—The subject of the verb ζῇ, *lives*, according to our translation, is, *the man*. The law bears rule over the individual man, so far as his civil relations are concerned, as long as he is in life. Some commentators (Or., Er., Beng.) understand as the subject of the verb *lives*, νόμος, *the law*. This would give the idea of the abolition of the law by the coming of Christ, in the sense of x. 4. But this sense is incompatible with the following verse, where the word ζῶντι (to the *living* husband) reproduces the idea of ζῇ, *liveth*, from ver. 1, as well as with the antithesis : "but if *the husband be dead*." Besides, the idea of the whole passage is not that of the objective abolition of the law by the coming of Christ ; the point in question is the believer's subjective emancipation from this external standard through faith in Christ's death. Philippi agrees with us in making ὁ ἄνθρωπος, *man*, the subject of the verb ζῇ, *liveth ;* but he applies the notion of *living* to life *in sin* (vi. 2), to which faith in Christ has put an end (vi. 2–11). The meaning of these last words of the verse would thus be : "The law has only power over the man as long as he continues in his own life, in his natural state of sin ; from the time he renounces it to enter into union with Christ, he is set free from the law." Hence it would follow that ver. 1, instead of citing an *example* taken from the law, with the view of illustrating the thought of the passage, would itself express this thought. But it is impossible thus to separate ver. 1 from the sequel. The *for* of ver. 2 shows that the latter is only the explanation of the article of the law quoted in ver. 1. Besides, how could the reader have suspected this extraordinary meaning of the word *live*, which would here designate neither common life nor life in God ? Finally, the words : "I speak to you as to those who know the law," forbid us to take the following maxim as anything else than an extract from the law. The first three verses form a whole : the example, namely, taken from the code relating to conjugal life. Ver. 4 will apply the general maxim contained in this example to the domain of religion.

Ver. 2. The maxim cited in ver. 1 is developed in ver. 2. The same law which renders the woman inseparable from the man as long as he lives, sets her free from this subjection as soon as he dies. In the first proposition the emphasis is on the word ζῶντι, *living ;* in the second, on the words : *if he be dead*. The precept Deut. xxiv. 2 expressly authorized the marriage of a woman *put away* by her first husband with a second ; and *a fortiori*, a new marriage after the first husband was *dead*. If, in the first proposition, the apostle does not speak of the case of divorce, it is because he is referring to the woman as the acting party, and because in any case it did not belong to the woman to put away her husband. The husband alone had the right to give a letter of divorce, Deut. xxiv. 1. The expression κατήργηται, literally: *is annulled, has ceased to be*, and hence, naturally, *is freed from*, is chosen to extend in a sense to the woman herself the notion of *death*, which applies in strictness only to the husband. The conjugal bond being broken by the husband's death, the wife dies also *as a wife*. Thus the formula of ver. 1, which seemed to apply only to the deceased, is found to apply likewise to the widow. She is dead (to the conjugal bond) in her dead husband. Some take the expression: *the law of the husband*, as meaning the article of the code concerning marriage, *lex ad maritum pertinens*. But it is more natural to understand by this law *the legal power* with which the husband is invested in relation to his wife.—The difficult question in this verse is why Paul takes as an example a wife losing her husband and free to remarry, rather than a husband losing his wife and enjoying the same right. For the two cases equally demonstrate the truth of the maxim of ver. 1. The fact that the law bound the woman more strictly than the husband, does not suffice to explain this preference. It is the application which Paul proposes to make of his example to the spiritual life which will give us the solution of the question. It shows, in point of fact, that Paul had in view not only the breaking of the believer's soul with the law (the first husband), but also its new union to the risen Christ (the second husband). Now in this figure of the second marriage, Christ could only represent the husband, and the believer, consequently, the wife. And this is what leads the apostle to take a step farther, and to attribute *death* to the wife herself. For Christ having died, the believing soul cannot espouse Him except as itself dead.

Ver. 3. " *So then if, while the husband liveth, she be married to another man, she shall be called an adulteress; but if the husband be dead, she is freed from the law, that she may not be an adulteress, though she be married to another man.*"—This verse is not a needless repetition of ver. 2. It serves to draw from the legal prescription explained in ver. 2 the conclusion which the apostle has to demonstrate—the *legitimacy* of a second union in the case supposed. What would be a crime during the husband's lifetime, becomes legitimate when he is dead.—The term χρηματίζειν strictly signifies *to do business*, and hence: to bear the name of the profession to which one is devoted. To this day a large number of our family names are names of some trade. Comp. also Acts xi. 26.—The expression: *freed from the law*, is defined by the context: it bears special reference to the law on the rule of marriage. But the expression is designedly kept up in all its generality to prepare for the absolute application of it to believers, which the apostle is about to make.—*That she may not be an adulteress* (if she marries again): the law was really intended to reserve for her such liberty.—Augustine, Beza, and Olshausen have attempted another explanation, according to which vv. 2 and 3 are not the development, but the *allegorical application* of the maxim of ver. 1. In its clearest form it is as follows, as it seems to me: The woman bound by the law to her living husband is the human soul subjected by the law to the dominion *of sin* (the first husband). The latter, sin, dying (through faith in Christ crucified), the soul is set free from his power, and enjoys the liberty of entering into union with Christ risen (the new husband). But this explanation would carry us back to the idea of the preceding passage (emancipation *from sin*), whereas ver. 6 shows clearly that Paul means to speak here of emancipation *from the law*. Then the relation between vv. 1 and 2 would require to be expressed, not by *for*, but by *so* (οὕτω), or *so that* (ὥστε). Finally, the ὥστε, *so that*, of ver. 4 shows it is not till then that the moral application begins.

Ver. 4. " *So that, my brethren, ye also are become dead to the law by the body of Christ; that ye should belong to another, even to Him who is raised from the dead, that we should bring forth fruit to God.*"—Coming to the application, the apostle approaches his readers anew, and more closely, addressing them as: *my brethren*. It is as if he were to say to them familiarly: Let us see! Now, then, is it not clear to you all?—The conjunction ὥστε, *so that*, cannot be taken, as some have sought to do, in the sense of *likewise*, or *so then*. The natural sense: *so that*, is perfectly suitable, if only the force of this conjunction is made to bear not exclusively on the following verb: *Ye are dead to the law*, but on the verb with its entire connection: *Ye are dead to the law; that ye should belong to another*. It is not the death of believers in Christ crucified whose legitimacy the apostle wished to show by the preceding example taken from the law, but the new union of which this death is the condition.—The same need of drawing close to his readers which suggests the form of address: *my brethren*, leads him also to use the second person, which is more in keeping with the direct application to which he is now coming.—*Ye also:* quite like this wife who is dead (as a wife) through her husband's death, and who thus has the right to marry again.—Ἐθανατώθητε, *ye are dead*, or more literally: *Ye have been put to death in relation to the law*. The first aorist passive here expresses, as usual, the highest degree of passivity. Jesus draws believers as it were violently into communion with Him in His sufferings. This participation in His violent death is not exactly the same in this passage as that spoken of in ver. 6 of the preceding chapter. The latter referred to the believer's death *to sin*, whereas Paul says here: "Ye are dead *to the law*." Christ on the cross died to the law, inasmuch as this punishment set Him free from the jurisdiction of the law, under which He had passed His life, and from the Jewish nationality which had determined the form of His earthly existence (Gal. iv. 4). The believer who appropriates this death appropriates also the glorious liberty which in the case of Christ was its consequence. Delivered in Him from the *law of ordinances* (Eph. ii. 15), he enters with Him into the higher life of communion with God. When Paul says: *by the body of Christ*, he reminds us that it was this body which formed the bond between Christ and the theocratic nation (i. 3); and that this bond once broken in His case by death, it is also broken in that of believers, who draw their life from Him. There is no reference in this context to the *gift* of His body as the *price* of our *redemption* (Gess).—The application of the idea of *death* to believers, in the words: *Ye are dead to the law*, agrees with the observation we have made on the expression κατήργηται, *she* (the wife) *is annulled, has ceased to be* (as a wife), at the end of ver. 2. As the new husband is a dead and risen Christ, the wife must necessarily be represented as dead (through the death of her first husband, the law), that she may be in a position to be united to Christ as one risen again. It is a marriage, as it were, beyond the tomb. And hence it is that the apostle is not content with saying: "Ye have been put to death in relation to the law; *that ye should belong to another*," but adds immediately: "*to Him who is raised from the dead.*"— We can now understand perfectly how Paul, with this application in view from the beginning, extended the notion of *death*, which, strictly speaking, applied only to the husband, to the wife, by the term κατήργηται, *she is abolished, has ceased to be*, ver. 2.—It is easy to see that this figure of a *marriage* between the soul dead in Christ crucified and Christ risen expresses exactly the same idea as we have found already in vi. 5, and as was developed in the whole passage vi. 6–10; only this idea is resumed here to deduce from it the believer's enfranchisement in regard to the law. We may therefore thus sum up the contents of these four verses: As by His death Christ entered upon an existence set free from every legal statute and determined by the life of God alone, so we, when we have died to sin, enter with Him into this same life in which, like a remarried widow, we have no other master than this new Spouse and His Spirit.

The object of this new union, says Paul, concluding this development, ver. 4, is, *that we may bring forth fruit unto God*. By this expression he unmistakably continues and completes the figure which he began, namely, that of marriage. The new issue which is to spring from this union between the Risen One and His church is an activity rich in holy works wrought in the service of God (καρποφορῆσαι τῷ Θεῷ, *to bear fruit unto God*). To reject this view of the figure is to show a prudery which is neither in harmony with the spirit of antiquity, nor with that of the gospel itself. It is, in fine, to put oneself in contradiction to the two following verses, which can leave no doubt as to the apostle's real meaning.—On what does the *that* depend? Hofmann and Schott hold that it must be connected solely with the last words: *to Him that is raised from the dead, that* . . . ; Christ is *raised* to a celestial life *that* He might communicate it to us, and render us active in God's service. But the aim of the resurrection cannot be thus restricted, and the sequel proves that the *that* depends, as is natural, on the principal idea: *that ye should be married to another*. It is not the resurrection, it is the union of the believer with the Risen One, which has for its end to give birth to a life of good works. This appears from the following verses, in which the apostle contrasts union with the law, which produced fruits of sin, with union with Christ, which results in the best fruits. What has led Hofmann to this false explanation is the desire to account for the transition from the second person plural: *ye have been put to death . . . ye were married . . .*, to the first: *we should bring forth fruit:* "*He is raised* for us, *believers*, that *we* should bring forth" . . . Some commentators, indeed (Meyer, to a certain extent), suppose that the verb in the second person and the pronoun ὑμᾶς (*you*) were written from the viewpoint of Judeo-Christians; for, it is said, only people formerly subject to the law could *become dead in relation to it*. The last verb in the first person is, on the contrary, it is said, written from the standpoint of all Christians. But the author of these lines, being himself of Jewish origin, would require to say, and especially when speaking of Judeo-Christians, *we*, rather than *ye*. Comp. Gal. iii. 13, where, speaking in the name of believers of Jewish origin, he says *we*, to contrast with them afterward, in ver. 14, *the Gentiles*, and in the end to combine both in a final *we*. The true explanation of the contrast between *ye* and *we* in our passage is simpler. At the beginning of this passage, Paul, to get near to his readers, had passed from the didactic tone to the direct address: *brethren!* It was a way of saying to them: "Understand thoroughly, brethren; it is your own history which was contained beforehand in this legal prescription." A new and still more urgent apostrophe had followed in ver. 4 (*my brethren*), at the point where from the explanation Paul was passing to the application. And now the application being made by the: *Ye became dead, that ye should belong*, the didactic tone of the treatise recommenced with the: *that we should bring forth fruit*, which is true not only of the Roman readers, but of the whole Church; and the first person continues (vv. 5, 6); comp. viii. 12, 13 (the inverse change). In ver. 6 he also affirms, as well as in ver. 4, things which at first sight can only suit believers of Jewish origin: "*that* (the law) *under the power of which we were held*." This is because the apostle does not forget that the experiment of the effects of the law made by the Jews is to the benefit of all mankind. For if the law had continued for the Jews, its maintenance must have issued in extending the reign of the law to the rest of the world; and so it was indeed that Paul's adversaries understood it (*the Judaizing false brethren*), so that it is when addressing all believers that he can say: "Ye became dead to the law by the body of Christ, that ye should be married to the Risen One." Calvin also says, speaking of every Christian: "From hand to hand, *passing from the power of the law*, we were given over to Christ." Apart from Christ, the Gentiles would have no other religious future than subjection to the

Jewish law.—The apostle had just proved by the law itself that believers, in consequence of the death which they have undergone, may *without unfaithfulness* cast off the yoke of the law, and contract a new union with Christ. He now points out the grave reason which they have for using this right and preferring this new union to the previous one. The fruits which shall issue from it will be as excellent as those which proceeded from the former were detestable. This expression : *fruits*, recalls the conclusion of the preceding passage, vi. 20-23, where the moral result of the two *servitudes* was described. Here the subject is two *marriages*. The contents of the two verses 5 and 6 were announced in the last words of ver. 4. And first, ver. 5 : the first marriage and its fruits.

Ver. 5. "*For when we were in the flesh, the affections of sins, excited by the law, did work in our members to bring forth fruit unto death ;*"—The *for* evidently bears not on ver. 5 only, but on vv. 5 and 6 together.—The expression : *to be in the flesh*, is very far from being synonymous with *living in the body ;* comp. Gal. ii. 20. The term *flesh*, denoting literally the soft parts of the body, which are the usual seat of agreeable or painful sensations, is applied in biblical language to the whole natural man, in so far as he is yet under the dominion of the love of pleasure and the fear of pain, that is to say, of the tendency to self-satisfaction. The natural complacency of the ego with itself—such is the idea of the word *flesh* in the moral sense in which it is so often used in Scripture. Now, what part does the law play in the moral development of man in this state ? The *affections of sins*, παθήματα ἁμαρτιῶν, are, says Paul, *excited by it*. The Greek term, which may be rendered by *affection* or *passion*, denotes an essentially passive state. And, indeed, the affections of sense, which correspond to certain external objects fitted to satisfy them, are less of the nature of spontaneous determinations of the will, than the effect of impressions received. As to the complement : *of sins*, it might be taken either as the genitive of *cause* (produced by sins), or of *quality* (which have the character of sins). But in both senses the singular : *of sin*, would have been more natural. This complement might also be explained as the genitive *of apposition :* the affections *in which* the varied inward forms of sin *consist*, such emotions as are intemperate or impure, interested or proud, selfish or violent. But is it not more natural to see in this complement : *of sins*, the genitive of *effect ?* the affections which do not fail to produce every kind of sins, as soon as, being strongly excited, they seek their gratification.—The regimen : *by the law*, depends directly on the word παθήματα, *the affections ;* it cannot signify : *produced* by the law, which would be to say too much ; for they result from the natural state which Paul designated by the expression : *to be in the flesh*. We must therefore explain : *excited* by the law ; this coming into collision with those instincts which were asleep, makes them pass into the active and violent state. Why as a fact do we find man degrading himself so often, by passing beyond the simple satisfaction of his wants, and plunging into excesses to which the brute does not descend ? There is not in the latter case that arrest of law which seems so often nothing more to man than an incitement to evil-doing.—The term ἐνηργεῖτο, *acted, operated*, literally, *worked within*, denotes that sort of inward fermentation which is produced when the passions, excited by the resistance of the commandment, seek to master the body in order to their gratification. The verb ἐνεργεῖσθαι, *to act, operate*, is always taken by Paul in the middle sense, which we give to it here, never in the passive sense : *to be put in action ;* comp. 1 Thess. ii. 13 ; 2 Thess. ii. 7 ; Gal. v. 6 ; 2 Cor. i. 6, iv. 12, etc. etc. The word : *the members*, corresponds to the expression : *of the sins*. Every evil instinct has, so to speak, an agent corresponding to it in one of the members of the body. The result of this impure working, caused by the shock of the holy law against the carnal heart of the natural man, is an abundance of evil *fruits* which produce *death* in man ; comp. Jas. i. 14, 15.

The εἰς, *to*, *in order to*, contains, as it always does, the notion of *end*, and not only of effect. In the affections of the flesh, it is said, viii. 6, there is a secret aspiration after death. The man who acts without God tends to separate himself ever more profoundly from God.

Ver. 6. "*But now we are delivered from the law, being dead*[1] *to him under whom we were held ; so that we serve in newness of spirit, and not in oldness of the letter.*"—The contrast between this *but now* and the *when we were* of ver. 5, corresponds exactly, both as to form and substance, with the contrast between the *when•ye were* and the *but now*, vi. 20 and 22 ; only with an application to another domain (that of the law). In the κατηργήθημεν, literally, *we were annulled*, we again find the form already explained in ver. 2, where it was said of the woman deprived of her standing as a married wife by the death of her husband : κατήργηται, *she is abolished*, she *has ceased to be* (as a wife). Here, as in the former case, this verb, construed with the preposition ἀπό, *from*, contains the idea of the most complete deliverance. We have seen in ver. 4 that this deliverance resulted from the death undergone in Christ (*ye were put to death*). It is this last idea which is recalled by the *being dead*, ἀποθανόντες. The reading of the T. R. : ἀποθανόντος, *that under which we were held* (the law) *being dead*, arises, according to Tischendorf, from a mistake of Beza, who followed Erasmus in a false interpretation which he gives of a passage from Chrysostom. In point of fact, as we have seen, the idea of the abolition *of the law* is foreign to this passage. As to the reading τοῦ θανάτου of the Greco-Latins : "We are delivered from *the law of death* under which we were held," it has probably been occasioned by the expression : *to bring forth fruit unto death*, ver. 5 ; but this qualification of the law is equally foreign to the passage before us.— Could the master, under whom we were held, possibly be, as Hofmann would have it, *the flesh*, taking the ἐν ᾧ as a *neuter* pronoun ? But the whole context, as well as the parallel passage, ver. 4, shows clearly that the subject in question is *the law*. The antecedent of ἐν ᾧ is the demonstrative pronoun τούτῳ (*him*, that is to say, *the master*) understood. The last words : *under whom we were* . . ., appear superfluous at first sight ; but they are intended to remind us of the example taken from the law, which was the starting point of this demonstration (vv. 1–3).

But this liberation does not tend to license. On the contrary, it is to issue in a δουλεύειν, a new *servitude* of the noblest and most glorious nature, which alone indeed deserves the name of liberty. This term δουλεύειν, *to serve*, is chosen as alone applicable to the two states about to be characterized.—*In newness of spirit*, says the apostle ; he thus designates the *new* state into which the Holy Spirit introduces the believer, when He establishes a full harmony between the inclination of the heart and moral obligation ; when to do good and renounce self for God has become a joy. With this state, of which he gives us a glimpse, and which he reserves for description (chap. viii.), the apostle in closing contrasts the former state. This he puts second, because it is the state which he proposes to describe immediately, vv. 7–25. He calls it *oldness of the letter :* there may be in this expression an allusion to the *old man*, παλαιὸς ἄνθρωπος, vi. 6 ; but anyhow Paul wishes to designate this state as now past for the believer ; it is from the viewpoint of his new state that he can characterize it thus. *The letter* is the moral obligation written in the code, imposing itself on man as a foreign law, and opposed to his inward dispositions. Is it not legitimate (vv. 1–4) and advantageous (vv. 5, 6) to break with such a state, and enter upon the other, as soon as this possibility is presented by God Himself ?[2]

[1] T. R., without any authority whatever, reads αποθανοντος'; ℵ A B C K L P, Syr.: αποθανοντες; D E F G, It.: του θανατου.
[2] The sense of the concluding clause is well given by Riddle (Pop. Com. *l. c.*) : "The new service is the only true service ; under the law such a service was not possible. The law said, 'Do this and live ;' the gospel says, 'Live and do this ;' and the doing is of a different character from all the previous attempts to earn eternal life."—T. W. C.

The apostle has shown in the first section that the gospel has the power to sanctify, and thereby to put an end at once to the reign of sin and law, which are one and the same state. He proceeds to explain that the law need not be an object of regret, since it is powerless to sanctify. It has therefore no well-founded protest to raise against the judgment which falls on it. Such is the subject of the following section.

SECOND SECTION (7:7-25)

POWERLESSNESS OF THE LAW TO SANCTIFY MAN

SIXTEENTH PASSAGE (Vers. 7-25)

The essential ideas of this passage are the following : After having involved man in death (vv. 7-13), the law leaves him to struggle in this state which cleaves to his nature, and from which it has no power to extricate him (vv. 14-23). It cannot bring him farther than to sigh for deliverance (vv. 24, 25).

But in developing this theme of the powerlessness of the law, is not the apostle turning backward ? Was not this subject treated already in chap. iii. ? It seems so, and this is one of the reasons why Reuss thinks that our Epistle is deficient in systematic order. But what Paul proved in chap. iii. was the insufficiency of the law to *justify ;* the demonstration to be given in the part relative to justification by faith. What he proves here is its powerlessness to *sanctify*, which is entirely different, at least in the eyes of the apostle, and of all those who do not confound justification and sanctification.

It is perfectly intelligible how, after displaying the sanctifying power of the gospel (vi.-vii. 6), the apostle should take a look backward to consider the work of the law, and describe it from this point of view. This retrospective glance at the part played by an institution which he regards as divine, and which had ruled so important a part of his life, does not at all, as has been thought, assume Judaizing readers, or even such as were of Jewish-Christian origin. The question of the influence of the law was of general interest ; for the new gospel revelation appeared everywhere as a competitor with the ancient revelation of the law, and it concerned all to know their respective value in the work of man's sanctification ; some, on the one side, wishing to know if they should *remain* under the law ; others, if they should *place themselves* under its discipline.

The following section consists of only one passage, divided into two parts. In the first (vv. 7-13), the apostle proves from experience that the law can only *kill* man morally—that is to say, separate him from God ; in the second, from ver. 14, he shows its powerlessness to extricate him from the sad state into which he is plunged. The passage has this peculiarity, that the theses demonstrated are not expounded in a general way, but in a purely personal form ; ver. 7 : "*I* had not known" . . . ; ver. 8 : " Sin wrought in *me*" . . . ; ver. 9 : "*I* was alive . . . *I* died " . . . ; ver. 11 : " Sin deceived *me ;*" ver. 14 : "*I* am carnal ;" ver. 15 : " What *I* would, that *I* do not ;" ver. 22 : "*I* delight in the law of God ;" ver. 24 : " Who shall deliver *me ?*" ver. 25 : "*I* thank God." This style continues even into the beginning of the following chapter, viii. 2 : " The law of the spirit of life hath made *me* free." The question is, who is the personage denoted throughout this whole piece by the ἐγώ, *I ?* Commentators have indulged in the most varied suppositions on this point.

1. Some Greek commentators (Theoph., Theod. of Mops.) have thought that Paul was here speaking of himself as representing the whole race of mankind from the beginning of its existence, and was thus relating the great moral experiences of the *human race* up to the time of its redemption.

2. Others (Chrys., Grot., Turret., Wetst., Fritzs.) apply this description to the *Jewish nation*. *Apostolus hic sub primâ personâ describit hebræum genus*, says Grotius. The experiences here described (see below) are referred to the different phases of their history.

3. A large number of commentators (most of the Fathers, Er., the Pietistic school, the rationalistic critics, Beng., Thol., Neand., Olsh., Baur, Mey., Th. Schott, Holst., Bonnet, etc.), consulting the context more strictly, think that the apostle, in virtue of his past history, is here introducing himself as the personification of the *legal Jew*, the man who, being neither hardened in self-righteousness, nor given over to a profane and carnal spirit, seeks sincerely to fulfil the law without ever being successful in satisfying his conscience.

4. After his dispute with Pelagius, Augustine, who had formerly adhered to the previous opinion, gave currency to another explanation. He expounded the passage, especially from ver. 14, as referring to the *converted Christian ;* for he only can be so profoundly in sympathy with the divine law as Paul describes himself in the passage, and on the other hand every believer in the course of his life has those profound experiences of his misery which are here described by the apostle. This opinion was followed by Jerome, then adopted by the Reformers, and defended in our time by Philippi, Delitzsch, Hodge, etc.

5. Only two commentators, so far as known to us, restrict the application of the passage to the apostle's own person. Hofmann, who, if we understand rightly, refers it to Paul as a Christian, but such as he finds himself when he abstracts for a moment from his faith, and Pearsall Smith,[1] who thinks that Paul is here relating a painful experience of his Christian life, in consequence of a relapse under the yoke of the law ; after which chap. viii., he thinks, sets forth his return to the full light of grace.

We shall not pronounce on what we believe to be the true sense of the apostle till we have studied this controverted passage in all its details. The first part extends to the end of ver. 13. It explains the effects of the first living contact between the divine law and the carnal heart of man. Sin is unveiled, ver. 7, and in consequence of this discovery it gathers strength and grows (vv. 8, 9), so that man, instead of finding life in his relation to the law, finds death (vv. 10, 11). But this tragical result must be ascribed not to the law itself, but to sin, which uses the law to this end.

Vv. 7–13

This whole exposition is introduced by the objection which consists in identifying the law with sin. But it must not be thought that the apostle's aim is really to exonerate the law from such a suspicion. Who, in the circle in which he taught, could have pronounced such a blasphemy against an institution recognized to be divine ? What the apostle wishes to justify is not the law ; it is his own teaching, from which it seemed to follow that the two things, law and sin, are inseparably united, or even identical. Had he not just proved that to be set free from sin is to be so also from the law ? Does it not seem to follow that the law and sin are one and the same thing ? It is this impious consequence from which he proceeds to clear his gospel. He shows that if the law plays so active a part in the history of

---

[1] *Bondage and liberty*, by M. P. Smith, 1875.

272 / Sanctification

sin, it is by no means because of its own nature, which would be wicked, but because of the exceedingly sinful nature of sin.

Ver. 7. "*What shall we say then? Is the law sin? Let it not be! Nay, I did not learn to know sin, but by the law; for I had not known lust, if the law had not said, Thou shalt not covet.*"—Some commentators think that in the second question the word *sin* should be taken in the sense of *a cause* of sin. But Paul would easily have found a way of expressing this thought more precisely. The simple meaning of the terms which he uses is this: Is the law something bad in itself, contrary to the essence and will of God, and consequently malignant? And this meaning suits the context still better than the preceding one, which, however, does not imply that we should paraphrase ἁμαρτία, *sin*, by ἁμαρτωλός, *sinner* (Mey., Philip.), a term which can only be applied to a personal agent.—While repelling with indignation the conclusion ascribed to him, the apostle nevertheless points out the measure of truth which it contains. The law does not produce sin, but it is the law which reveals it. There might be given to the word ἀλλά, *but*, which follows the: *Let it not be!* the meaning of a strong contrast: *Nay, but on the contrary.* To unveil sin is in reality, in some respects, the opposite of producing it. But the apostle has already in view what he proceeds to expound in ver. 8, the fact of the growth of sin as an effect of its detection by means of the law. And hence we think it better to give to the word ἀλλά, *but*, a *restrictive* sense, in relation to the strong negation which precedes. No, assuredly! *But at least* this cannot be denied.—It is unnecessary to give to οὐκ ἔγνων, literally: *I did not learn to know*, the meaning of the conditional (understanding ἄν): I should not have known. The indicative is perfectly suitable. It is a fact: "I did not learn to judge of sin otherwise than by the light of the law."—The notion of *knowledge*, contained in ἔγνων, has been here explained in many ways. Fritzsche applies it to the *existence* of sin, as when it is said: I did not know pain; for I had not yet suffered. But this meaning would throw the responsibility of sin on the law, the very thing which Paul wishes to avoid. Meyer thinks that the law *made* sin *known* by calling forth its violence, and so rendering it more easily perceived. But in this sense the idea of ver. 7 would not differ from that of ver. 8; now this is precluded by the δέ, progressive or adversative, at the beginning of the verse (see the strait to which Meyer is reduced to explain this transition). Tholuck and Philippi give an entirely different sense to the word *know*. The point in question is not the proof of the fact of sin, but the understanding of its culpability: "It was by the law that I knew sin as an act contrary to the will of God." But why in this way force the application of the word *know*, when its simple meaning is perfectly sufficient: "I did not perceive in myself the presence of the evil instinct of sin, except by means of the law;" comp. the ἔγνων, Luke viii. 46: I became aware of, I became conscious. This sentence is absolutely parallel, whatever Meyer may say, to that in iii. 20: "By the law is the knowledge of sin."—And how was this discovery, made by means of the law, effected? This is what the apostle explains in the following proposition: "*For also I had not known lust if*" . . . He explains by a concrete fact what he has just stated more abstractly in the preceding proposition. If he discovered sin by the law, it was because one of the commandments made palpable to him the presence of lust, of whose abnormal existence in his inner man he would otherwise have remained forever ignorant.—This τὲ γάρ, *for also, and in fact*, denotes two things: 1st, a *second* fact of the same kind as the preceding (τέ, *also*); and 2d, the second fact serving as a proof or explanation to the first (γάρ, *for*). Paul might have remained ignorant forever of the state of sin in which his heart was sunk, if lust had not made it palpable to him. And the presence of lust would have forever escaped him, if the tenth commandment had not made it known to him. Ἐπιθυμία, *lust*, denotes that involuntary motion of the soul (θυμός) toward (ἐπί) the external object which presents itself as corresponding to its desire. This motion of the soul toward the objects which can satisfy it is so natural to the human heart, that it would be absolutely lost in the general current of life, and would not fall specially under the eye of conscience, unless the law said: *Thou shalt not covet.* This prohibition is needed to bring man to fix his attention on this spontaneous movement of the soul, and to discover in this fact the symptom of an inward revolt against the divine will.—The pluperfect ᾔδειν has, strictly speaking, the meaning of an imperfect: *I had learned* to know, and hence: *I knew*. But in consequence of the *if* (if not=except) which follows, this verb can only be taken logically in the sense of a conditional (understanding, as is frequently done, the ἄν which indicates this mood): *I should know* (present), or: *I should have known* (past). It may therefore be translated in two ways: "I should not know lust (present), except the law said to me (ἔλεγεν, imperfect)." Or: "I should not have known (I should not have been aware of) lust, except the law had said" (extending the ellipsis of the ἄν to the second verb). In the second case, Paul goes back in thought to the previous time denoted by ἔγνων: "I did not know except by . . . ; and in fact I should not have been made aware of . . . except" . . . What seems to me to decide in favor of the latter sense, which places the action in the past, is the relation indicated between the two propositions, and expressed by the τὲ γάρ, *for also*, or *and in fact*. For the abstract terms: *sin* and *law* (in the first proposition), there are substituted in the second the two concrete terms: *lust* and *commandment*. Sin *appears* in lust, as law in the commandment. This is what is signified in reality by the τὲ γάρ, the τέ denoting the transition from the general to the particular, and the γάρ characterizing the particular fact as a *proof* or explanation in relation to the general: "I did not learn to know sin except by the law; for in fact I should not have been aware of lust (in which sin is revealed), had there not been a positive commandment saying to me: Lust not." With this sense also agrees the difference between the two verbs: ἔγνων, from γιγνώσκειν, *to learn to know*, and ᾔδειν, from ἰδεῖν, *to perceive* (a fact). It was through the tenth commandment that Paul discovered lust, and it was by finding out this inward fact of lust that he became conscious of his state of sin.—In this picture of his inner life Paul gives us, without intending it, a very high idea of the purity of his life as a child and a young man. He might, when confronted with the nine commandments, have to the letter claimed for himself the verdict, Not guilty, like the young man who said to Jesus: "All these have I kept from my youth up." But the tenth commandment cut short all this self-righteousness, and under this ray of the divine holiness, he was compelled to pass sentence of condemnation. Thus there was wrought in him, Pharisee though he was, without his suspecting it, a profound separation from ordinary Pharisaism, and a moral preparation which was to lead him to the arms of Christ and His righteousness. To this so mournful discovery there was added (δέ, ver. 8) by and by a second and still more painful experience.

Ver. 8. "*Then sin, taking occasion, wrought in me by the commandment all manner of concupiscence; for without the law sin is dead.*"—After revealing to him the presence of sin, the law itself intensified in him the force of this evil principle. This idea of progress is indicated by the δέ, *now, then*, which makes the fact described in ver. 8 a sequel to that of which we are reminded in ver. 7. The word ἀφορμή, which we translate by *occasion*, strictly signifies *the point of support* from which the spring or flight proceeds (ἀπό, ὁρμάω). Some critics make the words διὰ τῆς ἐντολῆς, *by the commandment*, dependent on the participle λαβοῦσα, *having taken*. In this case we should not have to translate: "Taking occasion *from* the commandment," which would require one of the prepositions ἀπό or ἐκ usual in such a case. The meaning would be: "Taking occasion *by means of* the commandment." But it is more natural to make this clause depend on the principal verb *wrought*. For, in the other sense, there would have been no reason for inserting the subject between this clause and the participle which depended on it. The analogous construction of ver. 11 also leads us to make the clause : *by the commandment*, dependent on the principal verb *wrought*.—What is the *occasion* meant by the apostle ? The usual answer is, the commandment itself : *"In lege* est occasio," says Calvin. This meaning is not inadmissible. Sin, finding a series of prohibitions enumerated in the commandment, made use of this means to enkindle desire for the forbidden objects. But is it not more probable that Paul finds *the occasion* of which sin makes use, in those forbidden objects themselves, when they appear to the eye or imagination ? " Sin finding an occasion, in the view of one of those objects in regard to which God says to me : Thou shalt not covet, took advantage of the circumstance to kindle in my heart, through this very prohibition, the manifold lusts which are related to those different objects." The point in question here is the well-known experience already remarked by the ancients, that man always inclines to forbidden fruit. Comp. Prov. ix. 17. The prohibition has for its effect to fix the object strongly on the imagination, and thereby to lend it a new charm. The heart is as it were fascinated by it, and the latent desire changes into intense aspiration. Thus every word of the commandment has, so to speak, the property of awakening in the heart a new lust. But it must be constantly borne in mind that this is only so because sin, the egoistic instinct, already exists in the heart. The commandment of itself does not produce this result ; it is sin which, so to speak, trades upon the commandment for its own profit. On a sound nature, the commandment would not have acted thus ; witness the first temptation in which a foreign agent required to play the part here ascribed to sin.—Calvin, in his eagerness to exculpate the apostle completely from the charge of ascribing to the law the aggravation of sin, gives this verse a purely logical meaning. Paul means, according to him, that the law *manifested* the various lusts already present. *Detexit in me omnem concupiscentiam*. This is evidently to distort the meaning of the apostle's words.

And in what state, then, was sin before the law had thus made it abound in all manner of particular lusts ? *It was dead*, says Paul. This expression, far from signifying that it did not *exist*, proves, on the contrary, its presence, but, virtually, like the germ of a disease still slumbering, which the least circumstance may cause to break out so as to bring the malady to the acute state. And it is this malignant principle, already in existence, which bears all the responsibility of the disagreeable effects of the law. The literal translation would be : *Without law sin is dead.* It is not as Mosaic law, but as *law*, that is to say, as an external letter, that the code produces this pernicious effect on the sinful soul. And this is what warrants us in applying this description to the law of nature, and what explains how the *nitimur in vetitum* may also be a confession of the heathen conscience.—We must beware of understanding with Beza the verb ἦν, *was :* " Without law sin *was* dead." The very ellipsis of the verb proves that we have here a general proposition.—The verses which follow initiate us more deeply still into the apostle's moral experiences, when he was *under the law*.

Vv. 9, 10*a*. *"And I was alive when I was formerly without law ; but when the commandment came, sin revived, and I died ;"*—Calvin well expresses the rhythm of these verses : " The death of sin is the life of man ; and, on the contrary, the life of sin is the death of man."—The *Vatic.* reads ἔζην instead of ἔζων : both forms are classical. What is this *life* which the apostle enjoyed when he was yet *without law ?* Augustine, the Reformers, and some modern commentators (Bengel, Bonnet) think that the time in question is when, sunk in his Pharisaical delusions, filled with self-righteousness, Paul *thought himself* in possession of the life of God, of true righteousness. They understand the : *I was alive*, in the sense of : *I thought myself alive*. This interpretation is in itself forced ; but there is more against it. Could Paul really say of himself that, as a Pharisee, *he was without law?* It was, on the contrary, the time when he was absolutely *under the law*, ὑπὸ νόμον, according to 1 Cor. ix. 20, kept under the charge of the schoolmaster, who was to bring him to Christ, according to Gal. iii. 24. Then if it was his Pharisee life which he wished to characterize in the words : *when I was formerly without law*, what would be the time denoted by the following words : *when the commandment came?* Will it be said : the time of his conversion, when the law took its inmost meaning for him, *in Christ*, its full spiritual bearing ? " Though before his eyes," says Calvin, when speaking of his life as a Pharisee, " the law did not seriously affect his heart with the conviction of the judgment of God." It was only by the Spirit of Christ that his eyes were opened, and that the commandment truly humbled and condemned him. But where, then, is this idea of the interposition of Christ, and of the profound crisis of which he speaks elsewhere as a *new creation?* And was the understanding of the commandment then the sole or even the principal character of this transformation ? Certainly, if these words refer to his conversion, some indication or other would not be wanting to designate this transition to a new faith. To discover a period in Paul's life to which the words : *formerly when I was under the law*, really apply, we must go back to the days which preceded the awakening of his moral consciousness under the operation of the law. We are thereby led to the period of his childhood, before he was subjected to the Pharisaic ordinances and the exact discipline of the law. From the age of twelve, young Israelites were subjected to the legal institutes, and became, as was said, *sons of the law, bené hattorah*. This stage of his outward life was undoubtedly for the young Saul the signal of the inward crisis described from ver. 7 onward. From the moment he found himself called to apply the prescriptions of the law seriously to his conduct, he was not slow to discover sin within him ; for in the depths of his heart he found lust ; and not only did the law unveil this evil principle to him, but it intensified its power. The torrent bubbled and boiled on meeting with the obstacle which came in its way. Till then Saul *was alive*, morally and religiously, which does not mean merely that he thought himself alive ; nor does it denote merely the innocent and pure sprightliness of childhood, yet untroubled by any remorse. The word *live*, when used by Paul, always includes something more profound. It refers here to the state of a young and pious Israelitish child, trained in the knowledge and love of Jehovah, tasting by faith in the promises of His word the blessings of the covenant, awaking and going to sleep in the arms of the God of his fathers, and seeking not to displease Him in his conduct. There was here a real beginning of *life in God*, a pure flame, which was extinguished no doubt afterward by self-righteousness and by the inward strife inseparable from it, but which burst forth at last magnificently at the breath of faith in Jesus Christ.

The words : *when the commandment came*, after what precedes, refer simply to the appearance of the commandment, with its holy majesty, in the conscience of young Saul. Then began in him the serious attempt to put it fully into practice. The term *commandment* is used instead of *law*, because, as ver. 7 shows, it is specially the tenth commandment which is in question. It is by it above all that the work here described is effected in him. This work was, as Paul tells us, to make sin *live* or *revive*. The term *live* forms an antithesis to the other : *sin is dead* (ver. 8). It is a somewhat difficult question which of its two meanings is to be attached to the preposition ἀνά in the composition of the verb ἀναζῆν, that of *anew* (like our *re* in revive) : *recovered life;* or whether, according to its strict signification,

276 / Sanctification

above, it merely denotes here the transition from the passive to the active state : *took life*. Meyer, in favor of the first sense, insists on the fact that it is impossible to quote, either in the N. T. or in the classics, a single case in which this verb or its analogues (ἀναβιόω, ἀναβιώσκομαι) signifies anything else than *revive* (Luke xv. 24, for example). This cannot be denied. Nevertheless it is true that many verbs compounded with ἀνά do not at all include the idea of a *return* to a previous state ; thus ἀνατέλλω, *to spring* (speaking of plants), and *to rise* (speaking of the stars) ; ἀναβοάω, *to raise the voice, to cry ;* ἀναζέω, *to bubble up*. The verb ἀναβλέπω is taken in both senses : *to look above* (Matt. xiv. 19 ; Mark vii. 34 ; Luke xix. 5), and *to see anew* (Acts ix. 12, 17, 18). In John ix. 11, the meaning is doubtful. If we translate : "*recovered* life," what is the previous life of sin present to the mind of the apostle ? Origen discovers here his system of the preexistence of souls, and of a fall anterior to this present life. Hilgenfeld also ascribes this idea to the apostle. But how obscurely would it be expressed, and how would it come about that no other trace of it is found in his writings ? Rom. v. 12 is anything but favorable to this theory. Augustine and Bengel think of the first appearance of sin in paradise ; but this fact is too remote to furnish us with the explanation of the word *revive* here. It would be better to hold that Paul was thinking of sin as it had lived in his parents before *reviving* in him. But what is simpler still is to abandon this idea of the renewal of the life of sin, and to explain ἀναζῆν in the sense of : to awake to active life.—The commentators who have applied the preceding words to the Pharisaic epoch of the apostle's life, are embarrassed by the declaration : *Sin revived, and I died* (10*a*). Would such be the terms in which he would characterize his new birth ? Impossible ! But they apply, it will be said, to the most advanced stage of his Pharisaism. M. Bonnet says in this direction : "Sin, pursued to its last intrenchments, manifested its power by a desperate resistance . . . ; and, on the other hand, the man saw the nothingness of his moral life, and succumbed to the sentence of death executed by the law within the depths of his consciousness." But where in Paul's Epistles do we find the evidences of such a crisis ? It seems to me more natural to carry it back to the time when his moral consciousness was first developed, and to hold that this state was gradually increasing during the whole time of his Pharisaism.

Ver. 10*a*. The transition of sin from its latent state to that of an active force was to Saul a mortal stroke. The internal divorce between God and him was consummated : to infantine liberty there succeeded fear, to filial feeling the revolt of the heart and servile obedience, two equally sure symptoms of death. A weight henceforth repressed the impulse of his soul Godward.

The words which follow serve to bring out the unforeseen character of this effect (ver. 10*b*), and give the true explanation of it (ver. 11).

Vv. 10*b*, 11. "*And the commandment, which should have guided me to life, was found to turn me to death ; for sin, taking occasion, deceived me by the commandment, and by it slew me.*"—This coming into activity on the part of sin, which Paul felt as if he were the object of a spiritual murder, was occasioned by a gift of God, the commandment ; for this was the instrument of it, the commandment which God had given to the faithful Israelite with the words : "This do and *thou shalt live*" (Lev. xviii. 5) ! Instead of guiding him to holiness and peace, or *giving life*, it did the opposite, by revealing sin to him and increasing its power, it raised a thick wall between God and him, and involved him in death ! The feeling of *surprise* which so unexpected a result produced is expressed by the word εὑρέθη, *was found.*—Meyer understands the term *death* (end of the verse) of *eternal death*, in the sense that the man who passes through such experiences is doomed to final perdition (apart, of course, from redemption). But Paul is speaking of a more immediate result, a separation from God, that spiritual death which he describes himself, Eph. ii. 1 et seq.

Undoubtedly this description of the effects of the law exhibits only one aspect of the truth, that which had been particularly experienced by Saul the Pharisee. For he then regarded the law as the means of *establishing his own righteousness* (x. 3), and not as the pathway opened to divine grace. The psalmists frequently describe the effects of the law in a wholly different light (Ps. xix., cxix., etc.), and we cannot doubt that Jesus Himself, during the period of His development up to His baptism, found in it the fulness of what God had promised : *Doing these things, thou shalt live by them*, or what is expressed by the words of Paul : " The commandment which was given me *to guide me to life.*" Only, if it is to display this beneficent effect, the law must be received either by a heart free from sin, or otherwise by a heart which does not separate the commandment from the grace accompanying the law, a heart which seeks in it not the means of acquiring self-merit and gratifying its pride, but the way of union to the God of the covenant by sacrifice and prayer : as an illustration, let the parable of the Pharisee and the publican serve !

Ver. 11 is intended to explain what *really* took place. It throws back the blame of the sad experience related, on its true author, *sin*, as was already done in ver. 8, while reproducing this explanation more forcibly after the fuller development of the experience itself in vv. 9 and 10. The word ἡ ἁμαρτία, *sin*, is placed foremost ; for it is the true culprit, not the law ; it is this depraved instinct which the commandment encountered, and which caused the latter to produce a result diametrically opposed to that for which it was given.—The words *taking occasion* refer, as in ver. 8, to the external objects corresponding to our various lusts. The commandment, by raising a barrier between these objects and us, makes them appear so much the more desirable ; we cannot get rid of the impression that a jealous God takes pleasure in refusing them to us, for the very reason that they would promote our happiness. Such is the mirage which sin produces in us *by the commandment* itself. The words : *deceived me by the commandment*, certainly contain an allusion to the part played by the serpent in Gen. iii., where, as we have said, it fills the office here ascribed to sin in relation to man in innocence. It deceives and seduces Eve by ascribing hatred to God, love to itself ; and hence murder, separation from God, either by internal revolt or external disobedience.—The repetition of the clause : *by the commandment . . . by it*, with each of the two verbs, expresses forcibly how contrary to the nature of the commandment is the part which sin makes it play.—The verb ἐξαπατᾷν includes the two ideas of *deceiving*, and of thus causing *to deviate* from the right road (ἐκ, *out of*). Deception causes to deviate, and deviation leads to *death : by it slew me.* It is incomprehensible how Calvin should take the liberty of giving a purely logical sense to the terms *deceived* and *slew :* " Sin was unveiled by the law as a seducer and murderer (*Ergo verbum* ἐξεπάτησεν *non de re ipsâ, sed de notitiâ exponi debet*).''

It remained to conclude by finally formulating the result of this profound psychological analysis contained in the passage vv. 7–11. This is what is done in vv. 12 and 13. The ὥστε, *so that*, ver. 12, announces a conclusion.

Vv. 12, 13. "*So that the law assuredly is holy, and the commandment holy, just, and good. Did then that which is good become*[1] *death unto me ? Let it not be so ! But sin, that it might appear sin, wrought death in me by that which is good ; that sin by the commandment might become exceeding sinful.*"— The result formulated in these two verses is this : The holier the law is, the more does sin, which has used it to produce evil, appear thereby in the

---

[1] T. R. reads γέγονεν, with K L, instead of ἐγένετο, which is read by ℵ A B C D E P.

blackness of its nature.—The apostle begins, in view of the result indicated, by removing from the law all suspicion of blame. The μέν, *undoubtedly*, has no corresponding δέ, *but*. So far as the sense goes, the δέ is found in ver. 13*b*. This μέν is intended to guard beforehand the unassailable character of the law. Whatever may be said afterward, nothing shall invalidate the character of *holiness* belonging to the law. *The law*, ὁ νόμος, here denotes the Mosaic system in its entirety, and the commandment ἡ ἐντολή, each article of the code in particular. The term ἅγιος, *holy*, is the word which in Scripture denotes *the perfect love of good;* when it is applied to God, it is the identity of His will with goodness ; when it is applied to the creature, it is his voluntary consecration to God, the one Being essentially good. The law is *holy*, precisely because it demands this consecration, and the commandment also, because each commandment only demands this consecration in a particular relation. The two characteristics *just* and *good* flow from and are included in that of holiness. The commandment is *just* (δικαία), because it regulates in a normal way the relations between different beings. It is *good* (ἀγαθή), in the sense of *beneficent;* this epithet is explained by the preceding words : *fitted to give life* (ver. 10).

Ver. 13. Here was the place strictly speaking for the *but* (δέ), answering to the μέν, *assuredly*, of ver. 12. But Paul interrupts himself ; he feels the need of yet again stating the problem in all its difficulty. This is what he does in the question beginning ver. 13. The difference between the reading of the majority of the Mjj., ἐγένετο (aorist), and that of the T. R., γέγονε (perfect), is this : The first expresses the act by which this whole internal history was brought about ; the second, the permanent state which resulted from that act. The first is therefore rather connected with what precedes, the second with what follows. From the internal point of view both may consequently be defended ; but the authorities are rather[1] in favor of the first.—The problem being thus put afresh in all its rigor, the second part of ver. 13 gives its solution precisely as the μέν of ver. 12 leads us to expect, and as we have stated it at the beginning of that verse.—The second part of the verse has been construed in many ways. And first, what is the verb of the subject ἡ ἁμαρτία, *sin*, which begins the sentence ? Either it is derived from the preceding sentence, by understanding ἐγένετο θάνατος : " But sin (not the law) *became my death*," or " turned me to death." But is not this ellipsis somewhat serious ? Or the verb is found in the following participle κατεργαζομένη, by making it a finite verb : " But sin, that it may appear sin, *works my death* (Calvin : *operatur* mihi mortem) by that which is good." To this meaning there has been objected the form of the participle. But if the apostle means to denote rather a quality than an act of the subject, the participle may be suitable : " Sin (*is*) *working* death," that is to say, *is capable of working*, or *wicked enough to* work it. But this return to the *present* tense would be singular after the past ἐγένετο ; then it would require rather the present φαίνῃ, *may appear*, than the aorist φανῇ, *might appear*. Paul is not speaking of what *is*, he is reflecting on what has *taken place*. The first of the two constructions would therefore be preferable ; but there is still room for hesitation between two alternatives : (*a*) Either the participle κατεργαζομένη is taken as in explanatory apposition to the principal subject ἡ ἁμαρτία, *sin*, by making the three words ἵνα φανῇ ἁμαρτία a short parenthetical proposition : " But sin, that it might appear sin, *turned me to death, working* my death by what was good." The participle κατεργαζομένη would have the force of the Latin gerund. Only the general sense suffers from an awkward tautology : to turn to death by working death ! (*b*) Or the participle κατεργαζομένη is joined to the proposition ἵνα φανῇ ἁμαρτία : " But sin (turned me to death), that *it might appear sin by working* my death by that which is good." This second sense is

---

[1] One might better say, decidedly.—T. W. C.

evidently preferable. As to making the second ἁμαρτία the subject of this dependent proposition : " But sin turned me to death that *sin might appear* (to all eyes) *working* my death by what is good," it cannot be thought of ; this construction would require the article ἡ before the second ἁμαρτία. We should therefore range ourselves without hesitation on the side of construction No. 1*b*, were it not for two grave difficulties, the one arising from the thought itself, the other from the connection between the two ἵνα, *in order that*, which follow one another in this verse. Could Paul say : Sin turned me to death, that it might appear sin slaying me by a good thing ? The idea is rather this : Sin *caused my death by a good thing*, that it might appear so much the more sin. Then what relation are we to establish in this sense between the two *thats?* Are they parallel as two distinct and simultaneous ends : Sin turned me to death, 1st, that it *might appear* sin ; 2d, that it *might become* exceeding sinful ? But the fact of *becoming* is not parallel to that of *appearing ;* the latter is rather the result of the former. Or should we give to γένηται, *become*, a purely *logical* sense, as is done by many commentators : that it might appear exceedingly sinful *in the view of my conscience ?* But this verb would only serve in this sense to repeat the idea of the verb φανῇ, *might appear ;* and then why change the term ? Or should we see in the second *that* a more remote end in relation to which the first *that* would only be the means ? But *appearing* is not the means of *becoming ;* on the contrary, *appearing* is the result of becoming. It is clear that none of those constructions is wholly satisfactory.

It seems to me that to obtain a result in harmony both with the requirements of language and of logic, it is enough to modify construction No. 1, and combine it so modified with No. 2. We need to understand not ἐγένετο θάνατος, but merely the verb ἐγένετο, then to make of this finite verb the point of support for the participle κατεργαζομένη : " But sin, that it might appear sin, *turned to* [became] *working* (ἐγένετο κατεργαζομένη) my death by what was good." We have thus a simple ellipsis, a meaning exact, clear, and in keeping with the context ; we keep up the *past* tense (ἐγένετο), which suits the aorist φανῇ ; we get an analytic form (ἐγένετο κατεργαζομένη) which, while leaving the fact in the past, serves to bring out (by the *present* participle) the permanent *attribute*, and not merely the initial *act*, as the aorist κατειργάσατο (ver. 8) would have done. Finally, in this way we get without difficulty at the explanation of the two *thats*. The verb ἐγένετο κατεργαζομένη, *became working*, becomes the point of support for the second *that*, which gives a clear meaning : sin wrought death by goodness, that it *might become* as sinful as possible. God *willed* that sin, by *killing* by means of that which was ordained to give *life*, should commit a true masterpiece of perversity. Hence the second *that :* it applies to the fact in itself (γένηται, *might become*). And why did God will that it should be so ? This is what we are told *in the outset* by the first *that : that sin* might appear fully what it is, *sin* (ἵνα φανῇ ἁμαρτία). These three words form a parenthetical proposition put at the beginning to indicate from the first the *final* aim of this whole unexpected dispensation. It was necessary that *to manifest* completely its evil nature (the first *that*), sin should inflict death on me, not by something evil (which would throw part of the odium of this murder on the means employed), but by something good (the commandment), that the crime *might be* completely the work of sin (the second *that*).

Thus we have three ideas—(1) sin slays by that which is good ; (2) *that* thereby it *may accomplish* an act worthy of its nature ; (3) *and that* thereby (final end) this nature *may be manifested* clearly. It is obvious from this progression that we must beware of taking γένηται, *might become*, in the logical sense, and of identifying as far as the sense goes the two *thats*, as Meyer does.

On vv. 7–13.—The commentators who apply the moral experiences described by the apostle in this passage (p. 270) *to mankind* in general, apply the words *I was alive* (ver. 9) to the period of paradise; those which follow: *when the commandment came*, to the prohibition to eat of the tree of the knowledge of good and evil, and the rest of the passage, extending to the end of the chapter, to the fall and its consequences. By the question: *What shall we say then* (ver. 7)? Paul would thus invite his readers to a general contemplation of the history of our race from the beginning, to justify what he has been expounding in regard to emancipation from the law (vv. 1–6). But this interpretation is excluded first by the words ἁμαρτία νεκρά, *sin is dead* (ver. 8). In paradise, according to St. Paul, sin was not *dead;* it did not exist (ch. v. 12). Then neither would the term ἀνέζησεν, as understood, be suitable to designate the first appearance of sin. Finally, the commandment expressly quoted (ver. 7) belongs to the code of Sinai, and thus brings us face to face with the *Jewish* law.

Those who, from Chrysostom to our day (p. 271), apply this passage to the *Jewish people*, find in the words *I was alive* an indication of the patriarchal period when the promise was the bond between God and man, and in *the coming of the commandment*, the epoch of Moses, when the law broke this relation, and produced the great national revolts. This interpretation connects itself more easily with the context than the preceding. But neither is it tenable. When we think of the shameful sins of the patriarchal period, can we apply to that time the descriptions of *sin being dead*, and *I was alive?* Then is it historically demonstrable that through the giving of the law, the state of the nation was made sensibly worse, and that its relation to Jehovah was broken? Do not the words of Paul apply to an inward event (*covetousness*, revelation of sin), rather than to a great national experience? Finally, what subtleties are we led into by this explanation, when we attempt to apply it in a consequent way to the end of the section! When we come to the passage 14–25, we must then, with Reiche, apply the first of the two *I*'s which are in conflict, to the ideal Jew, the Jew such as he ought to be, and the other, to the real Jew, such as he shows himself in practice! We do not deny that the human conscience in general, and the Jewish conscience in particular, may recognize their experiences in those which are here described. But that is natural; is not Paul a man and a Jew? The truth is, the whole is narrated about *himself*, but with the conviction that his experience will infallibly be that of every Israelite, and of every man who will seriously use the moral or Mosaic law as a means of sanctification.

The point in question now is to trace this experience to its profound cause. Such is the study to which the following section (vv. 14–25) is devoted (*for*, ver. 14).

Vv. 14–25

It is from this ver. 14 especially that the difference between the two explanations of the passage comes out: that which applies it to the state of man regenerate, and that which regards it as depicting the impotent struggles of a sincere and serious man, but one still under the yoke of the law, and ignorant of deliverance by the Holy Spirit.

The principal reasons advanced in favor of the first opinion are the following (best developed perhaps by Hodge): 1. The transition from the *past* tense in the preceding passage to the *present* in this; 2. The impossibility of ascribing to unregenerate man sentiments so elevated in their nature as those which are here professed: cordial assent to the law, vv. 16 and 22, and profound hatred of evil, vv. 15, 19, etc.; 3. Ver. 25, where the apostle seems expressly to appropriate to himself at the present time the entire description which he has just traced: thus far the objections whose validity or groundlessness it belongs to exegesis alone to determine.

The only side of the question which we can exhaust here is that of the connection of this passage with the preceding, and with the section to which it belongs taken as a whole.

1. Paul has just delineated, vv. 7–13, the deadly action of the law upon him, from the time it established its supremacy in his inmost soul, and from that period during the whole time of his Pharisaism. How should he now pass all at once from this description, to that of his inward struggles as a *regenerate* man? Hodge and Philippi explain this transition by an *a fortiori*. The law is powerless to regenerate the natural man, it only serves to increase the power of sin, vv. 7–13. And the proof is, that it does not act otherwise, even on the believer's heart, when, forgetting his faith for the time, he finds himself as a naturally carnal man face to face with the law. Even with the profound sympathy which his renewed heart feels for the law, he cannot find in it the means of sanctification which he needs ; how much less can it deliver from sin a heart still unregenerate ? This attempt to construe the passage in keeping with what precedes is ingenious, but inadmissible. Exactly what it was most essential to say in this case, to make the argument intelligible, would be understood : " Even since I have become a new creature in Christ, I cannot find any assistance in the law ; on the contrary, when I put myself under its yoke, it renders me worse." This must have been said in order to be clear. Paul says nothing of the kind between vv. 13 and 14.

2. Another omission, not less inexplicable, would be his passing over the profound change which was effected in him by regeneration. He would pass from the period of his Pharisaism (vv. 7–13) to his Christian state, as it were on the same level, and without making the least allusion to the profound crisis which made all things, and the law in particular, *new* to him (2 Cor. v. 17). And it would not be till chap. viii., and by an afterthought, that he would come to his experiences as a Christian. The author of the Epistle to the Romans has not accustomed us hitherto to a style of writing so far from clear. Hodge says no doubt that the apostle is here speaking of the believer from the viewpoint of his relations to the law, abstracting from his faith. But a believer, apart from his faith . . ., that surely resembles a non-believer. So understood the description of the miserable state, vv. 14–25, would be the demonstration not of the impotence of the law, but of that of the gospel.

3. How explain the contrast between the delineation of chap. vii. and that of chap. viii., a contrast infinitely *sharper* than we find between the section vv. 7–13 (description of Saul as a Pharisee) and vv. 14–25, a passage which they would refer to Paul the Christian ? Is there, then, a greater difference between Christian and Christian, than between Pharisee and Christian ? Philippi alleges that the apostle describes successively in the two passages, vv. 14–25 and viii. 1 et seq., the two *opposite aspects of the Christian life*, the believer *without* and the believer *with* the breath of the Spirit. But once again the great crisis would require to be put in this case, not in vv. 24 and 25, between the *two aspects* of the *same state*, but between vv. 13 and 14, where the new state is contrasted with the old, *newness of spirit* with *oldness of the letter*, to use Paul's own words.—The direction of the apostle's thought is clearly marked out by the section as a whole ; it may serve as a guiding thread in all that follows. After showing that there is in faith a new principle of sanctification (vi. 1-14), which is a sufficiently firm standard for moral life (vv. 15–23), and which renders emancipation from the law possible and desirable (vii. 1-6), he explains what the intervention of the law produced in his own life (vv. 7–13), and the state in which, despite his sincere and persevering efforts, it left him (vv. 14–23), to issue in that desperate cry of distress in which this state of continual defeats finally expresses itself : *Who shall deliver me?* Of this liberator he does not know the name at the time when he utters the cry

(a fact which proves that he is not yet in the faith); but he anticipates, he hopes for, he appeals to him without knowing him. And heaven gives him the answer. Chap. viii. contains this answer: *The Spirit of Christ hath set me free*, ver. 2; He it is who works in me all that the law demanded, without giving me power to do it (ver. 4).—This series of ideas is unimpeachable; it only remains to see whether in this way we shall account for all the details of the following passage, and succeed in overcoming the objections mentioned above, which have been raised in opposition to this view.

This passage seems to me to fall into three cycles, each of which closes with a sort of refrain. It is like a dirge; the most sorrowful elegy which ever proceeded from a human heart.

The first cycle embraces vv. 14–17. The second, which begins and ends almost in the same way as the first, is contained in vv. 18–20. The third differs from the first two in form, but is identical with them in substance; it is contained in vv. 21–23, and its conclusion, vv. 24 and 25, is at the same time that of the whole passage.

It has been sought to find a gradation between these three cycles. Lange thinks that the first refers rather to the *understanding*, the second to the *feelings*, the third to the *conscience*. But this distinction is artificial, and useless as well. For the power of this passage lies in its very monotony. The repetition of the same thoughts and expressions is, as it were, the echo of the desperate repetition of the same experiences, in that legal state wherein man can only shake his chains without succeeding in breaking them. Powerless he writhes to and fro in the prison in which sin and the law have confined him, and in the end of the day can only utter that cry of distress whereby, having exhausted his force for the struggle, he appeals, without knowing him, to the deliverer.

First Cycle: Vv. 14–17

Ver. 14. "*For*[1] *we know that the law is spiritual; but I am carnal,*[2] *sold under the power of sin.*"—We have in this cycle, ver. 14, an affirmation: "I acknowledge that the law . . . but I am captive;" then the demonstration of this fact (vv. 15 and 16); finally, ver. 17, the conclusion, which is merely the reaffirmation of the thesis now demonstrated.

The reading of some MSS. οἴδαμεν δέ, *then*, or *but we know*, has no meaning. We must read γάρ, *for*, with the majority of the Mjj. and versions. This *for* might signify: The case was really so; for witness my state as it *resulted* from this fatal crisis. The law slew me, and what proves it is the state of death in which I found myself involved from that time. But it is more natural to understand the transition from the preceding passage to this somewhat differently. Holstein seems to me to put it well when he says: From the historical phenomenon, described vv. 7–13, Paul now ascends to its real moral nature, which explains it: "The law produced on me the effect which I have just described, because there is an opposition between its nature which is holy, and mine which is corrupt." This transition includes what we have presented in the first place, for the state in which the law involves us is only the continuation of that in which it had found us. It finds us diseased, and leaves us so. If this is the explanation of the *for*, we need not be surprised at the use of the *present* in the verbs which follow. We do not certainly say with Hodge: Paul speaks of the regenerate man abstractly from his faith for the time; but we say: Paul

---

[1] A D E L read οιδαμεν δε instead of οιδαμεν γαρ, which T. R. reads with all the other Mjj., It., Syr.

[2] ℵ A B C D E F G read σαρκινος instead of σαρκικοσ, which T. R. reads with K L P.

speaks of the unregenerate man without concerning himself with the question how far the unregenerate heart still remains in the regenerate believer. He describes man *as he is* by nature, man as he knew him, and still finds him in himself, every time that his natural character shows itself. Here is *the permanent essence* of human nature since the fall outside the action of faith. Thus is explained the use of the *present*, without our saying that Paul describes his present state.—Some commentators, such as Jerome, Hofm., Schott, write οἶδα μέν : *I know undoubtedly*. But after that should we not have had simply εἰμι δέ, *but I am*, instead of ἐγὼ δὲ . . . εἰμι : "but *as for me*, I am" . . . ? In point of fact, this form implies a very marked contrast between the *I* thus emphasized, and some other subject in the preceding context. And this subject to which the *I*, ἐγώ, forms an antithesis, can only be the subject of the preceding verb *we*. We are thus led to regard the ordinary reading as necessary : οἴδαμεν, *we know*. In this *we*, Paul no doubt includes with himself all believers who have passed through the same experiences, and even the Jews who are at one with Christians regarding the truth affirmed by him.—The *knowing*, of which he here speaks, is more than a matter of understanding ; the sequel shows that it implies a cordial adhesion to that truth (comp. the verbs σύμφημι, συνήδομαι, vv. 16 and 22) : "We know and heartily own that the law is excellent."—The epithet *spiritual*, applied to the law, has been understood by many, Beza for example, in this sense, that the law is suited to the spiritual nature of man (the πνεῦμα, *the spirit*, in man) ; whence it follows that it demands not only external observance, but also the obedience of the heart. But the term πνευματικός, *spiritual*, is usually connected with the idea of the Divine Spirit ; and as in chap. viii. 4, Paul says himself that what is demanded by the law is wrought in them who walk *after the Spirit* (evidently God's Spirit), it is more exact to understand here by *spiritual:* agreeable to the impulse or tendency of the Divine Spirit. What the law commands is nothing else than what the Holy Spirit works in the heart where He dwells. There is a complete identity between the external precept of the law and the internal working of the Spirit. The idea found here by Calvin, that the law *cannot* be fulfilled *except* through the Spirit, follows indeed from the expression used by Paul, but does not express its meaning.

But, says Paul, returning upon himself, of what avail practically is this knowledge which we all have of the holy spirituality of the law ? By the use of the pronoun *I*, he here contrasts with this collective acknowledgment (*we know*) the wholly individual experience of his carnal state ; and in this latter he finds the invincible obstacle to the fulfilment of the law, however it may be recognized, as perfect in theory. The reading of the T. R. and of the Byzs., σαρκικός, and that of the Mjj. of the two other families, σαρκινός, have almost the same meaning : *carnal*. But the first adjective denotes carnal *activity*, the second the carnal *substance*, and by metonymy the carnal *nature*. As the apostle in this passage is contrasting with the *essentially* good law not only his own sinful *action*, but his corrupt *nature*, the form σαρκινός is certainly preferable.—The notion *flesh* is here taken in its moral sense, and embraces, as it does in all cases where *the flesh* is opposed to *God*, or to what is divine, the whole *human person*. Paul feels his natural self controlled by the flesh, that is to say, by self-complacency, the inclination to seek self-satisfaction in everything. This tendency is what determines his natural will. And hence the incompatibility between his nature and that of the law, which demands absolute self-consecration. —He adds in explanation of the term *carnal*, the words : *sold to sin*, literally, "*under* sin." Thereby he compares himself to a slave bought for money. The seller is the flesh, and the buyer, who has become his master, *sin*. In fact, a fatal contract, as it were, has taken effect on us, whereby the violence of the flesh has given over our will to the power of sin. The expression *sold under* is stronger than the usual form *sold to;* it includes the idea of the shameful state of *servitude* which has followed the act of sale.

Ver. 15. "*Indeed what I perform I know not: for what I would, that do I not; but what I hate, that do I.*"—This verse contains the proof from fact of the state of slavery which Paul has just affirmed. The slave knows not what he does, for he does the will of another. So Paul complains that his work is not the result of a distinct view in which he has, as it were, intellectually possessed himself beforehand of what he was going to do ; it is the result of blind instinct, which drags him along as if without his knowledge, so that when he sees it realized, it is not what he wished ; it is, on the contrary, what he detests. The expression : *I know not*, should not be taken in the sense : " I do not own *as good*," a forced sense, and one which is not necessary.—The θέλειν, *will*, which Paul does not execute, is of course the willing of good, and what he *hates* and yet executes is certainly evil. The moral tendency of his will to purpose good and hate evil, is connected with the acknowledgment of the perfection of the law of which he spoke in ver. 14. But this will which puts itself on the side of the law is nothing more than a desire, a wish, a simple *I should like*, which gives way in practice. Such, indeed, is the frequent meaning of θέλειν, *to will*, in Paul (1 Cor. vii. 7 ; 2 Cor. v. 4, xii. 20 ; Col. ii. 18).—The term πράσσειν, *to do*, has the meaning of *working at*, and expresses the idea that his practical activity does not follow the direction of his will.—Μισεῖν, *to hate*, here denotes moral reprobation ; and ποιεῖν, *to do*, which has the sense of *accomplishing*, realizing, refers not to activity in exercise (πράσσειν), but to the *product* of the activity, so that the exact paraphrase of the two last propositions would be this : " At the time when I act, I am not working in the direction of my desire to fulfil the law ; and when I have acted, I find myself face to face with a result which my moral instinct condemns."—It is asked how Paul could ascribe to himself this desire of good and hatred of evil, while speaking of the time when he was yet under the law ? but we ask in turn of those who refer this verse to Paul in his regenerate state, how he could in this state ascribe to himself the powerlessness with which he charges himself, especially if we compare the contrast he brings out between the state described here and the delineation of the Christian he draws in chap. viii. ? In fact, what this verse expresses is nothing else than what is contained in the words of Jesus, John iii. 24 : " He that *doeth truth* cometh to the light." To do the truth certainly denotes the loyal desire of goodness ; and this disposition *precedes* faith in the case of the men of whom Jesus is speaking, since the latter is its consequence : *cometh to the light*. We meet with the same thought in the parable of the sower, Luke viii. 15, when Jesus speaks of the *honest and good heart* in which the gospel seed produces its fruit ; comp. also Rom. ii. 7 and Acts x. 34, 35. It is understood, of course, that such a disposition exists only as the work of Him who is *alone good*. But there is a way of regarding the corruption of human nature contrary to the gospel, and which when thoroughly weighed is self-destructive.

Vv. 16, 17. "*If then I do that which I would not, I consent with the law that it is good. And now it is no more I that perform it, but sin that dwelleth*[1] *in me.*"—These two verses draw the conclusion from the fact mentioned ver. 15, a conclusion which is the reaffirmation of the thesis laid down in ver. 14.—The reprobation with which Paul's conscience visits his own work, is a solemn homage rendered by him to the law, for thereby he takes part with the law against himself. The preposition σύν, *with*, in the verb σύμφημι, *I give testimony*, I applaud *with*, can only bear on the regimen τῷ νόμῳ, *the law:* " I declare, *in concert with the law*, that the contents of the

---

[1] ℵ B read οικουσα instead of ενοικουσα, which all the others read.

law are good." It is the reproduction of the assertion : " We know that the law is spiritual."

Ver. 16 likewise reproduces the second part of ver. 14 ; it is, so to speak, the paraphrase of the words : *sold to sin*. It is not to be thought that Paul wishes to exculpate himself in the least when he says : " It is not I who do it, but sin." On the contrary, he wishes to make the miserable state of bondage to which he is reduced the more palpable ; he is not master even in his own house ; there he finds a tyrant who forces him to act in opposition to his better wishes. What humiliation ! What misery ! It is the state of sin regarded from its painful rather than its culpable point of view.—The adverbs *now*, νυνί, and *no more*, οὐκέτι, cannot have a temporal meaning here ; Paul states the moral *conclusion* drawn from the facts which he has just recorded. Their meaning is therefore logical. *Now* means : " Things being so ;" *no more:* " not as if the normal state, that of full moral liberty, *still* existed in me."

Second Cycle: Vv. 18–20

The first verse again contains a thesis parallel to that of ver. 14. This thesis is demonstrated by experience in the second part of the verse and in ver. 19, which thus correspond to vv. 15 and 16 of the first cycle. Finally, in ver. 20 we find as a conclusion the reaffirmation of the thesis ; it is the parallel of ver. 17.

Ver. 18*a*. " *For I know that in me, that is, in my flesh, dwelleth no good thing.*"—This thesis, reproducing that of ver. 14 : *I am carnal*, connects itself, by terms used, with the last words of ver. 17 ; comp. the two expressions : " Sin dwelling in me," and " in me dwelleth no good thing." The γάρ, *for*, is explanatory rather than demonstrative. It is the same experience which is again expounded more precisely ; comp. the similar *for*, ver. 10. It might seem, when Paul said, ver. 14 : *I am carnal*, that he left nothing subsisting in the *ego* which was not flesh. The contrary appeared, however, from the *we know* preceding ; for he who recognizes that the law is spiritual, must possess in himself something spiritual. This distinction between the *ego*, the *I*, and the *flesh*, is emphasized still more fully in ver. 18. For it is obvious that the phrase *that is* has a restrictive sense, and that Paul means : in me, so far at least as my person is carnal. He therefore gives it to be understood that there is something more in him besides the flesh. This something is precisely that in him which recognizes the spirituality of the law, and pays it homage. We thereby understand what *the flesh* is in his eyes, the complacent care of his person, in the form of pride or sensuality. Now this is precisely the active power which in practice determines the activity of the unregenerate man. The flesh thus understood does not exclude the knowledge, and even the admiration of goodness ; but it renders this noble faculty fruitless in ordinary life, by enslaving to itself the active principle, the will. There is therefore really, as Paul gives it to be understood, good in the *ego*, but in the understanding only, the contemplative faculty, not in the flesh which gives the active impulse. See this contrast exactly stated in ver. 25.—The proof from fact follows.

Vv. 18*b*, 19. " *For to will is present with me ; but how to perform that which is good I find*[1] *not. For the good that I would I do not ; but the evil which I would not, that I do.*"—In what precedes, Paul had already claimed a certain will in relation to good ; he here affirms the same thing more expressly. This will *is present ;* παράκεισθαι, to be *beside*, and as it were within reach. The verb θέλειν, *to wish*, denotes, as in vv. 15 and 16, a simple desire, an

---

[1] ℵ A B C read ου instead of ουχ ευρισκω, which T. R. reads with all the others, Syr., Vulg.

intention rather than a fixed and deliberate decision ; comp. the passages quoted. Paul means : as to good intentions, *they are present* and in abundance ; but the execution . . . that is what I find not. *Not finding* is the opposite of *being within reach*. Instead of οὐχ εὑρίσκω, *I find not*, read by the Byzs. and the Greco-Lats., there is found in the four Alex. a simple οὐ, *not:* " But the doing of good, not !" (οὐ παράκειται). This reading has something harsh and abrupt which renders it suspicious. Whence could this word εὑρίσκω, *I find*, have come into the text, corresponding so well with the term παράκεισθαι, *to be present?* Has not Meyer ground for suspecting a copyist of having passed carelessly from the οὐχ, ver. 18, to the following οὐ, ver. 19 ?[1]

Ver. 19. The *I find not* was the proof that no good whatever dwelt in the flesh ; it is demonstrated in turn by the two facts stated in ver. 19. The only difference between this verse and ver. 15*b*, is that here the verb ποιεῖν, *to do*, accomplish, is applied to good, while the verb πράσσειν, *to work at*, is applied to evil ; which leads to this sense : " I do not succeed in *realizing* the good which I would, while I find myself *working at* the evil which I would not."—The two notions of good and evil must of course be taken in their deepest sense, embracing the inward disposition as well as the external act. Even in doing the external task, one may himself, and in the eyes of God, find that he is doing *evil.*—The conclusion is expressed in ver. 20.

Ver. 20. "*Now if I do that I would not, I myself,*[2] *it is no more I that do it, but sin that dwelleth in me.*"—A conclusion uniform with that before enunciated, vv. 16 and 17 : " I am not master of myself ; a stranger has forced his way into my house and holds me captive."—This is really the proof of the *sold unto sin*, ver. 14. Paul does not say so by way of excuse, but to describe a state of the profoundest misery. And every time he repeats this confession, it is as if he felt himself seized with a stronger conviction of its truth. The ἐγώ, *I* (after *that I would not*), is rejected by important authorities, and condemned by Meyer. But Tischendorf seems to me to be right in preserving it.[3] It stands in a moral relation to the ἐγώ, *I*, which follows : " What I would not, *I myself*, it is not really I who do it."

Third Cycle : Vv. 21-25.

This cycle, while repeating the same experiences, stamps them as the abiding and definitive *result* of the state of things described throughout the whole passage (ἄρα, *consequently*). The following cycle really contains the full picture of man's state under the law. Like the others, it first expresses the general thesis, ver. 21, parallel to vv. 18 and 14 ; then the proof from fact, vv. 22 and 23 as above ; and finally, the conclusion, vv. 24 and 25, which, while reproducing that of the other cycles, goes beyond it and forms the transition to the description of the new state which has replaced the former in the regenerate (chap. viii.).

Ver. 21. "*I find then, this law, that, when I would do good, evil cleaves to me.*"—Always the same two characteristics of his moral state : will for good, but powerless ; evil carrying him away in practice.—We have frequently seen the term νόμος, *law*, taking the general sense of a *governing principle of life ;* any rule whatever imposing itself authoritatively on the will (νόμος πίστεως, the law of faith ; νόμος ἔργων, the law of works, iii. 27 ; νόμος πνεύματος, τῆς ἁμαρτίας, the law of the spirit, of sin, viii. 2, etc.). Such, undoubtedly, is the meaning of the word here. Paul is summing up *the mode of his existence* since the time when the law came in to affect his

---

[1] All the recent editors favor the shorter reading.—T. W. C.
[2] B C D E F G, It. Syr. here omit ἐγω.
[3] Lachman, Tregelles, Westcott, and Hort agree in rejecting it."—T. W. C.

inward life, and from which the law gives him no means of escape. This is what he calls τὸν νόμον, *this law*. This general and abstract meaning of the term *law* follows first from the expression : the law *of God*, ver. 22, where by this complement *of God* the law of which he speaks here is contrasted with the moral and Mosaic law ; and next from ver. 23, where Paul again applies the general idea of *law*, speaking, in contrast to the law of God, of *another law*.—This mode of existence appears with two opposite characteristics ; the will for good : *to me who would do good*, and the doing of evil : *evil cleaves to me*. The dative τῷ θέλοντι, *to me who would*, is the object of τὸν νόμον, *the law ;* for this word has here a very active sense : " The law which imposes itself on me who would do" . . . We have taken the liberty of translating the words thus : *with me, when I would do*. The ὅτι, *that*, depends also on τὸν νόμον, *the law :* this law which I find in me *consisting in the fact that* . . .—The verb παράκεισθαι, *to be present with*, is taken here in the same sense as in ver. 18 : to be within reach, to present itself at once : " As to me, when I wish to do good, evil is present first." —The two ἐμοί, *to me*, serve to bring out strongly the *unity* of the subject who has the misfortune to wish one thing and to do its opposite.

The numerous critics who have begun with taking the term *law* in this verse in the sense of the *Mosaic law*, have thereby involved themselves in inextricable difficulties. Witness the following :—1. Knapp and Olshausen take τὸ καλόν, *good*, as in apposition to τὸν νόμον, *the law ;* then ὅτι, *that*, as the object of *I find :* " As to me who would perform the law, that is, good, I find that evil is present with me." But this apposition is very strange, and the participle τῷ θέλοντι would require to be placed before τὸν νόμον.—2. Chrysostom and the Peshitto take the words τῷ θέλοντι, *to me wishing*, as the dative of favor, and the conjunction ὅτι in the sense of *because :* " I find the law coming to my aid, to mine who would do good, and that because evil is present with me." The law coming to Paul's help in the struggle against evil ! The idea is the antipodes of what Paul teaches throughout this whole chapter.—3. Ewald obtains a directly opposite sense, by taking τὸ κακόν, *evil*, as the apposition to τὸν νόμον, *the law :* " I find the law, that is, evil, present with me when I would do good."— Not only is this construction forced grammatically, but above all this identification of the law and of evil would be an evident exaggeration (comp. vii. 7). Only Marcion could have expressed himself thus.—4. Meyer gives as the object of the participle θέλοντι, *wishing*, the substantive *law*, and takes ποιεῖν, *to do*, as the infinitive of aim : " I find that with me when I wish the law with the view of doing good, evil is present." But the object τὸν νόμον would require to be placed between τῷ and θέλοντι ; and the term *wishing the law* is unsupported by example. Finally, it is far from natural to take the infinitive ποιεῖν, *to do*, as the infinitive of aim ; it is evidently the object of θέλοντι, *wishing*.—5. The masterpiece of all these explanations is that of Hofmann ; according to him the verb ποιεῖν, *to do*, has no object ; it must be taken in the sense of *acting ;* τὸ καλόν, *good*, is an attribute of τὸν νόμον, *the law*, and ὅτι signifies *because :* " I discover that the law is goodness for me when I would act, because evil is present with me ;" meaning : that evil, by arresting me in my eagerness to act when good is before me, serves to prove to me by this resistance that it is really the law which I intend to realize. Is it possible to imagine a more tortuous thought and a more artificial construction ? The active verb ποιεῖν, *to do*, without an object ; the attribute separated from its substantive, etc. !—The true meaning of the word νόμος, *law*, which we have established, delivers this poor verse from all those tortures to which it has been subjected. Our meaning is found in a goodly number of commentators (Calvin, Tholuck, Philippi, etc.). If after that confirmation were needed, it would be found in the two following verses, the one of which demonstrates the : *in me when I would do good* (ver. 21*a*), the other the : *evil is present with me* (ver. 21*b*).

Vv. 22, 23. "*For I applaud the law of God after the inward man: but I see another[1] law in my members, warring against the law of my mind, and bringing me into captivity to*[2] *the law of sin which is in my members.*"—The verb συνήδομαι strictly signifies: *I rejoice with*. Does it mean, as van Hengel thinks: with *other persons*, who like me take pleasure in the law? Or as Meyer understands it, with *the law itself*, which as well as myself takes pleasure in the good it prescribes? The first idea is not supported by the context, and the second is unnatural; for the law is not the subject, but *the object* of συνήδεσθαι, of the feeling of joy spoken of by the apostle. We must therefore apply the σύν, *with*, to *the inwardness* of the feeling experienced: I rejoice *in* and *with myself*, that is to say, in the inmost chamber of my being. This term is still stronger than the σύμφημι, *to agree with*, of ver. 16. The latter merely signified: "What the law declares good, I declare good along with it," while here we have an eager and even delighted adherence.—The complement *of God*, added to *the law*, brings out the moral elevation of the rule, and so justifies the assent indicated by the verb συνήδομαι, *I applaud*.—The last words: *after the inward man*, expressly remind us that it is only to a part of his being that we must apply what Paul here says of himself. We must beware of confounding *the inward man* with the *new man* (καινὸς ἄνθρωπος). Paul means to speak only of that which he calls, vv. 23 and 25, *the understanding*, the νοῦς, the organ with which the human soul is endowed to perceive the true and good, and to distinguish them from the bad and false. Here especially is the action of the moral consciousness, that faculty which has little more than a theoretic character, and which in practice exercises no control over the will sufficient to constrain it to do what it approves. The *outward* man, the acting phenomenal personality, remains under the dominion of another power which draws it on the other side (ver. 23). Again, in 2 Cor. iv. 16 we come upon the contrast between the *inward* and the *outward* man, but modified by the context. The first in this passage denotes the whole man morally regarded, the will as well as the understanding, and the second, physical man only.— We have already shown, on occasion of the expressions used, ver. 16, that nothing affirmed by Paul here passes in the least beyond what Jesus Christ Himself ascribes to man unconverted, but desirous of goodness and placed under the influence of the divine law and of the prevenient grace which always accompanies it; comp. John iii. 21. St. Paul in chap. ii. had already recognized not only the existence of moral conscience in the Gentiles, but the comparative rightness with which they often apply this divine rule in the practice of life.

Ver. 23. This verse is the development of 21*b*: *Evil is present with me*. All the expressions of this verse refer to the same figure and form a picture. At the moment when the speaker starts to follow the law of God which attracts him, he beholds (βλέπω, *I see*) an armed adversary advancing against him to bar his passage; such is the literal meaning of the term ἀντιστρατεύεσθαι, *to set oneself in battle against*. This enemy is *a law* opposed to that *of God* dwelling in *his* own *members*. Thereby Paul denotes the egoistical instincts attached to the members of the body, and which seek their gratification through them, in spite of the assent the understanding gives to the law which labors to repress them. Thus two adversaries find themselves as it were face to face, the law of the mind and that which dwells in the members. The prize of the contest is the *I*, the ego which both seek; and its ordinary result, the taking of the *ego* by the second.— The words: *bringing me into captivity to the law of sin*, represent the *ego* at the moment when it is dragged captive (αἰχμαλωτίζειν, *to make prisoner*) by the law of the members, and so given over to the power of sin. St. Paul

---

[1] The original term means not simply *another*, but a *different* law.—T. W. C.
[2] ℵ B D E F G K P, It. read εν before τω νομω; this εν is omitted by T. R. with A C L, Syr.

calls this master *the law of sin which is in my members.* These last words appear at first sight like a repetition. But they are added to show in these members, which strive so faithfully against the law of the mind to wrest the *ego* from it, the army equipped as it were by sin to fight in its service and pay.

In the two verses, 22 and 23, we thus find four particular laws mentioned, in which there is summed up the general law, or the entire mode of living belonging to the natural man. Two of these laws are *objective*, and are imposed on the will as it were from without. The one is the *law of God*, the moral law written or unwritten; the other is the *law of sin*, that egoistical instinct which hereditarily reigns over mankind since the fall. To these two objective laws there correspond two *subjective* ones, which are, so to speak, the representatives of the two former in the individual: *the law of the mind*, which is nothing else than the moral sense in man, appropriating the law of God, and making it the rule of the individual; and *the law of the members*, which is, on the other hand, the subjective organ by which the individual falls under the law of sin. And the four laws combined, the habitual fact being added of the victory which the latter two gained over the former two, constitute the general law of our existence before regeneration, that order of life which Paul recognizes within him when he examines himself, the νόμος of ver. 21.—If the apostle were merely a cold moralist, dissecting our state of moral misery with the scalpel of psychological analysis, he would have passed directly from ver. 23 to the second part of ver. 25, where in a precise antithesis he sums up once more the result of this whole investigation. But he writes as an apostle, not as a philosopher. In drawing the picture of this state, the question he feels weighing on his heart is one of salvation. Anguish seizes him as if he were still in the heat of this struggle. He utters the cry of distress (ver. 24), then immediately that of thanksgiving, because now when he is writing he knows of deliverance (ver. 25*a*); after which he resumes the course of exposition in the second part of ver. 25.

Vv. 24, 25. " *O wretched man that I am! who shall deliver me from the body of this death? I thank God*[1] *through Jesus Christ our Lord! So then with the mind*[2] *I myself serve the law of God; but with the flesh the law of sin.*"
—The figure of the preceding verse continues in this; these two exclamations are those of the inward man, who, feeling himself led captive to the law of sin, utters a groan and then cries for help. The term ἄνθρωπος, *man*, is fitted to remind *every* reader that the state described is really *his own*, so long as the deliverer has not appeared for him.—Why does Paul here call himself *wretched*, rather than guilty? Because the point in question is not the condemnation resulting from guilt; this subject was treated in the first part, chaps. i.-v. The innate power of evil, against which that of the law is shattered, is a hereditary disease, a misfortune which only becomes a fault in proportion as we consent to it personally by not struggling against it with the aids appropriate to the economy in which we live. Thus undoubtedly is explained the cry of the apostle: ταλαίπωρος, *wretched!*[3] —The term ῥύεσθαι, *to deliver*, is used to denote the act of the soldier who runs at his comrade's cry to rescue him from the hands of the enemy. It too belongs to the same order of figures as the two verbs ἀντιστρατεύεσθαι and αἰχμαλωτίζειν in the preceding verse.—The enemy who keeps the prisoner bound is here called *the body of this death*. The term *body* has sometimes been taken as a figurative expression, signifying merely *mass, load.* Thus Calvin says: *Corpus mortis vocat massam peccati vel congeriem, ex quâ*

---

[1] Three readings: T. R. with ℵ A K L P, Syr.: ευχαριστω τω θεω; B. Or.: χαρισ τω θεω (ℵ*a* χαρις δε . . .); D E F G: η χαρις του θεου (F G: του κυριου).
[2] ℵ F G, It. omit μεν between τω and νοι.
[3] It does not seem that any explanation was needed. Paul's wretchedness was simply the burden of his indwelling sin.—T. W. C.

totus homo conflatus est. But there occurs the mention in ver. 23 of the μέλη, *members,* of the body in the strict sense ; and such a figure is far from natural. Chrysostom, followed by several, takes *the body* in the strict sense ; but in the cry he finds a call for death, also in the strict sense : How long shall I be obliged to live in this miserable body ? Calvin's explanation of the apostle's cry amounts to the same thing : " He teaches us, to ask for death as the only remedy of evil ; and such indeed is the only end which can make the desire of death lawful." It is impossible to mistake the meaning of this saying more completely. Does not the apostle give thanks in the following sentence for the deliverance obtained ? And is this deliverance then death ? Assuredly not ; it is the spiritual emancipation described in chap. viii. It is then *the body* strictly so called which is in question, but the body in a sense analogous to that in which it was called, vi. 6, *the body of sin.* It is the body regarded as the principal instrument of which sin makes use to enslave the soul and involve it in spiritual death, estrangement from God, the life of sin (ver. 5 : *to bring forth fruit unto death*). The body continues with the Christian, but to be to his soul an instrument of righteousness, *to bring forth fruit unto God* (ver. 4) ; comp. vi. 12, 13. Those who applied the whole passage, vii. 14–23, to the regenerate believer, were of course led to the explanation either of Chrysostom or Calvin.—Should the adjective τούτου be connected with σώματος, *the body* (*this* body of death), or with θανάτου, *death* (the body of *this* death) ? The Greek phrase would give rise to an almost inevitable misunderstanding, if the first construction were the true one ; and Meyer rightly observes that the sigh for deliverance does not arise from the fact that the body is *this* earthly body, but from the fact that the body is the instrument of *this* state of death in which the soul is sunk (ver. 11). This observation seems to us to decide the question.

There are two things in the form of the second question of ver. 24 which do not harmonize well with the supposition that Paul is here speaking as the representative of *regenerate* humanity. There is the indefinite pronoun τίς, *who.* A Christian may find himself in distress ; but he knows at least the name of his deliverer. Then there is the future : *will deliver me.* In speaking as a Christian, Paul says, viii. 2 : *hath made me free ;* for to the believer there is a deliverance accomplished once for all, as the basis of all the particular deliverances which he may yet ask. He does not pray, therefore, like the man who utters the cry of our verse, and who evidently does not yet know this great fundamental fact. Finally, let us reflect on the opposite exclamation in the following words : *I thank God through Jesus Christ.* If, as is manifest, we have here the regenerate believer's cry of deliverance, corresponding to the cry of distress uttered in ver. 24, it follows as a matter of course that the latter cannot be the apostle's, except in so far as he throws himself back in thought into a state anterior to the present time.

Ver. 25. Of the three readings presented by the documents in the first part of this verse, we must first set aside the Greco-Latin : ἡ χάρις τοῦ Θεοῦ, *the grace of God.* This would be the answer to the τίς in the preceding question : " Who shall deliver me ?" Answer : " The grace of God." This reading evidently arises from the desire to find an immediate answer to the question in the words which followed it. According to the reading of the Vatic. and Origen : χάρις τῷ Θεῷ, *thanks to God !* the exclamation would be a triumphant one, corresponding to the previous cry of pain. The copyists might easily yield to the temptation of thus contrasting cry with cry ; but would not this change of mood be somewhat abrupt ? Is it not probable that the analogous passage, 1 Cor. xv. 57, has exercised some influence on the form thus given to our text ? We therefore hold to the received reading, notwithstanding the authority of Tischendorf : εὐχαριστῶ τῷ Θεῷ, *I thank God,* not only because it has representatives in the three families of documents, but also because, having a more peaceful character, it contrasts better both in form and matter with the agonizing agitation which characterizes the two preceding questions.—Is the mediation of Jesus Christ, referred to in the following words, to be applied to *the giving of thanks* itself, of which He is the mediator and instrument in the presence of God, or to *the deliverance*, which is the understood ground of the giving of thanks, and of which Jesus Christ was the instrument ? The first meaning is defended by Hofmann ; but it is not supported by the general idea, while the second is demanded by the context ; comp. 1 Cor. xv. 57.—The special feature in the deliverance, of which the apostle is here thinking, is not the pardon of sins through the blood of Christ, but victory over sin through Christ crucified and risen, communicated to faith by the Holy Spirit ; comp. the contrast established by Paul himself between these two means of grace contained in Christ, chap. v. 1, 2.—If Paul does not develop the mode of deliverance, it is because every reader can and should supply it on the instant from the preceding passage, vi. 1–vii. 6. The apostle indeed may satisfy himself at this point with few words, because, as Schott well says, he is merely recalling what he has been expounding at great length ; we shall add : and announcing what he is about fully to develop, viii. 1 et seq.

After this interruption in the description of his state of misery previously to faith, Paul returns to his subject in the second part of ver. 25, which is a sort of summary of the whole passage, vv. 14–23. It seems to me that the ἄρα οὖν, *so then*, has the double office of taking up the broken thread (ἄρα) and of marking that there is here a conclusion (οὖν). This conclusion might be regarded as the consequence of the : *I thank through Jesus Christ*, in this sense, that without Christ Paul's state would still be that which is about to be expressed in the two following propositions ; so Meyer thinks. But this connection has the awkwardness of making an idea, which has only been expressed in passing, control the general thought of the whole piece. I am therefore more inclined to agree with Rückert, in connecting the *then* with the entire piece, which is about to be recapitulated in two striking sentences. We have already found more than once, at the close of a development, a pointed antithesis intended to sum it up by recalling the two sides of the question ; comp. chap. v. 21 and vi. 23.—The two particles μέν and δέ, the first of which is not often used in the N. T., forcibly bring out the contrast. The rejection of the μέν in the *Sinaït*, and two Greco-Latins is a pure negligence. This form (μέν and δέ) shows that the first of the two thoughts is mentioned only in passing and with the view of *reserving* a side of the truth which is not to be forgotten, but that the mind should dwell especially on the second.—The pronoun αὐτὸς ἐγώ, *I, myself*, has been variously understood. Some (Beza, Er.) have taken it in the sense of *I, the same* man, *ego idem:* "I, one and the same man, am therefore torn in two." This meaning, whatever Meyer may say, would suit the context perfectly ; but it would rather require the form ἐγὼ ὁ αὐτός. The examples quoted to justify it are taken wholly from the language of poetry. Others (Grot., Thol., Philip.) understand it : *I, I myself, ipse ego ;* "I, *that same man* who have thus been deploring my misery." But this meaning would only be suitable if what Paul proceeds to say of himself formed a contrast (or at least a gradation) to the preceding description. Now, as we shall immediately see, far from saying anything new or different, he simply sums up in order to conclude. This pronoun has also been explained in the sense of *I alone, ego solus*, that is, isolating my person from every other. This sense would be the true one if it had not the awkwardness of substituting a numerical notion (*one* only) for the purely *qualitative* idea of the pronoun. As Hofmann says, "the αὐτός, *self*, serves to restrict the *I* to himself ;" that is, to what Paul is in and by himself. The undoubted antithesis is : I in what I am *through Christ* (ver. 24) or *in Christ*

(viii. 1). By this statement of his case he replaces himself in the position described from ver. 14. The instant he abstracts from the interposition of Christ the deliverer in his moral life, he sees only two things in himself, those mentioned in the immediate sequel. On the one hand, a man who *with the mind serves the law of God*. The term νοῦς, *the mind*, is strangely tortured by Hodge, who paraphrases it thus : " the heart so far, as regenerated ;" and by Calvin and Olshausen, the one of whom takes it as : " the rational element of the soul enlightened by God's Spirit ;" the other : " the understanding set free [by regeneration] to fulfil the law." But where is there a word of God's Spirit in the passage ? Do we not again meet here with the same expression as in ver. 23 : *the law of my mind*, equivalent to the term : *the inward man*, ver. 22 ? True, Calvin makes bold to say that " it is *the Spirit* which is there called the inward man !" Paul's language is more strict, and it is enough to prove that this specially Christian sense, which is sought to be given to the term *mind*, is false ; that, as Meyer observes, if it were the regenerate man who is here in question, the order of the two propositions would necessarily require to be inverted. Paul would have required to say : " With the flesh no doubt I serve the law of sin, but with the mind the law of God ;" for it is on the latter side that victory remains in the Christian life. The mind here therefore simply denotes, as in ver. 22, that natural organ of the human soul whereby it contemplates and discerns good and gives to it its assent. If this organ did not exist in the natural man, he would no longer be morally responsible, and his very condemnation would thus fall to the ground.— The expression seems extraordinarily strong : "*serve* the law of God !" But comp. vii. 6 : "*serve* in oldness of the letter," and Phil. iii. 6 : " as to the righteousness of the law blameless." It is impossible to overlook a gradation from the *we know*, or *we acknowledge*, ver. 14, to the *I agree with* (σύμφημι), ver. 16 ; from this term to the *I rejoice in* (συνήδομαι), ver. 22 ; and finally from this last to the *I serve*, ver. 25 ; Paul thus passes from knowledge to assent, from that to joyful approbation, and from this, finally, to the sincere effort to put it in practice. He therefore emphasizes more and more the sympathetic relation between his inmost being and the divine law.

As the first of the two antithetical propositions sums up the one aspect of his relation to the law, vv. 14-23 (the goodwill of the mind), the second sums up the opposite aspect, the victory gained by the flesh in the practice of life. And this is the point at which human life would remain indefinitely, if man received no answer to the cry of distress uttered, ver. 24. Olshausen and Schott have thought right to begin the new section (the description of the state of the regenerate man) at ver. 25. But this obliges us either to admit an immediate interruption from the second part of this verse onward, or to give to the term νοῦς, *the mind*, the forced meaning given to it by Olshausen. Hofmann succeeds no better in his attempt to begin the new section with the ἄρα οὖν, *so then* (25*b*). How would a second ἄρα, *then*, viii. 1, immediately follow the first ? And, besides, the contrast which must be admitted between 25*b* and viii. 1 would require an adversative particle (δέ, *but*), much more than a *then*.

Conclusion regarding the passage vv. 14-25.—Before entering on the study of this passage, we had concluded from the context, and from the section taken as a whole, that this part could only refer to Paul's state as a *Pharisee*. It was the natural consequence of the identity of the subject of the passage vv. 7-13 (on which all, or nearly all, are agreed) with that of the section vv. 14-25. This view seems to us to have been confirmed by the detailed study of the whole passage. Paul has avoided, with evident design, every expression specially belonging to the Christian sphere, and the term πνεῦμα, the *Spirit*, in particular, to make use only of terms denoting the natural faculties of the human soul, like that of νοῦς, the mind. The contrast in this respect with viii. 1–11 is striking. We can thus understand why this is the passage in all Paul's Epistles which presents the most points of contact with profane literature.[1] The state of the pious Jew under the law does not differ essentially from that of the sincere heathen seeking to practice goodness as it is revealed to him by conscience (ii. 14, 15).—Neither has it seemed to us that the verbs in the present offer an insurmountable obstacle to this explanation. Not only did ver. 24 prove with what liveliness Paul in writing this passage recalled his impressions of former days. But it must also be remembered, and Paul cannot forget it, that what for him is a past, is a present for all his sincere fellow-countrymen of whom he is himself the normal representative. Finally, does he not feel profoundly, that as soon as he abstracts from Christ and his union with Him, he himself becomes the natural man, and consequently also the legal Jew, struggling with sin in his own strength, without other aid than the law, and consequently overcome by the evil instinct, the flesh? What he describes then is the law grappling with the evil nature, *where these two adversaries encounter one another* without the grace of the gospel interposing between them. No doubt this is what explains the analogy between this picture and so many Christian experiences, and which has misled so many excellent commentators. How often does it happen that the believer finds nothing more in the gospel than a law, and a law more burdensome still than that of Sinai! For the demands of the cross go infinitely deeper than those of the Israelitish law. They penetrate, as a sacred writer says, "even to the dividing asunder of soul and spirit, and of the joints and marrow, and discerning even the thoughts and intents of the heart" (Heb. iv. 12). Now as soon as the Christian has allowed the bond between Christ and his heart to be relaxed, however little, he finds himself face to face with the gospel, exactly like the Jew face to face with the law. Obliged to carry into effect the injunctions of Jesus and the apostles in his own strength, since Christ no longer lives in him, is it surprising that he should make the same, and even more bitter experiences, than the Jew under the yoke of the Decalogue? Faith in Christ is usually supposed to be a fact accomplished once for all, and which should necessarily and naturally display its consequences, as a tree produces its fruits. It is forgotten that in the spiritual domain nothing *is done* which does not require to be continually *done again*, and that what is not done again to-day, will to-morrow begin to be undone. Thus it is that the bond of the soul to Christ, whereby we have become *His branches*, relaxes the instant we do not re-form it with new active force and begins to break with every unpardoned act of infidelity. The branch becomes barren, and yet Christ's law demanding its fruitfulness remains (John xv.). Thus, then, he recommences the experience of the Jew. And this state is the more frequent and natural because we Christians of the present day have not passed, like Paul, from the law to faith through that profound and radical crisis which had made the one dispensation in him *succeed* to the other. From the fact of our Christian education, it happens rather that we learn to know the gospel at once as law and grace, and that we make, so to speak, the experiences of Jew and Christian simultaneously, and that very often (when there has been no marked conversion) to the end of our life. But we must beware

---

[1] ... Aliudque cupido
Mens aliud suadet.
(*Desire counsels me in one direction, reason in another.*)—OVID.

... Video meliora proboque
Deteriora sequor.
(*I see the better part. and approve it; but I follow the worse.*)—OVID.

Scibam ut esse me deceret, facere non quibam miser.
(*I knew what I ought to be, but, unhappy that I am, I could not do it.*)—PLAUTUS.

Quid est quod nos aliò tendentes aliò trahit.
(*What then is it that, when we would go in one direction, drags us in the other?*)
SENECA.

Ὁ ἁμαρτάνων ὃ μὲνθ ἔλει, οὐ ποιεῖ, καὶ ὃ μὴ θέλει, ποιεῖ.
(*He who sins does not what he would. and does what he would not.*—EPICTETUS.)

We need scarcely add the well-known comparison of Plato, which represents the human soul as like a chariot drawn by two horses, the one of which draws it upward, the other downward.

of concluding therefrom that this state of half Jew half Christian is normal, and may be justified by the passage, Rom. vii. It is against this enervating view, resting on a false interpretation of our chapter, that the most recent religious movement has just sought to protest. It has brought out forcibly the difference between the spiritual state described in chap. vii. and that which chap. viii. describes, and claimed for the latter only the name of Christian. Is not the one in fact what Paul calls *oldness of the letter*, the other, *newness of Spirit* (vii. 6)? These cannot be, as Philippi would have it, the two aspects of one and the same state; they are two opposite states. We ought to humble ourselves because of the last traces of the former, when we find them in ourselves, as for something abnormal, and aspire after the complete possession of the glorious privileges which constitute the second.

Of the various explanations mentioned above (pp. 15, 16), we therefore set aside the application of this passage : 1. *To mankind* in general ; 2. To the *Jewish people*, considered in their external and national history ; 3. To Paul, as the representative of *regenerate* Christians ; 4. Neither can we share Hofmann's opinion, who finds here only the entirely *personal* experiences of Paul. How would those experiences interest the Church, and deserve a place in the description of the *method of salvation*, given in the Epistle to the Romans, if they had not something of a prototypical character? Paul himself ascribes to them this character, Eph. iii. 8–10, and 1 Tim. i. 12–16. He regards himself as the normal example of what must happen to every man who, in ignorance of Christ, or thinking to dispense with Him, will yet take the law in earnest. It is only as such that he can think of presenting himself prominently in the pronoun *I*, in a work of supreme importance like our Epistle. —As little can we accept the explanation proposed in the treatise of Pearsall Smith : *Bondage and Liberty*. According to this writer, as we have said, the apostle is here giving the account of a sad experience through which he passed, some time after his conversion, by yielding to the attempt to "render himself perfect by his own efforts," so that in consequence of this aberration sin recovered life in him ; he saw himself deprived of his intimate communion with Christ, and consequently also of victory over sin (see p. 14). This idea assuredly does not merit refutation, especially when this example of the apostle's alleged aberration is contrasted with that of an American preacher, who for forty years had known only the experience of chaps. vi. and viii. of the Romans, those of triumph, and never the experience of chap. vii., that of defeat (p. 28) ! We cannot express our conclusion better than in these words of M. Bonnet (*Comment.* p. 85) : "The apostle is speaking here neither *of the natural man* in his state of voluntary ignorance and sin, nor *of the child of God*, born anew, set free by grace, and animated by the Spirit of Christ; but of the man whose conscience, awakened by the law, has entered sincerely, with fear and trembling, but still *in his own strength,* into the desperate struggle against evil ;"—merely adding that in our actual circumstances the law which thus awakens the conscience and summons it to the struggle against sin, is the law in the form of the Gospel, and of the example of Jesus Christ, taken apart from justification in Him and sanctification by Him.[1]

THIRD SECTION (8:1-39)

THE WORK OF THE HOLY SPIRIT IN THE JUSTIFIED BELIEVER

At the close of the preceding section, the apostle had contrasted the *oldness of letter*, a term by which he denotes the state of the sincere Jew under the law, with the *newness of Spirit*, by which he understands the state of the regenerate Christian. He has just described from his own experience the former of these two states, in order to show how little reason the Christian has to regret the passing away of subjection to a principle of morality so external and inefficacious as the law. He now turns the page of his spiritual life, and describes the latter of these two states, the work of the Holy Spirit. This divine principle does not impose good from with-

[1] See Appendix B.

out; He inspires it; He causes it to penetrate into the very will, by radically transforming its direction. The consequences of this life of the Spirit are displayed from this time onward from stage to stage, till the perfect accomplishment of God's plan in behalf of redeemed humanity. Such is the subject developed in this admirable chapter, which has been called: "The chapter beginning with *no condemnation*, and ending with *no separation!*" Spener is reported to have said that if holy Scripture was a ring, and the Epistle to the Romans its precious stone, chap. viii. would be the sparkling point of the jewel.

This chapter may be divided into four sections:

In the first, vv. 1–11, the Holy Spirit is represented as the principle of the *moral and bodily resurrection* of believers.

In the second, vv. 12–17, the new state into which the Holy Spirit has brought the believer, is represented as the state of *adoption*, which confers on him the dignity of an *heir*.

The third, vv. 18–30, contrasts with the misery still attaching to the present state of things the assured realization of *glory*, to which believers have been *eternally destined*.

Finally, in the fourth section, vv. 31–39, the hymn of the *assurance of salvation* crowns this exposition of sanctification, adoption, and glorification by the Spirit.

Before beginning the study of this incomparable chapter, we must again take account of its connection with chap. vi. In the latter, the apostle had showed how *the object* of justifying faith, Christ justified and risen, becomes to the believer, who appropriates it, a principle of death to sin and life to God. But there it was yet nothing more than a state of the *will*, contained implicitly in the act of faith. That this new will may have the power of realizing itself in the life, there is needed a *force from above* to communicate to the human will creative efficacy, and overturn the internal and external obstacles which oppose its realization. This force, as the apostle now unfolds, is the Holy Spirit, by whom Christ crucified and risen reproduces Himself in the believer (Phil. iii. 10).

SEVENTEENTH PASSAGE (8:1-11)

The Victory of the Holy Spirit over Sin and Death

Vv. 1–4 describe the restoration of *holiness* by the Holy Spirit; and vv. 5–11 show how from this destruction of *sin* there follows that of *death*. Thus are destroyed the two last enemies of salvation.

Vv. 1, 2. "*There is therefore now no condemnation to them which are in Christ Jesus.*[1] *For the law of the Spirit of life in Christ Jesus hath made me*[2] *free from the law of sin and of death.*"—The word *now* has here its temporal, and not its logical sense, as Philippi would have it (to be in keeping with the application which he makes of vii. 7–25 to the regenerate). By this word Paul contrasts the new state with the old, which had passed away.— The *therefore* is not merely connected, as Meyer thinks, with the preceding verse: "As I am no more in myself, but in Christ, there is no" . . .; for then *but* would have been required rather than *therefore*. This *therefore* takes up the thread, which had been for the moment broken, of the exposition of Christian sanctification; for the passage vii. 7–25 was, as we have seen, a retrospective glance at the moral effects of the law in fallen

---

[1] T. R. adds here, with E K L P : μη κατα σαρκα περιπατουσιν, αλλα κατα πνευμα : A, Syr^{sch} add only the words : μη κατα σαρκα περιπατουσιν ; the reading followed in the translation is found in ℵ B C D F G.
[2] ℵ B F G, Syr^{sch} read σε (*thee*) instead of με (*me*).

man, and consequently a sort of parenthesis. Now Paul resumes at the point where he had interrupted himself, that is, at vii. 6, and raises the superstructure, the foundation of which he had laid in the section vi. 1–vii. 6. Hence the *therefore:* "Since ye are dead to sin and alive to God, and so subject to grace, and made free from the law, all condemnation has disappeared." The expression: *no condemnation*, does not apply to any one form of condemnation, and, indeed, Paul takes into view first that which has been lifted off by the grace of justification, chaps. i.–v.: the abolition of *guilt;* and next, that which is made to disappear by the destruction of *sin* itself (chaps. vi. 1–vii. 6). After *therefore* the believer has found reconciliation with God, and thereby death to sin, he can really exclaim: "There is now *no* condemnation." Only sin must not recover its dominion; otherwise condemnation would infallibly revive. For we have seen at the close of chap. vi. that sin entails death on the justified, in whom it regains the upper hand, as well as on the unjustified (viii. 12, 13). There is therefore only one way of preventing sin from causing us to perish, that is, that it perish itself. Grace does not save by patronizing sin, but by destroying it. And hence the apostle can draw from what has been proved in chap. vi. the conclusion: that there is no condemnation. It ought to be so after sin is pardoned as guilt and destroyed as a power, if always this power remains broken. The view of Paul extends even it would seem to a third condemnation, of which he has not yet spoken, that which has overtaken the body, *death*, the abolition of which he proceeds also to explain, ver. 11.—The words: *them which are in Christ Jesus*, form a contrast to the expression αὐτὸς ἐγώ, *I, as I am in myself*, vii. 25.—Our translations, following the received text, give us at the end of the verse this addition: *who walk not after the flesh, but after the Spirit*. These words are, according to numerous authorities, and according to the context itself, an interpolation borrowed by anticipation from ver. 4: "A precautionary gloss against the freeness of salvation," says M. Bonnet very happily. It was needful to proclaim deliverance before explaining it.—*How* has it been effected? This is what is expounded vv. 2–4.

Ver. 2. It is strange that Paul should speak of the *law of the Spirit*. Are these two expressions not contradictory? We shall not understand the phrase unless we bear in mind what has been said (iii. 27, vii. 21, etc.) of the general sense which the word *law* often takes in Paul's writings: a controlling power imposing itself on the will, or, as in the case before us, appropriating the very will. The complement τῆς ζωῆς, *of life*, may be understood as the genitive of *cause:* "The Spirit which proceeds from the life (that of Jesus Himself);" or as the gen. of *effect:* "The Spirit which produces life (in the believer)." But is it possible wholly to sever these two relations? If the Spirit produces spiritual life in the believer's heart, is it not because he is the breath of the living and glorified Christ? He *takes of that which belongs to Jesus*, John xvi. 15, and communicates it to us. —The clause: *in Jesus Christ*, is connected by several commentators with the verb *hath made free:* "The Spirit of life made us free as soon as we entered into communion with Jesus Christ." But in this sense would not Paul rather have said in him, ἐν αὐτῷ, simply referring to the *in Christ Jesus* of the previous verse? It is therefore more natural to make the clause dependent on the immediately preceding phrase: the law of the Spirit of life. The only question is what article is to be understood, to serve as the link of this clause. Should it be ὁ, relating to νόμος, *the law*, or τοῦ, referring to πνεύματος, *the Spirit*, or finally τῆς, referring to ζωῆς, *life?* The first connection, that adopted by Calvin, seems to us the preferable one. The apostle has no special reason for recalling here that *life* or *the Spirit* are given *in Jesus Christ*, which is understood otherwise of itself. But it is important for him to remind us that, in opposition to the reign of the letter, which made us slaves, the *reign* of the Spirit of life, which sets us free, was inaugurated in Jesus Christ. The absence of the article ὁ before the clause ἐν Χ. ʼΙ. arises from the fact that the latter is regarded as forming only one and the same idea with the phrase on which it depends. —Instead of the pronoun μέ, *me*, read by the T. R. with the majority of the Mss., there is found in the *Sinaït.* and the *Vatic.*, as well as in two Greco-Latins, σέ, *thee:* "hath made *thee* free." This reading must be very ancient, for it is found so early as in the Peshitto and Tertullian. It has been admitted by Tischendorf in his eighth edition. But it is nevertheless very improbable. Why the sudden appearance of the second person at the very close of this argument? This σέ has evidently arisen, as Meyer thinks, from the repetition of the last syllable of ἠλευθέρωσε. The μέ, *me*, is the continuation of the form of expression which the apostle had used throughout the whole of the second part of chap. vii. Indeed, the figure used by him in vv. 23 and 24, that of a prisoner calling for help, with the cry: "Who shall deliver me?" still continues and reaches its close in our verse, as is seen by the choice of the term ἠλευθέρωσε, *hath made free.* Our ver. 2 is the true answer to this cry of distress, ver. 23. It is *the breath of life* communicated in Jesus to the justified Christian which causes the chains of sin and death to fall from him.—We must beware of following several commentators in applying the phrase: *the law of sin and of death*, to the law of Moses. Paul has just called the latter *the law of God*, and has declared that he *took pleasure in it after the inward man;* this would not be the time to abuse it in this fashion. The true explanation follows from ver. 23, where he has spoken of the *law which is in his members*, and which renders him the captive *of sin*. The word *law* is therefore still used here in that general sense in which we have just seen it taken in the beginning of the verse. The apostle deliberately contrasts *law* with *law*, that is to say here: power with power.—The two combined terms, *sin* and *death*, form the antithesis to *life;* for the latter includes the notions of holiness and resurrection. *Death* is the state of separation from God in which sin involves us, but with the understanding that physical death is the transition to eternal death. The two words: *sin* and *death*, control the following development down to ver. 11. And first! deliverance from sin, vv. 3 and 4.

Vv. 3, 4. "*For—what the law could not do, in that it was weak through the flesh—God sending His own Son in the likeness of a flesh of sin, and for sin, condemned sin in the flesh, that the righteousness prescribed by the law might be fulfilled in us, who walk not after the flesh, but after the Spirit.*"—The *fact* and *agent* of the deliverance had just been mentioned in ver. 2; vv. 3 and 4 describe its *mode;* ver. 3 its condition, ver. 4 its realization. The *for* of ver. 3 extends its force to the close of ver. 4.—Our translation shows to what construction we hold in explaining the words: *what the law could not do.* We make them, with Meyer, Philippi, and others, a nominative, in apposition to the divine act, to be enunciated immediately afterward: "God condemned sin, a thing which the law was powerless to accomplish." This construction is to be preferred for its simplicity and clearness to all others: to that of Schott, who, by means of a harsh inversion, thus explains the words: "seeing that (ἐν ᾧ) the impotence of the law was weak through the flesh;" that is to say, the weakness of the law was still further increased through the influence of the flesh—the meaning is as forced as the construction;—or to that of Hofmann, who understands the verb ἦν, *was*, and makes the whole a principal proposition; "The weakness of the law *was* (consisted) in that it was weak through the flesh." But such an ellipsis is inadmissible, and the asyndeton between this and the following proposition is without explanation. It would be better to understand, with Luther (comp. the translations of Ostervald and Oltramare), the words ἐποίησε τοῦτο: "What the law could not do, God *did* by sending"... When Paul was about to write this verb, he is held to have substituted the mention of the

act itself thus announced : "What was impossible ... God condemned."
But does not that bring us back to Meyer's construction, which reaches the
goal by a shorter course? Comp. Heb. viii. 1.—The powerlessness of the
law to accomplish this work did not come from any intrinsic imperfection,
but from the fact that it found resistance in man's sinful nature : διὰ τῆς
σαρκός, *by reason of the flesh*. The law could certainly condemn sin in writing, by engraving its condemnation on stone ; but not by displaying this
condemnation in a real human life. And yet this was the necessary condition of the destruction of the sinful tendency in mankind, and in order to
the restoration of holiness. The expression : *the powerlessness* or *impossibility of the law*, is easily understood, notwithstanding Hofmann's objection,
in the sense of : "What it is impossible for the law to realize." Meyer
quotes the expression of Xenophon : τὸ δύνατον τῆς πόλεως, *what the city can
make or give*.—The words ἐν ᾧ, *in this that*, evidently open up the explanation of this weakness. The depraved instinct which the law encounters in
man, *the flesh*, prevents it from obtaining the cordial obedience which the
law demands from him. *The flesh* here as so frequently, in the moral sense
which rests on the physical : self-complacency. The participle πέμψας,
sending, though an aorist, nevertheless expresses an act simultaneous with
that of the finite verb *condemned* (see Meyer) : "condemned by sending."
The term *sending* by itself would not necessarily imply the pre-existence of
Christ ; for it may apply to the appearance of a mere man charged with a
divine mission ; comp. John i. 6. But the notion of pre-existence necessarily follows from the relation of this verb to the expression : *His own Son*,
especially if we take account of the clause : *in the likeness of sinful flesh*.
It is evident that, in the view of one who speaks thus, the existence of this
Son preceded His human existence (comp. the more emphatic term ἐξαπέσ-
τειλεν, Gal. iv. 4).—The expression : *His own Son*, literally, *the Son of Himself*, forbids us to give to the title *Son*, either the meaning of *eminent man*,
or *theocratic king*, or even *Messiah*. It necessarily refers to this Son's
personal relation to God, and indicates that Him whom God sends, He takes
from *His own bosom ;* comp. John i. 18. Paul marks the contrast between
the *nature* of the envoy (*the true Son* of God) and the manner of His appearing here below : *in the likeness of sinful flesh*.—This expression : *sinful flesh*
(strictly *flesh of sin*), has been understood by many, especially most recently by Holsten, as implying the idea that sin is inherent in the flesh,
that is to say, in the bodily nature. It would follow therefrom—and this
critic accepts the consequence—that Jesus Himself, according to Paul, was
not exempt from the natural sin inseparable from the substance of the body.
Only Holsten adds that this *objective* sin never controlled the will of Jesus,
nor led Him to a positive *transgression* (παράβασις) : the pre-existing divine
Spirit of Christ constantly kept the flesh in obedience. We have already seen,
vi. 6, that if the body is to the soul a cause of its fall, it is only so because the
will itself is no longer in its normal state. If by union with God it were
inwardly upright and firm, it would control the body completely ; but being
itself since the fall controlled by selfishness, it seeks a means of satisfaction
in the body, and the latter takes advantage therefrom to usurp a malignant
dominion over it. Thus, and thus only, can Paul connect the notion of sin
so closely with that of *body* or *flesh*. Otherwise he would be obliged to
make God Himself, as the creator of the body, the author of sin. What
proves in our very passage that he is not at all regarding sin as an attribute
inseparable from the flesh, is the expression he uses in speaking of Jesus :
in the likeness of a flesh of sin. Had he meant to express the idea ascribed
to him by Holsten, why speak of likeness ? Why not say simply : *in a flesh
of sin*, that is to say, sinful like ours? While affirming similarity of *substance* between the flesh of Jesus and ours, the very thing the apostle wishes
here is to set aside the idea of likeness in *quality* (in respect of *sin*). This
is done clearly by the expression which he has chosen. It will be asked,

might he not have said more briefly: *in the likeness of flesh* or *of our flesh* (ἐν ὁμοιώματι σαρκός)? But by expressing himself thus, he would have favored the idea that the body of Jesus was a mere *appearance*. And this is the very consequence which Marcion has sought to draw from our passage. One cannot help admiring the nicety of the phrase formed by the apostle, and the pliability of the language which lent itself so readily to the analysis and expression of such delicate shades.—Wendt, while rightly criticising Holsten's opinion, escapes it only by another inadmissible explanation. He understands the word *flesh* in the sense in which it is taken in that frequent expression: *all flesh*, that is to say, every man, every creature. Paul means here, he thinks, that Jesus appeared on the earth in the likeness *of the sinful creature*.[1] But should we then require to take the word *flesh* in the preceding proposition: "The law was weak *through the flesh*," in the sense of creature? It seems to us that M. Sabatier is right in saying:[2] "No doubt the word *flesh* sometimes denotes man taken in his entirety. But even then it never absolutely loses its original signification; the notion of the material organism always remains the fundamental notion." We have no need of Wendt's expedient to account for the phrase of the apostle. Here is its meaning, as it seems to us: God, by sending His Son, meant to provide a human life in that same flesh under the influence of which we sin so habitually, such that it might complete this dangerous career without sin (χωρὶς ἁμαρτίας, Heb. iv. 15); comp. 2 Cor. v. 21: "He who knew no sin" . . .—What then was the reason why God sent His Son in this form? Jesus, Paul tells us in Philippians, might in virtue of His *God-form*, of His *divine state* in the presence of God, have appeared here below as the equal of God. The reason it was not so is explained by the words καὶ περὶ ἁμαρτίας, *and for sin*. If man had still been in his normal state, the appearance of the Son would also have had a normal character. But there was an extraordinary thing to be destroyed, sin. And hence the necessity for the coming of the Son in a flesh like our sinful flesh. As the expression: *for sin*, is sometimes taken in the O. T. (LXX. version) as a substantive, in the sense of *sacrifice for sin* (Ps. xl. 6, *e.g.*), and has passed thence into the N. T. (Heb. x. 6–18), some commentators have thought that Paul was here appropriating this Alexandrine form. But there are two reasons opposed to this idea: 1. This very special sense, which might present itself naturally to the mind of the readers of such a book as the Epistle to the Hebrews, filled throughout with allusions to the ceremonies of the Levitical worship, could hardly have been understood, without explanation, by the Christians of Rome, who were for the most part Gentiles. 2. The context does not require the idea of *sacrifice*, because the matter in question is not guilt to be expiated, but solely the evil tendency to be uprooted. Not that the notion of expiation should be wholly excluded from the contents of so general an expression as *for sin*. It is undoubtedly contained in it, but it is not here the leading idea.[3] Paul means in a wide sense, that it is the fact of *sin*, and especially the intention to *destroy* it (by every means, *expiation* and *sanctification*), which have caused the coming of Christ here below, in this form, so unlike His glorious nature.

This coming is only the means of the means; the latter is the decisive act expressed by the words: *He condemned sin*. To condemn, is to declare evil, and devote to destruction; and we see no occasion to depart from this simple and usual meaning. Most commentators have thought it inapplicable, and have substituted for it the meaning of *conquering, overwhelming, destroying*, Chrys.: ἐνίκησεν ἁμαρτίαν; Theod.: κατέλυσεν; Beza: *abolevit;* Calvin: *abrogavit regnum;* Grot.: *interfecit;* Beng.: *virtute privavit;* so

---

[1] *Die Begriffe Fleisch und Geist*, p. 190 et seq.
[2] *L'Apôtre Paul*, p. 252.
[3] It must, moreover, be taken in the same sense as the τὴν ἁμαρτίαν following, which, of course, has the literal signification.—T. W. C.

also Thol., Fritzs., De Wette, Mey., etc. But Paul has a word consecrated to this idea; it is the term καταργεῖν, *to abolish, annul;* comp. vi. 6; 1 Cor. xv. 24, etc. There is in the word κατακρίνειν, *to condemn,* the notion of a judicial sentence which is not contained in the sense indicated by these authors. Other commentators have felt this, and have again found here the idea of *expiation,* developed in chap. iii.: God condemned sin in Christ crucified, as its representative, on the cross (Rück., Olsh., Philip., Hofm., Gess); to this idea many add that of the *destruction* of sin, evidently demanded by the context; so Philippi: "*to destroy by expiating;*" Gess: "a destruction of the power of sin founded on a judicial sentence," which is included in "Christ's expiatory death." But that powerlessness of the law in consequence of the flesh, of which Paul was speaking, did not consist in not being able to condemn sin; for it did condemn and even punish it; but it was powerless to destroy it, to render man victorious over its power. Besides, would it not be surprising to find Paul, after developing the subject of expiation in its place in chap. iii., returning to it here, in very unlike terms! We are therefore led to a wholly different explanation. Paul has in view neither the *destruction* of sin by the Holy Spirit (ver. 4), nor its *condemnation* on the cross; he is regarding *Christ's holy life* as a living condemnation of sin. The flesh in Him was like a door constantly open to the temptations both of pleasure and pain; and yet He constantly refused sin any entrance into His will and action. By this persevering and absolute exclusion He declared it evil and unworthy of existing in humanity. This is what the law, *because of the flesh,* which naturally sways every human will, could not realize in any man. This meaning, with an important shade of difference, was that to which Menken was led; it is that of Wendt; it was certainly the idea of Theophylact when he said: "He sanctified the flesh, and crowned it by condemning sin in the flesh which He had appropriated, and by showing that the flesh is not sinful in its nature" (see the passage in De Wette). Perhaps Irenæus even had the same thought when he thus expressed himself: *Condemnavit peccatum* (in the inner chamber of His heart) *et jam quasi condemnatum ejecit extra carnem.*—It is evident that if this meaning corresponds exactly to the thought of the apostle, the question whether we should connect the following clause: ἐν τῇ σαρκί, *in the flesh,* with the substantive τὴν ἁμαρτίαν, *sin* ("sin *which is* in the flesh"), or with the verb κατέκρινε, *condemned* ("He *condemned in* the flesh"), is decided. Not only, indeed, in the former case would the article τήν be necessary after ἁμαρτίαν; but still more this clause: *in the flesh,* would be superfluous, when connected with the word *sin;* now it becomes very significant if it refers to the verb. It might even be said that the whole pith of the thought centres in the clause thus understood. In fact, the law could undoubtedly overwhelm sin with its sentences, and, so to speak, *on paper.* But Christ accomplished what it could not do, by condemning sin *in the flesh,* in a real, living, human nature, in a humanity subject to those same conditions of bodily existence under which we all are. Hence the reason why He must appear here below *in flesh.* For it was in the very fortress where sin had established its seat, that it behooved to be attacked and conquered. We must beware of translating with several: "in *His* flesh," as if there were the pronoun αὐτοῦ, *of Him.* In this case the pronoun could not be wanting; and the thought itself would be misrepresented. For the expression: in *His* flesh, would only denote the particular historical fact, whereas the latter: in *the* flesh, while reminding us of the particular fact, expresses the general notion which brings out its necessity. Like the hero spoken of in the fable, He required, if one may venture so to speak, Himself to descend into the infected place which He was commissioned to cleanse.—Thus from the perfectly holy life of Jesus there proceeds a conspicuous condemnation of sin; and it is this moral fact, the greatest of the miracles that distinguished this life, which the Holy Spirit goes on reproducing in the life of every believer, and propagating throughout the entire race. This will be the victory gained over the law *of sin* (ver. 2). Thus we understand the connection between the *condemned* of ver. 3, and the *no condemnation,* ver. 1. In His life He condemned that sin, which by remaining master of ours, would have brought into it condemnation. The relation between vv. 3 and 4 becomes also very simple : The condemnation of sin in Christ's life is the *means* appointed by God to effect its destruction in ours.[1]

Ver. 4. The relation we have just indicated between vv. 3 and 4 forbids us to give here to δικαίωμα, *what the law lays down as just*, the meaning of : *sentence of absolution*, which some, and Philippi most recently, have given to it. The matter in question here is not *guilt* to be removed ; and to say that the law itself can henceforth declare as just, the term πληρωθῆναι, *to be fulfilled*, would not be very suitable. The matter in question, according to the context and the terms employed, is *what the law demands* of man. All the postulates contained in the righteousness demanded by the law (comp. the Sermon on the Mount, for example) are *fulfilled in us*, as soon as we *walk*, no more *after the flesh*, but *after the Spirit*. For, as we have seen, the law being *spiritual*, must coincide at all points in its statutes with the impulses of the Spirit. The participle περιπατοῦσιν, *who walk*, expresses the condition on which Paul can affirm of believers what he has just said (comp. the τοῖς πιστεύουσιν, John i. 12).—Commentators differ as to the meaning of the word πνεῦμα, *spirit*. Does it denote, as Lange thinks, the *spiritual life* in believers ? But would this be a very sure standard, and does ver. 2 admit of this subjective sense ? Most, therefore, understand by the expression : *the Holy Spirit*. This meaning does not seem to us open to question (comp. also vv. 9 and 11). Only from the use of the word *spirit* in the sequel (vv. 5–8), it follows that the apostle is not speaking of the Holy Spirit, independently of His union with the human πνεῦμα, but of the former as dwelling in the latter, or of the latter as wholly directed by the former. And hence the reason why the one and the other idea becomes alternately the dominant one in the following passage.

But the most important word in this verse is the conjunction *that.* In this word is contained Paul's real notion of sanctification How does the fulfilment of the law in believers follow from the fact expounded in ver. 3 : the condemnation of sin wrought in the person of Christ ? The strangest answer to this question is that of Holsten : "The power of the flesh in humanity was destroyed by the death-blow which slew the flesh of Christ on the cross." But how could sin of nature, *objective* sin, in humanity, be destroyed by the fact of Christ's death ? If sin is inherent in *the flesh*, the flesh which needs to be destroyed is not only Christ's, but that of the entire human race. As Wendt rightly observes, nothing but *the death of all men* could secure the desired result.—Gess thinks that the part played by Christ's death in sanctification was to render possible the gift of the Spirit, who alone has power to sanctify (comp. Gal. iii. 13, 14). But Paul does not say in ver. 4 : "that the Spirit might be given" (as he does Gal. iii. 14 : *that we might receive the Spirit*). He passes directly from the condemnation of sin in Christ (ver. 3) to the fulfilment of the law in believers (ver. 4). This mode of expression supposes another relation. And this relation is easy to comprehend if the right meaning of ver. 3 has been taken. The

---

[1] Menken and Wendt, as well as Theophylact, think that, according to Paul, Christ's holy life in the flesh was intended to *justify* the flesh, and thereby humanity itself. from the reproach of having sin inherent in its essence. But this pretended justification is not directly enough connected with the context, and it would prove at most the *possibility* of sanctification ; the apostle evidently goes further.—Menken and others seem to have concluded from this passage, like Holsten, that sin, in so far as it is a fact of *nature*, must have belonged in some way to Christ's flesh, that so it might be vanquished by our Lord. But to secure the reality of victory it was enough that He should endure *temptation*. It is possible to conquer sin, not only by forcing it to go out, but also by preventing it from entering.

believer's holiness is nothing else than that which Jesus Himself realized during His earthly existence. "For their sakes I sanctify myself," says Jesus, John xvii. 19, "that they also might be sanctified through the truth." Here, as in other respects, the Spirit only *takes what is His*, to communicate it to us (John xvi. 14). Our Lord's holy life on the earth is the type which the Holy Spirit is commissioned to reproduce in us, the treasure from which He draws the renewing of our life (Col. iii. 10 ; 2 Cor. iii. 17, 18). The holiness of all of us is only this unique holiness which the Spirit makes ours : *He is our sanctification* as well as *our righteousness*, the latter by His death (which faith makes our death), the former by *His* holy *life* (which the Spirit makes our life). Witness the two διά, *through, by*, of v. 1, 2 ; and the mysterious *by His life*, ἐν τῇ ζωῇ αὐτοῦ, of v. 10. Such is the rich and profound sense of the *that*, v. 4.—The expression ἐν ἡμῖν, *in us*, perfectly suits this meaning. It says first, that therein we are receptive ; then it contains also the *by us*.—The term περιπατεῖν, *to walk*, is Paul's usual figure for moral conduct.—The subjective negation μή is used because Paul is speaking not of the fact in itself, but of the fact as being the *assumed condition* of the preceding affirmation.

Thus the first idea of this passage has been developed : emancipation from the *law of sin*. What the law condemns was condemned in Christ, that henceforth through His Spirit the law might be fully carried out in us. No doubt the power of sin is not annihilated within, but it cannot control the active part of our being and determine the περιπατεῖν (*the walk*). There remains the second idea : deliverance from the last condemnation, that of *death:* death *spiritual*, vv. 5–10, and finally also from *bodily* death, ver. 11.

Vv. 5, 6. "*For they that are after the flesh aspire after the things of the flesh ; but they that are after the Spirit aspire after the things of the Spirit. For the aspiration of the flesh is death ; but the aspiration of the Spirit is life and peace.*"—To understand the *for* which connects this verse with the preceding, we must begin with paraphrasing the first clause by adding : "For, *while* they that are after the flesh," . . . then complete the second clause by adding to the words : "aspire after the things of the Spirit," the following : "and consequently *walk after the Spirit*, with the view of obtaining those spiritual blessings."—*To be after the flesh*, is to be inwardly governed by it, as the natural man always is. The part here referred to is the deepest source of the moral life, whence the will is constantly drawing its impulses and direction. Hence the consequence : τὰ τῆς σαρκὸς φρονοῦσιν : they are preoccupied with the things of the flesh, aspire after them. The word φρονεῖν is one of those terms which it is difficult to render in French, [1] because it includes at once *thinking* and *willing*. Comp. the well-known Greek expressions ὑψηλοφρονεῖν, μεγαφρονεῖν, *to aim high, to have a high self-regard*. The φρονεῖν, *the aspiration*, of which our verse speaks, proceeds from the εἶναι, *being*, and produces the περιπατεῖν, *the walking*, of ver. 4, the moral necessity of which Paul wishes to demonstrate, whether it be on the side of the flesh or on that of the Spirit.—The *I, ego*, is distinct from both tendencies ; but it yields itself without fail to the one or the other—to the former, as the *I* of the natural man ; to the latter, as the *I* of the regenerate man. As its state, so is its tendency ; as its tendency, so is its conduct.

Ver. 6 explains (γάρ, *for*) the moral necessity with which this motion constantly proceeds, from the inward moral state to aspiration, and from aspiration to action. There is on both sides, as it were, a fated end to be reached, which acts at a distance on the will by an attraction like that which is exercised by a precipice on the current of a river as it approaches it. No doubt one might take the words *death* and *life* as characterizing the two tendencies themselves. But the argument does not find so natural an

---

[1] The same difficulty occurs in English. The meaning is, think of, care for, strive to obtain.—T. W. C.

explanation thus, as if we take the two words to express the inevitable *goal* to which man is inwardly impelled in both ways. This goal is *death* on the one hand, *life* on the other. The *flesh* tends to the former; for to gain the complete liberty after which it aspires, it needs a more and more complete separation from God; and this is death. The Spirit, on the contrary, thirsts for life in God, which is its element, and sacrifices everything to succeed in enjoying it perfectly. Neither of these two powers leaves a man at rest till it has brought him to its goal, whether to that state of death in which not a spark of life remains, or to that perfect life from which the last vestige of death has disappeared.—*Death* is here, as in ver. 2, separation from God, which by a course of daily development at length terminates through physical death in eternal perdition (vi. 23). *Life*, in Scripture, denotes a fully satisfied existence, in which all the faculties find their full exercise and their true occupation. Man's spirit, become the abode and organ of the Divine Spirit, realizes this life with a growing perfection to eternal life. *Peace* is the inward feeling of tranquillity which accompanies such an existence; it shows itself particularly in the absence of all fear in regard to death and judgment (v. 1). There is no changing the *nature* of these two states and walks (ver. 5), and no arresting the latter in its onward march (ver. 6). The way of salvation is to pass from the first to the second, and not to relapse thereafter from the second to the first.

The two theses of ver. 6 are justified in the following verses, the former in vv. 7 and 8, the latter in vv. 9 to 11.

Vv. 7, 8. "*Because the aspiration of the flesh is enmity against God: for it doth not submit itself to the law of God, neither indeed can it. And they that are in the flesh cannot please God.*"—The flesh tends to death (ver. 6); for it is in its essence *hatred of God*. The conjunction διότι, literally, *because of the fact that*, announces an explanation which indeed follows. The flesh, the life of the *I* for itself, must be hostile to God; for it feels that all it gives its idol it takes from God, and all it would bestow on God it would take away from its idol. Enmity to God is therefore only the reverse side of its attachment to itself, that is to say, it belongs to its essence. This enmity is proved by two facts, the one belonging to man as related to God (ver. 7*b*), the other to God as related to man (ver. 8). The first is the revolt of the flesh against the divine will; this feeling is mentioned first as a simple fact. The flesh wishes to satisfy itself: most frequently the law withstands it; hence inward revolt always, and often external revolt. And this fact need not surprise us. The flesh is what it is; it cannot change its nature, any more than God can change the nature of His law. Hence an inevitable and perpetual conflict, which can only come to an end with the dominion of the flesh over the will. Now this conflict is the way of death; comp. Gal. vi. 8.

Ver. 8. On the other hand, God is no more the friend of the flesh than the flesh is of Him. The δέ has been understood in all sorts of ways, from Meyer, who understands it in the sense of *now then*, to Calvin and Flatt, who give it the sense of *therefore (ergo)!* It is a simple adversative: *and on the other hand*. The enmity is as it were natural. For the abstract principle, *the flesh*, Paul here substitutes the carnal individuals; he thus approaches the direct application to his readers which follows in ver. 9.— *To be in the flesh* is a still stronger expression than *to be after the flesh*, ver. 5. According to this latter, the flesh is the *standard* of moral existence; according to the former, it is its *principle*[1] or source. Now, how could God take pleasure in beings who have as the principle of their life the pursuit of self? Is this not the principle opposed to His essence?—Thus, then, carnal beings, already involved in spiritual death, plunge themselves

---

[1] Rather, according to the usual force of the preposition, the sphere in which man lives.— T. W. C.

in it ever deeper and deeper; and consequently for them condemnation remains, and is all that remains; while spiritual men rise on the ladder of life to that perfect existence wherein the last trace of condemnation, physical *death* itself, will disappear (vv. 9 to 11).

Ver. 9. "*But as for you, ye are not under the dominion of the flesh, but under that of the Spirit, if the Spirit of God really dwell in you. But if any man have not the Spirit of Christ, he is none of His.*"—In thus apostrophizing his readers directly, the apostle wishes to bring them to examine themselves, in order to know which of these two currents they are obeying; for we easily apprehend these truths with the understanding, but we are slow to apply them to ourselves personally. He begins with expressing a feeling of confidence in regard to their state; but he adds a restriction fitted to excite their vigilance: εἴπερ, *if really*. This word does not positively express a doubt, as εἴγε would do, *if at least* (Col. i. 23). Paul proceeds on their Christian profession to draw from it a sure consequence in the supposed case of their profession being serious. To them it belongs to verify the truth of the supposition. The expression: *to dwell in you*, denotes a permanent fact; it is not enough to have some seasons of impulse, some outbursts of enthusiasm, mingled with practical infidelities.—This first proposition of ver. 9 is the foundation of an argument which will be prolonged to the close of ver. 11. Before continuing it the apostle throws in by the way the serious warning contained in ver. 9*b*, which raises the supposition contrary to that of the εἴπερ, *if really*, and shows also the consequence which would flow from it. It is remarkable that *the Spirit of Christ* is here used as the equivalent of *the Spirit of God* in the preceding proposition.[1] The Spirit of Jesus is that of God Himself, which He has so perfectly appropriated here below as to make it His personal life, so that He can communicate it to His own. It is in this form that the Holy Spirit henceforth acts in the Church. Where this vital bond does not exist between a soul and Christ, it remains a stranger to Him and His salvation. After this observation, which every one is expected to apply to himself, the argument recommences, connecting itself with the favorable supposition enunciated ver. 9*a*.

Ver. 10. "*Now if Christ be in you, the body is indeed dead because of sin; but the Spirit is life because of righteousness.*"—As the apostle had substituted *the Spirit of Christ* for the *Spirit of God*, he now substitutes for the Spirit of Christ His person: *Now if Christ be in you*. "Where the Spirit of Christ is," says Hofmann, "there he is also Himself." In fact, as the Spirit proceeds from Christ, His action tends to make Christ live in us. "I shall come again to you," said Jesus (John xiv. 17, 18), when He was describing the work of the Spirit. This new expression brings out more forcibly than the preceding the solidarity between the *person* of Jesus and *ours*, and so prepares for ver. 11, in which the resurrection of Jesus is set forth as the pledge of ours.—This hope of sharing His resurrection rests on the fact that even now His life has penetrated the spiritual part of our being (ver. 10*b*). No doubt this spiritual life will not prevent the body from dying; but it is the earnest of its participation in the resurrection of Christ. From chap. v. 12, 15, and 17, we know the apostle's view respecting the cause of death: "Through one man's offence *many* are dead." The fact of universal death does not therefore arise from the sins of individuals, but from the original transgression. The meaning of these words: *because of sin*, is thus fixed; they refer to Adam's sin. It is sometimes asked why believers still die if Christ really died for them; and an argument is drawn hence against the doctrine of expiation. But it is forgotten that, death not being an individual punishment, there is no connection

---

[1] "This is a proof text not only for the deity of Christ, but for the doctrine of the procession of the Holy Spirit from both the Father and the Son." Shedd *in lo.*—T. W. C.

between this fact and the pardon of sins granted to believing individuals. Death, as a judgment on humanity, bearing on the *species* as such, remains till the general consummation of Christ's work; comp. 1 Cor. xv. 26.— The term *dead* here signifies: irrevocably smitten with death. The human body bears within itself from its formation the germ of death; it begins to die the instant it begins to live. Commentators who, like Chrys., Er., Grot., explain this term *dead*, as *dead unto sin* (in a good sense), evidently do not understand the course of thought in these verses, 9–11.—But if the believer's death cannot be prevented, there is a domain in him where life has already established its reign, *the spirit* in which Christ dwells. Hofmann insists strongly that the term *spirit* should here be applied to the Spirit of God. In that case the words: *the spirit is life*, must be understood in the sense: the spirit produces and sustains life in the soul. But this sense is unnatural, and the contrast between *spirit* and *body* leads us rather to apply the former term to the spiritual element in the believer. In the passage, 1 Thess. v. 23, Paul distinguishes these three elements in man: *body, soul,* and *spirit.*[1] By the third term he denotes the organ with which the soul of man, and of man alone of all animated beings, is endowed, whereby he perceives and appropriates the divine; by this spiritual faculty it is that the Spirit of God can penetrate into the soul, and by it rule the body. Hence arises the sanctification of the body (vi. 11–13), not its deliverance from death. But Paul can already say, nevertheless, that in consequence of its union with the Spirit of God the spirit of the believer *is life*. This expression no doubt sounds somewhat strong; why not say simply: *living?* This peculiarity seems to have been observed very early; it is certainly the origin of the reading ζῇ, *lives*, instead of ζωή, *life*, in two Greco-Latin mss.; but Paul's thought went further. The life of God does not become merely an *attribute* of the spirit in man through the Holy Spirit; it becomes his *nature*, so that it can pass from the spirit to his whole person, psychical and bodily (ver. 11).—The last words: *because of righteousness*, cannot refer to the restoration of *holiness* in the believer; not that the word *righteousness* cannot have this meaning in Paul's writings (comp. vi. 13 and 19), but because it is impossible to say life exists because of holiness; for in reality the one is identical with the other. We must therefore take the word *righteousness* in the sense of *justification*, as in chaps. i.–v. To this meaning we are also led by the meaning of the clause which forms an antithesis to this in the first proposition: *because of sin.* As the body dies because of a sin which is not ours individually, so the spirit lives in consequence of a righteousness which is not ours.—But will this body, given over to death, be abandoned to it forever? No; the last trace of condemnation behoves to be effaced.

Ver. 11. "*Now, if the Spirit of Him that raised up Jesus from the dead dwell in you, He that raised up Christ Jesus*[2] *from the dead shall quicken also*[3] *your mortal bodies, because of His Spirit that dwelleth*[4] *in you.*"—The δέ, *now*, denotes the progress of the life which, after penetrating the spirit, takes hold even of the body. That body in which, as well as in Jesus, the Spirit of God has dwelt, will be judged worthy of the same honor as the body of Jesus Himself.—In the first proposition the apostle uses the name *Jesus*, because the reference is to His *person* merely; in the second he says *Christ*, or *Christ Jesus*, because the subject in question is the office He fills as *Me-*

---

[1] This passage is not a philosophical analysis of man's constitution, but a rhetorical statement of the whole inner and outer man, just as in the analogous utterance of our Lord Matt. xxii. 37.—T. W. C.
[2] Three principal readings: T. R., with K L P: τον Χριστον; B E F G: Χριστον; ℵ A D: Χριστον Ιησουν (C, Syr^sch: Ιησουν Χριστον).
[3] ℵ B omit και.
[4] The 3d ed. of Stephens, with B D E F G K L P, 10 Mnn. It. Syr^sch Ir. Or., reads: δια το ενοικουν αυτου πνευμα; T. R., with ℵ A C, many Mnn. Cop. Clem, Athan. Epiph. etc., read: δια του ενοικουντος αυτου πνευματος.

diator between God and us. As Hofmann remarks, the personal resurrection of Jesus merely assures us that God *can* raise us ; but His resurrection, regarded as that *of the Christ,* assures us that He *will do* so actually. Once again we see how carefully Paul weighs every term he uses. We have a new proof of the same in the use of the two expressions ἐγείρειν, *to awake* (applied to Jesus), and ζωοποιεῖν, *to quicken* (applied to believers). The death of Jesus was a sleep, unaccompanied with any dissolution of the body . . .; it was therefore enough to *awake* Him. In our case, the body, being given over to destruction, must be entirely reconstituted ; this is well expressed by the word *quicken.*—The word καί, *also,* omitted by the *Sinaït.* and the *Vatic.,* suits the context well : the spirit is already quickened ; the body must be so *also.*—The apostle had said of the body in ver. 10, it is *dead,* νεκρόν. Why does he here substitute the term *mortal,* θνητόν ? It has been thought that he used this word, which has a wider meaning, to embrace those who *shall be alive* at the Lord's coming, and whose bodies shall be not raised, but transformed. Hofmann takes the term *mortal,* of ver. 10, as referring to the *future* state of the body, the state of death to which it is still only destined, and from which the resurrection will rescue it. The true explanation of the term seems to me simpler : In ver. 10, Paul means to speak of the *fact* (death) ; in ver. 11, of the *quality* (mortal). For the resurrection will not only change the *fact* of death into that of life, but it will transform the *nature* of the body, which from being mortal will become incorruptible (1 Cor. xv. 43, 44).

The last words of this verse played a somewhat important part dogmatically in the first ages of the church. Those who maintained the divinity and personality of the Holy Spirit were more inclined to read, as is done by some ancient Alex. Mjj., διὰ τοῦ ἐνοικοῦντος αὐτοῦ πνεύματος . . ., "*by* the Holy Spirit who dwelleth in you."—In fact, by this mode of expression the apostle would ascribe the *divine* operation of raising from the dead (John v. 21) to the Holy Spirit, which would imply His power of free causation as well as divinity. The opponents of this doctrine alleged the other reading, which is that of Stephens, and which differs here from the received reading : διὰ τὸ ἐνοικοῦν αὐτοῦ πνεῦμα, "*because of the Spirit that dwelleth in you.*" This reading is found in authorities of the three families in the oldest versions, the *Itala* and the *Peshito,* and in some very ancient Fathers, such as Irenæus and Origen. Such being the case, we can only ascribe it to Tischendorf's provoking predilection for the *Sinaït.,* that he adopts the first reading in his eighth edition. Indeed, so far as external authorities are concerned, the decisive fact is the well-attested existence of a reading in the documents of the various countries of the church ; now in this case we find the reading διὰ τὸ . . ., *because of,* in Egypt (Vatic.), in the West (It. Fathers), in Syria (Peshito), and in the Byzantine Church (K L P, Mnn.), while the received reading is represented by little more than three Alexandrines and a Father of the same country (Clement). The meaning also decides in favor of the best supported reading. The διά with the accusative, *because of,* follows quite naturally the two similar διά of ver. 10 : "because of sin, death ; because of righteousness, the life of the Spirit ;" and because of the life of the Spirit, the resurrection of the body. The entire course of thought is summed up in this thrice repeated *because of.* Besides, Paul is not concerned to explain here by what agent the resurrection is effected. What is of importance in the line of the ideas presented from ver. 5 onward, is to indicate the *moral state* in consequence of which the granting of resurrection will be possible. That to which God will have respect, is the dwelling of His own Spirit in the believer ; the holy use which he shall have made of his body to glorify Him ; the dignity to which the Spirit shall have raised the body by making it a *temple of God* (1 Cor. vi. 19). Such a body he will treat as He has treated that of His own Son. This is the glorious thought with which the apostle closes this passage and completes the development of the word: *no condemnation.*—This difference of reading is the only one in the whole Epistle to the Romans which is fitted to exercise any influence on Christian doctrine.[1] And yet we do not think that the question whether the resurrection of the body takes place *by* the operation of the Holy Spirit, or *because of* His dwelling in us, has been very often discussed in our Dogmatics or treated in our Catechisms.

The apostle does not speak of the lot reserved for the bodies of unbelievers, or of unsanctified believers. The same is the case in the passage 1 Cor. xv. 20-28. But the word of ver. 13: "If ye live after the flesh, ye shall die," should suffice. That is not, especially after all that precedes, a word of salvation. Besides, what would be meant by the sharp contrast between the two propositions of vv. 5 and 6? We have to explain his silence by his aim, which was to expound the work *of salvation* to its completion. It is the same with 1 Cor. xv. 20-28.—We believe, finally, that after that it is quite unnecessary to refute the opinion of those who, like De Wette, Philippi, Holsten, think the expression: *to quicken the body,* ver. 11, should be applied in whole or in part to the *sanctification* of the Christian's body; Paul does not mix up questions so; he spoke, in ver. 2, of two laws to be destroyed, that of *sin* and that of *death.* And he has rigorously followed the order which he traced for himself.

EIGHTEENTH PASSAGE (8:12:17)

Freed from Sin and Death, the Christian becomes Son and Heir

Victory over sin and death once decided by the reign of the Holy Spirit, condemnation is not only taken away, it is replaced by the benediction which is given to us in all its degrees: in the present, the filial state, adoption; in the future, the divine inheritance.

Vv. 12 and 13 form the transition from the preceding passage to this. The life of the Spirit is not realized in the believer without his concurrence merely from the fact that the Spirit has once been communicated to him. There is needed on man's part a persevering decision, an active docility in giving himself over to the guidance of the Spirit. For the guidamce of the Spirit tends constantly to the sacrifice of the flesh; and if the believer refuses to follow it on this path, he renounces the life of the Spirit and its glorious privileges.

Vv. 12, 13. "*Thus then, brethren, we are under obligation, not to the flesh to live after the flesh; for if ye live after the flesh, ye must die; but if ye through the Spirit do mortify the deeds of the body,[2] ye shall live.*"—It is not enough to have received the Spirit; it is also necessary to walk according to Him. The *thus then* refers to the thought of the preceding passage: "Since the Spirit has set you free from the law of sin and death, do not replace yourselves under this curse." The address: *brethren,* reappears every time the apostle wishes to bring home to his readers a practical and personal warning.—When saying: *we are under obligation,* literally *debtors,* Paul meant to continue in the words: to the Spirit, to live according to Him. As soon as the Spirit comes to dwell in our heart, we owe to Him, ourselves, and a life wholly conformed to His wishes. But the apostle breaks off his sentence to set aside the opposite supposition, one unfortunately which cannot be passed over in silence, and he makes haste to add:

---

[1] The doubtful state of the question is shown by the fact that while Lachman (2d ed.) and Tregelles sustain one reading, Tischendorf and Westcott and Hort sustain the other, which is adopted by English Revision of 1881.—T. W. C..

[2] D E F G, It. Ir. Or. read της σαρκος instead of του σωματος.

not to the flesh. "The natural man," Hofmann observes, "imagines that he owes it to his flesh to satisfy it." The care of his person, from the most earthly point of view, appears to him the first and most important of his obligations. Now it is this tendency which is combated by the Spirit as soon as He takes possession of us (Gal. v. 17). This is the debt which should neither be acknowledged nor paid. The apostle says why in the following verse.

Ver. 13. In this way the regenerate man himself would go on to death. So the flesh will reward us for our fidelity in discharging our debt to it. —Μέλλετε: "there is nothing for you but to die; such is the only future which awaits you." Now was the time to resume the sentence which had been begun: "Ye are under obligation . . . *to the Spirit.*" But the apostle supposes this idea to come out clearly enough from the expressed contrast: *not to the flesh*, and continues as if he had expressed it: "*But if through the Spirit,*" etc. Whither does this principle, whose impelling power takes the place of the flesh, lead us? To death also; to the death of the flesh, and thereby *to life: ye shall live.* The rhythm of this verse is quite similar to that observed by Calvin in vii. 9, 10; 13*a*, the life of the flesh is the death of man; 13*b*, the death of the flesh is the life of man. Why does the apostle say: *the works of the body*, and not *of the flesh?* This difference already struck certain Greco-Latin copyists, who have sought to correct the text in this direction. But it is unnecessary. The complement: *of the body*, is not here the genitive of *the instrument*, but that of *the author.* The acts of which the body is the simple *instrument* are not its own. Paul would suppress those of which it is the independent author, and wherein, consequently, it withdraws from the dominion of the Spirit. These should come to an end, because in the Christian the Spirit should direct and penetrate *all*, even *his eating and drinking*, according to the example quoted by the apostle, 1 Cor. x. 31. In all these acts of life the body should not guide, but be guided. Every act of sacrifice whereby the independence of the body is denied, and its submission to the spirit forcibly asserted, secures a growth of spiritual life in man. It is only as a void is cleared in the domain of the flesh, that the efficacy of the Spirit shows itself with new force. Thus is explained the *ye shall live*, which applies to every moment of the believer's existence on to the state of perfection.— This last word: *ye shall live*, becomes the theme of the following passage. For the two attributes *son* and *heir* of God, which are about to be developed, the one in vv. 14–16, the other in ver. 17, exhaust the notion of *life.*

Vv. 14, 15. "*For all they who are led by the Spirit of God, they are the sons of God. For ye have not received a spirit of bondage to fall back into fear; but ye have received a Spirit of adoption, whereby we cry: Abba, Father!*"—Ὅσοι, literally: "*as many as there are of them who are led . . . they are*" . . . The *for* refers to the promise: *ye shall live.* It is impossible for one who is a Son of God, the source of life, not to live. Now he who gives himself to be guided by the Spirit of God, is certainly a son of God. The thought expressed in this verse may be understood in two ways. Does Paul mean that living according to the Spirit is the *proof* that one possesses the rank of a child of God? In that case this would follow from the grace of justification; and the gift of the Spirit would be a subsequent gift coming to seal this glorious acquired position. In favor of this view there might be quoted Gal. iv. 6: "*Because* ye are sons, God hath sent forth the Spirit of His Son into your hearts." But it must not be forgotten that Paul is not here speaking of the *gift* of the Spirit, but of the believer's *surrender* to His influences. The reference therefore is to a more advanced stage of the Christian life. The other possible meaning is this: "Ye have a right to the title of *sons* as soon as ye let yourselves be led by the Spirit." And this meaning evidently suits the context better. Though one become a *son* by justification, he does not possess the filial *state*, he does not really enjoy *adoption* until he has become loyally submissive to the operation of the Spirit. The meaning is therefore this: "If ye let yourselves be led by the Spirit, ye are *ipso facto sons of God*."—Meyer gives the pronoun οὑτοι, *they*, an exclusive sense: "they *only*." But we are no longer at the warning; the apostle is now proving the: *ye shall live (for)*. The restrictive intention is therefore foreign to his thought, he is making a strong affirmation. —In the term ἀγονται, *are led*, there is something like a notion of holy violence; the Spirit drags the man where the flesh would fain not go. The verb may be taken in the passive: *are driven*, or in the middle: *let themselves be driven*.—The intentional repetition of the word *God* establishes a close connection between the two ideas: obeying the Spirit and being sons. A son obeys his father. The term υἱός, *son*, implies community of nature and all the privileges which flow from it; consequently, when God is the father, participation in *life*.—The apostle gives in what follows two proofs of the reality of this state of sonship: the one, partly subjective, the filial feeling toward God experienced by the believer, ver. 15; the other, objective, the testimony of the Divine Spirit proclaiming the divine fatherhood within his heart, ver. 16.

Ver. 15. The ancients were much perplexed to explain this expression: *Ye have not received a spirit of bondage*. It seemed to them to imply the idea, that a servile spirit had been given to the readers previously by God Himself. Hence the explanation of Chrysostom, who applied the spirit of bondage to the *law*. This meaning is inadmissible. It would be preferable to understand it of the mercenary and timid spirit which accompanied legal obedience. But could Paul possibly ascribe this to a divine communication? If we connect the adverb πάλιν, *again*, as we should do, not with the verb ἐλάβετε, *ye received*, but only with the regimen εἰς φόβον, *to fear*, there is nothing in the expression obliging us to hold that Paul has in view an anterior divine communication; for the meaning is this: "The Spirit which ye have received of God is not a servile spirit throwing you back into the fear in which ye formerly lived." Comp. 2 Tim. i. 7. The character of heathen religions is in fact the sentiment of fear (δεισιδαιμονία, Acts xvii. 22). And was it not in some respects the same among the Jews, though with them the fear of Jehovah took a more elevated character than the fear of the gods among the Gentiles? The feeling with which the Spirit of God fills the believer's heart is not fear, suited to the condition of a slave, but the confidence and liberty which become a son.—The word *spirit* might here be regarded as denoting simply a subjective disposition; as in that word of the Lord in reference to Sennacherib (Isa. xxxvii. 7): "I will put *such a spirit* in him, that he will return to his own land;" comp. 1 Cor. iv. 21: a *spirit of meekness*; Rom. xi. 8: a *spirit of slumber*. Here it would be the *filial sentiment* in relation to God. What might support this subjective meaning of the word *spirit*, is the strongly emphasized contrast between this verse and the following, where the objective meaning is evident: "The *Spirit Himself* beareth witness" . . . Nevertheless it is impossible, if we consider the connection between ver. 15 and the preceding verse, not to see in *the Spirit of adoption*, of which Paul here speaks, the Spirit of God Himself; comp. especially Gal. iv. 6, a passage so like ours, and where there is no room for uncertainty. The difference between vv. 15 and 16, so far as the meaning of the word *spirit* is concerned, is not the difference between an inward disposition and the Spirit of God, but rather that which distinguishes two different modes of acting, followed by one and the same Holy Spirit. In the former case, the operation of the Spirit makes itself felt by means of a personal disposition which He produces in us; in the second case it is still more direct (see on ver. 16).—The *Spirit of adoption* is the Spirit of God, in so far as producing the spiritual state corresponding to sonship; He may even be called: the Spirit of the Son Himself, Gal. iv. 6. He puts us relatively to God in the same position as Jesus, when He said: Father! The term υἱοθεσία, *adoption*, reminds us of the fact that Jesus alone is *Son* in essence (υἱὸς μονογενής, *only son*). To become sons, we must be incorporated into Him by faith (Eph. i. 5).—The pronoun ἐν ᾧ, *in whom*, shows that it is *under the inspiration* of the filial sentiment produced in us by this Spirit that we thus pray, and the term *cry* expresses the profound emotion with which this cry of adoration goes forth from the believing heart.—*Abba* is the form which the Hebrew word *ab*, *father*, had taken in the Aramaic language, commonly spoken in Palestine in the time of Jesus. It was thus Jesus spoke to God when He called Him *Father;* comp. Mark xiv. 36. It has been thought Paul employed the form here, because he made use of it habitually in his own prayers, and that he added the Greek translation: ὁ πατήρ, *father*, in writing to the Romans and to the Galatians, because the Aramaic was unintelligible to them as former Gentiles. But the employment of the expression (which occurs in three writings of the N. T.) must rest on a more general usage. Like the terms *Amen*, *Hosanna*, *Hallelujah*, this word *Abba* had no doubt passed from the liturgical language of the primitive Judeo-Christian church into general ecclesiastical language.[1] By adapting this sacred form of address, which had passed through the mouth of Jesus Himself, to the worship of Christians, not only was there a compliance with the command: "When ye pray, say: *Our Abba* (*our Father*), who art in heaven," but the feeling of the whole church seemed to blend with that of its High Priest, who had prayed, using the same term for Himself and His brethren. From regard to Greek-speaking Christians, and neophytes in particular, the custom was probably followed of adding the Greek translation: ὁ πατήρ, *father*, as is done by Mark. Augustine and Calvin suppose that it was meant, by using these two forms in juxtaposition, to express the union of Jewish and Gentile Christians in one spiritual body. This hypothesis has no great probability.

Vv. 16, 17. "*The Spirit itself beareth witness to our spirit, that we are children of God. Now if children, then heirs of God, and joint-heirs with Christ; if so be that we suffer with Him, that we may be also glorified with Him.*"—The asyndeton form (the absence of a connecting particle) between vv. 15 and 16 indicates here, as always, profound emotion; it announces the more forcible reaffirmation of the same fact, but presented in a new aspect. The expression αὐτὸ τὸ πνεῦμα does not signify *the same Spirit* (-ὸ αὐτὸ πνεῦμα), but *the Spirit Himself*, as the immediate organ of God. All who are not strangers to the experience of divine things, know that there is a difference between a state formed in us by the Divine Spirit, and expressing itself in the form of prayer (ver. 15), and the language in which God answers us directly by means of the Spirit. This difference comes out in the following passage, when the apostle expressly distinguishes the groaning of the Spirit Himself in those who have received the first-fruits of the Spirit (ver. 26), from their own groaning (ver. 23). We observe a similar difference in the life of Jesus Himself when it is He who says: *my Father* (Luke ii. 49, *et al.*), or when it is God who says to Him: *Thou art my Son* (Luke iii. 12). So, in this case the apostle means that we are *sons of God*, not only because our heart cherishes a filial disposition toward God, and inspires us with the cry of love: *my Father;* but—and this is still more sublime—because from the heart of God Himself there comes down the answer by the voice of the Holy Spirit: *my child*. It is not only our arms which are stretched out to take hold of God who gives Himself to us in Christ, but His at the same time which embrace us and draw us to His bosom.—The σύν, *with*, in the verb συμμαρτυρεῖν, *to bear witness with*, should evidently preserve its natural meaning: "bears witness

---

[1] So that it became a proper name, just as was the case with Messiah, Christ, etc.—T. W. C.

conjointly with our spirit," the feeling of which was expressed in ver. 15. But the dative: τῷ πνεύματι ἡμῶν, *to our spirit*, is not to be regarded as the regimen of σύν, *with* ("bears witness *with our spirit*"); it is our spirit which here receives the divine testimony.[1] The term τέκνον, *child*, differs from υἱός, *son*, ver. 14, in this, that the latter expresses rather the personal dignity and independence, the official character of the representative of a family, while the second has a more inward sense, and indicates rather community of life. In the one what is expressed is the position of honor, in the other the relation of nature.

Ver. 17. The apostle has proved the fact of our being sons or children, first by the filial feeling produced in us by the Spirit, and then by the direct witness of the Spirit Himself. He can now conclude his argument; for even in expressing the most exalted sentiments, his exposition always assumes a logical form. He had said, vv. 13 and 14: "Ye shall live, for ye are sons;" then he demonstrated the reality of this title *son;* and he now infers from it the condition of *heirship.* Thus the reasoning is concluded; for to be an heir of God is identical with being a possessor of life.—No doubt God does not die, like those who leave an inheritance; it is from the heart of His glory that He enriches his sons by communicating it to them, that is, by imparting Himself to them. For, rightly taken, His heritage is Himself. The best He can give His children is to dwell in them. St. Paul expresses it when he describes the perfect state in the words (1 Cor. xv. 28): *God all in all.*—But he here adds an expression particularly fitted to impress us with the sublimity of such a state: *co-heirs with Christ.* The loftiness of the title *heir of God* might easily be lost in vagueness, unless the apostle, with the view of making this abstract idea palpable, added a concrete fact. To be an heir with Christ is not to inherit in the second instance, to inherit from Him; it is to be put in the same rank as Himself; it is to share the divine possession *with* Him. To get a glimpse of what is meant by the title *heirs of God*, let us contemplate the relation between Christ and God, and we shall have an idea of what we are led to hope from our title *sons of God;* comp. ver. 29.—Only to reach the possession of the inheritance, there is yet one condition to be satisfied: *if we suffer with Him.* Paul knows well that, ambitious as we are of glory, we are equally ready to recoil from the necessary suffering. Now it is precisely in suffering that the bond between Christ and us, in virtue of which we shall be able to become His co-heirs, is closely drawn. We only enter into possession of the common heritage of glory, by accepting our part in the common inheritance of suffering; εἴπερ: "*if really*, as we are called to it, we have the courage to" . . . These last words are evidently the transition to the passage immediately following, in which are expounded, first the miserable state of the world in its present condition, but afterward the certainty of the glorious state which awaits us.

NINETEENTH PASSAGE (8:18-30)

Completion of the Plan of Salvation, notwithstanding the Miseries of our present Condition

In speaking of the full victory gained by the Spirit of Christ over the last remains of condemnation, Paul seemed to assume that the work had already reached its goal, and that nothing remained but to pass into glory. But in the words: "If so be we suffer with Him," he had already given it to be understood that there remained to the children of God a career of

---

[1] Still, the better translation is, *beareth witness with our spirit*, which necessarily involves the other.—T. W. C.

suffering to be gone through in communion with Christ, and that the era of glory would only open to them after this painful interval. These two thoughts: the present state of suffering, and the certain glory in which it is to issue, are the theme of the following passage. This piece, as it appears to me, is one of those, the tenor of which has been most misunderstood even in the latest commentaries. It has been regarded as a series of consolatory themes, presented by the apostle to suffering believers. They are the following three, according to Meyer: 1. The preponderance of future glory over present sufferings (vv. 18–25); 2. the aid of the Holy Spirit (vv. 26 and 27); 3. the working together of all things for the good of those who love God (vv. 28–30). M. Reuss says on reaching ver. 28: After *hope* (vv. 18–25) and the *Spirit* (vv. 26 and 27), the apostle mentions yet a *third fact* which is of a nature to support us, namely, "that everything contributes to the good of them that love God." A little further on he adds: "To this end Paul recapitulates the series of acts whereby God interposes in the salvation of the individual." *A third fact . . ., to this end!* Such expressions hardly suit our apostle's style; and when one is obliged to have recourse to them, it simply proves that he has not grasped the course of his thoughts. The same is the case with the division recently offered by Holsten, who here finds the hope of the Christian founded: 1. on the state of creation; 2. on the groaning of believers; 3. on the groaning of the Spirit; 4. on the consciousness of believers that their very sufferings must turn to their good. How can one imagine that he has understood St. Paul, when he lacerates his thoughts in this fashion?

The following passage develops two ideas: the world's state of misery in its present condition, a state demonstrated by the groaning of the whole creation, by that of believers themselves, and finally by that of the Holy Spirit; then in contrast, the certainty, notwithstanding all, of the perfect accomplishment of the glorious plan eternally conceived by God for our glory. The transition from the first idea to the second is found in the οἴδαμεν δέ, *but we know*, of ver. 28, where the adversative particle δέ, *but*, expressly establishes the contrast between the second idea and the first.

And first of all, the general theme, ver. 18, enunciating the two ideas to be developed: 1. *The sufferings of the present time* (the συυπάσχειν, *to suffer with*, ver. 17), and 2. *The glory yet to be revealed in us* (the συνδοξασθῆναι, *being glorified together with*, ver. 17).

Ver. 18. *"For I reckon that the sufferings of this present time are not worthy to be compared with the glory which shall be revealed in us."*—The term λογίζομαι, *I reckon*, here signifies: "I judge after calculation made." The expressions which follow imply, indeed, the idea of a calculation. The adjective ἄξιος, *worthy*, comes, as the old lexicographers say, from the verb ἄγω, *to drive, to cause to move*, and denotes strictly a thing which is heavy enough to produce motion in the scale of the balance. The preposition πρός is used here, as frequently, to denote proportion. Consequently, the apostle means that when he compares the miseries imposed on him by the present state of things with the glory awaiting him in the future, he does not find that the former can be of any weight whatever in the balance of his resolutions. Why does he use the first person singular, *I reckon*, instead of speaking in the name of all Christians? No doubt because he would have them verify his calculation themselves, each making it over again for himself. And he has good right to take the initiative in comparison with them, as evidently suffering more than all of them.—This *present time* denotes the actual conditions of our earthly life in contrast with those of the new world which succeeds it. These are, on the one hand, the miseries arising from bodily infirmities and the necessities of life; on the other, those caused by the enmity of man and the sins of believers themselves. Paul, who endured more than any other of these two kinds of sufferings, yet calls them, 2 Cor. iv. 17: *the light affliction of the present moment*, in opposition to the *eternal weight of glory* which he sees before him.—This *glory* is to be revealed ; it *is* therefore already ; and indeed it exists not only in the plan of God decreeing it to us, but also in the person of Christ glorified, with whose appearing it will be visibly displayed. The apostle adds εἰς ἡμᾶς, *in* and *for us*. He might have written ἐν ἡμῖν, *in us ;* but this expression would have been insufficient. For the glory will not consist only in *our* own transformation, but also in the coming of the Lord Himself, and the transformation of the universe. Thus it will be displayed at once *for* us and *in* us ; this is expressed by the εἰς ἡμᾶς. Being unable to render the two relations into French by a single preposition, we have preferred to express the second, which is the most comprehensive.

Ver. 19 begins the development of this general state of misery and waiting in which the church still participates, and which was denoted by the term : *the sufferings of this present time* (ver. 18).

Ver. 19. "*For the earnest expectation of the creation longeth for the manifestation of the sons of God.*"—The *for* is usually made to refer to the idea of *the glory yet to be revealed*, ver. 18. And this view is supported either by the *greatness* of this glory (De W., Hofmann), or by its *certainty* (Meyer), or by its *futurity* (Philip.), or by the imminence of its manifestation (Reiche). But not one of these affirmations is really *proved* in what follows. What Paul demonstrates is simply the fact, that if we are already saved spiritually, we are far from being so also outwardly. In biblical language : As to the spirit, we are in the *age to come ;* as to the body, in the *present age*. The *for* therefore refers to *the sufferings of this present time*. This strange discord forms the basis of our present condition ; and this is what ver. 19 demonstrates by the waiting attitude which all nature betrays. Holsten, ever preoccupied with the alleged application of our Epistle to the Judeo-Christians of Rome, thus introduces the subject : "The Judeo-Christians ask : But, if all wrath is taken away, why so much suffering still ?" We in turn ask : Is it only Judeo-Christians, is it not every Christian conscience which asks the question ?

The Greek term which we have translated by the word *expectation*, is one of those admirable words which the Greek language easily forms. It is composed of three elements : κάρα, *the head ;* δοκέω, δοκάω, δοκεύω, *to wait for, espy ;* and ἀπό, *from, from afar ;* so : "to wait with the head raised, and the eye fixed on that point of the horizon from which the expected object is to come." What a plastic representation ! An artist might make a statue of hope out of this Greek term. The verb ἀπεκδέχεται, which we have translated by *longeth for*, is not less remarkable ; it is composed of the simple verb δέχομαι, *to receive*, and two prepositions : ἐκ, *out of the hands of*, and ἀπό, *from, from afar ;* so : "to receive something from the hands of one who extends it to you from afar." This substantive and verb together vividly describe the attitude of the suffering creation, which in its entirety turns as it were an impatient look to the expected future.—What is to be understood here by *the creation* (Eng. version, *the creature*) ? There is an astonishing variety of answers given to this question by commentators. The word ἡ κτίσις itself denotes either the creative act, or its result, the totality of created things. But very often it takes a more restricted meaning, which is indicated by the sense of the whole passage. Thus in this context we must begin with excluding *believers* from the creation. For in ver. 23 they are mentioned as forming a class by themselves. We must likewise cut off from it *unbelieving men*, whether Jews or Gentiles. For of two things one or other must happen : either they will be converted before the expected time, and in that case they will themselves be found among the children of God, and will not form part of the *creation* (end of the ver. and ver. 21). Or if they are not then converted, they will not participate (even indirectly) in the glorious condition of the children of God. Consequently, since there can be no question in this context either of good angels or devils, it only remains to us to restrict the application of the word *the creation* to all the unintelligent beings which we usually comprise in the expression *nature* (in opposition to *mankind*). Thus are excluded the explanation of St. Augustine, who understood by it *unconverted men*, and that of Locke and others, who applied it to unconverted *Jews;* that of Böhme, who applied it to the *heathen;* the Arminian explanation, which took the word *the creation* in the sense of *the new creation*, and applied this term to *Christians* only; that of Luther, who in some passages seems to have restricted it to *inanimate* nature; that of Zyro, who sees in this term a designation *of the flesh* in the regenerate, etc. The explanation we have given is that most generally adopted (Er., Calv., Grot., Thol., De Wette, Philip., Hofm., etc.). It is confirmed by the following parallels: Matt. xix. 28, where Jesus speaks of the *palingenesia*, or universal renovation which is to take place; Acts iii. 21, where Peter announces the restoration of all things; and Rev. xxi. 1, where this event is described as the substitution of a new heaven and a new earth for the present heaven and earth. The same perspective of a universal renovation in the last times is already opened up in the O. T. (Isa. xi. 1 et seq., lxv. 17; Ps. cii. 26, 27, civ. 34); it follows from the fact of the fall of man in which nature was involved. Solidarity in the matter of restoration is naturally associated with solidarity in the fall.—In this prophetico-poetical passage the destination of nature is represented as its own expectation. This figurative expression becomes a truth in proportion as the beings themselves suffer from the general disorder.—The hour of transformation is called the time of *the manifestation of the sons of God*. This expression is explained by Col. iii. 4 : " When Christ, our life, shall be manifested, then ye also shall be manifested with Him in glory." The appearing of the sons of God in their true sanctified nature, will break the bonds of the curse which still to this hour hold the creation in fetters; comp. Matt. xiii. 43; 1 John iii. 2. And nature herself is impatient to see those new guests arrive, because she knows that to receive them she will don her fairest apparel.—In the following verses, Paul develops more fully that abnormal character of the present creation which he has just declared in ver. 19.

Vv. 20–22. *" For the creation was made subject to vanity, not voluntarily, but by reason of him who hath subjected the same in hope, because*[1] *the creation itself also shall be delivered from the bondage of corruption into the glorious liberty of the children of God. For we know that the whole creation groaneth together and as it were travaileth until now."*—The *vanity* to which nature is now subject, is the state of frailty to which all earthly beings are subjected. "Everywhere," says M. Reuss, "our eyes meet images of death and decay; the scourge of barrenness, the fury of the elements, the destructive instincts of beasts, the very laws which govern vegetation, everything gives nature a sombre hue" . . . This reign of death which prevails over all that is born cannot be the normal state of a world created by God. Nature suffers from a curse which it cannot have brought upon itself, as it is not morally free. It is not *with its goodwill*, says the apostle, that it appears in this condition, but *because of him who hath subjected it to such a state*.—Whom does he mean? According to most modern commentators: God. Was it not He who pronounced the sentence of doom: "Cursed is the ground for thy sake" (Gen. iii. 17)? Yet if this were the apostle's meaning, it would be strange that he should use the expression: *by reason of* (διά with the accusative); for God is not the moral cause, but the efficient author of the curse on nature.[2] Then if the expression: *not with its goodwill*, signifies: not by its own fault, it is natural to seek in the contrasted term a designation of the person on whom the moral responsibility

---

[1] ℵ D F G read διότι instead of ὅτι, which is read by T. R. with all the other Mjj.
[2] He uses this expression in order reverently to remove this supreme will of God to a wider distance from corruption and vanity.—Alford.—T. W. C.

for this catastrophe rests; and we cannot be surprised at the explanation given by Chrysostom, Schneckenburger, Tholuck, who apply the term ὁ ὑποτάξας, *he who subjected,* to the *first man;* comp. the expression, Gen. iii. 17: "Cursed is the ground *for thy sake.*" It cannot be denied, however, that there is something strangely mysterious in the apostle's language, which he might easily have avoided by saying: by reason of the man, or by reason of us; then does the term: *he who subjected,* apply well to man, who in this event, so far as nature is concerned, played a purely passive part? This consideration has led one critic, Hammond, to apply the term to *Satan,* the prince of this world (as Jesus calls him), who, either by his own fall or by that of man, dragged the creation into the miserable state here described. The only room for hesitation, as it appears to me, is between the two latter meanings.—The regimen: *in hope,* can only refer to the term: *who hath subjected,* if we apply it to God, which, as we have seen, is unnatural. It depends therefore on the principal verb: *was made subject to vanity,* and signifies that from the first, when this chastisement was inflicted, it was so only with a future restoration in view. This hope, precisely like *the expectation,* ver. 19, is attributed to nature herself; she possesses in the feeling of her unmerited suffering a sort of presentiment of her future deliverance.

Ver. 21. The conjunction ὅτι *(that,* or *because)* may be made directly dependent on the words *in hope:* "in hope *that.*" Ver. 21 would then state wherein the hope itself consists. But we may also take it in the sense of *because,* and find in ver. 21 the *reason* of the hope: "I say: with hope, *because*"... This indeed would be the only possible meaning if, with Tischendorf, we adopted the reading of the Sinaït. and the Greco-Latins: διότι, *seeing that.* In any case it is the natural sense; for why otherwise would the apostle repeat *in extenso* the subject of the sentence: αὐτὴ ἡ κτίσις, *the creation itself?* No writer will say: nature was made subject in the hope that Nature herself would be delivered.[1]—The pronoun *itself* glances at a natural objection: one would not have expected such a fact in a being like Nature. The καί, *also, even,* refers to the same thought: the unintelligent creation *no less than men.*—In the expression: *the bondage of corruption,* the complement may signify: "the bondage *which consists* of corruption." But this complement may also be taken as the genitive of the object, subjection *to* corruption, *as a law.* This second meaning is undoubtedly better; for the idea of enslavement is thus rendered more emphatic, in opposition to the idea of liberty in what follows.—The term φθορά, *corruption, putrescence,* is more forcible than the word vanity, and serves to define it more exactly.—Paul does not say that nature will participate in *the glory,* but only in *the liberty* of the glory of the children of God. Liberty is one of the elements of their glorious state, and it is the only one to which nature can lay claim. It expresses the unchecked development of the free expansion of all the powers of life, beauty, and perfection, wherewith this new nature will be endowed. There is nothing to show that the apostle has in view the return to life of the individual beings composing the present system of nature. In the domains inferior to man, the individual is merely the temporary manifestation of the species. We have therefore to think here only of a new nature in its totality, differing from the old system in its constitution and laws.

Ver. 22. The hope expressed in ver. 21 is *justified* in ver. 22. By the word *we know,* Paul appeals, not as Ewald supposes, to an old book that has been lost, but to a book always open to those who have eyes to read it, nature itself, the daily sight of which proclaims loudly enough all the apostle here says. Is there not a cry of universal suffering, a woful sigh perpetually ascending from the whole life of nature? Have not poets

---

[1] Still, most of the recent expositors prefer to render the conjunction, *that.*—T. W. C.

caught this vast groaning in every age? has not their voice become its organ? As Schelling said : On the loveliest spring day, while Nature is displaying all her charms, does not the heart, when drinking in admiration, imbibe a poison of gnawing melancholy? The preposition σύν, *with,* which enters into the composition of the two verbs, can only refer to the *concurrence* of all the beings of nature in this common groaning. But there is more than groaning in the case; there is effort, travail. This is forcibly expressed by the second verb συνωδίνει, literally, *to travail in birth.* It seems as if old Nature bore in her bosom the germ of a more perfect nature, and, as the poet says, "*sente bondir en elle un nouvel univers*" (feels in her womb the leaping of a new universe).—We should beware of giving to the expression *until now* the meaning assigned to it by De Wette and Meyer : *from the first of time,* or *without interruption.* This would be a superfluous observation. The context shows what Paul means : Until now, *even after redemption is already accomplished.* The renovating principle has transformed the domain of the Spirit ; for it became penetrated therewith at Pentecost. But the domain of nature has remained till now outside of its action. Comp. the ἑως ἄρτι, 1 Cor. iv. 13. It is in this respect with the whole as with the individual ; comp. ver. 10.

On the passage viii. 18-22.—In following the exposition of the work of salvation, the apostle touches a domain, that, namely, of *nature,* where he comes into contact with the labors of science. Is there harmony or variance between his teaching and the results of scientific study? There is a first point on which the harmony is complete. For a century past the study of our globe has proved that the present condition of the earth is only the result of a series of profound and gradual transformations ; which leads us naturally to the conclusion that this state is not final, and should only be regarded as a temporary phase destined to pave the way for some other new transformation. So it is precisely that our earth appears to the view of the apostle enlightened by the Holy Spirit. But there is a second point on which the harmony does not seem so complete. The apostle traces the present state of suffering and death to a catastrophe which has intervened, first in the moral world, and which has reacted on external nature. Now modern science seems to prove that the present condition of the earth is a natural result of its whole previous development, and that the miseries belonging to it are rather remains of the primitive imperfection of matter than the effects of a fall which intervened at a given moment. Is death, for example, which reigns over mankind, anything else than the continuation of that to which the animal world was subject in the epochs anterior to man? This is a serious objection. Putting ourselves at the apostle's point of view, we may answer it in two ways. If we apply to man the expression ὁ ὑποτάξας, *he who subjected* (nature to vanity), it must be held that man placed in a privileged position, exempt from miseries in general and from death, with a body which life in God could raise above the law of dissolution, was called as the king of nature to free this magnificent domain from all the imperfections and miseries which it had inherited from previous ages. After developing all his faculties of knowledge and power in the favored place where he had been put for this purpose, man should have extended this prosperous condition to the whole earth, and changed it into a paradise. Natural history proves that a beneficial influence even on the animal world is not an impossibility. But in proportion as man failed in his civilizing mission to nature, if one may so speak, it fell back under that law of vanity from which it should have been freed by him, and which weighed on it only the more heavily in consequence of man's corruption. Thus the apostle's view may be justified on this explanation. But if the term ὁ ὑποτάξας, *he who subjected,* refers to Satan, there opens up to our mind a still vaster survey over the development of nature. Satan is called—and Jesus Himself gives him the title—*the prince of this world.* He who believes in the personal existence of Satan may therefore also hold that this earth belonged originally to his domain. Has it not been from the first steps of its development the theatre of the struggle between this revolted vassal and his divine liege-lord? The history of humanity is constantly showing us, both in great things and small, God taking the initiative and laying down some good, but that good hasting to alter its character by a progressive deviation, which leads slowly to the most enormous monstrosities. Might not primitive nature have been subject to a similar law, and the crisis of its development have resulted also from conflict between a beneficent force laying down a normal state, and that power of deviation which immediately takes hold of the divine product to guide it to the most abnormal result, till the salutary principle again interpose to establish a new point of departure superior to the former, and which the malignant spirit will corrupt anew? From this unceasing struggle proceeded the constant progress which terminated in man, and in the relatively perfect condition in which he originally appeared. But the power of deviation showed itself immediately anew on the very theatre of paradise, and in the domain of liberty produced *sin*, which involved all again under the law of death, which is not yet finally vanquished. It belongs to Christ, to the children of God, *the seed of the woman*, man victorious over the serpent, his temporary victor, to work out a deliverance which would have been the work of the race of mankind had it remained united to God.[1] Perhaps this second point of view explains more fully the thought of the apostle expressed in this passage.—There is a third point on which science seems to us to harmonize readily with St. Paul's view; I mean the close solidarity which exists between man and the whole of nature. The physiologist is forced to see in the human body the intended goal and masterpiece of animal organization which appears as nothing else than a long effort to reach this consummation. As the breaking of the bud renders sterile the branch which bore it, so the fall of man involved that of the world. As Schelling said in one of his admirable lectures on the philosophy of revelation: "Nature, with its melancholy charm, resembles a bride who, at the very moment when she was fully attired for marriage, saw the bridegroom to whom she was to be united die on the very day fixed for the marriage. She still stands with her fresh crown and in her bridal dress, but her eyes are full of tears."[2] The soul of the poet-philosopher here meets that of the apostle. The ancient thinkers spoke much of a soul of the world. The idea was not a vain dream. The soul of the world is man. The whole Bible, and this important passage in particular, rest on this profound idea.

The groaning of nature, of which the apostle has just spoken, is the expression and proof of the abnormal state to which it is subjected, with all the beings belonging to it. But it is not the only sufferer from this state of imperfection. Other beings of a higher order, and which have already been restored to their normal state, also suffer from the same, and mingle their groaning with that of nature. This is the truth developed in vv. 23–25.

Ver. 23. "*And not only only so, but we also,*[3] *which have the first-fruits of the Spirit, we ourselves also*[4] *groan within ourselves, waiting for the adoption,*[5] *the redemption of our body.*"—The connection between this passage and the preceding one is obvious at a glance; it is found in the idea of *groaning*. The groaning of believers themselves, men already animated with the breath of God, rises as it were on that of nature. Of the three or even four readings presented by the documents, we must first, whatever Volkmar may say to the contrary, set aside that of the *Vatic.*, which rejects the ἡμεῖς, *we*, in the middle of the verse; this pronoun is indispensable to emphasize the contrast between believers and nature. And whence could it have come into all the other texts? We may also set aside the Greco-Latin reading (D F G). By putting the pronoun: *we ourselves also*, at the beginning of the sentence, after the words: *not only but*, it obliterates the forcible re-

---

[1] This was the view-point of Steffens in his lectures on "Anthropology."
[2] We quote from memory.
[3] D E F G, It. read αλλα και ημεις αυτοι instead of και αυτοι.
[4] Three principal readings: 1. T. R., with K L P and Mnn.: εχοντες και ημεις αυτοι.—2. ℵ A C: εχοντες ημεις και αυτοι.—3. D F G: εχοντες αυτοι; B: εχοντες και αυτοι.
[5] D F G, It. omit υιοθεσιαν.

affirmation which these words contain when placed in the middle of the sentence : "*We also . . . we ourselves also*" . . . The two other readings differ only in this, that the Alexandrine (א A C) places the ἡμεῖς, *we*, before καὶ αὐτοί, while the Byzs. place it between the two words : *and we ourselves*. The difference of meaning is almost imperceptible (*we ourselves also ; also we ourselves*). It is probable that the Alexs. have displaced the ἡμεῖς, *we*, to bring it next the participle ἔχοντες. This is the reason why we have translated according to the received reading.—Several commentators have thought that in saying first *we*, then adding *we ourselves also*, the apostle meant to speak of two different subjects, for example, *Christians* and *apostles* (Mel.), or *Christians* and *Paul* himself (Reiche). But in this case the article οἱ before the participle ἔχοντες would be indispensable ; and what object could there be in such a distinction in the context?—The logical connection between the participle ἔχοντες, *having, possessing*, and the verb στενάζομεν, *we groan*, should be rendered by the conjunction *though:* "Though already possessing, we still groan (*ipsi nos habentes*)."—The expression : *the first-fruits of the Spirit*, is so clear that it is difficult to understand how it should have given rise to dispute. How has it occurred to commentators like De Wette, Olshausen, Meyer, to apply it specially to the Spirit bestowed on the *apostles* and *first* believers, to distinguish it from the Spirit afterward bestowed on other believers? What importance can this difference have for the spiritual life, and where is a trace of such a distinction to be found in the N. T. ? It would be preferable to regard the word *first-fruits* (with Chrys., Calv., Thol., Philip., Bonnet) as referring to the fact that Christians here below receive only a beginning, while there will be given to them above the entire fulness of the Spirit. In this sense the genitive would be the complement of the object : *The first-fruits of that gift which is the Spirit*. But the apostle is not here contrasting an imperfect with a more perfect spiritual state ; he is contrasting an *inward* state already relatively perfect, with an *outward* state which has not yet participated in the spiritual renewal ; this appears clearly from the last words : *waiting for the redemption of our body*. The genitive is therefore the complement of quality or apposition : "The first-fruits *which consist of* the Spirit Himself." This meaning is proved, besides, by the attentive comparison of 2 Cor. i. 22 and Eph. i. 14. The apostle means : " We ourselves, who by the possession of the Spirit have already entered inwardly into the new world, still groan, because there is a part of our being, the outer man, which does not yet enjoy this privilege."—Hofmann joins the regimen : *within ourselves*, to the participle ἔχοντες : *we who have within ourselves*. But is it not superfluous to say that the Holy Spirit is possessed inwardly ? This regimen is very significant, on the contrary, if we connect it, as is grammatically natural, with the verb *we groan:* " We groan often inwardly, even when others do not suspect it, and when they hear us proclaiming salvation as a fact already accomplished." The disharmony between *the child of God* and the child of the dust therefore still remains ; and hence we wait for something.—This something St. Paul calls *adoption*, and he explains it by the apposition : *the redemption of our body*. No doubt our adoption is in point of right an acquired fact (Gal. iv. 6). It is so in reality on its spiritual side, for we already possess the *Spirit of our Father*, as Paul has developed it, vv. 14-16. But the state of sons of God will not be fully realized in us until to the holiness of the Spirit there be added the glory and perfection of the body. It needs hardly be said that the expression : *the redemption of our body*, is not to be interpreted in the sense : that we are to be delivered *from* our body (Oltram.). For this idea, applied to the body itself, would be anti-biblical ; faith waits for a new body ; and if it applied to the body only as the body *of our humiliation*, as Paul says, Phil. iii. 21, this specification would require to be added, or at least Paul would require to say τοῦ σώματος τούτου, *of this present body*. The complement *of the body* is therefore evidently the genitive, not of the object, but of the subject: it is the body itself which is to be delivered from the miseries of its present corruption. We see from 2 Cor. v. 4 that Paul desired not to be *unclothed*, but *to be clothed upon:* that is, to receive his glorified body, by the power of which his mortal body was to be as it were swallowed up. It is by the transformation of the body only that we shall become completely *sons of God*. Comp. the affirmation, which is not identical, but analogous, made in reference to Christ Himself, i. 3, 4.

Vv. 24, 25. "*For we have been saved in hope; but hope that is seen is not hope; for what a man seeth, why would he yet* [1] *hope for? Now if we hope for that we see not, then do we with perseverance wait for it.*"—Ver. 24 uses one of the three constituent elements of the Christian life, namely *hope* (1 Cor. xiii. 13), to demonstrate the reality of that state of groaning and expectation which has just been ascribed to believers. On the one hand, undoubtedly salvation is a thing finished; this is indicated by the aorist ἐσώθημεν, *we have been saved*. But, on the other hand, this salvation having as yet penetrated only to the spiritual part of our being, is not fully realized, and leaves room for awaiting a more complete realization. Hence the restrictive specification τῇ ἐλπίδι, *in hope*. This word, from its position at the beginning of the sentence, evidently has the emphasis. This dative is, as Bengel says, a *dativus modi*, signifying: "*in the way of hope*." The meaning therefore is: "If we are saved, which is certain, this holds true only when we take account of the element of hope which continues always in our present state." We must not, like Chrys., De Wette, Rück, identify hope with faith, and find here the idea of salvation by faith. The whole context shows that it is really of *hope* in the strict and special meaning of the word that Paul is speaking. Already in the apostolic age we find persons who, intoxicated with a feeling of false spiritualism, gave out that salvation concerned only man's higher nature, and who abandoned the body to everlasting destruction; so those Christians of Corinth who denied the resurrection of the body (1 Cor. xv.), and those heretics of Asia Minor who alleged that *the resurrection was already past* (2 Tim. ii. 18), probably because they confounded it with moral regeneration. Were there such men at Rome? Paul must have had some reason for insisting, as he does here, on the outward and future consummation of the edifice of salvation. The meaning of the last two propositions of ver. 24 is clear: "Now, hope implies non-possession." In the words: *hope that is seen*, the term *hope* is taken for *the object hoped for*, as is often the case, Col. i. 5 for example. In the words following, the term resumes its subjective meaning. The last proposition has been amended by the copyists in all sorts of ways. In our translation we have rendered the T. R. The Greco-Latin text, rejecting the καί, *yet*, signifies: "For what one sees, why would he hope for?" The *Sinaït*.: "What one sees, he also hopes for," or "does he also hope for?" —a reading which in the context has no meaning. The *Vatic*.: "What one sees, does he hope for?" This is the reading which Volkmar prefers; for in regard to the *Vatic*. he gives himself up to the same predilection with which he rightly charges Tischendorf in regard to the *Sinaït*. This reading is impossible. It would require *when* instead of *what:* "When one sees, does he hope?"—The καί, *yet*, is by no means superfluous: *yet*, after sight has begun, along with sight, hope has no more place.

Ver. 25. This verse is not, as Meyer thinks, a deduction fitted to close the first reason of encouragement. In this case an οὖν, *therefore*, would have been necessary rather than δέ, *now*, or *but*. The meaning *but* (Osterv., Oltram.) well suits the contrast between the ideas of *hoping* (ver. 25) and *seeing* (ver. 24). Yet it seems to me that the meaning *now* is preferable. It

---

[1] T. R., with A C K L P, reads : τι και before ελπιζει ; D F G, It. Syr. : τι (without και) ; ℵ : και (without τι) ; B omits τι και ; ℵ A read υπομενει instead of ελπιζει.

320 / Sanctification

is not a conclusion ; it is a step in the argument intended to prove the painful state of waiting attaching even to believers. The emphasis is on the words δι' ὑπομονῆς, *with perseverance*, and the general meaning is this: "Now, obliged as we yet are to hope without seeing, waiting necessarily takes the character of *perseverance.*" To understand this thought, it is enough to recall the etymological meaning of the word ὑπομένειν : to hold out under a burden. *We wait with perseverance* amounts therefore to saying : "It is only by holding out under the burden of present sufferings that we can expect with certainty the hoped-for future." The conclusion is this : We are not therefore yet in our normal condition ; otherwise why *endurance?*

Vv. 26, 27. "*And likewise the Spirit also helpeth our infirmity ;*[1] *for we know not what we should ask*[2] *in order to pray as we ought, but the Spirit itself maketh intercession*[3] *with groanings which cannot be uttered. But He that searcheth the hearts knoweth what is the aspiration of the Spirit, because He maketh intercession for the saints according to God.*"—As the apostle had passed from the groaning of universal nature to that of the children of God, he now rises from the latter to that of the Holy Spirit Himself. This gradation is so evident that one is astonished it could have remained unobserved by so many commentators (see for example Meyer). But we must remark the significant difference between this second transition and the former. In passing from the groaning of nature to that of believers, he said : *not only . . . but also.* Now he simply says : *and likewise also.* There is no contrast indicated here ; for the groaning of the Spirit is homogeneous with that of believers (*likewise*), though distinct from it notwithstanding (*also*), and though there is a gradation from the one to the other (δέ, *now*, which we have rendered by *and*).—If, with the Byzs., we read the plural ταῖς ἀσθενείαις, *our infirmities*, the word would denote the moral infirmities of believers. But so general an idea is out of place in the context. We must therefore prefer the Alex. reading : τῇ ἀσθενείᾳ, *our infirmity.* This expression refers to a special infirmity, the fainting condition with which the believer is sometimes overtaken under the weight of present suffering ; it is the want which makes itself felt in his ὑπομονή, that *constancy*, the necessity of which had been affirmed in the previous verse. The reading of F G : *our weakness in prayer*, would refer to our ignorance as to what should be asked (the proposition following). But this so weakly supported reading is certainly a gloss. Infirmity in prayer enters into the weakness of which the apostle speaks, but does not constitute the whole of it. The verb συναντιλαμβάνεσθαι, *to support, come to the help of*, is one of those admirable words easily formed by the Greek language ; λαμβάνεσθαι (the middle) *to take a burden on oneself ;* σύν, *with* some one ; ἀντί, *in his place ;* so : to share a burden with one with the view of easing him ; comp. Luke x. 40. This verb is usually followed by a personal regimen, which leads us to take the abstract substantive here : *our weakness*, for : *us weak ones* (ἡμῖν ἀσθένεσιν). The Spirit supports us in the hour when we are ready to faint. The end of the verse will explain wherein this aid consists.— Before describing it the apostle yet further examines the notion : *our infirmity.* The case in question belongs to those times in which our tribulation is such that in praying we cannot express to God what the blessing is which would allay the distress of our heart. We ourselves have no remedy to propose. The article τό defines the whole following proposition taken as a substantive : "The: *what we should ask.*" This is what we know not ourselves. The words *as we ought* do not refer to the *manner* of prayer (this would require καθώς), but to its *object.* Jesus Himself was once

---

[1] T. R. reads, with K L P, ταις ασθενειαις ; ℵ A B C D F G, Syr.sch read τη ασθενεια, a word to which F G add : της δεησεως.
[2] T. R. reads, with ℵ A B C : προσευξωμεθα ; D K L P read προσευξομεθα ; and F G : προσευχομεθα.
[3] ℵ A B D F G omit the words : υπερ ημων (*for us*).

in the perplexity of which the apostle here speaks. "Now is my soul troubled," says He, John xii. 27, "and what shall I say? Father, save me from this hour : but for this cause came I unto this hour." After this moment of trouble and hesitation, his mind became fixed, and His prayer takes form : " Father, glorify Thy name." In our case the struggle usually lasts longer. Comp. a similar situation in the experience of Paul, 2 Cor. xii. 7–9.—In these extreme situations help is suddenly presented to us, a divine agent who raises us as it were above ourselves, *the Spirit*. The verb ὑπερεντυγχάνειν is again a term compounded of three words : τυγχάνειν, *to find oneself, to meet* with some one ; ἐν, *in* a place agreed on ; ὑπέρ, *in* one's *favor ;* hence : *to intercede in favor of*. It would seem that the regimen ὑπὲρ ἡμῶν, *for us*, in the Byz. text, should be rejected according to the two other families.—How are we to conceive of this *intercession* of the Spirit? It does not take place in the heavenly sanctuary, like that of the glorified Christ (Heb. vii. 25). It has for its theatre the believer's own heart. The very term *groaning* implies this, and ver. 27, by speaking of God *who searches the hearts*, confirms it.—The epithet ἀλάλητος, which we have translated *unutterable*, may be explained in three ways. 1. Beza and Grotius have given it the meaning of *mute*, that is to say, purely inward and spiritual. But what end would such a qualification serve here? 2. Others understand *inexpressible ;* such is the meaning of our translation ; that is to say, that the understanding cannot fully grasp its object, nor consequently express it in distinct terms. Only, 3, we should have preferred to translate, had the language permitted it, by the word *unformulated* or *unexpressed*.[1] In every particular case, he who is the object of this assistance feels that no distinct words fully express to God the infinite good after which he sighs. The fact proves that the aspiration is not his own, but that it is produced in his heart by the Spirit of Him of whom John said, "that He is greater than our heart" (1 John iii. 20). We here find ourselves in a domain analogous to that of the γλώσσαις λαλεῖν, *speaking in tongues*, to which 1 Cor. xiv. refers ; comp. vv. 14 and 15, where Paul says : "When I pray in a tongue, my spirit (πνεῦμα) prayeth indeed, but my understanding (νοῦς) is unfruitful." The understanding cannot control, nor even follow the movement of the spirit, which, exalted by the Spirit of God, plunges into the depths of the divine. Thus, at the moment when the believer already feels the impulse of hope failing within him, a groan more elevated, holy, and intense than anything which can go forth even from his renewed heart is uttered within him, coming from God and going to God, like a pure breath, and relieves the poor downcast heart.[2]

Ver. 27. The δέ, *but*, contrasts the knowledge of God, which thoroughly understands the object of this groaning, with the ignorance of the heart from which it proceeds. God is often called in the O. T. the καρδιογνώστης, the *searcher of hearts*. As to the blessing to which the aspiration of the Spirit goes forth in the believer's heart, he knows its nature, he discerns its sublime reality. Why? This is what is told us in the second part of the verse : Because this supreme object of the Spirit's aspiration is what God Himself has prepared for us. The groaning of the Spirit is κατὰ Θεόν, *according to God*. The preposition κατά, *according to*, denotes the standard ; God does not require the man who prays to express to Him the things he needs, since the groaning of the Spirit is in conformity with the plan of God which is to be realized. If it is so, how should not God understand such a groan? For the Spirit fathoms the divine plans to the bottom, 1 Cor. ii. 10. It is obvious how far Meyer and Hofmann are mistaken in al-

---

[1] There is some expression, but not an adequate one.—Shedd.—T. W. C.
[2] M. Renan (*St. Paul*, p. 469) thus interprets the words of Paul : "those indistinct and inarticulate groanings," as if the word ἀλαλήτοις referred to some physical stuttering like that of a child. Think what would be meant in this case by the phrase *praying as we ought*, and *knowing*, applied to God, ver. 27 ! it is to this also that many expositors bring down the *speaking with tongues* of 1 Cor. xiv. ; a miserable degradation of one of the most glorious phenomena.

leging that ὅτι should signify *that* and not *because*. They have not apprehended the bearing of the κατὰ Θεόν, *according to God ;* Paul has a reason for making this word the opening one of the proposition. What is according to Him cannot remain unintelligible to Him. It is impossible to conceive a more superfluous thought than the one here substituted by the two commentators referred to : " God knows that the Spirit intercedes, and that He does so according to Him for the saints." Did this *knowing* require to be affirmed ? The last words, ὑπὲρ ἁγίων, literally, "*for* saints," are very weighty. These *saints* are beings in whom the Spirit already dwells. After what He has already done in them, is it not natural for Him to interest Himself in the completion of their salvation ?—In the words : *according to God* and *for saints*, there is already enunciated a thought which is now to become that of the following passage, the thought of a *divine plan* conceived from all eternity in favor of the *elect*. It is to the accomplishment of this plan that the operation of the Spirit tends.

What a demonstration of the unutterable disorder which reigns throughout creation, and consequently of the state of imperfection in which it still is, notwithstanding the redemption which has been accomplished ! Nature throughout all her bounds has a confused feeling of it, and from her bosom there rises a continual lament claiming a renovation from heaven. The redeemed themselves are not exempt from this groaning, and wait for their own renewal which shall be the signal of universal restoration; and finally, the Spirit, who is intimate with the plans of God *for our glory* (1 Cor. ii. 7), and who distinctly beholds the ideal of which we have but glimpses, pursues its realization with ardor. Thus is exhausted the first of the two leading ideas of this passage, that of the συμπάσχειν, *suffering with Christ*. The apostle now passes to the second, that of the συνδοξασθῆναι, *being glorified with Him*. The first was the condition (εἴπερ, *if so be*, ver. 17) ; the second is the final aim.

Ver. 28. " *But we know that all things work together,*[1] *for good to them that love God, to them who are the called according to the design formed beforehand.*"
—We have shown how mistaken those expositors are who take the δέ as a simple particle of transition : *then*, and say : third or fourth ground of encouragement. The δέ is adversative : *but*. With this universal groaning which he has just described, and the source of which is in *the sufferings of the present time*, the apostle contrasts the full certainty already possessed by believers of the *glorious goal* marked out beforehand by the plan of God. This result, which they await with assurance, is the luminous point on which their eye is already fixed, and the brilliance of which is reflected on the obscurities of the way which they have yet to traverse : " We groan no doubt ; we know not how to pray . . ., *but we know*" . . . The regimen : *to them that love God*, is placed at the beginning, as expressing the condition under which the prerogative about to be enunciated is realized in man. This characteristic of love to God is associated with the attribute of *saints* which he ascribed to believers, ver. 27, and more particularly with the cry : *Abba, Father*, the expression of their filial feeling, ver. 15. Those who belong to this class will never fail to be strengthened, and even to gain progress, by everything which can happen them ; for in this normal path obstacles even become means of help. The end of the verse will explain why.—The term πάντα, *all things*, includes all that comes on us, especially everything painful in consequence of the miseries of the present time and of the sins of our neighbors. But it would be wrong to embrace under it what we may do ourselves in opposition to God's will, since that would contradict the idea : *them that love God*.—The σύν, *with*, in the verb συνεργεῖν, *to work together with*, has been variously explained. According to some, it means that all things work *in concert* (comp. the σύν, ver. 22) ; according to others, All things

---

[1] A B read ὁ θεός after συνεργει.

work *in common with God* under His direction. Others, finally: All things work in common with the believer who is their object, and who himself aspires after the good. This last sense, which is well developed by Philippi, is undoubtedly the most natural. The *Alex.* and the *Vatic.* have added ὁ Θεός, *God*, as the subject of the verb. In that case we must give to συνερ-γεῖν a causative sense: "God *makes* all things *work together*." But this meaning is foreign to the N. T., and probably to classic Greek; Passow does not quote a single example of it.—The regimen: εἰς ἀγαθόν, *for good*, has a more precise meaning in the apostle's language than that usually given to it. It means not only any good result whatever in which everything issues for the believer, but that constant progress to the final goal to which the plan of God leads us, and which constitutes our real destination. Everything is fitted to hasten our progress in this direction, when the heart has once been subjected to God. The last words of the verse give the reason. Those who have come to take God as the object of their life and activity, and to live for Him like Jesus Himself (vi. 10), are exactly those in whose favor God has formed the universal plan. All therefore which happens according to this plan must turn out in their favor. Two reasons explain the co-operation of all things for the believer's good: a subjective reason—he has entered into the true current (*loving God*); and an objective reason—all things are ordered in his favor in the plan of God; this is indicated by the second regimen.—The notion of the divine plan is expressed by the term πρόθεσις, *the design fixed beforehand*. Paul often uses this expression in a more or less extended sense; thus, 2 Tim. i. 9, he applies it specially to salvation *by grace* without works; Eph. i. 11, this term is applied to the *election* of the people of Israel; Rom. iii. 24, the design of God has for its object Christ's expiatory sacrifice. The classic passages, as they may be called, where this term is taken in its most general signification, are found in the Epistle to the Ephesians: i. 3–10 and iii. 11. We see here that the design of God is eternal (*before the ages*), for it rests on Christ (*in Jesus Christ*), and that is was conceived freely, solely on account of the divine love (the decree *of His will, according to His good pleasure*).— In this plan of salvation there were comprehended at the same time the individuals in whom it was to be realized; hence they are designated here as *the called according to His purpose*. The *call* is the invitation addressed by God to man, when by the preaching of His gospel He offers him salvation in Christ. This call by the Word is always accompanied with an inward operation of the Spirit which tends to render the preaching effectual. Those theologians who hold absolute predestination have no doubt denied the generality of this internal operation of grace; they have alleged that it does not accompany the outward call except in the case of the elect. Some have even gone the length of distinguishing between a *serious* and consequently effectual calling, and a *non-serious* and consequently ineffectual calling. But it will be asked, What could God have in view with a non-serious call, that is to say, one which He did not Himself seek to render effectual? It has been answered, that its object was to render those to whom it was addressed inexcusable. But if God Himself refuses to give the grace necessary for its acceptance, how is he who refuses thereby rendered more inexcusable? It must then be held that when the apostle in his Epistle speaks of the divine call, he always embraces under the term the two notions of an outward call by the Word and an inward call by grace, and that the apostle's expression: *the called according to His purpose*, is not at all intended to distinguish two classes of called persons, those who are so according to His purpose, and those who are not. All are alike seriously called. Only it happens that some consent to yield to the call and others refuse. This distinction is indicated by Jesus in the saying: "Many are called, but few are chosen," Matt. xxii 16.14 The *chosen* in this passage are those who accept the call, and who are thereby rescued from the midst of this perishing world; the *called* are those who, not accepting the call, remain *called* and nothing more, and that to their condemnation. In the Epistles, the apostles, addressing Christians, do not require to make this distinction, since the individuals whom they address are assumed to have *accepted* the call, from the very fact that they have voluntarily entered the church. The case is like that of a man who should say to his guests when assembled in his house: "Use everything that is here, for you are *my invited guests.*" It is obvious that by expressing himself thus, he would not be distinguishing invitation from acceptance, the latter being implied in the very fact of their presence; comp. 1 Cor. i. 23, 24. What the apostle means to say then is this: There is something prior to the present sufferings of believers, that is the eternal purpose in virtue of which their calling took place. It is not possible therefore but that all things should turn to their good.—The relation between the two clauses: *them that love God, and them that are the called according to His purpose,* reminds us of John's words: "We love Him because He first loved us" (1 John iv. 19).—The participle τοῖς οὖσι, *who are,* strongly expresses *the present reality* of this condition described by the word *called,* in opposition to the ideal nature of the decree, previously to its realization in time.—The Greek Fathers, Pelagius and others, in their desire to escape from the idea of an absolute predestination, applied the act indicated by the word πρόθεσις, *purpose,* to man, and understood thereby his *good will* to believe, as in Acts xi. 23. But in the context it is the *divine* side of salvation only which is meant to be emphasized, as it is the only side which is expounded in the two following verses. The ground of the calling could not really be the believer's disposition to accept it.

The idea of God's *purpose* is developed in the two verses, 29 and 30. Ver. 29 indicates its final aim; ver. 30 marks off, as it were, the path along which it reaches its realization.

Ver. 29. "*For whom He did foreknow, He also did predestinate to be conformed to the image of His Son, that He might be a first-born among many brethren.*"—The *for* bears on the principal idea of ver. 28: All things must turn to the good of them that are called according to God's eternal plan. Why so? Because once individually foreknown, He has determined to bring them to the glorious consummation of perfect likeness to His Son. This is the end with a view to which He has ordered the plan of all things beforehand.—By the οὓς προέγνω, *whom He did foreknow,* Paul evidently expresses the condition of the προώρισεν, *He predestinated.* The decree of *predestination* (προορισμός) is founded on the act of *foreknowledge* (πρόγνωσις). What does St. Paul understand by this last word? Some have given to the word *foreknow* the meaning of *elect, choose, destine, beforehand* (Mel., Calv., Rück., De Wette, etc.). Not only is this meaning arbitrary, as being without example in the N. T., and as even in profane Greek the word γινώσκειν, *to know,* has the meaning of *deciding* only when it applies to a *thing,* as when we say: *connaître d'une cause, to judge of a case,* and never when applied to a person; [in this case γινώσκειν περί would be absolutely necessary, *to decide regarding* (the person)]; but what is still more decidedly opposed to this meaning is what follows: *He also did predestinate;* for in that case the two verbs would be identical in meaning, and could not be connected by the particle of gradation καί, *also,* especially in view of ver. 30, where the successive degrees of divine action are strictly distinguished and graduated. Others give to the word *know* a sense borrowed from the shade of meaning which it sometimes has in the biblical style, that of *loving* (Er., Grot., Hofm.); comp. xi. 2; Jer. i. 5; Amos iii. 2; Hos. xiii. 5; Gal. iv. 9, etc. The meaning according to this view is: "whom He loved and privileged beforehand." With this class we may join those who, like Beza, give the word the meaning of *approving.* It is certain that with the idea of knowledge, Scripture readily joins that of approbation, intimate communion, and tender affection; for it is only through mutual love that intelligent beings really meet and know one another. Besides, no one can think of separating from the word *foreknow* here, any more than xi. 2, the notion of *love*. Only it is still less allowable to exclude from it the notion of *knowledge*, for this is the first and fundamental meaning ; the other is only secondary. There is not a passage in the N. T. where the word *know* does not above all contain the notion of *knowledge*, properly so called. The same is the case with the word *foreknow ;* comp. Acts xxvi. 5 ; 2 Pet. iii. 17. In the passage Acts ii. 23, foreknowledge is expressly distinguished from the *fixed decree*, and consequently can denote nothing but prescience ; and as to xi. 2 : "His people whom God foreknew," the idea of knowledge is the leading one in the word *foreknew ;* that of love is expressed in the pronoun *His*. The meaning then to which we are brought seems to me to be this : those on whom His eye fixed from all eternity with love ; whom He eternally contemplated and discerned *as His*. In what respect did God thus *foreknow* them? Obviously it is not as being one day *to exist*. For the foreknowledge in that case would apply to all men, and the apostle would not say : "*whom* He foreknew." Neither is it as future saved and glorified ones that He foreknew them ; for this is the object of the decree of *predestination* of which the apostle goes on to speak ; and this object cannot at the same time be that of the *foreknowledge*. There is but one answer : foreknown as sure to fulfil the condition of salvation, viz. *faith ;* so : foreknown as His *by faith*. Such is the meaning to which a host of commentators have been led, St. Augustine himself in early times, then the Lutheran expositors ; Philippi explains : *præcognovit prævisione fidei*. Only Philippi, after frankly acknowledging this meaning, instantly adds, that the faith which God foresees He also creates ; and so by this door a return is provided into the system of predestination which seemed to have been abandoned. But this view is not compatible with the true meaning of the word *know*, especially when this word is contrasted, as it is here, with the term *predestinate*. The act of *knowing*, exactly like that of seeing, supposes an object perceived by the person who knows or sees. It is not the act of seeing or knowing which creates this object ; it is this object, on the contrary, which determines the act of knowing or seeing. And the same is the case with divine prevision or foreknowledge ; for in the case of God who lives above time, foreseeing is seeing ; knowing what shall be is knowing what to Him already is. And therefore it is the believer's faith which, as a future fact, but in His sight already existing, which determines His foreknowledge. This faith does not exist because God sees it ; He sees it, on the contrary, because it will come into being at a given moment, in time. We thus get at the thought of the apostle : Whom God knew beforehand as certain to believe, whose faith He beheld eternally. He designated *predestined* ($\pi\rho oώρισεν$), as the objects of a grand decree, to wit, that He will not abandon them till He has brought them to the perfect likeness of His own Son.—It is clear from the οὕς and the τούτους, *whom* . . . *them*, that it was those individuals personally who were present to His thought when pronouncing the decree.—As the first verb contained an act of knowledge, the second denotes one of free will and authority. But will in God is neither arbitrary nor blind ; it is based on a principle of light, on knowledge. In relation to the man whose faith God *foresees, He decrees* salvation and glory. Reuss is certainly mistaken, therefore, in saying of these two verbs that substantially they denote "one and the same act." The object of the decree is not faith at all, as if God had said : As for thee, thou shalt believe ; as for thee, thou shalt not believe. The object of predestination is glory : " I see thee believing . . ., I will therefore that thou be glorified like my Son." Such is the meaning of the *decree*. The predestination of which Paul speaks is not a predestination *to* faith, but a predestination to glory, founded *on* the prevision of faith. Faith is in a sense the work of God ;

but it contains a factor, in virtue of which it reacts on God, as an object reacts on the mind which takes cognizance of it; this is the free adherence of man to the solicitation of God. Here is the element which distinguishes the act of foreknowledge from that of predestination, and because of which the former logically precedes the latter.—It is hardly necessary to refute the opinion of Meyer, who gives the verb *foreknow* the same object as the verb *predestinate:* " Whom He foreknew as conformed to the image of His Son, He also did predestinate to be conformed to the image of His Son." Has this any meaning? It would be more intelligible if the order were reversed : " Whom he *predestinated to* . . ., He also *did foreknow as*" . . .

What the decree of predestination embraces is the *realization of the image of the Son* in all foreknown believers. The adj. σύμμορφοι, *conformed*, is directly connected with the verb *He predestinated;* the ellipsis of the verb *to be*, or *to become*, is obvious and common. Paul does not say: "conformed or like *to His Son*," but : "to *the image* of His Son." By using this form of expression, he undoubtedly means that Christ has realized in Himself a higher *type of existence* (εἰκών, *image*), which we are to realize after Him. This is the existence of the God-man, as we behold it in Christ; such is the glorious vesture which God takes from the person of His Son, that therewith He may clothe believers. What, in point of fact, was the aim of God in the creation of man? He wished to have for Himself a family of sons; and therefore He determined in the first place to make His own Son our brother. Then in His person He raises our humanity to the divine state; and finally, He makes all believing men sharers in this glorious form of existence. Such are the contents of the decree. It is obvious that Christ Himself is its first object; and hence He is called *the Elect*, absolutely speaking, Isa. xlii. 1; Luke ix. 35 (most approved reading). His brethren are elect *in Him*, Eph. i. 4-6. The Father's intention in acting thus is to glorify the Son by causing His beauty to be reflected in a family of living likenesses.—The term πρωτότοκος, *first-born*, no doubt denotes primarily a relation of time: Jesus *preceded* all the others in glory, not only because of His eternal existence, but also as a man by His resurrection and ascension; comp. Col. i. 15 and 18. But the decree of predestination carries us into an eternal sphere, where the idea of priority has no more place, and is transformed into that of superiority. It will be vain for us to take on His likeness; we shall never be equal to Him; for the likeness which we shall bear will be *His*. Thus what comes out as the end of the divine decree is the creation of a great family of men made partakers of the divine existence and action, in the midst of which the glorified Jesus shines as the prototype.

But how are we, we sinful men, to be brought to this sublime state? Such a work could not be accomplished as it were by the wave of a magician's wand. A complete moral transformation required to be wrought in us, paving the way for our glorification. And hence God, after fixing the end, and pronouncing the decree in eternity, set His hand to the work in time to realize it. He beheld them at their haven, all these foreknown ones, before launching them on the sea; and once launched, *He acted;* such is the meaning of ver. 30.

Ver. 30. " *Moreover, whom He did predestinate, them He also called; and whom He called, them He also justified; and whom He justified, them He also glorified.*"—Here are the successive acts whereby the eternal decree is executed in time. They stand, as it were, between the eternity in which this decree is pronounced, and the eternity in which it is finished. It is to be remarked that the apostle only points out in its accomplishment the acts pertaining to God: *calling, justification, glorification*, because he is only setting forth that side of the work of salvation which is contained in the decree of predestination, and which consequently depends solely on divine causation. If his intention had been to explain *the order of salvation* in all its elements divine *and human*, he would have put *faith* between calling and justification, and *holiness* between justification and glorification.

The δέ, *then, moreover*, at the beginning of the verse is progressive; it indicates the transition from the eternal decree to its realization in time. He who wishes the end must employ the means; the first mean which God puts in operation is His *call*, which, as we have seen, embraces the outward invitation by preaching, and the inward drawing by the Spirit of grace. Paul does not mean that God addresses this call only to those whom He has predestined to glory, but he affirms that none of those who are predestinated fail to be also called in their day and hour. Not one of those foreknown shall be forgotten. They form a totality, which, once introduced from eternity into time, is faithfully led by God from step to step to the goal fixed beforehand. God would be inconsequent if He acted otherwise.—The plural pronouns *whom* . . . *them*, imply knowledge of the individuals as such. All were present to the mind of God when he decreed the height to which He would raise them.—The call once accepted—and it could not fail to be so, since we have to do here only with those whom God foreknew—a second divine act followed: *justification*. The καί, *also*, indicates the continuity of the divine work, the different acts of which follow, and mutually involve one another. Each successive grace is as it were implied in the preceding. *Grace upon grace*, says John i. 16. On those who have been called and have become believers, there has been passed the sentence which declares man righteous, that is to say, put relatively to God in the position of one who has never done any evil nor omitted any good.—The third step, *glorification*, is no longer connected with the preceding by καί, *also*, but by δέ, *moreover*. This change indicates a shade of difference in the thought. The apostle feels that he is nearing the goal, foreseen and announced in ver. 29; and this δέ consequently signifies: *and finally*. The feeling expressed is that of one who, after a painful and perilous journey, at length reaches the end.—We might be tempted to include holiness here in glorification; for, as has been said, holiness is only the inward side of glory, which is its outward manifestation. But when we remember chaps. vi.-viii., it seems to us more natural to make holiness the transition from justification to glory, and to regard it as implicitly contained in the former. Once justified, the believer receives the Spirit, who sanctifies him in the measure of his docility, and so prepares him for glory.—There is nothing surprising in the fact that verbs in the *past* are used to denote the first two divine acts, those of calling and justification; for at the time Paul wrote, these two acts were already realized in a multitude of individuals who were in a manner the representatives of all the rest. But how can he employ the same past tense to denote the act of glorification which is yet to come? Many expositors, Thol., Mey., Philip., think that this past expresses the absolute certainty of the event to come.[1] Others, like Reiche, refer this past to the eternal fulfilment of the decree in the divine understanding. Or again, it is taken as an aorist of anticipation, like that of which we have a striking example, John xv. 6 and 8. Hodge seems to have sought to combine those different senses when he says: "Paul uses the past as speaking from God's point of view, who sees the end of things from their beginning." But if it is true that the use of the two preceding aorists was founded on an already accomplished fact, should it not be the same with this? If believers are not yet glorified, their Head already is, and they are virtually so *in Him*. This is the completed historical fact which suffices to justify the use of the past. Does not Paul say, Eph. ii. 6: "We have been raised up together with Him, and made to sit together with Him in heavenly places"? When

---

[1] This is certainly a well-established usage of the Old Testament.—T. W. C.

the head of a body wears a crown, the whole body wears the same with it.

Paul has thus reached the goal he had set from the beginning, in the last words of the preceding passage (ver. 17) : "that we may be glorified together with Him." For he had proposed to himself (ver. 1) to show the final abolition of *all condemnation*, even of that of death, by the law of the Spirit of life which is in Jesus Christ ; and he has fulfilled this task. It only remains for him to celebrate in a hymn this unparalleled victory gained in our behalf.

It is obviously too narrow an interpretation of the passage to apply it merely, as Calvin does, to the victory over the sufferings of this present time (ver. 18). We have here the consummation of that *salvation* in Christ, the foundation of which Paul had laid (chaps. i.–v.) in the demonstration of the *righteousness of faith*, and the superstructure of which he had raised in the exposition of *sanctification* (chaps. vi.–viii.). Hereafter it will only remain to follow this salvation, thus studied in its essence, as it is unfolded on the theatre of history.

On predestination as taught vv. 28-30.— Wherein consists the divine predestination undoubtedly taught by the apostle in this passage ? Does it in his view exclude the free will of man, or, on the contrary, does it imply it ? Two reasons seem to us to decide the question in favor of the second alternative :—1. The act of *foreknowing*, which the apostle makes the basis of predestination, proves that the latter is determined by some fact or other, the object of this knowledge. It matters little that the knowledge is eternal, while the fact, which is its object, comes to pass only in time. It follows all the same from this relation, that the fact must be considered as due in some way to a factor distinct from divine causation, which can be nothing else than human liberty. 2. The apostle avoids making the act of *believing* the object of the decree of predestination. In the act of predestination faith is already assumed, and its sole object is, according to the apostle's words, the final participation of believers in *the glory of Christ*. Not only then does Paul's view imply that in the act of believing full human liberty is not excluded, but it is even implied. For it alone explains the distinction which he clearly establishes between the two divine acts of *foreknowledge* and *predestination*, both as to their *nature* (the one, an act of the understanding ; the other, of the will) and as to their *object* (in the one case, faith ; in the other, glory).

Human liberty in the acceptance of salvation being therefore admitted, in what will *predestination*, as understood by St. Paul, consist ? It contains, we think, the three following elements :

1. The *decree* (προορισμός) whereby God has determined to bring to the perfect likeness of His Son every one who shall believe. What more in keeping with His grace and wisdom than such a decree : "Thou dost adhere by faith to Him whom I give thee as thy Saviour ; He will therefore belong to thee wholly, and I shall not leave thee till I have rendered thee perfectly like Him, the God-man"?

2. The *prevision* (πρόγνωσις), in consequence of the divine foreknowledge, of *all the individuals* who shall freely adhere to the divine invitation to participate in this salvation. What more necessary than this second element? Would not God's plan run the risk of coming to nought if He did not foresee both the perfect fidelity of the Elect One on whom its realization rests, and the faith of those who shall believe in Him ? Without a Saviour and believers there would be no salvation. God's plan therefore assumes the assured foreknowledge of both.

3. The *arrangement* of all the laws and all the circumstances of *history* with a view to realizing the glorious plan conceived in favor of those foreknown. It is this arrangement which St Paul describes in ver. 28, when he says that "*all things must work together for good* to them who are the called according to the eternal purpose." What more magnificent ! Once believers, we may be tossed on the tempests of this present time ; not only do we know that no wave can

engulf us, but we are assured that every one of them has its place in the divine plan, and must hasten our course.

Thus we have three points : 1. The *end* indicated by the decree ; 2. The personally known *individuals* who are to reach it ; 3. The *way* by which they are to be led to it.

If any one does not find this predestination sufficient, he may make one to his taste ; but, according to our conviction, it will not be that of the apostle.[1]

TWENTIETH PASSAGE (8:31-39)

Hymn of the Assurance of Salvation

This passage is a conclusion. The *then* of ver. 31 indicates this. This conclusion is directly connected with the previous teaching on predestination (vv. 28–30) ; but as this passage only sums up all that the apostle had expounded before : 1st, on justification by faith (chaps. i.–v.), 2d, on sanctification by the Spirit of Christ (chaps. vi.–viii.), it follows that it is the conclusion of the entire portion of the Epistle now completed. It is presented in the form of questions which are, as it were, a challenge thrown out to all the adversaries of that salvation, the certainty of which Paul would here proclaim. This form has in it something of the nature of a triumph ; it gives us the idea of what was meant by him when he used the expression in the previous context : ἐν Θεῷ καυχᾶσθαι, *to glory in God.*

Vv. 31 and 32 contain a question of an entirely general character ; vv. 33–37 enumerate the different kinds of adversaries ; vv. 38 and 39 are as it were the shout of victory on the battle-field now abandoned by the enemy.

Vv. 31, 32. " *What shall we then say to these things? If God be for us, who can be against us? He that spared not His own Son, but delivered Him up for us all, how shall He not with Him also freely give us all things?*"—The question : *What shall we then say?* does not introduce an objection, as in other passages ; it invites the readers to take account of the position made theirs by the divine acts which have been thus far expounded, and to seek language adequate to such benefits (οὖν, *then*). It would be incorrect to give to the words πρὸς ταῦτα, *to these things*, the meaning of *besides*, as Bengel does ; this would have required πρὸς τούτοις. Πρός here signifies *in regard to :* " What shall we say when we consider these things ?" The apostle seeks to make himself and us thoroughly familiar with the nature of the new situation which is made ours. God has put Himself henceforth on our side . . . ; for that reason alone all adversaries will be powerless. " Not that there are none," says Calvin, " but with such a defender none of them is to be dreaded : *Hic murus nobis est aheneus.*"

Ver. 32. This absolute assurance in God, Paul derives from the great act of mercy toward us which has been accomplished. The expression ὅς γε, literally, *who at least*, is undoubtedly used in Greek in the sense of *who assuredly.* It is allowable, however, to seek the more precise sense of this restrictive form, and we think it may be expressed by the paraphrase : " Who though he had done *nothing else than that.*" There is a striking contrast between the expression : *His own Son*, and the verb *spared* not (so to say, did not treat delicately).—It is very clear here that the meaning of the word *Son* cannot be identified with that of Messiah—King. What would be meant by the expression : His own Messiah ? The being in question is evidently one who is united to Him personally and who shares His nature, whom He brings, as it were, from His own bowels (ἐκ τοῦ ἰδίου). The apostle's expressions certainly reproduce those of the angel of the Lord to Abraham, after the sacrifice of Isaac : " Because thou hast not spared thy

---

[1] See Appendix C.—T. W. C.

son, thine only son" (Gen. xxii. 12). Meyer denies this parallelism, but without sufficient reason. There was, as it were, a victory gained by God over Himself when He gave up His well-beloved to that career of pain and shame, just as there was a victory gained by Abraham over himself when with Isaac he climbed the mount of sacrifice. The inward sacrifice consummated, God *gave Him up* for us.—*For us all*, says Paul. These words might here embrace the totality of human beings. But the *us* ought undoubtedly to have the same meaning as that of ver. 31, unless, indeed, the word *all*, which is added here, be meant to indicate an extension to be given to the circle denoted by the preceding *us*. But is it not more natural to hold that this *all* contrasts the totality of believers with the *one* being whom God has given to be their Saviour? " One for all " (2 Cor. v. 14).— As *all* were the object of this sacrifice, so *all things* were comprehended in this gift. The word τὰ πάντα, *all things*, with the article, denotes a definite totality. This means all the gifts of grace previously enumerated. If, with the Greco-Lats.,[1] we reject the article, it is *all things*, absolutely speaking; which in the application amounts to the same thing. There is a very marked shade of difference between the verb : *freely give* (χαρίζεσθαι), and the preceding verbs : *not sparing, giving up*. While the latter express something painful, the former denotes an act full of pleasure to the heart of him who does it. How, after carrying through the sacrifice, would He not do the pleasant part of a gracious giver? Thus it is that all possible gifts, however great or small they may be, whether for this life or the next, are virtually comprised in the gift of the Son, just as the gift of all Abraham's possessions and of his person even were implicitly contained in that of Isaac. To give *all things* is a small matter after the best has been given. This is precisely what was expressed beforehand by the γέ, *at least*, at the beginning of the verse, and what is confirmed by the καί, *also*, added to the verb *shall give*. This particle indeed is connected with the verb, and not with the regimen *with Him* (see Philippi, in opposition to Meyer). He being once given, God *will also bestow* on us, in the course of our life, all other blessings.

The three questions which follow are only various applications of the question in ver. 31 : " Who can be against us?" The first two (vv. 33 and 34) refer to attacks of a judicial nature; they contemplate enemies who contest the believer's *right* to pardon and salvation. The third (vv. 35-37) refers to a violent attack in which the enemy has recourse to brute force, to break the bond between Christ and the believer. The whole passage vividly recalls the words of Isa. l. 7-9 : " I know that I shall not be ashamed. He is near that justifieth me : who will contend with me? Let us stand together : who is mine adversary? Let him come near to me! Behold, the Lord God will help me ; who is he that shall condemn me?"

Ver. 33. " *Who shall lay anything to the charge of God's elect? It is God that justifieth.*"—Paul is not ignorant how many accusers every believer has : conscience, the law, Satan, the accuser of the elect, the persons we have offended or scandalized by our faults : all so many voices rising against us. Did Paul himself, when writing these words, not think of the cries of pain uttered by the Christians whom he had cast into prison and scourged, and especially of the blood of Stephen, which, like that of Abel the righteous, called for vengeance against him? All these charges are only too real. But from the mouth of God there has gone forth a declaration which serves as a buckler to the believer, and against which those fiery darts are quenched, as soon as he takes shelter under the sentence : God *hath declared him just*. Here we clearly see the juridical meaning of the word *justify* as used by St. Paul. These words : *It is God that justifieth*, which paralyze every accusation uttered in His presence, are the sum-

---

[1] That is, D * F G and the Armenian version—a support hardly worth mentioning.—T. W. C.

mary of the whole first part of the Epistle (chaps. i.-v.). The expression: *the elect of God*, literally, *elect of God*, has an argumentative value ; it serves to demonstrate beforehand the powerlessness of the accusation. This expression recalls what has just been said (vv. 28-30) of the eternal predestination of believers to salvation and glory ; ἐκλεκτός, *elect*, from ἐκλέγεσθαι, *to draw out of*. Rescued by His own call from identification with a world plunged in evil, could God thrust them back into it?

From the time of St. Augustine several commentators (most lately Olshausen, De Wette, Reuss) have taken the last proposition of the verse in an interrogative sense : " Who will accuse ? Would it be God ? How could He do so, *He who justifieth?*" The apostle would thus be using an argument *ad absurdum*. This meaning is ingenious, and seems at the first glance to be more forcible. But can the part of *accuser* be ascribed, even by supposition, to God ? The function of God is more elevated. Besides, it is simpler, graver, and in reality more forcible to regard this proposition as a calm and decided affirmation. It is the rock against which every wave of accusation breaks ; compare also the parallel Isa. l., which speaks decidedly in favor of the affirmative form (Philippi).

The accusers are reduced to silence . . . for the present ; but will it also be so at the final moment when the tribunal will be set, in the day of the δικαιοκρισία, " of the just judgment of God," when sentence will be given without " acceptance of persons" and " according to every man's work" (ii. 5, 6, 11) ? Will the absolution of believers then still hold good ? Let it be remembered this was the question put at the close of the first part (vv. 9 and 10), and resolved in the second (vi.-viii.). St. Paul raises it again in this summary, but in a tone of triumph, because on this point also he knows that victory is won.

Ver. 34. " *Who is he that condemneth? It is Christ Jesus*[1] *that died, yea rather*,[2] *that is risen again*,[3] *who is also*,[4] *at the right hand of God, who also*[5] *maketh intercession for us.*"—The form τίς ὁ κατακρίνων, literally, *who* will be *the condemning one?* supposes only one judge possible, while the form of the previous question, *Who will accuse?* admitted a plurality of accusers. Why this difference ? When accusing is the matter in question, all creatures may raise their voice. But as to *judging?* One only is appointed for that office, He who is called (Acts x. 42) by St. Peter " the judge of quick and dead ;" comp. also Acts xvii. 31 and Rom. xiv. 10 ; so that the question put amounts to this : Will Christ, at the day of judgment, condemn us? The verb understood must be *will be*, not *is ;*[6] comp. vv. 33 and 35. The negative answer arises from the following enumeration of the acts done by Christ in our behalf. There would be a contradiction between this series of merciful interpositions and a final condemnation. It has excited surprise that when saying *Christ died*, Paul did not add *for us*. But he is not speaking here of the death of Christ from the viewpoint of expiation ; in this respect it was already implied in the answer to the previous question, " It is God that justifieth." The death of Christ is mentioned here from the same standpoint as in chap. vi., implying, for the man who appropriates it, death to sin. The article ὁ, literally, *the (one who died)*, reminds us that *one only* could condemn us, but that it is *that very one* who died that we might not be obliged to do it. The *resurrection* is likewise mentioned from the same point of view as in chap. vi., as the principle whereby a new life is communicated to believers, even the life of Christ Himself, of which, when once justified, we are made partakers (Eph. ii. 5 and 6).—*His sitting at the right hand of God* naturally follows, first as the principle of the out-

[1] ℵ A C F G L read Ιησους (after Χριστος), which is omitted by T. R. with B D E K, Syr.
[2] ℵ A B C reject και after μαλλον, which is read by T. R. with D E F G K L, It.
[3] ℵ A C add εκ νεκρων.
[4] ℵ A C omit και between ος and εστιν.
[5] Και is read in all the Mjj. and almost all the Mnn.
[6] So the late English Revision : *who is he that shall condemn ?*—T. W. C

pouring of the Holy Spirit, and then as having put into the hands of Christ the government of the world and the direction of all the events of our life.
—Finally, by His *intercession* we are assured of His precious interposition at such moments of spiritual weakness, as that in reference to which He declared to Peter : " I have prayed for thee, that thy faith fail not." How, with such support, should the Christian not become the conqueror of the sin which still cleaves to him, and how should he not succeed in presenting himself before the judgment-seat in a state which will not dishonor his Lord ? This is what the apostle had called (ver. 10), " being saved *by His life*," in contrast to " being reconciled by His death" (same verse).

After the example of Erasmus, Meyer divides the questions and answers contained in this passage quite differently. According to him, the words : *Who will be the condemner?* still form part of the answer to the question : *Who will accuse?* (ver. 33), as if it were : " Since God justifieth, who *then* will condemn ?" Then follows a second interrogation introduced by the affirmations : *Christ died*, etc., affirmations terminating in the conclusion expressed anew, ver. 35, in the interrogative form : *Who will separate?* that is to say : " who *then* will separate us ?" But this grouping of questions and answers seems to me inadmissible, for the following reasons :—1. The question : *Who will condemn?* cannot be the reproduction (negatively) of the previous question : *Who will accuse?* For *accusing* and *condemning* are two entirely different functions ; the one belongs to everybody, the other to one only. 2. A *then* would be indispensable in the two questions : *who shall condemn* (ver. 34) ? and *who shall separate* (ver. 35) ? intended, according to Meyer, to express the two conclusions. 3. The question : *Who shall separate* (ver. 35) ? is so far from being intended to express the conclusion from what precedes, that it finds its answer in all that follows, and particularly in the words of ver. 39, which close the whole passage : *Nothing shall separate us.* 4. This same question : *Who shall separate?* is followed by a long enumeration of the sufferings calculated to separate the believer from his Saviour, which absolutely prevents us from taking this question as expressing a conclusion.

A more seducing proposition is that of the expositors who, after taking the words Θεὸς ὁ δικαιῶν interrogatively : *God who justifieth?* give the same turn to ver. 34 : " Who is he that shall condemn ? Will it be Christ, He who died, who" . . . ? This form has something lively and piquant ; and if it applied only to a single question, one might be tempted to hold by it. But the series of questions which would then succeed one another in the same interrogative, and almost ironical sense, does not seem to us to be compatible with the profound feeling of this whole passage.

The numerous variants (ver. 34) which we have indicated in the note have no importance. The name *Jesus*, added to the title *Christ*, by several Mjj., is in thorough keeping with the context ; for in what follows there are summed up the phases of His existence as a historical person. It is the same with the καί, *also*, in the second and third proposition. It may even be said that the καί of the third does not admit of any doubt.

The apostle has defied accusers ; their voice is silenced by the sentence of justification which covers believers. He has asked if at the last day the judge will not condemn, and he has seen sin, the object of condemnation, disappear from the believer's life before the work of the crucified and glorified Christ. It remains to be known whether some hostile power will not succeed in violently breaking the bond which unites us to the Lord, and on which both our justification and sanctification rest. By this third question he reaches the subject treated in the last place, in this very chapter, from ver. 18 : τὰ παθήματα, *the sufferings of this present time;* and thus it is that in the three questions of this passage the entire Epistle is really summed up. It is clearly seen how the logical form does not for an instant slip from the mind of Paul, even at the time when the most overflowing feeling charges his pen.

Vv. 35–37. *"Who shall separate us from the love of Christ?*[1] *shall tribulation, or distress, or persecution, or famine, or nakedness, or peril, or sword? As it is written, For Thy sake we are killed all the day long; we are accounted as sheep for the slaughter. But in all these things we are more than conquerors through Him that loved*[2] *us."*—The pronoun τίς, *who*, refers properly to persons; here it is applied to all the sufferings about to be enumerated, as if Paul saw in each of them an enemy bearing a grudge at the bond uniting him to Christ.—*The love of Christ*, from which nothing will separate him, is not the love which we have to Him; for we are not separated from our own personal feeling. It is therefore the love which He has to us; and this is confirmed by the close of ver. 37: "through Him that loved us." We might, with Calv., Thol., Rück., understand; nothing will separate us *from the feeling we have* of the love of Jesus to us. But is not Paul rather representing this love itself as a force which takes hold of and possesses us? Comp. 2 Cor. v. 14: "The love of Christ constraineth us (holds us pressed)." Paul is thinking of the profound action which this love exercises through the Holy Spirit at once on our heart and will. Such is the mysterious power from the operation of which nothing will be able to withdraw us. — Θλίψις, *tribulation:* overwhelming external circumstances; στενοχωρια, *anguish*, literally, compression of heart, the inward effect produced by tribulation; διωγμός, *legal persecution.* To understand the words: *famine, nakedness, peril*, it is enough to refer to the sketch of St. Paul's life, given in 2 Cor. xi. 23 et seq. The *sword:* the symbol of capital punishment. When Paul writes this word, he designates, as Bengel observes, his own future mode of death.

Ver. 36. The apostle here quotes the sorrowful lament put by a psalmist in the mouth of the faithful under the old covenant, during a time of cruel oppression, Ps. xliv. 22. The quotation follows the LXX. *All the day:* every hour of the day (Meyer). Any hour is serviceable for dragging them to slaughter. *For the love of thee:* Jehovah in the O. T. corresponds to Christ in the New. *We are accounted:* it is long since sentence has been pronounced by hatred, and has hung over their head, though it is not yet executed.

Ver. 37. Paul expresses his certainty that none of these efforts will avail to tear the believer from the encircling arms of Christ's love. There is in this love a power which will overcome all the weaknesses of despondency, all the sinkings of doubt, all the fears of the flesh, all the horrors of execution. Paul does not say merely νικῶμεν, *we are conquerors*, but ὑπερνικῶμεν, *we are more than conquerors;* there is a surplus of force; we might surmount still worse trials if the Lord permitted them. And in what strength? The apostle, instead of saying: through the love of the Lord, expresses himself thus: *through the Lord that loved us.* It is His living person that acts in us. For it is He Himself in His love who sustains us. This love is not a simple thought of our mind; it is a force emanating from Him. The Greco-Latin reading: διὰ τὸν ἁγ., *on account of Him* ..., would make Jesus merely the moral cause of victory. This is evidently too weak. —It will perhaps be asked if a Christian has never been known to deny his faith in suffering and persecution. Yes, and it is not a mathematical certainty the apostle wishes to state here. It is a fact of the moral life which is in question, and in this life liberty has always its part to play, as it had from the first moment of faith. What Paul means is, that nothing will tear us from the arms of Christ against our will, and so long as we shall not refuse to abide in them ourselves; comp. John x. 28–30.[3]

---

[1] א B: του θεου instead of του Χριστου.
[2] D E F G, It.: δια τον αγαπησαντα instead of δια του αγαπησαντος.
[3] This explanation is a sad weakening of our Lord's words: *they shall never perish.* To add, *so long as they continue mine*, is to put in our Saviour's mouth what He does not say.— T. W. C.

Vv. 38–39. "*For I am persuaded, that neither death, nor life, nor angels,*[1] *nor principalities,*[2] *nor things present, nor things to come, nor powers,*[3] *nor height, nor depth, nor any other creation, shall be able to separate us from the love of God, which is in Christ Jesus our Lord.*"—The challenge which the apostle had just thrown out to condemnation, and sin and suffering of every kind, he now extends to all the hostile powers of the universe which could threaten the bond of love whereby Christ, and God Himself, are united to the believer. The *for* expresses an argument *a fortiori:* "none of the enemies mentioned is to be feared, for not even throughout the whole universe is there a being to be dreaded.—Paul reverts to the form *I*, which he had dropped after ver. 18 ; the reason being that here, as well as in ver. 38, the matter in question is a personal conviction of a moral rather than a systematic nature. We must not forget the : "*if at least* you persevere," which Paul himself wrote, Col. i. 23, nor examples such as that of Demas, 2 Tim. iv. 10. It is by ὑπομονή (ver. 25), perseverance in believing in the love of Christ to us, that this love exercises its irresistible power over us. The conviction here expressed by Paul does not apply to himself only, but to all believers (*us*, ver. 39).

The adversaries who rise before his view seem to advance in pairs. The first pair is *death* and *life.* Death is put first, in connection no doubt with vv. 35 and 36. The inverse order which we find 1 Cor. iii. 22, is occasioned there by the difference of the context. *Death:* the apostle is thinking of martyrdom, the fear of which may lead to apostasy. With death and its agonies, he contrasts *life* with its distractions, its interests and seductions, which may lead to lukewarmness and unfaithfulness, as in the case of Demas.—The second pair : *angels* and *principalities.* Undoubtedly *principalities,* ἀρχαί, might be regarded as an order of angels superior to common angels—archangels. But in the other pairs there is always found a contrast of character : it is therefore natural to apply these two terms to spirits of opposite kinds ; the first to *good* angels (though this sense is not exclusively the meaning of ἄγγελοι, as Meyer alleges ; comp. 1 Cor. iv. 9 and vi. 3) ; the second to malignant angels, as 1 Cor. xv. 24 and Eph. vi. 12 (Hofmann). It will be asked how good angels could labor to separate us from Christ ; but this may only be a hypothesis like that of Gal. i. 8. And may not what is of itself good contribute to lead us astray, if our attachment or admiration stops short at the creature, instead of rising to God ?—The Byzs. here read a third term almost synonymous : δυνάμεις, *powers;* and a Mj. (C) with some Mnn. even adds a fourth : ἐξουσίαι, *dominations.* This last term is evidently an interpolation to form a pair with the third. As to the latter, according to the Mjj. of the other two families, it has its place, if it is really authentic, after the following pair.—Third pair : *things present* and *things to come.* The first term embraces all earthly eventualities, death included ; the second, all that await us in the future life. The word ἐνεστῶτα, which strictly signifies what is *imminent*, when contrasted with *things to come*, takes the meaning : all that is already *present.*—If the term *powers* is authentic, it must be taken as embracing in one idea the two terms of the following pair : *height* and *depth.* These are all the powers of the invisible world, whether those which exalt us to the third heaven (*height*), but which in an instant, by reason of pride or even violently excited sensuality, may occasion the most frightful falls to the poor human heart ; or those which plunge us into the most mysterious and unspeakable agonies (*depth*), like that of Jesus at Gethsemane, when He exclaimed : "My soul is sorrowful even unto death ;" comp. what He added soon after : "This is your hour and *the power of darkness.*"[4] It is scarcely necessary to refute

---
[1] D E F G, It. : αγγελος instead of αγγελοι.
[2] T. R., with K L, Syr^sch, here puts ουτε δυναμεις (*powers*).
[3] א A B C D E F G, It. here put ουτε δυναμεις.
[4] Vaughan's exposition is worth citing : *Nothing lofty*, presenting a visible opposition, an open defiance, and *nothing profound*, working by insidious machination.—T. W. C.

the following interpretations which have been proposed : good fortune and bad ; or honor and disgrace ; the wisdom of heretics and vulgar prejudices (Mel.) ; the heights from which martyrs were precipitated, and the depths of the ocean where they were buried (Thomas Aquinas) ; or finally, the opposite dimensions of *space* (Meyer).—The last term, κτίσις ἑτερα, is usually translated by the expression : *any other creature*, and made a sort of *et cætera*. This meaning would certainly be rather poor after expressions of such ample comprehension as those which precede. But more than that, it hardly suits the word ἑτερα, which signifies *different*, and not merely *other*, as the word ἀλλη would do (for the distinction between these two adjectives, comp. 1 Cor. xv. 37–41). It seems, then, that the word κτίσις signifies here, not *creature*, as if the reference were to a particular being, to be put side by side with several others, but *creation*. Paul sees in thought this whole creation disappear, on the theatre of which there has been wrought the greatest wonder of divine love ; and he asks whether, if a new creation arise, and more magnificent marvels are displayed before the eyes of man, the cross in those new ages will not run the risk of being eclipsed, and the love of God in Jesus Christ of being relegated to the oblivion of the past. And he boldly affirms that whatever new creations may succeed one another, the first place in the heart of believers will ever remain for the redeeming love of which they have been the object here below.—Paul here speaks of the love of Jesus as being the love of God Himself ; for it is in the former that the latter is incarnated for us, and becomes the eternal anchor of which our faith lays hold for eternity ; comp. v. 15 and Luke xv., where the compassion of God is completely identified with the work of Jesus on the earth.

Nowhere has the feeling of St. Paul been displayed in such overflowing measure, and yet the thread of logical deduction is not broken for an instant. This passage sums up, as we have seen, all that Paul has hitherto expounded in this Epistle. He leaves us at the end of this chapter face to face with this divinely wrought salvation, which is complete, and assured, and founded on faith alone, to be apprehended, and ever apprehended anew by the same means. Then, after a moment of contemplation and rest, he takes us again by the hand to guide us to the theatre of history, and show us this divine work unfolding itself on a great scale in the human race.

SUPPLEMENTARY PART 2

9:1-11:36

THE REJECTION OF THE JEWS

IN stating the theme which he proposed to discuss (i. 16 and 17), the apostle had introduced an element of an historical nature which he could not fail to develop at some point or other of his treatise. It was this : " to the Jew *first*, and also to the Greek." In what relation did salvation, as set forth in his Gospel, stand to those two great sections of the human race looked at from the standpoint of its religious development ? And particularly, how did it happen that the Jewish people, to whom salvation was destined in the first place, showed themselves the most rebellious to this final revelation of divine mercy ? Did not the fact give rise to a grave objection to the truth of the gospel itself, and to the Messiahship ascribed to person of Jesus by the new faith ? A Jew might reason thus : Either the gospel is true and Jesus really the Messiah—but in this case the divine promises formerly made to this Jewish people who reject the Messiah and His salvation are nullified ;—or Israel is and remains forever, as should be the case in virtue of its election, the people of God, and in this case the gospel must be false and Jesus an impostor. Thus the dilemma seemed to be : Either to affirm God's faithfulness to His own election and deny the gospel, or to affirm the gospel, but give·the lie to the divine election and faithfulness.

The apostle must have found this problem in his way every time he bore testimony to the gospel of Christ ; and his demonstration of salvation by faith without the law would have contained a grave omission, if it had not presented a solution suitable to the nature of God of the greatest enigma in history : the *rejection* of the *elect* people.

Generally when a new doctrine presents itself, after demonstrating its intrinsic truth, it has a double task to discharge to mankind whom it professes to save—(1) to prove that it is capable of realizing what *ought to be*, moral good ; this Paul has done by showing, chaps. vi.–viii., that the doctrine of justification by faith (expounded chaps. i.–v.) was capable of producing holiness ; (2) to demonstrate that it can account satisfactorily for *what has been*, for history ; this the apostle proceeds to do, chaps. ix.–xi.

The domain upon which the apostle here enters is one of the most difficult and profound which can be presented to the mind of man. It is that of *theodicy*, or the justification of the divine government in the course of human affairs. But he does not enter on it as a philosopher, and in its totality ; he treats it in relation to a special point, the problem of the lot of Israel, and he does so as a part of his apostolic task.

There are two ways in which mistakes have been committed in expounding the thought of Paul in this passage. Some have taken it as a dogmatic and general statement of the doctrine of *election*, as an element of Christian teaching. This view finds its refutation in the entire course of this great exposition, in which the apostle constantly reverts to the people of Israel, the antecedents of their history (ix. 6 et seq.), the prophecies concerning them (ix. 27–29 and x. 19–21), and their present and future destiny (see the whole of chap. xi., and particularly the conclusion, vv. 25-31). It is therefore a problem of history and not of doctrine, strictly speaking, which he proposes to treat. Calvin himself is perfectly aware of this. Here is the dilemma which, according to him, St. Paul resolved in these chapters : " Either God is unfaithful to His promises (in regard to the Jews), or Jesus whom Paul preaches is not the Lord's Christ particularly promised to that people."

The other erroneous point of view in regard to these chapters is to take them as intended to reconcile the Judeo-Christian majority of the church of Rome to the apostle's mission to the Gentiles (Baur, Mangold, Holsten, Lipsius, with various shades). Weizsäcker, in his excellent work on the primitive Roman church,[1] asks with reason why, if the apostle was addressing Judeo-Christians, he should designate the Jews, ix. 3, " as *his* brethren," and not rather " as *our* brethren ;" and how it is that in xi. 1 he alleges as a proof of the fact that all Israel is not rejected, only his own conversion and not that of his readers. He likewise demonstrates beyond dispute, in our opinion, that in the passage, xi. 13, the words : " I speak unto you, Gentiles," are necessarily addressed to the whole church, not merely to a portion of the Christians of Rome (see on this passage). If it is so, it is impossible to hold that, addressing himself to former Gentiles, Paul should think himself obliged to demonstrate in three long chapters the legitimacy of his mission among the Gentiles. No ; it is not his mission, and still less his person, which Paul means to defend when he traces this vast scheme of the ways of God ; it is God Himself and His work in mankind by the gospel. He labors to dissipate the shadow which might be thrown on the character of God or the truth of the gospel by the unbelief of the elect people. The Tübingen school commits the same mistake in regard to this part of our Epistle as in regard to the Book of the Acts. This latter writing it views in general as the product of an ecclesiastical piece of management, intended to accredit Paul's person and ministry among Christians of Jewish origin, while it is meant to demonstrate by a simple statement of facts the painstaking and faithful manner in which God has proceeded toward His ancient people in the foundation of the church. Comp. besides, that remarkable passage in the Gospel of John, xii. 37-43, in which this apostle takes a general survey of the fact of Jewish unbelief, immediately after describing its development, and seeks to fathom its causes. This, indeed, was one of the most important questions at the period of the foundation of the church. In this question there was concentrated the subject of the connection between the two revelations.

How, at a given point in time, can God reject those whom He has elected ? Is the fact possible ? The apostle resolves this problem by putting himself successively at three points of view—1. That of God's absolute *liberty* in regard to every alleged *acquired* right, upon Him, on man's part ; this is the subject of chap. ix. 2. That of the legitimacy of the *use* which God has made of His liberty in the case in question ; such is the subject of chap. x., where Paul shows that Israel by their want of understanding drew upon themselves the lot which has overtaken them. 3. That of the *utility* of this so unexpected measure ; this forms the subject of chap. xi., where the beneficent consequences of Israel's rejection down to their glorious final result are unfolded.—This passage does not contain a complete philosophy of history ; but it is the finest specimen, and, so to speak, the masterpiece of this science.

---

[1] *Jahrbücher für deutsche Theologie*, 1876, p. 257 et seq.

TWENTY-FIRST PASSAGE (9:1-29)

The Liberty of God in regard to the Election of Israel

The apostle opens this passage with a preface expressing the profound grief he feels in view of the mysterious fact which is about to occupy him (vv. 1–5); then he shows how the liberty of God is set in its full light by the theocratical antecedents (vv. 6–13), and by the most unequivocal scriptural declarations (vv. 14–24); and finally, he calls to mind that the use which God is now making of this liberty in relation to the Jews, was clearly foretold (vv. 25–29). This last idea forms the transition to the following passage, which refers to the legitimacy of the application which God has made to the Jews of His sovereign right (chap. x.). Chap. x. ought strictly to begin at ver. 30 of chap. ix.

Vv. 1–5

Paul expresses all the intensity of his grief on account of his people (vv. 1–3), and he justifies it by the magnificent prerogatives wherewith this unique people had been honored (vv. 4 and 5).

Vv. 1, 2. "*I say the truth in Christ, I lie not, my conscience bearing me witness in the Holy Ghost, that I have a great grief and a continual lamentation*[1] *in my heart.*"—No connecting particle joins this part to the preceding. The *asyndeton* is here, as always, the evidence of a lively emotion which breaks, so to speak, the logical bond; but this form attests at the same time with all the more energy the profound relation of feeling which unites this piece to the preceding. And is it not in fact one and the same feeling in the two contrasted aspects, that emotion of triumphant joy expressed at the end of the previous chapter, when, after conducting poor condemned and lost creatures through the righteousness of faith and sanctification by the Spirit, he has brought them to the threshold of glory—and the grief which he feels at seeing his Israel loved above all, yet deprived of such blessings? He has just been following a people of elect and glorified ones rising from the midst of fallen humanity, and Israel is wanting from among the number! There is between these two parts a bitter contemplation in which the misery of rejected Israel appears to him like the sombre reverse of the incomparable blessedness of the faithful who are adopted in Jesus Christ.—The apostle does not pronounce the word which expresses the cause of his grief. It is not an oversight, as Reuss thinks; but it costs him too much to pronounce the fatal word; every reader will divine it from his very silence.—The words: *in Christ*, must be joined to the preceding: *I speak the truth*, and not to what follows: *I lie not*. To make Paul say: "in Christ I lie not," would be to put into his mouth a poor commonplace. Ver. 2, and especially ver. 3, will tell what the fact is which he is concerned to affirm so solemnly.—A man, even a truthful man, may exaggerate his own feelings; but in the eyes of Paul there is something so holy in Christ, that in the pure and luminous atmosphere of His felt presence no lie, and not even any exaggeration, is possible. The parenthesis following: "I lie not" . . ., might be taken as a second declaration in a negative form, parallel to the affirmation which precedes. But it is difficult in this case to understand what the testimony of *his conscience* and of the *Holy Spirit* can add to the security already given by the words *in Christ*. It seems to me, then, that this parenthesis should be

---

[1] Better, *pain*, ὀδύνη—T. W. C.

regarded as a confirmation of those first words themselves: "I do not lie in affirming that it is *under the view of Christ* that I declare what I there say." It is therefore on this declaration: "I speak in the communion of Christ," that the testimony of his conscience bears; and even this testimony, as too human, does not suffice. Paul declares that he feels at the same instant, through the Holy Spirit, the whole intimacy of this communion. The σύν, *with*, in the verb συμμαρτυρεῖν, *to testify with*, signifies: in concert with my own declaration. "In the mouth of two or three witnesses shall every word be established;" it seems as if Paul wished to confirm his affirmation by a double testimony, that of his conscience and that of the Holy Spirit. Why so much solemnity in entering on his subject? We understand the reason when we think what he has in view: the rejection of Israel. Was he not the man whom the Jews accused of being moved in his whole work by a spirit of hostility to his people? But here is the expression of his real feelings attested by all he counts sacred, however extraordinary what he is about to say (ver. 3) may appear.

Ver. 2. Vv. 2 and 3 contain the matter of that *truth* so solemnly announced in ver. 1. The parallelism of the two propositions of the verse, as always, is the indication of a rising feeling. A triple gradation has been remarked between the two propositions. First, between the two subjects: λύπη, *grief*, which denotes an inward sadness; ὀδύνη, *lamentation*, which refers to the violent outburst of grief, though it should only be inwardly; then a gradation between the two epithets μεγάλη, *great*, and ἀδιάλειπτος, *continual*: it is so *intense* that it accompanies *all* the moments of his life; finally, between the two regimens μοι, *to me*; and τῇ καρδίᾳ μου, *to my heart*, the latter term denoting the deepest spring of the emotions of the me.— Here still Paul leaves us to read between the lines the tragical word which expresses the cause of this grief.

Ver. 3. "*For I could wish that myself*[1] *were anathema away from*[2] *Christ for the sake of my brethren, my kinsmen according to the flesh.*"—This inward fact is the proof of the intensity of the feeling expressed in ver. 2 (*for*); and it is to this almost incredible fact that the exceptional affirmations of ver. 1 applied.—The imperfect indicative ηὐχόμην, literally, *I was wishing*, has in Greek the force of throwing this wish into the past, and into a past which remains always unfinished, so that this expression takes away from the wish all possibility of realization.[3] The meaning therefore is: "I should wish, if such a desire could be realized." If the apostle had meant to speak of a wish really formed by him, though under certain conditions, he would have expressed this idea by the present optative εὐχοίμην, or by the aorist εὐξαίμην with ἄν (Acts xxvi. 29); comp. Gal. iv. 20, and also Acts xxv. 22 (where Agrippa expresses his desire, while stating it as unrealizable, that he might not have the appearance of encroaching on the authority of Festus). It is from not understanding or applying the meaning of the Greek imperfect indicative that recourse has been had to so many unnatural explanations, intended to spare the apostle a wish which seemed to have in it something offensive to Christian feeling. Thus the interpretation of the *Itala* (*optabam*), Ambrosiaster, Pelagius, the *Vulgate*, Luther, Chalmers: "*I wished* (formerly when in my blind fanaticism I persecuted the church of Christ)." The apostle would, on this view, be recalling the fact that it was his ardent love for his people which had then driven him away from the Christ (who had appeared in Jesus). But it is not of what he was formerly, it is of what he is now, as the *apostle of the Gentiles*, that Paul wishes to bear testimony; and that the expression: *far from Christ*, may

---
[1] T. R. reads, with C K L, Syr^sch, αυτος εγω before αναθεμα ειναι, while all the rest put it after.
[2] D E G: υπο instead of απο
[3] Curtius, *Schulgramm.* § 109 and 110: "The indicative of the historical tenses expresses the contrast to reality in those *desires* which are to be expressly designated as impossible to be fulfilled; thus ἠβουλόμην, 'I should like certainly, but it cannot be.'"

prove the strength of his love to Israel, the testimony must go forth from a heart which has recognized Jesus as the Christ, and is able to appreciate Him at His proper value. Finally, some indication or other of the time when he formed this wish would have been necessary (ποτέ, *formerly*, vii. 9).—Some English expositors, among the last Morison and Tregelles, have made the first half of ver. 3 a parenthesis, and joined the end of the verse " for my brethren" . . ., with ver. 2.[1] What Paul, according to this view, meant to express by the wish, was the profound misery of Israel, a misery in which he himself also was formerly involved. But Morison has withdrawn this explanation, which is really inadmissible, and he now proposes to translate : *I might desire* (to go all that length).[2] The examples which he quotes to justify this meaning appear to me insufficient, and the idea itself lacks precision. Finally, Lange, after Michaelis, has made a still more unfortunate attempt. He translates : " I made a vow," and explains it of an engagement, accompanied no doubt with an imprecation, which he took, it is held, at the hands of the high priest when he was preparing to set out to Damascus, there to persecute the Christians (Acts ix. 2). He undertook in some way or other, at the peril of his Messianic blessedness, to save Judaism by extirpating the heresy. To set aside such an explanation it is enough to point to the imperfect ηὐχόμην, which would require, since the matter in question is a positive fact, to be replaced by the aorist ηὐξάμην, or at least accompanied with some kind of chronological definition.—It need not be asked how this vow could ever be realized. Paul himself declares that it is an impossibility ; but if its accomplishment depended only on his love, he would certainly express such a wish before the Lord.

The word ἀνάθεμα, *anathema*, from ἀνατίθημι, *to expose, to set in view*, always denotes an object consecrated to God. But this consecration may have in view either its preservation as a pious offering in a sanctuary (*donaria*)—in this case the LXX. and the N. T. use the form ἀνάθημα, for example 2 Macc. v. 16, and Luke xxi. 5—or it may be carried out by the destruction of the consecrated object, as in the case of the *ban* (*chérem*) ; the LXX. and the N. T. prefer in that sense using the form ἀνάθεμα (for example, Josh. vii. 12 ; Gal. i. 8, 9 ; 1 Cor. xvi. 22). This distinction between the two forms of the word did not exist in classic Greek. —The expression is so strong, especially with the regimen ἀπὸ Χριστοῦ, *away from Christ*, that it is impossible to apply it either, with Grotius, to ecclesiastical excommunication, or, with Jerome, to a violent death inflicted by Christ (substituting ὑπό, *by*, for ἀπό, *far from*). Paul has evidently in mind the breaking of the bond which unites him to Christ as his Saviour. He would consent, if it were possible, to fall back again forever into the state of *condemnation* in which he lived before his conversion, if by the sacrifice of his salvation he could bring about the conversion of his people Israel. The words : *away from Christ*, express the bitterness that such an anathema would have for his heart ; and yet he would face it, if it were possible thus to exchange lots with his people. Here is, as it were, the paroxysm of patriotic devotion. The pronoun *myself*, if placed, as in the Byz. text, before the term : *to be anathema*, sets Paul in contrast to the Jews who are really in this state : " I should *myself* like to be anathema (rather than they)." But if, with the other documents, it be placed after the words : *to be anathema*, it serves to contrast the real with the alleged Paul, who was made the mortal enemy of the Jews in consequence of the mission which he carried out among the Gentiles : " to be anathema *myself*, I who am represented as the despiser of my nation, and who have in fact the sad mission of consecrating the divorce between Israel and her God !" To the

---

[1] Morison, *An Exposition of the Ninth Chapter of Paul's Epistle to the Romans*, 1849.
[2] *The Expositor*, September, 1877.

notion of *spiritual* and theocratic *kinship* denoted by the title *brethren*, the expression : *kinsmen according to the flesh*, adds the idea of natural human kinship by *blood* and *nationality*.

Vv. 4 and 5 are intended to justify the wish expressed in ver. 3, by declaring the glorious prerogatives which are fitted to render this people supremely precious to a truly Israelitish heart.

Ver. 4. "*Who are Israelites ; to whom pertaineth the adoption, and the glory, and the covenants,*[1] *and the giving of the law and the service, and the promises.*"[2] —The pronoun οἵτινες, *who*, characterizes them in the context as persons for whom it would be worth while to accept even damnation.—The name *Israelites* is the name of honor belonging to the people ; it is a title resting on the glorious fact related Gen. xxxii. 28. It contains all the prerogatives which follow.—These prerogatives are enumerated in ver. 4, to the number of six, all connected by καί, *and*, a form expressing rising exaltation of feeling.—Υἱοθεσία, *the adoption:* Israel is always represented as the Lord's *son* or *first-born* among all peoples, Ex. iv. 22 ; Deut. xiv. 1 ; Hos. xi. 1.— Δόξα, *the glory:* this term does not at all express, as Reuss thinks, *the final glory* of the kingdom of God ; for this glory belongs to the Gentiles as well as to the Jews. The term is here taken in the special sense which it often has in the O. T. : *the visible*, luminous *appearance* of the Lord's presence, Ex. xxiv. 16, xxix. 43 ; 1 Kings viii. 11 ; Ezek. i. 28. The Rabbins had invented a particular term to denote this glorious appearance, the name *shekinah*, from *schakan, to dwell.*—Διαθῆκαι, *the covenants:* this word denotes the numerous covenants concluded by God with the patriarchs. The reading of some MSS. : *the covenant*, is a faulty correction. What led to it was the term : *the old covenant.*—Νομοθεσία, *the giving of the law:* this term embraces along with the gift of the law itself, the solemn promulgation of it on Mount Sinai ; comp. the saying of the psalmist, cxlvii. 20 : " He hath not dealt so with any nation."—Λατρεία, *the service (cultus)*, this is the sum-total of the Levitical services instituted by the law.—Ἐπαγγελίαι, *the promises:* this term carries our view from past benefits to the still greater blessings to come, which God promised to His people. The reading : *the promise*, in the Greco-Latin, is also an erroneous correction.

Ver. 5. "*Whose are the fathers, and of whom, as concerning the flesh, Christ came, who is God over all, blessed for ever, amen.*"—To blessings of an impersonal nature Paul adds, as crowning them, the gifts which consist in living persons, and which either preceded the above or followed them ; such are *the patriarchs*, from whom the people sprang, and who are as it were its root ; and *the Messiah*, who sprang from the people, and who is as it were its flower.—The first proposition literally signifies : " whose (Israelites') are the fathers," that is to say, to whom the fathers belong as national property. The heroes of a people are regarded by it as its most precious treasure.—But the apostle is careful not to apply the same form to the Messiah, which would signify that the Christ is the property of the Jews. He says here ἐξ ὧν, *from the midst of whom*. He proceeds from them as to origin, but He does not belong to them exclusively as to His destination. The antithesis between the two forms ὧν, *whose*, and ἐξ ὧν, *from among whom*, is certainly intentional.—But while fully recognizing that the Christ comes from the Jews, the apostle is well aware that this mode of origin refers only to the human and phenomenal side of His person ; and hence he immediately adds : *as to the flesh*. This expression should evidently be taken in the same sense as in ver. 3 ; for here as there the matter in question is a relation of filiation or origin. The term *flesh* therefore embraces *the human nature* in its totality ; and it is a mistake to seek here the contrast between the *flesh* and the *spirit*, σάρξ and πνεῦμα. We find this same

---

[1] B D E F G read η διαθηκη instead of αι διαθηκαι.
[2] D E F G read η επαγγελια instead of αι επαγγελιαι.

meaning of the word *flesh* again in ver. 8, where the human sonship is opposed to the divine (by faith in the promise). It is also in the same sense that John says (i. 14) : " The Word was made flesh." The antithesis to the word *flesh* in all these cases is not *spirit*, but *God ;* comp. Gal. i. 16 : " I conferred not with flesh and blood " (men in contrast to God) ; Matt. xxiv. 22 ; Rom. iii. 20 ; 1 Cor. i. 29, etc. The contrast is not, therefore, altogether the same in this passage as in i. 3 and 4. There, the point was the antithesis between the flesh and the spirit in the person of Jesus Himself ; here, it is the contrast between His *divine* origin (which was implied already in viii. 3) and His *human*, and more especially His Israelitish origin.

Many commentators close the sentence with the words: *according to the flesh* (Seml., Fritzs., Ew., van Heng., Meyer, Baur, Tischendorf, 8th edition). In that case it only remains to take the following words as an exclamation of thanksgiving to the praise of the God who has so highly privileged Israel ; so Oltramare translates : " Let Him who is over all things, God, be therefore blessed forever ! Amen." The epithet : ὁ ὢν ἐπὶ πάντων, *who is above all things*, or *above all*, would require to be regarded as paraphrasing the term παντοκράτωρ, *the universal sovereign*, by which the LXX. often render *Schaddaï*, *the All-powerful ;* comp. 2 Cor. vi. 18 ; Rev. i. 8, iv. 8. This thanksgiving in the context would apply either to the sovereign freedom with which God distributes His gifts to whom He pleases, or to His providence, which, always extending to all, favors one people only, with the view of bringing to Himself all the rest. On the other hand, it is impossible not to be surprised at a conclusion so abrupt and negative in form, at least as to sense, of an enumeration so magnificent as the preceding ; for there is evidently a limitation and, so to speak, a negation in the words : *as concerning the flesh*. They signify : "*At least* as concerning the flesh." This restriction goes in the teeth of the feeling which has inspired the whole passage thus far. It is a descent which, after the gradual ascent of the preceding lines, closes it with startling abruptness. Still more, the burst of gratitude which on this explanation would inspire this doxology, would be out of all harmony with the impression of profound grief which forms the basis of the whole passage. In fact, the privileges enumerated have been heaped up thus only to justify this painful impression ; and here is the apostle all at once breaking out into a song of praise because of those advantages which Israel have rendered unavailing by their unbelief ! (comp. Gess). If, besides, the participle ὁ ὤν, *who is*, referred to a subject not mentioned in the previous proposition (God), this transition from one subject to another would require to be indicated in some way, either by the addition of a δέ, *now*, as in xvi. 25, Jude ver. 24, etc., or by giving a turn to the sentence such as this : τῷ ἐπὶ πάντων Θεῷ, τῷ εὐλογημένῳ . . . δόξα, " to God ever blessed be glory !" comp. xi. 36 ; or simply : εὐλογητὸς ὁ Θεός, as in 2 Cor. i. 3 ; Eph. i. 3. In his truly classical dissertation on this passage,[1] Hermann Schultz vigorously develops the argument often alleged against the interpretation which we are examining, that the participle εὐλογημένος, *blessed*, would require to be placed not after, but before the substantive Θεός, *God*. The usage is, that in forms of thanksgiving the first word proceeding from the heart of the grateful worshipper is the term *blessed*, and that this word precedes the name of God ; comp. in the LXX. Gen. ix. 26 and xiv. 20 ; Ps. xviii. 46 ; xxviii. 6, xxxi. 21, xli. 13, lxvi. 20, lxviii. 35, lxxii. 18, 19, lxxxix. 52, etc. ; and in the N. T. Matt. xxiii. 39 ; Mark xi. 9 ; Luke i. 68, xiii. 35, xix. 38 ; 2 Cor. i. 3 ; Eph. i. 3 ; 1 Pet. i. 3. The only exception which can be quoted would be Ps. lxviii. 19, if the text of the LXX. were not probably corrupted in this passage, and if especially the verb to be understood were not the indicative ἐστί, *is*, instead of the imperative ἔστω, *let Him be ;* comp. ver. 34. Finally, it is difficult to un-

---

[1] *Jahrbücher für deutsche Theologie*, 1868.

derstand in our passage the object of the participle ὤν (*who is*, who is *really*) applied to God; the form ὁ ἐπὶ πάντων Θεός (without ὤν) would have been perfectly clear; and Paul could not have any reason for insisting in speaking of God on the *reality* of the divine sovereignty. For he was not concerned to combat idolatry, as in chap. i. for example.

Erasmus, who first proposed to end the period after σάρκα (*flesh*), had likewise put the question whether the sentence might not close with the word πάντων (*all things*, or *all*): "of whom is the Christ according to the flesh, who is over all things; God be blessed forever and ever!" Is this construction better than the preceding? Meyer thinks not. It seems to me that in the matter of improbability they are on a par. Yet the latter at least gives a more or less suitable conclusion to the proposition relative to the Christ. These last words: "who is over all," applied to Christ, contain up to a certain point the antithesis which we were led to expect from the restriction: *as concerning the flesh;* and by proclaiming the supreme dignity of the Christ, they bring out, as the context demands, the exceptional prerogative granted to the people of which He is a member. It would also be somewhat easier to explain the form of ὁ ὤν, *who is*, than on the previous construction. For the application to Christ of the idea of universal sovereignty might require this word ὤν, *who is really*. But independently of several difficulties which attach to the preceding explanation, and which remain in this one, there are new difficulties which belong to it, and which render it, if possible, still more inadmissible. The words: *who is over all things*, are not the natural antithesis of these: *as concerning the flesh*. The latter referred to origin; the former point only to position. Then, as Meyer observes, the doxology comes on us with intolerable abruptness: "God be blessed forever and ever!" And more than all, the sole reason which would make it possible to explain to a certain extent the position of the participle εὐλογημένος (*blessed*) after Θεός (*God*), contrary to the uniform usage of the sacred writers, is wholly lost; for this displacement can only arise (see Meyer) from the forcible description of *God* in the words: *who is over all things*.[1]

The entire primitive church seems to have had no hesitation as to the meaning to be given to our passage; comp. Irenæus, Tertullian, Origen, Chrysostom, Augustine, Jerome, Theodoret;[2] later, Luther, Calvin, Beza, Tholuck, Usteri, Olshausen, Philippi, Gess, Ritschl, Hofmann, Weiss, Delitzsch, Schultz.[3] In fact, in writing the restriction: τὸ κατὰ σάρκα, *as concerning the flesh*, Paul had evidently in view this peculiarity: that the Christ was something else and more than a Jew, and it is with this unparalleled fact that he rightly concludes the enumeration of Israel's prerogatives. No doubt the words: *who is over all things*, express in a certain measure the naturally expected idea of the supreme greatness of the Christ; but they are not enough for the apostle's object. For, if they connect themselves with the ἐξ ὧν, *from the midst of whom*, contrasting the *universal* supremacy of the Christ with His *national* origin, they bear no relation whatever to the still narrower restriction: *as concerning the flesh*. Now this latter leads us also to expect its antithesis, which appears only in the title *God*. This word is therefore the legitimate conclusion of the whole passage, as it forms its culminating point. Scripture frequently contrasts, as we have seen, *flesh* (human nature in its weakness) *with God;* comp. Isa. xxxi. 3. And if it is certain that Paul recognizes in the divine being who appeared in Jesus the creator of all things (1 Cor. viii. 6; Col. i. 16, 17), the Jehovah of the O. T. who led the people in the cloud (1 Cor.

---

[1] We need not point out the weakness of this reason alleged by Meyer to justify his own explanation; but it is certain that the difficulty tells with twofold force against the second construction.

[2] Theodore of Mopsuestia is the only dissentient.—T. W. C.

[3] Alford, Hodge, and Vaughan may be added. Meyer agrees with Erasmus and Tischendorf (8th ed.) in putting a period after *flesh*.—T. W. C.

x. 4), who before coming on the earth was *in the form of God* (Phil. ii. 6 et seq.), is it strange that he should have sometimes given the name of God to such a being, and that he should have done so especially in such a passage as this, where he is feeling in all its bitterness the contrast between the transcendent greatness of the gifts bestowed on Israel and the sad result in which they have terminated ? It seems to us difficult to avoid seeing in the benediction which follows the words : " who is God over all things," an expression of homage rendered to this God-Christ, and intended to wipe out the dishonor cast on Him by Jewish unbelief, as in chap. i. the form of adoration, pronounced in ver. 25, was a way of protesting against the outrage inflicted on the true God by Gentile idolatry.

But it is precisely because of this word *God* that objections are raised to the application of such utterances to the person of Christ. It is objected that nowhere else does Paul designate Jesus in this way (Meyer), and that even in 1 Cor. viii. 6, Christ, as only *Lord*, is expressly distinguished from the *Father*, as the one *God* (Reuss). It is added, that by the words : *over all things*, Christ would seem to be placed above God Himself, or at least made equal to the supreme God.—Suppose this passage were really the only one in which Jesus receives the name of God from Paul, is it not the same with John, in whose writings this name is not given to Christ confessedly more than once or twice (i. 1, xx. 28) ? As to the general question, I am unwilling to give judgment from the various passages which are alleged by many commentators with the view of proving that Paul has given Jesus the name of God, Θεός, more than once. I have carefully weighed the reasons of those who deny the fact ; and yet, after reading and re-reading Eph. v. 5 and Tit. ii. 13, I always come back to the first conviction which the Greek construction produces, viz. that Paul in these passages really meant to designate the Christ as Θεός. But this discussion would be out of place here, and could not in any case lead to an absolutely conclusive result.—As to the doxologies of the N. T. besides those of Revelation, which are addressed to the Lamb as well as to God, there is that of 2 Tim. iv. 13, which indisputably applies to Christ, and which must be assigned to St. Paul unless we deny to him the whole Epistle.—Let us add, that it would be wholly false to depend here on the rule (the correctness of which I do not examine), that when in the N. T. Christ is called Θεός, *God*, it is in every case without the article, and that the designation ὁ Θεός is reserved for the one God *and Father*. This rule does not apply to the case before us, for the article ὁ belongs not to the word Θεός, but to the participle ὤν. If Paul had meant here to use the form ὁ Θεός in application to God, he would have required to write : ὁ ὤν ὁ ἐπὶ πάντων Θεός. We have therefore the form Θεός without the article, as in John i. 1, that is to say, as a simple grammatical predicate.

Against our explanation Reuss with great assurance opposes 1 Cor. viii. 6. The reasoning of this critic may be valid against those who refuse to admit the subordination of the Son to the Father. But for those who prefer the true thought of Scripture to a theological formula, ancient, no doubt, but yet human, this argument does not affect them. The distinction between *the God and Father* and the God-Christ is in their eyes a perfectly established fact. And if there is nothing to hinder God the Father from frequently receiving the name Κύριος, *Lord*, neither is there anything to prevent the Lord Christ from receiving in certain cases the name Θεός, *God* (see Hofmann on this point).

The most singular objection is that which is taken from the words : *over all things* (or *over all*). Meyer says : " To all this there is added the insurmountable difficulty that Christ would not be simply called God, but *God over all;* which would designate Him the Θεὸς παντοκράτωρ, the *sovereign* God, and would contradict the general view maintained in the N. T. of the dependence of the Son in relation to the Father." Meyer argues as if ἐπὶ πάντων, *over all things*, was descriptive of the word Θεός, *God*, and here denoted the being called God as the *supreme* God. But what does he say himself two pages farther on: "ἐπί, *over*, denotes *government over all things.*" The *over all things*, according to Meyer himself, is not at all a determination of the word Θεός. We must not, as his objection assumed, connect ἐπὶ πάντων with Θεός, but with the participle ὤν, a word which otherwise would be unmeaning there: "He who is *exalted* over all things, as God blessed forever." Comp. Matt. xviii. 28. It is understood, of course, that to this πάντων, *all things*, the exception applies which is stated 1 Cor. xv. 27: "He is excepted which did put all things under Him." How could God be included in the πάντα, *all things?*

Gess, while holding with us that the conclusion of the verse applies to Christ, divides it into three clauses, placing a first comma after πάντων, and a second after Θεός, "who is above all things, (is) God, (is) blessed" ...; so that Paul is taken to affirm three things of Christ: first, that He is appointed universal sovereign; next, that He is God; finally—as follows from the two previous terms—that He is forever adored and blessed. I cannot agree with this explanation. The epithet *blessed* is too directly connected with the term *God* to be thus separated from it; and the expression: *God blessed*, seems, as well as the ἐπὶ πάντων, to be the attribute of the participle ὤν, and intended to form with this latter the complete antithesis to the restriction: *as to the flesh*. Besides, this breaking up of the proposition into three parallel clauses seems to me contrary to the gush of feeling which dictates this whole conclusion. Nearly the same reasons may be urged against the punctuation proposed by Hofmann (a comma after πάντων): "who is over all things, (who is) God blessed forever."

Schultz, after demonstrating with the tone of a master the necessity of applying this whole conclusion (from the word *flesh*) to Jesus Christ, insists notwithstanding on this point: that according to Paul's view this affirmation of Christ's divinity applies only to Jesus *glorified* (from the date of His exaltation at the close of His earthly life). Christ would thus be called God only in an inferior sense, as man raised to universal sovereignty. Three reasons render this explanation inadmissible—1. Paul requires to complete the idea of the Israelitish *origin* of Jesus by that of a higher *origin*. The matter in question, therefore, is not His *exaltation*, but His divine *pre-existence*. 2. The passages of the Epistles to the Corinthians, to the Colossians, and to the Philippians, which explain this name Θεός, *God*, relate to Christ before His incarnation, and not to Christ glorified by His ascension. 3. From the standpoint of biblical monotheism *to become* God, without *being* so by nature, is a monstrosity.

It seems to us, therefore, beyond doubt that Paul here points, as the crown of all the prerogatives granted to Israel, to their having produced for the world the Christ, who now, exalted above all things, is God blessed forever.[1] It only remains to say a word about the term πάντων. Some translate: *all*, and understand either all *men*, or all the *servants* of God, under the O. T.; others understand by the term *all things*, and apply it either to all the prerogatives bestowed on Israel, or to the universe in its entirety. This last meaning seems to us the most natural and the most agreeable to the context. What can form a people's supreme title to honor, if not the fact of having given to the world the universal monarch?

And yet such prerogatives did not exempt the Israelitish nation from the possibility of a rejection. In the very history of this people so peculiarly blessed there were antecedents fitted to put them on their guard against this terrible danger. This is the point the apostle brings out in the following passage, vv. 6-13, borrowing from Israelitish history two facts which

---

[1] In the *Journal of the Society of Biblical Literature and Exegesis*, June and December, 1881, will be found an exhaustive discussion of this doxology, by Prof. Tim. Dwight of New Haven and Prof. Ezra Abbot of Cambridge.—T. W. C.

prove that from the beginnings of this people God has proceeded by way of exclusion in regard to an entire portion of the elect race. Thus, when Isaac alone received the character of the chosen *seed*, to the exclusion of Ishmael, son of Abraham though he also was, vv. 6-9 ; and again, when of Isaac's two sons Jacob was preferred, and his eldest rejected, vv. 10-13.

Vv. 6-13

Vv. 6-9. *"Not as though the word of God were made of no effect ; for they are not all Israel,*[1] *which are of Israel. Neither because they are the seed of Abraham, are they all children ; but, 'In Isaac shall thy seed be called ; ' that is, they which are the children of the flesh, these are not the children of God; but the children of the promise are counted for a seed. For this is a word of promise, 'At this time will I return, and Sarah shall have a son.' "*—The δέ, *but*, between vv. 5 and 6, is strongly adversative : " But all those privileges, excellent as they were, could not assure to Israel what the word of God did not promise ;" that the divine election should apply to all the children of Abraham according to the flesh.—As the form οὐχ οἷόν τε signifies : *it is not possible*, this meaning has been adopted here by Beza and others : " *But it is not possible that* the word of God should be of no effect ;" which would imply that this word proclaimed the exclusion of the Jewish nation as inevitable, and that consequently this exclusion could not fail to come about some time or other. But the apostle does not go so far. In the demonstration which follows, he proves the *possibility* of the rejection of the mass of the people, but not its necessity ; then οἷον has only the meaning of *it is possible*, when it is followed by the particle τε ; and finally, when it has this meaning, the verb following is in the infinitive, whereas we have here the perfect ἐκπέπτωκεν. This meaning must therefore be given up, and we must abide by the ordinary signification of the word οἷος, *such that:* " The thing is not such that," that is to say, the rejection of Israel must not be so interpreted, that the word of God is thereby annulled. There is only a grammatical difficulty in the way of this explanation ; that is the conjunction ὅτι, *that*, which intervenes between οἷον and the verb ἐκπέπτωκεν : such as *that* it has been annulled. This *that* was already contained in οἷον, and forms a pleonasm. It has been variously explained ; it seems to me the simplest solution is to suppose that it depends on an idea understood : " such that *one might say* that" . . ., or : " that *it comes about* that" . . .—*The word of God* here denotes the promises by which Israel had been declared to be the people of God— promises which seemed to exclude the possibility of their rejection. Hofmann, followed in this case by Volkmar, interprets the transition from ver. 5 to ver. 6 somewhat differently. He applies the οὐχ οἷον, *not that the thing is such that*, to Paul's desire to be cast off for the love of his people, and gives to ver. 6 this meaning : " Not that my wish signifies that without the sacrifice of my salvation which I am ready to make, the promise of God to Abraham would be nullified." This meaning is more than forced. How could Paul suppose that the keeping of God's promise depends, even hypothetically, on the wish which he has expressed, especially when, in the very act of uttering it, he himself declares it to be impracticable ? Holsten makes the οὐχ οἷον bear on the grief itself : " not that I distress myself as if the word of God were made of no effect." This is less inadmissible, but far from natural. Could Paul suppose it possible for God to give man occasion to weep over the forgetfulness of His promises ? The verb ἐκπίπτειν, *to fall from*, denotes the non-realization of the promise, its being brought to nothing by facts. And it must be confessed that the present

---

[1] D E F G read Ισραηλιται instead of Ισραηλ.

rejection of Israel would be a giving of the lie to the divine election, if all the individuals composing the people of Israel really belonged to Israel, in the profound sense of the word. But that is precisely what is not the case, as the apostle declares in the second part of the verse. In this proposition Meyer applies the second *Israel* to the person of the patriarch Jacob ; the first, to the people descended from him. But it is not till later that Paul comes to Jacob personally. We must beware of destroying in this place the significant relation between the first and second *Israel*. The word is used both times collectively, and yet in two different applications. *They who are of Israel* denote all the members of the nation at a given moment, as descendants of the preceding generation. By the first words : *are not Israel*, Paul signalizes among the nation taken *en masse*, thus understood a *true* Israel, that elect people, that *holy remnant*, which is constantly spoken of in the O. T., and to which alone the decree of election refers, so that rejection may apply to the mass of *those who are of Israel*, without compromising the election of the *true Israel*.

This possibility of rejection for the mass of the people is what is proved by the two following examples. And first, that of Isaac :

Ver. 7. The first proposition of this verse has almost the same meaning as the second of ver. 6, but with a different shade intimated by the particle οὐδέ, *neither further*. The apostle, by way of transition to the following discussion, vv. 8 and 9, for the expression : *which are of Israel*, substitutes *seed of Abraham*. For he is going to speak of the lot of Abraham's two sons, Ishmael and Isaac. Both were *seed of Abraham ;* but they did not both for that reason deserve the title of *child*. This term, taken absolutely, combines the characteristic of a child of Abraham with that of a child of God ; for the subject in question is evidently that of the true members of God's family.—The simple fact of descending from Abraham is so far from making a man *his child*, in this exalted sense, that God, on the contrary, excludes from the divine family every other descendant of Abraham than Isaac and his seed, when He says to Abraham, Gen. xxi. 12 (literally) : " In Isaac shall thy seed be called." This last word evidently denotes the seed of Abraham properly so called, that which was to remain the depositary of the promise of salvation for the world. We might identify the person of Isaac with his seed, and understand the ἐν, *in*, in this sense : in the very person of Isaac (as containing in him all his descendants). The verb καλεῖν, *to call*, would be taken here, as in iv. 17, in the sense of : *to call into existence*. But as Isaac was already born, and as the verb καρά refers rather to the *name* to be given, it is more natural to distinguish Isaac from the seed, to understand καλεῖσθαι in the sense of : *to bear the name of*, and to explain the ἐν in the sense of *through :* " By Isaac it is that the race shall be born who shall truly bear the name of *seed*."

Ver. 8. In this verse Paul detaches the general principle from the particular fact which has just been cited. The τουτέστι, *that is*, exactly expresses his intention to derive from the historical fact the principle on which it rests. Ishmael's birth proceeded *from the flesh*, that is to say, had nothing in it except what was human. In Isaac's, God interposed with his promise ; and it was from this divine promise, according to chap. iv., that Abraham by faith drew the strength which rendered him capable of becoming father of the promised seed. In consequence of this higher element, only Isaac and his descendants can be regarded as *God's children*. This is what explains the second proposition of the verse, in which the name of the (promised) seed is expressly given to the descendants obtained by faith in the promise.—The first proposition of this verse implicitly legitimates the rejection of the Jews according to the flesh ; the second, the adoption of the believing Gentiles.

Ver. 9. This verse is simply intended to justify the expression : *children of the promise*, ver. 8. When the apostle says : *a word of promise*, he means: a word which had the free character of a promise, and which did not in the least imply the recognition of a right. The quotation is a combination of vv. 10 and 14 of Gen. xviii. according to the LXX. The term: *at this time*, signifies: "Next year, at the moment when this same time (this same epoch) will return."

But could Isaac and his race, though proceeding from Abraham, and that through the intervention of a divine factor, be regarded without any other condition as real children of God? Evidently not; for if the faith of Abraham himself ceased to belong to them, they became again a purely carnal seed. It must then be foreseen that the same law of exclusion which had been applied to Ishmael, in favor of Isaac, would anew assert its right even within the posterity of the latter. This is what came about immediately, as is seen in the second example quoted by the apostle, that of Esau and Jacob.

Vv. 10–13. "*And not only this; but when Rebecca also had conceived by one, even by our father Isaac (for the children being not yet born, neither having done any good or evil,[1] that the purpose of God according to election[2] may stand, not of works, but of Him that calleth); it was said unto her, The elder shall serve the younger, as it is written: Jacob have I loved, but Esau have I hated.*"—This second fact is still more significant than the former. We are now in the pure line of Abraham by Isaac, the ancestor from whom is the *promised* seed; and yet his wife sees that divine selection which had been exercised in regard to the sons of Abraham reproduced as between her own children.—The nominative *Rebecca*, in Greek, might be regarded as a provisional nominative, its true logical relation being expressed in ver. 12 by the dative αὐτῇ, *to her;* but it is more natural to find a verb in the preceding context, of which this nominative is the subject: She was treated in the same manner, or had to undergo the same lot, ἐπάθη τὸ αὐτό.—The expression *by one* is occasioned by the contrast here to the case of Isaac and Ishmael. There, there were two mothers, which might justify the preference accorded to Isaac. Here, where the children were of the same mother, the only possible difference would have been on the father's side. But as the case was one of twins, the commonness of origin was complete; no external motive of preference could therefore influence the divine choice. This is what is brought out once again by the last words: *Isaac, our father*. The *our*, no doubt, applies in the first place to the Jews, but also to Christians as children of Isaac by faith (iv. 1).

Ver. 11. Nay more, the preference given to Jacob was expressed even before the birth of the twins, before they had done any act whatever; so true is it, that it was not founded on any particular merit which Jacob might possess. The two subjective negations μήπω and μηδέ are used here because they contain a reflection of the author on the fact; as is expressed in the translation. No doubt it might have been said in answer to the apostle, that God foresaw the good works of Jacob and the evil acts of Esau, and that His predilection for the former was founded on this prevision. The view might even have been supported by a word used by the apostle, that of *foreknowledge*, viii. 29. But supposing the apostle had wished to discuss the question thoroughly, he might have replied in turn that the divine prevision, on which election rests, relates not to any *work* whatever as being able to establish some merit in favor of the elect, but on his faith, which cannot be a merit, since faith consists precisely in renouncing all merit, in the humble acceptance of the free gift. Faith foreseen is therefore a wholly different thing from works foreseen. The latter would really establish a right: the former contains only a moral condition, that, namely, which follows from the fact that possession in the case of a free

---

[1] א A B read φαυλον instead of κακον.
[2] T. R., with some Mnn. only, places του θεου before προθεσις, whereas all the Mjj., It., etc., place it after this word.

being supposes acceptance. Work foreseen would impose obligation on God and take away from the freedom of His grace ; faith foreseen only serves to direct its exercise.[1] *To accept* and *to merit* are two different things. But the apostle does not enter on this discussion, and simply states the fact that it was no *merit* on Jacob's part which constrained God to organize His plan as He did. This plan certainly was not arbitrarily conceived, but it contains nothing which gives it the character of an obligation or debt.—Before citing the oracle which he intends to quote here (ver. 12), the apostle explains the object of God's way of acting, announced in the oracle. What God meant by choosing the youngest of the two sons and setting aside the eldest was, that His liberty of organizing His plans in virtue of His free choice between individuals might remain perfectly intact.—We know already what the πρόθεσις is, the purpose formed beforehand (see on viii. 27). This purpose to be realized needs human instruments ; and it is to the choice of these individuals that the word ἐκλογή, *election,* refers. The expression : *the purpose of God according to election* (not as in the T. R. : *the purpose according to the election of God*), denotes therefore a plan of conduct in the preparation of salvation, which God draws out in virtue of a choice which He has made between certain individuals, in order to secure the man who best suits his purpose. Such a plan is the opposite of one founded on the right or merit of one or other of those individuals. God's free will indeed would be at an end if any man whatever might say to Him : " I have a *right* to be chosen, and used by Thee rather than that other." Suppose Saul had been chosen king in consequence of some merit of his own, when the time came for substituting David for him, God would have had His hands bound. In like manner, if in virtue of his right of seniority Esau must necessarily have become the heir of the promise, a man who suited His purposes less than another would have been imposed on God. The plan and choice of God must not therefore be tied up by any human merit, that the will of the only wise and good may be exercised without hindrance. This is the principle of His government which God wished to guard by choosing, in the case of which Paul speaks, the younger instead of the elder. It was easy for the Jews, who pretended to have a right to the divine election, to apply this principle to themselves.— The word μένῃ, *may stand,* may be understood in the logical sense : " may stand well established in the conscience ;" but is there not something more in Paul's thought ? Does he not mean : " may stand *in reality*" ? It is not only in the thought of man, but really that the liberty of God would be compromised if any human merit regulated His choice. God, who had determined to use Jacob and put aside Esau, might have caused Jacob to be born first. If He has not done so, it is precisely *that* His right of free choice may stand not only established, but intact.—Tholuck rightly observes that the apostle, by using the present μένῃ, *may stand,* instead of the aor. μείνῃ, *might stand,* extends this consequence of the fact to all times : it applies therefore also to the Jews of Paul's day.—The two regimens : "*not of works, but*" . . . might be made to depend on a participle understood : οὖσα, *being,* which would be a qualification of the verb μένῃ, *may stand.* But it is more natural to take this verb in an absolute sense, and to connect the two clauses with the subject of the sentence : *the purpose according to election.* Paul adds : " purpose not of works, but" . . . ; that is to say, the choice on which the plan rests was not made in accordance with a merit of works, but solely according to the will of the caller. Chap. viii. 29 has shown us that though this choice is unmerited, yet neither is it arbitrary.

---

[1] Notwithstanding the Professor's acute argumentation, it is still clear that "foreseen faith" makes the ground of the believer's salvation lie in himself, and not in "Him that calleth," which is opposed to all the apostle's teachings. As Augustine says: "God does not choose us because we believe, but that we may believe." Our salvation is not on account of faith, but through faith.—T. W. C.

Ver. 12. The oracle quoted is taken from Gen. xxv. 23. The question whether it refers to the two *brothers* personally, or to the two *peoples* who shall spring from them, is settled by the words preceding : " Two nations are in thy womb, and two manner of people shall issue from thee." Hence it follows that the oracle speaks neither of the two peoples separately from their fathers, nor of the two fathers separately from their descendants. Possibly Genesis gives greater weight to the idea of the two peoples, whereas Paul (ver. 11) thinks chiefly of the two fathers. It matters little : for a profound solidarity, at once physical and moral, connects the character of the race with that of the father.

The theocratic inferiority of Esau resulted historically from his profane spirit, which showed itself in the sale of his birthright ; it was sealed by the blessing of Jacob. As to the people who sprang from Esau, this same inferiority appeared, first, in the fact that their dwelling-place was assigned outside the promised land properly so called, then in their submission to Israel under David, and finally, after several alternations of subjection and independence, in their final incorporation with the Jewish state under John Hyrcanus, and their obliteration from the number of the nations.—The translation of the words μείζων and ἐλάσσων by *elder* and *younger*, is rejected by Meyer as opposed to the natural meaning of the two terms. But it is quite impossible to give a different meaning than *elder* to the word μείζων in the passage Gen. xxix. 16, where it is contrasted with the term ἡ νεωτέρα, *the younger*. Even in Hebrew the meaning of the narrative is not certainly that Leah was physically *greater* than her younger sister. And in our passage how can Meyer hold that the term *greater* signifies that Esau was the stronger of the twins in their mother's womb !

Ver. 13. A second quotation, meant to confirm the first ; it is taken from Mal. i. 2, 3. The conjunction *as* may be understood in two ways : either in the sense that God's love to Jacob and His hatred to Esau were the *cause* of the subjection of the latter to the former ; or it may be thought that Paul quotes this saying of Malachi as demonstrating by a striking fact in the later history of the two peoples the truth of the relation expressed in ver. 12. Malachi lived at a period when, in their return from exile, Israel had just received a marvellous proof of God's protection, while Edom was still plunged in the desolation into which it had been thrown by its eastern conquerors. Beholding those ruins on the one side and this restoration on the other, Malachi proclaims, as a fact of experience, the twofold divine feeling of love and hatred which breaks forth in these opposite modes of treatment. *I have loved* and *I have hated* do not signify merely : I have preferred the one to the other ; but : I have *taken* Jacob *to be mine*, while I have *set aside* Esau. Calvin here employs the two verbs *assumere* and *repellere*. God has made the one the depositary of His Messianic promise and of the salvation of the world, and denied to the other all co-operation in the establishment of His kingdom. And this difference of dealing is not accidental ; it rests on a difference of feeling in God Himself. On the one hand, a union founded on moral sympathy ; on the other, a rupture resulting from moral antipathy ; on *hating*, comp. Luke xiv. 26 : " If any man hate not his father and mother . . ., and his own life" . . .—God's love to Jacob is neither *merited* nor *arbitrary*. When we think of the patriarch's many grave sins, when we think of Israel's endless apostasies, it will be seen that *merit* cannot enter into the case. But when we take account of God's prevision of the power of faith, and of its final triumph in that man and people (the *foreknowing* of viii. 29), it will be seen—as follows otherwise from the divine essence itself—that neither is the prerogative bestowed on Jacob arbitrary.[1] As to Esau, let the three following facts be

---

[1] " While human goodness is the effect of divine love and grace, on the contrary, human wickedness is the cause of divine hatred and abhorrence ; and on that account alone can it be

remarked in regard to the *hatred* of which he is the object :—1. In speaking of Jacob and Esau, either as men or nations, neither Genesis nor Malachi nor St. Paul have *eternal salvation* in view ; the matter in question is the part they play regarded from the theocratic standpoint, as is proved by the word δουλεύειν, *to serve.* 2. Esau, though deprived of the promise and the inheritance, nevertheless obtained a blessing and an inheritance for himself and his descendants. 3. The national character inherited from the father of the race is not so impressed on his descendants that they cannot escape it. As there were in Israel many Edomites, profane hearts, there may also have been, as has been said, many Israelites, many spiritual hearts, in Edom. Comp. what is said of the *wise men* of Teman, Jer. xlix. 7, and the very respectable personage Eliphaz (notwithstanding his error) in the Book of Job.

The two examples of exclusion, given in the persons of Ishmael and Esau, have served to prove a fact which Israel embraced with their whole heart : God's right to endow them with privilege at the expense of the Arab (Ishmael) and Edomite (Esau) nations, by assigning to them in the history of redemption the preponderating part to which the right of primogeniture seemed to call those excluded. Now, if Israel approved the principle of divine liberty when it was followed in a way so strikingly in their favor, how could they repudiate it when it was turned against them !

To explain the apostle's view, we have added at each step the explanatory ideas fitted to complete and justify his thought ; this was the business of the commentator. But he himself has not done so ; he has been content with referring to the biblical facts, setting forth thereby the great truth of God's liberty. And hence this liberty, thus presented, might appear to degenerate into arbitrariness, and even into injustice. This gives rise to the objection which he puts in ver. 14, and treats down to ver. 24 ; this is the second part of this discussion : Does not liberty, such as thou claimest for God in His decrees and elections, do violence to His moral character, and especially to His justice ? It is to this question that vv. 14–18 give answer ; the apostle there proves that Scripture recognizes this liberty in God ; and as it can ascribe to Him nothing unworthy of Him, it must be admitted that this liberty is indisputable. Then in vv. 19–24 he shows by a figure that the superiority of God to man should impose silence on the proud pretensions of the latter, and he applies this principle to the relation between God and Israel.

Vv. 14–24

Vv. 14–16. "*What shall we say then ? Is there not unrighteousness with God ? Let it not be ! For He saith to Moses, I will have mercy on whom I have mercy, and I will have compassion on whom I have compassion. So then it is not of him that willeth, nor of him that runneth, but of God that showeth mercy.*"[1]—Several commentators, and Mangold among the last, have taken vv. 15–18 not as the answer to the objection raised in ver. 14, but as the continuation and justification of the objection itself. But nothing is needed to refute this opinion beyond the exclamation : μὴ γένοιτο, *let it not be,* which cannot be a simple parenthesis ; besides, the form of the question with the negation μή, in ver. 14, already assumes a negative answer, the development of which is necessarily expected in what follows.—The answer is taken solely from Scripture, which is an authority for Paul's opponent in the discussion as well as for himself. This opponent is a Jew, who thinks that the sovereign liberty which the apostle ascribes to God, and by which

the object of the primitive wrath and condemnatory decree of God."—Schaff in Lange.—T. W. C.

[1] T. R. reads, with K : ελεουντος, instead of ελεωντος, which is read in all the other Mjj.

he seeks to justify the rejection of Israel, wrongs the divine character. It must, indeed, be borne in mind that the Jewish conscience, being developed under the law, was accustomed to consider God's dealings with man as entirely dependent on human merit or demerit. Man's doings regulated those of God.

Ver. 15. Scripture itself, that foundation of all Israel's theocratic claims, demonstrates divine liberty as it is taught by Paul. This liberty therefore cannot involve any injustice. And first, a quotation proving the absence, in the case of man, of all right to God's favors. It is taken from Ex. xxxiii. 19, where God, when condescending to grant the bold request of Moses that he might behold His glory with his bodily eyes, gives him to understand that nothing in him, notwithstanding all he has been able to do up till now in God's service, merited such a favor. If God grants it to him, it is not because he is that Moses who asks it, or because there is any right in the matter; it is pure grace on God's part. The passage is cited according to the LXX. The only difference between it and the Hebrew is, that here in each proposition the first verb is in the past (present), the second in the future; while in the Greek the first is in the future, the second in the present. It matters little for the sense. The two verbs in the present (or past) express the internal feeling, the source, and the verbs in the future the external manifestations, the successive effects. But the emphasis is neither on the first nor on the second verbs; it is on the pronoun ὃν ἂν, *him, whosoever he may be*. It is the idea of God's free choice which reappears. The condescension of God to Moses is certainly not an arbitrary act; God knows why He grants it. But neither is it a right on the part of Moses, as if he would have been entitled to complain in case of refusal. The difference of meaning between the two verbs ἐλεεῖν and οἰκτείρειν is nearly the same as that between the two substantives λύπη and ὀδύνη, ver. 2. The first expresses the compassion of the heart, the second the manifestations of that feeling (cries or groans).

Ver. 16 enunciates the general principle to be derived from this divine utterance in the particular case of Moses. When God gives, it is not because a human *will* (*he that willeth*) or a human *work* (*he that runneth*) lays Him under obligation, and forces Him to give, in order not to be unjust by refusing. It is in Himself the initiative and the efficacy are (*Him that calleth*), whence the gift flows. He gives not as a thing due, but as a fruit of His love; which does not imply that therein He acts arbitrarily. Such a supposition is excluded, precisely because the giver in question is God, who is wisdom itself, and who *thinks* nothing good except what *is* good. The principle here laid down included God's right to call the Gentiles to salvation when He should be pleased to grant them this favor. The words: "of him that *willeth*, of him that *runneth*," have often been strangely understood. There have been found in them allusions to the *wish* of Isaac to make Esau the heir of the promise, and to Esau's *running* to bring the venison necessary for the feast of benediction. But Isaac and Esau are no longer in question, and we must remain by the example of Moses. It was neither the wish expressed in his prayer, nor the faithful care which he had taken of Israel in the wilderness, which could merit the favor he asked; and as no man will ever surpass him in respect either of pious willing or holy working, it follows that the rule applied to him is universal. So it will always be. Israel, in particular, should understand thereby that it is neither their fixed theocratic necessities, nor the multitude of their ceremonial or moral works, which can convert salvation into a debt contracted toward them by God, and take away from Him the right of rejecting them if He comes to think it good to do so for reasons which He alone appreciates.—But if the words of God to Moses prove that God does not *owe* His favors to any one whomsoever, must it also be held that He is free to *reject* whom He will? Yes. Scripture ascribes to Him even this right. Such is the truth following from another saying of God, in reference to the adversary of Moses, Pharaoh.

Vv. 17, 18. "*For the Scripture saith unto Pharoah, Even for this same purpose have I raised thee up, that I might show my power in thee, and that my name might be declared throughout all the earth. Therefore hath He mercy on whom He will, and whom He will He hardeneth.*"—Having given an instance of the liberty with which God dispenses grace, Paul gives an example of the way in which He hardens. This example is the more appropriately chosen, because the two personages brought on the scene are, in the Bible history, as it were the counterparts of one another. The logical connection expressed by *for* is this : There is nothing strange in Scripture ascribing to God the right of dispensing grace, since it ascribes to Him even the yet more incomprehensible right of condemning to hardness. These two rights indeed mutually suppose one another. The God who had not the one would not have the other. The passage quoted is Ex. ix. 16. God pronounces this sentence after the sixth plague. The verb ἐξεγείρειν (Osterv. : *I have called thee into being ;* Oltram. : *I have raised thee up*) signifies properly : to bring out of a state of insensibility or inaction ; from sleep, for example, as in Xenophon : " having seen this dream, *he awoke* (ἐξηγέρθη) ;" or from death, as 1 Cor. vi. 14 : " God will also raise up us by His power" (ἐξεγερεῖ). This passage is, with the one before us, the only place where this word is used in the N. T.—But it is employed in the LXX. in the sense of *raising up, causing to be born,* thus Zech. xi. 16 : " I raise you up (ἐξεγείρω) a shepherd ;" Hab. i. 6 : " I raise up (I cause to come) against you the Chaldeans." It is in this last sense that the simple ἐγείρειν is used in the N. T., Matt. xi. 11 : " There hath not been raised up (ἐγήγερται) . . . a greater than John the Baptist ;" John vii. 52 : " Out of Galilee no prophet hath been raised up (ἐγήγερται)." The simple verb ἐγείρειν is likewise used, Jas. v. 15, to signify *to cure* of a disease : " And the Lord will raise him up (ἐγερεῖ)." All these different shades of meaning have been applied by commentators to our passage. According to some (Aug., Fritzs., De Wette), the meaning is : " I aroused thee to resistance against me." Reuss also says : " Pharaoh acts as he does in regard to the Israelites, because *God excites him thereto.* In this case the apostle must have departed completely from the meaning of the Hebrew word *héemid* (not *héir*), which simply signifies : *to cause to stand up.* And would there not be something revolting to the conscience in supposing that God could have Himself impelled Pharaoh inwardly to evil ? Comp. Jas. i. 12. Others (Hofmann, Morison), fixing on the sense of the Hebrew word, according to which the LXX. have translated (διετηρήθης, *thou hast been preserved*), as on that of the simple verb ἐγείρειν, Jas. v. 15, think that God is thereby reminding Pharaoh that He could have left him to die (in one of the previous plagues), or that He could at that very moment visit him with death with all his people ; comp. ix. 15. But in the former case God would be made to allude to a fact which there is nothing to indicate ; and in the second, the verb employed would not be suitable ; for it expresses more than the idea of simple preservation, as is acknowledged by Hofmann himself. A third set give the word the meaning of : " I have established thee as *king*" (Flatt, for example). But so special a qualification as this would require to be expressed more precisely. This last meaning, however, comes near what seems to us to be the true one. We think, indeed, that we should here apply the meaning *raise up* in all its generality. " I have caused thee to appear at this time, in this place, in this position" (Theoph., Beza, Calv., Beng., Olsh., Rück., Thol., Philip., Beyschl.). The subject in question is not the *wicked* disposition which animates Pharaoh, but the entire situation in which he finds himself providentially placed. God might have caused Pharaoh to be born in a cabin, where his proud obstinacy would have been displayed with no less self-will, but without any notable historical consequence ; on the other hand, He might have placed on the throne of Egypt at that time a weak, easy-going man, who would have yielded at the first shock. What would have happened ? Pharaoh in his obscure position would not have been less arrogant and perverse ; but Israel would have gone forth from Egypt without *éclat*. No plagues one upon another, no Red Sea miraculously crossed, no Egyptian army destroyed ; nothing of all that made so deep a furrow in the Israelitish conscience, and which remained for the elect people the immovable foundation of their relation to Jehovah. And thereafter also no influence produced on the surrounding nations. The entire history would have taken another direction. God did not therefore create the indomitable pride of Pharaoh as it were to gain a point of resistance and reflect His glory ; He was content to use it for this purpose. This is what is expressed by the following words : ὅπως, *that thus*, not simply *that* (ἵνα). Comp. Ex. xv. 14, 15, those words of the song chanted after the passage of the Red Sea : " The nations heard it ; terror hath taken hold on the inhabitants of Palestina. The dukes of Edom have been amazed ; trembling hath taken hold upon the mighty men of Moab ; the inhabitants of Canaan have melted away." Also the words of Rahab to the spies sent by Joshua, Josh. ii. 9, 10 : " Terror hath taken hold of us, the inhabitants of the land have fainted ; for we have heard how the Lord dried up the waters of the Red Sea from before you . . . ; the Lord your God, He is God in heaven above and in earth beneath." Read also the words of the Gibeonites to Joshua, Josh. ix. 9 : " From a very far country thy servants are come, because of the name of the Lord thy God ; for we have heard the fame of Him, and all that He did in Egypt." Thus it was that the catastrophes which distinguished the going out from Egypt, provoked by Pharaoh's blind resistance, paved the way for the conquest of Canaan. And even to the present day, wherever throughout the world Exodus is read, the divine intention is realized : " to show my power, and make known my name throughout all the earth."

Ver. 18. From this particular example Paul deduces, as in ver. 16, the general principle, while reproducing by way of antithesis the maxim of ver. 16, so as to combine the two aspects in which he wishes here to present divine liberty : " No man can say either : I am, whatever I may do, safe from the judgment of God, or such another, whatever he may do, is unworthy of the divine favor."—The repetition of the words : *him that willeth*, as well as their position at the head of the two sentences, shows that the emphasis is on this idea. To a son who should complain of the favors granted to one of his brothers, and of the severe treatment to which he is himself subjected, might it not be said : " Thy father is free both to show favor and to chastise ;" it being understood that the man who answers thus does not confound liberty with caprice, and assumes that the father's character sufficiently secures the wise and just exercise of his liberty ? We must here cite the observation of Bengel, fixing the antithesis Paul has in view, and explaining his words : " The Jews thought that in no case could they be abandoned by God, and in no case could the Gentiles be received by God." The apostle breaks the iron circle within which this people claimed to confine the divine conduct toward themselves and the Gentiles, saying : to the Gentiles wrath ; to us, the only elect, clemency !

What is meant by the term *hardening*, and what leads the apostle to use the expression here ? The notion of hardening was not contained in the term *raised up*, but in its relation to the conjunction *that* which follows (see Meyer) ; besides, the narrative of Exodus was in the memory of every reader. God, in raising up Pharaoh, foresaw his proud resistance, and had in reserve to chastise it afterward by a complete blindness which was to be the means of reaching the desired result.—*To harden* signifies : to take from a man the sense of the true, the just, and even the useful, so that he is no longer open to the wise admonitions and significant circumstances which should turn him aside from the evil way on which he has entered. We need not therefore seek to weaken the force of the term, as Origen and Grotius do, who regard it as only a simple *permission* on the part of God (leaving the sinner to harden himself), or like Carpzov, Semler, etc., who explain it in the sense of *treating harshly*. The word *harden* cannot signify, in the account Ex. iv.-xiv., anything else, as God's act, than it signifies as the act of Pharaoh, when it is said that he *hardened himself*. But what must not be forgotten, and what appears distinctly from the whole narrative, is, that Pharaoh's hardening was at first *his own act*. Five times it is said of him that he himself hardened or made heavy his heart (vii. 13, 14, vii. 22, viii. 15, viii. 32, ix. 7 ; we do not speak here of iv. 21 and vii. 3, which are a prophecy), before the time when it is at last said that God hardened him (ix. 12) ; and even after that, as if a remnant of liberty still remained to him, it is said for a last time that he hardened himself (ix. 34, 35). It was a parallel act to that of Judas closing his heart to the last appeal. Then at length, as if by way of a terrible retribution, God hardened him five times (x. 1 and 20, x. 27, xi. 10, and xiv. 8). Thus he at first closed his heart obstinately against the influence exercised on him by the summonses of Moses and the first chastisements which overtook him ; that was his sin. And thereafter, but still within limits, God rendered him deaf not merely to the voice of justice, but to that of sound sense and simple prudence : that was his punishment. Far, then, from its having been God who urged him to evil, God punished him with the most terrible chastisements, for the evil to which he voluntarily gave himself up. In this expression *hardening* we find the same idea as in the παραδιδόναι ("God *gave* them *up*"), by which the apostle expressed God's judgment on the Gentiles for their refusal to welcome the revelation which He gave of Himself in nature and conscience (i. 24, 26, 28). When man has wilfully quenched the light he has received and the first rebukes of divine mercy, and when he persists in giving himself up to his evil instincts, there comes a time when God withdraws from him the beneficent action of His grace. Then the man becomes insensible even to the counsels of prudence. He is thenceforth like a horse with the bit in his teeth, running blindly to his destruction. He has rejected salvation for himself, he was free to do so ; but he cannot prevent God from now making use of him and of his ruin to advance the salvation of others. From being the *end*, he is degraded to the rank of *means*. Such was the lot of Pharaoh. Everybody in Egypt saw clearly whither his mad resistance tended. His magicians told him (Ex. viii. 19) : "This is the finger of God." His servants told him (Ex. x. 7) : "Let these people go." He himself, after every plague, felt his heart relent. He once went the length of crying out (ix. 27) : "I have sinned this time ; the Lord is righteous." Now was the decisive instant . . . for the last time after this moment of softening he hardened himself (ix. 33). Then the righteousness of God took hold of him. He had refused to glorify God actively, he must glorify Him passively. The Jews did not at all disapprove of this conduct on God's part as long as it concerned only Pharaoh or the Gentiles ; but what they affirmed, in virtue of their divine election, was, that never, and on no condition, could they themselves be the objects of such a judgment. They restricted the liberty of divine judgment on themselves, as they restricted the liberty of grace toward the Gentiles. Paul in our verse re-establishes both liberties, vindicating God's sole right to judge whether this or that man possesses the conditions on which He will think fit to show him favor, or those which will make it suitable for Him to punish by hardening him.—Thus understood—and we do not think that either the context of the apostle, or that of Exodus allows it to be understood otherwise—it offers nothing to shock the conscience ; it is entirely to the glory of the divine character, and Holsten has no right to paraphrase or rather to caricature the view of Paul by saying : " God shows grace, pure arbitrariness ; God hardens, pure arbitrariness."

Perhaps we shall be charged with introducing into the explanation of the apostolic text clauses which are not found in it. This charge is just ; only it is not against us that it comes. The reserves indicated in our interpretation arose of themselves, we think, from the *special case* the apostle had in view. For he was not here writing a philosophy or a system of Christian dogmatics ; he was combating a determined adversary, Jewish Pharisaism with its lofty pretensions both in relation to the Gentiles, and relatively to God Himself. Paul, therefore, only unveils the side of the truth overlooked by this adversary, that of divine liberty. Certainly if Paul had been disputing with an opponent who started from the opposite point of view, and who exaggerated divine liberty so as to make it a purely arbitrary and tyrannical will, he would have brought out the opposite side of the truth, that of the moral conditions which are taken into account by a wise and good sovereignty, like that of God.[1]— This occasional character of the apostle's teaching in this chapter has not always been considered ; men have sought in it a general and complete exposition of the doctrine of the divine decrees ; and so they have completely mistaken its meaning. And hence we have been forced to put ourselves at the general standpoint by supplying the clauses which the apostle took for granted, and the statement of which was not required by the particular application he had in view.

The apostle has proved from Scripture God's liberty to show grace when He thinks right, as well as His liberty to chastise by hardening when He thinks right. On this point the adversary can make no reply ; he is forced to accept the apostle's demonstration. But here is his rejoinder : " Granted ! says he, God has the right to harden me. But at least let Him not claim to complain of me after having hardened me." To this new rejoinder the apostle answers first by a *figure*, which he will afterward *apply* to the case in question. The figure of the potter :

Vv. 19-21. " *Thou wilt say then unto me, Why doth he yet*[2] *find fault? For*[3] *who can resist His will? Much rather,*[4] *O man, who art thou that repliest against God? Shall the vessel of clay say to him that formed it, Why hast thou made me thus? Or hath not the potter power over the clay, of the same lump to make one vessel unto honor, and another unto dishonor?* "—The word *then* proves that the interlocutor accepts the answer made to his first objection (ver. 14), but that he starts from it to raise a new one. The ἔτι, *yet*, after τί, signifies : *yet*, after hardening me. The verb μέμφεσθαι, *to find fault*, to speak with anger, applies to the perdition with which God threatens sinners who are hardened by Him. When He hardens any one, God cannot ask that he should not harden himself. The question, *Who can resist His will?* literally signifies, *Who hath resisted*, or rather *Who resisteth?* . . . For the perfect of the verb ἵστημι and its compounds has really the sense of the present : " I have placed myself there, and continue there." It is therefore clear that the question : " Who is he that resisteth Him ?" signifies : " Who is he that *can* resist Him ?" Hofmann thinks that the interlocutor means : Who, in this case (that of my hardening), *hath resisted* God ? Answer : " Nobody ; for in hardening myself I have done nothing but obey Him." This meaning is not impossible ; it is ingenious, but more far-fetched than the preceding.

---
[1] A sovereignty suspended on conditions which depend upon the acts of others is no sovereignty.—T. W. C.
[2] The ουν between τι and ετι is omitted by ℵ A K L P.
[3] The γαρ is omitted by T. R. (not by ς), with some Mnn. only.
[4] Μενουνγε is placed by T. R. with K L P, Syr., before ω ανϑρωπε ; by ℵ A B after these words ; it is omitted by D F G, It.

Ver. 20. Most commentators do not hold that in the following answer Paul comes seriously to discuss the objection. *Abrumpit quæstionem*, says Melanchthon. Holsten observes that Paul raises the question, not to resolve it, which would be impossible, but to crush it. We acknowledge that in vv. 19 and 20 Paul pleads solely man's incompetency to discuss the dealings of God. But we shall see that he does not stop there, and that he enters more profoundly into the marrow of the question than is generally thought. It would be surprising, indeed, if a conclusion not-to-be received should be found to be the last word of Paul's logic. It would have been better for him in that case not to have made his interlocutor bring him to such a strait.—The particle μενοῦνγε, translated by *much rather*, is omitted by the Greco-Latins ; wrongly, without doubt. It falls into three words : μέν, *certainly ;* οὖν, *therefore,* and γέ, *at least ;* that is to say, what follows remains in any case true, though all the rest should be false. Hence : *much more certainly still ;* comp. Phil. iii. 8 (*much more*).[1] It therefore signifies here : "I do not examine the intrinsic truth of what thou allegest ; but, however that may be, what is more certain is, that thou art not in a position to dispute with God." The address : *O man!* reminds the adversary of the reason of his incompetency ; it is his absolute inferiority in relation to the Creator. The exclamation ὦ ἄνθρωπε, *O man*, is placed by the Byzs. at the beginning of the sentence, but by the Alexs. after μενοῦνγε ; the former is undoubtedly preferable. For the address : *O man!* justifies the use of this particle ; and the two terms *man* and *God* placed, the one at the beginning of the sentence, the other at the end, form a better antithesis. The term ἀνταποκρίνεσθαι does not mean simply : *to reply ;* but, as is proved by the only parallel in the N. T. (Luke xiv. 6) : *to reply to a reply, to make rejoinder,* as it were. God, indeed, had already answered once in the previous sayings. This word implies the *spirit* of the contest.—The comparison of the relation between God and man to that between the vessel and the potter seems logically defective. Man free and responsible cannot be a mere instrument in the hands of God. Moreover, endowed as he is with sensibility to pleasure and pain, he cannot be manipulated like worthless matter. And certainly, if the question addressed by the vessel to the potter : "Why hast thou made me thus ?" signified : "Why hast thou created me good clay or bad clay ?" and in the application to man's relation to God : " Why hast thou created me with the disposition to good or to evil ?" the comparison would have no meaning. For the potter does not commit the absurdity of holding the clay *responsible* for its superior or inferior quality. But the question is not in the least about the *production* of the clay, and consequently about its *qualities*, but solely about the *use* which is made of it by the potter. He does not create the clay ; he takes it as he finds it, and adapts it as best he can to the different uses he proposes to himself. And besides, it is not the yet shapeless clay which asks : " Why hast thou made me thus (with or without such or such qualities) ?" it is the fully manufactured *vessel* (τὸ πλάσμα) which thus interrogates him *who has given it its* present *form* (τῷ πλάσαντι). Consequently, in the application made of this to the relation between man and God, this same question does not signify : " Why hast Thou *created* me good or evil ?"—in that case the question could not be summarily set aside by Paul—but : " Why, in the development of Thy work here below, hast Thou assigned me an honorable use (by favoring me with Thy grace, like Moses) or a vile use (by hardening me like Pharaoh) ? Why does such a man serve the end of Thy glory by his salvation ; such another the end of Thy glory by his dishonor ?" This is the question in regard to which Paul re-

---

[1] On μέν γε Passow says : "The matter of the sentence is thereby set forth as an acknowledged fact." On μὲν οὖν he says : "Most frequently in replies this expression confirms the saying of the interlocutor ; but sometimes also it distinctly sets it aside, and must be rendered by : *On the contrary.*" This is the case in our passage.

minds his Israelitish disputant of man's incompetency as before God. As it belongs only to the potter, in virtue of the knowledge he has of his art, to determine the use which he shall make of the different parts of the mass in his hands to extract from each the best result possible, so it belongs to God alone to assign to the different portions of humanity, to the Jews no less than to the rest of men, the use which suits Him best, with a view to His final aim. The question whether, in determining the use of one and another, He will act without rhyme or reason, or whether, on the contrary, He will adapt the use made of each to His moral predispositions,[1] finds no place in the mind of any one who understands that God's perfections always act in harmony, and that consequently His power is ever the servant of His goodness, justice, and wisdom. As that which justifies the power of the potter over the lump of clay is not only the superiority of his strength, but that of his understanding ; so, with stronger reason, what explains the sovereignty of God and His right over mankind is not only His almightiness, but His supreme understanding, and His infinite moral perfection. And what follows, vv. 22–24, proves that such is the view of the apostle. For to what purpose are the expressions $\theta\acute{\epsilon}\lambda\omega\nu$, *willing* (ver. 22), and $\emph{\'{\iota}}\nu\alpha$, *that* (ver. 23), if not to bring out, as we shall see, God's perfect wisdom in the choice of His ends and the employment of His means ? It is obvious, therefore, that the *use* God makes of man at a given moment (a Pharaoh, for example, as a vessel of dishonor), far from excluding his moral liberty, supposes and involves it. For the honor or dishonor to which God turns him in the execution of His work is not independent, as appears from this example, of the attitude taken by man in relation to God. The work of the skilful potter is not the emblem of an arbitrary use of strength ; but, on the contrary, of a deliberate and intelligent employment of the matter at his disposal. Such is the apostle's complete view. But it is quite true, as Lange says : " When man goes the length of making to himself a god whom he affects to bind by his own rights, God then puts on His majesty, and appears in all His reality as a free God, before whom man is a mere nothing, like the clay in the hand of the potter. Such was Paul's attitude when acting as God's advocate, in his suit with Jewish Pharisaism. This is the reason why he expresses only *one side* of the truth. The following passage, ver. 30–x. 21, will show that he is very far from mistaking or forgetting the other.

The $\mathring{\eta}$, *or*, of ver. 21, means : " Or, if it were otherwise, it must be admitted the potter has not ?" . . . Comp. Matt. xx. 15. The genitive $\tau o\tilde{v}$ $\pi\eta\lambda o\tilde{v}$, *of the lump of clay*, is dependent not on $\acute{o}$ $\kappa\epsilon\rho\alpha\mu\epsilon\acute{v}\varsigma$, *the potter*, but on $\acute{\epsilon}\xi o v\sigma\acute{\iota}\alpha\nu$, *power:* the power which he has to use the clay. The subject, the *potter*, is placed between the two words, the better, as it were, to command them.—What does the lump represent ? Some think that it is the *people of Israel*, and that God is described as having the right to make them either His elect people, or a rejected nation. This meaning breaks down on vv. 23 and 24, where we see that the vessels unto honor are elected from among the Gentiles as well as from among the Jews. The lump therefore represents the whole of *humanity*, not humanity as God creates it, but in the state in which He finds it every moment when He puts it to the service of His kingdom. This state includes for each individual the whole series of free determinations which have gone to make him what he is. Let not Israel therefore say to God : Thou hast no right to make of me anything else than a vessel of honor ; and Thou hast no right to make of that other body, the Gentiles, anything else than a base vessel. It belongs to God Himself to decide, according to His wisdom, the part which He will assign to every human being. Comp. 2 Tim. ii. 20, 21,

---

[1] The mention of these here is a gratuitous addition to the text. God never acts arbitrarily, but always for reasons. Those reasons, however, lie in Himself, and not in His creatures. It is the *same* lump that is fashioned into two different vessels.—T. W. C.

where the words : "If a man therefore purge himself from these, he shall be a vessel unto honor," show clearly the truth of the standpoint which we have just expounded.—The forms ὁ μέν, ὁ δέ, might be explained as a remnant of the most ancient form of the Greek article ; but it is perhaps more correct to admit an ellipsis : ὁ μὲν ποιεῖ εἰς τιμήν, εἰς τιμὴν ποιῆσαι, etc. —Let us add, that the figure here developed by Paul is familiar to the writers of the O. T. (Isa. xxix. 16, xlv. 9, 10 ; Jer. xviii. 6, etc.), and thus had the force of a quotation. Application of the figure, vv. 22–24.

Vv. 22–24. "*Now if God, willing*[1] *to show His wrath, and to make His power known, endured with much long-suffering the vessels of wrath fitted to destruction: And*[2] [*if*] *that He might make known the riches of His glo, y on the vessels of mercy, which he had afore prepared unto glory, us, whom he also called, not of the Jews only, but also of the Gentiles*" . . .—Many commentators, Tholuck for example, find in the δέ, *now*, which they translate by *but*, the indication of a strong contrast, and think that Paul is setting over against God's *abstract right*, expounded in vv. 19–21, the *real* use which He has made of it in the history of the Jewish people : Thou, O man, art in any case incompetent to dispute God's right ; but what, when I shall prove to thee that He has not used it rigorously, and that His conduct toward thee is still marked with the most wonderful long-suffering ! But such a contrast would have demanded a stronger adversative particle (ἀλλα, *but*) ; and this notion of a purely abstract right is rather philosophical than religious. Is it not simpler to take vv. 19–21 as giving the figure, and vv. 22–24 the application ? It is evident that the figure of *vessels unto dishonor*, ver. 21, finds its corresponding expression in *vessels of wrath*, ver. 22, as the figure of *vessels unto honor*, ver. 21, finds its corresponding term in *vessels of mercy*, ver. 23. It is equally obvious that to the liberty used by the potter over the lump of clay which is at his disposal, to make of it vessels of different destinations, ver. 21, there corresponds the power of God displayed either in the form of wrath or in that of grace in vv. 22 and 23. It is therefore the transition from the figure to the application which is indicated by the δέ, and the particle ought therefore to be translated by *now*. But in the form : *Now if*, there is at the same time contained a gradation. For Paul means thereby that God has not even dealt with Israel as the potter with his vessel. We seek the principal proposition on which depends the sentence : *Now, if willing* . . ., and we do not find it ; but it is easy to understand it from what precedes : " Wilt thou still find fault, O Jew ? wilt thou do what the vessel would not dare to do against the potter ? Wilt thou still accuse God of being unjustly angry ?" We shall see afterward the point in the following passage where this understood principal proposition finds its logical place.

Ver. 22 describes God's dealing with the vessels unto dishonor ; vv. 23 and 24 will describe His dealing with the vessels of value. The relation between the participle θέλων, *willing*, and the verb ἤνεγκεν, *He endured*, may be explained in three ways, expressed each by one or other of the conjunctions, *when, because*, or *though*. In the first connection the meaning would be : " When He had the intention of " . . . Instead of striking at once, as He already purposed doing, He bore with patience. The relation thus understood is only slightly different from that which would be expressed by *though*. The connection expressed by *because* (De Wette, Rück., and others), would signify that God's long-suffering had no other end than to bring about an accumulation of wrath ; but would such long-suffering deserve the name ? It is obvious from ii. 4 and 5 that if the long-suffering produces this painful result, this is not the *intention* of Him who bears long, but the fault of those who abuse His forbearance to harden themselves

---

[1] Better, *although willing*. See Riddle *in lo*.—T. W. C.
[2] B, Vulg. and some Mnn. omit καὶ.

the more. The true relation is consequently that expressed by the conjunction *though* (Fritz., Philip., Meyer). There is, in fact, a natural contrast between the long-suffering and the manifestation of wrath, and it is this contrast which is expressed by the *though*.—God's intention in regard to the Jews was moving on to the *display* of His wrath and the *manifestation* of His power. In these expressions there is an evident allusion to the saying of God regarding Pharaoh, as just quoted, ver. 17 ; comp. the expressions ἐνδείξασθαι τὴν ὀργήν, *to show wrath,* ver. 22, and ἐνδείξωμαι ἐν σοί, *to show in thee,* ver. 17 ; τὸ δυνατὸν αὐτοῦ, *His power,* ver. 22, τὴν δύναμίν μου, *my power,* ver. 17. This because unbelieving Judaism was playing toward the church, at the date of Paul's writing, exactly the same part as Pharaoh formerly played toward Israel themselves. As this tyrant sought to crush Israel in its cradle, so Israel was endeavoring to crush the church at its first steps in the world. And hence God's dealings with Pharaoh must be now reproduced in the judgment of Israel.—*The manifestation of wrath* refers at once to the doom of destruction which was already suspended over the head of the nation in general, and to the condemnation of all unbelieving Israelites in particular ; comp. ii. 5, and the saying of John the Baptist, Matt. iii. 10 and 12. We might refer the manifestation of God's *power* to the mighty efficacy of God's Spirit creating a new people in Israel from the day of Pentecost onward, and thus preparing the spiritual Israel, which was to replace the carnal Israel when the latter is to be rejected. But it is to vv. 23 and 24 that this idea belongs ; and the allusion to the power displayed in the destruction of Pharaoh and his army (ver. 17) leads us rather to apply this expression to the near destruction of Jerusalem and of the Jewish people by the arm of the Romans, which was to be in this unexampled catastrophe the instrument of God's wrath and power.—The execution of this destruction, long ago determined and clearly announced by Jesus Himself, God delayed for forty years ; that is the *long-suffering* of which the apostle here speaks. It seems as if, at the very moment when Israel was laying its deicidal arm on the person of the Messiah, God should have annihilated it by a thunderbolt. But, agreeably to the prayer of Him who said, " Father, forgive them," a whole period more of long-suffering was granted them, and not only of long-suffering, but of tender and urgent invitation by the preaching of the apostles. Is not Paul then right in characterizing God's dealings with Israel by the words : " Though He was already determined to . . . He endured with much long-suffering" ? Comp. the accumulated expressions of *goodness, forbearance,* and long-suffering. Chrysostom and De Wette have applied this word *endured* to God's patience with Pharaoh. This was to make a simple allusion the explanation ; Paul has finished with Pharaoh long ago. According to Meyer, Paul means that God put off the judgment of the Jewish people, because as the destruction of Jerusalem was to be the signal of the end of the world, if God had hastened this event there would have remained no more time for the conversion of the Gentiles. This idea is bound up with the explanation given by Meyer of the *that*, ver. 23. But it is difficult to suppose that Paul, who, according to 1 Thess. ii. 16, was expecting the destruction of the Jewish people as close at hand, and who yet, according to chap. xi., placed the conversion of all Gentile nations and the restoration of the Jews before the end of the world, could have imagined that all these phases of the great drama of humanity were to be accomplished in so brief a time. The meaning which we have given presents none of these difficulties.—But those Jews to whom God extends such marvellous long-suffering are none the less already *vessels of wrath fitted to destruction.* The term : *vessels of wrath,* signifies, according to Lange : " vessels on which wrath falls," that is to say, which He will break in His wrath. But ver. 21 and the completely parallel passage, 2 Tim. ii. 20, show that the point in question is the *use,* and consequently the *contents* of those vessels. The meaning is therefore : all saturated with wrath ; not for the purpose of emptying it on others, like the angels who hold the seven vials of divine wrath, Rev. xvi. (Lange's objection), but to taste all its bitterness themselves.—The perfect participle κατηρτισμένα, *prepared, fitted to*, has given rise to great discussions ; for the apostle does not tell us *by whom* this preparing was made. Meyer contends that it should be ascribed to *God Himself*. He supports his view by the regimen following : *to destruction*, which indicates a judgment *of God*. But we find in ii. 4 an authentic explanation from the apostle himself on this subject. If the Jews are actually ripe for judgment, he says, it is not the fault of God, who has faithfully pointed them to repentance and salvation ; it is the effect of their own *hardening* and *impenitent heart* which has changed the treasures of divine grace into treasures of wrath heaped on them. What answer does Meyer give to this ? He holds that the apostle moves between two irreconcilable theories. In chap. ii. Paul stood, it is true, at the viewpoint of human liberty ; but here he starts from the standpoint of absolute divine will. But is it probable that a mind so logical as Paul's should accept such an irreducible duality of views ? And what seems stranger still is, that from ver. 30 of our chapter onward, and in the whole of chap. x., he replaces himself anew at the standpoint of human liberty, and reproduces exactly the same explanation as in chap. ii. ! Finally, while in the following verse he directly ascribes to God the preparation of the elect for salvation : "*which He has* prepared unto glory," he deliberately avoids expressing himself thus in speaking of the preparation of the Jews for destruction. He here employs, instead of the active verb *prepare*, with God as its subject, the passive participle : *fitted to*. The understood subject of this action of *fitting* appears not only from ii. 4, but more clearly still if possible from the passage, 1 Thess. ii. 15, 16 : " The Jews, who both killed the Lord Jesus and their own prophets, and persecuted us ; and they please not God, and are contrary to all men : forbidding us to speak to the Gentiles that they might be saved, to fill up their sins alway ; but wrath is come upon them to make an end of them." It thus appears who is the author of the present ripeness of the Jews for judgment in Paul's view. It is not God assuredly who has Himself prepared vessels *which please Him not*, and of which *He is in haste to make an end*. De Wette even acknowledges that the apostle "*avoids saying* by whom they have been fitted to destruction."—The perfect participle used by the apostle denotes a *present state* which has been previously formed in a certain manner ; but this participle indicates absolutely nothing as to the mode in which this state has been produced ; hence the expressions *ripe* or *ready for* . . . very well render the thought contained in this term ; comp. Luke vi. 40. The choice of the verb καταρτίζειν, *to arrange perfectly, equip* (for example, a vessel, that it may be ready to set sail, see Passow), shows also that the point in question is not the beginning of this moral development (which would have required the term ἑτοιμάζειν, ver. 23), but its end. In using this term, Paul means to designate the *result* of the historical development of the people : their present state as being that of *full ripeness* for divine judgment. So this expression has been rightly explained by the Greek Fathers, Grot., Calov., Beng., Olsh., Hofm., etc. As to the manner in which St. Paul viewed the formation of this state of perdition, we may determine it with certainty by what he has said in chap. i. of the analogous development wrought among the Gentiles. First, they voluntarily extinguished the light which burned in them by natural revelation ; then, as a punishment, God *gave them up* to their evil propensities, and thereafter evil overflowed like a flood ; comp. i. 24, 26, and 28. The same was the case with Pharaoh ; he began by hardening himself when confronted with the first signs of the divine will ; then God hardened him ; again he hardened himself ; and finally, judgment took hold of him. Thus it is always that the two factors, the human and the divine, concur in the tragical development of such a moral state. As is admirably said by Lange : " These two points of view [which are alleged to be contradictory] fall into one, according to which every development in sin is a tissue of transgressions due to human responsibility, and of judgments coming from God." It is exactly so with Israel. The development of their state of perdition begins face to face with the Mosaic and prophetic revelations, whose sanctifying influence they reject ; it continues in presence of the appearance and work of Jesus Himself ; and now it reaches its goal with the rejection of the apostolical preaching and the perfidious obstacles raised by Israel against this preaching throughout the whole world. After such a history this people deserved the judgment of hardening which overtook them (xi. 8–10), more even than Pharaoh.—*Perdition*, ἀπώλεια, does not merely denote external punishment, the destruction of Jerusalem and the dispersion of the people ; it is also the condemnation of the wilfully unbelieving Israelites. It is quite obvious, indeed, that this ripeness of the people for condemnation did not prevent the individual conversion of any of its members, any more than the collective entrance of the Gentiles into the kingdom of God, ver. 27, prevents the unbelief and hardening of individuals among them. And this is what explains the object of God's *long-suffering* toward this people even when ripe for destruction ; He wished to allow all those who might yet separate from this mass time to respond to the gospel call (Acts ii. 40). To the long-suffering of God with the already devoted nation, there is added the merciful work whereby God draws from within it the foreknown believers to form the nucleus of the church (vv. 23, 24).

Ver. 23. Here God is presented to us as the potter, laboring to form the vessels of honor.—How are we to construe the proposition : *And that He might make known?* The most forced construction is that of Ewald, Hofmann, and Schott, who find here the principal clause on which depends the subordinate : Now, if God, willing . . . ver. 22. The sense would in that case be : " Now, if God, willing to show . . ., endured . . ., He also (καί) acted that (ἵνα)." Such an ellipsis seems inadmissible.—Calvin, Grotius, Meyer, Lange leave nothing to be understood, but make the καὶ ἵνα, *and that*, directly dependent on the : *He endured*, in the preceding sentence : " If, willing to show His wrath . . ., God endured . . ., *and also that* " . . . Here on this view would be a second aim in God's long-suffering, added by Paul as subsidiary to the first. The principal proposition on which the *if* depends would remain understood, as we said in the outset ; it would be : " What can be said ? Canst thou find fault ?" The meaning is nearly the same as in the previous construction ; only the grammatical form is a little more flowing. But it is difficult to believe that God's dealing with the vessels of honor should be given as a mere appendix, supplementary to His dealing with the vessels of wrath.[1] The two things ought at least to be put on an equal footing, as in ver. 21.—Beza, Rückert, and Beyschlag make the *that* dependent on κατηρτισμένα, *fitted to:* " Vessels of wrath fitted to destruction, and also that (καὶ ἵνα) God might make known the riches of His grace." But how make the manifestation of grace, which is one of the two fundamental ideas of the whole passage, dependent on an expression so subordinate as this participle ?—There remains only one possible construction, that of some ancients, and of Philippi, Reuss, and others, that is, to understand here the εἰ, *if*, of ver. 22, and to make ver. 23 a proposition parallel to the preceding : " If willing . . . God endured . . . and [if] that" . . . But where, in this case, is the verb dependent on this second *if* and parallel to *He endured ?* Either there must be held to be a new ellipsis to be added to that of the principal verb, —which is very clumsy—or this verb must be found in the ἐκάλεσεν, He

---

[1] But so far from being "supplementary" merely, it is the full carrying out of the forbearance stated in the previous clause.—T. W. C.

called, of ver. 24. Undoubtedly the relative pronoun οὕς, *whom,* "*whom* He called," seems to be opposed to this solution. But we have already seen—and it is a turn of expression not unusual in Greek—that Paul sometimes connects with a dependent proposition a member of the sentence which properly belonged to the principal proposition ; comp. iii. 8, and especially Gal. ii. 4, 5 : "*to whom* we did not give place," for : " we gave not place *to them.*" It is precisely for this reason, no doubt, that he here adds to the relative οὕς, *whom,* the pronoun ἡμᾶς, *us,* this apposition being, as it were, the last remnant of the regular construction which had been abandoned. And why this incorrectness ? Is it a piece of negligence ? By no means. By this relative οὕς, *whom,* as well as by the καί, *also,* added to the verb *He called,* ver. 24, the apostle means to bring out the close bond which connects with one another the two acts of *preparing beforehand,* ver. 23, and *calling,* ver. 24 ; comp. viii. 30, where the same relation of ideas is expressed under the same form : " Whom He did predestinate, them He *also called.*" Our translation has rendered (ver. 24) this turn of the original as exactly as our language permits.

By the words : *to make known the riches of His glory,* Paul alludes to the example of Moses, ver. 15, who had asked God to *show him His glory,* exactly as by the expression of ver. 22 he had reminded his readers of those relative to Pharaoh. These riches of glory are the manifestation of His mercy which heaps glory on the vessels of honor, as the manifestation of wrath brings down perdition on the vessels that are worthless. Glory is here particularly the splendor of divine love.— *Vessels of mercy :* Vessels that are to be filled with salvation by mercy.— *Which He prepared beforehand,* ἃ προητοίμασε. This expression means more than the *ready* or *fitted for* of the previous verse ; it was God Himself who had beforehand prepared everything to make those beings the objects of His grace. This saying is explained by the analogous expressions viii. 29, 30 ; comp. the πρό, *beforehand,* which enters into the composition of the verb, as into that of the two verbs viii. 29 ; then the relation of the verbs *prepared beforehand* and *call,* which is the same as that between the verbs *predestinate* and *call,* ver. 30 ; and, finally, the καί, *also,* before ἐκάλεσε, *called,* which reproduces that of viii. 30. Jesus expresses an idea analogous to this, Matt. xxv. 34 : " Inherit the kingdom *prepared for you* from the foundation of the world ;" with this difference, that in this saying it is the kingdom which is prepared in advance for believers, whereas here it is believers who are so for the kingdom. In this term : *prepared beforehand,* there are contained the two ideas of *foreknowledge* (prevision of faith) and *predestination* (destination to glory), expounded viii. 29.[1] Let us further remark these four striking differences between this expression and the corresponding term of the preceding verse (κατηρτισμένα) : 1. The preposition πρό, *beforehand,* is wanting in the participle of ver. 22. 2. There the passive form, instead of the active used here. 3. Here the aorist, referring to the eternal act, as in viii. 29, instead of the perfect (ver. 22), which denoted the present fact. 4. Here the verb ἑτοιμάζειν, *to prepare,* which indicates the beginning of the development, instead of that of ver. 21, which indicated its result. These four differences are not accidental, and leave no doubt as to the apostle's view.

Ver. 24. And those predestined to glory, He has drawn by long-suffering, not only from the midst of the lost mass of the Jews, but also from among the Gentiles. This was what Jesus had declared : " I have yet other sheep which are not of this fold " (John x. 16). And this Paul had in view in the words : *the riches of His glory.* While He gleaned among the Jews, He reaped a harvest among the Gentiles, and thus carried out, in spite of

---

[1] " The position of *prepared beforehand* (before *he called*), seems to show that the reference is rather to the purpose and choice of God than to the moral and spiritual preparation of the man."—Vaughan *in lo.*—T. W. C.

Jewish pretensions, the free and large plan of salvation which He had formed on the sole prevision of faith.—The καί, *also*, reminds us of the relation between the eternal decree and the call in time.—It is thus a new people of elect ones, composed of the believing portion of the old Israel and of the entire multitude of the believing Gentiles, whom the apostle sees rising to the divine call to take the place of that carnal Israel ; comp. Luke xiv. 15-24 and Rev. vii. 9 et seq. He cannot but think with a profound feeling of gratitude that it is by his own ministry this rich exercise of grace is effected ; that he is himself in a way the hand of God, to form out of the mass of the Gentile world that multitude of vessels unto honor !

Here should be placed logically the principal proposition, which is interrogative, but understood, on which rests the two preceding subordinate propositions, beginning with *now if*, ver. 22, and *and if*, ver. 23 : "And if those Jews, already ripe for perdition, are still borne with by God, who holds His arm ready to strike them and cast them far from Him, and if as to those believers whom He has prepared beforehand He does not confine Himself to take them from Israel, but goes in search of them to the very ends of the earth . . ., *will mankind be entitled to find fault with God who thus directs their destinies?* Will the Jewish people in particular be able to reproach God for the way in which He exercises His justice on them, seeing they have so justly brought this judgment upon them, and for the use which He at the same time makes of His mercy, calling His elect from the whole mass of mankind, without disturbing Himself about the reprobation which Israel is pleased to suspend over one whole part of this mass? . . . Yea, O Jew, who dost venture to dispute with God, what hast thou to say!" And I ask every reader who has attentively followed this explanation of the apostle's words, what can be said against this defence of God's dealings ? Do not all the divine perfections concur harmoniously in realizing God's plan, and has not the freedom of man its legitimate place in the course of history, in perfect harmony with God's sovereign freedom in His acts of grace as well as in His judgments ?

The word of God has not therefore been made of no effect by the fact of the rejection of the Israelitish nation (ver. 6). For, 1st, the principle of divine *selection* which controlled the early destinies of the patriarchal family is only realized anew in the distinction between believing Israelites and the carnal and rejected mass (vv. 6-13). 2d. God, when making choice of this people to prepare for the salvation of the world, did not abdicate His freedom to reject them on certain conditions, and if He came to think this good ; neither did He abdicate His liberty of calling other individuals not belonging to this people, on certain conditions, and if He came to see good reason. And the use which He actually makes of this liberty, in rejecting His obstinately rebellious people while sparing them as long as possible, and even after the greatest crimes, is not tantamount to the annulling of His word (vv. 14-24). But, 3d, more remains to be said : this double dispensation of the calling of the Gentiles and of the rejection of Israel is nothing else than the *fulfilling* of His very word ; for it was announced beforehand. This is what is proved by the third part of this discussion, vv. 25-29.

Vv. 25-29.

And, first, vv. 25 and 26 : the proclamation by the prophets of the calling of the Gentiles ; then vv. 27-29 : that of the rejection of the mass of the Jewish people.

Vv. 25, 26. "*As He saith also in Osee, I will call that my people, which was not my people ; and her beloved, which was not beloved. And it shall come to pass, that in the place where it was said unto them, Ye are not my people ; there shall they be called sons of the living God.*"—The words *as also* evidently refer to the last words of ver. 24 : " but also of the Gentiles." To facilitate the exposition of the following quotation, Hofmann has thought it best to apply this *as also* to the first words of ver. 24 : " not of the Jews only." But this reference is not in keeping with the apostle's thought ; for when he really passes to the prophecies relating to Israel, ver. 27, he expressly indicates this transition. The difficulty which has driven Hofmann to his view is this . Hosea, in the two passages quoted, ii. 23 and i. 10, is certainly speaking of the Israelites of the ten tribes scattered in distant lands, and not of Gentiles ; how can the apostle apply them to the latter ? St. Peter does exactly the same thing (1 Pet. ii. 10). Hodge remarks that the ten tribes having relapsed into idolatry, were thus in the same state as the Gentiles, so that what was said of the former could equally be applied to the latter. Then he cites the fact, as Tholuck does, that in Scripture a general truth enunciated in regard to a particular class of men is afterward applied to all those whose character and position are found to be the same. And, indeed, in the mouth of God the expressions : " that which is not of my people ;" " her which is not beloved ;" " I will call them my people . . ., beloved," express a principle of the divine government which comes into play everywhere when circumstances reappear similar to those to which they were originally applied. This was the case with the Gentiles yet more completely, if that is possible, than with the inhabitants of Samaria. We shall add, that the exiled Israelites being mingled with the Gentiles, and forming one homogeneous mass with them, cannot be brought to God separately from them. Isa. xlix. 22 represents the Gentiles as carrying the sons of Israel in their arms and their daughters on their shoulders, and consequently as being restored to grace along with them.—Instead of : *I will call*, Hosea simply says : *I will say to*. The meaning is the same ; for *I will call* applies to the *new name* which will be given them (see the full context of Hosea). Only by the form *I will call*, Paul alludes to the calling of the Gentiles *to salvation*.

Ver. 26. The second saying quoted (Hos. i. 10) is attached to the preceding as if it followed it immediately in the prophet. More than once in the following chapters we find this combination of originally distinct sayings. Some apply the expression in Hosea : *in the place where*, to the land of Samaria, in the meaning that God there *pronounced* the rejection of the people. In that case, Paul, in applying this saying to the Gentiles, would have perverted it entirely from its meaning. But is it not more natural to apply this word : *the place where*, to the strange land where the Jews were long captive, and as it were abandoned of God ? Was it not there God said to them by the voice of fact during long ages : " Ye are not my people" ? Is it not there that they will begin anew to feel the effects of grace when God shall visit them, and recall them as well as the Gentiles, with whom they are at present confounded ?

Vv. 27-29. "*But Isaiah crieth concerning Israel, Though the number of the sons of Israel be as the sand of the sea, the remnant*[1] [*only*] *shall be saved: for the Lord will make a short and summary reckoning on the earth:*[2] *and, as Esaias foretold, Except the Lord of hosts had left us a seed, we had become as Sodom, and been made like unto Gomorrha.*"— Δέ, on the other hand (but). Paul's object is not merely to contrast Israel with the Gentiles, for in that case the words *concerning Israel* would begin the sentence. He wishes at the same time to show how the one prophet completes the other. His meaning is this : " To the saying of Hosea regarding the Gentiles there is added, to complete the revelation of God's plan, the following declaration of Isaiah concerning Israel."—The expression κράζει, *cries*, indicates the threatening tone of the herald called to proclaim thus the judgment of the

---

[1] א B read υπολειμμα instead of καταλειμμα.
[2] We, along with א A B, Syr^sch, reject after συντεμνων the words following : εν δικαιοσυνη οτι λογον συντετμημενον.

Sovereign. In this relation the preposition ὑπέρ, *over*, might well have its local sense : this threat henceforth hangs *over the head* of Israel.—The quotation is taken from Isa. x. 22, 23. The article τό, *the*, before the word *remnant*, characterizes this remnant as a thing known ; and, indeed, one of the most frequent notions of the Book of Isaiah is that of the *holy remnant*, which survives all the chastisements of Israel, and which, coming forth purified from the crucible, becomes each time the germ of a better future. The T. R. reads κατάλειμμα, which is the term used by the LXX. ; we ought probably to read with the Alexs. ὑπόλειμμα. The view of the apostle is not, as Hofmann and others think, that this remnant will *certainly subsist* ; that is not the question. In the context, both of Isaiah and of the apostle, there is a contrast between the innumerable multitude which as it seemed ought to form Jehovah's people and which perishes, and the poor remnant which alone remains to enjoy the salvation.

Ver. 28 explains this idea of a *saved remnant*. This time, indeed, judgment will be carried out neither by halves nor over a long period. It will be, says Isaiah, a sudden and summary execution which will fall not upon this or that individual, but on the nation as a whole. Such is the meaning of the Hebrew and of the LXX., though the latter have somewhat modified the form of the original. Isaiah says literally : " Destruction is resolved on ; it makes righteousness overflow ; for the Lord works on the earth destruction and decree." The LXX. translate : " The Lord fulfils the sentence ; He cuts short righteously, because He will execute a summary reckoning upon all the earth." Paul reproduces this second form while abridging it ; for it is probable we should prefer the shortest reading, that of the oldest Mjj. and of the Peshito (see the note), since that of the T. R. merely restores the text of the LXX. The word λόγος might undoubtedly signify *decree ;* but in connection with the terms *number* and *remnant* of ver. 27, as well as with the two participles συντελῶν and συντέμνων, *consummating* and *cutting short*, the word ought here to preserve its natural meaning of *reckoning :* " God will this time make His reckoning with Israel by a short and summary process." In this threatening the feeling of indignation prevails. Paul subjoins to it a second saying, ver. 29, which rather breathes sadness and compassion ; it is taken from Isa. i. 9. He no longer quotes it with the word κράζει, *he cries ;* he uses the calmer term προείρηκεν, *he said before.* Some expositors explain this preposition πρό, *before*, contained in the verb, by the circumstance that in the Book of Isaiah this passage occurs before that which had just been quoted, vv. 27 and 28. This meaning is puerile ; for the position has no importance. Paul wishes to bring out the idea that the prophetical mouth of Isaiah having once declared the fact, it must be expected that one day or other it would be realized. The meaning of this saying is, that without a quite peculiar exercise of grace on the part of the Lord, the destruction announced vv. 27 and 28 would have been more radical still, as radical as that which overtook the cities of the plain, of which there remained not the slightest vestige.—Σπέρμα, *a germ, a shoot ;* this word expresses the same idea as ὑπόλειμμα, *the remnant*, ver. 27. But, as is well said by Lange, it adds to it the idea of the glorious future which is to spring from that remnant.—Instead of saying : *we should have been made like to*, Paul says, with the LXX., *made like as*, thus heaping up two forms of comparison, so as to express the most absolute assimilation. Such would have been the course of justice ; and if Israel will find fault, they have only one thing for which to blame God, that is, for not having annihilated them utterly.

No, certainly ; by concluding a special covenant with Israel, God had not abdicated the right of judging them, and alienated His liberty in respect of them and of the rest of mankind. His promise had never had this bearing, and the rejection of Israel does it no violence. But thus far the problem had been treated only from the formal point of view ; the question had been only as to God's *right*. The apostle now enters upon the matter involved. The right being established, it remains to examine what use God has made of it. This is the subject treated by the apostle in the following passage, which extends from ver. 30 to the end of chap. x.

TWENTY-SECOND PASSAGE (9:30-10:21)

Israel the Cause of their own Rejection

Vv. 30–33

In vv. 30-33 the apostle gives summarily the solution of the problem; then he develops it in chap. x.

Vv. 30, 31. "*What shall we say then? That the Gentiles, which followed not after righteousness, have obtained righteousness, but the righteousness which is of faith; and that Israel, which followed after the law of righteousness, hath not attained to the law of righteousness.*"[1]—The question: *What shall we say then?* has in the present case peculiar gravity: " The explanation of the fact not being found by saying, God has annulled His word; what, then, is the solution of the enigma?" Thus, after setting aside the false solution, Paul invites his reader to seek with him the true one; and this solution he expresses in ver. 31 in a declaration of painful solemnity, after prefacing it in ver. 30 with a saying relating to the lot of the Gentiles. While the latter have obtained what they sought not, the Jews have missed what they sought; the most poignant irony in the whole of history. Some expositors have thought that the proposition which follows the question, *What shall we say then?* was not the answer to the question, but a second question explanatory of the first. We must then prolong the interrogation to the end of ver. 31. But what do we find there? Instead of an answer, a new question, διατί, *wherefore?* This construction is clearly impossible. It is the same with the attempt of Schott, who makes a single question of the whole sentence from the τί οὖν to δικαιοσύνην (the second): What shall we say then of the fact that the Gentiles have obtained . . . ? and who finds the answer to this question in the last words of the verse: " but the righteousness of faith !"—The solution given by the apostle may be thus expressed: "That, whereas the Gentiles have obtained . . ., Israel, on the contrary, has failed " . . .—Ἔθνη, without article : Gentiles, beings having this characteristic. The subjective negative μή might be rendered: " *without their* seeking."—Δικαιοσύνην, without article, *a righteousness*. It is a mistake to give to this word here, as Meyer does, the moral sense of *holiness;* for it could not be said of the Greeks that they did not often aspire after a high morality. What they never sought was *righteousness*, in the religious sense of the word, justification. The idea which they formed of sin as a simple error, and of the Deity as not looking very narrowly at human actions, did not lead them to the pursuit of righteousness in this sense. And yet they obtained it, precisely because they were exempt from the false pretensions which barred access to it in the case of the Jews. They were like the man of whom Jesus speaks, who, crossing a field, discovers a treasure in it which he was not seeking, and without hesitating makes sure of its possession. The verb κατέλαβεν, literally, *put the hand on*, suits this mode of acquisition. It must, however, be further explained how the matter could transpire in this way; hence the last words: " but the righteousness which is of faith." The δέ, *but*, is explicative (as in iii.

---

[1] The word δικαιοσυνης, which is here read by the T. R., is found in F K L P, Syr.; it is omitted in ℵ A B D E G. [All the recent editors omit the word.—T. W. C.]

22) : "but the righteousness thus obtained could, of course, only be a righteousness of faith."

Ver. 31. The lot of the Gentiles presents a contrast fitted to bring out more clearly the tragical character of that of Israel. This people, which alone followed the law of righteousness, is precisely the one which has not succeeded in reaching it. Some (Chrys., Calv., Beng., etc.) have stumbled at this expression, *the law of righteousness*, and have translated it as if it were *the righteousness of the law*. They have not understood the apostle's expression. What Israel sought was not so much righteousness itself in its moral essence, as the law in all the detail of its external and manifold observances. The expression is therefore chosen deliberately, "to remind the reader," as Holsten well says, "of the weakness of the religious conscience of Israel, which was ever seeking an external standard." If the Jews in general had been seriously preoccupied, like young Saul, with true moral righteousness, the law thus applied would have become to them what it was in its destination, *the schoolmaster to bring them to Christ* (Gal. iii. 23, 24). But seeking only the letter, they neglected the spirit. Levitical prescriptions, minutiæ about Sabbaths and meats, fastings, tithes, washings of hands, of bodies, of furniture, etc., such were their sole pursuits. The object of their labor was thus really *the law*, from which *righteousness* should have proceeded, and not *righteousness* itself, as the true contents of the law. Therein there was a profound moral aberration which led them to the refusal of true righteousness when it was presented to them in the person of the Messiah.—By designating true righteousness in the same sentence by the same expression, *the law of righteousness*, the apostle wishes by the identity of terms to exhibit the contrast in the things : pursuing the shadow, they missed the reality.—The term *law* is taken the second time in that more general sense in which we have found it so often used in our Epistle (iii. 27, vii. 21 and 25, viii. 2) : a certain mode of being, fitted to determine the will. The reference is to the true mode of justification.—The strongly supported reading which rejects the word δικαιοσύνης, *of righteousness*, would signify : "they have not attained *to the law*." But what would that mean? They have not attained to the fulfilment of the law? The expression : "attain to the law," would be very strange taken in this sense. Or would it apply, as some have thought, to the law of the gospel? But where is the gospel thus called nakedly *the law?* This reading is therefore inadmissible, as Meyer himself acknowledges, notwithstanding his habitual predilection for the Alexandrine text, and in opposition to the opinion of Tischendorf.

Vv. 32, 33. "*Wherefore? Because [seeking] not by faith, but as it were by works,*[1] *they stumbled*[2] *at the stumbling-stone ; as it is written, Behold, I lay in Sion a stumbling-stone and rock of offence : and he*[3] *who believeth on Him shall not be ashamed.*"—The apostle has just declared (ver. 30) the moral fact which is the real cause of Israel's rejection, and he now asks how this fact could have come about. The question, *wherefore?* does not signify *for what end* (εἰς τί)? but *on account of what* (διὰ τί)? If, with the T. R. and some Byz. Mjj., we read γάρ, *for*, with *they stumbled*, this verb necessarily begins a new proposition, and a finite verb must be understood with the conjunction *because:* "because *they sought*, not by faith, but as it were by works." But this reading seems too slenderly supported to be admissible, and it is difficult to extract from it a rational meaning ; for the act of *stumbling* is rather the *effect* than the *cause*, or than the *proof* of seeking in a false way. It would require, consequently, to be, "they stumbled *therefore.*" If, with the most numerous and important documents, we reject the *for*, two possible constructions remain : Either the whole may be taken

[1] T. R. reads νομου after εργων, with D E K L P, Syr.
[2] T. R. reads γαρ after προσεκοψαν, with E K L P, Syr.
[3] T. R. reads πας after και, with K L P.

as a single proposition (see the translation); the two regimens: *not by faith* and *as it were by works*, depend in this case on *they stumbled*, the participle *seeking* being understood; this construction is somewhat analogous to that of ver. 11. The meaning is excellent. " Wherefore did they not find true righteousness ? Because, seeking it in the way of works, they ended in stumbling against the stumbling-stone, the Messiah who brought to them true righteousness, that of faith." Or it is possible, even without the *for*, to find here two propositions, as is done by most commentators; the first: " Because they sought not in the way of faith, but in that of works;" the second, which would follow by way of *asyndeton*, and which would require to be regarded as pronounced with emotion : " Yea ; they stumbled " . . . ! But what prevents us from adopting this last construction is, that the idea of *stumbling* thus comes on us too abruptly. It would require a καὶ οὕτως, *and so*, to establish the relation between the two acts of *seeking* in the false way and *stumbling*. We hold, therefore, by the preceding construction.—Paul can with good reason make it a *charge* against the Jews that they have not sought righteousness in the way of faith ; for he had shown (chap. iv.) by the example of Abraham that this way was already marked out in the O. T. ; comp. also the saying of Habakkuk quoted (i. 17), and that of Isaiah about to be referred to (ver. 33), etc. Every day the experiences made under the law should have brought the serious Jew to the feet of Jehovah in the way of repentance and faith to obtain pardon and help (see the Psalms). And following this course, they would have avoided stumbling at the Messianic righteousness ; they would, on the contrary, have grasped it greedily, as was done by the *élite* of the people. The *as it were*, added to the regimen *by works*, signifies quite naturally : " As if it were possible to find righteousness by this means." Meyer explains it somewhat differently. " To seek righteousness by a process *such as* that of works." But the first meaning much better describes the contrast between the real and the imaginary means.—The complement νόμου, *of the law*, in the T. R. is omitted by the Alexs. and the Greco-Latins ; it adds nothing to the idea. Seeking in this false way, they have ended by stumbling on the stone which made them fall. This stone was Jesus, who brought them a righteousness acquired by Himself and offered only to faith. The figure of *stumbling* is in keeping with all those that precede : *follow after, attain to, reach* (obtain). In their foolish course, Israel thought they were advancing on a clear path, and lo ! all at once there was found on this way an obstacle upon which they were broken. And this obstacle was the very Messiah whom they had so long invoked in all their prayers ! But even this result was foretold.

Ver. 33. Paul combines in this quotation Isa. xxvii. 16 and viii. 14, and that in such a way that he borrows the first and last words of his quotation from the former of these passages, and those of the middle from the latter. It is hard to conceive how a great number of commentators can apply the saying of Isaiah, xxviii. 16 : " Behold, I lay in Zion for a foundation a stone, a tried stone" . . . etc., to the theocracy itself (see Meyer). The theocracy is the edifice which is raised in Zion ; how should it be its foundation ? According to viii. 14, the foundation is Jehovah ; and it is on this stone that the unbelieving Israel of both kingdoms stumble, while on this rock he that believes takes refuge. In chap. xxviii. the figure is somewhat modified ; for Jehovah *is* no longer the foundation ; it is He who *lays* it. The foundation here is therefore Jehovah in His final manifestation, the Messiah. We thus understand why Paul has combined the two passages so closely ; the one explains the other. It is in the sense which we have just established that the same figure is applied to Christ, Luke ii. 34, xx. 17, 18 ; 1 Pet. ii. 4 (comp. *Bible annotée* on the two passages of Isaiah quoted by the apostle). The terms *stone, rock*, express the notion of consistency. We break ourselves struggling against the Messiah, rather than break Him.—The two words πρόσκομμα and σκάνδαλον, *stumbling* and *scandal*, are not wholly synonymous. The former denotes the shock, the latter the fall resulting from it ; and so the former, the moral conflict between Israel and the Messiah, and the latter, the people's unbelief. The first figure applies, therefore, to all the false judgments passed by the Jews on the conduct of Jesus—His healings on the Sabbath, His alleged contempt of the law, His blasphemies, etc. ; the second, to the rejection of the Messiah, and, in His person, of Jehovah Himself.—The adj. πᾶς, *every one*, which the T. R. adds to the word *he who believeth*, is omitted by the Alexs. and the Greco-Latins, and also by the Peshito. The context also condemns it. The point to be brought out here is not that *whosoever* believeth is saved, but : that *it is enough* to believe in order to be so. The word *every one* (which is not in Isaiah) has been imported from x. 11, where, as we shall see, it is in its place.—The Hebrew verb, which the LXX. have translated by : *shall not be confounded*, strictly signifies : *shall not make haste* (flee away), which gives the same meaning. There is no need, therefore, to hold, with several critics, a difference of reading in the Hebrew text (*jabisch* for *jakisch*).

General considerations on chap. ix.—Though we have not reached the end of the passage beginning with ver. 30, the essential thought being already expressed in vv. 30-33, we may from this point cast a glance backward at chap. ix. taken as a whole.—Three principal views as to the meaning of this chapter find expression in the numerous commentaries to which it has given rise :

1. Some think they can carry up the thought of Paul to complete logical unity, by maintaining that it boldly excludes human freedom, and makes all things proceed from one single factor, the sovereign will of God. Some of these are so sure of their view, that one of them, a Strasburg professor, wrote most lately : "As to determinism, it would be to carry water to the Rhine, to seek to prove that this point of view is that of St. Paul." [1]

2. Others think that the apostle expounds the two points of view side by side with one another—that of absolute predestination, to which speculative reflection leads, and that of human freedom, which experience teaches—without troubling himself to reconcile them logically. This opinion is perhaps the most widespread among theologians at the present hour.

3. Finally, a third class think that in Paul's view the fact of human freedom harmonizes logically with the principle of divine predestination, and think they can find in' his very exposition the elements necessary to harmonize the two points of view. Let us pass under review each of these opinions.

I. In the first, we immediately distinguish three groups. In the first place : the *particularistic predestinarians*, who, whether in the salvation of some or in the perdition of others, see only the effect of the divine decree. Such, essentially, are St. Augustine, the Reformers, the theologians of Dort, and the churches which have preserved this type of doctrine down to our day, whether pushing the consequence the length of ascribing the fall itself and sin to the divine will (*supralapsarians*), like Zwingle, who goes so far as to say, in speaking of Esau : "quem divina providentia creavit ut viveret *atque impie* viveret'' (see Th. p. 500) ; or whether they stop half way, and, while ascribing the fall to human freedom, make the divine decree of human election bear solely on those among lost men whom God is pleased to save (*infralapsarians*).—But, first, it is forgotten that the apostle does not think for a moment of speculating in a general way on the relation between human freedom and divine sovereignty, and that he is occupied solely with showing the harmony between the particular fact of the rejection of the Jews and the promises relating to their election. Then it would be impossible, if he really held this point of view, to acquit him of the charge of self-contradiction in all those sayings of his which assume—1st. Man's entire freedom in the acceptance or rejection of salvation (ii. 4, 6-10, vi. 12, 13) ; 2d. The possibility of one converted falling from the state of grace through want of vigilance or faithfulness (viii. 13 ; 1

---

[1] M. Adolphe Krauss, *Literatur-Zeit.* iii. 13.

Cor. x. 1-12 ; Gal. v. 4 ; Col. i. 23, a passage where he says expressly : "*if at least* ye persevere"). Comp. also the words of Jesus Himself, John v. 40 : "But ye will not come to me ;" Matt. xxiii. 37 : "How often would I . . . but ye would not." Finally, throughout the whole chapter which immediately follows, as well as in the four verses we have just expounded, vv. 30-33, the decree of the rejection of the Jews is explained, not by the impenetrable mystery of the divine will, but by the haughty tenacity with which the Jews, notwithstanding all God's warnings, affected to establish their own righteousness and perpetuate their purely temporary prerogative.

In this first class we meet, in the second place, with the group of the *latitudinarian determinists*, who seek to correct the harshness of the predestinarian point of departure by the width of the point reached ; the final goal, indeed, according to them, is *universal salvation*. The world is a theatre on which there is in reality but one actor, God, who plays the entire piece, but by means of a series of personages who act under his impulse as simple automata. If some have bad parts to play, they have not to blame or complain of themselves for that ; for their culpability is only apparent, and . . . the issue will be happy for them. All's well that ends well. Such is the view of Schleiermacher and his school ; it is that to which Farrar has just given his adherence in his great work on St. Paul.[1]—But how are we to reconcile this doctrine of universal salvation, I do not say only with declarations such as those of Jesus, Matt. xii. 23 ("neither in this world nor in the world to come"), xxvi. 24 ("it were better for that man that he had never been born"), Mark ix. 43-48, but also with the sayings of Paul himself, 2 Thess. i. 9 ; Rom. viii. 13 ? These declarations, indeed, seem incompatible with the idea of a universal final salvation. Neither does this idea seem to us to arise from the sayings of the apostle here and there whence it is thought possible to deduce it, such as 1 Cor. xv. 22 ("in Christ all made alive") and 28 ("God all in all") ; for these passages refer only to the development of the work of salvation in believers. It is impossible to allow that a system according to which sin would be the act of God Himself, remorse an illusion arising from our limited and subjective viewpoint, and the whole conflict, so serious as it is between guilty man and God, a simple apparent embroilment with a view of procuring to us in the end the liveliest sensation of re-established harmony—entered for a single moment the mind of the apostle.

We may say as much of the third form in which this determinist point of view presents itself, that of *pantheistic absorption*. No one will ever succeed in explaining the words of the apostle by such a formula. Paul emphasizes too forcibly the value and permanence of personality, as well as the moral responsibility of man ; and it must not be forgotten that if he says : "God shall be *all*," he adds : *in all*.—In none of these three forms, therefore, can the system which makes everything, even evil, proceed from divine causality, be ascribed to Paul.

II. Must we take refuge in the idea of an *internal contradiction* attaching to the apostle's mode of view, whether this contradiction be regarded as a logical inconsequence attributable to the weakness of his mind (so Reiche and Fritzsche, who go so far as to deplore that the apostle "was not at the school of Aristotle rather than that of Gamaliel") ; or with Meyer, Reuss, and a host of others, the problem be regarded as insoluble in its very nature, and in consequence of the limits of the human mind ; so that, as Meyer says, whenever we place ourselves at one of the two points of view, it is impossible to expound it without expressing ourselves in such a way as to deny the other, as has happened to Paul in this chapter?—We think that in the former case the most striking character of St. Paul's mind is mistaken, his logical power, which does not allow him to stop short in the study of a question till he has thoroughly completed its elucidation. This characteristic we have seen throughout the

---

[1] *The Life and Work of St. Paul*, vol. ii. p. 241 et seq. After saying that St. Paul does not recoil before the apparent contradiction of an eternal paradox—which would suppose that he allows the juxtaposition of two contradictory points of view—this writer arrives definitively at the solution of Schleiermacher. The rejection of some only serves to pave the way which leads to universal restoration. God wills the salvation of all. The duality of election resolves itself into a council of grace which embraces all men. Human sin is no more regarded except as a transitory step (a *moment*) leading to this absolute end : God all in all. Such are the ideas enunciated by Farrar, particularly in pp. 245 and 246.

whole of our Epistle. As to Meyer's point of view, if Paul had really thought thus, he would not have failed, in view of this insoluble difficulty, to stop at least once in the course of his exposition to exclaim, after the fashion of Calvin : *Mysterium horribile!*

III. It is therefore certain that the apostle was not without a glimpse of the real solution of the apparent contradiction on which he was bordering throughout this whole passage. Was this solution, then, that which has been proposed by Julius Müller in his *Sündenlehre*, and which is found in several critics, according to which Paul in chap. ix. explains the conduct of God from a purely *abstract* point of view, saying what God has the right to do, speaking absolutely, but what He does not do in reality? It is difficult to believe that the apostle would have thus isolated the abstract right from its historical execution, and we have seen in ver. 21 et. seq. that Paul directly applies to the concrete case the view of right expounded in the instance of the potter.—Must we prefer the solution defended by Beyschlag in the wake of many other critics, according to which the question here relates solely to *groups of men*, and to those groups of men solely as to the *providential part* assigned them in the general course of God's kingdom ; but not to the lot of *individuals*, and much less still as to the matter of their final salvation? That it is so in regard to Esau and Jacob, does not seem to us open to doubt, since in those cases we have to do with national dispensations in the course of the preparatory economy. But it seems to me impossible to apply this solution to the essential point treated in the chapter, the rejection of the Jews and the calling of the Gentiles. For among those rejected Jews, Paul proves an election of redeemed ones, who are certainly so, in virtue of their individual faith ; and among those Gentile nations who are called, he is very far from thinking there are none but saved individuals ; so that the vessels of wrath are not the Jewish nation as such, but the individual unbelievers in the nation ; and the vessels of mercy are not the Gentile peoples as such, but the individual believers among them. The point in question therefore is, the lot of individual Jews or Gentiles. When Paul says : "fitted to destruction" and "prepared unto glory," he is evidently thinking not only of a momentary rejection or acceptance, but of the final condemnation and salvation of those individuals. What is promised as to the final conversion of Israel has nothing to do with this question.—Neither can we adopt the attempt of Weiss to apply the right of God, expounded in chap. ix., solely to the competency belonging to God of *fixing the conditions* to which He chooses to attach the gift of His grace. The apostle's view evidently goes further ; the cases of Moses and Pharaoh, with the expressions *to show grace* and *to harden*, indicate not simple conditions on which the event may take place, but a real action on God's part to produce it.—A multitude of expositors, Origen, Chrysostom, the Arminians, several moderns, such as Tholuck, etc., have endeavored to find a formula whereby to combine the action of man's moral freedom (evidently assumed in vv. 30-33) with the divine predestination taught in the rest of the chapter. Without being able to say that they have entirely succeeded in showing the harmony between the two terms, we are convinced that it is only in this way that the true thought of the apostle can be explained ; and placing ourselves at this viewpoint, we submit to the reader the following considerations. already partly indicated in the course of the exegesis :

1. And first of all, the problem discussed by the apostle is not the speculative question of the relation between God's sovereign decree and man's free responsibility. This question appears indeed in the background of the discussion, but it is not its theme. This is simply and solely the fact of the *rejection* of Israel, the *elect* people ; a fact proved in particular by the preamble ix. 1-5, and the vv. 30-33, introduced as a conclusion from what precedes by the words : "What shall we say *then*?" We should not therefore seek here a theory of St. Paul, either regarding the divine decrees or human freedom ; he will not touch this great question, except in so far as it enters into the solution of the problem proposed.

2. We must beware of confounding *liberty* and *arbitrariness* on the part of God, and *aptitude* and *merit* on the part of man. To begin with this second distinction, the free acceptance of any divine favor whatever, and of salvation

in general, is an aptitude to receive and possess the gift of God, but does not at all constitute a merit conferring on man the right to claim it. We have already said: How can faith be a merit, that which in its essence is precisely the renunciation of all merit? This distinction once established, the other is easily explained. Face to face with human merit, God would no longer be *free*, and this is really all that Paul wishes to teach in our chapter. For his one concern is to destroy the false conclusion drawn by Israel from their special election, their law, their circumcision, their ceremonial works, their monotheism, their moral superiority. These were in their eyes so many bonds by which God was pledged to them beyond recall. God had no more the right to free Himself from the union once contracted with them, on any condition whatever. The apostle repels every *obligation* on God's part, and from this point of view he now vindicates the fulness of divine *liberty*. But he does not dream of teaching thereby divine *arbitrariness*. He does not mean for a moment that without rhyme or reason God resolved to divorce Himself from His people, and to contract alliance with the Gentiles. If God breaks with Israel, it is because they have obstinately refused to follow Him in the way which he wished the development of His kingdom henceforth to take (see the demonstration in chap. x.). If He now welcomes the Gentiles, it is because they enter with eagerness and confidence on the way which is opened to them by His mercy. There is thus no caprice on God's part in this double dispensation. God simply uses His liberty, but in accordance with the standard arising from His love, holiness, and wisdom. No anterior election can hinder Him either from showing grace to the man who was not embraced in it at the first, but whom he finds disposed to cast himself humbly on His favor; or to reject and harden the man to whom He was united, but who claims to set himself up proudly in opposition to the progress of His work. A free initiative on God's part in all things, but without a shadow of arbitrariness—such is the apostle's view. It is that of true monotheism.

3. As to the speculative question of the relation between God's eternal plan and the freedom of human determinations, it seems to me probable that Paul resolved it, so far as he was himself concerned, by means of the fact affirmed by him, of *divine foreknowledge*. He himself puts us on this way, viii. 29, 30, by making foreknowledge the basis of predestination. As a general, who is in full acquaintance with the plans of campaign adopted by the opposing general, would organize his own in keeping with this certain prevision, and would find means of turning all the marches and countermarches of his adversary to the success of his designs; so God, after fixing the supreme end, employs the free human actions, which He contemplates from the depths of His eternity, as factors to which He assigns a part, and which He makes so many means in the realization of His eternal design. Undoubtedly Paul did not think here of resolving the speculative question, for that did not enter into his task as an apostle; but his treatment furnishes us by the way with the necessary elements to convince us that if he had meant to do so, it would have been in this direction he would have guided our thoughts.

What are we to conclude from all this? That the apostle in this chapter, far from vindicating, as is ordinarily thought, the rights of divine election over against human freedom, vindicates, on the contrary, the rights of God's freedom in regard to His own election relating to Israel. His decree does not bind Him, as an external law imposed on His will would. He remains sovereignly free to direct His mode of acting at every moment according to the moral conditions which he meets with in humanity, showing grace when he finds good, even to men who were not in His covenant, rejecting, when He finds good, even men who were embraced in the circle which formed the object of His election. St. Paul did not therefore think of contending in behalf of divine sovereignty against human freedom; he contended for God's freedom in opposition to the chains which men sought to lay on Him in the name of His own election. We have here a treatise not *for*, but *against* unconditional election,[1]

[1] See Appendix D.

10:1-4

The apostle has summarily enunciated the real solution of the enigma in vv. 30-33. The proud claim of the people to uphold their own righteousness caused them to stumble at the true righteousness, that of faith, which God offered them in the person of the Messiah. Chap. x. develops and establishes this solution of the problem. Notwithstanding their religious zeal, the Israelitish nation, blinded by their self-righteousness, did not understand that *the end of the legal dispensation* must be the consequence of the coming of the Messiah (vv. 1-4); because he came to inaugurate a wholly new order of things, the characteristics of which were opposed to those of the legal system: 1st. The complete *freeness* of salvation (vv. 5-11); 2d. The *universality* of this free salvation (vv. 12-21).

In the act of unveiling the spiritual ignorance of the elect people, which forced God to separate from them for a time, Paul is seized with an emotion not less lively than that which he had felt when beginning to treat this whole matter (ix. 1 et seq.), and he interrupts himself to give vent to the feelings of his soul.

Vv. 1, 2. "*Brethren, my heart's good pleasure and the prayer*[1] *I address to God for them*[2] *are for their salvation.*[3] *For I bear them record that they have a zeal of God, but not according to knowledge.*"—The emotion with which the apostle's heart is filled betrays itself in the *asyndeton* between ver. 33 and ver. 1. By the word *brethren*, he joins his readers with him in that outburst of feeling to which he is about to give utterance.—The word εὐδοκία, *good pleasure, complacency of heart*, has been taken by many in the sense of *wish;* thus to make the term run parallel with the following: *my prayer.* But it is not necessary to give it this meaning, of which no example can be quoted. The apostle means that it is to this thought of Israel's salvation the regard of his heart rises with constant complacency; that therein, as it were, is found the ideal of his heart. To this idea there attaches quite naturally that of the prayer by which he asks the realization of the ideal. The three variants presented by the T. R. (indicated in the note) should be set aside. The two last arise no doubt from the circumstance that with this passage there began a public lesson, which made it necessary to complete the proposition.—The regimen ὑπὲρ αὐτῶν, *for them*, might depend on the verb *is*, or rather *are*, understood: my good pleasure and my prayer are *in their interest;* and this idea of interest, contained in the prep. ὑπέρ, would be afterward determined by the apposition εἰς σωτηρίαν: "are in their interest, that is to say, for their salvation." But why add this explanation, which seems superfluous? Is it not better to make the regimen *for them*, as well as the preceding one *to God*, dependent on the word *prayer*, which has an active and verbal meaning, and to make εἰς σωτηρίαν, *to salvation*, the regimen of the whole proposition: "My good pleasure . . . and my prayer for them (on their account) tend to their salvation"? It was a matter of course that Paul prayed on account of Israel; but did he pray for their chastisement or their salvation? That was the question which might have been asked.—Bengel here observes, "that Paul would not have prayed for the Jews if they had been absolutely reprobate." And this remark is quoted by some with approbation. I do not think it accurate, for an absolute reprobation might indeed overtake unbelieving individuals of Paul's time, without its being possible to conclude therefrom to the eternal objection of the people.[4] Even in this case, therefore, Paul could pray for their future conversion.

---

[1] The η which the T. R. places before δεησις is read only in K L and the Mnn.
[2] Instead of υπερ του Ισραηλ, which the T. R. reads with K L and Mnn., all the others read υπερ αυτων.
[3] Εστι of the T. R. is only read in K L P and Mnn.; omitted in all the rest.
[4] A better reason is found in the fact that their absolute reprobation was not revealed to Paul, and therefore could not be known by him.—T. W. C.

Ver. 2. In this verse Paul justifies his so lively interest in the lot of the Jews, expressed in ver. 1. What has not been done, what has not been suffered, by those Jews devoted to the cause of God, under successive Gentile powers? Notwithstanding the most frightful persecutions, have they not succeeded in maintaining their monotheistic worship for ages in all its purity? And at that very time what an admirable attachment did they show to the ceremonies of their worship and the adoration of Jehovah! When Paul says μαρτυρῶ, *I bear them witness*, he seems to be alluding to his conduct of other days, and to say : I know something of it, of that zeal! —Unhappily this impulse is not guided according to the standard (κατά) of a just *knowledge*, of a real discernment of things. And it is this want of understanding which has spoiled the effects of this admirable zeal. He does not use the word γνῶσις, *knowledge* (in the ordinary sense of the word), for the Jews certainly do not lack religious knowledge. The compound term ἐπίγνωσις, which he employs here, rather signifies *discernment*, that understanding which puts its finger on the true nature of the thing. They have failed to discern the true meaning and the true scope of the legal dispensation ; they are ardently attached to all its particular rites, but they have not grasped their moral end.

Vv. 3, 4. "*For they not knowing God's righteousness, and seeking to establish their own righteousness,*[1] *have not submitted themselves unto the righteousness of God. For Christ is the end of the law for righteousness to every one that believeth.*"—These verses are meant to explain the terrible misunderstanding which weighed on the mind of Israel, and which now brings about the separation between God and His people. Not understanding that it was from God their righteousness was to come, Israel were led to maintain their legal dispensation at any cost, and to mistake the limit which God had purposed to assign it.—The term ἀγνοοῦντες, *not knowing*, is directly related to the preceding expression : *not according to knowledge*. Under the discipline of the law, the discernment of true righteousness, that which God grants to faith, should have been formed in them. For, on the one hand, the conscientious effort to observe the law would have brought them to feel their weakness (comp. chap. vii.) ; and, on the other, the profound study of the Scriptures would have taught them, by the example of Abraham (Gen. xv. 5) and by sundry prophetic declarations (Isa. l. 8, 9 ; Hab. ii. 4), that "righteousness and strength come from the Lord." But through not using the law in this spirit of sincerity and humility, they proved unfit to understand the final revelation ; and their mind, carried in a false direction, stumbled at the divine truth manifested in the appearing of the Messiah (ver. 32). Several commentators understand ἀγνοοῦντες in a very forcible sense : *misconceiving*. Meyer insists on retaining the natural sense : *not knowing*. This latter sense may suffice, indeed, provided it be not forgotten that in this case, as in many others, the want of knowing is the result of previous unfaithfulnesses ; comp. 1 Cor. xiv. 38 and Acts xvii. 30.—Though we did not know from the first part of the Epistle the meaning of the term : *righteousness of God*, it would appear clearly here from the contrasted expression : *their own righteousness*. The latter is a sentence of justification which man obtains in virtue of the way in which he has fulfilled the law. God gives him nothing ; He simply attests and proclaims the fact. The *righteousness* of God, on the contrary, is the sentence of justification which He confers on faith of His own good will.—In the first proposition the subject in question is the *notion* of God's righteousness, which has not succeeded in finding an entrance into their mind ; in the second, the word is taken in the concrete sense ; the subject is righteousness, as it has been really offered them in Christ.—Στῆσαι, *to establish ;* this word means : **to cause to stand erect as a monument raised, not to the glory of God, but to their own**.—This proud attempt has issued in an open revolt, in the

---

[1] A B D E P omit the word δικαιοσυνην.

rejection of Christ and of the righteousness of God offered in Him. The verb οὐχ ὑπετάγησαν, *they have not submitted themselves*, characterizes the refusal to believe as a *disobedience*; it is the counterpart of the passages in which faith is called an *obedience* (i. 5, vi. 17). This verb may have the passive or middle sense; here it is evidently the second (viii. 7, xiii. 1).

But this voluntary revolt has cost Israel dear; for this is precisely the cause of their rejection.

Ver. 4. It is on this point, indeed, that their view and that of God have come into collision. The Messiah brought a free righteousness offered to faith; His coming consequently put an end to man's attempt to establish his own righteousness on the observance of the law; thus, then, fell the whole legal economy, which had now fulfilled its task. It was not so the Jews understood it. If they in a measure accepted the salvation of the Gentiles, they thought of it only as an annexation to Israel and a subjection to the sovereignty of Moses. It was under this idea "that they compassed sea and land, as Jesus says, to make proselytes" (Matt. xxiii. 15). The Messiah was simply to consummate this conquest of the world by Israel, destroying by judgment every Gentile who resisted. His reign was to be the perfect application of the legal institutes to the whole world. It is easy to understand the error and the irritation which could not fail to take possession of the people and their chiefs, when Jesus by His decided spirituality seemed to compromise the stability of the *law of ordinances* (Matt. v., ix. 11–17, xv. 1 et seq.); when He announced plainly that He came not to repair the old Jewish garment, but to substitute for that now antiquated regime, a garment completely new. In this familiar form He expressed the same profound truth as St. Paul declares in our verse: The law falls to the ground with the coming of Him who brings a completely made righteousness to the believer.—The word τέλος may signify *end* or *aim;* but not, as some have understood it here (Orig., Er.): *fulfilment* (τελείωσις), a meaning which the word cannot have. The meaning *aim*, adopted by Calov., Grot., Lange, and others, is in keeping with Gal. iii. 24, where the law is called *the pedagogue* to bring the Jews to Christ. But the context seems rather to require that of *end* (Aug., Mey., etc.). There is a contrast between this word τέλος and the term στῆσαι, *to hold erect* (ver. 3). This latter meaning, that of *end*, no doubt implies the notion of *aim;* for if the law terminates in Christ, it is only because in Him it has reached its aim. Nevertheless it is true that the contrast established in the following development between the righteousness of the law and that of faith requires, as an explanation properly so called, the meaning of *end*, and not *aim*. Of two contrary things, when the one appears, the other must take end.—This new fact which puts an end to the law, is the coming of Christ made righteousness to the believer. The εἰς indicates the destination and application: "in righteousness offered and given to the believer, whoever he may be, Jew or Gentile;" comp. 1 Cor. i. 30. These words: *every one that believeth*, express the two ideas which are about to be developed in the two following passages: that of the *freeness* of salvation, contained in the word *believeth* (vv. 5–11); and that of its *universality*, contained in the word *every one* (vv. 12–21).

Vv. 5–11

Ver. 5. "*For Moses describeth the righteousness which is of the law thus: The man who hath done [the law], shall live by it.*"[1]—In this translation we

---

[1] The numerous variants of this verse may be reduced to these three principal ones:
The ὅτι, *that*, is placed by T. R., with B E F G K L P, It. Syr. after the words τὴν ἐκ τοῦ νόμου, *the righteousness of the law*, while ℵ A D place it after γράφει, *writes*.
The αὐτά, *these things*, which T. R., with B F G K L P, gives as object to ὁ ποιήσας, *he who hath done*, is omitted by ℵ A D E.
Instead of ἐν αὐτοῖς, *by them*, (those things), which T. R. reads, with D E F G K L P, Syr., we find in ℵ A B: ἐν αὐτῇ, *by it* (righteousness).

have followed, for the first of the three variants indicated in the note, the reading of the T. R., which is supported not only by the Byz. documents, but also by the *Vatic.* and the two ancient Latin and Syriac versions. It is easy to explain the origin of the other reading which has transposed the ὅτι, *that*, by placing it immediately after the verb γράφει, *writes ;* it seemed that it should run : *Moses writes that.* As to the second variant, the authorities in favor of the T. R. ("he that hath done *those things*") are somewhat less strong, and especially it is probable that this object αὐτά (*those things*) was added under the influence of the text of the LXX. ; no reason can be imagined why this word should have been rejected. With regard to the third, we think the T. R. must also be abandoned, which reads at the end of the verse ἐν αὐτοῖς, *by them* (those things), and prefer the reading ἐν αὐτῇ, *by it* (this righteousness). This last reading has on its side the same reasons which have decided us in regard to the second variant, and the authority of the *Vaticanus* besides.—Accordingly, the object of the verb γράφει, *writes*, is not the saying of Moses quoted afterward, but the words : *the righteousness which is of the law*, so that we must here take the word γράφειν, with Calvin, in the sense of *describe* (Moses describit) : "Moses thus describes this way for him who would follow it." Then (second variant) the participle : *he who has done*, must be taken in an absolute sense ; for it has no expressed object ; comp. iv. 4 (*he that worketh*, ὁ ἐργαζόμενος), literally : "He who *has acted*" (in contrast to him who *has believed*). In the translation we have been obliged to supply an object ; that object is : what there was to be done, consequently the law. Finally, the ἐν αὐτῇ, *by it*, which we adopt (third variant), refers evidently to the whole phrase : "the righteousness which is of the law." This would be the means of salvation and life to him who should really do (the law).

But if it is certain that this way is impracticable for fallen man, how is it to be explained that Moses seriously proposed it to the people of God ? Or must it be thought that there was here a sort of irony : "Try, and thou shalt see that it is too hard for thee." It is enough to reperuse the passage of the law, Lev. xviii. 5, to be convinced that the latter cannot be the sense in which this invitation was addressed to the people by the lawgiver. Now, if this exhortation and promise were serious, the way thus traced out was practicable. And, in fact, the law of Jehovah rightly understood was not given independently of His grace. The law, taken in the full sense of the word, contained an entire provision of means of grace unceasingly offered to the pious Israelite. From the moment he sinned, he could have recourse humbly to the pardon of his God, either with or without sacrifice, as the case might be ; comp. Ps. li. 16, 17 : "Thou delightest not in sacrifice . . . ; the sacrifice of God is a broken spirit ;" vv. 10–12 : "Create in me a clean heart, O God ; let the spirit of freedom uphold me . . . ; restore unto me the joy of Thy salvation." The law thus humbly understood and sincerely applied was certainly the way of salvation for the believing Jew ; it led him to an ever closer communion with God, as we find exemplified so often in the O. T., and what was yet wanting to this theocratic pardon and salvation was to be granted one day in the Messianic pardon and salvation which closed the perspective of the national hope. There was nothing, then, more serious for the Israelite who understood and applied the law in its true spirit and in its full breadth than the saying of Moses. But, unfortunately, there was another way of understanding the law and using it. It was possible to take the law in a narrower sense, solely in the form of command, and to make this institution thus understood a means of self-righteousness, and of proud complacency in self-merit. Such was the spirit which reigned in Israel at the time when Paul wrote, and particularly that of the school in which he had been brought up. Pharisaism, separating the commandment from grace, deemed that its fulfilment, realized by man's own strength, was the true title to divine favor. It is against this point of view that Paul here turns the law itself. He takes it as it is regarded by those whom he wishes to convince, as simple law, *nuda lex* (Calvin), law properly so called. And he reasons thus: "You wish to be justified by your own *doing*. Well! But in that case let your *doing* be complete! If your obedience is to make you live, it must be worthy of Him to whom it is offered." Such is the hopeless pass into which the apostle had himself been driven by the law thus understood and practised, and into which he drives the Pharisees of his time. If man wishes to raise the edifice of his own righteousness, let him take out every element of grace in the law; for the instant he has recourse to grace for little or for much, it is all over with work : "work is no more work" (xi. 6). This is probably also the reason why the apostle expresses himself as he does according to the true reading, saying, not: "Moses writes that" . . ., but: "Moses thus describes the righteousness of the law, to wit, that" . . . The intention of Moses was not to urge to such righteousness. But in his saying there is formulated the programme of a righteousness that is of the law "as law." If the law be once reduced to commandment, the saying of Leviticus certainly implies a mode of justification such as that of which the apostle speaks. Calvin is therefore right in saying: *Lex bifariam accipitur;* that is to say, the law may be regarded in two aspects, according as we take the Mosaic institution in its fulness, comprehending therein the elements of grace which belonged to it in view of a previous justification and a real sanctification, or as we lose these elements of grace out of view to fasten only on the commandment and turn it to the satisfaction of human pride.

Vv. 6, 7. "*But the righteousness which is of faith speaketh on this wise, Say not in thine heart, Who shall ascend into heaven? that is, to bring Christ down. Or, who shall descend into the deep? that is, to bring up Christ again from the dead.*"—Few passages have been so variously understood as this. And, first, was the intention of the apostle to give a real *explanation* of the passage quoted (Aug., Abail., Buc., Cal., Olsh., Fritzs., Meyer, Reuss)— whether this explanation be regarded historically exact, or as a violence done to the text of Moses (as Meyer, who here finds an application of the Rabbinical method of seeking hidden meanings in the simplest texts; or Reuss, who expresses himself thus: "Paul finds a passage from which he extorts the desired sense . . . by means of explanations which contradict the meaning of the original")?—Or must it be held that the apostle only meant here *to employ* the expressions of which Moses made use, while giving them a new sense (Chrys., Beza, Beng., Thol., Rück., Philip., Hofm., etc.)? A third class may be formed of those who, like Calvin, Lange, Hodge, etc., find in Paul a fundamental thought identical with that of the text of Moses, but one which is expounded here with great freedom in form. It is clear that these three classes, the last two especially, cannot always be distinguished precisely.

Let us remark in the outset the change of subject as we pass from ver. 5 to ver. 6. Paul no longer says here: "*Moses* writes (or describes). It is no longer he who speaks either directly or indirectly. It is *the righteousness of faith* itself which takes the word, borrowing, in order to reveal its essence, certain expressions from the passage quoted, Deut. xxx. 11–14. Meyer endeavors in vain to weaken the bearing of this difference. It is clear that Paul is no longer *quoting* Moses himself as in ver. 5, but making another personage speak, while ascribing to him in a free way the language of Moses.—What now did the latter mean when uttering the words quoted here? The passage in the original context applies to the law which Moses had just been repeating to the people according to its spirit rather than according to its letter. Moses means that the people need not distress themselves about the possibility of understanding and practicing this law. They need not imagine that some one must be sent to heaven or beyond the seas, to bring back the explanation of its commandments, or make its fulfilment possible. This law has been so revealed by the Lord, that every Israelite is in a condition to understand it with the heart and profess it with the mouth ; its fulfilment even is within the reach of all. It is evident that in expressing himself thus the lawgiver is not taking up the standpoint of an independent morality, but of Israelitish faith, of confidence in the nearness of Jehovah, and in the promise of His grace and succor. It is not without meaning that the Decalogue began with the words : "I am the Lord thy God, who brought thee out of the land of Egypt," and that every series of laws terminated with the refrain : "I am the Lord." Consequently the understanding and fulfilling of the law which Moses declares possible, have nothing in common with meritorious work ; they are the fruits of a heart in the full communion of confidence and love with the God of the covenant. And how, indeed, could Moses, who had written of Abraham the words : "His faith was imputed to him for righteousness," have thought that the way of faith was to be replaced after a few centuries by that of meritorious work ? Comp. Gal. iii. 17 et seq. That element of grace which, according to Moses himself, formed the basis of the whole covenant throughout its different phases, patriarchal and Mosaic, is here disentangled by Paul from its temporary wrapping (in Deuteronomy), as Jesus in the Sermon on the Mount disentangles the spirit from the letter of the Decalogue. He does not put into the passage of Moses what is not there, but he draws from it, in order to set in relief its profoundest element, the grace of Jehovah wrapped up and attested in the commandment itself. This grace, already existing in the Jewish theocracy, was the fruitful germ deposited under the surface, which was one day to burst forth and become the peculiar character of the new covenant. The apostle therefore was perfectly right in taking this saying as the prelude of gospel grace. It is easy, however, to understand why, feeling himself at some distance from the letter, in this application, he has not introduced Moses himself, but the righteousness of faith emerging as it were itself in the expressions of the lawgiver.

The differences between the texts of Moses and that of Paul are numerous. Moses says: "This commandment is not in heaven above, saying (that is, thou shouldst say)" . . . Paul adds : *in thy heart*—an expression which, as Philippi says, commonly refers to an evil thought which one is afraid to utter. Comp. Matt. iii. 9 ; Rev. xviii. 7. Moses continues thus : "and having heard, we shall do it." Paul omits these words as not having to do directly with his object, namely, to bring out the element of grace contained in the passage. He does so also with the same expressions repeated vv. 13 and 14. Finally, for the phrase *beyond the sea*, he substitutes : *into the deep* (abyss), a word which evidently denotes here the abode of the dead ; comp. ver. 7. Did he understand the expression *beyond the sea* in the sense of the depth, or has he departed entirely from the figure supported by the fact that the word *abyss* sometimes denotes the immensity of the seas ? or, finally, is he alluding to the idea of antiquity, which placed the fields of the blessed beyond the ocean ? None of these is probable ; he has been led to the expression by the contrast so frequent in Scripture between heaven and Hades (Job xi. 8 ; Amos ix. 2 ; Ps. cvii. 26, cxxxix. 8). He wished to contrast what is *deepest* with what is *highest ;* to depict on the one hand the *condemnation* from which Christ rescues us (ver. 7), and on the other, the full *salvation* to which He raises us (ver. 6) ; and, keeping as close as possible to the figurative expressions of Moses, he has taken Sheol and heaven as types of these two states. By these slight transformations Paul substitutes for the yet imperfect grace attached by the Lord to the gift of the law, the perfect bestowals of grace belonging to the new covenant. In the application which he makes of the saying of Moses, he points out not only the help of Jehovah ever near the believer to sustain him *in the fulfilment* of the law, but the law already *completely fulfilled*, both in its prescriptions and threatenings, by the life and death of Christ, so that all that remains for him who seeks salvation is to appropriate and apply this fulfilment as his own. Moses reassured the sincere Jew by showing him that *doing* would follow easily from *believing*. Paul reassures every man desirous of salvation by offering to him a *doing* wrought by another, and which his *believing* has only to lay hold of. To penetrate, therefore, to the spirit of Moses' saying, and to prolong the lines of the figures used by him, are all that is needed to land us in the gospel. There was a piquancy in thus replying to Moses by Moses, and in showing that what the lawgiver had written was still more true of the gospel than of the law.

The meaning of this saying in Paul is not, therefore, as was believed by the Greek Fathers, and as is still thought by Meyer and a good many others : " Beware of being *unbelieving* toward Christ incarnate (ver. 6) and risen (ver. 7)." 1. This thought is foreign to the context, for Paul has no idea of contrasting *believing* with *not believing*, but *doing* with *believing*. 2. There would be no connection between the application of this saying by Paul, and its signification in Deuteronomy. 3. How could we suppose the apostle addressing this saying to *non-believers?* Has the righteousness of faith then the right to say to them : I prohibit your not believing ? What would be the use of such a prohibition ? The apostle is addressing Christians, who hold the supernatural facts of Christ's history, but who do not yet understand the full saving efficacy contained in them ; and this is what he would have them to perceive. The same objections apply equally to other explanations, such as that of Reiche : "Who shall ascend into heaven to convince himself that Jesus is really there ?" and : "Who shall descend into the abyss to assure himself that He has indeed risen from it ?" Or that of Grimm : "Who shall ascend to bring Christ down from heaven, and thus prove the reality of His glorified existence ?" Or that of Holsten : " Who shall go to convince himself in heaven and in the abyss that God has power to effect the incarnation of Christ and the resurrection of His body ?" In all these explanations the person dealt with is always one who has to be convinced of the facts of salvation. But we do not convince of a historical fact by giving command to believe it. He to whom the righteousness of faith speaks with this tone of authority is one who believes those facts, and whom it exhorts to draw the saving consequences which rationally flow from them.—Calvin already comes near the true practical bearing of the passage when he thus explains : " Who shall ascend into heaven to prepare our abode there ? Who shall descend into the abyss to rescue us from the sepulchre ?" Only the context proves that the subject in question is not our future resurrection and glorification, but our present justification by faith.—Philippi, Lange, and Reuss seem to us to come still nearer the truth when they take these words as indicating works which Christ has already really accomplished to save us, so that it only remains for us to accept this fully wrought salvation. But when Philippi and Lange apply the first question, that of ver. 6, to the fact of the *incarnation*, explaining it with Meyer : " Who shall ascend to bring Christ down (by incarnation) to work out our salvation ?" it is impossible for me to follow them ; first, because there is no need of an ascension, but prayer is enough to obtain a gift of grace from God ; and further, because in that case there would cease to be any real connection between the application made by Paul of this saying and its meaning in Moses.

If we start, as is natural, from this last point (the original meaning of the saying), the following is the explanation of vv. 6 and 7 : " O thou, who desirest to reach the heaven of communion with God, say not : How shall I ascend to it ? as if it were necessary for thee thyself to accomplish this ascent on the steps of thine own obedience. That of which thou sayest : Who will do it (how shall I do it) ? is a thing done ; to ask such a question is to deny that Christ has really done it. It is to undo, at least so far as thou art concerned, what He has done. Thou whom thy sins torment, say not any more: Who shall descend into the abyss, there to undergo my punishment? That of which thou sayest: Who will do it (how shall I do it)? is a thing done. To ask such a question is to deny that Christ has done it; it is to undo, at least so far as thou art concerned, what He has done. Expiation is accomplished; thou canst have it by faith.

The form τίς, *who*? has this meaning: it is not every man individually that is asked to fulfil these two conditions of salvation—obedience and expiation. In that case every man would be called to be his own Christ. The righteousness of faith forbids us to make such pretensions, which can only issue in our discouragement or embitterment. Instead of the part of Christs, it brings us down to that of believers; and hence the reason why Paul, in the following words, makes use twice of the name of *Christ*, and not that of *Jesus*, as he would certainly do if he meant to speak here of the historical facts as such: comp. viii. 11.

Twice the apostle interrupts his quotation of the Mosaic saying with one of those brief explanations which, in the Rabbins, get the name of *Midrasch*, and of which we find other examples in Paul, *e.g.* 1 Cor. xv. 55 and 56. To support his explanation of the questions vv. 6 and 7 (as addressed to an unbeliever), Meyer, with many others, has been obliged to make these two short explanations, interjected by the apostle, dependent on the two preceding questions, as if they were a continuation of them: "Who shall ascend into heaven, that is to say, *with the view* of bringing the Christ down? Who shall descend into the deep, that is to say, *with the view* of bringing the Christ up?" This meaning of τοῦτ' ἐστι, *that is to say*, is far from natural; for what we expect is the indication of the reason why the righteousness of faith forbids such speaking, not the mention of the motive which leads the interrogator to raise this question. Besides, there is a τοῦτ' ἐστι perfectly parallel in ver. 8; now, there it is impossible to take the phrase in the sense which Meyer here gives to it. The word is therefore directly connected with μὴ εἴπῃς, *say not*. "Say not: Who shall ascend? for that (speaking thus) *is* to bring down . . ., or: Who shall descend? for that (speaking thus) *is* to bring up" . . . And, in point of fact, to wish to do a thing oneself (or ask that some one should do it) is evidently equivalent to denying that it is already done. Consequently, to say: Who shall ascend to open heaven for us? is to deny that Christ has already ascended for this end; it is *logically* to bring Him down again to this earth. It is therefore impossible to follow the almost unanimous leading of commentators, and refer the here imagined descent of Christ to the incarnation; rather it is a giving of the lie to the fact of the *ascension* (as Glöckler has understood it): "What thou wouldst do, ascend to heaven by thine own obedience, thou canst not; but Christ, by His perfect obedience, has won heaven both for Himself and thee. To ask: How shall I do it? or: Who shall do it? is therefore equivalent to denying that He has ascended. If thou dost really believe in His ascension, as thou professest to do, thou canst not deal thus with it."—In the second question, ver. 7, De Wette and Meyer observe that there is no need of putting two points (:) after the ἤ, *or;* the quotation continues.—The *abyss* frequently denotes the abode of the dead and of fallen angels (Luke viii. 31). For as the azure of the sky represents perfect salvation, so the depth of the sea is the natural figure for the abode of death and the state of condemnation.—The meaning given by Meyer: τοῦτ' ἐστι, *that is to say*, is still more inadmissible here than above. In fact it is an impossible supposition, that of a man going down into hell to raise up Christ there. If He is the Christ, He will certainly rise of Himself: if He is not, He will not rise at all. And in whose mouth should we put such a question? In that of a believer? But a believer does not doubt the resurrection. In that of an unbeliever? But an unbeliever would say : Who shall descend? not certainly with the view of going to raise Him up, which has no meaning, but with the view of going to see whether He has risen, or of going to prove that he has not; and besides, such a man would not thus off-hand call Jesus *the Christ*. It seems to me that it is a mistake to refer the word ἀναγαγεῖν, *to bring up*, to cause to ascend, as is generally done, to the fact of the resurrection. This expression must of course be understood in a sense analogous to that of the word *bring down*, ver 6. Now this latter signified : to deny, by wishing to gain heaven oneself, that Christ has ascended thither to open it for us ; to replace things as they would be without the ascension. *To bring up* consequently signifies : to deny, by wishing oneself to undergo condemnation for his sins, that Christ has blotted them out ; to replace things as they would be without His expiatory death. Meyer objects that ver. 9 expressly speaks of the resurrection ; but he resolves this objection himself when he says, in the explanation of ver. 9 : "Without the resurrection, the death of Jesus would not be the expiatory death." What is in question here is not the historical fact of His death, but its expiatory value, of which the resurrection is the monument. It is by the resurrection that the death appears not merely as that of Jesus, but as that of the *Christ*. Meyer again objects, that the death would require to have been placed by Paul before the ascension. But Paul was following the order of the words of Moses, and this order really better suited the didactic meaning which he was introducing into them. First the conquest of heaven by Christ's holy life and perfect obedience ; then the abolition of condemnation by His expiatory death.

We may now sum up the general meaning of the passage : All the *doing* asked of man by the law (ver. 5), and which he could never accomplish otherwise than imperfectly, is now accomplished perfectly by the Christ, whether it relate to the conquest of heaven by holiness, or to the abolition of condemnation by expiation. All, therefore, that remains to man in order to be saved, is *to believe* in this work by applying it to himself ; and this is what is commanded us by the righteousness of faith, ver. 8, after it has forbidden us, vv. 6 and 7, to pretend ourselves to open heaven or to close hell. This argument showed at a glance, that Christ having charged Himself with the *doing*, and having left us only the *believing*, His work put an end to the legal dispensation, which the apostle wished to prove (ver. 4).

Ver. 8. "*But what saith it? The word is nigh thee, in thy mouth and in thy heart. Now, that is the word of faith which we preach.*"—In the passage quoted, Moses said : "Believe on him who is revealed to thee in the law. With Him in the heart and on the lips thou shalt understand it, and thou shalt certainly fulfil it." This saying was in the ancient economy a relative truth. It becomes in Christ absolute truth. In these words Moses had in a sense, without suspecting it, given the exact formula of the righteousness of faith ; and it is because the apostle was conscious of this fundamental identity of feeling between Moses and the gospel on this point, that he could venture, as he does here, to apply the saying of the one to the teaching of the other. There is therefore in this passage neither a simple *imitation* of the words of Moses, nor a false Rabbinical pretence to *interpret it* correctly. Paul has done what we do or should do in every sermon : 1st. Disentangle from the temporary application, which is the strict sense of the text, the fundamental and universal principle which it contains ; 2d. Apply freely this general principle to the circumstances in which we are ourselves speaking.

Nigh thee signifies (in the mouth of Moses) : of possible, and even easy accomplishment. The term is explained by the two expressions : *in thy mouth* and *in thy heart*, the former of which means : easy to be learned and repeated ; the second : easy to be loved ; of course : in communion with Jehovah and by the aid of His Spirit both promised to faithful Israelites.

"Such expressions, says Paul, are exactly those which find their full reality when they are applied to the *word of faith*, which forms the subject of gospel preaching." If faith is an emotion of the heart, and its profession a word of invocation: Jesus Lord! is it possible to realize this formula of Moses: *in thy mouth* and *in thy heart*, better than is done by the word of faith?—Salvation thus appears to us as a perfectly ripe fruit which divine grace places before us, and on which we have only to put the hand of faith. To Christ belongs the *doing*; to us the *believing*. This idea of the absolute nearness of the finished salvation is *analyzed* in vv. 9 and 10 (starting from the expressions of ver. 8), and *justified* once more by a scriptural quotation (ver. 11), which contains at the same time the transition to the following passage.

Vv. 9, 10. "*Seeing that if thou shalt confess with thy mouth the Lord Jesus, and shalt believe in thine heart that God hath raised Him from the dead, thou shalt be saved. For with the heart man believeth unto righteousness; and with the mouth confession is made unto salvation.*"—The two terms: *confessing with the mouth* and *believing with the heart*, reproduce the ideas *in thy mouth* and *in thy heart*, of ver. 8. These are the two conditions of salvation; for while faith suffices to take hold of the finished expiation, when this faith is living, it inevitably produces profession,[1] and from this follows incorporation into the flock already formed, by means of invocation and baptism. *Profession* is put first here, in keeping with the words of Moses (ver. 8: *in thy mouth*); the order is that which from the external ascends to the internal; it reminds us that profession would be nothing without faith.—The object of the profession is the title *Lord* given to Christ, as is done in the invocation by which we publicly declare ourselves subjects; comp. 1 Cor. xii. 3 (according to the true reading). Here again we find the idea of ver. 6, that of the glorified Christ. The same relation between the sovereignty of Christ and the Christian profession appears in Phil. ii. 9-11: "Wherefore God hath supremely exalted Him ... that every tongue should confess that He is Lord." This allusion to ver. 6 proves clearly that the reference there was not to the incarnation; for Jesus is called by the title of Lord, as the glorified, and not as the pre-existent Christ.—On the other hand, the special object of *faith* is Christ risen. The reason is clear: it is in the external fact of the resurrection that faith apprehends its essential object, the moral fact of justification; comp. iv. 25.—Paul concludes this long sentence with a brief summary word: σωθήσῃ, *thou shalt be saved*, as if he would say: After that all is done. Ver. 10 demonstrates in fact that these conditions once complied with, salvation was sure.

Ver. 10. The idea of *salvation* is analyzed; it embraces the two facts: *being justified* and *being saved* (in the full sense of the word). The former is especially connected with the act of *faith*, the latter with that of *profession*. Paul, in expressing himself thus, is not swayed, as De Wette believes, by the love of parallelism. There is in his eyes a real distinction to be made between *being justified* and *being saved*. We have already seen again and again, particularly in chap. v. 9 and 10, that justification is something of the present; for it introduces us from this time forth into reconciliation with God. But salvation includes, besides, sanctification and glory. Hence it is that while the former depends only on faith, the latter implies persevering fidelity in the profession of the faith, even to death and to glory. In this ver. 10, Paul returns to the natural and psychological order, according to which faith precedes profession. This is because he is here expounding his thought, without any longer binding himself to the order of the Mosaic quotation. And to put, as it were, a final period to this whole passage, the idea of which is the perfect freeness of salvation, he repeats once

---

[1] The translation conforms to the original French, but it is far better to use the word *confession*, by which one avoids the appearance of forwardness or ostentation thought by many to inhere in the fact of making *profession*.—T. W. C.

more the passage of Isaiah which had served him as a point of departure (ix. 33).

Ver. 11. *"For the Scripture saith, Whosoever believeth on Him shall not be confounded."*—That is to say, it suffices to believe in Him who has fulfilled all, to be saved exactly as if one had fulfilled all himself. Here again the apostle quotes according to the LXX. (see on ix. 33). The most miserable of believers will not be deceived in his hope, if only he believes. The apostle here adds the word πᾶς, *every one, whosoever*, which was not authentic (ix. 33), but which is not wanting in any document in our verse. He might, indeed, deduce it with reason from the idea of the verse taken as a whole. Yet he does not add it by accident ; for with the idea of the *freeness* of salvation he proceeds to connect that of its *universality*. This was the second point to which the ignorance of the Jews extended, and one of the two causes which rendered their rejection necessary for the execution of God's plan. Imagining that salvation was bound up with the fulfilment of the ordinances of the law, they monopolized it to their advantage, consenting to share it only with those of the Gentiles who would accept circumcision and the Mosaic dispensation, and thereby become members of the people of Israel. Through this conception, they came into conflict with the mind of God, which had in view the preaching of a free salvation to the whole world, and consequently the abolition of the legal system. This divine universalism, with its consequence, the free preaching of the gospel to all men, is the subject of the following passage. By introducing the word πᾶς, *every one, whosoever* (ver. 11), into the saying of Isaiah, the apostle announces this new idea which he proceeds to develop.

Vv. 12–21

Paul has justified the matter of his preaching, salvation by grace; he now justifies its *extension*. Not that, as Baur, Holsten, etc., think, he wishes thereby to remove the scruples of the Judeo-Christian conscience against his apostleship among the Gentiles ; but—as the context says clearly enough—to indicate the second point in regard to which the Jews have showed themselves *ignorant* (ver. 4) as to the plan of God, and because of which they have brought on themselves the rejection with which they are overtaken. When man would put himself against the plan of God, God does not stop ; He sets aside the obstacle. Such is the connection of ideas which leads to the following passage.

Vv. 12, 13. *"For there is no difference between the Jew and the Greek: for there is one and the same Lord for all, rich unto all that call upon Him. For whosoever shall call upon the name of the Lord shall be saved."*—Salvation being *free*, there is no longer any restriction to its application : it is necessarily *universal*. It is this logical consequence which the apostle expounds (ver. 12), and which he confirms (ver. 13) by a new Scripture passage.—What formed the separation between the two fractions of mankind, the Jews and the Greeks, was the law (Eph. ii. 14, the μεσότοιχον, the *partition wall*). This wall once broken down (as has just been proved) by the work of the Messiah, mankind no longer forms more than a single social body, and has throughout *the same Lord*, and a Lord *rich* enough to communicate the blessings of salvation to this whole multitude on one single condition : the *invocation* of faith. Israel had never imagined anything like this ; and yet it was so clearly announced, as is proved by ver. 13.—In the second proposition of ver. 12, the subject might be the pronoun ὁ αὐτός, *the same:* "the same (being) is Lord of all." It seems to me, however, more natural to join the word κύριος, *Lord*, to the subject, and then to understand it as the predicate : "The same Lord is (Lord) of all." See the same construction

ii. 29. In any case, there is no reason for making the participle πλουτῶν, *who is rich*, the principal verb in this sense : "The same Lord *is* rich for all ;" for the essential idea is not that of the Lord's riches, but that of His *universal* and identical sovereignty over all men. To us this idea is commonplace ; it was not so at the beginning. It strikes St. Peter like a sudden flash the first time he gets a glimpse of it (Acts x. 34-36).—The condition of *invocation* recalls the idea developed above of *profession* (the ὁμολογία) in vv. 9 and 10. The true profession of faith is, in fact, this cry of adoration : Lord Jesus ! And this cry may be equally uttered by every human heart, Jewish or Gentile, without the need of any law. Behold how the universalism founded on faith henceforth excludes the dominion of law.—The idea : *rich unto all*, establishes the full equality of believers in their participation of the blessings of salvation. The common Lord will give not less abundantly to one than to another ; comp. John i. 16 : " and of his fulness have *all* we received."

Ver. 13. Joel (ii. 32) had already announced this new fact : that salvation would depend only on the believing invocation of the name of Jehovah in His final Messianic manifestation. Legal rights had vanished from before his eyes ; there remained the adoration of Jehovah in His supreme revelation. Paul applies with full right this prophetic word to the coming of Jesus. Now, if the invocation of the name of Jehovah, revealed in the person of the Messiah Jesus, is to be the means of salvation for all, what follows therefrom ? The need of a universal preaching of the name which must be invoked by all.

Vv. 14, 15. "*How then shall they call*[1] *on Him in whom they have not believed? And how shall they believe*[2] *in Him of whom they have not heard? And how shall they hear*[3] *without a preacher? And how shall they preach,*[4] *except they be sent, as it is written, How beautiful are the feet of them that publish peace,*[5] *who announce*[6] *good things!*"—No invocation without faith ; no faith without hearing ; no hearing without preaching ; no preaching without sending. A universal apostolate is therefore the necessary corollary of a free and universal salvation. Such are the contents of our two verses, which are directed, not against Judeo-Christian prejudices, but against the ignorance of Israel, the final result of which was necessarily their rejection. Paul points out to the Jews, who took offence at the wide and universal character of his apostleship, the internal necessity on which it was based, and the positive prophetical texts which justified it. We are therefore still at the development of this theme : The ignorance of Israel the cause of their rejection.

And first, no invocation without faith. It is difficult to decide between the T. R. ἐπικαλέσονται, *shall they call on*, and the Alex. and Greco-Latin texts : ἐπικαλέσωνται, *shall they be able to call on*. This same variant reappears in the following verbs, and that without the critical authorities being consequent with themselves. The simple future is more natural, though the subjunctive may easily be defended.—No faith without the hearing of the gospel message. The pronoun οὗ, *whom*, presents a difficulty ; for the meaning is : "Him *whom* they have not heard." Now, men cannot hear Jesus Christ. Meyer answers, that they can hear Him by the mouth of His messengers : " whom they have not heard *preaching* by His apostles." But could this idea be left to be wholly understood ? Hofmann gives to οὗ a local meaning : *in the place where:* "How could He be invoked *in the place where* men have not heard (Him spoken of) ?" But the ellipsis of the last words would be very marked. It seems to me simpler to apply the

---
[1] T. R. reads, with K L P : επικαλεσονται ; all the others : επικαλεσωνται.
[2] T. R. reads, with A K L : πιστευσουσιν ; all the others : πιστευσωσιν.
[3] T. R. reads, with L : ακουσουσιν ; B : ακουσωσιν ; all the others : ακουσονται.
[4] T. R. says, with many Mnn. : κηρυξουσιν ; all the other Mjj. : κηρυξωσιν.
[5] א A B C omit the words των ευαγγελιζομενων ειρηνην.
[6] A B C D E F G omit the article τα before αγαθα.

pronoun οὗ to Jesus, not as *preaching* (Meyer), but as *preached ;* comp. Eph. iv. 21 : "If at least ye *have heard Him*, and have been taught by Him." It is true the pronoun which is the object of *have heard*, in this passage, is in the accusative (αὐτόν), and not, as here, in the genitive. But this difference is easily explained ; the act referred to in Ephesians is one of the understanding which penetrates the object, while here it is only a simple hearing, the condition of faith.

Ver. 15. No preaching without sending. Paul is not thinking here of some human association sending out missionaries. The term ἀποσταλῶσιν, *be sent*, evidently alludes to the *apostleship* properly so called, the normal mission established by the Lord Himself by the sending of the apostles. This mission included in principle all subsequent missions. At this thought of a universal apostleship the feeling of the apostle rises ; he sees them, those messengers of Jesus, traversing the world, and, to the joy of the nations who hear them, sowing everywhere the good news. The passage quoted is taken from Isa. lii. 7. A similar saying is found in Nahum (i.15), but in a briefer form : "Behold upon the mountains the feet of him that publisheth peace." In this prophet the saying applies to the messenger who comes to announce to Jerusalem the fall of Nineveh. In Isaiah, it is more in keeping with the text of Paul, and refers more directly to the preaching of salvation throughout the whole world. This message of grace is to be the consequence of the return from the captivity. The point of time referred to is when, as Isaiah says, xl. 5, "all flesh shall see the salvation of God." The words : "of them that publish peace," are wrongly omitted by the Alex. mss. The copyist has confounded the two εὐαγγελιζομένων, and thus omitted the intermediate words. It cannot be supposed that it is the T. R. and its documents which have added these words ; for they would have been copied more exactly from the text of the LXX. (comp. the substitution of the εἰρήνην for the ἀκοὴν εἰρήνης).[1] Besides, this is one of the passages in which Paul designedly abandons the translation of the LXX. to conform his quotation to the Hebrew text, the first words of which were utterly misrendered by the Greek version : ὡς ὥρα ἐπὶ τῶν ὀρέων, *as fair weather on the mountains* . . . The apostle at the same time allows himself some modifications even of Isaiah's text. He rejects the words : on the *mountains*, which did not apply to the preaching of the gospel ; and for the singular : *him that publisheth*, he substitutes the plural, which better suits the Christian apostleship.—We must naturally contrast the terms *peace* and *good things* (in our [French] translations : *good news*) with the establishment of the legal dispensation throughout the whole world ; comp. Eph. ii. 27, the thought and even expressions of which are so similar to those of our passage. If, with three Mjj., we read the article τά before ἀγαθά (*the* good things, instead of good things), Paul makes express allusion to those well-known foretold blessings which were to constitute the Messianic kingdom.

Such was to be the end of the old covenant : not the extension of the law to all nations, but a joyful and universal proclamation of peace and of heavenly grace on the part of a Saviour rich unto all. And if Israel had known the part assigned them, instead of making themselves the adversaries of this glorious dispensation, they would have become its voluntary instruments, and transformed themselves into that army of apostles who are charged with publishing the mercies of God. This divine plan was frustrated through their ignorance, both of the real nature of salvation and of its universal destination. Such is the force of the following verses.

Vv. 16, 17. "*But they have not all obeyed the gospel ; for Esaias saith, Lord, who hath believed our message* (prédication) ? *So then faith cometh of*

---

[1] The shorter reading rests on the four great uncials, and is preferred by all the recent editors.—T. W. C.

hearing, and hearing by the word of God."[1]—The word ἀλλά, *but*, contrasts strongly what has been produced (by the fact of Jewish unbelief) with with what should have been the result, faith and the salvation of Israel first of all.—Πάντες, *all*, denotes the totality of those who hear the word ; and the exception indicated by the οὐ πάντες, *not all*, applies in the context to the mass of the Jewish people who have formed an exception to the general faith which the gospel was finding in the world. The term : *have not obeyed*, reminds us of that in ver. 3 : *have not submitted themselves*. There is disobedience in not accepting what God offers. The term *gospel* (*evangel*) reproduces the word *evangelizing* (publishing good tidings), ver. 15.—But that was to be expected (*for*). This disobedience was in fact foreseen and proclaimed, Isa. liii. 1, without, however, the guilt of Israel being thereby diminished, divine foreknowledge not annulling human liberty.—Isaiah in this passage proclaims the unbelief of the people of Israel in regard to the Messiah, giving a description of His entire appearance in His state of humiliation and pain. He well knew that such a Messiah would not answer to the ambitious views of the people, and would be rejected by them. The subject of the unbelief thus proclaimed is not his prophecy only, but above all the fact in which it is to be realized.—The word ἀκοή, which we translated by *our message* signifies : *our hearing*, and may denote either : what we (prophets) hear from the mouth of God, and proclaim to you, Jews ; or : what you (Jews) hear *from us* (by our mouth). The second meaning is certainly more natural, and agrees better with the meaning of the same word in ver. 17.—In quoting this saying, the apostle has in mind not only the unbelief of the Jewish people in Palestine in regard to the preaching of the apostles, but also that of the synagogues of the whole world in relation to his own.

Ver. 17. There was no logical necessity obliging the apostle to return to the two ideas contained in this verse, and already expressed in ver. 14. But he takes them up again in passing, as confirmed by the words of Isaiah just quoted, and to give occasion more clearly to the objection about to follow in ver. 18. Ἄρα : *so then* (precisely as I was saying).—The meaning of ἀκοή, *hearing*, is not modified in passing from ver. 16 to ver. 17. It is still the hearing of what is preached as from God ; only Paul here distinguishes between the two ideas of *hearing* and *preaching* (*the word of God*), which were blended in the first of these two terms, ver. 16, in the passage of Isaiah (in consequence of the complement ἡμῶν, *of us* [*our*], prophets and apostles). It is unnecessary, therefore, to apply the expression *word of God*, as Meyer would, to *the command* by which God sends the preachers. This meaning has not the slightest support in the words of Isaiah, and it is contrary to the use of the term ῥῆμα, *word*, in vv. 8, 9, where it denotes the work of salvation as preached. It must be the same here. Ἐκ, *of* : faith *is born* of hearing ; διά, *by* : hearing *is wrought by* the word preached.—The complement *of God* in the T. R. denotes the *author* of the word, while the complement *of Christ* in the Alex. and Greco-Lat. reading would express its subject. The first reading agrees better with the context.[2]—The question is therefore relatively to the unbelief of the Jews : Has this double condition been fulfilled toward them ? If not, here would be a circumstance fitted to exculpate them, and to throw back on God the blame of their unbelief and rejection. The apostle does not fail, before closing, to raise this question.

Ver. 18. "*But I say, Have they not heard ? Yea, much more, their sound went into all the earth, and their words unto the ends of the world.*"—It is not God who has failed in His part. No ; they who have not believed (the majority of Israel) cannot excuse themselves by saying that the mission,

---
[1] T. R., with A K L P, Syr., reads θεου ; ℵ B C D E: Χριστου ; F G omit all regimen.
[2] But the second is much better sustained.—T. W. C.

which is an essential condition of faith, was not carried out in their case. As (according to Ps. xix. 1 et seq.) the heavens and their hosts proclaim God's existence and perfections to the whole universe, and, mute as they are, make their voice re-echo in the hearts of all men; so, says St. Paul, with a sort of enthusiasm at the memory of his own ministry, the voice of the preachers of the gospel has sounded in all countries and in all the cities of the known world. There is not a synagogue which has not been filled with it; not a Jew in the world who can justly plead ignorance on the subject.—Μὴ οὐκ ἤκουσαν: "It is not, however, the case that they have not heard, is it? Evidently the apostle is speaking of *those who have not believed*, consequently of the Jews. How can Origen and Calvin think here of the Gentiles? It is the case of the Jews which is being pleaded. The pronoun αὐτῶν, *their* (voice), refers not to the subject of the previous sentence, but to that of the sentence of the Psalm quoted by Paul: *the heavens*.—No one certainly will think that Paul meant here to give the explanation of this passage; it is an application of the Psalmist's words, which is still freer than that made of the passage from Deut. in vv. 6–8.

The apostle has just advanced, and then refuted, a first excuse which might be alleged in favor of the Jews; he proposes a second, the insufficiency of which he will also demonstrate.

Ver. 19. "*But I say, Did not Israel know?*[1] *First Moses saith, I will provoke you to jealousy by a people who are not a people, by a foolish nation I will anger you.*"—Μὴ οὐκ: "It is not the case, however, is it, that Israel did not know?" *Know* what, then? Critics answer the question differently. Some, from Chrysostom to Philippi and Hofmann, say: The gospel. But what difference in that case would there be between this excuse and the former? Philippi seeks to evade this difficulty by explaining the verb ἔγνω not in the sense of *know*, but in the sense of *understand*: "Is it credible that Israel did not understand what the Gentiles apprehended at once (the gospel)?" But in that case the answer would be: "Yes, certainly it is credible, for it is the fact." Now the form of the question (with μή) admits only of a negative answer. The object of the verb *did know* ought naturally to be taken from what precedes; it is therefore the essential idea of this whole passage, the universality of the preaching of the gospel.[2] Paul asks: It is not, however, the case, is it, that Israel did not know what was coming? that they were taken by surprise by this sending of the message of grace to the Gentiles throughout the whole world, as by an unexpected dispensation? If it were so, this might form an excuse for them. But no; Moses even (ver. 19), and again more distinctly Isaiah (vv. 20, 21), had warned them of what would happen, so that they cannot excuse themselves by saying that they are the victims of a surprise. The sequence and progress of the argument are thus vindicated in a way which is perfectly natural and well marked. It is not even necessary to introduce here, with Ewald and several others, the more special idea of the transference of the kingdom of God from the Jews to the Gentiles.—Moses is called *first* relatively to Isaiah (following verse), simply because he preceded him. Hofmann has attempted to connect this epithet with Israel: "Did Israel not hear the gospel *first*, as was their right?" But the answer would require to be affirmative; and this is excluded by the μή. It is clear that what Paul is concerned to bring out by this word *first* is not the simple fact of the priority of Moses in time to Isaiah, but the circumstance that from the very opening of the sacred volume the mind of God on the point in question was declared to Israel.— The words quoted are found in Deut. xxxii. 21: "As Israel have provoked the Lord to jealousy by worshipping that which is not God, so the

---

[1] T. R., with L, Syr., puts Ισραηλ after ουκ εγνω, while the rest put it before these words (after μη).
[2] So Fritzsche, DeWette, Meyer, Alford, Shedd, Riddle.—T. W. C.

Lord in His turn will provoke them to jealousy by those who are not His people." It is inconceivable how commentators like Meyer can apply these last words to the remains of the Canaanites whom the Israelites had allowed to remain among them, and whom God proposed to bless to such a degree as to render the Israelites jealous of their well-being. Such are the exegetical monstrosities to which a preconceived system of prophetical interpretation may lead. Moses certainly announces to the Jews in these words, as Paul recognizes, that the Gentiles will precede them in the possession of salvation, and that this will be the humiliating means whereby Israel themselves shall require at length to be brought back to their God.—The former of the two verbs (παραζηλοῦν) means that God will employ the stimulant of *jealousy;* and the latter (παροργίζειν), that this jealousy will be carried even to *anger;* but all in view of a favorable result, the conversion of Israel. The words : *by those who are not a people,* have been understood in the sense : that the Gentiles are not strictly *peoples,* but mere assemblages of men. This idea is forced, and foreign to the context. We must explain : *those who are not a people,* in the sense : those who are not a people, par excellence, *my* people.

What Moses had only announced darkly in these words, Isaiah proclaimed with open mouth. He declares unambiguously : God will one day manifest Himself to the Gentiles by a proclamation of grace, while the Jews will obstinately reject all the blessings which shall be offered to them.

Vv. 20, 21. *" But Esaias is very bold, and saith, I was found[1] of them that sought me not; I was made manifest unto them that asked not after me. But to Israel he saith, All the day long I have stretched forth my hands unto a disobedient and gainsaying people."*—'Ἀποτολμᾷ : " he declares without mincing matters." The passage quoted is Isa. lxv. 1. Most modern critics apply this saying of Isaiah to the *Jews* who did not seek the Lord, while Paul applies it to the Gentiles. Hofmann, while starting from the prevailing explanation, seeks to justify Paul's quotation ; but without success. Meyer acknowledges the difference between the two interpretations, Paul's and that of modern exegesis. But, he says, Paul saw in unbelieving Israel *a type* of the Gentile world. This solution is impossible ; for, as we shall see, Isaiah distinctly *contrasts* those of whom he is speaking in ver. 1 with unbelieving Israel, ver. 2. We think that the simple and unbiassed study of the passage from Isaiah leads irresistibly to the conclusion that the prophet really meant to speak in ver. 1 of the Gentiles reaching salvation notwithstanding their ignorance, and to contrast them with the Jews in their obstinate rebellion against God, who had long revealed Himself to them, ver. 2. In fact—1. The term *goï* expressly distinguishes as *Gentiles* those to whom ver. 1 refers, as the term *am (the people),* in ver. 2, positively describes Israel. 2. This contrast is the more certain that the prophet adds to the term *goï, the nation,* the commentary : " (the nation) which was not called by my name." Could he thus designate Israel ? 3. Is it possible to mistake the contrast established by the prophet between those who, not inquiring after the Lord, whom they do not yet know, find Him because He consents to manifest Himself to them spontaneously (ver. 1), and the people, properly so called, whom for ages He has not ceased to call to Him, who know Him as their God, but who obstinately reject His mercies (ver. 2) ? Let us add, 4, that the two ideas of the future unbelief of the Jews in relation to the Messiah, and of the calling of the Gentiles to fill for the time their place in the kingdom of God, are very distinctly expressed elsewhere in Isaiah ; so lii. 13–15 : the kings and peoples of the Gentiles, who had not heard any prophecy, believe in the suffering and exalted Messiah, while the Jews reject Him, though to them He had been clearly foretold (liii. 1) ; so again xlix. 4 :

---

[1] B D F G read εν after εὑρέθην.

the failure of the Messiah's work in Israel, forming a contrast to the rich indemnification which is bestowed on Him through the conversion of the Gentiles (ver. 6). It is clear that the alleged advances in the interpretation of the prophets may, after all, on certain points, be only retrogressions.

The thought of vv. 20 and 21 is analogous to that of x. 30 and 31. The unsophisticated ignorance and corruption of the Gentiles are an easier obstacle for the light of God to dissipate than the proud obduracy of the Jews, who have for long been visited by divine grace. The words: *I was made manifest*, are intended by the apostle to refer to that universal preaching which is the idea of the whole passage.

Ver. 21. What leads up to this verse is the lively feeling of the contrast between the conduct of Israel and that of the Gentiles. It sums up the idea of the whole chapter: the obstinate resistance of Israel to the ways of God. The Lord is represented, Isa. lxv. 2, under the figure of a father who, from morning to evening, stretches out his arms to his child, and experiences from him only refusal and contradiction. It is thus made clear that the apostle in no wise puts the rejection of Israel to the account of an unconditional divine decree, but that he ascribes the cause of it to Israel themselves.[1]—The preposition πρός might signify: *in relation to*, as in Luke xix. 9 and xx. 19. But yet the natural meaning is *to;* and this meaning is quite suitable: "He saith to Israel." For if in the prophetical discourse God spoke of Israel in the third person, in the book written for the people it is to them that he addresses this saying; comp. iii. 19.—*All the day long:* do not these words designate the whole theocratic epoch, which, in the eyes of the Lord, is like a long day of labor in behalf of His people? But what a response have they made to such fidelity! The words καὶ ἀντιλέγοντα, *and gainsaying*, were added to the Hebrew text by the LXX. They characterize the hair-splittings and sophisms whereby the Israelites seek to justify their persevering refusal to return to God; comp. in the Book of Malachi the refrain: "And ye say" . . . !

Thus Israel, blinded by the privileges bestowed on them, sought only one thing: to preserve their monopoly, and for this end to perpetuate their law (ver. 4). They have hardened themselves, consequently against the two essential features which constituted the Messianic dispensation, a free salvation (vv. 5-11) and a salvation offered to all by universal preaching (vv. 12-17). And to extenuate this sin, they are wholly without excuse. The messengers of salvation have followed them to the very ends of the earth to offer them grace as well as the Gentiles; neither had God failed to warn them beforehand, from the very beginning of their history, of the danger they ran of seeing themselves outstripped by the Gentiles (vv. 18-20). All to no purpose. They have held on in their resistance . . . (ver. 21). After this, is not the case fully ripe for trial? Do not the facts attest that it is not God who has arbitrarily excluded them, but themselves who have placed God under the necessity of pronouncing their rejection?

Yet there is a mercy which, where the sin of man abounds, yet more abounds. It has a last word to speak in this history. Its work toward the rebellious people seems closed; but it is far from being so. And chap. xi. proceeds to show us how God, in the overflowing of His grace, reserves to Himself the right to make this severe and painful dispensation issue in the most glorious result.

---

[1] We know of no Calvinist who would refuse assent to this proposition.—T. W. C.

TWENTY-THIRD PASSAGE (11:1-36)

God's Plan in Israel's Rejection

The apostle has proved in chap. ix. that when God elected Israel, He did not lose the *right* one day to take the severest course against them, if if it should be necessary. Then he has showed in chap. x. that *in fact* there was a real ground and moral necessity for this measure. He proceeds, finally, to establish in chap. xi. that it was taken with all due regard to the position of this people, and within the limits in which it should subserve the salvation of mankind and that of Israel themselves.

This chapter embraces the development of two principal ideas, and then a conclusion. The *first* idea is this : The rejection of Israel is not total, but *partial* (vv. 1-10). It bears only on that portion referred to in the demonstration of God's right, given in chap. ix. The *second:* This partial rejection even is not eternal, but *temporary* (vv. 11-32). For after it has served the various ends which God had in view in decreeing it, it shall come to an end, and the entire nation shall be restored, and with the Gentiles shall realize the final unity of the kingdom of God. The *conclusion* is a glance at this whole vast plan of God, and the expression of the feeling of adoration which is inspired by the contemplation, vv. 33-36.

Vv. 1-10

The *partial* character of the rejection of God's people is proved, first by the conversion of St. Paul himself (ver. 1) ; then by the existence of a whole Judeo-Christian church (vv. 2-6). And if this church does not contain the entire Jewish people, it is the effect of a judgment of a partial hardening rendered necessary by the moral state of the people (vv. 7-10).

Ver. 1. "*I say, then, Hath God cast away His people? Let it not be! For I also am an Israelite, of the seed of Abraham, of the tribe of Benjamin.*"— From all that preceded, chaps. ix. and x., the reader might have concluded that God had completely and finally broken with all that bore the name of Israel ; hence the *then*.—The form of the question is such ($\mu\acute{\eta}$) that only a negative answer can be expected. This is likewise indicated by the pronoun $\alpha\mathring{v}\tau o\tilde{v}$, *his*, which of itself implies the moral impossibility of such a measure.—The expression *His people* does not refer, as some have thought, to the *elect* part of the people only, but, as the expression itself shows, to the *nation* as a whole. It is evident, indeed, that the rest of the chapter treats not of the lot of the Israelites who have believed in Jesus, but of the lot of the nation in its entirety. Thus then, this question of ver. 1 is the theme of the whole chapter.—The apostle takes a first answer, by way of preface, from his own case. Is not he, a Jew of well-approved Israelitish descent, by the call which he has received from above, a living proof that God has not cast away *en masse* and without distinction the totality of His ancient people ? De Wette and Meyer give a wholly different meaning to this answer. According to them, Paul would say : " I am too good an Israelite, too zealous a patriot, to be capable of affirming a thing so contrary to the interests of my people." As if the interests of truth were not supreme, in Paul's view, over national affections ! And what in this case would be meant by the epithets *descendant of Abraham* and *of Benjamin*, which Meyer alleges against our explanation ? May not one, with his civil status as an Israelite perfectly unquestionable, comport himself as a bad patriot ? What Paul means by them is this : " It is nothing my being an Israelite of the purest blood ; God has nevertheless made of me such as you see me, a true believer." Meyer still urges the objection of the exceptional position of a man like Paul ; but the apostle does not confine himself to pleading this personal fact ; he adds to it immediately, from ver. 2 onward, the patent fact of the whole Judeo-Christian portion of the church.—Weizsäcker makes the important remark on this ver. 1 : "Paul could not possibly take his proof from his own person, if the mass of the Christians of Rome were Judeo-Christian, and so themselves the best refutation of the objection raised."

Vv. 2, 3. " *God hath not cast away His people which He foreknew. Or wot ye not what the Scripture saith in the passage about Elijah ; how he maketh intercession to God against Israel :* [1] *Lord, they have killed Thy prophets,* [2] *they have digged down Thine altars, and I am left alone, and they seek my life.*"— The formal denial which begins ver. 2 is intended to introduce the more general proof, the exposition of which begins with the words: *Or wot ye not ?* Several commentators (Or., Aug., Chrys., Luth., Calv., etc.) have explained the words : *whom He foreknew*, as a restriction narrowing the general notion of the people of Israel : "He could undoubtedly cast away the mass of the people, but not the *foreknown* elect who form, strictly speaking, *His people.*" This meaning is inadmissible ; for, as we have already seen in ver. 1, the matter in question here is not the lot of this elect portion, but that of the people as a whole. Is it not of the entire people that the apostle speaks when, in vv. 28 and 29, he says : "*As touching the election*, they are loved for the Father's sake ; for the gifts and calling of God are without repentance ?" These words are the authentic explanation of the expression in ver. 2 : *His people whom He foreknew.* Of all the peoples of the earth one only was chosen and known beforehand, by an act of divine foreknowledge and love, as the people whose history would be identified with the realization of salvation. In all others salvation is the affair of *individuals*, but here the notion of salvation is attached to the *nation* itself ; not that the liberty of individuals is in the least compromised by this collective destination. The Israelites contemporary with Jesus might reject Him ; an indefinite series of generations may for ages perpetuate this fact of national unbelief. God is under no pressure ; time can stretch out as long as He pleases. He will add, if need be, ages to ages, until there come at length the generation disposed to open their eyes and freely welcome their Messiah. God foreknew this *nation* as believing and saved, and sooner or later they cannot fail to be both.

As usual, the form : *or know ye not*, signifies : " Or if ye allege the contrary, do ye forget" . . .—The expression ἐν Ἠλίᾳ, literally, *in Elias*, is a form of quotation frequent in the N. T. (Mark xii. 26 ; Luke xx. 37) and in the Rabbins to denote : " in the passage of the Scriptures which contains the history of Elias."—The preposition κατά can signify nothing else here than *against.* To *intercede against* is a strange expression, but fitted to bring out the abnormal state of the people in regard to whom the prophet could only pray thus, that is to say, protesting before God against their conduct. Comp. 1 Kings xix. 10, 14, 18.

Ver. 3. In the Hebrew text the second clause of the verse is put first ; it is needless to seek an intention for this inversion.—Mention is made of " *altars* of God," though according to the law there was, properly speaking, only one legitimate altar, that of the sanctuary. But the law itself authorized, besides, the erection of altars in the places where God had visibly revealed Himself (Ex. xx. 24), as at Bethel, for example. Moreover, participation in the legitimate altar being interdicted within the kingdom of the ten tribes, it is probable that in such circumstances the faithful ventured to sacrifice elsewhere than at Jerusalem (1 Kings viii. 29).—Meyer interprets

---

[1] T. R. reads here λεγων, with ℵ L, Syr^sch.   [2] T. R. reads here και, with D E L, Syr.

the word *alone* in this sense: "alone of all the prophets." This meaning seems to us incompatible with God's answer. The *seven thousand* are not prophets, but simple worshippers. Elijah, in that state of deep discouragement into which foregoing events had plunged him, no longer saw in Israel any others than idolaters, or believers too cowardly to deserve the name.

Vv. 4, 5. "*But what saith the answer of God unto him? I have reserved to myself seven thousand men, who have not bowed the knee to Baal. Even so then, at this present time also there is a remnant according to the election of grace.*"—Χρηματισμός: the direction of a matter, and hence: a decision of authority; then: a divine declaration, an oracle (Matt. ii. 12).—It is impossible to apply the words: "I have reserved to myself," to the *temporal* preservation of this elect body of pious Israelites, in the midst of the judgments which are soon to burst on Israel. It is in the spiritual sense, as faithful worshippers in the midst of reigning idolatry, that God reserves them to Himself. They are the leaven kept by His faithfulness in the midst of His degenerate people.—It is impossible to understand what leads Hofmann to take κατέλιπον as the third person plural: "*They* (the persecutors) *have left me* seven thousand men." This cannot be the meaning in the Hebrew, where the grammar is opposed to it; and as little the sense meant by Paul, where the words *to myself* and *according to the election of grace*, ver. 5, prove that he is speaking of the action of God Himself. The pronoun *to myself* does not belong to the Hebrew text; it is added by Paul to bring more into relief the settled purpose of grace in this preservation.—The substantive Βάαλ, Baal, is preceded by the feminine τῇ: "*the* (female) Baal." This form is surprising, for Baal, the god of the sun among the Phœnicians, was a masculine divinity, to whom Astarte, the goddess of the moon, corresponded, as the female divinity. By the LXX. the name Baal is sometimes used as feminine, sometimes as masculine. In our passage this version uses it in the latter way. To explain the female form as used here by Paul, it has been thought that Baal was sometimes regarded as a hermaphrodite divinity. But in 1 Sam. vii. 4, we find Baal put along with Astarte, and both in the feminine form. It seems to us more natural simply to understand the feminine substantive εἰκόνι, *the image*, in the sense of: "the statue Baal." Meyer objects that in that case the article τοῦ would be required before Βάαλ. But the Jews took pleasure in identifying false gods with their images, as if to say that the god was nothing more than his material representation. The Rabbins, in this same contemptuous spirit, had invented the term *Elohoth* to designate idols, a feminine plural of Elohim, and several have been thereby led to suppose that our feminine article might be explained by a feeling of the same kind. This explanation is not impossible, but the previous one seems to me the more simple.

Ver. 5. This verse applies the case of the seven thousand to present circumstances. The *remnant*, of whom the apostle speaks, evidently denotes the small portion of the Jewish people who in Jesus have recognized the Messiah. The term λεῖμμα, *remnant*, is related to the preceding verb κατέλιπον, *I have reserved to myself*, *kept*. There is no reference whatever to the members of the Jewish people who shall survive the destruction of Jerusalem, and shall be preserved to go into exile. These form, on the contrary, the rejected portion to whom the words, vv. 7-10, apply.—The three particles which connect this verse with the preceding context: *so*, *then*, *also*, refer, the first to the internal *resemblance* of the two facts, for the same principle is realized in both; the second, to the moral *necessity* with which the one follows from the other in consequence of this analogy. The third simply indicates the addition of a new example to the former.—The words: *according to the election of grace*, might apply to the *individuals* more or less numerous who are embraced in this remnant, now become the nucleus of the church. The word *election* would in that case be explained, as in the case of the elect in general, viii. 29, 30, by the fact of the foreknowledge which God had of their faith. But the matter in question throughout the whole of this chapter is the lot of the Jewish *people* in general; it is therefore to them in their entirety that the idea of the divine election refers; comp. vv. 2 and 28. One thing indeed follows from the election of grace applied to the whole of Israel; not the salvation of such or such individuals, but the indestructible existence of a believing remnant at all periods of their history, even in the most disastrous crises of unbelief, as at the time of the ministry of Elias, or of the coming of Jesus Christ. The idea contained in the words: "according to the election of grace," is therefore this: In virtue of the election of Israel as the salvation-people, God has not left them in our days without a faithful remnant, any more than He did in the kingdom of the ten tribes at the period when a far grosser heathenism was triumphant.

Ver. 6. "*Now, if it is by grace, then is it no more of works; since grace would be no more grace.*"[1]—The apostle wishes to express the idea, that if Israel possess this privilege of always preserving within their bosom a faithful remnant, it is not because of any particular merit they have acquired before God by their works; it is purely a matter of grace on the part of Him who has chosen them.[2] The instant there was introduced into this dispensation a meritorious cause, whether for little or for much, there would be taken away from grace its character of freeness; it would no longer be what it is. Why add this idea here? Because it is only inasmuch as the maintenance of the faithful remnant is a matter of grace, that the rejection of the mass (of which Paul is about to speak, vv. 7-9) is not an injustice. If there were, on the part of Israel as a people, the least merit arising from work as the ground of their election, even that partial rejection, of which the apostle speaks, would be impossible.—The word οὐκέτι, *no more*, should be taken here in the logical sense: the principle of grace being once laid down. The verb γίνεται (literally, not *is*, but *becomes*) should be explained as Meyer does: Grace ceases to show itself as what it is, ceases to *become* in its realization what it is in its essence.

The second proposition, parallel to the former, which is found in the T. R., is entirely foreign to the context, and for this reason alone it must appear suspicious. But it is decidedly condemned by its omission in the greater number of documents, and in particular by the harmony on this point of the Alex. and Greco-Latin texts, excepting the *Vaticanus*. It is impossible to imagine a reason copyists could have had for rejecting it. Volkmar, in order to remain faithful to the *Vatic.* alleges this very fact of the want of relation to the context as that which struck copyists, and gave rise to its rejection. This is to do them too much honor. We should have had much graver and more numerous variants in the N. T. if copyists had proceeded so freely. It is much more probable that a reader composed a proposition parallel and antithetic to the former, and wrote it on the margin, whence it passed into the text. Cases of this kind are frequent.

It is obviously wholly unnecessary, in order to explain this verse, to hold, with the Tübingen school, that the apostle means to refute the Judeo-Christian principle of the mixing up of works and grace. Besides, would not the apostle have addressed himself directly in this case as he does to his Gentile-Christian readers in the passage vv. 13 and 14, which Volkmar himself puts parallel to this?

---

[1] T. R. here reads, with B L, the Mnn. and Syr.: ει δε εξ εργων, ουκετι εστι χαρις, επει το εργον ουκετι εστιν εργον (*but if it be of works it is no more grace, since work would be no more work*). These words are omitted in ℵ A C D E F G P, It. Vulg.; besides this, this sentence presents many variants.

[2] "Human salvation must be ascribed either to man or to God: it cannot be a mixed result of two different incommensurable and incongruous agencies."—Vaughan, *in lo.*—T. W. C.

Let us again remark the correlation between this passage, vv. 1–5, and the preceding, ix. 6–13. The latter referred to the carnal portion of the nation, and proved the right God had to reject them (as much as Ishmael and Esau); the present passage refers to the faithful portion, and establishes the fact that God has not failed to maintain a similar elect number in Israel. These two points of view taken together form the complete truth on the subject.

Reuss finds in this passage two theories placed side by side with one another, but "which logic deems contradictory." The one, he thinks, is that of unconditional *grace*, by which the holy remnant are kept in their fidelity; the other that of *works*, by which Paul explains the rejection of the nation in general. But there is no contradiction between these two points of view; for if the faithfulness of the elect supposes the initiative of grace, it nevertheless implies faith on their part,[1] and if the mass of the nation are rejected, this rejection only arises from their voluntary and persevering resistance to the solicitations of grace.

The apostle put the question whether the present relation between God and Israel was that of an absolute divorce; and he began by answering: no, in the sense that *a portion* at least of Israel have obtained grace, and form henceforth the nucleus of the church. But, he adds—for this is the other side of the truth—it is certainly true that the *greater part* of the people have been smitten with *hardness*. This is what he expounds in vv. 7–10, showing, as his habit is, that this severe measure was in keeping with the antecedents of the theocratic history and the declarations of Scripture.

Vv. 7, 8. "*What then? Israel hath not obtained that which he seeketh for,*[2] *while the election hath obtained it; but the rest were hardened. According*[3] *as it is written, God hath given them a spirit of torpor, eyes that they should not see, and ears that they should not hear, unto this day.*"—By the question: *What then?* Paul means: If Israel are not really rejected, what then? What has happened? As he has elucidated this question in chap. x., he confines himself to summing up in a word all that he had explained above regarding the foolish conduct of Israel. The object of their search, the justification to be obtained from God, having been pursued by them in a chimerical way (by means of human works), they have not attained the end which the elect have reached without trouble by faith. The present ἐπιζητεῖ, *seeketh*, for which there must not be substituted, with the oldest translations (see the critical note), the imperf. *sought*, indicates what Israel has done and is still doing at the very moment when the apostle is writing. —The elect then being once excepted, it is quite true that *all the rest*, οἱ λοιποί, have been rejected, and that in the severest way: a judgment of hardening with which God has visited them. The term πωροῦν, *to harden*, signifies in the strict sense: to deprive an organ of its natural sensibility; morally: to take away from the heart the faculty of being touched by what is good or divine, from the understanding, the faculty of discerning between the true and the false, the good and the bad. The sequel will explain how it is possible for such an effect to be ascribed to divine operation.

Ver. 8. Holy Scripture had already either witnessed to an operation of God in this direction in certain cases, or had raised the foreboding of it in regard to the Jews. So when Moses said to the people after their exodus from Egypt, Deut. xxix. 4: "The Lord hath not given you an heart to perceive, and eyes to see, and ears to hear, unto this day." And yet (ver. 2) "they had seen all that the Lord did before their eyes." All the

---

[1] Such an implication is by no means necessary, nor is it suggested by the words of Paul.—T. W. C.
[2] F G, It. Syr.: επεζητει (*sought*), instead of επιζητει (*seeketh*).
[3] ℵ B: καθαπερ instead of καθως.

wonders wrought in the wilderness they had seen in a sort without seeing them ; they had heard the daily admonitions of Moses without hearing them, because they were under the weight of a spirit of insensibility ; and this judgment which had weighed on them during the forty years of their rejection in the wilderness continued still at the time when Moses spoke to them in the plains of Moab, when they were preparing to enter Canaan : *until this day.* In quoting this remarkable saying, Paul modifies it slightly ; for the first words : "*God hath not given you* a heart to perceive," he substitutes a somewhat different expression, which he borrows from Isa. xxix. 10 : "The Lord hath poured upon you the spirit of deep sleep." The negative form of which Moses had made use ("God hath not given you" . . .) perfectly suited the epoch when this long judgment was about to close : "God hath not yet bestowed on you this gracious gift to this day ; but He is about to grant it at length !" While, when the apostle wrote, the affirmative form ed by Isaiah to express the same idea was much more appropriate : "God hath poured out on you " . . . The state of Israel indeed resembled in all respects that of the people when in Isaiah's time they ran blindfold into the punishment of captivity. Hence it is that Paul prefers for those first words the form of Isaiah to that of Moses.—There is something paradoxical in the expression : *a spirit of torpor ;* for usually the spirit rouses and awakens, instead of rendering insensible. But God can also put in operation a paralyzing force. It is so when He wills for a time to give over a man who perseveres in resisting Him to a blindness such that he punishes himself as it were with his own hand ; see the example of Pharaoh (ix. 17) and that of Saul (1 Sam. xviii. .10).—The term κατάνυξις, which is ordinarily translated by *stupefaction,* and which we prefer to render by the word *torpor,* may be explained etymologically in two ways : Either it is derived from νύσσω, the act of *piercing, rending, striking,* whence there would result, when the blow is violent, a state of stupor and momentary insensibility ; or it is taken to be from νύω, νύζω, νυστάζω, *to bend the head in order to sleep,* whence : *to fall asleep.* It is perhaps in this second sense that the LXX. have taken it, who use it pretty frequently, as in our passage, to translate the Hebrew term *mardema, deep sleep.* This second derivation is learnedly combated by Fritzsche ; but it has again quite recently been defended by Volkmar. If we bring into close connection, as St. Paul does here, the saying of Isaiah with that of Deuteronomy, we must prefer the notion of *torpor* or *stupor* to that of *sleep ;* for the subject in question in the context is not a man who is sleeping, but one who, while having his eyes open and seeing, sees not.—The works of God have two aspects, the one external, the material fact ; the other internal, the divine thought contained in the fact. And thus it comes about, that when the eye of the soul is paralyzed, one may see those works without seeing them ; comp. Isa. vi. 10 ; Matt. xiii. 14, 15 ; John xii. 40, etc. —The apostle adds in the following verses a second quotation, taken from Ps. lxix. 22 and 23.

Vv. 9, 10. "*And David saith, Let their table be made a snare and a trap and a stumbling-block, and* [*so*] *a just recompense unto them ! Let their eyes be darkened, that they may not see ; and bow down their back alway !* "—Paul ascribes this psalm to David, according to the title and Jewish tradition ; he does not meddle with criticism. Is this title erroneous, as is alleged by our modern savants ? They allege vv. 33–36, which close the psalm, and in which we have mention made of the liberated captives who shall rebuild and possess the cities of Judah, expressions which naturally apply to the time of the captivity. But, on the other hand, the author speaks " of that zeal for the house of God which eats him up ;" which supposes the existence of the temple. Nay more, the adversaries who oppress him are expressly designated as members of God's people : they are "his brethren, his mother's children" (ver. 8) ; they shall be blotted out of the book of life" (ver. 28); their name was therefore inscribed in it; they are not the Chaldeans. Finally, what is stronger: those enemies, his fellow-countrymen, enjoy perfect external well-being; while they give the Psalmist, the object of their hatred, gall to drink, they themselves sit at table and sing as they drink strong drink (vv. 22 and 11, 12); a singular description of the state of the Jews in captivity! It must therefore be held that the last verses of the psalm (vv. 33-36) were, like the last and perfectly similar verses of Ps. li. (vv. 18 and 19), added to the hymn later, when the exiled people applied it to their national sufferings.[1] The original description is that of the *righteous Israelite* suffering for the cause of God; and his adversaries, to whom the curses contained in the two verses quoted by Paul refer, are all the enemies of this just one within the theocracy itself, from Saul persecuting David down to the Jewish enemies of Jesus Christ and His Church.—The *table* is, in the Psalmist's sense, the emblem of the material pleasures in which the ungodly live. Their life of gross enjoyments is to become to them what the snares of all sorts with which men catch them are to the lower animals. It is difficult to avoid thinking that the apostle is here applying this figure in a spiritual sense; for the punishment which he has in view is of a spiritual nature; it is, moral hardening. The cause of such a judgment must therefore be something else than simple worldly enjoyment; it is, as we have seen, the proud confidence of Israel in their ceremonial works. The *table* is therefore, in Paul's sense, the emblem of presumptuous security founded on their fidelity to acts of worship, whether the reference be to the table of showbread as a symbol of the Levitical worship in general, or to the sacrificial feasts. These works, on which they reckoned to save them, are precisely what is ruining them.—The Psalmist expresses the idea of ruin only by two terms: those of *snare* and *net* (in the LXX. παγίς, *net*, and σκάνδαλον, *stumbling-block*). Paul adds a third, θήρα, strictly *prey*, and hence: every means of catching prey. This third term is taken from Ps. xxxv. 8 (in the LXX), where it is used as a parallel to παγίς, *net*, in a passage every way similar to that of Ps. lxix. By this accumulation of almost synonymous terms, Paul means forcibly to express the idea that it will be impossible for them to escape, because no kind of snare will be wanting; first the *net* (παγίς), then the weapons of the chase (θήρα), and finally the trap which causes the prey to fall into the pit (σκάνδαλον).—The Hebrew and the LXX., as we have said, contain only two of these terms, the first and the third. Instead of the second, the LXX. read another regimen: εἰς ἀνταπόδοσιν, *for a recompense*. Whence comes this expression? They have evidently meant thereby to render the word *lischelomim, for those who are in security*, which in the Hebrew text is put between the words *snare* and *stumbling-block*. Only to render it as they have done, they must have read *leschilloumim* (probably after another reading). This substantive is derived from the verb *schalam, to be complete*, whence in the Piel: *to recompense*. It therefore signifies *recompense*; hence this εἰς ἀνταπόδοσιν, *for a recompense*, in the LXX. Paul borrows from them this expression; but he puts it at the end as a sort of conclusion: "and so in just retribution." In ver. 10 the apostle continues to apply to the present judgment of Israel (hardening) the expressions of the Psalmist. The reference is to *the darkening* of the understanding which follows on the insensibility of the heart (ver. 9), to such a degree that the Gentiles, with their natural good sense, understand the gospel better than those Jews who have been instructed and cultivated by divine revelation.—The last words: *bow down their reins*, are an invocation; they refer to the state of slavish fear in which the Jews shall be held as long as this judgment of hardening which keeps them outside of the gospel shall last. They are slaves to their laws, to their Rabbins, and even to their God (viii. 15). We must beware of thinking,

---

[1] This is by no means necessary.—T. W. C.

as Meyer does, that this chastisement is their punishment for the rejection of the Messiah. It is, on the contrary, that rejection which is in the apostle's eyes the realization of the doom of hardening previously pronounced upon them. As St. John shows, xii. 37 et seq., the Jews would not have rejected Jesus if their eyes had not been already blinded and their ears stopped. It could only be under the weight of one of those judgments which visit man with a *spirit of torpor*, that any could fail to discern the raying forth of the glory of God in the person of Jesus Christ, as the apostle declares, 2 Cor. iv. 4. In this passage he ascribes the act of blinding to the *god of this world*, who has cast a veil over the spirit of his subjects. This means, as is seen in the book of Job, that God proves or punishes by leaving Satan to act, and it may be by the *spirit of torpor* mentioned in ver. 8, as with that spirit of lying whom the Lord sent to seduce Ahab in the vision of the prophet Micaiah, 1 Kings xxii. 10 et seq. However this may be, the rejection of Jesus by the Jews was the *effect*, not the *cause* of the hardening. The cause—Paul has clearly enough said, ix. 31-33—was the obstinacy of their self-righteousness.

Vv. 11-32

God has not then, absolutely speaking, rejected His people; but it is perfectly true that He has hardened and rejected a portion of them. Yet there are two restrictions to be noted here: This chastisement is only *partial*; and, besides, it is only *temporary*. It is this second idea which is developed in the following passage. It is obvious how far Reuss is mistaken when he calls this second passage, in relation to the former, "a *second* explanation." This critic's constant idea is that of contradictory points of view placed in juxtaposition in the apostle's writing. On the contrary, the following passage is the logical complement of the preceding: "And this chastisement, which has fallen on Israel only partially, is itself only for a time."

This passage includes four sections, having each a distinct subject.

The first, vv. 11-15, points out the two *ends*, the *proximate*, and the *final*, of the rejection of the Jews. The proximate end was to facilitate the conversion of the Gentiles, the final end is to restore the Jews themselves by means of the converted Gentiles, and that to bring down at length on the latter the fulness of divine blessing.

The second section, vv. 16-24, is intended to put the Gentiles on their guard against the pride with which they might be inspired by the position which is made theirs for the present in the kingdom of God, as well as against contempt of the Jews into which they might be carried.

In the third, vv. 25-29, Paul announces positively, as a matter of revelation, the fact of the final conversion of Israel.

Finally, the fourth, vv. 30-32, contains a general view of the course of divine work in the accomplishment of salvation.

It is impossible, in a subject so difficult, to imagine a simpler and more logical order.

Vv. 11-15

Vv. 11, 12. "*I say then, Have they stumbled that they should fall? Let it not be! But by their fall salvation is come unto the Gentiles, for to provoke them to jealousy. Now, if the fall of them be the riches of the world, and the diminishing of them the riches of the Gentiles, how much more will be their fulness!*"—The *then* indicates that this new question is occasioned by the preceding development: "A portion have been hardened; is it *then* forever ?" The question with μή anticipates a negative answer. According to many commentators, the two terms *stumble* and *fall* have almost the same meaning, and they make the question signify : "have they fallen solely for the end of falling ?" But this meaning would have required the adverb μόνον, *only*, and it is contrary besides, to the difference of meaning between the two verbs ; πταίειν, *to stumble*, expresses the shock against an obstacle; πίπτειν, *to fall*, the fall which follows from it. Consequently the meaning can only be this : "Have they stumbled so as to leave forever their position as God's people, and to remain as it were lying on the ground (plunged in perdition) ?" Comp. the figures of *striking against*, ix. 32, and *stumbling*, ver. 9.—"No," answers the apostle, "God has very different views. This dispensation tends to a first proximate aim, namely, to open to the Gentiles the gateway of salvation." According to Reuss, the apostle means to say, God "has for the present hardened the Jews *that* the gospel might be carried to the Gentiles." If by this the author means anew to ascribe to St. Paul the idea of the unconditional decree in virtue of which God disposes of men independently of their moral liberty, he completely mistakes the apostle's thought. It is through the fault of Israel that it has been impossible for the preaching of the gospel to the Gentiles to be carried out except by God's breaking with the chosen people. If, indeed, this people had lent themselves with intelligence and love to God's purpose toward the rest of mankind, they would willingly have let fall their theocratic pretensions ; and, substituting the righteousness of faith for that of the law, they would themselves have become God's instruments in offering to the Gentiles the grace they enjoyed. But as their national pride did not permit them to enter on this path, and as they wished at any cost to maintain their legal system, God was obliged to blind them, so that they should not in Jesus recognize their Messiah. Otherwise the gospel would have been Judaized ; believing Gentiles would have required to become the proselytes of Israel, and this would have been an end of salvation for the world, and of the world for salvation. Moreover, in consequence of the proud contempt of the Jews for the Gentiles, there would have been formed between them and the latter such a relation of enmity, that if Christianity offered itself to the world under cover of this detested Judaism, it would, no doubt, have gained some adherents, but it would have been the object of the antipathy which the Gentile world felt to the Jewish people. In these circumstances, God, who wished the salvation of the world, necessarily required to disentangle the cause of the gospel from that of Judaism, and even to oppose them to one another. And this is what was brought about by the refusal of Israel to recognize Jesus as the Messiah. The preaching of the Christ, delivered by this very separation, was able, free from all hindrance, to take its flight over the world. Once, then, Israel had become by their own fault what they were, God could evidently not act otherwise, if He would save the Gentiles ; but nothing forced Israel to become *such*. There is nothing here, therefore, of an unconditional decree ; it is ever the same law we meet with : God's plan embracing the vagaries of human liberty, and making them turn to its own fulfilment.

But that is not all. Wonderful result ! Israel, having been unwilling to concur with God in saving the Gentiles, must end by being themselves saved through their salvation. It is undoubtedly a humiliation for them to be the last to enter where they should have introduced all others ; but on God's part it is the height of mercy. Here is the more remote end (for which the conversion of the Gentiles becomes a means), which Paul indicates in the words borrowed from the passage of Moses quoted above, x. 19: "*to provoke* them *to jealousy*." Seeing all the blessings of the kingdom, pardon, justification, the Holy Spirit, adoption, shed down abundantly on the Gentile nations through faith in Him whom they have rejected, how can they help saying at length : These blessings are ours ?

And how can they help opening their eyes and recognizing that Jesus is the Messiah, since in Him the works predicted of the Messiah are accomplished ? How shall the elder son, seeing his younger brother seated and celebrating the feast at his father's table, fail to ask that he may re-enter the paternal home and come to sit down side by side with his brother, after throwing himself into the arms of their common father ? Such is the spectacle of which Paul gives us a glimpse in the words : *to provoke them to jealousy.* The sin of the Jews could modify the execution of God's plan, but by no means prevent it.

Ver. 12. The δέ is that of gradation : *well then.* It is a new and more joyous perspective still which the apostle opens up. If the exclusion of the Jews, by allowing the gospel to be presented to the world freed from every legal form, has opened for it a large entrance among the Gentiles, what will be the result of the restoration of this people, if it shall ever be realized ? What blessings of higher excellence for the whole world may not be expected from it ! Thus the apostle advances from step to step in the explanation of this mysterious decree of rejection.—*Their fall* or *their false step :* this expression, which refers back to the term πταίειν, *to stumble,* ver. 11, denotes Jewish unbelief.—By *the riches of the world,* Paul understands the state of grace into which the Gentiles are introduced by faith in a free salvation.—The two abstract expressions *fall* and *world* are reproduced in a more concrete way in a second proposition parallel to the first ; the former in the term ἥττημα, which we translate by *diminishing (reduction to a small number)* ; the latter in the plural word *the Gentiles.* The word ἥττημα comes from the verb ἡττᾶσθαι, the fundamental meaning of which is : *to be in a state of inferiority.* This inferiority may be one in relation to an enemy ; in this case the verb means : *to be overcome* (2 Pet. ii. 19), and the substantive derived from it signifies *defeat (clades).* Or the inferiority may refer to a state fixed on as normal, and below which one falls. The substantive in this case denotes a *deficit,* a fall. Of these two meanings the first is impossible here ; for the enemy by whom Israel would be beaten could be no other than God ; now in the context this thought is inapplicable. The second and only admissible sense may be applied either qualitatively or numerically. In the former case, the subject in question is a level of spiritual life beneath which Israel has fallen ; comp. 1 Cor. vi. 7 : "There is utterly an inferiority, ἥττημα (a moral deficit), among you because ye go to law one with another," and 2 Cor. xii. 13. Applied here, this meaning would lead to the following explanation : "The *moral degradation* of Israel has become the cause of the enriching of the Gentiles." But there is something repugnant in this idea, and, besides, we should be obliged by it to take the substantive πλήρωμα, *the fulness,* which corresponds to it, also in the moral sense : the *perfect spiritual state* to which the Jews shall one day be restored. Now this meaning is impossible in view of ver. 25, where this expression evidently denotes *the totality* of the Gentile nations. We are therefore led by this antithesis to the numerical meaning of ἥττημα, *diminishing to a small number* (of believers) : "If their diminishing as God's people to a very small number of individuals (those who have received the Messiah) has formed the riches of the world, how much more their restoration to the complete state of a people" . . .! But it is important to observe the shade of difference between this and the often repeated explanation of Chrysostom, which applies the word ἥττημα to the believing Jews themselves, which would lead to an idea foreign to the context, namely this : that if so small a number of believing Jews have already done so much good to the world by becoming the nucleus of the church, the entire nation once converted will do more still. The pronoun αὐτῶν (*their*) excludes this sense ; for in the three propositions it can only apply to the same subject, the Jewish people in general (Meyer).—Instead of "the riches *of the world,*" the apostle says the second time "the riches *of the Gentiles;*" because now there presents itself to his mind that indefinite series of Gentile nations who, ever as the preaching of the gospel shall reach them, shall enter successively into the church, and thus fill up the void arising from the reduction of Israel to so small a number of believers.—*Their fulness:* the totality of the then living members of the people of Israel. The term πλήρωμα, used apparently in such different acceptations by the N. T. writers, has but one fundamental signification, of which all the others are only various applications. It always denotes: that with which an empty space is filled (*id quo res impletur*); comp. Philippi simplifying Fritzsche. In the application of this term to the people of Israel, we must regard the abstract notion of a people as the empty frame to be filled, and the totality of the individuals in whom this notion is realized, as that which fills the frame.—From what we have said above, we must set aside meanings of a qualitative nature, such as: "the fulness of the Messianic salvation," or "the restoration of Israel to its normal position," or the state of spiritual perfection to which it is destined (Fritzs., Rück., Hofm.). Neither can the meaning be admitted which Philippi ascribes to the two words ἥττημα and πλήρωμα; he supplies as their understood complement the idea of the kingdom of God, and explains: "the blank produced in the kingdom of God by their rejection," and "the filling up of this blank by their readmission." This is to do violence to the meaning of the genitives αὐτῶν, and to introduce into the text an idea (that of the kingdom of God) which is nowhere indicated.

Vv. 13-15 are a more particular application to St. Paul's ministry of the ideas expounded vv. 11 and 12; for this ministry had a decisive part to play in accomplishing the plan of God sketched in these two last verses; and the feelings with which Paul discharged his apostleship must be in harmony with the course of God's work. This is exactly what he shows in these three verses.

Vv. 13-15. "*For* [1] *I say it to you Gentiles: Inasmuch* [2] *as I am an apostle of the Gentiles, I magnify mine office: if by any means I may provoke to emulation them which are my flesh, and might save some of them. For if the casting away of them be the reconciling of the world, what shall the restoring of them be, but a resurrection from the dead?*"—It is somewhat difficult to decide between the two readings γάρ (*for*) and δέ (*now then*). The authorities are balanced; but it is probable that the δέ, *now,* has been substituted for *for,* because the observation which begins ver. 13 was connected with the preceding verse in this sense: "Now I tell you that (the preceding) specially you Gentiles." And as this connection is decidedly mistaken, and the apostle's observation refers manifestly to what follows (vv. 13-15), there is reason to believe that the true connection is that which is expressed by *for*. And in fact the natural transition from vv. 11 and 12 to vv. 13-15 is this: "What I have just told you of the magnificent effects which will one day be produced among you Gentiles by the restoration of the Jews, is so true that it is even in your interest and as your apostle, the apostle to you Gentiles, that I strive to labor for the salvation of the Jews; for I know all that will one day accrue to you from their national conversion, a true spiritual resurrection (ver. 15)." There is a wholly different and widespread way of understanding the meaning of these three verses. It is to take vv. 13 and 14 as a sort of parenthesis or episode, and to regard ver. 15 as a somewhat more emphatic repetition of ver. 12; comp. for example, vv. 9 and 10 of chap. v. In that case, what the apostle would say in this parenthesis (vv. 13 and 14) would be this: "If I labor so ardently in my mission to the

---

[1] T. R. reads γαρ (*for*), with D E F G L, It., while ℵ A B P, Syr. read δε (*now then*), and C: ουν (*therefore*).
[2] T. R. reads μεν after οσον, with L and Mnn.; ℵ A B C P read μεν ουν; D E F G omit every particle.

Gentiles, it is that I may thereby stimulate my fellow-countrymen, the Jews, to seek conversion." It is the opposite thought from that which we have been expressing. This meaning occurs in almost all the commentaries. But, 1st. It is impossible to understand how Paul could say that *as the apostle of the Gentiles ;* he would rather say it *though* their apostle and *as* a Jew by birth. 2d, After an interruption like that of vv. 13 and 14, it would be unnatural to make the *for* of ver. 15 bear on ver. 12. This is what renders the case so different from that of chap. v. 9, 10. Let us study our text more closely, and we shall certainly be led to the first meaning which we have stated. The emphasis is not on the fact that in laboring for the conversion of the Gentiles he is laboring in the end for that of the Jews—which is undoubtedly true, vv. 13 and 14—but on the fact that in laboring thus for the conversion of the Jews he is in that very way laboring for the good of the Gentiles, who are his proper charge, vv. 13-15.

To you, Gentiles: Baur and his disciples (Volkmar, Holsten), and also Mangold, allege that this style of address embraces only a fraction of the church, the members of Gentile origin, who are only a weak minority. Meyer rightly answers that in that case Paul must have written : Τοῖς ἔθνεσιν ἐν ὑμῖν λέγω, "I address *those of you* who are of Gentile origin." Weizsäcker, in the often quoted work (p. 257), likewise observes with reason, that the form employed being the only direct style of address used to the readers in this whole passage, it is natural to apply it to the entire church ; that one may consequently conclude from these words with the utmost certainty that members of Gentile origin formed the preponderating element in this church. We shall ask further, if in the opposite case Paul could have called the Jews *my flesh,* as speaking in his own name only, while the great majority of his readers shared with him the characteristic of being Judeo-Christians.—And what does the apostle say to those Gentiles who have become believers ? The conjunction ἐφ᾿ ὅσον may signify *as long as,* or *inasmuch as.* It is clear that the notion of time has no application here, and that the second sense is the only possible one ; comp. Matt. xxv. 40. By this expression Paul distinguishes in his own person two men : one, in whose name he is here speaking ; that is, as he says, the *apostle of the Gentiles.* Who is the other ? That is understood of itself, and the following expression : μου τὴν σάρκα, which should be translated by : *my own flesh* (in consequence of the prominent position of the pronoun μου), reveals it clearly enough : it is *the Jew* in him. What does he mean then ? That if as a Jew who has become a believer he certainly feels the desire to labor for the salvation of his fellow-countrymen (*his flesh*), he strives all the more to do so as the apostle of the Gentiles, because the conversion of his people must end in loading the Gentiles with all the riches of the blessings of the gospel. The sequel will explain how (ver. 15). In this connection of ideas there is no doubt that the μέν, which the T. R. reads after ἐφ᾿ ὅσον, and which is rejected by the Greco-Latin reading, belongs really to the text. For this particle is intended to fix and bring out forcibly the character belonging to Paul of apostle to the Gentiles, in opposition to the other which he also possesses. The word is supported, besides, even by the Alexs., which read μὲν οὖν. As to this οὖν, *therefore,* added by the latter, it is evidently, as Meyer himself acknowledges, a gloss, occasioned by the fact that the first proposition was connected with ver. 12, in order to begin afterward a wholly new sentence.

What does Paul understand by the expression : *I magnify mine office?* These words might be applied to the defences which he was constantly obliged to make of his apostleship, to the narratives in which he proclaimed before the churches the marvellous successes which God granted him (Acts xv. 12, xxi. 19 ; 1 Cor. xv. 9, 10). But instead of contributing to bring the Jews to faith (ver. 14), such recitals could only embitter them. It is therefore of the zeal and activity displayed by him in the service of his mission that the apostle is thinking. *To magnify* his ministry as the apostle of the Gentiles, is to convert as many heathens as possible. And thereby at what remoter result is he aiming? He tells us in ver. 14.

Ver. 14. He would try *if in any way* (εἴπως; comp. Phil. iii. 11) he may reach the end, by dint of success, of awakening his people, whom he loves as *his own flesh*, from their torpor, should it only be by jealousy? Here, as in ver. 11, he uses the expression which Moses had employed (x. 19). No doubt he does not deceive himself; he does not reckon on a conversion of Israel *en masse* before the last times; but he would like at least, he adds, to save *some of them*, as first-fruits of the harvest. But we are not at the goal. That even is only a means. The *final* aim is declared in ver. 15.

Ver. 15. In truth, it will not be till the national conversion of Israel take place, that the work of God shall reach its perfection among the Gentiles themselves, and that the fruit of his labor as their apostle will break forth in all its beauty. Such is the explanation of the words of ver. 13: "inasmuch as I am the apostle of the Gentiles." As a Jew, he certainly desires the conversion of the Jews; but he desires it still more, if possible, as the apostle of the Gentiles, because he knows what this event will be for the entire church. It is clear how closely the *for* at the beginning of this verse joins it to vv. 13 and 14, and how needful it is to guard against making these two last a parenthesis, and ver. 15 a repetition of ver. 12. It is also clear how wide of the truth are Bauer and his school, when they find in these verses a clever artifice by which Paul seeks to render his mission among the Gentiles acceptable to the so-called Judeo-Christian church of Rome. According to this interpretation, his meaning would be: "You are wrong in taking offence at my mission to the Gentiles; it is entirely to the profit of the Jews, whom it must end by bringing to the gospel;" an adroit way, if one dared say so, of gilding the pill for them! Not only is such a supposition unworthy of the apostle's character, but it is just the opposite of his real thought.—Here it is as it results from the three verses combined: "To take it rightly, it is as your apostle, you Gentiles, that I labor in seeking to provoke the Jews to jealousy by your conversion; for it is not till they shall be restored to grace that you yourselves shall be crowned with fulness of life." This saying is not therefore a *captatio benevolentiæ* indirectly appealing to Judeo-Christian readers; it is a jet of light for the use of Gentile-Christians.

The term ἀποβολή strictly denotes the act of throwing far from oneself (Acts xxviii. 22: ἀποβολὴ ψυχῆς, *the loss of life*). How is the rejection of the Jews the reconciliation of the world? Inasmuch as it brings down that wall of law which kept the Gentiles outside of the divine covenant, and opens wide to them the door of grace by simple faith in the atonement. —Now, if such is the effect of their rejection, what shall be the effect of their *readmission?* The word πρόσληψις (translated by Osterv. *their recall*, by Oltram. *their restoration*, by Segond, *their admission*) strictly signifies the act of welcoming. When cursed, they have contributed to the restoration of the world; what will they not do when blessed? There seems to be here an allusion to what Christ Himself did for the world by His expiatory death and resurrection. In Christ's people there is always something of Christ Himself, *mutatis mutandis*.—A host of commentators, from Origen and Chrysostom down to Meyer and Hofmann (two men who do not often agree, and who unfortunately concur in this case), apply the expression: *a life from the dead*, to the *resurrection of the dead*, in the strict sense. But— 1st. Why use the expression *a life*, instead of saying as usual ἀνάστασις, *the resurrection?* 2d. Why omit the article before the word *life*, and not say as usual *the* life, life eternal, instead of *a* life? And more than all, 3d. What so close relation could there be between the fact of the conversion of the Jews and that of the bodily resurrection? Again, if Paul confined himself to saying that the second event will closely follow the first, this temporal relation would be intelligible, though according to him the signal for the resurrection is the return of the Lord (1 Cor. xv. 23), and not at all the conversion of Israel. But he goes the length of *identifying* the two facts of which he speaks : " What shall their return be but a life ?" It is evident, therefore, for all these reasons, that the expression : *a life from the dead*, must be applied to a powerful spiritual revolution which will be wrought in the heart of Gentile Christendom by the fact of the conversion of the Jews. So it has been understood by Theoph., Mel., Calv., Beza, Philip., etc. The light which converted Jews bring to the church, and the power of life which they have sometimes awakened in it, are the pledge of that spiritual renovation which will be produced in Gentile Christendom by their entrance *en masse*. Do we not then feel that in our present condition there is something, and that much, wanting to us that the promises of the gospel may be realized in all their fulness; that there is, as it were, a mysterious hindrance to the efficacy of preaching, a debility inherent in our spiritual life, a lack of joy and force which contrasts strangely with the joyful outbursts of prophets and psalmists; that, in fine, the feast in the father's house is not complete . . . why? because it cannot be so, so long as the family is not entirely reconstituted by the return of the elder son. Then shall come the Pentecost of the last times, the latter rain. We are little affected by the objection of Meyer, who alleges that, according to St. Paul, the last times will be times of tribulation (those of Antichrist), and not an epoch of spiritual prosperity. We do not know how the apostle conceived the succession of events; it seems to us that, according to the Apocalpyse, the conversion of the Jews (chap. xi. 13 and xiv. 1 et seq.) must *precede* the coming of the Antichrist, and consequently also Christ's coming again. Paul does not express himself on this point, because, as always, he only brings out what belongs rigorously to the subject he is treating.

Vv. 16-24

The apostle proves in this passage the perfect congruity, from the viewpoint of Israelitish antecedents, of the event which he has just announced as the consummation of Israel's history. Their future restoration is in conformity with the holy character impressed on them from the first; it is therefore not only possible, but morally necessary (ver. 16). This thought, he adds, should inspire the Gentiles, on the one hand, with a feeling of profound regard for Israel, even in their lapsed state (vv. 17, 18); on the other, with a feeling of watchful fear over themselves; for if a judgment of rejection overtook such a people, how much more easily may not the same chastisement descend on them (vv. 19-21)! He finishes with a conclusion confirming the principal idea of the passage (vv. 22-24).

Ver. 16. "*But if the first-fruit be holy, the lump is also holy; and if the root be holy, so are the branches.*"—The Jewish people are *consecrated to God* by their very origin—that is to say, by the call of Abraham, which included theirs (ver. 29).—According to Num. xv. 18-21, every time the Israelites ate of the bread of the land which God had given them, they were first of all to set aside a portion of the dough to make a cake intended for the priests. This cake bore the name of ἀπαρχή, *first-fruits;* it is to this usage the apostle alludes in the first part of our verse. It has sometimes been alleged that he took the figure used here from the custom of offering in the temple, on the 16th Nisan, on the morrow after the Passover, the sacred sheaf gathered in one of the fields of Jerusalem, as first-fruits and as a consecration of the entire harvest. But the subject in question here is a portion of *dough* (φύραμα), which necessarily leads to the first meaning. This cake offered to God's representative impressed the seal of consecration on the entire mass from which it had been taken. What is it that corresponds to this emblem in the apostle's view? Some answer: *the Jews converted* in the first times of the church; for they are the pledge of the final conversion of the whole people. But exactly the same thing might be said of the first Gentile converts, as being the pledge of the successive conversion of all the Gentiles. Now, by this figure Paul's very object is to express a characteristic peculiar to the Jews. Some Fathers (Or., Theod.) apply this emblem to *Christ*, as assuring the conversion of the people from whom He sprang. But this reasoning would apply equally to Gentile humanity, since Jesus is a man, not only a Jew. We must therefore, with the majority of commentators, take these holy first-fruits as *the patriarchs*, in whose person all their posterity are radically consecrated to the mission of being the salvation-people; comp. ix. 5 and xi. 28.

But this figure, by which the entire nation was compared to a lump of dough consecrated to God, did not furnish the apostle with the means of distinguishing between Jews and Jews, between those who had faithfully preserved this national character and those who had obliterated it by their personal unbelief. Thus he is obliged to add a second figure, that he may be able to make the distinction which he must here lay down between those two so different portions of the nation. There is therefore no need to seek a different meaning for the second figure from that of the first.—Origen, again, applies the emblem of the *root* to *Christ*, inasmuch as by His heavenly origin He is the true author of the Jewish people; but this notion of Christ's pre-existence is foreign to the context.—It follows from these two comparisons, that to obtain salvation the Jewish people had only to remain on the soil where they were naturally rooted, while the salvation of the Gentile demands a complete transplantation. Hence a double warning which Paul feels himself forced to give to the latter. And first the warning against indulging pride.

Vv. 17, 18. *"Now, if some of the branches be broken off, and thou, being a wild olive tree, wert grafted in their place, and with them partakest of the root*[1] *and fatness of the olive tree, boast not against the branches; and if thou boast, it is not thou that bearest the root, but the root thee."*—We might give δέ the sense of *but* ("*but* if, notwithstanding their natural consecration, the branches were broken off"); or that of *now*, which is better, as the argument continues down to the inference drawn in ver. 18.—Undoubtedly an event has happened which seems to be in contradiction to this people's character of holiness; a certain number of its members, like branches struck down with an ax, have been rejected. The term *some* indicates any fraction whatever, small or considerable matters not (see on iii. 3).—Σὺ δέ, *and if thou.* Some commentators think that this style of address applies to the Gentile-Christian *church* personified. But in that sense would not the article ὁ have been needed before ἀγριέλαιος, *the wild olive?* Without an article the word is an adjective, and denotes the quality, not the tree itself. Besides, it is not one tree that is engrafted on another. By this style of address, therefore, Paul speaks to *each Christian* of Gentile origin individually, and reminds him that it is in spite of his possessing the *quality* of a wild tree that he has been able to take a place in this blessed and consecrated organism to which he was originally a stranger.—The words ἐν αὐτοῖς, which we have translated: *in their place*, properly signify: *in them*, and may be understood in two ways: either in the sense of *among them*—that is to say, among the branches which have remained on the trunk, converts of Jewish origin—or: *in the place* which they occupied, and, as it were, in the stump which has been left by them, which would apply solely to the branches which have been cut down. The prep. ἐν, *in*, which enters into the composition of the verb, might favor this latter meaning, which is, however, somewhat forced.—Once engrafted on this stem, the wild

---

[1] א B C omit καὶ after ῥίζης; D F G, It. omit the words τῆς ῥίζης καὶ.

branches have become *co-participants* (συγκοινωνοί) of the root. This expression is explained by the following words: *and of the fatness of the olive*, of which the meaning is this: As there mounts up from the root into the whole tree a fruitful and unctuous sap which pervades all its branches, so the blessing assured to Abraham (ἡ εὐλογία τοῦ Ἀβραάμ, Gal. iii. 14) remains inherent in the national life of Israel, and is even communicated by believing Jews to those of the Gentiles who become children of the patriarch by faith; comp. Gal. iii. 5–9. The Alexs. reject the word καί, *and*, after ῥίζης, *root:* "the root *of* the fatness of the olive." It would be necessary in that case to give to the word *root* the meaning of *source*, which is impossible. This reading must therefore be rejected, as well as that of the Greco-Latins, which omit the words: *of the root and of:* "co-participant of the fatness of the olive." The meaning would be admissible; but this reading is only a correction of the text once altered by the Alex. reading.—This passage demonstrates in a remarkable way the complete harmony between St. Paul's view and that of the twelve apostles on the relation of the church to Israel. The Tübingen school persists in contrasting these two conceptions with one another. According to it, the Twelve regarded Christians of Gentile origin as simply members by admission, a sort of *plebs* in the church; while Paul made them members of the new people, perfectly equal to the old. The fact is, that in the view of Paul, as in that of the Twelve, the believers of Israel are the nucleus round which are grouped the converts from among the Gentiles, and God's ancient people, consequently, the flock with which the Gentiles are incorporated. "I have yet other sheep, said Jesus (John x. 16), who are not of this fold; them also I must bring, and there shall be one flock, one Shepherd." Excepting the figure, the thought is identical with our passage.

It has been objected to the figure used here by the apostle, that a gardener never engrafts a wild branch on a stem already brought under cultivation; but, on the contrary, a stem is taken which still possesses all the vigor of the wild state to insert in it the graft of the cultivated tree. There are two ways of answering this objection. It may be said that, according to the reports of some travellers, the course taken in the East is sometimes that supposed by the figure of the apostle. A wild young branch is engrafted in an old exhausted olive, and serves to revive it. But there is another more natural answer, viz. that the apostle uses the figure freely and without concern, to modify it in view of the application. What proves this, is the fact that in ver. 23 he represents the branches broken off as requiring to be engrafted anew. Now this is an impracticable process, taken in the strict sense.

Ver. 18. If it is so, Christians of Gentile origin have no cause to indulge pride as against the natural branches. The true translation would perhaps be: "*Do not despise the branches.* But if, nevertheless, *thou despisest*" . . . Must we understand by *the branches* those *broken off?* Certainly, for it is on them that the look of disdain might most easily be cast by those who had been called to fill their place. Do we not see Christians at the present day often treating with supreme contempt the members of the Jewish nation who dwell among them? But this contempt might easily extend even to Judeo-Christians; and this, perhaps, is the reason why Paul says simply *the branches*, without adding the epithet: *broken off*. It is all that bears the name of Jew which he wished to put under the protection of this warning. As to the idea Fritzsche had of applying this word *branches* to *Christians* of Jewish origin solely, it does not deserve refutation.

Yet the apostle supposes that the presumption of the Gentile-Christian continues, in spite of this warning. This is why he adds: "But if, notwithstanding, thou despisest" . . . We have not to understand a verb such as: *know that* or *think that*. The idea understood, if there is one, is to this effect : "Be it! despise! But this, nevertheless, remains the fact." And what is the fact that nothing can change, and with which such a feeling conflicts? It is, that the salvation enjoyed by this believer has been prepared by a divine history which is one with that of Israel, and that the Christian of Gentile origin enters into possession of a blessing already existing and inherent in this people. As Hodge says: "It is the Jews who are the channel of blessings to the Gentiles, and not inversely." The Gentiles become God's people by means of the Jews, not the Jews by the instrumentality of the Gentiles. In view of this fact, the contempt of the latter becomes absurd and even perilous.

Not only, indeed, should Gentile believers not *despise* the Jews; but if they understand their position rightly, the sight of this rejected people should lead them to tremble for themselves.

Vv. 19-21. "*Thou wilt say then, Branches*[1] *were broken off, that I might be grafted in. Well! because of unbelief they were broken off, and thou standest by faith; be not high-minded,*[2] *but fear! For if God spared not the natural branches, [it may be] that neither will He spare thee.*"[3]—The objection Paul puts in the mouth of his reader is taken from the very answer which he had just made to him in ver. 18; hence the *then:* "Since branches have been cut off the stem to make place for me, who was foreign to it by nature, the preference of God for me appears thereby still more striking than if God had confined Himself to engrafting me on the same stem with them."—The article οἱ, *the*, before the word *branches*, is to be rejected, according to the majority of the documents. Paul means, in reality: "beings who had the character of branches." The particular emphasis resting on the ἐγώ should be remarked; literally: "that *I* on my part should be grafted in." To make place for *me, even me*, God rejected branches!

Ver. 20. Paul grants the fact; but he denies the inference drawn from it. There is no arbitrary favor in God. If the Jews have been rejected, it is in consequence of their unbelief; and if thou fillest their place for the present, it is a consequence of faith—that is to say, of divine grace. For there is no merit in faith, since it consists only in opening the hand to receive the gift of God. The term: *thou standest*, alludes to the favored position of the engrafted branch which now rises on the stem, while those it has replaced lie on the ground.—The reading ὑψηλοφρόνει ought certainly to be preferred to the form ὑψηλὰ φρόνει, which is substituted for it by the Alexs., probably after xii. 16. In the passage 1 Tim. vi. 17, where this word again occurs, there is the same variant.—But it is not enough to avoid self-exaltation; there should be a positive fear.

Ver. 21. May not what has happened to the natural branches, happen to the engrafted branches? There is even here an *a fortiori:* For the engrafted branches being less homogeneous with the trunk than the natural branches, their rejection may take place more easily still, in case of unbelief. The Alex. reading rejects the conj. μήπως, *from fear that;* thus the meaning is: "neither will He spare thee." But the T. R., with the Greco-Latins, reads μήπως before οὐδὲ σοῦ, and should be translated by borrowing from the word *fear* in the preceding verse the notion of fear: "[fear] that He will no more spare thee." It is difficult to believe that a copyist would have introduced this form μήπως, *lest*, which softens the threat; it is more probable that this conjunction should have been omitted. Why? The other variant which the last word of this short proposition presents probably explains the reason. The future φείσεται, *will spare*, which is read in all the Mjj., seemed incompatible with the conj. μήπως, which usually gov-

---

[1] T. R. reads οἱ (*the*) before κλαδοι, with D only and several Mnn
[2] ℵ A B read υψηλα φρονει instead of υψηλοφρονει, which is read by all the others.
[3] T. R. reads μηπως ουδε σου, with D F G L, Syr.; but ℵ A B C P, Or. reject μηπως.—T. R. reads φεισηται, with some Mnn. only; all the Mjj. read φεισεται.

erns the subjunctive. Hence two kinds of corrections in opposite ways: the one (the Alex.) have rejected the conjunction, all the more that it was not dependent on any verb; and the others, the Byz. Mnn., have changed the indicative (φείσεται) into the subjunctive (φείσηται).

Vv. 22–24 derive for believers of Gentile origin the practical application of all they have been reminded of in vv. 17–21.

Ver. 22. *"Behold, therefore, the goodness and severity of God: on them which fell, severity;*[1] *but toward thee, goodness,*[2] *if thou continue in this goodness: otherwise thou also shalt be cut off."*—The readers have just been contemplating two examples, the one of severity, the other of grace; the first, in the person of the Jews; the second, in their own. Hence two lessons to be derived which the apostle entreats them not to neglect. In opposition to χρηστότης, *goodness*, from χρηστός (literally: *that may be handled*), the apostle uses the forcible term ἀποτομία (from ἀποτέμνω, *to cut right off*, to cut short): a rigor which does not bend. We may read in the second clause the two substantives in the nominative with the Alexs., and then we shall have either to understand the verb *is* ("severity is on those who"), which is excessively clumsy, or to make these two words absolute nominatives, as sometimes happens in Greek appositions. But the Received Reading puts these words in the accusative, which is much simpler. It is, besides, sufficiently supported.—In passing to the application of God's two modes of acting which he has just characterized, the apostle begins with the second; and he connects it directly with what precedes by this grave restriction: *"if thou continue in this goodness."* Continuance is effected by the same disposition whereby grace was appropriated at the first, humble faith. Unhappy is the believer for whom grace is no longer grace on the hundredth or the thousandth day, as it was on the first! For the slightest feeling of self-exaltation which may take possession of him on occasion of grace received or of its fruits, destroys in his case grace itself and paralyzes it. There is nothing more for him to expect in this condition than to be himself also cut off from the stem. Καὶ σύ, *thou also*, as well as the Jews. The future passive ἐκκοπήσῃ, *thou shalt be cut off*, abruptly closes the sentence, like the stroke of the axe cutting down this proud branch.—It is but too clear to any one who has eyes to see, that our Gentile Christendom has now reached the point here foreseen by St. Paul. In its pride it tramples under foot the very notion of that grace which has made it what it is. It moves on, therefore, to a judgment of rejection like that of Israel, but which shall not have to soften it a promise like that which accompanied the fall of the Jews.—For the rest, I do not think that any conclusion can be drawn from this passage against the doctrine of an unconditional decree relative to individuals; for the matter in question here is Gentile Christendom in general, and not such or such of its members in particular (see Hodge).

In vv. 23 and 24 the idea of *severity* is applied, as that of *goodness* was in the foregoing verse. As the goodness which the Gentiles have enjoyed may through their fault be transformed into severity, so the severity with which the Jews had been treated may be changed for them into compassionate goodness,—if they consent to believe as the Gentiles formerly did. With the close of this verse the apostle returns to his principal subject, the future of Israel.

Vv. 23, 24. *"And they also, if they abide not still in unbelief, shall be grafted in; for God is able to graft them in again. For if thou wert cut out of the olive tree which is wild by nature, and wert grafted contrary to nature into a good olive tree, how much more shall these, which be the natural branches, be grafted into their own olive tree!"*—Severity to the Jews was a threat to the Gentiles; so the goodness displayed to the Gentiles is a pledge, as it were,

---

[1] ℵ A B C read αποτομια instead of αποτομιαν.
[2] ℵ B C D read χρηστοτης instead of χρηστοτητα.—The same read θεου after χρηστοτης.

of mercy to the Jews. Let them only give up persisting in their unbelief (a contrast to the non-persistence of the Gentiles in faith, ver. 22), and on this one condition the power of God will restore them their place in His kingdom. It will engraft them on Christ, who will become to them a vivifying stem, as well as to the Gentiles. And this transplantation will be effected more easily still in their case than in the case of the Gentiles.

Ver. 24. There is, in fact, between the Jewish nation and the kingdom of God an essential affinity, a sort of pre-established harmony, so that when the hour has come, their restoration will be accomplished still more easily than the incorporation of the Gentiles.—The words: *how much more*, seem to us to signify naturally in the context: "How much more easily." It is objected, no doubt, that one thing is no easier to God than another. That is true in the physical world; but in the moral world God encounters a factor which He Himself respects—moral freedom. The Jewish people having been raised up only with a view to the kingdom of God, will not have an organic transformation to undergo in order to return to it; and if it is objected that a Jew is converted with more difficulty than a Gentile, that proves nothing as to the final and collective revolution which will be wrought in the nation at the end of the times. A veil will fall (1 Cor. iii. 14, 15), and all will be done.

Thus far the apostle has shown the moral congruity of the event which he has in view; now he announces the fact positively, and as matter of express revelation.

Vv. 25-32

Ver. 25 contains the announcement of the fact; vv. 26, 27 quote some prophecies bearing on it; vv. 28, 29 conclude as to Israel; finally, vv. 30-32 sum up the whole divine plan in relation to Israel and to the Gentiles.

Vv. 25, 26a. " *For I would not, brethren, that ye should be ignorant of this mystery, lest ye should be wise in own your conceits:*[1] *that a hardening in part hath befallen Israel, until the fulness of the Gentiles be come in; and so all Israel shall be saved.*"—The form of expression: "I would not that ye should be ignorant," always announces a communication the importance of which the apostle is concerned to impress. The style of address: *brethren*, leaves no room to doubt that the apostle is here speaking to the church as a whole. Now it is indubitable that in vv. 28 and 30 those readers whom he addresses with the word *ye* are of Gentile origin. This proof of a Gentile majority in the church of Rome seems to us incontrovertible.—Paul uses the word *mystery* to designate the fact he is about to announce. He does not mean by this, as might be thought from the meaning this term has taken in ecclesiastical language, that this fact presents something incomprehensible to reason. In the N. T. the word denotes a truth or fact which can only be known by man through a communication from above, but which, after this revelation has taken place, falls into the domain of the understanding. The two notions *mystery* and *revelation* are correlative; comp. Eph. iii. 3-6. The apostle therefore holds directly from above the knowledge of the event he proceeds to announce; comp. 1 Cor. xv. 51 and 1 Thess. iv. 15.—Before stating the fact he explains the object of this communication: "that ye be not wise in your own eyes." The reference here is not, as in ver. 19, to proud thoughts arising from the preference which God seems now to have given to the Gentiles. It is the *wisdom of self* whose inspirations Paul here sets aside. The converted Gentiles composing the church of Rome might form strange systems regarding Israel's rejection and future history. Paul is concerned to fix their ideas on this im-

---

[1] Instead of παρ' εαυτοις, A B read εν εαυτοις; F G : εαυτοις.

portant point, and leave no place in their minds for vain and presumptuous speculations. He borrows his expressions from Prov. iii. 7. Instead of παρ' ἑαυτοῖς, *beside yourselves,* two Alexs. read ἐν ἑαυτοῖς, *within yourselves.* The copyists may possibly have changed the original ἐν (*in*) into παρά, under the influence of the text of the LXX. The meaning is substantially the same.

The contents of the *mystery* are declared in the end of this verse and the first words of the following : "*hardness* is happened." Paul had already pointed out this, ver. 7 ; but he adds : *in part,* ἀπὸ μέρους. This word is explained, as it seems to me, by the expression of ver. 7 : "the *rest* were hardened," and by the term *some,* ver. 17. Hence it follows that we must here give the word *in part* a *numerical* sense. Judgment has not fallen on the *totality* of Israel, but on *a part* only ; such is also the meaning to which we are led by the antithesis of the *all Israel* of ver. 26 ; comp. 2 Cor. ii. 5. It is a mistake in Calvin to apply this word : *to the degree,* of the hardening which according to him still left room for partial blessings ; and in Hofmann, in a more forced way still, to apply it to the *restricted time* during which it is to last.—But even this judgment, which has overtaken one entire portion of the nation, will have an end : to make it cease, God waits till the totality of the Gentile nations shall have made their entry into the kingdom of God. This is the people which should have introduced all the other peoples into it ; and for their punishment the opposite is what will take place, as Jesus had declared : "The first shall be last." It is almost incredible how our Reformers could have have held out obstinately, as they have done, against a thought so clearly expressed. But they showed themselves in general rather indifferent about points of eschatology, and they dreaded in particular everything that appeared to favor the expectation of the thousand years' reign which had been so much abused in their time. Calvin has attempted to give to the conj. ἄχρις οὗ, *until that,* the impossible meaning of *in order that ;* which in sense amounted simply to the idea of vv. 11 and 12. Others gave to this conjunction the meaning of *as long as,* to get this idea : that *while* the Gentiles are entering successively into the church, a part of the Jews undoubtedly remain hardened, but yet a certain number of individuals are converted, from which it will follow that in the end the totality of God's people, Jews and Gentiles (*all Israel,* ver. 26), will be made up. This explanation was only an expedient to get rid of the idea of the final conversion of the Jewish people. It is of course untenable —1st. From the grammatical point of view the conj. ἄχρις οὗ could only signify *as long as,* if the verb were a present indicative. With the verb in the aor. subjunctive the only possible meaning is : *until.* 2d. Viewed in connection with the context, the word *Israel* has only one possible meaning, its strict meaning : for throughout the whole chapter the subject in question is the future of the Israelitish *nation.* 3d. How could the apostle announce in a manner so particular, and as a fact of revelation, the perfectly simple idea that at the same time as the preaching of the gospel shall sound in the ears of the Gentiles, some individual Jews will also be converted ? Comp. Hodge.—The expression : *the fulness of the Gentiles,* denotes the totality of the Gentile nations passing successively into the church through the preaching of the gospel. This same whole epoch of the conversion of the Gentile world is that which Jesus designates, Luke xxi. 24, by the remarkable expression : καιροὶ ἐθνῶν, *the times of the Gentiles,* which he tacitly contrasts with the theocratic epoch : *the times of the Jews* (xix. 42, 44). Jesus adds, absolutely in the same sense as Paul, "that Jerusalem shall be trodden down *until* those times of the Gentiles be fulfilled ;" which evidently signifies that after those times had elapsed, Jerusalem shall be delivered and restored. In this discourse of Jesus, as reported by Matthew (xxiv. 14) and Mark (xiii. 10), it is said : "The gospel of the kingdom shall be preached unto the Gentiles throughout all the earth ; and then shall the end come." This *end* includes the final salvation of the Jewish people.—Olshausen and Philippi suppose that the complement of the word πλήρωμα, *fulness*, is : " of the kingdom of God," and that the genitive ἐθνῶν, *of the Gentiles*, is only a complement of apposition : "Until the full number of Gentiles necessary to fill up the void in the kingdom of God, made by the loss of Israel, be complete." This is to torture at will the words of the apostle ; their meaning is clear : Till the accomplishment of the conversion of the Gentiles, there will be among the Jews only individual conversions ; but this goal reached, their conversion *en masse* will take place.

Ver. 26*a*. Καὶ οὕτως cannot be translated "and then ;" the natural meaning is : *and thus ;* and it is quite suitable. Thus, that is to say, *by means of* the entrance of the Gentiles into the church, comp. ver. 31. When Israel shall see the promises of the O. T., which ascribe to the Messiah the conversion of the Gentiles to the God of Abraham, fulfilled throughout the whole world by Jesus Christ, and the Gentiles through His mediation loaded with the blessings which they themselves covet, they will be forced to own that Jesus is the Messiah ; for if the latter were to be a different personage, what would this other have to do, Jesus having already done all that is expected of the Messiah?—Πᾶς 'Ισραήλ, *all Israel*, evidently signifies *Israel taken in its entirety*. It seems, it is true, that the Greek expression in this sense is not correct, and that it should be 'Ισραὴλ ὅλος. But the term πᾶς, *all* (*every*), denotes here, as it often does, every element of which the totality of the object is composed (comp. 2 Chron. xii. 1 : πᾶς 'Ισραὴλ μετ' αὐτοῦ, *all Israel was with him*) ; Acts. ii. 36 ; Eph. ii. 21. We have already said that there can be no question here of applying the term *Israel* to the *spiritual* Israel in the sense of Gal. vi. 16. It is no less impossible to limit its application, with Bengel and Olshausen, to *the elect portion* of Israel, which would lead to a tautology with the verb *shall be saved*, and would suppose, besides, the resurrection of all the Israelites who had died before. And what would there be worthy of the term *mystery* (ver. 25) in the idea of the salvation of all the elect Israelites !—Paul. in expressing himself as he does, does not mean to suppress individual liberty in the Israelites who shall live at that epoch. He speaks of a collective movement which shall take hold of *the nation in general*, and bring them as such to the feet of their Messiah. Individual resistance remains possible. Compare the admirable delineation of this period in the prophet Zechariah (xii. 10–14).[1]—Two prophetic sayings are alleged as containing the revelation of this mystery.

Vv. 26*b*, 27. " *As it is written, There shall come out of Sion*[2] *the Deliverer, and shall turn away ungodliness from Jacob : and this is the covenant I will make with them when I shall take away their sins*."—Two passages are combined in this quotation, as we have already found so often ; these are Isa. lix. 20 and xxvii. 9. As far as the word *when*, all belong to the first passage ; with this conjunction the second begins. Both in Isaiah refer to the *last times*, and have consequently a Messianic bearing. Paul follows the LXX. in quoting, with this difference, that instead of ἐκ Σιών, *from Sion*, they read ἕνεκεν Σιών, "in favor of Sion." The form of the LXX. would have as well suited the object of the apostle as that which he employs himself. Why, then, this change ? Perhaps the prep. ἕνεκεν, *in favor of*, was contracted in some MSS. of the LXX. so as to be easily confounded with ἐκ, *from*. Or perhaps the apostle was thinking of some other passage, such as Ps. cx. 2, where the Messiah is represented as setting out *from Sion* to establish His kingdom. But what is singular is, that neither the one nor the other form corresponds exactly to the Hebrew text,

---

[1] See Appendix E.—T. W. C.
[2] T. R. reads καὶ here, with E L, Syr. only.

which says: "There shall come *to* Sion (*the Zion*), and to them who turn from their sins in Jacob." It is probable that instead of *leschavē* ("them that turn") the LXX. read *leschov* (*to turn away*); and they have rendered this infinitive of aim by the future: *he will turn away*. Hence the form of our quotation. However that may be, the meaning is that He who shall deliver Sion from its long oppression, will do so by taking away iniquity from the *entire people*. Such is, in fact, the bearing of the term 'Ιακώβ, *Jacob*, which denotes the whole nation collectively. It is therefore on this second proposition of ver. 26 that the weight of the quotation properly rests. As to the first proposition, it may be regarded as a simple introduction; or we may find in it the idea, that after setting out *from Sion*, the preaching of the gospel, having made the round of the world, will return *to Israel* to purify it, after all the other nations; or, finally, it may be held, with Hofmann, that the words *from Sion* denote the place whence the Lord will make His glory shine forth, when He shall fulfil this last promise on the earth.

Ver. 27. The first proposition of this verse belongs also to the first of the two passages quoted; but, singular to say, it is almost identical with the clause with which Isaiah begins the second saying used here (xxvii. 9): "And this is the blessing which I shall put on them when" ... This is no doubt what has given rise to the combination of these two passages in our quotation. The meaning is: "Once the sin of Israel (their unbelief in the Messiah) has been pardoned, I shall renew with them my broken covenant." The pronoun αὐτῶν, *their*, refers to the individuals, as the word *Jacob* denoted the totality of the people.

In the two following verses the apostle draws from what precedes the conclusion relative to Israel. In ver. 28 he expresses it in a striking antithesis, and in ver. 29 he justifies the final result (28*b*) by a general principle of the divine government.

Vv. 28, 29. "*As touching the gospel, they are, it is true, enemies for your sakes; but as touching the election, they are beloved for the fathers' sake; for the gifts and calling of God are irrevocable.*"—To sum up, Israel are in a twofold relation to God, at once enemies and beloved; but the latter character will carry it in the end over the former. The term ἐχθρός, *hated*, opposed as it is here to ἀγαπητός, *beloved*, can only be taken in the passive sense: an object of the hatred, that is to say, of the just wrath of God; comp. chap. v. 10. It needs not be said that when the feeling of *hatred* is applied to God, we must eliminate from it all admixture of personal resentment, or of the spirit of revenge. God hates the sinner in the same sense in which the sinner ought to hate himself, that is to say, *his own life*. This sentiment is only the hatred of holiness to evil; and then to the wicked man in so far as he is identified with evil.—The words: *as concerning the gospel*, refer to what was said above: that the Jews being once determined not to abandon their law and their monopoly founded on it, needed to be struck with blindness, so that they might not discern in Jesus their Messiah; otherwise a Judaized gospel would have hindered the offer of salvation to the Gentile nations. The apostle might therefore well add to the words: *as concerning the gospel*, the further clause: *for your sakes*.—But in every Jew there is not only an object of the wrath of God, there is an object of His love. If it is asked how these two sentiments can co-exist in the heart of God, we must remark, first, that the same is the case up to a certain point with respect to every man. In every man there co-exist a being whom God hates, the sinner, and a being whom He still loves, the man created in His image, and for whom His Son died. Then it must be considered that this duality of feelings is only transitory, and must issue finally either in absolute hatred or perfect love; for every man must arrive at the goal either absolutely good or absolutely bad of his moral development, and then the divine feeling will be simplified (see on chaps. v. 9, 10).—The words: *as touching the election*, must not be referred, as Meyer will have it, to the *elect remnant*, as if Paul meant that it is in consequence of this indestructible elect that God always loves Israel. The antithesis to the expression: *as concerning the gospel*, leads us rather to see in *election* the divine act by which God chose this people as the salvation people. This idea is reproduced in the following verse by the expression: ἡ κλῆσις τοῦ Θεοῦ, *the calling of God*.—This notion of election is closely connected with the explanatory regimen: *for the fathers' sake*. It was in the persons of Abraham, Isaac, and Jacob that the divine election of Israel was originally realized, and through them that it was transmitted to the whole people. The love with which God loved the fathers continues toward their descendants "even to a thousand generations" (Ex. xx. 6). Only let the hearts of the children return to their fathers, that is to say, let them return to the sentiments of their fathers (Mal. iv. 6 ; Luke i. 17), and the beneficent cloud which is always spread over their head will again distil its dew on them.

Ver. 29. This verse justifies the assurance of salvation expressed in favor of Israel in the second proposition of ver. 28. The *gifts of God* might denote divine favors in general ; but it seems to us more in harmony with the context, which refers throughout to the destination of Israel, to give this term the special meaning which it usually has in St. Paul's Epistles. He there uses the word to denote the moral and intellectual aptitudes with which God endows a man with a view to the task committed to him. And who can fail to see that the people of Israel are really endowed with singular qualities for their mission as the salvation-people ? The Greeks, the Romans, the Phœnicians had their special gifts in the different domains of science and art, law and politics, industry and commerce. Israel, without being destitute of the powers related to those spheres of mundane activity, have received a higher gift, the organ for the divine and the intuition of holiness. The *calling of God* is on the one hand the cause, on the other the effect of those gifts. It is because God called this people in His eternal counsel that He entrusted the gifts to them ; and it is because he enriched them with those gifts that in the course of time He called them to fulfil the task of initiating the world in the way of salvation, and of preparing salvation for the world. Of this august mission they have for the time been deprived : instead of entering first, they will enter last. But their destination is nevertheless irrevocable ; and through the overflowing of divine mercy (chap. v. 20) it will be realized in them at the period announced by the apostle, when, saved themselves, they will cause a stream of life from above to flow into the heart of Gentile Christendom (xv. 12, 15, and 25, 26).—This *irrevocable* character of Israel's destination has nothing in it contrary to individual liberty ; no constraint will be exercised. God will let unbelieving generations succeed one another as long as shall be necessary, until that generation come which shall at length open its eyes and return freely to Him. And even then the movement in question will only be a national and collective one, from which those shall be able to withdraw who refuse decidedly to take part in it. Only it is impossible that the divine foreknowledge in regard to Israel as a people ("the people whom God foreknew," ver. 2) should terminate otherwise than by being realized in history.

There is nothing in this passage pointing to a *temporal* restoration of the Jewish nation, or to an Israelitish monarchy having its seat in Palestine. The apostle speaks only of a spiritual restoration by means of a general pardon, and the outpouring of the graces which shall flow from it. Will there be a political restoration connected with this general conversion of the people? Or will it not even precede the latter ? Will not the principle of the reconstitution of races, which in our day has produced Italian unity, German unity, and which is tending to the unity of the Slavs, also bring about Israelitish unity ?

These questions do not belong to exegesis, which confines itself to establishing these two things—(1) That, according to apostolical revelation, Israel will be converted in a body ; (2) That this event will be the signal of an indescribable spiritual commotion throughout the whole church.

The theme of the chapter is properly exhausted ; we are furnished with light from all points of view, that of *right*, that of *cause*, and that of *aim*, on the mysterious dispensation of the rejection of Israel. Nothing remains but to gather up what has been said of the past and future of this elect people into a general view of God's plan as to the religious progress of humanity. This is what the apostle does in vv. 30–32.

Vv. 30, 31. "*For as ye also*[1] *in time past disobeyed God, but have now obtained mercy by their disobedience ; even so have these also*[2] *now been disobedient, that by the mercy shown to you they also*[3] *may obtain mercy.*"—The entire course of the religious history of the world is determined by the antagonism created among mankind by the calling of Abraham, between a people specially destined by God to receive His revelations, and the other nations given over to themselves. From that moment (Gen. xii.) there begin to be described those two immense curves which traverse the ages of antiquity in opposite directions, and which, crossing one another at the advent of Christianity, are prolonged from that period in inverse directions, and shall terminate by uniting and losing themselves in one another at the goal of history.—Ver. 30 describes the rebellion of the Gentiles, then their salvation determined by the rebellion of the Jews ; and ver. 31, the rebellion of the Jews, then their salvation arising from the salvation of the Gentiles.

Ver. 30. The Gentiles first had their time of disobedience. The expression *in time past* carries the reader back to the contents of chap. i., to those times of idolatry when the Gentiles voluntarily extinguished the light of natural revelation, to abandon themselves more freely to their evil propensities. This epoch of disobedience is what the apostle calls at Athens (Acts xvii. 30) by a less severe name : "the times of ignorance." Perhaps we should read with the T. R. καί, *also*, after *for*. This little word might easily be omitted ; it reminds the Gentiles from the first that they *also*, like the Jews, had their time of rebellion.—That time of disobedience has now taken end ; the Gentiles have found grace. But at what price ? By means of the disobedience of the Jews. We have seen this indeed : God needed to make the temporary sacrifice of His elect people in order to disentangle the gospel from the legal forms in which they wished to keep it imprisoned. Hence it was that Israel required to be given up to unbelief in regard to their Messiah ; hence their rejection, which opened the world to the gospel. Now then, wonderful to tell, an analogous, though in a certain sense opposite, dispensation will take effect in the case of the Jews.

Ver. 31. The word νῦν, *now*, strongly contrasts the present period (since the coming of Christ) with the former, ver. 30. Now it is the Jews who are passing through their time of disobedience, while the Gentiles enjoy the sun of grace. But to what end ? That by the grace which is now granted to the latter, grace may also one day be accorded to the Jews. This time, then, it will not be the disobedience of the one which shall produce the conversion of the others. A new discord in the kingdom of God will not be necessary to bring about the final harmony. In this last phase, the good of the one will not result from the evil of the other, but from their very blessedness. Israel went out that the Gentiles might enter. But the Gentiles shall not go out to make place for the Jews ; they will open the door to them from within. Thus are explained at once the analogy and the contrast expressed by the conjunctions ὥσπερ, *as*, and οὕτω,

---

[1] T. R. reads καί after γαρ, with L, Mnn., Syr. ; the others omit it.
[2] D F G read και αυτοι instead of και ουτοι.
[3] B D read νυν again before ελεηθωσιν.

even so, which begin and form a close connection between vv. 30 and 31. It cannot be doubted that the clause τῷ ὑμετέρῳ ἐλέει, *by your mercy* (that which has been shown to you), depends on the following verb ἐλεηθῶσι, *may obtain mercy*, and not on the preceding proposition. The apostle places this clause before the conj. ἵνα, *that*, to set it more in relief; for it expresses the essential idea of the proposition. Compare the similar inversions, xii. 3; 1 Cor. iii. 5, ix. 15, etc. —For the form καὶ οὗτοι, *these also*, in the first proposition, there is substituted in the second the form καὶ αὐτοί, *they*, or *they themselves also*, to bring out the identity of the subject to which those two so opposite dispensations apply. It is impossible to admit the Greco-Latin reading, which has καὶ αὐτοὶ both times. We must also reject the reading of some Alex. and of some ancient translations, which in the second proposition repeat the νῦν, *now*. These last words refer evidently to the future.

Ver. 32. "*For God hath included all in disobedience, that He might have mercy upon all.*"—Here we have, as it were, the full period put to all that precedes the last word in explanation of the whole plan of God, the principal phases of which have just been sketched (*for*). The term συγκλείειν, *to shut up together*, applies to a plurality of individuals, enclosed in such a way that they have only one exit, through which they are all forced to pass. The prep. σύν, *with*, which enters into the composition of the verb, describes the enclosure as subsisting on all sides at once. Some commentators have thought that there must be given to this verb a simply *declarative* sense, as in Gal. iii. 22, where it is said: "The Scripture hath concluded all under sin," in this sense, that it *declares* all men to be subject to sin and condemnation. But in our passage the action is not ascribed to an impersonal subject like Scripture; the subject is God Himself; it is His dispensations in the course of history which are explained. The verb can therefore only refer to a *real* act, in virtue of which the two portions of mankind just spoken of have each had their period of disobedience. And the act whereby God has brought about this result, as we know from all that precedes, is the judgment denoted in the case of the Gentiles by the term παρέδωκεν, *He gave them up*, thrice repeated, i. 24, 26, and 28, and in the case of the Jews by the word ἐπωρώθησαν, *they were hardened*, xi. 7. Only it must be remarked that this divine action had been provoked in both cases by man's sin; on the part of the Gentiles through their ingratitude toward the revelation of God in nature, and on the part of the Jews by their ignorant obstinacy in maintaining beyond the fixed time their legal particularism. The Danish theologian Nielsen says with good reason, in his short and spiritual exposition of the Epistle to the Romans: "The sinful nature already existed in all; but that the conviction of it might be savingly awakened in individuals, this latent sin required to be manifested historically on a great scale in the lot of nations." To be complete, however, it must be added that this latent sin was already manifested actively and freely on the part both of Gentiles and Jews before taking the form of a passive dispensation and of a judgment from God. Thus the act of συγκλείειν, *shutting up together*, is already justified from the viewpoint of cause; but how much more magnificently still from the viewpoint of end! This end is to make those Jews and Gentiles the objects of universal mercy. The word τοὺς πάντας, *all*, is applied by Olshausen solely to the totality of the *elect* in these two parts of mankind; and by Meyer, to all the individuals comprehended in these two masses, but solely, according to this author, in respect of their *destination*, in the divine mind. For that this destination may be realized, there is needed the free act of faith. But it should not be forgotten that this saying does not refer to the time of the last judgment and the eternal future, which would necessarily suppose the resurrection of the dead, of which there is no question here. According to the whole context, the apostle has in view an epoch in the history of the kingdom of

416 / Rejection of the Jews

God *on this earth*, an epoch, consequently, which comprehends only the individuals who shall then be in life. Hence it is that he puts the article τούς, *the*, before πάντας, *all;* for the subject in question is a determined and already known totality, that which comprehends the two portions of mankind which Paul has been contrasting with one another throughout the whole chapter.—The domain of disobedience, within which God has successively shut them all up, leaves both in the end only one issue, that of humbly accepting salvation from the hand of mercy. As Nielsen again says: "Divine impartiality, after having been temporarily veiled by two opposite particularisms, shines forth in the final universalism which embraces in a common salvation all those whom these great judgments have successively humbled and abased." There is therefore no inference to be drawn from this passage in favor of a final universal salvation (De Wette, Farrar, and so many others), or even of a determinist system, in virtue of which human liberty would be nothing more in the eyes of the apostle than a form of divine action. St. Paul teaches only one thing here: that at the close of the history of mankind on this earth there will be an economy of grace in which salvation will be extended to the totality of the nations living here below, and that this magnificent result will be the effect of the humiliating dispensations through which the two halves of mankind shall have successively passed. The apostle had begun this vast exposition of salvation with the fact of universal condemnation; he closes it with that of universal mercy. What could remain to him thereafter but to strike the hymn of adoration and praise? This is what he does in vv. 33-36.

Vv. 33-36

Ver. 33. "*O the depth of the riches both of the wisdom and knowledge of God! How unsearchable are His judgments, and His ways past finding out!*" —Like a traveller who has reached the summit of an Alpine ascent, the apostle turns and contemplates. Depths are at his feet; but waves of light illumine them, and there spreads all around an immense horizon which his eye commands. The plan of God in the government of mankind spreads out before him, and he expresses the feelings of admiration and gratitude with which the prospect fills his heart.—The word βάθος, *depth*, applies precisely to that abyss which he has just been exploring. The genitive πλούτου, *of riches*, by which the word *depth* is qualified, is regarded by most commentators as a first complement, co-ordinate with the two following: *of wisdom* and *of knowledge*. In this case it must be held that the abstract term *riches* applies to a special divine attribute which can be no other than divine mercy; comp. x. 12; Eph. ii. 4, etc. The two καί, *and* . . . *and*, which follow, would furnish an instance of a construction like that of Luke v. 17. And one might make these three complements, *riches, wisdom, knowledge*, parallel to the three questions which follow, vv. 34 and 35, as in fact the first refers rather to knowledge, the second to wisdom, and the third to grace. But if this latter relation really existed in the apostle's mind, why should the questions be arranged in an opposite order to that of the three terms corresponding to them in our verse? Then is not the notion of *mercy* too diverse in kind from those of *wisdom* and *knowledge* to allow of the first being thus co-ordinated with the other two? Finally, would not the abstract term *riches* have required to be determined by a complement such as ἐλέους or χάριτος (mercy, grace)? The apostle is not afraid of such accumulations of genitives (ii. 5 and Eph. i. 19). It rather seems to me, therefore, that the second of these two abstract terms (*depth* and *riches*) ought to be regarded as a complement of the other: *a depth of riches*, for: an infinitely rich depth, that is to say, one which, instead of being an immense void, presents itself as embracing contents of inexhaustible fulness. Calvin has well caught this meaning : " This is why," says he, " I doubt not that the apostle exalts the *deep riches* of wisdom and knowledge which are in God."—This depth is rich, not in darkness, but in light ; it is a depth *both of wisdom and knowledge.*—The two καί, *both . . . and . . .*, have the disjunctive sense ; they distinguish the two following substantives very precisely, however closely allied their meaning may be. The second, γνῶσις, *knowledge*, refers especially in the context to divine *foreknowledge*, and in general to the complete view which God has of all the free determinations of men, whether as individuals or as nations. The former, σοφία, *wisdom*, denotes the admirable skill with which God weaves into His plan the free actions of man, and transforms them into so many *means* for the accomplishment of the excellent end which He set originally before Him.[1] We cannot reflect, however[1] little, without seeing that the very marked difference which Paul here establishes between these two divine perfections, is by no means indifferent ; it is nothing less than the safeguard of human liberty. If the omniscience of God, especially His foreknowledge, were counfounded with His wisdom, everything in the universe would be directly the work of God, and the creatures would be nothing more than blind instruments in His hands.

Paul sees these two attributes of God shine forth in two orders of things which, combined, constitute the whole government of the world : *judgments*, κρίματα, and *ways* or *paths*, ὁδοί. Here the general sense of *decree* is sometimes given to the former of these terms. But the word in every case implies the idea of a *judicial* decree ; and what Paul has just been referring to, those severe dispensations whereby God has successively chastised the ingratitude of the Gentiles (chap. i.) and the haughty presumption of the Jews (chap. x.), shows clearly that we are to keep to its strict sense.— *Ways*, ὁδοί, do not really denote different things from *judgments ;* but the term presents them in a different and more favorable light, as so many advances toward the final aim. The term *judgments* expresses, if one may so speak, the *because* of the things, as the word *ways* points to their *in order that*. We may thus understand the twofold relation of the events of history to *knowledge* on the one hand, and *wisdom* on the other. From the *knowledge* which God possesses, there follow from the free decisions of man the *judgments* which He decrees, and these judgments become the *ways* which His *wisdom* employs for the realization of His plan (Isa. xl. 14 : κρίματα, ὁδοί).[2] —These two orders of things are characterized by the most extraordinary epithets which the most pliant of languages can furnish : ἀνεξερεύνητος, *what cannot be searched to the bottom ;* ἀνεξιχνίαστος, *the traces of which cannot be followed to the end*. The former of these epithets applies to the supreme principle which the mind seeks to approach, but which it does not reach ; the latter to an abundance of ramifications and of details in execution which the understanding cannot follow to the end. These epithets are often quoted with the view of demonstrating the incomprehensibility to man of the divine decrees, and in particular of that of predestination (Aug.). But it must not be forgotten that St. Paul's exclamation is called forth, not by the obscurity of God's plans, but, on the contrary, by their dazzling clearness. If they are incomprehensible and unfathomable, it is to man's natural understanding, and until they have been revealed ; but, says the apostle, 1 Cor. ii. 10 : " God hath revealed them unto us by His Spirit ; for the Spirit searcheth (ἐρευνᾷ) all things, even the deep things (τὰ βάθη) of God." It is therefore in view of the *unveiled* mystery that the exclamation is raised, as is done by Paul here : " O the depth of the riches !" A fact which does not prevent the mind which understands

---

[1] "*Wisdom* refers to the end aimed at by the divine mind ; *knowledge* to the means employed for the attainment of the end."—Shedd.—T. W. C.
[2] *Judgments* means decisions, not necessarily judicial. See Ps. xxxvi. 6 in the Septuagint. *Ways* are methods of acting.—T. W. C.

them in part from having always to discover in them new laws or applications.

Vv. 34, 35. *"For who hath known the mind of the Lord, or who hath been His counsellor? Or who hath first given to Him, and it shall be recompensed unto Him again?"*—Here is the Scripture proof that God's designs are impenetrable until He reveal them Himself to His apostles and prophets, and by them to His people. The first passage quoted is Isa. xl. 13, which Paul uses as if it were his own saying. This question in the mouth of the prophet applies to the wonders of creation. Paul extends it to those of the divine government in general, for the works of God in history are only the continuation of those of nature.—The question: *Who hath known?* is a challenge thrown down to the *natural* understanding. As to those whom God has enlightened on the subject of His designs, Paul himself says, 1 Cor. ii. 16: "But we have the mind of Christ."—This first question contrasts the always limited knowledge of man with the infinite *knowledge* of God (γνῶσις τοῦ Θεοῦ, ver. 33). The second goes further, it bears on the relation between human and divine *wisdom*. It is no longer merely the *discovery* of the secrets of God by the study of His works which is in question, but some *good counsel* which man might have been called to give to the Creator in the organizing of His plans. The word σύμβουλος denotes one who *deliberates with* another, and can communicate to him something of his wisdom. It is therefore a more exalted position than that supposed by the previous question.

The third question, ver. 35, would imply a still more exalted part. The matter in question is a *service* rendered to God, a present which man is supposed to have made to Him so as to merit a gift in return. Such, indeed, is the position which the Jews were taking, and by which they claimed especially to limit the freedom of God in the government of the world on account of their meritorious works. "There is no difference," said the Jews of Malachi's day pettishly, "between the man who serveth God and him who serveth Him not. What have we gained by keeping His commandments?" This spirit of pride had been growing; it had reached its apogee in Pharisaism. The preposition πρό, *in advance*, which enters into the composition of the first verb, and the preposition ἀντί, *in exchange*, which enters into that of the second, perfectly describe the relation of dependence on man in which God would be placed, if the former could really be the first to do something for God and thereby constitute Him his debtor. With this third question Paul evidently returns to the special subject of this whole dissertation on the divine government: the rejection of the Jews. By the first question he denied to man the power of understanding God and judging Him till God had explained Himself; by the second, the power of co-operating with Him; by the third, he refuses to him the power of imposing on Him any obligation whatever. Thus is fully vindicated the liberty of God, that last principle of the mysterious fact to be explained.

This question of ver. 35 is also a Scripture quotation which Paul weaves into his own text. It is taken from Job xli. 11, which the LXX. translate strangely (xli. 2): "Or who is he that will resist me and abide?" It is true that in the two MSS. *Sinait.* and *Alex.* there is found at the close of Isa. xl. 14 a saying similar to the apostle's translation. But there it is certainly an interpolation taken from our epistle itself.

Ver. 36. *"For of Him, and through Him, and to Him are all things: To whom be glory for ever! Amen."*—God's absolute independence, man's total dependence in everything which might be a matter of glory to him: such is the thought of this verse, the termination of this vast survey of the plan of God. The first prep. ἐκ, *of*, refers to God as Creator; it is of Him that man holds everything: "life, breath, and all things," Acts xvii. 25. The second, διά, *through*, refers to the government of mankind. Everything, even the free determinations of the human will, are executed only through

Him, and are turned immediately to the accomplishment of His designs. The third, εἰς, *to*, refers to the final goal. The word *to Him* does not refer to God's personal satisfaction, an idea which might undoubtedly be supported ; for, as Beck says, " the egoism of God is the life of the world." But it is more natural to apply the term *to Him* to the accomplishment of His will, in which His own glory and the happiness of His sanctified creatures blend together as one and the same thing. It has been sometimes attempted to apply these three prepositional clauses to the three persons of the divine Trinity ; modern exegesis (Mey., Gess, Hofm.) has in general departed from this parallel ; and rightly. When Paul speaks of *God*, absolutely considered, it is always the *God and Father* he intends, without, of course, excluding His revelation through Christ and His communication by the Holy Spirit. But this distinction is not raised here, and had no place in the context. What the apostle was concerned to say in closing, was that all things proceeding from the creative will of God, advancing through His wisdom and terminating in the manifestation of His holiness, must one day celebrate His glory, and His glory only.—The application of the word *all things* might be restricted to the two portions of mankind spoken of (as in ver. 32). But Paul rises here to the general principle of which ver. 32 was only a particular application, and hence also he substitutes the neuter *all things* for the masculine *all*. What is meant, therefore, is the totality of created things, visible and invisible.—The glory of God, the reflection of His perfections in all that exists, that glory, now veiled, in so many respects in the universe, must shine forth magnificently and perfectly forever and ever. For, as Hodge says, " the highest end for which all things can exist and be ordered, is to display the character of God." This goal of history is, as it were, anticipated by the wish and prayer of the apostle : " To Him be glory !" [1]

The first part of the doctrinal treatise had terminated in the parallel between the two heads of mankind, a passage in which there was already heard a more exalted note. The second part closed, at the end of chap. viii., with a sort of lyrical passage, in which the apostle celebrated the blessing of sanctification crowning the grace of justification, and thus assuring the state of glory. The third, that which we are concluding here, terminates in a passage of the same kind, a hymn of adoration in honor of the divine plan realized in spite of, and even by means of, human unfaithfulness. After thus finishing the exposition of salvation in its foundation (justification), in its internal development (sanctification), and in its historical course among mankind (the successive calling of the different nations, and their final union in the kingdom of God), the apostle puts, as it were, a full period, the *Amen* which closes this part of the epistle.

Never was survey more vast taken of the divine plan of the world's history. First, the epoch of primitive unity, in which the human family forms still only one unbroken whole ; then the antagonism between the two religious portions of the race, created by the special call of Abraham : the Jews continuing in the father's house, but with a legal and servile spirit, the Gentiles walking in their own ways. At the close of this period, the manifestation of Christ determining the return of the latter to the domestic hearth, but at the same time the departure of the former. Finally, the Jews, yielding to the divine solicitations and to the spectacle of salvation enjoyed by the Gentiles as children of grace ; and so the final universalism in which all previous discords are resolved, restoring in an infinitely higher form the original unity, and setting before the view of the universe the family of God fully constituted.

The contrast between the Jews and Gentiles appears therefore as the

---

[1] This doxology, Alford says, is the sublimest apostrophe existing even in the pages of inspiration itself.—T. W. C.

essential moving spring of history. It is the actions and reactions arising from this primary fact which form its key. This is what no philosophy of history has dreamed of, and what makes these chaps. ix.-xi. the highest theodicy.

If criticism has thought it could deduce from this passage the hypothesis of a Judeo-Christian majority in the church of Rome, if it has sought to explain it, as well as the whole of our epistle, by the desire felt by Paul to reconcile this church to his missionary activity among the Gentiles, it is easy to see from the passage, rightly understood, how remote such criticism is from the real thought which inspired this treatise. The conclusion from an altogether *general* application, vv. 30–32, in which he addresses the whole church as former Gentiles whom he expressly distinguishes from Jews, can leave no doubt as to the origin of the Christians of Rome. Supposing even that in ver. 13 he had divided his readers into two classes, which we have found to be a mistake, from ver. 25 he would in any case be again addressing all his readers. And as to the intention of the whole passage, it is evidently to show that those who should have been *first*, though now put *last*, are not, however, *excluded*, as the Gentiles might proudly imagine, and that if the πρῶτον, *firstly*, ascribed to the Jews by God's original plan (i. 16) has not been historically realized (through their own fault), the divine programme in regard to mankind will nevertheless, though in another way, have its complete execution. Ver. 32 is the counterpart of i. 16. It is therefore to impair the meaning of this passage to see in it an apology for Paul's mission. The thought is more elevated : it is the defence of the plan of God Himself addressed to the whole church.

SECOND PART OF THE EPISTLE

PRACTICAL TREATISE

THE LIFE OF THE JUSTIFIED BELIEVER

12:1-15:13

In the doctrinal part which we have just finished, the apostle has expounded the *way of salvation*. This way is no other than justification by faith, whereby the sinner is reconciled to God (chaps. i.-v.), then sanctified in Christ by the communication of the Spirit (vi.-viii.) ; and it is precisely the refusal to follow this way which has drawn down on Israel their rejection (chaps. ix.-xi.). What now will be the life of the justified believer—*life in salvation?* The apostle sketches it in a general way in chaps. xii. and xiii. ; then he applies the moral principles which he has just established to a particular circumstance peculiar to the church of Rome (xiv. 1-xv. 13). We can therefore distinguish two parts in this course of practical doctrine, the one general, the other special.

GENERAL PART

12:1-13:14

There exists in regard to these two chapters a general prejudice which has completely falsified their interpretation. They have been regarded as giving, according to the expression used even by Schultz, " a series of practical precepts," in other words : a collection of moral exhortations without systematic order, and guided merely by more or less accidental associations of ideas. This view, especially in recent times, has brought graver consequences in its train than could have been expected. It has been asked whether those details in regard to practical life were in keeping with a whole so systematically arranged as the didactic treatise contained in the first eleven chapters. And Renan and Schultz have been led in this way to the critical hypotheses which we have summarily expounded at the end of the Introduction (I. pp. 66 and 67), and which we must now study more closely.

According to the former of these writers, chaps. xii. xiii. and xiv. formed no part of the Epistle as it was sent to the church of Rome. These chapters were only in the copies despatched to the churches of Ephesus and Thessalonica, and an unknown church, for whose benefit Paul is held to have composed our Epistle. The conclusion, in the copy destined for the church of Rome, was composed solely of chap. xv. Nor did chap. xvi. belong to it. Here we have to do only with chaps. xii and xiii. The reasons which lead Renan to doubt the original connection of these chapters with the first eleven, in the copy sent to Rome, are the two following :

422 / Life of the Justified Believer

(1) Paul would be departing here from his habitual principle : " Every one in his own domain ;" in fact, he would be giving imperative counsels to a church which he had not founded, he who rebuked so sharply the impertinence of those who sought to build on the foundations laid by others.[1] The first word of chap. xii., the term παρακαλῶ, *I exhort*, is no doubt habitual to him when he is giving a command to his disciples ; but it is unsuitable here, where the apostle is addressing believers whom he did not bring to the faith.[2] (2) The first part of chap. xv., which, according to Renan, is really addressed to the church of Rome, forbids the thought that chaps. xii. xiii. and xiv. were composed for the same church ; for it would form a duplicate of those three chapters of which it is a simple summary, composed for Judeo-Christian readers, such as those at Rome.

The viewpoint at which Schultz places himself is somewhat different. In his eyes, we possess from chap. xii. a considerable fragment of a wholly different epistle from that which the apostle had composed for the church of Rome. This letter, of which we have not the beginning, was addressed to the church of Ephesus, and must have been written in the last period of St. Paul's life, that of his Roman captivity. To it belong the three chapters, xii. xiii. and xiv., as well as the first seven verses of chap. xv., then the salutations of chap. xvi. (vv. 3–16), and finally, the warning against Judaizers, xvi. 17–20. The true conclusion of the Epistle to the Romans is to be found, according to him, in chap. xv., from ver. 7 to the end, adding thereto the recommendation of Phœbe, xvi. 1 and 2, and the salutations of Paul's companions, xvi. 21–24. How has the fusion of those two letters in one come about ? It is rather difficult to explain, as the one went to the East, the other to the West. Schultz thinks that a copy of this Epistle to the Ephesians, written from Rome, remained without address in the archives of this church, and that the editors of the Epistle to the Romans, finding this short epistle of practical contents, and thinking that it had been written to the Romans, published it with the large one. Only they omitted the beginning, and mixed up the two conclusions.

The following are the reasons which lead Schultz to separate chaps. xii. and xiii. from what precedes :—1. The exhortation to humility, at the beginning of chap. xii., would be somewhat offensive if addressed to a church which the apostle did not know. 2. The exhortation to beneficence toward the saints, and the practice of hospitality, supposes a church in connection with many other churches, which was rather the case with the church of Ephesus than with that of Rome. 3. It is impossible to connect the beginning of chap. xii. (οὖν, *therefore*) naturally with chap. xi. ; for *the mercies of God* spoken of chap. xii. 1, are not at all identical with the *mercy* of God spoken of xi. 32. 4. The whole moral side of the gospel having been expounded in chap. vi., it was not necessary to go back on it in chap. xii. 5. There was no reason for reminding the Judeo-Christians of the church of Rome, as Paul does in chap. xiii., of the duty of submission to the Roman authorities ; for the Jews were quite happy at Rome about the year 58, during the first years of Nero's reign. Such a recommendation was much more applicable to the Jews of Asia, disposed, as the Apocalypse proves, to regard the imperial power as that of Antichrist.

Are we mistaken in saying that the reasons alleged by these two writers produce rather the impression of being painfully sought after than of having presented themselves naturally to the mind ? What ! Paul cannot give imperative moral counsels and use the term παρακαλεῖν, *exhort*, when writing to a church which he does not know ? But what did he do in chaps. vi. and viii., when he said to his Roman readers : " Yield not your members as instruments unto sin ;" " If ye live after the flesh, ye shall die," etc. ? And as to the term which seems unsuitable to Renan, does

---

[1] *Saint Paul*, p. lxiii.   [2] *Ibid.* pp. lxv. and lxix.

not Paul use it, as Lacheret[1] observes, in chap. xv. 30, which this writer himself supposes addressed to the church of Rome? The objection which Renan draws from the sort of pleonasm which the first part of chap. xv. would form, if it appeared in the same writing as chap. xii., will easily be resolved when we come to the passage. On the contrary, what a difficulty there would be in holding that a doctrinal treatise, composed by the apostle with a view to Gentile-Christian churches, such as Ephesus or Thessalonica, for the purpose of giving them a complete exposition of the faith, could have been addressed just as it was to a Judeo-Christian church like that of Rome (according to Renan) for the purpose of gaining it to the apostle's point of view! This consideration, says Lacheret with reason, suffices to overthrow from the foundation the whole structure of Renan.[2] And what a factitious procedure is that which Renan invites us to witness: " the disciples of Paul occupied for several days copying this manifesto for the different churches," and then later editors collecting at the end of the chief (*princeps*) copy the parts which varied in the different copies, because they scrupled to lose anything of what dropped from the apostle's pen![3]

The reasons of Schultz inspire as little confidence. Paul is careful himself to explain his exhortation to humility in chap. xii., as in chap. i., and in chap. xv. he explains his whole letter, on the ground of his apostleship, and especially his apostleship to the Gentiles, which gives him authority over the church of Rome, though he has not personally founded it: " I say, *through the grace given unto me*, to every man that is among you" (xii. 3).—Why would, not the exhortation to beneficence and hospitality have been in place at Rome, where the poor and strangers abounded, as well as at Ephesus?—And as to the warning relative to submission to the authorities, had it not its reason in the general position of Christians over against pagan power, without any need of special oppression to give the apostle occasion to address it to this church? Had not the Emperor Claudius not long before expelled the Jews from Rome because of their continual risings? And what church could more suitably than that of the capital receive instruction on the relation between Christians and the State?— Chap. xii. forms by no means a reduplication of chap. vi. ; for in the latter the apostle had merely laid down *the principle* of Christian sanctification, showing how it was implied in the very fact of justification, while in chap. xii. he gives the description of all the fruits into which this new life should expand. We shall immediately see what is the relation between chap. xii. and all that precedes, as well as the true meaning of the *therefore* in ver. 1.

We think, therefore, we are entitled to continue the interpretation of our Epistle, taking it as it has been transmitted to us by Christian antiquity. It would need strokes of very different power to sunder the parts of so well-compacted an edifice.

In the theme of the treatise: " The just shall live by faith," there was a word whose whole contents had not yet been entirely developed : *shall live*. This word contained not only the whole matter of chaps. vi.-viii., but also that of chaps, xii. and xiii. ; and this matter is not less systematically arranged in these chapters than that of the whole doctrinal part in the preceding eleven. The essentially logical character of Paul's mind would of itself suffice to set aside the idea of an inorganic juxtaposition of moral precepts, placed at haphazard one after the other. We no sooner examine these two chapters more closely, than we discover the idea which governed their arrangement. We are struck first of all with the contrast between the two spheres of activity in which the apostle successively places the believer, the *religious* sphere and the *civil* sphere—the former in chap. xii., the latter in chap. xiii. These are the two domains in which he is called to manifest the life of holiness which has been put within him ; he acts in

---

[1] *Revue Théologique*, 1878, p. 85. [2] *Ibid.* p. 76. [3] *Saint Paul*, pp. 462 and 481.

the world as a member of the church and as a member of the state. But this twofold course has one point of departure and one point of aim. The point of departure is *the consecration of his body*, under the direction of the renewed understanding ; this is the basis of the believer's entire activity, which Paul lays down in the first two verses of chap. xii. The point of aim is *the Lord's coming again* constantly expected ; this advent Paul causes to shine in splendor at the goal of the course in the last four verses of chap. xiii. So : one point of departure, two spheres to be simultaneously traversed, one point of arrival ; such, in the view of the apostle, is the system of the believer's practical life. Such are also the four sections of this general part : xii. 1, 2, xii. 3-21, xiii. 1-10, xiii. 11-14.

This moral instruction is therefore the pendant of the doctrinal instruction It is its necessary complement. The two taken together form the apostle's *complete catechism*. It is because the rational relation between the different sections of this part has not been understood that it has been possible for the connection of this whole second part with the first to be so completely mistaken.

Some one will ask, perhaps, if the apostle, in thus tracing the model of Christian conduct, does not seem to distrust somewhat the sanctifying power of faith so well expounded by him in chaps. vi.-viii. If the state of justification produces holiness with a sort of moral necessity, why seek still to secure this object by all sorts of precepts and exhortations ? Should not the tree, once planted, bear its fruits of itself ? But let us not forget that moral life is subject to quite different laws from physical life. Liberty is and remains to the end one of its essential factors. It is by a series of acts of freedom that the justified man appropriates the Spirit at every moment, in order to realize with His aid the moral ideal. And who does not know that at every moment also an opposite power weighs on his will ? The believer is *dead unto sin*, no doubt ; he has broken with that perfidious friend ; but sin is not dead in him, and it strives continually to restore the broken relation. By calling the believer to the conflict against it, as well as to the positive practice of Christian duty, the apostle is not relapsing into Jewish legalism. He assumes the inward consecration of the believer as an already consummated fact ; and it is from this fact, implicitly contained in his faith, that he proceeds to call him to realize his Christian obligation.

TWENTY-FOURTH PASSAGE (12:1, 2)

The Basis of Christian Conduct

Ver 1. "*I exhort you, therefore, brethren, by the mercies of God, that ye present your bodies a living victim, holy, acceptable unto God,*[1] *which is your rational service.*"—How are we to explain the οὖν, *therefore*, which joins this verse to what precedes ? We fully concur with Schultz in holding that it is impossible to connect chap. xii. directly with the idea of chap. xi., and to identify the *mercies of God* (ver. 1) with the *mercy* displayed in the course of salvation across the field of history (xi. 32). The true connection with what precedes is much wider ; it is nothing less than the relation between the two parts of the Epistle. Religion among the ancients was service (*cultus*) ; and cultus had for its centre sacrifice. The Jewish service counted four kinds of sacrifice, which might be reduced to two : the first, comprising the sacrifices offered *before* reconciliation and to obtain it (sacrifice *for sin* and *for trespass*) ; the second, the sacrifices offered *after*

---

[1] T. R., with the majority of documents, puts τω θεω after ευαρεστον, while ℵ A P put it before.

the obtaining of reconciliation and serving to celebrate it (the *whole burnt-offering* and the *peace-offering*). The great division of the Epistle to the Romans to which we have come is explained by this contrast. The fundamental idea of the first part, chaps. i.–xi., was that of the sacrifice offered by God for the sin and transgression of mankind ; witness the central passage, iii. 25 and 26. These are *the mercies of God* to which Paul appeals here, and the development of which has filled the first eleven chapters. The practical part which we are beginning corresponds to the second kind of sacrifice, which was the symbol of consecration after pardon had been received (the holocaust, in which the victim was entirely burned), and of the communion re-established between Jehovah and the believer (the peace-offering, followed by a feast in the court of the temple). The sacrifice of expiation offered by God in the person of His Son should now find its response in the believer in the sacrifice of complete consecration and intimate communion.

Such is the force of these first words : " I exhort you, *therefore*, by the mercies of God." This word *therefore* gathers up the whole doctrinal part, and includes the whole practical part. Comp. the entirely similar *therefore*, Eph. iv. 1. So true is it that the relation of ideas just expounded is that which fills the apostle's mind, that to designate the believer's conduct in response to the work of God he employs the expression *victim* and *living* victim, which pointedly alludes to the Jewish sacrifices.

The term παρακαλῶ, *I exhort*, differs from the legal commandment, in that it appeals to a sentiment already existing in the heart, faith in God's mercies. It is by this term, also, that Paul, in the Epistle to the Ephesians, iv. 1, passes from the doctrinal teaching to the practical part. And as this Epistle (notwithstanding its title) is addressed to Christians whom Paul did not know personally (i. 15, iii. 2, iv. 21), we there find a new proof of the mistake of Renan, who thinks that this expression would be out of place addressed to others than the apostle's personal disciples.—The διά, *by*, gives the reader to understand that the divine mercies are the power by means of which this exhortation should take possession of his will. The word παριστάναι, *to present*, is the technical term to denote the presentation of victims and offerings in the Levitical cultus (Luke ii. 22).—The victim to be offered is *the body* of the believer. Many regard *the body* as representing the entire person. But why not in that case say ὑμᾶς αὐτούς, *yourselves?* comp. vi. 13. De Wette thought that Paul meant by the word to remind his readers that the body is the seat of sin. But this intention would suppose that the question about to be discussed was the destruction of this hostile principle, while the apostle speaks rather of the active consecration of the body. Olshausen supposes that, by recommending the sacrifice of the lower part of our being, Paul meant to say : all the more everything that is in you of a more exalted nature. But he could not have passed over all the rest in silence ; comp. 1 Thess. v. 23. Meyer distinguishes between the consecration *of the body*, ver. 1, and that *of the mind*, which, according to him, is referred to in ver. 2. But this contrast between the two parts of our being does not come out in the least in the sequel ; and we shall see, in point of fact, that the relation between the two verses is wholly different. Let us not forget that those whom the apostle here addresses (ἀδελφοί, *brethren*), and whom he exhorts, are believers already inwardly consecrated. Chap. vi. has shown how justification by faith provides the principle of sanctification. It is in the name of this finished work that Paul now invites them to lead the life of consecrated victims. Now, the indispensable instrument for this purpose is *the body*. And hence it is that the apostle, supposing the will already gained, does not require more than the consecration of the body.—The expression θυσία ζῶσα, *living victim*, refers to the animal victims which were offered in the Levitical cultus by putting them to death. The sacrifice required by Paul is the opposite of these. The victim must live to become, at every moment of his existence, the active agent of the divine will. The term *living* has not here, therefore, a spiritual sense, but should be taken in the strict sense. The word θυσία is often translated *sacrifice*. It may have this meaning ; but the meaning *victim* better agrees with the term παραστῆσαι, *to present*. The epithet ἁγία, *holy*, might express the idea of *real* holiness, in opposition to the merely ritual purity of the Levitical victims. But would not Paul have said, in that sense, ὄντως or ἀληθῶς ἁγία, *truly* holy ? He means rather to contrast the new employment of the body in the service of God with its previous use under the dominion of sin.—This body, full of life and constantly employed for good, will present a *well-pleasing* spectacle to the eye of God ; it will be an " offering of sweet-smelling (well-pleasing) savor" in the N. T. sense. And this is what is expressed by the third epithet. Some have connected the regimen τῷ Θεῷ, *to God*, with the verb παραστῆσαι, *to present*. But this would be a tautology, and too many important words separate the two terms.—The last words of the verse certainly establish a contrast between the external service of the Old Testament and the spiritual service of the New. Hence several commentators have been led to give the word λογικήν, *reasonable*, the sense of *spiritual ;* comp. 1 Pet. ii. 2, where, in consequence of the understood antithesis (material milk), there can be no doubt as to the meaning of this word. But why would not Paul have rather used in our passage the ordinary term πνευματικήν, *spiritual ?* Calvin takes the epithet *reasonable* as opposed to the superstitious practices of the heathen ; and Grotius contrasts it with the ignorance of animal victims. It seems to me that in all these explanations it is forgotten to take account of an important word, the complement ὑμῶν, *of you*—that is to say, " of such people as you." Is it not this pronoun which explains the choice of the word λογικήν, *reasonable*, of which, undoubtedly, the true meaning is this : " the service which rationally corresponds to the moral premises contained in the faith which you profess" ?

It will be asked whether Paul, by requiring simply that service (*cultus*) which consists of a life devoted to good, means to exclude as irrational, *acts of worship* properly so called. Assuredly not, a host of passages prove the contrary ; comp. for example, 1 Cor. xi.-xiv. Only the acts of external service have no value in his eyes except as means of nourishing and stimulating the truly rational service of which he speaks here. Every act of service which does not issue in the holy consecration of him who takes part in it, is christianly illogical.—But what use is to be made of this consecrated body ? Ver. 2 proceeds to answer this question.

Ver. 2. "*And be not fashioned*[1] *after this age, but be ye transformed*[2] *by the renewing of your mind,*[3] *that ye may discern what is the will of God, that good, acceptable, and perfect will.*"—We have already said that we are not to seek in this verse, as Meyer does, the idea of the sanctification of the soul, as completing the consecration of the body. This idea would have been placed first, and the term *soul* or *spirit* would certainly have been used instead of νοῦς, *the mind*, which denotes only one of the faculties of the soul, and that the faculty of simple perception. The relation between the two verses is quite different. Paul has just pointed to the believer's body as a consecrated instrument. What remains to him to indicate, except the *rule* according to which the believer ought to make use of it ? The καί, *and*, therefore signifies here : *and in order to that*. The T. R., with several ancient documents and the two oldest versions, reads the two verbs in the imperative : *conform ye, transform ye*, while the Greco-Latin MSS. read them in the infinitive. It is probable that the copyists by this latter reading meant to continue the construction of ver. 1, and to make these two

---
[1] T. R., with א B L P, It., reads συσχηματιζεσθε ; A D F G: συσχηματιζεσθαι.
[2] T. R., with B L P, It. Syr., reads μεταμορφουσθε ; א A D F G: μεταμορφουσθαι.
[3] A B D F G here omit υμων, which T. R. reads with all the rest.

verbs dependent on παρακαλῶ, *I exhort you.* The authorities speak in favor of the imperative. But even if the other reading were adopted, we should have to give to the infinitive the meaning of the imperative, as is so often the case in Greek ; comp. in this very chapter, ver. 15. For the relation of dependence on παρακαλῶ is in any case forced.—In the use of his consecrated body, the believer has first an everywhere present model to be rejected, then a new type to be discerned and realized. The model to be rejected is that presented to him by *the present world*, or, as we should say, the reigning *fashion*, taking this word in its widest sense. The term σχῆμα denotes the manner of holding oneself, attitude, pose ; and the verb σχηματίζεσθαι, derived from it, the adoption or imitation of this pose or received mode of conduct. The term (this) *present world* is used in the Rabbins to denote the whole state of things which precedes the epoch of the Messiah ; in the N. T. it describes the course of life followed by those who have not yet undergone the renewing wrought by Christ in human life. It is this mode of living anterior to regeneration which the believer is not to imitate in the use which he makes of his body. And what is he to do ? To seek a new model, a superior type, to be realized by means of a power acting within him. He is to be *transformed*, literally, *metamorphosed*. The term μορφή, *form*, strictly denotes, not an external pose suitable for imitation, like σχῆμα, *attitude*, but an *organic form*, the natural product of a principle of life which manifests itself thus. It is not by looking around him, to the right and left, that the believer is to learn to use his body, but by putting himself under the dominion of a new power which will by an inward necessity transform this use. It is true that Meyer, Hofmann, and others refuse to acknowledge this difference of meaning between the substantives σχῆμα and μορφή, and between the two verbs derived from them, alleging that it is not confirmed by usage. But if Phil. ii. 5 et seq. be adduced, the example proves precisely the contrary. Etymology leads naturally to the distinction indicated, and Paul evidently contrasts the two terms of set purpose.[1]—It should be remarked, also, that the two imperatives are in the *present*. The subject in question is two continuous incessant acts which take place on the basis of our consecration performed once for all (the aorist παραστῆσαι, ver. 1).—And what will be the internal principle of this metamorphosis of the believer in the use of his body ? *The renewing of his mind*, answers St. Paul. The νοῦς, *the mind*, is the faculty by which the soul perceives and discerns the good and the true. But in our natural state this faculty is impaired ; the reigning love of self darkens the mind, and makes it see things in a purely personal light The natural mind, thus misled, is what Paul calls νοῦς τῆς σαρκός, the carnal mind (under the dominion of the flesh), Col. ii. 18. This is why the apostle speaks of the *renewing* of the mind as a condition of the organic transformation which he requires. This faculty, freed from the power of the flesh, and replaced under the power of the Spirit, must recover the capacity for discerning the new model to be realized, the most excellent and sublime type, the will of God : *to appreciate* (discern exactly) *the will of God.* The verb δοκιμάζειν does not signify here, as it has often been translated (Osterv., Seg.) : *to prove, to make experience of.* For *the experience* of the excellence of the divine will would not be an affair of the mind only ; the whole man would take part in it. The meaning of the word here, as usually, is *to appreciate, discern.* By means of his renewed mind the believer studies and recognizes in every given position the divine will toward him in the circumstances, the duty of the situation. He lifts his eyes, and, like Christ Himself (John v. 19, 20), " he sees what his Father shows him" to be done. This per-

---

[1] The difference between these two words may be judged of by the use which we ourselves make of the following terms derived from them : *scheme, Schematism ; amorphous, morphology.*

ception evidently requires a renewed mind. In order to it we require to be raised to the viewpoint of God Himself.—It is against the rules of grammar to translate the following words, either in the sense of : " *that the will of God is good* " (Osterv., Seg.), or in the sense : " *how good it is*" (Oltram.). The only possible meaning is : " *what is the* good, acceptable . . . will of God." It is not always easy for the Christian who lives in the world, even with a heart sincerely consecrated, to discern clearly *what is* the will of God concerning him, especially in regard to the externals of life. This delicate appreciation demands a continual perfecting, even of the transformed mind.—And why is the model to be studied and reproduced in the life not the present world's mode of acting, but the will of God ? The apostle explains by the three epithets with which he qualifies this will ; literally : *the good, the acceptable, the perfect.* Such, then, is the normal type to which, in all circumstances, we must seek to rise with the mind first, then with the conduct. *Good:* in that its directions are free from all connivance with evil, in any form whatever. *Acceptable:* this adjective is not accompanied here with the words *to God,* as in ver. 1 ; it refers, consequently, to the impression produced on men when they contemplate this will realized in the believer's life. They cannot help paying it a tribute of admiration, and finding it beautiful as well as good. Have not devotion, disinterestedness, self-forgetfulness, and self-sacrifice, a charm which subdues every human heart ? *Perfect:* this characteristic follows from the combination of the two preceding. For perfection is goodness united to beauty. The meaning would not be very different if, with some commentators, we regarded these three adjectives as three substantives forming an apposition to the term : *the will of God.* " The will of God, to wit, the good, the acceptable, the perfect." But the article τό would require to be repeated before each of the terms if they were used substantively.

The following, then, is the *résumé* of the apostle's thought : To the false model, presented in every age by the mundane kind of life, there is opposed a perfect type, that of the will of God, which is discerned by the renewed mind of the believer, and which he strives to realize by means of his God-consecrated body, at every moment and in all the relations of his life ; thus is laid down the principle of life in salvation. This life he now proceeds to show as manifesting itself simultaneously in two spheres, that of the church, chap. xii., and that of the state, chap. xiii.

TWENTY-FIFTH PASSAGE (12:3-21)

The Life of the Believer as a Member of the Church.

The notion of consecration is still the prevailing one in this passage. This consecration is realized in life : 1st, in the form of *humility* (vv. 3–8) ; 2d, in that of *love* (vv. 9–21).

Vv. 3–8

The natural tendency of man is to exalt himself. Here is the first point at which the will of God, discerned by the renewed mind of the believer, impresses on his conduct a completely opposite character to that of secular conduct. He recognizes the limit which God imposes on him, and modestly confines himself within it.

Ver. 3. "*For I say, through the grace given unto me, to every man that is among you, not to aspire beyond that to which he ought to lay claim ; but to aspire to regulate himself, according to the measure of faith which God hath allotted to every man.*"—It is with this that he who forms part of the church ought to begin, the sacrifice of himself ; instead of seeking to make himself great, as is done in the world, he should aspire to moderate and control himself in conformity with the standard traced for him by the new type which he consults, the will of God. Thus we see how this verse should be joined to the preceding by the word *for*. It is an application which confirms the principle.—The authority with which Paul traces this line of conduct rests on *the grace given unto him*. This grace is that of the apostleship and of the light accompanying it. In virtue of his office, he has not only the gift of teaching the way of salvation, as he has done in the doctrinal part of this Epistle (chaps. i.-ix.). He has also that of marking out the true direction for moral action, as he proceeds to do in this practical part.—The term λέγω, *I say, I declare*, has a more marked character of authority than the *I exhort* of ver. 1. Religious impulse ought to be regulated by a higher authority. 1 Cor. xii.-xiv. shows the necessity of apostolical direction on that very point which is about to occupy us, that of *spiritual gifts*. It is not without reason that Paul here calls to mind his *office;* comp. i. 1-7. Apostle to the Gentiles, he had the task not only of founding churches among them, but also of guiding them when founded. This charge Paul had, in virtue of his apostleship also, in relation to the church of Rome.—The expression : παντὶ τῷ ὄντι ἐν ὑμῖν, *to every man that is among you*, would be superfluous, if it were merely intended to denote the members of the church *present at Rome*. It is necessary to give the words : *every man that is*, a more special and forcible meaning : " Every man that is *in office*, engaged in ministry in some form or other among you ; every one that plays a part int he life of the church."[1] See the enumeration which follows. Perhaps the apostle is led to use this expression by his own absence from Rome. He who with his apostolic gift is absent, addresses all those who, being present, can exercise an influence on the progress of the church, to say to them on what condition this influence shall be a blessed one.—Ὑπερφρονεῖν : "*to aspire beyond one's measure.*" The measure of each man is denoted by the words : ὃ δεῖ φρονεῖν, *that which he has a right to claim*. In the believer's case it consists in his wishing only to be that which God, by the gift committed to him, calls him to be. The gift received should be the limit of every man's claim and action, for it is thereby that the will of God regarding him is revealed (ver. 2).—The following expression : φρονεῖν εἰς τὸ σωφρονεῖν, contains a sort of play on words : "to turn the φρονεῖν, the energy of the mind, into a σωφρονεῖν, to recognize its limits and respect them." The man of the world enters into conflict with others, to exceed his measure, to make himself prominent, to rule. The Christian enters into conflict with himself, that he may gain self-rule and self-restraint. He aspires to continue within or return to his measure. Such is a wholly new type of conduct which appears with the gospel.—The rule of this voluntary limitation ought to be *the measure of faith* as it is imparted to each. Paul does not mean to speak of *the quantity* of faith which we possess ; for this measure depends in part on human freedom.[2] The genitive : *of faith*, should be regarded not as a partitive complement, but as denoting quality or cause : " the capacity assigned to each man in the domain of faith ; the particular form of activity for which each has been fitted as a believer ; the special gift which constitutes his appanage in virtue of his faith." This gift, the measure of the action to which we are called, is a divine limit which the Christian's renewed mind should discern, and by which he should regulate his aspirations in regard to the part he has to play in the church.

---

[1] Surely it is better to take the phrase as meaning each and all without exception. The author's limitation is arbitrary.—T. W. C.
[2] But this is just what the apostle's phrase denies. Faith is of God's apportioning.—T. W. C.

430 / Life of the Justified Believer

Vv. 4, 5. *"For as*[1] *we have many members in one body, and all members have not the same office; so we, who are many, are one body in Christ, and severally*[2] *members one of another."*—The organization of the human body should be an example to the believer to make him perceive the necessity of limiting himself to the function assigned him. Not only, indeed, is there a plurality of members in one body, but these members also possess special functions, varied capacities (ver. 4). So in the church, which is the organ of Christ's life on the earth (*His body*), there is not only a multiplicity of members, but also a *diversity* of functions, every believer having a particular gift whereby he ought to become the auxiliary of all the rest, their member. Hence it follows that every one should remain in his function, on the one hand that he may be able to render to the rest the help which he owes them, on the other that he may not disturb these in the exercise of their gift. See the same figure more completely developed, 1 Cor. xii.— The form καθ' εἷς, instead of καθ' ἕνα, occurs only in the later Greek writers. —Instead of ὁ δέ (in the Byzs.), which is the pronoun in the nominative, the Alexs. and Greco-Latins read τὸ δέ, which may be taken as an adverbial phrase : *relatively to*, or better, as a pronoun, in the sense : " *and that*, as members of one another.

Vv. 6–8. *"Having then gifts differing according to the grace that is given to us* [*let us exercise them*], *whether prophecy, according to the proportion of faith; or ministry, in ministering; or he that teacheth, in teaching; or he that exhorteth, in exhortation; he that giveth, with simplicity; he that ruleth, with zeal; he that doeth works of mercy, with cheerfulness."*—There is no occasion for making the participle ἔχοντες, *having*, as De Wette and Lachmann do, the continuation of the preceding proposition : " We are one body, *but that while having* different gifts." This idea of the diversity of gifts has been sufficiently explained in the previous verses. And if this participle still belonged to the previous proposition we should require to take all the subordinate clauses which immediately follow : according to the proportion . . . in ministering . . . in teaching . . . etc., as simple descriptive appendices, which would be tautological and superfluous. The words *having then* are therefore certainly the beginning of a new proposition. Paul takes up the last thought of the previous verse, to make it the point of departure for all the particular precepts which are to follow : " As, then, we have different gifts, let us exercise them every one as I proceed to tell you : confining our activity modestly within the limits of the gift itself." As to the meaning, it is always the σωφρονεῖν, *self-rule*, which remains the fundamental idea. Grammatically, the principal verb should be taken from the participle *having:* " Having then different gifts, let us have (exercise) them by abiding simply in them, by not seeking to go out of them."—The term χάρισμα, *gift*, denotes in the language of Paul a spiritual aptitude communicated to the believer with faith, and by which he can aid in the development of spiritual life in the church. Most frequently it is a natural talent which God's Spirit appropriates, increasing its power and sanctifying its exercise.—The gift which holds the first place in the enumerations of 1 Cor. xii. and Eph. iv. is *apostleship.* Paul does not mention it here; he pointed to it in ver. 3 fulfilling its task.

After the apostolate there comes *prophecy* in all these lists. The prophet is, as it were, the eye of the church to receive new revelations. In the passages, Eph. ii. 20 and iii. 5, it is closely connected with the apostolate, which without this gift would be incomplete. But it may also be separate from it; and hence prophets are often spoken of as persons distinct from apostles in the primitive church, for example, Acts xiii. 1, and 1 Cor. xiv. Prophets differed from teachers, in that the latter gathered up into a con-

---

[1] D E F G read ωσπερ instead of καθαπερ.
[2] T. R. reads, with E L : ο δε ; all the others : το δε.

secutive body of doctrine the new truths revealed to the church by the prophets.—Wherein, then, will the voluntary limitation consist which the prophet should impose on himself in the exercise of his gift (his σωφρονεῖν)? He should prophesy *according to the analogy of faith*. The word ἀναλογία is a mathematical term; it signifies *proportion*. The prophet is not absolutely free; he ought to proportion his prophecy to faith. What faith? Many (Hofmann, for example) answer: his own. He should take care in speaking not to exceed the limit of confidence, of real hope communicated to him by the Spirit, not to let himself be carried away by self-love to mingle some human alloy with the holy emotion with which he is filled from above. But, in that case, would not the apostle have required to add the pronoun αὐτοῦ: "*his* faith"? And would not the term *revelation* have been more suitable than that of *faith?* Others think it possible to give the term *faith* the objective meaning which it took later in ecclesiastical language, as when we speak of the evangelical faith or the Christian faith; so Philippi. The prophet in his addresses should respect the foundations of the faith already laid, the Christian facts and the truths which flow from them. But the word faith never in the N. T. denotes doctrine itself; it has always a reference to the subjective feeling of self-surrender, confidence in God, or in Christ as the revealer of God. And may not we here preserve this subjective meaning, while applying it also to the faith of the whole church? The prophet should develop the divine work of faith in the heart of believers, by starting from the point it has already reached, and humbly attaching himself to the work of his predecessors; he should not, by giving scope to his individual speculations, imprudently disturb the course of the work begun within souls already gained. In a word, the revelations which he sets forth should not tend to make himself shine, but solely to edify the church, whose present state is a sort of standard for new instructions. It is obvious how, in the exercise of this gift, it would be easy for one to let himself go beyond the measure of his revelations, and thus add heterogeneous elements to the faith and hope of the church itself. No more in the New Testament than in the Old does it belong to every prophet to recommence the whole work. Hence no doubt the *judgment* to be pronounced on prophesyings, mentioned 1 Cor. xiv. 29.

Ver. 7. The term διακονία, which we translate by *ministry*, denotes generally in the N. T. a charge, an office confided to some one by the church. Such an office undoubtedly supposes a spiritual aptitude; but the holder is responsible for its discharge, not only in relation to God from whom the gift comes, but also to the church which has confided to him the office. Such is the difference between the functions denoted by this name and the ministry of the prophet, or of him who *speaks with tongues*. These are pure gifts, which man cannot transform into a charge. In our passage this term *ministry*, placed as it is between prophecy and the function of teaching, can only designate an activity of a practical nature, exerted in action, not in word. It is almost in the same sense that in 1 Pet. iv. 11 the term διακονεῖν, *serving*, is opposed to λαλεῖν, *speaking*. We think it probable, therefore, that this term here denotes the two ecclesiastical offices of the *pastorate* (bishop or presbyter) and of the *diaconate* properly so called. *Bishops* or *presbyters* were established in the church of Jerusalem from the first times of the church, Acts xi. 30. Paul instituted this office in the churches which he had just founded, Acts xiv. 23; comp. Phil. i. 1; 1 Tim. iii. 1 et seq.; Tit. i. 5 et seq. They presided over the assemblies of the church, and directed its course and that of its members in respect of spiritual matters; comp. 1 Thess. v. 12 and 13. Hence their title ποιμένες, *pastors*, Eph. iv. 11.—*Deacons* appear even before elders in the church of Jerusalem (Acts vi. 1 et seq.). They were occupied especially with the care of the poor. This office, which emanates so directly from Christian charity, never ceased in the church; we find it again mentioned Phil. i. 1;

1 Tim. iii. 12.—Each of these functionaries, says the apostle, should keep to his part, confine himself within the administration committed to him. The elder should not desire to mount the tripod of prophet, nor the deacon aspire to play the part of bishop or teacher. It is ever that voluntary limitation which the apostle had recommended, vv. 3–5.

In the passage from the first to the second part of this verse, we observe a slight change of construction. Instead of mentioning the gift or the office, as in the two preceding terms, Paul addresses himself directly to the man who is invested with it. This is not a real grammatical incorrectness ; for, as the preceding accusatives : προφητείαν (*prophecy*), διακονίαν (*ministry*), were placed in apposition to the object χαρίσματα, *gifts* (ver. 6), so the nominatives : ὁ διδάσκων, *he that teacheth*, ὁ παρακαλῶν, *he that exhorteth*, are in apposition to the participle ἔχοντες, *having* (same verse).—As to the following clauses : *in teaching*, *in exhortation*, they continue to depend on the understood verb ἔχωμεν, *let us have*, exercise, abide in.—*He that teacheth* (the teacher, ὁ διδάσκαλος), like the prophet, exercises his gift by speech ; but while the latter receives by revelations granted to him new views which enrich the faith of the church, the teacher confines himself to an orderly and clear exposition of the truths already brought to light, and to bringing out their connection with one another. He it is who, by *the word of knowledge* or *of wisdom* (1 Cor. xii. 8), shows the harmony of all the parts of the divine plan. In the enumeration, Eph. iv. 11, the teacher is at once associated with and distinguished from the *pastor*. In fact, the gift of teaching was not yet essentially connected with the pastorate. But more and more it appeared desirable that the pastor should be endowed with it, 1 Tim. v. 17 ; Tit. i. 9.

Ver. 8. In 1 Cor. xiv. 3, the function of *exhorting* is ascribed to the prophet, and the surname Barnabas, *son of prophecy*, Acts iv. 36, is translated into Greek by υἱὸς παρακλήσεως, *son of exhortation*. The prophet therefore had certainly the gift of exhorting, stimulating, consoling. But it does not follow from the fact that the prophet exhorts and consoles, that, as some have sought to persuade themselves in our day, any one, man or woman, who has the gift of exhorting or consoling, is a *prophet*, and may claim the advantage of all that is said of the prophets in other apostolical declarations. Our passage proves clearly that the gift of exhorting may be absolutely distinct from that of prophecy. So it is also from that of *teaching*. The teacher acts especially on the understanding ; he would be in our modern language the catechist or dogmatic theologian. He that *exhorts* acts on the heart, and thereby on *t*he will ; he would rather be the Christian poet. Also in 1 Cor. xiv. 26, Paul, bringing these two ministries together as he does here, says : " Hath any one a *doctrine*, hath any one a *psalm ?*"

The three last functions mentioned in this verse are no longer exercised in the assemblies of the church ; they come, to a certain point, under the exercise of private *virtues*. It is wrong, indeed, to regard the μεταδιδούς, *he that distributeth*, as has been done, to indicate the official deacon, and the προϊστάμενος; *he that ruleth*, the elder or bishop. The verb μεταδιδόναι does not signify *to make a distribution* on behalf of the church (this would require διαδιδόναι, Acts iv. 35) ;. but : *to communicate* to others of one's own wealth ; comp. Luke iii. 11 ; Eph. iv. 28. And as to the bishop, the position here assigned to this ministry would not be in keeping with his elevated rank in the church ; and the matter in question is especially works of beneficence. The first term : *he that giveth* (communicateth), therefore denotes the believer, who by his fortune and a natural aptitude sanctified by faith, feels himself particularly called to succor the indigent around him. Paul recommends him to do so *with simplicity*. The Greek term might be translated : *with generosity*, with large-heartedness ; such is the meaning which the word ἁπλότης (2 Cor. viii. 2, ix. 13) often has. According to its etymological meaning, the word signifies: the disposition not to turn back on oneself ; and it is obvious that from this first meaning there may follow either that of *generosity*, when a man gives without letting himself be arrested by any selfish calculation, or that of *simplicity*, when he gives without his left hand knowing what his right does—that is to say, without any vain going back on himself, and without any air of haughtiness. This second meaning seems to us preferable here, because the prevailing idea throughout the entire passage is that of σωφρονεῖν, *self-limiting*, self-regulating.—The second term : *he that ruleth*, should be explained by the sense which the verb προΐστασθαι frequently has in Greek : *to be at the head of;* hence : *to direct a business*. So, in profane Greek, the term is applied to the physician who directs the treatment of a disease, to the magistrate who watches over the execution of the laws. In the Epistle to Titus, iii. 8, there occurs the expression : προΐστασθαι καλῶν ἔργων, *to be occupied with good works;* [1] whence the term προστάτις, *patroness*, protectress, benefactress, used in our Epistle, xvi. 2, to express what Phœbe had been to many believers and to Paul himself. Think of the numerous works of private charity which believers then had to found and maintain! Pagan society had neither hospitals nor orphanages, free schools or refuges, like those of our day. The church, impelled by the instinct of Christian charity, had to introduce all these institutions into the world ; hence no doubt, in every community, spontaneous gatherings of devout men and women who, like our present Christian committees, took up one or other of these needful objects, and had of course at their head directors charged with the responsibility of the work. Such are the persons certainly whom the apostle has in view in our passage. Thus is explained the position of this term between the preceding : *he that giveth*, and the following : *he that showeth mercy*. The same explanation applies to the following clause ἐν σπουδῇ, *with zeal*. This recommendation would hardly be suitable for one presiding over an assembly. How many presidents, on the contrary, would require to have the call addressed to them : Only no zeal ! But the recommendation is perfectly suitable to one who is directing a Christian work, and who ought to engage in it with a sort of exclusiveness, to personify it after a manner in himself.—The last term : ὁ ἐλεῶν, *he that showeth mercy*, denotes the believer who feels called to devote himself to the visiting of the sick and afflicted. There is a gift of sympathy which particularly fits for this sort of work, and which is, as it were, the key to open the heart of the sufferer. The phrase ἐν ἱλαρότητι, literally, *with hilarity*, denotes the joyful eagerness, the amiable grace, the affability going the length of gayety, which make the visitor, whether man or woman, a sunbeam penetrating into the sick-chamber and to the heart of the afflicted.

In the preceding enumeration, the recommendation of the apostle had in view especially *humility* in those who have to exercise a gift. But in the last terms we feel that his thought is already bordering on the virtue of *love*. It is the spectacle of this Christian virtue in full activity in the church and in the world which now fills his mind, and which he presents in the following description, vv. 9–21 : First, self-limiting, self-possessing : this is what he has just been recommending ; then self-giving : this is what he proceeds to expound.

Vv. 9–21

The χαρίσματα, *gifts*, are different, as we have just seen. But there is a gift which is at the root of all the rest, and which ought to be common to all believers, that of all those who have no other, viz. love. The church,

---

[1] In every other case in which it occurs in the N. T., its meaning is to hold an office of rule over others. See 1 Thess. v. 12. ; 1 Tim. iii. 4, 5, 12, v. 17.—T. W. C.

gained by faith in divine love, lives by love. All who believe, love. When this love is sincere, it produces in every believer a spontaneous ministry, which is carried out in his whole life by the manifold activity of love. This beneficent activity is exercised, first, toward the *sympathetic* elements the believer finds around him, vv. 9–16 ; then toward the *hostile* elements which he happens to meet, whether within the church itself or without, vv. 17–21.

Vv. 9–16.

Vv. 9, 10. "*Let love be without dissimulation. Abhor that which is evil, cleave to that which is good. As to brotherly love, being full of tenderness one toward another ; as to honor, each making others to pass before him.*"—In these two verses the apostle speaks of three dispositions, and first, ver. 9, of the fundamental feeling, the principle of all the activity about to be described, as well as of the two characteristics which alone guarantee its sincerity : *love*, in the general sense of the word. There follow in ver. 10 two immediate manifestations of love : *brotherly* love and mutual *respect*.— *Without dissimulation*, literally, *without mask*. The heart ought to feel really the whole measure of affection which it testifies. There is also here something of the σωφρονεῖν, *self-ruling*, the controlling idea of the preceding passage, in opposition to the ὑπερφρονεῖν, *self-exalting*.—The two following verbs : *abhor* and *cleave*, are in the participle in Greek : *abhorring, cleaving*. These participles relate grammatically to the subject of the verb *love*, contained in the substantive *love*. It follows from this construction that the two participles : "abhorring, cleaving," are intended to *qualify* the love unfeigned, by reminding us of the characteristics in virtue of which it deserves the title. This is not here a commonplace recommendation to detest evil and love good. Paul means that love is not *pure* except when it is the declared enemy of evil, even in the person of those whom we love, and that it applies all its energy to labor for their progress in goodness. Destitute of this moral rectitude, which is the spirit of holiness, love is only a form of selfishness.

Ver. 10. The two datives : τῇ φιλαδελφίᾳ, τῇ τιμῇ, which we have translated by : "*as to* brotherly love," "*as to* honor," might be regarded as datives of means : *by*, or *in virtue of*. But it is more natural to take them as a sort of headings in the catalogue of Christian virtues. They are the well-known categories forming the believer's moral catechism. The article τῇ, (*the*) precisely characterizes those virtues as supposed present in the heart. The adjective and participle which follow, show how they are to be realized in the life. The word φιλόστοργος, *full of tenderness*, comes from the verb στέργω, which denotes the delicate attentions mutually rendered by those who cherish one another with natural affection, as parents and children, brothers and sisters, etc. The apostle, by using this term, wishes to give to the love of the members of the church to one another the tender character of a family affection.—The term τιμή denotes the feeling of *respect* which every believer feels for his brother, as one redeemed by Christ and a child of God, like himself.—The verb προηγεῖσθαι strictly signifies : "to put oneself at the head in order to guide." Hence may be deduced the meanings : *to give example* (Meyer), or *to anticipate, to be beforehand with kindness* (Vulg., Luth., Osterv., Oltram., Seg.), or *to surpass* (Chrys.). But in all these meanings we should expect from the usage of the language to find the regimen in the genitive or dative rather than the accusative. Erasmus, Hofmann, etc., proceeding on the sense which the simple verb ἡγεῖσθαι often has : *to esteem, regard* (Phil. ii. 3), translate : "each esteeming others better than himself." This meaning is evidently forced ; but it may be rendered more natural by taking ἡγεῖσθαι in its primitive signification of *con*-

ducting: "Conducting others before you," that is to say, making them pass in all circumstances before yourselves.

There follows a second group of three dispositions which are naturally connected with the preceding and with one another.

Ver. 11. "*As to zeal, being not indolent; fervent in spirit; taking advantage of opportunity.*"[1]—With respectful consideration, ver. 10, there is easily connected the disposition to render service, which is here denoted by the word: *not indolent.*—This in its turn, in order to overcome the resistance of selfishness, in cases where to oblige requires self-sacrifice, and must be, not a natural disposition only, but a powerful movement, due to the impulse of the Divine Spirit, and like an inner fire kept up unceasingly by action from above: *fervent in spirit.* The word *spirit* undoubtedly refers here to the spiritual element in man himself, but that as penetrated and quickened by the Divine Spirit. In reading these words, we see the believer hastening, with his heart on fire, wherever there is any good to be done.—The third proposition presents an important variant. The Alex. and Byz. documents read τῷ Κυρίῳ (*serving*) *the Lord*. The Greco-Lat. text reads τῷ καιρῷ (*serving*) *the time*, the season, the occasion; adapting yourselves to the opportunity. This expression is somewhat strange, but it is common enough in profane Greek; comp. the καιρῷ λατρεύειν (see Meyer), and in Latin the *tempori servire* (Cicero). The very fact that this phrase is without example in the N. T. may speak in favor of its authenticity. For it is far from probable that any one would have replaced so common an expression as that of *serving the Lord* by that of *serving the time*, while the opposite might easily happen, especially if abbreviations were used in writing. The context must therefore decide, and it seems to me that it decides in favor of the Greco-Latin reading. The precept: *serve the Lord*, is too general to find a place in a series of recommendations so particular. The only means of finding a certain suitableness for it would be to understand it thus: "While employing yourselves for men, do it always *with a view to the Lord* and His cause." But it would be necessary to supply precisely the essential idea. On the contrary, the meaning: "serving the opportunity," or "adapting yourselves to the need of the time," admirably completes the two preceding precepts. Zeal, according to God, confines itself to espying providential occasion, and suiting our activity to them; it does not impose itself either on men or things.

There follows a third group, the three elements of which form a small well-connected whole.

Ver. 12. "*Rejoicing in hope, patient in tribulation, persevering in prayer.*" —The fervor of devotion, referred to in ver. 11, has no more powerful auxiliary than *joy;* for joy disposes us to kindness and even to self-sacrifice. But this applies only to Christian joy, to that which is kept up in the heart by the glorious *hopes* of faith.—The passage, chap. v. 3, 4, shows the intimate bond which unites this joy of hope with the *patient endurance* which the believer should display in the midst of trial; comp. 1 Thess. i. 3.—And what are we to do to keep up in the heart the joyful spring of hope, and that firmness of endurance which holds out? *Persevere in prayer*, says the apostle; such is the fruitful principle of those admirable dispositions. The following is Hofmann's paraphrase of the verse: "In so far as we have cause to hope, let us be joyful; in so far as we have cause of pain, let us hold out; in so far as the door of prayer is open to us, let us continue to use it." The force of the datives which head the three propositions could not be better rendered.

Paul came down from charity and its external manifestations to the depths of the inner life; he now returns to the practical manifestations of

---

[1] T. R. reads τα Κυριω (*the Lord*), with ℵ A B E L P, Mnn. Italiq. Syr. But D F G read τω καιρω (*the fitting time*). [Plainly, the external evidence is in favor of the T. R.—T. W. C.]

this feeling, and points out the blessings of active charity extending to three classes of persons: brethren, strangers, enemies.

Vv. 13, 14. "*Distributing to the necessities* [1] *of saints; eager to show hospitality. Bless them that persecute you;* [2] *bless and curse not.*"—The saints are not only the families of the church of Rome, but also all the churches whose wants come to the knowledge of the Christians of the capital. The Byz. and Alex. documents read χρείαις, *the necessities;* while the Greco-Latins read μνείαις, *the remembrances.* Would this term denote the anniversary days consecrated to the memory of martyrs? This meaning would suffice to prove the later origin of this reading. Or should the expression *remembrances* be applied to the pecuniary help which the churches of the Gentiles sent from time to time to the Christians of Jerusalem (Hofmann)? This meaning of μνείαις, in itself far from natural, is not at all justified by Phil. i. 3. The Received reading is the only possible one. The verb κοινωνεῖν strictly signifies *to take part;* then, as a consequence, *to assist effectively.*—There is a gradation from saints to *strangers.* The virtue of hospitality is frequently recommended in the N. T. (1 Pet. iv. 9; Heb. xiii. 2; 1 Tim. v. 10; Tit. i. 8).—The term διώκειν, literally, "*pursue* (hospitality)," shows that we are not to confine ourselves to according it when it is asked, but that we should even seek opportunities of exercising it.

Ver. 14. A new gradation from strangers to them *that persecute.* The act to be done by love becomes more and more energetic, and this is no doubt the reason why the apostle passes abruptly to the imperative, after this long series of participles. Here we have no longer a manifestation which, supposing love, is in a manner understood as a matter of course. To act as the apostle demands, requires a powerful effort of the will, which the imperative expressly intended to call forth. This is also the reason why this order is repeated, then completed in a negative form; for the persecuted one ought, as it were, to say no to the natural feeling which rises in his heart. The omission of the pronoun *you* in the *Vatic.* serves well to bring out the odiousness of persecution in itself, whoever the person may be to whom it is applied.—We do not know whether the apostle had before him the Sermon on the Mount, already published in some document; in any case, he must have known it by oral tradition, for he evidently alludes to the saying of Jesus, Matt v. 44; Luke vi. 28. This discourse of Jesus is the one which has left the most marked traces in the Epistles; comp. Rom. ii. 19; 1 Cor. iv. 12 and 13, vi. 7, vii. 10; Jas. iv. 9, v. 12; 1 Pet. iii. 9 and 14. This recommendation, relating to love toward malevolent persons, is here an anticipation; Paul will return to it immediately.

Now comes a group of four precepts, the moral relation of which is equally manifest.

Vv. 15, 16. "*Rejoice with them that do rejoice,* [3] *weep with them that weep: aspiring after the same aim for one another; not minding high things, but associating with men of low estate. Be not wise in your own eyes.*"—The connection between vv. 14 and 15 is the idea of self-forgetfulness. As self-forgetting is needed to bless him who hates us, we must also be freed from self to identify ourselves with the joy of others when our heart is full of grief, and with his grief when we ourselves are filled with joy. In Greek the two verbs are in the infinitive. This form is rightly explained by understanding δεῖ, *it is necessary.* But here we may be permitted to mark a shade of distinction; the infinitive is the indication of an accidental fact: to act thus every time that the case presents itself. It is less pressing than the imperative; it is, as it were, a virtue of the time being.—The following precept is commonly applied to good feeling between the members of the

---

[1] T. R. reads χρειαις, with ℵ B E L P, Mnn. It. Syr.; D F G read μνειαις.
[2] B omits υμας (*you*).
[3] T. R. reads και between the two propositions, with A E L P, Syr^sch; this word is omitted, ℵ B D F G, It.

church. But in that case there would require to be ἐν ἀλλήλοις, *among you*, and not εἰς ἀλλήλους, *in relation to one another*, and the following precept would have no natural connection with this. The only possible meaning is: "aiming at the same object for one another as for yourselves;" that is to say, having each the same solicitude for the temporal and spiritual well-being of his brethren as for his own; comp. Phil. ii. 4. As this common disinterested aspiration naturally connects itself with sympathy, ver. 15, so it is easily associated with the feeling of *equality* recommended in the following verse. There frequently forms in the congregations of believers an aristocratic tendency, every one striving by means of the Christian brotherhood to associate with those who, by their gifts or fortune, occupy a higher position. Hence small coteries, animated by a proud spirit, and having for their result chilling exclusiveness. The apostle knows these littlenesses, and wishes to prevent them; he recommends the members of the church to attach themselves to all alike, and if they will yield to a preference, to show it rather for the humble. The term ὑψηλά therefore denotes distinctions, high relations, ecclesiastical honors. This neuter term does not at all oblige us, as Meyer thinks, to give a neuter sense to the word ταπεινοῖς in the following proposition: "humble *things;*" the inferior functions in the church. The prep. *with*, in the verb συναπαγόμενοι, *letting yourselves be drawn with*, does not admit of this meaning. The reference is to the most indigent and ignorant, and least influential in the church. It is to them the believer ought to feel most drawn.—The antipathy felt by the apostle to every sort of spiritual aristocracy, to every caste distinction within the church, breaks out again in the last word. Whence come those little coteries, if it is not from the presumptuous feeling each one has of *his own wisdom?* It is this feeling which leads you to seek contact especially with those who flatter you, and whose familiar intercourse does you honor. —This precept is taken from Prov. iii. 7, but it evidently borrows a more special sense from the context.

Already, in ver. 14, the apostle had made, as it were, an incursion into the domain of relations to the hostile elements which the believer encounters around him. He returns to this subject to treat it more thoroughly; here is the culminating point in the manifestations of love. He has in view not merely the enmity of the unbelieving world. He knew only too well from experience, that within the church itself one may meet with ill-will, injustice, jealousy, hatred. In the following verses the apostle describes to us the victory of love over malevolent feelings and practices, from whatever quarter they come, Christians or non-Christians. And first, vv. 17-19, in the passive form of *forbearance;* then, vv. 20, 21, in the active form of generous beneficence.

Vv. 17-19. "*Recompensing to no man evil for evil; being preoccupied with good in the sight of all men. If it be possible, as much as lieth in you, living peaceably with all men. Dearly beloved, avenging not yourselves; but give place unto wrath; for it is written: Vengeance is mine; I will repay, saith the Lord.*"—There is a close connection between the abnegation described in the preceding verses and the love which pardons. Hence it is that the apostle continues, in ver. 17, with a simple participle; for vengeance is very often the effect of wounded pride. But why add the second precept, taken from Prov. iii. 4? Probably the apostle means to contrast preoccupation *with good*, as an antidote, with those sombre thoughts and hostile projects which are cherished under the dominion of resentment. The clause: *before all men*, depends of course on the participle προνοούμενοι, *preoccupying yourselves,*[1] not on the object καλά, *good things*, as Hofmann thinks. Paul would have the believer's inward preoccupation with good to be so manifest in his conduct, even toward his adversaries or enemies, that no

---

[1] Better, Taking thought for what is honorable.—T.W.C.

one shall be able to suspect in him any working of the mind inspired by a contrary disposition. The meaning of the Hebrew is rather different from that of the Alex. version, which the apostle here follows. The original ought probably to be translated thus: "Thou shalt find favor and success before men." The LXX. have translated: "Thou shalt find favor; and do thou consider good before all men."

Ver. 18. This spirit of goodwill is necessarily *pacific;* not only does it not do nor mediate anything which can trouble, but it strives to remove what disunites. The first restriction: *if it be possible,* refers to our neighbor's conduct; for we are not master of his feelings. The second: *as much as lieth in you,* refers to our own; for we can exercise discipline over ourselves. If it does not depend on us to bring our neighbor to pacific dispositions toward us, it depends on us to be always disposed to make peace.

Ver. 19. But this notwithstanding, there is in the heart of man an ineffaceable feeling of justice which the apostle respects. He only desires to give this sentiment its true direction. Evil ought to be punished, that is certain. Only, if thou wouldest not thyself become unjust, think not thou shouldest make thyself the instrument of justice, and peacefully resign this care to God, the just Judge. The apostle knows that he is here requiring a difficult sacrifice. Hence the style of address: *dearly beloved,* by which he reminds his readers of the tender love which dictates this recommendation, a love which is only an emanation of that which God Himself bears to them. *To give place unto wrath,* is to refrain from avenging oneself, in order to give free course to the justice which God Himself will exercise when and how He thinks good. To seek to anticipate His judgment is to bar the way against it. Comp. what is said of Jesus Himself, 1 Pet. ii. 23. It is needless to refute explanations such as the following: "Let your wrath have time to calm down," or: "Let the wrath of the enemy pass." The passage quoted is Deut. xxxii. 35, but modified in conformity with the version of the LXX. The Hebrew text says: "To me belong vengeance and retribution." The LXX. translate: "In the day of punishment I will repay." Either they read *aschallem, I will repay,* instead of *schillem, retribution;* or they freely paraphrased the meaning of the substantive. Paul appropriates the verb: *I will repay,* as they introduced it; and it is remarkable that the author of the Epistle to the Hebrews does exactly the same. The same form is also found in the paraphrase of *Onkelos* (*vaani aschallem*), which seems to prove that this way of quoting the verse was common. It is impossible, therefore, to conclude anything from this analogy as concerning the author of the Epistle to the Hebrews. —But forbearance alone would only be a half victory. It is not enough to refrain from meeting evil with evil; the ambition of love must go the length of wishing to transform evil into good.

Vv. 20, 21. "*Therefore, if*[1] *thine enemy hunger, feed him; if he thirst, give him drink; for in so doing thou shalt heap coals of fire on his head. Be not overcome of evil, but overcome evil with good.*"—The connection: *But if,* in the Alex., would signify: "But, far from avenging thyself, if the opportunity of doing good to thine enemy present itself, seize it." The connection: *Therefore if,* in the Byzs., is somewhat more difficult to apprehend; but it is precisely this fact which speaks in its favor: "Thou oughtest not to avenge thyself; *consequently,* if the occasion present itself of doing good to thine enemy, seize it; for to neglect it would in itself be an act of revenge." The Greco-Latin reading: *if* (simply), merely adds doing good to forbearance; it is the least probable.—The precept is taken, like so many others in this chapter, from the Book of Proverbs; comp.

---

[1] T. R., with E L, reads εαν ουν (*therefore if*); ℵ A B P, Mnn. read εαν δε (*but if*); D F G: ει (*if*) simply.

xxv. 21, 22. It is impossible to suppose that in this book the precept is an encouragement to heap benefits on the head of the evil-doer in order to aggravate the punishment with which God shall visit him (Chrys., Grot., Hengst., etc.). For we read in the same book, xxiv. 17 : "Rejoice not when thine enemy falleth ; and let not thine heart be glad when he stumbleth." Not to be guilty of a self-contradiction, the author would therefore have required to add in our passage : "if thine enemy repent not." In any case, Paul could not quote this saying in such a sense. For how would acting thus be "to overcome evil with good " (ver. 21) ? There is here, therefore, rather a fine irony at the expense of him who would cherish in his heart a desire of vengeance : "Thou wouldst avenge thyself ? Be it ; and here is the way in which God permits thee to do so : Heap benefits on thine enemy ; for thereby thou shalt cause him the salutary pain of shame and regret for all the evil he has done thee ; and thou shalt light up in his heart the fire of gratitude instead of that of hatred." The figure *coals of fire* is common among the Arabs and Hebrews to denote a vehement pain ; but, as Meyer observes, it contains no allusion whatever to the idea of melting or softening the object.

Ver. 21. To render evil for evil, is to let evil have the victory ; to confine oneself to not rendering evil is, if it may be so said, neither to be conqueror nor conquered, though in reality this also is to be conquered. The true victory over evil consists in transforming a hostile relation into one of love by the magnanimity of the benefits bestowed. Thereby it is that good has the last word, that evil itself serves it as an instrument : such is the masterpiece of love.

TWENTY-SIXTH PASSAGE (13:1-10)

The Life of the Believer as a Member of the State

Meyer and many others find no connection whatever between the subject treated in this chapter and that of the foregoing. "A new subject," says this author, " placed here without relation to what precedes." It must be confessed that the connections proposed by commentators are not very satisfactory, and afford some ground for this judgment of Meyer. Tholuck says : The apostle passes here from *private* offences to official persecutions proceeding from the heathen state. But in what follows the state is not regarded as a persecutor ; it is represented, on the contrary, as the guardian of justice. Hofmann sees in the legally-ordered social life one of the aspects of that *good* by which evil ought to be overcome (ver. 21). Schott finds the link between the two passages in the idea of the *vengeance* which God will one day take by the judgment (xii. 19), and which He is taking now by the power of the state (xiii. 4). Better give up every connection than suppose such as these.

As for us, the difficulty is wholly resolved. We have seen that Paul, after pointing to the Christian consecrating his body to God's service, places him successively in the two domains in which he is to realize the sacrifice of himself : that of *spiritual* life properly so called, and that of *civil* life. And what proves that we are really in the track of his thought, is that we discover in the development of this new subject an order exactly parallel to that of the preceding exposition. Paul had pointed to the Christian, first, *limiting* himself by humility, then *giving* himself by love. He follows the same plan in the subsequent passage. In vv. 1–7, he inculcates the duty of *submission* by which the believer controls and limits himself in relation to the state ; then, in vv. 8–10, he enters into the domain of private relations, and points to the Christian giving himself to all in the exercise of *righteousness*. We therefore find here the counterpart of the two passages, xiii. 3–8 and 9–21, the former of which presented the believer in his relations to the church as such ; the latter, in his conduct in the midst of society in general.

If such is the nexus between the subjects treated in these two chapters, there is no necessity for seeking in the local circumstances of the church of Rome for a particular reason to explain this passage. Bauer, proceeding on the idea of a Judeo-Christian majority in this church, has alleged that the apostle meant here to combat the Jewish prejudice which held heathen authorities to be only delegates of Satan, as the prince of this world. But Hofmann justly remarks, that if such were the polemic of the apostle, he would have confined himself to proving that it is *allowable* for the Christian to submit himself to a heathen power, without going the length of making this submission a duty, and a duty not of expediency only, but one of conscience. Weizsäcker also replies to Baur, that if the matter in question were a Jewish prejudice to be combated, the apostle would require especially to remind his readers that the Christian faith does not at all imply, as the Jewish Messianic viewpoint did, the expectation of an earthly kingdom ; whence it follows that nothing is opposed from this side to the submission of believers to the power of the state. It is in this line he argues, in the *First Epistle to the Corinthians*, vii. 21 et seq., when he shows that there is no incompatibility between the position of slave and Christian.[1] Besides, we have seen the error of Baur's hypothesis regarding the Judeo-Christian composition of the church of Rome too clearly to make it necessary for us to spend more time in refuting this explanation. If it were thought absolutely needful to find in the state of this church a particular reason for the following precepts, we should certainly have to prefer Ewald's hypothesis. This critic thinks that the spirit of insubordination which broke out soon after in the Jewish nation in the revolt against the Romans, was already agitating this people, and making itself felt even at Rome. The apostle's intention was therefore, he thinks, to protect the church of the capital from this contagion emanating from the synagogue. This supposition can no more be proved than it can be refuted by positive facts. All that we can say is, that it is not needed to explain the following passage. Expounding the gospel didactically, and the life which flows from it, the apostle must naturally, especially when writing to the church resident in the heart of the empire, develop a duty which was soon to become one of the most important and difficult in the conflicts for which it was necessary to prepare with the heathen power, that of submission to the state on the ground of conscience, and independently of the character of those who wield the power for the time. Weizsäcker thinks that all Paul says here to Christians supposes no persecution to have yet taken place. We think on this point he is mistaken, and that in any state of the case Paul would have spoken as he does. For, as we shall see, he treats the question from the viewpoint of moral principle, which remains always the standard for the Christian. And what is a clear proof of it is, that the course traced by him has been ratified by the conscience of Christians in all epochs, even in times of persecution. It was followed, in particular, by the whole primitive church, and by the Christians of the Reformed Church of France ; and if there was a time when the latter, driven to extremity by extraordinary sufferings, deviated from this line of conduct, their action certainly did not turn out a blessing to them. Moreover, comp. the sayings analogous to those of Paul in Matt. xxvi. 52, Rev. xiii. 10, and the whole of the First Epistle of Peter, especially chap. ii.—We cannot help

---

[1] *Jahrbücher für deutsche Theologie*, 1876, pp. 18 and 19. This author, in another article published in the same journal, the same year, p. 262 et seq., points out how the remarkable prayer for the authorities of the state, which is found in the manuscript of the *First Epistle of Clement of Rome*, recently published by Archbishop Bryennius, chap. 61, furnishes the most striking proof of the *purely Christian* need which is met by the exhortation of St. Paul in our Epistle.

quoting here, as a specimen of Renan's manner, the observation with which he accompanies the precept of the apostle: "Paul had too much tact to be a mover of sedition. He wished the name of Christian to be of good standing" (p. 477).

In vv. 1–7, the apostle points out the Christian's duty in regard to the state (1a), and explains the ground of it (1b). He points out its penal sanction (ver. 2), and justifies it (vv. 3 and 4). Ver. 5 draws the general consequence from these principles; finally, vv. 6 and 7 apply this consequence to the details of social life.

Ver. 1. "*Let every soul submit itself unto the higher powers; for there is no power but of God,*[1] *and the powers*[2] *that be are ordained of God.*"—Why does the apostle say: *every soul*, instead of every man, or rather every believer? Is he alluding to the fact that submission ought to proceed from the inmost sanctuary of the human being (the conscience, ver. 5)? The word *every* does not correspond well with this explanation; it leads rather to the thought that the apostle means to express that a duty is involved which is naturally incumbent on every human being. This is not an obligation on the believer arising from his spiritual life, like the precepts of chap. xii.; it is an obligation of the *psychical* life which is the common domain of mankind. Every free and reasonable being should recognize its suitableness.—The present imperative, $\dot{\upsilon}\pi\omicron\tau\alpha\sigma\sigma\acute{\epsilon}\sigma\theta\omega$, *let it submit itself*, indicates a reflex action, exercised by the man on himself, and that permanently. This expression is, indeed, the counterpart of the term $\sigma\omega\phi\rho\omicron\nu\epsilon\tilde{\iota}\nu$, *to control oneself*, in chap. xii.—The term *higher powers* does not denote merely the highest class of authorities in the state. It is all those powers in general and of all degrees; they are thus designated as being raised above the simple citizen; comp. ver. 7.

The second part of this verse justifies the duty of submission, and that for two reasons: the first is the divine origin of the state as an institution; the second, the will of God which controls the raising of individuals to office at any given time. The first proposition has the character of a general principle. This appears—(1) from the singular $\dot{\epsilon}\xi\omicron\upsilon\sigma\acute{\iota}\alpha$, *power*; comp. the same word in the plural before and, after, in the same verse, which proves that Paul means to speak of power *in itself*, and not of its historical and particular realizations; (2) from the negative form of the proposition: "there is not but of" . . .; this form corresponds also to the enunciation of an abstract principle; (3) from the choice of the preposition $\dot{\alpha}\pi\acute{o}$, *of*, or *on the part of*, which indicates the origin and essence of the fact. It is true the Alexs. and Byzs. read $\dot{\upsilon}\pi\acute{o}$, *by*, in this proposition as well as in the following. But this is one of the cases in which the Greco-Latin text has certainly preserved the true reading. It is clear, whatever Tischendorf may think, that the copyists have changed the first preposition according to that of the following clause.[3] Meyer himself acknowledges this. We shall see that as thoroughly as $\dot{\alpha}\pi\acute{o}$ corresponds to the idea of the first proposition, so thoroughly does $\dot{\upsilon}\pi\acute{o}$ apply to that of the second. Paul means, therefore, first, that the institution of the state is according to the plan of God who created man as a social being; so that we are called to recognize in the existence of a power (authority) the realization of a divine thought. In the second proposition he goes further ($\delta\acute{\epsilon}$, *and, moreover*). He declares that at each time the very persons who are established in office occupy this exalted position only in virtue of a divine dispensation. This gradation from the first idea to the second appears—(1) from the particle $\delta\acute{\epsilon}$; (2) from the participle $\omicron\tilde{\upsilon}\sigma\alpha\iota$, *those who are*, that is to say, who are there; this term added here would be superfluous if it did not denote the historical

---

[1] T. R., with D E F G: απο θεου; ℵ A B L P, Mnn. read υπο θεου.
[2] ℵ A B D F G omit εξουσιαι.
[3] Here again the author differs, not only from Tischendorf, but also from all the modern editors.—T. W. C.

fact in opposition to the idea; (3) from the return to the plural (*the powers*), which proves that Paul means again to designate here, as in the first part of the verse, the manifold realizations of social power; (4) from the affirmative form of the proposition, which applies to the real fact; (5) from the preposition ὑπό, *by*, which more naturally describes the historical fact than would be done by the preposition ἀπό, *on the part of*.—The word ἐξουσίαι in the T. R. is probably only a copyist's addition.

But for the very reason of this precept it is asked: If it is not merely the state in itself which is a thought of God, but if the very individuals who possess the power at a given time are set up by His will, what are we to do in a period of revolution, when a new power is violently substituted for another? This question, which the apostle does not raise, may, according to the principles he lays down, be resolved thus: The Christian will submit to the new power as soon as the resistance of the old shall have ceased. In the actual state of matters he will recognize the manifestation of God's will, and will take no part whatever in any reactionary plot. But should the Christian support the power of the state even in its unjust measures? No, there is nothing to show that the submission required by Paul includes active co-operation; it may even show itself in the form of passive resistance, and it does not at all exclude protestation in word and even resistance in deed, provided that to this latter there be joined the calm acceptance of the punishment inflicted; comp. the conduct of the apostles and Peter's answer, Acts v. 29, 40-42.[1] This submissive but at the same time firm conduct is also a homage to the inviolability of authority; and experience proves that it is in this way all tyrannies have been morally broken, and all true progress in the history of humanity effected.

Ver. 2. "*Whosoever, therefore, rebelleth against the power, resisteth the ordinance of God; now, they that resist shall receive to themselves a judgment.*"— This verse exhibits the guilt, and, as a consequence, the inevitable punishment of revolt. The term ἀντιτασσόμενος is the counterpart of ὑποτάσσεσθαι, ver. 1. The perfect ἀνθέστηκεν, as well as the participle which follows, has the meaning of the present.—The term διαταγή, *ordinance*, includes the two ideas expressed in 1*b*: an institution, and a fact of which God Himself is the ordainer. This term etymologically and logically recalls the three preceding: ὑποτασσέσθω, ἀντιτασσόμενος, and τεταγμέναι.—The application of the principle laid down here remains always the same, whatever may be the form of government, Monarchical or Republican. Every revolt has for its effect to shake for a longer or shorter time the feeling of respect due to a divine institution; and hence the judgment of God cannot fail to overtake him who becomes guilty.—Undoubtedly the term κρίμα, *judgment*, without article, does not refer to eternal perdition; but neither should we apply it, with many critics, solely to the punishment which will be inflicted by the authority attacked. Most certainly, in the mind of the apostle, it is God who will put forth His hand to avenge *His institution* which has been compromised, whether he do so directly or by some human instrumentality. Paul here reproduces in a certain sense, but in another form, the saying of Jesus, Matt. xxvi. 52: "All they that take the sword shall perish by the sword." Volkmar has thought good, in connection with this precept, to advance a supposition which resembles a wicked piece of pleasantry. He alleges that when the author of the Apocalypse represents the false prophet seeking to induce men to submit to the beast (the Antichrist), he meant to designate Paul himself, who, in our passage, teaches the Christians of Rome to submit to the emperor. But the author of this ingenious hypothesis will yet acknowledge that *to submit* is not the equivalent of *to worship* (Rev.

---

[1] "The Christian's duty is to obey until the duty of resistance is clearly proven."—Riddle. —T. W. C.

xiii. 12). And to give this application any probability whatever, the Apocalypse must have avoided reproducing exactly the saying of Jesus which we have just quoted, and the precept of Paul himself, by cautioning Christians against revolt, and saying to them, xiii. 10: "He that killeth with the sword must be killed with the sword ; here is the patience and the faith of the saints." It is obvious that Jesus, Paul, and John have only one and the same watchword to give to the believer in regard to his relations to the state : submission, and, when necessary, patience.

Vv. 3, 4. "*For rulers are not a terror to good works, but to the evil.*[1] *Now wouldest thou not be afraid of the power? do that which is good, and thou shalt have praise from the same ; for he is the minister of God to thee for good. But if thou do that which is evil, be afraid ; for it is not in vain that he beareth the sword, for he is a minister of God, to execute just wrath upon him that doeth evil.*"—If revolt is a crime, and a crime which cannot fail to receive punishment, it is because the power whose authority it attacks is a *divine delegation* in the midst of human society, and is charged with a moral mission of the highest importance ; hence the *for.*—The *good work* is not submission, and the *evil work* is not revolt. Paul means by the one the practice of justice, and by the other that of injustice, in general, in the whole social life. The state is called to encourage the doing of good, and to repress the doing of evil in the domain which is confided to it. This domain is not that of the inward feelings, it is that of external deeds, of *work* or *works*, as the apostle says. It matters little which of the two readings (the dative singular or the genitive plural) is preferred ; the first is better supported.—After this general declaration, the apostle takes up again each of the two alternatives. And first that of *well-doing*, vv. 3*b* and 4*a*. The verses have been badly divided here. The first proposition of ver. 4 belongs still to the idea of ver. 3, that of well-doing.—No doubt it may happen, contrary to what the apostle says, that the virtuous man falls under the vengeance of the laws, or becomes a butt for the unjust dealings of the magistracy. But it remains true that in this case good is not punished *as good*. An unjust law or a tyrannical power make it appear falsely as evil ; and the result of this suffering unjustly endured will certainly be the reform of the law and the fall of the power. Never has any power whatever laid down as a principle the punishment of good and the reward of evil, for thereby it would be its own destroyer.—The *praise* of which the apostle speaks consists, no doubt, in the consideration which the man of probity generally enjoys in the eyes of the magistracy, as well as in the honorable functions which he is called by it to fill.

Ver. 4*a*. If it is so, it is because magistracy is a divine ministry, instituted for the good of every citizen (σοί, *to thee*), and because, though it may err in the application, it cannot in principle deny its charge to assert justice.

Ver. 4*b*. The other alternative : *evil-doing*. The power of the state is not to be feared except by him who acts unjustly.—The verb φορεῖν, a frequentative from φέρειν, *to carry*, denotes official and habitual bearing.—The term μάχαιρα, *sword*, denotes (in opposition to ξίφος, the poniard or straight-edged sword) a large knife with bent blade, like that carried by the chiefs in the *Iliad*, and with which they cut the neck of the victims, similar to our *sabre*. Paul by this expression does not here denote the weapon which the emperor and his pretorian prefect carried as a sign of their power of life and death—the application would be too restricted—but that which was worn at their side, in the provinces, by the superior magistrates, to whom belonged the right of capital punishment, and which they caused to be borne solemnly before them in public processions. It has been said that this expression was not intended by the apostle to convey the notion of the

---

[1] T. R. reads, with E L., Mnn. Syr. : των αγαθων εργων . . . των κακων ; but א A B D F G P, It. read τω αγαθω εργω . . . τω κακω.

punishment of death. The sword, it is said, was simply the emblem of the right to punish in general, without involving anything as to the punishment of death in particular. Is not Philippi right in answering to this: that it is impossible to exclude from the right of punishing the very kind of punishment from which the emblem representing this right is taken? It is improper to bring in here the idea of the grace of the gospel. For at the very time when the state is carrying out on the criminal the work of justice to which it is called, the church may, without the least contradiction, carry out toward the same man the work of mercy which is divinely confided to it. Thus Paul devotes to the *destruction of the flesh* (1 Cor. v. 4, 5) the same man whose salvation he labors to procure against the day of Christ. And Peter tells us of men who perished when *judged according to the flesh*, but to whom the gospel is preached that they may live *in spirit* according to God. Experience even proves that the last punishment of the law is very often the means of opening up in the heart of the malefactor a way for divine grace. The penalty of death was the first duty imposed on the state at the time of its divine founding, Gen. ix. 6: " Whoso sheddeth man's blood, *by man* shall his blood be shed ; for God made man after His image." It is profound respect for human life which in certain cases enjoins the sacrifice of human life. The question involved is not that of simple social expediency, but that of keeping up the human conscience to the level of the value which God Himself attaches to the human person.—The last proposition is exactly parallel to that with which the apostle had concluded the first alternative, that of good (ver. 4*a*). When the magistracy punishes, no less than when it rewards, it does so as God's agent and vicegerent on the earth (διάκονος, *servant*).—In the expression ἔκδικος εἰς ὀργήν, *an avenger for wrath*, there is not, as might be thought, an unmeaning pleonasm. The meaning is : *an avenger by office* to satisfy the demands of *wrath*, that of God, the only wrath perfectly holy. The expression ἔκδικος might be used here in a favorable sense : to render justice to him who is trampled on ; comp. Luke xviii. 3, 5, 7, and 8.

Ver. 5. " *Wherefore ye must needs be subject*,[1] *not only because of the wrath, but also for conscience' sake.*"—If the state were only armed with means of punishing, it would be enough to regard it with fear ; but it is the representative of God to assert justice among men ; and hence it is from a principle of *conscience* that submission must be given to it. It is obvious that the apostle has a much nobler idea of the state than those who make this institution rest on utilitarian grounds. As its foundation he lays down a divine principle, and sees in it an essentially moral institution. This teaching was the more necessary as the Christians were daily witnesses of the corruption which reigned in heathen administration, and might be led to involve in one common reprobation both the institution and its abuses. But it must not be forgotten that, in assigning conscience as a ground for obedience, the apostle is in the very act indirectly tracing the limit of this obedience. For the very reason that the state governs in God's name, when it comes to order something contrary to God's law, there is nothing else to be done than to make it feel the contradiction between its conduct and its commission (see above, the example of the apostles), and that while still rendering homage to the divine principle of the state by the respect with which the protest in the case is expressed and the calmness with which the punishment inflicted is borne.

In the two following verses the apostle confirms by a particular fact of public life the notion of the state which he has just been expounding (ver. 6), and passes from the principle to its practical applications (ver. 7).

Vv. 6, 7. " *For it is for this cause also that ye pay tribute; for they are God's ministers for this very thing, attending thereto continually. Render*[2] *to*

---

[1] D E F G reject ἀνάγκη and read ὑποτασσεσθε.
[2] T. R. reads here ουν, *therefore ;* this word is omitted by ℵ A B D.

all their dues: tribute to whom tribute; custom to whom custom; fear to whom fear; honor to whom honor.''—There is a usage universally practised, and whose propriety no one disputes: that is, the payment of tribute for the support of the state. How are we to explain the origin of such a usage, except by the general conviction of the indispensable necessity of the state? The: *for this cause*, does not refer specially to the idea of ver. 5, but to the whole preceding development from ver. 1. The *for* makes the practical consequence (the payment of tribute) the proof of the principle, and the *also* refers to the agreement between the general idea and the particular fact. It is unnecessary, therefore, with Hofmann, to make the verb τελεῖτε, *ye pay*, an imperative: *Pay*. It is a simple fact which Paul states. —The apostle, to designate the divine character of the state, here uses a still graver term than that of *servant*, ver. 4. He calls him λειτουργός, *minister*. This term, compounded of the words λαός, *people*, and ἔργον, *work*, denotes one who labors for the people, who fills a *public office*, and with the complement Θεοῦ, *of God*, a public office in the religious sphere, like the priests and Levites in the theocracy. Among the Jews these divine functionaries were supported by means of the tithe; the same principle, in the view of the apostle, explains the tribute paid by citizens to the state: for the state performs a function for God.—Some have translated: "For ministers are *of God*." The meaning is impossible grammatically; it would require the article before λειτουργοί.—The clause which follows: *for this very thing*, might depend on the participle προσκαρτεροῦντες, *applying themselves to*. But it is more natural to make it depend on the expression λειτουργοί: "ministers for this very thing"—that is to say, to make justice reign by checking evil and upholding good. Olshausen and Philippi apply the words: *for this very thing*, to the payment of tribute, which would signify that the state is God's minister to levy tribute, or that it may watch continually on this levying. Neither the one nor the other of these two ideas rises to the height of the notion of the state as it has just been expounded. This appendix: προσκαρτεροῦντες, *attending thereto continually*, seems at the first glance superfluous; but it is intended to account for the payment of tribute because the magistrates, devoting *their whole time* to the maintenance of public order and the well-being of the citizens, cannot themselves provide for their support, and ought consequently to be maintained at the expense of the nation.

Ver. 7. After thus confirming the notion of the state which he has enunciated, the apostle deduces from it some practical applications. Four MSS. reject the *therefore*, which is read in all the others. We may indeed be content to understand this particle. The imperative *render* thus becomes somewhat livelier.—Foremost is placed the general obligation which is afterward specified. The verb ἀπόδοτε, *render*, belongs to the four principal propositions which follow. The verb of the four dependent propositions is understood; it is ὀφείλετε, *ye owe*, to be taken from the substantive ὀφειλάς: "him to whom ye [*owe*] tribute, [*render*] tribute."—Πᾶσι, *to all*, denotes all persons in office.—The term, φόρος, *tribute*, refers to a personal impost, the annual capitation (the *tributum*); the word is connected with συμφέρειν, to contribute regularly to a common expenditure; the word τέλος, *custom*, denotes the custom duty on goods (*vectigal*); it comes from the verb τελεῖν, *to pay* (occasionally); φόβος, *fear*, expresses the feeling due to the highest authorities, to supreme magistrates before whom the lictor walks, and who are invested with the power of life and death; τιμή, *honor*, applies generally to all men in office.

The church did not neglect the faithful discharge of all these obligations. The author of the Epistle to Diognetus, describing in the second century the conduct of Christians during a time of persecution, characterizes it by these two words: "They are outraged, and honor (ὑβρίζονται καὶ τιμῶσι)." The passage, 1 Pet. ii. 13–17, presents, especially in ver. 14, a striking resemblance to ours. The Apostle Paul is too original to allow us to suppose that he imitated Peter. Could the latter, on the other hand, know the Epistle to the Romans? Yes, if he wrote from Rome; hardly, if he wrote from Babylon. But it is probable that the two apostles, when they lived together at Jerusalem or Antioch, conversed on a subject so important for the guidance of the church, and so the thoughts, and even the most striking expressions of the Apostle Paul, might have been impressed on the mind of Peter.

From the duty of submission to the state, Paul passes to that of justice in private relations.

Ver. 8. "*Owe no man anything, save to love one another ; for he that loveth another hath fulfilled the law.*"—The expression *anything* and *no man* clearly indicate a transition to the private sphere. Most commentators think that Paul here returns to the duty of love; Meyer, for example, says at the beginning of vv. 8–14: "Exhortation to *love* and to Christian conduct in general." As if the apostle were in the habit of thus resuming without cause a subject already treated, and as if, wishing to describe the task of love, he could have contented himself with saying, as he does in ver. 10: "Love *worketh no ill* to his neighbor !" No, the apostle does not wander from his subject: the duty of *justice*. Only he is not ignorant that there is no perfectly sure pledge for the exercise of this duty except love. This is what leads him to speak again of love, and what explains at the same time the purely negative form he uses: "not to do wrong," an expression which is the formula of justice, much more than that of love. Love is therefore not mentioned here except as the solid support of justice.—The believer should keep no other debt in his life than that which a man can never discharge, the debt which is renewed and even grows in proportion as it is discharged: that of loving. In fact, the task of love is infinite. The more active love is, the more it sees its task enlarge; for, inventive as it is, it is ever discovering new objects for its activity. This debt the believer therefore carries with him throughout all his life (chap. xii.). But he can bear no other debt against him; and loving thus, he finds that in the very act he has fulfilled all the obligations belonging to the domain of justice, and which the law could have imposed.—How could it have occurred to the mind of Hofmann to refer the words τὸν ἕτερον, *the other*, to νόμον, *the law :* "He that loveth hath fulfilled *the other* law"—that is to say, the rest of the law, what the law contains other than the commandment of love? Love is not in the law a commandment *side by side* with all the rest; it is itself the essence of the law.—The perfect πεπλήρωκεν. *hath fulfilled*, denotes that in the one act of loving there is virtually contained the fulfilment of all the duties prescribed by the law. For a man does not offend, or kill, or calumniate, or rob those whom he loves. Such is the idea developed in the two following verses.

Vv. 9, 10. "*For this : Thou shalt not commit adultery, thou shalt not kill, thou shalt not steal,*[1] *thou shalt not covet ; and if there be any other commandment, it is summed up in this saying, namely,*[2] *Thou shalt love thy neighbor as thyself. Love worketh no ill to his neighbor; therefore*[3] *love is the fulfilling of the law.*"—It has been asked why the apostle only mentioned here the commandments of the second table. Simply because he does not make ethics at will, and because he keeps strictly to his subject. Duties to God do not belong to *justice ;* the obligations which constitute the latter are therefore found solely in the second table of the law, which was, so to speak, the civil code of the Jewish people. It is this also which explains the *negative* form of the commandments. Justice does not require the positive doing of good, but only the abstaining from doing *wrong* to others. Paul begins like

---

[1] T. R. here reads ου ψευδομαρτυρησεισ, but with ℵ P only.
[2] B F G, It. omit the words εν τω.
[3] D F G, It. read δε instead of ουν.

Jesus, Mark x. 19, Luke xviii. 20, and Jas. ii. 11, with the commandment forbidding adultery; Philo does the same. Hofmann thinks this order arises from the fact that the relation between man and wife is anterior to the relation which a man holds to all his neighbors. This solution is not so inadmissible as Meyer thinks. The latter believes that the apostle simply follows the order which he finds in his manuscript of the LXX.; for such inversions are observed in the MSS. of this version.—According to the most of the documents belonging to the three families, the words: "Thou shalt not bear false witness," are unauthentic. This is possible; for Paul closes the enumeration with the general expression: "and if there be any other commandment." The commandment which forbids *covetousness* is mentioned here, because it puts the finger on the secret principle of the violation of all the rest. It is really in the struggle with this internal source of all injustices that love appears as the indispensable auxiliary of justice; what other feeling than love could extinguish covetousness?—The word ἕτερον, *different*, is not, strictly speaking, used for ἄλλον, *other;* it reminds us that every article of the code protects our neighbor on a different side from the preceding.—The apposition ἐν τῷ, *in the* (namely), though wanting in some MSS., is certainly authentic; it might easily be forgotten after the preceding substantive (ἐν τῷ λόγῳ). Like the τὸ γάρ, *for this*, at the beginning of the verse, it points to the saying quoted as something familiar to all readers.—The quotation is taken from Lev. xix. 18; as true as it is that one does not wrong himself, so true is it that it contains all the duties of justice to our neighbor. Ἀνακεφαλαιοῦν: to gather up a plurality in a unity; Eph. i. 10.—The Alexs. have thought right to correct the ἑαυτόν, *himself*, by σεαυτόν, *thyself*. It was not in the least necessary; comp. John xviii. 34.

Ver. 10. The *asyndeton* between these two verses arises from the vividness with which the author perceives their logical relation: "No, *certainly!* love cannot do wrong"... It has been asked why the apostle speaks here only of the evil which love does not do, and not of the good which it does. "The good to be done," answers Hofmann, "was understood as a matter of course." But the evil not to be done was still more so. The explanation of the fact arises from what precedes. Love is spoken of here only as the means and pledge of the fulfilment of justice. Now, the functions of justice have a negative character (not to do wrong).—The second proposition of this verse serves only to express as a conclusion (*therefore*, true reading) the maxim laid down as a thesis in ver. 8, and regarded as demonstrated.—Πλήρωμα, *the fulfilment;* strictly: what fills a void; the void here is the commandment to be fulfilled.

Paul has thus closed his exposition of the Christian's duties as a member of civil society. It only remains for him to direct the minds of his readers to the solemn expectation which can sustain their zeal and perseverance in the discharge of all those religious and social obligations.

The nature of the state, according to Rom. xiii.—The apostle's doctrine on this important subject occupies the mean between two opposite errors, both equally dangerous: that which *opposes* the state to the church, and that which *confounds* them. The first view is that which is expressed in the famous maxim: "The state is godless" (Odillon Barrot). Bordering on this saying, as it seems, was Vinet's thought when he wrote the words: "The state is the flesh," thus contrasting it with the church, which would be the incarnation of the Spirit. This opinion appears to us false, because the state represents the natural man, and the natural man is neither "godless," nor "the flesh" pure and simple. There is in him a moral element, the law written in the heart (chap. ii. 14 and 15), and even a religious element, God's natural revelation to the human soul (i. 19 –21). And these two elements superior to the flesh ought to enter also into the society of natural men organized as a state. This is what St. Paul has thoroughly marked, and what, according to him, gives a moral and even religious character to the institution of the state, as we have just seen in explaining this passage. But, on the other hand, we must beware of confounding this religious character of the state with the Christian character. It is impossible to distinguish the Christian sphere from the civil more exactly than Paul does in these two chapters, xii. and xiii. The one belongs to the psychical order; hence the πᾶσα ψυχή, *every human soul*, xiii. 1 ; the other is spiritual or pneumatic, and supposes faith (xii. 1-6). The one has justice as its principle of obligation, the other love. To the one belong means of constraint, for we have the right to demand of every man that he discharge the duties of justice ; the other is the reign of liberty, because love is essentially spontaneous, and cannot be exacted from any one. There is therefore a profound *distinction* between the state and the church, according to Paul's teaching, but not *opposition*, any more than between law and grace, or between justice and love. As the law paves the way for grace, and as the conscientious practice of justice prepares the soul for the exercise of love, so the state, by repressing crime, preserves public order, and thereby the condition in which the church can tranquilly pursue her work, that of transforming the citizens of the earth into citizens of the kingdom of heaven. There is thus a reciprocal service which the two institutions render to one another. But we must beware of going further ; the church has nothing more to ask of the state than her freedom of action, that is to say, the common right. So Paul himself declares, 1 Tim. ii. 1 and 2. And on its side the state has not to espouse the interests of the church, nor consequently to impose on this society, which it has not contributed to form, any belief or procedure whatever. The essence and origin of the two societies being different, their administration ought to remain distinct.—Such is the result of the exposition which we have just studied in chaps. xii. and xiii. In tracing these outlines of the philosophy of right and of the theory of the state, by how many centuries was St. Paul ahead of his own age, and perhaps of ours? We have palpable proof of the truth of the saying with which he introduces this whole moral doctrine (xii. 3) : "I declare unto you by the grace given unto me."

TWENTY-SEVENTH PASSAGE (13:11-14)

The Expectation of Christ's coming again a Motive to Christian Sanctification.

This passage is the counterpart of that with which the apostle had begun his moral teaching, xii. 1 and 2. There he had laid down the principle : a living consecration of the body to God under the guidance of a mind renewed by faith in the mercies of God. This was, as it were, the impelling force which should sustain the believer in his twofold spiritual and civil walk. But that this course may be firm and persevering, there must be joined to the impelling force a power of attraction exercised on the believer's heart by an aim, a hope constantly presented to him by faith. This glorious expectation is what the apostle reminds us of in the following passage. The passage, xii. 1, 2, was the foundation ; this, xiii. 11-14, is the corner-stone of the edifice of Christian sanctification.

Vv. 11, 12. "*And this, knowing the season, that now it is high time for you*[1] *to awake out of sleep ; for now is salvation nearer to us than when we believed. The night is far spent, the day is at hand ; let us therefore cast off the works of darkness, and*[2] *let us put on the instruments of light.*"—The somewhat abrupt transition from ver. 10 to ver. 11 has been differently understood. What is the principal verb on which the participle εἰδότες, *knowing*, rests? Meyer thinks that we must go back on ὀφείλετε (ver. 8), " Owe no man anything."

---
[1] T. R. reads ημας, with D E F G L, It. Syr^sch the reading is υμας in ℵ in A B C P.
[2] A B C D E P read δε instead of και.

But there is no *special* relation to be observed between the duty of justice, ver. 8, and the following passage. Lange has recourse to a strong ellipsis; he derives from the participle *knowing* the understood verb *we know* (comp. xii. 6), which leads to this meaning: "and knowing this (that love is the fulfilling of the law), we know also the importance of the present moment (the nearness of final salvation)." The logical connection between these two ideas would thus be this: When once love is present, perfect salvation cannot be far off. This meaning is ingenious, but very far-fetched, and this construction is not sufficiently justified by xii. 6. Hofmann, feeling the impossibility of these explanations, has recourse to the following expedient: he gives τοῦτο, *that*, an abverbial meaning: *in that way*, or *in that respect*. The clause would therefore signify: "Knowing the time *thus far*, that the hour is come for you to awake"—that is to say, the true meaning of the present moment is the obligation to awake. This strange construction is its own condemnation.—After the exposition which we have given of the plan of this whole moral part, we are not embarrassed by this transition. In the words: *And this*, Paul sums up all the foregoing precepts, all the duties of love and justice, enumerated chaps. xii. and xiii., with the view of passing to the fourth and last section of this part: "And all that [we fulfil], knowing" . . . The idea of fulfilling did not need to be specially expressed, because the foregoing precepts along with the idea of duties included that of their execution.—Faithfulness in the realization of such a life rests on the knowledge which Christians have of the present situation of the world and of its significance: "The hour is solemn; time is short; we shall soon be no longer able to labor on the work of our sanctification; there is not an instant to lose." In the following proposition: "It is high time for you to awake out of sleep," the apostle compares the Christian's position to that of a man who has begun to awake from the sleep in which he was plunged, and who, by an energetic act, requires to overcome the last remnant of sleepiness. *Sleep* is the state of forgetfulness of God and of estrangement from Him, and the carnal security of the man of the world in this state. *Awaking* is the act by which man reaches the lively conviction of his responsibility, gives himself to the impulse of prayer drawing him to God, and enters into communication with Him to obtain through Christ the pardon of his sins and divine help. As to awakening, his readers had already experienced it; but the most awakened in the church has still need of awakening; and hence the apostle reminds his readers that the meaning of the present situation is the duty of awakening thoroughly. The word ἤδη, *already (now)*, is well explained by Philippi: *at length*, "high time."—The reading ὑμᾶς, *you*, is to be preferred to the reading ἡμᾶς, *us*. The latter evidently arises from the following verb, which is in the first person plural.

The need of a complete awakening arises from the rapidity with which *the day* is approaching to which we are moving on. Paul understands by this day the decisive moment of *Christ's coming again*, which he proceeds to compare (ver. 12) to the rising of the sun in nature. He here calls it *salvation*, because this will be the hour of complete redemption for believers; comp. v. 10, viii. 23-25, x. 10.—The march of events to this goal, or of this goal to us, is so rapid, says the apostle, that the interval which separates us from it has already sensibly diminished since he and his readers were brought to the faith. To understand this saying, which is somewhat surprising when we think of the eighteen centuries which have followed the time when it was written, it must be remembered, 1st. That the Lord had promised His return at the time when all the nations of the earth had heard His Gospel; and 2d. That the apostle, looking back on his own career, and seeing in a sense the whole known world evangelized by his efforts (Col. i. 6), might well say without exaggeration that the history of the kingdom of God had made a step in advance during the course of his ministry. Of course this saying supposes that the apostle had no idea of the ages which should yet elapse before the advent of Christ. The revelation of the Lord had taught him *that* He would return, but not *when* He would return.[1] And when it was sought to fix this time, the apostle himself opposed the attempt (1 Thess. v. 1, 2 ; 2 Thess. ii. 1 et seq.). He expresses himself sometimes as a possible witness of it (1 Thess. iv. 17 ; 1 Cor. xv. 52) ; sometimes as if he were not to have part in it ; 1 Cor. vi. 14 (ἡμᾶς, *us*, the undoubted reading) ; 2 Tim. iv. 18. And is it not thus we ought to live constantly, waiting without ceasing? Is not this attitude the most favorable to progress in sanctification? Did not Jesus claim this of His own when He said, Luke xii. 36 : " Be ye like unto men that wait for their lord when he will return from the wedding, that when he cometh and knocketh, they may open unto him immediately" ? And if it is not He who comes to us in the Parousia, is it not we who shall go to Him in death? Is not death for the individual what the Parousia is for the church as a whole, meeting with the Lord?—The interval between the time when the readers had come to the faith and that of this solemn meeting, individual or collective, was therefore sensibly shortened since the day of their conversion.

Ver. 12. On the one hand the night advanced, on the other the day drew near. The former of these figures signifies that the time granted to the present world to continue its life without God had moved on, was shortened ; the latter, that the appearing of the kingdom of Christ had approached. Hence a double inference : As the night is dissipated, there should be an end of the works of the night ; and as the day begins to shine, awaking should be completed, and there should be effected what may be called the toilet worthy of full day.—The *works of darkness:* all that dare not be done by day, and which is reserved for night (ver. 13). The term ὅπλα may be translated in two ways : the *instruments* or *arms* of light. The parallel, 1 Thess. v. 4–11, speaks in favor of the second sense. In that case the reference would be to the breastplate, the helmet, the sandals of the Roman soldiery, *arms* which may be regarded as garments fitted on in the morning to replace the dress of night. But the delineation as a whole does not seem to apply to a day of battle ; rather it appears that the day in question is one of peaceful labor. And for this reason we think it more natural to apply the expression ὅπλα here to the *garments* of the laborious workman who, from early morning, holds himself in readiness for the hour when his master waits to give him his task. These figures are applied in vv. 13 and 14 : the *works of night*, in ver. 13 ; the *instruments of light*, in ver. 14.

Vv. 13, 14. " *Let us walk becomingly, as in the day, not in revelling and drunkenness, not in chambering and wantonness, not in strife and passion ; but put ye on the Lord Jesus Christ, and be not preoccupied with the flesh to excite its lusts.*"[2]—The words ὡς ἐν ἡμέρᾳ signify : "as is done in full day ;" but not without allusion to the fact that the light which shines in the believer's soul is the very light which shall break on the world in the *day* of salvation, in the hour of the Parousia ; comp. 1 Thess. v. 5 and 8.—Christian holiness is represented here as the highest decency (εὐσχημόνως, *decently*), to be compared with that full attitude of dignity which the rising of the sun enjoins on the man who respects himself. Worldly conduct resembles, on the contrary, those indecencies to which men dare not give themselves up except by burying them in the shades of night. Such a mode of acting is therefore incompatible with the situation of a man who is already enlightened by the first rays of the great day.—The *works of night* are enumerated in pairs : first, sensuality in the forms of eating and drinking ; then im-

---

[1] " He himself knew that he could not know the time."—Riddle.—T. W. C.
[2] A C read εις επιθυμιαν ; F G It. : εν επιθυμιαις ; all the others : εις επιθυμιας.

purity, those of brutal libertinism and wanton lightness; finally, the passions which break out either in personal disputes or party quarrels. This last term seems to me to express the meaning of the word $\zeta\tilde{\eta}\lambda o\varsigma$, in this passage, better than the translations *jealousy* or *envy*. Comp. 1 Cor. iii. 3; 2 Cor. xii. 20; Gal. v. 20.

Ver. 14. To lay aside what belongs to the night of worldly life, is only the first part of the preparation to which we are called by the rising of the great day. Our concern must be, besides, to put on the dispositions which are in keeping with so holy and brilliant a light. What is this new equipment which we must haste to substitute for the old? Paul indicates it in the expression : *to put on Jesus Christ*. He certainly speaks of Christ here not as our *righteousness*, but as our *sanctification*, 1 Cor. i. 30. The toilet of the believer, if one may venture so to speak, in view of the approaching salvation, consists solely in putting on Christ, in appropriating by habitual communion with Him all His sentiments and all His manner of acting. He thus becomes for His redeemed ones Himself the robe for the marriage-feast. The Christian will be unable to stand before Him except in so far as he is "found *in Him*" (Phil. iii. 9).

It seemed as if this forcible recommendation : "But put ye on the Lord Jesus Christ," should close the passage. But the apostle adds a last word, which is certainly intended to form the transition to the following passage.

This pure garment of the believer (Christ's holiness which he appropriates) should be kept free from every stain. But the apostle here perceives a very common infirmity, which is not made greatly matter of self-reproach, and against which he feels the need of putting his readers particularly on their guard. It is a sensuality which has not the gross character of the works of night, and which may even assume a lawful form. The body being an indispensable servant, is it not just to take care of it? The apostle does not deny this. But to take care of the body and *to be preoccupied* with its satisfaction are two different things. The expression $\pi\rho\acute{o}\nu o\iota a\nu$ $\pi o\iota\varepsilon\tilde{\iota}\sigma\theta a\iota$, *to give oneself up to preoccupation*, clearly indicates a thought directed with a certain intensity toward sensual enjoyment. I do not think the notion of sin is contained in the word *flesh*, which simply denotes here our sensitive nature ; it is rather to be found in the term : *to preoccupy oneself with*. Paul does not forbid the believer to accept a pleasure which comes of itself ; comp. the touching expression, Acts xxvii. 3, where it is said of Julius the centurion that he allowed Paul to repair to his friends *to enjoy their attentions* ($\varepsilon\pi\iota\mu\varepsilon\lambda\varepsilon\acute{\iota}a\varsigma$ $\tau\upsilon\chi\varepsilon\tilde{\iota}\nu$). But to accept with pleasure the satisfaction which God gives, is quite another thing from going in quest of pleasure. In this second case there is a weakness, or, to speak more properly, a defilement which spoils the marriage garments of many Christians.—The last words : $\varepsilon\iota\varsigma$ $\dot{\varepsilon}\pi\iota\theta\upsilon\mu\acute{\iota}a\varsigma$, literally, *for lusts*, may be regarded either as expressing the aim of the preoccupation : "Do not preoccupy yourselves *with a view to* satisfying lusts," or, as a reflection of Paul himself, intended to justify the previous warning : "Do not preoccupy yourselves with the satisfaction of the flesh *so as to* (or : which would not fail to) give rise to lusts." Both constructions are possible. But the second meaning seems to us simpler. The clause $\varepsilon\iota\varsigma$ $\dot{\varepsilon}\pi\iota\theta\upsilon\mu\acute{\iota}a\varsigma$ thus understood well justifies the warning : "Be not preoccupied with" . . .—These verses, 13 and 14, have acquired a sort of historical celebrity ; for, as related by St. Augustine in the eighth book of the *Confessions*, they were the occasion of his conversion, already prepared for by his relations with St. Ambrose. If ver. 13 had been the inscription of his past life, ver. 14 became that of his new life.

We may now be convinced that the practical treatise, which serves as a complement to the doctrinal, is not less systematically arranged than the latter was. The four parts of which it is composed : faith in the mercies of God as the basis of Christian life (xii. 1, 2) ; the realization of this life in the two spheres, religious and civil, under the supreme law of love (xii. 3-21 and xiii. 1-10) ; finally, the eye of hope constantly fixed on the coming of Christ as the spring of progress in sanctification (xiii. 11-14 ;— these four parts, we say, which may be reduced to three, bring us without straining to Paul's ordinary *triad :* faith, love, and hope (1 Thess. i. 3 ; 1 Cor. xiii. 13, etc.). It might be asked, no doubt, how it comes that in this summary of Christian morals he omits family duties, so well set forth in the Epistles to the Colossians and Ephesians. But perhaps the subject of domestic life appeared to him too particular to find a place in so general an exposition.

TWENTY-EIGHTH PASSAGE (14:1-15:13)

Exhortation relative to a particular Difference of View in the Church of Rome.

The following passage is a practical application of the law of love expounded, chaps. xii. and xiii. It is an immediate illustration of the self-sacrifice which Paul has just been requiring. This passage, from its connection with a local circumstance, is at the same time the first step of return from the *treatise* to the *letter* form ; it is, consequently, the transition to the epistolary conclusion of the entire writing. Thus it is that everything is organically bound together in the compositions of the apostle.

What was the subject of the difference of view to which the instruction following refers ? Ver. 2 proves that a certain number of Christians at Rome thought they should abstain from the use of meats and of wine ; and it is probable, from vv. 5 and 6, that the same men joined to this abstinence the scrupulous observance of certain days which seemed to them more holy than others. This party does not appear to have been considerable or influential ; and Paul, far from treating it as he treated those who corrupted the pure gospel in Galatia, at Corinth, or at Colosse, seems rather inclined to take it under his protection as against the rest of the church. The subject is one on which somewhat divergent views have been expressed. It is difficult to explain the principle which led these people to act thus.

Eichhorn regarded the *weak* as former Gentiles, who had belonged previously to a school of philosophy with an ascetic tendency, the Neo-Pythagoreans, for example. They imported into the gospel, according to him, certain principles pertaining to their former philosophy.—This opinion is now generally rejected. 1st. There are manifest indications of the Jewish origin of this party. Thus vv. 5 and 6 appear to prove that these same men observed the Jewish feast days, like the heretics of Colosse (see the exegesis). Besides, if the passage, xv. 1-13, still forms part of this section, as appears to us unquestionable, it follows that we have to do with a Judeo-Christian party. For this whole passage closes with the celebration of the union of Christians *of both origins* in one and the same salvation. 2d. Such men would not have taken the modest and timid attitude at Rome which seems to have been that of the *weak*. On the ground of their pretended superiority, either in holiness or in culture, they would much rather have affected haughty airs in relation to the rest of the church.

Origen and Chrysostom regarded these people as Christians of Jewish origin, and ascribe their kind of life to their attachment to the Mosaic law. But the law did not forbid the eating of flesh, except that of certain (unclean) animals, nor the use of wine, except to certain persons and in certain particular cases. It would therefore be difficult to explain how they could have come by the way of the Levitical ordinances to the principle of entire abstinence.

This reflection and comparison with the passage, 1 Cor. viii.–x., have led many commentators (Clem. of Alex., Flatt, Neand., Philip., etc.) to explain the abstinence of the *weak* by the fear they felt of unwittingly eating flesh and drinking wines which had been *offered to idols*. Rather than run such a risk, they preferred to dispense with them altogether. But it should have been easy to find means of avoiding this danger, at least in private meals; and it would be hard to understand how, if the ideas of these people had been the same as those of their scrupulous brethren in the church of Corinth, Paul should not give them any of those explanations which he had given to the latter, and should content himself with striving to preserve peace within the church of Rome. It appears to us very doubtful, besides, whether the *weak* at Corinth were of Jewish origin. The more we have examined the question, the more have we been led to regard them rather as formerly Gentiles. Finally, the text of ver. 14 is incompatible with this opinion. Paul says: "I am persuaded in the Lord that there is nothing unclean *of itself.*" These words: *of itself*, prove that the pollution appeared to the weak as attaching to the very nature of the meats, and not merely contracted by accident.

Baur, in his *Apostel Paulus* (I. p. 361 et seq.), has attempted to connect the party of the *weak* with the *Ebionites*, who, according to the description given by Epiphanius, abstained from all animal food, or even from food prepared with animal matter. He also cites the *Clementine Homilies* (dating from Rome in the last third of the second century), in which the Apostle Peter thus describes his mode of life: "I use only bread and oil and a little pulse," and where it is taught that the use of flesh is contrary to nature, and of diabolical origin. He cites also the saying of Hegesippus regarding James the brother of our Lord: "He ate nothing ἐμψυχον (*animated*)." As to wine, this critic refers to the fact that according to Epiphanius, the most austere of the Ebionites celebrated the Eucharist only with unleavened bread and water; which seems to prove that they abstained wholly from wine.

Ritschl (*Enst. der altkath. Kirche*, 2d ed. p. 184 et seq.) has given out a somewhat different hypothesis, which has been adopted by many moderns (Mey., Mang., etc.). Our party of the *weak* at Rome was composed, it is said, of former *Essenes*. According to this critic, the fundamental idea of the Essene order was to realize a permanent priestly life. Now, it is known that the priests were forbidden (Lev. x. 9) to drink wine while they were officiating; the Essene must therefore have abstained from it entirely. Moreover, the priests, being required to eat only food consecrated to God, and Essenism rejecting at the same time the practice of bloody sacrifices, it followed that they could eat no flesh. If, therefore, such men had been sold as prisoners, and carried to Rome as the result of previous wars, then set free and converted to the gospel, they might have carried with them into the church their former mode of life as superior in holiness to that of ordinary Christians. An analogous origin ought probably to be assigned to the sect which some years later troubled the church of Colosse. In general, it is clear that a certain ascetic dualism was in the air at this period. And this was the common source of all the different tendencies which we have mentioned.— Only the question arises—(1) Whether, supposing *the weak* had belonged to one of these parties, Paul could have attached so little importance to the question considered in itself (comp. his polemic in the Epistle to the Colossians); and (2) whether the attitude of such Christians would have been so modest as the following passage supposes?

Perhaps there is a simpler way of explaining the origin of such ideas. We must go back even beyond the law. According to the narrative of Genesis, animal food was not originally allowed to man (Gen. i. 29). It was not till after the deluge that it was expressly authorized (ix. 3). The invention of wine dates also from this latter epoch, and the abuse of this drink was immediately connected with its discovery. It is easy to understand how such biblical precedents might have taken hold of serious readers of the O. T., and led them to the abstinence of which our text speaks. In this conduct no Christian principle was seriously compromised. It was simply an attempt to return to the primitive regimen, which easily presented itself to the mind as the most normal. And thus is explained why the apostle does not even touch the root of the question, and treats it solely on the side on which it concerns the maintenance of harmony between the members of the church.—To finish at once the exposition of our view, we shall add that, as appears to us, it was in the love-feasts that the difference broke out and gave rise to certain painful manifestations to which the apostle desired to put an end. We think we can give the proof of this as we study chap. xiv.

It has been sometimes thought that in the first part of this chapter, vv. 1-12, the apostle was addressing the *weak*, with the view of checking their unjust judgments upon the strong ; and in the second, vv. 13–23, the *strong*, to call them to the exercise of charity toward the weak. This view does not seem to me exact, at least as to the first part. Rather Paul begins by addressing both in this part, in order to point out to them the duty of *mutual toleration ;* then he turns specially to the strong in the second part, to remind them of the *considerate bearing* which love claims of them toward the weak.

Vv. 1–12

The first three verses are a sort of heading, in which the apostle expounds the ground of difference, and gives the solution of it provisionally.

Vv. 1, 2. "*Him that is weak in the faith receive ye, yet not to enter into discussions of opinions. One hath faith to eat all things ; but another, who is weak, eateth herbs.*"—The participle ἀσθενῶν, *being weak*, is not altogether synonymous with the adjective ἀσθενής, *weak ;* it denotes one whose faith falters (becomes weak) at a given moment and in a special case. This expression better spares the sensibilities of those here spoken of. The imperative προσλαμβάνεσθε, *receive*, addressed to the whole church, evidently assumes that those who are recommended to this favorable reception form only a very weak minority at Rome. The Greek expression signifies *to take to oneself with tenderness ;* comp. xv. 7 and John xiv. 3, where it is applied to Christ's conduct in relation to believers.—The last words of the verse have been explained in a multitude of ways. Luther, Olsh. : "but not so as to excite doubts (διακρίσεις) in your neighbor's inward thoughts (διαλογισμῶν)." There are two reasons opposed to this meaning ; διάκρισις does not signify *doubt*, and διαλογισμός cannot mean simply *thought*. The word always denotes in the N. T. the activity of the understanding in the service of evil ; comp. Luke ii. 35, v. 22 ; 1 Cor. iii. 20 ; and in our Epistle, i. 21.—Beza, Vulgate : "but not to dispute with them (διακρίσεις) regarding the ideas which they form of things (διαλογισμῶν)." But διαλογισμός does not denote an *idea ;* it is a *reasoning*.—Rückert : "but not to reach a still profounder separation of opinions." But how could it be thought that this would be the result of the reception recommended ; and how should the idea : *still profounder*, have been omitted by the apostle ?—Meyer : "but not so as to criticise the thoughts (of your weak brethren)." This meaning would require the singular διάκρισις, *criticism*, and it does not harmonize with the term διαλογισμός, which applies rather to the reasonings of a proud wisdom than to pious scruples.—The following is the meaning which alone seems to me natural : "but not to get by this very reception into debates (διακρίσεις), which would terminate in the end only in vain reasonings (διαλογισμοί)." This meaning suits the two substantives used, as well as the plural form of both. After this general recommendation the apostle formulates the point of the question.

Ver. 2. The meaning of πιστεύειν, to believe, is determined by its opposition to ἀσθενῶν, being weak: "who has a faith firm enough to be able to eat anything without scruple."—Eateth herbs, that is to say, nothing else.

Ver. 3. "Let not him that eateth, despise him that eateth not; and[1] let not him which eateth not, judge him that eateth; for God hath received him."—This verse contains the theme which is about to be developed down to ver. 12. The two propositions are connected in the T. R. by and, and in the Alex. by but. The second reading more strongly, perhaps too strongly, contrasts the two views. The term despise applies well to one who feels himself strong, and regards with a disdainful eye the timid attitude of the weak; the term judge suits the latter, who, not understanding the liberty used by the strong, is disposed to confound it with license.—The last words: God hath received him, may refer to both, or to the latter only (the strong). The following verses being addressed more particularly to the weak, it may possibly be the divine reception of the strong only to which Paul wishes here to refer. A being whom God has taken to Him, whom He has made one of His own, ought not to be judged lightly by his brother, as if he were without master. This is what is developed in the following verse.

Ver. 4. "Who art thou that judgest another man's servant? To his own master he standeth or falleth. Yea, he shall stand; for God[2] is powerful[3] to hold him up."—The idea is: It is to the advantage or disadvantage of his master, not of his fellow-servants, that a servant fulfils or neglects his task. The terms standing and falling refer, not to the servant's absolution or condemnation at the judgment, but to his daily faithfulness or unfaithfulness, and to the strengthening or weakening of his inward relation to Christ. What proves this, is the ground for confidence indicated in the words: "Yea, he shall stand; for God is powerful to hold him up." There is no more need of being held up, or at least of being so by the power of God, in the judgment day. Of course the servant's sincerity, in the line of conduct which he has adopted, is assumed, even if he were in error on a particular point. Paul affirms that the Lord will be able to hold him in communion with Himself.—Here the Lord is probably, as generally in the N. T., Christ. It is He, indeed, who is Master of the house, and for whom the servants labor (Luke xii. 41–48).—There is a slight touch of irony in this reason: "Yea, he shall be held up." It is as if Paul said to the weak: "thou mayest assure thyself about him; for, even if he is mistaken, his Master is powerful enough to avert the bad effects of a piece of flesh." This argument applies, of course, only to things which arise exclusively on the domain of the individual conscience.—In the last proposition, the Greco-Lat. reading ὁ Θεός, God, it seems to me, ought to be preferred to that of the other documents: ὁ κύριος, the Lord; for the act in question is that of strengthening, which is naturally ascribed to God. The reading ὁ κύριος has probably arisen from the τῷ κυρίῳ which precedes.—How easily do these verses find their explanation, if we imagine the church assembled for the love-feast! The majority gives an affectionate welcome to the minority. They sit down altogether for the feast; then immediately the difference breaks out between neighbors. It is the moment for watching: "Well!" says the apostle, "no perverse debates on this occasion; but let each beware of the danger which threatens him at this instant, the one of despising, the other of judging.

Vv. 5, 6. "One man[4] distinguisheth one day from another, the other esteemeth every day alike: let every man be fully persuaded in his own mind. He

---

[1] T. R., with E L P, Syr., reads και ο μη; ℵ A B read ο δε μη.
[2] T. R., with D E F G L. It. reads ο θεος; ℵ A B C P: ο κυριος.
[3] T. R., with L P and Mnn., reads δυνατος γαρ εστιν; ℵ A B C D F G: δυνατει γαρ.
[4] ℵ A C P read γαρ after ος μεν.

that regardeth the day, regardeth it unto the Lord; and he that regardeth not the day, to the Lord[1] *he does not regard it. He that eateth, eateth to the Lord, for he giveth God thanks; and he that eateth not, to the Lord he eateth not, and giveth God thanks.*"—Paul here adduces an example taken from the same domain of external practices, and in which the two opposite lines of conduct may be also followed with equal fidelity. The *days* are those of the Jewish feasts, which Judeo-Christians continued for the most part to observe: Sabbaths, new moons, etc. (Col. ii. 15). Did this example really exist at Rome, or did the apostle choose it from the life of the church in general, to have the opportunity of better explaining his thought? The first is the more natural supposition. For there must have been in the church of Rome a certain number of Judeo-Christians, though they did not form the majority.—The *for*, which is read in some mss., is probably owing to a copyist's habit. The word κρίνειν, *to judge*, frequently takes the sense of *distinguishing*. *To judge one day among others*, may therefore signify: to distinguish it favorably from the others; to set it apart as more worthy to be sanctified. There is a little irony in the second alternative: to discern *every* day. For it is evident that there is no longer any distinction when all are distinguished. To set apart every day as holy, is no longer to sanctify any one specially. Between the two modes of acting thus expressed, the apostle does not decide. All he asks of any one is, that his practice should obey a personal and deliberate conviction. The expression ἐν τῷ νοΐ, *in his mind*, contains the idea of a serious examination; and the term πληροφορεῖσθαι, strictly: *to be filled to the brim*, denotes a state of conviction which leaves no more room for the least hesitation.

Ver. 6. The apostle states the reason why the two lines of conduct are equally admissible. It is because, opposed as they are, they are inspired by one and the same desire, that of *serving the Lord*. The second proposition: "He that regardeth not the day" . . ., is omitted in the Alex. and Greco-Lat. texts. Notwithstanding all the efforts of commentators, and of Hofmann in particular, to justify the absence of this parallel proposition, this reading appears to me untenable. It is necessary strangely to force the meaning of the first alternative: "He that regardeth . . . regardeth untó the Lord," to bring it into logical relation to the two ways of acting explained in ver. 5. And it is impossible to refer it only to one of them. The confounding of the two φρονεῖ by a careless copyist must have caused the omission, as in so many other similar cases.—The apostle means that the man who, in his religious practice, keeps the Jewish feast-days, does so for the purpose of doing homage to the Lord by resting in Him, as the man who does not observe them does so for the purpose of laboring actively for Him.

It has been concluded from these sayings of Paul, that the obligation to observe *Sunday* as a day divinely instituted, was not compatible with Christian spirituality, as this was understood by St. Paul. The context does not allow us to draw such a conclusion. The believer who observes Sunday does not in the least do so under the thought of ascribing to this day a *superior holiness* to that of other days. To him all days are, as the apostle thinks, equal in holy consecration. As rest is not holier than work, no more is Sunday holier than other days.[2] It is another form of consecration, the periodical return of which, like the alternations of sleep and waking, arises from the conditions of our physico-psychical existence. The Christian does not cease to be a man by becoming a spiritual man. And as one day of rest in seven was divinely instituted at the creation in behalf of natural humanity, one does not see why the believer should not require this periodical rest as well as the unregenerate

---

[1] The whole proposition ο μη φρον. την ημ. κυρ. ου φρονει, which T. R. reads, with L P Syr., is omitted by ℵ A B C D E F G, It.
[2] How can this be if Sunday, or the Lord's Day, takes the spiritual place now which the seventh day, or Sabbath, had in the Old Dispensation, and which Jehovah is said expressly to have *hallowed*?—T. W. C.

man. "The Sabbath was made *for man;*" so long as the Christian preserves his earthly nature, this saying applies to him, and should turn not to the detriment, but to the profit of his spiritual life. The keeping of Sunday thus understood has nothing in common with the Sabbatical observance which divides life into two parts, the one holy, the other profane. It is this legal distinction which Paul excludes in our ver. 5 and Col. ii.

In the second part of ver. 6, Paul returns to the principal case. He does so simply by the copula καί, *and*, and not by a ὡσαύτως, *likewise;* which seems to prove that the example taken from the keeping of days was not a simple comparison chosen at pleasure from the general life of the church, but a case which was really found at Rome itself. As a proof that he who eats (of everything), eats to the Lord, the apostle adduces (*for*) the fact that he gives thanks *for those meats*. The object of this giving of thanks is God, as the author of nature.—In speaking of him who does not eat (of everything), Paul does not say, as in the previous case: "*for* he giveth thanks," but: "*and* he giveth thanks." It was unnecessary, indeed, *to prove* that by abstaining he did so for the Lord; that was understood of itself. The real meaning of this proposition is therefore: "And he does not the less give thanks, he too, for this frugal repast."—As to these two thanksgivings, which mark the two different ways of acting with a seal of equal holiness, how much more of a dramatic character do they take when we imagine them as offered by these two classes of believers at the same moment and at the same table!

This so remarkable saying of the apostle furnishes us with the true means of deciding all those questions of casuistry which so often arise in Christian life, and cause the believer so much embarrassment: May I allow myself this or that pleasure? Yes, if I can enjoy it to the Lord, and while giving Him thanks for it; no, if I cannot receive it as a gift from His hand, and bless Him for it. This mode of solution respects at once the rights of the Lord and those of individual liberty.

The contrast between these two ways of acting, partaking and abstaining, which we must beware of converting into a contrast of faithfulness and unfaithfulness, was only the special application of a more general contrast which pervades the whole of human life: that between living and dying. Paul, always under the necessity of embracing questions in all their width, extends in the following verses that which he has just been treating to the entire domain of life and death.

Vv. 7, 8. "*For none of us liveth to himself, and no man dieth to himself. For, whether we live, we live unto the Lord; whether we die,[1] we die[2] unto the Lord. Whether we live, therefore, or die,[3] we are the Lord's.*"—In everything that concerns the active use of life (such as the enjoyment of a kind of food), as well as in everything connected with the wasting of it, of which death is the termination (such as abstinence), the Christian depends not on his own will, but on the Lord's. Paul does not mean to say thereby how we *ought* to act. For in that case the following verse would require to be connected with this one by *therefore*, and not by *for*. It is a *fact* which he expresses; he supposes it realized in the life of his readers. The truth of this supposition follows from the meaning of the word ἡμῶν, *us*, us believers. Faith, if it is real, implies this consequence. Once we are believers, the current of life with all it embraces, and the current of death with all that accelerates it, tend no longer self-ward, as in our natural existence. Consequently we cannot be called by men to give account of our conduct, though it may differ from theirs.

Ver. 8. The proof of ver. 7 is given in ver. 8 (*for*). Our life and death being through the fact of faith at the Lord's service, the contrast between

---

[1] T. R., with ℵ B, reads αποθνησκωμεν; A D E F G P: αποθνησκομεν.
[2] ℵ C L read αποθνησκομεν instead of αποθνησκωμεν, which T. R. has, with all the rest.
[3] T. R. reads, with ℵ B C L: αποθνησκωμεν; A D E F G P: αποθνησκομεν.

living and dying is thus completely dependent on the higher direction impressed on our being. Comp. 2 Cor. v. 15 and Rom. xii. 1. For the believer to live, is to serve Christ; to die, is to be united to Him more perfectly (Phil. i. 21–24; 2 Cor. v. 6–9). Hence it follows (*οὖν, therefore*) that he remains in every state of the case the Lord's *property*. As the dative τῷ κυρίῳ, *to the Lord*, in the first part of the verse, expressed consecration; so the genitive τοῦ κυρίου, literally, *of the Lord*, in the last proposition, expresses possession. We remain *His* in both cases. The bond which unites us to Him can only be strengthened by the so varied circumstances summed up in the two words: life and death.—The first and third time we should probably read the subjunctive ἀποθνήσκωμεν; for ἐάν, *if, whether*, is construed in the N. T. only with the subjunctive. But the second time the indicative ἀποθνήσκομεν must certainly be read; for it is a fact which Paul is stating. Those who have read the subjunctive, have mistaken it for an exhortation.

The solidity of the bond of possession which unites the believer to the Lord, rests on his side on the subjective fact of faith, but on the Lord's side on an objective fact which nothing can shake: the sovereignty of the glorified Christ, in virtue of which He evermore controls the contrast between life and death (ver. 9).

Ver. 9. "*For to this end Christ*[1] *died and revived;*[2] *that He might be Lord both of the dead and living.*"—With the view of securing the possession of His own, whether as living or dead, Jesus began by resolving in His own person the contrast between life and death. He did so by dying and reviving.—For what is one raised again except *a dead man living?* Thus it is that He reigns simultaneously over the two domains of being through which His own are called to pass, and that He can fulfil His promise to them, John x. 28: "None shall pluck them out of my hand." Comp. also John xi. 25, 26. Of the three principal readings presented by the documents, the simplest and most agreeable to the context is certainly the Alexandrine reading: "He died and revived." These two terms correspond to *the living* and *the dead*. This very simple relation has been changed in the other readings. The word *rose again*, in the Byz. reading, has evidently been introduced to form the transition between these: *died* and *revived*. The reading of two Greco-Lats. and of Irenæus: "lived, died, and rose again," has certainly arisen from the desire to call up here the earthly life of Jesus; which was not necessary, since the domain of the living belongs now to Jesus, not in virtue of His earthly existence, but in consequence of His present life as the glorified One. To understand this saying rightly, Eph. iv. 10 should be compared, where the apostle, after pointing to Christ "descended into the lowest parts (the abode of the dead)," then "ascended to the highest heavens," adds: "that He might fill all things." Which signifies that by traversing all the domains of existence Himself, He has so won them, that in passing through them in our turn as believers, we never cease to be His, and to have Him as our Lord. Hence the inference expressed ver. 10.

Ver. 10. "*But thou, why dost thou judge thy brother? or thou also, why dost thou set at nought thy brother? For we shall all stand at the judgment-seat of Christ.*"[3]—The δέ, *but*, contrasts the incompetent judgment of a *brother*, with the judgment of this one *Lord*.—The first question is addressed to the weak; comp. ver. 3. The second, connected by: *or thou also*, to the strong. The

---

[1] T. R., with L Syr., reads και before απεθανεν.
[2] Three principal readings with variants:
 1. T. R.. with Syr_sch. and the Mnn.: απεθανεν και ανεστη και ανεζησεν, *died and rose again and revived* (L P: καιεζησεν, *and revived*).
 2. ℵ A B C: απεθανεν και εζησεν, *died and revived* (F G: απεθανεν και ανεστη, *died and rose again*).
 3. D E, It.: εζησεν και απεθανεν και ανεστη, *lived and died and rose again*.
[3] T. R., with L P, Syr., reads του Χριστου (*of the Christ*); all the rest: του θεου (*of God*).

also is explained by the fact that contempt is likewise a mode of judging. No one ought to be withdrawn from his rightful judge, who is the Lord alone.—The *all* is prefixed to remind us that no one will escape from that judge. It is well said, no doubt, John v. 24, that the believer "shall not come into judgment;" but that does not mean that he shall not appear before the tribunal (2 Cor. v. 10). Only he will appear there to be owned as one who has already voluntarily judged himself by the light of Christ's word and under the discipline of His Spirit; comp. John xii. 48 and 1 Cor. xi. 31.—The Alexs. and Greco-Lats. read τοῦ Θεοῦ : "the judgment-seat *of God.*" This expression must then be explained in the sense: *the divine tribunal,* where Christ will s t as God's representative. For never is God Himself represented as seated on the judgment throne. But is it not the two following verses which have given rise to this reading?

Vv. 11, 12. "*For it is written, As I live, saith the Lord, every knee shall bow to me, and every tongue shall confess to God. . So then,*[1] *every one of us shall give account of himself to God.*"[2]—In ver. 11, Paul quotes Isa. xlv. 23, where the universal homage is described, which all creatures will render to God at the end of the world. This homage supposes and implies the judgment, by which they shall all have been brought to His feet. If we read *of Christ,* and not *of God,* at the end of ver. 10, it must be held that the apostle sees this last royal manifestation of Jehovah, proclaimed by Isaiah, finding its realization *in Christ;* comp., indeed, Phil. ii. 10, 11, where the words of Isaiah in our verse are applied to Jesus glorified.—The form of affirmation in the original text is: *I have sworn by myself.* Paul substitutes, unintentionally no doubt, a somewhat different form of oath, but one which is also frequent in the O. T.: "I am living that" . . . the meaning of which is: "As truly as I am the eternally living One, so truly shall this come to pass." The words: *saith the Lord,* are here added by the apostle. Then he substitutes for the expression: *shall swear by me* (as the one true God), the term "shall do me homage" (ἐξομολογεῖσθαι). This word, which strictly signifies *to confess,* might allude to the judgment which will lay every man low in the conviction of his guilt, and draw forth from the heart of all an acknowledgment of God's holiness and righteousness. But all that this term expresses may simply be the homage of adoration, which proclaims God as the one being worthy to be glorified; comp. Luke ii. 38; Phil. ii. 11.—The words *to God* are the paraphrase of the *to me,* in Isaiah.

In ver. 12, Paul applies to every individual in particular what has just been said of all in general. The preceding context signified: "Judge not thy brother, for God will judge *him;*" this verse signifies: "Judge thyself, for God will judge *thee.*"—Paul here repeats the expression τῷ Θεῷ, *to God,* rather than say τῷ Χριστῷ, *to Christ,* because he wishes to contrast in a general way divine, the alone truly just judgment, with human judgments.

Vv. 13–23.

After having addressed the strong and the weak simultaneously, the apostle further addresses a warning to the former, to induce them not to use their liberty except in conformity with the law of love. As is observed by Hofmann, he had nothing similar to recommend to the weak; for he who is inwardly bound cannot change his conduct, while the strong man who feels himself free may at pleasure make use of his right or waive it in practice. To induce the strong believer to make sacrifice of his liberty, the apostle brings to bear on him the two following motives: 1st. Vv. 13–19*a*, the duty of not wounding the heart of the weak or producing inward irritation; 2d. Vv. 19*b*–23, the fear of destroying God's work within him by leading him to do something against his conscience.

---

[1] B D F G P, Syr^sch. omit ουν, *then.* [2] B F G omit τω θεω, *to God.*

Ver. 13. "*Let us not, therefore, judge one another any more, but judge this rather: that no man put a stumbling-block or an occasion to fall in his brother's way.*"—The first proposition sums up the whole of the first part of the chapter; for it is still addressed to both parties; it forms at the same time the transition to the second. The object of the verb: *one another*, proves that the term *judge* here includes the contempt of the strong for the weak, as well as the condemnation which these take the liberty of pronouncing on the former.—From the second proposition of the verse onward, the apostle turns to the strong exclusively. He makes a sort of play on the meaning of the word κρίνειν, *to judge :* "Do not judge one another; but, if you will judge absolutely, judge as follows." *Judge* the second time has the meaning of *decide ;* comp. Tit. iii. 12.—The wise decision to take is, according to Paul, to avoid anything that might cause a *shock* (πρόσκομμα), or even a *fall* (σκάνδαλον), to your neighbor. There must be, whatever Meyer may say, a difference of meaning between the two substantives; not only because Paul does not use pleonasms, but also on account of the particle ἤ, *or*, which undoubtedly expresses a gradation: *or even*. One *strikes against* (προσκόπτειν), the result is a *wound ;* but one stumbles against an obstacle (σκανδαλίζεσθαι), the result is a *fall.* The second case is evidently graver than the first. It is easy even to recognize in these two terms the theme of the two following developments: the first relates to the *wounded feeling* of the weak, with all its vexing consequences; the second to the *sin* which one is in danger of making him commit by leading him into an act contrary to his conscience. The first of these evils, as we have said, is referred to in vv. 14–19*a*.

Vv. 14, 15. "*I know, and am persuaded in the Lord Jesus, that nothing is unclean of itself :*[1] *except that to him that esteemeth anything to be unclean, it is unclean. Now*[2] *if thy brother be grieved because of food, thou walkest no more charitably. Destroy not by thy food, him for whom Christ died.*"—Paul does not wish to discuss the matter; but yet he cannot conceal his conviction; and he expresses it in passing, in ver. 14, as a concession he must make on the side of the strong. At bottom, it is they who are right. Οἶδα, *I know*, indicates a rational, theoretic conviction, such as even a Jew, trained by the O. T. to a true spirituality, might reach. The second verb πέπεισμαι, *I am persuaded*, goes further; it indicates that this conviction has penetrated to his very conscience, and set it practically free from all perplexity. The words: *in the Lord Jesus*, remind us that it is He who has put an end to the obligations imposed by the ceremonial law. The emancipation which faith finds in Him arises not only from His doctrine (Matt. xv. 11, for example), but above all from the redemption wrought by Him. This clause: *in the Lord Jesus*, bears on the second verb; there is nothing except the possession of salvation which can practically give full liberty to the soul.—Several ancient commentators have referred the words δι' αὐτοῦ, to Jesus Christ: "Through Him there is no longer anything unclean." But the negative form of the proposition is not favorable to this sense. Paul would rather have said: "everything is clean through Him." It is more natural to understand this δι' αὐτοῦ in the sense of: *of itself* (as would obviously be the case with the reading δι' ἑαυτοῦ): "Nothing is unclean in its own nature (in the matter of food) ;" comp. 1 Cor. x. 26; 1 Tim. iv. 4, 5; Tit. i. 15.—The restriction εἰ μή, *except*, applies to the idea of uncleanness in general, without taking account of the limitation *of itself.* This slightly incorrect use of εἰ μή has given rise, though erroneously, to the belief that this particle might signify *but ;* comp. Matt. xii. 4; Luke iv. 26, 27; John v. 19; Gal. i. 19, ii. 16, etc.—This restriction, whereby Paul reminds us that what is regarded as unclean becomes really so to him

---

[1] T. R., with ℵ B C, reads δι' εαυτον instead of δι' αυτου, which is read in all the others.
[2] T. R., with L, Mnn. Syr^sch., reads δε instead of γαρ, which all the others read.

who uses it under this idea, paves the way for indicating the voluntary limits which the strong should be able to impose on himself in the exercise of his liberty.

Ver. 15. If this verse be connected with the preceding by *for*, with the majority of the Mjj., it is very difficult to understand their logical relation. Meyer paraprhases thus: "It is not without reason that I remind you of that (the preceding restriction); *for* love is bound to take account of such a scruple." Hofmann rightly judges this explanation of the *for* impossible; but is his own less so? He takes the phrase following in the interrogative sense: "*For*, if thy brother is grieved thereby, wouldest thou for this error on his part henceforth cease to walk toward him in love?" It is difficult to imagine anything more forced. We must therefore, though the T. R. δέ, *now then* or *but*, has only a single Mj. (L) in its favor, prefer this reading (Reiche, Rück., De W., Philip.). This δέ may be taken in the sense of *now then*, or in that of *but*. The adversative sense seems to me preferable. The *but* refers to the first part of ver. 14: "I know that nothing is unclean . . ., but if, nevertheless . . . The meaning is excellent, and the construction the more admissible because the second part of ver. 14 was a simple parenthesis.—Λυπεῖται, *is grieved, hurt;* this word expresses the painful and bitter feeling produced in the heart of the weak by the spectacle of the free and bold eating of the strong.—With the words: "Thou walkest *no more* (οὐκέτι) charitably," we must evidently understand the idea: when thou actest thus. The threat, added by the apostle, of compromising thereby our neighbor's salvation, is so grave, that it is not explicable at the first glance, and one is tempted to refer it to the sin which the weak believer would commit by imitating the strong; comp. ver. 20. But it is not till afterward that Paul comes to this side of the question, and it is far from probable that the weak man, at the very time when he is *wounded* by the conduct of the strong, could be tempted to imitate him. These words therefore refer to the profound irritation, the hurtful judgments, the breach of brotherly ties, which must result from such wounding. The *asyndeton* is striking: it shows Paul's emotion when writing these last words . . . : " By thy meat make him perish whom Christ saved by His death !" The whole scene supposed by this verse is infinitely better understood if it is placed in the full love-feast, than if the strong and the weak are supposed taking their meal at their own houses. The following verses (16–19a) complete by some secondary considerations the principal motive which has been expressed at the end of ver. 15.

Ver. 16. "*Let not, then, the good you*[1] *enjoy be evil spoken of.*"—The expression *your good* has been applied to the kingdom of God (Meyer), or to faith (De Wette), or to the gospel (Philip.), or to the superiority of the Christian to the non-Christian (Hofmann). But all these meanings want appropriateness. The context itself shows that the subject in question is *Christian liberty* (Orig., Calv., Thol., etc.). The *you* applies not to all believers, but to the strong only. Paul recommends them not to use their liberty so as to provoke the indignation and blame of their weaker brethren. The blessing they enjoy ought not to be changed by their lack of charity into a source of cursing. Carefully comp. 1 Cor. viii. 9–11, and x. 29, 30.

Ver. 17. "*For the kingdom of God is not food or drink, but righteousness and peace and joy in the Holy Spirit.*"—Nothing could be simpler than the connection of this verse with the preceding. The force from above, which is the essence of the kingdom of God, does not consist in being able to eat or drink more or less freely and regardlessly toward our neighbor, but in realizing in life the three dispositions mentioned, by triumphing over our own tastes and vanity. The three terms: *righteousness, peace, joy*, ought, according to the context, to be taken in the social sense, which is only an

---

[1] D E F G, It. Syr^sch. read ἡμῶν instead of ὑμῶν.

application of their religious sense. *Righteousness:* moral rectitude whereby we render to our neighbor what is his due—here particularly respect for his convictions. *Peace:* good harmony between all the members of the church. *Joy:* that individual and collective exultation which prevails among believers when brotherly communion makes its sweetness felt, and no one is saddened. By such dispositions the soul finds itself raised to a sphere where all sacrifices become easy, and charity reigns without obstacle. Such is the reality of the kingdom of God on the earth. Would it not then be folly to seek it in the inconsiderate use of some meat or drink, at the expense of those the only true blessings?—By the words: *in the Holy Spirit,* Paul indicates the source of these virtues: it is this divine guest who, by His presence, produces them in the church ; the instant He retires grieved, He carries them with Him.—It is incomprehensible how this passage has not succeeded in moving Meyer from the interpretation of the term *kingdom of God,* which he has adopted once for all in his commentary, applying it invariably to the *future* Messianic kingdom.

Ver. 18. "*For he that in these things*[1] *serveth Christ, is acceptable to God and approved of men.*"—So true is it that it is in these dispositions the kingdom of God consists, that the goodwill of God and men rests only on him who cultivates them. If we read ἐν τούτῳ, we may refer the pronoun (*him* or *that*) either to the *principle* expressed in ver. 17 ("thus"), or to the *Holy Spirit.* The first meaning is forced ; it would have required κατὰ τοῦτο, *according to* (this principle). Nor is the second less so ; for it would be the merest commonplace to say that he who serves Christ in the Holy Spirit is acceptable to God. We must therefore read, with the T. R. and the Byzs., ἐν τούτοις, *in these dispositions.* Such a man is acceptable to *God,* who reads the heart, and he enjoys merited consideration even in the judgment of *men.* Every one, Christian or non-Christian, recognizes him to be a man really animated with power from above, the opposite of a fool or a boaster ; δόκιμος: an approved Christian, who has stood the test of trial.

Vv. 19, 20. "*Let us therefore follow after*[2] *the things which make for peace, and things which pertain to mutual edification.*[3] *For food destroy not the work of God ; all things indeed are pure, but a thing becomes evil for that man who eateth in a state of scandal.*"—Ver. 19 forms the transition from the first to the second reason ; 19*a* repeats the first : the obligation to preserve harmony in the church ? 19*b* introduces the second : the obligation to do nothing which might be injurious to our neighbor's edification. The call, therefore, is no longer merely to avoid what may wound and vex our neighbor, but also to respect and not compromise the *work of God* already wrought in his heart. It is obvious, as Meyer acknowledges, that we must read διώκωμεν, *let us seek,* and not διώκομεν, *we seek.* The Greco-Latin reading, according to which we should require to read φυλάξωμεν, *let us keep,* as the verb of the last proposition of the verse: "Let us keep the things which are for edification," may very probably be authentic. The omission of this verb would be explained by the fact that the copyists did not understand that the apostle was passing to a new reason.

Ver. 20. The *asyndeton* between vv. 19 and 20 proves how acutely the apostle is alive to the responsibility of the strong : destroy the work of God ! In ver. 14, where it was personal pain, wounding, which was referred to, the apostle spoke of making *the brother* himself perish. Here, where the occasioning of a *scandal* is the matter in question, he does not speak any more of the person, but of the *work* of God in the person.—It matters not that food is free from uncleanness in itself ; it is no longer so as soon as man uses it against his conscience. Rückert has taken the

---

[1] T. R., with E L, Mnn. Syr., reads εν τουτοις (*in these things*) : all the rest read εν τουτω (*in this*).
[2] T. R. reads, with C D E, Mnn. It., διωκωμεν ; all the rest : διωκομεν.
[3] D E F G, It. read after αλληλους, φυλαξωμεν (*let us keep*).

word κακόν, *evil*, as the attribute of a verb understood : "*Eating* becomes *evil* for the man who does it against his conscience." Meyer prefers to take from the preceding proposition the understood subject τὸ καθαρόν, what is clean in itself : "Even *the food which is clean of itself* becomes evil when it is eaten thus." But it seems to me simpler to make κακόν the subject : "*There is evil* (sin) for him who eateth in such circumstances."—Διὰ προσκόμματος, *in a state of scandal*. On this use of the διά, comp. ii. 27. Is the reference to the strong man, who eats while *occasioning* scandal, or to the weak brother, who lets himself be drawn into eating by *succumbing* to the scandal? Evidently the second. Paul is not speaking here of the evil which the strong believer does to himself, but of that which he does to his brother carried away into sin.—We may be astonished to find the apostle regarding the salvation of the weak as compromised by this one trespass. But is not one voluntary sin interposing between Christ and the believer enough to disunite them, and if this sin is not blotted out, and the state is prolonged, to plunge him again in death?
Ver. 21 is the summing up of the whole warning addressed to the strong from ver. 13.
Ver. 21. "*It is good not to eat flesh and not to drink wine, and [to do nothing] whereby thy brother stumbleth, or is offended, or even is made weak.*"[1] —The word καλόν, *it is good, honorable*, is tacitly opposed to the notion of humiliation, which in the eyes of the strong attached to abstinence. There is nothing, except what is honorable, Paul means, in abstaining when we sacrifice our liberty to charity.—Before the pronoun ἐν ᾧ, *wherein*, we must understand the verb ποιεῖν τι, *to do anything*.—Of the three verbs which the T. R. reads, the first refers to the *wounding* of the heart caused to our neighbor by conduct which he disapproves; the second, to the *sin* which he would be led to commit by being drawn away to do what his conscience condemns; the third, to the want of regard for the scruples with which he is affected through weakness of faith. So : to make him judge ill of you; to make him do what he condemns; or to do in his presence something which raises a scruple in him. The ἤ, *or*, which connects the two last verbs, should be translated by : *or even only*.—The reading λυπεῖται, *is grieved*, instead of προσκόπτει, *is offended*, in the *Sinaït.*, is certainly mistaken. As to the omission of the last two verbs in the Alex. text, it is probably the effect of an oversight; for the verb προσκόπτειν, *to be offended*, would not completely sum up the warning given to the strong (see at ver. 13).

The last two verses are the conclusion and summary of the entire chapter. Ver. 22 applies to the strong; ver. 23 to the weak.

Vv. 22, 23. "*As to thee, thou hast faith ;*[2] *have it to thyself before God. Happy is he that judgeth not himself in that thing which he approveth! But he that doubteth is condemned if he eat, because he eateth not of faith. Whatsoever is not done by faith is sin.*"[3]—The proposition : *thou hast faith*, might be taken in the interrogative sense ; but there is more force in the simple affirmation. The Alexs. read ἥν, *which*, after πίστιν, *faith*. The meaning in that case is : "The faith which thou hast, keep." The ancient versions do not favor this reading, and neither is it in keeping with the context, which requires that the two cases treated should be put expressly face to face with one another, with a view to the definite counsel to be stated for each. The words *keep*, etc. allude to the sacrifice which Paul had asked the strong to make in his external conduct. Paul reminds him that he does not in the least ask the abandonment of his internal conviction, and invites

---

[1] א P read λυπειται instead of προσκοπτει, and א A C Syr^sch. reject the words η σκανδαλιζεται ηασθενει.
[2] א A B C read ην before εχεις.
[3] L, 200, Mnn. and the *Lectionaria* here add the three verses which in other documents form the conclusion of the Epistle, xvi. 25-27 ; G g here have a blank space ; A P have these three verses here and at the end of chap. xvi.

him to preserve it intact in his heart under the eye of God.—By the last words: *Happy* . . ., he gives him to understand that it is a feeling of gratitude and not of pride, with which he ought to be inspired by the degree of faith, and of liberty in faith, to which he has attained. Here, as elsewhere, the word κρίνειν must be translated by *judge*, and not by *condemn*. "To condemn oneself in what he adopts as good," would be a contradictory idea. The subject in question is a simple *inquiry* as to the course which has been adopted once for all. Happy the man who no longer feels any scruple, nor puts any question of conscience to himself regarding the resolution he has taken. Δοκιμάζειν, *to find good after examination*.

Ver. 23 applies to the opposite case: that of doubt in regard to the line to be followed. Conscience has not reached oneness with itself; hence the term διακρίνεσθαι, *to be divided* into two men, the one of whom says yes, the other no.—Many give to the word πίστις, *faith*, the abstract sense of *conviction*.[1] But there is nothing to authorize us to take from the word so common in Paul its religious signification. It refers, as always, to the acceptance of the salvation won by Christ. What a man cannot do as His redeemed one and in the joy of His salvation, must not be done at all. Otherwise this act, of which faith is not the soul, becomes sin, and may lead to the result indicated ver. 20: the total destruction of God's work in us.

Of the position of the doxology, xvi. 25–27, *at the end of chap.* xiv.—A considerable number of documents place here, after ver. 23, the three doxological verses which, in the generally Received text, close the Epistle (xvi. 25–27). These are the Mj. L, nearly 220 Mnn., the *Lectionaria*, the Philoxenian Syriac version, some ancient MSS. mentioned by Origen, finally, the Fathers of the Greek Church (Chrysostom, Cyril, Theodoret, etc. There may be added the MS. G and the Latin translation which accompanies it (g), which leave a blank here, as well as the Mjj. A and P and three Mnn., which read these three verses in *both* places. We shall complete these indications when we come to xvi. 25. Should it be held that these verses have their original place here, and were afterward transposed from it to the end of the Epistle? Or did they, on the contrary, form originally the conclusion of the letter, and have certain copyists transferred them to this place for some reason or other? Or, finally, should we regard this passage as a later interpolation, which was placed sometimes at the end of chap. xiv., sometimes at the end of chap. xvi.? There might be a fourth supposition, viz., that the apostle himself *repeated* at the end of his letter this passage, placed originally at the end of our chapter. But such a repetition would be without example or object. As to the apostolic origin of the passage, we shall examine it at xvi. 27.

The question has more importance than appears at the first glance; for it has a somewhat close connection with that of the authenticity of chaps. xv. xvi. If the apostle closed chap. xiv. with this formula of adoration, it is probable that he meant thereby to terminate his Epistle; consequently all that follows would be open to the suspicion of being unauthentic. True, Reuss says, that even though the last three verses were placed at the end of chap xiv., "there would arise therefrom no prejudice unfavorable to the authenticity of chap. xv.;" the apostle might have intended "to lay down the pen and close his discourse with a short prayer; then he bethought himself to add a few pages." We doubt, however, whether a real example of such procedure can be quoted, and we think that if the true position of these three verses was indeed at the end of chap. xiv., the fact would prove indirectly either that chaps. xv. and xvi. are the work of an interpolator, or that, if they proceeded from the apostle's pen, they belonged originally to some other writing, whence they were transferred to this.

[1] So Chrys., De Wette, Hodge, Vaughan, and Shedd (who, however, combines the two interpretations), and Gifford in Speaker's Comm., who argues the case, and argues it well.—T. W. C.

Let us examine the different hypotheses made on this subject :

1st. Hofmann has attempted to bring these three verses into the apostolic text by making them the transition from chap. xiv. to chap. xv. According to him, the expression : "To Him that is of power to stablish you" (xvi. 25), is in close connection with the discussion of chap. xiv. relative to the strong and the weak ; and the dative τῷ δυναμένῳ, *to Him that is of power* . . . is dependent on the verb ὀφείλομεν, *we owe* (xv. 1) : "We owe to Him that is of power to stablish us to concur in His work by bearing the burdens of the weak." The relation is ingeniously discovered ; but this explanation is nevertheless inadmissible. Not only would this dative : *to Him that is of power*, be separated from the verb on which it depends by a doxological amplification out of all proportion, but especially the δέ, *now then*, which accompanies the verb *we owe*, indicates clearly the beginning of a new sentence.

2d. Baur, Volkmar, Lucht, place the doxology here, but as a later interpolation, and infer from this fact the total or almost total unauthenticity of chaps. xv. and xvi. According to Lucht, the true conclusion of the Epistle, which immediately followed xiv. 23, was suppressed by the elders of the church of Rome as too severe for the weak of chap. xiv. But it was discovered again afterward in the archives of this church, and amplified in two different ways, in the form of the doxology xvi. 25-27, and in the more extended form of the passage xv. 1–xvi. 24 ; these two conclusions, at first distinct, were afterward fused into one, which produced the now generally received form. Volkmar enters still more into detail. The true apostolic conclusion may, according to him, be found with certainty and in a complete form in chaps. xv. and xvi. It consists of the two passages xv. 33–xvi. 2, and xvi. 21-24. The rest of these two chapters embraces additions intended to co-operate in the pacification of the church. They proceed principally from two authors, the one in the east, who added the doxology about 145 ; the other in the west, who composed nearly all the rest about 120.—We are struck at once with the arbitrariness there is in the hypothesis of Lucht. What ! elders take the liberty of suppressing the end of the apostolic writing ! Then they preserve it in the archives of the church, and it becomes in the hands of some writer or other, along with some fragments of an Epistle to the Ephesians, the theme of our last two chapters ! This is a romance which in any case could only gain some historical probability if we were to discover in chaps. xv. and xvi. very positive proofs of their unauthenticity. Volkmar holds that the authentic conclusion has been wholly preserved, though mixed with a conglomerate of diverse interpolations. But would this close be sufficient ? The apostle had introduced his didactic treatise with a long preamble in the letter form (i. 1-15). Was it possible that in closing the writing he should not return, at least for a few moments, to the epistolary form with which he had begun ? Now it is evident that the few words which Volkmar preserves as authentic by no means correspond to a preamble at once so grave and affectionate as the beginning of the Epistle. And it is impossible to understand how Paul could pass suddenly from the end of the practical treatise : "Whatsoever is not of faith is sin" (xiv. 23), to the words which, according to Volkmar, immediately followed : "The God of peace be with you all ! Amen. I commend unto you Phœbe" . . . No, it was not thus the apostle composed.

3d. Since, then, it is impossible to find a place for this doxology in the didactic tissue of chaps. xiv. and xv. ; and since, on the other hand, it cannot be held that it indicates the conclusion of the Epistle (at the end of chap. xiv.) —it only remains to have recourse to a third solution. The weight of critical authorities makes the balance incline in favor of the position of these three verses at the end of chap. xvi. What circumstance could have led to their migration, in a certain number of documents, to the end of chap. xiv. ? If we keep account of the fact demonstrated by the study of the text of the whole N. T., that most of the errors of the Byz. documents arise from the tendency to adapt the text to the necessities of public reading, we shall be led to the supposition that in very ancient times the reading of our Epistle in the assemblies of the church stopped at the end of chap. xiv., because from that point the didactic part, properly so called, terminated. But the reading could not end so abruptly. There was written therefore on the margin, for the use of the reader, the doxology which closed the entire Epistle ; and, as has so often happened, it passed from the margin into the text at this place. So it has come about that it is found here in the documents of Byz. origin, and particularly in the *Lectionaria*, or collections of passages intended for public reading. It is objected, no doubt, that chaps. xv. and xvi. appear in all our ancient lectionaries. But the period at which the omission of these two chapters would have taken place is long anterior to the date of the collections of pericopes which have been preserved to us. This way of explaining the transposition of the doxology seems to us preferable to the reasons stated by Meyer. If it is so, we understand how this doxology is found in both places at once in some documents, and how it is wholly wanting in some others. Certain copyists, doubtful about the position to be given to it, put it in both places ; certain others, made suspicious by this double position, rejected it altogether. It is singular, we acknowledge, that it was not rather placed after ver. 13 of chap. xv., so as to embrace also in the public reading the passage we are now going to study (xv. 1-13). It is impossible at this date to discover the circumstance which has led to the choice rather of the end of chap. xiv.

15:1-13

Here, according to M. Renan, we return to the text of the copy addressed to the church of Rome ; for, according to him, chap. xv. formed the conclusion of the Epistle destined for this church. If this view were well grounded, the first verse of chap. xv. must have immediately followed the last of chap. xi. ; for chaps. xii. xiii. and xiv. only belonged to the copies intended for other churches. Is this hypothesis probable ? What connection is there between the end of chap. xi., celebrating the wisdom of God in the course of history, and this distinction between the strong and the weak with which chap. xv. begins ? This contrast fits in, on the contrary, in the closest possible way to the subject of chap. xiv. Schultz feels this so much, that though sharing Renan's opinion in regard to the three preceding chapters, up to a certain point, he still makes the first six verses of chap. xv. the continuation and conclusion of the passage chap. xiv., and not till ver. 7 does he find the resumption of the true Epistle to the Romans, which closed, according to him, with our ver. 13. Thus in the apostolic copy it was ver. 7 : " Wherefore receive ye one another as Christ also received you," which immediately followed the close of chap. xi. But this sudden transition to a hortatory application, after so vast a development as that of chap. xi., is somewhat too abrupt to be probable ; and especially when we recognize, as this author does, the close connection between the first six verses of chap. xv. and the whole development of chap. xiv., it must also be seen that the exhortation : " Wherefore receive ye one another" (ver. 7), is only the resumption of that which began chap. xiv. in these terms : " Receive ye him that is weak in faith." Not only is it in both cases the same verb that is used : προσλαμβάνεσθαι, *to take to oneself*. But, moreover, the following words of ver. 7 : " As Christ took you to Himself," reproduce exactly the end of xiv. 3 : " For God hath taken him to Himself," (thy brother, weak or strong). Our ver. 7 is therefore the close of the cycle of teaching opened xiv. 1-3 ; and Paul sums up in ver. 7 the general exhortation to connect with it the invitation to union between the two parts of the church which forms the subject of vv. 8–13. Thus is closed the practical part begun in chap. xii. Everything is so strongly compacted, and forms so fine a whole, that it is hard to understand how it should have entered the mind of intelligent commentators to break such an organism.

We have already said that with chap. xv. there begins, according to Baur, the unauthentic part of our Epistle. We shall examine step by step the objections to which the composition of these two chapters by the

Apostle Paul seems to him to be exposed. We shall have to study likewise the reasons which have led a great number of critics, such as Semler, Griesbach, Eichhorn, Reuss, Schultz, Ewald, and others to dispute, not the apostolic origin of the whole or part of the last two chapters, but their original connection with the Epistle to the Romans. As we have stated these very diverse opinions in the Introduction, vol. i. pp. 66–69, we think it unnecessary to reproduce them here.

From the particular question which has just occupied the apostle, he now passes to a more general subject, that of the perfect union which, notwithstanding the difference between the two elements of which it is composed, ought to unite the whole church in a common song of praise to the God of salvation. The goodwill with which all, Jews and Gentiles, have been received by God, ought to make them, as it were, one heart and one mouth to magnify the Lord, while awaiting patiently the consummation of the work He has begun. Such are the contents of this passage, which admirably crowns the practical part. It is really impossible to understand Baur's affirmation : " This piece contains nothing which had not been much better said before," or that of M. Renan, who, adhering to this judgment, thus expresses himself : " Thĕse verses repeat and weakly sum up what precedes." The particular question treated in chap. xiv. broadens ; the point of view rises, and the tone is gradually heightened even to the elevation of a hymn, as at the end of all the great parts preceding (chap. v. 12 et seq., viii. 31 et seq., xi. 33 et seq.).—Paul first exhorts, by the example of Christ, to mutual condescension, vv. 1–3 ; he points out, vv. 4–7, as an end to be reached the common adoration to which such conduct will bring the church ; finally, vv. 8–13, he indicates the special part given to Jews and to Gentiles in this song of the whole redeemed race. He has not before expressed anything like this.

Ver. 1. " *We then that are strong ought to bear the infirmities of the weak, and not to please ourselves.*"—The δέ, *then,* is progressive. The domain enlarges ; it is no longer simply the question of meats, but in general of the relation between Judeo-Christianity more or less legal, of which the party of the weak, chap. xiv., was a branch, and that pure spirituality, which is the proper character of Paul's gospel. This tendency to enlarge the subject had already appeared in the preceding chapter, in vv. 5 and 6, where the example taken from the observance of feast *days* was evidently borrowed from a more general domain. The apostle now expresses his entire thought regarding the relation between a Christianity still allied to the legal spirit, and that which is wholly exempt from it. Since the two elements co-existed in the church of Rome, Paul must once at least before closing utter his thought as to their normal relation, and he does so here quite naturally by applying that law of love in which he has just pointed out that the soul of the Christian life is to be found. It is this gradation in the subject treated which is indicated by the δέ progressive (*then*) of ver. 1. It is no doubt for the same reason he changes the expression which he had used to designate *the weak* in chap. xiv. He now employs the terms δυνατός and ἀδύνατος, *able, unable*, whereas he had made use of the term ἀσθενής. It would be improper, however, completely to identify the contrast expressed by these two terms, employed ver. 1, with that between Judeo-Christians and believers of Gentile origin. For by saying ἡμεῖς, *we*, the apostle shows clearly that he puts himself among *the strong*, and not only himself, but all those also of his Jewish fellow-countrymen who, like Aquilas and Priscilla, for example, have risen to the height of Christian spirituality. Among the weak, on the other hand, might be found a goodly number of former proselytes who had brought with them into the gospel their attachment to the law. We acknowledge then, with Mangold, that the contrast between the strong and the weak in chap. xv. does not coincide absolutely with that of chap. xiv. There the matter in question was only a special feature of Judeo-Christian formalism; here the apostle speaks of the conduct to be observed toward the formalist spirit in itself. But, on the other hand, it is impossible to adopt the opinion of the same author, when he represents the strong and the weak here as two small minorities, two *ultra* parties of the right and left, the one of extreme Gentile-Christians, the other of particularly narrow Judeo-Christians, whom Paul contrasted with the in general moderate Judeo-Christian mass of the church of Rome. How could Paul himself, by saying: *we, the strong*, take his place in one of these extreme parties, which, according to Mangold, wished even (see at ver. 7) to excommunicate the weak! This construction, whereby it is sought in the face of this whole passage to save the hypothesis of a Judeo-Christian majority in the church of Rome, is an expedient which all critics have hitherto judged untenable.—'Ασθενήματα, *the infirmities* or *weaknesses;* these are, as Hodge says, "the prejudices, errors, and faults which arise from weakness of faith." The strong ought to show his strength, not by humiliating the weak and triumphing in the feeling of his superiority, but by bearing the burden of his weakness with love and tenderness. To serve is always in the gospel the true sign of strength (Gal. vi. 2).—But to be able to act thus, there is an enemy that must be swept out of our own heart: self-complacency. The man who boasts of his superiority in understanding and in Christian liberty, is not fitted to assist the weak; rather he estranges and revolts them.

Vv. 2, 3. "*Let every one*[1] *of us*[2] *please his neighbor in what is good to edification. For also Christ pleased not Himself; but, as it is written, The reproaches of them that reproached thee fell on me.*"—The γάρ, *for*, in the T. R., is certainly unauthentic: the *asyndeton* implies a more emphatic reproduction of the thought of ver. 1. The word *every one* seems to us to extend the exhortation to all the members of the church, weak or strong; it is as if it ran: "Yes, let every one of us in general" . . .—There are two ways of seeking to *please our neighbor*. In the one we are self-seeking; we seek to satisfy our interest or self-love. In the other, we seek the good of our neighbor himself. It is this latter way only which the apostle recommends: such is the force of the first clause: *in good;* for good, not from egoism. Then this abstract notion is positively determined by the second clause: *to edification*. The life of Paul was all through the realization of this precept; comp. 1 Cor. x. 33, 34.

Ver. 3. The example of Christ is to the believer the new law to be realized (Gal. vi. 2); hence the *for also*. If, as man, Christ had pleased Himself in the use of His liberty, or in the enjoyment of the rights and privileges which His own righteousness had acquired, what would have come of our salvation? But He had only one thought: to struggle for the destruction of sin, without concerning Himself about His own well-being, or sparing Himself even for an instant. In this bold and persevering struggle against our enemy, evil, He drew on Him the hatred of all God's adversaries here below, so that the lamentation of the Psalmist, lxix. 9, became as it were the motto of His life. In laboring thus for the glory of God and the salvation of men, He recoiled, as Isaiah had prophesied, "neither before shame nor spitting." This certainly is the antipodes of *pleasing ourselves*. Ps. lxix. applies only indirectly to the Messiah (ver. 5: "*My sins* are not hid"); it describes the righteous Israelite suffering for the cause of God. But this is precisely the type of which Jesus was the supreme realization.—We need not say, with Meyer, that Paul adopts the saying of the Psalmist directly into his own text. It is more natural, seeing the total change of construction, like Grotius, to supply this idea: "*but he did* as is written;" comp. John xiii. 18.—Paul, vv. 1 and 2, had

---

[1] T. R. reads γαρ after εκαστος, with some Mnn. only.
[2] F G P, Italiq. read υμων instead of ημων.

said *us;* it is difficult, indeed, to believe, that in writing these last sayings he could avoid thinking of his own apostolic life.

But divine succor is needed to enable us to follow this line of conduct unflinchingly ; and this succor the believer finds only in the constant use of the Scriptures, and in the help of God which accompanies it (vv. 4–6).

Vv. 4–6. "*For whatsoever things were written aforetime*[1] *were written*[2] *for our learning, that we, through patience and through*[3] *comfort of the Scriptures, might have hope. Now the God of patience*[4] *and of comfort grant you to be like-minded one toward another according to Christ Jesus;*[5] *that with one accord ye may with one mouth glorify the God and Father of our Lord Jesus Christ.*"— The transition from ver. 3 to ver. 4 is this : "If I thus apply this saying of the Psalmist to Christ and ourselves, it is because, in general, all Scripture was written to instruct and strengthen us." It is certain that in the case of the first verb we should read προεγράφη, *was written aforetime;* and probably we should read for the second the simple ἐγράφη, *was written* (comp. the critical note). The new light which Scripture revelation throws on all things, and particularly on the events of human life, diffuses in the heart the strength which makes us *hold out* (ὑπομονή, *patience*), and even hold out joyously (παράκλησις, *comfort*). Whether we read or reject the second διά, *through,* the genitive τῶν γραφῶν, *of the Scriptures,* equally depends on both the preceding substantives : the patience and comfort of which the Scriptures are the source.—And it is by these dispositions that we are kept at the height of Christian *hope* which anticipates the joy of perfect salvation. We need not give the verb ἔχωμεν the exceptional meaning of *holding fast* (κατέχειν) ; the simple sense of *possessing* is enough.— Baur has found in this verse an evidence of the unauthenticity of the whole piece. How could the apostle, on occasion of the passage quoted (ver. 3), set himself to speak all at once of the entire O. T. ? But he forgets that this whole piece is a practical exhortation, and that in such circumstances the particular recommendation of the use of the Scriptures is quite in place. The inspiration thereto was probably given by the apostle's own daily experience.—But he knows well himself that Scripture is ineffectual without the direct help of the God of the Scriptures. It is therefore to Him that he lifts his eyes, ver. 5.

Ver. 5. By the double description of God as the *God of patience* and *of consolation,* He is characterized as the true source of these two graces which are communicated to us through the channel of the Scriptures. To get them we must therefore go not only to the Scriptures, but to Himself. —There is a close relation in a church between the consolation and the union of its members. When all are inwardly consoled from above, the way is paved for communion of hearts, all together aspiring vehemently after the same supreme good. It is this *common impulse* which is expressed by Paul's term (φρονεῖν ἐν ἀλλ). He thus returns to the principal idea of the passage, which he had left for an instant to speak of the Scriptures.— On the difference between *Christ Jesus* and *Jesus Christ,* see at i. 1.

Ver. 6. When one common aspiration reigns in the church, secondary diversities no longer separate hearts ; and from the internal communion there results common adoration like pure harmony from a concert of well-tuned instruments. All hearts being melted in one, all mouths become only one. And how so ? Because one being only appears henceforth to all as worthy of being glorified.—It seems obvious to us, since the two words *God* and *Father* are joined in Greek by one and the same article, that the complement : *of our Lord Jesus Christ,* must depend on both. Comp. Eph. i. 17

---

[1] B. It. read εγραφη instead of προεγραφη.
[2] T. R., with A L P, reads προεγραφη instead of εγραφη.
[3] D E F G P omit the second διa.
[4] The French original here has *d'esperance,* but this must be an error of the printer or the copyist.—T. W. C.
[5] T. R., with B D E G L, It. reads Χριστον Ιησουν ; ℵ A C E P, Syr. : Ιησουν Χριστον.

("the God of Jesus Christ"); Matt. xxvii. 46 ("my God, my God"); John xx. 17 ("my Father and your Father, my God and your God"). The expression: *God of Jesus Christ*, denotes the relation of complete dependence; and the expression: *Father of Jesus Christ*, the relation of perfect intimacy. The ideal here described by the apostle, and which is the supreme object of the prayer which he has just formed, ver. 5, is therefore that of the union of the entire church, composed of Jews and Gentiles, in the adoration of the God and Father who has redeemed and sanctified it by Jesus Christ. This union was in a sense his personal work, and the prize of his apostolic labors. How his heart must have leaped, hearing already by the anticipation of faith, the hymn of saved humanity! It is the part of every believer, therefore, to make all the advances and all the sacrifices which love demands in order to work for so magnificent a result. So there is added, as the conclusion of all that precedes (from xiv. 1), ver. 7.

Ver. 7. "*Wherefore receive ye one another, as Christ also received us,*[1] *to the glory of God.*"—The compassionate welcome which Christ has given to all the members of the church individually ought to be perpetually reproduced in the welcome of goodwill and tenderness which they give one another in all the relations of life. And if there is some concession to make, some antipathy to surmount, some difference of opinion to allow, some injury to forgive, one thing ought to lift us above all these annoyances—the thought that we are thereby laboring for the glory of God, who received us in grace through Jesus Christ. Mutual love ought to reign supremely in a church wholly composed of the Lord's well-beloved. We should probably read ἡμᾶς, *us, us believers* in general, rather than ὑμᾶς *you* (the Christians of Rome). This latter reading has no doubt arisen from the verb in the second person plural: *receive ye*. The words: *to the glory of God*, depend rather on the first than on the second verb; for they are intended to explain the recommendation.—Mangold finds himself led by his peculiar point of view, according to which the strong in this chapter are merely the small number of extreme Paulinists, to give to the word *receive* a wholly different sense from that which it had xiv. 1, where the same recommendation was addressed to the entire (according to him, Judeo-Christian) church. The party of the strong mentioned here had, according to this critic, pushed opposition to the weak the length of regarding them as a burden to the life of the church, and of demanding their excommunication. And this is what Paul would prevent. It is very obvious how arbitrary is this difference laid down in the notion of *receiving*. Not only can the προσλαμβάνεσθαι (*receive*) signify nothing else than in xiv. 1, but, moreover, the apostle would never have consented to rank himself, as he would do by the word *us* (vv. 1 and 2), in a party so violent.

The apostle would seem, by this conclusion, to have reached the end of the whole development begun xiv. 1. But he has still an explanation to add: If Christ has received us with equal goodness, there has yet been a difference in the mode of this receiving. Unity in the works of God is never uniformity. Rather harmony implies variety. This common adoration, in which all presently existing contrasts in the church are to be fused, does not prevent each group in the new people of God from bringing with it its own experiences, and playing its particular part in the final concert.

Vv. 8, 9a. "*Now*[2] *I say that Christ*[3] *was*[4] *made a minister of the circumcision for the truth of God, to confirm the promises made unto the fathers, but that the Gentiles glorify God for His mercy;*"—The gracious acceptance which Jesus Christ has given to men has taken place in two principal ways. In

---

[1] T. R. reads, with B D P: ημας; all the rest: υμας.
[2] T. R., with L, Syr., reads δε (*now*); all the rest: γαρ (*for*).
[3] T. R., with D E F G, It. Syr., reads Ιησουν Χριστον; L P: Χριστον Ιησουν; א A B C: Χριστον.
[4] T. R., with א A E L P: γεγενησθαι; B C D E F G: γενεσθαι.

His relation to the Jews, God has above all displayed *His truth*, His fidelity to His ancient promises ; in His relation to the Gentiles, He has more particularly manifested *His mercy ;* for, without having promised them anything directly, He has given everything to them as well as to the Jews. And hence it is, that with the voice which rises from the people of Israel to celebrate God's faithfulness, there should henceforth be joined that of the Gentile world magnifying His grace. Such is the meaning of this admirable passage, which extends to ver. 13.—The reading γάρ, *for*, would introduce the demonstration of the προσελάβετο, *He received us*. But what follows is rather an explanation than a proof ; the latter would have been superfluous. We must therefore read λέγω δέ : "*Now*, here is my whole thought regarding this receiving on the part of Christ, and the duty of union arising from it."—What attracts the Jew to Christ is not exactly the same as that which gains for Him the heart of the Gentile. The Jew is struck with the fulfilment of the prophecies in His person (comp. the Gospel of St. Matthew) ; the heart of the Gentile is taken by the view of His mercy (comp. the Gospel of Luke).—Bauer has thought that the expression : *minister of the circumcision*, could not be ascribed to the apostle, and that it betrayed a writer disposed to carry concessions to Judaism much further than St. Paul could have done. But what is there in this expression which goes beyond the contents of Gal. iv. 4 and 5 : " Born of a woman, born under the law, to redeem them that are under the law" ? All the Gospels prove that Jesus submitted to the strictest observance of the law, and that from His circumcision to His death He enveloped Himself as it were in the national form of Israelitish life. It is a gratuitous error of commentators to think that he ever violated the Sabbath, even in His works of healing. He simply freed it from the Pharisaical prescriptions which had greatly exaggerated Sabbatical strictness. And when Paul says, Phil. ii. 8 : "He became obedient, even to the death of the cross," he exactly expresses the idea contained in the term with which Baur finds fault. Hilgenfeld himself acknowledges the error of the master of his school on this point : "This passage," says he, " contains nothing more than was already contained in chap. xi. of our Epistle."—Several MSS. substitute the aorist γένεσθαι for the perfect γεγενῆσθαι ; erroneously, without doubt, for the fact in question is one which remains forever in its results, as is proved in the sequel.—*To establish* a promise is to confirm by fulfilling it. Comp. 2 Cor. i. 19, 20, a passage which is, as it were, the exegesis of ours.

Ver. 9*a*. The Gentiles, indeed, occupied a place in the prophecies committed to Israel ; but God had never promised them anything directly. This circumstance gave to the salvation which was granted to them as well as to the Jews a more marked character of freeness.—The verb δοξάσαι, *to glorify*, is not an optative, as Hofmann thinks ; the change of construction would be too abrupt. It is the aorist infinitive ; and this infinitive is not to be regarded as parallel to βεβαιῶσαι, to establish, and consequently as dependent on εἰς, *in order to :* "in order to confirm the promises . . ., and in order that the Gentiles might glorify" . . ., as Meyer thinks. For the work of God for the Gentiles would thus be made dependent on the act by which Jesus became a minister of the law in behalf of the Jews, which, in this passage at least, would have no meaning. The simple construction is to make this infinitive, as well as the preceding γεγενῆσθαι, the object of λέγω, *I say :* "Now, I say that Jesus became a minister . . . for the truth of God. . . . ; and that the Gentiles glorify [have in Him a cause for glorifying] God for His mercy." Thus is formed the sublime duet in which there is uttered henceforth the thanksgiving of the entire race.—In support of this idea Paul now quotes a series of O. T. passages which announced the future participation of the Gentiles in the eternal hallelujah.

Vv. 9*b*, 10. "*According as it is written, For this cause I will praise Thee* among the Gentiles, and sing unto Thy name. And again He saith, Rejoice, ye Gentiles, with His people."—The first passage quoted is Ps. xviii. 49: David, victorious over all his enemies, declares that he will make his hymn of thanksgiving resound even in the heathen countries subject to his sceptre, in order to associate these nations in celebrating the work of Jehovah. In the application, Paul starts from the idea that what was accomplished in David's person must be more magnificently realized in that of his antitype the Messiah.

The second passage (ver. 10) is found in Deut. xxxii. 43. Moses, in his final hymn, describes Israel's future deliverance and the judgment of their adversaries; then he invites the Gentiles who have escaped punishment to join their song of rejoicing with that of Israel glorified. The apostle follows the version of the LXX. The latter translates from a form of the text which is not that of our Masoretic text, but which has been proved by Kennicott as a variant. According to this reading, the preposition *eth* (*with*) stands before *ammo* (*His people*), which leads to the meaning of the LXX. and of the apostle: "Rejoice, ye Gentiles, *with* His people." If this *eth* be rejected, as in the ordinary text, we may translate: "Rejoice, ye nations, His people," either, with De Wette, applying the term nations (*gojim*) to the twelve tribes of Israel, or holding, with Aquilas, Theodotion, Ostervald, Hofmann, that it is the Gentiles themselves who are here designated as the people of God. In the sense of De Wette, the application Paul makes of this saying would have no connection with the thought which is really expressed. But this meaning is not admissible, for Moses could not designate the people of Israel as *gojim*, *Gentiles*, especially in a song which turns throughout on the antagonism between Israel and the heathen. The second explanation would be possible; it would be in harmony with the object of the apostolic quotation. Only it must be confessed that the idea of the *transformation* of the Gentiles into God's people has not been so much as hinted by the rest of the song.—Again, it may be translated, as by the Vulgate and Segond: "Nations, praise His people," or, "Sing the praises of His people." But is it natural to direct praise to Israel rather than to Jehovah? Besides, Meyer rightly observes that the Hiphil *hirenin, to sing*, either has no regimen (Ps. xxxii. 11), or it is construed with the dative (Ps. lxxxi. 1).—Lange and others hold yet a different translation: "Gentiles, *make* His people *sing with joy* (by turning to the Lord)." *Hirenin* has really this causative sense, Ps. lxv. 8. But there is no question here of making Israel rejoice, but of celebrating the glory of Jehovah. If the meaning defended by Hofmann (see above) is inadmissible, it only remains to follow the reading adopted by the LXX., and which has passed into the text of the apostle. The idea of these two quotations, as well as of the two following, is the announcement of the great fact: that a day will come when the Gentiles shall celebrate Jehovah in concert with Israel.

Vv. 11, 12. "*And again*,[1] *Praise the Lord, all ye Gentiles; and let all the peoples laud Him!*[2] *And again, Isaiah saith, There shall be the root of Jesse, and He that ariseth to reign over the Gentiles; in him shall the Gentiles hope.*"—The third passage is taken from Ps. cxvii. 1. This hymn in honor of Jehovah, ascribed to the Gentiles, naturally supposes their conversion and their entrance into the kingdom of God. We prefer the reading ἐπαινεσάτωσαν, *let them laud*, to the T. R. ἐπαινέσατε, *laud ye*. The second person is probably a correction after the preceding proposition. The MSS. of the LXX. present the same variant.

Ver. 12. Quotation from Isa. xi. 10. The literal meaning of the Hebrew is: "And in that day there shall be a shoot of Jesse, which shall be set up as a banner for the peoples." . . . For the figure of an erected *banner*,

---

[1] B D E F, It. Syr. read λεγει after παλιν.
[2] T. R., with F G L P, reads επαινεσατε (*laud ye*) instead of επαινεσατωσαν (*let them laud*), which all the others read.

the LXX. have substituted the idea of a person rising up to reign; Paul quotes after them. In meaning it comes to the same thing.—With what emotion does St. Paul refer to all these passages, each of which was the motto, as it were, of his own work among the Gentiles! One understands, in reading such quotations, what he said in ver. 4, undoubtedly from his own experience, of the patience and consolation which are kept up in the believer by the daily use of the Scriptures, as well as of the ever new hope which they inspire. This idea of *hope* is that which is expressed in the prayer uttered ver. 13. For this adoration of the Gentiles, to which the four preceding quotations refer, is the fruit not only of the enjoyment of present blessings, but also, and above all, of the hope of future blessings.

Ver. 13. "*Now the God of hope fill you with every kind of joy and peace in believing, that ye may abound in hope through the power of the Holy Spirit!*" —God is described here as the *God of hope*, evidently in relation to the last words of the preceding quotation: "In Him shall the Gentiles hope." The apostle could not more clearly designate his readers as former Gentiles, than he does by this connection.—The richer the possession of present blessings (*peace and joy*) which the believer derives by the ever-renewed act of faith (ἐν τῷ πιστεύειν, literally, *by believing*), the more does his soul rise to the lively view of future blessings, and according to the expression of the apostle, superabounds or overflows with hope.—The last words: *the power of the Holy Spirit*, point out to the reader once more, as in xiv. 17, the true power which they ought to seek, in opposition to the factitious power by which one exalts himself so easily above others. The former unites, for it strives to serve (xv. 1), whereas the second disunites.

From the very marked connection of this whole last passage with the apostle's ministry, it forms at once the conclusion of the didactic part of the Epistle to the Romans and the transition to the epistolary conclusion in which Paul proceeds to treat of the present situation of his apostolic work.

The reasons alleged by Baur against the authenticity of the first part of this chapter have appeared to us without force. The spirit of conciliation in regard to Judaism, which Baur judges incompatible with Paul's character, never ceased to be that which inspired his work. It was because he felt the need of keeping up union with the Twelve, that after each of his missions he returned to Jerusalem, "lest," as he says himself, Gal. ii. 2, "he had run in vain." The collections which he made in the churches of the Gentile world in behalf of the Judeo-Christians of Palestine had the same object. This was also the object of the personal concessions of which he speaks 1 Cor. ix. 21, 22, and by which he became "to the weak as weak," exactly as he recommends to the strong in this passage. Hilgenfeld rightly says: "What is looked upon as not possibly Paul's, to my conviction only proves one thing: that since the days of Marcion there has been formed an inexact idea of the apostle to which it is still sought at the present day to conform the real Paul" (*Einleit.* p. 323). It will be seen that this observation applies equally to the criticism of Baur and Lucht in regard to the second part of this chapter.

According to Schultz, it is from ver. 7 that the real Epistle to the Romans recommences, to which the whole moral treatise, xii. 1–xv. 6, was originally foreign. It would follow therefrom that the *wherefore* of ver. 7 was immediately connected with the end of chap. xi. There is something seductive at first glance in this combination. The mercy shown both to the Gentiles and to the Jews (xi. 32) is well adapted to justify the invitation to the mutual receiving spoken of in our ver. 7. But it is nevertheless true that this relation is factitious—1st. Because the object of chap. xi. was to justify God's dispensations toward the people of Israel, and not to endeavor the union of Jews and Gentiles in the church; 2d. Because ver. 7 is in evident, and we might say literal correlation, not with any saying whatever of chap. xi., but with the first three verses of chap. xiv.

Finally, we have an inference to draw from this whole piece, xiv. 1–xv. 13, as to the composition of the church of Rome. We appropriate the observation of Hilgenfeld, who declares that in this passage, as nowhere else, there is revealed the true composition of this church ; but we apply it in a very different sense from his. While confessing, indeed, that Paul is addressing the Roman Christians in a body as *strong* (xiv. 1 and xv. 1), this critic refuses to conclude therefrom that the majority of the church were Pauline by conviction and Gentile-Christian by origin. How does he escape from this consequence, which is yet so evident ? By supposing that Paul expresses himself thus : "as conceiving good hopes of them"—that is to say, describing them here not as they are, but as he hopes they will become. This critical subterfuge will deceive no one.

M. Reuss experiences no less embarrassment in view of our passage. In his *Histoire des écrits du N. T.* he expressed himself thus : "This passage is cleverly turned, so as to make believe that the freer opinion was dominant at Rome, while the contrary was assuredly the case." Reuss thus ascribed tactics to the apostle unworthy of his character, rather than abandon his preconceived opinion of a Judeo-Christian majority in this church. In his *Commentaire sur les épîtres pauliennes* he expresses himself somewhat differently : " It is thus evident," he says, "that the author considers the Christian community of Rome as not being exclusively composed of Jews." That is certainly very evident, and no one ever denied that there were at Rome other Christians than those of Jewish origin. But this confession is altogether insufficient. Instead of *not exclusively*, he should have said *not essentially*, to deal fairly with the text before us. The violent expedient attempted by Mangold, in his desire to evade this conclusion, demonstrates it better than anything else. And when Schultz, acknowledging that the strong are Paulinists, and at the same time that they form the majority in the church, concludes therefrom that the whole passage, xiv. 1–xv. 6, cannot have been addressed to the church of Rome, *seeing that the majority of it was Jewish-Christian*, he will allow us to regard this simply as a naive confession of the falsity of the latter opinion, and to conclude by saying, to the contrary effect : As this passage cannot have been written to a Jewish-Christian church, and as it is addressed to the church of Rome, the majority of this church was not Jewish-Christian.

EPISTOLARY CONCLUSION

15:14-16:27

WE have said that the Epistle to the Romans is a didactic treatise, doctrinal and practical, contained in a letter. The treatise is now closed, and the letter begins again. It is easy to show, indeed, that the part about to follow is closely correlated to the epistolary preface which preceded the treatise (i. 1–15). The apostle apologizes for the liberty with which he writes to the Christians of Rome, by reminding them of his mission to the Gentiles (xv. 14–16). This passage corresponds to i. 14 and 15, where he declares himself a *debtor* for the gospel to all Gentiles, the Romans included. He explains (xv. 17–24) what has kept him hitherto in the east. Thus he completes what he had said, i. 11–13, of the impossibility he had before found in the way of visiting Rome. The personal salutations which we find in the first part of chap. xvi. correspond to the address, i. 7 : "To all that are at Rome, beloved of God." Finally, the doxology which closes at once chap. xvi. and the whole Epistle (vv. 25–27) brings us back to the idea with which the letter had opened (i. 1, 2) : that of the fulfilment of the divine plan by the gospel promised beforehand in the O. T. Thus the circle is completed ; on every other view (whether the end of the Epistle be put at chap. xi. or at chap. xiv.) it is broken.

This conclusion contains the following passages :

(1) xv. 14–33, where the apostle gives explanations of a personal nature regarding his letter, his work in general, his approaching visit to Rome, and the journey which he must first make to Jerusalem.

(2) xvi. 1–16 : Recommendations and salutations of the apostle.

(3) Vv. 17–20 : A warning in regard to the probable arrival of Judaizers in the church of Rome.

(4) Vv. 21–24 : The salutations of his fellow-workers.

(5) Vv. 25–27 : The doxology which closes the Epistle.

TWENTY-NINTH PASSAGE (15:14-33)

Personal Explanations.

This passage is intended to convey to the minds of his readers full light as to the apostle's conduct toward them. These explanations relate first to this letter itself.

Vv. 14–16

Vv. 14, 15. "*Now I myself also am persuaded of you, my brethren, that ye also*[1] *yourselves are full of goodness, filled with all knowledge, able also to admonish one another.*[2] *But brethren,*[3] *I have written the more boldly*[4] *unto you, as in some measure to put you in remembrance again of these things, because of*

---

[1] The words και αυτοι are omitted by D E F G, It.
[2] L Syr. read αλλους instead of αλληλους.
[3] ℵ A B C omit αδελφοι.
[4] A B τολμηροτερως instead of τολμηροτερον.

the grace that is given to me of God;"[1]—The form of address: *my brethren*, is occasioned by the return to the epistolary style.—By saying: *myself also*, the apostle hints that the very full instruction which he has given them in this Epistle is not caused by a want of confidence in their Christian attainments; *myself:* "though my letter might make you suppose the contrary." This meaning seems to me more natural than that of many commentators who suppose that Paul means: " I, as well as others," or : " without needing any one to remind me of what you are."—The καὶ αὐτοί, *ye also*, is certainly authentic, notwithstanding the omission of the words by the Greco-Latins; the meaning is: "you to whom I am thus writing." The qualities on which the apostle rests this favorable judgment are at once of a moral and intellectual nature. They are full of *goodness*, ἀγαθωσύνη; this word denotes practical solidity, the full maturity of spiritual life; then they possess in abundance every kind of Christian *knowledge*, πᾶσα γνῶσις. We may remark the difference between this testimony and the eulogium passed on the Corinthians (1st Ep. i. 5), where Paul brings out only this second sort of gifts (*knowledge and speech*).—From these two kinds of qualities it followed that there was among them the capacity for providing in a certain measure for their own edification and their mutual instruction. The true reading is ἀλλήλους, *one another*, and not as it is in one Mj. and the Syriac version, ἄλλους, *others*. The καί, *also* or *even*, which accompanies this pronoun, means: even among yourselves, without the help of any master from without. There is nothing in the expressions of this verse which goes beyond what the apostle could say with all sincerity, nor anything to support the judgment of Baur: that these sayings are the work of a later writer, who, seeing the bad effect produced by this letter on the Judeo-Christians of Rome, sought to soothe them by adding these chaps. xv. and xvi. The apostle might well think the church of Rome very advanced in all respects, without its following that a letter like this was a work of supererogation. He himself (i. 8) gave thanks for the faith of his readers, "which is spoken of throughout the whole world;" and if the terms which he uses in our verse could not be applied fully to all the individuals composing the church, they were nevertheless strictly true when applied to the church as a whole; for, as chap. xvi. will show, it possessed a very great abundance of teachers and evangelists who could carry out within it the functions of instruction and admonition.

Ver. 15. The δέ is adversative: *but;* nevertheless; and the comparative τολμηρότερον, *more boldly*, is explained precisely by this contrast with ver. 1: " more freely than it seemed I should do in the case of such a church." The repetition of the form of address: *brethren*, is perfectly natural in these conditions; it expresses anew the feeling of equality with which the apostle loves to approach them.—In the explanation of what follows, everything depends on the grammatical meaning and construction of ἀπὸ μέρους, which we have translated by: *in some measure*, and which literally signifies: *in part*. Some refer this restriction to the verb: *I wrote you* (Meyer, for example), and apply it solely to some particularly forcible passages of the letter, such as xi. 17–25, xii. 2, xiv. 1 et seq. But what is there in these passages so different from the rest of the Epistle, and which should have called forth a special apology? Hofmann refers this "in part" to what is fragmentary in the teaching of the Epistle to the Romans. But in no letter does Paul give a statement of evangelic doctrine which less deserves to be called fragmentary. It is impossible to get an appropriate meaning for ἀπὸ μέρους, *in part*, except by referring this restriction to ἐπαναμιμνήσκων, *putting you in remembrance*, and applying it, not to the extent and contents of the teaching, as if the readers had had certain parts of the truth present to their mind, and not others, but to the *mode* of giv-

---

[1] T. R. reads, with 7 Mjj., υπο instead of απο, which is the reading of ℵ B F.

ing instruction. The apostle has written to them, not with the view of teaching them things that were *new* to them, but to bring back to their memory, in a way not to be forgotten, things which he knew to be already known to them *to a certain degree*. Thus is explained the ὡς, *as;* it is much more as *reminding* than as instructing them that he has written. He wished to treat them not as catechumens, but as Christians and brethren.— And if he has taken the liberty of acting thus toward them, it is not arbitrarily and at his own hand, it is in virtue of the mission which he has received and of the gift which has been bestowed on him in order to its fulfilment. Such is the meaning of the διὰ τὴν χάριν, *on account of the grace,* an expression which we must beware of rendering "*through* the grace," which is forbidden by the regimen in the accusative. The thing referred to, as is shown by the following verse, is his commission as apostle of the Gentiles, which he has only been obeying by writing thus to the church of Rome. Thus he apologizes for his letter :—(1) By declaring that he wished merely to remind his readers of what they already knew ; and (2) by tracing his right of acting thus to the apostleship which he has received. There is room for hesitating between the two readings, ὑπό, "*by* God," and ἀπό, "*on the part of* God." The former is perhaps preferable in the context, as denoting a more direct divine interposition.

The right understanding of these two verses suffices to set aside Baur's view regarding the entire Epistle to the Romans. According to this critic, the apostle aimed at nothing less than to bring over the church from the Judeo-Christian legal standpoint to his own evangelical conception. Now, to say that all he did was only *to bring back to the memory* of his readers what they already knew, would, if such had been his aim, be an act of gross hypocrisy ; to make one change his opinion is not to remind him of what he knows. It is true that Baur has sought to give a quite different meaning to the expression : " as putting you in mind." He applies it, not to the contents of the Epistle, but solely to the communications which are about to follow regarding the work which Paul has accomplished in the world. But such is not the natural meaning of the word ἔγραψα, *I have written unto you ;* and the restriction : ἀπὸ μέρους, *in part,* no longer in that case admits of explanation. It is with good reason that Mangold himself declares that it is impossible to found a hypothesis on exegetical processes of such violence.

Ver. 16. " *That I should be a minister of Jesus Christ to the Gentiles, ministering as a priest in the gospel of God, that the offering of the Gentiles might be made acceptable, being sanctified by the Holy Spirit.*"—The grace of apostleship had been given to Paul for the accomplishment of a sublime task. The word λειτουργός denotes a public functionary. In this case the function involved is nothing less than presenting to God the Gentile world as an offering which may be acceptable to Him. This world-wide service to which Jesus Christ Himself had called St. Paul was not only that of a preacher, it had a priestly character. This is certainly what is expressed by the term ἱερουργεῖν (see Meyer) : " to offer as a priest ;" not that the preacher of the gospel is in any sense a mediator who comes between God and the believer ; but his function does not consist in simple teaching ; each time it is an act of consecration whereby the messenger of salvation offers to God his own person as well as the persons of all his hearers. We know how Paul prayed constantly for the churches which he had already founded (comp. i. 8–10, and the beginning of all the Epistles), and we can thus imagine what the work of their founding was. Thus was his whole apostolate a priestly function. In the expression : " to fulfil sacerdotally (minister) the gospel of God," we must understand, here as elsewhere (see on i. 8), by " the gospel," not the contents, but the *act* of preaching.—The end of this priestly office confided to the apostle is to transform the world of the Gentiles into an *offering well-pleasing to God.* Comp. Phil. ii. 17.—Τῶν ἐθνῶν, *of the Gentiles*, is a genitive of apposition : the offering which consists of the persons of the Gentiles. The verb γένηται, *might be (become)*, indicates progress ; this progress does not consist only in the growing extension of the work ; but also, and especially, as is shown by the following words, in the transformation of those who are its subjects : *being sanctified by the Holy Spirit*. The word of salvation received with faith must be sealed in the heart by power from on high, that the soul may be truly gained, and that it may belong to God ; comp. Eph. i. 13. The apostle probably alludes to the Levitical ordinance, according to which the sprinkling of salt over the meat-offering was the condition of its acceptance on the part of God.

If it is true, according to the natural meaning of these verses 14–16, that the apostle justifies his Epistle to the Romans by his commission to be the apostle of the Gentiles, it clearly follows that the majority of the Christians of Rome were of Gentile origin. The defenders of the Jewish-Christian composition of this church have had to seek to parry this decisive blow. They have tried to do so in two ways. Mangold explains these verses in this sense : "I have required, as apostle of the Gentiles, to express myself more than once in this letter more forcibly than seemed fitting in addressing Jewish-Christians like you ; but I had to uphold the rights of those of whom God made me the apostle."[1] But what is there to give us the right to restrict the application of the word τολμηρότερον, *more boldly*, to a few passages of the Epistle relative to the calling of the Gentiles? This expression bears on the character of the entire writing as a doctrinal composition ; this is shown by the connection of ver. 15 with ver. 14. Filled with knowledge, as the Romans were, they seemed to have no need of this complete instruction. Then the description of Paul's apostolate, from ver. 16 to ver. 20, proves that we have here the positive indication of the motive which led him to write this Epistle, and not only the justification of some passages of his letter. Weizsäcker correctly observes that the apostle explains his letter by the duty which his task of providing for the edification of the Gentiles imposed on him, and not by the right which he has to uphold their cause before Jewish-Christians.—Volkmar, who pursues the same object as Mangold, has attempted another explanation :[2] "I do not forget, Paul would say, that I am only the apostle of the Gentiles, and I have no thought, in writing you as I do, to intrude on a church which does not belong to me, since it is of Jewish-Christian origin ; and that is the very reason which has prevented me hitherto from visiting you, for my intention is not to build on a foundation laid by another ; but now that I have no more place in the countries of the east, I am about to proceed to Spain, and I shall see you in passing " (vv. 17–24). This construction is ingenious, but impossible. The διὰ τὴν χάριν, "*because of* the grace given unto me," depending on ἔγραψα, *I have written unto you*, is absolutely opposed to it ; and in what follows the apostle does not for a moment say that he has not yet visited Rome because of the Judeo-Christian character of the church, but that he has not done so because he was still detained in the east by nearer duties. Whether the founders of the church of Rome were or were not Judeo-Christians, whether the believers gathered in by them were or were not of this character, the apostle makes no allusion to this side of the question ; a proof that it was not this which concerned his inference.—Lucht has attempted to find a proof of unauthenticity in the absence of the title *apostle*, ver. 16. The forger sought, he holds, by avoiding this title, to spare the susceptibilities of the Jewish-Christians of Rome. But, answers Hilgenfeld, "If the word is not there, the thing is." And, in fact, ver. 16 is nothing else than the paraphrase of the term : *apostle of the Gentiles*. And if Paul has here preferred the paraphrase to the title itself, it is because it was much more suitable than the latter to explain the course which he had followed in writing such a letter to this church which he had not founded, and which he did not even yet know.

As to this mission to the Gentile world with which he has been invested, God has crowned it with such successes that it is now finished in the east,

---

[1] *Der Römerbrief*, etc., pp. 70 and 71.   [2] *Paulus Römerbrief*, pp. 60 and 61.

and that it only remains to the apostle to continue it in the west, which will lead him next to Rome. Such are the contents of the following verses, 17-24, the somewhat free connection of which with what precedes is not hard to understand.

Vv. 17-24

Vv. 17-19. *"I have therefore whereof I may glory[1] through Jesus Christ in the service of God. For I will not dare to speak[2] of any of those things which Christ hath not wrought by me, for the obedience of the Gentiles, by word and by deed, in the power[3] of signs and wonders, in the power of the Spirit of God ;[4] so that from Jerusalem, and the countries round about, as far as Illyria, I have accomplished [the preaching of] the gospel of Christ."*—*Therefore :* in virtue of that weighty commission by which I have felt myself authorized to write you as I have done. If we read the article τήν before καύχησιν, "*the* glorying," the meaning is : "I have therefore *this* cause of glorying (that of being Christ's minister to the Gentiles)." But the last words : *in the service of God*, are thus made superfluous. The article must therefore be rejected ; the meaning is this : "I have truly occasion to glory in what concerns the service of God." The expression τὰ πρὸς Θεόν, literally, "what concerns God," is a sort of technical phrase in the Jewish liturgical language to denote the functions of worship (Heb. ii. 17, v. 1, etc.). This term therefore belongs to the same order of ideas as all those of the preceding verse (ἱερουργεῖν, λειτουργός, προσφορά, ἡγιασμένη).—The words : *through Jesus Christ*, soften the too startling force which the term *glorying* might have. This verse, while recalling the work already done by Paul in God's service, completes the justification of what Paul had called the τολμηρότερον, the somewhat bold character of his conduct. Nothing assuredly could have a more authentic character than such a passage.

This ver. 17 is at the same time the transition to what follows. As a confirmation of his apostolic mission to the Gentiles, Paul expounds the extraordinary results which he has obtained—(1) from the viewpoint of the nature of the work, vv. 18, 19a ; (2) from the viewpoint of the extension of the work accomplished, ver. 19b.

Ver. 18. The words : "I will not dare to speak of any of those things," signify, according to Meyer and others, that to exalt himself he will not take the liberty of inventing facts which Christ had not really wrought by him. But did this odious supposition need to be denied ? Such a defence of his veracity might be in place in the Epistles to the Corinthians, but not in that to the Romans. Besides, the expression τι ὧν, *any of the things which*, naturally refers only to real facts. To designate fictitious facts, he must have used, not τι ὧν, but τι ὃ, *anything which*. Finally, all the following qualifications : *"for the obedience . . ., by word* and *by deed"* . . ., can be applied only to real facts. Hofmann thinks Paul means that he will not take advantage here of any other grounds of glorying than those which enter into the service of Christ ; that he will omit, for example, all those he enumerates (Phil. iii. 4 ct seq.). But in that case the subject Χριστός, *Christ*, should be at the head of the proposition. And what motive could the apostle have to allude in this passage to the advantages which he might have possessed before being a Christian ? The only possible meaning of these words : *I will not dare*, is this : "It would imply some hardihood on my part to indicate a single mark of apostleship whereby God has not deigned to set His seal on my ministry to the Gentiles." It is a very delicate form of saying, that it would be easier to convict him of false-

---

[1] B C D E F G read την (before καυχησιν), which is rejected by א A L P and the Mnn.
[2] D E F G read ειπειν instead of λαλειν.
[3] D E F G read αυτου after δυναμει.
[4] T. R., with א L P, Syr^{sch}., reads πνευματος θεοῦ ; A C D E F G, It. read πνευματος αγιου : B : πνευματος alone.

hood in the signs of apostolic power which he might omit in speaking of his work, than in those which he enumerates here. This : *I will not dare*, is, as it were, the acme of the καύχησις, of that *glorying* of which he spoke in ver. 17. It would be vain for him to seek a divine manifestation which Christ has not wrought by him; he would not discover it. This mode of speaking does not come of boastfulness; it is the expression of a holy jealousy in behalf of the Gentiles, that domain which God has assigned him, and which He has privileged by the apostleship of Paul, no less than the Jewish world has been by the apostleship of the Twelve; comp. 2 Cor. xii. 11, 12.—In the expression : *by word*, are embraced all his teachings, public and private; and in the expression : *by deed*, his labors, journeys, collections, sufferings, sacrifices of all kinds, and even miracles, though these are mentioned afterward as a category by themselves.—The expression : *the power of signs*, is explained by Meyer in this sense : "the power (my power over men) arising from signs." It seems to me more natural to understand : "the (divine) power breaking forth in signs." Miraculous facts are called *signs* in relation to the meaning which God attaches to them and which men ought to see in them, and *wonders* (τέρας) in relation to nature and its laws, on the regular basis of which the miracle is an inroad.—*The power of the Spirit* may designate the creative virtue inherent in this divine breath; but here the complement seems to me to be the person of Paul : "the power with which the Spirit fills me."—It is better to read, with the T. R., the Spirit *of God* than the *Holy* Spirit (with 6 Mjj.), for it is force that is in question rather than holiness.

In the second part of the verse Paul passes from the nature of his activity to the extent of the results obtained. The latter is the effect of the former; hence the ὥστε, *so that*. For the previous subject, *Christ*, there is substituted the personal pronoun *I*, because in the act of preaching it is the human agent who is in view. There has been found (by Hofmann and others) in the word κύκλῳ, *in a circle*, an indication of the course followed by the apostle in his work of evangelizing, to the effect that Paul did not proceed from Jerusalem to Illyria by a straight line, but by describing a vast ellipse. This idea is far from natural, and would have a shade of boastfulness. It is much simpler to understand the word *in a circle* (or *with its surroundings*) as intended to widen the point of departure indicated by the word *Jerusalem :* "Jerusalem, with the surrounding countries." In fact, it was strictly at Damascus, then in Arabia, that Paul had begun to evangelize. But Jerusalem being the point best known to western Christians, he names only this capital.—If we refuse, with Meyer, to give to the word εὐαγγέλιον the meaning of *preaching of the gospel*, it is impossible to find a natural meaning here for the word πληροῦν, *to fill*. To translate, with Luther : "to fill every place *with* the gospel," is contrary to grammar. Meyer understands : to give the gospel its full development (by spreading it everywhere). But one feels how forced this manner of expression would be in this sense. We have only to represent to ourselves the *act of preaching* the gospel in the east as a task to be fulfilled or an ideal to be reached, and the meaning of πληροῦν becomes clear. It is in this same sense that we have seen πλήρωμα νόμου signify *the fulfilment of the law*, xiii. 10. Baur has here found manifest exaggeration, and therein a sign of unauthenticity. But it is clear that Paul was not claiming to have finished the work of preaching in relation to the small towns and country districts of the lands he had evangelized. He regarded his apostolic task as entirely fulfilled when he had lighted the torch in the great centres, such as Thessalonica, Corinth, and Ephesus. That done, he reckoned on the churches founded in those capitals continuing the evangelization of the provinces. The same critic has pronounced the fact here mentioned of the apostle's preaching *in Illyria* to be inadmissible. None of the apostle's journeys known to us had led him into this "rude and inhospitable country." The rudeness of a country did not arrest St. Paul. From the fact that this mission is not mentioned in the Book of Acts, must it be concluded that it is a fable? But this book does not speak of the *three years* passed by Paul in Arabia, according to Gal. i. 17; must it therefore be concluded that the statement is false, and that the Epistle to the Galatians is unauthentic? A forger would have taken good care, on the contrary, not to implicate himself in other facts of the apostle's life than those which were generally known. Besides, what is there improbable in the statement that during the time which elapsed from his leaving Ephesus (Pentecost 57 or 58) till his arrival at Corinth (December 58) the apostle, who spent that time in Macedonia, should have made an excursion to the shores of the Adriatic? For that only a few days were needed. The Book of Acts is not at all intended to relate in detail the life of Peter or of Paul.

Vv. 20, 21. "*And that while making it my ambition*[1] *to preach the gospel, not where Christ was already named, lest I should build upon another man's foundation: but as it is written, They to whom nothing was said of Him shall see Him; and they that have not heard shall know Him.*"—To confirm the reality of his apostleship to the Gentiles, Paul has referred to the successes with which his activity thus far has been crowned in the east; and now, to pass to the idea of his future work in the west and of his visit to Rome, he recalls the principle by which he has always been guided in the direction of his labors. The participle $\varphi\iota\lambda o\tau\iota\mu o\acute{\upsilon}\mu\epsilon\nu o\nu$ has something of the force of a gerund: *while making it my ambition*. The reading $\varphi\iota\lambda o\tau\iota\mu o\tilde{\upsilon}\mu a\iota$, *I make it my ambition*, must be unhesitatingly rejected; for the apostle does not mean here to express a new idea, but merely to define the manner of his procedure in the work to the goal of which he is now approaching. The term $\varphi\iota\lambda o\tau\iota\mu\epsilon\tilde{\iota}\sigma\theta a\iota$ should not be generalized in the sense of: *to strive* or *bind myself to;* it must be kept in its strict sense: *to esteem it a matter of* honor. Not that Paul sought his personal honor in the method followed by him: what he was concerned about was his apostolic dignity. An apostle is not a simple pastor or evangelist; his mission is, as Paul himself says, 1 Cor. iii. 10, to "*lay* the foundation" on which others after him may build, consequently to preach where others have not yet come. Paul might have said: "to preach the gospel where Christ has not yet been named," but he prefers to give his expression a still more negative turn, and to say more precisely: "to preach the gospel, not where He has been named." He wishes to preach the gospel, but not where any one has done so before him.

Ver. 21. This conduct rested, as we have just said, on the exalted feeling which he had of the apostolic mission; and, moreover, he found, as it were, the programme for it in a prophetical saying, Isa. lii. 15. The prophet speaks here of the Gentile kings and peoples to whom the declaration of the Messiah's work shall come for the first time.—The expression: "as it is written," depends, as in ver. 3, on a verb understood: "*but doing* as it is written." Volkmar here finds proof of the Jewish-Christian character of the church of Rome, since this church is to Paul like a foreign domain on which he has denied himself the satisfaction of entering. Weizsäcker shows indeed that Paul's words contain nothing of the kind; for what he says refers in general to every church not founded by him, whether of Jewish or Gentile origin. But it may be questioned if Paul is even alluding to the reason which has kept him hitherto from visiting Rome. Does not Paul by this digression, vv. 20 and 21, simply mean to say that so long as there still remained unevangelized countries in the east, it was his duty to remain in that part of the world? In vv. 22–24, he calls to mind that now circumstances are changed, and that the application of the same principle

---

[1] T. R. reads, with ℵ A C E L, the Mnn., Syr., $\varphi\iota\lambda o\tau\iota\mu o\upsilon\mu\epsilon\nu o\nu$; B D F G P: $\varphi\iota\lambda o\tau\iota\mu o\upsilon\mu a\iota$.

which had hitherto detained him in the east, henceforth impels him to the west, which will bring him at the same time to Rome.—Baur has asked, if to write a letter of so considerable compass as this to a Jewish-Christian church not founded by him, was not to build on the foundation laid by another ? We first remove from the objection the word Jewish-Christian ; then we call to mind that the founders of the church of Rome were chiefly disciples of St. Paul, who came from churches founded by him in the east ; and finally, we cannot put on the same footing a letter written by Paul, and his personal intervention as a preacher. He wrote to the Colossians and the Laodiceans, though he had not personally founded and known those churches (Col. ii. 1). It is precisely for this reason that in beginning his Epistle (i. 1–7), and then again in closing it (xv. 16), he has referred to his mission to the Gentiles which imposes on him duties to all churches of Gentile origin.

Vv. 22–24. *"From which cause also I have been hindered*[1] *often*[2] *from coming to you; but now, having no more place in these regions, and having a great desire for many*[3] *years to come unto you, when*[4] *I take my journey unto Spain,*[5] *I trust*[6] *to see you in passing, and to be brought on my way thitherward by you,*[7] *if first I have somewhat satisfied the need I have of seeing you."*—The "for which cause also" might be connected with vv. 20 and 21 in this sense : because I still found parts in the east where Christ had not been preached. But vv. 20 and 21 may also be regarded as a disgression, and the "for which cause" connected with the idea of ver. 19. The immense labor to which Paul had to give himself to preach the gospel from Jerusalem to Illyria has not allowed him to carry out his often formed project of going to preach it at Rome (i. 13).—The imperfect ἐνεκοπτόμην is the true reading. It is an imperfect of duration : "Ever and again I was hindered."— Τὰ πολλά might signify : *by many things ;* but it is more natural to understand it in the sense : *many times,* like πολλάκις, which is read by the *Vatic.* and the Greco-Lats.

Vv. 23, 24. Yet, agreeably to the principle expounded vv. 20 and 21, his journey to Rome will not, strictly speaking, be a mission, but rather a visit as it were in passing, for the church already exists in this capital. When, Acts xix. 21, Paul at Ephesus was forming his plans for the future, it indeed was *to Rome* that he wished to proceed ; but afterward he had no doubt heard of the foundation of a church in that city, and therefore he now no longer says : to *Rome,* but : *to Spain by way of Rome.* The unevangelized country, Spain, is the goal (the εἰς) ; Rome is now only the way (the διά). Yet it would be easy to go directly by sea from Asia to Spain. But this is what he will take good care not to do, for he hungers and thirsts to enter into personal communication with the Christians of Rome, and he will make a detour to visit them in passing. Such is the perfectly obvious meaning of these two verses.

The text of ver. 24 comes to us in three forms. The T. R. and the Byzs. read after the words : "into Spain," a principal clause : "*I will come to you ;* " which leads them to add a *for* with the following verb : *"for* I trust." The clause is simple, the sense clear ; only these words : *I will come to you,* are wanting in the documents of the two other texts.—The Alex. is much less intelligible. It begins at ver. 23 with two participles : "having no more place . . . but having the desire" . . . ; then it continues with a subordinate proposition : " when I shall go into Spain ;" and instead

---

[1] D E F G : ενεκοπην instead of ενεκοπτομην.
[2] B D E F G : πολλακις instead of τα πολλα.
[3] B G : ικανων instead of πολλων.
[4] T. R., with L, Mnn. reads ως εαν ; all the others : ως αν.
[5] T. R., with L, Mnn., reads (after Σπανιαν), ελευσομαι προς υμας, *I will come to you.* These words are omitted by ℵ A B C D E F G P, It. Syr^{sch}.
[6] T. R., with ℵ A B C D E L P. reads γαρ after ελπιζω ; this γαρ is omitted by F G It. Syr.
[7] Instead of υφ' υμων, B D E F G read αφ υμων.

of the principal verb expected, it closes by saying : "for I hope to see you in passing" . . . ; and in ver. 25 : "now then I go to Jerusalem." There would be but one way of justifying this text, to make a long parenthesis from : *for I trust*, to the end of the verse, and to find the principal verb on which the two participles of ver. 23 depend in ver. 25 : "now I go to Jerusalem." But this would require us to reject the δέ, *but* or *now*, at the beginning of ver. 25, contrary to the authority of *all* the documents ; then, there is no logical relation between the idea of these two participles : *having no more place, having the desire to come to you*, and the verb : *I go to Jerusalem*. To render this reading admissible, it is absolutely necessary to reject the γάρ, *for*, after ἐλπίζω, *I trust*, and thus to make this the principal verb.—This is precisely what is done by the Greco-Lat. reading, which is supported by the ancient Syriac version. This is not the only time that the Greco-Latin text has the superiority over the other two. We have already met with some similar cases in the Epistle to the Romans (xiii. 1, for example), and we beg the reader specially to compare 1 Cor. ix. 10, which is not intelligible except in the form preserved by the Greco-Latin documents. The meaning which we get by means of this text is faultless : " Having no more place . . ., but having the desire to see you . . ., when I go into Spain, I hope to see you in passing."—The διά in διαπορευόμενος alludes to the idea that Rome will only be a place of rest and passage ; the reason of this has been explained. The church is already founded there.—The verb προπεμφθῆναι, *to be conducted farther*, contains these two ideas : to be accompanied by some of theirs, and to be provided with everything necessary for the journey ; comp. Tit. iii. 13 and 3 John 6.— The reading ὑφ' ὑμῶν, *by you*, which contains the idea of the solicitude of the Romans about Paul, is much to be preferred to the reading ἀφ' ὑμῶν, *from among you*, which makes the church only a point of departure.—'Εκεῖ, the adverb of rest, is used, as it often is, instead of ἐκεῖσε, the adverb of motion ; the goal is considered as reached : "to go *thither* and be *there*." Comp. John xi. 8.—'Εμπλησθῆναι, literally to *saturate himself with them*, a very lively expression of the need he feels to make their personal acquaintance, and of the pleasure which this relation will bring him ; comp. i. 12. The word *somewhat* is not a poor compliment which he pays to the Romans, as if he meant to say that his stay among them will only half satisfy him ; Paul means, on the contrary, that he will never see them enough to satisfy *completely* the want he feels of spiritual communion with them.—Baur suspects this whole passage, for the reason that this journey to Spain is a pure fiction ; a notion, the realization of which is wholly without attestation. But the Fragment of Muratori says expressly : "the departure of Paul, setting out from Rome to Spain." For the very reason, answers Hilgenfeld, that this journey never took place, a forger would not have mentioned it. And without examining the question of fact, how is it possible to prove that Paul could not have formed such a project, which corresponded so well with his noble ambition, even though he had not been able to realize it ?

But before setting out for the west, the apostle has yet a task to fulfil ; he proposes to seal by a solemn act the union between the two portions of the church in that part of the world which he is about to leave. Such is the object of a last visit which he yet reckons on making to Jerusalem. He must transmit to the mother church of Jerusalem, on behalf of the churches of Greece, the fruits of a collection which they have made spontaneously for it. The apostle is concerned to inform the Christians of Rome on this point, not only because this journey will detain him some time yet in the east, but especially because it may involve him in dangers, and because he has a request to address to them in this relation. Such are the perfectly natural contents of the end of the chapter.

Vv. 25–33

Vv. 25–27. *"But now I go unto Jerusalem ministering*[1] *unto the saints. For it hath seemed good to them of Macedonia and Achaia to make a contribution for the poor saints which are at Jerusalem. For it hath seemed good to them, and verily their debtors they are; for if the Gentiles have been made partakers of their spiritual things, they ought also to minister unto them in carnal things."*—The *νυνὶ δέ*, *but now*, does not contrast, as that of ver. 22 did, his approaching journey to Rome with certain anterior obstacles; the matter in question now is a near hindrance which still retards his visit to Rome. The word *διακονῶν*, *putting myself at the service of* (ministering), shows that the apostle is referring to a task which is sacred in his eyes. The participle present *διακονῶν* is preferable to the participle future or to the infinitive aorist: "in order to serve," which is read by some documents. For the service is not only the object of the journey; it consists of the journey itself.

Ver. 26. The expression: *the saints*, characterizes the church of Jerusalem as the most venerable of Christendom; comp. 1 Cor. xvi. 1. But it is not to all the church, it is the most indigent of its members, that this service is destined. The idea has often been advanced, that the cause of the poverty of so large a number of believers at Jerusalem was the community of goods which is thought to have prevailed at the origin of this church. This is to exaggerate and mistake the import of the facts related in the narrative of the Acts on this subject. The state of things is quite naturally explained in the following way. From the beginning, the preaching of Christ found but little access except to the poorer classes; "Blessed are *the poor*," said Jesus (Luke vi. 20). The indigence of those first believers must have been increased day by day by the violent hatred of the Jewish authorities and of the upper classes; comp. Jas. ii. 4–6. What easier for rich and powerful families than to deprive poor artisans, who had become the objects of their reprobation, of their means of subsistence! This is an event which is reproduced everywhere when there is a transition from one religious form to another; so in Catholic countries where Protestantism is preached; among the Jews, among the heathen of India or China, etc., when one of their own becomes a Christian. Thus are naturally explained the meals in common (the service of tables) to which the whole church was invited in the first times, the collection made at Antioch (Acts xi. 29) in behalf of the church of Jerusalem, and the request which the apostles addressed to Paul and Barnabas, Gal. ii. 10.—*Κοινωνία*, strictly *communion*, and hence material communication so far as it arises from communion of hearts; comp. Heb. xiii. 16. The word *τινά*, "*some communication*," brings out with delicacy the free and at the same time accidental character of this collection, both as to the thing in itself and as to its amount. It is the churches which have spontaneously taxed themselves for this purpose. It is surprising that Paul speaks only of the churches of Greece, for Acts xx. 4 and 1 Cor. xvi. 1 put beyond doubt the participation of the churches of Asia and Galatia.

Ver. 27. The repetition of the: "it seemed good to them," emphasizes still more forcibly the free-will of the churches in this course. They felt themselves impelled to pay this homage to the church from which the gift of salvation had come to them; they even judged that it was a small matter to act thus in a lower domain in behalf of those to whom they owed blessings of an infinitely more precious nature. Paul evidently enlarges thus on this subject, not only to praise the churches of Greece, or with the view of leading the church of Rome immediately to carry out a similar work, but with the intention of awaking in the hearts of his hearers the

---

[1] ℵ reads διακονησων; D E F G: διακονησαι; all the rest: διακονων.

feeling of a duty which they shall also have the opportunity of fulfilling some time or other. After this episode Paul returns to his principal subject.

Vv. 28–29. "*When, therefore, I have accomplished this and have sealed to them this fruit, I will go on by you unto Spain. Now I know that when I come unto you, I shall come in the fulness*[1] *of the blessing of Christ.*"[2]—The term σφραγίζεσθαι, *to seal*, has been understood here in many ways. Erasmus explained it thus: "when I have delivered to them this money well enclosed and sealed." This meaning is grammatically impossible, and the idea is rather vulgar. Theodoret thought Paul was alluding to the duly signed and sealed receipt which should be given him by the receivers to be transmitted to the donors. But the αὐτοῖς, *to them*, can only apply to the former, while in this sense it would require to refer to the latter. Hofmann applies the idea of the *seal* to the signed and sealed deed by which the churches of Greece charged Paul to take to Jerusalem the deputies who were bearers of the collection. But how could all that be included in the simple expression: to seal? The term σφραγίζεσθαι is frequently taken in a metaphorical sense: *to keep closed, to keep secret, attest, confirm, consent*. It is in this wide sense that it must be explained here. The word denotes the delivery officially and in due form of the sum collected. We can see, Acts xxi. 18, how Paul, arrived at Jerusalem, repaired to the assembly of the elders called together in the house of James, as to a solemn reception. It was then no doubt that the letter of commission from the churches was communicated, with the sums accompanying it, and that a receipt duly signed was given by the elders.—Paul declares that this formality once accomplished, he will haste to take up his project of a journey to the west (ver. 29); and if things can be so brought about, he is perfectly sure of the happiness he will enjoy among his brethren of the church of Rome. Would a forger, writing in the apostle's name in the second century, have made him pen a plan of the future so different from the way in which things really fell out?—The Greco-Latin reading πληροφορία, instead of πληρώματι (*fulness*), is evidently erroneous; for this word signifies only "fulness *of conviction*," a meaning which does not suit the context. The words τοῦ εὐαγγελίου τοῦ, *of the gospel of* (Christ), in the Byz. documents, must be regarded as an interpolation, unless we choose to explain their omission in the other Mjj. by the four terminations in ου which follow one another consecutively.

The more assured the mind of the apostle is when it is turned to Rome, the more does disquiet take possession of his heart when he thinks of Jerusalem.

Vv. 30–32. "*Now I exhort you, brethren,*[3] *by our Lord Jesus Christ, and by the love of the Spirit, that ye strive together with me before God for me in your prayers, that I may be delivered from the disobedient in Judea, and that this aid*[4] *which I have for*[5] *Jerusalem may be acceptable to the saints; that coming*[6] *with joy among you by the will of God,*[7] *I may with you find rest.*"—The δέ might be adversative (*but*); it would thus express the contrasted impressions which we have just indicated. But it is better to take it simply as progressive: *now*. The form of address: *brethren*, which the *Vatic.* wrongly rejects, makes a pressing appeal to the sympathy of the readers. This appeal is addressed in the name of Christ Himself, whom Paul serves, then of the affection by

---

[1] D F G: πληροφορια instead of πληρωματι.
[2] T. R., with L. Mnn. Syr., reads του ευαγγελιου του Χριστου (*of the Gospel of Christ*); all the rest: Χριστου (*of Christ*) only.
[3] B omits αδελφοι.
[4] B D F G read δωροφορια instead of διακονια.
[5] B D F G read εν instead of εις.
[6] T. R., with D E F G L P, reads ελθω with και before συναναπαυσωμαι; א A C read ελθων, and reject the και.
[7] T. R., with A C L P, Mnn. Syr., reads θεου; א: Ιησου Χριστου; B: κυριου Ιησου; D E F G, It.: Χριστου Ιησου.

which he feels himself bound to the Romans by the operation of the Holy Spirit. *The love of the Spirit* is opposed to that which exists between persons who know one another personally; "who have seen my face in the flesh," as Paul himself says, Col. ii. 1 (in opposition to i. 8).—The request so solemnly prefaced is one for a common *struggle;* for there are hostile powers to be combated (ver. 31). The two phrases: *for me* (in my behalf) and *before God*, are often joined to the substantive προσευχαῖς: "your prayers for me before God. But would not the regimen *before God* connected with the word *prayers* be superfluous, and would not the expression *your prayers for me* imply a thing which Paul has no right to assume: viz. that they make prayer for him continually? The two regimens, therefore, depend rather on the verb *strive*. To strive *before God*, whose arm can alone cover the apostle in this journey with an impenetrable buckler; and *by your prayers*, since they are the efficacious means of moving this almighty arm. —The phrase: *with me*, reminds the Romans how he is himself striving for the same end.

Ver. 31. The enemies to be removed are, above all, the unbelieving Jews. It is to them the first *that* refers; the second intimates that there are other adversaries within the church itself; they are "those thousands of Jews who have believed," Acts xxi. 20 and 21, and who have been filled with prejudices against Paul's person and work. All those hearts must be prepared by God Himself to receive well the offering which is about to be brought them. The reading δωροφορία (*offering of a present*) instead of διακονία (*service*), in the *Vatic.* and the Greco-Lats., seems to me probable enough, considering the rareness of the expression.—The kind of anxiety which breathes throughout this whole passage is in keeping with the painful presentiments felt by all the churches about this journey to Jerusalem, and which found utterance shortly afterward by the mouth of the prophets wherever Paul stopped (Acts xx. 22, 23, xxi. 4 et seq., 11 et seq.).

Ver. 32. If with ℵ A C we read: "*that coming* (ἐλθών) . . . *I may find rest* (συναναπαύσωμαι)," the two clauses: *with joy and by the will of God*, might refer to the principal verb: "that I may find rest." But it seems to me that this relation is unnatural, for the idea of *joy* is already contained in that of *finding rest*, and the *will of God* more naturally determines the matter of *arriving* than that of resting. It is therefore preferable to apply these two clauses to the idea of *coming*. Of the two readings ἐλθών or ἔλθω . . . καί, the former is more in keeping with the simplicity of the apostle's style; the latter, more elegant, seems to be an Alexandrine correction.— We think we see the apostle, after happily finishing his mission in Palestine, embarking full of joy and guided by the will of God, then arriving at Rome there to rest his weary heart among his brethren in the joy of the common salvation, and to recover new strength for a new work.—The reading "By the will *of God*" is preferable to all the others: Paul ordinarily rises to God whenever the subject involved is providential dispensations.

Ver. 33. "*The God of peace*[1] *be with you all! Amen.*"[2]—The apostle's heart seems constrained, in proportion as he approaches the end, to transform every particular subject he touches into a prayer or request. The special prayer contained in this verse is suggested to him by his conviction of the hostilities and dangers lying before himself, and by the need of soon being in full peace in the midst of his readers.—The authenticity of the word ἀμήν, *amen*, is doubtful. It is found, no doubt, in most of the Mjj., but it is wanting in three of them, and it is easier to explain its addition by copyists than its omission.

The authenticity of vv. 30-33 is acknowledged by Lucht. Volkmar admits only that of ver. 33, adding the first two verses of chap. xvi. We have seen how

---

[1] D E F G, It. Syr^sch. read ητω after ειρηνης.   [2] A F G omit the word αμην.

little weight belongs to the objections raised by Baur and those critics to the authenticity of chap. xv. in general ; we have not therefore to return to them. As to the opinions formerly given out by Semler and Paulus, according to which this whole chapter is only a particular leaf intended by the apostle either for the persons saluted in chap. xvi., or for the most enlightened members of the church of Rome, they are now abandoned. The apostle was no friend of religious aristocracies, as we have seen in chap. xii. ; and he would have done nothing to favor such a tendency. Besides, what is there in this chapter which could not be read with advantage by the whole church ? We have proved the intimate connection between the first part of the chapter and the subject treated in chap. xiv., as well as the connection between the second part and the Epistle as a whole, more particularly the preface, i. 1–15. The style and ideas are in all points in keeping with what one would expect from the pen of Paul. As Hilgenfeld says : "It is impossible in this offhand way to reject chaps. xv. and xvi. ; the Epistle to the Romans cannot have closed with xiv. 23, unless it remained without a conclusion." M. Reuss expresses himself to the same effect, and we have pleasure in quoting the following lines from him in closing this subject : "The lessons contained in the first half of the text (chap. xv.) are absolutely harmonious with those of the previous chapter, and of the parallel passages of other Epistles, and the statement of the apostle's plans is the most natural expression of his mind and antecedents, as well as the reflection of the situation of the moment. There is not the slightest trace of the aim of a forged composition, nor certainly of the possibility that the Epistle closed with chap. xiv."

THIRTIETH PASSAGE (16:1-24)

Recommendations, Salutations, Warning

It is the apostle's custom, when closing his letters, to treat a number of particular subjects of a more or less personal nature, such as special salutations, commissions, or warnings ; comp. 1 Cor. xvi. 10–22 (particularly ver. 22) ; 2 Cor. xiii. 11–13 ; Col. iv. 7–18 ; Phil. iv. 10–23 ; 1 Thess. v. 25–28. He does so in our Epistle.

And first, vv. 1 and 2, the recommendation of the deaconess Phœbe.

Vv. 1, 2. "*Now*[1] *I commend unto you Phœbe, our sister, which is a deaconess of the church of Cenchrea, that ye receive her in the Lord as becometh saints, and that ye assist her in whatsoever business she may have need of you ; for also she hath been a succorer of many and of myself.*"—Here, according to some, begins a private note entrusted by the apostle to the bearers (Semler), or to the female bearer (Eichhorn), of this Epistle, to indicate the principal persons to be saluted in the churches which were to be visited by the way. Some moderns, D. Schulz, Reuss, Ewald, Laurent, Renan, etc., even think they can, either from the starting-point (Cenchrea), or from certain names in the salutations which follow, positively determine the church for which this note was composed. It was, they hold, the church of Ephesus. We shall examine step by step as we proceed the reasons alleged in favor of this supposition. We only remark here, that many of those who reject the salutations, vv. 3–16, from the Epistle to the Romans, yet regard vv. 1 and 2 as having belonged to it (Scholten, Volkmar, Schultz). We note besides, as to the rest of this chapter, the following observation of Schultz : "As long as the destination to the church of Rome of all the parts of chap. xvi. *can be maintained,* this view ought to be preferred to every other." And, indeed, it will always be difficult to understand how a leaf of salutations intended for the church of Ephesus, or any other, should have strayed into the copy of our Epistle deposited in the archives of the church of Rome (see the remarks at the end of this chapter).

[1] D F G omit the δέ.

It has generally been admitted that Phœbe was the bearer of our Epistle, and no doubt with reason. For otherwise how are we to explain this so special personal recommendation? Comp. Col. iv. 7; Eph. vi. 21. Paul mentions two titles which point her out for the interest of the Christians of Rome; she is *a sister*, and, moreover, *a servant of the Lord*, invested consequently with an ecclesiastical office. It has been denied that at so remote a period the office of deaconess could already be in existence. But why, if there were *deacons* (xii. 7; Acts vi. 1 et seq.; Phil. i. 1), should there not have been also from primitive times a similar office discharged by women, members of the church? With what right can we allege that the office mentioned xii. 8 belonged only to men? It seems to us impossible to think that *the widows* spoken of, 1 Tim. v. 3 et seq., were not persons invested with an ecclesiastical office. And in any case, the ministrations of beneficence of a private nature, mentioned in our Epistle (xii. 7), must have been carried out in good measure by *sisters*. And why should not a rich and devoted woman, who had for a time occupied herself with such work, have borne, even without ecclesiastical consecration, the title of deaconess? If our passage had a later origin than the first century, there would certainly have been introduced here, instead of the word διάκονος (*deacon*), which is the masculine term originally applied to both sexes, the feminine title διακόνισσα (*deaconess*), already in use in the second century. Comp. the letter in which Pliny relates that he has been obliged to torture two of those *servants* who are called *ministræ* (evidently a translation of διακόνισσαι). There were so many services to be rendered to the poor, to orphans, to strangers, to the sick, which women only could discharge! As is observed by Schaff, the profound separation between the sexes in the East must also have contributed to render a female diaconate altogether indispensable.—The participle οὖσαν, *who is*, expressly denotes that Phœbe is still, at the time of Paul's writing, invested with this office.—Cenchrea was the port of Corinth toward the east, on the Egean Sea; and hence it has been inferred that Phœbe was going rather to Ephesus than to Rome. The proof is far from convincing. "The person in question," says Schultz himself, "is not a Corinthian who is passing through Cenchrea, but, on the contrary, a woman of Cenchrea who is passing through Corinth, and who is consequently on her way to the west." A good answer as an argument *ad hominem*. But, speaking freely, what a puerility is criticism thus handled.

Ver. 2. *In the Lord:* in the profound feeling of the communion with Him, which binds into one body all the members of the church.—The expression: *as becometh saints*, may signify, becoming saints who are received, like Phœbe, or saints who are called to receive, like the Romans. Is it absolutely necessary to choose between the two meanings?—There is a correlation between the two terms παριστάναι, *to stand beside in order to hold up*, and προστάτις (*protectress, patroness*), one who stands before in order to guide or protect. Hence it appears that Phœbe had bestowed care on Paul himself, perhaps during his stay at Cenchrea, mentioned Acts xviii. 18, and on occasion of an illness. M. Renan informs us that "this poor woman started on a wild winter journey across the Archipelago without any other resource than Paul's recommendation." Then he adds: "It is more natural to suppose that Paul recommended Phœbe to the Ephesians, whom he knew, than to the Romans, whom he did not know." As if the titles given to Phœbe, cited vv. 1 and 2, were not enough to interest any church whatever in her!

Vv. 3–16

To the recommendation of Phœbe, the apostle joins a list of *salutations*, which might indeed still be called recommendations; for the imperative ἀσπάσασθε, *greet*, fifteen times repeated, is addressed to the whole church. It is, in fact, the church itself which he charges to transmit this mark of affection to its different objects. How was this commission carried out? Probably, at the time when the letter was read in full assembly of the church, the president expressed to the person designated, in some way or other, the mark of distinction which the apostle had bestowed on him. Most critics of the present day hold that this list of salutations cannot have been written by Paul with a view to the church of Rome, which he had not yet visited. How then could he have known so many persons in it? The persons in question, therefore, were friends of the apostle in a church which he had himself founded, and, to all appearance, in the church of Ephesus. Accident has willed that this list should be joined afterward to the Epistle to the Romans (see especially Reuss, *Epîtres Pauliniennes*, pp. 19, 20). Bauer, Lucht, etc., go still further: they think that this list was composed later by a forger, who thought good to make Paul pen the names of several notable persons of the church of Rome, in order to produce an advantageous impression on this church, which was always somewhat unfavorably disposed toward the apostle. "A very improbable procedure," observes Schultz. "And how," asks this writer with reason, "would the forger in this case have forgotten Clement," who should surely have figured at the head? For the rest, let us study the list itself.

Vv. 3-5a. "*Salute Prisca*[1] *and Aquilas, my fellow-workers in Christ Jesus, who have for my life laid down their own necks—unto whom not only I give thanks, but also all the churches of the Gentiles—and the church that meets in their house.*"—Aquilas and his wife Prisca (or Priscilla) were Jews, natives of Pontus, in Asia Minor. They were established at Rome as tent-makers, when the edict of Claudius, which expelled Israelites from the capital, obliged them to emigrate. They had been settled for a short time at Corinth, when Paul arrived there for the first time in the year 53. Their common occupation drew them together, and Paul soon brought them to the knowledge of Christ (Acts xviii. 2). For it is absolutely arbitrary to represent them as already Christians when they left Rome. This opinion arises only from the tendency to derive the propagation of the gospel at Rome from the Jewish synagogue. But it is excluded by the expression of the Acts: τινὰ 'Ιουδαῖον, *a certain Jew*. Luke would have added the epithet μαθητήν, *disciple;* comp. Acts xvi. 1. When, two years later, the apostle left Corinth with the intention of going to found a mission at Ephesus, Aquilas and his wife repaired to the latter city, while Paul proceeded first to visit Jerusalem and Antioch. Their intention certainly was to prepare the way for him in the capital of the province of Asia, then to support his ministry there, as they had done at Corinth; comp. Acts xviii. 18-21.—It is this salutation more than anything else which has given rise to the supposition that our entire list was addressed to Ephesus. But could not this husband and wife, who had emigrated from Pontus to Rome, then from Rome to Corinth, and lastly, from Corinth to Ephesus, have returned to Rome, their former domicile, after the imperial edict had fallen into desuetude? This is the more admissible as the object of this return is easily understood. We know from Acts xix. 21, that even at Ephesus Paul had already formed the plan of proceeding to Rome as soon as he had finished his work in Asia and Greece. Aquilas and Priscilla, who had been so useful to him at Corinth, who had even gone to Ephesus with him with a view to his approaching mission, might a second time, by proceeding from Ephesus to Rome, do for him what they had done by leaving Corinth for Ephesus. The passage, Jas. iv. 13, shows with what ease rich Jewish traders travelled from one large city to another. "To-day or to-morrow we will go into such a city, and buy and sell and get gain." Objection is taken from the short time which had elapsed since the end of Paul's sojourn at Ephesus: ten

---

[1] T. R. reads Πρισκιλλαν, with several Mnn. Syr.

months only, it is said, from the spring of the year 57, when at Ephesus he wrote the First Epistle to the Corinthians (chap. xvi. 8), and when he conveys greetings from Aquilas and Priscilla (xvi. 19), to the beginning of 58, when it is alleged he wrote the Epistle to the Romans from Corinth. But we think there is a mistake in putting only ten months' interval between the First Epistle to the Corinthians and the Epistle to the Romans. A profound study of the Second Epistle to the Corinthians, as well as of the Acts, leads to a wholly different result. From the spring of the year 57, when Paul left Ephesus, to the time when he made the stay at Corinth, during which he composed our Epistle, there elapsed, we think, nearly two years, from Easter 57 to February 59. Such an interval fully suffices to explain the new change of Aquilas and Priscilla, and their return to Rome. In the fact that many years later, about the year 66, and perhaps on occasion of the persecution of Nero (in 64), they are again settled at Ephesus, where Paul sends them a salutation, 2 Tim. iv. 19, there is nothing to surprise us.—The form *Prisca* is certainly authentic in the Epistle to the Romans; the diminutive *Priscilla*, which is read in the T. R., is found only in some Mnn. In the Acts (xviii. 2, 18, 26, and 1 Cor. xvi. 19), the latter form is found in all the documents. In 2 Tim. iv. 19, the two readings exist, but the majority are in favor of Prisca, as in Romans. There is also variation in the reciprocal position of the two names. The wife is placed here first, as in Acts xviii. 18 and 2 Tim. iv. 19. Probably she was superior to her husband, either in ability or Christian activity.

Ver. 4. The qualitative pronoun οἵτινες signifies : *as people who* . . . The expression : *to put the neck under (the axe)*, is no doubt figurative ; but in any case it implies the act of exposing one's life. We do not know where or when this event took place. Was it at Corinth, on occasion of the scene described Acts xviii. 12 et seq. ? or was it not rather at Ephesus, in one or other of the cases to which allusion is made in the words, 1 Cor. xv. 32 and 2 Cor. i. 8 ? The apostle reminds the Romans that they had thereby rendered service to all the churches of the Gentile world, and consequently to them also. This passage proves two things—1st. That these words, intended to recommend Aquilas and Priscilla, were not addressed to the church of Ephesus, where the event referred to probably too place ; for Paul undoubtedly means to give his readers information. 2d. That the church to which he addressed them was itself one of those churches of the Gentile world whose gratitude these two persons had deserved ; a new proof of the Gentile origin of the Christians of Rome.

Ver. 5a. The expression : *the church that is in their house*, may have three meanings. Either it denotes the entire assembly of the servants and workpeople residing and working with them ; or it applies to that *portion* of the church which had its usual place of meeting in their house ; or finally, the words apply to the whole church of the capital, which held its plenary meetings at their house ; comp. 1 Cor. xiv. 23. This last sense is incompatible with the preposition κατά, the meaning of which is distributive, and supposes other places of worship (vv. 14 and 15). The first is improbable, for the term ἐκκλησία, *church*, would not suit a purely private gathering. The second is therefore the only possible one ; comp. 1 Cor. xvi. 19. Schultz thinks we may conclude from these words that Aquilas was invested with the office of elder in the church of Ephesus where he lived, and that, consequently, he could not so easily change his domicile. One must surely be at a loss for good reasons to imagine such a one as this.—What is certain is, that these two persons are saluted here, not only as particular friends of St. Paul, but because of the important part they played in the work of his apostleship. The passage, Acts xviii. 24-28, presents an example of their activity, and of the powerful influence they exercised ; and it is most probable that what they had been at Ephesus, they had also been at Rome, from the day when they returned to it. In a word, they were evangelists of the first order. This is what recommends them to the respectful attention of the church, and assigns them the first rank in this list of apostolic salutations. This circumstance throws light on the character of the whole list.

Vv. 5b, 6. "*Salute my well-beloved Epenetus, who was the first-fruits of Asia*[1] *unto Christ.*[2] *Salute Mary,*[3] *who bestowed much labor on us.*"[4]—Epenetus is to us an unknown personage. According to the Received reading, he would be the first convert of *Achaia*, consequently a native of Corinth, which could hardly be reconciled with 1 Cor. xvi. 15. This reading probably arises from the copyist thinking that Paul meant to speak of the country from which he was writing. The true reading is certainly *of Asia*. Meyer concludes, from the fact that Epenetus was the first convert in this province, that he must have been a Jew, because Paul preached first of all in the synagogue ; as if Aquilas and Priscilla, who had preceded Paul at Ephesus, might not have met with and converted a Gentile in that city before Paul arrived, and proclaimed the gospel in full synagogue ! The Greek name of Epenetus would rather lead us to think him a Gentile ; he was *the first-fruits of the Gentiles* converted at Ephesus. Here again the critics find an undeniable proof of the destination of this list to the church of Ephesus. But if, as is probable, Epenetus was the fruit of the labors of Aquilas, anterior even to those of Paul, he might very naturally have accompanied the evangelist-pair from Ephesus to Rome, to take part in their work in that great city. Hence the intimate relation which the apostle here establishes between these three persons ; hence also the honorable title which he gives to this last before all the church.—The regimen εἰς Χριστόν, *unto Christ,* makes Christ the person to whom the first-fruits are offered.

Ver. 6. We know nothing of this *Mary* saluted in ver. 6 ; her name indicates her Jewish origin, even if, with some Mjj., we read Μαρίαν.—If, with almost all the Mjj., we read εἰς ὑμᾶς, *on you,* Mary would be one who had rendered herself particularly useful in the church of Rome, perhaps by her devotion during some epidemic which had raged in the church. But would Paul thus remind the church of a thing which, in that case, it knew much better than himself ? Besides, all the persons saluted here are so because of some connection or other with the apostle ; this is what makes us prefer the reading εἰς ἡμᾶς, *on us.* Like Phœbe, like Aquilas and Priscilla, she had actively taken part in the work of Paul, and occupied herself by ministering to those who surrounded him ; and now from the east she had gone to Rome, like so many others.

Vv. 7, 8. "*Salute Andronicus and Junias, my countrymen and my fellow-prisoners, who are of note among the apostles,· and who also have been in Christ before me.*[5] *Salute Ampliatus,*[6] *my beloved in the Lord.*"—The word *Junian* might be taken as the accusative of a female name, *Junia,* to denote the sister or wife of Andronicus. But the end of the verse leads us rather to think of a man of the name of *Junias.*—The expression συγγενεῖς μου may signify : *my kinsmen,* or *my countrymen* (ix. 3). The first meaning seems, in itself, the more natural ; but in vv. 11 and 21 this term is applied to other persons, two of whom (Jason and Sosipater) appear to be Macedonians (Acts xvii. 5, and xx. 4). The wider meaning, that of *countrymen,* thus becomes the more probable. Even Schultz finds a proof in these words that Paul wrote these lines to a church of Gentile origin ("*my* countrymen"). Hence it has been concluded that these salutations could not be addressed to the church of Rome. From the same circumstance we, for

---

[1] T. R. reads, with L P, Syr., Αχαιας (*of Achaia*) instead of Ασιας (*of Asia*).
[2] D E F G read εν Χριστω (*in Christ*) instead of εις Χριστον (*unto Christ*).
[3] A B C D: Μαριαν instead of Μαριαμ.
[4] T. R., with L, Mnn., reads εις ημας (*on us*) ; all the rest : εις υμας (*on you*).
[5] D E F G, It. read τοις προ εμου instead of οι και προ εμου γεγονασι.
[6] D E L P, Syr. : Αμπλιαν instead of Αμπλιατον.

our part, on the contrary, conclude that the church of Rome was not Jewish-Christian. It has been asked when these two Christians of Jewish origin could have been imprisoned with St. Paul ? Neither the Acts nor the previous Epistles furnish an answer to this question. But the descriptions in 2 Cor. vi. 5 et seq., and xi. 23 et seq., allude to so many unknown circumstances in the apostle's life, that this ignorance ought not to excite our surprise. In chap. xv. of his Epistle to the Corinthians, Clement of Rome enumerates seven captivities of the apostle, and we know of only four (Philippi, Jerusalem, Cæsarea, Rome). Probably the event in question belongs to a period anterior to his missionary journeys (comp. the end of the verse).— Most critics of the present day agree in explaining the following words in this sense : " well known by the apostles" (the Twelve). But what a strange title of honor : the apostles know them ! And can the $\dot{\varepsilon}\nu$, *in*, have such a meaning : " illustrious *with*, that is to say, in the opinion of the apostles." Meyer quotes the phrase of Euripides : $\dot{\varepsilon}\pi i\sigma\eta\mu o\varsigma$ $\dot{\varepsilon}\nu$ $\beta\rho o\tau o\tilde{\iota}\varsigma$, illustrious with mortals, or in their eyes. But why not translate quite simply : illustrious *amidst* or *among* mortals ? And similarly, and with still more reason, here : illustrious among those numerous evangelists who, by their missionary labors in the countries of the East, have merited the name of *apostles*. This title, indeed, could in certain cases have a wider sense than it has in our Gospels ; thus, Acts xiv. 4 and 14, it is applied to Barnabas, as it is indirectly, 1 Cor. ix. 5. So we call the missionary Brainerd, the apostle of the Indians. Such another, the apostle of China or of the Indies.—A last title of honor : these two men preceded Paul himself in the faith. They belong, therefore, to that primitive church of Jerusalem whose members, as years elapse, take ever a more venerable character in the eyes of all the churches. The Greco-Latin reading : " the apostles *who were before me*," is an evident corruption of the text.

Ver. 8. The Alexs. : *Ampliaton;* the others, following an abridged form : *Amplian.* Paul, having no special distinction to mention as belonging to this person, contents himself with pointing him out to the respect of the church by the expression of his affection ; and that is enough, for it is an affection *in the Lord*, which consequently implies in Amplias devotion to His service.

Vv. 9, 10. " *Salute Urbanus, our fellow-worker in Christ, and Stachys my beloved. Salute Apelles [the brother] approved in Christ. Salute them which are of Aristobulus' household.*"—Urbanus, a Latin name signifying *citizen;* Stachys, a Greek name signifying *an ear of corn.* In speaking of the former as his fellow-worker, Paul says : *our* (comp. the *on us*, ver. 6), because it is the apostolic *work* which is in question with all the workers who engage in it along with him ; speaking of his personal friendship, he says : *my.*

Ver. 10. *Apelles :* a frequent name for freedmen at Rome, especially among Jews. Every one knows the *Credat judæus Apella* of Horace.—Δόκιμος, the Christian who has passed his trials, who has shown himself steadfast in his course.—The last words may denote the Christians who are of the number of Aristobulus' *children,* or those who belong to his house as *servants.* The expression used agrees better with the second meaning. It was a large house, Jewish perhaps, to which the gospel had found access.

Vv. 11, 12. " *Salute Herodion my countryman. Salute them that be of the household of Narcissus, which are in the Lord. Salute Tryphena and Tryphosa, who labor in the Lord. Salute Persis the beloved, which labored much in the Lord.*"—Here, again, συγγενής may signify either *countryman* or *kinsman* (see ver. 7). The Roman writers Suetonius, Pliny, Tacitus, speak of a freedman of Claudius, of the name of Narcissus. Is it the house of this imperial favorite which is here referred to ? He himself had been executed four years before the composition of our Epistle ; but his house might still exist at Rome.

Ver. 12. Paul speaks here of three women, the two former of whom were distinguished at this time, and the third had been distinguished previously in the service of the Lord and of the church, like Priscilla and Mary. The two former were probably sisters; their almost identical names come from the verb τρυφᾶν, *to live voluptuously.* Paul wishes evidently to contrast this meaning of their name with that of the epithet κοπιώσας, *who work laboriously.* They are in Christ the opposite of what their name expresses.— Persis, a woman of Persia. Foreigners were often designated by the name of their native country (Lydia, a Lydian). Meyer points out the delicacy with which Paul here omits the pronoun μου (*my*). Probably she was an aged woman: Paul says: *labored.*

Ver. 13. "*Salute Rufus, chosen in the Lord, and his mother and mine.*"— The term *chosen* cannot be taken here in the sense in which it applies to all Christians: it must denote something special. Hofmann, judging from what follows, understands: " The man whom I have specially chosen as my brother in the Lord." But in this sense the pronoun μου (*my*) could not be wanting. As what is the better is willingly chosen, the word ἐκλεκτός, *chosen,* takes the sense of *distinguished, excellent.* This is certainly the meaning of the epithet here, as in 2 John 1 and 13. The following words: " his mother and mine," prove that Paul was united to this family by the closest ties—that he had even lived in it. And if we remember that Mark, writing his Gospel at Rome, was pleased to designate Simon of Cyrene, who carried the cross of Jesus, as " the father of Alexander and *Rufus,*" we shall be naturally led to hold that this family had removed from Jerusalem to Rome, where Rufus occupied a distinguished place in the church. It was therefore during the years of his youth, when he was studying at Jerusalem, that Paul had lived in the bosom of this family, and had enjoyed the motherly care of Simon's wife.

Vv. 14, 15. " *Salute Asyncritus, Phlegon, Hermes, Patrobas, Hermas, and the brethren which are with them. Salute Philologus, and Julia,[1] Nereus, and his sister, and Olympas, and all the saints which are with them.*"—The personages whose names follow are not designated by any epithet of distinction; but it was honor enough to be marked out, were it only by name, to the respectful attention of the whole church of Rome.—The last words of both of the verses 14 and 15: *and the brethren who are with them,* prove that the persons just named are so, not simply as believers, but as directors of a whole assembly which is accustomed to meet around them. They lived, no doubt, in different quarters, and formed, besides the group which met in the house of Aquilas, two distinct assemblies.—Hermas was regarded by Origen as the author of the work famous in the primitive church, entitled the *Pastor* of Hermas. But it seems now established by the Fragment of Muratori that this writing dates only from the second half of the second century, and that Hermas is a wholly different person from the man who is here saluted by the apostle.—*Olympas* (perhaps an abbreviation of Olympiodorus) is certainly here a *man's* name.

Ver. 15. *Julia* (for such is the true reading) is undoubtedly the wife of Philologus.

Ver. 16. "*Salute one another with an holy kiss. All[2] the churches of Christ salute you.*"[3]—The apostle has just saluted in his own name the influential members of the different flocks of the church of Rome; but he naturally feels the need of also testifying his affection to the whole church; and he charges all its members to do so for him toward another. For this purpose they are to use the customary form of the *brotherly kiss.* If we did not know positively from the Fathers, particularly Tertullian (*osculum pacis*) in the *De Oratione,* c. 14 (comp. 1 Pet. v. 14) that the reference here is to an external rite, we should be tempted to hold the opinion of Calvin and Phi-

---

[1] C F G read Ιουνιαν instead of Ιουλιαν.
[2] T. R., with several Mnn. only, omits πασαι (*all*).
[3] D E F G, It. omit all the second part of ver. 16 (see on ver. 21).

lippi, according to which we must give the term *holy kiss* a purely spiritual meaning: the salutation of brotherly love. But we learn from the *Apostolic Constitutions* that at a later time rules were laid down to remove from this custom all that might be offensive in it, so that it is more probable the term ought to be taken literally. We may be assured that in the apostolic churches all was done with order and dignity. This is what is expressed by the epithet ἅγιον, *holy*, which recurs 1 Cor. xvi. 20, 2 Cor. xiii. 12, and 1 Thess. v. 26. Probably the president of the assembly gave the kiss to the brother who sat next him, and he to his neighbor, while the same thing took place on the part of the women.

While the apostle in thought sees the Christians of Rome saluting one another by this sign of brotherhood, a greater spectacle is presented to his mind, that of all the churches already composing Christendom, and which are likewise united by the bond of communion in Christ. He has just himself traversed the churches of Greece and Asia; he has spoken to them of his already formed plan of proceeding to Rome (Acts xix. 21, xx. 25), and they have all charged him with their salutations to their sister in the capital of the world. Now is the time for him to discharge this commission. Through his instrumentality, the members of Christ's body scattered over the earth salute one another with a holy kiss, just like the members of the church which he is addressing. The T. R. has rejected the word *all*, no doubt because it was not understood how Paul could send greetings from other churches than those among which he was at the time.—The Greco-Latin text has transferred this second half of the verse to the end of ver. 21, with the evident intention of connecting it with the salutations of Paul's companions. But these have too private and personal a character to allow of the apostle appending to them so solemn a message as that of all the churches of the East to the church of Rome. This message must form an integral part of the letter; it is quite otherwise with these salutations (see below).

We are now in a position to judge of the question whether this passage belongs to our Epistle. In it twenty-six persons are individually designated —twenty-four by their names. Of these names it may be said that one or two are Hebrew, five or six Latin, fifteen to sixteen Greek; three Christian communities assembling in different localities are mentioned (vv. 5, 14, 15); besides two groups having more of a private character (vv. 10 and 11). It appears evident to us that the apostle feels the need of paying homage to all the faithful servants and all the devoted handmaids of the Lord who had aided in the foundation and development of this church, and before his arrival completed the task of the apostolate in this great city. Not only is the apostle concerned to testify to them his personal feelings; but he expresses himself in such a way as to force the church, so to speak, to take part as a whole in this public testimony of gratitude toward those to whom it owes its existence and prosperity. If such is the meaning of this truly unique passage in St. Paul's letters, does it not apply infinitely better to a church which, like that of Rome, had not yet seen an apostle within it, than to those of Ephesus or Corinth, where the entire activity of laying the foundation was, as it were, personified in a single individual? Hence those different expressions used by the apostle: "fellow-worker in the Lord," "who labored," or "who labor," "all those who are with them," and even once the use of the title *apostle*. We seem, as we read these numerous salutations, to have before us the spectacle of a beehive swarming on all sides with activity and labor in the midst of the vast field of the capital of the world, and we understand better the whole passage of chap. xii. relative to the varied gifts and numerous ministries, as well as the remarkable expression: πάντι τῷ ὄντι ἐν ὑμῖν, *every man that is* [as a worker] *among you* (ver. 3). "Here is," says Gaussen,[1] "a picture to the life of a primitive

[1] *Théopneustie*, pp. 468 and 474.

church; we can see to what height the most ignorant and weak of its members can rise. . . . We wonder at the progress already made by the word of God, solely through the labors of travellers, artisans, merchants, women, slaves, and freedmen who resided in Rome." Not only did the apostle know a large number of these workers, because he had been connected with them in the East (Andronicus and Junias, Rufus and his mother, for example), or because he had converted them himself (Aquilas and Priscilla); but he also received news from Rome, as is proved by the intimate details into which he entered in chap. xiv.; and he might thus know of the labors of many of those saluted, whom he did not know personally. Such is probably the case with the last persons designated, and to whose names he adds no description. The Greek origin of the most of these names constitutes no objection to the *Roman* domicile of those who bear them. What matters it to us that, as M. Renan says, after Father Garucci, the names in *Jewish* inscriptions at Rome are mostly of Latin origin? If there is any room for surprise, five or six Latin names would perhaps be more astonishing at Ephesus than fifteen or sixteen Greek names at Rome. Have we not proved over and over that this church was recruited much more largely from Gentiles than from Jews, and that especially it was founded by missionaries who had come from Syria, Asia, and Greece? M. Reuss no doubt asks what became of all those friends of Paul, when, some years later, he wrote from Rome his Epistles to the Colossians and Philippians; and later still, the Second to Timothy. But, in writing from Rome to the churches of Colosse and Philippi, he could only send salutations from individuals who knew them. And a little before the Second to Timothy, there occurred the persecution of Nero, which had for the time dispersed and almost annihilated the church of Rome. Our conclusion, therefore, is not only that this passage of salutations may have been written to the church of Rome, but that it could not have been addressed to any other more suitably. As at the present day, Paris or even Rome is a sort of rendezvous for numerous foreign Christians of both sexes, who go thither to found evangelistic works; so the great pagan Rome attracted at that time the religious attention and zeal of all the Christians of the East.

Let us remark, in closing, the exquisite delicacy and courtesy which guide the apostle in those distinguishing epithets with which he accompanies the names of the servants or handmaids of Christ whom he mentions.[1] Each of those descriptive titles is as it were the rough draft of the *new name* which those persons shall bear in glory. Thus understood, this enumeration is no longer a dry nomenclature; it resembles a bouquet of newly-blown flowers, which diffuse refreshing odors.

Vv. 17–20

In the First Epistle to the Corinthians, the apostle, after a passage of salutations, xvi. 19–21, stops all at once to address to the church, as in the form of a postscript, a solemn warning (ver. 22). It is as if the salutation which he had just written awoke in him once more before closing the feeling of the danger which lies in the way of his readers. It is the same here, with this difference, that at Corinth the danger was present and pressing, as is shown by the whole Epistle, whereas at Rome it is still remote, though inevitable. The tone also of the warning is distinctly different in the two cases; for Corinth a threatening, for Rome a simple putting on their guard in the most affectionate and fatherly tone.—Renan, Weizsäcker, Schultz, agree in thinking that this passage can only have been addressed by Paul to a church which he had himself founded—that of Ephesus, for

---

[1] See on this subject the whole beautiful passage in M. Gaussen's work just quoted, pp. 468–471.

example. We shall examine their reasons as we study this passage. In the eyes of Baur, Lucht, Volkmar, it is not even St. Paul's; it falls under the judgment of condemnation which, according to these critics, is due to the two chaps. xv. and xvi. mostly or totally.

Vv. 17, 18. *"Now I exhort you, brethren, to mark them which cause [the] divisions and offences contrary to the doctrine which ye have learned; and turn away from them. For these persons serve not Christ our Lord, but their own belly; and by fair speeches and benedictions*[1] *deceive the hearts of the simple."* —As observed by Hofmann, the apostle had regulated (chaps. xiv. and xv.) all that related to the internal differences which might exist in the church of Rome. But now the unity of all Christendom has just presented itself vividly to his mind; and remembering the divisions which trouble it in other churches, he thinks that they might penetrate from without into the bosom of this one. He has evidently in view those Judaizers who from Jerusalem had come down to trouble the church of Antioch, who from Syria had followed Paul step by step to Galatia, and even to Corinth, and who would be sure as soon as they heard of a church founded at Rome, to arrive on the spot, seeking to monopolize it for themselves. Facts proved that the anticipation of Paul was well founded. The beginning of the Epistle to the Philippians, written from Rome four or five years after ours, proves the pernicious activity of those fanatical partisans of the law in the church of Rome. Probably the party of the *weak*, chap. xiv., had opened it to their entrance.

The description which follows contains details which are too minute to allow us, with Hofmann, to apply this warning to all false teachers in general, Gentile or Jew.—The article before the words *divisions* and *offences*, shows that the apostle has in view facts already known. But it does not follow that they had transpired in the church to which he was writing, as is alleged by those who maintain that this passage cannot have been addressed to the church of Rome. It was enough that these disorders were facts of notoriety in other churches, to warrant St. Paul in speaking as he does. And how could those who had labored with him in the churches of the East, and whom he has just been saluting in such numbers, Aquilas and Priscilla, for example, who had shared with him at Ephesus all the agonies of the great Corinthian conflict, have failed to know intimately the burning enmity with which the apostle was regarded by a certain number of Judeo-Christians? The term *divisions* refers to ecclesiastical divisions; the term *offences*, to the moral disorders which had so often accompanied them, particularly at Corinth; comp. 2 Cor. x.-xiii.—It is entirely false to conclude from the words: "contrary to the doctrine which ye have learned," that Paul himself was the founder of the church to which this passage was addressed. He would have said more clearly in that case: "which ye learned *of me;*" comp. Phil. iv. 9. This passage says nothing more than vi. 17, where Paul gives thanks "because the Romans have obeyed from the heart the form of doctrine according to which they were taught." The reference, here as there, is to Paul's gospel which had been taught to the Romans, not by himself, but by those of his fellow-laborers whom he has just saluted. The teaching opposed to this gospel is the legal system, which, according to this passage, as well as i. 8, 11, 12, vi. 17, and the whole Epistle in general, had not yet got a footing at Rome.—These words are obviously sufficient, if they were really addressed to this church, to overthrow Baur's opinion as to its composition and tendency. As the expression: *to mark, have the eyes open to* (σκοπεῖν), refers to an enemy expected rather than present, we must apply the last words of the verse: *avoid them,* to the time when they shall be present, and shall seek to do their work. Then there will be no need even to enter into communication with them;

---

[1] D E F G, It. omit the words και ευλογιας.

all that is necessary will be simply to turn the back to them ; and why ? The following verse answers this question.

Ver. 18. The parties referred to are men at once sensual and hypocritical ; it is therefore under the influence of a deep moral aversion that the Christians of Rome are called to avoid them. They serve their sensual appetites, and not Christ. This feature reminds us of Phil. iii. 19, words which apply to the same individuals : " whose god is their belly, and who mind earthly things ;" comp. also 2 Cor. xi. 20 and 21 : " If a man bring you into bondage, devour you, take of you, ye suffer it." It is this sensual and insolent conduct which Paul characterizes, Phil. iii. 2, in the severe terms : " Beware of dogs ; beware of evil workers." The gospel ministry was to these people a means of gain, and gain the means of satisfying their gross passions. They were the Tartuffes of the period. Another point of resemblance identifies them more completely still with the type drawn by Molière : they present themselves with a benignant style of speech (χρηστολογία), and with fatherly benedictions (εὐλογίαι) ; and *the simple* (ἄκακοι, literally, *the innocent*), who suspect no evil, allow themselves to be caught with these devout airs and paternal tone. Was it necessary, as Schultz holds, that these men should be already present to account for Paul speaking thus in regard to them ? Had he not learned to know them in this light in Galatia and at Corinth, and could he not portray them to the church of Rome, that they might be recognized immediately on their appearing ?

Ver. 19. "*For the report of your obedience is come abroad unto all ; I am glad therefore on your behalf.*[1] *But yet I would have you wise*[2] *unto that which is good, and simple unto that which is evil.*"—This verse has been connected with the preceding in different ways. Thol., Mey., Philip. find in it a reason for peace : " You will be able to resist them ; for every one knows your obedience to the pure gospel." But the *for* in this sense cannot be explained except in a forced way (see Meyer), and Paul would have required to say in any case : " For *I* know" . . ., and not : " For *all* know" . . . Origen explains : " I warn you thus ; for ye are yourselves of the number of those simple (ἄκακοι), whose obedient docility is well known." But how are we to reconcile such a statement with the eulogies bestowed on the knowledge and experience of the readers, xv. 14 and 15 ? It is to no purpose to answer that this very saying proves that the passage is not addressed to the Romans. For the Ephesians, who had for three years enjoyed Paul's presence and his teaching in public and private, and who had been witnesses of his most strenuous conflicts with the Judaizers, might far less be designated ἄκακοι, *innocent*, than the Christians of Rome, who had never seen an apostle. Calvin and others understand thus : " I warn you in this way, because I desire that to your obedience, universally known, you would add both the wisdom and simplicity which shall secure you from seduction." This meaning is good ; but it does not account for the idea placed at the head of the verse : " Your obedience has come abroad unto all." It is on these words that Rückert has with good reason rested his explanation ; for they are the key to the following sentences. He explains : " If I warn you as I have just done (vv. 17, 18), it is because the report of your obedience to the gospel having already spread everywhere, those men will not fail to hear your church spoken of, and to break in on you to make gain of your faith, as they have done elsewhere." Taken in this sense, the saying is a repetition of i. 8 : " Your faith is spoken of throughout the whole world." The apostle adds how rejoiced he is because of their evangelical convictions, but how indispensable it is that in order to preserve them, they should join to the wise discernment of

---

[1] T. R., with E, Mnn , reads χαιρω ουν το εφ' υμιν ; D F G likewise, while rejecting the το ; א A B C L P read εφ' υμιν ουν χαιρω.
[2] T. R , with א A C P, reads μεν after σοφους ; the rest omit this particle.

498 / Epistolary Conclusion

what it is good to do, the simple and hearty horror of what is evil.—The reading of the T. R. : τὸ ἐφ᾽ ὑμῖν, *in that which concerns you*, must be set aside. It is too slenderly supported, and there is no reason for here contrasting the Romans with other churches. Of the two other readings, the Greco-Lat., which places the verb χαίρω, *I rejoice*, first, ought to give place to that of the Alexs., which begins with the words : ἐφ᾽ ὑμῖν οὖν, *on your behalf therefore*. This clause connects the sentence closely with the preceding. Their attachment to evangelical truth rejoices the apostle (comp. the : *Thanks be to God*, vi. 17). Only they must persevere, and for that end the apostle desires that to their obedience to the truth they should add two things : discernment and simplicity.—A moralist writing on this subject would probably have said : " wisdom *as concerning evil*, and simplicity *as concerning good.*" St. Paul does the opposite. And here again we can show that he is speaking " by the grace given unto him." In regard to what is evil, there are no two questions. The sentence once pronounced in the conscience : it is evil ! everything is said. Woe to him who thereafter still disputes and reasons ? An abler than he (comp. ver. 20) will not fail to take him in the snare. There is but one thing to be done : *to turn from it* (ver. 17). Hence, as concerns evil, the one thing needed is simplicity. It is not so in regard to good. When a thing is recognized as good, all has not yet been said. Here, on the contrary, it is that there is need of prudence not to spoil a good thing by the unwise or unskilful way in which it is gone about. Different questions present themselves : Is it the time for doing it ? How should one address himself to it to succeed ? Who should put his hand to the work ? etc., etc. All, questions which demand a certain measure of wisdom, of discernment, of practical ability, of σοφία. In the case of evil, woe to the able ! Ability makes dupes. In the case of good, woe to the simple ! Simplicity is the parent of mistakes. —The T. R. places μέν, *without doubt*, after the word σοφούς, *wise;* which would lead to the sense : " I would, that *while ye are* wise in good, ye should be simple as regards evil." This form makes all the weight of the recommendation fall on the second proposition. But the word *wise*, σοφούς, too evidently forms a contrast to the word ἄκακοι, *innocent*, to allow us to give it so secondary a position. The first proposition should, in Paul's recommendation, be on the same line as the second. As much clear-sightedness is needed to discern the corruption of adversaries under their fair exteriors, as of simplicity to avoid them after having discerned them.—It is to be remarked, that to denote *simplicity*, Paul in this verse uses quite a different term from that in the preceding. There he had in view men ignorant of evil, who are easily duped ; hence the use of the term ἄκακοι, *innocent*. Here Paul wishes to speak of the moral rectitude which, the instant it knows evil, breaks with it. Hence the term ἀκέραιος, literally, *not mixed*, exempt from impure alloy. This saying of the apostle may serve to explain the precept of Jesus, Matt. x. 16 : " simple as doves, wise as serpents." Comp. also 1 Cor. xiv. 20 and 2 Cor. xi. 3.—We should like to know what forger would have hit on such a word ?

Ver. 20. *"Now, the God of peace shall bruise Satan under your feet quickly. The grace of our Lord Jesus Christ*[1] *be with you."* [2]—From the visible enemy who threatens, the apostle's eye turns to thine visible world, where he discovers on the one side the more formidable enemy of whom his earthly adversaries are the instruments, and on the other, the all-powerful ally on whose succor the church can reckon in this struggle. The connection between vv. 19 and 20 may find its explanation in vv. 13–15 of 2 Cor. xi., where the apostle thus expresses himself in regard to Judaizing disturbers : " Such are false apostles, deceitful workers, transforming themselves into

---

[1] ℵ B read Ιησου simply.
[2] D E F G, It. omit the second proposition of the verse.—T. R., with some Mnn. adds αμην.

apostles of Christ ; and no marvel, for Satan himself is transformed into an angel of light. Therefore it is no great thing if his ministers also be transformed as the ministers of righteousness. Their end shall be according to their works."—The expression : *God of peace*, is designedly chosen to describe God as one who, if the church fulfils its task well in these circumstances, will take care to overthrow the designs of its adversaries, and preserve harmony among the faithful.—The term συντρίψει, *shall bruise*, is evidently an allusion to the ancient promise, Gen. iii. 15, which—strange to say —is referred to nowhere else in the N. T.—The words ἐν τάχει are ordinarily translated by *soon*, which would signify : " at a time near this when I write you." It is because of this translation that Schultz and many others find here the idea of Christ's near return. But the word ταχύς and its derivatives do not denote the imminence, the nearness of the event. They denote the celerity with which it is accomplished. The ταχέες πόδες, in Homer, are feet which move *quickly* and not *soon ;* a *tachygraph* is a man who writes quickly and not near one. The Greek has the word εὐθύς (*straight*, who goes right to his end) and its derivatives to express imminence.[1] Paul means, therefore, not that the victory will be near, but that it will be *speedily* gained, once the conflict is begun. When the believer fights with the armor of God (Eph. vi.), the conflict is never long.—Victory will result from two factors, the one divine (*God shall bruise*), the other human (*under your feet*). God communicates strength ; but it passes through the man who accepts and uses it.

To this warning there is attached in the T. R. and in the Alexs. a prayer of benediction, with this difference, that in the former this prayer is repeated word for word in ver. 24. The Greco-Lats. place it only in ver. 24. Of these three forms, that of the Alex. is the most probable ; for it easily explains the other two. The Greco-Lats. have transposed this prayer, putting it after the salutations, vv. 21-23, to conform to the ordinary usage of the apostle ; the Byz. text has combined the two forms. What confirms this supposition is, that the Greco-Lats. in general omit the doxology at the end of our chapter ; now, they could not close the Epistle to the Romans with the words : " and Quartus our brother." They were therefore obliged to transfer thither the prayer of ver. 20. Regarded here as authentic, this prayer is the counterpart of that which we find 1 Cor. xvi. 23. It forms the general conclusion of the Epistle ; for it has nothing sufficiently special to be applied only to the preceding warning. But why the salutations which still follow, vv. 21-23, and the final doxology, vv. 25-27 ? This is what we shall have to explain.

Critical conclusion regarding the passage, vv. 17-20.—The objections of Baur and Lucht to the composition of this passage by the Apostle Paul are of no weight. The only serious question is, whether the warning forms part of the Epistle to the Romans, or whether it was addressed, as is thought by so large a number of our modern critics, to the church of Ephesus. First of all, we have a right to ask how it could have happened that a warning addressed to Ephesus, and which had no force except in relation to those whom it personally concerned, made the journey from Ephesus to Rome, and was incorporated into the Epistle to the Romans? For ourselves, we know no probable explanation of such a phenomenon, nor any example of such a migration. But it is still more the intrinsic reasons which prevent us from holding this supposition. This passage applies more naturally to a church which was not instructed by the apostle personally, than to a church founded by him. He rejoices in its docile attitude to the gospel, as in a thing which ne has learned, and the news of which will spread to many other ears than his (ver. 19). This is not how one writes to his own disciples. Besides, is it conceivable that he would ad-

---

[1] We think also that it is wrong to translate Rev. xxii. 20: "I come *soon* (my arrival is near) ;" the meaning is rather : "I come quickly," that is to say, I move *rapidly* (even though my arrival may yet be long delayed).

dress to the church of Ephesus, that church within which he had recently passed three whole years, and where he had composed the Epistle to the Galatians and the First to the Corinthians, a passage in which the readers are reckoned as still strangers to the manœuvres of the Judaizing adversaries, and ignorant of their character? What! Paul pass all this time in this church, between Galatia on the one side and Corinth on the other, and speak to them of those parties as persons against whom they still require to be put on their guard! No, such a warning can only concern a church situated at a distance from the theatre of conflict. This church is therefore quite naturally that of Rome.—If it is so, Weizsäcker's opinion as to the state of this church and the object of our letter is at once set aside. This critic thinks that the Epistle to the Romans was called forth by the necessity of combating a Judaizing movement which at that very time showed itself in the church. But our passage evidently points to the danger as yet to come. The letter may not have been written without the intention of forearming the church; but it cannot have had the intention of combating the enemy as already present.

Vv. 21-23. "*Timothy my fellow-worker, saluteth you, and Lucius, and Jason, and Sosipater, my countrymen.*[1] *I Tertius, who wrote this Epistle, salute you in the Lord. Gaius mine host, and of the whole church, saluteth you. Erastus the treasurer of the city saluteth you, and the brother Quartus.*"[2] —After the farewell prayer, ver. 20, this passage of salutations excites surprise; for usually the salutations of Paul's fellow-laborers are placed before the final prayer. But there is a circumstance fitted to throw light on this exceptional fact; the mention of Timothy, ver. 21. Ordinarily, when Paul has this faithful fellow-laborer beside him, he mentions him in the *address* of the letter, as if to associate him in the very composition of the writing; comp. 1 and 2 Thess., 2 Cor., Col., Philip., Phil. If he does not do so in 1 Cor., it is because, according to the letter itself, Timothy was absent. In the Epistle to the Galatians, Timothy is embraced no doubt pre-eminently in the general expression: "And all the brethren who are with me" (ver. 2). There remain, therefore, only Ephesians and Romans. This conjunction serves exactly to explain the particular fact which we are pointing out. For these two letters have this in common: that Paul wrote them in his capacity of *apostle to the Gentiles*, a dignity which he shared with no one; for it followed from a personal and special call (i. 1). And hence it is, that though Timothy was with him at the time he composed them (as appears in the case of the Romans from ver. 21, and in the case of the Ephesians from the addresses to the Colossians and Philemon written at the same time), he could not associate his disciple with him in an act so solemn, and which had a sort of official character. Now this is also the reason why those salutations from his fellow-laborers have been in this case placed outside of the letter properly so called. The official Epistle must first be closed before a place could be granted to a communication of an entirely private character.—We know that *Timothy* was at that moment at Corinth with the apostle, ready to join him in the journey to Jerusalem; this appears from Acts xx. 4. This same passage explains to us the presence in this city, and at the same time, of another of the three fellow-laborers afterward named, *Sosipater* of Berea, in Macedonia. This name, which is probably identical with that of Sopater, Acts xx. 4, belonged to one of the deputies delegated by the churches of Macedonia to represent them in the mission which Paul was about to carry out for them at Jerusalem (2 Cor. viii. 18 et seq.).—*Jason* was also of that province; for he is probably identical with Paul's host at Thessalonica, of whom mention is made, Acts xviii. 1-7. He had accompanied the deputies of Thessalonica and Berea whom Paul had appointed

---

[1] F G read here και ολαι αι εκκλησιαι (transposed from ver. 16).
[2] T. R. reads here, with D E F G L, Mnn. It., η χαρις του Κυριου ημων I.X. μετα παντων υμων αμην (transposed from ver. 20). These words are omitted by ℵ A B C, Or.

to meet together at Corinth, because he reckoned on embarking there for Palestine (Acts xx. 3). The third person, *Lucius*, cannot be, as Origen thought, the evangelist Luke ; for the Greek name of the latter (*Lucas*) is an abbreviation of Lucanus, while Lucius certainly comes from the word *lux*. But it is not improbable that we have here again the Lucius of Cyrene, who had played an important part as prophet or teacher in the church of Antioch soon after its foundation. He was now fulfilling the same ministry in other churches, and so had come to Corinth. Paul designates these three last as his countrymen ; for the meaning *kinsmen*, which some give to συγγενεῖς, cannot, as we have already seen, apply to so large a number of persons (comp. vv. 7 and 11).—Very probably these four fellow-laborers of the apostle had come into contact in the East with many of the persons whom Paul had just saluted at Rome in his own name—for example, Aquilas, Epenetus, and the first of those who follow. Delicacy accordingly required Paul to add to his own, the salutations of these brethren who surrounded him.

Ver. 22. But Paul had beside him at this very time a fellow-laborer of a different kind, to whom he must also give a place. This was the friend who had lent him the help of his pen in his long work, the *Tertius* of this verse. Only, could he dictate to him his own salutation as he had dictated the preceding ? No, that would have been to treat him as a simple machine. The apostle had too exquisite a sense of propriety to follow such a course. He ceases to dictate, and leaves Tertius himself to salute in his own name : "I Tertius." This detail, insignificant in appearance, is not without its value. It lets us see what St. Paul was better than many graver actions. Here we have what may be called the politeness of the heart. Would a forger have thought of this ?

Ver. 23. Yet another fellow-laborer, but of a wholly different kind : he is Paul's host, under whose roof he is composing this work. This *Gaius* can neither be the Gaius of Derbe in Asia Minor, Acts xx. 4, nor the Gaius of a church in the neighborhood of Ephesus, 3 John 1. He is evidently the person of whom Paul speaks 1 Cor. i. 14, one of the first believers of Corinth whom he had baptized with his own hand before the arrival of Silas and Timothy. Paul calls him at once *his* host and that of *the whole* church. These last words might signify that when the church of Corinth held a full meeting (1 Cor. xiv. 23), it was at the house of Gaius that these assemblies took place. But there attaches to the term ξένος, *host*, rather the idea of welcome given to strangers. Paul means, therefore, no doubt that the house of Gaius is the place of hospitality by way of eminence, that which at Corinth is ever open to receive Christian strangers. From Gaius, the first member of the church of Corinth named here, the apostle naturally passes to two other distinguished Christians of the same church, and who had personal relations to some of the Christians of Rome. *Erastus*, occupying an exalted post in the administration of the city (probably as treasurer), cannot be the evangelist of this name mentioned Acts xix. 22 ; he is more likely the person of whom Paul speaks 2 Tim. iv. 20. We know nothing of *Quartus*.—One sees, then, that all these persons are placed with the order, tact, and discernment which never failed the apostle, even in the minutest details of his letters.

Ver. 24 in the T. R. is certainly unauthentic. Meyer quotes, to defend it, the repetition of the apostolic prayer, 2 Thess. iii. 5 and 18 ; but there no MS. omits it, while here it is not found in any of the four oldest MSS. It is easy to see that certain copyists have transposed it hither from ver. 20, to place it, as is customary, at the close of the salutations.

Critical conclusion regarding the passage, vv. 21-24.—This short passage is acknowledged to be authentic, and to belong to the Epistle to the Romans, by Volkmar and Schultz. The latter has brought out forcibly the proof in its favor arising from the enumeration of the deputies of Macedonia, Acts xx. 4. He also rebuts the objection taken from the Latin origin of several of these names, by recalling the fact that Macedonia was peopled throughout with Roman colonists, which explains the propagation of Latin names in this province.—M. Renan infers from the salutations addressed in the name of several Macedonians, that we have here the conclusion of the copy intended for the church of Thessalonica. In arguing thus, he does not take account of the assembling in the city of Corinth of all the deputies of Greece and Asia who were to accompany Paul to Jerusalem.—We cannot discover in this passage the least word calculated to inspire doubts either as to its being composed by the apostle, or as to its original connection with the Epistle to the Romans.

THIRTY-FIRST PASSAGE (16:25-27)

The Look Upward

Could the apostle have closed such an Epistle with the words : " and the brother Quartus" ? After the final benediction, he had added the salutations of some eminent brethren who surrounded him, and who were connected with certain members of the church of Rome. But could he, having reached the close of such a writing, fail once more to lift his eye upward and invoke on this work, the gravity of which he knew, and on the church for which it was intended, the blessing of Him who alone truly builds up and strengthens ? He had done so several times, in the course of his writing, when concluding some important development. How could he avoid doing it with stronger reason at the close of the entire Epistle ? In the somewhat exceptional presence of a doxology at the end of this letter, there is therefore nothing which of itself can inspire the least suspicion.

Our one task is to examine whether this passage comes up to the elevation of the apostle's mind, and agrees with his mode of writing ; and then, if as a whole and in its details it possesses satisfactory appropriateness.

Vv. 25-27.[1] *"Now to him that is able to stablish you according to my gospel, and the preaching of Jesus Christ, according to the revelation of the mystery, which was kept secret during the eternal times, but now is made manifest, and*[2] *by prophetical writings, according to the commandment of the eternal God, published to all the Gentiles for the obedience of faith: to God only wise . . ., by Jesus Christ, whose*[3] *is the glory for ever and ever.*[4] *Amen."*—Paul had in the preface of the Epistle expressed his desire to visit the Christians of Rome, that they might receive by his means an increase of *strength*, "εἰς τὸ στηριχθῆναι ὑμᾶς." This desire he has partly gratified by addressing to them this letter of instruction. But what are man's words when the obtaining of a true spiritual result is in question ? A sounding brass. Hence the need of lifting his soul to Him who *can do* what man is incapable of producing : τῷ δυναμένῳ, *to Him that is able.* The particle δέ, *now*, serves here to form the transition from the weak man who has just been writing, to the Almighty God, who can act. It is exactly the same connection as in the discourse of Paul at Miletus, Acts xx. 31 and 32.—We shall afterward inquire after the verb, expressed or understood, on which this dative depends : *to Him that is of power.* The verb στηρίζειν, *to stablish*, is absolute. There is no special reference to stablishing in faith or love. Paul means to speak of the firmness of the inner life in general, of that spiritual consistency against which all attacks from within and from without are

---

[1] ℵ B C D E, some Mnn. It. Syr^{sch}. read here, and here only, the doxology, vv. 25-27.—A P read it here and after xiv. 23.—L, more than 200 Mnn., and the Lectionaries read it only after xiv. 23.—F G omit it altogether. This was also done by Marcion, according to the testimony of Origen : " Caput hoc Marcion . . . de hac epistolâ penitus abstulit.'
[2] The τε is wanting in D E, Syr.
[3] B Syr^{sch}. omit ω.
[4] T. R., with B C, omit των αιωνων *(of the ages).*

defeated. He would have them all to become of the number of those *strong*, δυνατοί, of whom he has spoken, xv. 1. This strength embraces both inward emancipation of conscience in relation to legal forms, and new life by the power of the Holy Spirit.—The increasing communication of this spiritual strength is connected by the apostle with a definite standard : *my gospel.*—He means thus to indicate the type of Christian doctrine which had been personally revealed to him (Gal. i. 11–16), and the two characteristic features of which were, as we have seen throughout this Epistle, the perfect *freeness*, and, as a consequence, the absolute *universality* of salvation. Salvation without any condition of previous *working*, salvation offered without distinction *to all:* such is, in two words, what Paul called *his gospel;* an expression which is found only in our Epistle (ii. 16) and 2 Tim. ii. 8. The power of God can act only in agreement with the thought of God. Now, Paul's gospel being the supreme thought of God, it follows that God's power can only be put forth in the heart of man in so far as this gospel is by it received and understood. Such is the meaning of the preposition κατά, *according to*, which must not be confounded either with ἐν, *in* (stablish *in the faith of* . . .), or with διά, *through* (stablish *by means of* . . .).—The following words : *and according to the preaching of Jesus Christ*, have been understood in this sense : " the preaching of which Jesus Christ is the author ;" some, like Meyer, understanding thereby the preaching which Christ causes to sound through the world by the mouth of Paul ; others, like Hofmann : the word as Christ preached it while He was on the earth. This last meaning is inadmissible ; for Paul never alludes to the earthly preaching of Jesus Christ, which had been circumscribed within limits traced by His pedagogical condescension toward Israel. But neither does Meyer's meaning commend itself. Paul has no motive for here raising the particular idea that it is Christ Himself who preaches by his mouth. If we consider that the words : " the preaching of Jesus Christ," depend equally with the preceding term : " my gospel," on the preposition κατά, *according to*, we shall easily see that this complement : *of Jesus Christ*, can only designate here the *subject* of the preaching. The apostle wishes to efface what seemed too strongly personal in the standard : " according to *my gospel.*" Hence it is that he takes care to add : " and (in general) according to the preaching of which Christ is the subject." Indeed, the Christ proclaimed by the Twelve is the same whom Paul preaches ; comp. 1 Cor. xv. 11. It is Christ crucified and risen for us. And if the peculiar revelation which Paul received had for its effect to unveil new and unexpected consequences of the work of this Christ, it is nevertheless true that the Christ preached by him is the same as the Christ of apostolic preaching in general. We are not diverted from this so natural sense by the objection which Lucht draws from it : that this expression reveals a conciliatory tendency in regard to the Twelve which is incompatible with St. Paul's character. For we have found that this spirit of union was that of the apostle's whole ministry. Paul and Peter felt themselves radically at one, whatever even M. Renan may say, for each acknowledged the other's ministry as proceeding *from the same* God, who had confided to each what was peculiarly his own (Gal. ii. 7, 8).

We again find a clause dependent on the preposition κατά, *according to: according to the revelation of the mystery* . . . And the question is, whether this clause is parallel to those which precede, or whether, on the contrary, it depends on them. In the former case, it might be made to depend on the verb *stablish* (Meyer), or on the whole phrase : *to Him that is of power to stablish you* (Philippi). But in either construction it is impossible to escape from a sort of tautology with the preceding regimen. And it cannot be allowed that Paul would have thus co-ordinated two κατά, *according to,* without joining them by a copula. I think, therefore, that the second regimen must be regarded as dependent on the first. There is in the words εὐαγγέλιον and κήρυγμα (*gospel* and *preaching*) an active verbal notion : "*the act* of evangelizing, preaching," which allows this grammatical relation. The act of preaching is subject to a standard. The man does not discharge it in an independent and arbitrary manner. So Paul is careful to conform his evangelic preaching to the revelation he has received of the divine mind for the salvation of mankind. The clause : *according to the revelation*, depends therefore on the two previous substantives.—God from eternity has conceived a plan on our behalf (1 Cor. ii. 7). This plan was *kept secret* for ages ; and so long as man was not initiated into it, it remained a *mystery*, a thing inaccessible to man left to himself ; comp. xi. 25. But now this eternal plan has been unveiled. Realized through the appearing and work of Jesus Christ, it has been revealed by the Holy Spirit (1 Cor. ii. 7–12) to those who are called to make it known to the world, and specially to Paul, so far as concerns the Gentiles (Eph. iii. 2 and 3).—The contents of this *mystery* are, generally speaking, salvation in Christ, but more particularly in our passage, that salvation as it is to be preached to the Gentiles (Gal. i. 16)—to wit, that through faith they become *one body* in Christ with Jewish believers (Eph. iii. 4–6).—*The eternal times* are the numerous ages which have elapsed between the creation of man and the appearing of Christ ; comp. Tit. i. 2.

Ver. 26. With these times of silence there is contrasted that of divine speaking. The word νῦν, *now*, strongly expresses this contrast. The participle φανερωθέντος, *manifested*, refers to the inward revelation of the divine mystery by the Holy Spirit, which the apostles have received ; comp. the perfectly similar expressions, Eph. iii. 5.—This act of revelation must necessarily be completed by another, as is indicated by the following participle : γνωρισθέντος, *published*, *divulged*. What the apostles received by revelation, they are not to keep to themselves ; they are called to proclaim it throughout the whole world. These two participles are joined by the particle τέ, *and*. This mode of connection applies in Greek only to things of a homogeneous nature, and the one of which serves to complete the other. This peculiarity of the τέ suffices to set aside Hofmann's explanation, who translates : "manifested *now and by* the prophetical writings." For the two notions of the time and mode of revelation are too heterogeneous to be thus connected. And, moreover, it would follow from this explanation that the second participle (γνωρισθέντος, *published*) would be unconnected with the first by any conjunction, which is impossible. The Greco-Lats. and some versions omit the particle τέ. But it is a copyist's error well explained by Meyer. The words : *by prophetical writings*, were connected with the preceding participle (φανερωθέντος, *manifested*), as nearer than the following one, and from this false connection arose the suppression of the τέ.—The second participle, γνωρισθέντος, *made known*, is *defined* by four clauses. The first refers to the *cause:* the divine command ; the second to the *means:* the prophetical writings ; the third to the *end:* the obedience of the faith ; the fourth to the *object:* all the Gentiles.

The *command of God* sounded forth by the mouth of Jesus when He said : "Go ye and teach all nations." This command was not the expression of a transient or secondary thought ; it was the immutable and eternal thought, to which all the rest were subordinated, even the decree of creation. This is what the epithet *eternal*, given to God, is intended to remind us of. He remains exalted above all the phases through which the execution of His designs passes.

By the *prophetical Scriptures*, which are the *means* of the making known, all critics understand the prophetical books of the O. T. But how could Paul say : The gospel is proclaimed *by* these books ? He has just declared, on the contrary, that they mystery had been kept secret up to the present time. It is answered, that the apostle is alluding to the use made of the writings of the prophets in apostolic preaching. But though these writings were a means of demonstration, they were not a means of making known; and yet this is what is expressed by the participle λvωρισθέντος. And, besides, why in this case reject the article which was necessary to designate these prophetical books as *well-known* writings; why say: " by *writings*" . . . and not: " by *the* writings of the prophets ?" It might be answered, that Paul expresses himself in the same way in the passage i. 2; but there, the term *prophets* which precedes, and the epithet *holy* which accompanies, the word *Scriptures*, sufficiently determine the idea. It is not so here, where these writings are represented as the means of propagating a new revelation, and should consequently designate new prophetical writings. I think that the only explanation of this term in harmony with the apostle's thought is got from the passage which we have already quoted, Eph. iii. 3–6 : " For God by revelation made known unto me the mystery, *as I wrote afore* in few words, whereby when ye read ye may understand my knowledge in the mystery of Christ, which in other ages was not made known unto the sons of men, as it is now revealed unto His holy apostles *and prophets* by the Spirit, that the Gentiles are fellow-heirs, and of the same body, and partakers of His promise in Christ by the gospel." The apostles are here called *prophets*, inasmuch as they are bearers of a new revelation. What then are their writings, if not *prophetical writings?* Paul himself feels that the letter which he has just written has this character, and that it ranks among the means which God is using to carry out the publication of the new revelation. It is therefore of this very letter, as well as of the other letters which had proceeded from his pen, or from that of his colleagues, that he is speaking in our passage. And from this point of view the absence of the article is easily explained. Paul really means: " by prophetical writings." It is as it were a new series of inspired writings coming to complete the collection of the ancient and well-known books, even as the new revelation is the completion of the old.—The *end* is denoted by the words : *for the obedience of faith;* an expression which reproduces that of i. 5, and the meaning of which is, as we have proved there, the obedience to God *which consists of* faith itself.—Finally, *the object* of the publication : *to all the Gentiles* (nations); an expression similar to that of i. 5 : *among all the Gentiles.* Paul thus ends where he had begun : with his apostleship to the Gentiles, which follows from the appearance of a new and final revelation, and of the full realization of God's eternal plan. The return to the ideas of i. 1–5 is evident.

Ver. 27. The dative τῷ δυναμένῳ, *to Him that is able*, in ver. 25, has not yet found the verb on which it depends. It is evidently this same dative which, after the long developments contained in vv. 25 and 26, reappears in the words : *to God only wise.* The idea of God's power in ver. 25 was naturally connected with that of *stablishing;* and so the idea of the divine *wisdom* is joined here with the notion of the divine plan and its accomplishment, expounded in vv. 25 and 26. But on what does this dative of ver. 27, as well as that of ver. 25 which it takes up again, depend ? Some answer : on the proposition following : " To Him is (or be) the glory !" But why in this case introduce the relative pronoun ᾧ, *to whom?* Why not say simply αὐτῷ, *to Him?* (Eph. iv. 20, 21). To make this construction admissible, all that would be necessary would be to reject this pronoun, as is done by the *Vatic.* and some Mnn. But these authorities are insufficient. And the reason of the omission is so easy to understand ! Must it then be held, as Meyer and many others do, that we have here, exactly in the last sentence of the Epistle, an inaccuracy ? It is supposed that Paul, carried away by the great thoughts expressed in vv. 25 and 26, forgot the dative with which he had begun the sentence in ver. 25, and continues as if the preceding proposition were finished. But this remote dative, which Paul is thought to have forgotten, is evidently reproduced in this one : *to God only wise!* He has it therefore still present to his mind. Tholuck, Philippi, and others refer the relative pronoun ᾧ, *to whom*, not to *God*, but to *Jesus Christ;* they hold that, according to the apostle's intention, the doxology was originally meant to apply to God, the author of the plan of salvation, but that Paul, on reaching the close of the period, applied it to Christ, who executes the plan : " To God powerful . . . and wise [be glory], by Jesus Christ, to whom be glory forever." This explanation would certainly be more tolerable than Meyer's. But we doubt whether the apostle's real meaning is thereby obtained. In fact, when he began his period with the words : *To Him that is of power to stablish you*, his intention was certainly not to terminate with this idea : To Him be glory ! We glorify Him who *has done* the work ; but as concerning Him who *is able* to do it, we look to Him to do it ; we ask His succor ; we express our confidence in Him and in His strength. Such was the inward direction of the apostle's heart when he began ver. 25 by saying : " To Him that is of power" . . ., exactly as when he closed his discourse to the elders of Ephesus, Acts xx. 32, by saying : " And now *I commend you to God* and to the word of His grace, *to Him that is of power* (τῷ δυναμένῳ) to build you up and give you the inheritance" . . . The idea understood, on which the dative of ver. 25 depends, is therefore that of commendation and confidence : " My eye, in closing, turns to Him who *is able*, and from whom I expect everything." This impulse Godward, in which he desires his readers to join him, is so lively within his soul that he does not even feel the need of expressing it ; he includes it in this reduplicated dative τῷ δυναμένῳ and μόνῳ σοφῷ Θεῷ). And hence the proposition may be regarded as complete, and as terminating without any real inaccuracy in the doxological formula which closes the period and the whole Epistle : " whose is the glory" . . . The full form would be : " I look with you all to Him who can stablish you . . . to God only wise, through Jesus Christ whose is [or be] the glory !"

The clause : *through Jesus Christ*, is connected by Meyer with the word *wise:* " to God whose wisdom is manifested in Jesus Christ, in His person and work." But the expression : *only wise through Christ*, would not signify : who *has shown himself* wise through Christ, but : who *is* really wise through Christ. And that is an idea which Paul could not enunciate. The words : *through Jesus Christ*, must therefore be referred to the understood thought which forms the basis of the whole preceding sentence : " I look to God, I wait on Him, for all that concerns you, through Jesus Christ." It is through Jesus Christ that the apostle sends up his supplication, as it is through Jesus Christ that there will come down on the Romans the help of God only strong and only wise.—If it is so, the relative pronoun *to whom* refers rather to Jesus Christ than to God. But it must be added that in his view the author and executor of the plan of salvation are so closely united, that it is difficult in this final homage to separate God to whom He looks, from Jesus Christ in whose name he looks. In the passage i. 7, the two substantives : *God* and *Jesus Christ*, are placed under the government of one and the same preposition ; they may therefore be embraced here in one and the same pronoun.—The verb to be understood in the last proposition would certainly be ἐστω, *let it be*, if Paul had used the word δόξα, *glory*, without article. But with the article (" *the* glory") the verb ἐστί, *is*, must be preferred : " whose *is the* glory." It belongs to Him wholly throughout all eternity. For He has done everything in that work of salvation just expounded in the writing now closed.

Critical conclusion regarding the doxology, vv. 25-27, and regarding chaps. xv. *and* xvi.—The *authenticity* of vv. 25-27 has been combated in a thoroughgoing way by Reiche, Lucht, and Holtzmann.[1] Hilgenfeld, who against these critics

[1] Reiche in his critical Commentary.—Lucht, *Ueber die beiden letzten Kap. des Römerbr.* 1871.—Holtzmann, *Epheser und Colosser Brief*, pp. 307-310.

Critical Conclusion Regarding the Doxology / 507

defends the authenticity of chaps. xv. and xvi. in general, agrees with them on this point. M. Renan, on the contrary, ascribes the composition of this passage to the apostle; but he regards it as the final particular of the copy addressed to a church unknown. In this copy these verses joined on immediately, according to him, to the end of chap. xiv. M. Reuss also supports their authenticity, and regards them as the conclusion of our Epistle, with which, according to him, they are intimately connected.

The following are the principal reasons alleged against the authenticity of the passage :—(1) The entire omission of these verses in Marcion and in two Mjj., and their transposal to the end of chap. xiv. in three Mjj. and in most of the Mnn. (2) The absence of similar sayings at the end of St. Paul's other Epistles. (3) The emphasis of the style and the heaping up of expressions which contrast with the ordinary sobriety of the Pauline language. (4) Certain echoes of expressions in use in the Gnostic systems of the second century. (5) The want of appropriateness and of all definite object.

1. As to Marcion, it is not surprising that he suppressed this passage, as well as so many others, in the letters of the one apostle whose authority he recognized. For this passage, by mentioning the *prophetical writings*, appeared to Marcion to connect the new revelation closely with that of the O. T., which absolutely contradicted his system.—We think we have explained at the end of chap. xiv. the transference of these verses to that place in some documents, as well as their omission or repetition in a very few documents. The position of the doxology at the end of the Epistle certainly rests on the concurrence of the most numerous and weighty authorities. 2. It is not surprising that in a letter so exceptionally important as this the apostle should not be satisfied with concluding, as usual, with a simple benediction, but that he should feel the need of raising his soul heavenward in a solemn invocation on behalf of his readers. This writing embraced the first full exposition of the plan of salvation. If, on closing the different parts of the statement of this plan, his heart had been carried away by an impulse of adoration, this feeling must break forth in him still more powerfully at the moment when he is laying down his pen. 3. It is true the heaping up of clauses is great; but it arises from the strength of this inward impulse, and has nothing which exceeds the natural measure of Paul's style. The participle γνωρισθέντος, *made known*, ver. 26, is accompanied by four regimens; but in that there is nothing suspicious. The participle ὁρισθέντος, *established* (i. 4), has three, and an attribute besides; and the verb ἐλάβομεν, *we received* (i, 5), has three also, and, moreover, two objects. The passage, chap. v. 15-17, has given us a specimen of the way in which Paul's nimble and fertile mind succeeded in cramming into a single sentence a wonderful mass of expressions and ideas. The one question, therefore, is whether there is a superfluous accumulation of identical expressions ; now this is what cannot be proved. We have established the deliberate intention and precise import of every term in these verses, 25-27, as well as throughout the rest of the Epistle. 4. The analogies which Lucht thinks he has discovered with certain Gnostic terms are purely imaginary. The reader will judge of this from the examples quoted by Meyer. The expression *eternal ages*, Lucht would have it, refers to the æons of the Valentinian system. The term σεσιγημένον, *kept secret*, is related to the divine principle designated by the name σιγή, *silence*, in this same system. In speaking of *prophetical writings*, the author is alluding to the allegorical exegesis in use among the Gnostics.—Such criticism belongs to the domain of fancy, not of science. 5. The absence of definite aim cannot be charged against this passage, except in so far as the critic fails to understand the act of having recourse to God, which forms its essence, and which is intended to bring the whole church to the footstool of the throne from which strength comes down.

According to Reiche, the author of this doxology was an anagnost (public reader), who composed it with the help of the end of Jude's Epistle (vv. 24, 25), and of the last words of Heb. xiii. 21. But when from the parallel in Jude there is removed the word σοφῷ, *wise*, which is unauthentic, and the τῷ δυναμένῳ, which proves nothing (Acts xx. 32 ; Eph. iv. 20), what remains to justify the supposition of its being borrowed? The liturgical formula, Heb. xiii. 21, is so common that it can prove nothing. Would a compiler so servile as the one supposed by Reiche have composed a piece of such originality as this, in which there are found united as in a final harmony, corresponding to the opening one (i. 1–7), all the principal ideas of the preceding composition?—Holtzmann, in his treatise on the letters to the Ephesians and to the Colossians, supposes this passage to be the work of the unknown author, who, about the end of the first century, took to collecting St. Paul's Epistles. He began by giving in the Epistle to the Ephesians an amplification of a very short Epistle addressed by Paul to the Colossians; then he revised this latter by means of his previous work; finally, he set himself also to complete the Epistle to the Romans by this doxology by means of some passages of Ephesians and Colossians, where the same hymnological tone and the same tendency to amplification are to be remarked. The parallels which we have quoted in the course of exegesis undoubtedly prove a certain analogy of thought and expression between our passage and these letters. But if Paul himself composed the latter three years after our Epistle, there is nothing wonderful in this coincidence. If, on the contrary, their author is a forger of the end of the first century, he must have had some point of departure in Paul's authentic writings for a composition of this kind, and the authenticity of our doxology is thus rendered probable by this very forgery. In any case, a forger would hardly have committed the apparent inaccuracy which is remarked in ver. 27. For it supposes an exaltation of feeling and thought which is at variance with a composition in cold blood.—Finally, to refute M. Renan's supposition, to which we have referred above, it is enough to read again the last verse of chap. xiv. : " What is not of faith is sin," and to attempt to follow it up with our ver. 25 : "To Him that is of power to stablish you," etc., to measure the diametrical distance of ideas which separate these two verses, the one of which on this theory would be the sequel of the other!

There is but little more for us to add on chaps. xv. and xvi. taken as a whole. We have stated the numerous and contradictory hypotheses in which critics have indulged for more than a century in regard to these chapters. We have examined them passage by passage; they have appeared to us of little weight in detail; is it possible they have more force when applied to the whole? That Marcion rejected all, or perhaps only some parts of these chapters,[1] is of no importance; for the dogmatic nature of the motives which guided him is evident. As to the fact that the Tübingen school feel themselves obliged to follow this example, by rejecting the whole or nearly the whole, the reason of this critical procedure is not less clear; for these chapters, accepted as authentic, overturn Baur's hypothesis regarding the composition of the church of Rome, the aim of our Epistle, and in general the position taken up by Paul in relation to Judaism.—If Irenæus and Tertullian do not yet quote any passage from these last two chapters, it may only be an accident, like the absence of any quotation from the Epistle to Philemon in Irenæus or in Clement of Alexandria.—The apparent multiplicity of conclusions is the thing which seems to have told most forcibly on the mind of modern critics. Some have even been led by this circumstance to regard the whole closing part of our Epistle as an accidental collection of detached leaves, unrelated to one another. We think this impression superficial; it is dissipated by a profounder study. We have found that the conclusion, xv. 13, is intended to close the exhortation to union begun in chap. xiv., and that the prayer, xv. 33, is occasioned by the details which Paul has just given about his personal situation, and by the anxious fears he has expressed in regard to the journey which still lies between him and his arrival at Rome. The salutation of the churches, xv. 16, naturally attaches itself to those of the apostle. The prayer, xvi. 20a, is closely connected with the warning, in the form of a postscript, by which he has just put

---

[1] There is room, indeed, for hesitation as to the meaning of the word *dissecuit* (*he mutilated*) in the passage in which Origen explains the course taken by Marcion (*ad Rom.* xvi. 25), a passage which we have only in Latin. Must this term be regarded as synonymous with *desecuit* (*he rejected*), a meaning which *dissecare* sometimes has in the vulgar Latin of that period? It is possible, but yet doubtful. What makes me think that the thing intended was a simple *mutilation*, is the to me evident contrast to the preceding expression relative to the doxology, vv. 25–27 : *penitus abstulit* (*he wholly rejected*). Marcion, then, suppressed the doxology, and made simple rejections here and there in the rest of the two chapters; comp. Intro l. I. p. 65.

the church on its guard against the disturbers whose coming cannot be distant. Finally, the prayer which closes this verse is that which in all the other letters concludes the Epistle. As to the passage, vv. 23, 24, it is an appendix containing salutations of a private nature, of a very secondary character, and which lie, strictly speaking, beyond the Epistle itself. The prayer, ver. 24, is certainly unauthentic. Finally, the doxology is a last word fitted to sum up the whole work, by raising the eyes of the readers, with those of St. Paul himself, to the heavenly source of all grace and strength. This forms a natural whole; if we examine the details closely, there is nothing in them betraying a conglomerate. Besides, when indulging in such suppositions as those before us, sufficient account is not taken of the respect with which the churches cherished the apostolic writings which they might possess. They preserved them as precious treasures in their archives, and it would not have been so easy for an individual to introduce into them unobserved changes. The Epistle of Clement of Rome [1] was regularly read at Corinth in the second century. It was therefore always in hand. As much certainly was done for the apostolic writings. We know from declarations of the Fathers that these writings were kept at the house of one of the presbyters,[2] and that they were copied and reproduced for other churches, which asked to have them, only under strict control, and with the sort of attestation formally given: *correctly copied.*[3] We are therefore entitled to say, that so long as peremptory reasons do not force us to suspect the *general* tenor of the transmitted text, it has on its side the right of the first occupant.[4]

[1] "This Sunday we have read your letter (that of Soter, Bishop of Rome), and by reading it regularly again hereafter, as well as that formerly written to us by Clement, we shall not fail to be well exhorted."
[2] Irenæus (*Hær.* iv. 26. 2) says: "Every question shall be decided for him as soon as he reads with care the Scriptures in the keeping of those who are presbyters in the church."
[3] Tertullian (*Cont. Marc.* iv. 4) thus describes the mode in which the Gospels were communicated from one church to another: "the Gospels which we possess *per illas* through the apostolic churches) *et secundum illas*) according to the copy which they caused to be made and collated for us)."
[4] The reader may find a further and very elaborate discussion of this theme by the eminent scholars, Bishop Lightfoot and Professor Hort, in the English *Journal of Philology*, 1870-1871. T. W. C.

CONCLUSIONS

I ANNOUNCED a chapter of conclusions, in which the results of the exegesis should be summed up. These conclusions will bear on three points—
1. The critical questions stated and left open in the Introduction.
2. The importance of the writing.
3. Its true character.

1 —CRITICAL RESULTS

The *integrity of the commonly transmitted text* has been verified as a whole. We have found, in particular, how little weight there is in the numerous and contradictory suppositions by which modern criticism seeks to dismember the last part of the Epistle from chap. xii. But we have pointed out in detail a considerable number of variants ; about 270 in all, and among them a certain number on which it has been impossible for us to pronounce with certainty. We have remarked with tolerable distinctness three principal varieties of text : that which bears the name of Alexandrine ; that which represents the form received in the countries of the West ; and the third, which reproduces the text adopted in the Byzantine Church. The comparison of these three forms of the text has not made it possible for us to give in a general way the preference to any one over the two others. In every particular case in which they diverge we have been obliged to try them by the context, without being unduly influenced either by antiquity or number ; and that all the more because we have frequently found the representatives of each of the three groups at variance with one another, and allying themselves capriciously with some members of the two other families to support one and the same variant. In the few cases in which the three texts are well distinguished, and the witnesses of each precisely grouped, if our exegetical appreciation has not deceived us, the preference must be given to the Alexandrine text. In fourteen cases in which some documents of the three texts are at one, the true reading has, in every case, been preserved by their means. . The Alexandrines are found in twenty-one cases in harmony with the Greco-Latin against the Byzantine, which in these cases has been judged thrice only superior to the two others. The Greco-Latins and the Byzantines are agreed eighteen times in opposition to the Alexandrine, which has proved in six cases superior to its two rivals. The Alexandrines and Byzantines harmonize thirty-five times against the Greco-Latin, which in four cases appears to us to have preserved the better reading.—In many cases experience has proved that a weakly supported and apparently more recent reading may be that which exegetical tact forces us to prefer.—In no case has a variant appeared to us of a nature to modify the apostolic conception of the gospel.[1]

Relatively to the founding, composition, and religious tendency of the

---

[1] We subjoin some special observations. The Received text in eleven cases agrees with the Mnn. only, and always erroneously.—It rests eight times on the Mj. L, and the Mnn. only, and five times, if we are not mistaken, with good reason. The MS. P, the form of which is somewhat indecisive, agrees sixteen times with the Byzantines, five times with the Greco-Latins, and four times with the Alexandrines : it is therefore rather Byzantine.

church of Rome, we have found in the way of exegesis the confirmation of the results to which we were led in the Introduction by the historical data.

Though we knew absolutely nothing of the history of the church of Rome during the first two centuries, we should be forced by our Epistle itself, impartially consulted, to recognize in its founding the work of Paul's disciples and friends, in the majority of its members Gentiles by birth, and in its religious conception the type of the apostle to the Gentiles. For the first point we refer especially to xvi. 3 et seq.—For the second, to i. 5 and 6, 13–15, vii. 1, xi. 1, 13, 14, 28, 30, 31, xv. 12, 13, 15, 16, xvi. 26. —For the third, to i. 8, 11, 12, vi. 17, xiv. 1, xv. 1, 14, 15, xvi. 25.[1]—The manner in which Paul expresses himself in these passages forces us to choose between two alternatives : to accept the results which we have just expressed, or to ascribe tactics to the apostle according to which he would deliberately represent the state of things in such a way as to make it appear different from what it really was. Who would not judge such procedure unworthy of the character of such a man ?

A third critical result is consequently this : The aim of our Epistle cannot have been to transform the convictions and tendency of the majority of the church of Rome, but solely, as St. Paul himself declares, both in beginning and concluding (i. 11 and xvi. 25), to *strengthen* them. He wished to confirm the believers of Rome by making the church rest on the foundation of solid and thorough instruction.—Neither does the Epistle present the least trace of a struggle already existing within the church. For this name cannot be given to the secondary ground of difference to which chap. xiv. applies ; and the only passage which is directed against the Judaizing adversaries is found quite at the end of the Epistle (xvi. 17–20), and speaks of them as of enemies still at a distance. But it follows from this same passage that St. Paul foresaw their arrival as a thing certain, which naturally explains the need he felt of putting the church in a condition to resist such an attack. He had just seen his most flourishing creations in Galatia and Achaia threatened with destruction by these relentless disturbers ; and yet he had lived among those churches ; he had himself founded and instructed them ; what, then, was there not to be dreaded for the church of the capital of the world, founded merely by apostolic fellow-workers, when once it was put to the proof ? It is also quite natural that before setting out for Jersualem he should calmly propound his dogmatical and practical catechism, as he teaches it in all the churches which he is called to found, the gospel of salvation by faith which was revealed to him personally by the Lord, and that while taking account of the experiences made in the hot conflict which he has just been maintaining. The Epistle to the Romans is thus found to be at once the most perfect expression of his preaching and of his inner life, the triumphal arch raised on the battle-field after his recent victory, the normal conclusion of that period of his apostleship now brought to an end, and, if one may so speak, the *Ebenezer* of the apostle of the Gentiles.

[1] I am glad to find these general results accepted and confirmed in the interesting article of Professor Chapuis (*Revue de théologie et de philosophie*, "L'Eglise de Rome au 1er siècle," Janvier 1880). The only point of any importance which divides us is the following : M. Chapuis thinks that the gospel brought to Rome by Christians of the churches of the East, was first preached there, as well as at Antioch (see the καί, Acts xi. 20), in the synagogue. The agitations which led to the decree of Claudius were, he thinks, the effect of this preaching ; and as to the chief of the synagogue (Acts xxviii.), who pretend not to know what this new doctrine is, we must regard their words as only "a prudent reserve on their part" in regard to Paul, who was to them a stranger. It would also follow that the founding of the church of Rome took place earlier than I think.—I do not believe that the conduct of the Jews of Rome can be explained thus. Neither do I think that the καί, *also*, Acts xi. 20, necessarily implies a public preaching in the *synagogue* of Antioch. And the passage Rom. i. 8, which so strikingly recalls the saying, 1 Thess. i. 7, 8, seems rather to allude to a somewhat recent founding, which is not at all contradicted by other statements such as i. 13 and xv. 23.—But however that may be, I eagerly embrace the present occasion to thank Professor Chapuis for the kind and courteous tone which characterizes his whole article.

2 — Importance of the Epistle

From the theological point of view, the Epistle to the Romans appears to us as the first powerful effort of human thought to embrace in one survey the divine salvation realized in Jesus Christ, and to sum it up in a few fundamental points connected with one another by the closest possible rational and moral bond. It is not only the first *Dogmatic* which has continued to be the basis of all others, but also the first Christian *Ethic*. For, as we have seen, the practical part is not less systematically arranged than the doctrinal part. The plan of both is perfectly logical. Salvation in its objectivity *in Christ*, and as it is freely apprehended by faith ; salvation realized in the *individual* by sanctification, the work of the Holy Spirit ; salvation wrought out in the whole of *humanity* through the great passages of history, the plan of which God's finger has traced ;—such is the doctrinal part. The life of the saved believer, explained first in its inward principle : *consecration to God* by the sacrifice of the body ; this life manifesting itself in the two spheres, the *religious* and *civil*, there by humility and love, here by submission and righteousness ; this life finally moving on to its glorious *goal:* the return of Him who is to impress on it the seal of perfection ;—such is the practical part. We doubt whether the precision of this primordial conception of Christ's work has ever been surpassed.

Apologetic also finds in this Epistle the most precious materials. Twenty-nine years after our Lord's death, Christianity had traversed continents and seas, and created a new society at Rome. What power of expansion and renovation !—A quarter of a century after the earthly existence of Jesus, His life was regarded as that of the second Adam, as the appearance of a new personal centre of the human species, as the principle of a universal restoration. The contemporaries of Jesus were still living, and His death was, in the eyes of the church, the expiatory sacrifice offered for all mankind, the supreme manifestation at once of God's righteousness and mercy. The fact of His resurrection was not only accepted and believed without question, but regarded as the revelation of a justification virtually pronounced in favor of every sinful man. Jesus had scarcely disappeared when already the eye of faith followed Him to the invisible world, and contemplated Him there as the Sovereign who, from the midst of His glory, filled all things, from heaven to the very place of the dead (chap. xiv.) ; the expectation of His return was the soul of the collective and individual life of all believers. The facts of His human life were still present to all minds, and already from Jerusalem to Rome the church recognized Him as a being whose *name* was to be *invoked* like that of God Himself (Rom. x. 12), and to whom the title of God could be applied without blasphemy (ix. 5). What an impression, then, must have been produced by that public activity of two or three years ! And what must He have been, who in so short a time had graven so profound a mark in the consciousness of humanity ?

It is not theology only, but human thought in general, which, by coming to this writing of Paul, drinks from new fountains. In the first two chapters, the *Philosophy of religion* can learn these two decisive truths : primitive revelation and human responsibility in the origin of polytheism. In chap. v. *Anthropology* can gather the fruitful propositions of the unity of the human species and of the successive concentration of our race in two manifestations of a character at once generic and individual, the one issuing in ruin, the other in salvation. In pondering chap. vi., *Psychology* finds itself face to face with the terrible law in consequence of which man is every moment alienating something of his liberty of choice, by spontaneously subjecting himself to the good or bad principle to which he surrenders himself, and which will not fail henceforth to control him ever more completely. Chap. vii. furnishes the same science with an incomparable analysis of the natural state of the human soul created for good, and yet the slave of evil. Chap. viii. hands over to the *Philosophy of nature* the great idea of a future renovation of the universe, proceeding from the physical and moral regeneration of humanity. In chap. xi. there are traced the great lines of the *Philosophy of history*, and chap. xiii. is a no less sure guide for the *Philosophy of law* in investigating its fundamental notion, that of the state. On all these points, in regard to which human thought labors in all directions, the thought of Paul goes straight to the mark. The entire domain of truth seems to lie unveiled before him, while that of error seems on all sides to be closed to him.

But the essential matter, when it is sought to estimate the importance of such writing, is the full light which it casts on the *way of salvation* opened to sinful man. The apostle knows the unrest which troubles the depths of the human heart, and which keeps it separate from God and imprisoned in evil. And he understands that it is within those depths of the conscience, where the echo of divine condemnation resounds, that a saving transformation must first of all be wrought. Hence the first gift of grace which the gospel offers to man is, according to him, the gift of his justification, without any other condition than that which every one may fulfil at once—faith. This first act done, man is free from his guilt in relation to his God ; no cloud any longer troubles his relation to Him ; peace takes the place of the inward unrest ; and in this state of inward tranquillity there may be sown *the fruit of righteousness*, sanctification. The reconciled man becomes open to the communication of the Divine Spirit. As naturally as this guest must withdraw from a condemned heart, so necessarily does He come to dwell in the man whom nothing any longer separates from God ; and he realizes within him Christ's life and death in the measure in which this life and death have been apprehended by his faith. Finally, to him who walks in this way there opens up in the distance a new gift, the renewing of his body and the inheritance of glory, through his complete transformation into the likeness of the glorified Christ. What clearer, what simpler, what at once more really divine and human, than this *order of salvation* traced by the apostle ; and what a seal has not the experience of ages impressed on this exposition contained in the first eight chapters of our Epistle ! Let not him who desires to see such a work accomplished within himself, or who proposes to carry it out in others, emancipation from guilt and victory over sin, take to the task in any other way, if he would not fail miserably !

3 —The True Nature of this Apostolic Writing

There remains to us a last question to be examined : Is the conception of the way of salvation, which St. Paul has expounded in the Epistle to the Romans, a creation of his powerful understanding, or a revelation of God's mind on the subject ? This dilemma may be thought imperfect ; it may be said that a certain divine illumination does not exclude the exercise of the understanding, and that inward meditation is a means of bringing help from above. Of this there is no doubt, and yet in the case before us the question must be pressed more closely. Does Paul give us here a view to which he has raised himself by the exercise of his mind, or, on the contrary, the thought of God which was communicated to him by a direct operation of the Spirit for the purpose of initiating him, and through him the world, into the eternal plan of divine salvation ? In the latter case we have a *witness* speaking, in the former a genius speculating. In this case we find here a sublime thought, but a thought which may some day be surpassed by one more elevated still ; in the former case, it is the thought of God re-thought and expounded by man at a given time, not to be perfected in the future, but to be appropriated as it is by every soul desirous of salvation. In the first case, the Epistle of Paul deserves our admiration ; in the second, our faith. It is clear that the difference is great, and that the question cannot be declared idle.

We know of no peremptory answer to this question except that which Paul's own consciousness gives to it. With the first words of his Epistle, he places the contents of this writing under the warrant of the Christ who called him to it, that Christ who, born a son of David, has by His resurrection recovered His essential dignity as the Son of God, by means of which He embraces in His salvation not only the Jews, but the whole Gentile world. His apostleship is the work of this universal Lord, and his writing the fruit of this apostleship. To this first word of the Epistle must be added the last, xvi. 25 : "according to my gospel and the preaching of Jesus Christ, *according to the revelation* of the mystery which was kept secret during eternal ages, and now is made manifest." The evangelical conception which the apostle develops is therefore, according to him, God's eternal thought, which He had kept secret from the creation, and which, after the coming of Jesus Christ, was revealed to him—to him, Paul—with the mission to make it known to the Gentiles whom it more directly concerned ; and hence it is that he can justly call it *his gospel*. Such is the apostle's inward conviction. It is likewise expressed, Gal. i. 11 and 12 : " I certify you that the gospel which was preached of me is not after man ; for I neither received it of man, neither was I taught it, but by the revelation of Jesus Christ." And hence he writes to the Thessalonians (First Epistle, iv. 8) : " He that despiseth us, despiseth not man, but God ;" and to the Ephesians (iii. 2-4) : " It was by revelation God made known unto me the mystery, as I wrote afore in few words ;" and this is what constitutes the allotment of evangelical grace and light which God has specially imparted to him for the accomplishment of his task within the apostleship common to him and to the Twelve (ver. 2). By appearing to him on the way to Damascus, Christ made Saul an apostle ; and by the revelation which followed, He bestowed on him the endowment necessary for the fulfilling of his apostleship.

In all this, could Paul have been the victim of an illusion ? Could this divine calling, this supernatural revelation, be only a fruit of his pious imagination ? We have examined this question in the Introduction of this commentary, and from the historical viewpoint at least we have not to return to it. But there are two points which we feel bound to bring out here, which seem to us in a peculiarly striking way to characterize the Epistle to the Romans. The first is the penetrating logic, the sure sweep of vision which the apostle shows in the discussion of the different subjects which he takes up. Not an exaggeration, not a digression. The hot conflict which he had been maintaining in the previous years with the partisans of the legal system, might have predisposed him to go beyond the limit of truth on some points in estimating Judaism The incline was slippery ; of this we may easily convince ourselves, by seeing into what errors it carried the authors of the so-called Epistle of Barnabas and of the letter to Diognetus, and finally Marcion. And yet these men had guides before them, Paul's writings and the Epistle to the Hebrews, which might have helped them to weigh their judgments. Paul had none but himself ; he was under the influence of the strong reaction against the law into which his sudden change had thrown him, and of the violent resentment which must have been produced in him by the injustice and hatred of his Judaizing adversaries. And yet he moves, without wavering for an instant, on the straight line of truth, exhibiting the divinity of the ancient dispensation, and at the same time its profound contrast to the new, so that the result of his exposition is a complete view both of the difference and of the harmony between the two economies of salvation. And the same is the case, as we have seen, in all the questions which he touches. In matters where we still detect our modern writers, even the most sagacious and Christian, flagrantly guilty of exaggeration to the right or to the left, we discover in the apostle's view a fulness of truth which constantly excludes error.—The second feature which strikes us in his writing is the perfect calmness with which he seems to handle truth. He does not seek it, he has it. Compare the Epistle to the Romans with Pascal's *Thoughts*, and the distance will be seen between the apostle and the thinker of genius. It is also evident that the apostle himself draws his life from the faith which he preaches; he has faith in his faith as one cannot have in his thought, for the very simple reason that this faith is not his discovery, but the gift of God. Besides, St. Paul was not unaware of the illusions which a man may form in regard to false inspirations. If we bear in mind how he has put the Corinthians on their guard against the abuse of the gifts of the Spirit (First Epistle, xiv.), it will suffice to show us that in such a domain he could not easily be the dupe of his imagination.

And let us not forget that the experience of ages has spoken. It has put its seal to the conviction which the apostle bore within him, that in *his Gospel* he was giving to the world, not his own thought, but that of God. For history shows that a truly powerful and healthy Christianity has never developed except on the way of salvation traced by St. Paul. Where can we find a sinner who has found full relief for his conscience in relation to God, otherwise than by the gift of free justification? A sinner who has been put in possession of a sanctification decisively cutting short the dominion of sin over the heart and body, otherwise than through the spirit of life bestowed in Jesus Christ on the sinner justified by Him?

The New Testament contains two writings which admirably complete one another, the Epistle to the Romans and the fourth Gospel. The one presents for our contemplation the object of faith in its grander and perfect beauty: the union of man with God realized in One, in order to be at length realized through Him, in all; the other initiates us into the means of apprehending the salvation thus realized in one for all, and of appropriating it: the act of faith. There, the ideal realized, shining as on a celestial summit; here, the arduous pathway by which sinful man may succeed in reaching it. Let the church constantly possess herself of the Christ of John by means of the faith of Paul—and she will be preserved, not from persecution, but from a more terrible enemy, death.

APPENDIX

by Talbot W. Chambers

A. *Probation after Death*   (P. 119.)

THE author appends some peculiar views to his discussion of the apostle's assurance of eternal life to those who continue in well doing (ii. 7). He remarks, justly enough, that the apostle does not here treat of the means of attaining to well doing, but merely affirms that no one will be saved apart from the doing of good. But then he adds that Paul " assumes that the man who is animated with this persistent desire will not fail, some time or other, in the journey of life, to meet with the means of attaining an end so holy and glorious. This means is faith in the gospel." But how does Professor Godet know that Paul makes this assumption ? It is not expressed or implied anywhere in his writings. If it had been, doubtless the author would have quoted the words. But he has not done so, and we are compelled to think that he has attributed to the apostle what is only his own assumption. There was no call in this portion of the Epistle to consider the question as to the dependence of salvation upon faith. That matter was not before the apostle's mind at this time. He is treating not of the gospel, but of the law. In the entire section from the 6th verse to the 16th he is describing the legal position of the race by their creation, quite irrespective both of apostasy and of redemption. He simply sets forth the principles of divine legislation for moral beings. At first blush the utterances do seem to be inconsistent with the doctrine of gratuitous salvation by faith. But the answer to an objection made on this ground is not the weak and illogical escape of our author, but the simple and truthful affirmation that the apostle treats one thing at a time, that the whole Epistle is an emphatic denial of the notion that fallen man can attain salvation as the reward of his merits, and that here there was no necessity of interposing a *caveat* on the point, since the single theme is the ethical ground of judgment for the whole human race. This is given in the 6th verse with the 11th : " Who will render to every man according to his deeds : . . . for there is no respect of persons with God." All that Dr. Godet says about " the love of goodness which is the spring of life" is quite aside from any utterance of the apostle. It is not implied in his words, or even suggested by them. The whole atmosphere of the passage is filled with the strict administration of law, nor is there even a hint that " the desire of goodness is the acceptance of the gospel by anticipation."

There is then no room for the corollary which the author draws, that the gospel is to be preached " before the judgment to every human soul, either in this life or next." That position does not rest upon anything said by the apostle Paul, here or elsewhere. Yet if it has anything like the importance attached to it in our day, it ought to have been enunciated clearly and unequivocally, or at least we should naturally expect such a distinct statement. It assumes that every human being is entitled to an offer of the divine mercy. But this reverses the very idea of mercy, which is the bestowment of that to which there is no claim. Mercy that may be demanded is no longer mercy. And every unsophisticated conscience speaks to the contrary. Such a conscience condemns a man for violating his own sense of duty without any regard to the fact whether he had or had not access to any remedial provision. A healthy moral nature acknowledges at once that sin deserves punishment *per se*. And this is what the apostle affirms: "As many as have sinned without law shall also perish without law." Not having possession of the written or Mosaic law, they will of course not be judged by it, but still having violated the law of conscience they must suffer its penalty, and therefore perish. If hereafter they are to have an offer of salvation, this was the place to mention it. The silence of the author of the Epistle on this point is unaccountable if he held the view of Dr. Godet. His *theodicy* would be different from what it is if this feature belonged to it, and I submit that it is not reasonable to interpret into his utterances a sentiment which contradicts their general tenor and their underlying principles, and which, moreover, is not reasonable in itself, and has never in any age found admission into the creeds of the church.

The author finding no citation from Paul suitable to his purpose gives us two from Peter. The first one (I. iii. 19, 20), as given in the Revised Version, speaks of our Lord as "being put to death in the flesh, but quickened in the spirit; in which also he went and preached to the spirits in prison, which aforetime were disobedient when the long-suffering of God waited in the days of Noah while the ark was a preparing." The meaning of these words has long been stoutly contested, but there is a general agreement now among critical expositors that the translation above given is correct, and indeed the only one possible of the true text (which omits the article before *pneumati*). They hold therefore that the passage relates an experience of our Lord's human soul after death, and cannot be explained consistently or grammatically of the preaching of the pre-existent Logos through the agency of Noah, although that opinion has been held by eminent men in all ages, such as Augustine, Thomas Aquinas, Beza, Pearson, and Hofmann. These scholars seem to have been influenced more by their theological views, or what is called the analogy of faith, than by the laws of exegesis. It may be said in opposition to this explanation, that (1) it is not the natural sense of the passage, that which would occur to an unprejudiced person on first reading it. (2) It is inconsistent with the word πνεύματι as contrasted with σαρκί; not that these two words do not at times denote respectively the divine side of Christ's person and the human, but that here the exact balance of the clauses requires both datives to be rendered in the same way. If the one is to be understood as meaning in the flesh or as to the flesh, then the other must be, in the spirit or as to the spirit. Consequently, the latter cannot be interpreted of Christ's divine nature or of the Holy Spirit, for in no conceivable sense could He be said to be made alive *in* either of these. (3) No account is made of πορευθεὶς which here, just as in verse 22, "who is on the right hand of God, *having gone* into heaven," must refer to a local transfer, a real change of place, which certainly did not occur in what was done through Noah. (4) There is an unauthorized and capricious separation of ποτε from the word ἀπειθήσασί, to which it must belong by Greek usage (="which aforetime were disobedient"), and an equally capricious connection of it with ἐκήρυξεν (="aforetime preached"). Followed as ποτε is immediately by ὅτε, it is impossible to allow such a violent disjunction as is here proposed. (5) Moreover, the occurrence of πνεύμασι in verse 19, in the undoubted sense of human spirits, gives a very strong probability that the same noun in the singular in verse 18 is used in the same sense.

On the other hand, it must be admitted that there is a difficulty in the word ζωοποιηθεὶς on the modern critical view. For how could Christ's human be said to be made alive, when as we all believe it never died? Some escape the difficulty by rendering "preserved alive," but this is not the fair, natural sense of the word. It is better to regard the term as stating that while Christ did really die as to the flesh—*i.e.*, ceased to live any longer in the body—yet as to his human soul he was quickened to fresh energies, to a higher spiritual life than was compatible with an existence hampered by flesh and blood.—It may be added that any reference to our Lord's resurrection is out of the question, for that change takes place in the body and not in the spirit, which alone is spoken of in this clause.

This is the view taken by Alford, by Froumüller in Lange, by Hüther in Meyer, by the Speaker's Commentary, and by Ellicott's Commentary. Nor can it well be doubted by any one who will consider the well-marked antithesis of the two modal datives and the force of the participle represented by the verb "went." The act reported must have been performed by our Lord in person—*i.e.*, by his disembodied spirit—and therefore took place between His death and His resurrection. But as the statement stands alone in the New Testament, and we have no aid from parallel passages, it must be interpreted strictly, neither adding to nor taking from the natural force of the words employed. The "spirits in prison" of course were those of the persons who perished in the flood, and it is of little consequence whether we consider them as being in penal durance as condemned criminals, or simply in custody as prisoners awaiting the day of doom. It is enough to know that they were persons who had died in sin. The question is, What did Christ do to them? Prof. Godet would answer at once, He preached the gospel. But this is by no means clear. It is true that the Greek word κηρυσσω is often employed without an object to denote preaching the gospel, but in all such cases the omitted object is easily or rather necessarily supplied from the connection. There are, however, other instances in which it neither has nor can have such a meaning. Matthew x. 27: "What ye hear in the ear, *proclaim* upon the housetops." Mark i. 46: "He went out and began to *publish* it much;" vii. 36: "So much the more a great deal they *published* it." Rev. v. 2: "I saw a strong angel *proclaiming* with a great voice." It is certain, therefore, that our Lord made a proclamation in the unseen world, but what the tenor of that proclamation was is not said, nor is it necessarily implied. To assume that it was the gospel is to beg the question. Some have said that he went there to proclaim his own triumph, or to predict his deliverance from Sheol, or to announce the completion of the work for which he became incarnate. But no man can pronounce authoritatively in favor of any of these views. The materials for a decision are not at hand.

But whatever may be concluded on this point, it is very certain that the parties our Lord addressed were not of the class who had been left to themselves, and who had sinned only against the law written on their hearts. For they had enjoyed the teaching of Noah, whom the apostle (II. ii. 5) expressly styles a preacher of righteousness (δικαιοσύνης κερυκα). It is obvious then that their experience can shed no light upon the fate of others differently situated, such as the heathen. And it is very singular that they who insist that every man must have the opportunity of learning God's revealed will, appeal to a case which is not at all in point, even if their interpretation of its meaning be correct. For the impenitent in the antediluvian world had a very prolonged space in which to obtain the divine favor. The long-suffering of God waited upon them for more than a century. "His days [*i.e.*, the days of the race then existing] shall be an hundred and twenty years." During all this period Noah uttered the warning message by his voice, by his walking with God, and still more by his patient perseverance in the building of the ark. But all was vain. Even the very workmen who labored upon the singular vessel gave no heed to its purpose. All filled up the measure of their iniquity, and when the appointed time was accomplished, the overwhelming flood came, and every soul perished. And that this was final and irrevocable seems to be plain from the use which our Lord twice makes of the fact, as recorded in the address given by Luke (xvii. 26, 27), and also that given by Matthew (xxiv. 37-39). The former runs thus : "And as it was in the days of Noah, even so shall it be also in the days of the Son of man. They ate, they drank, they married, they were given in marriage, until the day that Noah entered into the ark, and the flood came and destroyed (ἀπώλεσεν) them all." It is impossible to see the force of this historical reference if it does not imply the spiritual overthrow of the antediluvians. If our Lord intended, and knew that He intended, to give them another opportunity of salvation by a personal summons made after His death in the unseen world, how could He with any show of reason adduce their case as an example of the danger of neglecting spiritual things and giving oneself up to the pursuit of the earthly and the perishing? Such a course would seem like trifling with his hearers.

But again, even admitting (which, however, is not admitted) that the words do mean or may mean that our Lord proclaimed a gospel to the spirits in prison, this proves nothing in respect to the case of others, before or since the time of the proclamation in question, for the simple reason that then the circumstances were peculiar and extraordinary. And what is done on momentous occasions is no precedent for ordinary days. Because the conduits run wine instead of water when the king receives his crown, we are not to expect that they will do the same after the coronation is over. If on the completion of our Lord's humiliation by His death, His disembodied spirit passed the interval before his resurrection in setting forth the fruits of His now finished work to some of the other disembodied spirits to be found in Hades, what reason is there for thinking that such an exceptional experience will ever be repeated, much less become a normal feature in the administration of the divine government? Exceptional procedures are to be confined to exceptional occasions.

Still further, there is no intimation anywhere that the preaching, if made was successful, nor is it at all necessary for the purposes of the connection of the passage that it should have been. The apostle is setting forth the sufferings of Christ together with His subsequent exaltation, and He simply intercalates between the death on the cross and the exaltation to God's right hand, something that was done in the intermediate state. Our Lord's disembodied spirit did not, even in the short interval during which it was fitting that His flesh should dwell in the grave, lie in a state of unconsciousness, or simply be in expectancy of the victory of the third day, but, in triumphant and assured conviction of that victory, did make announcement to other disembodied spirits of the work of redemption. The point in question is not what *they* did, but what *He* did ; and even if, as we suppose and as other Scriptures show, they neither received nor accepted an offer of salvation, yet the other fact remains, that our Lord's human soul did while apart from the body make statements to other like souls ; and the reason why this particular class of sinners—viz., the antediluvians—is mentioned, is that the flood was to be cited presently as a figure of baptism. The cause, therefore, of Peter's silence as to the result of the proclamation is that that result had no bearing upon the matter in hand. It may then, upon all these grounds, be safely asserted that this solitary text cannot be made to bear the huge weight of dogma attached to it ; that the premises are far too small for the conclusion that is drawn, and that therefore the question of a new probation after death must be determined altogether by other Scriptures in detail or the general tenor of revelation as a whole.

Nor is the case otherwise in respect to the other obscure utterance of the apostle, in the 6th verse of the next chapter : "For unto this end was the gospel preached even to the dead, that they might be judged according to men in the flesh, but live according to God in the spirit." It is argued that here is a plain case of the preaching of the gospel to the dead. But if so, how could it be said of these dead persons thus preached to and converted that they should be judged according to men in the flesh? How can such a result in the case of any be made known on earth so as to be followed by any kind of judgment here ? It is therefore far more reasonable and consistent to understand the passage as referring to what took place during the life-time of the dead. They had the good news efficaciously declared to them, so that they might indeed be condemned by their fellows in "the fiery trial" (verse 12), but nevertheless their spirits enjoyed immortal life with God. If, however, it be insisted that "the dead" here spoken of were dead when the gospel was preached unto them, then the rest of the verse is made to teach that these and all the dead of preceding generations (for there is no limit annexed) not only heard the gospel offer, but accepted it and were saved—a conclusion at war with all the teachings of our Lord and His apostles. The same reasoning would apply to all the dead of following generations, and so we would reach the conclusion that the day of judgment is a day of general jail-delivery. None are condemned. And then what becomes of our Lord's solemn utterance : " These shall go away into everlasting punishment" ?

The only other passage of Scripture referred to is the well-known utterance of our Lord in Matthew (xii. 32) : " Whosoever shall speak against the Holy Spirit, it shall not be forgiven him, neither in this world, nor in that which is to come." From this it is inferred that there are sins which if not forgiven in this world may be in the next. To which the answer is, that this is turning rhetoric into logic. The 32d verse is merely a repetition in concrete form of what was said in the 31st verse, but in that verse the Lord simply says that " blasphemy against the Spirit shall not be forgiven," an utterance that is complete and states the whole point at issue— viz., whether for a certain class of sins there was or was not forgiveness. What is added in the 32d verse is an emphatic rhetorical expansion of the foregoing. This is made apparent by considering the origin of the phrase. The Jews divided time into two portions (עוֹלָם הַבָּא ,עוֹלָם הַזֶּה = ὁ αἰὼν οὗτος, ὁ αἰὼν μέλλων), this world or age, and the world or age that is to come. In the former they comprehended all duration up to the time of the Messiah's appearance, and in the latter all that followed up to the judgment day. Now our Lord avails Himself of this usage in order to give force and vividness to His declaration. He combines these two great periods in order to express an absolute negation, and show that the sin He is speaking of shall never be forgiven.

Nor does it make any difference if we take the age to come (αἰὼν μέλλων) as referring to the period that follows the general judgment—a reference which it and its equivalents undoubtedly have in the New Testament. Mark x. 30, Luke xviii. 30 : " In the world to come (αἰὼν. τῷ ἐρχομ.), eternal life." In Luke xx. 34 our Lord contrasts the children of this age or world with those counted worthy to obtain that age or world and the resurrection from the dead. 1 Tim. iv. 8, Paul speaks of the life that now is and of that which is to come. Even in this view of the words, it is still apparent that our Lord is not using them with exegetical exactness. The question He was considering was not the time of forgiveness, but the fact whether there was forgiveness at all in certain cases. First, he says there is no forgiveness ; then he adds that there never shall be. This view is confirmed by the parallel passage in Mark (iii. 29), where it is said, according to the accurate rendering of the New Revision, " Whosoever shall blaspheme against the Holy Spirit hath never forgiveness, but is guilty of an eternal sin." No one would infer from the language of Mark any idea of the kind which has been drawn from Matthew's, and we have a right to interpret the obscure passage by that which is plain, and to conclude that both evangelists mean the same thing, though they express it in somewhat different ways. That is, to say that a sin hath never forgiveness is precisely equivalent to saying that it shall not be forgiven, neither in this world nor in that which is to come.

It is further to be said that this notion of a possible forgiveness after death, or a fresh probation in the unseen world, stands opposed to the whole current of gospel teaching. Take as an illustration the commencement of the gospel. John the Baptist began, saying, "Repent, for the kingdom of heaven is at hand." Our Lord followed him with the very same words (Matt. iii. 1, iv. 17). Now what John meant is very plain from his reference to the threshing-floor and the winnowing shovel. Wheat is destined to the garner, but the chaff to the fire unquenchable. The ground, the urgency of the call, lies in the consequences of neglect. To repent means escape, but to refuse and turn away means irretrievable ruin. And what John said our Saviour approves. But if forgiveness is possible after death, how are we to explain the solemn warning of the Baptist? All the life is taken out of his tremendous imagery. There is a new seed-time, a new harvest, a new cleansing of the threshing-floor. Such a view strikes out the entire underpinning of the gospel. Again, Paul in 2 Cor. v. 10 says that in the judgment each one is to "receive the things done in the body, according to what he hath done, whether good or bad." But persons in the intermediate state are not "in the body," and therefore cannot do or receive anything to interfere with the result determined by their previous lives. So, in Hebrews ix. 24, it is said, "It is appointed unto men once to die, but after this cometh judgment," an appointment which leaves no room for a fresh probation between these two dread events.

In truth, the whole subject is treated in the wrong way. Men conclude from their subjective views of what is right and becoming on the part of their Maker and Judge, that every human soul must hear the gospel in this life or the next, and then look around for Scripture to buttress up this view. Yet it appears that the passage to which all with one consent first turn is one that says nothing about persons who lived and died without a revelation, but is confined to those who heard an inspired preacher of righteousness, and which therefore, if it proves anything, proves, not a probation to those who had none before, but a second to those who had one and abused it. Then they appeal to another divine utterance, which, if it means what they say it means, teaches that to all the dead, past, present, and future, the gospel is preached, and therefore the next life, instead of being a period of retribution, merely reproduces the characteristic features of the present. Finally, recurrence is had to an utterance of our Lord, which, interpreted without reference to its connection or to its form in the second Gospel, might allow the vague and dubious inference that there is some kind of forgiveness in the life to come, although our Lord's parabolic teachings, especially that of the Rich Man and Lazarus, are clear and strong against any such inference. It is proper, therefore, to insist that the provisions of mercy being purely matter of revelation, the divine oracles are to be consulted in the first instance as decisive. They are to be regarded as original and all-sufficient sources of truth, and not to be employed merely as lending support to conclusions reached in some other way.

B. *The Christian Conflict* (P. 176.)

The precise application of this remarkable passage has been a subject of dispute for fifteen hundred years. It was hotly debated in the days of Augustine, and many centuries afterward was the pivotal point in the conflict between the Remonstrants and the Contra-Remonstrants in Holland. And the division of opinion still continues. Prof. Shedd's able exposition (1879) and Dr. Sanday in Ellicott's Commentary for English Readers (1880) take one view, while Dr. Gifford in the Speaker's Commentary (1881) takes the other—viz., that which is presented with so much force by Prof. Godet. In a matter of so much difficulty, one in which men of equal

Appendix / 523

learning, acuteness, and piety have differed so widely, it does not become any to speak with dogmatism. Having, however, come to a conclusion different from that reached by the author of this book, I venture to suggest some considerations in reply to the argument with which he closes the seventh chapter.

1. The Professor speaks of the studied avoidance by the apostle of every expression specially belonging to the Christian sphere. Such avoidance certainly occurs, but it is to be accounted for by the nature of the case. The object of the apostle was to show the impossibility of securing sanctification by the law. Being occupied with this negative side of the subject, he does not anticipate what is to be said afterward in setting forth the positive side. This is done in the eighth chapter, which continues and completes his view of the relation between justification and progressive sanctification.

2. As to the very striking parallels found in profane literature, their aptness and force are just the same whether we compare them with the struggle between inclination and duty in an unregenerate man, or with that between the new nature and the old in the regenerate.

3. The change of tense in this passage is very remarkable, and is by no means explained away by Prof. Godet's reasoning. In the former part of the chapter (vv. 7-14) the apostle uses past tenses describing a former condition—viz., that of one still unregenerate, as all admit—but in the remainder he persistently uses the present, "I *am* carnal," "sin *is* present," etc. It is hardly conceivable that this sudden and total change of the tenses can have been accidental, and if it was intentional, then the only explanation of it is a change of the point of view. Before, the apostle was discussing his condition prior to conversion; now, he is setting forth his condition after that change.

4. This view suits admirably the general scope of the Epistle and the course of the argument. The apostle, having shown that the law is helpless as a means of justification, proceeds to set forth its utter inability as a method of sanctification. This is done in the seventh chapter by a vigorous statement of its working, first in relation to original sin in man in a state of nature (vv. 7-14), and then in relation to indwelling sin in one who is in a state of grace. In neither case does the law manifest any power to conquer depravity. A new element is necessary, which is introduced with great fulness in the eighth chapter, where the inward struggle is once more described, but with growing assurances of success which finally culminate in a song of unmingled triumph.

5. Particular expressions occur in the section which cannot without great violence be applied to the natural man. For example, the words with which v. 22 opens: "For I delight in the law of God after the inward man." The force of the verb here is very inadequately given in Prof. Godet's translation, "I applaud" (*j'applaudis*). To praise a person or a thing is by no means the same as to delight in them. Natural men may and often do admire and commend the law of God, but they do not have pleasure in it. Nay, the full approbation of the conscience may coexist with deadly hatred in the heart. Again, in the last verse, the apostle says, "With the mind I serve the law of God." The word *serve* (δουλεύω) is very strong, denoting a total subjection of the will. The man voluntarily enslaves himself to righteousness. Can this be said of any mere natural man?

6. The view which denies that this section describes a Christian experience goes to wreck on the Scripture account of man's condition apart from grace. That view supposes an element of holiness, slight and weak but real, still remaining in man after the fall, which accounts for the struggle here recounted. But there is no basis for this opinion. Fallen man's condition is one of total alienation from God. The fearful ungodliness and

immorality described in the first chapter is the natural development of the evil heart cut off from God and seeking its gratification in the creature. Now this inborn corruption, however veiled or qualified by outward graces, or domestic affections, or civic virtues, or actings of conscience, cannot possibly be the subject of such a conflict as is here described. Consent to sin, the act and dominion of sin, is the permanent condition of the unregenerate. Hence the Scripture defines so sharply everything truly spiritual in man as a supernatural, gracious effect. What is born of the flesh only is flesh (John iii. 6); the psychical (or natural) man understands nothing of spiritual things (1 Cor. ii. 13); he is one having not the Spirit (Jude 19); his mind is enmity against God. No such man in the innermost centre of his personality is at one with the law of God. He neither knows nor feels what is its interior essence, the very secret of its excellence, its exact reflection of the nature of its divine author.

7. On the other hand, the view of the passage here contended for puts it in harmony with the frequent representation of S. S. that there is a remnant of corruption in the believer and that this occasions a continual conflict. Witness the outcry of the prophet beholding the heavenly vision (Is. vi. 5): "Woe is me! for I am undone," or the pleading of David (Ps. xix.): "Cleanse thou me from secret faults: keep back thy servant from presumptuous sins." The same writer who says (Ps. cxxxix.): "How precious are thy thoughts unto me, O God!" adds the entreaty, "Search me and know my heart, and see if there be any wicked way in me." Our Lord said to the Twelve, "The spirit indeed is willing, but the flesh is weak," and in Gal. v. 17 the apostle sets forth this perpetual struggle in very plain words: "The flesh lusteth against the Spirit, and the Spirit against the flesh; for these are contrary one to the other; that ye may not do the things that ye would." As Lightfoot (*in lo.*) says, "Between the spirit and the flesh there is not only no alliance, there is an interminable feud. You feel these antagonistic forces working in you: you would fain follow the guidance of your conscience, and you are dragged back by an opposing power."

It may be added in conclusion that while mediatizing views are apt to be a snare, yet there is one given in this case by Prof. M. B. Riddle (Schaff's Pop. Com. III. 74), which is worthy of attention. It is here subjoined in the author's own words: "It seems best to hold that the apostle does not have in mind any sharp distinction between the unregenerate and regenerate states, but gives the experience of man attempting to become better through the law; of an awakened man, before he comes to Christ; but also of a Christian man so far as he feels the pressure of law rather than the power of the Spirit. Hence it is not always possible to discriminate, if the distinction between the regenerate and unregenerate states is emphasized. Yet the apostle himself, as a Jew, before his conversion, probably passed through this entire experience."

C. *Foreordination* (P. 329.)

The learned author says that some may hold a different view of predestination from the one he advocates, but if so, he frankly expresses his conviction that "it will not be that of the apostle." To which it may be replied with equal frankness that the great objection to his view is that it is not Pauline, being opposed alike to the words of the great apostle and to the general tenor of his teaching. The opinion which resolves divine foreordination into a mere prescience of human volition makes man the originator of his own salvation—a doctrine contradicted on every page of Scripture, and nowhere more directly than in the utterances of Paul. With him God is ever on the throne. Of Him and through Him and to Him are all things. Salvation is by grace from beginning to end, and the apostle delights to trace its origin back to a period before the foundation of the world (Eph. i. 4). He is not concerned about any metaphysical difficulties, but presses the divine efficiency even where one would least expect it, as when he tells the Philippians, "Work out your own salvation with fear and trembling, for it is God which worketh in you both to will and to work for his good pleasure." Repentance is a divine gift, faith results from divine illumination, every excellence of the Christian is a fruit of the Spirit, and no man has anything which he has not received. It is therefore in exact consistency with the unvarying purport of the apostle's doctrine that the Agent who is supreme in all the believer's history in this life should have the same pre-eminence in all that preceded. He who is sovereign in bestowing grace is equally sovereign in the determination to bestow it. And that determination runs back to the ages before time, indeed is pronounced strictly eternal (Eph. iii. 11). The difficulty with Prof. Godet is that he cannot reconcile this view with human liberty. But he is under no necessity of doing this, any more than he is obliged to explain how Peter's assertion at Pentecost that Christ was delivered up by God's deliberate counsel and foreknowledge is consistent with his charge in the same breath that his death was effected by the hand of lawless men. As Prof. Riddle well says, "The difficulty which arises in reconciling God's sovereignty and man's free will confronts us whenever we accept the existence of a Personal God, and is not peculiar to Christianity, much less to some one school of Christian theology." (Pop. Com. III. 39.) It is every way better to take the Scripture just as we find it, boldly insisting in all cases on the two factors, divine causation and human freedom, but refusing to draw the line between them or to insist that we have the means of adjusting their respective claims.

In the passage immediately before us the entire difficulty arises in the first clause, *Whom He did foreknow* (ver. 29). Of course it cannot mean that prescience of which all men and all things are the objects. For then it would say nothing, and the bitterest of Paul's enemies never charged him with writing nonsense. Nor can the phrase mean *whom he determined upon*, both because there is nothing in the usage of the word to sustain this meaning, and because in this way it would be confounded with the next verb, whereas the Scripture keeps the two ideas of foreknowledge and election distinct, as in 1 Peter i. 2 : "Elect according to the foreknowledge of God." Nor can it mean, as Godet says, that God foreknows those who were sure to fulfil the condition of salvation—viz., faith. For this adds an idea which is contained neither in the word itself nor in the context. And besides, this would directly contradict what Paul says elsewhere. For example (1 Tim. i. 9) : "Who hath called us not according to our works, but according to His own purpose and grace, given us in Christ Jesus, before the world began." Nor is it of any avail to say that faith is not a work, but rather a renunciation of all merit ; for it certainly is an act or work, and, according to the Professor, is a free adherence of man to the solicitation of God. And if it be assumed here, it puts as the ground of our calling and election something in ourselves, which is just what the Scripture emphatically denies. Cremer in his Biblico-Theological Lexicon suggests a meaning drawn from the word itself. He says that γινωσκω in New Testament Greek often denotes a personal relation between the person knowing and the object known = to suffer oneself to be determined thereby ; for anything is known only so far as it is of importance to the person knowing and has an influence upon him, so that a personal relationship is established between the knowing subject and the object known. The prefix of προ to this word simply carries us back to an anterior period, and here it denotes that the γινωσκειν is already present in the divine decree before its manifestation in history—*i.e.*, the union takes place between God and the objects of his sovereign grace. Hence we may render, "Whom God had beforehand entered into fellowship with." Thus the word is a conception complete in itself and needing no addition from without. This view preserves the distinction between foreknowledge and foreordination, the former being an act of conscious perception, the latter one of specific volition. Augustine insists upon this distinction: *Prædestinatio . . . sine præscientia non potest esse; potest autem esse sine prædestinatione præscientia* (De Præd. Sanctorum, cap. 4.). Whatever is implied in God's knowing His people now ("The Lord knoweth them that are His." 2 Tim. ii. 19) existed from all ages in the divine mind, and was the ground of His gracious decree. That decree depended upon something in God, but in no sense or degree upon anything in man.

And this is the uniform voice of Christian experience. Whatever the devout believer's head may say, his heart is right, and he feels instinctively that he owes everything to God and nothing to himself. The simple but touching stanzas of Faber express the religious consciousness of Christendom in every age from the apostle's to our own.

> " O gift of gifts ! O grace of faith !
> My God ! how can it be
> That Thou who hast discerning love
> Shouldst give that gift to me ?
>
> " How many hearts Thou mightest have had
> More innocent than mine ;
> How many souls more worthy far
> Of that sweet touch of Thine ! "

The author's conception of foreordination, if I understand him rightly, limits the divine purpose to the future glory of the redeemed as its object. That is, it secures to them who endure to the end a blessed reward in the life to come. But their repenting and believing, their calling and justification, their growth in grace, their victory over sin and death and the devil—all these are outside of the divine decree, and depend simply upon the due exercise of their freedom. At any moment they may be lost. There is nothing to secure the believer that he shall not one day fall into the hand of the Philistines. Surely such a truncated election as this, such a bald and useless foreordination, is not what the apostle is laboring upon. Something larger, grander, more comprehensive is required to reach the full meaning of his fervid rhetoric, his profound thought, his acute dialectic. His vision takes in the whole range of the believer's experience from first to last. In his view foreknowledge, foreordination, calling, justification and glorification are simply successive links in one and the same chain, stretching from before times eternal down to the ages of ages, world without end. The child of God delights to trace each step of his progress to "the sweet will of God," conceived in eternity but manifested in time, choosing alike the means and the end, and securing not simply future glory to those who are worthy, but the grace that renders them worthy, thus making the crown of life only the natural culmination of all that had gone before.

D. *Freedom and Sovereignty* (P. 373.)

The ingenious statement of the author in this résumé of opinions seems to require some further notice. All admit that the apostle teaches a predestination of some kind, and the only, or certainly the chief, question is in respect to its nature ? Is it absolute or conditional ? The former is the common faith of the Reformed. This is not quite accurately expressed by the author when he says that in the salvation of some and the perdition of others it sees only the effect of the divine decree. A more correct statement is that the decree is the direct and efficient cause of the salvation of the saved; it is only negatively concerned with the perdition of the lost, since it simply passes them by.. Their own sin is the direct cause of their ruin. A sovereign God leaves them to themselves. It is different with the others. These he foreordains not simply to glory, as Prof. Godet says, but to salvation, that term comprehending their whole experience from the first act of saving faith to the final acquittal in the great day. This foreordination is absolute, *i.e.*, depending only on God, but is not therefore arbitrary or capricious, *i.e.*, exercised without reason. The nature of God forbids such a thought. The infinite Mind always acts in accordance with its own perfections. But here, as in many other cases, the Lord does not see fit to inform us of the ground of His procedures, but that there is such a ground seems a just and necessary inference from His own very being as a God of infinite wisdom and holiness.

Now that the apostle teaches such a self-determination on the part of God, entirely independent of anything external to himself, is apparent alike from a cursory and a critical reading of his words. This is the natural meaning of his language, and it is confirmed by careful and prolonged study, as is shown by the fact that many of the learned who reject the doctrine yet admit that Paul taught it. An opinion held by such scholars as De Wette and Meyer must have some basis, and cannot be so unceremoniously dismissed.

It is declared that the future of Jacob and Esau (and of the peoples who sprang from them) was decided before they were born, and that the very reason of this was that it might be seen that God's purpose was not founded on works, but on His own good pleasure. For neither of the two had done either good or evil, and the choice of the one and the rejection of the other was determined by the will of "Him that calleth." Prof. Godet says that the matter of eternal salvation was not in view in this case. Even if this were true it would not affect the principle involved, for the point at issue is whether God's sovereignty is unconditional or not, and that can be determined as well in reference to temporal as to spiritual benefits. And besides, the choice to the means is usually a choice to the end, and the blessings by which Jacob was distinguished were the *sine qua non* of eternal life to multitudes of his descendants. But the assertion is incorrect. For what reason did the apostle cite the case except to show the liberty of God to choose whom He pleases to be the recipients of His blessing? Apart from its illustration of this principle, the case had no bearing upon his argument.

So again (verse 16) it is expressly declared that salvation is not the result of human will or human effort, but simply the fruit of God's mercy. Now mercy is indeed a necessary feeling in the divine nature, but its manifestation in any given case is optional. As Charnock finely says: "God is not like the sun, which shines indiscriminately because it has no choice in the matter, being an unintelligent agent, whereas God, as a being of infinite understanding, has a sovereign right to choose His own subjects, nor would His goodness be supreme unless it were voluntary." Indeed: the whole doctrine is but the expansion of the words in our Saviour's parable, "Is it not lawful for me to do what I will with mine own" (Matt. xx. 15)? The entire race being involved in guilt and ruin, God is pleased for reasons known only to Himself to have mercy upon some, and to leave others to the just and natural result of their evil ways.

The same thing appears from the character of the objections raised against the doctrine. "Why doth He yet find fault, for who hath resisted His will?" A reference to the original here shows that it is the will of decree and not the will of desire that is intended. Now this question evidently implies that it is God's sovereignty that is complained of. If it were otherwise, how easily could the apostle have set aside the objection by showing that God was not the final arbiter in the case. But he does no such thing, but rather reaffirms his previous assertions. After rebuking the folly which leads weak and erring man to call to account his infinite Creator, he introduces the striking figure of the potter, as if to say, the sovereignty I claim is inherent in the commonest artificer, how much more in the Lord of all! The potter claims not only the power but the right (*exousian*) to put the clay to a noble or an ignoble use at his pleasure, and the form it is to take rests solely with him. Now, the apostle reasons, fallen humanity is before God just as the clay is before the potter. All sinners are alike destitute of claim; they are "the same lump." If God chooses to save some and not others, He does no injustice to those who are left. He did not make them sin. But when they had sinned and became guilty, He, acting as a moral governor, forbore to interpose, and so they became vessels of wrath. And so far from His procedure here being questionable, it displays His glory. For on one hand He endures with much long-suffering and patience the evil courses of some, long delaying their punishment, and on the other He magnifies the riches of His mercy in the salvation of the rest.

The chief difficulty which Prof. Godet finds in accepting the Augustinian view, which, as shown above, is the correct exegetical view, of the apostle's reasoning, is philosophical and speculative. He says that it cannot be reconciled with "man's entire freedom in the acceptance or rejection of salvation" (ii. 4, 6–10, vi. 12, 13). But this is no reason for denying the plain meaning of words. The apostle may have seen and felt this antinomy, and have decided not to touch it. The Professor indeed thinks that Paul's logical power would not have allowed him "to stop short in the study of a question until he has thoroughly completed its elucidation." But it is much safer to reason from what he did say than from what our view of the nature of his mind would lead us to deem him likely to say. He does touch the very point at issue (verses 19, 20), but how? Not by a metaphysical inquiry into the nature and limits of human freedom, but by an animated declaration that the created being cannot investigate the causes which may have determined the will of his Creator. His language implies that man is compelled by the constitution of his nature to acknowledge that certain actions are sinful and deserve punishment, and this being so, no view of his dependence upon God can make these actions innocent; hence it is vain to argue against incontrovertible facts. And this is all that need be said on the subject. "Scripture considers men under two points of view: first as created by God, and secondly, as free moral agents themselves. These two points of view are, to the intellect of man, irreconcilable; yet both must be true, since the reason convinces us of the one, and the conscience of the other" (Conybeare). It is necessary therefore to hold both, whether we can frame a system of reconciliation or not. In fact, the serious errors on the subject have arisen from the tendency to neglect or deny one side of the complex facts for the sake of making a consistent theory. Pelagians and Arminians have denied the dependence of man's will on God, and Fatalists have denied the freedom of moral agency. Our author sides with the former by making certain "moral conditions" in men the ground of their election. We prefer the method of the apostle, who sides with neither.

Another of his arguments is "the possibility of one converted falling from the state of grace through want of vigilance or faithfulness" (viii. 13; 1 Cor. x. 1–12; Gal. v. 4; Col. i. 23; a passage where he says expressly: "*if at least* ye persevere"). This he thinks wholly inconsistent with an unconditional decree of election. But the particle in the case last cited (which he thinks decisive), "*If indeed*," does not express doubt (compare Eph. iii. 2, iv. 21, where it rather means certainty by challenging the opposite), but is simply intended to call attention to the necessity of faith to secure the result spoken of in the preceding verse. And so with all the hypothetical statements and promises in the Scripture. These are simply parts of the series of means by which the Lord carries out His eternal purpose. That purpose cannot fail, simply because it is God's purpose. If it rested upon man's strength or resources, it would utterly fail. But believers are kept by the power of God through faith unto salvation, ready to be revealed in the last time.

"Finally," the Professor says, "the decree of the rejection of the Jews is explained, not by the impenetrable mystery of the divine will, but by the haughty tenacity with which they affected to establish their own righteousness," etc. This is very true, but nothing to the purpose. The rejection of the Jews and the perdition of any that are lost are the just results of their own sin. This is a real and sufficient cause, and none farther need be sought. The relation of sovereignty to the event is simply negative. God refuses to interfere, and justice takes its course.

E. *The Mystery respecting Israel's Future.*—xi. 25, 26   (P. 411.)

The importance of this utterance of the apostle in its bearing upon eschatology suggests some further remark. It is not an incidental statement, nor a burst of rhetoric, nor yet a lofty poetical expression like viii. 19-23, but a link in a sustained argument carried all through the chapter, and is therefore to be interpreted strictly. It is the explanation of what is called a *mystery*, *i.e.*, as well stated by our author, not a truth incomprehensible by reason, which is the accepted theological sense of the word, but one which can be known only by revelation from above, yet when revealed can be fully understood by those who receive it. It is stated in plain words, without the use of metaphor, by one who well knew the force of language. It treats of a point in the future which man's unaided faculties could never have discovered, and it was intended to vindicate the divine purpose in the application of redemption, and to furnish guidance and admonition to the believers not of the stock of Israel. Occurring, then, as it does in the course of the most didactic portion of the New Testament, and being the last utterance in that book on the subject, it is not to be explained by other preceding Scriptures, but to be used to explain them, and this the more as the inspired author was fully acquainted with the prophecies of the Old Testament, and indeed proceeds at once to cite from them in confirmation of his views. So that we have here in brief a divine interpretation of what is contained in the writings of the holy men of old.

The passage asserts (*a*) a fact, (*b*) a limitation of the time of its continuance, and (*c*) the final result. The fact is that Israel in part has been hardened against the gospel, or rather are subjects of a process going on in this direction, a process in which God judicially withdraws the providential and gracious influences by which men are restrained. Now there are cases in which this hardening is allowed to work out its natural result in the utter destruction of its subjects, as is seen in the cities of the plain, in Tyre and Sidon, in Nineveh, etc. But in the case of the Jews it is otherwise. Their induration has a limit. It will come to an end upon the occurrence of a certain event: *until the fulness of the Gentiles come in*—*i.e.*, to the church or people of God. (Comp. Luke xiii. 24, where the verb is used absolutely, as it is here.) The meaning of the phrase rendered *until* is clear and certain. But the Reformers were led, by their fears of Chiliastic ideas, which in their age assumed a very dangerous form, to depart from the natural sense and give the meanings, *in order that*, or *as long as*, which, however, are now universally repudiated on the ground of both etymology and usage. And, as the author shows, such a rendering is against the whole sense of the passage. The event, then, which is to limit the hardening of

Israel is the coming in of the fulness of the Gentiles. The term *fulness* may be understood, like the verb from which it is derived, either relatively, as complementum, that which fills up what is lacking, like the patch put upon a rent in a garment (Mark ii. 21), or absolutely, as totality, completeness. It is in this latter sense that it is usually employed by the apostle, as in Colos. ii. 9 : " All the fulness of the Godhead." Eph. i. 23 : " The fulness of him that filleth all in all." Here, then, the meaning must be the totality [1] of the Gentiles, not necessarily including every individual, but the nations as a whole. It will not do to render it " a great multitude" (*magna caterva*), for this is a limitation for which there is no warrant. It is " the full number," " the whole body," as contrasted with the part which had already been gathered into the church. Opinions may reasonably differ as to the *intensive* force of this expression—*i.e.*, to what degree the coming in of the Gentiles reaches in respect to their practical appropriation of saving truth—but as to the *extensive* import there can be little or no doubt. The gospel must extend its sway over the peoples who sit in darkness ; it must penetrate every continent ; it must be spoken in every tongue, and have its adherents in every nation and tribe. Nothing less than this would seem to answer the legitimate scope of the apostle's words.

When this takes place, a blessed result is to follow—viz., the salvation of all Israel. This does not deny the occurrence of conversions among the Jews previously. Such are to be expected, but not any widespread or general movement. Dogmatic views and perhaps anti-Semitic prejudices have led many to endeavor to limit the natural meaning of the words : " And so all Israel shall be saved." Sometimes, and that even by such astute men as Augustine and Calvin, the term has been understood spiritually as denoting the whole number of believers, Jews and Gentiles, a sense which Israel certainly has in certain cases (as in Rom. ix. 6 ; Gal. vi. 16), but which here is simply impossible, since there is an express contrast between Jews and Gentiles in the immediate connection. Nor can the term when understood of the national Israel be narrowed down to " the remnant according to the election of grace," understanding by this the number of those who from time to time in the course of the ages shall be brought into the fold. Had this been the meaning, the apostle would have expressed it otherwise. Nor, on the other hand, can the phrase be extended so as to include the whole nation numerically without any exception. For this would be contrary to usage. When Rehoboam went to Shechem, all Israel came there to make him king (1 Kings xii. 1), and when David brought up the ark from Kirjath Jearim (1 Chron. xiii. 5), it is said that he gathered all Israel together ; but in neither case is it necessary or even possible to hold that every individual of the nation was included. It was enough that the people as a whole could be thus described. And so the passage before us must be understood as indicating a national conversion, forever ending the old division into " an elect remnant" and " the rest who were hardened," and uniting the entire body with the Gentiles as fellow-heirs in the grace of life. Nothing less than this can be the meaning of the apostle, and certainly it is sustained by that great miracle of Providence, the preservation of the nation in its distinctive life amid defeats, exiles, dispersions, persecutions, and enmities, such as in any other case would have caused an utter extermination of the sufferers.

But with this conversion of the Jews as a nation there have often been conjoined other views which receive no countenance from this passage, such as their restoration to Palestine, the renewal of the theocratic royalty, and the re-erection of the temple with its priesthood and its ritual just as in the palmiest days of the old Covenant. There is not a word of this in the New Testament, but much that points the other way. As Meyer well

---

[1] See an admirable discussion of πλήρωμα in Bp. Lightfoot on Colossians, p. 323.

says, "Israel does not take in the church, but the church takes in Israel." And this is all that need be asked. The self-invoked curse which has rested upon the race is to be removed, and dawn breaks in at last upon the long, long night of affliction. If all Israel is to be saved, if anti-Semitic prejudices and hatreds are to be removed, if the old distinction which has outlived all other differences of nation or of race and run the deepest groove in human society the world has seen, is to be forever effaced, and Jew and Gentile are to become really one in Christ Jesus, then the domicile of the covenant people is of small consequence. Whether they live in Canaan or elsewhere, they still would retain the ancestral glories recited by the apostle (ix. 4. 5), would still be beloved for their fathers' sakes, and would still feel the tie of the elder brother more than any others, because as to His human nature He too was of the stock of Israel. No earthly priority, no civil distinctions, no headship in ritual services, no national privilege of any kind, would be anything more than a wretched exchange for the adoption and the blessed hope which belong to all Christians as fellow-heirs and fellow-members of the body and fellow-partakers of the promise in Christ Jesus.